CANADIAN
GLOBAL
ALMANAC
2000

Macmillan Canada
Toronto

Contents

CANADIAN GLOBAL ALMANAC 2000

Publisher and Editor-in-Chief	**SUSAN GIRVAN**
Contributing Editors	**LIBA BERRY** *(Index)*
	ANDREW BORKOWSKI *(Arts and Entertainment)*
	FRANKLIN CARTER *(Politics, News Events)*
	SHI DAVIDI *(Sports)*
	DAWN HUNTER *(Statistics)*
	DAVID PHILLIPS *(Climate)*
	DONNA WILLIAMS *(Hall of Fame, Obituaries)*
Design/Typesetting	**LINDA MACKEY**
Researchers	**SONJA RUTHARD**
	ELENA SIMONETTI
Cover Design	**GORD ROBERTSON**
Maps	**MAPPING SPECIALISTS**

Comments and Suggestions

Please feel free to send us your comments and any suggestions for subsequent editions. Many readers took the time to drop us notes and letters last year and the correspondence is most welcome, although it is not always possible to respond personally to each writer. Address all correspondence to the Publisher, *The Canadian Global Almanac*, c/o CDG Books Canada Inc., Suite 400, 99 Yorkville Avenue, Toronto, Ontario M5R 3K5.
You can also e-mail us. The address is almanac@cdgbooks.com. We look forward to hearing from you.

A portion of the information in this pub-lication is made available through the co-operation of Statistics Canada. Integral and/or adapted reproductions are published with permission of the Minister of Industry, Science and Technology. Readers wishing further information on any of the subjects credited "Statistics Canada" may obtain copies of related publications by contacting Publications Sales, Statistics Canada, Ottawa, Ontario, Canada K1A 0T6 or by calling (toll free in Canada) 1-800-267-6677; outside Canada, 1-613-951-7277. Readers may also facsimile orders by dialing 1-613-951-1584.

Canadian Cataloguing in Publication Data

The National Library of Canada has cata-logued this publication as follows:

Main entry under title:

The Canadian global almanac

Annual
1992–
"A book of facts".
Continues: Canadian world almanac and book of facts, ISSN 0833-532X.
ISSN 1187-4570
ISBN 0-7715-7658-7 (1999)

1. Almanacs, Canadian (English).*
2. Almanacs.

AY414.C36   031.02   C92-031173-3

Macmillan Canada, an imprint of
CDG Books Canada Inc., Toronto

Printed in Canada

CANADA

(as of October 1999)

Confederation:	July 1, 1867
Governor General:	Her Excellency, the Right Honourable Adrienne Clarkson
Prime Minister:	The Right Honourable Jean Chrétien
Motto:	A Mari Usque ad Mare (From Sea to Sea)
National Symbols:	the Maple Leaf and the Beaver (both official)
National Game:	lacrosse (summer), hockey (winter)
Official Languages:	English and French
Anthem:	O Canada (National), God Save the Queen (Royal)
Population:	30 482 900 (April 1, 1999 projection)
Capital City:	Ottawa, Ontario

■ GEOGRAPHY

Area:	9 970 610 sq. km
Length of coastline:	243 791 km (longest in the world)
Length of border with U.S. inc. Alaska:	8 890 km
Longitudinal centre of Canada:	97°W (close to Winnipeg)
Latitudinal centre of Canada:	62°N (close to Yellowknife, NWT)
Geographic centre of Canada:	Arviat, NWT (60°06'30"N, 94°03'30"W)
Greatest distance east to west:	5 514 km (Cape Spear, Nfld. to the Yukon/Alaska border)
Greatest distance north to south:	4 634 km (Cape Columbia, Ellesmere Is. to Middle Is., Lake Erie)

Superlative Canadian Facts

Largest province		Quebec	1 540 680 sq. km
Smallest province		Prince Edward Island	5 660 sq. km
Largest city[1]	by area	Timmins, Ont.	3 004.3 sq. km
	by population	Montreal, Que.	1 016 376 people
	by density	Montreal-Nord, Que.	7 396.3 people/sq. km
Smallest city[1]	by area	L'Ile-Dorval, Que.	0.18 sq. km
	by population	L'Ile-Dorval, Que.	2 people
	by density	Moisie, Que.	0.6 people/sq. km
Largest island		Baffin Island, NT[2]	507 451 sq. km
Northernmost point		Cape Columbia, Ellesmere Island, NT	83° 06'N.–69°57'W.
Southernmost point		Middle Island, Lake Erie, Ont.	41° 41'N.–82°40"W.
Easternmost point		Cape Spear, Nfld.	47° 31'N.–52° 37'W.
Westernmost point		Yukon-Alaska boundary	141° 00'W.
Northernmost community		Grise Fiord, Ellesmere Island, NT	76° 25'N.–82°54'W.
Southernmost community		Pelee Island South, Ont.	41° 45'N.–82°38'W.
Easternmost community		Blackhead, Nfld.	47°32'N.–52° 39'W.
Westernmost community		Beaver Creek, YT	62°23'N.–140° 52'W.
Highest city		Kimberley, BC	1 128 m
Highest community		Lake Louise, Alta.	1 540 m
Northernmost ice-free port		Stewart, BC	55°56'N.
Longest river		Mackenzie River, NWT	4 241 km
Largest lake (entirely) in Canada		Great Bear Lake, NWT	31 328 sq. km
Deepest lake		Great Slave Lake, NWT	614 m
Highest mountain		Mt. Logan, YT	5 959 m
Highest waterfall		Della Falls, BC	440 m (more than one leap)

Source: *Natural Resources Canada; Statistics Canada*

(1) As of 1996 Census. Based on the municipal status of census subdivisions; definition varies by province and, for Quebec, includes "ville."
(2) Nunavut

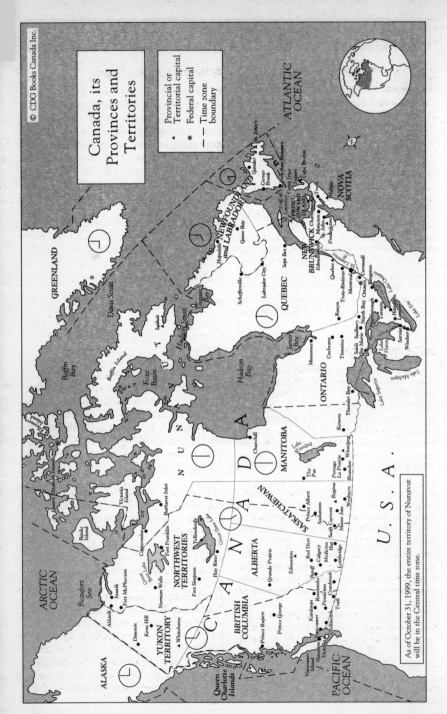

© CDG Books Canada Inc.

Canada, its Provinces and Territories

▲ Provincial or Territorial capital
* Federal capital
– – – Time zone boundary

As of October 31, 1999, the entire territory of Nunavut will be in the Central time zone.

2

LANDFORMS OF CANADA

Canada is the largest country in the Western Hemisphere and the second largest in the world, with a total area of 9,970,610 sq. km. It stretches north to south from Cape Columbia on Ellesmere Island to Middle Island in Lake Erie, a distance of 4,634 km. The greatest east-west distance is 5,514 km from Cape Spear, Nfld, to the Yukon-Alaska border. Within this vast expanse, Canada contains an extremely wide variety of geographical features: the towering peaks of the Rockies, the flat Prairies, the rugged north and the gently rolling landscape of the east. But within this seemingly wide range of features, five areas with common characteristics are found. These physiographic regions are generally used to describe Canada and form the basis of Canada's geographical landforms and geological regions.

■ The Canadian Shield

Also known as the Precambrian Shield, this area is located in the central part of the continent. Viewed from the air it is a vast, inhospitable land of rocks, lakes and trees. It makes up roughly half of Canada's surface area, sweeping around Hudson Bay like a giant horseshoe, but also is the foundation for the rest of the continent.

The Canadian Shield has not always looked as it does today. Early in the Earth's history this area was the site of towering mountains, deep valleys and mighty rivers. The mountains were thrust up by volcanic activity as long as 3.8 billion years ago, during the Precambrian era. Over time, the forces of erosion—wind, water, freezing temperatures, ice—wore down the rocks that formed the mountain peaks and carried the materials away. Now all that remains are the roots of the once-mighty mountains.

The processes of volcanism present at the time of mountain-building caused minerals to form in the cooling rock of the Precambrian mountains. Deep inside the mountains, minerals such as gold, silver, copper and nickel came together into veins of ore. These ore bodies make the Shield a rich storehouse of mineral wealth.

■ The Appalachian Region

To the east of the Shield, this region was also once the site of massive mountain peaks. The rock that forms these peaks is not as old as the rock of the Shield, and is of a type that is more easily eroded. The Appalachian Region runs in a northeasterly direction from the southern United States to Newfoundland.

The mineral deposits found in the region reflect the complexity of the geology, and include gypsum, barite, salt, copper, zinc, lead, gold and silver. Since the end of the mountain-building period, erosion has worn off the tops of the mountains and filled the valleys with sediments, which gives the area its present-day less rugged appearance.

■ The Interior Plains

West of the Shield, rock which formed at the bottom of ancient lakes and seas gives the Prairies their distinctive flatness.

The Interior Plains occupy the central portion of the continent. Minerals found in the Interior Plains include potash, a substance produced when lakes and shallow seas evaporate, leaving deposits. Potash deposits in Saskatchewan are among the largest in the world. Coal, oil and natural gas were formed from organic materials trapped by the sedimentary layers during Palaeozoic times. An extension of the Interior Plains thrusts up between the Canadian Shield and the Appalachian Region, forming the Great Lakes-St. Lawrence Lowlands landform area. Soils throughout the Interior Plains are fertile, since the sedimentary materials that are found in the Plains break down easily.

Other lowland areas were formed during the Palaeozoic era as a result of the deposit of sediment which created the Interior Plains. The Hudson Bay Lowlands on the southwestern edge of Hudson Bay are relatively thin layers of sedimentary rock on top of the Precambrian Shield. The Arctic Lowlands, between the Shield and the Innuition Mountains of the high Arctic, are similar in age and characteristics to the material of the Interior Plains.

■ The Western Cordillera

As the Precambrian mountains eroded, the sedimentary layers were deposited over a great distance and formed the Appalachian Region to the east. These deposits also provided the material from which future landforms would be built to the west. These landforms are now known as the Western Cordillera.

When the continent started its westward movement about 200 million years ago, its leading edge was forced against the adjacent oceanic plate and the land moved overtop the ocean. Geologists speculate that the tremendous pressure exerted during this process caused the sedimentary layers of the plate's edge to buckle into a massive dome. Magma, the hot fluid substance below the Earth's crust, flowed into the dome and formed a core which eventually collapsed between 65 and 160 million years ago, breaking the rock layers. This core stretches along the edge of the continental plate and absorbs the pressure of the two plates as they press upon each other.

The Western Cordillera is an area of great complexity; rocks composed of different materials and through different processes are thoroughly mixed. The Coast Ranges which form the leading western edge of the continent are composed of both igneous and metamorphic rock. The interior of the Cordillera is a jumble of plateaus, folded and broken rock layers and recent volcanoes. The sedimentary materials of the Rockies on the eastern edge of the Cordillera were folded and broken during a period of mountain-building in Eocene times, some 40-65 million years ago.

The Cordillera contains minerals associated with all the processes involved in its creation. The igneous rocks of the western part of the Cordillera are a major source of minerals including lead, zinc, silver, copper and gold. The sedimentary deposits of the eastern Cordillera are responsible for the coal and petroleum found there.

■ Innuitian Region

Mountain-building shaped the landforms of the high Arctic during the Devonian period (about 405 million years ago). The most recent activities appear to have occurred about 30 million years ago, which was long after the mountain-building period that thrust up the Rocky Mountains in the Cordillera.

Little detail is known about this region because research is so difficult in the inhospitable climate, but some geologists have suggested mountain-building is the result of the North American plate advancing on the Eurasian plate.

The topography of this region is characterized by low plateau mountains, with ridges as high as 3,000 m. The area is composed mainly of sedimentary rocks but includes some metamorphic and volcanic rocks.

For more information on geological time periods, see the chart in the Science and Nature section.

Highest Point in Each Province and Territory

Province/Territory	Highest Point	Elev. (m)
Newfoundland	Mt. Caubvick[1]	1 652
Prince Edward Island	46° 20'—63° 25' (Queen's County)	142
Nova Scotia	46° 42'—60° 36' (Cape Breton Highlands)	532
New Brunswick	Mt. Carleton	817
Quebec	Mont D'Iberville[2]	1 652
Ontario	Ishpatina Ridge	693
Manitoba	Baldy Mtn.	832
Saskatchewan	Cypress Hills	1 468
Alberta	Mt. Columbia	3 747
British Columbia	Fairweather Mtn.	4 663
Yukon Territory	Mt. Logan	5 959
Northwest Territories	61° 52'—127° 42' (unnamed peak, Mackenzie Mtns.)	2 773
Nunavut	Barbeau Peak (Ellesmere Island)	2 616

Source: *Natural Resources Canada*

(1) On the Nfld/Que. border; also known as Mt. D'Iberville in Quebec; next highest point in Nfld is Cirque Mt. at 1,568 m. (2) On the Nfld/ Que. border; also known as Mt. Caubvick in Newfoundland; next highest point in Que. is Mont Jacques-Cartier at 1,268 m.

The Great Lakes

The Great Lakes form the largest body of fresh water in the world and with their connecting waterways are the largest inland water transportation unit. They enable shipping to reach the Atlantic via the St. Lawrence River; the Gulf of Mexico via the Illinois Waterway, from Lake Michigan to the Mississippi River; a third outlet connects with the Hudson River and thence the Atlantic via the New York State Barge Canal System.

	Superior	Michigan	Huron	Erie	Ontario
Length in km	563	494	332	388	311
Breadth in km	257	190	295	92	85
Deepest soundings in metres	405	281	229	64	244
Volume of water in cubic km	12 100	4 920	3 540	484	1 640
Area[1] (sq. km) in US	53 400	57 800	23 600	12 900	8 960
Area[1] (sq. km) in Canada	28 700	0	36 000	12 800	10 000
Total Area[1] (sq. km) US and Canada	**82 100**	**57 800**	**59 600**	**25 700**	**18 960**
National boundary line in km	430	0	446	404	281

Source: *Natural Resources Canada*

(1) Does not include islands larger than 0.052 sq. km.

Largest Lakes in Canada

Lake	Area[1] (sq. km)	Lake	Area[1] (sq. km)
Superior, Ont.[2]	82 100	Nettilling, NT*	5 542
Huron, Ont [3]	59 600	Winnipegosis, Man.	5 374
Great Bear, NWT	31 328	Nipigon, Ont.	4 848
Great Slave, NWT	28 568	Manitoba, Man.	4 624
Erie, Ont.[4]	25 700	Dubawnt, NT*	3 833
Winnipeg, Man.	24 387	Lake of the Woods, Ont./Man.[6]	4 472
Ontario, Ont.[5]	18 960	Amadjuak, NT*	3 115
Athabasca, Sask.	7 935	Melville, Nfld	3 069
Reindeer, Sask./Man.	6 650	Wollaston, Sask.	2 681
Smallwood Reservoir, Nfld	6 527	Lac Mistassini, Que.	2 335

Source: *Natural Resources Canada*

*Nunavut

(1) Total area, including islands except for the Great Lakes, where area does not include islands larger than 0.052 sq. km. (2) Includes 53,400 sq. km in US (3) Includes 23,600 sq. km in US (4) Includes 12,900 sq. km in US (5) Includes 8 960 sq. km in US (6) Includes 1,322 sq. km in US.

Largest Islands in Canada

Island	Area (sq. km)	Island	Area (sq. km)
Baffin, NT*	507 451	Prince Patrick, NWT	15 848
Victoria, NT*	217 291	King William, NT*	13 111
Ellesmere, NT*	196 236	Ellef Ringnes, NT*	11 295
Newfoundland (main island)	108 860	Bylot, NT*	11 067
Banks, NWT	70 028	Cape Breton, N.S.	10 311
Devon, NT*	55 247	Prince Charles, NT*	9 521
Axel Heiberg, NT*	43 178	Anticosti Island, Que.	7 941
Melville, NT*	42 149	Cornwallis, NT*	6 995
Southampton, NT*	41 214	Graham, BC	6 361
Prince of Wales, NT*	33 339	Prince Edward Island (main island)	5 620
Vancouver, BC	31 285	Coats, NT*	5 498
Somerset, NT*	24 786	Amund Ringnes, NT*	5 255
Bathurst, NT*	16 042		

Source: *Natural Resources Canada*

*Nunavut

Canada's Highest Waterfalls

Name	Vertical drop (metres)	Location	Latitude	Longitude
Della Falls[1]	440	Della Lake, BC	49° 27'	125° 32'
Takakkaw Falls[1]	254	From the Daly Glacier, BC	51° 30'	116° 28'
Hunlen Falls	253	Atnarko River, BC	52° 17'	125° 46'
Panther Falls	183	Nigel Creek, Alta	52° 10'	117° 03'
Helmcken Falls	137	Murtle River, BC	51° 57'	120° 11'
Bridal Veil Falls	122	Bridal Creek, BC	49° 11'	121° 44'
Virginia Falls	90	South Nahanni River, NWT	61° 36'	125° 44'
Montmorency, Chute	84	Rivière Montmorency, Que.	46° 53'	71° 09'
Ouiatchouan, Chute	79	Rivière Ouiatchouaniche, Que.	48° 26'	72° 10'
Churchill Falls	75	Churchill River, Nfld	53° 36'	64° 19'

Source: *Natural Resources Canada*   (1) Falls with more than one leap

Longest Rivers in Canada

River	Length (km)	Flows Into
Mackenzie	4 241	Arctic Ocean
Yukon	3 185	Bering Sea
St. Lawrence	3 058	Gulf of St. Lawrence
Nelson	2 575	Hudson Bay
Columbia	2 000	Pacific Ocean
Saskatchewan	1 939	Lake Winnipeg (via Cedar Lake)
Peace	1 923	Lake Athabasca
Churchill (Man.)	1 609	Hudson Bay
South Saskatchewan	1 392	Saskatchewan R.
Fraser	1 370	Pacific Ocean

River	Length (km)	Flows Into
North Saskatchewan	1 287	Saskatchewan R.
Ottawa	1 271	St Lawrence R.
Athabasca	1 231	Lake Athabasca
Liard	1 115	Mackenzie R.
Assiniboine	1 070	Red R.
Severn	982	Hudson Bay
Albany	982	James Bay
Back	974	Arctic Ocean
Thelon	904	Hudson Bay
La Grande Rivière	893	James Bay

Source: *Natural Resources Canada*

Highest Peaks in Canada

Mountain	Range	Prov./Terr.	Elev. (m)
Mt. Logan	St. Elias Mtns	YT	5 959
Mt. St. Elias	St. Elias Mtns	YT/Alaska	5 489
Mt. Lucania	St. Elias Mtns	YT	5 226
King Peak	St. Elias Mtns	YT	5 173
Mt. Steele	St. Elias Mtns	YT	5 067
Mt. Wood	St. Elias Mtns	YT	4 838
Mt. Vancouver	St. Elias Mtns	YT/Alaska	4 785
Mt. Macaulay	St. Elias Mtns	YT	4 663
Mt. Slaggard	St. Elias Mtns	YT	4 663
Fairweather Mtn.	St. Elias Mtns	BC/Alaska	4 663

Mountain	Range	Prov./Terr.	Elev. (m)
Mt. Cook	St. Elias Mtns	YT/Alaska	4 194
Mt. Hubbard	St. Elias Mtns	YT/Alaska	4 577
Mt. Walsh	St. Elias Mtns	YT	4 505
Mt. Alverstone	St. Elias Mtns	YT/Alaska	4 439
McArthur Peak	St. Elias Mtns	YT	4 344
Mt. Augusta	St. Elias Mtns	YT/Alaska	4 289
Mt. Kennedy	St. Elias Mtns	YT	4 235
Avalanche Peak	St. Elias Mtns	YT	4 212
Mt. Strickland	St. Elias Mtns	YT	4 212
Mt. Newton	St. Elias Mtns	YT	4 210

Source: *Natural Resources Canada*

VEGETATION

Coniferous forests dominated by spruce, fir and pine cover much of the Canadian landscape, sweeping across the continent in a broad band. Through the rest of the country there is a range of forest conditions. To the north, cold temperatures limit growth and the trees become small and fewer in number. At the tree line, trees grow only in sheltered river valleys. The tree line marks the northern extent of forests and the beginning of tundra conditions (moss, lichens and dwarf vegetation with permanent frozen subsoil).

The massive spruce, fir and pine of the forests along the coast of British Columbia are encouraged by a friendly climate. The moisture-laden winds from the Pacific Ocean keep the land well-supplied with rain. Under these conditions tree growth is rapid: the soils are constantly being replenished with minerals by the rains, and plant decay is also rapid in the damp conditions, thereby releasing more minerals for tree growth. With average monthly temperatures seldom going below freezing, the growing season is long. Coniferous trees thrive under such conditions.

The Interior Plains is one region of Canada that is not covered by forests because there is not enough precipitation, or available moisture, to sustain tree growth. In Alberta, Saskatchewan and Manitoba, forests gradually give way from north to south through a transitional area called the park belt, which contains both trees and grassland, before yielding to grasslands. Within these provinces, there are areas where moisture levels are insufficient to support grasslands and even hardy grasses have difficulty growing. During the 1930s, the lack of rainfall in the Interior Plains led to "dust bowl" conditions because vegetation could not grow enough to anchor the soil.

The forests of southeastern Canada are mixed, containing both coniferous and deciduous trees. Adequate rainfall and warm temperatures allow the less hardy species such as oak, maple, hickory and walnut to flourish in southern Ontario and Quebec and the Maritime provinces.

The Arctic tundra is so very dry and cold that the growing season is extremely limited. The vegetation of the tundra consists of mosses, lichen, dwarf bushes and heather. These plants are able to grow because they have adapted to the difficult conditions through characteristics such as small size and slow growth. Some shrubs and lichen grow so slowly that their development must be measured in centimetres per century.

AGRICULTURE

There are four main types of farms in Canada: livestock farms, grain farms producing such crops as wheat and oats, mixed farms producing both grain and livestock, and special crop farms producing vegetables, fruits, tobacco and other products. Both the type and amount of farming within Canada are affected by climate and location.

■ The Atlantic Region

The Atlantic region is an area of diverse agricultural activity. Newfoundland, because of poorly developed soils and a difficult climate, has a limited agricultural industry supplying only local markets. Encouraged by a moist climate and silty, stone-free soils, farming is the leading industry on Prince Edward Island; potatoes are the main crop. The land also supports mixed grains and dairy farms.

Nova Scotia's main agricultural areas surround the Bay of Fundy and Northumberland Strait where they are protected from Atlantic gales; dairy farming and poultry production are common. Nova Scotia's Annapolis Valley is famous for fruit, mainly apples. In New Brunswick, potatoes and livestock are produced in the Saint John River valley, and there is mixed farming in the northwest of the province.

■ The Central Region

In Canada's central region, the fertile soils and moist climate of southern Ontario and Quebec support a thriving agricultural industry. Although these growing conditions allow a variety of crops, the population concentration in this area encourages specialization in products with high transportation costs. Dairy farms are concentrated around Montreal and in southwestern Ontario, supplying milk, butter and cheese to the major centres such as London, Hamilton, Toronto, Kingston, ▶

Montreal and Quebec City. Vegetable crops are also grown near these centres. Farms specializing in poultry and egg production, sheep and hogs are also common.

The Niagara Peninsula, between Lakes Ontario and Erie, is a major fruit-growing centre. The moderating effects of the lakes delay the growth of the fruit trees in the spring until the danger of frost is past. Tender fruit crops—peaches, pears, plums and cherries—as well as grapes thrive in these conditions. Tobacco (and now ginseng) grow well on the glacially-created sand plains of southwestern Ontario.

■ The Prairie Provinces

Manitoba, Saskatchewan and Alberta contain 80 percent of Canada's farmland. Here, a combination of flat, easily-worked land, fertile soils, long sunny summer days and sufficient precipitation encourages the healthy growth of high-quality grains. This area grows most of Canada's wheat, about 90 percent of its barley and rye, and more than 75 percent of its oats.

Manitoba grows canola and flax in addition to wheat and other grains. Mixed farming in the province emphasizes beef cattle. Dairy farms are common around Winnipeg. Saskatchewan grows about 60 percent of Canada's wheat and large quantities of other grains. Mixed farming, poultry, egg and livestock production contribute to the provincial economy. Alberta, also a major grain producer, has more beef cattle ranches than any other province. They are located mainly in the south of the province and in the foothills of the Rocky Mountains where the steep slopes and dry land is unsuited to growing crops.

■ The Pacific Region

In the Pacific region, only 2 percent of British Columbia is agricultural land. But the pockets of farmland are extremely productive. The lower mainland and the southern tip of Vancouver Island comprise the Georgia Strait agricultural region, an area concentrating on dairy farming and poultry raising to supply the province's population centres. Other crops include raspberries, strawberries, peas, tomatoes and flowers.

The Okanagan Valley contains 90 percent of British Columbia's orchards, producing grapes, apples and tender fruit such as peaches, plums, apricots and cherries. Here, local climatic and physiographic characteristics have resulted in conditions suitable for the orchard industry, although irrigation is often necessary and frost damage is a hazard. Beef cattle and sheep are raised in the interior of the province, where growing conditions are not suitable for crops requiring cultivation, but grazing can be carried out.

■ The North

Canada's North generally has soil and climatic conditions unsuited to agriculture. A small number of farms produce some dairy products, beef cattle and vegetables for the local market.

Canadian Rural Partnership

*I*n 1998, the federal government, through Agriculture and Agri-Food Canada, committed $20 million over four years for the Canadian Rural Partnership. The program is concerned with fostering cooperative approaches and practices that will help solve rural development issues.

In the first phase, May to July 31, 1998, rural issues were identified through consultation with individuals and groups—close to 7,000 rural Canadians took part. The responses were analysed and presented at the National Rural Workshop in Belleville, Ontario, held Oct. 2 to 4, 1998. Participants identified 11 priorities for the government to consider in developing a long-term, flexible policy for rural and remote communities. The Federal Framework for Action in Rural Canada, announced May 14, 1999 is the result of that process. (The next National Rural Conference will be in Magog-Orford, Quebec, April 28-30, 2000.)

A copy of the long-term policy is posted for review at the web site for the Canadian Rural Partnership: http://www.rural.gc.ca Copies can also be obtained by contacting the Canadian Rural Information Service at the Canadian Agriculture Library, Sir John Carling Building, 930 Carling Avenue, ON K1A 0C5 Toll free: 1-888-757-8725 or fax: 613-759-6763 The web site gives participants an overview of program initiatives to date and pages such as "Rural Canadians on the Internet" encourage an exchange of ideas among rural people across the country.

CLIMATE

Within Canada, climate is primarily affected by surrounding landforms, proximity to large bodies of water and the degree of latitude.

Landforms Air masses are forced to rise over mountains which lie in their path. As this happens, the air cools and its ability to retain moisture is reduced. Condensation then occurs and precipitation falls in the form of snow or rain. For instance, Prince Rupert on the western side (windward) of the Coastal Mountains receives over 2,500 mm of precipitation annually.

On the leeward side of the mountains (the side away from the wind), the air mass descends, warms and is able to once again retain moisture. Moreover, there may be little moisture left in the air mass. Thus precipitation is light and a rain-shadow effect is created. In a rain-shadow area, such as near Kamloops, BC, desert-like conditions exist.

Water Parts of Canada near large bodies of water have more moderate climates due to the differing abilities of land and water to gain or lose heat. Whereas water can act like a heat bank, releasing accumulated heat through the fall and early winter and warming the land nearby, the reverse is also true. In the spring and early summer, the water is cooler than the land and can keep the land temperature lower. [*see also*: Ocean Currents, p.11.]

Wind direction also determines the degree to which this influence is felt. On the Pacific coast the prevailing westerlies blow off the water onto the land and the influence of the Pacific Ocean is keenly felt. On the Atlantic coast, the westerlies blow off the land onto the water so the effect of the Atlantic Ocean is not as pronounced. Victoria's lowest monthly average temperature is 4.6°C in Jan. with an annual range of only 11°C between the warmest and coldest months while Halifax's lowest monthly average is -4.8°C in Feb. with an annual range of 22.7°C.

Latitude Latitude is the distance north or south of the equator and is expressed in degrees. Its effects on climate are twofold. Firstly, the further north the location, the more the curvature of the earth results in the sunlight spreading over a greater surface area. This decreases the solar radiation per unit area of ground so that less warmth from the sun is felt. Secondly, solar radiation has to travel a greater distance through the atmosphere at higher latitudes which again reduces the amount of energy reaching the earth.

Other Factors Because the prevailing wind direction is from west to east, the air masses move eastward across the continent picking up moisture from lakes and rivers and releasing it further along. Therefore, generally, precipitation increases with greater distance eastward from the central continent: the average precipitation in Winnipeg is 504 mm, Toronto 781 mm, Montreal 940 mm and Halifax 1 474 mm.

Also, the Labrador Current affects climate on the Atlantic coast. This cold current within the Atlantic Ocean flows south along the coast of Newfoundland and Labrador and reduces the moderating effect of the ocean on the land. It also causes the thick Newfoundland fog when relatively warm air is cooled from below on contact with the cold waters.

Where did the word "meteorology" come from?

*W*hy is the study of weather called meteorology—when a meteor is a mass from outer space? The term goes back to the Greek philosopher Aristotle, who wrote a book on natural philosophy around 350 BC entitled Meteorologica. The Greek word "meteor" meant all substances that fell from the sky or anything seen in the air. Hence, the study of anything "in the sky" was referred to as meteorology.

Aristotle included a wide range of natural phenomena in his study—anything that had its location below the level of the stars. The natural phenomena he classified as meteors included shooting stars, aurora borealis, comets, and the Milky Way, as well as familiar atmospheric phenomena such as clouds, winds, rainbow, thunder and rain. Even surface features like earthquakes, rivers and the oceans were considered meteors.

Nowadays, meteorology is the science of the atmosphere and its phenomena—not nearly as broad in its scope as ancient peoples thought. The domain of the meteorologist ends at the upper limit of the earth's atmosphere, about 60 to 80 km up. The space beyond with its constellations, meteors and shooting stars comes under the jurisdiction of the astronomer.

Average Weather Data for Selected Airports in Canada

| | Temperature °C | | | | Precipitation | |
| | Winter | | Summer | | Annual Snowfall cm | Total Precipitation mm |
Airport	High	Low	High	Low		
Vancouver	5.7	0.1	21.7	12.7	55	1 167
Calgary	-3.6	-15.7	23.2	9.5	135	399
Edmonton	-8.7	-19.8	22.5	9.4	127	466
Regina	-11.0	-22.1	26.3	11.9	107	364
Winnipeg	-13.2	-23.6	26.1	13.4	115	504
Toronto	-2.5	-11.1	26.8	14.2	124	781
Ottawa	-6.3	-15.5	26.4	15.1	222	911
Montreal	-5.8	-14.9	26.2	15.4	214	940
Saint John	-2.8	-13.6	22.1	11.6	283	1 433
Halifax	-1.5	-10.3	23.4	13.2	261	1 474
Charlottetown	-3.4	-12.2	23.1	13.6	339	1 201
St. John's	-0.7	-7.9	20.2	10.5	322	1 482
Iqaluit	-21.5	-30.0	11.6	3.7	257	424
Yellowknife	-23.9	-32.2	20.8	12.0	144	267
Whitehorse	-14.4	-23.2	20.3	7.6	145	269

| | Wind | | | Sunshine | |
Airport	Average Speed km/hr	Prevailing Direction	Peak Wind km/hr	Bright Sunshine hours	Possible Sunshine hours
Vancouver	12	E	129	1 919	4 475
Calgary	16	N	127	2 395	4 483
Edmonton	13	S	146	2 303	4 488
Regina	20	SE	153	2 365	4 483
Winnipeg	18	S	129	2 377	4 482
Toronto	15	W	135	2 038	4 464
Ottawa	14	W	135	2 054	4 469
Montreal	15	W	161	2 015	4 465
Saint John	18	S	146	1 894	4 452
Halifax	18	S	132	1 949	4 488
Charlottetown	19	W	177	1 844	4 467
St. John's	24	W	193	1 527	4 470
Iqaluit	16	NW	141	1 508	4 563
Yellowknife	15	E	113	2 277	4 546
Whitehorse	14	S	106	1 852	4 523

| | Annual Number of Days | | | | | | |
Airport	Frost	Wet Weather	Thunder-storms	Freezing Precipitation	Smoke/ Haze	Blowing Snow	Fog
Vancouver	55	164	6	1	120	—	34
Calgary	201	111	25	6	22	9	22
Edmonton	210	122	25	8	16	7	18
Regina	204	109	23	14	3	28	28
Winnipeg	195	119	28	13	20	24	17
Toronto	165	141	28	10	104	9	34
Ottawa	165	159	24	17	80	13	36
Montreal	156	162	26	13	75	12	18
Saint John	173	164	11	12	22	13	102
Halifax	163	170	10	16	17	14	122
Charlottetown	169	177	9	17	20	26	47
St. John's	176	217	4	38	19	27	121
Iqaluit	273	152	<1	5	<1	61	15
Yellowknife	226	118	6	11	6	9	19
Whitehorse	224	122	6	2	1	3	15

Source: *Environment Canada*

Ocean Currents

Oceans or large bodies of water like the Great Lakes affect the climate of the land nearby because they act as heat reservoirs and heat exchangers. Water heats up more slowly than land, and it holds that heat for a longer time. Because of this, the climate in the areas closest to water is more moderate than the climate inland: even though the air over the coastal land is warmer in summer and colder in winter than the air over water at the same latitude, it won't be as hot (or as cold) as the air over land that is far away from the coast.

These water bodies also affect rainfall, wind and clouds: when the water is warmer than the air above it, it generates clouds, rain and wind; when the water is colder than the air above, the opposite happens—there is likely to be fog, less rain, and winds are reduced.

As the ocean currents move heat and cold around the world, Canada is affected by the warm Gulf Stream on the Atlantic coast and the weaker but still warm Alaska Current on the Pacific side; both of these flow northward. Cold currents like the West Greenland Current and the Labrador Current flow south from the Arctic on the east side; the banks of fog off the southeast coast of Newfoundland mark the spot where the Labrador Current meets the Gulf Stream. In general though, because our weather flows from west to east, it is the currents on the Pacific side that have the most effect on Canada's climate.

Inland, the Great Lakes and Hudson Bay are two vast areas of water that affect the climate around them: the Great Lakes act as a huge heat reservoir that moderates the weather in southern Ontario and Quebec, while Hudson Bay is frozen over for six months, and even during the summer months melting ice keeps the surface water temperature close to freezing. Hudson Bay's most common effect is fog in summer and precipitation, cloud and strong winds during the rest of the year.

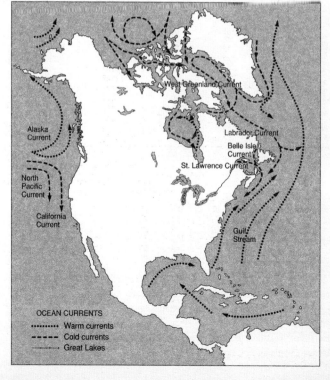

West Greenland Current

Alaska Current

Labrador Current

Belle Isle Current

St. Lawrence Current

North Pacific Current

California Current

Gulf Stream

OCEAN CURRENTS
.... Warm currents
- - - - - Cold currents
———— Great Lakes

SUMMER AIR MASSES AND CIRCULATION

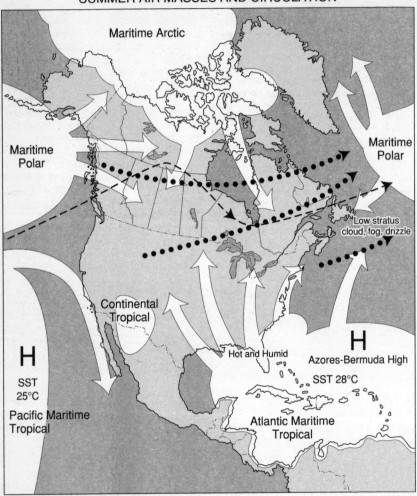

Maritime Arctic

Maritime Polar

Maritime Polar

Low stratus cloud, fog, drizzle

Continental Tropical

H

SST 25°C

Pacific Maritime Tropical

H

Hot and Humid

Azores-Bermuda High

SST 28°C

Atlantic Maritime Tropical

– – – – Polar jet stream

•••• Primary storm tracks

SST   Sea Surface Temperature

Pacific Maritime Tropical: high pressure precludes moist air
Atlantic Maritime Tropical: very hot, humid, unstable
Maritime Arctic: modified by water
Maritime Polar: warmer, more stable than Maritime Arctic air
Continental Tropical: hot, dry, unstable

WINTER AIR MASSES AND CIRCULATION

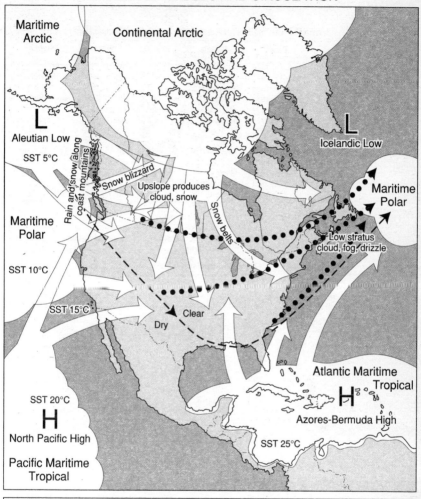

- – – – Polar jet stream
- •••• Primary storm tracks
- SST   Sea Surface Temperature

Continental Arctic: very cold, dry, stable
Maritime Arctic: very unstable, clouds, frequent showers or flurries
Maritime Polar: milder, more stable than Arctic air
Pacific Maritime Tropical: stable in lower 1000m
Atlantic Maritime Tropical: warm and humid

Provincial Weather Facts

Province	Warmest Temperature Ever Recorded			Coldest Temperature Ever Recorded		
	°C	Date	Station	°C	Date	Station
Newfoundland ...	41.7	Aug. 11, 1914	Northwest River	-51.1	Feb. 17, 1973	Esker 2
P.E.I.	36.7	Aug. 19, 1935	Charlottetown	-37.2	Jan. 26, 1884	Kilmahumaig
New Brunswick ..	39.4	Aug. 18, 1935	Nepisiguit Falls	-47.2	Feb. 2, 1955	Sisson Dam
Nova Scotia	38.3	Aug. 19, 1935	Collegeville	-41.1	Jan. 31, 1920	Upper Stewiacke
Quebec	40.0	July 6, 1921	Ville Marie	-54.4	Feb. 5, 1923	Doucet
Ontario	42.2	July 20, 1919	Biscotasing	-58.3	Jan. 23, 1935	Iroquois Falls
Manitoba	44.4	July 11, 1936	St. Albans	-52.8	Jan. 9, 1899	Norway House
Saskatchewan ...	45.0	July 5, 1937	Midale	-56.7	Feb. 1, 1893	Prince Albert
Alberta	43.3	July 21, 1931	Bassano Dam	-61.1	Jan. 11, 1911	Fort Vermilion
British Columbia .	44.4	July 16, 1941	Lillooet	-58.9	Jan. 31, 1947	Smith River
Yukon Territory ..	36.1	June 14, 1969	Mayo	-63.0	Feb. 3, 1947	Snag
Northwest Territories..	39.4	July 18, 1941	Fort Smith	-57.2	Dec. 26, 1917	Fort Smith
Nunavut	33.9	July 22, 1973	Arviat	-57.8	Feb. 13, 1973	Shepherd Bay

Source: *Environment Canada*

Province	Warmest Annual Temperature On Average		Coldest Annual Temperature On Average	
	°C	Station	°C	Station
Newfoundland	6.3	Holyrood Ultramar	-3.8	Wabush Lake A
Prince Edward Island	5.9	Charlottetown CDA	4.8	O'Leary
New Brunswick	6.2	St. Andrews	1.6	Upsalquitch Lake
Nova Scotia	7.6	Sable Island	4.9	Trafalgar
Quebec	7.6	Montreal Lafontaine	-7.2	Koartak
Ontario	9.7	Windsor University	-5.5	Winisk A
Manitoba	3.3	Morden CDA	-7.2	Churchill A
Saskatchewan	5.0	Maple Creek North	-4.6	Collins Bay
Alberta	5.9	Bow Island Rivers	-2.7	Fort Chipewyan A
British Columbia	10.7	Sumas Canal	-3.2	Cassiar Yukon
Yukon Territory	-1.0	Whitehorse Riverdale	-11.4	Komakuk Beach A
Northwest Territories.............	-2.2	Fort Liard	-12.4	Cape Parry
Nunavut	-6.4	Resolution Island	-19.7	Eureka

Source: *Environment Canada*

Average Annual Bright Sunshine

Province	Greatest		Least	
	hrs	Station	hrs	Station
Newfoundland	1 572	Churchill Falls A	1 303	St. Shotts
Prince Edward Island	1 967	Tignish	1 817	East Baltic
New Brunswick	2 010	Chatham A	1 373	Summit Depot
Nova Scotia	1 969	Shearwater A	1 449	Sable Island
Quebec	2 054	Montreal Int'l. A	1 158	Mont Logan
Ontario	2 203	Thunder Bay A	1 635	New Liskeard
Manitoba	2 460	Delta U	1 828	Churchill A
Saskatchewan	2 537	Estevan A	2 073	Cree Lake
Alberta	2 490	Coronation A	1 724	Banff
British Columbia	2 244	Cranbrook A	949	Stewart A
Yukon Territory	1 844	Whitehorse A	1 789	Watson Lake A
Northwest Territories	2 277	Yellowknife A	1 899	Inuvik
Nunavut	2 091	Eureka	1 443	Mould Bay A

Source: *Environment Canada*

Average Annual Precipitation

Province	Greatest		Least	
	mm	Station	mm	Station
Newfoundland	1 699.7	Burgeo	739.8	Nain
Prince Edward Island	1 169.4	Charlottetown A	921.0	Montague
New Brunswick	1 444.4	Saint John A	909.6	Upsalquitch Lake
Nova Scotia	1 630.7	Ingonish Beach	973.7	Pugwash
Quebec	1 559.8	Mont Logan	295.9	Cape Hopes Advance
Ontario	1 191.1	West Guilford	569.0	Kenora TCPL
Manitoba	696.1	Peace Gardens	402.3	Churchill A
Saskatchewan	530.1	Brabant Lake	287.9	Nashlyn
Alberta	1 072.0	Waterton Park HQ	270.8	Empress
British Columbia	6 655.0	Henderson Lake	205.6	Ashcroft
Yukon Territory	590.6	Tuchitua	135.9	Komakuk Beach A
Northwest Territories	663.2	Cape Dyer A	137.6	Tuktoyaktuk
Nunavut	355.1	Fort Simpson	61.0	Rea Point

Source: *Environment Canada*

Average Annual Snowfall

Province	Greatest		Least	
	cm	Station	cm	Station
Newfoundland	322.8	Woody Point	91.6	St. Shotts
Prince Edward Island	330.6	Charlottetown A	173.3	Montague
New Brunswick	448.8	Dawson Settlement	176.2	Southwest Head
Nova Scotia	406.7	Cheticamp	104.1	Baccaro
Quebec	648.4	Mont Logan	161.6	Havre aux Maisons
Ontario	430.0	Searchmount	74.0	Lakeview MOE
Manitoba	332.7	Island Lake	94.9	Lundar
Saskatchewan	348.6	Collins Bay	58.0	Aylesbury
Alberta	642.9	Columbia Icefield	59.9	Empress
British Columbia	1 433.0	Glacier NP Mt. Fidelity	20.4	Carnation Creek
Yukon Territory	365.7	Keno Hill	60.1	Komakuk Beach A
Northwest Territories.	234.5	Fort McPherson	65.2	Tuktoyaktuk
Nunavut	602.4	Cape Dyer A	28.6	Rea Point

Source: *Environment Canada*

Greatest Snow on the Ground Any Month

Province	Depth (cm)	Station	Province	Depth (cm)	Station
Newfoundland	313	Hopedale	Manitoba	175	Glenlea
Prince Edward Island . . .	156	Charlottetown	Saskatchewan	224	Hudson Bay
New Brunswick	252	Harvey Station	Alberta	179	Parker Ridge
Nova Scotia	183	Nappan	British Columbia	450	Whistler Roundhouse
Quebec	259	Blanc-Sablon	Yukon Territory	149	Hour Lake
Ontario	219	Gravenhurst	Northwest Territories	206	Fort Good Hope
			Nunavut	241	Cape Dyer

Source: *Environment Canada*

What is a severe thunderstorm?

*E*nvironment Canada classes a thunderstorm as severe when one or more of the following occurs: wind gusts of 90 km/h or more; hail of two cm in diameter or larger; rainfall of 50 mm or more within one hour or 75 mm or more within three hours.

*   When the weather service issues a severe thunderstorm watch conditions are favourable for severe storm development. A severe thunderstorm warning means the storms are highly probable.

Wind

Province	Highest Wind Speed		Highest % of Calms	
	km/hr	Station	%	Station
Newfoundland	28.0 (W)	Bonavista	17.1	Wabush Lake A
Prince Edward Island	22.4 (SSW)	Summerside A	4.4	Summerside A
New Brunswick	22.4 (W)	Miscou Island (AUT)	11.8	Fredericton A
Nova Scotia	25.7 (W)	Sable Island	16.9	Greenwood A
Quebec	32.0 (NW)	Grindstone Island	20.4	Gaspé A
Ontario	21.0 (SW)	Bruce Ontario Hydro	30.2	White River
Manitoba	22.7 (WNW)	Churchill A	21.0	Norway House A
Saskatchewan	22.9 (W)	Swift Current A	12.8	La Ronge A
Alberta	21.5 (W)	Pincher Creek	39.7	High Level A
British Columbia	33.7 (NW)	Cape St. James	48.5	Quesnel A
Yukon Territory	14.1 (SSE)	Whitehorse A	57.5	Dawson A
Northwest Territories	19.9 (E)	Nicholson Peninsula	18.9	Fort Simpson
Nunavut	35.3 (NW)	Resolution Island	35.1	Eureka

Source: *Environment Canada*

"Coldest Days" (Wind Chill)

Province	ET/WCF[1]	Location	Date	Temp (°C)	Wind (km/hr)
Newfoundland	-71/2814	Wabush Lake	Jan. 20, 1975	-41	40
Prince Edward Island	-57/2450	Charlottetown	Jan. 18, 1982	-32	37
Nova Scotia	-53/2309	Sydney	Jan. 18, 1982	-25	59
New Brunswick	-61/2547	Charlo	Jan. 18, 1982	-31	54
Quebec	-77/3001	Nitchequon	Jan. 20, 1975	-42	56
Ontario	-70/2753	Thunder Bay	Jan. 10, 1982	-36	54
Manitoba	-76/2938	Churchill	Jan. 18, 1975	-41	56
Saskatchewan	-70/2757	Swift Current	Dec. 15, 1964	-34	89
Alberta	-68/2740	Red Deer	Dec. 15, 1964	-35	61
British Columbia	-69/2749	Old Glory Mtn.	Dec. 15, 1964	-36	58
Yukon Territory	-83/3152	Komakuk Beach	Feb. 12, 1975	-50	40
NWT/Nunavut	-92/3357	Pelly Bay	Jan. 13, 1975	-51	56

Source: *Environment Canada*

(1) ET is equivalent wind chill temperature in °C. WCF is wind chill factor in watts/square metre

Weather Summaries for 1998-1999

JULY 1998: The average temperature across Canada in July was 15°C. This was the highest, nation-wide average in over a half-century of records. Every province and both territories experienced 30°C at some time during the month. The hot spot was Osoyoos, BC with a high of 42.8°C on July 27. Vancouver's high on the 28th was 32°C—only the second time the city has ever reached that mark. High humidity and surplus heat fuelled an active summer severe weather season, especially in Ontario and the western Prairies. Calgary saw thunderstorms on 8 of the first 10 days in July, with a record 43 mm of rain falling in six hours on July 4, breaking one set in 1909. On the 5th much of the city was flooded by heavy rain and golfball-size hail.

For the second consecutive year, farmers in NS's Annapolis Valley faced a drought. Farmers accustomed to 80 to 90 mm of monthly rain had to make do with as little as 5 to 10 mm.

AUGUST 1998: It was another month of warm, dry weather. By month end, Canada had recorded its warmest summer since records began in 1948.

The high temperatures and low rainfall created potential for major forest fires in the west, particularly east of Kamloops. At Salmon Arm, out-of-control fires forced the evacuation of over 7,000. Each region had bouts of violent summer weather. Mid-month, thunderstorm winds downed trees on an Edmonton golf course, killing one woman. One storm cell struck Saskatoon dumping as much as 70 mm of rain. On the 24th, there were reports of hail—ranging in size from walnut to tennis ball—in an area from Cobourg to just north of Kingston ON. Many orchards along the NE shore of Lake Ontario were hard hit, some having their entire crop destroyed.

SEPTEMBER 1998: For the third month, a new average national high temperature was set. Dry weather also persisted across most of the country. The only areas with any significant moisture were northern Ontario, where over 120 mm of rain fell, and NFLD which received close to 200 mm. Forest fires continued unabated across BC and the northern Prairies. More than $700 million was spent extinguishing forest fires—twice the normal cost.

OCTOBER 1998: October was also warmer than usual across Canada. Along the Pacific coast and in the Maritimes, several locations received ample rainfall, however, in southern ON most communities received less than 40 mm, and several had only 20, about a quarter to a third of normal amount. For the Great Lakes-St. Lawrence basin, the previous 12 months were the third driest in 51 years, 12.4% below normal. Lake Superior had its lowest water level in 73 years. In some inland waterways, such as the Grand River in southern ON, water levels sank to their lowest in nearly 40 years.

In SK one of the worst fall snowstorms on record dumped 25 to 70 cm across southern and central districts at Thanksgiving. Prince Albert took the worst hit with 42 cm, a new one-day snowfall record. In Saskatoon, snow-laden trees collapsed onto power lines, knocking out electricity to 30,000 homes.

NOVEMBER 1998: The national average temperature for Sept., Oct. and Nov. was 2.3° above normal. El Niño's residual heat remained; in the Arctic, the ocean was slow to freeze over. Ice concentration in the Western Arctic remained at a record-breaking minimum. On November 30, Ottawa, ON reached 16.4°, and in St. Catharines 18.9°—15 degrees above normal.

On the west coast, storms pushed rainfall totals well over 200 mm and strong winds caused blackouts and disrupted ferry sailings. A November 23 storm left about 200,000 without power; on the 24th winds measured 85 km/h with gusts of 102 km/h—the most severe wind storm to hit the area according to BC Hydro. Several intense storms raced across the Great Lakes in Nov. The storm on the 10th-11th bore a remarkable resemblance to the storm that hit Lake Superior on the same day and path in 1975 and downed the *Edmund Fitzgerald* ore carrier.

DECEMBER 1998: For the first half of the month, very mild weather prevailed. Temperatures were generally 8 to 10° above normal. In southern AB, daytime highs hit the mid-teens; near the lower Great Lakes they reached the upper teens. As Christmas week began, overnight lows from AB to northern ON plunged below -30° and -10° eastward. Even SW BC had temperatures several degrees below the freezing mark.

The first significant snowfalls came with the colder weather. On the 18th, blowing snow caused traffic accidents in AB, and the storm dumped another 25 cm in MB. As the cold air moved SE across the Great Lakes, snow squalls resulted in the closure of a 250-km stretch of the Trans-Canada Highway near Sault Ste. Marie. Atlantic Canada received as much as 25 cm across southern NB and eastern NS.

Overall, snowfall was scanty. By mid-Dec., Montreal and Ottawa, two of the snowiest cities in the world, had snowfall totals to Dec. 16 of a trace amount and 1.6 cm, respectively, compared to a normal of 55 cm.

JANUARY 1999: Across most of Canada, mean temperatures were within a degree of normal. In Whitehorse, the temperature fell to -40° for two days and visibility was about one block due to thick ice fog. In central YT, the temperature was -53° and falling. Above-normal amounts of snow fell from AB to the Atlantic. On Jan. 1, an avalanche swept down onto Kangiqsualujjuaq, a village 1,500 km north of Montreal, killing nine and injuring 25.

On Jan. 2, very heavy snow spread across the lower Great Lakes. During the first half of Jan., several small storms hit the Toronto area. On the 13th and 14th, lake-enhanced snows of 25 cm or more fell along the north shore of Lake Ontario. By storm's end, Toronto had 65 cm of snow on the ground—more than any time since the late-1800s. Montreal also set an all-time monthly record snowfall total for Jan.: 95.1 cm. A week later, mild weather and rain moved into southern ON.

FEBRUARY 1999: From eastern BC to the Atlantic, mean temperatures were 3 to 5° or more above normal, and as much as 6 to 8° above normal from SE MB to the south-central Arctic. Several storms slammed into the Pacific coast. A storm on the 11th stalled near the

Alaska panhandle. A southerly flow of mild air overran a shallow layer of Arctic air resulting in enormous snowfalls in the Terrace-Kitimat area. Tahtsa Lake West, located about 120 km SSE of Terrace, broke the record for the greatest one-day snowfall in Canada: 145 cm. The two-day total was 210 cm.

In ON, several communities experienced temperatures in the teens mid-month, only to plunge back into winter. In the transition, severe thunderstorm watches were issued north of Lake Superior while a flash freeze warning was in effect. Southern BC experienced its windiest, wettest, and dullest winter in about two decades. Local ski resorts reported near-record snowpacks; Seymour had more than 500 cm.

MARCH 1999: Milder than normal temperatures were the norm with the greatest anomalies along the Nunavut-NWT border-to-be. The Atlantic and Pacific coasts and BC interior were wetter than normal; elsewhere was unseasonably dry. On Mar. 4 a winter storm with vicious winds and drifting snow hit southern ON; about 400 truckers spent the night snowbound on the 401 between Trenton and Kingston. An intense winter storm battered Atlantic Canada on Mar. 7-8. Moncton recorded a record one-day snowfall of 65 cm with two-metre deep snowdrifts and zero visibility. In NS, the province had up to 40 cm of snow and bouts of rain, freezing rain and fog.

Residents of BC's lower mainland had another stormy, wet dreary month. From Nov. to Mar. in Vancouver, there were 18 days when gusts reached or exceeded 60 km/h; the city had a record high 116 wet days and the fewest sunshine total (297 hours).

APRIL 1999: Most of Canada experienced warmer than normal temperatures, and anomalies were as much as 3 to 7 degrees above normal across the northern Prairies. Generally, conditions were drier than normal in the east. St. John's was an exception with 285 mm of precipitation—more than twice the normal level.

For the 17th month in a row, locations in southern ON reported warmer than normal temperatures—causing concern in sectors from farming to forestry. Spring precipitation to the end of April was 40 to 60% of normal in ON.

Two winter storms over the Easter weekend spread a heavy snow cover across parts of southern SK and MB raising fears of flooding. In Winnipeg, officials raised the gates of the Red River Floodway to divert riverflow around the city. Also on the Easter weekend an intense winter storm with high winds and heavy snow caused major power outages in NS. That same storm slammed into St. John's dumping a record one-day snowfall of 69 cm and a total storm total of 80 cm over 16 hours.

MAY 1999: Central ON to NFLD was warmer and drier than normal. In the west, the weather was colder than normal in BC and AB and much wetter, especially in SK and MB. At Brandon 200 mm of rain fell, more than a half a year's total.

May 2 saw the first heat wave and smog alert from Windsor to Ottawa and Sudbury. Forest fire crews were busy in northern ON around the community of Beardmore and Bearskin and in inter-lake communities in MB. A tornado ripped through Hull on May 8, causing an estimated $2 million in damages, and sending six people to hospital. On the 18th, three tornadoes touched down west of Saskatoon. The city was lashed by a spectacular lightning storm with heavy rain, 95-km hour winds and marble-sized hail. Many in the eastern prairies received up to four times the normal amount of rain, delaying seeding. Fields in SE SK and SW MB were submerged, roads washed out and basements took in water. Meanwhile, farmers in southern ON, QC and the Maritimes were talking drought. The Great Lakes recorded the lowest water levels since the mid-1960s. In the Port of Montreal, water levels were nearly two metres below average, forcing shipping companies to reduce loads.

Visit http://www.ec.gc.ca — The Green Lane

*E**nvironment Canada offers a wealth of information here in both official languages. Browsers can access weather and environmental data updated with the latest press releases and studies. The site includes pages on Climate Change, Clean Air, Clean Water, Nature, and Weather and Environmental Predictions. There are links to the Canadian Hurricane Centre and the Science and Environment Bulletin, among others.*

The Canadian Hurricane Centre was established in Halifax in 1985 after Hurricane Gloria demonstrated the need for Canadian-based hurricane information. Its meteorologists work with the U.S. National Centre in Miami and the World Meteorological Organization's Hurricane Committee.

The Science and Environment Bulletin is a bi-monthly publication providing information on environmental science and technology. It is posted on-line, with links to other relevant sites. Bulletin material can be reproduced with proper credit, and browsers can contact the related departmental scientists.

Average Number of Days Per Year With the Most...

Province	Average # Days	Frost Station	Average # Days	Smoke or Haze Station
Newfoundland	259	Nain	25	St. John's A
Prince Edward Island ...	175	O'Leary	34	Summerside A
New Brunswick	215	Nine Mile Brk. (Camp 68)	42	Chatham A
Nova Scotia	194	Northeast Margaree	29	Greenwood A
Quebec	296	Cape Hopes Advance	118	St. Hubert A
Ontario	254	Winisk A	228	Windsor A
Manitoba	258	Churchill A	30	Winnipeg Int'l. A
Saskatchewan	238	Stony Rapids	8	Saskatoon
Alberta	269	Lake Louise	34	Edmonton Municipal A
British Columbia	280	Alexis Creek Tautri Creek	187	Vancouver Int'l. A
Yukon Territory	296	Komakuk Beach A	3	Dawson
Northwest Territories ...	295	Nicholson Peninsula	7	Fort Smith A
Nunavut	340	Isachsen	2	Ennadai Lake

Province	Average # Days	Fog Station	Average # Days	Hail Station
Newfoundland	206	Argentia A	0	—
Prince Edward Island ..	47	Charlottetown A	0	—
New Brunswick	106	Saint John A	0	—
Nova Scotia	127	Sable Island	0	—
Quebec	85	Cape Hopes Advance	2	Matagami A
Ontario	76	Mount Forest	1	Red Lake
Manitoba	48	Churchill A	3	Winnipeg Int'l. A
Saskatchewan	37	Collins Bay	2	Estevan A
Alberta	39	Whitecourt	7	Edson A
British Columbia	226	Old Glory Mountain	18	Cape Scott
Yukon Territory	61	Komakuk Beach A	2	Dawson A
Northwest Territories	70	Nicholson Peninsula	0	—
Nunavut	196	Resolution Island	0	—

Province	Average # Days	Thunderstorms Station	Average # Days	Blowing Snow Station
Newfoundland	7	Daniels Harbour	45	Hopedale
Prince Edward Island ..	11	Summerside A	26	Summerside A
New Brunswick	13	Fredericton A	16	Chatham A
Nova Scotia	12	Debert A	21	Greenwood A
Quebec	27	St. Hubert	90	Border A
Ontario	36	London A	38	Winisk A
Manitoba	26	Rivers A	64	Churchill A
Saskatchewan	25	Wynyard	32	Regina A
Alberta	26	Edmonton Int'l. A	15	Coronation A
British Columbia	24	Prince George	25	Old Glory Mountain
Yukon Territory	11	Snag	82	Komakuk Beach A
Northwest Territories ..	12	Fort Smith A	48	Holman
Nunavut	2	Baker Lake	91	Resolute A

Source: *Environment Canada*

Seasonal Temperature and Precipitation in Canada

All figures are based on the thirty-year period 1961 to 1990 inclusive.
*Airport station unless * designates city office station.*

	January			April		
	Average Temperature (°C)		Total	Average Temperature (°C)		Total
Station	Mid Afternoon	Early Morning	Precipitation (mm)	Mid Afternoon	Early Morning	Precipitation (mm)
Calgary, Alta.	-3.6	-15.7	12.2	10.6	-2.4	25.1
Charlottetown, PEI	-3.4	-12.2	106.3	6.3	-1.8	81.6
Churchill, Man. ...	-22.9	-30.9	17.3	-5.2	-14.8	22.6
Dawson, Yukon* ..	-27.1	-34.2	16.5	5.9	-9.7	9.4
Edmonton, Alta.	-8.7	-19.8	22.9	9.9	-2.7	21.8
Fredericton, NB ...	-4.0	-15.4	93.3	9.4	-1.4	83.4
Iqaluit, NT	-21.7	-30.0	21.8	-9.9	-19.6	28.4
Halifax, NS	-1.5	-10.3	146.9	8.0	-0.9	124.4
Hamilton, Ont.	-2.6	-10.0	61.3	11.3	1.2	74.3
Kitchener, Ont.* ..	-3.3	-11.4	54.3	11.2	0.4	72.6
London, Ont.	-2.8	-10.7	69.0	11.7	0.7	79.2
Moncton, NB	-3.7	-13.9	119.7	7.7	-2.0	100.9
Montreal, Que.	-5.8	-14.9	63.3	10.7	0.6	74.8
Ottawa, Ont.	-6.3	-15.5	58.0	10.8	0.3	69.0
Quebec, Que.	-7.7	-17.3	90.0	7.9	-1.5	75.5
Regina, Sask.	-11.0	-22.1	14.7	10.5	-2.4	20.4
Saint John, NB	-2.8	-13.6	128.3	7.9	-1.5	109.7
St. John's, Nfld ...	-0.7	-7.9	147.8	4.8	-2.2	110.4
Saskatoon, Sask. .	-12.3	-22.9	15.9	10.0	-2.2	25.7
Sault Ste. Marie, Ont.	-5.5	-15.4	74.4	8.5	-2.0	65.2
Toronto, Ont.	-2.5	-11.1	45.6	11.5	0.6	64.0
Vancouver, BC	5.7	0.1	149.8	12.7	4.9	75.4
Victoria, BC	6.5	0.3	141.1	12.9	3.8	41.9
Whitehorse, Yukon	-14.4	-23.2	16.9	5.7	-5.1	8.3
Windsor, Ont.	-1.3	-8.8	50.3	13.4	2.7	80.3
Winnipeg, Man. ...	-13.2	-23.6	19.3	9.8	-2.3	35.9
Yellowknife, NWT .	-23.9	-32.2	14.9	-0.5	-12.0	10.3

It Does Rain More on Weekends

*S*cientists are starting to prove what most people have always known: what follows two days of rain? Monday. Analyzing rainfall records from cities along the east coast of North America, climatologists from Arizona State University found that weekly rainfall and accumulated pollution levels both peak on Saturday and dip noticeably on Monday. Overall, Saturday receives an average of 22% more rainfall than Monday.

The massive drift of pollution generated by many cities creates a natural cloud-seeding effect. As traffic builds and office air-conditioners and factories crank up between Monday and Friday, pollution levels in the area grow, spawning the clouds for a wet weekend. Saturdays in Canada are not the wettest day everywhere though:

	Wettest Day	Driest Day		Wettest Day	Driest Day
Ottawa	Saturday	Friday	Calgary	Friday	Monday
Montreal	Monday	Wednesday/Thursday	Winnipeg	Saturday	Monday
Hamilton	Sunday	Tuesday			

Station	July Average Temperature (°C) Mid Afternoon	July Average Temperature (°C) Early Morning	July Total Precipitation (mm)	October Average Temperature (°C) Mid Afternoon	October Average Temperature (°C) Early Morning	October Total Precipitation (mm)
Calgary, Alta.	23.2	9.5	69.9	12.6	-1.2	15.5
Charlottetown, PEI	23.1	13.6	81.6	12.1	4.0	111.7
Churchill, Man. . . .	16.9	6.8	50.7	1.4	-4.3	46.5
Dawson, Yukon* .	22.8	6.5	33.9	0.5	-10.4	27.9
Edmonton, Alta. . .	22.5	9.4	101.0	11.3	-2.2	17.7
Fredericton, NB . . .	25.6	12.9	84.5	13.1	1.5	93.1
Iqaluit, NT	11.6	3.7	58.2	-2.1	-7.8	42.4
Halifax, NS	23.4	13.2	96.8	13.0	4.0	128.9
Hamilton, Ont.	26.4	15.1	81.0	13.9	4.7	66.3
Kitchener, Ont.* . .	26.1	13.6	90.4	13.2	2.9	70.4
London, Ont.	26.4	14.2	76.7	14.2	3.9	76.4
Moncton, NB	24.4	12.5	102.6	12.7	2.1	106.4
Montreal, Que. . . .	26.2	15.4	85.6	13.0	3.6	75.4
Ottawa, Ont.	26.4	15.1	88.1	12.8	3.0	74.8
Quebec, Que.	24.9	13.2	118.5	11.0	2.0	96.0
Regina, Sask.	26.3	11.9	58.9	11.9	-1.7	20.3
Saint John, NB . . .	22.1	11.6	103.7	12.1	2.9	122.5
St. John's, Nfld . . .	20.2	10.5	121.2	10.6	3.4	151.7
Saskatoon, Sask. .	25.4	11.7	58.0	11.1	-1.5	16.9
Sault Ste. Marie, Ont.	24.3	11.2	65.6	11.8	2.9	83.2
Toronto, Ont.	26.8	14.2	76.6	14.1	3.6	63.0
Vancouver, BC . . .	21.7	12.7	36.1	13.5	6.4	115.3
Victoria, BC	21.8	10.7	17.6	14.1	5.3	74.4
Whitehorse, Yukon	20.3	7.6	39.3	4.3	-3.1	23.0
Windsor, Ont.	27.7	17.0	85.3	15.8	6.0	57.9
Winnipeg, Man. . .	26.1	13.4	72.0	11.3	0.1	29.5
Yellowknife, NWT .	20.8	12.0	35.2	1.3	-4.2	34.8

Source: *Environment Canada*

Beware Black Ice

*B*lack ice is the bane of motorists and pedestrians alike. It's not really black. It's transparent; an invisible, very thin covering of ice that takes on the colour of the material it's on. On a dark road, it looks black; on cement, it looks grey or the surface may just look wet.

Black ice develops on road surfaces when the temperature is near the freezing mark. In those conditions, supercooled fog droplets can coat the surface with slick black ice; water from vehicle tailpipes may freeze directly on the roadway or frost can form when the temperature of the road surface falls below freezing and the air above moist.

The most common form of black ice occurs when rain or drizzle falls from warm, moist air through a shallow freezing layer of air near the ground. The raindrops reach the surface as supercooled liquid. Upon striking the cold pavement, the unfrozen water spreads over the pavement before freezing into a thin, dangerous glaze. Glaze contains no air bubbles and is smooth and shiny as glass. It is heavy, hard and bonds tenaciously to the underlying surface.

Another common way black ice forms on road surfaces follows a sunny winter day when the black asphalt absorbs the heat and there is enough traffic to keep the road surface just above freezing adding to the daytime thaw. Any snow or ice near or on the road melts and the pavement becomes damp. At night, temperatures dip back below freezing—the result is transparent and slippery.

Surfaces that are especially vulnerable include: shaded sections of road; bridges, overpasses and ramps because they lose heat faster than the ground around them; areas adjacent to lakes or rivers; and low points in the road surface

Spring and Fall Frost Dates in Canada

Frost occurs whenever temperatures fall to 0°C or lower. All frost dates and values are based on the available data during the period 1951-1980.

Growing degree-day data are from the period 1961-90. Data reported from airport stations unless * designates city office station.

	1 in 10 Chance Last Spring Frost After Date	1 in 10 Chance First Fall Frost Before Date	Frost-free Period (days)	Growing Degree-Days Above 5°C[1]
Newfoundland				
Corner Brook*	June 10	Sept. 8	139	1 432
St. John's*	June 24	Sept. 19	131	1 262
Prince Edward Island				
Charlottetown	May 27	Oct. 6	151	1 636
Nova Scotia				
Halifax	May 28	Sept. 30	155	1 707
New Brunswick				
Fredericton	June 10	Sept. 13	126	1 760
Moncton	June 10	Sept. 14	124	1 649
Saint John	June 10	Sept. 18	139	1 499
Quebec				
Chicoutimi*	June 4	Sept. 18	135	1 575
Gaspé*	June 12	Sept. 11	123	1 336
Montreal	May 19	Sept. 26	157	2 079
Quebec	May 28	Sept. 14	137	1 688
Schefferville	June 27	Aug. 22	77	604
Ontario				
Kitchener*	May 25	Sept. 17	151	1 992
London	May 25	Sept. 23	147	2 121
Moosonee*	July 6	July 30	70	1 078
Ottawa	May 25	Sept. 21	147	2 045
St. Catharines*	May 18	Oct. 5	173	2 451
Sudbury	June 11	Sept. 11	128	1 680
Thunder Bay	June 13	Aug. 29	104	1 427
Timmins	June 23	Aug. 19	91	1 395
Toronto	May 25	Sept. 18	149	2 090
Windsor	May 10	Oct. 3	177	2 544
Manitoba				
Brandon	June 9	Aug. 31	108	1 652
Churchill	July 7	Aug. 20	76	562
Flin Flon	June 10	Sept. 2	115	1 379
Winnipeg	June 10	Sept. 11	121	1 802
Saskatchewan				
Prince Albert	June 21	Aug. 17	95	1 455
Regina	June 14	Aug. 27	109	1 723
Saskatoon	June 10	Sept. 1	117	1 658
Alberta				
Banff*	June 30	Aug. 6	89	1 124
Calgary	June 10	Aug. 27	112	1 435
Edmonton	June 14	Aug. 13	105	1 352
Fort McMurray	June 30	Aug. 2	84	1 352
Lethbridge	May 31	Sept. 2	124	1 779
Medicine Hat	May 27	Sept. 8	129	1 971
Peace River	June 23	Aug. 13	93	1 276
British Columbia				
Fort Nelson	June 7	Aug. 14	106	1 289
Kamloops	May 18	Sept. 19	149	2 259
Penticton	May 23	Sept. 14	148	2 163
Prince George	July 1	Aug. 11	85	1 238
Prince Rupert	May 25	Sept. 28	156	1 181
Vancouver	Apr. 21	Oct. 13	216	2 018
Victoria	Apr. 30	Oct. 17	201	1 864

▶

	1 in 10 Chance Last Spring Frost After Date	1 in 10 Chance First Fall Frost Before Date	Frost-free Period (days)	Growing Degree-Days Above 5°C[1]
▶ **Yukon**				
Dawson*	June 16	Aug. 6	91	1 015
Whitehorse	June 24	Aug. 13	82	871
Northwest Territories				
Yellowknife	June 9	Sept. 3	111	1 039
Nunavut				
Alert*	July 15	July 16	4	30
Iqaluit	July 12	July 26	59	177
Resolute	July 15	July 16	9	29

Source: *Environment Canada*
(1) Growing degree days represent the average total number of heat units (daily mean temp. -5°C) during the growing season

Plant Hardiness Zones in Canada

A plant's hardiness rating is related to its ability to survive in specific climate conditions. Plant hardiness zones were originally based on average minimum winter temperatures in a location, and first developed by the US Department of Agriculture (USDA).

The USDA created 11 zones, each of which have since been split into subzones a and b. Canada's Department of Agriculture and Agri-Food took the concept of hardiness further by including other factors besides minimum temperature in designating Canada's plant hardiness zones. They created a weighted equation that took into account such factors as the average minimum temperature of the coldest month; the average length of the frost-free period; average rainfall between June and November; the average maximum temperature in the hottest month; the amount of snow; and the maximum windspeeds in the last 30 years in any given area.

Canada's zones range from 0a in our coldest regions to 9a in our most temperate locations, and the minimum temperature equivalents are shown below. Canadian gardeners may find themselves in micro-climates that differ from the conditions the zone map indicates, however most should choose perennials based on the zone the garden is in and the hardiness rating of the plant. (A plant can survive in the zone it's rated for or a higher/warmer one.)

To find out what zone you're in, consult a local nursery or visit the map at http://res.agr.ca/CANSIS/SYSTEMS/online_maps.html

Hardiness Zone	Average Minimum Temperature (°C)
0a - 0b	-46 or colder
1a - 1b	-46 to -37
2a - 2b	-37 to -29
3a - 3b	-29 to -23
4a - 4b	-23 to -20

Hardiness Zone	Average Minimum Temperature (°C)
5a - 5b	-20 to -15
6a - 6b	-15 to -12
7a - 7b	-12 to -6
8a - 8b	-6 to -1
9a	-1 to 4 or warmer

Source: *Agriculture and Agri-Food Canada*

It's Warmer and Spring Arrives Earlier

*S**omething, maybe global warming, appears to be causing birds in the UK to lay their eggs earlier. Ornithologists report that birds now lay their eggs some nine days earlier in the spring than they did in 1971.*

Spring is also springing eight days earlier than it did a decade ago in the Arctic according to satellite measurements of vegetation cover. The satellite data confirms what scientists in Environment Canada have observed since the 1970s. Ice on many lakes, mainly in western Canada and the Mackenzie Basin, is breaking up one to two weeks earlier than it did two decades ago.

The warming trend is not confined to spring and it has been noticeable right across the country. Above-normal average temperatures have been reported nation-wide for nine consecutive seasons—from summer 1997 to summer 1999. The data has been compared to that from the past 52 years and reveals that seven of the ten warmest summers on record happened in the last 20 years, while only three of the ten coolest have occurred in that span. The summers in question have also featured more precipitation—eight of the ten wettest summers also happened in the last 20 years.

PROVINCES AND TERRITORIES

Latitude, Longitude, Elevation of Canadian Cities

City	Lat. N °	Lat. N ′	Long.W °	Long.W ′	Elev. (m)	City	Lat. N °	Lat. N ′	Long.W °	Long.W ′	Elev. (m)
Alert, NT*	82	30	62	22	31	Moose Jaw, Sask.	50	23	105	32	544
Brandon, Man.	49	51	99	57	409	Niagara Falls, Ont.	43	06	79	03	180
Brantford, Ont.	43	08	80	15	215	North Bay, Ont.	46	18	79	27	204
Burlington, Ont.	43	19	79	47	87	Ottawa, Ont.	45	26	75	41	56
Calgary, Alta.	51	02	114	03	1 045	Peterborough, Ont.	44	18	78	19	205
Charlottetown, PEI	46	14	63	07	9	Prince Rupert, BC	54	19	130	19	38
Churchill, Man.	58	45	94	10	29	Quebec, Que.	46	48	71	12	50
Dartmouth, NS	44	39	63	34	7	Regina, Sask.	50	27	104	36	577
Dawson, Yukon	64	03	139	26	369	Saint John, NB	45	16	66	03	8
Edmonton, Alta.	53	32	113	29	666	St. John's, Nfld	47	34	52	43	61
Fredericton, NB	45	57	66	38	9	Saskatoon, Sask.	52	07	106	39	484
Guelph, Ont.	43	32	80	14	325	Sault Ste. Marie, Ont.	46	30	84	20	180
Halifax, NS	44	38	63	34	18	Sherbrooke, Que.	45	24	71	53	191
Hamilton, Ont.	43	15	79	52	100	Sudbury, Ont.	46	29	80	59	347
Hull, Que.	45	25	75	42	56	Sydney, NS	46	08	60	11	62
Iqaluit, NT*	63	45	68	31	34	Thunder Bay, Ont.	48	22	89	14	188
Kingston, Ont.	44	13	76	28	80	Toronto, Ont.	43	39	79	23	91
Kitchener, Ont.	43	26	80	29	335	Trois-Rivières, Que.	46	21	72	33	35
LaSalle, Que.	45	25	73	39	34	Vancouver, BC	49	18	123	04	43
Laval, Que.	45	33	73	44	43	Victoria, BC	48	25	123	21	17
Lethbridge, Alta.	49	41	112	49	910	Whitehorse, Yukon	60	43	135	03	703
London, Ont.	42	59	81	14	251	Winnipeg, Man.	49	53	97	08	232
Moncton, NB	46	05	64	46	12	Yellowknife, NWT	62	28	114	22	205
Montreal, Que.	45	30	73	33	27						

Source: *Natural Resources Canada*

*Nunavut

Area[1] of Canadian Provinces and Territories

(sq. km)

	Land	Water	Total	% of Total Area of Canada
Newfoundland and Labrador	373 872	31 340	405 212	4.06
Prince Edward Island	5 660	—	5 660	0.06
Nova Scotia	53 338	1 946	55 284	0.55
New Brunswick	71 450	1 458	72 908	0.73
Quebec	1 365 128	176 928	1 542 056	15.44
Ontario	917 741	158 654	1 076 395	10.78
Manitoba	553 556	94 241	647 797	6.49
Saskatchewan	591 670	59 366	651 036	6.52
Alberta	642 317	19 531	661 848	6.63
British Columbia	925 186	19 549	944 735	9.46
Yukon Territory	474 391	8 052	482 443	4.83
Northwest Territories	1 183 085	163 021	1 346 106	13.48
Nunavut	1 936 113	157 077	2 093 190	20.96
Canada	**9 093 507**	**891 163**	**9 984 670**	**100.0**

Source: *Natural Resources Canada*

(1) Calculated from the National Atlas of Canada 1:1000000 scale hydrology base. (—) = zero

Newfoundland

□ **CAPITAL:** St. John's, metro pop. (1996) 124 175. **Date entered Confederation:** Mar. 31, 1949.

□ **POPULATION (1996): 551 792; Pop. density:** 1.4 per sq. km. **Pop. growth:** (1991-6): -2.9%; **Pop. urban** (1996): 56.9%. **Official Languages** (1996): 96% English; 3.9% bilingual. **Net interprovincial migration** (1999): –11 434.

□ **VITAL STATISTICS: Rates** (per 1000 pop. 1997–98): **Birth:** 9.7; **Death:** 7.2; **Life expectancy at birth** (1996): male 75; female: 81.

□ **GEOGRAPHY: Total area** 405 720 sq. km; **Land area** 371 690 sq. km; **Forested land** 142 000 sq. km; **Length of coastline** 19 720 km. **Climate:** ranges from subarctic in Labrador and northern tip of island to humid continental with cool summers and heavy precipitation. **Topography:** Island of Newfoundland: highlands of the Long Range Mtns. (elev. 900 m) along w. coast; barren and rocky central plateau descends to lowlands towards the n. east; coast is deeply indented with bays and fjords. Labrador: mountainous in the n.; rugged coast and interior plateau.

□ **ECONOMY: Gross Domestic Product** (1997): $10 880 million. **% change GDP** (1996–97): 1.9%. **Per capita GDP** (1997): $19 603. **Employment distrib.** (1997): goods-producing industries (agriculture, primary ind., mfg, construction) 24%; service-producing industries (transpt., trade, finance, service, pub. admin, unclassified) 76%. **Unemployment rate** (1998): 17.9%. **Principal industries:** mining, manufacturing, fishing, logging and forestry, electricity production, tourism.

□ **EDUCATION (1996–97): No. of schools:** 462 elem. and sec.; 11 post-sec. **Enrolment:** 106 494 elem. and sec.; 21 865 post-sec.

□ **INTERNATIONAL AIRPORTS:** Gander.

□ **NATIONAL PARKS:** Gros Morne, Terra Nova.

□ **PROVINCIAL DATA: Motto:** *Quaerite Prime Regnum Dei:* "Seek Ye First the Kingdom of God." **Flower:** Pitcher plant. **Bird:** Atlantic Puffin (unofficial). **Anthem:** Ode to Newfoundland. **Tartan:** Newfoundland Tartan.

□ **POLITICS: Premier:** Brian Tobin (Lib.). **Leaders, opposition parties:** Jack Harris (NDP), Ed Byrne (Prog. Cons.). **Date of last general election:** Feb. 9, 1999. **Lt. Governor:** A.M. House.

Prince Edward Island

□ **CAPITAL:** Charlottetown, metro pop. (1996) 36 990. **Date entered Confederation:** July 1, 1873.

□ **POPULATION (1996): 134 557; Pop. density:** 23.8 per sq. km. **Pop. growth:** (1991-6): 3.7%; **Pop. urban** (1996): 44.2%. **Official Languages** (1996): 88.9% English; 0.1% French; 11.0% bilingual. **Net interprovincial migration** (1999): –851.

□ **VITAL STATISTICS: Rates** (per 1000 pop. 1997–98): **Birth:** 12.4; **Death:** 9.2; **Life expectancy at birth** (1996): male 74; female: 81.

□ **GEOGRAPHY: Total area** 5 660 sq. km; **Land area** 5 660 sq. km; **Forested land** 3 000 sq. km; **Length of coastline** 1 107 km. **Climate:** humid continental with temperatures moderated by maritime location. **Topography:** flat through gently rolling hills; sharply indented coastline; many streams but only small rivers and lakes.

□ **ECONOMY: Gross Domestic Product** (1997) $2 943 million. **% change GDP** (1996–97): 2.7%. **Per capita GDP** (1997): $21 482. **Employment distrib.** (1997): goods-producing industries (agriculture, primary ind., mfg, construction) 31%; service-producing industries (transpt., trade, finance, service, pub. admin, unclassified) 69%. **Unemployment rate** (1998): 13.8%. **Principal industries:** agriculture, tourism, fishing, manufacturing.

□ **EDUCATION (1996–97): No. of schools:** 70 elem. and sec.; 3 post-sec. **Enrolment:** 24 814 elem. and sec.; 4 156 post-sec.

□ **INTERNATIONAL AIRPORTS:** none.

□ **NATIONAL PARKS:** Prince Edward Island (north shore).

□ **PROVINCIAL DATA: Motto:** *Parva Sub Ingenti:* "The small under the protection of the great." **Flower:** Lady's slipper. **Bird:** Blue Jay. **Tree:** Red Oak.

□ **POLITICS: Premier:** Pat Binns (Prog. Cons.) **Leaders, opposition parties:** Wayne Carew (Lib.), Dr. H. Dickieson (NDP). **Date of last general election:** Nov.18, 1996. **Lt. Governor:** Gilbert R. Clements.

Nova Scotia

☐ **CAPITAL:** Halifax, metro pop. (1996) 265 610. **Date entered Confederation:** July 1, 1867.

☐ **POPULATION (1996): 909 282; Pop. density:** 16.4 per sq. km. **Pop. growth:** (1991-6): 1.0%; **Pop. urban** (1996): 54.8%. **Official Languages** (1996): 90.4% English; 0.2% French; 9.3% bilingual. **Net interprovincial migration** (1999): −5 040.

☐ **VITAL STATISTICS: Rates** (per 1000 pop. 1997–98): **Birth:** 11.0; **Death:** 8.5; **Life expectancy at birth** (1996): male 75; female: 81.

☐ **GEOGRAPHY: Total area** 55 490 sq. km; **Land area** 52 840 sq. km; **Forested land** 41,000 sq. km; **Length of coastline** 5 934 km. **Climate:** humid continental with some moderating effects due to maritime location. **Topography:** Atlantic Uplands are segmented by river valleys; Cape Breton Is. rises from lowland in the s. to a high plateau; many rivers, lakes and jagged coastline.

☐ **ECONOMY: Gross Domestic Product** (1997): $20 322 million. **% change GDP** (1996–97): 3.4%. **Per capita GDP**(1997): $21 482. **Employment distrib.** (1997): goods-producing industries (agriculture, primary ind., mfg, construction) 24%; service-producing industries (transpt., trade, finance, service, pub. admin, unclassified) 76%. **Unemployment rate** (1998): 10.7%. **Principal industries:** manufacturing, fishing and trapping, mining, agriculture, pulp and paper.

☐ **EDUCATION (1996–97): No. of schools:** 494 elem. and sec.; 21 post-sec. **Enrolment:** 167 162 elem. and sec.; 44 078 post-sec.

☐ **INTERNATIONAL AIRPORTS:** Halifax

☐ **NATIONAL PARKS:** Cape Breton Highlands, Kejimkujik.

☐ **PROVINCIAL DATA: Motto:** *Munit Haec et Altera Vincit:* "One defends and the other conquers." **Flower:** Mayflower. **Bird:** Osprey. **Tree:** Red Spruce. **Gem:** Agate.

☐ **POLITICS: Premier:** Dr. John Hamm (Prog. Cons.). **Leaders, opposition parties:** Russell MacLellan (Lib.), Robert Chisholm (NDP). **Date of last general election:** July 27, 1999. **Lt. Governor:** J. James Kinley.

New Brunswick

☐ **CAPITAL:** Fredericton, metro pop. (1996) 48 233. **Date entered Confederation:** July 1, 1867.

☐ **POPULATION (1996): 738 133; Pop. density:** 10.1 per sq. km. **Pop. growth:** (1991-6): 2.0%; **Pop. urban** (1996): 48.8%. **Official Languages** (1996): 57.3% English; 10.1% French; 32.6% bilingual. **Net interprovincial migration** (1999): −3 056.

☐ **VITAL STATISTICS: Rates** (per 1000 pop. 1997–98): **Birth:** 10.3; **Death:** 7.9; **Life expectancy at birth** (1996): male 75; female: 81.

☐ **GEOGRAPHY: Total area** 73 440 sq. km; **Land area** 72 090 sq. km; **Forested land** 61,000 sq. km; **Length of coastline** 1 524 km. **Climate:** humid continental climate except along the shores where there is a marked maritime effect. **Topography:** northern upland; rolling central plateau; southern lowland plain with many rivers.

☐ **ECONOMY: Gross Domestic Product** (1997): $17 061 million. **% change GDP** (1996–97): 2.1%. **Per capita GDP**(1997): $22 449. **Employment distrib.** (1997): goods-producing industries (agriculture, primary ind., mfg, construction) 25%; service-producing industries (transpt., trade, finance, service, pub. admin, unclassified) 75%. **Unemployment rate** (1998): 12.1%. **Principal industries:** manufacturing, fishing, mining, forestry, pulp and paper, agriculture.

☐ **EDUCATION (1996–97): No. of schools:** 403 elem. and sec.; 8 post-sec. **Enrolment:** 135 254 elem. and sec.; 28 607 post-sec.

☐ **INTERNATIONAL AIRPORTS:** none.

☐ **NATIONAL PARKS:** Fundy, Kouchibouguac.

☐ **PROVINCIAL DATA: Motto:** *Spem Reduxit:* "Hope was restored." **Flower:** Purple Violet. **Bird:** Black-capped Chickadee. **Tree:** Balsam Fir.

☐ **POLITICS: Premier:** Bernard Lord (Prog. Cons.). **Leaders, opposition parties:** Camille Thériault (Lib.), Elizabeth Weir (NDP). **Date of last general election:** June 7, 1999. **Lt. Governor:** Marilyn Trenholme Counsell.

Quebec

□ **CAPITAL:** Quebec, metro pop. (1996) 609 353. **Date entered Confederation:** July 1, 1867.

□ **POPULATION (1996):** 7 138 795; **Pop. density:** 4.6 per sq. km. **Pop. growth:** (1991-6): 3.5%; **Pop. urban** (1996): 78.4%. **Official Languages** (1996): 56.1% French; 5.1% English; 37.8% bilingual; 1.0% neither French nor English. **Net interprovincial migration** (1999): –17 454.

□ **VITAL STATISTICS: Rates** (per 1000 pop. 1997–98): **Birth:** 10.5; **Death:** 7.3; **Life expectancy at birth** (1996): male 75; female: 81.

□ **GEOGRAPHY: Total area** 1 540 680 sq. km; **Land area** 1 356 790 sq. km; **Forested land** 940 000 sq. km; **Length of coastline** 10 839 km. **Climate:** varies from subarctic to continental. **Topography:** lowlands along the St. Lawrence R. valley separate the Laurentian Mtns. to the n. and the Appalachian Mtns. to the s.; Canadian Shield landscape dominates north.

□ **ECONOMY: Gross Domestic Product** (1997): $185 366 million. **% change GDP** (1996–97): 3.6%. **Per capita GDP** (1997): $24 885. **Employment distrib.** (1997): goods-producing industries (agriculture, primary ind., mfg, construction) 26%; service-producing industries (transpt., trade, finance, service, pub. admin, unclassified) 74%. **Unemployment rate** (1998): 10.4%. **Principal industries:** manufacturing, electric power, mining, pulp and paper, transportation equipment.

□ **EDUCATION (1996–97): No. of schools:** 3047 elem. and sec.; 97 post-sec. **Enrolment:** 1 137 122 elem. and sec.; 413 560 post-sec.

□ **INTERNATIONAL AIRPORTS:** Dorval; Mirabel.

□ **NATIONAL PARKS:** Forillon, La Mauricie, Mingan Archipelago, Saguenay-St. Lawrence Marine Park.

□ **PROVINCIAL DATA: Motto:** *Je me souviens:* "I remember." **Flower:** Lys blanc de jardin (White Garden (Madonna) Lily). **Bird:** Harfang des neiges (Snowy Owl).

□ **POLITICS: Premier:** Lucien Bouchard (Parti Québécois). **Leader, opposition parties:** Jean Charest (Lib.), Mario Dumont (A.D.). **Date of last general election:** Nov. 30, 1998. **Lt. Governor:** Lise Thibault.

Ontario

□ **CAPITAL:** Toronto, metro pop. (1996) 3 921 897. **Date entered Confederation:** July 1, 1867.

□ **POPULATION (1996):** 10 753 573; **Pop. density:** 10.1 per sq. km. **Pop. growth:** (1991-6): 6.6%; **Pop. urban** (1996): 83.3%. **Official Languages** (1996): 85.7% English; 0.4% French; 11.6% bilingual; 2.3% neither English nor French. **Net interprovincial migration** (1999): 6 662.

□ **VITAL STATISTICS: Rates** (per 1000 pop. 1997–98): **Birth:** 12.2; **Death:** 7.2; **Life expectancy at birth** (1996): male 76; female: 81.

□ **GEOGRAPHY: Total area** 1 068 580 sq. km; **Land area** 891 190 sq. km; **Forested land** 807 000 sq. km; **Length of coastline** 1 210 km. **Climate:** ranges from humid continental in south to subarctic in far north; westerly winds bring winter storms; the Great Lakes moderate winter temperatures. **Topography:** Rugged, rocky Canadian Shield plateau is broken by lowlands around Great Lakes, St. Lawrence R. and Hudson Bay.

□ **ECONOMY: Gross Domestic Product** (1997): $347 149 million. **% change GDP** (1996–97): 4.9%. **Per capita GDP** (1997): $30 116. **Employment distrib.** (1997): goods-producing industries (agriculture, primary ind., mfg, construction) 26%; service-producing industries (transpt., trade, finance, service, pub. admin, unclassified) 74%. **Unemployment rate** (1998): 7.2%. **Principal industries:** manufacturing, construction, agriculture, forestry, mining.

□ **EDUCATION (1996–97): No. of schools:** 5751 elem. and sec.; 62 post-sec. **Enrolment:** 2 161 483 elem. and sec.; 526 709 post-sec.

□ **INTERNATIONAL AIRPORTS:** Pearson (Toronto); Ottawa.

□ **NATIONAL PARKS:** Bruce Peninsula, Fathom Five Marine Park, Georgian Bay Islands, Point Pelee, Pukaskwa, St. Lawrence Islands.

□ **PROVINCIAL DATA: Motto:** *Ut Incepit Fidelis Sic Permanet:* "Loyal she began, loyal she remains." **Flower:** White trillium. **Bird:** Common Loon. **Tree:** Eastern White Pine. **Gem:** Amethyst.

□ **POLITICS: Premier:** Mike Harris (Prog. Cons.). **Leaders, opposition parties:** Dalton McGinty (Lib.); Howard Hampton (NDP). **Date of last general election:** June 21, 1999. **Lt. Governor:** Hilary Weston.

Manitoba

□ **CAPITAL:** Winnipeg, metro pop. (1996) 621 887. **Date entered Confederation:** July 15, 1870.

□ **POPULATION (1996): 1 113 898;** Pop. density: 1.7 per sq. km. **Pop. growth:** (1991-6): 2.0%; **Pop. urban** (1996): 71.8%. **Official Languages** (1996): 89.4% English; 0.1% French; 9.4% bilingual; 1.1% neither English nor French. **Net interprovincial migration** (1999): –5 383.

□ **VITAL STATISTICS: Rates** (per 1000 pop. 1997–98): **Birth:** 13.5; **Death:** 8.6; **Life expectancy at birth** (1996): male 75; female: 81.

□ **GEOGRAPHY: Total area** 649 950 sq. km; **Land area** 548 360 sq. km; **Forested land** 349 000 sq. km; **Length of coastline** 917 km. **Climate:** continental with seasonal extremes. **Topography:** the land rises gradually south and west from Hudson Bay; flat plateau through south central region; countless lakes, streams and bogs.

□ **ECONOMY: Gross Domestic Product** (1997): $29 246 million. **% change GDP** (1996–97): 3.2%. **Per capita GDP** (1997): $25 587. **Employment distrib.** (1997): goods-producing industries (agriculture, primary ind., mfg, construction) 25%; service-producing industries (transpt., trade, finance, service, pub. admin, unclassified) 75%. **Unemployment rate** (1998): 5.7%. **Principal industries:** manufacturing, agriculture, food industry, mining, construction.

□ **EDUCATION (1996–97): No. of schools:** 850 elem. and sec.; 11 post-sec. **Enrolment:** 223 826 elem. and sec.; 37 798 post-sec.

□ **INTERNATIONAL AIRPORTS:** Winnipeg.

□ **NATIONAL PARKS:** Riding Mountain, Wapusk.

□ **PROVINCIAL DATA: Motto:** Glorious and Free. **Flower:** Prairie Crocus. **Bird:** Great Gray Owl. **Tartan:** Manitoba Tartan.

□ **POLITICS: Premier:** Gary Doer (NDP). **Leaders, opposition parties:** Gary Filmon (Prog. Cons.), Jon Gerrard (Lib.). **Date of last general election:** Sept. 21, 1999. **Lt. Governor:** Peter M. Liba.

Saskatchewan

□ **CAPITAL:** Regina, metro pop. (1996) 180 400. **Date entered Confederation:** Sept. 1, 1905.

□ **POPULATION (1996): 990 237;** Pop. density: 1.5 per sq. km. **Pop. growth:** (1991-6): 0.1%; **Pop. urban** (1996): 63.3%. **Official Languages** (1996): 94.3% English; 5.2% bilingual; 0.5% neither English nor French. **Net interprovincial migration** (1999): –3 367.

□ **VITAL STATISTICS: Rates** (per 1000 pop. 1997–98): **Birth:** 12.5; **Death:** 8.2; **Life expectancy at birth** (1996): male 75; female: 82.

□ **GEOGRAPHY: Total area** 652 330 sq. km; **Land area** 570 700 sq. km; **Forested land** 178 000 sq. km; **Climate:** continental, with cold winters and hot summers. **Topography:** gently rolling plains through south; higher, hilly plateaus in the s.w.; north is rugged Canadian Shield.

□ **ECONOMY: Gross Domestic Product** (1997): $28 260 million. **% change GDP** (1996–97): 6.8%. **Per capita GDP** (1997): $27 625. **Employment distrib.** (1997): goods-producing industries (agriculture, primary ind., mfg, construction) 29%; service-producing industries (transpt., trade, finance, service, pub. admin, unclassified) 71%. **Unemployment rate** (1998): 5.9%. **Principal industries:** agriculture, mining, manufacturing, electric power, construction, chemical prod.

□ **EDUCATION (1996–97): No. of schools:** 925 elem. and sec.; 8 post-sec. **Enrolment:** 212 941 elem. and sec.; 34 265 post-sec.

□ **INTERNATIONAL AIRPORTS:** none.

□ **NATIONAL PARKS:** Grasslands, Prince Albert.

□ **PROVINCIAL DATA: Motto:** *Multis E Gentibus Vires:* "from many peoples strength". **Flower:** Western Red Lily. **Bird:** Prairie sharp-tailed grouse. **Tree:** White Birch. **Tartan:** Saskatchewan Tartan.

□ **POLITICS: Premier:** Roy Romanow (NDP). **Leaders, opposition parties:** Elwin Hermanson (Sask.), Jim Melenchuk (Lib.). **Date of last general election:** Sept. 16, 1999. **Lt. Governor:** John Wiebe.

Alberta

☐ **CAPITAL:** Edmonton, metro pop. (1996) 716 014. **Date entered Confederation:** Sept. 1, 1905.

☐ **POPULATION (1996): 2 696 826; Pop. density:** 4.1 per sq. km. **Pop. growth:** (1991-6): 5.9%; **Pop. urban** (1996): 79.5%. **Official Languages** (1996): 91.9% English; 0.1% French; 6.7% bilingual; 1.3% neither English nor French. **Net interprovincial migration** (1999): 46 787.

☐ **VITAL STATISTICS: Rates** (per 1000 pop. 1997–98): **Birth:** 13.3; **Death:** 5.9; **Life** expectancy at birth (1996): male 76; female: 81.

☐ **GEOGRAPHY: Total area** 661 190 sq. km; **Land area** 644 390 sq. km; **Forested land** 349 000 sq. km. **Climate:** great variance in temperatures between regions and seasons; summer highs between 16°C and 32°C; winters as low as -45°C. **Topography:** Rocky Mtns. in s.w. to rolling prairie throughout southern region; far north is a forested plateau.

☐ **ECONOMY: Gross Domestic Product** (1997): $101 069 million. **% change GDP** (1996–97): 8.0%. **Per capita GDP** (1997): $34 936. **Employment distrib.** (1997): goods-producing industries (agriculture, primary ind., mfg, construction) 27%; service-producing industries (transpt., trade, finance, service, pub. admin, unclassified) 73%. **Unemployment rate** (1998): 5.7%. **Principal industries:** chemical products, mining, agriculture, food, manufacturing, construction, oil prod. and refinement.

☐ **EDUCATION (1996–97): No. of schools:** 1865 elem. and sec.; 26 post-sec. **Enrolment:** 553 726 elem. and sec.; 114 802 post-sec.

☐ **INTERNATIONAL AIRPORTS:** Edmonton; Calgary.

☐ **NATIONAL PARKS:** Banff, Elk Island, Jasper, Waterton Lakes, Wood Buffalo (shared with Northwest Territories).

☐ **PROVINCIAL DATA: Motto:** *Fortis et Liber:* "Strong and free." **Flower:** Wild Rose. **Bird:** Great horned owl. **Tree:** Lodge pole pine. **Tartan:** Alberta Tartan. **Stone:** Petrified wood.

☐ **POLITICS: Premier:** Ralph Klein (Prog. Cons.). **Leaders, opposition parties:** Nancy McBeth (Lib.), Pam Barrett (NDP). **Date of last general election:** March 11, 1997. **Lt. Governor:** H. (Bud) Olson.

British Columbia

☐ **CAPITAL:** Victoria, metro pop. (1996) 279 138. **Date entered Confederation:** July 20, 1871.

☐ **POPULATION (1996): 3 724 500; Pop. density:** 3.9 per sq. km. **Pop. growth:** (1991-6): 13.5%; **Pop. urban** (1996): 82.1%. **Official Languages** (1996): 90.6% English; 6.7% bilingual; 2.6% neither French nor English. **Net interprovincial migration** (1999): –4 230.

☐ **VITAL STATISTICS: Rates** (per 1000 pop. 1997–98): **Birth:** 11.6; **Death:** 7.2; **Life** expectancy at birth (1996): male 76; female: 82.

☐ **GEOGRAPHY: Total area** 947 800 sq. km; **Land area** 929 730 sq. km; **Forested land** 633 000 sq. km; **Length of coastline** 17 856 km. **Climate:** maritime with mild temperatures and abundant rainfall in the coastal areas; continental climate with temperature extremes in the interior and northeast. **Topography:** mostly mountainous; deep river valleys and gorges, except for the n.e. area which is an extension of the Great Plains; indented coast with numerous bays and islands.

☐ **ECONOMY: Gross Domestic Product** (1997): $109 347 million. **% change GDP** (1996–97): 3.3%. **Per capita GDP** (1997): $27 620. **Employment distrib.** (1997): goods-producing industries (agriculture, primary ind., mfg, construction) 23%; service-producing industries (transpt., trade, finance, service, pub. admin, unclassified) 78%. **Unemployment rate** (1998): 8.9%. **Principal industries:** forestry, wood and paper, mining, tourism, agriculture, fishing, manufacturing.

☐ **EDUCATION (1996–97): No. of schools:** 2053 elem. and sec.; 29 post-sec. **Enrolment:** 667 070 elem. and sec.; 151 660 post-sec.

☐ **INTERNATIONAL AIRPORTS:** Vancouver; Victoria.

☐ **NATIONAL PARKS:** Glacier, Kootenay, Mount Revelstoke, Pacific Rim, South Moresby, Yoho.

☐ **PROVINCIAL DATA: Motto:** *Splendor Sine Occasu:* "Splendor without Diminishment." **Flower:** Dogwood. **Bird:** Stellar's Jay.

☐ **POLITICS: Premier:** Dan Miller (interim) (NDP). **Leader, opposition parties:** Gordon Campbell (Lib.), Bill Vander Zalm (Reform). **Date of last general election:** May 28, 1996. **Lt. Governor:** Garde B. Gardom.

Yukon Territory

☐ **CAPITAL:** Whitehorse, metro pop. (1996) 17 196. **Date entered Confederation:** June 13, 1898.

☐ **POPULATION (1996): 30 766; Pop. density:** .06 per sq. km. **Pop. growth: (1991-6):** 10.7%; **Pop. urban** (1996): 60.0%. **Official Languages** (1996): 89.2% English; 0.2% French; 10.5% bilingual; 0.2% neither French nor English. **Net interprovincial migration** (1999): –929.

☐ **VITAL STATISTICS: Rates** (per 1000 pop. 1997–98): **Birth:** 14.2; **Death:** 4.2; **Life expectancy at birth** (1996): male 71; female: 84.

☐ **GEOGRAPHY: Total area** 483 450 sq. km; **Land area** 478 970 sq. km; **Forested land** 242 000 sq. km; **Length of coastline** 343 km. **Climate:** great variance in temperatures; warm summers, very cold winters; low precipitation. **Topography:** main feature is the Yukon plateau with 21 peaks exceeding 3 300 m; open tundra in the far north.

☐ **ECONOMY: Gross Domestic Product** (1997): $1 131 million. **% change GDP** (1996–97): -4.2%. **Per capita GDP** (1997): $36 484. **Unemployment rate** (1999): n.a.. **Principal industries:** mining, tourism.

☐ **EDUCATION (1996–97): No. of schools:** 30 elem. and sec.; 1 post-sec. **Enrolment:** 6 132 elem. and sec.; 654 post-sec.

☐ **INTERNATIONAL AIRPORTS:** Whitehorse.

☐ **NATIONAL PARKS:** Ivvavik, Kluane, Vuntut.

☐ **PROVINCIAL DATA: Flower:** Fireweed. **Bird:** Common Raven.

☐ **POLITICS: Govt. Leader:** Piers McDonald (NDP). **Leader, opposition party:** John Ostashek (Yukon Party). **Date of last general election:** Sept. 30, 1996. **Commissioner:** Judy Gingell.

Northwest Territories[1]

☐ **CAPITAL:** Yellowknife, metro pop. (1996) 14 027. **Date entered Confederation:** July 15, 1870.

☐ **POPULATION (1996): 64 402; Pop. density:** .02 per sq. km. **Pop. growth:** (1991-6): 11.7%; **Pop. urban** (1996): 42.5%. **Official Languages** (1996): 87.1% English; 6.3% bilingual; 6.5% neither French nor English. **Net interprovincial migration** (1999):[1] –1 705.

☐ **VITAL STATISTICS: Rates** (per 1000 pop. 1997–98): **Birth:** 22.6; **Death:** 3.5; **Life expectancy at birth** (1996): male 70; female: 76.

☐ **GEOGRAPHY: Total area** 3 426 320 sq. km; **Land area** 3 293 020 sq. km; **Forested land** 615 000 sq. km; **Length of coastline** 111 249 km. **Climate:** extreme temperatures and low precipitation; arctic and sub-arctic. **Topography:** mostly tundra plains formed on the rocks of the Canadian Shield; the Mackenzie Lowland is a continuation of the Great Plains; the Mackenzie River Valley is forested.

☐ **ECONOMY: Gross Domestic Product** (1997): $2 915 million. **% change GDP** (1996–97): 0.8%. **Per capita GDP** (1997): $43 507. **Unemployment rate** (1999): n.a. **Principal industries:** construction, utilities, services, tourism.

☐ **EDUCATION (1996–97): No. of schools:** 47 elem. and sec.; 1 post-sec. **Enrolment:** 17 625 elem. and sec.; 676 post-sec.

☐ **INTERNATIONAL AIRPORTS:** none.

☐ **NATIONAL PARKS:** Aulavik, Nahanni, Tuktut Nogait, Wood Buffalo (shared with Alberta).

☐ **PROVINCIAL DATA: Flower:** Mountain Avens. **Bird:** Gyrfalcon. **Tree:** Jack pine.

☐ **POLITICS: Premier:** James L. Antoine. **Date of last general election:** Oct. 16, 1995. **Commissioner:** Daniel T. Marion.

(1) Divided into Nunavut and Northwest Territories April 1, 1999. Some statistics remain combined.

Provinces on the Web

Newfoundland: http://www.nf.ca
Prince Edward Island: http://www2.gov.pe.ca
Nova Scotia: http://www.gov.ns.ca
New Brunswick: http://www.gov.nb.ca
Quebec: http://www.gouv.qc.ca
Ontario: http://www.gov.on.ca
Manitoba: http://www.gov.mb.ca

Saskatchewan: http://www.gov.sk.ca
Alberta: http://www.gov.ab.ca
British Columbia: http://www.gov.bc.ca
Nunavut: http://www.gov.nu.ca
Northwest Territories: http://www.gov.nt.ca
Yukon Territory: http://www.gov.yk.ca

Nunavut

☐ **CAPITAL:** Iqaluit, metro pop. (1996): 4220. **Date became province:** April 1, 1999.

☐ **POPULATION (1996):** 24 730. **Pop. Density:** 0.1 per sq. km. **Pop. growth:** (1991–96): n.a.. **Pop. Urban** (1996): 25.4%. **Official languages** (1996): 71.4% Inukitut; 23.6% English; 1.6% French.

☐ **VITAL STATISTICS: Rates** (per 1000 pop., 1996): **Birth:** 22.6; **Death:** 3.5. **Life expectancy at birth** (1996): male: 70; female: 76.

☐ **GEOGRAPHY: Total area:** 2 million sq. km. **Climate:** extreme temperatures and low precipitation; arctic. **Topography:** rocky tundra with stunted vegetation located above the tree-line; snow-covered most of the year.

☐ **ECONOMY: Gross Domestic Product** (1997): n.a. **% change GDP** (1996–97): n.a. **Per capita GDP** (1997): n.a. **Principal industries:** mining, tourism, shrimp and scallop fishing, hunting and trapping, arts and crafts production. **Unemployment rate:** 15.4.

☐ **EDUCATION (1997–98):** No. of schools: 38 elem. and sec.; 1 post-sec. **Enrolment:** 7 770.

☐ **INTERNATIONAL AIRPORTS:** Iqaluit Airport.

☐ **NATIONAL PARKS:** Auyuittuq, Ellesmere Island.

☐ **PROVINCIAL DATA:** n.a.

☐ **POLITICS: Premier:** Paul Okalik. **Date of last general election:** Feb. 9, 1999. **Commissioner:** Hon. Helen Maksagak.

CANADIAN CITIES

Calgary, Alta

Year Incorporated: 1893. **Area:** 5 083 sq. km.

☐ **DEMOGRAPHICS: CMA Population** (1996 Census): 821 628; **Pop. density:** 161.6 per sq. km. **Pop. growth** (1991–1996): 9.0%. **Immigrant pop.** (1996) 170 880, 20.8%. **Age Structure:** (1996) Male pop.: under 25: 35.8%, over 65: 7.4%; Female pop.: under 25: 34.1%, over 65: 10.0%.

☐ **OFFICIAL LANGUAGES (1996):** 90.7% English; 0.1% French; 7.3% bilingual; 1.9% neither.

☐ **FAMILIES: Ave. family size (1996):** 3.2. **Lone-parent families (1996):** 13.2% of families.

☐ **INCOME: Ave. Employment Income:** (1995) $28 991. **Ave. Family Income:** (1995) $63 586. **Incidence of low income:** (1995) 19.8%.

☐ **LABOUR FORCE (1998): Employed (000s):** 495.4. **Unemployed (000s):** 27.5. **Unemployment rate:** 5.3%. **Participation rate:** 74.0%. **Employment rate:** 70.1%.

☐ **CLIMATE: Avg. day/night temps.** -3.6°/-15.7° (Jan.); 23.2°/9.5° (July). **Avg. annual sunshine:** 2 395 h. **Avg. annual precip.** 398.8 mm. **Avg. annual snowfall:** 135.4 cm.

Chicoutimi–Jonquière, Que.

Year Incorporated: 1976. **Area:** 1 723 sq. km.

☐ **DEMOGRAPHICS: CMA Population** (1996 Census): 160 454; **Pop. density:** 93 per sq. km. **Pop. growth** (1991–1996): -0.3%. **Immigrant pop.** (1996) 1 165, 0.7%. **Age Structure:** (1996) Male pop.: under 25: 36.3%, over 65: 8.8%; Female pop.: under 25: 33.0%, over 65: 12.6%.

☐ **OFFICIAL LANGUAGES (1996):** 0.1% English; 82.5% French; 17.4% bilingual.

☐ **FAMILIES: Ave. family size (1996):** 3.1. **Lone-parent families (1996):** 15.0% of families.

☐ **INCOME: Ave. Employment Income:** (1995) $25 127. **Ave. Family Income:** (1995) $46 656. **Incidence of low income:** (1995) 20.7%.

☐ **LABOUR FORCE (1998): Employed (000s):** 65.8. **Unemployed (000s):** 9.5. **Unemployment rate:** 12.6%. **Participation rate:** 55.7%. **Employment rate:** 48.7%.

☐ **CLIMATE: Avg. day/night temps.** -10.2°/-21.5° (Jan.); 24.2°/11.8° (July). **Avg. annual sunshine:** 1 676 h. **Avg. annual precip.** 929.7 mm. **Avg. annual snowfall:** 345 cm.

Edmonton, Alta

Year Incorporated: 1904. **Area:** 9 537 sq. km.

☐ **DEMOGRAPHICS: CMA Population** (1996 Census): 862 597; **Pop. density:** 90.5 per sq. km. **Pop. growth** (1991–1996): 2.6%. **Immigrant pop.** (1996) 158 370, 18.4%. **Age Structure:** (1996)

Male pop.: under 25: 37.0%, over 65: 8.4%; Female pop.: under 25: 35.1%, over 65: 11.1%.

☐ **OFFICIAL LANGUAGES (1996):** 90.9% English; 0.1% French; 7.5% bilingual; 1.6% neither.

☐ **FAMILIES: Ave. family size (1996):** 3.2. Lone-parent families (1996): 15.0% of families.

☐ **INCOME: Ave. Employment Income:** (1995) $25 974. **Ave. Family Income:** (1995) $56 090. **Incidence of low income:** (1995) 21.3%.

☐ **LABOUR FORCE (1998): Employed (000s):** 482.1. **Unemployed (000s):** 32.1. **Unemployment rate:** 6.2%. **Participation rate:** 70.6%. **Employment rate:** 66.2%.

☐ **CLIMATE: Avg. day/night temps.** -8.7°/-19.8° (Jan.); 22.5°/9.4° (July). **Avg. annual sunshine:** 2 303 h. **Avg. annual precip.** 465.8 mm. **Avg. annual snowfall:** 127.1 cm.

Halifax, NS

Year Incorporated: 1841. **Area:** 2 503 sq. km.

☐ **DEMOGRAPHICS: CMA Population** (1996 Census): 332 518; **Pop. density:** 133 per sq. km. **Pop. growth** (1991–1996): 3.7%. **Immigrant pop.** (1996) 23 635, 7.1%. **Age Structure:** (1996) Male pop.: under 25: 35.0%, over 65: 8.3%; Female pop.: under 25: 32.4%, over 65: 11.8%.

☐ **OFFICIAL LANGUAGES (1996):** 88.9% English; 0.1% French; 10.7% bilingual; 0.3% neither.

☐ **FAMILIES: Ave. family size (1996):** 3.1. Lone-parent families (1996): 15.9% of families.

☐ **INCOME: Ave. Employment Income:** (1995) $25 419. **Ave. Family Income:** (1995) $54 241. **Incidence of low income:** (1995) 17.8%.

☐ **LABOUR FORCE (1998): Employed (000s):** 175.4. **Unemployed (000s):** 14.1. **Unemployment rate:** 7.4%. **Participation rate:** 68.4%. **Employment rate:** 63.3%.

☐ **CLIMATE: Avg. day/night temps.** -1.5°/-10.3° (Jan.); 23.4°/13.2° (July). **Avg. annual sunshine:** 1 949 h. **Avg. annual precip.** 1 473.5 mm. **Avg. annual snowfall:** 261.4 cm.

Hamilton, Ont.

Year Incorporated: 1846. **Area:** 1 359 sq. km.

☐ **DEMOGRAPHICS: CMA Population** (1996 Census): 624 360; **Pop. density:** 460 per sq. km. **Pop. growth** (1991–1996): 4.1%. **Immigrant pop.** (1996) 145 660, 23.3%. **Age Structure:** (1996) Male pop.: under 25: 34.2%, over 65: 12.0%;

Female pop.: under 25: 31.3%, over 65: 15.7%.

☐ **OFFICIAL LANGUAGES (1996):** 91.7% English; 0.1% French; 6.8% bilingual; 1.5% neither.

☐ **FAMILIES: Ave. family size (1996):** 3.1. Lone-parent families (1996): 14.3% of families.

☐ **INCOME: Ave. Employment Income:** (1995) $29 455. **Ave. Family Income:** (1995) $60 899. **Incidence of low income:** (1995) 19.0%.

☐ **LABOUR FORCE (1998): Employed (000s):** 328.5. **Unemployed (000s):** 17.9. **Unemployment rate:** 5.2%. **Participation rate:** 65.8%. **Employment rate:** 62.4%.

☐ **CLIMATE: Avg. day/night temps.** -2.6°/-10.0° (Jan.); 26.4°/15.1° (July). **Avg. annual sunshine:** 2 079 h. **Avg. annual precip.** 890.4 mm. **Avg. annual snowfall:** 152.4 cm.

Kitchener, Ont.

Year Incorporated: 1912. **Area:** 824 sq. km.

☐ **DEMOGRAPHICS: CMA Population** (1996 Census): 382 940; **Pop. density:** 465 per sq. km. **Pop. growth** (1991–1996): 7.4%. **Immigrant pop.** (1996) 82 760, 21.6%. **Age Structure:** (1996) Male pop.: under 25: 37.0%, over 65: 8.9%; Female pop.: under 25: 34.5%, over 65: 12.8%.

☐ **OFFICIAL LANGUAGES (1996):** 91.4% English; 0.1% French; 6.9% bilingual; 1.6% neither.

☐ **FAMILIES: Ave. family size (1996):** 3.2. Lone-parent families (1996): 13.7% of families.

☐ **INCOME: Ave. Employment Income:** (1995) $27 893. **Ave. Family Income:** (1995) $59 658. **Incidence of low income:** (1995) 14.6%.

☐ **LABOUR FORCE (1998): Employed (000s):** 212.4. **Unemployed (000s):** 14.8. **Unemployment rate:** 6.5%. **Participation rate:** 70.0%. **Employment rate:** 65.4%.

☐ **CLIMATE: Avg. day/night temps.** -3.3°/-11.4° (Jan.); 26.1°/13.6° (July). **Avg. annual sunshine:** 1 969 h. **Avg. annual precip.** 917.0 mm. **Avg. annual snowfall:** 158.0 cm.

London, Ont.

Year Incorporated: 1855. **Area:** 2 105 sq. km.

☐ **DEMOGRAPHICS: CMA Population** (1996 Census): 398 616; **Pop. density:** 189.4 per sq. km. **Pop. growth** (1991–1996): 4.5%. **Immigrant pop.** (1996) 75 975, 19.1%. **Age Structure:** (1996) Male pop.: under 25: 35.9%, over 65: 10.6%; Female pop.: under 25: 32.6%, over 65: 14.5%.

☐ **OFFICIAL LANGUAGES (1996):** 92.2% English; 6.6% bilingual; 1.1% neither.

☐ **FAMILIES:** Ave. family size **(1996):** 3.1. Lone-parent families **(1996):** 15.5% of families.

☐ **INCOME:** Ave. Employment Income: (1995) $27 289. Ave. Family Income: (1995) $58 671. Incidence of low income: (1995) 17.3%.

☐ **LABOUR FORCE (1998):** Employed (000s): 210.2. Unemployed (000s): 13.7. **Unemployment rate:** 6.1%. **Participation rate:** 65.5%. **Employment rate:** 61.4%.

☐ **CLIMATE:** Avg. day/night temps. -2.8°/-10.7° (Jan.); 26.4°/14.2° (July). **Avg. annual sunshine:** 1 858 h. **Avg. annual precip.** 955.1 mm. **Avg. annual snowfall:** 212.3 cm.

Montreal, Que.

Year Incorporated: 1832. **Area:** 4 024 sq. km.

☐ **DEMOGRAPHICS:** CMA Population (1996 Census): 3 326 510 **Pop. density:** 827 per sq. km. **Pop. growth** (1991–1996): 3.7%. **Immigrant pop.** (1996) 586 470, 17.6%. **Age Structure:** (1996) Male pop.: under 25: 33.3%, over 65: 9.8%; Female pop.: under 25: 30.3%, ,over 65: 14.1%.

☐ **OFFICIAL LANGUAGES (1996):** 8.5% English; 39.8% French; 49.7% bilingual; 1.9% neither.

☐ **FAMILIES:** Ave. family size **(1996):** 3.1. Lone-parent families **(1996):** 17.4% of families.

☐ **INCOME:** Ave. Employment Income: (1995) $26 918. Ave. Family Income: (1995) $52 795. Incidence of low income: (1995) 27.3%.

☐ **LABOUR FORCE (1998):** Employed (000s): 1636.7. Unemployed (000s): 176.4. **Unemployment rate:** 9.7%. **Participation rate:** 64.7%. **Employment rate:** 58.4%.

☐ **CLIMATE:** Avg. day/night temps. -5.8°/-14.9° (Jan.); 26.2°/15.4° (July). **Avg. annual sunshine:** 2 015 h. **Avg. annual precip.** 939.7 mm. **Avg. annual snowfall:** 214.2 cm.

Oshawa, Ont.

Year Incorporated: 1924. **Area:** 894 sq. km.

☐ **DEMOGRAPHICS:** CMA Population (1996 Census): 268 773 **Pop. density:** 301 per sq. km. **Pop. growth** (1991–1996): 11.9%. **Immigrant pop.** (1996) 44 105, 16.4%. **Age Structure:** (1996) Male pop.: under 25: 37.6%, over 65: 8.4%; Female pop.: under 25: 35.1%, over 65: 11.2%.

☐ **OFFICIAL LANGUAGES (1996):** 92.8% English; 0.1% French; 6.7% bilingual; 0.5% neither.

☐ **FAMILIES:** Ave. family size **(1996):** 3.2. Lone-parent families **(1996):** 14.1% of families.

☐ **INCOME:** Ave. Employment Income: (1995) $31 332. Ave. Family Income: (1995) $62 101. Incidence of low income: (1995) 12.4%.

☐ **LABOUR FORCE (1998):** Employed (000s): 140.4. Unemployed (000s): 11.2. **Unemployment rate:** 7.4%. **Participation rate:** 69.5%. **Employment rate:** 64.3%.

☐ **CLIMATE:** Avg. day/night temps. -1.7°/-9.9° (Jan.); 25.2°/15.3° (July). **Avg. annual sunshine:** 2 025 h. **Avg. annual precip.** 880.3 mm. **Avg. annual snowfall:** 125.7 cm.

Ottawa-Hull

Year Incorporated: 1854 (Ottawa). **Area:** 5 686 sq. km.

☐ **DEMOGRAPHICS:** CMA Population (1996 Census): 1 010 498 **Pop. density:** 177.7 per sq. km. **Pop. growth** (1991–1996): 7.3%. **Immigrant pop.** (1996) 161 885, 16.0%. **Age Structure:** (1996) Male pop.: under 25: 35.1%, over 65: 8.4%; Female pop.: under 25: 32 3%, over 65: 11.9%.

☐ **OFFICIAL LANGUAGES (1996):** 45.8% English; 9.0% French; 44.0% bilingual.

☐ **FAMILIES:** Ave. family size **(1996):** 3.1. Lone-parent families **(1996):** 15.6% of families.

☐ **INCOME:** Ave. Employment Income: (1995) $30 633. Ave. Family Income: (1995) $64 243. Incidence of low income: (1995) 18.9%.

☐ **LABOUR FORCE (1998):** Employed (000s): 545.1. Unemployed (000s): 41.4. **Unemployment rate:** 7.1%. **Participation rate:** 67.1%. **Employment rate:** 62.3%.

☐ **CLIMATE:** Avg. day/night temps. -6.3°/-15.5° (Jan.); 26.4°/15.1° (July). **Avg. annual sunshine:** 2 054 h. **Avg. annual precip.** 910.5 mm. **Avg. annual snowfall:** 221.5 cm.

Quebec, Que.

Year Incorporated: 1832. **Area:** 3 150 sq. km.

☐ **DEMOGRAPHICS:** CMA Population (1996 Census): 671 889 **Pop. density:** 213.3 per sq. km. **Pop. growth** (1991–1996): 4.1%. **Immigrant pop.** (1996) 17 390, 2.6%. **Age Structure:** (1996) Male pop.: under 25: 33.1%, over 65: 9.1%; Female pop.: under 25: 30.0%, over 65: 14.0%.

☐ **OFFICIAL LANGUAGES (1996):** 0.2% English; 69.6% French; 30.0% bilingual; 0.2% neither.

☐ **FAMILIES:** Ave. family size **(1996):** 3.0. Lone-parent families **(1996):** 16.1% of families.

☐ **INCOME:** Ave. Employment Income: (1995) $26 039. Ave. Family Income: (1995) $52 570. Incidence of low income: (1995) 22.8%.

☐ **LABOUR FORCE (1998):** Employed (000s): 335.8. Unemployed (000s): 31.7. **Unemployment rate:** 8.6%. **Participation rate: 63.1%. Employment rate:** 57.6%.

☐ **CLIMATE:** Avg. day/night temps. -7.7°/-17.3° (Jan.); 24.9°/13.2° (July). **Avg. annual sunshine:** 1 910 h. **Avg. annual precip.** 1 207.7 mm. **Avg. annual snowfall:** 337.0 cm.

Regina, Sask.

Year Incorporated: 1903. **Area:** 3 422 sq. km.

☐ **DEMOGRAPHICS:** CMA Population (1996 Census): 193 652 **Pop. density:** 57 per sq. km. **Pop. growth** (1991–1996): 1.0%. **Immigrant pop.** (1996) 15 230, 7.9%. **Age Structure:** (1996) Male pop.: under 25: 38.5%, over 65: 9.8%; Female pop.: under 25: 35.5%, over 65: 13.6%.

☐ **OFFICIAL LANGUAGES (1996):** 93.9% English; 0.1% French; 5.6% bilingual; 0.4% neither.

☐ **FAMILIES:** Ave. family size **(1996):** 3.2. Lone-parent families **(1996):** 16.6% of families.

☐ **INCOME:** Ave. Employment Income: (1995) $25 918. Ave. Family Income: (1995) $56 844. Incidence of low income: (1995) 17.6%.

☐ **LABOUR FORCE (1998):** Employed (000s): 108.1. Unemployed (000s): 5.9. **Unemployment rate:** 5.2%. **Participation rate:** 71.2%. **Employment rate:** 67.5%.

☐ **CLIMATE:** Avg. day/night temps. -11.0°/-22.1° (Jan.); 26.3°/11.9° (July). **Avg. annual sunshine:** 2 365 h. **Avg. annual precip.** 364.0 mm. **Avg. annual snowfall:** 107.4 cm.

St. Catharines–Niagara, Ont.

Year Incorporated: 1876. **Area:** 1 400 sq. km.

☐ **DEMOGRAPHICS:** CMA Population (1996 Census): 372 406 **Pop. density:** 266 per sq. km. **Pop. growth** (1991–1996): 2.2%. **Immigrant pop.** (1996) 67 290, 18.1%. **Age Structure:** (1996) Male pop.: under 25: 33.8%, over 65: 14.2%; Female pop.: under 25: 30.2%, over 65: 18.3%.

☐ **OFFICIAL LANGUAGES (1996):** 90.8% English; 0.2% French; 8.3% bilingual; 0.7% neither.

☐ **FAMILIES:** Ave. family size **(1996):** 3.0. Lone-parent families **(1996):** 14.8% of families.

☐ **INCOME:** Ave. Employment Income: (1995) $25 749. Ave. Family Income: (1995) $53 674. Incidence of low income: (1995) 16.1%.

☐ **LABOUR FORCE (1998):** Employed (000s): 170.7. Unemployed (000s): 14.1. **Unemployment rate:** 7.6%. **Participation rate:** 62.5%. **Employment rate:** 57.8%.

☐ **CLIMATE:** Avg. day/night temps. -1.3°/-8.4° (Jan.); 27.2°/15.8° (July). **Avg. annual sunshine:** 2 079 h. **Avg. annual precip.** 953.1 mm. **Avg. annual snowfall:** 163.7 cm.

Saint John, NB

Year Incorporated: 1785. **Area:** 3 509 sq. km.

☐ **DEMOGRAPHICS:** CMA Population (1996 Census): 125 705 **Pop. density:** 35.8 per sq. km. **Pop. growth** (1991–1996): -0.1%. **Immigrant pop.** (1996) 4 915, 3.9%. **Age Structure:** (1996) Male pop.: under 25: 36.4%, over 65: 10.4%; Female pop.: under 25: 32.9%, over 65: 14.7%.

☐ **OFFICIAL LANGUAGES (1996):** 87.5% English; 0.1% French; 12.3% bilingual; 0.1% neither.

☐ **FAMILIES:** Ave. family size **(1996):** 3.1. Lone-parent families **(1996):** 16.9% of families.

☐ **INCOME:** Ave. Employment Income: (1995) $24 201. Ave. Family Income: (1995) $49 138. Incidence of low income: (1995) 20.0%.

☐ **LABOUR FORCE (1998):** Employed (000s): 59.7. Unemployed (000s): 6.5. **Unemployment rate:** 9.8%. **Participation rate:** 62.7%. **Employment rate:** 56.5%.

☐ **CLIMATE:** Avg. day/night temps. -2.8°/-13.6° (Jan.); 22.1°/11.6° (July). **Avg. annual sunshine:** 1 894 h. **Avg. annual precip.** 1 432.8 mm. **Avg. annual snowfall:** 283.2 cm.

St. John's, Nfld

Year Incorporated: 1888. **Area:** 790 sq. km.

☐ **DEMOGRAPHICS:** CMA Population (1996 Census): 174 051 **Pop. density:** 220 per sq. km. **Pop. growth** (1991–1996): 1.3%. **Immigrant pop.** (1996) 5 065, 2.9%. **Age Structure:** (1996) Male pop.: under 25: 37.4%, over 65: 8.2%; Female pop.: under 25: 34.4%, over 65: 11.7%.

☐ **OFFICIAL LANGUAGES (1996):** 94.5% English; 0% French; 5.4% bilingual; 0.1% neither.

☐ **FAMILIES:** Ave. family size **(1996):** 3.2. Lone-parent families **(1996):** 16.8% of families.

☐ **INCOME:** **Ave. Employment Income:** (1995) $24 717. **Ave. Family Income:** (1995) $52 054. **Incidence of low income:** (1995) 19.5%.

☐ **LABOUR FORCE (1998):** Employed (000s): 81.6. Unemployed (000s): 11.2. Unemployment rate: 12.1. **Participation rate:** 64.6%. **Employment rate:** 56.9%.

☐ **CLIMATE:** **Avg. day/night temps.** -0.7°/-7.9° (Jan.); 20.2°/10.5° (July). **Avg. annual sunshine:** 1 527 h. **Avg. annual precip.** 1 481.7 mm. **Avg. annual snowfall:** 322.1 cm.

Saskatoon, Sask.

Year Incorporated: 1906. **Area:** 5 322 sq. km.

☐ **DEMOGRAPHICS:** CMA **Population** (1996 Census): 219 056 **Pop. density:** 41.2 per sq. km. **Pop. growth** (1991–1996): 3.8%. **Immigrant pop.** (1996) 16 455, 7.5%. **Age Structure:** (1996) Male pop.: under 25: 39.5%, over 65: 9.4%; Female pop.: under 25: 37.0%, over 65: 12.8%.

☐ **OFFICIAL LANGUAGES (1996):** 92.9% English; 0.0% French; 6.5% bilingual; 0.5% neither.

☐ **FAMILIES:** **Ave. family size (1996):** 3.2. **Lone-parent families (1996):** 15.9% of families.

☐ **INCOME:** **Ave. Employment Income:** (1995) $24 033. **Ave. Family Income:** (1995) $53 196. **Incidence of low income:** (1995) 21.4%.

☐ **LABOUR FORCE (1998):** Employed (000s): 112.8. Unemployed (000s): 8.7. Unemployment rate: 7.2%. **Participation rate:** 68.1%. **Employment rate:** 63.2%.

☐ **CLIMATE:** **Avg. day/night temps.** -12.3°/-22.9° (Jan.); 25.4°/11.7° (July). **Avg. annual sunshine:** 2 381 h. **Avg. annual precip.** 347.2 mm. **Avg. annual snowfall:** 105.4 cm.

Sherbrooke, Que.

Year Incorporated: 1875. **Area:** 980 sq. km.

☐ **DEMOGRAPHICS:** CMA **Population** (1996 Census): 147 384 **Pop. density:** 150 per sq. km. **Pop. growth** (1991–1996): 4.7%. **Immigrant pop.** (1996) 6 225, 4.2%. **Age Structure:** (1996) Male pop.: under 25: 35.7%, over 65: 9.6%; Female pop.: under 25: 32.5%, over 65: 14.7%.

☐ **OFFICIAL LANGUAGES (1996):** 1.9% English; 58.8% French; 39.1% bilingual; 0.3% neither.

☐ **FAMILIES:** **Ave. family size (1996):** 3.0. **Lone-parent families (1996):** 17.0% of families.

☐ **INCOME:** **Ave. Employment Income:** (1995) $23 410. **Ave. Family Income:** (1995) $47 198. **Incidence of low income:** (1995) 22.8%.

☐ **LABOUR FORCE (1998):** Employed (000s): 66.4. Unemployed (000s): 8.2. Unemployment rate: 11.0%. **Participation rate:** 60.2%. **Employment rate:** 53.5%.

☐ **CLIMATE:** **Avg. day/night temps.** -5.6°/-17.7° (Jan.); 24.7°/11.2° (July). **Avg. annual sunshine** 1 901 h. **Avg. annual precip.** 1 108.9 mm. **Avg. annual snowfall:** 288.2 cm.

Sudbury, Ont.

Year Incorporated: 1930. **Area:** 2 612 sq. km.

☐ **DEMOGRAPHICS:** CMA **Population** (1996 Census):160 488 **Pop. density:** 61 per sq. km. **Pop. growth** (1991–1996): 1.8%. **Immigrant pop.** (1991): 12 840, 8.1%. **Age Structure:** (1996) Male pop.: under 25: 35.8%, over 65: 10.4%; Female pop.: under 25: 33.5%, over 65: 13.0%.

☐ **OFFICIAL LANGUAGES (1996):** 58.0% English; 1.5% French; 40.1% bilingual; 0.3% neither.

☐ **FAMILIES:** **Ave. family size (1996):** 3.1. **Lone-parent families (1996):** 15.2% of families.

☐ **INCOME:** **Ave. Employment Income:** (1995) $28 345. **Ave. Family Income:** (1995) $57 109. **Incidence of low income:** (1995) 17.3%.

☐ **LABOUR FORCE (1998):** Employed (000s): 78.0. Unemployed (000s): 9.9. Unemployment rate: 11.3%. **Participation rate:** 61.9%. **Employment rate:** 54.9%.

☐ **CLIMATE:** **Avg. day/night temps.** -8.5°/-18.7° (Jan.); 24.8°/13.3° (July). **Avg. annual sunshine:** 1 960 h. **Avg. annual precip.** 871.8 mm. **Avg. annual snowfall:** 266.6 cm.

Thunder Bay, Ont.

Year Incorporated: 1970. **Area:** 2 295 sq. km.

☐ **DEMOGRAPHICS:** CMA **Population** (1996 Census): 125 562 **Pop. density:** 54.7 per sq. km. **Pop. growth** (1991–1996): 0.5%. **Immigrant pop.** (1996) 15 275, 12.2%. **Age Structure:** (1996) Male pop.: under 25: 34.3%, over 65: 12.2%; Female pop.: under 25: 32.0%, over 65: 15.9%.

☐ **OFFICIAL LANGUAGES (1996):** 91.7% English; 0.1% French; 7.4% bilingual; 0.7% neither.

☐ **FAMILIES:** **Ave. family size (1996):** 3.1. **Lone-parent families (1996):** 16.0% of families.

☐ **INCOME:** **Ave. Employment Income:** (1995)

$27 649. **Ave. Family Income:** (1995) $58 731. **Incidence of low income:** (1995) 14.5%.

☐ **LABOUR FORCE (1998): Employed (000s):** 59.7. **Unemployed (000s):** 6.0. **Unemployment rate:** 9.1%. **Participation rate:** 62.2%. **Employment rate:** 56.6%.

☐ **CLIMATE:** Avg. day/night temps. -8.9°/-21.3° (Jan.); 24.4°/11.0° (July). **Avg. annual sunshine:** 2 183 h. **Avg. annual precip.** 703.5 mm. **Avg. annual snowfall:** 195.5 cm.

Toronto, Ont.

Year Incorporated: 1834. **Area:** 5 568 sq. km.

☐ **DEMOGRAPHICS: CMA Population** (1996 Census): 4 263 757 **Pop. density:** 727 per sq. km. **Pop. growth** (1991–1996): 9.4%. **Immigrant pop.** (1996) 1 772 905, 41.6%. **Age Structure:** (1996) Male pop.: under 25: 34.7%, over 65: 9.5%; Female pop.: under 25: 31.6%, over 65: 12.4%.

☐ **OFFICIAL LANGUAGES (1996):** 87.4% English; 0.1% French; 8.0% bilingual; 4.5% neither.

☐ **FAMILIES:** Ave. family size **(1996):** 3.3. **Lone-parent families (1996):** 15.5% of families.

☐ **INCOME:** Ave. Employment Income: (1995) $31 264. **Ave. Family Income:** (1995) $64 044. **Incidence of low income:** (1995) 21.1%.

☐ **LABOUR FORCE (1998): Employed (000s):** 2329.8. **Unemployed (000s):** 175.6. **Unemployment rate:** 7.0%. **Participation rate:** 68.4%. **Employment rate:** 63.6%.

☐ **CLIMATE:** Avg. day/night temps. -2.5°/-11.1° (Jan.); 26.8°/14.2° (July). **Avg. annual sunshine:** 2 038 h. **Avg. annual precip.** 780.8 mm. **Avg. annual snowfall:** 124.2 cm.

Trois–Rivières, Que.

Year Incorporated: 1857. **Area:** 872 sq. km.

☐ **DEMOGRAPHICS: CMA Population** (1996 Census): 139 956 **Pop. density:** 161 per sq. km. **Pop. growth** (1991–1996): 2.7%. **Immigrant pop.** (1996) 2 220, 1.6%. **Age Structure:** (1996) Male pop.: under 25: 33.2%, over 65: 10.5%; Female pop.: under 25: 30.1%, over 65: 15.6%.

☐ **OFFICIAL LANGUAGES (1996):** 0.1% English; 75.4% French; 24.4% bilingual.

☐ **FAMILIES:** Ave. family size **(1996):** 3.0. **Lone-parent families (1996):** 16.1% of families.

☐ **INCOME:** Ave. Employment Income: (1995) $24 763. **Ave. Family Income:** (1995) $47 242.

Incidence of low income: (1995) 23.4%.

☐ **LABOUR FORCE (1998): Employed (000s):** 62.0. **Unemployed (000s):** 9.2. **Unemployment rate:** 12.9%. **Participation rate:** 59.4%. **Employment rate:** 51.8%.

☐ **CLIMATE:** Avg. day/night temps. -7.5°/-17.7° (Jan.); 25.6°/14.1° (July). **Avg. annual sunshine:** 1 910 h. **Avg. annual precip.** 1 046.7 mm. **Avg. annual snowfall:** 242.0 cm.

Vancouver, BC

Year Incorporated: 1886. **Area:** 2 821 sq. km.

☐ **DEMOGRAPHICS: CMA Population** (1996 Census): 1 831 665 **Pop. density:** 649 per sq. km. **Pop. growth** (1991–1996): 14.3%. **Immigrant pop.** (1996) 633 740, 34.6%. **Age Structure:** (1996) Male pop.: under 25: 32.8%, over 65: 10.1%; Female pop.: under 25: 30.6%, over 65: 13.5%.

☐ **OFFICIAL LANGUAGES (1996):** 87.9% English; 0.1% French; 7.4% bilingual; 4.7% neither.

☐ **FAMILIES:** Ave. family size **(1996):** 3.2. **Lone-parent families (1996):** 13.9% of families.

☐ **INCOME:** Ave. Employment Income: (1995) $29 122. **Ave. Family Income:** (1995) $60 438. **Incidence of low income:** (1995) 23.3%.

☐ **LABOUR FORCE (1998): Employed (000s):** 960.3. **Unemployed (000s):** 84.8. **Unemployment rate:** 8.1%. **Participation rate:** 65.8%. **Employment rate:** 60.4%.

☐ **CLIMATE:** Avg. day/night temps. 5.7°/0.1° (Jan.); 21.7°/12.7° (July). **Avg. annual sunshine:** 1 919 h. **Avg. annual precip.** 1 167.4 mm. **Avg. annual snowfall:** 54.9 cm.

Victoria, BC

Year Incorporated: 1862. **Area:** 633 sq. km.

☐ **DEMOGRAPHICS: CMA Population** (1996 Census): 304 287 **Pop. density:** 480 per sq. km. **Pop. growth** (1991–1996): 5.7%. **Immigrant pop.** (1996) 57 795, 19.0%. **Age Structure:** (1996) Male pop.: under 25: 30.7%, over 65: 15.1%; Female pop.: under 25: 27.6%, over 65: 20.4%.

☐ **OFFICIAL LANGUAGES (1996):** 90.6% English; 0.0% French; 8.6% bilingual; 0.7% neither.

☐ **FAMILIES:** Ave. family size **(1996):** 2.9. **Lone-parent families (1996):** 14.1% of families.

☐ **INCOME:** Ave. Employment Income: (1995) $27 038. **Ave. Family Income:** (1995) $59 585. **Incidence of low income:** (1995) 15.4%.

☐ **LABOUR FORCE (1998):** Employed (000s): 150.4. **Unemployed (000s):** 14.6. **Unemployment rate:** 8.8%. **Participation rate:** 62.9%. **Employment rate:** 57.4%.

☐ **CLIMATE:** Avg. day/night temps. 6.5°/0.3° (Jan.); 21.8°/10.7° (July). **Avg. annual sunshine:** 2 082 h. **Avg. annual precip.** 857.9 mm. **Avg. annual snowfall:** 46.9 cm.

Windsor, Ont.

Year Incorporated: 1892. **Area:** 862 sq. km.

☐ **DEMOGRAPHICS:** CMA Population (1996 Census)s: 278 685 **Pop. density:** 323 per sq. km. **Pop. growth** (1991–1996): 6.3%. **Immigrant pop.** (1996) 56 990, 20.4%. **Age Structure:** (1996) Male pop.: under 25: 35.7%, over 65: 10.8%; Female pop.: under 25: 32.9%, over 65: 15.0%.

☐ **OFFICIAL LANGUAGES (1996):** 87.8% English; 0.2% French; 10.5% bilingual; 1.5% neither.

☐ **FAMILIES:** Ave. family size (1996): 3.2. **Lone-parent families (1996):** 16.0% of families.

☐ **INCOME:** Ave. Employment Income: (1995) $30 048. **Ave. Family Income:** (1995) $62 244. **Incidence of low income:** (1995) 15.7%.

☐ **LABOUR FORCE (1998):** Employed (000s): 138.3. **Unemployed (000s):** 13.4. **Unemployment rate:** 8.8%. **Participation rate:** 65.8%. **Employment rate:** 59.9%.

☐ **CLIMATE:** Avg. day/night temps. -1.3°/-8.8° (Jan.); 27.7°/17.0° (July). **Avg. annual sunshine:** 2 045 h. **Avg. annual precip.** 901.6 mm. **Avg. annual snowfall:** 123.3 cm

Winnipeg, Man.

Year Incorporated: 1873. **Area:** 4 078 sq. km.

☐ **DEMOGRAPHICS:** CMA Population (1996 Census): 667 209 **Pop. density:** 167 per sq. km. **Pop. growth** (1991–1996): 1.0%. **Immigrant pop.** (1996) 111 690, 16.7%. **Age Structure:** (1996) Male pop.: under 25: 35.4%, over 65: 10.9%; Female pop.: under 25: 32.5%, over 65: 15.6%.

☐ **OFFICIAL LANGUAGES (1996):** 87.9% English; 0.1% French; 10.9% bilingual; 1.1% neither.

☐ **FAMILIES:** Ave. family size (1996): 3.1. **Lone-parent families (1996):** 15.8% of families.

☐ **INCOME:** Ave. Employment Income: (1995) $30 048. **Ave. Family Income:** (1995) $62 244. **Incidence of low income:** (1995) 15.7%.

☐ **LABOUR FORCE (1998):** Employed (000s): 362.2. **Unemployed (000s):** 22.7. **Unemployment rate:** 5.9%. **Participation rate:** 68.4%. **Employment rate:** 64.4%.

☐ **CLIMATE:** Avg. day/night temps. -13.2°/-23.6° (Jan.); 26.1°/13.4° (July). **Avg. annual sunshine:** 2 377 h. **Avg. annual precip.** 504.4 mm. **Avg. annual snowfall:** 114.8 cm.

NATIONAL PARKS

Canada's national parks are protected by law to preserve representative natural areas throughout the country. The parks are maintained to enhance public understanding, appreciation and enjoyment of the country's natural heritage, and increasingly, park management efforts are being directed to protect Canada's wide variety of ecosystems for the long term.

In 1988, the National Parks Act was amended to ensure that each park's management plan would maintain the ecological integrity of the area, that is, that the structure and function of the existing ecosystem would not be harmed by human activity. This amendment was made as it became increasingly clear that many ecological features, such as grizzly bear populations, require very large areas and very long time lines if they are to survive, if not thrive. The host of modern environmental stresses also affect protected areas and their inhabitants, and mere protection is not enough; a co-operative parks management structure—including public, corporate, environmental and Aboriginal interest groups—and an ecosystem management approach is the preferred management model to minimize damage.

The goal of the national parks policy is to create at least one national park in each of Canada's 39 natural regions. Thirty-eight national parks and national park reserves currently exist, however to achieve the goal, 17 more national parks are needed. Once completed, the parks system will preserve just over 3 percent of the country's land mass. ▶

Park	Location	Size (sq. km)	Year est.	Description
Aulavik	northern portion of Banks Is., NWT	12 200	(1992)[1]	Thomsen River forms core of a park marked by deep river canyons and desert-like badlands. Area supports high concentration of musk oxen. The Thomsen River is Canada's most northerly navigable river.
Auyuittuq[2]	Cumberland Peninsula, Baffin Is., NT	21 469	1976	Located on the Arctic Circle; this is an isolated and very rugged wilderness area with mountains, fjords, tundra and permafrost. Park protects part of Northern Davis Strait Natural Region and portions of Baffin Island Shelf Marine region. Contains prehistoric and historic resources from ancient Thule settlements.
Banff	Banff, Alta.	6 641	1885	Our first national park is noted for ice-capped peaks, canyons, glaciers, hot springs, and hoodoos (rock pillars, often in fantastic shapes). Wildlife includes bighorn sheep, black and grizzly bears, elk and caribou. Banff is part of UNESCO's Rocky Mountain Parks World Heritage Site.
Bruce Peninsula, including Fathom Five National Marine Park	299 km northwest of Toronto, between Lake Huron and Georgian Bay	154	(1987)[1]	This park was created to protect the Niagara Escarpment and the limestone cliffs on Georgian Bay; contains mixed forests, wetlands and limestone cliffs. Fathom Five National Marine Park includes 19 islands, over 20 shipwrecks, clear water and distinctive underwater geological features.
Cape Breton Highlands	across northern Cape Breton Is., NS	948	1936	The scenic Cabot Trail is characterized by a rugged shoreline with plunging cliffs.
Elk Island	45 km east of Edmonton, Alta.	194	1913	A large population of plains and wood bison, elk and moose inhabit the rolling woodlands and lakes. Other wildlife include bear, beaver and coyote.
Ellesmere Island[2]	northern tip of Canada	37 775	1988	Vast isolated high Arctic wilderness park. Mountains, glaciers, musk-oxen, Peary's caribou. Fragile permafrost environments. Historic sites and artifacts from early Arctic explorers
Forillon	northeast tip of Gaspé Peninsula, Que.	244	1970	Protects parts of the Notre-Dame and Mégantic mountains and some of the Gulf of St. Lawrence marine area. This seaside park features a rich variety of seabirds and animals, limestone cliffs, Arctic-alpine plants and the highest mountains in eastern Canada.
Fundy	southeastern shore on the Bay of Fundy, NB	206	1948	The giant tides of the Bay of Fundy, among the highest in the world, and a bold, irregular coastline.
Georgian Bay Islands	160 km northwest of Toronto, Ont.	25	1929	59 glacier swept islands are home to endangered species, limestone cliffs, caves and archaeological sites. This area was the inspiration for many of the Group of Seven artists.

Park	Location	Size (sq. km)	Year est.	Description
Glacier	45 km east of Revelstoke, BC	1 349	1886	Protects a section of the Columbia Mountains Natural Region that includes habitats for grizzly bear and mountain caribou. Steep angular mountains, deep valleys, icefields, glaciers, waterfalls, avalanche paths and high precipitation characterise the area.
Grasslands	100 km south of Swift Current, Sask.	906	(1975)[1]	Unique natural habitat of short-grass prairie; blacktailed prairie dogs, pronghorn antelope and the prairie falcon are found.
Gros Morne	west coast of Nfld	1 805	(1970)[1]	Park is dominated by a coastal lowland and an alpine plateau that each boast a variety of land mammals, bird species, fish and trees, ferns and flowers. The park has been declared a UNESCO World Heritage Site because of its spectacular geology.
Ivvavik	northern tip of Yukon	10 168	1984	Migration route for Porcupine caribou herd; major North American waterfowl area; home to grizzly, black and polar bears. Contains unique non-glaciated landscape.
Jasper	340 km west of Edmonton, Alta.	10 878	1907	Contains the largest icefield in the Canadian Rockies—Columbia Icefield—and preserves the headwaters of major rivers, particularly the Athabasca.
Kejimkujik	central southwestern NS	404	1974	Gently rolling country with many lakes and rivers; provides good canoeing and camping. The earliest inhabitants—Maritime Archaic Indians—arrived about 4,500 years ago.
Kluane[2]	southwest corner of Yukon	22 013	1976	Features Mount Logan, Canada's highest peak, Kluane Lake (Yukon's largest), grizzly bears, dall sheep and whitewater rivers.
Kootenay	1 km east of Radium Hot Springs, BC	1 406	1920	The park contains Rocky Mountain wilderness and is part of UNESCO's Rocky Mountain Parks World Heritage Site. Hot springs, alpine lakes, canyons, glaciers, two river valleys; home to bighorn sheep, mountain goats.
Kouchibouguac	eastern NB	239	1979	Swimming and sunbathing on the beaches and sand dunes; cycling, hiking trails; windsurfing.
La Mauricie	55 km north of Trois-Rivières, Que.	536	1977	Hilly terrain at the edge of the Canadian Shield with transitional forest vegetation from evergreens to deciduous. Beaver, moose and the common loon; an area filled with brooks, lakes and waterfalls.
Mingan Archipelago[2]	N of Anticosti Is. along the St. Lawrence shore, QC	151	1984	This is a limestone environment that is home to diversified plant species, nesting seabirds and whales, seals and porpoises.

Park	Location	Size (sq. km)	Year est.	Description
Mount Revelstoke	Revelstoke, BC	260	1914	Columbia Mountain ranges form first tall barrier east of the Coastal Mountains and intercept westward moving air masses laden with moisture. The park is characterised by deep snow accumulation and high annual precipitation. The area contains three ecoregions: Interior Alpine Tundra, Interior Sub-alpine Tundra and Interior Cedar Hemlock. Each is packed with their own variety of vegetation and wildlife.
Nahanni[2]	southwestern NWT	4 765	1976	The wild and spectacular South Nahanni river passes through this long, narrow part. The route contains four canyons and the river plunges from twice the height of Niagara Falls at Virginia Falls. Park contains sulphur hotsprings, alpine tundra and vast forests, plus numerous species of birds, mammals and fish.
Pacific Rim [2]	west coast of Vancouver Island	500	(1970)[1]	3 sections—Long Beach, Broken Group Islands and West Coast Trail—offer rainforest, beaches and scenic, rugged hiking. Park contains native archaeological sites that indicate settlement for at least 4,300 years.
Point Pelee	southernmost point of Ont.	15	1918	Extensive marshlands and beaches provide refuge for many migratory birds and butterflies. The temperate climate allows over 70 species of tree to survive, as well as a huge variety of reptiles, birds, amphibians, insects and spiders.
Prince Albert	200 km north of Saskatoon, Sask.	3 875	1927	This mixture of forest land and lakes is home to woodland caribou, bison and a pelican nesting colony. Archaeological digs indicate that the area has been inhabited by Aboriginal cultures for at least 6,000 years.
Prince Edward Island	north shore of PEI	22	1937	40 km of fine saltwater beaches, sand dunes, high coastal cliffs, marshes, ponds and woodlands. Green Gables in located in this park.
Pukaskwa	northeastern shore of Lake Superior	1 878	(1971)[1]	Hilly terrain is characterised by ridges and cliffs, and lakes on rocky shores with shallow soil. Park interior features spruce, fir, cedar, aspen and birch. Wildlife includes moose, wolves, black bears and woodland caribou. This park is also the site of rare Arctic plants.
Riding Mountain	270 km northwest of Winnipeg, Man.	2 973	1929	Wildlife—wolf, elk, moose, black bear and beaver—abound.
St. Lawrence Islands	Thousand Islands	8	1904	Park includes over 21 islands and 90 islets between Kingston and Brockville, with 100 acres on the mainland at Mallorytown Landing. The area features Thousand Islands landscape and the St. Lawrence River. The Great Lakes moderate the climate, allowing many animals and plants to exist further north than might otherwise be possible.

Park	Location	Size (sq. km)	Year est.	Description
South Moresby (Gwaii Haanas)[2]	southern part of Queen Charlotte Islands, BC	1 495	(1987)[1]	Canada's "Galapagos," home to 39 unique plants, an estimated 750,000 seabirds which come to nest, and animals such as black bear, pine marten, deer mice, shrews and weasels. Geography features deep fjords, rugged mountains, and one of the finest old-growth temperate rainforest left on Pacific coast.
Terra Nova	east coast of Nfld on Bonavista Bay	400	1957	Rolling forested hills are remnants of the ancient Appalachian Mountains. Rugged cliffs and sheltered inlets are featured on the coast; the interior has spongy bogs, rolling hills covered with forest and inland ponds.
Tuktut Nogait	east of Inuvik in NWT	16 340	1996	Spectacular river canyons and cliffs are dotted by hundreds of archaeological sites that bear testimony to thousands of years of human history. Park protects calving grounds of Bluenose caribou and contains one of the highest concentrations of birds of prey in North America.
Vuntut	Old Crow Flats, northern Yukon	4 345	(1993)[1]	This wetland area is Yukon's most important waterfowl habitat and home to porcupine caribou, grizzly bear, moose, muskrat and several species of fish. Vertebrate fossils found at over 56 sites within park. The area is only 300 m in elevation and features over 2,000 shallow lakes.
Wapusk	northeast corner of Manitoba	11 475	1996	This region of flat inland expanse of tundra, eskers and permafrost includes one of the world's largest known polar bear denning areas.
Waterton Lakes	southwest corner of Alta.	505	1895	Officially renamed the Waterton-Glacier International Peace Park in 1932, it became the world's first park established jointly by two governments. Protects transition from prairie grasslands to Rocky Mountains and features a rich variety of wildlife.
Wood Buffalo	straddles the Alta.-NWT border	44 802	1922	Canada's largest national park is also a UNESCO World Heritage Site. Home to the largest free-roaming herd of bison; only site of naturally nesting whooping cranes, peregrine falcons and red-sided garter snakes. Geography features sinkholes, underground rivers, caves and sunken valleys.
Yoho	25 km east of Golden, BC	1 313	1886	Contains several of the highest peaks in the Rocky Mountains, icefields, waterfalls and a varied plant and animal life.

Source: *Canadian Heritage, Parks Canada*

(1) Park created by federal/provincial/territorial agreement rather than federal enactment and administered by special legislation. (2) Park reserve, set aside for national park and under jurisdiction of National Parks Act, but lands, fish and wildlife are subject to future settlement of native land claims.

THE PEOPLE

POPULATION

Population of Provinces and Territories

(thousands of persons)

	Canada	Nfld	PEI	NS	NB	Que	Ont	Man	Sask	Alta	BC	YT	NWT
1861[1]	3 230	n.a.	81	331	252	1 112	1 396	*	n.a.	n.a.	52	*	7
1871	3 689	n.a.	94	388	286	1 192	1 621	25	n.a.	n.a.	36	*	48
1881	4 325	n.a.	109	441	321	1 360	1 927	62	n.a.	n.a.	49	*	56
1891	4 833	n.a.	109	450	321	1 489	2 114	153	*	*	98	*	99
1901	5 371	n.a.	103	460	331	1 649	2 183	255	91	73	179	27	20
1911	7 207	n.a.	94	492	352	2 006	2 527	461	492	374	393	9	7
1921	8 788	n.a.	89	524	388	2 361	2 934	610	758	588	525	4	8
1931	10 377	n.a.	88	513	408	2 875	3 432	700	922	732	694	4	9
1941	11 507	n.a.	95	578	457	3 332	3 788	730	896	796	818	5	12
1951	14 009	361	98	643	516	4 056	4 598	777	832	940	1 165	9	16
1961	18 238	458	105	737	598	5 259	6 236	922	925	1 332	1 629	15	23
1971	21 962	531	113	797	643	6 137	7 849	999	932	1 666	2 241	19	36
1981	24 820	575	124	855	706	6 548	8 811	1 036	976	2 294	2 824	24	48
1986[2]	26 101	577	128	889	725	6 708	9 438	1 092	1 029	2 431	3 004	25	55
1991	28 031	580	130	915	746	7 065	10 428	1 110	1 003	2 593	3 373	29	61
1996	29 672	561	136	931	753	7 274	11 101	1 134	1 020	2 781	3 882	32	68
1997[3]	30 287	564	137	948	762	7 420	11 408	1 145	1 024	2 847	3 933	32	68
1998[4]	30 300	544	136	935	753	7 333	11 412	1 139	1 024	2 915	4 010	32	67

Source: © *Census of Canada, Statistics Canada*

(n.a.) Not applicable. (*) Included with the Northwest Territories. (1) Pre-Confederation. (2) includes estimates rather than actual counts for the population of some Indian reserves and settlements that were not completely enumerated. (3) Intercensal estimate. (4) Estimate as of July 1, 1998.

Age Structure of the Population[1]

	Total (000s)	% Under 5 Years	% 5–19 Years	% 20–44 Years	% 45–64 Years	% 65+ Years
1851	2 436	18.51	37.81	31.65	9.40	2.67
1861	3 230	16.81	37.21	32.66	10.15	3.03
1871	3 689	14.67	38.03	32.58	11.14	3.66
1881	4 325	13.85	36.02	33.94	12.14	4.12
1891	4 833	12.64	34.49	35.40	12.91	4.55
1901	5 371	12.03	32.73	36.19	14.00	5.05
1911	7 207	12.35	30.15	38.81	14.06	4.66
1921	8 788	12.05	31.51	36.63	15.02	4.78
1931	10 377	10.36	31.29	36.07	16.74	5.55
1941	11 507	9.14	28.39	37.19	18.61	6.67
1951	14 009	12.29	25.60	36.63	17.74	7.75
1961	18 238	12.37	29.44	33.19	17.37	7.63
1971	21 568	8.42	30.97	33.87	18.66	8.09
1981	24 343	7.32	24.70	39.14	19.13	9.70
1991	27 297	6.99	20.42	41.33	19.66	11.61
1996	28 847	6.65	20.60	39.03	21.49	12.23
1998[2]	30 300	6.26	20.26	38.97	22.18	12.33

Source: © *Census of Canada, Statistics Canada*   (1) Total percentage for census year may not equal 100 due to rounding. (2) Preliminary numbers.

Male and Female Population by Age Group

(thousands of persons)

		Total Population	Under 5 Years	5–9 Years	10–14 Years	15–24 Years	25–34 Years	35–44 Years	45–54 Years	55–64 Years	65 Years and Over
1851	MALE	1 250	233	173	152	248	168	116	78	46	35
	FEMALE	1 186	218	173	146	252	161	103	67	38	30
1861	MALE	1 660	277	218	203	341	232	156	107	70	54
	FEMALE	1 570	266	211	196	337	222	141	92	59	44
1871	MALE	1 869	276	264	243	374	249	175	132	86	74
	FEMALE	1 820	265	255	233	385	256	171	120	73	61
1881	MALE	2 189	304	284	262	455	302	217	161	111	94
	FEMALE	2 136	295	278	251	464	301	212	153	100	84
1891	MALE	2 460	309	300	282	504	366	263	191	131	115
	FEMALE	2 373	302	292	272	499	354	246	180	122	105
1901	MALE	2 752	326	313	297	543	412	331	234	157	139
	FEMALE	2 620	320	306	285	530	386	299	214	148	133
1911	MALE	3 822	450	396	356	745	687	475	334	209	171
	FEMALE	3 385	440	389	346	653	535	388	286	184	165
1921	MALE	4 530	534	529	462	757	693	630	434	276	215
	FEMALE	4 258	525	521	452	761	650	532	366	246	206
1931	MALE	5 375	543	573	543	990	778	707	590	356	295
	FEMALE	5 002	531	560	531	962	717	627	485	306	281
1941	MALE	5 901	534	529	556	1 083	920	745	649	494	391
	FEMALE	5 606	518	517	545	1 069	891	691	579	421	377
1951	MALE	7 089	879	714	575	1 070	1 066	950	728	557	551
	FEMALE	6 921	843	684	556	1 077	1 108	919	679	520	535
1961	MALE	9 219	1 154	1 064	948	1 316	1 258	1 191	959	655	074
	FEMALE	9 019	1 102	1 016	908	1 301	1 222	1 199	920	635	717
1971	MALE	10 795	930	1 152	1 181	2 016	1 462	1 286	1 132	854	782
	FEMALE	10 773	887	1 102	1 129	1 988	1 428	1 241	1 160	877	963
1981	MALE	12 068	914	912	985	2 356	2 106	1 497	1 256	1 031	1 011
	FEMALE	12 275	869	865	936	2 303	2 110	1 471	1 242	1 128	1 350
1991	MALE	13 455	976	978	963	1 944	2 420	2 176	1 487	1 180	1 330
	FEMALE	13 842	931	930	915	1 887	2 446	2 196	1 479	1 220	1 840
1996	MALE	14 170	983	1 019	1 023	1 955	2 227	2 403	1 848	1 224	1 487
	FEMALE	14 677	935	971	970	1 902	2 272	2 459	1 863	1 265	2 040
1998[2]	MALE	14 998	972	1 060	1 038	2 090	2 302	2 612	2 028	1 306	1 589
	FEMALE	15 303	924	1 009	984	1 994	2 255	2 603	2 041	1 345	2 147

Source: © *Census, Statistics Canada*
(1) Excludes incompletely enumerated Indian reserves. (2) Estimate as of July 1, 1998.

Canadian Population Projections[1] by Age Group

(thousands of persons)

	Total Population	Under 5 Years	5–9 Years	10–14 Years	15–24 Years	25–34 Years	35–44 Years	45–54 Years	55–64 Years	65-74 Years	75 Yrs and Over
2001											
MALE	15 781.2	988.2	1 069.0	1 089.2	2 168.1	2 295.9	2 740.0	2 263.7	1 456.9	1 024.8	685.3
FEMALE	16 096.1	936.2	1 013.1	1 035.6	2 071.4	2 248.1	2 699.6	2 276.0	1 493.3	1 156.3	1 164.4
2006											
MALE	16 674.3	988.4	1 035.9	1 115.0	2 280.1	2 329.0	2 651.0	2 555.6	1 839.7	1 087.0	792.8
FEMALE	17 003.2	936.2	980.1	1 055.2	2 176.6	2 265.3	2 611.3	2 569.6	1 889.4	1 211.7	1 307.8
2011											
MALE	17 541.8	1 017.0	1 036.4	1 082.3	2 353.8	2 441.1	2 511.6	2 769.7	2 173.6	1 274.4	881.8
FEMALE	17 878.5	963.1	980.3	1 022.5	2 237.7	2 367.8	2 475.8	2 754.2	2 252.2	1 403.5	1 412.4
2016											
MALE	18 387.5	1 054.4	1 065.0	1 082.9	2 347.8	2 552.2	2 546.3	2 689.7	2 457.8	1 613.6	977.6
FEMALE	18 732.2	998.4	1 007.2	1 022.8	2 225.3	2 471.4	2 494.0	2 671.2	2 539.0	1 778.6	1 524.3

Source: © *Statistics Canada* — (1) Based on 1993 population estimates and medium-growth projections.

Canadian Population by Country of Birth

	1931	1951	1971	1991	1996
Total Population	10 376 786	14 009 429	21 568 310	27 296 855	28 846 760
Total Foreign Born	2 307 525[11]	2 059 911[11]	3 295 530[11]	4 342 885[11]	4 971 070[11]
Afghanistan[1]	—	—	—	5 545	10 915
Africa - Other............................	—	—	—	26 355	43 160
Algeria[1]	—	—	—	3 900	8 005
Argentina[1]	—	—	—	11 110	11 740
Asia - Other	6 310	6 740	52 795	24 310	47 940
Australia	3 565	4 161	14 335	13 955	14 660
Austria[2]	37 391	37 598	40 450	26 680	24 600
Barbados[3]	—	—	—	14 825	15 225
Belgium......................................	17 033	17 251	25 770	22 480	21 805
Brazil[1]	—	—	—	7 330	9 360
Cambodia[1]	—	—	—	17 960	19 355
Caribbean & Bermuda - Other .	—	—	—	25 995	36 965
Central America - Other...........	—	—	—	5 745	9 025
Chile[1]	—	—	—	22 870	23 880
China..	42 037	24 166	57 150	157 405	231 055
Colombia[1]	—	—	—	7 865	9 465
Czech and Slovak Federal Republic, former[12]	22 835	29 546	43 100	42 615	41 225
Denmark[14]	17 217	15 679	28 045	—	—
Ecuador[1]	—	—	—	8 015	9 640
Egypt[1]	—	—	—	28 020	33 930
El Salvador[1]	—	—	—	28 295	39 020
Ethiopia, former[1]	—	—	—	11 060	18 595
Europe - Other[5]	10 657	10 858	87 255	8 665	7 980
Fiji[3]	—	—	—	15 995	20 580
Finland[14]..................................	30 354	22 035	24 930	—	—
France	16 756	15 650	51 655	55 159	62 600
Germany[6]	39 163	42 693	211 060	180 525	181 650
Ghana1	—	—	—	6 675	13 085
Greece.......................................	5 579	8 594	78 780	83 680	79 695
Guatemala[1]	—	—	—	8 920	13 270
Guyana[3]	—	—	—	66 060	77 700
Haiti[1]	—	—	—	39 880	49 395
Hong Kong[3]	—	—	—	152 405	241 095
Hungary	28 523	32 929	68 495	57 010	54 225
India[3,7]	4 672	3 934	43 645	173 675	235 930
Indonesia	—	—	—	7 610	8 515
Iran[1]	—	—	—	30 710	47 405
Iraq[1]	—	—	—	7 165	16 795
Ireland	—	24 110	38 490	28 405	28 940
Israel (and Palestine/ West Bank/Gaza Strip)[1]	—	—	—	16 770	20 390
Italy...	42 578	57 789	385 755	351 615	332 110
Jamaica[3]	—	—	—	102 440	115 800
Japan	12 261	6 239	9 485	12 280	14 990
Kenya[3]	—	—	—	16 585	18 005
Korea[4,13]	—	—	—	33 170	46 025
Laos[4]	—	—	—	14 445	14 765
Lebanon[1]	—	—	—	54 600	63 130
Malaysia[4]	—	—	—	16 100	19 460
Malta[3]	—	—	—	10 185	9 445
Mexico[1]	—	—	—	19 400	27 480
Morocco[1]	—	—	—	16 790	20 435
Netherlands................................	10 736	41 457	133 525	129 615	124 545
Nicaragua[1]	—	—	—	6 460	8 545
Norway[14]	32 679	22 969	16 350	—	—
Oceania - Other[15]	—	—	—	16 305	13 780

	1931	1951	1971	1991	1996
▶ Pakistan[7]	—	—	—	25 180	39 245
Peru[1]	—	—	—	11 480	15 235
Philippines[4]	—	—	—	123 295	184 550
Poland[8]	171 169	164 474	160 040	184 695	193 375
Portugal[8]	—	—	—	161 180	158 815
Romania[9]	40 322	19 733	24 405	33 785	46 400
Scandanavia	—	—	—	54 980	50 145
Singapore[1]	—	—	—	6 285	7 970
Somalia[1]	—	—	—	5 290	16 740
South America - Other	—	—	—	15 840	19 445
South Africa[3]	2 235	2 057	—	24 730	28 465
Spain[8]	—	—	—	11 170	11 240
Sri Lanka[4]	—	—	—	25 435	67 425
Syria[1]	—	—	—	11 005	13 105
Sweden[14]	34 415	22 635	14 110	—	—
Switzerland[8]	6 076	6 414	13 895	16 330	19 310
Taiwan[4]	—	—	—	17 770	49 290
Tanzania[1]	—	—	—	17 820	18 130
Thailand[1]	—	—	—	5 815	7 710
Trinidad/Tobago[3]	—	—	—	49 385	62 020
Turkey[8]	—	—	—	12 180	14 430
Uganda[1]	—	—	—	8 960	10 755
USSR, Former[10]	133 869	188 292	160 120	99 355	108 390
United Kingdom	1 138 942	912 482	933 040	717 750	655 535
UK possessions / dependencies[5]	35 416	10 415	112 120	—	—
United States	344 574	282 010	309 640	249 075	244 695
Viet Nam[4]	—	—	—	113 595	139 325
Yugoslavia, Former[8]	17 110	20 912	78 285	88 815	121 975

Source: ©*Statistics Canada, Census of Canada*
(1) Included in "Other countries" until 1986 census. (2) Includes Hungary (Austria-Hungary) in 1911 census. (3) British possessions/dependencies (see UK possessions) during various census years could include African, Asian, Caribbean, Mediterranean and Pacific possessions as well as any territory in British North America prior to Confederation with Canada (in the case of Newfoundland, this was not until 1949); many not reported separately until 1986 census. (4) Included in "Asia - Other" until 1986 census. (5) More detailed breakdown given in subsequent census data. (6) Total for Germany includes both East and West Germany. (7) Totals for India before 1986 include Pakistan. (8) Where not reported, included in "Europe - Other." (9) For 1911 census, also includes Bulgaria. (10) Includes Russia. (11) Totals include those where country unknown or not noted: 1931: 3 051; 1951: 6 089;1971: 78 805; 1991: 65; 1996: 20. (12) Includes Czech and Slovak Federal Republics. (13) Includes North and South Korea. (14) After 1986, reported as Scandanavia. (15) Includes New Zealand. (—) = not reported.

Honouring Immigrants at Pier 21

B *etween 1928 and 1971,one million immigrants arrived in Canada through Pier 21 in Halifax. The Pier 21 Society was created to revitalize Pier 21and create a permanent site honouring the contributions of immigrant Canadians. Pier 21 will also spur the development of a historic Canadian immigration database.*

The restoration project was given its start when Prime Minister Jean Chrétien announced that the government had set aside $4.5 million for the project at Pier 21 as a legacy from the Halifax G7 Summit. The Pier 21 Centre will consist of four main components:

1. **The Immigration Exhibition:** *A highly interactive exhibition tracing the physical and emotional experience of immigrants and refugees who came to Canada through Pier 21.*

2. **The Welcome Pavilion:** *An international centre with boutiques, a waterside ethnic café and tourist information kiosks. The Welcome Pavilion includes the **Pier 21 Resource and Virtual Outreach Centre**, which will be accessible on the Internet.*

3. **The In Transit Theatre:** *An exciting show focusing on the in transit experience of immigrants and refugees who came to Canada through Pier 21, and the role Pier 21 played in World War II.*

4. **The Multicultural Hall:** *A large, multifunctional space that will become a meeting place for Canadians to explore and better understand the multicultural character of Canada.*
For more information contact the Pier 21 Society at (902) 425-7770.

Top 15 Ethnic Origins in Canada, 1996

Ethnic origin as defined in the census refers to the ethnic or cultural group(s) to which an individual's ancestors belonged. In other words, it refers to the ancestral roots of the population, not place of birth, citizenship or nationality.

In the 1996 census respondents were given four blank spaces to indicate single or multiple ethnic origins. Over 35% of them (10.2 million) reported more than one ethnic origin, reflecting intermarriage among those who have been in Canada for several generations.

The table below shows the 15 most commonly cited ethnic origins, either as the sole ethnic origin or as part of a mixed heritage.

	Total Responses	Single Ethnic Origin	Multiple Ethnic Origins
Total population	**28 528 125**	**18 303 625**	**10 224 495**
Canadian	8 806 275	5 326 995	3 479 285
English	6 832 095	2 048 275	4 783 820
French	5 597 845	2 665 250	2 932 595
Scottish	4 260 840	642 970	3 617 870
Irish	3 767 610	504 030	3 263 580
German	2 757 140	726 145	2 030 990
Italian	1 207 475	729 455	478 025
Aboriginal	1 101 955	477 630	624 330
Ukrainian	1 026 475	331 680	694 790
Chinese	921 585	800 470	121 115
Dutch	916 215	313 880	602 335
Polish	786 735	265 930	520 805
South Asian	723 345	590 145	133 200
Jewish	351 705	195 810	155 900
Norwegian	346 310	47 805	298 500

Source: © *Census of Canada, Statistics Canada*

Visible Minority Population by Group, 1996

The 1996 Census also gathered information on the number of people in Canada who are members of a visible minority, as defined by the Employment Equity Act: "persons, other than Aboriginal peoples, who are non-Caucasian in race or non-white in colour." According to the 1996 census, these groups accounted for 11.2 percent of the population (3,197,480 people).

The visible minorities are represented by the following groups:

	Total Number	% of Total Population
Total visible minority population	**3 197 480**	**11.2**
Chinese	860 150	3.0
South Asian	670 585	2.4
Black	573 860	2.0
Arab/West Asian	244 665	0.9
Filipino	234 200	0.8
Latin American	176 975	0.6
Southeast Asian	172 765	0.6
Japanese	68 135	0.2
Korean	64 835	0.2
Visible minority not included elsewhere	69 745	0.2
Multiple visible minority	61 570	0.2

Source: © *Census of Canada, Statistics Canada*

(1) Total population in 1996 was 28 528 125.

Canadian Population by Mother Tongue[1]

As Canada's population has become more diverse, so have the mother tongues reported at census time. The table below shows all languages reported to be the mother tongue of 10,000 Canadians or more in the 1996 Census, with historical comparisons.

(thousands of persons and percent of total population)

	1941	%	1951	%	1961	%	1971	%	1991	%	1996	%
Total Population .	**11 507**		**14 009**		**18 238**		**21 568**		**27 297**		**28 847**	
English	6 448	56.0	8 281	59.1	10 661	58.5	12 974	60.2	16 170	59.2	16 891	58.6
French	3 355	29.2	4 069	29.0	5 123	28.1	5 794	26.9	6 503	23.8	6 637	23.0
Chinese	34	0.3	28	0.2	49	0.3	95	0.4	499	1.8	716	2.5
Italian	80	0.7	92	0.7	340	1.9	538	2.5	511	1.9	485	1.7
German	322	2.8	329	2.3	564	3.1	561	2.6	466	1.7	450	1.6
Spanish	1	...	2	...	7	...	24	0.1	177	0.6	213	0.7
Polish	129	1.1	129	0.9	162	0.9	135	0.6	190	0.7	213	0.7
Portugese	n.a.		n.a.		18	0.1	87	0.4	212	0.8	211	0.7
Punjabi	n.a.		n.a.		n.a.		n.a.	n.a.	136	0.5	202	0.7
Ukranian	313	2.7	352	2.5	361	2.0	310	1.4	187	0.7.	163	0.6
Arabic	8	0.1	5	...	13	0.1	29	0.1	108	0.4	149	0.5
Dutch	53	0.5	88	0.6	170	0.9	145	0.7	139	0.5	134	0.5
Tagalog (Philipino)	n.a.		n.a.		n.a.		n.a.		100	0.4	133	0.5
Greek	9	0.1	8	0.1	40	0.2	104	0.5	126	0.5	121	0.4
Vietnamese ...	n.a.		n.a.		n.a.		n.a.		79	0.3	107	0.4
Hungarian	46	0.4	42	0.3	86	0.5	87	0.4	80	0.3	77	0.3
Cree	n.a.		n.a.		n.a.		n.a.		74	0.3	77	0.3
Tamil	n.a.		n.a.		n.a.		n.a.		31	0.1	67	0.2
Persian (Farsi) .	n.a.		n.a.		n.a.		n.a.		41	0.2	60	0.2
Russian	52	0.5	39	0.3	43	0.2	32	0.1	35	0.1	58	0.2
Korean	n.a.		n.a.		n.a.		n.a.		36	0.1	55	0.2
Croatian	n.a.		n.a.		n.a.		n.a.		40	0.1	50	0.2
Gujarati	n.a.		n.a.		n.a.		n.a.		38	0.1	45	0.2
Hindi	n.a.		n.a.		n.a.		n.a.		35	0.1	43	0.2
Urdu	n.a.		n.a.		n.a.		n.a.		25	0.1	40	0.1
Romanian	n.a.		n.a.		n.a.		n.a.		22	0.1	36	0.1
Creoles	n.a.		n.a.		n.a.		n.a.		28	0.1	35	0.1
Japanese	22	0.2	18	0.1	18	0.1	17	0.1	30	0.1	34	0.1
Serbian	n.a.		n.a.		n.a.		n.a.		11	...	29	0.1
Inuktitut	n.a.		n.a.		n.a.		n.a.		24	0.1	27	0.1
Armenian	n.a.		n.a.		n.a.		n.a.		26	0.1	26	0.1
Czech[2]	30	0.3	46	0.3	51	0.3	45	0.2	27	0.1	25	0.1
Finnish	37	0.3	32	0.2	45	0.2	37	0.2	28	0.1	25	0.1
Somali	n.a.		n.a.		n.a.		n.a.		—		25	0.1
Ojibway	n.a.		n.a.		n.a.		n.a.		22	0.1	23	0.1
Yiddish	130	1.1	104	0.7	82	0.4	50	0.2	25	0.1	21	0.1
Danish	19	0.2	16	0.1	35	0.2	27	0.1	22	0.1	20	0.1
Macedonian ...	n.a.		n.a.		n.a.		n.a.		15	0.1	19	0.1
Serbo-Croatian .	n.a.		n.a.		n.a.		n.a.		5	...	18	0.1
Slovak	n.a.		n.a.		n.a.		n.a.		18	0.1	18	0.1
Bengali	n.a.		n.a.		n.a.		n.a.		8	...	16	0.1
Khmer	n.a.		n.a.		n.a.		n.a.		14	...	15	0.1
Slovenian	n.a.		n.a.		n.a.		n.a.		9	...	14	...
Hebrew	n.a.		n.a.		n.a.		n.a.		12	...	13	...
Lao	n.a.		n.a.		n.a.		n.a.		12	...	13	...
Turkish	n.a.		n.a.		n.a.		n.a.		9	...	12	...
Estonian	n.a.		n.a.		n.a.		n.a.		12	...	11	...
Norwegian	60	0.5	44	0.3	40	0.2	27	0.1	13	...	10	...
Swedish	50	0.4	36	0.3	33	0.2	22	0.1	12	...	10	...
Latvian	n.a.		n.a.		n.a.		n.a.		10	...	10	...
Lithuanian	n.a.		n.a.		n.a.		n.a.		11	...	9	...

Source: © Census of Canada, Statistics Canada

(n.a.) Not available. (...) = Too small to be included. (1) The language first spoken in childhood and still understood. (2) Prior to 1996, includes Slovak.

Native Population of Canada

	1991				1996[2]			
	Total Popu-lation with Aboriginal Origins[1,4]	Native Indian	Métis	Inuit	Total Aboriginal Population[3]	Native Indian	Métis	Inuit
Canada	1 002 675	783 980	212 650	49 255	799 010	554 290	210 190	41 080
Newfoundland	13 110	5 845	1 605	6 460	14 205	5 430	4 685	4 265
Prince Edward Island	1 880	1 665	185	75	950	825	120	15
Nova Scotia	21 885	19 950	1 590	770	12 380	11 340	860	210
New Brunswick	12 815	11 835	975	450	10 250	9 180	975	120
Quebec	137 615	112 590	19 480	8 480	71 415	47 600	16 075	8 300
Ontario	243 550	220 135	26 905	5 250	141 525	118 830	22 790	1 300
Manitoba	116 200	76 370	45 575	900	128 685	82 990	46 195	360
Saskatchewan	96 580	69 385	32 840	540	111 245	75 205	36 535	190
Alberta	148 220	99 650	56 310	2 825	122 840	72 645	50 745	795
British Columbia	169 035	149 570	22 295	1 990	139 655	113 315	26 750	815
Yukon	6 390	5 870	565	170	6 175	5 530	565	110
Northwest Territories	35 390	11 100	4 310	21 355	39 690	11 400	3 895	24 600
Nunavut	n.a.	n.a.	n.a.	n.a.	20 690	90	80	20 490

Source: © *Census of Canada*

(n.a.): Not applicable (1) The 1991 census question on ethnic or cultural origins gathered information on the number of people who reported North American Indian, Métis or Inuit origin as either a single response or in combination with other origins. (2) The numbers shown may exceed the total population as 6 400 respondents counted themselves as belonging to more than one group. (3) The 1996 data examined the responses to both an ancestry and an identity question, and the resulting information is a compilation of the two. The identity question included a more direct inquiry into whether the person considered him or herself to have an Aboriginal identity in addition to an Aboriginal ancestry. (4) In the 1991 census, 78 reserves were incompletely enumerated, representing 37 000 individuals. (5) Data from the 1996 Census was used to create a profile for Nunavut.

Status Indian Population,[1] 1998

	Total Indian Population	On Reserve	Off Reserve	On Crown Land	Number of Bands
Canada............................	627 435	341 825	261 629	23 981	608
Atlantic Provinces	24 610	16 080	8 514	16	31
Quebec.................................	59 881	40 524	18 178	1 179	39
Ontario.................................	142 408	70 185	69 825	2 398	126
Manitoba..............................	98 197	62 262	34 158	1 777	61
Saskatchewan......................	97 776	48 770	47 329	1 677	70
Alberta.................................	78 495	49 331	26 380	2 784	43
British Columbia...................	104 411	53 763	49 818	830	197
Yukon Territory.....................	7 330	696	3 555	3 079	15
Northwest Territories............	14 327	214	3 872	10 241	26

Source: *Indian and Northern Affairs Canada*

(1) Status Indians are those individuals registered with the Department of Indian and Northern Affairs Canada under the Indian Act.

Largest Native Bands in Canada, 1998

Band, Province	Population[1]	Band, Province	Population[1]
Six Nations of the Grand River,[2] Ontario ...	19 894	Mohawks of the Bay of Quinte, Ontario ...	6 768
Mohawks of Akwesasne, Ontario	9 046	Lac la Ronge, Saskatchewan	6 757
Blood, Alberta	8 689	Peguis, Manitoba	6 703
Kahnawake, Quebec	8 649	Peter Ballantyne Cree Nation, Saskatchewan ..	6 444
Saddle Lake, Alberta	7 261	Wikwemikong, Ontario	6 153

Source: *Indian and Northern Affairs Canada*

(1) Registered Indian population as of December 31. (2) This band consists of the following 13 registry groups: The bay of Qunite mohawks, Bearfoot Onondaga, Delaware, Konadaha Seneca, Lower Cayuga, Lower Mohawk, Niharondasa Seneca, Onondaga Clear Sky, Tuscarora, Upper Cayuga, Upper Mohawk and Walker Mohawk.

Canadian Urban and Rural Population

(thousands)

Year	Urban		Rural						
	Total	%	Non-Farm	%	+	Farm	%	=	Total	%
1871	722	19.6	n.a.	n.a.		n.a.	n.a.		2 967	80.4
1881	1 110	25.7	n.a.	n.a.		n.a.	n.a.		3 215	74.3
1891	1 537	31.8	n.a.	n.a.		n.a.	n.a.		3 296	68.2
1901	2 014	37.5	n.a.	n.a.		n.a.	n.a.		3 357	62.5
1911	3 273	45.4	n.a.	n.a.		n.a.	n.a.		3 934	54.6
1921	4 352	49.5	n.a.	n.a.		n.a.	n.a.		4 436	50.5
1931	5 469	52.7	1 670	16.1		3 238	31.2		4 908	47.3
1941	6 271	54.5	2 123	18.4		3 113	27.1		5 236	45.5
1951	8 817	62.9	2 423	17.3		2 769	19.8		5 192	37.1
1956	10 715	66.6	2 734	17.0		2 632	16.4		5 366	33.4
1961	12 700	69.6	3 465	19.0		2 073	11.4		5 538	30.4
1966	14 727	73.6	3 374	16.9		1 914	9.6		5 288	26.4
1971	16 410	76.1	3 738	17.3		1 420	6.6		5 158	23.9
1976	17 367	75.5	4 591	20.0		1 035	4.5		5 626	24.5
1981	18 436	75.7	4 867	20.0		1 040	4.3		5 907	24.3
1986	19 352	76.5	5 067	20.0		890	3.5		5 957	23.5
1991	20 907	76.6	5 583	20.5		807	3.0		6 390	23.4
1996	22 461	77.9	n.a.	n.a.		n.a.	n.a.		6 386	22.1

Source: © *Census of Canada, Statistics Canada*   (n.a.) not available

Definitions: Urban: persons living in a built-up area having a population of 1 000 or more and a population density of 400 or more per sq. km; **Rural:** persons living outside "urban areas"; **Rural Farm:** persons living in rural areas who are members of households of farm operators; **Rural Non-Farm:** persons living in rural areas who are not members of households of farm operators..

Urban and Rural Population by Province

Province	1951		1991		1996	
	Rural	Urban	Rural	Urban	Rural	Urban
Canada	5 174 555	8 473 458	6 389 724	20 907 135	6 385 551	22 461 210
Newfoundland[1]	n.a.	n.a.	264 023	304 451	237 973	313 819
Prince Edward Island	73 744	24 685	77 952	51 813	75 097	59 460
Nova Scotia	297 753	344 831	418 434	481 508	411 424	497 858
New Brunswick	300 686	215 011	378 686	345 214	377 712	360 421
Quebec	1 358 363	2 697 318	1 544 752	5 351 211	1 541 170	5 597 625
Ontario	1 346 443	3 251 099	1 831 043	8 253 842	1 794 832	8 958 741
Manitoba	336 961	439 580	304 767	787 175	313 835	800 063
Saskatchewan	579 258	252 470	365 531	623 397	363 059	627 178
Alberta	489 826	449 675	514 660	2 030 893	554 011	2 142 815
British Columbia	371 739	793 471	641 922	2 640 139	667 112	3 057 388
Yukon Territory	6 502	2 594	11 462	16 335	12 319	18 447
Northwest Territories	13 280[2]	2 724[2]	36 492[2]	21 157[2]	37 007	27 395
Nunavut[3]	n.a.	n.a.	n.a.	n.a.	18 452	6 278

Source: © *Census of Canada, Statistics Canada*
(1) Newfoundland joined confederation in 1949 and urban/rural split in population was not included in 1951 census data. (2) Includes Nunavut. (3) Nunavut became a province in 1999, but data from the 1996 census was used to create a profile.

Preparing for 2001 Census

Statistics Canada was asked to further delineate rural areas in Canada. The 2001 Census will help users analyze the socioeconomic features of rural Canada to a greater degree.

Population of Canadian Towns and Cities

(more than 5,000 inhabitants)

Town or city classification is made according to the official designations adopted by provincial or federal authority. *Indicates a city or *ville* in Quebec; all others are towns.

	POPULATION 1991	1996	AREA (sq. km)
■ NEWFOUNDLAND			
Bay Roberts	5 474	5 472	24.15
Carbonear	5 259	5 168	11.81
Channel-Port aux Basques	5 644	5 243	37.83
Clarenville	4 473	5 335	139.98
Conception Bay South	17 590	19 265	59.40
Corner Brook*	22 410	21 893	147.55
Deer Lake	5 161	5 222	71.75
Gander	10 339	10 364	101.16
Grand Falls-Windsor	14 693	14 160	56.66
Happy Valley-Goose Bay	8 610	8 655	306.42
Labrador City	9 061	8 455	6.47
Marystown	6 739	6 742	59.27
Mount Pearl*	23 676	25 519	15.06
Paradise	7 358	7 960	27.83
Placentia	5 515	5 013	58.00
Portugal Cove-St. Philip's	5 459	5 773	56.43
St. John's*	104 659	101 936	431.75
Stephenville	7 621	7 764	34.80
Torbay	4 707	5 230	36.04
■ PRINCE EDWARD ISLAND			
Charlottetown*	31 541	32 531	42.64
Stratford	5 427	5 869	22.14
Summerside*	13 636	14 525	27.71
■ NOVA SCOTIA			
Amherst	9 742	9 669	16.65
Bedford	11 618	13 638	39.79
Bridgewater	7 248	7 351	13.35
Dartmouth*	67 798	65 629	58.57
Halifax*	114 455	113 910	79.22
Kentville	5 506	5 551	17.12
New Glasgow	9 905	9 812	10.36
Truro	11 683	11 938	38.09
Yarmouth	7 781	7 568	11.14
■ NEW BRUNSWICK			
Bathurst*	14 409	13 815	90.94
Campbellton*	8 699	8 404	17.30
Dieppe	10 650	12 497	51.62
Edmunston*	10 835	11 033	34.58
Fredericton*	46 466	46 507	129.58
Grand Falls (Grand-Sault)	6 083	6 133	17.73
Miramichi	21 165	19 241	175.07

	POPULATION 1991	1996	AREA (sq. km)
Moncton*	56 823	59 313	142.37
Oromocto	9 325	9 194	22.08
Quispamsis	8 446	8 839	39.98
Riverview	16 270	16 653	34.26
Sackville	5 494	5 393	74.42
Saint John*	74 969	72 494	322.88
Woodstock	4 782	5 092	14.08
■ QUEBEC			
Alma*	25 910	26 127	109.27
Amos*	13 783	13 632	428.72
Amqui*	6 518	6 800	120.82
Anjou*	37 207	37 308	13.64
Asbestos*	6 487	6 271	13.47
Aylmer*	32 244	34 901	91.21
Baie-Comeau*	26 012	25 554	352.27
Beaconsfield*	19 616	19 414	10.64
Beauharnois*	6 449	6 435	40.44
Beauport*	69 158	72 920	71.32
Bécancour*	10 911	11 489	434.29
Beloeil*	18 516	19 294	24.01
Bernieres-Saint-Nicholas	14 431	15 594	94.12
Blainville*	22 679	29 603	55.20
Boisbriand*	21 124	25 227	27.32
Bois-des-Filion*	6 337	7 124	3.92
Boucherville*	33 796	34 989	69.33
Brossard*	64 793	65 927	44.98
Buckingham*	10 548	11 678	14.59
Candiac*	10 765	11 805	16.54
Cap-de-la-Madeleine*	33 716	33 438	17.30
Cap-Rouge*	14 105	14 163	6.39
Carignan*	5 386	5 614	62.35
Chambly*	15 893	19 716	25.06
Charlemagne*	5 598	5 739	1.76
Charlesbourg*	70 792	70 942	67.53
Charny*	10 239	10 661	8.80
Chateauguay*	39 833	41 423	35.40
Chibougamau*	8 855	8 664	754.08
Chicoutimi*	62 670	63 061	156.66
Coaticook*	6 637	6 653	12.60
Cote-Saint-Luc*	30 126	29 705	7.40
Cowansville*	11 986	12 051	49.12
Delson*	6 063	6 703	7.15
Deux-Montagnes*	13 035	15 953	6.05
Dolbeau*	8 181	8 310	46.32 ▶

	POPULATION		AREA		POPULATION		AREA
	1991	**1996**	(sq. km)		**1991**	**1996**	(sq. km)
Dollard-des-Ormeaux*	46 922	47 826	15.05	Mont-Saint-Hilaire*	12 267	13 064	43.39
Donnacona*	5 659	5 739	20.12	Montmagny*	11 861	11 885	125.77
Dorval*	17 249	17 572	20.76	Montréal*	1 017 669	1 016 376	177.10
Drummondville*	43 171	44 882	70.25	Montréal-Nord*	85 516	81 581	11.03
Farnham*	6 146	6 044	25.07	Montréal-Ouest*	5 180	5 254	1.63
Fleurimont*	14 727	16 262	34.77	Outremont*	22 935	22 571	3.68
Gaspé*	16 402	16 517	1 105.11	Pierrefonds*	48 735	52 986	24.39
Gatineau*	92 284	100 702	140.62	Pincourt*	9 749	10 023	9.24
Granby*	42 804	43 316	72.73	Plessisville*	6 952	6 810	4.34
Grand-Mere*	14 287	14 223	70.79	Point-Claire*	27 647	28 435	19.19
Greenfield Park*	17 652	17 337	4.58	Port-Cartier*	7 383	7 070	87.34
Hampstead*	7 219	6 986	1.77	Québec*	167 517	167 264	88.86
Hull*	60 707	62 339	37.35	Repentigny*	49 630	53 824	24.42
Iberville*	9 352	9 635	4.90	Rimouski*	30 873	31 773	76.02
Joliette*	17 396	17 541	22.52	Riviere-du-Loup*	14 017	14 721	16.94
Jonquiere*	57 933	56 503	209.62	Roberval*	11 628	11 640	147.24
Kirkland*	17 495	18 678	10.34	Rock Forest*	14 551	16 604	51.34
L'Ancienne-L'orette*	15 242	15 895	7.87	Rosemere*	11 198	12 025	10.20
L'Assomption*	10 817	11 366	66.44	Rouyn-Noranda*	28 958	28 819	210.79
L'Ile Bizard*	11 352	13 038	22.69	Roxboro*	5 879	5 950	2.23
L'Ile Perrot*	8 065	9 178	4.92	Saint-Antoine*	10 232	10 806	9.90
La Baie*	20 995	21 057	261.69	Saint-Basile-le-Grand*	10 127	11 771	34.84
La Plaine*	10 576	14 413	39.70	Saint-Bruno-de-Montarville*	23 849	23 714	41.79
La Prairie*	15 237	17 128	43.33	Saint-Constant*	18 424	21 993	57.32
La Sarre*	8 513	8 345	148.30	Saint-Emile*	6 916	9 889	8.77
La Tuque*	12 577	12 102	599.07	Saint-Eustache*	37 278	39 848	70.03
Lac-Mégantic*	5 852	5 864	20.97	Saint-Félicien*	9 340	9 599	168.56
Lachenaie*	15 052	18 489	42.75	Saint-Georges*	19 583	20 057	24.94
Lachine*	35 266	35 171	17.38	Saint-Hubert*	74 093	77 042	63.05
Lachute*	11 730	11 493	96.24	Saint-Hyacinthe*	39 292	38 981	36.63
LaSalle*	73 804	72 029	16 42	Saint-Jean-Chrysostome* ..	12 717	16 161	82.90
Laval*	314 398	330 393	245.40	Saint-Jean-sur-Richelieu* ..	37 607	36 435	47.42
Le Gardeur*	13 814	16 853	44.00	Saint-Jérome*	23 384	23 916	15.79
LeMoyne*	5 412	5 052	0.96	Saint-Lambert*	20 976	20 971	6.43
Lévis*	39 417	40 407	44.0	Saint-Laurent*	72 402	74 240	46.17
Longueuil*	129 808	127 997	42.85	Saint-Leonard*	73 120	71 327	12.93
Loretteville*	14 219	14 168	6.94	Saint-Louis-de-France	6 747	7 327	61.54
Lorraine*	8 410	8 876	5.46	Saint-Luc*	15 008	18 371	51.20
Louiseville*	8 000	7 911	62.57	Saint-Raymond*	8 126	8 773	671.22
Magog*	14 034	14 050	15.28	Saint-Rédempteur*	5 862	6 358	3.46
Marieville*	5 128	5 510	3.42	Saint-Rémi*	5 768	5 707	79.67
Mascouche*	25 828	28 097	107.95	Saint-Romuald*	9 830	10 604	18.34
Masson-Angers*	5 753	7 989	55.60	Saint-Timothée*	8 292	8 495	68.02
Matane*	12 756	12 364	24.35	Sainte-Agathe-des-Monts* ..	5 452	5 669	15.58
Mercier*	8 227	9 059	45.89	Sainte-Anne-des-Monts* ...	5 652	5 617	106.06
Mirabel*	17 971	22 689	492.20	Sainte-Anne-des-Plaines* ..	10 787	12 908	92.23
Mistassini*	6 842	6 904	248.50	Sainte-Catherine*	9 805	13 724	9.06
Mont-Joli*	6 265	6 267	9.59	Sainte-Foy*	71 133	72 330	83.86
Mont-Laurier*	7 862	8 007	82.05	Sainte-Julie*	20 632	24 030	47.91
Mont-Royal*	18 212	18 282	7.43	Sainte-Marie*	10 513	10 966	105.31 ▶

	POPULATION		AREA
	1991	1996	(sq. km)
Sainte-Marthe-sur-le-Lac* ..	7 410	8 295	9.01
Sainte-Thérèse*	24 158	23 477	10.09
Salaberry-de-Valleyfield* ...	27 598	26 600	27.47
Sept-Iles*	24 848	25 224	298.93
Shawinigan*	19 931	18 678	26.27
Shawinigan-Sud*	11 584	11 804	51.52
Sherbrooke*	76 431	76 786	57.77
Sillery*	12 519	12 003	6.73
Sorel*	24 253	23 248	38.04
Terrebonne*	39 700	42 214	73.21
Thetford Mines*	18 251	17 635	33.91
Tracy*	13 181	12 773	19.11
Trois-Rivières*	49 426	48 419	77.81
Trois-Rivières-Ouest*	20 076	22 886	28.75
Val-Belair*	17 181	20 176	68.52
Val d'Or*	23 842	24 285	1 206.60
Vanier*	10 833	11 174	4.66
Varennes*	14 758	18 842	93.96
Vaudreuil-Dorion*	17 109	18 466	73.13
Verdun*	61 307	59 714	8.15
Victoriaville*	36 392	38 174	83.49
Westmount*	20 239	20 420	3.96

■ ONTARIO

Ajax	57 350	64 430	67.70
Amherstburg	8 921	10 245	11.26
Ancaster	21 988	23 403	174.55
Arnprior	6 679	7 113	13.63
Aurora	29 454	34 857	49.16
Aylmer	6 244	7 018	5.85
Barrie*	62 278	79 191	76.79
Belleville*	37 243	37 083	29.13
Bracebridge	12 308	13 223	632.09
Bradford-West Gwillimbury .	17 702	20 213	197.26
Brampton*	234 445	268 251	265.04
Brantford*	81 997	84 764	71.22
Brockville*	21 582	21 752	20.25
Burlington*	129 575	136 976	177.40
Caledon	34 965	39 893	686.16
Cambridge*	92 772	101 429	115.64
Carleton Place	7 432	8 450	7.30
Chatham*	43 632	43 409	30.86
Clarington	49 479	60 615	607.79
Cobourg	15 079	16 027	15.89
Collingwood	14 382	15 596	33.60
Cornwall*	47 137	47 403	63.49
Dryden	6 505	6 711	16.86
Dundas	21 868	23 125	24.20
Dunnville	12 131	12 471	302.92
East Gwillimbury	18 637	19 770	245.14
Elliot Lake*	14 089	13 588	756.79

	POPULATION		AREA
	1991	1996	(sq. km)
Espanola	5 527	5 454	17.66
Essex	6 759	6 785	6.48
Etobicoke*	309 993	328 718	123.93
Fergus	7 940	8 884	7.23
Flamborough	29 616	34 037	489.90
Fort Erie	26 006	27 183	168.30
Fort Frances	8 891	8 790	26.05
Gananoque	5 209	5 219	9.01
Georgina	29 746	34 777	286.27
Gloucester*	101 677	104 022	293.86
Goderich	7 452	7 553	6.97
Gravenhurst	9 988	10 030	524.06
Grimsby	18 520	19 585	68.12
Guelph*	88 444	95 821	87.12
Haldimand	20 573	22 128	638.15
Halton Hills	36 816	42 390	275.86
Hamilton*	318 499	322 352	122.99
Hanover	6 711	6 844	6.49
Hawkesbury	9 713	10 162	8.71
Hearst	6 079	6 049	96.85
Huntsville	14 997	15 918	700.90
Ingersoll	9 378	9 849	10.21
Innisfil	21 249	24 711	284.10
Iroquois Falls	5 999	5 714	689.94
Kanata*	37 344	47 909	132.21
Kapuskasing	10 344	10 036	83.92
Kenora	9 782	10 063	15.33
Kincardine	6 601	6 620	10.25
Kingston*	56 597	55 947	29.64
Kingsville	5 716	5 991	4.27
Kirkland Lake	10 440	9 905	270.01
Kitchener*	168 282	178 420	135.15
LaSalle	16 628	20 566	65.61
Leamington	14 140	16 188	10.63
Lincoln	17 149	18 801	163.43
Lindsay	16 696	17 638	15.19
Listowel	5 404	5 467	6.19
London*	311 620	325 646	437.99
Markham	153 811	173 383	211.53
Midland	14 485	15 035	21.75
Milton	32 075	32 104	367.20
Mississauga*	463 388	544 382	273.86
Nanticoke*	22 727	23 485	674.72
Napanee	5 179	5 450	4.41
Nepean*	107 627	115 100	217.00
New Liskeard	5 431	5 112	6.42
New Tecumseth	20 344	22 902	274.83
Newmarket	45 474	57 125	35.91
Niagara Falls*	75 399	76 917	212.02
Niagara-on-the-Lake	12 945	13 238	131.11
Nickel Centre	12 332	13 017	378.36 ▶

	POPULATION		AREA
	1991	1996	(sq. km)
North Bay*	55 405	54 332	312.88
North York*	563 270	589 653	176.87
Oakville	114 670	128 405	138.18
Onaping Falls	5 402	5 277	228.98
Orangeville	17 921	21 498	14.07
Orillia*	25 925	27 846	28.55
Oshawa*	129 344	134 364	143.41
Ottawa*	313 987	323 340	110.15
Owen Sound*	21 674	21 390	23.69
Paris	8 600	8 987	13.64
Parry Sound	6 125	6 326	14.98
Pelham	13 328	14 343	124.52
Pembroke*	13 997	14 177	15.33
Penetanguishene	6 862	7 291	12.58
Perth	5 576	5 886	9.18
Peterborough*	68 379	69 535	53.99
Pickering*	68 631	78 989	226.52
Port Colborne*	18 766	18 451	122.82
Port Elgin	6 857	7 041	5.92
Port Hope	11 505	11 698	13.00
Rayside-Balfour	15 039	16 050	328.21
Renfrew	8 134	8 125	12.25
Richmond Hill	00 142	101 725	99.42
Rockland	6 771	8 070	8.49
Sarnia*	74 167	72 738	163.73
Sault Ste. Marie*	81 476	80 054	221.52
Scarborough*	524 598	558 960	187.70
Simcoe	15 539	15 380	40.51
Smiths Falls	9 439	9 131	8.20
St. Catharines*	129 300	130 926	94.43
St. Marys	5 496	5 952	12.14
St. Thomas*	30 332	32 275	32.22
Stoney Creek*	49 968	54 318	98.60
Stratford*	27 666	28 987	20.33
Strathroy	10 566	11 852	13.89
Sturgeon Falls	5 837	6 162	5.79
Sudbury*	92 884	92 059	262.73
Tecumseh	10 495	12 828	6.17
Thorold*	17 542	17 883	84.54
Thunder Bay*	113 496	113 662	322.87
Tillsonburg	12 019	13 211	21.99
Timmins*	47 461	47 499	3 004.39
Toronto*	635 395	653 734	97.15
Trenton*	16 908	17 179	11.68
Valley East	21 939	23 537	518.03
Vanier*	18 150	17 247	2.93
Vaughan*	111 359	132 549	275.34
Walden	9 805	10 292	718.62
Wallaceburg	11 846	11 772	10.71
Wasaga Beach	6 457	8 698	55.62

	POPULATION		AREA
	1991	1996	(sq. km)
Waterloo*	71 181	77 949	64.43
Welland*	47 914	48 411	81.23
Whitby	61 281	73 794	142.99
Whitchurch-Stouffville	18 357	19 835	206.85
Windsor*	191 435	197 694	120.29
Woodstock*	30 075	32 086	24.78
York*	139 819	146 534	23.18
■ MANITOBA			
Brandon*	38 575	39 175	74.85
Dauphin	8 453	8 266	11.94
Flin Flon* (part in Man. balance in Sask.)	7 119	6 572	11.55
Morden	5 273	5 689	12.44
Portage La Prairie*	13 186	13 077	24.03
Selkirk	9 815	9 881	24.71
Steinbach	8 213	8 478	25.24
The Pas	6 166	5 945	28.46
Thompson*	14 977	14 385	16.85
Winkler	6 397	7 241	16.33
Winnipeg*	615 215	618 477	464.13
■ SASKATCHEWAN			
Estevan*	10 240	10 752	17.67
Humboldt	4 989	5 074	11.92
Lloydminster*(part in Sask)	7 241	7 636	17.37
Melfort*	5 628	5 759	14.66
Melville*	4 905	4 646	15.41
Moose Jaw*	33 593	32 973	46.64
North Battleford*	14 348	14 051	35.48
Prince Albert*	34 181	34 777	64.98
Regina*	179 183	180 400	114.06
Saskatoon*	186 067	193 647	136.79
Swift Current*	14 824	14 890	22.87
Weyburn*	9 673	9 723	14.04
Yorkton*	15 315	15 154	23.82
■ ALBERTA			
Airdrie*	12 456	15 946	21.02
Banff	5 688	6 098	4.86
Beaumont	5 042	5 810	5.59
Bonnyville	5 132	5 100	14.39
Brooks	9 433	10 093	15.81
Calgary*	710 795	768 082	716.79
Camrose*	13 420	13 728	26.10
Canmore	5 681	8 354	67.08
Coaldale	5 310	5 731	7.06
Cochrane	5 267	7 424	16.09
Crowsnest Pass	6 680	6 356	379.19
Drayton Valley	5 983	5 883	7.95
Drumheller*	6 263	6 587	26.24

	POPULATION		AREA
	1991	1996	(sq. km)
Edmonton*	616 741	616 306	670.08
Edson	7 323	7 399	25.89
Fort Saskatchewan*	12 092	12 408	45.10
Grande Prairie*	28 271	31 140	41.83
High River	6 269	7 359	11.58
Hinton	9 046	9 961	22.27
Innisfail	5 700	6 116	9.82
Lacombe	6 934	8 018	12.45
Leduc*	13 970	14 305	25.49
Lethbridge*	60 974	63 053	119.90
Lloydminster (part)*	10 042	11 317	23.93
Medicine Hat*	43 625	46 783	112.96
Morinville	6 104	6 226	12.32
Okotoks	6 723	8 510	15.76
Olds	5 549	5 815	10.14
Peace River	6 717	6 536	21.20
Ponoka	5 861	6 149	10.07
Red Deer*	58 145	60 075	58.18
Rocky Mountain House	5 641	5 805	10.82
Slave Lake	5 607	6 553	18.00
Spruce Grove	12 908	14 271	25.57
St. Albert*	42 146	46 888	33.97
Stettler	4 947	5 220	9 35
Stony Plain	7 226	8 274	26.51
Sylvan Lake	4 210	5 178	8.18
Taber	6 664	7 214	15.66
Vegreville	5 138	5 337	13.86
Wainwright	4 732	5 079	8.16
Wetaskiwin*	10 657	10 959	16.45
Whitecourt	6 938	7 783	25.40

■ **BRITISH COLUMBIA**

Abbotsford	86 928	105 403	343.85
Burnaby	158 858	179 209	88.45
Castlegar*	6 579	7 027	16.16
Colwood*	13 468	13 848	17.87
Comox	9 477	11 069	14.47
Coquitlam*	84 021	101 820	123.36
Courtenay*	11 698	17 335	15.49
Cranbrook*	16 447	18 131	17.18

	POPULATION		AREA
	1991	1996	(sq. km)
Dawson Creek*	10 981	11 125	20.30
Fort St. John*	14 156	15 021	21.73
Kamloops*	67 057	76 394	296.06
Kelowna*	75 953	89 442	212.57
Kimberley*	6 531	6 738	58.19
Ladysmith	4 875	6 456	7.53
Langley*	19 765	22 523	10.18
Merritt*	6 898	7 631	23.74
Nanaimo*	60 129	70 130	88.19
Nelson*	8 849	9 585	7.71
New Westminster*	43 585	49 350	15.38
North Vancouver*	38 436	41 475	10.77
Parksville	7 381	9 472	15.93
Penticton*	27 258	30 987	40.80
Port Alberni*	18 523	18 468	17.81
Port Coquitlam*	36 773	46 682	28.76
Port Moody*	17 756	20 847	26.21
Prince George*	69 653	75 150	315.94
Prince Rupert*	16 620	16 714	53.56
Qualicum Beach	5 137	6 728	11.14
Quesnel*	8 208	8 468	23.00
Revelstoke*	7 729	8 047	34.09
Richmond*	126 624	148 867	124.20
Sidney	10 082	10 701	5.02
Smithers	5 029	5 624	13.63
Surrey*	245 173	304 477	301.76
Terrace*	11 433	12 779	19.21
Trail*	7 921	7 696	18.74
Vancouver*	471 844	514 008	113.09
Vernon*	27 722	31 817	75.09
Victoria*	71 228	73 504	18.78
View Royal	5 996	6 441	15.42
White Rock*	16 314	17 210	5.05
Williams Lake*	10 395	10 472	23.45

■ **YUKON TERRITORY**

Whitehorse*	17 925	19 157	413.48

■ **NORTHWEST TERRITORIES**

Yellowknife*	15 179	17 275	102.38

Source: © *Census of Canada, Statistics Canada*

A Statistical Profile of Canadian Communities

A Statistical Profile of Canadian Communities *is a popular component of Statistics Canada's Web site (www.statcan.ca). Users can obtain statistical information for 6000 Canadian cities, towns, villages and Aboriginal communities using a mapping feature to pinpoint the community of interest. Information is based on the 1996 Census and is given for five major topics: population; education; income and work; and families and dwellings; and health.*

Population of Census Metropolitan Areas in Canada

Statistics Canada defines a census metropolitan area (CMA) as a very large urban area, together with neighbouring urban and rural areas that have a high degree of economic and social integration with that large urban area. The urban area itself (or urbanized core) must have a population of at least 100,000 based on the previous census. For a more detailed look at these cities, see "Canadian Cities" pages 34-8.

CMA	Population[1] (000s)					Land Area
	1966	1976	1986	1996	1998[2]	1996[1]
Calgary, Alta.	330 575	469 917	671 453	821 628	907 112	5 083.28 sq. km
Chicoutimi, Que.	109 142	128 643	158 468	160 454	161 982	1 723.31 sq. km
Edmonton, Alta.	401 299	554 228	774 026	862 597	917 536	9 536.63 sq. km
Halifax, N.S.	198 193	267 991	295 922	332 518	347 984	2 503.10 sq. km
Hamilton, Ont.	449 116	529 371	557 029	624 360	658 618	1 358.50 sq. km
Kitchener, Ont.	192 275	272 158	311 195	382 940	409 520	823.64 sq. km
London, Ont.	207 396	270 383	342 302	398 616	418 180	2 105.07 sq. km
Montreal, Que.	2 436 817	2 802 485	2 921 357	3 326 510	3 428 304	4 024.21 sq. km
Oshawa, Ont.	100 255	135 196	203 543	268 773	289 192	894.19 sq. km
Ottawa-Hull, Ont.-Que.	494 535	693 288	819 263	1 010 498	1 056 748	5 686.45 sq. km
Quebec, Que.	413 397	542 158	603 267	671 889	687 155	3 149.65 sq. km
Regina, Sask.	131 127	151 191	186 521	193 652	199 539	3 421.58 sq. km
St.Catharines-N, Ont.	109 418	301 921	343 258	372 406	389 081	1 399.80 sq. km
St. John's, Nfld.	101 161	143 390	161 901	174 051	173 586	789.66 sq. km
Saint John, N.B.	101 192	112 974	121 265	125 705	127 280	3 509.34 sq. km
Saskatoon, Sask.	115 892	133 750	200 665	219 056	229 302	5 322.09 sq. km
Sherbrooke, Que.	79 667	104 505	129 960	147 384	152 655	979.94 sq. km
Sudbury, Ont.	117 075	157 030	148 877	160 488	163 313	2 612.11 sq. km
Thunder Bay, Ont.	143 673	119 253	122 217	125 562	128 607	2 295.27 sq. km
Toronto, Ont.	2 158 496	2 803 101	3 431 981	4 263 757	4 594 880	5 867.73 sq. km
Trois Rivières, Que.	94 476	98 583	128 888	139 956	142 448	871.91 sq. km
Vancouver, B.C.	892 286	1 166 348	1 380 729	1 831 665	1 995 927	2 820.66 sq. km
Victoria, B.C.	173 455	218 250	255 225	304 287	318 124	633.44 sq. km
Windsor, Ont.	211 697	247 582	253 988	278 685	296 726	861.66 sq. km
Winnipeg, Man.	508 759	578 217	625 304	667 209	676 432	4 077.64 sq. km

Source: © *Census of Canada, Statistics Canada*

* Indicates a Census Agglomeration; all others are Census Metropolitan Areas.

Census Agglomeration: A large urban area (population at least 10 000) together with adjacent urban and rural areas that have a high degree of social and economic integration.

(1) Total land area considered to be part of CMA varied from census to census. (2) Estimate of total population.

VITAL STATISTICS

Births in Canada, 1921–98

	Live Births	Birth Rate[1]		Live Births	Birth Rate[1]
1921	264 879	29.3	1960	478 551	26.8
1922	259 825	28.3	1961	475 700	26.1
1923	247 404	26.7	1962	469 693	25.3
1924	251 351	26.7	1963	465 767	24.6
1925	249 365	26.1	1964	452 915	23.5
1926	240 015	24.7	1965	418 595	21.3
1927	241 149	24.3	1966	387 710	19.4
1928	243 616	24.1	1967	370 894	18.2
1929	242 226	23.5	1968	364 310	17.6
1930	250 335	23.9	1969	369 647	17.6
1931	247 205	23.2	1970	371 988	17.5
1932	242 698	22.5	1971	362 187	16.8
1933	229 791	21.0	1972	347 319	15.9
1934	228 296	20.7	1973	343 373	15.5
1935	228 396	20.5	1974	350 650	15.4
1936	227 980	20.3	1975	359 323	15.8
1937	227 869	20.1	1976	359 987	15.7
1938	237 091	20.7	1977	361 400	15.5
1939	237 991	20.6	1978	358 852	15.3
1940	252 577	21.6	1979	366 064	15.9
1941	263 993	22.4	1980	370 709	15.5
1942	281 569	23.5	1981	371 346	15.3
1943	292 943	24.2	1982	373 082	15.0
1944	293 967	24.0	1983	373 689	15.0
1945	300 587	24.3	1984	377 031	15.0
1946	343 504	27.2	1985	375 727	14.8
1947	372 589	28.9	1986	372 913	14.2
1948	359 860	27.3	1987	369 742	13.9
1949	367 092	27.3	1988	376 795	14.0
1950	372 009	27.1	1989	392 661	14.3
1951	381 092	27.2	1990	405 486	14.6
1952	403 559	27.9	1991	402 528	14.3
1953	417 884	28.1	1992	398 642	14.0
1954	436 198	28.5	1993	388 394	13.4
1955	442 937	28.2	1994	385 110	13.2
1956	450 739	28.0	1995	384 571	13.1
1957	469 093	28.2	1996	371 270	12.5
1958	470 118	27.5	1997	364 765	12.1
1959	479 275	27.4	1998[2]	355 290	11.8

Source: © *Statistics Canada*   (1) Per 1 000 population. (2) Based on preliminary figures.

Births by Province, 1998

	Live Births	Birth Rate[1]		Live Births	Birth Rate[1]
Canada	**355 290**	**11.8**	Manitoba	15 305	13.5
Newfoundland	5 320	9.7	Saskatchewan	12 740	12.5
Prince Edward Island	1 695	12.4	Alberta	38 390	13.3
Nova Scotia	10 290	11.0	British Columbia	46 245	11.6
New Brunswick	7 795	10.3	Yukon	455	14.2
Quebec	77 020	10.5	Northwest Territories	1 530	22.6
Ontario	138 505	12.2			

Source: © *Statistics Canada*   (1) Rate per 1 000 population.

Expected Years of Life Remaining, by Age, 1991

	Male		Female			Male		Female	
Age	% Dying[1]	Years of Life Remaining	% Dying[1]	Years of Life Remaining	Age	% Dying[1]	Years of Life Remaining	% Dying[1]	Years of Life Remaining
0	.71	74.55	.58	80.89	56	.84	22.53	.48	27.42
1	.05	74.08	.05	80.36	57	.93	21.71	.52	26.55
2	.04	73.12	.03	79.40	58	1.03	20.91	.57	25.69
3	.03	72.15	.02	78.42	59	1.15	20.12	.62	24.83
4	.03	71.18	.02	77.44	60	1.13	19.35	.68	23.98
5	.02	70.19	.01	76.46	61	1.41	18.59	.74	23.15
6	.02	69.21	.01	75.47	62	1.56	17.85	.81	22.31
7	.02	68.22	.01	74.48	63	1.71	17.13	.89	21.49
8	.01	67.23	.01	73.48	64	1.87	16.42	.97	20.68
9	.01	66.24	.01	72.49	65	2.04	15.72	1.06	19.88
10	.02	65.25	.01	71.50	66	2.23	15.04	1.16	19.09
11	.02	64.26	.01	70.51	67	2.44	14.37	1.28	18.31
12	.02	63.27	.02	69.52	68	2.68	13.72	1.40	17.54
13	.03	62.28	.02	68.53	69	2.93	13.08	1.53	16.78
14	.05	61.30	.02	67.54	70	3.20	12.46	1.67	16.03
15	.07	60.33	.03	66.56	71	3.50	11.85	1.84	15.30
16	.08	59.37	.03	65.58	72	3.84	11.27	2.04	14.57
17	.09	58.42	.04	64.60	73	4.22	10.70	2.26	13.87
18	.10	57.47	.04	63.62	74	4.62	10.15	2.51	13.18
19	.11	56.53	.04	62.64	75	5.06	9.61	2.78	12.50
20	.11	55.58	.04	61.67	76	5.54	9.10	3.09	11.05
21	.11	54.64	.04	60.69	77	6.08	8.60	3.45	11.21
22	.11	53.70	.04	59.71	78	6.67	8.13	3.84	10.59
23	.12	52.77	.04	58.73	79	7.31	7.67	4.27	9.99
24	.12	51.83	.04	57.75	80	7.99	7.24	4.74	9.42
25	.11	50.89	.04	56.77	81	8.73	6.82	5.27	8.86
26	.11	49.94	.04	55.80	82	9.53	6.43	5.87	8.32
27	.11	49.00	.04	54.82	83	10.39	6.05	6.53	7.81
28	.12	48.05	.04	53.84	84	11.31	5.70	7.25	7.32
29	.12	47.11	.05	52.86	85	12.28	5.36	8.03	6.85
30	.12	46.17	.05	51.89	86	13.32	5.04	8.90	6.41
31	.13	45.22	.05	50.91	87	14.43	4.74	9.85	5.99
32	.13	44.28	.05	49.94	88	15.60	4.45	10.90	5.59
33	.14	43.34	.06	48.96	89	16.84	4.18	12.02	5.21
34	.14	42.39	.06	47.99	90	18.15	3.93	13.22	4.85
35	.15	41.45	.07	47.02	91	19.52	3.69	14.53	4.51
36	.16	40.51	.07	46.05	92	20.98	3.46	15.96	4.20
37	.16	39.58	.08	45.09	93	22.52	3.25	17.49	3.90
38	.17	38.64	.09	44.12	94	24.12	3.05	19.13	3.62
39	.18	37.71	.09	43.16	95	25.80	2.86	20.87	3.35
40	.19	36.77	.10	42.20	96	27.57	2.68	22.74	3.11
41	.20	35.84	.11	41.24	97	29.42	2.51	24.74	2.87
42	.21	34.91	.12	40.28	98	31.36	2.35	26.88	2.66
43	.23	33.98	.13	39.33	99	33.37	2.20	29.13	2.45
44	.25	33.06	.15	38.38	100	35.48	2.05	31.52	2.25
45	.28	32.14	.17	37.44	101	37.67	1.90	34.05	2.05
46	.31	31.23	.19	36.50	102	39.96	1.74	36.75	1.85
47	.34	30.32	.21	35.57	103	42.34	1.56	39.59	1.64
48	.37	29.42	.23	34.64	104	44.82	1.34	42.58	1.39
49	.41	28.53	.25	33.72	105	47.38	1.03	45.73	1.04
50	.45	27.65	.27	32.80	106	100.00	0.50	100.00	0.50
51	.50	26.77	.30	31.89					
52	.55	25.90	.33	30.98					
53	.61	25.04	.36	30.08					
54	.68	24.19	.40	29.19					
55	.75	23.35	.43	28.30					

Source: © *Census of Canada, Statistics Canada*

(1) Represents the percentage of the population that will die before reaching the next age; in some cases totals do not equal 100% due to rounding.

Health Improvement Measures

The following table shows the results of a survey of Canadians over the age of 15 who were asked what steps they had taken to try to improve their health, and, if yes, what they did.

| | 1985 | | 1990 | | 1996–97 | |
	% Male	% Female	% Male	% Female	% Male	% Female
Total..	100.0	100.0	100.0	100.0	100.0	100.0
Nothing..	39.2	35.1	52.8	46.9	54.9	49.5
Increase Exercise........................	31.5	26.8	18.9	16.8	28.2	30.1
Improve eating habits..................	8.0	15.0	10.2	16.4	3.9	6.2
Quit smoking/reduce amount smoked	4.9	3.0	4.5	3.7	2.5	2.5
Lose weight.................................	2.3	5.6	2.6	4.3	4.5	6.5
Learn to manage stress and reduce stress level...........................	1.0	1.5	1.5	1.5	n.a.	n.a.
Receive medical treatment..........	3.0	4.1	1.2	1.8	1.0	1.4
Drink less alchohol	1.6	...	1.2	...	...	...
Reduce drug/medication use	...	...	...	...	n.a.	n.a.
Control blood pressure/have blood pressure checked....................................	1.1	1.0	...	...	n.a.	n.a.
Take vitamins..............................	n.a.	n.a.	n.a.	n.a.	...	...
Other..	5.8	5.9	4.3	5.3	1.0	1.0
Not stated...................................	1.2	1.2	2.6	2.5	2.8	1.6

Source: © Statistics Canada (...) Less than 1 percent. (n.a.) Not asked. (1) Population 15 and over.

Exercise Frequency (percentage)

In 1994–95 and in 1996–97, The General Social Survey asked Canadians how frequently they exercised. Not all respondents replied, however the table below shows the percentage of respondents who indicated their exercise level.

"Exercise" was defined as including vigorous activities such as calisthenics, jogging or racquet sports, team sports, dance classes or brisk walking for a period of at least 15 minutes.

| | 1994–95 | | | 1996–97 | | |
| | Three or more times weekly | Once or twice weekly | Less than once a week or never | Three or more times weekly | Once or twice weekly | Less than once a week or never |
	% of Respondents			% of Respondents		
Men[1]						
15–19 years....................	68.3	12.4	6.9	73.0	15.1	8.8
20–24 years....................	57.3	18.5	16.3	61.8	17.1	17.2
25–34 years....................	53.2	22.2	18.2	55.3	22.4	20.4
35–44 years....................	47.6	23.7	22.1	53.2	23.4	20.8
45–54 years....................	45.4	22.1	25.0	50.8	20.8	24.3
55–64 years....................	48.7	20.8	23.5	55.9	17.1	23.6
65 years and over	49.9	12.3	27.0	52.7	12.0	26.7
Women[1]						
15–19 years....................	61.6	19.3	10.2	65.6	18.4	14.0
20–24 years....................	56.9	18.9	18.4	63.5	19.7	16.0
25–34 years....................	50.6	22.6	24.5	61.0	20.2	17.4
35–44 years....................	49.8	22.4	25.6	59.1	18.4	21.2
45–54 years....................	49.9	23.1	24.9	58.3	18.2	22.1
55–64 years....................	58.1	14.4	24.2	57.7	17.4	23.0
65 years and over	44.5	14.7	36.2	46.3	11.4	35.2

Source: © Statistics Canada
(1) Components may not add to 100 percent as frequency was not stated for up to 1 percent of respondents.

Percent of Total Deaths due to Cardiovascular Diseases, 1997

Age Group	% All Deaths due to All Cardiovascular Diseases		% All Deaths due to Heart Disease[1]		% All Deaths due to Heart Attack[1]		% All Deaths due to Stroke[1]	
	Male	Female	Male	Female	Male	Female	Male	Female
> 35	0.6	0.4	0.5	0.3	0.2	0.01	0.6	0.5
35–44	1.8	0.8	1.9	0.6	2.1	0.6	1.3	1.2
45–54	5.3	1.8	5.8	1.6	7.2	2.2	3.6	2.1
55–64	11.1	4.3	12.1	4.5	14.5	5.5	7.5	3.7
65–74	25.1	14.4	25.7	15.1	27.8	18.9	21.4	11.7
75–84	34.8	34.2	33.7	34.4	33.6	39.2	38.7	34.0
85+	21.4	44.2	20.2	43.5	14.6	33.5	26.8	46.9
All ages........	18.2	18.2	13.53	12.1	5.7	4.3	3.1	4.3

Source: *Statistics Canada*

(1) Selected subcategories of cardiovascular diseases.

Percentage of Canadians Smoking Daily

	Both Sexes			Men			Women		
	1989	1995	1996–97	1989	1995	1996–97	1989	1995	1996–97
12 years of age and over	**30**	**25**	**23.6**	**31**	**27**	**25.9**	**29**	**23**	**21.3**
12–19 years....................................	22	23	15.8	21	21	14.9	23	25	16.6
20–44 years....................................	34	29	28.9	34	31	31.7	33	28	26.2
45–64 years....................................	32	25	23.8	33	27	26.0	30	22	21.6
65 years and over	17	11	12.3	20	14	15.1	15	10	10

Source: © *Statistics Canada*

The Battle Against Cancer Continues

*A*n estimated 129,300 new cases of cancer and 63,400 deaths from cancer occurred in Canada in 1999. The most frequently diagnosed cancers continue to be breast cancer for women and prostate cancer for men, but lung cancer remains the leading cause of cancer deaths for both men and women. Almost one-third of the cancer deaths in men and almost one-quarter of cancer deaths in women are due to lung cancer.

Among men, the cancer mortality rate for all cancers combined has been declining slowly since 1988. Among women, cancer incidence and mortality rates have remained relatively stable. However, when lung cancer rates are excluded, the mortality rate for women has dropped by 15 percent since 1971.

Lung cancer incidence and mortality rates among women are now almost five times higher than the 1969 rates; however, they remain only half as high as the mortality rates for men. One in 21 women will develop lung cancer in their lifetimes, and one in 11 men will develop lung cancer in their lifetimes.

Cancer is the leading cause of premature death in Canada, being responsible for almost one-third of all potential years of life lost. Lung cancer is by far the leading cause of premature death due to cancer.

Smoking is responsible for about one-third of potential years of life lost (PYLL) due to cancer. Smoking is responsible for about one-quarter of PYLL due to diseases of the heart and for about one-half of PYLL due to respiratory diseases.

Source: National Cancer Institute of Canada: *Canadian Cancer Statistics 1999*

Expected Years of Life Remaining, 1921–91

	At Birth Male	At Birth Female	At Age 20 Male	At Age 20 Female	At Age 40 Male	At Age 40 Female	At Age 60 Male	At Age 60 Female	At Age 80 Male	At Age 80 Female
1921[1]	n.a.	n.a.	49.1	49.2	32.2	33.0	16.6	17.1	6.0	6.1
1931	60.0	62.1	49.1	49.8	32.0	33.0	16.3	17.2	5.6	5.9
1941	63.0	66.3	49.6	51.8	31.9	34.0	16.1	17.6	5.5	6.0
1951	66.3	70.8	50.8	54.4	32.5	35.6	16.5	18.6	5.8	6.4
1956	67.6	72.9	51.2	55.8	32.7	36.7	16.5	19.3	5.9	6.8
1961	68.4	74.2	51.5	56.7	33.0	37.5	16.7	19.9	6.1	6.9
1966	68.8	75.2	51.5	57.4	33.0	38.2	16.8	20.6	6.4	7.3
1971	69.3	76.4	51.7	58.2	33.2	39.0	17.0	21.4	6.4	7.9
1976	70.2	77.5	52.1	59.0	33.6	39.7	17.2	22.0	6.4	8.2
1981	71.9	79.0	53.4	60.1	34.7	40.7	18.0	22.9	6.9	8.8
1986	73.0	79.7	54.3	60.7	35.5	41.2	18.4	23.2	6.9	8.9
1991	74.6	80.9	55.6	61.7	36.8	42.2	19.4	24.0	7.2	9.4

Source: © *Census Canada, Statistics Canada*   (n.a.) Not available. (1) Excludes Quebec.

Deaths in Canada, 1921–98

	Deaths	Death Rates[1] Both Sexes	Males	Females		Deaths	Death Rates[1] Both Sexes	Males	Females
1921[2]	104 531	11.6	11.9	11.2	1980	171 473	7.0	8.0	6.0
1926[2]	111 055	11.4	11.9	10.9	1981	171 029	6.9	7.8	5.9
1931[3]	108 446	10.2	10.5	9.6	1982	174 413	6.9	7.8	6.0
1936[3]	111 111	9.9	10.3	9.3	1983	174 484	6.9	7.7	6.0
1941[3]	118 797	10.1	10.9	9.1	1984	175 727	6.8	7.7	6.0
1946	118 785	9.4	10.3	8.4	1985	181 323	7.0	7.8	6.2
1951	125 823	9.0	10.1	7.8	1986	184 224	7.0	7.8	6.3
1956	131 961	8.2	9.4	7.0	1987	184 953	7.0	7.7	6.3
1961	140 985	7.7	9.0	6.5	1988	190 011	7.1	7.8	6.3
1966	149 863	7.5	8.7	6.2	1989	190 965	7.0	7.7	6.3
1971	157 272	7.3	8.5	6.1	1990	191 973	6.9	7.5	6.3
1972	162 413	7.4	8.7	6.2	1991	195 568	7.0	7.6	6.4
1973	164 039	7.4	8.6	6.2	1992	196 535	6.9	7.5	6.3
1974	166 794	7.3	8.4	6.2	1993	204 909	7.1	7.6	6.5
1975	167 404	7.2	8.3	6.1	1994	207 077	7.1	7.6	6.6
1976	167 009	7.1	8.2	6.0	1995	209 435	7.1	7.6	6.6
1977	167 498	7.0	8.1	5.9	1996	212 880	6.7	8.6	5.3
1978	168 179	7.0	8.1	5.9	1997	215 669	6.5	8.2	4.8
1979	168 183	6.9	8.0	5.9	1998	217 860	7.2	n.a.	n.a.

Source: © *Statistics Canada*
(1) Per 1 000 population. (2) Excludes Que., Nfld, Yukon and NWT. (3) Excludes Nfld, Yukon and NWT.

Deaths by Province, 1998

	Deaths	Death Rate[1]		Deaths	Death Rate[1]
Canada	**217 860**	**7.2**	Manitoba	9 765	8.6
Newfoundland	3 395	7.2	Saskatchewan	8 410	8.2
Prince Edward Island	1 255	9.2	Alberta	16 930	5.9
Nova Scotia	7 915	8.5	British Columbia	28 710	7.2
New Brunswick	5 970	7.9	Yukon Territory	135	4.2
Quebec	53 410	7.3	Northwest Territories	235	3.5
Ontario	81 175	7.2			

Source: © *Statistics Canada*   (1) Rate per 1 000 population.

Leading Causes of Death, Men, All Ages

	1977		1997	
	No. of Deaths	Rate[1]	No. of Deaths	Rate[1]
All Causes	96 872	875.5	111 1971	753.8
Diseases of the Circulatory System	45 760	413.6	39 834	268.2
- Ischaemic Heart Disease	31 180	281.8	23 822	160.4
- Stroke	7 160	64.7	6 673	44.9
Cancer	20 378	184.2	31 550	212.4
- Lung	6 142	55.5	9 725	65.5
- Prostate	1 833	16.6	3 622	24.4
Respiratory Diseases	6 828	61.7	10 608	71.4
- Other Chronic Airway Obstructions	2 584	23.4	4 517	30.4
- Pneumonia and Influenza	2 764	25.0	3 747	25.2
External Causes of Injury and Poisoning	11 366	102.7	8 724	58.7
- Suicide	2 459	22.2	2 914	19.6
- Motor Vehicle Accidents	3 831	34.6	2 110	14.2
Diseases of the Digestive System	3 742	33.8	3 791	25.5
- Chronic Liver Disease and Cirrhosis	1 924	17.4	1 310	8.8
- Noninfective Enteritis and Colitis	n.a.	n.a.	422	2.8
Endocrine Diseases	1 616	14.6	3 489	23.5
- Diabetes Mellitus	1 289	11.7	2 767	18.6
- Fluid, Electrolyte and Acid-Base Balance	85	0.8	192	1.3
Diseases of the Nervous System	1 023	9.3	2 843	19.1
- Alzheimer's Disease	n.a.	n.a.	928	6.2
- Parkinson's Disease	n.a.	n.a.	0.6	4.7
Mental Disorders	763	6.9	2 253	15.2
- Senile and Presenile Dementia	n.a.	n.a.	831	5.6
- Psychoses, including Alcoholic	154	1.4	511	3.4
All Other Causes	5 396	48.8	0 079	59.8

Source: © *Statistics Canada*   (1) Per 100 000 population by gender.

Leading Causes of Death, Women, All Ages

	1977		1997	
	No. of Deaths	Rate[1]	No. of Deaths	Rate[1]
All Causes	70 626	644.3	103 668	684.3
Diseases of the Circulatory System	35 714	325.8	39 614	261.5
- Ischaemic Heart Disease	20 228	184.6	19 699	130.0
- Stroke	8 362	76.3	9 375	61.9
Cancer	16 041	146.5	27 142	179.1
- Lung	1 519	13.9	5 713	37.7
- Breast	3 321	30.3	4 945	32.6
Respiratory Diseases	4 005	36.5	9 425	62.2
- Pneumonia and Influenza	2 392	21.8	4 283	28.3
- Other Chronic Airway Obstructions	2 213	20.2	3 028	20.0
External Causes of Injury and Poisoning	4 635	43.4	4 324	28.5
- Accidental Falls	829	7.6	1 538	10.2
- Motor Vehicle Accidents	1 424	13.0	945	6.2
Endocrine Diseases	2 103	19.2	3 839	25.3
- Diabetes Mellitus	1 721	15.7	2 932	19.4
- Fluid, Electrolyte and Acid-Base Balance	98	0.9	323	2.1
Diseases of the Digestive System	2 388	21.8	3 839	25.3
- Chronic Liver Disease and Cirrhosis	838	7.7	720	4.8
- Noninfective Enteritis and Colitis	n.a.	n.a.	648	4.3
Diseases of the Nervous System	786	7.2	3 713	24.5
- Alzheimer's Disease	n.a.	n.a.	1 885	12.4
- Parkinson's Disease	n.a.	n.a.	578	3.8
Mental Disorders	382	3.57	3 601	23.8
- Senile and Presenile Dementia	n.a.	n.a.	1 725	11.4
- Psychoses, including Alcoholic	161	1.47	161	1.1
All Other Causes	4 572	41.71	8 171	54.1

Source: © *Statistics Canada*   (1) Per 100 000 population by gender.

MIGRATION

FOCUS ON...

How to Become a Canadian Citizen

To become a Canadian citizen, you must be at least 18 years of age, a permanent resident and in Canada legally.

If you are a permanent resident, you must have lived in Canada for at least three of the four years before the date of your application. If you lived in Canada before becoming a permanent resident, that time is counted at half the rate if it was during the four years before your application date.

You must be able to speak and understand spoken English or French, or be able to read and write in simple English or French.

If you are between 18 and 59 years of age, you must learn about Canada before becoming a citizen. When you apply for citizenship, you'll be sent a free publication called *A Look at Canada* on which your citizenship test will be based.

Children under 18 don't need to meet the three-year residency requirement; however, you must already be a Canadian citizen or be applying to become one. Children don't write a citizenship test.

Who Doesn't Qualify

Not everyone can become a Canadian citizen. You cannot become a citizen if

- you were convicted of an indictable offence in the past three years
- you are under a deportation order
- you were in prison, on parole or on probation in the past four years
- you have been charged with an indictable offence
- you are now charged with an offence under the Citizenship Act
- your Canadian citizenship has been revoked in the past five years
- you are under investigation for war crimes or crimes against humanity

Applying

1. **Get the correct application form.** It should be the "Application for Citizenship." Each child for whom you are applying needs a separate form.

2. **Read the form.** The cost to process your forms isn't refundable, so be sure you are ready to become a citizen and fill the form out carefully. The current fee for citizenship for adults is $200, and the fee for children under 18 is $100.

3. **Complete the application and attach necessary documents.** Photocopies of documents are acceptable, but you may need to bring the original when you take the test. The application form comes with detailed instructions.

4. **Mail the completed application.** Check that you have included all documentation and filled in the application completely.

5. **Prepare for your test.** Read the book *A Look at Canada* that will be sent to you. You may want to take a citizenship class if one is being held near you. A notice detailing the date and time of your citizenship test will be sent to you. The test may be oral or written.

6. **Take the oath.** Once you have met all the requirements, you will receive a notice detailing when and where the citizenship ceremony will take place.

Call Centres and Citizenship Offices

You can get more information on any of the topics discussed here by contacting one of the call centres listed below.

Montreal: (514) 496-1010
Toronto: (416) 973-4444
Vancouver: (604) 666-2171
Toll-free: 1-888-242-2100

Case Processing Centre

P.O. Box 7000
Sydney, NS B1P 6V6

Source: *Citizenship and Immigration Canada*

Canadian Immigration Totals, 1852–1998

Year	Total	Year	Total	Year	Total	Year	Total
1852*	29 307	1889	91 600	1926	135 982	1963	93 151
1853*	29 464	1890	75 067	1927	158 886	1964	112 606
1854*	37 263	1891	82 165	1928	166 783	1965	146 758
1855*	25 296	1892	30 996	1929	164 993	1966	194 743
1856*	22 544	1893	29 633	1930	104 806	1967	222 876
1857*	33 854	1894	20 829	1931	27 530	1968	183 974
1858*	12 339	1895	18 790	1932	20 591	1969	161 531
1859*	6 300	1896	16 835	1933	14 382	1970	147 713
1860*	6 276	1897	21 716	1934	12 476	1971	121 900
1861*	13 589	1898	31 900	1935	11 277	1972	122 006
1862*	18 294	1899	44 543	1936	11 643	1973	184 200
1863*	21 000	1900	41 681	1937	15 101	1974	218 465
1864*	24 779	1901	55 747	1938	17 244	1975	187 881
1865*	18 958	1902	89 102	1939	16 994	1976	149 429
1866*	11 427	1903	138 660	1940	11 324	1977	114 914
1867	10 666	1904	131 252	1941	9 329	1978	86 313
1868	12 765	1905	141 465	1942	7 576	1979	112 096
1869	18 630	1906	211 653	1943	8 504	1980	143 117
1870	24 706	1907	272 409	1944	12 801	1981	128 618
1871	27 773	1908	143 326	1945	22 722	1982	121 147
1872	36 578	1909	173 694	1946	71 719	1983	89 157
1873	50 050	1910	286 839	1947	64 127	1984	88 239
1874	39 373	1911	331 288	1948	125 414	1985	84 302
1875	27 382	1912	375 756	1949	95 217	1986	99 219
1876	25 633	1913	400 870	1950	73 912	1987	152 098
1877	27 082	1914	150 484	1951	194 391	1988	161 929
1878	29 807	1915	36 665	1952	164 498	1989	192 001
1879	40 492	1916	55 914	1953	168 868	1990	214 230
1880	38 505	1917	72 910	1954	154 227	1991	232 020
1881	47 991	1918	41 845	1955	109 946	1992	253 345
1882	112 458	1919	107 698	1956	164 857	1993	255 935
1883	133 624	1920	138 824	1957	282 164	1994	223 912
1884	103 824	1921	91 728	1958	124 851	1995	212 463
1885	79 169	1922	64 224	1959	106 928	1996	226 050
1886	69 152	1923	133 729	1960	104 111	1997[1]	216 042
1887	84 526	1924	124 164	1961	71 689	1998[1]	174 130
1888	88 766	1925	84 907	1962	74 586		

Source: *Citizenship and Immigration Canada*

(1) Preliminary figure. (*) Pre-Confederation.

An Active Immigration Program

*C*anada accepts more immigrants in proportion to its population than any other country and is one of the few countries in the world with an active program for permanent immigration. One out of every six residents was born outside Canada.

Since 1967, Citizenship and Immigration Canada has assessed immigrants on standards that do not discriminate on the basis of race, national or ethnic origin, colour, religion or sex. Applicants from every country are assessed against the same criteria.

The Immigration Act sets out three basic goals for the immigration program:

- to foster the development of a strong viable economy in all regions
- to facilitate the reunion of Canadian residents with family members from abroad
- to uphold Canada's humanitarian tradition

The Act also states that the immigration program should protect the health and safety of Canadians, and prevent the entry of criminals, spies, terrorists and subversives.

Immigration[1] to Canada, 1956–98

	Total Immigrants	United States	Asia[2]	Europe	Caribbean[3]	South America	Africa	Oceania
1956	164 857	9 777	3 537	145 554	1 351	1 551	1 079	1 924
1957	282 164	11 008	3 244	257 540	1 586	2 376	2 970	3 345
1958	124 851	10 846	4 223	102 279	1 519	2 168	1 355	2 344
1959	106 928	11 338	5 368	84 517	1 529	1 750	8 43	1 512
1960	104 111	11 247	4 002	82 922	1 542	1 823	8 33	1 657
1961	71 689	11 516	2 706	52 132	1 454	1 301	1 0 88	1 432
1962	74 586	11 643	2 593	53 790	1 842	1 103	2 1 71	1 384
1963	93 151	11 736	3 553	69 069	2 611	1 779	2 4 31	1 692
1964	112 606	12 565	6 121	82 798	2 467	2 257	3 8 74	2 303
1965	146 758	15 143	11 215	108 285	3 420	2 471	3 196	2 711
1966	194 743	17 514	13 835	148 410	4 357	2 604	3 661	4 057
1967	222 876	19 038	20 740	159 979	9 004	3 090	4 608	6 168
1968	183 974	20 422	21 686	120 702	8 129	2 693	5 204	4 815
1969	161 531	22 785	23 319	88 363	13 908	4 767	3 297	4 411
1970	147 713	24 424	21 170	75 609	13 371	4 943	2 863	4 385
1971	121 900	24 366	22 171	52 031	11 653	5 058	2 841	2 902
1972	122 006	22 618	23 325	51 293	9 218	4 309	8 3 08	2 143
1973	184 200	25 242	43 193	71 883	20 704	11 057	8 307	2 671
1974	218 465	26 541	50 566	88 694	25 276	12 528	10 450	2 594
1975	187 881	20 155	47 382	72 898	19 483	13 270	9 867	2 174
1976	149 429	17 315	44 328	49 903	16 198	10 628	7 752	1 886
1977	114 914	12 888	31 368	40 748	13 187	7 840	6 372	1 545
1978	86 313	9 945	24 007	30 075	9 240	6 782	4 2 61	1 233
1979	112 096	9 617	50 540	32 858	7 060	5 898	3 9 58	1 395
1980	143 117	9 926	71 602	41 168	8 141	5 433	4 3 30	2 497
1981	128 618	10 559	48 831	46 299	9 625	6 163	4 8 89	2 253
1982	121 147	9 360	41 686	46 156	10 317	6 871	4 513	2 119
1983	89 157	7 381	36 906	24 312	10 864	4 816	3 659	1 213
1984	88 239	6 922	41 920	20 901	9 706	4 085	3 5 52	1 151
1985	84 302	6 669	38 597	18 859	11 143	4 356	3 545	1 128
1986	99 219	7 275	41 600	22 709	14 947	6 686	4 770	1 227
1987	152 098	7 967	67 337	37 563	18 100	10 801	8 50 1	1 827
1988	161 929	6 537	81 136	40 689	15 108	7 255	9 380	1 822
1989	192 001	6 931	93 261	52 105	16 764	8 685	12 199	2 041
1990	213 334	6 057	111 195	51 667	19 459	8 888	13 426	2 642
1991	232 020	20 122[4]	120 736	48 232	12 978	10 632	16 175	3 145[5]
1992	253 345	20 123[4]	139 546	44 933	14 993	10 415	19 669	3 666[5]
1993	255 935	8 025	147 378	46 622	24 315	9 588	16 922	3 085[5]
1994	223 912	6 242	141 600	38 652	13 486	7 919	13 708	2 305[5]
1995	212 463[6]	5 199	128 534	41 127	13 352	7 485	14 560	1 873[5]
1996	226 050[6]	5 896	143 956	40 009	12 958	6 115	14 836	2 058[5]
1997[7]	216 042[6]	5 043	138 091	38 673	11 828	5 691	14 489	2 024[5]
1998[7]	174 130[6]	4 764	101 157	38 475	9 035	4 953	13 654	1 644[5]

Source: *Citizenship and Immigration Canada*

(1) By country of last permanent residence. (2) Includes China and Hong Kong. (3) Includes Central America, Greenland and St. Pierre & Miquelon for 1956–76; except for 1991, 1992 when N and Central America were included with U.S. figures (4) Includes North and Central America. (5) Includes Australia and other islands. (6) Includes those whose country of last permanent residence was not stated. (7) Preliminary numbers.

Deciding How Many Immigrants to Accept

A legislative requirement of Canada's immigration policy is to set the number and categories of immigrants who can come to Canada each year. Targets are announced annually in Parliament by November 1. The federal government has made agreements with several provincial governments for federal–provincial cooperation with respect to immigration. The most recent was with Newfoundland in 1999, but the Canada-Quebec Accord remains the most comprehensive.

Immigration by Province of Intended Destination

	Total immigrants[1]	Nfld	PEI	NS	NB	Que	Ont	Man	Sask	Alta	BC	YK	NWT
1956 ...	164 857	426	112	1 639	852	31 396	90 662	5 796	2 202	9 959	17 812	n.a.	n.a.
1960 ...	104 111	306	83	1 210	634	23 774	54 491	4 337	2 087	6 949	10 120	n.a.	n.a.
1965 ...	146 758	604	137	1 612	1 074	30 346	79 702	3 948	2 649	8 049	18 502	n.a.	n.a.
1970 ...	147 713	630	185	2 007	1 070	23 261	80 732	5 826	1 709	10 405	21 683	n.a.	n.a.
1975 ...	187 881	1106	235	2 124	2 093	28 042	98 471	7 134	2 837	16 277	29 272	n.a.	n.a.
1980 ...	143 117	541	190	1 616	1 207	22 538	62 257	7 683	3 603	18 839	24 437	n.a.	n.a.
1981 ...	128 618	483	128	1 405	990	21 182	55 032	5 370	2 402	19 330	22 095	n.a.	n.a.
1982 ...	121147	406	165	1 256	751	21 336	53 049	4 931	2 125	17 949	18 999	n.a.	n.a.
1983 ...	89 157	275	105	833	554	16 374	40 036	3 978	1 735	10 688	14 447	n.a.	n.a.
1984 ...	88 239	299	109	1 034	600	14 641	41 527	3 903	2 150	10 670	13 190	n.a.	n.a.
1985 ...	84 302	325	113	974	609	14 884	40 730	3 415	1 905	9 001	12 239	n.a.	n.a.
1986 ...	99 219	274	168	1 097	641	19 459	49 630	3 749	1 860	9 673	12 552	49	67
1987 ...	152 098	458	159	1 227	642	26 822	84 807	4 799	2 119	11 975	18 913	80	72
1988 ...	161 929	408	153	1 299	679	25 789	88 996	5 009	2 223	14 025	23 204	68	76
1989 ...	192 001	468	159	1 473	905	34 171	104 799	6 138	2 142	16 211	25 335	100	100
1990 ...	214 230	546	176	1 563	842	40 842	113 438	6 637	2 361	18 994	28 723	83	75
1991 ...	232 020	641	150	1 504	685	52 155	119 257	5 659	2 455	17 043	32 263	84	124
1992 ...	253 345	787	151	2 359	754	48 597	138 453	5 084	2 511	17 696	36 709	133	111
1993 ...	255 935	807	165	3 021	702	44 964	134 420	4 874	2 403	18 580	45 724	104	171
1995...	212 463	585	167	3 581	639	27 182	115 681	3 603	1 949	14 329	44 541	108	91
1996...	226 050	584	153	3 223	716	29 800	119 682	3 923	1 824	13 898	52 021	94	97
1997[2]...	216 042	437	151	2 891	664	27 684	118 063	3 765	1 743	12 918	47 506	86	100
1998[2]...	174 130	432	130	2 086	765	26 221	92 617	3 000	1 582	11 207	35 876	57	66

Source: *Citizenship and Immigration Canada*

(1) Includes those where destination not stated. (2) Preliminary figures.

Persons Granted Canadian Citizenship, 1920–1998[1]

1920	3 004	**1946**	9 047	**1972**	80 866
1921	10 507	**1947**	15 335	**1973**	104 697
1922	10 360	**1948**	11 410	**1974**	130 278
1923	7 589	**1949**	11 991[2]	**1975**	137 507
1924	7 659	**1950**	10 441	**1976**	117 276
1925	13 288	**1951**	10 301	**1977**	123 655
1926	15 403	**1952**	10 888	**1978**	223 214
1927	16 917	**1953**	13 562	**1979**	156 699
1928	13 466	**1954**	19 545	**1980**	118 590
1929	13 099	**1955**	58 711	**1981**	94 457
1930	21 221	**1956**	55 404	**1982**	87 468
1931	21 392	**1957**	95 462	**1983**	90 328
1932	32 517	**1958**	84 183	**1984**	109 504
1933	23 613	**1959**	71 280	**1985**	126 466
1934	21 908	**1960**	62 378	**1986**	103 800
1935	20 903	**1961**	56 476	**1987**	73 638
1936	30 679	**1962**	72 082	**1988**	58 810
1937	31 744	**1963**	69 468	**1989**	87 478
1938	27 455	**1964**	64 334	**1990**	104 267
1939	21 418	**1965**	63 844	**1991**	118 630
1940	18 207	**1966**	60 852	**1992**	115 757
1941	15 594	**1967**	59 968	**1993**	150 543
1942	14 213	**1968**	60 055	**1994**	217 320
1943	12 533	**1969**	59 900	**1995**	227 720
1944	12 827	**1970**	57 556	**1996**	166 627
1945	13 562	**1971**	63 669	**1997**	140 241
				1998	134 485
				1999[3]	180 000

Source: *Citizenship and Immigration Canada*

(1) For fiscal year ending Mar 31 for 1920 to 1951; calendar years 1952 onwards. (2) Does not include approx 359 000 Newfoundlanders who became Canadian citizens when Newfoundland became Canada's 10th province in 1949. (3) Preliminary number.

Refugees[1] to Canada, 1960–98

1960 .... 2 329	**1970** 1 361	**1980** 40 638	**1990** 36 093
1961 .... 1 813	**1971** 614	**1981** 15 058	**1991** 35 891
1962 .... 1 733	**1972** 5 204	**1982** 17 000	**1992** 36 943
1963 .... 2 024	**1973** 2 381	**1983** 14 062	**1993** 24 835
1964 .... 2 279	**1974** 1 656	**1984** 15 553	**1994** 19 739
1965 .... 2 131	**1975** 6 109	**1985** 17 000	**1995** 26 789
1966 .... 2 058	**1976** 5 576	**1986** 19 485	**1996** 28 552
1967 .... 1 499	**1977** 3 670	**1987** 21 950	**1997** 25 324
1968 .... 9 971	**1978** 3 038	**1988** 27 230	**1998** 22 831
1969 .... 3 604	**1979** 27 894	**1989** 37 361	

Source: *Refugees Branch, Citizenship and Immigration Canada*

(1) Includes persons admitted from abroad as Convention Refugees or members of Designated Classes, as well as persons recognized in Canada as Convention Refugees or members of the special Backlog Clearance Designated Class. Does not include special humanitarian movements of other persons.

Refugees by Province of Destination, 1979–98

	Total[1]	Nfld	PEI	NS	NB	Que	Ont	Man	Sask	Alta	BC	YK	NWT
1979......	27 825	182	100	372	397	6 077	10 758	1 749	1 485	3 732	2 895	51	27
1980......	40 631	145	40	669	422	8 110	15 460	2 829	2 148	5 567	5 185	29	27
1981......	14 997	28	11	119	76	3 257	5 544	822	657	2 751	1 722	6	4
1982......	16 991	40	28	161	47	3 200	7 013	1 031	644	3 112	1 706	7	2
1983......	14 062	11	17	89	61	2 184	6 100	844	574	2 488	1 692	0	2
1984......	15 553	40	20	175	85	2 228	6 900	1 032	773	2 446	1 848	1	5
1985......	17 000	55	33	206	165	1 906	8 301	1 131	749	2 529	1 919	1	5
1986......	19 485	77	43	253	170	2 530	9 580	1 350	777	2 677	2 018	5	5
1987......	21 921	87	45	241	192	3 216	11 026	1 366	791	2 673	2 277	3	4
1988......	27 230	93	48	290	208	3 690	14 716	1 653	806	3 265	2 453	7	1
1989......	37 361	94	49	329	194	5 137	21 585	1 929	815	4 535	2 679	9	6
1990......	36 093	94	50	361	182	5 085	20 644	2 325	776	4 118	2 447	6	5
1991......	35 891	265	40	337	211	6 284	21 342	1 579	706	2 738	2 382	4	3
1992......	36 943	220	28	176	95	7 111	22 894	1 048	568	2 428	2 374	1	0
1993......	24 835	243	41	189	100	5 776	14 433	692	375	1 649	1 325	1	11
1994......	19 739	225	64	173	137	4 430	10 485	582	515	1 606	1 520	2	0
1995......	26 789	198	59	213	166	5 610	16 122	628	546	1 423	1 816	8	0
1996......	28 552	155	74	232	186	9 246	13 719	655	587	1 308	2 257	133	0
1997......	25 324	153	81	238	189	7 542	12 391	665	597	1 315	2 096	57	0
1998......	22 831	116	58	235	162	6 226	11 550	649	532	1 274	2 028	0	1

Source: *Refugees Branch, Citizenship and Immigration Canada*   (1) Shows only those whose destination was identified.

Canadian Emigration by Province

(number of persons moving from Canada)

	Canada	Nfld	PEI	NS	NB	Que	Ont	Man	Sask	Alta	BC	YK	NWT
1976–81[1]	278 228	1 812	434	2 509	4 643	46 110	131 672	9 873	4 982	37 891	37 773	384	145
1981–86[1]	277 579	2 274	483	2 413	4 651	43 062	125 735	9 305	5 778	42 666	40 540	363	309
1986–91[1]	212 532	1 378	283	2 860	4 366	28 496	91 635	10 799	4 527	35 105	32 446	254	383
1991–96[1]	227 612	1 343	378	4 196	4 715	30 733	96 519	10 980	4 851	38 378	34 805	333	381
1996–97[1,2]	49 633	287	78	893	1 030	6 687	21 012	2 485	1 076	8 313	7 603	68	101
1997–98[1,2]	49 696	293	74	890	1 032	6 694	21 059	2 480	1 075	8 322	7 616	65	96

Source: © *Statistics Canada*   (1) Year end June 30. (2) Preliminary numbers.

Where Canadians Move Within Canada

When Canadians move from one province to another, it tends to be directly related to economic conditions. This trend was most apparent during 1977–81 when the resource boom in Alberta caused a large influx from other provinces. But falling international oil prices in the early 1980s led to a reversal of this trend as Canadians moved east,

especially to Ontario. In recent years, those moving to another province have been heading west again to B.C. and Alberta.

The following table shows net interprovincial migration—(the number of persons moving into a province minus the number of persons moving out of that province.

	Nfld	PEI	NS	NB	Que	Ont	Man	Sask	Alta	BC	YT	NWT
1977-81	-21 086	-1 451	-8 185	-13 680	-156 817	-60 890	-42 115	-11 729	190 719	131 176	-2 363	-3 579
1982-86	-14 117	811	7 442	835	-67 235	165 460	-2 395	-7 057	-82 737	3 226	-2 393	-1 840
1987-91	-11 355	-65	-607	-2 063	-45 406	28 876	-39 533	-69 397	-13 198	154 126	871	-2 249
1992	-2 563	232	355	-1 087	-9 785	-13 530	-6 417	-7 727	1 030	39 578	215	-301
1993	-3 397	532	-1 143	-492	-7 426	-12 771	-5 206	-4 543	-2 355	37 595	-755	-39
1994	-6 204	694	-2 694	-505	-10 252	-4 527	-4 010	-3 958	-2 684	34 449	-245	-64
1995	-6 566	368	-1 972	-931	-10 248	-1 764	-3 344	-3 190	4 251	23 414	656	-674
1996[1]	-7 945	401	-1 064	-910	-15 358	-1 706	-3 738	-1 871	15 069	17 798	215	-891
1997[1,2]	-9 279	-466	-3 355	-1 688	-17 789	5 149	-7 008	-3 288	33 834	5 554	-433	-1 231

Source: © *Statistics Canada*
(1) Year end June 30. (2) Preliminary numbers.

Canadians on the Move

*J*ust under 1.2 million Canadian residents moved within Canada between 1996 and 1997. Movement between provinces and territories was virtually unchanged from 1995–96 (+0.4 percent) and was offset by a slight decrease (–0.5 percent) in the number of residents who moved within their own province.

For overall net migration (interprovincial plus international), Ontario had the largest net increase (114,800), while Newfoundland had the largest net decrease from migration (–7800).

For people moving within Canada, Alberta was the most popular choice. The province had a net interprovincial migration more than triple the gain of 1995–96. Alberta's growing economy (demonstrated in the record increase in the number of drilled oil wells, the increased production of crude oil and natural gas and the oil industry's spin-off activity to engineering services and manufacturing(enticed a large number of job seekers into the province and few people left. British Columbia had the second largest interprovincial net gain, but this was down significantly from the net gain in 1995–96.

Quebec had the largest net decrease of people moving to other provinces and territories. Newfoundland had the second largest net decrease due to interprovincial migration, offset only slightly by a small number of immigrants.

For census metropolitan areas (CMAs), the Toronto CMA and the Vancouver CMA continued to experience the largest inflows and outflows of migration. (Moves between census divisions are considered migration.) In total, 265,000 people moved into or out of the Toronto CMA, while total movement for the Vancouver CMA was 156,000. Of Vancouver's arrivals, 52 percent were from outside Canada, 27 percent from other provinces and the rest from elsewhere in the province. The Toronto CMA accounted for one-fifth of Canada's international outflow, while 11 percent of this migration came from the Vancouver CMA.

Calgary had the third largest net gain of migrants (+21,200) among CMAs. After three consecutive periods of negative net migration, Edmonton benefited from the increase in job opportunities related to natural resource industries and recorded a net gain of 6100 people due to migration.

The Montreal CMA had a net gain from migration of 6,500. The interprovincial net migration decline of Montreal residents (–14,500) was offset by a net gain of 22,700 international arrivals.

Ten of the CMAs had net declines due to migration, all of which were less than 1 percent of their total population.

Population Growth Components

(thousands of persons)

Population growth is made up of natural increase (births minus deaths) plus net migration (immigration minus emigration). As the birth rate in Canada falls and the death rate continues to rise, the role of immigration becomes an increasingly important factor in population growth.

By 2030, natural increase is projected to be close to zero, and immigration will become Canada's sole source of population growth.

	Total Population Growth	Natural Increase		Net Migration		Census population at the end of the period
		Births	Deaths	Immigration	Emigration	
1851–61	793	1 281	670	352	170	3 230
1861–71	459	1 370	760	260	411	3 689
1871–81	636	1 480	790	350	404	4 325
1881–91	508	1 524	870	680	826	4 833
1891–1901	538	1 548	880	250	380	5 371
1901–11	1 836	1 925	900	1 550	739	7 207
1911–21	1 581	2 340	1 070	1 400	1 089	8 788
1921–31	1 589	2 415	1 055	1 200	971	10 377
1931–41	1 130	2 294	1 072	149	241	11 507
1941–51	2 141	3 186	1 214	548	379	13 648
1951–56	2 072	2 106	633	783	184	16 081
1956–61	2 157	2 362	687	760	278	18 238
1961–66	1 777	2 249	731	539	280	20 015
1966–71	1 553	1 856	766	890	427	21 568
1971–76	1 492	1 755	824	1 053	492	23 518
1976–81	1 382	1 820	843	771	366	24 900
1981–86	1 304	1 872	885	677	360	26 204
1986–91	1 907	1 933	946	1 199	279	28 111
1991–96	1 848	1 935	1 027	1 170	230	29 959
1997	332	365	218	225	50	30 276
1998	296	355	218	194	50	30 572

Source: © *Statistics Canada*

Canada's Declining Birth Rate

*T*he birth rate in Canada has been declining since the 1950s. As the death rate continues to rise, it is likely that, by the year 2020, Canada's natural growth in the population will approach zero. Population growth in Canada now depends on immigration. Canada's natural growth rate declined from 7.7 to 5.7 per 1000 between 1990 and 1995. By 1996, immigration had passed natural growth. Why?

The fertility rate has remained around 1.6 children per woman for several years. Fewer women of child-bearing age were born during the baby bust years following the baby boom generation, and voluntary sterilization is also playing a role.

In comparison to other Western countries, Canada's rate of sterilization stands out. According to the General Social Survey, 4.5 million Canadian couples with a woman was under age 50 (46 percent of all couples in their reproductive years) were sterile for either natural, medical or contraceptive reasons.

An estimated 2.7 million women under the age of 50 who were living with a male partner had been surgically sterilized. About 250,000 Canadian women were also sterile for natural reasons.

About 47 percent of couples with two children undergo sterilization, compared with only 14 percent of couples with one child. Of the women born between 1927 and 1931, 60 percent had a third birth but only 25 percent of those born between 1952 and 1956 did so.

SOCIAL TRENDS

Marriages and Divorces in Canada

	Marriages				Divorces		
			Average Age at Marriage				Average Length of Marriage[2]
	Total	Rate[1]	Brides[3]	Grooms[3]	Total	Rate[1]	
1925	66 378	6.9	25.3	29.8	550	0.06	n.a.
1930	73 341	7.0	25.0	29.2	875	0.09	n.a.
1935	78 908	7.1	25.0	29.0	1 431	0.13	n.a.
1940	125 797	10.8	25.2	28.9	2 416	0.21	n.a.
1945	111 376	9.0	25.5	29.0	5 101	0.42	n.a.
1950	125 083	9.1	25.3	28.5	5 386	0.39	n.a.
1955	128 029	8.2	25.1	28.0	6 053	0.39	n.a.
1960	130 338	7.3	24.7	27.7	6 980	0.39	n.a.
1965	145 519	7.4	24.5	27.2	8 974	0.46	n.a.
1970	188 428	8.8	24.9	27.3	29 775	1.40	n.a.
1975	197 585	8.5	22.0	24.4	50 611	2.22	11.1
1980	191 069	7.8	22.8	25.0	62 019	2.59	11.5
1981	190 082	7.6	23.0	25.2	67 671	2.78	11.5
1982	188 360	7.5	23.2	25.4	70 436	2.86	11.5
1983	184 675	7.3	23.5	25.7	68 567	2.76	11.4
1984	185 597	7.2	23.8	26.0	65 172	2.59	11.6
1985	184 096	7.1	24.1	26.2	61 980	2.44	11.6
1986	175 518	6.7	24.3	26.5	78 160	3.09	11.5
1987	182 151	6.9	24.7	26.9	90 985	3.55	11.4
1988	187 728	7.0	25.0	27.1	80 507	0.11	11.0
1989	190 640	7.0	25.2	27.3	80 998	2.96	11.2
1990	187 737	6.8	25.5	27.4	78 463	2.82	11.1
1991	172 251	6.1	25.7	27.7	77 020	2.74	11.0
1992	164 573	5.8	26.0	28.0	79 034	2.77	10.9
1993	159 316	5.5	26.8	28.7	78 226	2.70	10.7
1994	159 959	5.5	26.9	28.8	78 880	2.70	10.7
1995	160 251	5.4	27.1	29.0	77 636	2.62	10.7
1996	156 691	5.2	27.3	29.3	71 528	2.41	10.8
1997	159 350	n.a.	n.a.	n.a.	67 408	2.23	n.a.

Source: © *Statistics Canada*

(1) Rate per 1 000 population. (2) Refers to the average length (in years) of those marriages ending in divorce during the year stated.
(3) Data after 1975 represents average age of bride and groom at first marriage. (n.a.) not available.

Marriages and Divorces by Province

	Marriages		Divorces			
	1996		1996		1997	
	Total	Rate[1]	Total	Rate[2]	Total	Rate[2]
Canada	**156 692**	**5.2**	**71 528**	**36.9**	**67 408**	**34.8**
Newfoundland	3 194	5.6	1 060	26.3	822	20.2
Prince Edward Island	924	6.7	237	24.0	243	24.2
Nova Scotia	5 392	5.7	2 228	32.4	1 983	38.2
New Brunswick	4 366	5.7	1 450	25.9	1 373	24.8
Quebec	23 968	3.2	18 078	45.7	17 478	44.8
Ontario	66 208	5.9	25 035	32.9	23 629	31.0
Manitoba	6 448	5.6	2 603	30.9	2 625	31.3
Saskatchewan	5 671	5.5	2 216	30.6	2 198	30.6
Alberta	17 283	6.2	7 509	38.3	7 185	36.5
British Columbia	22 834	5.9	10 898	45.0	9 692	39.5
Yukon Territory	198	6.3	115	56.1	101	47.7
Northwest Territories	206	3.1	99	38.9	79	32.5

Source: © *Statistics Canada* (1) Rate per 1 000 population. (2) Rate per 100 marriages.

Marital Status of the Canadian Population, 1997

	Total Population		Single		Married		Widowed		Divorced	
Age Group	**Male (000s)**	**Female (000s)**	**Male (%)**	**Female (%)**	**Male (%)**	**Female (%)**	**Male (%)**	**Female (%)**	**Male (%)**	**Female (%)**
Total Population 15+	**11 927.7**	**12 385.6**	**32.0**	**34.5**	**78.7**	**58.9**	**2.2**	**9.9**	**5.0**	**7.5**
15–19	1 051.1	996.7	99.7	98.7	0.3	1.2	...	...	...	...
20–24	1 039.0	997.7	89.5	76.8	10.3	22.6	...	0.1	0.2	0.5
25–29	1 076.4	1 052.9	56.7	38.9	41.6	58.4	0.1	0.2	1.6	2.5
30–34	1 225.6	1 202.3	32.2	21.1	63.9	74.5	0.1	0.3	3.8	5.1
35–39	1 353.0	1 340.0	21.3	14.0	72.8	78.2	0.2	0.6	5.8	5.1
40–44	1 259.5	1 262.5	21.3	14.0	72.8	78.2	0.2	0.6	5.8	7.2
45–49	1 095.1	1 100.2	14.6	10.4	77.5	78.8	0.3	1.2	7.7	9.7
50–54	933.4	940.7	10.3	8.1	80.3	78.2	0.6	2.2	8.9	11.5
55–59	711.5	726.6	7.6	6.4	82.5	77.4	1.0	4.2	9.0	12.0
60–64	594.6	618.7	6.1	5.2	83.3	70.8	3.4	15.0	7.2	9.0
65–69	547.0	594.7	6.2	5.4	82.0	62.6	5.8	24.7	6.0	7.3
70–74	439.3	543.7	6.2	5.7	79.7	51.8	9.6	37.2	4.4	5.2
75–79	312.5	447.3	5.7	6.3	75.9	38.9	15.2	51.1	3.2	3.7
80–84	175.1	295.8	5.7	7.3	68.1	24.3	23.7	65.8	2.4	2.3
85–89	83.2	172.9	6.3	8.9	56.7	13.0	35.2	76.7	1.8	1.4
90+	31.5	92.7	6.8	10.1	40.1	5.1	51.7	84.1	1.3	0.7

Source: © Statistics Canada

(...) = Less than 0.1 percent.

Canadian Attitudes to Divorce, by Age

The 1995 General Social Survey on family and social support collected data from nearly 11,000 Canadians aged 15 and over living in the 10 provinces. In addition to gathering information about the respondent's family and marital history, the survey also asked: "...if you think the following reasons are sufficient for splitting up a marriage or common-law relationship."

Ten reasons were included in three general categories: fundamental issues, experiential issues, and fertility issues. Respondents were also asked if they themselves would stay in a union for the sake of their children.

Reasons for Divorce	**% of Total Respondents**	**% of Respondents Aged 15-29**	**% of Respondents Aged 30-49**	**% of Respondents Aged 50+**
FUNDAMENTAL ISSUES				
Abusive behaviour from partner	95	95	95	94
Unfaithful behaviour from partner	88	89	85	89
Lack of love and respect from partner	88	86	87	87
Partner drinks excessively	74	68	73	80
EXPERIENTIAL ISSUES				
Constant disagreement about family finances	40	28	40	49
Unsatisfactory sexual relationship	35	21	37	45
Unsatisfactory division of household tasks	17	12	16	21
Conflict over how children are raised	17	14	17	21
FERTILITY ISSUES				
Inability to have children with partner	13	8	12	17
Disagreement over number of children to have	7	3	6	11
WOULD STAY FOR THE CHILDREN	43	44	39	52

Source: © Statistics Canada

Lone-Parent Families by Province, 1998

Province	Lone-Parent Families	Male Parent	Average Family Size	Female Parent	Average Family Size
Canada......................	1 227 537	204 793	2.4	1 022 744	2.6
Newfoundland..................	21 445	3 241	2.4	18 204	2.5
Prince Edward Island........	5 589	940	2.5	4 649	2.6
Nova Scotia......................	42 451	6 355	2.4	36 096	2.6
New Brunswick	31 021	5 033	2.4	25 988	2.5
Quebec............................	328 514	60 783	2.4	267 731	2.5
Ontario............................	463 366	71 180	2.5	392 186	2.6
Manitoba..........................	43 137	7 015	2.5	36 122	2.7
Saskatchewan	37 687	5 923	2.6	31 764	2.7
Alberta.............................	100 606	18 164	2.5	82 442	2.6
British Columbia	153 721	26 159	2.4	127 562	2.6

Source: © *Statistics Canada*

Lone-Parent Families by Age, 1998

	Total Families	Size of Families		
		2 Members	3 Members	4 or more Members
Headed by Male Parent	**204 793**	**137 636**	**52 300**	**14 857**
Age 15–24..	1 696	1 662	248	59
25–34...	21 092	13 929	5 690	1 473
35–44...	64 898	38 335	20 479	6 084
45–54...	65 029	42 409	17 613	5 007
55–64...	25 270	18 916	5 057	1 297
65+..	26 535	22 385	3 213	937
Headed by Female Parent	**1 022 744**	**592 530**	**310 735**	**119 479**
Age 15–24..	63 813	46 543	14 475	2 795
25–34...	223 806	109 028	79 150	35 628
35–44...	325 836	144 623	126 113	55 100
45–54...	212 022	128 353	64 195	19 474
55–64...	79 938	62 560	13 840	3 538
65+..	117 329	101 423	12 962	2 944

Source: © *Statistics Canada*

Income Increasing for Lone-Parent Families

*T*he highest median income in 1997 for husband-wife families was in the Northwest Territories ($72,200), excluding Nunavut, followed by the Yukon ($60,200) and Ontario ($55,300).

The median total income of lone-parent families was $21,300 in 1997, up 1.3 percent from 1996 after adjusting for inflation. An increase in median total income in Alberta came from the province posting the second-highest median income for lone-parent families ($22,400), just behind Ontario ($23,000).

Husband-wife families received $42.7 billion of the total government transfers of $75.8 billion, and lone-parent families received $9.1 billion. Twenty-six percent of lone-parent family income came from transfers, while transfers made up 10 percent of income to husband-wife families.

Taxes and transfers reduced the income disparity between family types. On a pre-transfer basis, two-parent families with two earners received an average of $3 for each $1 received by female lone-parent families. This was reduced to just over $2 for each $1 after tax.

Two-parent families had an average income of $64,814 in 1997. Average income for lone-parent families headed by women increased 4.1 percent to $25,445, as higher employment earnings were accompanied by increased Child Tax Benefits.

Composition of Canadian Families

(thousands)

	1971		1981		1991		1996	
	No. of Families	%	No. of Families	%	No. of Families	%	No. of Families	%
Total families[1]	5 071	100.0	6 325	100.0	7 356	100.0	7 838	100.0
Without children at home	1 545	30.5	2 013	31.8	2 580	35.1	2 730	35.0
With children at home	3 526	69.5	4 312	68.2	4 776	64.9	5 108	65.2
With one child	1 045	20.6	1 580	25.0	1 945	26.4	2 106	27.0
two children	1 077	21.2	1 648	26.1	1 927	26.2	2 047	26.1
three children	677	13.4	730	11.5	691	9.4	729	9.3
four children	367	7.2	243	3.8	165	2.2	175	2.2
five children or more	360	7.1	112	1.8	48	0.5	51	0.6
Lone parent families	471	9.3	653	10.3	955	13.0	1 137	14.5
lone female parent	371	7.3	541	8.6	786	10.7	945	12.1
lone male parent	100	2.0	112	1.8	168	2.3	192	2.5

Source: © *Census of Canada, Statistics Canada*

(1) Based on the census family definition: a husband and wife (without children or with children who never married) or a parent with one or more children who never married, living together in the same home.

Size of Families in Canada

(thousands of families)

	1961		1971		1981		1991		1996	
	No. of Families	Avg. Size	No. of Families	Avg. Size	No. of Families	Avg. Size	No. of Families	Avg. Size	No. of Families	Avg. Size
Canada	4 147	3.9	5 071	3.7	6 325	3.3	7 356	3.1	7 838	3.1
Newfoundland	89	4.7	108	4.4	135	3.8	151	3.3	156	3.1
Prince Edward Island	22	4.2	24	4.0	30	3.5	34	3.2	36	3.2
Nova Scotia	162	4.0	181	3.8	216	3.3	245	3.1	254	3.0
New Brunswick	125	4.3	140	4.0	177	3.4	198	3.1	207	3.0
Quebec	1 104	4.2	1 357	3.9	1 672	3.3	1 883	3.0	1 950	3.0
Ontario	1 511	3.6	1 882	3.6	2 279	3.2	2 727	3.1	2 933	3.1
Manitoba	216	3.7	236	3.6	262	3.2	286	3.1	293	3.1
Saskatchewan	212	3.8	216	3.7	246	3.3	258	3.2	260	3.1
Alberta	306	3.8	382	3.7	566	3.3	668	3.1	718	3.1
British Columbia	394	3.6	534	3.5	728	3.1	888	3.0	1 008	3.0
Yukon	7[1]	4.3[1]	11[1]	4.3[1]	6	3.3	7	3.1	8	3.1
Northwest Territories	7[1]	4.3[1]	11[1]	4.3[1]	9	4.0	13	3.7	15	3.6

Source: © *Census of Canada, Statistics Canada*   (1) Includes both the Yukon and Northwest Territories.

Estimates of Family Size, 1998

Statistics Canada estimates that the size of Canadian families has continued to drop during the 1990's. Compare these estimates with the chart above:

	No. of Families (000's)	Avg. Size		No. of Families (000's)	Avg. Size
Canada	8 116 905	3.0	Ontario	3 067 351	3.1
Newfoundland	156 326	3.1	Manitoba	297 370	3.1
Prince Edward Island	36 709	3.1	Saskatchewan	267 362	3.1
Nova Scotia	257 624	3.0	Alberta	768 577	3.1
New Brunswick	213 075	3.0	British Columbia	1 062 703	3.0
Quebec	1 989 808	3.0			

Source: © *Statistics Canada*

Home Electronics and Appliances Owned by Canadians

(percentage of households owning item)

	1965	1970	1975	1980	1985	1990	1996	1997
Air conditioners	2.2	4.3	12.4	16.7	18.0	24.4	29.3	29.1
Automobiles	75.0	77.7	78.9	79.8	77.3	77.8	73.9	74.6
Camcorders	n.a.	n.a.	n.a.	n.a.	n.a.	5.6	16.1	17.7
Cellular Telephones	n.a	n.a.	n.a.	n.a.	n.a.	n.a.	14.1	18.6
Clothes dryers	25.2	40.8	48.1	63.2	68.4	73.4	76.5	76.7
Compact disc players	n.a.	n.a.	n.a.	n.a.	n.a.	15.4	53.4	58.1
Computer modems	n.a.	n.a.	n.a.	n.a.	n.a.	n.a.	15.5	21.5
Dishwashers	2.7	7.5	15.2	28.6	37.1	42.0	47.7	48.5
Electric stoves	69.0	78.6	85.1	89.4	92.3	93.8	93.7	93.5
Electric washers	86.2	83.7	76.9	77.3	77.3	78.6	79.6	80.0
Freezers	22.6	33.2	41.8	51.0	57.0	57.6	57.1	56.0
Gas barbecues	n.a.	n.a.	n.a.	n.a.	19.9[1]	45.9	53.2	53.9
Home computers	n.a.	n.a.	n.a.	n.a.	n.a.	16.3	31.6	36.0
Microwave ovens	n.a.	n.a.	0.8	8.0[2]	23.0	68.2	85.2	86.2
Radios	96.1	97.2	98.3	98.7	98.7	99.1	98.6	98.7
Refrigerators	95.8	98.4	99.3	99.6	99.2	99.5	99.6	99.8
Smoke detectors	n.a.	n.a.	n.a.	n.a.	n.a.	n.a.	95.7	96.1
Telephones	89.4	93.9	96.4	97.6	98.2	98.5	98.7	98.6
Television, cable	n.a.	n.a.	40.4	54.8	62.5	71.4	74.0	73.7
Televisions	92.6	96.0	96.8	97.7	98.3	99.0	99.1	99.1
Televisions, color	n.a.	12.1	53.4	81.1	91.4	96.9	98.5	98.7
Video cassette recorders	n.a.	n.a.	n.a.	n.a.	23.5	66.3	83.5	84.7
Number of households[3]	**5 000**	**5 784**	**6 721**	**7 787**	**8 762**	**9 624**	**11 412**	**11 580**

Source: © *Statistics Canada*

(n.a.) Not available. (1) 1984 figure. (2) 1981 figure. (3) In thousands.

The Internet and Electronic Commerce

*A*CNielsen began surveying Canadians about Internet access in 1996 and the data show that the Internet population in Canada is growing rapidly. In 1996, 23 percent of Canadians used the Internet. By the spring of 1997, this user group had grown to 28.5 percent of Canadians, and in the fall of 1997 it was 31 percent.

Connectedness increases substantially with education, according to the 1998 Household Internet Use Survey. In 1998, the rate of connectedness for households where the head has a university degree (68.1 percent) was more than five times higher than the rate for households where the head did not complete high school (12.6 percent).

Growth in electronic commerce has been more dramatic. According to a study by the Organisation for Economic Co-operation and Development (OECD), in 1995 the amount spend in international electronic commerce was tiny. By 1997 electronic commerce had grown to US$26 billion. Optimistic projections for 2001–03 are US$330 billion, and US$1 trillion in 2003–05.

Business-to-business electronic commerce leads the way, accounting for 80 percent the total. Business-to-consumer e-commerce has moved more slowly. Only 13 percent of Canadian Internet users have made a purchase on-line.

According to research by the Office of Consumer Affairs in June 1998, consumers who do shop online buy from companies with whom they are familiar and with whom they have had previous dealings. Purchasers are usually male, have higher household incomes than average and see themselves as financial risk takers. The most popular Internet purchases are computer software and hardware, books and magazines and CDs or cassettes.

Consumers cite three reasons for buying something through the Internet rather than in a store: the item they bought was inexpensive, they bought from a company they knew and trusted or they couldn't find the product or service through their usual retailers. Canadian Internet shoppers say they are aware of the risks involved in buying online, but see those risks as the tradeoff for getting what they want.

Average Annual Income in Canada

The following figures have been adjusted for inflation; they are expressed in constant 1997 dollars for the purpose of comparison.

	1991	1992	1993	1994	1995	1996	1997
Economic families[1]	57 537	57 222	56 045	57 095	56 997	57 544	57 146
Elderly families[2]	43 398	41 976	42 763	42 366	44 283	43 450	43 351
Married couples only	38 947	38 305	39 495	39 399	40 092	40 228	40 047
All other elderly families	54 065	50 989	50 340	50 003	55 113	52 581	53 092
Non-elderly families[3]	59 970	59 915	58 373	59 706	59 336	59 986	59 583
Married couples, no children	57 911	60 053	57 029	57 084	57 409	57 590	56 889
One earner	44 514	45 611	46 502	46 051	45 390	47 786	43 963
Two earners	65 633	68 121	64 588	64 830	65 378	65 409	65 352
Two-parent families with children[4]	64 141	64 589	63 049	64 424	64 048	65 015	64 814
One earner	46 772	46 825	45 774	48 062	45 650	46 054	46 308
Two earners	65 061	66 415	64 569	66 541	66 590	67 311	66 998
Three or more earners	81 623	80 529	81 486	81 612	81 441	84 099	83 337
Married couples with other relatives[5]	79 990	79 439	79 439	80 730	78 759	82 495	80 830
Lone-parent families[4]	26 218	27 593	26 146	26 975	27 577	26 569	27 576
Male lone-parent families	40 314	42 583	36 705	36 764	37 640	40 065	39 371
Female lone-parent families	24 145	25 551	24 403	25 364	25 881	24 432	25 445
No earner	14 385	14 690	15 408	15 020	15 473	13 948	13 373
One earner	26 413	28 598	26 950	28 215	28 447	28 154	28 550
All other families	47 712	43 496	45 597	47 309	46 324	49 603	49 996
Unattached individuals	24 918	25 273	24 823	25 036	24 931	24 828	25 005
Elderly	19 888	20 009	18 890	19 800	20 639	20 346	19 944
Male	22 345	23 652	22 007	25 074	24 516	25 424	24 340
Female	19 074	18 807	17 806	18 035	19 335	18 432	18 399
Non-elderly	26 766	27 164	27 075	26 995	26 518	26 641	26 976
Male	28 727	28 976	28 673	29 381	28 233	28 613	28 754
Female	24 148	24 528	24 709	23 516	24 159	23 811	24 430

Source: © *Statistics Canada*

(1) An economic family is a group of individuals sharing a common dwelling unit who are related by blood, marriage (including common-law relationships) or adoption. (2) Head aged 65 or over. (3) Head aged under 65. (4) With single children less than 18. (Children 18 or over and other relatives may also be present.) (5) Children less than 18 are not present, but children over 18 may be present.

Average Family Income[1]

	1980	1985	1990	1995	1996	1997
Canada	**28 006**	**38 059**	**51 633**	**55 247**	**56 629**	**57 146**
Newfoundland	21 794	29 629	40 770	43 753	43 564	41 850
Prince Edward Island	23 264	30 943	39 701	46 170	47 414	45 639
Nova Scotia	22 471	34 349	44 385	45 715	45 087	45 731
New Brunswick	21 873	31 473	42 356	45 516	46 284	46 480
Quebec	25 842	35 068	47 158	49 851	50 935	51 256
Ontario	29 248	41 775	57 027	60 923	62 614	65 503
Manitoba	26 092	34 829	47 178	52 149	52 132	54 316
Saskatchewan	26 705	34 866	44 234	50 797	50 847	50 368
Alberta	32 506	40 736	51 985	54 092	57 735	58 562
British Columbia	31 200	37 968	54 448	57 046	59 440	59 453

Source: © *Statistics Canada*   (1) Not adjusted for inflation.

Incidence of Low Income for Selected Types of Families

(percent)

The following has been calculated using low-income cutoffs, 1992 base, for the purposes of comparison. It shows the percentage of families that fall into the low income category.

	1980	1990	1993	1994	1995	1996	1997
Economic families, two persons or more[1]	13.2	12.3	14.6	13.5	14.2	14.5	14.0
Elderly families[2]	19.2	7.6	9.7	7.1	7.8	8.7	6.8
Married couples only	20.1	7.6	8.8	5.9	6.7	7.9	6.0
All other elderly families	17.3	7.7	11.8	9.9	10.4	10.7	9.2
Non-elderly families[3]	12.4	13.1	15.5	14.6	15.4	15.5	15.3
Married couples, no children	6.7	8.1	9.6	9.4	10.1	10.0	10.6
One earner	11.9	11.6	13.1	11.4	15.0	12.8	13.9
Two earners	1.6	3.4	3.9	4.1	4.0	4.0	4.2
Two-parent families with children[4]	9.7	9.8	12.2	11.5	12.8	11.8	12.0
One earner	16.6	23.2	24.4	23.5	27.4	25.0	25.6
Two earners	5.8	6.5	7.1	6.1	7.3	6.6	6.6
Three or more earners	3.6	2.6	3.5	3.7	4.0	3.4	4.1
Married couples with other relatives[5]	4.1	3.2	3.6	5.5	5.2	5.3	5.3
Lone-parent families[4]	52.9	54.4	55.0	53.0	53.0	56.8	51.1
Male lone-parent families	25.4	25.5	30.9	32.3	30.7	31.3	23.5
Female lone-parent families	57.3	59.5	59.0	56.4	56.8	60.8	56.0
No earner	96.4	95.7	92.3	93.5	91.7	96.9	95.7
One earner	49.0	49.6	45.4	40.4	43.1	45.4	42.6
All other families	25.2	18.4	19.9	19.3	18.8	17.8	18.3
Unattached individuals	40.0	07.4	40.5	40.0	39.3	40.2	39.0
Elderly	68.6	50.7	51.9	47.6	45.1	47.9	45.0
Male	60.7	41.0	39.0	31.8	28.7	33.3	33.3
Female	71.6	53.8	56.4	52.9	50.6	53.4	49.1
Non-elderly	34.5	32.4	36.2	38.0	37.2	37.1	37.5
Male	29.0	29.0	33.5	33.3	34.8	34.0	35.1
Female	41.1	37.1	40.1	44.9	40.4	41.7	40.9

Source: © *Statistics Canada*

(1) An economic family is a group of individuals sharing a common dwelling unit who are related by blood, marriage (including common-law relationships) or adoption. (2) Head aged 65 or over. (3) Head aged under 65. (4) With single children less than 18. (Children 18 or over and other relatives may also be present.) (5) Children less than 18 are not present, but children over 18 may be present.

Percentage Income Distribution by Gender[1]

(percent)

	1980		1985		1990		1995		1997	
	male	female	male	female	male	female	male	female	male	female
under $1,000	3.9	9.4	3.0	6.2	—	—	—	—	—	—
under $2,500	13.5	31.1	9.2	19.5	4.8	8.2	4.9	7.6	2.9	2.5
$2,500–4,999	*	*	*	*	4.1	7.7	3.5	6.8	2.7	1.7
$5,000–7,499	16.5	26.9	14.6	27.0	5.2	9.7	4.7	8.4	7.2	5.4
$7,500–9,999	*	*	*	*	5.1	9.5	4.7	7.8	5.8	6.1
$10,000–14,999	14.8	17.3	13.2	16.0	10.9	18.8	11.0	18.4	15.0	26.8
$15,000–19,999	16.3	8.1	11.2	12.1	10.0	12.5	10.2	11.9	11.4	17.1
$20,000–24,999	14.4	4.2	10.8	7.9	9.4	10.3	9.0	9.9	9.7	8.9
$25,000–29,999	8.9	2.0	9.4	4.6	9.7	7.7	8.6	7.9	7.2	8.5
$30,000–39,999	11.8	1.2	28.6	6.7	16.1	9.0	15.2	11.1	14.9	10.9
$40,000–49,999	*	*	*	*	10.6	3.5	11.1	5.2	9.8	5.4
$50,000+	*	*	*	*	14.1	3.0	17.2	5.2	13.4	6.7

Source: © *Census of Canada*

(*) Included in previous category. (—) Not reported. (1) Data represents income of unattached individuals (i.e., not family income).

Household Environmental Practices, 1994

(% of households)

	Canada	Nfld	PEI	NS	NB	Que	Ont	Man	Sask	Alta	BC
Access to recycling programs											
Paper	69.6	19.7	20.8	50.3	46.7	57.2	83.5	61.0	69.3	71.2	74.5
Metal cans	67.2	21.3	16.7	47.6	69.8	48.9	82.3	61.0	77.3	72.2	69.6
Glass bottles	67.4	12.0	18.8	47.3	72.9	50.1	82.0	58.9	74.8	72.6	70.7
Plastics	62.8	18.6	16.7	42.5	61.2	49.5	77.7	61.0	73.7	66.2	55.7
Special disposal	40.2	3.3	10.4	12.0	12.2	41.8	45.9	29.0	34.9	56.9	32.2
Use of recycling programs											
Paper	83.1	44.4	70.0	72.5	58.8	74.0	92.9	48.3	73.2	75.8	88.2
Metal cans	83.5	48.7	62.5	69.6	81.5	70.7	93.3	51.2	81.0	78.7	86.0
Glass bottles	83.5	40.9	66.7	68.8	82.8	70.9	93.3	46.2	81.1	78.8	86.1
Plastics	81.7	47.1	62.5	67.4	77.6	71.4	92.2	51.2	80.8	70.8	82.4
Special disposal	57.1	66.7	80.0	65.0	64.5	54.5	60.1	48.7	46.8	53.8	59.1
Use of disposable diapers											
All of the time	76.9	92.3	100.0	68.2	82.4	81.9	79.0	70.4	62.5	67.1	73.2
Most of the time	9.5	7.7	—	13.6	5.9	10.2	7.6	7.4	12.5	11.8	13.4
Sometimes	11.1	—	—	—	—	—	11.3	—	25.0	19.7	12.2
Never	2.0	—	—	4.5	5.9	1.7	2.1	—	—	—	—
Children not in diapers	—	—	—	—	—	—	—	—	—	—	—
Other Environmental Practices											
Regularly purchase paper towels or toilet paper made from recycled paper	58.3	68.3	56.3	65.7	66.3	60.7	59.9	48.6	49.3	51.5	53.9
Regularly take their own bag when shopping	24.4	4.4	12.5	14.8	22.7	17.6	25.4	35.0	32.7	31.3	31.1
Use a compost heap, compost container or composting service	22.7	9.3	16.7	19.0	16.1	7.9	30.3	18.1	21.6	21.2	37.9
Use chemical pesticides	31.1	9.4	11.6	18.7	19.7	29.8	34.3	30.1	37.2	36.1	29.6
Use chemical fertilizer	46.8	26.4	23.3	35.3	35.8	41.4	50.7	38.5	57.0	58.1	47.2
Have programmable thermostat	16.0	5.6	6.7	9.4	9.1	9.7	23.6	14.9	10.2	15.1	15.3
Regularly lower temperature	71.1	82.1	87.8	82.4	75.3	70.5	64.4	65.9	77.0	72.0	81.0
Use energy efficient compat fluorescent light bulbs	18.9	8.2	20.8	13.3	17.6	14.2	24.6	13.1	14.1	15.9	20.0
Have water-saving, low-flow or modified shower-head	42.3	27.9	33.3	40.7	42.4	46.0	44.9	34.0	26.6	32.2	43.4 ▶

	Canada	Nfld	PEI	NS	NB	Que	Ont	Man	Sask	Alta	BC
Have water-saving, low-volume toilet	14.8	6.0	6.3	12.7	11.4	8.7	18.0	19.4	12.5	20.6	15.9
Have water filter or purifier for drinking water	19.5	9.8	2.1	16.3	14.1	9.7	24.9	18.4	22.7	16.4	29.1
Purchase bottled water	21.9	8.7	6.3	18.1	16.9	33.4	19.6	13.4	8.9	15.3	19.9
Principal method of travel to work											
Public transit	13.7	—	—	6.7	2.7	14.9	16.3	10.1	3.7	11.2	14.4
Motor vehicle as driver	78.8	79.3	85.7	80.0	82.7	76.6	79.7	78.5	80.4	80.3	77.8
Motor vehicle as passenger	10.6	18.5	17.9	16.9	17.3	9.6	10.0	13.4	11.0	9.5	10.7
Bicycle	2.3	—	—	—	—	2.0	1.9	5.3	4.1	2.4	3.7
Walk only	7.8	12.0	—	8.7	6.7	8.5	6.3	11.3	11.4	7.4	8.7
Other	0.3	—	—	—	—	—	—	—	—	—	—
Not ascertained	5.8	5.4	—	6.7	6.7	6.2	5.5	5.3	7.3	6.3	5.2

Source: © *Statistics Canada*

If there's a Blue Box program in your neighbourhood...

Blue Box recycling programs have grown in popularity over the last five years and the variety of materials that can be recycled has also grown. The Blue Box itself can carry certain recyclables; other items can be bundled up and set out separately. (Check with your local Blue Box program for local variations.)

What can a Blue Box hold?
- **glass bottles and jars.** They should be rinsed; their lids can also go in the box.
- **aluminum and steel food and beverage containers.** They should be rinsed; their lids can be placed inside, if applicable. There is no need to flatten the cans.
- **plastic containers.** Look for the ones with the recycling triangle and the number 1, 2 or 4 inside. Clean the bottles out and remove the caps and lids. The caps and lids of plastic containers should go in the regular garbage; do not try to recycle them.
- **aluminum foil wrap and containers.** Rinse the items first.
- **empty aerosol and paint cans.** They must be empty. Paint can lids should be removed, but they can go in the box as well.

What else can be recycled?
- **newspapers, inserts, magazines and phone books.** They should be bagged together.
- **plastic film.** These can be stuffed into one bag. (Remember to remove any contents— including old cash register tapes.)
- **boxboard and fine paper.** All wrap, spouts and liners should be removed. These can be flattened and placed inside one of the boxes.
- **corrugated cardboard.** This should be bundled separately from boxboard and flattened if the box is larger than 3 ft x 3 ft x 3 ft.

Leftover paint, paint thinners, cleaners, finishes, gasoline, oils and other toxic or flammable substances can usually be taken to a central depot for disposal. DO NOT dump this material into your local sewer system (or simply store it all together somewhere it can be ignored).

Large items such as old appliances or fixtures can also be used by someone for another project or for parts. Make a concerted effort to find a new home or a secondary use for an item before you add it to the landfill.

Low Income in Canada, 1997[1]

The low-income cutoff level is set by Statistics Canada, using a standard that families or individuals who spend 54.7 percent or more of their pre-tax income on food, clothing and shelter are in financial difficulty.

The table below shows the minimum income level necessary to avoid financial hardship. It varies according to changes in the cost of living, family size and place of residence. For instance, in 1996 the poverty line for a family of four living in Fredricton was $27,459; for a family of four living in a rural area it was $22,279.

Family size[2]	Urban Areas				Rural Areas
	Pop. Under 30 000	Pop. 30 000 to 99 999	Pop. 100 000 to 499 999	Pop. 500 000 or more	
1 person	13 924	14 965	15 070	17 571	12 142
2 persons	17 405	18 706	18 837	21 962	15 178
3 persons	21 647	23 264	23 429	27 315	18 877
4 persons	26 205	28 162	28 359	33 063	22 877
5 persons	29 293	31 481	31 701	36 958	25 542
6 persons	32 379	34 798	35 043	40 855	28 235
7 or more persons	35 467	38 117	38 385	44 751	30 928

Source: © *Statistics Canada*

(1) 1992 base. (2) Does not distinguish between adults and children as family members.

Canadian Residents Living Below the Poverty Line

While there is no official definition of "poverty line," as noted in the above table it is generally accepted that those spending more than 54.7 percent of their pre-tax income on food, clothing and shelter are likely to be in financial difficulty.

Another way of defining low income (or the poverty line) is to take 50 percent of the median family income considered to be necessary to cover a family's needs. Defining a family's "needs" is not easy. For the purposes of assessing low income, Statistics Canada has set a figure for the needs of one adult and then

assumed that family needs increase in proportion to the size of the family. Each additional adult is assumed to increase the family's needs by 40 percent of the first figure, and each additional child increases the needs by 30 percent. These income figures were then compared to the actual incomes of families and individuals and used to calculate how many Canadians, living as family members or single individuals, failed to generate enough income to cover their basic needs for food, clothing, shelter and other expenses.

(thousands of persons)

	1985	1987	1989	1991	1993	1995	1996
Total	**3 840**	**3 767**	**3 784**	**4 067**	**4 276**	**4 408**	**5 294**
Children under 18	1 175	1 125	1 083	1 250	1 330	1 358	1 498
Adults, 18 to 65	2 211	2 173	2 123	2 400	2 538	2 713	3 074
Adults, 65 and over	455	470	579	417	409	337	722
Family Members, total	**2 889**	**2 760**	**2 741**	**2 977**	**3 163**	**3 276**	**3 707**
Children under 18	1 175	1 125	1 083	1 250	1 330	1 358	1 498
Adults, 18 to 65	1 566	1 480	1 459	1 614	1 716	1 833	2 031
Adults, 65 and over	149	156	199	114	117	85	178
Single individuals, total	**951**	**1 007**	**1 043**	**1 090**	**1 113**	**1 132**	**1 587**
Adults, 18 to 65	645	693	664	786	822	880	1 043
Adults, 65 and over	305	314	380	304	291	252	544

Source: © *Statistics Canada*

EDUCATION

Canadian Population[1] by Highest Level of Schooling

(percentage)

	1976	1981	1986	1991	1996
Less than grade 9	25.4	20.7	17.7	14.3	12.4
Grades 9 to 13	44.1	43.7	42.5	42.6	40.4
Some postsecondary education	24.1	27.6	30.2	31.7	33.9
University degree	6.4	8.0	9.6	11.4	13.3

Source: © *Census of Canada, Statistics Canada* (1) Over the age of 15.

Canadian Population[1] by Highest Level of Schooling, by Province, 1996

(percentage)

	Elementary-Secondary Schooling Only	Postsecondary, Non-university Education	University Without a Degree	University With a Degree
Canada	**52.8**	**24.2**	**9.7**	**13.3**
Newfoundland	58.2	23.0	10.7	8.1
Prince Edward Island	55.4	22.5	11.5	10.6
Nova Scotia	52.8	23.8	11.2	12.2
New Brunswick	58.3	21.6	9.9	10.2
Quebec	57.5	22.3	8.0	12.2
Ontario	51.1	24.6	9.4	14.9
Manitoba	55.9	21.0	11.5	11.6
Saskatchewan	56.8	21.6	11.8	9.8
Alberta	48.7	27.8	10.2	13.3
British Columbia	47.5	27.0	11.9	13.6
Yukon Territory	40.0	33.5	12.0	14.5
Northwest Territories	53.3	28.7	7.5	10.5

Source: © *Census of Canada, Statistics Canada* (1) Over the age of 15.

Enrolment in Canadian Schools

(000s)

	1971	1981	1991	1996	1997[1]	1998[1]
Elementary/secondary schools	5 805.8	5 024.2	5 218.2	5 433.1	5 459.5	5 497.0
- percent in private schools	2.4	4.3	4.7	5.3	5.3	5.15.3
Public college/trade/vocational (full time)	167.3	n.a.	275.9	266.4	264.5	n.a.
College/postsecondary, full-time	173.8	273.4	349.1	395.3	396.7	397.7
College/postsecondary, part-time	n.a.	n.a.	216.8	153.7	149.1	n.a.
University (full-time)	323.0	401.9	554.0	573.6	573.0	578.6
University (part-time)	n.a.	251.9	313.3	256.1	249.7	243.0
Adult education and training	n.a.	n.a.	5 504	n.a.	6 069	n.a.

Source: © *Statistics Canada* (n.a.) Not available. (1) Based on preliminary numbers.

University Enrolment by Field of Study, 1997–98

	Undergraduate			Graduate		
	Male	Female	Total	Male	Female	Total
Full-time						
Agricultural/biological sciences ..	13 511	19 067	32 578	2 572	2 156	4 728
Arts/science	63 111	70 176	133 287	5 917	3 818	9 735
Education	8 199	24 804	33 003	554	1 360	1 914
Engineering/applied sciences	34 798	9 172	43 970	6 311	1 643	7 954
Fine/applied arts	13 652	18 454	32 106	1 317	1 612	2 929
Health professions	10 193	23 286	33 479	7 952	7 405	15 357
Humanities	27 601	46 817	74 418	7 888	9 830	17 718
Mathematics/physical sciences ..	28 981	16 863	45 844	6 265	3 540	9 805
Social sciences	10 405	35 681	46 086	1 621	4 182	5 803
Not applicable	5 430	6 714	12 144	1 129	1 244	2 373
Not reported	1 434	2 096	3 530	133	159	292
Interdisciplinary	1 071	1 950	3 021	195	319	514
Total full-time enrolment	**218 386**	**275 080**	**493 466**	**41 854**	**37 268**	**79 122**
Part-time						
Agricultural/biological sciences ..	1 616	3 762	5 378	353	315	668
Arts/science	19 124	26 375	45 499	8 792	11 286	20 078
Education	4 175	10 686	14 861	1 398	4 225	5 623
Engineering/applied sciences	4 840	1 003	5 843	2 498	554	3 052
Fine/applied arts	2 328	4 297	6 625	1 852	2 018	3 870
Health professions	1 207	8 573	9 780	758	2 594	3 352
Humanities	8 623	15 961	24 584	3 949	6 676	10 625
Mathematics/physical sciences ..	7 698	3 892	11 590	2 550	1 924	4 474
Social sciences	3 818	13 040	16 858	664	1 969	2 633
Not applicable	13 905	23 643	37 548	32 346	5 290	37 636
Not reported	1 453	2 119	3 572	214	387	601
Interdisciplinary	766	2 610	3 376	96	224	320
Total part-time enrolment	**69 553**	**115 961**	**185 514**	**55 470**	**37 462**	**92 932**

Source: © *Statistics Canada*

Statistics Canada on the Internet

*S*tatistics Canada has been an active participant on the Internet for over four years and has established a web site of information for all Internet users—be they Canadian or international. The web service has been designed in two parts, providing two types of service: a public good service and a commercial service.

The public good service is extensive and growing. This offering includes Statistics Canada's "The Daily," the notification of first release. "The Daily" contains information on the latest data releases in the form of excerpts and details of the publications themselves, including catalogue numbers. Internet users can view "The Daily" in HTML, PDF or ASCII formats. It is also obtainable via e-mail through Stats Can's listserver subscription service. A fully searchable archive of previous issues of "The Daily" is also accessible.

The public good service also includes a public information databank containing data tables on all aspects of Canada. Under the heading "Canadian Dimensions" there are over 160 updated and down-loadable tables available on topics including geography, population, government and the economy. The table of Economic Indicators is updated at 8:30 every business day.

The commercial service allows clients to purchase data and publications over the Internet. Two databases now available for commercial access are CANSIM—a time series database containing over 700,000 times series, and a trade database providing detailed data on imports and exports between Canada and other countries. CANSIM contains information on many aspects of population and consumption, collected over a number of years. Clients can establish accounts or purchase data anonymously. All data can be purchased without the need to contact a Statistics Canada representative.

The Statistics Canada's web service can be accessed at **http://www.statcan.ca.**

University Graduates by Field of Study, 1997

Field of Study	Bachelor's/ First Professional Degree	Diploma and Certificate	Men	Women	Total Undergraduate
Education	20 319	2 937	6 670	16 586	23 256
Fine/applied arts	4 047	514	1 458	3 103	4 561
Humanities	14 869	2 911	6 431	11 349	17 780
Social sciences	47 054	8 684	22 744	32 994	55 738
Agricultural/biological sciences . .	9 538	586	3 951	6 173	10 124
Engineering/applied sciences	9 030	722	7 691	2 061	9 752
Health professions	8 701	1 752	2 529	7 924	10 453
Mathematics/physical sciences . .	6 992	559	5 124	2 427	7 551
Other	3 474	1 836	1 663	3 647	5 310
Total	**124 024**	**20 501**	**58 261**	**86 264**	**144 525**

Field of Study	Masters	Doctoral	Graduate Diploma and Certificate	Men	Women	Total Graduate
Education	3 266	326	557	1 241	2 908	4 149
Fine/applied arts	503	47	25	214	361	575
Humanities	2 714	160	240	1 520	1 890	3 410
Social sciences	8 405	674	989	5 322	4 746	10 068
Agricultural/biological sciences . .	977	469	57	765	738	1 503
Engineering/applied sciences	2 134	673	54	2 313	548	2 861
Health professions	1 576	482	390	896	1 552	2 448
Mathematics/physical sciences . .	1 320	687	54	1 541	570	2 111
Other	63	25	48	47	89	136
Total	**20 958**	**3 836**	**2 417**	**13 859**	**13 402**	**27 261**

Source: © *Statistics Canada*

Brain Drain

*A*bout 1.5 percent of the more than 300,000 men and women who graduated from a Canadian postsecondary institution in 1995 moved to the United States after graduation, but nearly half of the graduates who relocated ranked near the top of their graduating class in their field of study. Those who left Canada were more likely to have received scholarships or other academic awards than their counterparts.

Just over 4600 postsecondary graduates from the class of 1995 were living in the U.S. in 1997. By March 1999, about 830 (18 percent) had moved back to Canada. Fifteen percent of those who moved had a master's degree and 8 percent had a doctorate. Among graduates who stayed in Canada, 7 percent had a master's degree and 1 percent had a doctorate. Twelve percent of PhDs and 3 percent of master's graduates moved to the United States.

Among the 1995 graduates still living in the U.S. in March 1999, four in 10 planned to return to Canada, three in 10 did not plan to return and three in 10 were uncertain. Approximately 44 percent of the graduates still in the U.S. planned to obtain permanent residence status within two years.

Education Expenditures in Canada

(millions of dollars)

	1971	1976	1981	1986	1991	1996	1998
Elementary/secondary..........	5 387.5	10 070.9	16 703.2	22 968.0	33 444.9	36 387.4	37 736.2
Vocational..........................	565.9	959.9	1 601.2	3 275.1	4 573.8	6 250.8	6 297.9
College...............................	539.4	1 081.5	2 088.1	2 999.0	3 870.7	4 091.7	4 669.3
University............................	1 864.5	2 987.5	4 980.7	7 368.7	11 254.8	11 452.1	11 788.7
Total	**8 357.4**	**15 099.7**	**25 373.1**	**37 074.5**	**53 144.3**	**58 182.0**	**60 492.1**
Spending as a % of GDP......	8.7	7.6	7.1	7.3	7.9	7.3	6.8

Source: © Statistics Canada

How We Compare: Education Spending, G-7 Countries, 1996

	Canada	United States	France	United Kingdom	Germany	Italy	Japan
Education spending as a percentage of total public expenditures	13.6	14.4	11.1	n.a	9.5	9.0	9.8
Public spending as a percentage of GDP	5.8	5.0	5.8	4.6	4.5	4.5	3.6
Participation rate in formal education (percentage)[1]	68.2	68.8	64.5	66.8	61.8	53.8	57.0
Ratio of Secondary School Graduates to Population (percentage)	73	72	85	n.a.	86	79	99
Ratio of First University Degree to Population (percentage).........................	32	35	n.a.	34	n.a.	1	23
Labour Force Participation by Education Attainment (percentage) secondary education							
- men	89	88	90	89	85	80	n.a.
-women..............................	72	72	76	74	69	61	n.a.
university education							
- men	92	93	92	94	93	92	n.a.
- women..............................	85	82	83	86	83	81	n.a.
Unemployment Rate by Level of Educational Attainment (percentage) upper secondary education							
- men	9	6	8	8	8	6	n.a.
- women..............................	9	4	12	6	10	11	n.a.
university education							
- men	5	2	6	4	5	5	n.a.
- women..............................	6	2	9	3	5	10	n.a.

Source: © Statistics Canada

(1) Total number of students enrolled in formal education as a percentage of the population aged 5–29. (n.a.) Not available.

Elementary and Secondary School Pupils per Educator

(pupil/teacher ratio)

1976	1981	1986	1991	1992	1993	1994	1995	1996	1997	1998
18.1	17.0	16.5	15.5	15.7	16.1	16.1	16.1	16.2	16.4	16.5

Source: © Statistics Canada

The National Anthem: O Canada

The music of *O Canada* was composed by Calixa Lavallée and the lyrics were written in French by Adolphe-Basile Routhier in Quebec City. Originally called *Chant National*, it was first performed at a banquet in Quebec City on June 24, 1880. The anthem grew in popularity in Quebec but was not heard in English until the early 1900s. There have been several English versions of the work, the most popular of which was written in 1908 by Robert Stanley Weir. In 1967 a Special Joint Committee of the Senate and the House of Commons was formed to recommend official versions of Canada's National and Royal Anthems. With a few minor changes, the official English version of *O Canada* is based on Weir's lyrics. On June 27, 1980 the House of Commons passed Bill C-36 designating both the music and lyrics of *O Canada* as Canada's national anthem. It was proclaimed July 1, 1980.

O Canada

O Canada! Terre de nos aïeux,

Ton front est ceint de fleurons glorieux!

Car ton bras sait porter l'épée,

Il sait porter la croix!

Ton histoire est une épopée

Des plus brillants exploits,

Et ta valeur, de foi trempée,

Protégera nos foyers et nos droits,

Protégera nos foyers et nos droits.

O Canada

O Canada! Our home and native land!

True patriot love in all thy sons command.

With glowing hearts we see thee rise,

The True North strong and free!

From far and wide, O Canada,

We stand on guard for thee.

God keep our land glorious and free!

O Canada, we stand on guard for thee.

O Canada, we stand on guard for thee!

The National Flag

The National Flag was adopted by Parliament December 15, 1964 and proclaimed by Queen Elizabeth II. It was inaugurated on Feb. 15, 1965.

It is a red flag of the proportions two by length and one by width, containing in its centre a white square, the width of the flag, bearing a single, red, stylized maple leaf. The maple leaf has been looked upon as an emblem of Canada since the early 1700s. Red and white were declared Canada's official colours by King George V on Nov. 21, 1921.

The National Flag is to be flown daily at all federal government buildings, airports and military bases and establishments within and outside Canada. When flown with other flags, it should be given a place of honour.

The National Coat of Arms

The creation of coats of arms dates back to the Middle Ages. Centuries ago few could read, nor did they have access to print material, pictures or the other means we now use to identify people. Heraldry was developed as a form of picture-writing, used in the Middle Ages to create visual emblems that identified individuals or members of a community or nation, particularly on the field of battle.

Over time, the development of such symbols became quite sophisticated; a coat of arms could identify not only the individual but tell if his father was still alive, his birth order, whether or not he was married and the prestige of his branch of the family. In war, the device was painted on a shield; in peace, it would be embroidered on a coat or banner. Because of its significance, heraldry came to be carefully regulated; colleges of arms controlled the grant and use of them.

At the time of Confederation, Canada did not have a coat of arms and used the Royal Arms of the United Kingdom to identify the offices of the Government of Canada. By 1868, however, a Great Seal was required and the government adopted a design that was also used as the Arms of Canada. The design showed the emblems of the original four provinces of the federation—Nova Scotia, New Brunswick, Quebec and Ontario—on a shield. When new provinces joined the federation, their emblems were added to the shield and the design became fragmented and confusing as the provinces multiplied. In 1919, the governor general convened a special committee to study the question of a Canadian coat of arms; a request for a grant of arms was later submitted to the sovereign.

Canada's Coat of Arms was granted by a royal proclamation of King George V on November 21, 1921. Although simplified in 1957, the coat of arms we have now is faithful to that original design.

The most important part of the design is the shield, which shows the emblems of the four founding peoples (English, Scottish, Irish and French) with an added sprig of distinctly Canadian maple leaves. The shield is supported on one side by the lion of England holding the Royal Union flag and the unicorn of Scotland holding a banner of royalist France on the other. A royal helmet and mantle sit above the shield, with a crest showing a royal lion holding a maple leaf on top of the helmet. (The crest is the symbol used on the Governor General's standard.) The imperial crown above the crest represents the monarch as Canada's head of state.

Below the shield is Canada's motto, "A Mari usque ad Mare" (from sea to sea) which is based on a verse from Psalm 72 of the Bible: "He shall have dominion from sea to sea and from the river unto the ends of the earth." The floral emblems of the four founding nations are found at the base of the design: the English rose, the Scottish thistle, the French fleur-de-lis and the shamrock of Ireland.

Canada's coat of arms represents national sovereignty and is used on federal government property such as buildings, official seals, money, passports, proclamations and publications as well as badges of some members of the armed forces. This national symbol is protected from unauthorized commercial use by the Trade Marks Act.

Canada's Changing Boundaries

In **1867**, when the British North America Act was proclaimed and the Dominion of Canada was created, the four "provinces" of Ontario, Quebec, Nova Scotia and New Brunswick were the only members—and the boundaries of at least two were very different from what exists now. While New Brunswick and Nova Scotia were recognizable, the territory divided between Quebec and Ontario included only the land near the Gulf of St. Lawrence (on both sides), the St. Lawrence River and the land north of the Great Lakes. The British government, through the Hudson's Bay Company, controlled most of the rest of the territory we know as Canada today.

In **1870**, the British government gave control of what was known as the North-Western Territory (including the fertile prairies) to Canada, and at the same time the Hudson's Bay Company sold Rupert's Land to the Canadian government. Rupert's Land included all land drained by rivers flowing into Hudson Bay— about 40 percent of the country, nearly 2.8 million ha. It also included the land around the company's trading posts (another 18,000 ha.) The purchase price was £300,000. The two pieces of land were combined into a huge area called the Northwest Territories. The province of Manitoba was carved out of a tiny part around the Red River. It was originally only 36,000 sq. km.—it's now nearly 650,000 sq. km.

In **1871**, after the promise of a railway to link it with the rest of the country, the British colony of British Columbia joined.

Prince Edward Island became the 7th province in **1873**, but only after promises to establish year-round "efficient steam service for the conveyance of mail and passengers" between the island and the mainland. The ability to deliver on this promise was often jeopardized by severe winter weather; the Confederation Bridge, opened in 1997, is yet another attempt to make the promise good.

In **1874** Ontario's boundaries were pushed farther north, but not west; the District of Keewatin was created in the Northwest Territories in **1876**, including part of present-day Ontario and Manitoba and extending north to the Gulf of Boothia. Ownership of the islands of the Arctic archipelago was transferred from Britain to Canada in **1880**, and in **1881** Manitoba's boundaries were extended, giving that province some land claimed by Ontario.

The Northwest Territories was subdivided, with the Districts of Saskatchewan, Assiniboia, Alberta and Athabaska making an appearance on the maps in **1882**. In **1895**, further subdivision created the Districts of Ungava (northern Quebec), Franklin (the Arctic Islands), and Mackenzie (western Northwest Territories) and Yukon. The Yukon District became a separate territory in **1898**.

Also in **1898**, Quebec's boundaries were extended farther north, but the province still shared the area with the District of Ungava, and the District of Keewatin continued to grow, taking in much of present-day Manitoba and Ontario.

By **1905**, as the prairies began to fill with settlers, the provinces of Saskatchewan and Alberta were created out of the Districts of Athabaska, Alberta, Saskatchewan and Assiniboia. The District of Keewatin was transferred to the shrinking (but still vast) Northwest Territories.

In **1912**, the boundaries of Quebec, Ontario and Manitoba were extended north to Hudson Bay and Hudson Strait, assuming the boundaries that we recognize today. In **1920**, the Districts of Mackenzie, Franklin and Keewatin became identified as the Northwest Territories.

The Judicial Committee of the British Privy Council was called on to mediate a boundary dispute between Quebec and Labrador in 1927 and the boundary for present-day Labrador was established. This territory belonged to Newfoundland which was still a British colony. It did not join the union until **1949**, after extensive debate and two closely fought referenda.

On Apr. 1, 1999, the Northwest Territories was divided again into two units. The western part, which kept the name Northwest Territories, was reduced to 1,171,918 sq. km. The eastern Arctic, however, was renamed Nunavut. (The name is Inuktitut for "our land.") Nunavut covers one fifth of Canada's land mass or about 2 million sq. km. The new territory also includes seven of Canada's 12 largest islands and two thirds of Canada's coastline.

CANADIAN HISTORY

■ Exploration and First Settlements

The first people who came to North America arrived during the last Ice Age which began about 80,000 years ago and ended about 12,000 years ago. These Native People were hunters who crosssed from Asia via a land bridge that is now submerged beneath the Bering Sea. Although there is continuing debate among archeologists as to how early humans might have settled in what is now Canada, the earliest accepted occupation site is at the Bluefish Caves in the Yukon; artifacts at least 12,000 to 17,000 years old have been found there. As the glaciers of the Ice Age retreated, human settlements spread across Canada and gradually, these first Canadians developed lifestyles based on the environments in which they lived. They obtained their food by hunting, fishing, gathering, and in the case of Eastern Woodland tribes, by farming. By the time explorers from Europe reached Canada, the Native People had well developed trading patterns, arts and crafts, languages, writing, religious beliefs, laws and government.

There has been much conjecture as to who the first Europeans to come to Canada were. The claim that an Irish monk, St. Brendan, arrived about the year 550 has not been proven. However, the theory that Vikings settled in Newfoundland was confirmed by archeological excavations at L'Anse aux Meadows during the 1960s and 1970s.

A burst of European exploration didn't take place until the Age of Discovery in the 15th and 16th centuries. Explorers found what they called a New World while in search of a route to the Far East. In 1497, Giovanni Caboto (John Cabot), an Italian sailing for England, landed on the Canadian coast, likely in Cape Breton or Newfoundland, and claimed the land for Henry VII. Although Cabot probably died on a second expedition in 1498, his voyages helped open up the rich fishing grounds of the Grand Banks.

European navigators and fishermen continued to visit the shores of Canada, but the first serious exploration of the area was undertaken by Jacques Cartier, who discovered the Gulf of St. Lawrence while searching for a passage to Asia, in 1534. The next year he travelled up the St. Lawrence River as far as the native settlements of Stadacona (Quebec) and Hochelaga (Montreal). On this voyage, Cartier picked up the Iroquoian word for village, Kanata (thought to be the origin of "Canada"), and used it to apply to the whole region he had discovered. Cartier's discoveries gave France a claim to Canada and led to the first French settlements.

In 1541–42, Cartier and the Sieur de Roberval established a short-lived settlement at Charlesbourg-Royal just above Quebec. In 1605, the Sieur de Monts and Samuel de Champlain established the colony of Port Royal in what is now Nova Scotia. Champlain went on to establish a settlement at Quebec in 1608, to explore the interior and to draw maps of New France. Champlain also started a fur-trading network (mostly in beaver pelts) with the Algonquins and the Hurons who inhabited the St. Lawrence and Great Lakes regions. This trade relationship became a military alliance as Champlain supported these groups against the Iroquois. This enmity between the French and the Iroquois prevailed throughout most of the history of New France.

Circa 1000 **Leif Ericsson** and other **Vikings** visit Labrador and Newfoundland.

1497 **John Cabot** (Giovanni Caboto) claims Cape Breton Island (or possibly Newfoundland or Labrador) for Henry VII of England (June 24).

1498 **Cabot** makes his second voyage to North America.

1534 **Jacques Cartier** visits the Strait of Belle Isle (Newfoundland), and charts the Gulf of St Lawrence (landing in Gaspé July 14).

1535 **Cartier** sails up the St Lawrence River to **Quebec** and **Montreal**.

1541 Cartier and the Sieur de Roberval found Charlesbourg-Royal, the **first French settlement** in America.

1577 **Martin Frobisher** of England makes the first of his three attempts to find a northwest passage, sailing as far as Hudson Strait.

1600 King Henry IV of France grants a **fur-trading monopoly** in the Gulf of St Lawrence to a group of French merchants.

1605 **Samuel de Champlain** and the Sieur de Monts found Port Royal (Annapolis, NS).

1608 **Champlain** founds Quebec.

1609 Champlain supports the Algonquins against the Iroquois at Lake Champlain.

1610 **Étienne Brûlé** goes to live among the Huron and eventually becomes the first European to see Lakes Ontario, Huron and Superior. **Henry Hudson** explores Hudson Bay.

1617 Louis Hébert, the **first habitant (farmer),** arrives in Quebec.

1625 Jesuits arrive in Quebec to begin missionary work among the Indians.

1627 The **Company of One Hundred Associates** is founded (Apr. 29) to establish a French empire in North America.

■ The Growth of New France (1627-1660)

The economic foundation of New France was the fur trade. In fact, the French kings were content to let fur-trading companies run the colony. Although these companies expanded the territory's boundaries, they failed to encourage settlement. One of King Louis XIII's most able advisers, Cardinal Richelieu, tried to remedy this problem by granting a fur-trading monopoly to the Company of One Hundred Associates in 1627, on condition that it bring out several hundred settlers each year. However, war between England and France broke out and Quebec was captured in 1629. Even after peace was restored in 1633, the Company of One Hundred Associates failed to honor its commitment to bring out settlers.

Despite the lack of settlers, the colony was expanding in other ways. As governor, Champlain encouraged the expansion of the fur trade. The Jesuits had arrived in 1625 and were vigorously pursuing their missionary work among the Hurons.

Champlain died in 1635, just two years after the colony was restored to France. No leader possessing his vision or drive emerged to replace him. Next, despite their conviction, the French missionaries made few converts among the native people. Even Sainte-Marie among the Hurons, their central mission-post, was abandoned in 1649 in the face of invasion by the Iroquois, who dispersed the Hurons and disrupted the French fur-trading network. Finally, the security of the centre of the fur trade, Montreal (founded in 1642), and the rest of the colony was threatened by the wars against the Iroquois. When the wars were renewed in 1659-1660, after a brief peace, there were still only about 3,000 French settlers in the colony. Clearly, the French king would have to act to secure France's foothold in North America.

1629 **David Kirke** captures Quebec for Britain (July 19).

1632 The **Treaty of Saint-Germain-en-Laye** returns Quebec to France.

1634–40 The **Huron nation** is reduced by half from European diseases (smallpox epidemic, 1639).

1637 **Kirke** is named first governor of Newfoundland.

1642 **Montreal** is founded (May 18) by the Sieur **de Maisonneuve**.

1649 The Jesuit Father **Jean de Brébeuf** is martyred by the **Iroquois** at St-Ignace (Mar. 16). The Iroquois disperse the Huron nation (1648–49).

1659 **François de Laval,** later to become Canada's first bishop, arrives in Quebec (June).

1660 **Adam Dollard des Ormeaux** makes his last stand against the Iroquois at Long Sault (May). The small party of French fights so well that the Iroquois decide not to attack Montreal.

■ Royal Government in New France (1663-1700)

In 1663 King Louis XIV made New France a crown colony. Regular troops were sent out and undertook a successful campaign against the Iroquois, which resulted in the signing of a peace treaty in 1667. Several hundred of these regulars stayed on as settlers, thereby adding to the security of the colony. A system of government headed by a governor, an intendant and a bishop was instituted. The governor, who was the king's representative, was charged with defence. The intendant was responsible for industry, trade and administrative affairs. The bishop looked after religious matters, which included education. In theory, this system provided for a clear separation of powers; but, in practice, there were frequent disputes among the three officials. Still, this system survived intact for the remainder of the colony's history, and it provided New France with some remarkably dynamic officials. Two of these arrived in the first years of the Royal Government.

The first intendant of New France, Jean Talon (1665–1672), introduced innovative measures, including awards for early marriage, to boost the population. As well, he tried to build a diversified economy on the St. Lawrence by promoting crafts, farming and local industry. Few subsequent officials in New France shared Talon's concern for settlement or economic diversity. Most were more interested in profits from the fur trade. Count Frontenac, governor for all but seven years between 1672 and 1698, threw his support behind the fur trade, not only raising profits but also encouraging exploration. Under his rule, French adventurers explored the Mississippi River from its upper reaches to the Gulf of Mexico, greatly expanding the fur-trading boundaries of New France. Frontenac gained more fame when he withstood the attack of an English army which besieged Quebec in 1690.

But Frontenac had not only exceeded his powers in promoting territorial expansion, he had also undermined the security of the colony. With its limited population, New France now found itself competing for the fur trade with the more populous English colonies around them. In the north, there was rivalry with the Hudson's Bay Company, founded in 1670. To the south, there was border warfare between French fur traders and their Indian allies, and the English with their Iroquois allies. New France fared well in the limited warfare of the 1680s and 1690s; but in the 18th century there was a series of major wars which resulted in disaster for the colony.

1663 Quebec becomes a **royal province**.

1665 The Carignan-Salières regiment is sent from France to Quebec to deal with the Iroquois. **Jean Talon** becomes Quebec's intendant.

1666 Canada's **first census** counts 3,215 non-native inhabitants in 668 families.

1670 The **Hudson's Bay Company** is formed and granted trade rights over all territory draining into Hudson Bay (May 2).

1672 Count **Frontenac** becomes Governor of Quebec.

1673 **Marquette** and **Jolliet** explore the Mississippi to its junction with the Arkansas.

1674 **Laval** becomes first Bishop of Quebec.

1678–79 Dulhut explores the headwaters of the Mississippi.

1682   La Salle explores the Mississippi to its mouth.

1686   De Troyes and **D'Iberville** capture the English posts of Moose Fort (June 20), Rupert House (July 3) and Fort Albany (July 26) on James Bay.

1689 The Iroquois kill many French settlers at Lachine.

1690   Sir William Phips captures Port Royal (May 11). Frontenac repels Phips's attack on Quebec (Oct.).

1697 The **Treaty of Ryswick** restores the status quo in the struggle between England and France. All captured territory is returned.

■ The Collapse of New France (1701-1763)

In the early years of the 18th century, New France stretched from Hudson Bay to the Gulf of Mexico, and from Newfoundland to the Great Lakes. Its population was thinly scattered in the north, south and west but its fur-trading posts in these regions gave legitimacy to its territorial claims. In the Atlantic region, there were several hundred colonists in Newfoundland and another 1,500 in Acadia. The heartland of New France was the settlement of about 20,000 colonists in Montreal, Quebec and in the small communities along the St. Lawrence. The prosperity of the French settlements was to be hurt by long periods of war.

The first of these was the war of the Spanish Succession fought between France and Austria (and their allies) between 1701-1714. Although the British failed to capture their main objective in the North American campaign, the fortress city of Quebec, they made other gains at the bargaining table. In the Treaty of Utrecht, which ended the conflict, France gave up claims to the Hudson Bay territory, all of Acadia except Cape Breton, and Newfoundland.

During a 30-year period of peace, New France enjoyed limited prosperity. The populaton grew, farm yields increased, some industry was established and furs were still exported. But military expenditure necessary to protect the colony was turning it into a financial burden for France. Much of that expenditure went into the huge fortress of Louisbourg, built on Cape Breton Island to protect the offshore fisheries and guard the St. Lawrence.

Prussia, France, Spain, Naples, Bavaria and Saxony fought Austria and England when the war of Austrian Succession broke out in 1740 and Louisbourg was a natural target. The fortress fell to the British, although it was returned to France at the war's end in 1748. The British established their own military and naval base at Halifax in 1749.

The fragile peace was broken in 1754, when fighting broke out between the English and French colonists in the Ohio Valley. Within two years, Britain and France were officially at war again in what became known as the Seven Years' War. Despite some early victories, the French suffered the loss of Louisbourg in 1758. In the following year, General Wolfe defeated General Montcalm on the Plains of Abraham above the St. Lawrence at Quebec. Although Montreal did not fall until the next year, the loss of Quebec was an irreversible setback. The British army occupied New France, and in 1763 the treaty ending the Seven Years' War confirmed British sovereignty.

New France had fallen because of decisive military defeats at Louisbourg and Quebec, but more significant was the inability of France to supply its colony in the face of British naval supremacy. The British were now masters in North America.

1701 The **War of the Spanish Succession** begins in Europe; the conflict spreads to North America the following year.

1710 Francis Nicholson captures Port Royal for England.

1713 The **Treaty of Utrecht** confirms British possession of Hudson Bay, Newfoundland and Acadia (except Cape Breton Island). France starts building Fort **Louisbourg**.

1739 La Vérendrye expedition explores Lake Winnipeg.

1740 The **War of the Austrian Succession** pits Britain against France; the European conflict spreads to North America (**King George's War**) in **1744**.

1745 Massachusetts Governor William Shirley takes the French fortress of **Louisbourg**.

1748 Louisbourg is returned to France by the **Treaty of Aix-la-Chapelle**.

1749 Britain founds **Halifax** to counter the French presence at Louisbourg.

1752 Canada's **first newspaper**, the Halifax *Gazette,* appears (Mar. 25).

1753 **George Washington**'s military expedition to the Monogahela is defeated by the French.

1754 Beginning of **French and Indian War** in America. Although war is not officially declared for another two years, this marks the final phase in the struggle between France and Britain in North America.

1755 Britain expels the **Acadians** from Nova Scotia, scattering them throughout her other North American colonies.

1756 Beginning of the **Seven Years' War** in Europe pits Britain against France. The Marquis **de Montcalm** assumes command of French troops in North America.

1758 The British under Generals Amherst and Wolfe take Louisbourg.

1759 **Wolfe takes Quebec**, defeating Montcalm on the Plains of Abraham (Sept. 13). Both generals are killed.

1760 General **James Murray** is appointed military governor of Quebec; he becomes civil governor in **1764**.

■ The First Years of British Rule (1763-1812)

The British had been active on the continent during their search for a northwest passage to the far east; however, their victory over the French encouraged a shift from exploration and fur trading to settlement and the strengthening of British customs in the new territory.

In 1763 a Royal Proclamation was imposed by the British government on the newly-acquired territories of New France. The intent of this proclamation was clear. By encouraging the establishment of Protestant schools, by promoting the Church of England, and by stipulating that an assembly be elected, the proclamation aimed at Anglicization. The intent was most visible in the matter of the assembly. Although the French inhabitants were in the majority, under British law no Roman Catholic could hold office. If an assembly were elected, a few hundred British settlers would control about 65,000 Canadiens.

Fortunately for the French in Canada, James Murray, the governor of Quebec from 1760 to

1768, felt that the loyalty of the French colonists could more likely be gained by fair treatment. Murray refused to call elections for the assembly, and allowed French legal practices to continue. Murray's sympathies provoked a storm of protest from the British colonists in Quebec and he was recalled. But his successor, Guy Carleton, also realized that the Royal Proclamation of 1763 would only alienate the recently-defeated colonists. Carleton saw that even if Anglicization were carried out, few colonists from the Thirteen Colonies in America or immigrants from Britain would be lured to the rugged colony of Quebec. Consequently, Carleton advised the government in London to replace the proclamation with more liberal legislation.

The result was the Quebec Act of 1774, which dropped the assembly in favour of an appointed council on which Catholics might serve. As well, the French system of civil law and the seigneurial system of land tenure were both guaranteed. Finally, the Quebec Act expanded the borders of the colony to include the rich lands of the Ohio Valley. The British had acted to win the support of the Canadiens. In doing so, however, the British government angered the citizens of the Thirteen Colonies, who resented the special treatment given to their former enemies. These English colonists were especially upset over the loss of the Ohio Valley, a region into which they expected to expand.

The Quebec Act was not the only cause for complaint in the Thirteen Colonies. Protests over British taxation policies and trade restriction led to talk of revolution. That talk led to action, and in 1775 an invading American army took Montreal. Quebec held out against the American siege until relieved by British forces. Although there was some sympathy for the American cause in both Quebec and Nova Scotia, it was not a strong enough sentiment to cause these two colonies to join the revolution.

During and immediately after the American Revolution, some American colonists who wished to retain their British ties fled from the newly-created United States into the Maritimes and Quebec. The arrival of about 30,000 of these Loyalists in Nova Scotia resulted in the creation of a new colony, New Brunswick, in 1784. Similarly, the influx of 10,000 Loyalists into Quebec led to division of the colony, and in 1791, the western part of the colony became Upper Canada. The remainder of the old colony was known as Lower Canada.

Despite these changes, fur trading remained an important economic activity in the interior of British North America. In fact, there was keen rivalry for furs between the Hudson's Bay Company and the newly-formed (1784) North West Company based in Montreal which led to a flurry of western exploration. Alexander Mackenzie, a partner in the North West Company, explored a river (now known as the Mackenzie) to its mouth on the Beaufort Sea in 1789, and found a route to the Pacific via the Fraser and Bella Coola Rivers in 1793. Two other North West Company employees, Simon Fraser and David Thompson, also carried out voyages of discovery. Fraser followed the river named after him to the Pacific in 1808, and Thompson travelled down the Columbia River to the coast in 1811. These voyages, along with the earlier coastal explorations of James Cook in 1778 and George Vancouver in 1792-1795, helped establish Britain's claim to the northwest part of the continent.

1763 France cedes its North American possessions to Britain by the **Treaty of Paris.** A Royal Proclamation imposes British institutions on Quebec (Oct.). This proclamation also serves as the cornerstone for relations between Canadian aboriginal peoples and the Canadian government, preserving land for their use and giving the government exclusive right to negotiate treaties.

1768 **Guy Carleton** succeeds Murray as governor of Quebec.

1769 Frances Brooke publishes *The History of Emily Montague*, a novel with descriptions of geography, climate and social culture in the New World.

1774 The **Quebec Act** provides for British criminal law but restores French civil law and guarantees religious freedom for Roman Catholic colonists.

1775 Americans under Montgomery capture Montreal (Nov.) and attack Quebec (Dec. 31).

1776 Under Carleton, Quebec withstands American siege until the appearance of a British fleet (May 6).

1778 Captain **James Cook** anchors in Nootka Sound, Vancouver Island (Mar. 29–Apr. 26).

1783 The American Revolutionary War ends; the border between Canada and the US is accepted between the Atlantic Ocean and Lake of the Woods.

1784 **United Empire Loyalists** arrive in Canada. The province of **New Brunswick** is created. The **North West Company** is formed.

1789 **Alexander Mackenzie** journeys to the Beaufort Sea, following what would later be named the Mackenzie River.

1791 **Constitutional Act** divides Quebec into Upper and Lower Canada.

1792 **George Vancouver** begins his explorations of the Pacific coast.

1793 **Alexander Mackenzie** reaches the **Pacific**.

1794 **Jay's Treaty** (Nov. 19) between the US and Britain promises British evacuation of the Ohio Valley forts. The treaty's appointment of officials to settle boundary disputes marks the beginning of international arbitration through its provisions for boundary settlements.

1797 **David Thompson** joins the North West Company as a surveyor and mapmaker.

1806 *Le Canadien*, Quebec nationalist newspaper, is founded.

1808 **Simon Fraser**, a North West Company employee, travels the river named after him to the Pacific.

1811 **David Thompson** charts the Columbia River to the Pacific coast.

■ The War of 1812

Although the British and Americans signed a peace treaty in 1783 to end the American War of Independence, there was still friction between them. One source of conflict was the British fur-trading posts in the Ohio Valley which now belonged to the United States. Although Britain surrendered these posts in 1796 as stipulated by Jay's Treaty (1794), there were still American complaints that the British were arming the local native people. At the same time there was growing American resentment over British interference with shipping. The British, who were at war with France, claimed the right to search American ships for cargoes bound for the enemy. In the process, the British often forced American sailors on these ships to join the British navy. Resentment grew among Americans until June 1812, when the United States declared war on Britain.

In the first year of the war, the Americans under General William Hull crossed the Detroit River to invade Upper Canada. Hull expected Canadian sympathizers to flock to his cause but he was disappointed. Without fighting a major battle, he retreated to Detroit. British General Isaac Brock and the Shawnees, under Chief Tecumseh, moved against Detroit and General Hull surrendered. This British and Canadian victory was followed by a victory at Queenston Heights on the Niagara River. Brock was killed in this battle which nevertheless gave confidence to the defenders of the British colonies.

In 1813, the Americans carried out a successful raid on York (now Toronto), and also gained a foothold in the Niagara district. But by the summer of that year the Americans had been pushed back across the Niagara River by British victories at Stoney Creek and Beaver Dam. Meanwhile, the Americans were building up a large fleet on the Great Lakes, and in September 1813 the Americans won control of Lake Erie at the Battle of Put-in-Bay. This victory prompted the British under General Proctor to abandon Fort Malden on the Detroit River. However, the American General Harrison caught the retreating forces at Moraviantown on the Thames River and defeated Proctor. Tecumseh was killed in this battle. In the east, a two-pronged attack on Montreal was repulsed. The American invaders were defeated on the Chateauguay River and at Crysler's Farm near Cornwall in the fall of 1813.

In 1814, the Americans again invaded the Niagara district but were halted at the Battle of Lundy's Lane. From Halifax, British forces attacked targets in Maine, and occupied most of that state. Another attack from Halifax was launched on the American capital, Washington. The British raiders burned the government buildings there in retaliation for the destruction of York the previous year. Despite these successes, a major British offensive against Plattsburgh on Lake Champlain failed. By now the war was in stalemate and both sides were tired. British and American negotiators signed the Treaty of Ghent in Dec. 1814, to end the war.

In the aftermath of the war, the two sides made an effort to settle outstanding differences. The Rush-Bagot Agreement of 1817 provided for naval disarmament on the Great Lakes. In the following year Britain and the United States agreed to accept the 49th parallel as the international boundary from the Lake of the Woods to the Rocky Mountains. In addition, they agreed to the joint occupation of the Oregon Territory for 10 years.

1812 The US declares war on Britain (June 18), beginning the **War of 1812**. Americans under General William Hull invade Canada from Detroit (July 11). The Red River settlement is begun in Canada's northwest (Aug.–Oct.). Battle of Queenston Heights (Oct. 13): Canadian victory. British **General Isaac Brock** is killed in this battle.

1813 Americans burn York (Apr. 27). Battle of Stoney Creek (June 5): Canadian victory. Battle of Beaver Dams (June 23): Canadian victory. **Laura Secord**, driving a cow, passes American sentries and walks 32 km through dense bush to warn of American attack. Battle of Put-in-Bay, Lake Erie (Sept. 10): American victory. Battle of Moraviantown (Oct. 5): American victory; the Indian Chief **Tecumseh** is killed. Battle of Chateauguay (Oct. 25): Canadian victory. Battle of Crysler's Farm (Nov. 11): Canadian victory.

1814 Battle of Chippewa (July 5): American victory. Battle of Lundy's Lane (July 25): Canadian victory. A British naval force takes Washington (Aug. 24). Battle of Lake Champlain (Sept. 6–11): American victory. The **Treaty of Ghent** ends the War of 1812 (Dec. 24).

■ **Rebellion and Reform (1814-1839)**

In the years after the War of 1812, there was considerable growth in British North America. The population increased as immigrants from both the United States and Britain arrived to take up land that was free or inexpensive. The economy became more diversified as lumbering, farming and shipbuilding developed in the Canadas and in the Maritimes. Finally, a sense of nationalism began to grow in parts of British North America. This feeling arose partly out of postwar patriotism and partly out of the shared experiences of a demanding colonial life.

As the colonies became more populous, political interest increased. In both the Canadas and the Maritimes friction between ruling elites and the ordinary colonists developed and was partially fueled by the form of government in each colony. British governors or lieutenant-governors picked their own officials, including the members of legislative or executive councils. There were elected assemblies in each colony, but their powers were limited. Legislation might pass in the assembly but be turned down by the legislative council. The assemblies, the voice of the people, found themselves frustrated by the power of appointed officials.

By the mid-1830s, economic distress increased the discontent that had been building during the 1820s. In Lower Canada, where cultural prejudice against the Canadiens added to the tension, Louis Joseph Papineau emerged as leader of the radical Patriote Party. When the colonial authorities would not grant the reforms called for by Papineau and his followers, rebellion broke out in November 1837. But loyalist forces quickly defeated the badly-organized and poorly-led rebels. Papineau and other leaders fled to the United States.

In Upper Canada, the reform movement was able to gain a majority in the assembly in several elections. Still, the reformers could not turn their program into legislation because of Tory control of the Legislative Council. When an anti-reform lieutenant-governor, Sir Francis Bond Head, took over in 1836, some reformers became more radical. Their leader was William Lyon Mackenzie, a newspaper editor and member of the assembly. The Tories won the election of 1836, when Head directly intervened in the campaign. Mackenzie and his followers, spurred on by events in Lower Canada, took up arms in early December of 1837. Mackenzie's disorganization, and lack of widespread support among the colonists, doomed the rebellion. After a skirmish north of Toronto the main body of rebels fled. An uprising in the western districts of Upper Canada was equally unsuccessful. Throughout the following year some rebels and American sympathizers mounted raids on Upper Canada from the United States, but these received no popular support.

In the aftermath of the rebellions came political change. The British government sent out Lord Durham to act as Governor General of British North America and investigate the rebellion. The Durham Report of 1839 contained two main recommendations: the first called for the union of Upper and Lower Canada as a first step in the eventual assimilation of the French Canadians; the second recommended the granting of responsible government (in which the executive is responsible to the assembly), a key demand of reformers.

1816 Agents of the North West Company kill Robert Semple, governor of the Hudson's Bay Company's Red River colony, and 21 others at White Oaks (June 19).

1817 The **Rush-Bagot** agreement limits the number of battleships on the Great Lakes.

1818 The **49th parallel** is accepted as **Canada's border** with the US from Lake of the Woods to the Rocky Mountains.

1821 The Hudson's Bay Company and the North West Company are amalgamated as the HBC.

1829 The **Lachine** and **Welland Canals** are completed.

1835 **William Lyon Mackenzie** becomes the first mayor of Toronto.

1836 Opening of Canada's **first railway line,** from St. Johns, Que., to La Prairie, Que.

1837 Unsuccessful **rebellions** in Upper and Lower Canada are led by Mackenzie and Louis-Joseph Papineau.

1839 **Lord Durham's Report** recommends union of Upper and Lower Canada and the establishment of responsible government.

■ The Road to Confederation (1840-1867)

The middle years of the 19th century were both satisfying and disturbing for British North Americans. Immigrants from Europe streamed into the colonies, more land was cleared and towns grew. Local industries were started while lumbering and shipbuilding activities increased. Montreal and Toronto became commercial centres and the ports of the Maritimes were prosperous, fuelled by ship building and trade. Transportation improved as roads, canals and, by the 1850s, railways were built. Some British North Americans looked beyond their borders and began to think of a federation of British colonies that included not only Canada and the Maritimes, but the Red River settlement and the colonies in British Columbia.

Despite the prosperity, there were reasons to consider such an alliance. Until the mid-1840s, the colonies had enjoyed a preferential trading relationship whereby Britain reduced tariffs on colonial products. This advantage was lost in 1846 when Britain adopted free trade. At first, the colonies found some advantage in entering into a limited free trade arrangement with the United States. But the Americans allowed this Reciprocity Treaty of 1854 to lapse in 1866. British North Americans would have to look to themselves as trading partners.

There was also concern in British North America about the United States. That country seemed intent on fulfilling its "Manifest Destiny" to take over North America. The threat was especially clear during and after the American Civil War (1861-65). During the war, the Northern States were angered by British support for the South, and after the war, there was a fear that the large Northern army might march into British territory.

As well, there was a serious political problem in the colony of Canada. The union of Upper and Lower Canada in 1841 had resulted in the creation of a single legislature for the new colony, Canada. By the 1860s, however, this legislature was barely functioning. No single party could gain enough support from both Francophones and Anglophones to gain a majority. There had been 12 different governments in 15 years, and Canadian politicians were desperate for a solution.

Three powerful figures in Canada's legislature, John A. Macdonald, George Brown and George-Étienne Cartier formed a coalition and proposed a larger union of British North America as a way to end the political deadlock. In addition, this proposal would solve the problem of trade and provide security against the American threat. Meanwhile, on the east coast there was interest in a union too, a union of the Maritimes. A conference had been called for Charlottetown in September 1864 to discuss that topic. When the leaders of the new Canadian coalition heard of this meeting, they asked for an invitation. At Charlottetown the British North American delegates decided on a federation of all the colonies. A second conference at Quebec in October 1864 resulted in a plan for federal union. A federal government would control defence, trade and other matters of national interest. Provincial governments would have power over local matters such as roads and education. The final details were hammered out at another conference in London, England, in 1866.

The British government, which supported this colonial initiative, passed the British North America Act in March of 1867. On July 1, 1867, the provinces of Nova Scotia, New Brunswick, Ontario (formerly Canada West) and Quebec (formerly Canada East), became the Dominion of Canada.

1841   The **Act of Union** unites Upper and Lower Canada.

1842   The Ashburton-Webster Treaty settles the Maine-New Brunswick border dispute.

1843   Fort Victoria is built to bolster Britain's claim to Vancouver Island.

1846   Great Britain ends a preferential trading policy with the British North American colonies and enters into a **limited free trade agreement** with the United States.

1848   Responsible government is achieved in the Canadas and in the Maritimes, thanks to the work of **Robert Baldwin** and **Joseph Howe**.

1849   The boundary of the 49th parallel is extended to the Pacific Ocean. Canada begins its policy of **official bilingualism**. All bills of the United Canada Parliament, now Quebec and Ontario, are given assent in both English and French.

1851   Britain transfers control of the colonial postal system to Canada.

1854   The **Reciprocity Treaty** between Canada and the US is signed (June 6).

1857   Ottawa is named **Canada's capital** by Queen Victoria.

1860   Cornerstone of the **Parliament Buildings** is laid (Sept. 1).

1861   The **Grand Trunk Railway** through the length of the Province of Canada and as far as the City of Halifax is completed.

1864   The **Charlottetown Conference** (Sept. 1–9) takes the first steps toward **Confederation**. The **Quebec Conference** (Oct. 10–27) sets out the basis for union.

1866   The **London Conference** (Dec. 4) passes resolutions which are redrafted to become the **British North America Act**. First raid into Canada by the **Fenians**, a radical Irish-American anti-British group, takes place

(June 2). The American government allows the **Reciprocity Treaty of 1854** to lapse.

1867   Confederation.   Britain's   North American colonies are united by means of the **BNA Act** to become the **Dominion of Canada** (July 1). **Sir John A. Macdonald** is Canada's first prime minister. The BNA Act, now the **Constitution Act, 1867**, confirms the practice of **official bilingualism**, guaranteeing the use of French and English in the debates of the House of Commons and in the Senate, in federal courts and in publications of federal statutes. The provincial legislature, statutes and courts of Quebec are also made bilingual.

■ The Nation Expands (1867-1885)

Soon after the Confederation of Ontario, Quebec, New Brunswick and Nova Scotia in 1867, the new nation of Canada began to acquire more territory. In 1869, guided by the national vision of Prime Minister John A. Macdonald, the federal government bought Rupert's Land from the Hudson's Bay Company. This was a huge territory which included most of modern Manitoba, as well as parts of Saskatchewan, Alberta and the Northwest Territories. The few Ontario immigrants in the Red River Settlement there welcomed this move; but the far more numerous Métis (descendants of French fur traders and native people) were suspicious, especially because they had not been consulted beforehand. When newly-appointed Lieutenant-Governor William McDougall tried to enter the settlement before the territory had officially been transferred to Canada, the Métis turned him back. In the absence of a legitimate government, the Métis, under their leader Louis Riel, seized Fort Garry on the Red River and proclaimed a provisional government. The Métis demanded the right to vote, land laws, the official use of both French and English, and the provision of both Roman Catholic and Protestant schools. The Métis list of rights became the terms for negotiating Manitoba's entry into Confederation in 1870.

In the same year, representatives from the colony of British Columbia arrived in Ottawa to discuss union. With the promise from Ottawa to build a transcontinental railway, British Columbia entered Confederation in 1871. Canada now stretched from sea to sea, but the work of nation building was still not complete.

In 1868, Nova Scotia elected an anti-Confederation provincial government and sent a delegation, led by veteran politician Joseph Howe, to London to seek a repeal of the union. But Britain was unsympathetic, and in 1869 Macdonald seized the opportunity to offer Nova Scotia better terms and Howe a cabinet position. With the Nova Scotia situation resolved, Macdonald turned his attention to Prince Edward Island. The Islanders were more attracted to the idea of union after an expensive railway project nearly bankrupted the colony. Macdonald agreed to assume the colony's debts, offered a cash subsidy, and promised a steamer service to the mainland. In 1873, Prince Edward Island agreed to the terms and became Canada's 7th province.

In the 1870s and 1880s railways were built to link the provinces of the new nation. The Intercolonial Railway, joining central Canada to the Maritimes, was completed in 1876, but construction of a rail link to British Columbia ran into several delays. First, Macdonald's government was defeated in 1873 over charges of corruption associated with the railway project. The new prime minister, Alexander Mackenzie, refused to fund railway projects because the country was in the midst of a depression. However, after Macdonald's re-election in 1878, railway building began in earnest. In February 1881, the Canadian Pacific Railway Company (CPR) was incorporated, and in November 1885 the last spike was driven at Craigellachie in British Columbia to complete the link to the Pacific.

Even before it was fully completed, the CPR was used to carry troops to quell a rebellion in the spring of 1885. Trouble had started several years earlier when settlers in the North-West Territory (modern Alberta and Saskatchewan) complained to the government about land titles, shipping rates, and their lack of an elected government. Among those who complained were the Métis, some of whom had moved farther west after the Red River troubles of 1870. When the federal government was slow to respond, the Métis, again under Louis Riel, rose up in March 1885 against the territorial council appointed by Ottawa. By late April, 5,000 Canadian soldiers, who had travelled by the new railway, were on the march against Riel and his Métis and native followers. At the Battle of Batoche in May, the forces of General Middleton defeated the rebels. Riel was found guilty of treason by an English-speaking jury and executed.

1868 Confederationist **Thomas D'Arcy McGee** is **assassinated** by a Fenian in Canada's first political assassination.

1869 Canada purchases Rupert's Land from the Hudson's Bay Company for £300,000.

1870 **Louis Riel** leads the Métis in resisting Canadian authority in Canada's northwest. The Métis negotiate with the Canadian government over the right to vote, land laws, the official use of both French and English and the provision of Roman Catholic and Protestant schools. The Manitoba Act creates the province of **Manitoba**.

1871 **British Columbia** joins Confederation upon the promise from Ottawa to build a **transcontinental railway**.

1872 Macdonald's Conservatives win federal re-election.

1873 **Prince Edward Island** joins Confederation. A period of economic depression begins. The North-West Mounted Police are formed. **Alexander Mackenzie** becomes Canada's second prime minister after **Macdonald resigns** over the **Pacific Scandal**.

1874 **Liberals** win federal election.

1875 The **Supreme Court of Canada** is established.

1876 The **Intercolonial Railway** linking central Canada and the Maritimes is completed (July 1). The **Indian Act of 1876** defines special status for aboriginal people living on land reserves and sets out land regulations. Status Indians have no vote in Canadian elections and are exempted from taxation.

1878 Conservatives under Macdonald win federal election.

1879 Macdonald introduces **protective tariffs** as part of his **National Policy**.

1880 **Emily Stowe** receives her medical licence after practising medicine in Toronto since her graduation from a New York medical school in 1867.

1881 The **Canadian Pacific Railway** is incorporated.

1884 **Riel returns** to Canada.

1885 Métis and the NWMP clash at Duck Lake (Mar. 26). The Métis are defeated at Batoche (May 9–12). The **last spike of the transcontinental railway** is driven at Craigellachie in Eagle Pass, BC, by Donald

Smith (Nov. 7). **Louis Riel** is **hanged** in Regina (Nov. 16).

1887 Conservatives win federal election. Liberals choose **Wilfrid Laurier** as leader. The **first provincial premiers' conference** takes place in Quebec City.

1889 The **Dominion Women's Enfranchisement Association** is created to campaign for female voting rights in Canada.

1890 Manitoba Liberals under Thomas Greenway halt public funding of Catholic schools in Manitoba (Mar.).

1891 Conservatives win federal election. **Sir John A. Macdonald dies**. **Sir John Abbott** takes office as prime minister (June 16).

1892 Abbott resigns (Nov. 24). **Sir John Thompson** becomes prime minister (Dec. 5). He establishes the **Canadian Criminal Code**.

1894 Thompson dies (Dec. 12). **Sir Mackenzie Bowell** is asked by the governor general, the Earl of Aberdeen, to form the fourth Conservative government since 1891.

■ The Laurier Era (1896-1911)

Conservative Prime Minister John A. Macdonald died in 1891, soon after winning a federal election. The Conservatives could not find a suitable successor and by 1896 there had been four prime ministers—John Abbott, John Thompson, Mackenzie Bowell and Charles Tupper. During this period, the Conservatives had to deal with a crisis over school legislation introduced in Manitoba. The Manitoba legislature had replaced the dual school system (both Protestant and Catholic schools) which had been guaranteed in the terms of union, with a single Protestant system. Francophone Catholics across Canada were already bitter about Louis Riel's execution. Now the Manitoba schools legislation convinced them that English Protestant Canadians wanted to stamp out French Catholic rights. Extremists on both sides inflamed the issue, and the Conservatives' inability to settle the matter hurt them in the election of 1896. The Liberals, under Wilfrid Laurier, formed a government.

Laurier settled the Manitoba school question by adopting a compromise approach. Religious instruction would be allowed within the single system, and instruction in French could take place where numbers warranted.

The issue died down, but Laurier remained sensitive to the tensions between Anglophone Protestants and Francophone Catholics. Many English Canadians were swept up in a great wave of pro-imperial sentiment associated with the Diamond Jubilee of Queen Victoria. In Britain the event was seen as an opportunity to strengthen ties within the British Empire. Laurier acknowledged Canada's support for the Empire, but resisted proposals for a closer relationship with Britain and the other colonies. The prime minister did not wish to yield Canadian autonomy, nor did he wish to lose support in French Canada. The issue of Canada's role in the Empire came to a head in 1899 during the Boer War when the South African Republic (Transvaal) and the Orange Free State fought against Britain. Once again steering a middle course, Laurier agreed to equip and transport Canadian volunteers to South Africa, but sent no official troops. Although this compromise did not satisfy all Canadians, it avoided a bitter dispute. For a time, imperial issues were forgotten, as Canadians enjoyed boom times after the turn of the century.

Laurier summed up the nation's mood when he declared that the "twentieth century is Canada's century." Impressive growth in both industrial and agricultural production provided support for his words. Canada's prospects appealed to immigrants who flocked to the industrial cities and to the farmland of the Prairies. Many of them were attracted by an extensive government advertising campaign and by the lure of free land in the west. As a result of this influx, two new provinces, Alberta and Saskatchewan, were created in 1905. The immigrant tide boosted Canada's population from 5,371,315 in 1901 to 7,206,643 in 1911. The mood of the country was so confident that two new transcontinental railway building projects got under way in the early years of the century.

The international scene, however, was not so bright. In 1903, the British sided with the Americans in the Alaska Boundary Dispute, a disagreement over the international boundary near the Klondike gold fields. Canadians were dismayed, but Britain was less concerned about the Canadian claim than for the need to maintain good relations with the United States. Tension in Europe was increasing and Britain found itself outside of the complicated system of alliances which had developed there. This same concern led both the British government and the Canadian pro-imperialists to pressure Laurier into providing money to build British warships. Again, Laurier staked out a middle position by introducing a Naval Service Act which created a Canadian navy that could help Britain where the need arose.

Laurier's compromise on naval policy satisfied neither side. Some French Canadians supported the views of Quebec nationalist Henri Bourassa who claimed Laurier had betrayed his people. Anglophone pro-imperialists complained that Laurier's "tin pot navy" was not enough. Canada's naval policy became an issue in the 1911 election, as did the Liberal plan for free trade with the United States. Conservative leader Robert Borden was able to use both to characterize Laurier as not only disloyal to Britain but favoring annexation to the United States. The Conservatives won the election. Borden became prime minister and Laurier stayed on as leader of the Opposition, continuing to advocate conciliatory policies when the interests of French and English Canadians clashed.

1896 The economic depression ends. Bowell resigns, calling his cabinet a "nest of traitors" (Apr. 27). **Sir Charles Tupper** leads an interim government until the Liberals under Laurier win federal election on **Manitoba Schools Question** (June 23). Canada's minister of the interior, **Clifford Sifton,** develops an immigration plan that will bring farmers from central and eastern Europe to settle on the Prairies. Gold is discovered in the Klondike (Aug. 16).

1897 **Gold Rush** begins in the Klondike. **Clara Brett Martin** is the first woman admitted to the bar of Ontario.

1898 Yukon becomes a separate entity from the Northwest Territories. **Kit Coleman**, the first female Canadian war correspondent, covers the Spanish-American War for a Toronto newspaper.

1899 The first **Canadian troops** ever sent overseas are dispatched to the **Boer War** (Oct. 30).

1901 Marconi receives the **first transatlantic radio message** at St. John's, Newfoundland.

1903 Canada loses the **Alaska Boundary Dispute** when British tribunal representative Lord Alverstone sides with the US (Oct. 20).

In northern Ontario, Fred LaRose throws hammer at what he thinks are fox's eyes and hits world's richest silver vein.

1904 Liberals win federal election.

1905 The provinces of **Alberta** and **Saskatchewan** are formed.

1907 The **National Council of Women** calls for "equal pay for equal work."

1908 Liberals win federal election.

1909 The Department of External Affairs is formed. John McCurdy's Silver Dart is first heavier-than-air machine to achieve powered flight in Canada at Baddeck, NS. University of Toronto wins **first Grey Cup** football match.

1910 Laurier creates a Canadian navy via the Naval Service Bill.

1911 **Robert Borden** and the Conservatives win federal election, defeating Laurier on the reciprocity issue.

■ Canada and the First World War (1914-1918)

In August 1914, Britain declared war on Germany and Austria–Hungary. The declaration automatically applied to Canada, as part of the British Empire. At first, there was an enthusiastic response, especially among recent British immigrants. When the minister of militia, Sam Hughes, called for 25,000 volunteers, nearly 33,000 appeared. In 1915, when the government asked the Canadian public to buy $50 million in war bonds, they bought $100 million. But enthusiasm for war began to fade as the casualties mounted and the realities of trench warfare became known.

Canadian troops sailed for Europe in October 1914 and, after training in Britain, went into action at Ypres, Belgium, in April 1915. There they gained a reputation for courage, holding their positions in the face of a poison gas attack, a new weapon at the time. Canadians took part in the costly battles at St. Eloi and Mont Sorrel in 1916. By the Battle of the Somme, in late summer of 1916, Canada had four army divisions in France; in the spring of 1917, all four were deployed in the attack on Vimy Ridge, which resulted in the first real Canadian victory of the war. But by now it was clear that every battle would result in terrible losses. At Passchendaele in October 1917, the Canadians sustained more than 15,000 casualties.

Voluntary recruitment could not keep pace with the high casualty rates. Prime Minister Borden was forced to consider conscription to draft soldiers into the army and took the question to the electorate in 1917, unleashing one of the most bitterly fought campaigns in Canadian history. In Quebec, Henri Bourassa rallied anti-conscription supporters and argued that Canada had done enough. In Ontario, Borden's supporters condemned French-Canadian anti-conscriptionists as traitors. For his part Borden introduced the Wartime Elections Act to help secure victory. This act removed the right to vote from enemy aliens, even though some were Canadian citizens. It also gave the right to vote to women relatives of soldiers. In the election Borden won in every province except Quebec where he was soundly rejected. Conscription had created a deep division between Quebec and the rest of Canada and once in practice, it had little impact on the course of the war. When the first 400,000 conscripts were called up, 90 percent of them appealed for exemption, and by the war's end only about 24,000 conscripts had reached the front.

While the conscription crisis raged at home, Canadian soldiers played a major role in the events leading to an Allied victory. They took part in the successful battle at Amiens in August 1918 and helped to roll the Germans back to Mons by November. The Canadians were still fighting at Mons when the armistice was signed Nov. 11, 1918.

Canadians also served with distinction in other theatres of war. By 1918, Canadians made up almost 25 percent of the pilots in Britain's Royal Flying Corps. Other Canadians served in the Royal Navy or on coastal patrol in Canada's own small navy. Some served in forestry corps overseas and others operated the railways behind the British lines. Some, including women, served as ambulance drivers at the front. Many Canadian women also played key roles as nurses overseas and in the munitions factories in Canada.

Canada's war effort won the country a place in the Imperial War Cabinet during the war, and a seat in the League of Nations afterwards. There were other benefits, too. Women's contributions to the war effort helped them win the right to vote in federal elections and in provincial elections in seven of the provinces by 1919. Yet these advances came at a terrible cost. Overseas, 68,300 Canadians had died. At home, bitterness over the conscription issue had created a division between French and English Canadians that would be remembered for decades.

1914 CP ship *Empress of Ireland* sinks in the St Lawrence in 14 minutes after being rammed in fog, with the loss of 1,014 lives (May 29). **Canada is automatically at war** with Germany when Britain declares war (Aug. 4). The first Canadian troops leave for England (Oct. 3). Parliament passes the **War Measures Act**, allowing suspension of civil rights during periods of emergency. European immigration to Canada increases. Over one million settlers come between 1911 and 1913, bringing total immigration to three million since 1891.

1915 Canadians face German gas attack at **Ypres,** Belgium (Apr. 22). John McCrae writes "In Flanders Fields."

1916 **Nellie McClung** succeeds in persuading the Manitoba government to grant women the right to vote and to hold office (Jan.). The Parliament Buildings are destroyed by fire (Feb. 3). Canadian troops fight in the Battle of the **Somme** (July to Nov.); 24,713 Canadians and Newfoundlanders are killed. The unreliable, Canadian-made Ross rifle is withdrawn from war service (Aug.). **Emily Gowan Murphy** is the first woman magistrate appointed within the British Empire.

1917 **Income tax** is introduced as a "temporary wartime measure." Prime Minister Sir Robert Borden sits as a member of the Imperial War Cabinet (Feb. 23), giving Canada a voice in war policy. The Military Service Bill is introduced (June 11), leading to the **Conscription Crisis** between Quebec and English Canada. Unionist government under Borden wins federal election, in which **women vote** for the first time. **Louise McKinney** is elected to the Alberta legislature, the first woman in the British Commonwealth to hold such office. Canadians capture **Vimy Ridge,** France (Apr. 9–12). Canadians take **Passchendaele,** Belgium, (Nov. 7) in one of the war's worst battles; of the 20,000 Canadian troops sent into the two-week battle, 15,654 are killed or wounded. Explosion of a munitions ship in **Halifax harbour** wipes out two square miles (5.2 sq. km) of Halifax, killing almost 2,000 and injuring 9,000 (Dec. 6).

1918 Canadians break through German trenches at Amiens (Aug. 8), "the black day of the German army." The period from this date until the end of the war becomes known as "Canada's Hundred Days." Armistice ends war (Nov. 11).

■ Canada in the 1920s

As the soldiers returned home, many expected to find a Canada ready to reward them for their sacrifices. What they found was a nation in the midst of painful postwar readjustment. Industry had to convert to peacetime production, but interest rates were so high investment capital was scarce. Jobs were hard to find and wages were low, and tariffs on imported goods kept prices high. By 1921, 300,000 men and women—more than 15% of the work force—were unemployed. Farmers, especially on the Prairies, also suffered. During the war, the west had become the world's breadbasket: wheat prices had soared and many farmers had borrowed heavily to expand their production. But with the war's end, world markets collapsed; wheat prices fell by almost half within two years.

These conditions, along with resentment over wartime profiteering by big business, created unrest. The One Big Union movement, centred in western Canada, attempted to create a single union to represent all workers. The Winnipeg General Strike of 1919 grew out of the organizers' efforts and the general discontent. Although the Winnipeg workers were striking over such issues as the right to collective bargaining, better wages and improved working conditions, the opponents of the general strike characterized it as a communist conspiracy by raising the spectre of a revolution similar to the one in Russia two years earlier. The federal government sided with the anti-strike forces. Immigration laws were amended to deport "alien" labour radicals, the strike leaders were arrested and the Royal North West Mounted Police fired into a rioting crowd on June 21, 1919— "Bloody Sunday"—killing 1 and wounding 30. The six-week strike was over and so was the growth of labor unions. In 1919 alone there were more than 400 strikes, but after the Winnipeg General Strike, the federal government and most governments at the provincial level opposed union activities. Throughout the 1920s there was a decline in union membership.

The reasons for unrest and discontent varied from region to region in the 1920s. The government takeover of five financially troubled railways had led to the creation of the Canadian National Railways in 1919 and railway rates in the Maritimes were raised 40% to bring them up to central Canadian levels. Angry over the rail rates and feeling that Ottawa was making decisions on the basis of central Canada's interests, many Maritimers protested by forming the Maritimes Rights movement, aimed at winning transportation concessions and federal subsidies. At the same time it promoted regional rights and pride.

Canadian farmers, resentful over low prices for farm products, high rail rates and high prices for manufactured goods, formed the United Farmers' movement. United Farmers' parties won provincial elections in Ontario in 1919, in Alberta in 1921, and in Manitoba in 1922. At the federal level, the Progressive Party embraced some of the program of the United Farmers' movement. The Progressives called for free trade, nationalization (especially in the case of railways) and more direct democracy (such as the use of a referendum to decide a controversial issue). Although they were a new party, the Progressives were to play an important role in politics in the 1920s.

The election of 1921 marked new directions in Canadian politics. Both major parties had new leaders: Arthur Meighen had replaced Borden as prime minister; William Lyon Mackenzie King had taken over as Liberal leader after Laurier's death. Of even greater significance was that for the first time, Canadians could vote for one of three parties at the federal level: the Liberals, the Conservatives or the Progressives. The Liberals won the 1921 election, but the Progressives finished second and formed the opposition. Their position in the House of Commons was even more important after the 1925 election in which the Conservatives under Meighen won the most seats, but King remained in power by claiming the support of the Progressives. After 1925 the Progressives declined, and many of their supporters voted Liberal in King's 1926 election victory. But the influence of the Progressive movement was felt as King's government, anxious to keep their support, passed Canada's first Old Age Pension Act in 1927.

In foreign affairs, King made sure that Canada played a cautious role in the League of

Nations, because he feared that Canada would be drawn into international disputes. In imperial matters, his insistence on autonomy contributed to a redefinition of the empire at the Imperial Conference of 1926. There it was acknowledged that Canada and the other British dominions were autonomous even in their external affairs. As a result, by 1929, Canada had diplomatic posts in Washington, Paris and Tokyo and Britain had a high commissioner in Ottawa. The Governor General became a symbolic representative of the Crown rather than a representative of the British government.

At home, there were many signs that good times had finally come to Canada. World markets for Canadian manufactured goods had revived, and wheat prices were soaring to new levels. New mining and lumbering areas were developed. By 1928, more than a billion dollars' worth of products were being extracted from the newly-developed primary industries of the Canadian Shield. Immigrants poured into Canada by the hundreds of thousands to provide labour in the growing industrial cities. Cars, radios, telephones, electrical appliances and other consumer goods were being bought, especially by middle-class Canadians, often using credit plans. Credit was also used to buy shares on the stock market, as the country became increasingly optimistic about its future. On both sides of the Canadian-American border, the Roaring Twenties were in full swing and there seemed no end in sight to the good times.

1919   Alcock and Brown take off from St. John's, Nfld, (June 14) on the first successful flight across the Atlantic to Cliften, Ireland. A **general strike paralyzes Winnipeg** (May–June), where an armed charge by the RCMP kills one person and injures 30 (June 21).

1920   **Canada joins** the **League of Nations** at its inception (Jan. 10). The flow of emigrants from the British Isles and Europe resumes, many going to urban centres. Federal legislation makes **women eligible** to sit in the **House of Commons**. The Northwest Mounted Police became the Royal Canadian Mounted Police (RCMP).

1921   Liberals under **Mackenzie King** defeat Conservatives under Arthur Meighen in federal election; the Progressive Party comes in

second. **Agnes Macphail** becomes the first woman elected to Parliament. The world's fastest fishing schooner, the ***Bluenose,*** is launched at Lunenburg, NS. (Mar. 26). **Postwar economic depression** puts 300,000 men and women out of work—more than 15% of the work force.

1922   Canada declines to rally to Britain's side during the Chanak Crisis. Sir Frederick **Banting**, Dr Charles **Best**, Dr J.J.R. MacLeod and J.B. Collip share Nobel Prize for the **discovery of insulin**.

1923   The Canadian Northern and Canadian Transcontinental are merged to form the **Canadian National Railways**. Canada signs the Halibut Treaty with the US without a corroborating British signature. Mackenzie King leads opposition to a common imperial policy ("one voice for the empire") at an Imperial Conference in London.

1924   The Saskatchewan Wheat Pool begins operations.

1925   Although Conservatives win more seats in federal election, Mackenzie King's Liberals remain in power with the support of the Progressives.

1926   King's Liberals win federal election. An Imperial Conference defines British dominions as autonomous (Balfour Report).

1927   Britain's Privy Council awards Labrador to Newfoundland instead of to Quebec (Mar. 1). The Diamond Jubilee of Confederation (July 1) is marked by Canada's first coast-to-coast radio network broadcast. King's government, with the support of the Progressive Party, passes Canada's first **Old Age Pension Act**.

1928   The Supreme Court of Canada rules that, according to the British North America Act, women are not "persons" who could hold public office. This decision is reversed by British Privy Council in 1929.

■ The Great Depression (1929-1939)

In 1929, Canadians looked with confidence toward the next decade and that confidence made the effects of the Great Depression of the 1930s even more bitter. The Depression was worldwide, but the effects were especially felt in Canada because about a third of the nation's gross national product was based on exports. The first signs of Canadian economic collapse appeared in October 1929 when wheat prices began to fall. In the same month the stock market collapsed, ruining thousands of shareholders, some of whom, on paper at least, had been millionaires. By 1930, the number of unemployed had doubled and the Conservatives, under R.B. Bennett, won the 1930 federal election decisively as voters hoped a change in government would bring a change in fortune. However by 1933, one in five Canadians was unemployed.

Western Canada was hardest hit in "The Dirty Thirties" because of its reliance on wheat. The Prairie provinces also suffered from a drought which led to crop failure during these hard times. The combined results were devastating. In Saskatchewan, provincial income fell by 90% and two-thirds of the province's population had to go on welfare. In the 1930s, welfare, or "relief" as it was then known, became a burden for municipal and provincial governments across the country. By 1935, 10% of Canadians were on relief.

Bennett's government did not intervene to rebuild the economy. In the 1930s, politicians, economists and business leaders assumed that the Depression, like other downswings in the business cycle, would soon be followed by a recovery. Their experience, and most economic theory at the time, did not encourage them to consider major government spending as a way to stimulate a depressed economy.

One of the few federally financed programs created involved sending single unemployed men to camps where they did manual work in return for their keep and a small allowance. Working in isolated conditions, often at meaningless tasks, did nothing to satisfy the men and those in the British Columbia camps took action. In 1935, about 1,500 camp inmates decided to present their complaints directly to Bennett in Ottawa. They began the "On to Ottawa" trek by taking over freight trains heading east. By the time they reached Regina, there were about 2,000 protesters and the railway refused to provide further transportation. Representatives of the Trekkers met with Prime Minister Bennett in Ottawa, but the talks were inconclusive. When the delegation returned to Regina, Bennett decided to arrest the protest leaders. On July 1, there was a bloody riot in Regina involving the Trekkers, local police and the RCMP, which left one policeman dead and several dozen rioters, constables and local citizens injured. The Trek was over and the protesters

returned home over the next few days; but Bennett's handling of the affair hurt his image. In the election of 1935, the people turned to King again, in the hope that this time he could deal with the Depression.

After 1935, economic conditions began to improve slowly, yet federal politicians did little to speed this recovery. The failure of the Liberals and the Conservatives to deal with the Depression led to the rise of reform parties. A socialist party, the Co-operative Commonwealth Federation (CCF) won seven seats in the 1935 election and elected members to several provincial legislatures. Other new parties appeared at the provincial level. In Alberta, the Social Credit Party promised $25 prosperity certificates to each resident; but the plan fell flat because the province did not have the power to issue currency. In Quebec, Maurice Duplessis established the Union Nationale and promised economic reform. But the Union Nationale, like the other parties, could not end the Depression, the effects of which faded only with the outbreak of World War II in 1939.

1929 The **Great Depression** begins.

1930 **Cairine Wilson** is appointed Canada's first woman senator (Feb. 20). The Canadian Federation of Business and Professional Women's Clubs is organized. Conservatives under **R.B. Bennett** win federal election (Aug. 7).

1931 The **Statute of Westminster** (Dec. 11) grants Canada full legislative authority domestically and in external affairs. The Governor General becomes a representative of the Crown.

1932 Ottawa Agreements provide for preferential trade between Canada and other Commonwealth nations. The **Co-operative Commonwealth Federation (CCF)** is founded at Calgary.

1933 One in five Canadians is unemployed.

1934 The Bank of Canada is formed. The **Dionne quintuplets** are born in Callander, Ont.

1935 Ten percent of Canadians rely on welfare or "relief." The **On to Ottawa Trek** by young men from government work camps ends in a riot at Regina (July 1). Liberals under Mackenzie King win federal election. The CCF win seven seats. Social Credit claims 17. **William Aberhart** leads Social Credit into office in Alberta. The Canadian Wheat Board is created.

1936 Union Nationale under **Maurice Duplessis** wins its first election in Quebec.

1937 The **Rowell-Sirois Commission** is appointed to investigate the financial relationship between the federal government and the provinces. First regular flight of **Trans Canada Air Lines** (Sept. 1).

1938 Franklin D. Roosevelt becomes first US President in office to visit Canada, meeting Mackenzie King at Kingston.

■ Canada in World War II (1939-1945)

While most Canadians focused attention on the effects of the Depression at home, events in Europe during the 1930s were moving the world closer to another global conflict. After taking over Austria and Czechoslovakia (present-day Czech and Slovak republics), Germany invaded Poland in 1939; Britain and France responded by declaring war. Following Britain's action, King quickly summoned Parliament. On Sept. 10, one week after Britain had entered the conflict, the Canadian Parliament declared war on Germany and its allies.

Parliamentary support for the war declaration was based in part on King's known preference for a limited Canadian role and his assurance that there would be no conscription. Initially, only one Canadian division was sent to Britain. But by 1940, France had fallen and Britain faced invasion. King abandoned the concept of limited participation and decided to dispatch more troops. By late 1942, Canada had five divisions overseas. Canadian soldiers first saw action in December 1941 during the unsuccessful defence of Hong Kong. In August 1942, 5,000 Canadians took part in the disastrous raid on the French port of Dieppe, suffering casualties of 2,200 killed or captured. Despite these setbacks, the Canadian army played a major role in defeating enemy forces in Italy and took part in the Allied landings at Normandy in June of 1944. After taking key targets in France, Canadian soldiers moved northward to liberate Holland in 1945.

Canadians contributed to the war effort in other important ways. The Royal Canadian Navy grew from six destroyers and less than 2,000 personnel in 1939 to 471 warships, 99,688 men and 6,500 women by the war's

end in 1945. The navy helped win the Battle of the Atlantic against German submarines by providing protection to the convoys of merchant ships carrying essential supplies from North America to Britain. (Despite the protection German U-boats sank 5,150 merchant ships.) Canadians also fought in the air as members of Britain's Royal Air Force, and, in increasing numbers throughout the war, in the Royal Canadian Air Force (RCAF). By 1945, there were 48 RCAF squadrons overseas. Other members of the RCAF were involved in the British Commonwealth Air Training Plan. Operating from Canadian airfields, this plan trained 131,000 aircrew from around the Commonwealth.

Canada also produced a wide variety of munitions, and provided important food supplies to the Allied war effort. Much of Canada's war production went directly to Britain, so did more than $3 billion in financial assistance.

While the contributions of Canadian men and women to the war effort were significant, the conflict raised disturbing issues at home. In reversing his earlier stand against conscription, Prime Minister King called for a national plebiscite on the issue in 1942. In all provinces except Quebec the electorate voted for conscription; relations between Quebec and the rest of Canada were strained, although not as severely as in World War I.

In a move that would later become controversial, Japanese–Canadians were interned and their property was confiscated in the name of national security after the Japanese attack on Pearl Harbor in 1941. The interned included Japanese–Canadians who had fought for Canada in World War I and more than 40 years later the Canadian government would officially apologize to the interned and their families.

By the war's end, more than a million Canadians had served in the armed forces and more than 42,000 had died. Canada's war effort enhanced its international image. At the same time, Canada had developed closer ties with the United States as the country's interests shifted away from Britain and Europe.

1939 Canada declares war on Germany (Sept. 10) after remaining neutral for a week following the British declaration. Quebec Premier Maurice Duplessis, who opposed Quebec participation in the war, is defeated by the provincial Liberals on that issue (Oct. 26).

1940 **Unemployment insurance** is **introduced**. Liberals win federal election (Mar. 26). The Permanent Joint Board of Defence is formed between Canada and the US. **Thérèse Casgrain** wins women in Quebec the right to vote and to hold provincial office.

1941 Canadians are captured when Hong Kong falls to Japanese (Dec. 25); about 500 of the POWs subsequently die in Japanese camps. Immigration has changed Canadian demographic structure. Canadians of British ancestry now make up 49.7% of the population, of French descent 30.3% and of other ethnic backgrounds 20%.

1942 In the Canadian army's first European war action, many soldiers are captured or killed in the disastrous **Dieppe** raid (Aug. 19). Canadians of Japanese descent are moved inland from the coast of British Columbia as "security risks"; their property is confiscated. A national plebiscite releases Mackenzie King from his pledge of no conscription but reveals deep divisions between Quebec and the rest of Canada.

1943 Canadians participate in the invasion of Sicily (July 10). Canadians win the Battle of Ortona (Dec. 20–28). **Ernest C. Manning** wins first of nine successive elections for the Social Credit in Alberta.

1944 Canadian troops push further inland than any other Allied unit on D-Day (June 6). Canadian forces fight as a separate army (July 23). Saskatchewan elects Tommy Douglas's CCF, the first socialist government in North America. Maurice Duplessis regains office for the Union Nationale in Quebec.

1945 War in Europe ends (May 8). One million Canadians fought in WW II; 42,042 were killed. Canadians killed while fighting for other Allied forces numbered 4,500. Liberals win federal election (June 11). First **family allowance payments** are **made** (June 20). Canada joins the **United Nations** (June 26). Igor Gouzenko defects from the Soviet Embassy in Ottawa (Sept. 5) and reveals the existence in Canada of a Soviet spy network. Canada's first nuclear reactor begins operations at Chalk River, Ontario.

■ Postwar Canada: 1945-1968

In the years following World War II, Canadians enjoyed a standard of living that was in stark contrast to the Depression years.

The economy had boomed during the war and the gross national product had doubled. The war had prompted development in new industries which continued to expand in peacetime. Consumer spending had increased dramatically during the war, and continued to rise with the postwar baby boom. This boom, along with large numbers of European immigrants, resulted in a 40% population increase between the war's end and 1958. In Canada's quickly growing cities and suburbs, home ownership was made easier by the National Housing Act, designed to make mortgages easier to obtain. This example of government involvement in the economy was characteristic of the times. By 1945, unemployment insurance and family allowance legislation had been passed and other social welfare measures were being discussed.

Prime Minister King retired in 1948, and was followed as Liberal leader by Louis St. Laurent. One of St. Laurent's first achievements was the entry of Newfoundland into Confederation in 1949. In 1951, his government increased old age pensions and, in 1957, introduced a hospital insurance plan. St. Laurent negotiated with the United States to build the St. Lawrence Seaway, an impressive feat of engineering completed in 1959. In 1956, however, the government used closure (a limit on debate) to cut off the parliamentary debate concerning the building of the trans-Canada pipeline for oil and gas. In the election the following year, the Conservatives under John Diefenbaker won a minority victory. In 1958, Diefenbaker called another election to consolidate his position. This time the Conservatives swept the country, winning 208 of 265 seats.

Western agriculture found huge new markets when the government arranged wheat sales to China. In 1960, Diefenbaker's government introduced the Bill of Rights to protect the rights of all Canadians, and granted Native Canadians the right to vote in federal elections.

Despite continuing popular support for the British Commonwealth, the government of Canada signed the North American Air Defence Agreement (NORAD) with the United States to increase security during a time of international tension. But it could not deal with an economic recession that led to a devalued dollar and high unemployment. Also, the prime minister dealt Canada's fledgling aircraft industry a serious blow when he cancelled production of the Canadian-made Avro Arrow fighter jet, and his refusal to allow nuclear warheads on the American missiles based in Canada earned him the emnity of the US government. In the election of 1962, his government was returned to power, but in a minority situation that forced another election in 1963. The 1963 election also resulted in a minority government, but this time, the Liberals, under Lester B. Pearson, were in power.

As prime minister, Pearson, a career diplomat, concentrated on domestic matters. His government relied on the support of the New Democratic Party (formerly the CCF) to hold a majority in the House of Commons, and the partnership produced legislation that broadened social welfare by introducing Medicare, the Canada Pension Plan and the Canada Assistance Plan. Canadian nationalism was heightened with the adoption of the maple leaf flag in 1965, and in the same year another federal election produced a Liberal government one seat short of a clear majority. The opening of the world's fair, Expo in Montreal, in Canada's centennial year, 1967, marked a year of celebration across the country.

During the 1960s, Pearson was sensitive to growing nationalism in Quebec. His government established a Royal Commission on Bilingualism and Biculturalism in 1963, to demonstrate that Quebec's interests could be served by federalism, and he encouraged some of those closely associated with the Quiet Revolution to run for federal office. Quebec had been transformed from traditional to modern attitudes towards education, social reform and industrialization, a movement known as the Quiet Revolution, under Premier Jean Lesage. The Quebec government was implementing the ideas of the Quiet Revolution, and championed provincial rights with its slogan *maîtres chez nous* (masters in our own house). This sentiment took centre stage during Centennial celebrations. Visiting French President Charles de Gaulle ended a Montreal speech with the cry *"Vive le Québec libre!"* ("Long live free Quebec") which set off a storm of diplomatic protest and delighted local nationalists. Despite growing nationalist sentiment, many Quebeckers, including Pierre Trudeau, went to Ottawa. Trudeau was elected to the House of Commons in 1965, and was named minister of justice in 1967. In 1968,

following Pearson's retirement, Trudeau became Liberal leader.

1947 Imperial Oil discovers the **Leduc oil field** (Feb. 13).

1948 Louis St. Laurent succeeds Mackenzie King as prime minister (Nov. 15).

1949 Under Premier **Joey Smallwood**, **Newfoundland** becomes Canada's 10th province (Mar. 31). Canada joins NATO. Canadian appeals to Britain's Judicial Committee of the Privy Council are abolished: Canada's Supreme Court becomes final court of appeal. Liberals under St Laurent defeat Conservatives under George Drew in federal election (June 3).

1950 The Korean War begins (June 25); Canadian troops participate in the conflict as part of a United Nations force.

1951 The midcentury census reports Canada's population as 14,009,429. **Postwar immigration** to Canada exceeds 100,000 annually during the 1950s, primarily moving from central and eastern Europe to hold manufacturing jobs in urban centres. The Massey Royal Commission reports that Canadian cultural life is dominated by American influences. Revisions to the **Indian Act**, beginning in 1951, limit its coverage of aboriginal people. Indian women married to non-Indian men are excluded from the act. This provision was removed in 1985 after much protest of discrimination. **Charlotte Whitton**, the first woman to be mayor of a major Canadian city, is elected in Ottawa.

1952 Vincent Massey becomes the first native-born Governor General of Canada. Canada's **first television** stations begin broadcasting in Montreal (Sept. 6) and Toronto (Sept. 8). **W.A.C. Bennett** begins **Social Credit**'s administration in British Columbia.

1953 Canada's National Library is established in Ottawa (Jan. 1). The Stratford Festival opens (July 13). The **Korean War ends** (July 27); total Canadian casualties are 314 killed and 1,211 wounded. Liberals under St Laurent defeat Conservatives under Drew in federal election (Aug. 10).

1954 An economic slump interrupts the postwar boom. Canada's **first subway** opens in Toronto (Mar. 30). Roger Bannister and John Landy run the "miracle mile" at the British Empire Games in Vancouver (Aug.), the first to run a mile in less than four minutes. Sixteen-year-old Marilyn Bell becomes the first person to swim Lake Ontario (Sept. 9). **Hurricane Hazel** hits Toronto, killing 83 people (Oct. 15). The Geneva Conference on the Far East invites Canada to join India and Poland in **supervising peace in Indochina**. This peacekeeping commitment continues for nearly 20 years to 1973.

1955 The Canadian Labour Congress is formed. The suspension of Montreal Canadiens' hockey star Maurice (Rocket) Richard leads to rioting in Montreal (Mar. 17).

1956 The Liberals use closure to limit the **Pipeline Debate** (May 8–June 6), a manoeuvre that contributes to their electoral defeat the following year.

1957 Conservatives under **John Diefenbaker** win federal election (June 10) and form minority government. Ellen Fairclough becomes the first woman federal cabinet minister. The Canada Council is created to help foster Canadian cultural life. **Lester B. Pearson wins Nobel Prize** (Oct. 12) for his role in resolving the Suez Crisis. Canadian supply and services troops are sent to work with a multinational UN force around the **Gulf of Aqaba**. They stay until 1967 and return there in 1973.

1958 Conservatives under Diefenbaker win 208 seats in federal election (Mar. 31). Coal mine disaster at Springhill, NS, results in death of 74 miners.

1959 The **Avro Arrow** project is terminated, with a loss of almost 14,000 jobs (Feb. 20). The **St. Lawrence Seaway** is **opened** (June 26).

1960 Liberals under **Jean Lesage** win provincial election in Quebec (June 22), inaugurating the **Quiet Revolution**. A **Canadian Bill of Rights** is approved by Parliament. Native people get the right to vote in federal elections. During the 1960s French is recognized as a language of instruction in elementary and secondary schools in New Brunswick, Ontario and Manitoba. It is recognized subsequently in other provincial jurisdictions.

1961 The **New Democratic Party** replaces the CCF.

1962 Conservatives are reduced to minority status in federal election (June 18). Social Credit wins 30 seats and NDP take 19 to control the balance of power in the House of Commons. The Saskatchewan NDP introduces the first Canadian **Medicare** plan (July 1), and is opposed by a doctors' strike. **Trans-Canada Highway** officially opens (Sept. 3). Canadian-made satellite *Alouette* is launched (Sept. 29), making Canada the third nation in space. Canada's last execution, the double hanging of Ronald Turpin and Arthur Lucas, takes place (Dec. 11), at the Don Jail in Toronto.

1963 Liberals under Pearson win federal election (Apr. 8), and form a minority government. The Quebec separatist group **Front de libération du Québec (FLQ)** sets off a series of bombs in Montreal (Apr.–May). A TCA flight crashes in Quebec, killing all 118 people aboard (Nov. 29). The **Royal Commission on Bilingualism and Biculturalism** begins its work.

1964 Canadians get social insurance cards (Apr.). Canada ends difficult peacekeeping duties in the Congo (Zaïre) after four years of service with heavy casualties. Canadian troops join UN forces in Cyprus.

1965 Canada gets a new flag (Feb. 15). The **Autopact** between Canada and the US is signed. Canadian Roman Catholic Churches begin to celebrate mass in English (Mar. 7). Liberals win federal election (Nov. 8) to continue as a minority government. Failure of an Ontario Hydro relay device at Queenston plunges eastern North America into a power blackout (Nov. 9).

1966 The Munsinger Affair becomes Canada's first major parliamentary sex scandal (Mar. 4). The **Canada Pension Plan** is established. The CBC begins colour television broadcasting (Oct. 1).

1967 The Canadian army, navy and air forces are **unified** to become the Canadian **Armed Forces** (Apr. 25). Montreal hosts a world's fair, **Expo 67** (opened Apr. 27). Canada celebrates its **Centennial** (July 1). French President Charles **de Gaulle** delivers his "Vive le Québec Libre" speech in Montreal (July 24). The federal Department of Manpower and Immigration establishes the "points system" for immigrants. Patterns shift in the 1960s from European to Third World immigration as humanitarian objectives and family reunification policies increase multicultural immigration.

■ The Trudeau Years (1968-1984)

The Liberals won a majority victory in the election of 1968. Trudeau was a strong federalist, determined to show that Ottawa could promote the rights of French Canada. The Official Languages Act of 1969 recognized both English and French as official languages, and required federal institutions to provide services in both languages. Although the legislation was supported by all parties, it was not universally popular, even in Quebec.

In the October Crisis of 1970 separatist extremists belonging to the FLQ (Front de libération du Québec) kidnapped British Trade Commissioner James Cross, and killed Quebec cabinet minister Pierre Laporte. Trudeau used the War Measures Act to apply emergency measures of arrest, detention and martial law. This move was generally accepted but was criticized by advocates of civil rights, especially since the FLQ had little real support and the Act was in effect across the country.

In his early years in power, Trudeau attempted to concentrate decision-making in Ottawa, and his newly created Prime Minister's Office led to western Canadian accusations of an eastern-dominated federal government. At the same time opposition parties charged that Trudeau was undermining both the power of the cabinet and of Parliament. The Liberals were almost defeated in the election of 1972, but retained office through a minority government that saw the New Democrats, under David Lewis, hold the balance of power. During this period the Foreign Investment Review Agency was set up (1973) to protect the Canadian economy against foreign domination; business critics claimed that it discouraged investment.

By 1974, the Liberals had regained a majority; their agenda was dominated by an economy battered by inflation. The government tried a variety of economic measures, including a three-year imposition of wage and price controls under the Anti-Inflation Act of 1975. Although the controls may have had some effect, world conditions, especially the international oil crisis, kept inflation high.

In 1976, the separatist Parti Québécois under René Lévesque defeated the provincial Liberals, led by Robert Bourassa in the Quebec election. This election fueled public uncertainty over the future of Quebec (and Canada), while continuing inflation and western alienation also undermined Liberal support. In the 1979 election, the Liberals lost, and Conservative leader Joe Clark took office as head of a minority government. Clark's government was short-lived as it suffered defeat in the House of Commons that same year.

The Liberals won the election of 1980, and Trudeau, lured out of planned retirement by the sudden election, embarked on an eventful term of office. He and members of his government actively campaigned on the victorious NO side in the 1980 Quebec referendum on sovereignty association. The Liberals brought in the National Energy Program in the same year, again attempting to regulate ownership and control in part of the economy, and again succeeding in alienating foreign and local business interests. Resistance to the NEP, particularly in the west, was deep and persistent.

Then, after a long (18 months) and difficult campaign waged in Parliament, at federal-provincial meetings and in the media, Trudeau succeeded in getting an agreement on patriating the Canadian constitution amongst all provinces except Quebec. Patriation officially took place when Queen Elizabeth II proclaimed the new Constitution Act in Ottawa on Apr. 17, 1982. The Charter of Rights and Freedoms was also proclaimed, entrenching bilingualism in the federal jurisdiction and providing for minority language education rights across Canada.

By 1984 the country was mired in a recession and in no mood for the international interest Trudeau was pursuing; he retired and John Turner became Liberal leader and prime minister for a brief period. The Liberal government was at the end of its mandate and parliament was dissolved. After nearly 16 years of Liberal government, the voters were eager for a change.

1968 **Pierre Elliott Trudeau** succeeds Pearson as prime minister (Apr. 6), and leads Liberals to majority in federal election (June 25). A Royal Commission on the Status of Women is appointed. Canadian divorce law is reformed.

1969 Saturday postal deliveries end. Abortion law is liberalized (May). English and French become **official languages** of federal administration (July 9). New Brunswick declares official bilingualism. The breathalizer comes into use as a test for alcohol-impaired drivers (Dec. 1).

1970 The FLQ kidnaps British trade commissioner James Cross (Oct. 5), precipitating the **October Crisis**. Quebec labour and immigration minister Pierre Laporte is kidnapped (Oct. 10), and found murdered (Oct. 17). The federal government invokes the **War Measures Act** (Oct. 16), leading to the arrest of 465 people.

1971 A policy of **multiculturalism** is adopted by the federal government. Canadian Gerhard Herzberg wins the Nobel Prize in chemistry for his studies of chemical reactions that help produce smog.

1972 Canada defeats the USSR in the first hockey series between the Soviets and Canadian professionals (Aug.–Sept.). Liberals win federal election with 109 seats to the Conservatives 107, with the NDP holding the balance of power at 31 (Oct. 30).

1973 The separatist Parti Québécois becomes the official Opposition in Quebec. Canadian troops are sent to the Middle East and serve with the United Nations Emergency Task Force there until 1979.

1974 Liberals under Trudeau win federal election and form majority government (July 8). **Pauline McGibbon** becomes the first female lieutenant-governor (Ontario) in the British Commonwealth.

1975 The **CN Tower**, the world's tallest free-standing structure at 553.339 metres, is completed in Toronto (Apr. 2). Federal government announces (July 18) its intention to screen foreign investment in Canada, via the Foreign Investment Review Agency (FIRA). Television cameras are allowed inside the House of Commons for the first time. Federal government imposes **wage and price controls** in an effort to fight inflation (Oct. 14). **Grace Hartman** is elected president of the Canadian Union of Public Employees.

1976 Canada announces 200-nautical-mile coastal fishing zone (June 4). **Death penalty** is **abolished** in a free vote (130–124) in Parliament (July 14). Montreal hosts **Olympic Games** (July 17–31). Team Canada wins the first **Canada Cup** hockey series (Sept. 15). The **Parti Québécois** under René Lévesque wins provincial election in Quebec (Nov. 15).

1977 Quebec government pases Bill 101, restricting English-language schooling to children whose mother or father had attended English elementary school in Quebec (Aug. 26). Highway signs in most of Canada become metric (Sept. 6).

1978 **Soviet nuclear-powered satellite crashes** in Canadian north (Jan. 24). Sun Life Assurance Co. announces a head office move from Montreal to Toronto because of language laws and political instability in Quebec. **Hilda Watson**, first woman to lead a political party in Canada, wins leadership of Yukon Progressive Conservative party.

1979 Conservatives under **Joe Clark** win federal election (May 22). Canada's first gold bullion coin, the Maple Leaf, goes on sale (Sept. 5). Supreme Court of Canada declares Manitoba and Quebec legislation creating unilingual courts and legislatures unconstitutional (Dec. 13). Federal Conservatives lose non-confidence vote on budget (Dec. 13), forcing the government's resignation. **Antonine Maillet** wins the prestigious French literary prize, the Prix Goncourt, for her novel *Pélagie-la-Charette*.

1980 Canada's ambassador to Iran, Ken Taylor, arranges the successful **escape of six American Embassy staff** from Tehran while their colleagues are held hostage (Jan. 28). Liberals win federal election (Feb. 18). Canada boycotts the Olympic Games in Moscow because of the Soviet invasion of Afghanistan. **Jeanne Sauvé** becomes the first female Speaker of the House of Commons (Apr. 14). **Quebec votes "no"** to "sovereignty-association" in a **referendum** (May 22). **"O Canada"** becomes Canada's national anthem (June 27). The Supreme Court awards Rosa Becker half the assets accumulated during a 19-year common-law relationship. **National Energy Program** is created to encourage oil self-sufficiency, increase Canadian ownership in the oil industry and obtain a larger share of Canadian energy revenues.

1981 Quebec bans public signs in English (Sept. 23). The federal government and every province except Quebec reach agreement on a method for patriating Canada's constitution (Nov. 5). The 1981 census indicates significant increases in the percentage of new Canadians from Asia, the Caribbean and Latin America.

1982 Bertha Wilson becomes Canada's first woman to be appointed a justice of the Supreme Court (Mar. 4). The Quebec Court of Appeal rejects the Quebec government's claim of veto power over constitutional change (Apr. 7). Canada gains a new **Constitution** and **Charter of Rights and Freedoms** (Apr. 17). Canada's GNP falls 4.8% in the worst recession since the Great Depression of the 1930s.

1983 Canadian pay-TV channels begin operation (Feb. 1). **Jeanne Sauvé** is Canada's first woman to be appointed Governor General (Dec. 23). Canada approves a US plan to test unarmed **cruise missiles** in western Canada beginning in 1984.

■ Mulroney in Power (1984-1993)

In the 1984 general election, the Conservatives, under Brian Mulroney, won a decisive victory, taking 211 of 282 seats in the House of Commons, including 58 seats in Quebec, a former Liberal stronghold. In contrast to the previous government, the Conservatives sought to strengthen ties with the United States and took steps to attract more foreign investment to Canada. The recession of the early 80s was over and business and government were both ready to expand.

One of the goals of the Mulroney government was to amend the Constitution Act of 1982 to obtain the support of Quebec. The prime minister and 10 provincial premiers reached an agreement, which became known as the Meech Lake Accord, on such an amendment in 1987; the agreement was to be taken to provincial legislatures and to parliament for approval by June 23, 1990. Also in 1987, the government negotiated a Canada-US free trade agreement (FTA) which provided for the elimination of all cross-border tariffs over 10 years. But the deal was rejected by both opposition parties and Liberal leader John Turner announced that the Liberal-dominated Senate would not approve free trade unless the Conservatives obtained public support in a general election. Mulroney called an election for November 1988. The campaign that followed was fractious;

emotions ran high and there were wide fluctuations in public opinion. Anti-FTA sentiment was split between the opposition parties and the Conservatives won a second majority government. The FTA was approved in December and took effect Jan. 1, 1989.

As the deadline for ratification of the Meech Lake Accord approached, its confirmation became increasingly uncertain. Provincial governments had changed in the interim and both Manitoba and Newfoundland indicated that they had reservations about the agreement. Despite a last-minute first ministers' conference and a great deal of political pressure, the Manitoba legislature failed to ratify the accord and Newfoundland withdrew its consent; the deal lapsed on June 23, 1990. The following years were marked by numerous federal-provincial conferences, a variety of proposals and pressure from Quebec to include recognition of its distinct society. In August 1992 a new federal-provincial agreement was reached (the Charlottetown Accord) in time to be considered in a referendum Quebec Premier Robert Bourassa had pledged to hold on the future of Quebec. The other provinces also took part in a national referendum on the terms of the accord, which included not only recognition of Quebec as a distinct society, but also provisions to transfer mining, forestry, telecommunications and many other jurisdictions to the provinces. Canadians from all walks of life grappled with the issues raised by the terms of the Charlottetown Accord and the question dominated national media, (aside from the sports pages which were distracted by the prospect of a Canadian team, the Toronto Blue Jays, winning the 1992 World Series). The referendum was held on Oct. 26, 1992 and the deal was rejected by 54.8% of the voters.

The Conservatives' second term of office was also marked by the introduction of the Goods and Services Tax (GST), a tax designed to replace the manufacturers' tax and spread the tax burden more evenly across the economy. This tax was deeply unpopular and the Liberal-appointed members of the Senate vowed to block its passage in the upper chamber. Mulroney responded by temporarily increasing the number of senators to 112, with new appointees who would support the measure. The tax was the subject of heated debate and much protest across the country as Canadians transferred their frustration over the endless constitutional discussion, the now faltering economy and disappointment over the results of FTA to the government.

The GST took effect on Jan. 1, 1991, and the Conservative government continued to pursue wider trade agreements by joining the US and Mexico in negotiations for a North American Free Trade Agreement that would supersede the FTA. Amid much controversy, the deal was signed in December and the government's popularity continued to plumb the depths of the popularity polls. In February, Mulroney announced his decision to step aside as leader; Kim Campbell became the new leader of the Conservatives and the country's first female prime minister after a June leadership convention. As the Conservative mandate drew to a close, Campbell attempted to present herself as a brand-new prime minister at the head of a brand-new government. In the election in October 1993, Canadian voters made it clear they did not accept this stance: the Liberals under Jean Chrétien won a lopsided victory in an election that changed the political map of the country. The new government took office with a record number of rookie MPs, the Loyal Opposition was made up of members of the separatist Bloc Québécois, with the Reform Party from western Canada nearly matching the BQ's number of seats. The Conservatives elected only two members and the NDP also fared poorly at the hands of the electorate.

1984 Trudeau is succeeded as prime minister by **John Turner** (June 30). Conservatives under **Brian Mulroney** win federal election with 211 seats, the largest majority in Canada's history (Sept. 4). The **Pope visits Canada** (Sept. 9–20). **Marc Garneau** becomes the first Canadian in space, aboard US space shuttle *Challenger* (Oct. 5). Council for the Northwest Territories recognizes the use of **aboriginal languages** as well as English and French.

1985 The voyage through the Northwest Passage of US icebreaker *Polar Sea* challenges Canada's **Arctic sovereignty**. Prime Minister Mulroney and US President Reagan declare mutual support for **Star Wars research** and **free trade** between the two nations at "Shamrock Summit" (Mar. 18) in Quebec City. The Quebec provincial Liberals under Robert Bourassa defeat the Parti Québécois (Dec. 2).

1986 The Canadian dollar hits a then all-time low of 70.20 cents US (Jan. 31). The **Expo 86** world's fair is held in Vancouver (May 2–Oct. 13). Canada joins other Commonwealth nations (Aug. 5) in adopting **economic sanctions against South Africa** because of its apartheid policy. Canada receives a United Nations award (Oct. 6) for providing a haven for world refugees. Canadian John Polanyi shares the Nobel Prize for chemistry.

1987 The Bank of Canada rate drops to a 13-year low of 7.49% (Jan. 28); 6-month residential mortgages are as low as 7.5%. The **Meech Lake Accord**, proposing major constitutional amendments, is agreed to by Prime Minister Brian Mulroney and the 10 provincial premiers (Apr. 30). Ontario passes the first **pay equity legislation** for the private sector enacted in North America (June). A free vote in Parliament on restoration of **capital punishment** defeats the proposal 148–127 (June). A **free trade** agreement between Canada and the United States is set out. (Oct. 3). **Stock prices tumble** (Oct. 19) in Canada and throughout the world. The founding assembly of the **Reform Party of Canada** is held (Nov.)

1988 Canada is left without an **abortion law** (Jan. 28) when the Supreme Court rules that existing legislation is unconstitutional. Canadian sprinter **Ben Johnson** sets a world record and wins a gold medal at the Summer Olympics in Seoul (Sept. 24) but is stripped of both (Sept. 26) after testing positive for steroids. Yukon Territory passes language legislation recognizing the use of aboriginal languages. Brian Mulroney's Progressive Conservatives win a second consecutive majority in the **federal election** (Nov. 21), a bitter campaign fought over the free trade agreement with the US. Quebec's **French-only sign law** is struck down by the Supreme Court (Dec. 15) but is re-instated by Quebec (Dec. 21) using the "notwithstanding" clause in the Charter of Rights and Freedoms. Free trade legislation passes the House of Commons (Dec. 24) and the Senate (Dec. 30). The "Kamloops Amendment" to the Indian Act grants band councils jurisdiction over all reserve land, including the power to impose taxes.

1989 The Free Trade Agreement takes effect (Jan. 1). The federal government announces a new **goods and services tax** (GST) to take effect Jan. 1991. Audrey McLaughlin becomes Canada's **first female national party leader** as the NDP chooses a successor to Ed Broadbent (Dec. 2).

1990 Revisions to the Criminal Code provide choice of language in criminal hearings (Jan.). Several Quebec Conservative MPs, led by cabinet minister Lucien Bouchard (May 21), leave the government to form the pro-independence **Bloc Québécois**. The **Meech Lake Accord dies** when both Newfoundland and Manitoba fail to ratify the constitutional agreement by the deadline (June 23). Manitoba MLA **Elijah Harper** refuses the unanimous consent required for debate and a vote on the Meech Lake Accord because the accord does not provide special status for aboriginal peoples as it does for Quebec. Jean Chrétien becomes leader of the federal Liberal party. A land dispute leads to a 78-day armed confrontation between Mohawk warriors and government forces at the Kanesatake reserve near **Oka**, Quebec. **Canada sends warships** to the Persian Gulf as part of the multinational force being assembled to force Iraq to withdraw from occupied Kuwait. Brian Mulroney's Conservative government stacks the Senate (Sept. 27) with new appointees to ensure passage of the federal **goods and services tax (GST)**, which becomes law Dec. 17 to take effect Jan. 1.

1991 Canadian military personnel participate with the Allied forces in the assault against Iraq beginning Jan. 16 (the **Gulf War**). Prime Minister Brian Mulroney and US President George Bush sign an **acid rain accord** with the goal of ending acid rain within 10 years. **Rita Johnston** succeeds BC Premier **William Vander Zalm** as premier, the first woman to enter the provincial premier's office in Canada. Mulroney's government announces a **new constitutional reform package** promising aboriginal self-government within 10 years and guaranteeing aboriginal representation in an elected Senate. **Gun control** bill is passed, imposing tougher controls and banning imported military assault weapons; **Yukon First Nations** sign umbrella agreement on land claims and self-government; agreement reached on creation of Nunavut in Northwest Territories.

1992 A year-long crisis in the Atlantic **fisheries** results in a two-year shutdown of the cod fishery (July 2), a five-year ban on commercial salmon fishing in Newfoundland (Mar. 6) and

international negotiations to protect the fish stocks; **Gwich'in Indians** sign a deal with Ottawa, giving them title to nearly 24,000 sq. km of land in the NWT and Yukon (Apr. 22); details of North American Free Trade Agreement (**NAFTA**) are announced Aug. 12, Prime Min. Mulroney signs the deal on Dec. 17; negotiations on **constitutional reform** take place throughout the year and an agreement (the Charlottetown Accord) that has Quebec's approval is announced Aug. 19 (proposals include Senate reform, an enlarged House of Commons and self-government for native people); a national referendum on the accord is held Oct. 26 and No side claims victory, killing the deal.

1993 The **Sahtu Tribe** of the Great Bear Lake region in the NWT settled a land claim to 41,437 sq. km; the **Cree** in northern Quebec win compensation from Hydro-Quebec for damage done around James Bay. Jan. 19 Canadian troops begin the planned pull-out from NATO bases. On Feb. 24 Prime Min. Mulroney announces his resignation, to take effect in June. Four members of the **Canadian Airborne Regiment**, in Somalia since Jan. on a peacekeeping mission, are charged in the death of a Somali civilian. NAFTA legislation passes in the House of Commons on May 27. Yukon's 14 First Nations sign the **Umbrella Final Agreement** in Whitehorse on May 29; the settlement includes 41,400 sq. km of land and $280 million. On June 15, Canada officially ends its role in Cyprus after 29 years of peacekeeping duties on the island. Defence Min. **Kim Campbell** takes over the reins of the Conservative government after a second ballot victory at the leadership convention on June 25. On Oct. 25 the Liberal Party wins a decisive victory in a federal election that sees the emergence of **two new parties**—the Bloc Québécois and the Reform party—and the near demise of the Progressive Conservatives. The cod moratorium of 1992 is extended to include the Gulf of St. Lawrence and is slated to last until the end of the decade.

1994 Most of the country west of the Rockies endures the coldest winter since the 1950s. **Cigarette taxes** are cut federally and provincially in an effort to curb a black market in cigarettes. The Liberals first budget forecasts cuts in defence spending, UI benefits, tax deductions and foreign aid and freezes transfer payments and public sector salaries. The **Canada Pension Plan** posts a deficit for the first time in 28 years. Members of the **Saskatchewan Wheat Pool** vote to transform the organization, formed in 1924, into a public company. The prime minister and provincial premiers sign an agreement to end trade barriers among the provinces. The Inuit of Quebec sign a self-government deal with the Quebec government. **Canadian troops leave CFB Lahr**, officially ending 27 years of Canadian service for NATO in Europe. The **Algonquins** of Gold Lake, Ontario, sign an agreement to begin negotiating an 8.5 million acre land claim in southern Canada. Canadian sports fans are left hockey-less until the new year by a labour dispute and **NHL lock-out**.

1995 The Canadian Airborne Regiment is disbanded (Jan.) after a new scandal compounds damage done by the **Somalia Affair**. Federal fisheries officials seize the Spanish fishing vessel *Estai* in Mar., in a battle over fishing rights on the Grand Banks. A settlement of the dispute in Apr. gives the **North Atlantic Fishing Organization** greater powers; in the same month Canada loses its triple A bond rating courtesy of Moody's Investors Service of New York. In June the worst forest fire season in northern parts of central Canada begins, while torrential rains trigger flooding along major rivers in Alberta. BC's Fraser River salmon run is shut down in Aug., because fish stocks are too low. In Sept., Newfoundland voters approve a proposal to shift control of education from the church to the province. In Oct. **Alexa McDonough** is elected leader of the federal NDP. On Oct. 30, after a bruising campaign that sees federal Opposition Leader Bouchard take over the YES side, the **proposal that Quebec separate from Canada** to form a sovereign state is narrowly defeated in a referendum—49.4% Yes, and 50.6% against. In early Nov., security at 24 Sussex Drive is breached as an intruder armed with a knife accosts the prime minister's wife in the hall outside their bedroom. In Dec. consumer exhaustion and caution make the Christmas retail season one of the poorest on record.

1996 **Brian Tobin** sworn in as premier of Nfld (Jan. 26). **Lucien Bouchard** sworn in as Quebec premier (Jan. 29). The Mint unveiled the new $2 coin (Feb. 19). **Glen Clark** was sworn in as premier of BC (Feb. 22). A major land claims agreement in principle was signed with the **Nisga'a** of BC. (Mar. 22) The **ANIK** E-1 satellite suffered irreparable damage and

displaced traffic was transferred to ANIK E-2 (Mar. 26). On May 2, PEI replaced its dual-member riding system with single members representing each of 27 ridings. On May 29, Canada and the US signed a **softwood lumber agreement** after 15 years of controversy. In late May, the worst floods in 36 years hit northern Ontario towns. **Bob Thirsk** blasted off on *Columbia* for a 17-day mission (June 7). On July 9, the **Innu** of Davis Inlet agreed to relocate their community to Sango Bay. On July 20-21, **devastating floods** hit the Saguenay valley in Quebec. Ten people were killed, businesses and homes were swept away and property damage amounted to about $365 million. On July 31, Canada and Israel signed a free trade deal. The *Irving Whale* was raised from the bottom of the Gulf of St. Lawrence (Aug.) to prevent environmental damage. In Sept., Canada's Insurance Bureau announced July 1996 was the worst month on record for insurance losses, citing hailstorms and tornadoes in the west and the floods in the Saguenay. Shortly after that announcement, an intense storm swept through Manitoba. On Oct. 2, former Quebec premier Robert Bourassa died. On Oct. 8, Gen. Jean Boyle resigned as head of Canada's armed forces after controversial evidence arose at the Somalia inquiry; Vice-Admiral Larry Murray was appointed as acting chief of defence. On Oct. 10, Keith Milligan was sworn in as premier of PEI, replacing Catherine Callbeck five days after a leadership convention. On Nov. 1, an agreement between native bands, federal and territorial governments and BHP Diamonds Inc. cleared the way for Canada's first diamond mine. On Nov. 5, Quebec's controversial Lt. Gov. Jean-Louis Roux resigned after apologizing for his participation in an anti-Semitic protest in 1942. On Nov. 18, PEI Conservatives, led by Pat Binns, scored a major election victory after 10 years of Liberal rule. On the same day, Canada and Chile signed a free trade deal. In Dec., Canada signed a $4 billion contract with China for two CANDU reactors. On Dec. 17, Tupac Amaru guerrillas took four Canadians hostage at a Christmas party hosted by the Japanese ambassador in Lima, Peru; the hostages were later released unharmed. The Ontario government announced plans to merge

Toronto and five surrounding municipalities into a single "mega-city" (Dec. 17).

1997 Rules for applying for **Employment Insurance** (formerly Unemployment Insurance) changed (Jan. 4), including the elimination of weekly minimum and maximum benefits and stricter penalties for fraud. The federal government announced an out-of-court settlement with former prime minister Mulroney in his libel suit launched during the **Airbus investigation** (Jan. 6). Several provincial finance ministers had good news to go along with their Feb. budgets as Ontario announced a slowing of cuts, Alberta acknowledged a surplus and Saskatchewan increased spending. On Feb. 14 federal Finance Min. Martin announced a plan to sharply increase contributions to **CPP** over the next 6 years, in order to prepare the plan for the demands of retiring Baby Boomers. The Feb. 18 federal budget announced set aside $1 billion for jobs and social programs, a much lower forecasted deficit and tax breaks for some parts of the economy. The New York debt rating agency, Standard and Poor's, upgraded its ratings of Canada's foreign currency debt and bonds in response to the cost cutting measures instituted to reduce the deficit (Feb. 24). Voters in Alberta gave Premier **Ralph Klein** another majority (Mar. 11). Manitoba became the third province to make a payment on its debt (Mar. 14); On Mar. 6 the federal government's **anti-smoking bill**, including the controversial provisions to severely limit tobacco funding of arts and sports activities, was passed in the House of Commons. **Industry Canada** announced that business and consumer bankruptcies were 20% higher in 1996 than in 1995 (Mar. 14). **Gilles Duceppe** was elected the new leader of the Bloc Québécois (Mar. 15). NS Premier **John Savage** made a surprise resignation announcement (Mar. 21). Saskatchewan's finance minister cut PST by 2% as the province. A freight train plunged into a sinkhole in the Fraser Canyon and exploded, killing the conductor and the engineer (Mar. 26). The first of the population and dwelling count data from the 1996 census was released (Apr. 15); Quebec's share of the population had fallen below 25% for the first time since 1867. Manitoba premier **Gary Filmon** declared a state of emergency in the southern portion of his province as the crest of the **Red River** headed across the US border (Apr. 22).

A small cod fishery re-opened on the east coast of Newfoundland after a moratorium that began in 1993 (May 1). An independent auditor confirmed that the gold in samples from the **Bre-X claim** in Indonesia was "negligible" (May 4). May 13 Canadian Forces headed out of Winnipeg, having assisted residents in battling the "flood of the century." On May 31, The **Confederation bridge** officially opened to traffic between Prince Edward Island and the mainland (May 31). The Liberals were re-elected, but with a reduced majority; the Reform party became the official opposition (June 2). The **Somalia inquiry** handed in its report, placing most of the blame for the military's problems on poor leadership (July 12). Nova Scotia Liberals elected **Russell MacLellan** as their new leader (July 12). Manitoba chief **Phil Fontaine** was elected as the national chief of the Assembly of First nations (July 30). On August 7, Canadian astronaut **Bjarni Tryggvason** blasted off on the space shuttle *Columbia*. 73% of Newfoundland voters casting ballots in a second referendum on creating a secular school system supported the change (Sept. 2). A VIA train headed west derailed near Biggar, Saskatchewan; one passenger was killed and numerous others injured (Sept. 3). Nova Scotia premier **Frank McKenna** announced his resignation (Oct. 7), effective Oct. 13. **Red Cross** was deemed negligent in tainted blood scandal by a judge's ruling (Oct. 8). A bus crash in Quebec killed 43, in the worst road accident in Canadian history (Oct. 13). Teachers in Ontario staged a province-wide strike to protest changes in the education system (Oct. 27-Nov. 10). **Saskatchewan Conservatives** voted to mothball their party for at least two provincial elections (Nov. 9). Nation-wide postal strike shut down mail delivery (Nov. 20-Dec. 5). Annual **APEC conference** was held in Vancouver (Nov. 21-25). In Dec, Canada's six biggest banks announced huge profits, with Royal Bank on top with $1.68 billion in net income. Canada came to an agreement with parties to the **Kyoto convention** on greenhouse gas emissions (Dec. 11). An Air Canada flight from Toronto to Fredericton crashed on landing, skidding off the runway into snow and bush; all passengers and crew survived (Dec. 16).

1998 An **ice storm** crippled Que. and eastern Ont., leaving one million people without power and food (Jan. 6). Ottawa apologized to Canada's aboriginals for past mistreatment (Jan. 7). On Feb. 17, **Ontario Hydro** reported a loss of $6.32 billion in 1997–the largest business loss in Canadian history. By Feb. 22, Canadian athletes at the **Nagano Winter Olympics** had won a record 15 medals. Finance Min. Paul Martin forecast a balanced budget for two fiscal years (Feb. 24). Que. Liberal leader **Daniel Johnson** announced his resignation (Mar. 2). On Mar. 6, the Ont. government offered the three surviving **Dionne quintuplets** $4 million and an apology for government actions during their childhood. **BC doctors** launched the first of three province-wide office closings to protest medicare shortages (Mar. 6). After signing a $12 billion deal, Nfld and Que. began talks for a new Churchill Falls power project. **Mutual Life** of Canada acquired MetLife, becoming the second largest life insurer in Canada (Mar. 12). Absentee Sen. **Andrew Thompson** resigned on Mar. 23 after the Senate voted in Feb. to suspend him. The **NS election** resulted in the Liberals and NDP winning 19 seats each; the Conservatives won 14 (Mar. 24). On Mar. 27, federal Conservative leader **Jean Charest** said he would run for leader of Que.'s Liberal party. On the same day, federal and provincial governments announced $1.1 billion in compensation for victims who contracted hepatitis C from tainted blood in 1986-90. Floods forced 2,000 Quebecers from their homes (Apr. 1). In late Apr., a standoff between the NB government and natives occurred over logging. Prime Min. Chrétien visited Cuba (Apr. 26-28). **Camille Theriault** replaced Frank McKenna as NB Liberal party leader and premier (May 14). Ottawa banned coho fishing in BC, citing low fish stocks (May 21). The military announced plans to investigate or reopen up to 24 cases of alleged rape within its ranks (May 26). The Supreme Court of Canada struck down a ban on publishing opinion poll results 24 hours before federal elections (May 29). In June, fishermen in St John's protested when federal ministers said they would buy back fishing licences, pay

lump sums and end the **TAGS program** earlier than anticipated. **Macmillan Bloedel** said it would phase out clearcutting old-growth forests. Alta used a budget surplus to pay off $2.6 billion of the province's debt (June 24). Ottawa and Washington agreed to save Pacific salmon. In July, wildfires forced 1,000 people in northern Man. and Ont. to leave their homes. The **Nisga'a** people and the BC government signed a historic land claim treaty (July 15). On July 20, the **Canadian Red Cross** gained bankruptcy protection; the agency faced $8 billion in lawsuits from tainted blood victims. The **Human Rights Tribunal** endorsed the **Public Service Alliance of Canada**'s claim to $5 billion in pay equity (July 29). On Aug. 11, one of several BC fires threatened Salmon Arm, forcing the evacuation of 8,000 people. Federal officials re-opened the Fraser River fishery after finding one million more salmon than anticipated and after announcing new fishing restrictions. The Supreme Court of Canada ruled on Que.'s proposed secession from Canada: Canada-Que. talks must begin after a majority in Que. votes for independence in a referendum with an unambiguous question (Aug. 20). The Canadian dollar hit its lowest point of US$.6402 (Aug. 28). On Sept. 1, a new blood collection agency replaced the Canadian Red Cross. Air Canada pilots began a national 13-day strike; **Swissair Flight 111** crashed off the coast of NS, killing all 229 passengers (Sept. 2). The Supreme Court said carriers of sexually transmitted diseases must tell partners about their condition or face criminal charges (Sept. 3). Ten thousand gun owners met on Parliament Hill to protest firearm registration (Sept. 22). The Canadian Radio-television and Telecommunications Commission ended **Teleglobe**'s monopoly, removing the last barrier to full competition in Canada's telephone market (Oct. 1). **Bombardier** landed a $1.5 billion contract for building 50 jets (Oct. 1). Canada won a seat on the UN Security Council (Oct. 8). Finance Min. Martin ruled out big tax cuts after returning from talks in Washington on the global economic crisis (Oct. 14). Ottawa confirmed its plan to cut half the West Coast commercial salmon fleet within three years (Oct. 14). Man. joined an Alta-led coalition of provinces and territories opposing federal gun registration; Canada's first diamond mine opened in NWT (Oct. 14). BC Liberal leader **Gordon Campbell** went to court to block BC's treaty with the Nisga'a (Oct. 19). Statistics Canada reported that inflation had sunk to 1960s levels (Oct. 21). The *National Post* published its first edition (Oct. 27). Ont. passed the **Energy Competition Act** to end Ontario Hydro's monopoly in 2001 (Oct. 29). A month-long strike at Pearson International Airport ended (Nov. 8). Former Prime Min. **Joe Clark** was elected leader of the federal Conservative party (Nov. 14). **George Kosich** resigned as president of Eaton's (Nov. 16). Workers at **Abitibi-Consolidated** went back to work after a four-month strike (Nov. 19). Federal Solicitor-General **Andy Scott** resigned on Nov. 23 after weeks of criticism over his comments about the pepper spraying of demonstrators at the 1997 APEC conference in Vancouver. **Don Morin** resigned as NWT's premier, vowing to fight conflict of interest charges (Nov. 26). Premier **Lucien Bouchard** handily won re-election in Que. (Nov. 30) and promised another referendum of Que.'s sovereignty (Dec. 7). On Dec. 1, federal Justice Minister **Anne McLellan** officially launched Canada's new gun control law three years after Parliament had passed the bill. On Dec. 4, the **International Court of Justice** rejected Spain's attempt to punish Canada for seizing Spanish turbot fishing vessels in 1995. Statistics Canada reported the national jobless rate fell to eight percent in Nov.–the lowest level this decade (Dec. 4). Ont. offered $100 million to aid hospitals running deficits after cutting $860 million from health care for two years (Dec. 10). Finance Min. Martin prohibited Canadian **bank mergers**, saying they would concentrate economic power in the hands of fewer bankers and reduce competition as well (Dec. 14).

Fathers of Confederation

Union of the British North American colonies into the Dominion of Canada was discussed and its terms negotiated at three confederation conferences held at Charlottetown (C), Sept. 1, 1864; Quebec (Q), Oct. 10, 1864; and London (L), Dec. 4, 1866. The names of delegates are followed by the provinces they represented; Canada refers to what are now the provinces of Ontario and Quebec.

Adams G. Archibald, NS	C,Q,L
George Brown, Canada	C,Q
Alexander Campbell, Canada	C,Q
Frederick B.T. Carter, Nfld	Q
George-Étienne Cartier, Canada	C,Q,L
Edward B. Chandler, NB	C,Q
Jean-Charles Chapais, Canada	Q
James Cockburn, Canada	Q
George H. Coles, PEI	C,Q
Robert B. Dickey, NS	Q
Charles Fisher, NB	Q,L
Alexander T. Galt, Canada	C,Q,L
John Hamilton Gray, NB	C,Q
John Hamilton Gray, PEI	C,Q
Thomas Heath Haviland, PEI	Q
William A. Henry, NS	C,Q,L
William P. Howland, Canada	L
John M. Johnson, NB	C,Q,L
Hector L. Langevin, Canada	C,Q,L
Jonathan McCully, NS	C,Q,L
A.A. Macdonald, PEI	C,Q
John A. Macdonald, Canada	C,Q,L
William McDougall, Canada	C,Q,L
Thomas D'Arcy McGee, Canada	C,Q
Peter Mitchell, NB	Q,L
Oliver Mowat, Canada	Q
Edward Palmer, PEI	C,Q
William H. Pope, PEI	C,Q
John W. Ritchie, NS	L
J. Ambrose Shea, Nfld	Q
William H. Steeves, NB	C,Q
Sir Étienne-Paschal Taché, Canada	Q
Samuel Leonard Tilley, NB	C,Q,L
Charles Tupper, NS	C,Q,L
Edward Whelan, PEI	Q
R.D. Wilmot, NB	L

Canadian Disasters

Aug. 29, 1583: Canada's first recorded marine disaster took 85 lives when the *Delight* was wrecked on Sable Island.

Aug. 23, 1711: As many as 950 drowned when ships attached to the British fleet preparing to attack Quebec were grounded and sank on the rocks of Ile-aux-Oeufs.

Oct. 5, 1825: The Miramichi fire, north of New Brunswick's Miramichi River, destroyed the towns of Newcastle and Douglastown, and killed between 200–500 people.

June 10-27, 1832: A cholera epidemic peaked in Montreal when at least 947 people died. The epidemic, which first appeared in Quebec City, killed hundreds more throughout Lower Canada during the summer. A second cholera epidemic broke out in 1834.

May 17, 1841: On this date, several large boulders from Cap Diamant tumbled down the precipitous cliffs above the Lower Town of Quebec City and demolished eight houses, killing 32 people.

Oct. 27, 1854: In one of the earliest Canadian train disasters, a gravel train running near Baptiste Creek, 24 km west of Chatham, Ont., was hit by an express train on the same line. In the collision, 52 persons were killed and 48 seriously injured.

June 29, 1864: Near St-Hilaire, Que., a passenger train was unable to stop for an open drawbridge at the Beloeil bridge on the Richelieu River. The train plunged through the opening onto passing barges, killing 99 and injuring 100 people.

Apr. 1, 1873: Sailing from Liverpool to New York, the steamer *Atlantic* struck Meager's Rock off the coast of Nova Scotia and sank with the loss of 535 people.

May 13, 1873: Sixty men died when a fire and subsequent explosion in a coal mine at Westville, Pictou County, NS, trapped firemen and workers. The mine was eventually sealed to starve the fire of oxygen and it was two years before all the bodies were recovered.

Aug. 25, 1873: The Great Nova Scotia Cyclone swept over Cape Breton Island. The hurricane destroyed 1,200 vessels and 900 buildings, demolished dykes, wharves and bridges and claimed 500 lives.

May 3, 1887: An explosion at the Number One mine in Nanaimo, BC owned by the Vancouver Coal Mining and Land Company, killed 148 miners.

Jan. 24, 1888: Seventy-seven men lost their lives in a fire in the Number Five Mine at Wellington, just outside of Nanaimo, BC.

Feb. 21, 1891: In the first of several major disasters in the coal mines of Springhill, NS, 125 men were killed in an explosion.

May 26, 1896: Fifty-five people were killed when a bridge at Point Ellice in Victoria, BC, collapsed while a streetcar was passing over it. The bridge was too weak to support the weight of a recently built tramline.

Sept. 19, 1899: A massive rockslide from the cliffs above Quebec City's Lower Town demolished most of Champlain St, killing 45 people.

Apr. 29, 1903: Parts of the town of Frank, Alta., were obliterated by a sudden landslide when over 90 million tonnes of limestone came crashing down Turtle Mountain, crossed the four-km-wide valley floor and rolled up the other side of the valley. Approximately 75 people were killed. The landslide also sealed a mine entrance at the foot of the mountain and trapped 17 miners inside. The men were able to escape by digging a new tunnel to the surface.

Aug. 29, 1907: The Quebec Bridge, 11 km north of Quebec City, was the largest cantilevered bridge in the world at the time. As the bridge was nearing completion, the southern cantilever span collapsed, killing 75 workmen.

Aug. 2, 1908: A fire in BC's Kootenay Valley caused $5 million in damages and killed 70 people.

Mar. 5, 1910: A CPR work crew clearing the tracks from a previous snow slide in Rogers Pass, BC, was hit by an avalanche. Sixty-two men were killed; one survived.

June 30, 1912: The worst tornado in Canadian history swept through Regina, Sask., killing 28 residents, injuring hundreds and causing $75 million damage (est. 1990 dollars).

May 29, 1914: The Canadian Pacific liner *Empress of Ireland* collided with a Norwegian coal ship in the St Lawrence River near Rimouski, Que., and sank in only 14 minutes with the loss of 1,014 lives. This was one of the worst naval disasters in history, with the eighth largest loss of life for a naval accident.

June 19, 1914: The worst coal mine disaster in Canadian history occurred at Hillcrest, Alta, when dust explosions killed 189 men.

July 29, 1916: A forest fire in northern Ontario, thought to have been started by lightning and locomotive sparks, engulfed the towns of Cochrane and Matheson, killing at least 233 persons.

Sept. 11, 1916: The Quebec Bridge was the scene of further tragedy when a new centre span being hoisted into position fell into the river below. Thirteen men were killed, bringing the loss of life during construction of the bridge to 88.

Dec. 6, 1917: Halifax was the scene of Canada's worst single disaster when a French munitions ship filled with explosives collided with a freighter in Halifax harbour. The French ship, the *Mont Blanc*, was split to the waterline; fuel oil spilled over its explosive cargo and started a fire in the hold. The crew abandoned ship without attempting to extinguish the fire.

In the explosion that followed, the *Mont Blanc* was tossed more than 1,000 m into the air. The explosion levelled homes and businesses in a large part of the city and set off explosives stockpiled on shore. The blast, heard as far away as Prince Edward Island, is thought to be the largest-ever accidental explosion, and the largest non-nuclear blast in history. More than 1,600 people were killed, 9,000 injured, and 6,000 left homeless. Property damage was estimated at $35 million.

Oct. 23, 1918: The Canadian Pacific steamship *Princess Sophia* ran onto Vanderbilt Reef while sailing from Alaska to Vancouver. The ship sank two days later on Oct. 25. All 343 aboard were drowned.

Jan. 9, 1927: A small fire that broke out in Montreal's Laurier Palace Theatre was quickly extinguished, but in the panic that ensued 12 people were crushed to death and 64 were asphyxiated, including many children.

Apr. 14, 1928: The 18-gun sloop *Acorn* sank near Halifax with 115 men on board.

Nov. 18, 1929: Newfoundland's Burin Peninsula was struck by a 4.5 m tidal wave. Property damage was extensive and 27 were killed.

Dec. 12, 1942: An arsonist set fire to the Knights of Columbus hostel in St John's. Because the hostel had no emergency lighting, the doors opened inwards and exits were restricted, 99 people died and another 100 were seriously injured.

Sept. 17, 1949: Seven hundred people were aboard the Great Lakes excursion ship *Noronic* when it caught fire and burned at its pier in Toronto harbour. The ship's fire hydrants were dry and no alarm was sent to the city fire department until 15 minutes after the blaze was discovered. In the meantime, the single exit became blocked by fire and 118 lives were lost.

Oct. 15, 1954: During the worst inland storm in Canadian history, Hurricane Hazel, over 10 cm of rain fell in Toronto in 12 hours. At that time, many houses in Toronto were built on low-lying flood plains. The storm and resulting floods caused 83 deaths and widespread property damage.

Nov. 1, 1956: A second major tragedy struck the coal mines at Springhill, NS, when an accident killed 39 men.

Dec. 9, 1956: A DC-4 North Star flown by Trans-Canada Airways (later Air Canada) crashed into the east face of Mount Slesse, killing all 62 on board.

June 17, 1958: Design errors in Vancouver's Second Narrows Bridge caused one section to collapse. The accident killed 18 men, including the two engineers that an investigation later determined were responsible for the errors.

Oct. 23, 1958: A third mining accident in Springhill, NS, killed 75 when a tunnel collapsed.

Nov. 19, 1963: A Trans Canada Airlines DC-8F crashed after takeoff from Dorval in Montreal, killing 118.

July 5, 1970: At Toronto International Airport, an Air Canada DC-8 lost one starboard engine during a landing attempt. During the pilot's effort to take off and land again, the remaining starboard engine fell off. The aircraft crashed, killing all 109 persons aboard.

May 4, 1971: During a prolonged rainstorm in St-Jean-Vianney, Que., a giant sinkhole appeared in the ground. The hole swallowed 40 houses, several cars and a bus, and 31 people were killed.

Nov. 10, 1975: The 218-m ore carrier *Edmund Fitzgerald*, based in Sault Ste Marie, broke apart during a storm on Lake Superior and sank in 156 m of water with all 29 members of the crew aboard. Two days later only two rubber rafts and some life preservers from the ship were found.

June 21, 1977: A fire that broke out in the cell block of the city police headquarters of St John, NB, was so hot that the locks on several cell doors were fused. Twenty prisoners were killed and 12 police officers who attempted to rescue the prisoners were injured.

Feb. 11, 1978: A Pacific Western Airlines aircraft crashed at Cranbrook, BC, killing 43 people.

Aug. 4, 1978: The brakes on a chartered bus failed near Eastman, Que. The bus plunged into a lake, and 41 passengers were killed.

Dec. 31, 1979: Forty-four persons were killed during New Year's Eve celebrations at a social club in Chapais, Que., in a fire caused by a man playing with a lighter who set decorations ablaze.

Feb. 15, 1982: The ocean drilling rig *Ocean Ranger* overturned and sank during a storm while operating 265 km east of Newfoundland, killing 84 men. Inadequate safety procedures and equipment were later blamed for the accident.

May 31, 1985: A midafternoon tornado struck Barrie, Ont., killing 12, including four children. Property damage was in the hundreds of millions of dollars.

Dec. 12, 1985: In the worst air crash in Canada, an Arrow Airlines DC-8, after refueling in Gander en route to Hopkinsville, Ky., crashed seconds after takeoff, killing 256 passengers and crew.

Feb. 8, 1986: A 16-unit VIA Rail passenger train slammed head-on into a 118-unit CN freight train near Hinton, Alta. Twenty-six people were killed and dozens were seriously injured.

July 31, 1987: A tornado touched down in Edmonton, Alta, killing 26 people, injuring 250 others and causing an estimated $250 million damage.

Mar. 10, 1989: An Air Ontario jet crashed immediately after takeoff from Dryden, Ont., killing 24 people.

Feb. 12, 1990: One of the worst tire fires in North America broke out near Hagersville, Ont., spewing oil and toxic smoke. The dump, which stored 14 million tires for recycling, burned for 16 days; the blaze was extinguished at a cost of $1.5 million.

May 9, 1992: Twenty-six miners died underground in the Westray coal mine near Plymouth, NS, after a methane gas explosion. Fifteen bodies were recovered but the bodies of the remaining victims could not be reached in the debris.

July 16, 1993: Nineteen people died when a truck towing tanks of diesel fuel collided with a van carrying senior citizens near Lac-Bouchette, Que.

July 19-20, 1996: Ten people died in the Lac-St-Jean Saguenay Region when flash floods from overflowing dams and reservoirs wiped out communities along the Saguenay River.

Oct. 13, 1997: Forty-four passengers were killed when the brakes failed on their sightseeing bus; the vehicle missed a turn at the bottom of a steep hill and crashed into a ravine in Les Eboulements, 110 km northeast of Quebec City.

Sept. 2, 1998: All 229 passengers were killed when a Swissair MD-11 en route from New York to Geneva crashed in the Atlantic near Peggy's Cove, NS. The accident was the second worst in Canadian aviation history.

Canadian Crimes

July 17, 1771: Samuel Hearne, an Arctic explorer working for the Hudson's Bay Co., witnessed the unprovoked Chipewyan massacre of an Inuit community at Bloody Fall on the Coppermine River. More than 20 Inuit were killed.

June 19, 1816: Métis raiders massacred Gov. Robert Semple and 21 Anglo-Scottish militiamen at Seven Oaks in the North-Western Territory. Tensions had been growing between Métis hunters and Anglo-Scottish settlers over land use in the Red River region.

Apr. 7, 1868: Thomas D'Arcy McGee, a member of Parliament and a Father of Confederation, was shot at his home in Ottawa. McGee's death was the first political murder in the newly united Canada. James Whelan, an Irish nationalist, was convicted and hanged for the shooting.

Mar. 4, 1870: A Métis firing squad at Fort Garry shot Thomas Scott, an Irish settler, for threatening the life of Louis Riel. The execution, which enraged Protestant Ontarians, prompted Ottawa to draft the Manitoba Act and send troops to Fort Garry.

July 1871: Axe murderess Phoebe Campbell chopped up her husband George in their farmhouse near London, Ont. She had been having an affair with another man and sought to inherit her husband's property. Campbell was convicted and hanged in 1872.

Late May 1873: Seeking revenge for a series of horse thefts, a party of white plainsmen attacked an Assiniboine encampment in the Cypress Hills. The resulting massacre left 30 Assiniboine Indians and one white man dead.

Feb. 3, 1880: A mob of at least 31 farmers, including a police constable, massacred five members of the Donnelly clan in their farmhouses in Lucan, Ont. The killings climaxed a blood feud dating back to 1855. No one was convicted for the killings.

Feb. 17, 1890: Reginald Birchall shot and killed Frederick Benwell in a swamp near Woodstock, Ont. Birchall had lured Benwell from Britain with the false promise of making him an investor in a farm. Birchall's trial and hanging received international press coverage.

Apr. 1916: John Mychaluk shot and killed six members of the Manchur family at their farm in Wakaw, Sask. Mychaluk also burned down the Manchur's house and barn before shooting himself dead.

1928-46: Lila and William Young, owners of the Ideal Maternity Home in East Chester, NS, sold about 1,500 babies from unwed mothers to couples in the US and Canada. Between 100 and 400 babies deemed unfit for adoption were allowed to die and buried nearby in wooden butterboxes.

Feb. 17, 1932: A posse of RCMP officers killed Albert Johnson, the Mad Trapper of Rat River, in a shoot-out near Eagle River, YT. Johnson had been wanted for killing an RCMP officer on Jan. 29 and wounding another in Dec. The manhunt was the longest in Canadian Arctic history.

Sept. 9, 1949: All 23 passengers aboard a Quebec Airways DC-3 were killed when a bomb exploded in mid-flight and the plane crashed near St. Joachim, Que. Police uncovered a conspiracy to kill one passenger, Rita Guay. Husband Albert Guay and two accomplices were convicted and hanged.

Mar. 6, 1952: Two members of Edwin Alonzo Boyd's gang shot two police officers, killing one, in Toronto. The shootings climaxed a two-and-a-half-year spree of armed bank robberies in Toronto. All four gang members were caught and imprisoned within the year.

Mar. 1, 1966: Thieves disguised in Air Canada uniforms hijacked 12 crates of gold bullion at Winnipeg airport. The haul, worth $383,497, was the largest gold robbery in Canadian history. The thieves were subsequently caught; most of the gold was recovered.

Aug. 15, 1967: Victor Hoffman shot and killed nine members of the Peterson family–a family he did not know–near Shell Lake, Sask. Hoffman was caught, diagnosed as schizophrenic and confined to a mental hospital.

Sept. 5, 1970: In a drunken rampage, Dale Nelson killed eight people in Creston Valley, BC. His victims were either beaten, stabbed or shot to death; one girl was dismembered in the woods. The RCMP caught Nelson; he was sentenced to life imprisonment.

Oct. 5, 1970: The Front de libération du Quebec (FLQ) kidnapped James Cross, the British trade commissioner, in Montreal. In Dec., the kidnappers exchanged Cross for safe passage to Cuba. Years later, after returning to Canada, the kidnappers stood trial and were convicted.

Oct. 17, 1970: The FLQ murdered Pierre Laporte, Quebec's labour minister, and left his body in the trunk of a car. Laporte had been kidnapped at his home on Oct. 10. In Dec., the killers were caught at a country house; they received long prison sentences.

Sept. 1, 1972: The Blue Bird Bar in Montreal was torched by three disgruntled patrons who had been ejected from the bar earlier in the evening. The blaze killed 37.

July 1977: Four men participated in the 12-hour rape and eventual drowning of Emanuel Jaques, a 12-year-old shoeshine boy, above a body rub parlour in Toronto. Three were convicted and drew life imprisonment. One man was found not guilty.

1980-82: Clifford Olson, a construction worker from Coquitlam, BC, raped and killed eight girls and three boys aged nine to 18 between Nov. 17, 1980, and Olson's arrest on Aug. 12, 1982. Olson drew life imprisonment, but the government paid $90,000 into a trust fund for Olson's wife and son to learn where Olson had buried the bodies of his victims.

Apr. 27, 1982: Police in Toronto arrested Brian Molony, an employee of the CIBC, for embezzling almost $17 million from the bank in 93 separate frauds beginning in Sept. 1980. Molony had gambled away the money in US casinos. He was convicted in 1983.

Jan. 21, 1983: Colin Thatcher, a wealthy Moose Jaw rancher and former provincial Conservative cabinet minister, had his ex-wife murdered in Regina, Sask. He was convicted of first-degree murder and sentenced to life imprisonment.

Nov. 14, 1983: The body of organized crime boss Paul Volpe was found in the trunk of his wife's car at Toronto International Airport. His throat had been slashed.

May 8, 1984: Outraged by the Parti Québécois, Cpl. Denis Lortie killed three people and injured 13 more with machinegun fire in Quebec's national assembly. Rene Jalbert, the assembly's unarmed sergeant-at-arms, talked Lortie into surrendering. Lortie was sentenced to life in prison in 1987.

Mar. 12, 1985: Three Armenian terrorists carrying shotguns, revolvers and explosives attacked the Turkish embassy in Ottawa. They killed one security guard and held 12 hostages for four hours. All were caught and given life sentences.

June 23, 1985: 280 Canadians were killed when an Air India 747 flying from Toronto to London, England, crashed into the Atlantic Ocean. A bomb on board is thought to have caused the disaster.

May 25, 1986: A Punjabi cabinet minister, Malkiat Singh Sidhu, was shot while visiting Vancouver. Police suspected Sikh militants were responsible for the shooting.

Sept. 30, 1988: Newfoundlanders learned that Christian brothers had been sexually abusing altar boys since the 1970s at the Mount Cashel orphanage near St John's. By 1992, nine sex offenders had been convicted, receiving sentences of one to 13 years imprisonment. A public inquiry revealed a cover-up in 1975 involving public officials.

May-Nov. 1989: Escaped convict Allan Legere terrorized Miramichi, NB, killing victims at random while eluding a massive police search. Legere was eventually caught and convicted for four killings; he drew life imprisonment.

Dec. 6, 1989: Gunman Marc Lepine shot and killed 14 women and wounded 13 others at Montreal's l'école Polytechnique before killing himself. Lepine left a letter claiming he had attacked the students because they were feminists.

1990-92: Paul Bernardo and Karla Homolka, a young couple in Port Dalhousie, Ont., committed the sex-slayings of three girls between Dec. 23, 1990 and Apr. 29, 1992. Both killers were convicted, but Homolka got a lighter sentence in exchange for testimony against her husband. Bernardo also admitted to 14 rapes in Scarborough, Ont., in the 1980s.

Sept. 18, 1992: A bomb exploded underground at the Giant goldmine in Yellowknife, NWT, killing nine workers. Striking workers had been locked out since May; disgruntled miner Roger Warren was convicted of murder and sentenced to 20 years.

Prime Ministers of Canada

■ Sir John A. Macdonald

Canada's first prime minister, Sir John A. Macdonald, was born in Glasgow, Scotland, Jan. 11, 1815. At age five he came to Canada with his parents who settled at Kingston, Upper Canada.

Called to the bar in 1836, Macdonald practised law in Kingston and then in Toronto. He established a reputation as a corporate lawyer, company director and businessman.

He was elected to the Legislative Assembly of the Province of Canada in 1844 and was re- elected in 1848, 1851, 1854, 1857, 1861 and 1863. In 1864, he joined a coalition with George Brown, leader of the Upper Canadian reformers, dedicated to bringing about Confederation. That same year, Macdonald was a delegate to the Charlottetown and Quebec Conferences, and became the principal author of the Confederation resolutions agreed upon in Quebec. He was chairman of the London Conference (1866–67) and played a pivotal role in bringing about Confederation.

Macdonald became Canada's first prime minister when the Conservative party won a majority of seats in Parliament following the first post-Confederation general election in 1867. Though he was re-elected in 1872, Macdonald's second administration was marred by the "Pacific Scandal" in 1873, when the Liberal opposition charged that his government had awarded the CPR contract to Sir Hugh Allan in return for political contributions. An investigation into these charges was held, and the government resigned on Nov. 5, 1873.

Macdonald's Liberal-Conservatives were re-elected Sept. 17, 1878, and Macdonald remained prime minister until his death in Ottawa on June 6, 1891.

During his first administration, the Dominion of Canada expanded to include the provinces of British Columbia, Prince Edward Island and the newly created Manitoba.

The building of the transcontinental railway is the most memorable feature of his second administration, but other accomplishments include the establishment of the "National Policy"—a system of tariff protection to aid the development of Canadian industries (1879)—and the increased settlement of the Western provinces that followed the construction of the railway.

■ Alexander Mackenzie

Alexander Mackenzie was born on Jan. 28, 1822 near Dunkeld, Perthshire, Scotland. He left school and became a stonemason at the age of 14.

He emigrated to Canada in 1842 and became a contractor at Lambton, Ontario, and then editor of the *Lambton Shield*. From 1866–74, he was a major in the 27th Lambton Battalion Volunteer Infantry.

In 1861, Mackenzie was elected to the Legislative Assembly of the Province of Canada, where he gave his support to the Confederation plan. When George Brown was defeated in the 1867 election, Mackenzie became *de facto* leader of the Opposition, though it was not until after the 1872 elections that he formally accepted this title.

It was Mackenzie who led the attack on the Macdonald administration over the "Pacific Scandal"; when Macdonald resigned on Nov. 5, 1873, Mackenzie became prime minister.

During his 5-year term of office, Mackenzie introduced changes to election laws that included the secret ballot and universal male suffrage. The Supreme Court of Canada was established under Mackenzie's rule, and Wilfrid Laurier was brought into Mackenzie's cabinet.

Severe economic depression plagued Canada during the Mackenzie years, and in 1878, his Liberal party was routed at the polls.

Mackenzie retained his own seat, however, and was still a member of Parliament when he died Apr. 17, 1892, in Toronto.

■ Sir John Abbott

Sir John Joseph Caldwell Abbott was born Mar. 12, 1821, at St. Andrews, Lower Canada—the first prime minister to be born on Canadian soil.

After taking his law degree from University of McGill College, he was admitted to the bar

in 1847 and practised law in Montreal. From 1855–80 he was dean of the Faculty of Law, McGill University.

Abbott was elected to the Legislative Assembly of the Province of Canada in 1857, re-elected in 1861 and 1863, and sat until Confederation. He was then elected to the House of Commons in 1867, 1872 and 1874. He was last elected in 1882 and appointed to the Senate on May 12, 1887.

When Sir John A. Macdonald died in 1891, Abbott—though a senator—inherited the Conservative leadership. The three other leading Conservatives—Langevin, Tupper and Thompson—were unwilling or unable to assume the post. Abbott held the office of prime minister from June 16, 1891, until his resignation on Nov. 24, 1892. He died in Montreal on Oct. 30, 1893.

■ Sir John Thompson

Sir John Sparrow David Thompson was born in Halifax, NS, on Nov. 10, 1845.

Thompson was called to the Nova Scotia bar in 1865, and was instrumental in founding Dalhousie Law School in 1883, where he eventually became a lecturer.

In May 1882, Thompson became premier of Nova Scotia, but when his government was defeated two months later, he retired from politics and became a judge of the Supreme Court of Nova Scotia.

Prime Minister Macdonald coaxed Thompson back into politics, making him Minister of

Justice in 1885. When Macdonald died in 1891, Thompson declined the leadership, fearing that his conversion to Roman Catholicism in 1870 would hinder his party's fortunes. However, the following year, Thompson changed his mind, and on Dec. 5, 1892, he became prime minister.

Though prime minister for just over 2 years, Thompson was largely responsible for the establishment of the Criminal Code and penetentiary reforms. He very nearly succeeded in bringing Newfoundland into Confederation in 1894, and successfully negotiated fisheries clauses in the Treaty of Washington.

He died while still in office on Dec. 12, 1894.

■ Sir Mackenzie Bowell

Mackenzie Bowell was born at Rickinghall, Suffolk, England, on Dec. 27, 1823, and came to Canada in 1832. In 1834, he became an

apprentice printer at Belleville, Upper Canada and was later editor and proprietor of the Belleville *Intelligencer*. He served in the militia of the United Province of Canada during the American Civil War and the Fenian raids of 1866.

Bowell was elected to the House of Commons in 1867 for Hastings North, Ont., and was re-elected in 1872, 1874, 1878, 1887 and 1891.

As spokesman for the Orange Association of British America, Bowell was instrumental in having Louis Riel expelled from the Commons in 1874.

On Dec. 5, 1892, Bowell was appointed to the Senate and, after Thompson's death in 1894, was invited by the Governor General to form a government.

Perhaps the thorniest problem facing Prime Minister Bowell was the Manitoba Schools question. In 1890, Manitoba legislation had withdrawn school privileges from the Roman Catholic and primarily French minority in that province. By the time Bowell assumed office, attempts were being made to restore those lost school privileges by federal remedial legislation. Bowell was not equal to the political challenges facing him; he lost control of his cabinet ministers, several of whom eventually called for his resignation. Bowell denounced this cabinet rebellion as a "nest of traitors," but eventually he resigned on Apr. 27, 1896. He died in Belleville, Ont., on Dec. 10, 1917, at age 93.

■ Sir Charles Tupper

Charles Tupper was born at Amherst, NS, July 2, 1821. He took a degree in medicine at Edinburgh University. At the age of 22, he began practising medicine in Amherst and became the first president of the Canadian Medical Association (1867–70).

The 1855 election that brought him to the Legislative Assembly of Nova Scotia was declared void on Feb. 24, 1857. He was subsequently re-elected in a by-election that same year and was elected again in 1859 and 1863.

Tupper was active in the Confederation movement, and was a delegate to the

Charlottetown, Quebec and London Conferences. He was elected to the House of Commons in 1867 and re-elected 1870, 1872, 1874, 1878 and 1882. He resigned in 1884 and served as High Commissioner for Canada in the United Kingdom from May 28 of that year to Jan. 26, 1887. In 1887, he was re-elected to the House of Commons, but resigned the following year and again served as High Commissioner from May 23, 1888, to Jan. 14, 1896.

In 1896, following the rebellion of Bowell's cabinet, Tupper became *de facto* leader of the administration until Bowell formally resigned on Apr. 27, 1896. At that time, the Governor General invited Tupper to form the government. Parliament was dissolved shortly thereafter and in the election that followed on June 23, Tupper's Conservatives were defeated. Tupper stayed on as leader of the Opposition until Feb. 5, 1901, then retired from public life. He died Oct. 30, 1915 at Bexley Heath, Kent, England.

■ Sir Wilfrid Laurier

Wilfrid Laurier was born at St-Lin, Canada East, Nov. 20, 1841. He first attended College de l'Assomption and then took his degree from McGill University.

He was called to the bar of Lower Canada in 1865. He practised law at Montreal and at Arthabaskaville, Que.

First elected to the Legislative Assembly of Quebec in 1871, Laurier resigned in Jan. 1874 and later that year was elected to the House of Commons. He became leader of the Liberal Opposition in June 1887. Then, following the 1896 election that gave his party a 23-seat majority, Laurier became Canada's first French-speaking prime minister on July 11, 1896. The Liberals retained power in 1900 and won a landslide election victory in 1904.

Immigration increased during his time in office as Clifford Sifton, Laurier's minister of the interior from 1896–1905, mounted a powerful campaign to attract immigrants from Britain, the United States and Europe. In 1905, Laurier created the provinces of Alberta and Saskatchewan and established the boundaries of Manitoba. During Laurier's years in power the Canadian West became a major world wheat producer. In 1909, Laurier established the External Affairs Department.

His government's controversial support for the creation of a Canadian navy, and his unpopular attempt to enter into a reciprocal trade agreement with the United States (an agreement that would have reduced or eliminated duties on many imported goods) spelled trouble for Laurier in 1911. His party was

defeated in the Sept. 21 election. He remained an Opposition M.P. until his death on Feb. 17, 1919, in Ottawa.

■ Sir Robert Borden

Robert Laird Borden was born at Grand Pré, NS, June 26, 1854. At age 14 he gave up formal schooling to become an assistant master in classical studies. He taught classics and mathematics in New Jersey in 1873, before returning to Nova Scotia to study law. He was admitted to the Nova Scotia bar in 1878 and practised first in Halifax, then in Kentville, NS.

Borden was elected to the House of Commons in 1896 and 1900 and became leader of the Conservative party on Feb. 6, 1901. He served as leader of the Opposition until 1911, when he led his party to victory in the Sept. 21 election.

Borden was prime minister throughout World War I, and during the war years his government was accused of scandal over British munitions contracts and its staunch support of the Ross Rifle—a weapon known to jam in battle. Borden's government introduced the first federal income tax, nationalized Canadian railways and introduced conscription in 1917.

In the election of Dec. 17, 1917, Borden led a re-organized Union Government made up of

Conservatives and pro-conscription Liberals to victory. Borden headed the Canadian delegation at the Paris Peace Conference in 1919, where the autonomy of Canada and other dominions within the British Commonwealth was successfully established. He resigned on July 10, 1920, and died in Ottawa June 10, 1937.

■ Arthur Meighen

Arthur Meighen was born at Anderson, Ont., June 16, 1874. Following his graduation from university in 1896, Meighen taught high school for a year, then moved to Winnipeg in 1898 to study law. He was called to the Manitoba bar in 1902, and practised at Portage La Prairie.

He was first elected to the House of Commons in 1908, re-elected in 1911, 1913 and 1917, defeated in 1921, and re-elected in 1922 and 1925.

Meighen first achieved national prominence in 1913 when he helped devise a closure rule which permitted the government to end debate on a bill which was to effect a $35-million contribution to the British navy. Prior to closure, the bill had been obstructed by a fierce and protracted Opposition party blockade.

Prime Minister Borden appointed Meighen his solicitor general on Oct. 2, 1915, and

Meighen held this post for two years. A strong supporter of conscription, Meighen essentially drafted Canada's 1917 conscription bill, and put it into operation. He was also the chief draughtsman of the Wartime Elections Act.

When Borden resigned on July 10, 1920, Meighen succeeded him as prime minister. In the general election of Dec. 6, 1921, Meighen's party was defeated. Though his Conservatives won the most seats in the election of Oct. 29, 1925, the Liberals were able to stay in power with the support of Progressive and Labour members.

Following the resignation of William Lyon Mackenzie King's government on June 28, 1926, the Governor General invited Meighen to form a new ministry. This government was less than three months old, however, when it was defeated in the House of Commons (by only one vote) and Canadians again went to the polls.

Following a Liberal victory in the election of Sept. 14, 1926, Meighen resigned as Conservative leader in the House of Commons. He was appointed to the Senate on Feb. 3, 1932, during Richard Bennett's ministry and became government leader in the Senate. Then, following King's victory in 1935, he became Senate Opposition leader.

On Nov. 12, 1941, he once again became leader of the Conservative party, but failed in his bid to win a seat in the Commons in a federal by-election on Feb. 2, 1942. Following this defeat, he retired from politics and resumed his law practice in Toronto where he died Aug. 5, 1960.

■ Mackenzie King

William Lyon Mackenzie King, grandson of William Lyon Mackenzie, was born in Kitchener (then called Berlin) on Dec. 17, 1874.

He took his B.A. and law degrees from the University of Toronto and also studied at the University of Chicago and Harvard University.

He served as deputy minister of labour from 1900–08.

He was first elected to the House of Commons in 1908, and succeeded Laurier as leader of the Liberal party in 1919. King became prime minister when the Liberals won the general election of Dec. 6, 1921.

Though Meighen's Conservatives won a majority of seats in the general election of Oct. 29, 1925, King stayed in office with the help of Progressive and Labour members who supported his proposed tariff reductions and old-age pension legislation. King had lost his York North seat in the 1925 election but returned to the House of Commons as the member for Prince Albert, Sask., following a by-election on Feb. 15, 1926. King's government was shaken in 1926 by the revelation that the customs department was tainted with corruption and incompetence. In the furor that followed, King lost the support of many members of Parliament and, although never technically defeated in the House of Commons, decided that he could no longer hold his minority government. He appealed to Governor General Lord Byng to dissolve Parliament, even though the government had not been defeated. Byng refused. King subsequently resigned on June 28, 1926, and the Governor General invited Arthur Meighen to form a government which was subsequently defeated in the House of Commons.

In the general election of Sept. 14, 1926, King's Liberals regained power and held it until 1930. But the disastrous fall in the price of wheat and other Canadian exports in 1929 soured Canadians on their government, and King was defeated by R.B. Bennett's Conservatives in the election of July 28, 1930.

Five years later, King was back in the prime minister's office, following the Liberal victory in the general election of Oct. 14, 1935. In the coming years, King, an ardent supporter of Canada's autonomy within the British Commonwealth, was faced with the issue of Canada's participation in an impending European war. To soothe French-Canadian concerns over Canadian support of Great Britain, King promised there would be no conscription; Canada declared war in September 1939. Later, however, heavy casualties in France and Italy in 1944 prompted King to break his promise and send conscripts overseas.

King's government began introducing postwar recovery legislation even before peace was declared. These measures included recon-

struction plans and social security schemes such as mother's allowances.

King resigned as prime minister on Nov. 15, 1948, supporting Louis St Laurent as his successor. In poor health in his final years, King died July 22, 1950, at Kingsmere, his estate in Wright County, Que.

■ Richard Bennett

Richard Bedford Bennett was born at Hopewell, NB, July 3, 1870. Bennett studied law at Dalhousie University. He read and practised law in Chatham, NB, from 1893–97, before moving to Calgary where he entered a legal partnership with Senator James A. Lougheed.

Bennett was first elected to the House of Commons in 1911. He served as minister of justice in Arthur Meighen's 1921 cabinet, and minister of finance and minister of mines in Meighen's 1926 government.

Bennett was chosen to replace Meighen as Conservative leader at the party convention in

Winnipeg in 1927. He became prime minister following the Conservative victory in the election of July 28, 1930.

Bennett had the task of governing Canada during the worst years of the Depression. Virtually every measure his government attempted ended in failure. High unemployment levels continued despite Bennett's efforts to reduce them. Negotiations for a reciprocity treaty with the United States did not succeed. A plan of preferential tariffs agreed to in 1930 at the Imperial Conference did little to ease Canada's economic woes.

Then, in 1935, near the end of his term, Bennett took an unexpected step to the political left. He proclaimed that "the old order is gone" and that it was time for a new economic system. That new system was to include a state-planned economy, new unemployment and health insurance legislation and old-age pension laws.

In the election of Oct. 14, 1935, Bennett's Conservatives suffered a devastating defeat, winning just 39 seats. Bennett remained in Opposition until 1937, when he retired to England. There he was given the title Viscount Bennett of Mickelham, Hopewell and Calgary.

Despite the overwhelming problems of the Great Depression, Bennett's term saw the creation of the Canadian Radio Broadcasting Corporation (the predecessor to the CBC) and the Bank of Canada. As well, it was during Bennett's tenure that the Statute of Westminster gave Canada increased autonomy in 1931.

Bennett died June 27, 1947.

■ Louis St Laurent

Louis Stephen St Laurent was born at Compton, Que., Feb. 1, 1882. Called to the Quebec bar in 1905, he practised law in Quebec City, and became Professor of Law at Université Laval. He was elected president of the Canadian Bar Association in 1930.

St Laurent became justice minister in Mackenzie King's cabinet on Dec. 10, 1941. On Feb. 9, 1942, he was elected to the House of Commons in a by-election for Quebec East.

Originally planning to hold his cabinet post only during the war, St Laurent was persuaded to stay on. On Dec. 10, 1946, he became secretary of state for external affairs. A firm believer in collective security, St Laurent was one of the architects of the North Atlantic Treaty Organization (NATO). On Aug. 7, 1948, he accepted his party's nomination to be King's successor, and on Nov. 15 became prime minister.

While in power St Laurent ended the practice of appealing court cases to the Judicial Committee of the Privy Council in England, and made the Supreme Court of Canada the final Canadian court of appeal. He won the acceptance of a new apportionment of taxes in 1956 and, in negotiation with President Truman, laid the foundation for a US–Canada agreement to develop the St Lawrence Seaway.

In 1958, he retired and returned to Quebec City to practise law. He died July 25, 1973.

■ John Diefenbaker

John George Diefenbaker was born at Neustadt, Ont., Sept. 18, 1895. He received his B.A. from the University of Saskatchewan in 1915 and his M.A. one year later.

After the outbreak of World War I, he joined the Canadian Officers' Training Corps, and served overseas as a lieutenant with the 105th 'Saskatoon Fusiliers' Regiment from 1916 to 1917.

Returning to Saskatchewan, he took his law degree from the University of Saskatchewan in 1919 and established a law practice at Wakaw. He later moved to Prince Albert.

After several unsuccessful attempts to gain a seat, first in the federal, then in Saskatchewan's provincial parliament, Diefenbaker was finally elected to the House of Commons in 1940. He was a candidate for leadership of the Progressive Conservative Party at the 1942 and 1948 conventions, but did not win the nomination until Dec. 14, 1956.

The PCs won the election of June 10, 1957 by a slim margin, and on June 21, John Diefenbaker officially became prime minister. A year later, he called an election, hoping to turn his Conservative minority government into a clear majority. He was overwhelmingly successful, winning 208 of the 265 seats in the Mar. 31, 1958, election. He fared less well in the 1962 election, when only 116 PCs were elected, and in the general election of 1963, a Liberal victory relegated Diefenbaker to the role of Opposition leader. Diefenbaker remained Conservative leader until Sept. 1967, when he was replaced by Robert Stanfield.

The Diefenbaker years (1957–63) saw the passage of the Canadian Bill of Rights, a "roads-to- resources" program to encourage the development of northern resources, legislation providing support for agriculture, encouragement of technical training and improved health and welfare programs. Regional development was emphasized by significant public works such as construction of the South Saskatchewan Dam, and simultaneous translation was introduced in the House of Commons.

Diefenbaker died Aug. 16, 1979, at his home in Rockliffe Park, Ottawa.

■ Lester Pearson

Lester Bowles Pearson was born at Newtonbrook, Ont., on Apr. 23, 1897. He took his B.A. at the University of Toronto and his M.A. at Oxford University.

After serving overseas in World War I, he became a history professor at the University of Toronto, where he taught from 1924–1928. He joined Canada's foreign service in 1928, became Canada's ambassador to the UN in 1945, was appointed under-secretary of state for external affairs in 1946 and accepted the invitations of King and St Laurent to become minister of external affairs in Sept. 1948.

In 1956, following the Anglo-French-Israeli invasion of Egypt, Pearson's work at the United Nations helped establish a UN Emergency Force which kept peace on the Israeli–Egyptian border for the next decade. His settlement of the Suez crisis brought him the Nobel Peace Prize in 1957—the only time a Canadian has been so honoured.

Pearson was chosen leader of the Liberal party Jan. 15, 1958. In the general election of

Apr. 8, 1963, the Liberals won 129 seats in the House of Commons, and Pearson became the leader of a minority government.

In the 1965 election, the Liberals made slight gains, but were still short of a majority. Pearson announced his resignation in Dec. 1967 and, in Apr. 1968, was succeeded by Pierre Trudeau.

Under Pearson, the old age pension was extended and a national health plan created. He secured the adoption of a national flag and established the Royal Commission on Bilingualism and Biculturalism.

Though he retired in 1968, his international reputation prompted the World Bank to commission him to prepare a report on international aid programs.

He died in Ottawa, Dec. 27, 1972.

■ Pierre Trudeau

Pierre Elliott Trudeau was born in Montreal on Oct. 18, 1919. He attended the University of Montreal, Harvard University, Université de Paris and the London School of Economics. He was called to the Quebec bar in 1943. From 1949–51, he was a member of the Privy Council staff in Ottawa. In 1950, he co-founded the magazine *Cité Libre*. From 1952–62, he practised law and was a journalist and broadcaster in Montreal. From 1962–65, he was a law professor at the University of Montreal.

First elected to the House of Commons in 1965, Trudeau was named justice minister in Lester Pearson's cabinet in 1967. The following year, he won the Liberal leadership and became prime minister Apr. 19, 1968. In the general election of the same year, the Liberals won a solid majority.

During his first four years in power, Trudeau faced the "FLQ Crisis"—the kidnapping of British diplomat James Cross and Quebec cabinet minister Pierre Laporte by the radical separatist organization Front de libération du Québec. (Laporte was later murdered.) In response he invoked the War Measures Act, a statute giving the state broad powers of arrest and detention.

In the general election of 1972, Trudeau returned to power with a minority government. In 1974, he regained a majority.

In the general election of 1979, the Progressive Conservatives under Joe Clark won a narrow victory and were able to form a minority government. Trudeau announced his intention to retire, but when the Clark government fell later that year, Trudeau led the Liberals in the election and won a majority on Feb. 18, 1980.

Trudeau's final term in office was devoted to constitutional reform which, for the first time, allowed Canada's Parliament to amend the constitution without appeal to the UK government. A constitutionally-entrenched Charter of Rights and Freedoms was also introduced.

Trudeau's introduction of a National Energy Program led to bitter disputes between the federal government and the energy-producing provinces, particularly Alberta. The NEP was aimed at increasing Canadian control of the oil industry, promoting energy self-sufficiency and generating more federal revenues in the energy sector.

During his final year as prime minister Trudeau launched a world peace initiative, visiting more than 40 world leaders to appeal for peace and an end to the nuclear arms race.

In June of 1984, Trudeau resigned. He was succeeded by John Turner and left politics, eventually joining a Montreal law firm.

■ Joe Clark

Charles Joseph "Joe" Clark was born at High River, Alta., on June 5, 1939. He was educated at the University of Alberta.

Clark was first elected to the House of Commons in 1972. In 1976 he became leader of the Progressive Conservative party and, in the general election of 1979, won enough seats to form a minority government. At 39, Clark was Canada's youngest prime minister. But his minority government fell in Dec. 1979 on a vote of non-confidence on its proposed budget. In the Feb. 1980 election that followed, the Liberals returned to power.

At a national general meeting of the Conservative party in Jan. 1983, Clark received the support of only two-thirds of the delegates and called for a national party leadership convention. In June 1983, Clark lost the leadership to Brian Mulroney on the 4th ballot. He remained an MP and, when Mulroney became prime minister in 1984, Clark joined the cabinet as secretary of state for external affairs.

In 1991, he was appointed as minister responsible for constitutional affairs and given the task of succeeding where the Meech Lake Accord had failed. Late 1991 and the first half of 1992 were marked by weeks of cross-country constitutional negotiations under Clark's guidance. In August 1992 the Charlottetown Accord—an agreement to amend the Constitution Act of 1982—was agreed upon by all first ministers. The text of the agreement was presented to Canadians and a national referendum was held on Oct. 26, 1992, on the issue of whether or not to approve the deal. The agreement was rejected by the majority of voters across the country.

Clark left federal politics after the 1993 election. In 1998, he re-entered public life when Jean Charest vacated the federal Conservative leadership to run in Quebec's provincial election. On Nov. 14, 1998, Clark was re-elected federal Conservative leader.

■ John Turner

John Napier Turner was born at Richmond, Surrey, England on June 7, 1929. He attended the University of British Columbia, Oxford University and Université de Paris. He was called to the bar in England in 1953 and the bar in Quebec in 1954. He lectured for a time in the Faculty of Commerce at Sir George Williams University.

First elected to the House of Commons in 1962, Turner entered Lester Pearson's cabinet in 1965. He became minister of consumer and corporate affairs in 1967. In 1968, he was a candidate for the Liberal leadership, finishing 3rd on the final ballot.

In 1968, Turner was appointed minister of justice in Pierre Trudeau's cabinet. In 1972, he became minister of finance, a post he held until his resignation in Sept. 1975. In Feb. 1976 he left politics and joined a Toronto law firm.

Turner remained in private practice until Trudeau's retirement in 1984, when he successfully ran for leader of the Liberal party and became prime minister on June 30, though he did not have a seat in the House of Commons. He dissolved Parliament July 9, and in the ensuing general election the Liberals were overwhelmingly defeated by the Progressive Conservatives.

As leader of the Opposition, Turner used the Liberal majority in the Senate to block passage of the Conservatives' free trade legislation and force an election on the issue in 1988. The Conservatives won the election and were able to form another majority government.

Early in 1989, Turner announced plans to step down as leader; in June 1990, he was succeeded by Jean Chrétien.

■ Brian Mulroney

Martin Brian Mulroney was born at Baie Comeau, Que., Mar. 20, 1939. He attended St. Francis Xavier University and Université Laval. Called to the bar of Quebec in 1965, Mulroney practised law in Montreal. In 1976, he joined the Iron Ore Company of Canada as executive vice-president and was elected company president the following year.

Mulroney made an unsuccessful bid for the Progressive Conservative party leadership in 1976. In 1983 he ran again, defeating the incumbent leader, Joe Clark, on the 4th ballot.

A by-election for the Maritime riding of Central Nova brought Mulroney into Parliament as leader of the Opposition. In the general election of 1984, he led the Conservatives to victory, winning the largest number of seats (211) in Canadian history.

Mulroney's major initiatives between 1984 and 1988 were the Meech Lake Accord—a package of constitutional changes designed to end Quebec's boycott of the 1982 constitutional reform—and the negotiation of a free trade agreement with the United States.

In 1988, with free trade the central election issue, Mulroney won a second majority government. The free trade agreement subsequently received final approval and took effect in 1989.

His term from 1988 to 1993 was marked by intense negotiations to bring about a new constitutional agreement to replace the Meech Lake Accord which was not ratified by all provinces by the June 1990 deadline. Agreement was reached amongst federal and provincial officials in what became known as the Charlottetown Accord, but the proposals were rejected in a national referendum held on Oct. 26, 1992.

The Conservatives under Mulroney continued their free trade initiative and finalized a North American free trade deal (NAFTA) with the US and Mexico.

Mulroney announced his intention to retire in February 1993 and on June 25, 1993 he was replaced by Kim Campbell, newly-elected leader of the Conservative party.

■ Kim Campbell

Avril Phaedra (Kim) Campbell was born Mar. 10, 1947 in Port Alberni, BC. She attended the University of British Columbia, earning an honours degree in political science.

After an academic career in BC, she studied law at UBC. In Sept. 1985, she joined BC Premier William Bennett's office as a policy advisor. In May 1986, Campbell ran in the provincial election and won a seat in the legislature, representing Vancouver/Point Grey. She served in the provincial legislature until October 1988 when she resigned her seat to contest the federal riding of Vancouver Centre. An ardent defender of free trade, Campbell joined Prime Minister Mulroney's cabinet with the Indian Affairs and Northern Development portfolio.

In 1990 Campbell became the first woman promoted to the Attorney General and Justice post. In January of 1993 she became Canada's first female defence minister and a candidate in the Conservative leadership contest that year. On June 13, 1993, she was elected leader on the second ballot; on June 25, she was sworn in as Canada's first female prime minister. In the election of Oct. 1993, however, the Conservatives lost all but two seats in the House of Commons. Campbell's tenure as prime minister ended on Nov. 4; she stepped down as federal Conservative leader on Dec. 14, 1993.

■ Jean Chrétien

Jean Chrétien was born in Shawinigan, Quebec, on Jan. 11, 1934. He studied law at Laval University and was called to the bar of Quebec in 1958.

Chrétien was first elected to the House of Commons in 1963 and after re-election in 1965 served as parliamentary secretary to the prime minister (1965) and the finance minister (1966). He became minister of national revenue in 1968; after the June 1968 election, he became responsible for Indian affairs and northern development. In 1974, he was appointed president of the treasury board; in 1976, he served as minister of industry, trade and commerce. In 1977, he was named finance minister; in 1980 he became justice minister and attorney general and also served as minister of state for social development. Chrétien played an important role in patriating the Constitution. In 1982, he became minister of energy, mines and resources; in 1984, he became deputy prime minister and secretary of state for external affairs.

In 1986, Chrétien left public life, returning after his election as Liberal leader in 1990. After his re-election to the House in a December by-election in Beausejour, he took his seat as leader of the Opposition. In the federal election of October 1993, Chrétien led his party to a majority victory.

FOCUS ON...

Power in Ottawa

Selected politicians, civil servants and judges wield great power in the nation's capital: the prime minister and cabinet ministers, deputy ministers and their assistants, and the nine justices of the Supreme Court.

The **prime minister** is the most powerful figure in government: head of government; leader of the majority party in the House of Commons (when a majority government has been elected); and chair of the Cabinet. The prime minister's authority also derives from unwritten conventions such as those related to party discipline. (Party discipline in particular ensures that all members of the governing party—from cabinet ministers to backbenchers—unanimously support the government's policies and legislative agenda. The prime minister's power to enforce this—and expel members who do not support the government—ensures that majority governments will stay in power during their mandate.)

The prime minister also has the power to fill government posts, including appointments to the Cabinet, the Senate, Canadian embassies and the judiciary. Heads of royal commissions, Crown corporations and federal regulatory agencies are also appointed by the prime minister. In addition, the prime minister recommends candidates for Governor General and the lieutenant-governors to the Queen.

The prime minister and staff set Parliament's legislative agenda, selecting the issues to be addressed. The PM can create, reform and abolish cabinet posts, royal commissions, Crown corporations and federal civil service departments. The prime minister also decides (within a five year period) when to dissolve Parliament and call elections.

Cabinet ministers rank below the prime minister in importance. They act as the chief executives of assigned federal departments and approve all government policies coming from their department. Cabinet ministers direct their staff to write new departmental policies, draft bills for debate in Parliament and pass orders-in-council—laws approved by the Governor General but never debated in Parliament. Collectively, cabinet shapes the federal budget, raising, allocating and spending billions of tax dollars annually. Within the Cabinet, some ministers wield more power than others. These include the heads of the departments that affect all citizens (e.g., finance, industry, justice and national revenue). The **deputy prime minister** stands in for the prime minister when the PM is absent. The **government house leader** ensures the timely passage of bills through the House of Commons and the **whip** supervises the attendance of MPs.

Deputy ministers are the most important federal civil servants. They are appointed career bureaucrats who manage their departments, draft the laws and policy that affect their departments, and advise cabinet ministers on management and policy proposals. Deputy ministers possess years of experience, specialized knowledge and the resources of large organizations. They also control access to their minister.

The chief justice and eight associate justices of the **Supreme Court of Canada** are the most powerful judges in the land. Independent of Parliament's executives and legislators, the Supreme Court interprets and applies the law as set down by the legislators. Since 1875, the justices have ruled on the division of federal and provincial powers; since 1949 they have constituted Canada's highest court of appeal. Before the passage of the Canadian Charter of Rights and Freedoms in 1982, Parliament was supreme and the Supreme Court rarely overturned laws. After 1982, the provisions of the Charter gave the justices the power to interpret and enforce Charter guarantees in relation to federal and provincial legislation. The justices now strike down unconstitutional provisions in federal and provincial laws.

GOVERNMENT OF CANADA

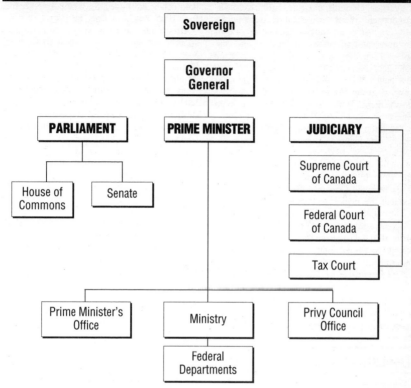

Canada is an independent, self-governing democracy whose form of government is a constitutional monarchy. There are three types of government power: legislative, executive and judicial. In Canada the legislative and executive powers are joined, while the judiciary remains separate. The executive proposes legislation, presents budgets and implements laws; the legislature adopts laws and votes on recommendations for taxes or other revenue; the judiciary interprets the laws.

■ The Monarchy

The British monarch (since June 2, 1953 Queen Elizabeth II) is Canada's official head of state through which the entire authority of the government is set in motion and in whose name laws are enacted. The Queen's role is set out in the *Constitution Act,* (formerly the *British North America Act, 1867),* and that same act gives the monarch ultimate

authority over Canada's armed forces.

In practice, however, the Queen has little or no part to play in Canadian government. She appoints the Governor General, but does so only on the prime minister's recommendation. Once appointed, it is the Governor General who performs the monarch's duties, and these duties have been mainly ceremonial for many years. Only during royal visits does the Queen carry out those functions normally performed in her name by the Governor General, such as the opening of Parliament.

■ The Governor General

The Governor General is selected by the prime minister and formally appointed by the Queen to act as her representative in Canada. The appointment is usually for five years but has sometimes been extended to seven.

Bills passed in the House of Commons and

Senate do not become law until the Governor General has given them royal assent. The Governor General executes all orders-in-council and other state documents, appoints all superior court judges (on the advice of Cabinet) and summons, prorogues and dissolves Parliament (on the advice of the prime minister). Also, the Governor General invites the leader of the political party with the most support in the House of Commons to form a government. Thus, that leader becomes prime minister.

The Imperial Conferences of 1926 and 1930 established that the Governor General was not the representative or agent of the British government and should act only on the advice of the Canadian prime minister and Cabinet. Therefore, the Governor General is obliged to respect the principle of responsible government and to follow the wishes of Canada's elected representatives. Because of this, the role of the Governor General has become largely symbolic, with duties that are chiefly ceremonial.

Two members of the Royal Family have held the post: the Duke of Connaught (1911–16) and the Earl of Athlone (1940–46). The first Canadian Governor General was Vincent Massey (1952– 59).

The Legislature

Canada's legislature or Parliament consists of the Queen, an upper house, known as the Senate, and the House of Commons. Senators are appointed by the Governor General on the advice of the prime minister; the seats in the Senate are distributed on a regional basis; originally, there were 72 senators, but through the years the Senate has increased as the number of provinces and the population have grown. In 1975 the Senate was increased to 104 members; in 1990 Prime Minister Brian Mulroney employed a never-before-used section of the *Constitution Act* to increase the number to temporarily 112. The House of Commons is an elected assembly in which each member represents one of 301 electoral districts distributed according to population.

■ The Senate

The Senate is the Upper House of the Canadian Parliament through which all legislation must pass before it becomes law. Its members, appointed by the Governor General on the recommendation of the prime minister, hold office until age 75. (If appointed before June 1965 they hold office for life).

After 1999, there were 105 Senate seats apportioned on a regional basis: 24 from the Maritime provinces (Nova Scotia, 10; New Brunswick, 10; Prince Edward Island, 4); 24 from Quebec; 24 from Ontario; 24 from the Western provinces (Manitoba, 6; Saskatchewan, 6; Alberta, 6; British Columbia, 6); 6 from Newfoundland; 1 each from the Yukon, Northwest Territories and Nunavut.

To be eligible for Senate appointment, a person must be a Canadian citizen, at least 30 years old, a resident of the province for which he or she is appointed, possess land in that province with an unencumbered value of $4 000 and have a net estate of $4 000. A Senator for Quebec must either be resident in the division for which he or she is appointed, or have property qualification there.

Technically, the Senate's legislative powers are equal to those of the House of Commons with two restrictions: first, on certain constitutional amendments, the Senate may delay resolutions of the House of Commons for up to 180 days, but cannot defeat them; second, the Senate cannot initiate money bills.

In practice, however, the Senate's chief role is to provide technical reviews of legislation proposed in the House of Commons rather than to initiate political action. These reviews are done by Senate committees, which inspect each bill clause-by-clause and hear evidence from groups or individuals who may be affected by the proposed legislation.

Historically, the Senate rarely used its powers to impede legislation originating from the elected House of Commons. From 1984 to 1990, however, the Liberal-dominated Senate attempted several times to stall or block legislation approved by the Conservative majority in the House of Commons. In 1990, when the Senate blocked his government's goods and services tax, Mulroney temporarily increased the size of the Senate and added eight new Conservatives, ensuring that the measure would be made law.

In recent years, there have been repeated calls, especially from the West, for constitutional reform which would include an elected Senate with more representation from the Western provinces and Newfoundland. Plans for discussions leading to a Senate overhaul are now part of other constitutional discussions.

■ The House of Commons

The House of Commons is Canada's 301-member elected federal assembly. Its members are chosen in general elections held at least once every five years. By-elections are held if a member dies or resigns between general elections.

All bills governing matters within federal jurisdiction must be passed by a majority of members of Parliament to become law.

Members of Parliament usually belong to a political party and will normally vote with that party on any proposed legislation. Occasionally, members will break with their party on a vote and will sometimes leave the party they were affiliated with when elected to sit as independents or to join another political party within the House. Members of Parliament can also be elected as independent candidates who do not belong to a political party.

The **prime minister** is the leader of the political party able to command the support of a majority of the members of the House of Commons. If no party holds a clear majority of seats, a "minority government" is formed, usually led by the party with the most seats in Parliament, provided it has enough support from the other parties to enable it to pass legislation.

When the House of Commons is in session it convenes at two o'clock daily and 11 o'clock on Fridays when the Speaker of the House takes the chair. After the mace is laid on the table in front of the Speaker and the daily prayer is read, business commences. Members of the government sit to the Speaker's right and the Opposition sits on the left. The leaders of other opposition parties sit on the left farther away from the Speaker's chair.

An important feature of Parliament is the daily question period at which time members question Cabinet ministers about their policies and actions. But most of Parliament's time is spent discussing proposed legislation introduced as "bills". Any member may introduce a bill, although this is usually done by a member of Cabinet. After readings in the House and detailed examination in committee, the bill will go for "third reading" in the House and if passed, will be forwarded to the Senate.

When a major piece of legislation introduced by the government is defeated in the House of Commons, the government is obliged to resign. The Governor General may then call on the leader of the Opposition to form a government but, in most cases, will call a general election so that the electorate can decide which party has the most public support for its policies.

The Executive

■ The Prime Minister

The prime minister is the pre-eminent figure in Canadian politics. The power and authority of the office come from the fact that the prime minister is the leader of the party (or group of parties) that has control of, if not a clear majority of seats in the House of Commons, at least more seats than any of the other parties. The prime minister is an elected member of parliament as well as national party leader and as such has a mandate to govern via programs and policies and to speak on behalf of Canada.

The prime minister has control over appointments, including appointing (and shifting) cabinet members, senior staff in the public service and parliamentary secretaries; and appointing senators, judges, lieutenant governors, privy councillors, provincial administrators, and speakers of the senate. In addition, the prime minister recommends to the monarchy the appointment of the governor general. The prime minister has the authority to dissolve parliament and can therefore control the timing of an election. The prime minister also controls the organization of government, including the power to: create or shut down crown corporations; create, modify or merge cabinet portfolios and bureaucratic agencies; and appoint royal commissions.

■ The Cabinet

The Cabinet is a group of government ministers who, chosen and led by the prime minister, determine executive policies and are responsible for them to the House of Commons. Cabinet members are usually given responsibility for heading specific areas of the government such as finance or foreign policy and will introduce legislation pertaining to them in the House of Commons. They will also explain or defend government actions when questioned in the House.

Cabinet ministers are generally chosen from members of the government's party in the House of Commons, although Senators are sometimes appointed to provide Cabinet representation from all parts of the country. When Senators join the Cabinet they do not usually head a government department because a Senator is constitutionally forbidden to introduce tax or "money bill" legislation.

There are five categories of cabinet ministers:

1. Department Ministers who assume responsibility for running one or more government departments.

2. Ministers with special parliamentary responsibilities.

3. Ministers without portfolios who do not have responsibility for running a department and are often appointed to balance regional representation in the Cabinet.

4. Ministers of state for designated purposes who formulate and develop new policies outside normal departmental responsibilities.

5. Other ministers of state who may assist departmental ministers, though the departmental minister remains legally responsible for the duties and functions performed by the minister of state.

■ The Privy Council Office

The Privy Council Office is directed by the senior member of the public service, the Clerk of the Privy Council, who also serves as the Secretary to the Cabinet. As part of the executive branch of government, the Office staffs the Cabinet secretariat and provides services to ensure the smooth functioning of the Cabinet and Cabinet meetings. In its advisory capacity, the Privy Council Office advises the Prime Minister on government appointments, relations with Parliament and the Monarchy, the roles and responsibilities of ministers and the organization of government. The Office assists in the co-ordination of policy, ensuring that new proposals are compatible both with existing policy and the government's objectives. During a transition period between governments, the Privy Council Office assists in the winding down of outgoing administrations and the startup of the newly-elected government.

The Privy Council Office's primary responsibilities are to ensure the smooth functioning of the machinery of government and the decision-making process, provide support to the Cabinet, monitor developments throughout the government, and act as a broker to resolve governmental problems.

■ The Treasury Board

The Treasury Board is a committee of the Privy Council that reviews planned expenditures and programs proposed by the various government departments, and assigns priorities to each. The Board is responsible for preparing a long-range and comprehensive fiscal plan that projects government income and expenses for up to four years; it also prepares operational plans for departmental programs. The Board's estimates of the costs of existing programs, major statutory payments (such as transfer payments) and public debt charges form the basis of the Main Estimates, which are tabled by the first of March each year for review by various House committees.

The Treasury Board is also responsible for administrative policy; organization of the public service; and financial, expenditure and personnel management. In 1988, the Board was also given responsibility for the policies and programs of the Official Languages Act. The Board's Secretariat negotiates collective agreements with the federal public service, acting as employer on the government's behalf.

■ Departments

Legislation and government policies are administered through departments, departmental branches and corporations, corporations owned or controlled by the government, special boards and various commissions and advisory bodies. Departments and departmental corporations are accountable to a Cabinet minister and ultimately to Parliament; they perform research, administrative, advisory, supervisory or regulatory roles. Crown corporations usually operate in a competitive or commercial environment and some are accountable to Parliament through a minister as well.

The Canadian Judiciary

■ The Supreme Court of Canada

The Supreme Court of Canada is Canada's highest court of law. It was created by federal statute in 1875. Originally, Supreme Court decisions could be appealed to a special tribunal in England, but such appeals were abolished for criminal cases in 1933 and for civil cases in 1949. Since then, the Supreme Court of Canada has been the court of last resort for every case—criminal or civil— commenced in a Canadian court.

The Supreme Court has jurisdiction to hear appeals from the courts of appeal of each province, as well as from the Federal Court of Canada. The Court is also empowered to consider questions referred to it by the federal cabinet, and to rule on the legality of bills submitted by the government.

The *Constitution Act, 1982,* with its new Canadian Charter of Rights and Freedoms, has expanded the role of the courts in general, and of the Supreme Court in particular. Though it has always been within the power of Canadian courts to declare laws or other government actions invalid, this power had narrow limits prior to 1982. Legislation could only be struck down if the government introducing it had exceeded its legislative authority as defined in the *Constitution Act, 1867* (the BNA Act). In other words, the federal government was not permitted to legislate on matters within provincial legislative authority, and the provincial governments were not permitted to legislate on matters within federal legislative authority. As long as the legislation satisfied that test, it was valid.

But since the *Constitution Act* became law in 1982, the courts have had the power to strike down legislation or invalidate other government actions if they infringe or deny any of the fundamental rights and freedoms recognized by the Charter of Rights and Freedoms. This new power has made Supreme Court judges the watchdogs of Parliament and, ultimately, the guardians of our constitutionally-guaranteed rights. As the highest court in the land, it is the Supreme Court of Canada that has the final word on whether laws violate the Constitution.

The Supreme Court consists of 9 judges, including the Chief Justice. Three of the judges must be appointed from Quebec. By convention (although it is not legally required) 3 have usually been appointed from Ontario, 2 from the West and one from Atlantic Canada. All judges are appointed and paid by the federal government, and may hold office until age 75.

■ Federal Court of Canada

This Court consists of a trial division and a court of appeal and has jurisdiction over a small range of specialized areas such as admiralty law, income tax, patents and customs. Once called the Exchequer Court, the Federal Court is administered by the federal government.

■ Appellate Courts

When a decision of the provincial superior courts is to be appealed, these courts hear the appeal and decide upon it. An appeal is not a new trial; there are rarely any witnesses called and the judges do not rehear the whole case. Instead, they examine written transcripts of the trial and listen to legal arguments presented by the parties' lawyers. The appellate courts are provincial institutions and are called either the Court of Appeal, the Supreme Court Appeal Division or Appellate Division; the judges are appointed by the federal government.

■ Superior Court of Original Jurisdiction

This is the highest court at the provincial level, with jurisdiction to hear all civil and criminal cases, unless a statute specifically says otherwise. The name of the superior court differs among provinces. It can be called either the Court of Queen's Bench, the High Court of Justice or the Supreme Court Trial Division. The judges of these courts are appointed and paid by the federal government.

■ District or County Courts

These trial courts hear all but the most serious criminal matters and civil matters up to a certain dollar value. The judges of these courts are also appointed by the federal government.

■ Provincial Courts

This is the lowest rung of the judicial ladder. The jurisdiction of the provincial courts is limited by statute to the less serious criminal matters and civil cases involving relatively small sums of money. These judges are appointed and paid by the province in which they serve.

■ Federal and Provincial Legislative Authority

Because Canada is a federal state, legislative powers are divided between 2 levels of government: federal and provincial. (Municipal governments only exercise powers delegated to them by the provincial government).

Each level of government has a distinct sphere of authority. With a few exceptions, neither level is permitted to encroach on the legislative authority of the other.

The Constitution Act, 1867 (formerly called the British North America Act, 1867), lists the classes of subject over which the federal and provincial governments have exclusive authority. The federal government, in addition to a general power to make laws for the "peace, order and good government of Canada," has exclusive power in a number of areas including criminal law, unemployment insurance, postal service, regulation of trade, external relations, money and banking, transportation, citizenship, Indian affairs and defence. Matters exclusively within provincial legislative authority include property and civil rights, administration of justice, education, health and welfare, municipal institutions and matters of a merely local or private nature.

Many of the subject classes set out in the Constitution Act, 1867, are broadly worded, and considerable debate has arisen over which level of government has authority to pass certain laws. Confusion has also arisen over the proper distribution of powers to regulate matters that could not have been foreseen by the Fathers of Confederation, such as air travel, radio and television broadcasting, etc. These difficulties have led to long political debates and frequently to court challenges which arise when a person adversely affected by a particular law claims that the law is invalid because it is *ultra vires*—beyond the powers of the level of government that enacted it. Prior to the passing of the Constitution Act, 1982, only statutes found to be *ultra vires* could be declared inoperative by the Constitution. Now, there is an additional restraint on the federal parliament and the provincial legisla-

tures to comply with constitutional provisions, including the Canadian Charter of Rights and Freedoms.

■ The Provincial Governments

Canada's provinces have a system of government which parallels that of the federal government in several ways. A premier, like the prime minister, leads the government by virtue of being leader of the party with the most support in the provincial legislature and forms a Cabinet from the elected members of the governing party. Members of a provincial legislature, like members of the federal Parliament, represent constituencies and approve legislation within their constitutional jurisdiction. A lieutenant-governor, like the Governor General, gives royal assent to the laws passed by the legislature.

The major difference between the provincial and federal systems is that the provinces have no equivalent body to Canada's Senate.

■ Government in the Yukon, Northwest Territories and Nunavut

The Yukon, Northwest Territories and Nunavut are governed by elected representatives. Although the administration of each territory is technically in the hands of a commissioner appointed by the federal government, in practice, the commissioners' role has become much like that of the provincial lieutenant-governors' in that they follow the wishes of the territories elected representatives when exercising their authority.

In the Northwest Territories, the legislature consists of 14 elected members who run for office as independents rather than as members of political parties. This assembly selects the territory's political executives: a premier, who must win more than 50 per cent of the vote, and five other cabinet ministers.

In Nunavut, the legislature consists of 19 elected members who also run for office as independents rather than as members of political parties. The territory's executive, which is drawn from this assembly, consists of a premier and seven cabinet ministers.

Yukon has a 17-member legislative assembly which features political parties. The leader of the party supported by a majority of the assembly's elected representatives is named government leader. Executive power is in the hands of an executive council, which functions like a provincial cabinet. Its members are appointed by Yukon's commissioner on the advice of the government leader.

In the territories, the elected bodies have jurisdiction over such areas as education, housing, social services and renewable resources.

In 1990, the Northwest Territories established six aboriginal languages (Dogrib, Chipewyan, Gwich'in, Cree, Slavey and Inuktitut) as Official Languages, in addition to English and French.

■ Mechanics of Government

Formation of Government   General elections to choose House of Commons members occur at least every five years. But they may take place more often if the prime minister decides to call an election or if the governing party loses the support of the majority of members of the House.

Following an election, the Governor General calls upon the leader of the party with the greatest House of Commons support to become prime minister. This is almost always the leader of the party with the most seats in the House but, under unusual circumstances, it could be the leader of another party which is able to gain majority support in Parliament.

The prime minister selects the cabinet, usually from members of his party in the House of Commons. Formally, the prime minister and cabinet act as advisors to the Governor General. In practice, however, they wield executive power and the Governor General's role is mainly ceremonial.

Passage of Legislation   To become law, proposed legislation (known as bills) must be passed by a majority of members in both the House of Commons and the Senate and must then be given royal assent by the Governor General. Most bills are introduced by members of the government in the House of Commons. Typically, a bill is given three "readings" in the House. The first reading is simply to introduce the bill. The second reading is accompanied by debate on the principle of the bill. The bill is then voted on and, if approved, is sent to a House committee composed of representatives of all parties to be considered clause-by-clause. The committee prepares a report and submits it to the House of Commons along with any proposed amendments. These amendments, plus any others moved by any member of Parliament, are debated and usually voted on. A motion is then brought for the bill to be given third reading. If the vote is favorable, the bill is then introduced in the Senate where it undergoes a similar process. After a bill has been approved by both Houses, the Governor General gives it royal assent in a ceremony that takes place in the Senate chamber.

Defeat of a Government   Between elections, a government can be forced to resign if it is defeated in a vote on a major government bill. When this happens the government is considered to have lost the support of the majority of Parliament's elected representatives. This typically occurs only when the party in power has formed a minority government—that is, if it holds more seats than any other single party but fewer seats than the combined Opposition parties. This last happened federally in 1979 when a minority Conservative government, elected earlier that year, introduced a budget which was defeated by the combined votes of the Liberal and New Democratic Party members in the House. Parliament was dissolved, an election was called and the Liberals regained power.

■ The Constitution of Canada

Canada's constitution consists of written documents and unwritten conventions. The written constitution is embodied in the *Constitution Acts 1867–1982*. The 1867 legislation (originally titled the British North America Act) was a British statute that established a federal state with a Parliament modelled on the British system. That Act assembled the colonies of Nova Scotia, New Brunswick and Canada (Ontario and Quebec) into the "Dominion of Canada," created a federal government in Ottawa, and divided the powers of government between Ottawa and the provinces.

The BNA Act gave Ottawa broad jurisdiction over internal matters, including unlimited powers of taxation, while allowing the provinces only a narrow field of local control. In general, the Canadian constitution of the late 19th century was a centralist document.

Under the BNA Act, Britain still had the power to veto Canadian laws or to enact statutes affecting Canada. But the British had no desire to raise revenue in Canada, for example, or to tax Canadians directly. This approach extended to trade and tariffs. Gradually, the practice was established that where money was involved, even in trade treaties, Canada would determine its own policy.

The same was not true of political foreign policy. When Britain declared war on Germany in 1914, Canada, as part of the British Empire, was automatically at war. During this period, British courts also interpreted Canadian statutes, especially those involving the division of power between Ottawa and the provinces. Through this process, the constitution's strong centralist thrust was altered to give more authority to the provinces.

The constitution was also adjusted more directly, through amendments. But because the BNA Act was a British statute, Canada could make formal changes to it only with the consent of the British Parliament. Ottawa tended to seek such amendments only when they did not affect provincial powers or when the provinces agreed with the changes. This process worked at least some of the time: 29 times, in fact, between 1870 and 1975. In 1940, for example, unemployment insurance became a federal responsibility through an amendment to the BNA Act.

In 1931, Britain attempted to tidy up relations with Canada and other self-governing dominions within the Commonwealth by passing the Statute of Westminster. The Statute ceded full powers over foreign affairs and trade to Canada. But because the federal and provincial governments could not agree on a method for amending the BNA Act at home, the British Parliament retained ultimate power over Canada's constitution. Until 1949, British courts continued to review Canadian constitutional cases.

From 1927 until 1982, a succession of federal governments attempted to resolve the problem by getting the provinces to agree to an amending formula. These negotiations failed as the provinces used them as a means to gain concessions from Ottawa.

The catalyst in constitutional discussions during the late 20th century has been the province of Quebec, where provincial governments since 1960 have sought to expand the province's jurisdiction. To protect French culture, the Quebec government requested more powers, over culture itself, and over the economy and social institutions.

Ottawa resisted the move under prime ministers Lester Pearson and Pierre Trudeau. Trudeau argued that without a strong central power a country as sprawling and diverse as Canada would be fatally weakened and might disintegrate.

In lengthy negotiations with the provinces, Trudeau was unable to gain agreement on an amending formula, even when he offered increased powers in return. In 1976, the election of the separatist Parti Québécois in Quebec made constitutional compromise even more unlikely and the matter was set aside.

After Quebec's 1980 referendum on the question of sovereignty association was won by the "No" side, constitutional renewal was back on the agenda. However, federal-provincial discussions became mired in disagreement through the summer of 1980. In September, Trudeau announced that the federal government, with the support of only Ontario and New Brunswick, would ask the British parliament to amend the BNA Act to patriate the constitution and establish a *Charter of Rights and Freedoms* to protect individual liberties. The *Charter* would also protect minority rights in education and the mobility rights of Canadian citizens, and change the name of the constitution: the BNA Act became the *Constitution Act, 1982*.

It took 18 months to get the new amendments approved by the Canadian Parliament, resolve the concerns of eight provincial governments, and get the act through the British Parliament. But, in April 1982, the *Constitution Act* was proclaimed—although the consent of the Quebec government was never given.

The *Constitution Act, 1982*, consolidated all the previous BNA Acts and added an amending formula and a *Charter of Rights and Freedoms*. The Charter, which provided for basic democratic rights, also contained a "notwithstanding" clause that allowed Parliament or any provincial legislature to over-ride its provisions.

The amending formula provided for two types of constitutional change: the division of powers between the federal and provincial governments could be modified with the consent of the federal Parliament and seven provincial legislatures in provinces totalling more than 50 percent of the Canadian population; matters such as the composition of the Supreme Court or the status of English or French, however, required unanimous consent. It also stipulated that no amendment could take longer than three years to be ratified by Ottawa and all 10 provinces.

FOCUS ON...

Government of Canada Primary Internet Site

The Canada Site is the official Web site of the Canadian government. It provides Internet access to information and services about Canada and Canadian governments. The starting point is http://canada.gc.ca and the information appears in French and English.

As of September 1999, what did browsers find there?

WHAT'S NEW?: This link connects you to an archive of government press releases, advisories and reports about conferences, politics, health, science, technology and business. A calendar lists forthcoming events across Canada. You can read *The Canada Gazette,* Statistics Canada's *The Daily* and recent debates in Parliament. You can also connect to the Governor General's Web site for awards given to outstanding Canadians.

DIRECTORIES: This link connects you to three directories. The *Government of Canada Employees Directory* lists federal public servants. A search engine allows you to find information by surname, telephone number, job title and organization; this site also provides online help and a "frequently asked questions" page. The *Government of Canada Internet Addresses Directory* links you to the Web sites of various federal institutions from Agriculture and Agri-Food Canada to the Yukon Territory Water Board. The *Members of Parliament Directory* organizes information on all 301 MPs by surname, party, province and territory. It gives you MPs' telephone and fax numbers and e-mail addresses.

PROGRAMS AND SERVICES: *Info/Centre Subject Categories* links you to sites on business, customs and tariffs, education, employment insurance, the environment, health, immigration, social programs and tourism. *Jobs and Employment* connects you to information on jobs for youth and aboriginals and applications for public service work. Other links provide access to programs for

seniors, students, rural residents, women, minorities and people with disabilities. *On-line Services* links you to commonly requested government forms (e.g., passport applications and GST/HST remittance forms), services provided by Canada Post and online forums on public issues.

ABOUT CANADA: *Facts and History* connects you to sites about Canada, the provinces and the territories; information covers basic geography, history and economics. Related links point you toward sites on Canadian culture, French, industry, law, multiculturism, police, sports and women. *Canadian Symbols* provides information about the coat of arms, historical flags and other national emblems. *Test Your Knowledge* quizzes you on history and geography. There's even aid for people planning visits to Canada.

ABOUT GOVERNMENT: *Government at a Glance* provides an overview of Canada's federal system including Web pages for the Governor General, the Prime Minister, the Cabinet, the Senate and the Supreme Court. Related links provide information on orders-in-council and legislative procedures. *Other Governments* connects you to the official Web sites of the provinces, the territories and international organizations. *Frequently Requested Acts* provides links to federal laws (e.g., the Canada Pension Plan) and the Department of Justice. A final link, *Miscellaneous,* features Web pages on Canadian municipalities, linguistic minorities and global climate changes.

PUBLICATIONS AND FORMS: This site connects you to lists of books and CD-ROMs on the constitution, health, labour, natural resources and technology. You can find publications listed by subject or sponsoring institution. You can order online; some publications are free. The site also provides access to *Hansard,* the official record of Parliament, and another link to frequently requested government forms.

If You're Not on the Internet...

*R**eference Canada is a telephone inquiry service that is available toll-free within Canada. 1 (800) 667–3355 will connect callers to a service that will either supply the necessary information or direct the caller to the department that has the answer.*

Text of the Canadian Charter of Rights and Freedoms

*W*hereas Canada is founded upon principles that recognize the supremacy of God and the rule of law:

■ Guarantee of Rights and Freedoms

1 The Canadian Charter of Rights and Freedoms guarantees the rights and freedoms set out in it subject only to such reasonable limits prescribed by law as can be demonstrably justified in a free and democratic society.

■ Fundamental Freedoms

2 Everyone has the following fundamental freedoms: (a) freedom of conscience and religion; (b) freedom of thought, belief, opinion and expression, including freedom of the press and other media of communication; (c) freedom of peaceful assembly; and (d) freedom of association.

■ Democratic Rights

3 Every citizen of Canada has the right to vote in an election of members of the House of Commons or of a legislative assembly and to be qualified for membership therein.

4 (1) No House of Commons and no legislative assembly shall continue for longer than five years from the date fixed for the return of the writs at a general election of its members. (2) In time of real or apprehended war, invasion or insurrection, a House of Commons may be continued by Parliament and a legislative assembly may be continued by the legislature beyond five years if such continuation is not opposed by the votes of more than one-third of the members of the House of Commons or the legislative assembly, as the case may be.

5 There shall be a sitting of Parliament and of each legislature at least once every twelve months.

■ Mobility Rights

6 (1) Every citizen of Canada has the right to enter, remain in and leave Canada. (2) Every citizen of Canada and every person who has the status of a permanent resident of Canada has the right (a) to move to and take up residence in any province; and (b) to pursue the gaining of a livelihood in any province. (3) The rights specified in subsection (2) are subject to (a) any laws or practices of general application in force in a province other than those that discriminate among persons primarily on the basis of province of present or previous residence; and (b) any laws providing for reasonable residency requirements as a qualification for the receipt of publicly provided social services. (4) Subsections (2) and (3) do not preclude any law, program or activity that has as its object the amelioration in a province of conditions of individuals in that province who are socially or economically disadvantaged if the rate of employment in that province is below the rate of employment in Canada.

■ Legal Rights

7 Everyone has the right to life, liberty and security of the person and the right not to be deprived thereof except in accordance with the principles of fundamental justice.

8 Everyone has the right to be secure against unreasonable search or seizure.

9 Everyone has the right not to be arbitrarily detained or imprisoned.

10 Everyone has the right on arrest or detention (a) to be informed promptly of the reasons therefor; (b) to retain and instruct counsel without delay and to be informed of that right; and (c) to have the validity of the detention determined by way of *habeas corpus* and to be released if the detention is not lawful.

11 Any person charged with an offence has the right (a) to be informed without unreasonable delay of the specific offence; (b) to be tried within a reasonable time; (c) not to be compelled to be a witness in proceedings against that person in respect of the offence; (d) to be presumed innocent until proven guilty according to law in a fair and public hearing by an independent

and impartial tribunal; (e) not to be denied reasonable bail without just cause; (f) except in the case of an offence under military law tried before a military tribunal, to the benefit of trial by jury where the maximum punishment for the offence is imprisonment for five years or a more severe punishment; (g) not to be found guilty on account of any act or omission unless, at the time of the act or omission, it constituted an offence under Canadian or international law or was criminal according to the general principles of law recognized by the community of nations; (h) if finally acquitted of the offence, not to be tried for it again and, if finally found guilty and punished for the offence, not to be tried or punished for it again; and (i) if found guilty of the offence and if the punishment for the offence has been varied between the time of commission and the time of sentencing, to the benefit of the lesser punishment.

12 Everyone has the right not to be subjected to any cruel and unusual treatment or punishment.

13 A witness who testifies in any proceedings has the right not to have any incriminating evidence so given used to incriminate that witness in any other proceedings, except in a prosecution for perjury or for the giving of contradictory evidence.

14 A party or witness in any proceedings who does not understand or speak the language in which the proceedings are conducted or who is deaf has the right to the assistance of an interpreter.

■ Equality Rights

15 (1) Every individual is equal before and under the law and has the right to the equal protection and equal benefit of the law without discrimination and, in particular, without discrimination based on race, national or ethnic origin, colour, religion, sex, age or mental or physical disability. (2) Subsection (1) does not preclude any law, program or activity that has as its object the amelioration of conditions of disadvantaged individuals or groups including those that are disadvantaged because of race, national or ethnic origin,

colour, religion, sex, age or mental or physical disability.

■ Official Languages of Canada

16 (1) English and French are the official languages of Canada and have equality of status and equal rights and privileges as to their use in all institutions of the Parliament and government of Canada. (2) English and French are the official languages of New Brunswick and have equality of status and equal rights and privileges as to their use in all institutions of the legislature and government of New Brunswick. (3) Nothing in this Charter limits the authority of Parliament or a legislature to advance the equality of status or use of English and French.

17 (1) Everyone has the right to use English or French in any debates and other proceedings of Parliament. (2) Everyone has the right to use English or French in any debates and other proceedings of the legislature of New Brunswick.

18 (1) The statutes, records and journals of Parliament shall be printed and published in English and French and both language versions are equally authoritative. (2) The statutes, records and journals of the legislature of New Brunswick shall be printed and published in English and French and both language versions are equally authoritative.

19 (1) Either English or French may be used by any person in, or in any pleading in or process issuing from, any court established by Parliament. (2) Either English or French may be used by any person in, or in any pleading in or process issuing from, any court of New Brunswick.

20 (1) Any member of the public in Canada has the right to communicate with, and to receive available services from, any head or central office of an institution of the Parliament or government of Canada in English or French, and has the same right with respect to any other office of any such institution where (a) there is a significant demand for communications with and services from that office in such language; or (b) due to the nature of the office, it is reasonable that communications with and services from that office be available in both English and French. (2) Any member of the public in New Brunswick has the right to communicate with, and to receive available services from, any office of an institution of the legislature or government of New Brunswick in English or French.

21 Nothing in sections 16 to 20 abrogates or derogates from any right, privilege or obligation with respect to the English and French languages, or either of them, that exists or is continued by virtue of any other provision of the Constitution of Canada.

22 Nothing in sections 16 to 20 abrogates or derogates from any legal or customary right or privilege acquired or enjoyed either before or after the coming into force of this Charter with respect to any language that is not English or French.

◼ Minority Language Educational Rights

23 (1) Citizens of Canada (a) whose first language learned and still understood is that of the English or French linguistic minority population of the province in which they reside, or (b) who have received their primary school instruction in Canada in English or French and reside in a province where the language in which they received that instruction is the language of the English or French linguistic minority population of the province, have the right to have their children receive primary and secondary school instruction in that language in that province. (2) Citizens of Canada of whom any child has received or is receiving primary or secondary school instruction in English or French in Canada, have the right to have all their children receive primary and secondary school instruction in the same language. (3) The right of citizens of Canada under subsections (1) and (2) to have their children receive primary and secondary school instruction in the language of the English or French linguistic minority population of a province (a) applies wherever in the province the number of children of citizens who have such a right is sufficient to warrant the provision to them out of public funds of minority language instruction; and (b) includes, where the number of those children so warrants, the right to have them receive that instruction in minority language educational facilities provided out of public funds.

◼ Enforcement

24. (1) Anyone whose rights or freedoms, as guaranteed by this Charter, have been infringed or denied may apply to a court of competent jurisdiction to obtain such remedy as the court considers appropriate and just in the circumstances. (2) Where, in proceedings under subsection (1), a court concludes that evidence was obtained in a manner that infringed or denied any rights or freedoms guaranteed by this Charter, the evidence shall be excluded if it is established that, having regard to all the circumstances, the admission of it in the proceedings would bring the administration of justice into disrepute.

◼ General

25 The guarantee in this Charter of certain rights and freedoms shall not be construed so as to abrogate or derogate from any aboriginal, treaty or other rights or freedoms that pertain to the aboriginal peoples of Canada including (a) any rights or freedoms that have been recognized by the Royal Proclamation of October 7, 1763; and (b) any rights or freedoms that now exist by way of land claims agreements or may be so acquired. (SI/84-102)

26 The guarantee in this Charter of certain rights and freedoms shall not be construed as denying the existence of any other rights or freedoms that exist in Canada.

27 This Charter shall be interpreted in a manner consistent with the preservation and enhancement of the multicultural heritage of Canadians.

28 Notwithstanding anything in this Charter, the rights and freedoms referred to in it are guaranteed equally to male and female persons.

29 Nothing in this Charter abrogates or derogates from any rights or privileges guaranteed by or under the Constitution of Canada in respect of denominational, separate or dissentient schools.

30 A reference in this Charter to a province or to the legislative assembly or legislature or a province shall be deemed to include a reference to the Yukon Territory and the Northwest Territories, or to the appropriate legislative authority thereof, as the case may be.

31 Nothing in this Charter extends the legislative powers of any body or authority.

■ Application of Charter

32 (1) This Charter applies (a) to the Parliament and government of Canada in respect of all matters within the authority of Parliament including all matters relating to the Yukon Territory and Northwest Territories; and (b) to the legislature and government of each province in respect of all matters within the authority of the legislature of each province. (2) Notwithstanding subsection (1), section 15 shall not have effect until three years after this section comes into force.

33 (1) Parliament or the legislature of a province may expressly declare in an Act of Parliament or of the legislature, as the case may be, that the Act or a provision thereof shall operate notwithstanding a provision included in section 2 or sections 7 to 15 of this Charter. (2) An Act or a provision of an Act in respect of which a declaration made under this section is in effect shall have such operation as it would have but for the provision of this Charter referred to in the declaration. (3) A declaration made under subsection (1) shall cease to have effect five years after it comes into force or on such earlier date as may be specified in the declaration. (4) Parliament or the legislature of a province may re-enact a declaration made under subsection (1). (5) Subsection (3) applies in respect of a re-enactment made under subsection (4).

■ Citation

34 This Part may be cited as the Canadian Charter of Rights and Freedoms.

Canadian Orders and Decorations

Detailed information about Canada's orders and decorations can be found in the Web site of the Governor General of Canada at http://www.gg.ca/honour_e.html. Information is available in French and English. Supplementary information on Canadian honours can be found at http://www.vac-acc.gc.ca/collections/cmdp/mainmenu/group02.html.

■ National Orders

■ The Order of Canada

History   Creation of the Order of Canada was announced by Prime Minister Lester B. Pearson in 1967. It was instituted on the centennial of Canadian Confederation, July 1, 1967.

Basis of Award   To honour Canadians for outstanding achievement and service to their country or humanity. Appointments are announced twice annually, around July 1 and Jan. 1. Investitures occur three times a year, in February, April and October when the awards are given by the Governor General.

Eligibility   Every living Canadian is eligible to become a member. Federal and provincial politicians and judges are ineligible while in office.

Membership   There are three categories of membership. The first is Companion of the Order of Canada (C.C.). No more than 15 companions may be appointed in any one year, and no more than 165 living companions may hold the order at one time.

The second is Officer of the Order of Canada (O.C.). No more than 52 appointments may be made annually.

The third is Member of the Order of Canada (C.M.)., which recognizes service in a locality or a field of activity. No more than 106 appointments may be made annually.

Badge   A stylized snowflake bearing the crown with a ribbon in the same proportions of white and red which appear on the Canadian flag and the Latin motto *Desiderantes Meliorem Patriam*—"They Desire a Better Country." Worn at the neck by companions and officers and on the left breast by members.

■ The Order of Military Merit

History   The Order of Military Merit was instituted on July 1, 1972.

Basis of Award   To recognize exceptional service and conspicuous merit by regular and reserve members of Canada's Armed Forces.

Appointments are made by the Governor General on the recommendation of the Chief of Defence Staff.

Eligibility   Active members of the Canadian Armed Forces, regular and reserve. A formula limits the number of annual appointments per year to one-tenth of one per cent of the average number of persons who were members of the Armed Forces during the previous year.

Membership   There are three categories of membership. The first is Commander of the Order of Military Merit (C.M.M.). Six percent of annual appointments go to this category of membership.

The second is Officer of the Order of Military Merit (O.M.M.). Thirty percent of annual appointments go to this category of membership.

The third is Member of the Order of Military Merit (M.M.M.). The balance of annual appointments go to this category of membership.

Badge   In the form of an enamelled blue cross having expanded arms, with a blue ribbon edged in gold. Bears the words "Merit Merite Canada." Worn at the neck by commanders and on the left breast by officers and members.

■ Medals for Military Valour

The Military Valour Decorations, consisting of the Victoria Cross (Canadian), the Star of Military Valour and the Medal of Military Valour, enable Canada to recognize members of the Canadian Forces, or members of an allied armed force serving with the Canadian Forces, for deeds of military valour.

■ Victoria Cross (V.C.) (Canadian)

History   Approved by Queen Elizabeth II on Feb. 2, 1993. The British Victoria Cross was created by Queen Victoria in 1856 and was awarded to Canadians in all wars until 1945. There have been 93 Canadian recipients of the British V.C. and none of the Canadian version.

Basis of Award   In recognition of "the most conspicuous bravery, a daring or pre-eminent act of valour or self-sacrifice or extreme devotion to duty, in the presence of the enemy." The V.C. will be awarded by the Governor General on the advice of the Military Valour Advisory Committee. It is the highest in the order of precedence in Canadian honours.

Eligibility   Members of the Canadian Forces or a member of an allied armed force that is serving with or in conjunction with the Canadian Forces on or after Jan. 1, 1993. The V.C. may be awarded posthumously.

Badge   The Cross is a bronze straight armed cross, suspended from a crimson ribbon. The

face has, in the middle of the cross, a lion guardant standing on the Royal Crown, with the Latin inscription *Pro Valore*—"For Valour". The date of the act for which the decoration is bestowed is engraved in a raised circle on the reverse.

■ The Star of Military Valour (S.M.V.)

History   Approved by Queen Elizabeth II on Feb. 2, 1993.

Basis of Award   Awarded for distinguished and valiant service in the presence of the enemy.

Eligibility   Members of the Canadian Forces or a member of an allied armed force that is serving with or in conjunction with the Canadian Forces on or after Jan. 1, 1993. The S.M.V. may be awarded posthumously.

Badge   A gold star with four points with a maple leaf in each of the angles, on the face of which a gold maple leaf is superimposed in the centre of a sanguine field surrounded by a silver wreath of laurel and on the reverse of which the Royal Cypher and Crown and the Latin inscription *Pro Valore*—"For Valour" shall appear. The Star shall be worn, suspended from a crimson ribbon with two white stripes, immediately after any order and before the Star of Courage.

■ The Medal of Military Valour (M.M.V.)

History   Approved by Queen Elizabeth II on Feb. 2, 1993.

Basis of Award   Awarded for an act of valour or devotion to duty in the presence of the enemy.

Eligibility   Members of the Canadian Forces or a member of an allied armed force that is serving with or in conjunction with the Canadian Forces on or after Jan. 1, 1993. The M.M.V. may be awarded posthumously.

Badge   A circular gold medal, on the face of which there shall be a maple leaf surrounded by a wreath of laurel and on the reverse of which the Royal Cypher and Crown and the Latin inscription *Pro Valore*—"For Valour" will appear. The medal shall be worn, from a crimson ribbon with three white stripes, immediately after the Meritorious Service Cross and before the Medal of Bravery.

■ Decorations for Bravery

The Decorations for Bravery, consisting of the Cross of Valour, the Star of Courage and the Medal of Bravery honour those who have risked their lives to save or protect others.

These three Canadian decorations replaced the following non-combatant Commonwealth medals: the George Cross, the George Medal and the Queen's Gallantry Medal, respectively.

■ The Cross of Valour (C.V.)

History Created in 1972, the Cross of Valour takes precedence before all orders and other decorations except the Victoria Cross.

Basis of Award Awarded for acts of the most conspicuous courage in circumstances of extreme peril.

Eligibility May be awarded to civilians or members of the Armed Forces. Only 19 have been awarded. May be awarded posthumously.

Badge A gold cross bearing the words "Valour Vaillance."

■ The Star of Courage (S.C.)

History Created in 1972.

Basis of Award Awarded for acts of conspicuous courage in circumstances of great peril.

Eligibility May be awarded to civilians or members of the Armed Forces. May be awarded posthumously.

Badge A four-pointed silver star with the word "Courage."

■ The Medal of Bravery (M.B.)

History Created in 1972.

Basis of Award Awarded for acts of bravery in hazardous circumstances.

Eligibility May be awarded to civilians or members of the Armed Forces. May be awarded posthumously.

Badge A circular silver medal with the words "Bravery Bravoure."

■ The Meritorious Service Cross (M.S.C.) (military and civilian)

History Military division created in 1984; civilian division created in 1991.

Basis of Award *Military division*: awarded in recognition of a military deed or activity that has been performed in an outstandingly professional manner, according to a rare high standard that brings considerable benefit or great honour to the Canadian Forces. *Civilian division*: awarded in recognition of the performance of a deed or activity performed in an outstandingly professional manner or according to an uncommonly high standard that brings considerable benefit or great honour to Canada.

Eligibility A member of the Canadian and allied forces, persons serving in conjunction with the Canadian Forces or other persons, Canadian and foreigners.

Badge A Greek cross of silver, ends splayed and convexed, ensigned with the Royal Crown. On the face appear a maple leaf within a circle and a laurel wreath between the arms. Recipients are entitled to use the letters "M.S.C." after their names.

■ The Meritorious Service Medal (M.S.M.) (military and civilian)

History Created in 1991.

Basis of Award *Military division*: awarded in recognition of a military deed or activity that has been performed in a highly professional manner or is of a very high standard that brings benefit or honour to the Canadian Forces. *Civilian division*: awarded in recognition of the performance of a deed or activity performed in a highly professional manner or of a very high standard that brings benefit or honour to Canada.

Eligibility A member of the Canadian and allied forces, persons serving in conjunction with the Canadian Forces or other persons, Canadian and foreigners.

Badge A circular medal of silver ensigned with the Royal Crown. On the face appears the design of the cross. On the reverse appears the Royal Cypher and, within a double circle, the words "Meritorious Service Méritoire." Recipients are entitled to use the letters "M.S.M." after their names.

■ Other Notable Awards

The Governor General bestows the following awards for scholastic excellence and community service.

■ The Academic Medal

History Created in 1873 by Lord Dufferin, Canada's third Governor General after Confederation.

Basis of Award Awarded for academic excellence. Awards are distributed in March to colleges and universities and in April to secondary schools.

Eligibility The student with the highest average graduating from an approved program in a Canadian high school, college or university.

Award A circular medal bearing the profiles of the current Governor General and spouse on the face and the Coat of Arms of the Governor General on the reverse as well as a certificate signed by the Governor General. Medals are awarded at four levels: bronze at the secondary school level; collegiate bronze at the post-secondary diploma level; silver at the postsecondary undergraduate level; and gold at the postsecondary graduate level.

■ The Governor General's Caring Canadian Award

History Created on April 29, 1996.

Basis of Award Awarded to unpaid volunteers for their extraordinary contributions, performed behind the scenes and for several years, in support of family, community or humanitarian causes.

Eligibility Living Canadian citizens who have not previously won national or provincial honours. Public officials are ineligible while in office.

Award A framed certificate and a lapel pin. The award symbol depicts a helping hand and a heart supporting a maple leaf.

■ Governor General's Canadian History Medal for the Millennium

History Announced on May 12, 1999.

Basis of Award Awarded for academic excellence in Canadian history or Canadian studies.

Eligibility Secondary school students recording the highest final marks in the 1999-2000 school year. Award to be given only once, in the year 2000.

Award A certificate signed by the Governor General and a bronze medal. The medal's face shows a map of Canada surmounted by a compass rose; the reverse shows a Canadian flag flying in the breeze.

FOCUS ON...

The Order of Canada

The Order of Canada is bestowed on many Canadians. How is the honour awarded?

First, someone nominates a candidate. The nomination form requests the candidate's name, address, sex, citizenship, profession, official language, birthdate and place of birth. It requests the names and addresses of three other people who support the nomination. The reason the candidate deserves the honour and the candidate's resum(must be included.

Canadian citizens are eligible for the honour. Federal and provincial politicians and judges are ineligible while in office. Deceased persons are ineligible.

The nomination goes to the Chancellery of the Governor General:

> Director, Honours
> The Chancellery, Rideau Hall
> 1 Sussex Drive
> Ottawa, Ontario
> K1A 0A1

A council recommends nominees to the governor general. It consists of the clerk of the Privy Council, the deputy minister of Canadian heritage, the chair of the Canada Council, the president of the Royal Society of Canada, the chair of the Board of Directors of the Association of Universities and Colleges in Canada and two people who may be members of the Order of Canada. The chief justice of Canada chairs the council.

The council's deliberations are secret. Sometimes the deputy minister of foreign affairs and international trade reviews nominations. The governor general approves the final appointments.

The chancellery receives more than 900 nominations per year, but no more than 15 companions, 52 officers and 106 members of the order may be appointed annually. The governor general may appoint non-Canadians for outstanding service to Canada or humanity; the governor general may promote members within the order.

Call 1 (800) 465-6890 or visit http://www.gg.ca/honours/order_e.html.

Governors General of Canada

Name	Date Appointed	Assumed Office	Term
Sir Charles Stanley, Viscount Monck	June 1, 1867	July 1, 1867	1867–69
Sir John Young, Baron Lisgar	Dec. 29, 1868	Feb. 2, 1869	1869–72
Frederick Temple Hamilton Blackwood, Earl of Dufferin	May 22, 1872	June 25, 1872	1872–78
John Douglas Sutherland Campbell, Marquess of Lorne	Oct. 5, 1878	Nov. 20, 1878	1878–83
Henry Charles Keith Petty-Fitzmaurice, Marquess of Lansdowne	Aug. 18, 1883	Oct. 23, 1883	1883–88
Frederick Arthur Stanley, Baron Stanley of Preston	May 1, 1888	June 11, 1888	1888–93
John Campbell Hamilton-Gordon, Earl of Aberdeen	May 22, 1893	Nov. 18, 1893	1893–98
Gilbert John Elliott Murray-Kynynmound, Earl of Minto	July 30, 1898	Nov. 12, 1898	1898–1904
Albert Henry George Grey, Earl Grey	Sept. 26, 1904	Dec. 10, 1904	1904–11
His Royal Highness The Prince Arthur, Field Marshal Duke of Connaught	Mar. 21, 1911	Oct. 13, 1911	1911–16
Victor Christian William Cavendish, Duke of Devonshire	Aug. 19, 1916	Nov. 11, 1916	1916–21
Julian Byng, General Baron Byng of Vimy and of Thorpe	Aug. 2, 1921	Aug. 11, 1921	1921–26
Freeman Freeman-Thomas, Baron Willingdon of Ratton	Aug. 5, 1926	Nov. 2, 1926	1926–31
Vere Brabazon Ponsonby, Earl of Bessborough	Feb. 9, 1931	Apr. 4, 1931	1931–35
John Buchan, Baron Tweedsmuir	Aug. 10, 1935	Nov. 2, 935	1935–40
Alexander George Cambridge, Major General Earl of Athlone	Apr. 3, 1940	June 21, 1940	1940–46
Sir Harold George Alexander, Field Marshal Viscount Alexander of Tunis	Aug. 1, 1945	Apr. 18, 1946	1946–52
The Right Honourable Vincent Massey	Jan. 24, 1952	Feb. 22, 1952	1952–59
General the Right Honourable Georges P. Vanier	Aug. 1, 1959	Sept. 15, 1959	1959–67
The Right Honourable Daniel Roland Michener	Mar. 25, 1967	Apr. 15, 1967	1967–73
The Right Honourable Jules Léger	Oct. 5, 1973	Jan. 14, 1974	1973–79
The Right Honourable Edward Richard Schreyer	Dec. 7, 1978	Jan. 22, 1979	1979–83
The Right Honourable Jeanne Sauvé	Dec. 23, 1983	May 14, 1984	1984–90
The Right Honourable Ramon John Hnatyshyn	Oct. 6, 1989	Jan. 21, 1990	1990–95
The Right Honourable Roméo LeBlanc	Nov. 22, 1994	Feb. 8, 1995	1995–99
The Right Honourable Adrienne Clarkson	Sept 8, 1999	Oct. 7, 1999	1999—

Prime Ministers of Canada

Prime Minister	Party	Term(s)	Born	P.M. at age	Died
Sir John A. Macdonald	Conservative	July 1, 1867–Nov. 5, 1873 Oct. 9, 1878–June 6, 1891	Jan. 11, 1815	52	June 6, 1891
Alexander Mackenzie	Liberal	Nov. 5, 1873–Oct. 9, 1878	Jan. 28, 1822	51	Apr. 17, 1092
Sir John Abbott	Conservative	June 15, 1891–Nov. 24, 1892	Mar. 12, 1821	70	Oct. 30, 1893
Sir John Thompson	Conservative	Nov. 25, 1892–Dec. 12, 1894	Nov. 10, 1845	48	Dec. 12, 1894
Sir Mackenzie Bowell	Conservative	Dec. 13, 1894–Apr. 27, 1896	Dec. 27, 1823	70	Dec. 10, 1917
Sir Charles Tupper	Conservative	Apr. 27, 1896–July 8, 1896	July 2, 1821	74	Oct. 30, 1915
Sir Wilfrid Laurier	Liberal	July 11, 1896–Oct. 6, 1911	Nov. 20, 1841	54	Feb. 17, 1919
Sir Robert Borden	Conservative/ Unionist	Oct. 12, 1917–July 10, 1920 Oct. 10, 1911–Oct. 12, 1917	June 26, 1854	57	June 10, 1937
Arthur Meighen	Unionist/ Conservative	June 29, 1926–Sept. 25, 1926 July 10, 1920–Dec. 29, 1921	June 16, 1874	46	Aug. 5, 1960
Mackenzie King	Liberal	Dec. 29, 1921–June 28, 1926 Sept. 25, 1926–Aug. 6, 1930 Oct. 23, 1935–Nov. 15, 1948	Dec. 17, 1874	47	July 22, 1950
Richard B. Bennett	Conservative	Aug. 7, 1930–Oct. 23, 1935	July 3, 1870	60	June 27, 1947
Louis St. Laurent	Liberal	Nov. 15, 1948–June 21, 1957	Feb. 1, 1882	66	July 25, 1973
John Diefenbaker	Prog. Cons.	June 21, 1957–Apr. 22, 1963	Sept. 18, 1895	61	Aug. 16, 1979
Lester Pearson	Liberal	Apr. 22, 1963–Apr. 20, 1968	Apr. 23, 1897	65	Dec. 27, 1972
Pierre Trudeau	Liberal	Apr. 20, 1968–June 4, 1979 Mar. 3, 1980–June 30, 1984	Oct. 18, 1919	48	
Joe Clark	Prog. Cons.	June 4, 1979–Mar. 3, 1980	June 5, 1939	39	
John Turner	Liberal	June 30, 1984–Sept. 17, 1984	June 7, 1929	55	
Brian Mulroney	Prog. Cons.	Sept. 17, 1984–June 25, 1993	Mar. 20, 1939	45	
Kim Campbell	Prog. Cons.	June 25, 1993–Nov. 4, 1993	Mar. 10, 1947	46	
Jean Chrétien	Liberal	Nov. 4, 1993–	Jan. 11, 1934	59	

Canadian Cabinet Ministers and Secretaries of State

(as of Oct. 1999)

Cabinet ministers are the most powerful elected officials in government. They are sworn to the Privy Council and are bound by collective responsibility. They work with their staffs to set policies for their ministries and present (or defend) those policies in the House of Commons. They shepherd their bills through various readings and committees before having their bills voted into law.

Secretaries of state, although sworn to the Privy Council and bound by collective responsibility as well, are not members of the Cabinet. Secretaries of state are assigned to support specific Cabinet ministers; they also get smaller staffs and less pay than Cabinet ministers. Prime Minister Jean Chrétien introduced the distinction between these "senior" and "junior" officials on Nov. 4, 1993.

■ The Cabinet

The Prime Minister of Canada
The Right Hon. Jean Chrétien
(Saint-Maurice, Quebec)
Telephone: (613) 992-4211
Fax: (613) 941-6900
E-mail: ChretJ@parl.gc.ca

The Deputy Prime Minister of Canada
The Hon. Herbert Eser Gray
(Windsor West, Ontario)
Telephone: (613) 995-7548
Fax: (613) 995-3259
E-mail: GrayH@parl.gc.ca

The Leader of the Government in the Senate
Represents the Cabinet in the Senate.
The Hon. Alasdair Graham
(The Highlands, Nova Scotia)
Telephone: (613) 992-3770
Fax: (613) 995-5217

The Minister of Agriculture and Agri-Food
Responsible for nearly all aspects of production, processing, marketing and protection of crops and livestock, including research and technology; soil conservation; food processing and inspection; and trade policies and support programs.
The Hon. Lyle Vanclief
(Prince Edward-Hastings, Ontario)
Telephone: (613) 992-5321
Fax: (613) 996-8652
E-mail: VancilL@parl.gc.ca

The Minister of Canadian Heritage
Responsible for both Canada's natural heritage (parks) and our historic and cultural heritage, including the arts, sports and multiculturalism.
The Hon. Sheila M. Copps
(Hamilton East, Ontario)
Telephone: (613) 995-2772
Fax: (613) 992-2727
E-mail: CoppsS@parl.gc.ca

The Minister of Citizenship and Immigration
Administers policies and procedures for citizenship and immigration.
The Hon. Elinor Caplan
(Thornhill, Ontario)
Telephone: (613) 992-0253
Fax: (613) 992-0887
E-mail: CaplaE@parl.gc.ca

The Minister of the Environment
Protects and conserves Canada's air and water; monitors climate and pollution.
The Hon. David Anderson
(Victoria, British Columbia)
Telephone: (613) 996-2358
Fax: (613) 952-1458
E-mail: AnderD@parl.gc.ca

The Minister of Finance
Provides the federal government with an annual budget; provides research and advice on financial issues; regularly monitors the performance of Canada's economy.
The Hon. Paul Martin
(LaSalle-Émard, Quebec)
Telephone: (613) 992-4284
Fax: (613) 992-4291
E-mail: MartiP@parl.gc.ca

▶

The Minister of Fisheries and Oceans

Manages Canada's resources in the water, particularly in the ocean, when outside other jurisdictions; oversees public harbours and coastal and inland fisheries.
The Hon. Harbance Singh Dhaliwal
(Vancouver South–Burnaby, British Columbia)
Telephone: (613) 995-7052
Fax: (613) 995-2962
E-mail: DhaliH@parl.gc.ca

The Minister of Foreign Affairs

Creates foreign policy; promotes and protects Canada's interests abroad; manages Canadian embassies and diplomatic staff; ensures Canadian citizens abroad receive fair treatment under foreign laws.
The Hon. Lloyd Axworthy
(Winnipeg South Centre, Manitoba)
Telephone: (613) 995-0153
Fax: (613) 947-4442
E-mail: AxworL@parl.gc.ca

The Minister of Health

Provides funding and policies for a national health care system; sets and enforces health standards.
The Hon. Allan Rock
(Etobicoke Centre, Ontario)
Telephone: (613) 947-5000
Fax: (613) 947-4276
E-mail: RockA@parl.gc.ca

The Minister of Human Resources Development

Fosters an educated and mobile workforce; provides income as necessary for seniors, the unemployed and the disabled.
The Hon. Jane Stewart
(Brant, Ontario)
Telephone: (613) 992-3118
Fax: (613) 992-6382
E-mail: StewaJ@parl.gc.ca

The Minister of Indian Affairs and Northern Development

Meets the federal government's treaty obligations to Inuit and First Nations people, including the provision of basic services; negotiates and oversees claims settlements.
The Hon. Robert Daniel Nault
(Kenora–Rainy River, Ontario)
Telephone: (613) 996-1161
Fax: (613) 996-1759
E-mail: NaultR@parl.gc.ca

The Minister of Industry

Drafts major federal bills and programs for consumer and business groups; provides policy advice, business services and industrial information. The minister is also responsible for Western Economic Diversification.
The Hon. John Manley
(Ottawa South, Ontario)
Telephone: (613) 992-3269
Fax: (613) 995-1534
E-mail: ManleJ@parl.gc.ca

The Minister for International Cooperation

Administers economic and technical aid to the developing world through CIDA.
The Hon. Maria Minna
(Beaches–East York, Ontario)
Telephone: (613) 992-2115
Fax: (613) 996-7942
E-mail: MinnaM@parl.gc.ca

The Minister for International Trade

Takes part in international trade talks and institutions to promote Canadian business abroad and to resolve trade disputes.
The Hon. Pierre S. Pettigrew
(Papineau–Saint-Denis, Quebec)
Telephone: (613) 995-8872
Fax: (613) 995-9926
E-mail: PettiP@parl.gc.ca

The Minister of Justice and Attorney General of Canada

Provides legal services to all government departments and agencies; supervises the administration of justice.
The Hon. Anne McLellan
(Edmonton West, Alberta)
Telephone: (613) 992-4524
Fax: (613) 943-0044
E-mail: McLelA@parl.gc.ca

The Minister of Labour

Enforces the labour code including health and safety in the workplace; promotes fairness and cooperation between labour and management; provides mediation and conciliation in labour disputes.
The Hon. Claudette Bradshaw
(Moncton–Riverview–Dieppe, New Brunswick)
Telephone: (613) 992-8072
Fax: (613) 992-8083
E-mail: BradsC@parl.gc.ca

▶

The Minister of National Defence

Administers Canada's armed forces, defends citizens at home and meets Canada's military obligations abroad.
The Hon. Arthur C. Eggleton
(York Centre, Ontario)
Telephone: (613) 941-6339
Fax: (613) 941-2421
E-mail: EggleA@parl.gc.ca

The Minister of National Revenue and Secretary of State (Economic Development Agency of Canada for the Regions of Quebec)

Administers the Customs and Excise Acts as well as import and export taxes and permits.
The Hon. Martin Cauchon
(Outremont, Quebec)
Telephone: (613) 995-7691
Fax: (613) 995-0114
E-mail: CauchM@parl.gc.ca

The Minister of Natural Resources and Minister responsible for Canadian Wheat Board

Proposes and plans national policies for energy, mines and resources (renewable and nonrenewable); researches conservation and development strategies.
The Hon. Ralph E. Goodale
(Wascana, Saskatchewan)
Telephone: (613) 996-3843
Fax: (613) 992-5098
E-mail: GoodaR@parl.gc.ca

The Minister of Public Works and Government Services

Buys services to support the daily operation of government; provides office space and maintains public buildings; provides telecommunications and information services; prepares public audits and disburses public monies.
The Hon. Alfonso Gagliano
(Saint-Léonard–Saint Michel, Quebec)
Telephone: (613) 995-9414
Fax: (613) 992-8523
E-mail: GagliA@parl.gc.ca

The Minister of State and Leader of the Government in the House of Commons

Plans and manages the government's legislative agenda in its pre-parliamentary and parliamentary stages; maintains relations with the Opposition.
The Hon. Don Boudria
(Glengarry–Prescott–Russell, Ontario)
Telephone: (613) 996-2907
Fax: (613) 996-9123
E-mail: BoudrD@parl.gc.ca

The Minister of Transport

Oversees national policies to ensure competitive, safe and environmentally sustainable transportation.
The Hon. David Michael Collenette
(Don Valley East, Ontario)
Telephone: (613) 995-4988
Fax: (613) 995-1686
E-mail: ColleD@parl.gc.ca

The Minister of Veterans Affairs and Secretary of State (Atlantic Canada Opportunities Agency)

Provides Canadian combat veterans and their families with benefits; preserves the memory veterans' sacrifices and achievements.
The Hon. George S. Baker
(Gander–Grand Falls, Newfoundland)
Telephone: (613) 996-1541
Fax: (613) 992-5397
E-mail: BakerG@parl.gc.ca

The President of the Queen's Privy Council for Canada and Minister of Intergovernmental Affairs

Manages federal-provincial relations; provides legal advice on constitutional issues and national unity.
The Hon. Stéphane Dion
(Saint-Laurent–Cartierville, Quebec)
Telephone: (613) 996-5789
Fax: (613) 996-6562
E-mail: DionS@parl.gc.ca

The President of the Treasury Board and Minister responsible for Infrastructure

Functions as the government's chief employer and general manager; responsible for finances, personnel and administration.
The Hon. Lucienne Robillard
(Westmount-Ville Marie, Quebec)
Telephone: (613) 996-7267
Fax: (613) 995-8632
E-mail: RobilL@parl.gc.ca

The Solicitor General of Canada

Responsible for prisons, the RCMP, CSIS, parole boards and everything within Parliament's jurisdiction that is not legally assigned somewhere else.
The Hon. Lawrence MacAuley
(Cardigan, Prince Edward Island)
Telephone: (613) 995-9325
Fax: (613) 995-2754
E-mail: MacAuL@parl.gc.ca

▶

■ Secretaries of State

Secretary of State (Amateur Sport)
The Hon. Denis Coderre
(Bourassa, Quebec)
Telephone: (613) 995-6108
Fax: (613) 995-9755
E-mail: CoderD@parl.gc.ca

Secretary of State (Asia-Pacific)
The Hon. Raymond Chan
(Richmond, British Columbia)
Telephone: (613) 996-1995
Fax: (613) 996-1560
E-mail: ChanR@parl.gc.ca

Secretary of State (Children and Youth)
The Hon. Ethel Blondin-Andrew
(Western Arctic, Northwest Territories)
Telephone: (613) 992-4587
Fax: (613) 992-7411
E-mail: BlondE@parl.gc.ca

Secretary of State (Federal Economic Development Initiative for Northern Ontario) (Rural Development)
The Hon. Andrew Mitchell
(Parry Sound–Muskoka, Ontario)
Telephone: (613) 996-3434
Fax: (613) 991-2147
E-mail: MitchA@parl.gc.ca

Secretary of State (Francophonie) (Western Economic Diversification)
The Hon. Ronald J. Duhamel
(Saint Boniface, Manitoba)
Telephone: (613) 995-0579
Fax: (613) 996-7571
E-mail: DuhamR@parl.gc.ca

Secretary of State (International Financial Institutions)
The Hon. James Scott Peterson
(Willowdale, Ontario)
Telephone: (613) 992-4964
Fax: (613) 992-1158
E-mail: PeterJ@parl.gc.ca

Secretary of State (Latin America and Africa)
The Hon. David Kilgour
(Edmonton Southeast, Alberta)
Telephone: (613) 995-8695
Fax: (613) 995-6465
E-mail: KilgouR@parl.gc.ca

Secretary of State (Multiculturalism) (Status of Women)
The Hon. Hedy Fry
(Vancouver Centre, British Columbia)
Telephone: (613) 992-3213
Fax: (613) 995-0056
E-mail: FryH@parl.gc.ca

Secretary of State (Science, Research and Development)
The Hon. Gilbert Normand
(Bellechasse–Etchemins–Montmagny–L'Islet, Quebec)
Telephone: (613) 992-2289
Fax: (613) 992-6864
E-mail: NormaG@parl.gc.ca

Canada's Most Recent Federal Cabinet Shuffle

*O**n Aug. 3, 1999, Prime Minister Jean Chrétien shuffled the Cabinet. He welcomed five new ministers, changed responsibilities for another five ministers and retired five more.*

The newest ministers are George Baker (veterans' affairs), Elinor Caplan (citizenship and immigration), Martin Cauchon (national revenue), Maria Minna (international cooperation) and Robert Nault (Indian affairs and northern development)

David Anderson moved from fisheries and oceans to the environment; Harbance Dhaliwal traded national revenue for fisheries and oceans; Pierre Pettigrew shifted from human resources development to international trade; Lucienne Robillard moved from citizenship and immigration to the treasury board and infrastructure; Jane Stewart shifted from Indian affairs and northern development to human resources development.

Sergio Marchi departed from international trade; Diane Marleau left international cooperation and Francophonie; Marcel Massé retired from the treasury board and infrastructure; Fred Mifflin left veterans' affairs; Christine Stewart departed from environment.

Federal Opposition Critics

(as of Oct. 1999)

The role of Opposition MPs in the House of Commons is to present opposing and minority viewpoints to the Government's policies and decisions. Opposition MPs direct their criticism at Cabinet ministers during question period.

To make criticism more effective, Opposition parties appoint their leading MPs to focus on specific Cabinet ministers during the parliamentary session. These Opposition critics, listed below, are sometimes called "the shadow cabinet."

Party Affiliation	Cabinet Critic	Specific Area of Expertise	Telephone	Fax Number
Prime Minister of Canada				
Ref.	Preston Manning	....	(613) 996-6740	(613) 947-0310
BQ	Gilles Duceppe	....	(613) 992-6779	(613) 954-2121
BQ	Louis Plamondon	Official Languages, ... Francophones Outside Quebec	(613) 995-9241	(613) 995-6784
NDP	Alexa McDonough	....	(613) 995-7224	(613) 995-4565
PC	Elsie Wayne	....	(613) 947-4571	(613) 947-4574
Deputy Prime Minister of Canada				
Ref.	Deborah Grey	....	(613) 996-9778	(613) 996-0785
BQ	Louis Plamondon	Official Languages, ... Francophones Outside Quebec	(613) 995-9241	(613) 995-6784
PC	André Bachand	....	(613) 992-4473	(613) 995-2026
Agriculture and Agri-Food				
Ref.	Howard Hilstrom	....	(613) 992-2032	(613) 992-6224
BQ	Hélène Alarie	....	(613) 995-4995	(613) 996-8292
NDP	Dick Proctor	....	(613) 992-9115	(613) 992-0131
PC	Rick Borotsik	....	(613) 995-9372	(613) 992-1265
Canadian Heritage				
Ref.	Inky Mark	....	(613) 992-3176	(613) 992-0930
BQ	Suzanne Tremblay	....	(613) 992-5302	(613) 996-8298
BQ	Claude Bachand	Cultural Industries	(613) 992-5296	(613) 992-9849
BQ	Caroline St-Hilaire	Status of Women	(613) 992-8514	(613) 992-2744
NDP	Michelle Dockrill	Status of Women	(613) 992-6756	(613) 992-4053
NDP	Gordon Earle	Multiculturalism	(613) 996-3085	(613) 996-6988
NDP	Rick Laliberte	Parks	(613) 995-8321	(613) 995-7697
NDP	Wendy Lill	Communications, Cultural Industries	(613) 995-9378	(613) 995-9379
PC	Mark Muise	Status of Women	(613) 995-5711	(613) 996-9857
Citizenship and Immigration				
BQ	Réal Ménard	....	(613) 947-4576	(613) 947-4579
NDP	Louise Hardy	....	(613) 995-9368	(613) 995-0945
PC	Norman Doyle	....	(613) 996-7269	(613) 992-2178
Environment				
Ref.	Rick Casson	....	(613) 996-0633	(613) 995-5752
BQ	Jocelyne Girard-Bujold	....	(613) 992-2617	(613) 992-6069
NDP	Rick Laliberte	....	(613) 995-8321	(613) 995-7697
PC	John Herron	....	(613) 996-2332	(613) 995-4286
Finance				
Ref.	Monte Solberg	....	(613) 992-4516	(613) 992-6181
BQ	Yvan Loubier	....	(613) 996-4585	(613) 992-1815
BQ	Antoine Dubé	Regional Development	(613) 992-7434	(613) 995-6856
NDP	Lorne Nystrom	Banks	(613) 992-4593	(613) 996-3120
NDP	Nelson Riis	International Financial Institutions	(613) 995-6931	(613) 995-9897
PC	Scott Brison	....	(613) 995-8231	(613) 996-9349 ▶

Party Affiliation	Cabinet Critic	Specific Area of Expertise	Telephone	Fax Number
▶ **Fisheries and Oceans**				
Ref.	Gary Lunn	....	(613) 996-1119	(613) 996-0850
BQ	Yvan Bernier	....	(613) 992-6188	(613) 992-6194
NDP	Peter Stoffer	....	(613) 995-5822	(613) 996-9655
NDP	Svend Robinson	West Coast Fisheries	(613) 996-5597	(613) 992-5501
Foreign Affairs				
Ref.	Bob Mills	....	(613) 995-0590	(613) 995-6831
BQ	Daniel Turp	....	(613) 992-5036	(613) 995-7821
BQ	Maud Debien	Asia-Pacific; Latin America ... and Africa	(613) 992-0611	(613) 992-8556
NDP	Svend Robinson	International Affairs; .... International Human Rights	(613) 996-5597	(613) 992-5501
PC	André Bachand	....	(613) 992-4473	(613) 995-2026
Francophonie				
Ref.	Inky Mark	....	(613) 992-3176	(613) 992-0930
BQ	Monique Guay	....	(613) 992-3257	(613) 992-2156
PC	Diane St-Jacques	....	(613) 992-5279	(613) 992-7871
Health				
Ref.	Grant Hill	....	(613) 995-8471	(613) 996-9770
BQ	Pauline Picard	....	(613) 947-4550	(613) 947-4551
NDP	Judy Wasylycia-Leis	....	(613) 996-6417	(613) 996-9713
PC	Gregory Thompson	....	(613) 995-5550	(613) 995-5226
Human Resources Development				
Ref.	Diane Ablonczy	....	(613) 996-2750	(613) 992-2537
BQ	Paul Crête	....	(613) 995-0265	(613) 943-1229
BQ	Bernard Bigras	Children and Youth	(613) 992-0423	(613) 992-0878
BQ	Madeleine Dalphond-Guiral	Persons with Disabilities	(613) 995-7398	(613) 996-1195
BQ	Maurice Dumas	Seniors	(613) 992-0902	(613) 992-2935
NDP	Libby Davies	Children and Youth; .... Post Secondary Education; Social Programs	(613) 992-6030	(613) 995-7412
NDP	Michelle Dockrill	Seniors	(613) 992-6756	(613) 992-4053
NDP	Yvon Godin	Employment Insurance	(613) 992-2165	(613) 992-4558
NDP	Wendy Lill	Persons with Disabilities	(613) 995-9378	(613) 995-9379
NDP	Lorne Nystrom	Pension Reform	(613) 992-4593	(613) 996-3120
PC	Jean Dubé	....	(613) 995-0581	(613) 996-9736
PC	Charlie Power	Children and Youth	(613) 992-0927	(613) 995-7858
PC	Diane St-Jacques	Children and Youth	(613) 992-5279	(613) 992-7871
Indian Affairs and Northern Development				
Ref.	Mike Scott	....	(613) 993-6654	(613) 993-9007
BQ	Claude Bachand	....	(613) 992-5296	(613) 992-9849
NDP	Louise Hardy	....	(613) 995-9368	(613) 995-0945
PC	Gerald Keddy	....	(613) 996-0877	(613) 996-0878
Industry				
Ref.	Rahim Jaffer	....	(613) 995-7325	(613) 995-5342
BQ	Francine Lalonde	....	(613) 995-6327	(613) 996-5173
BQ	Hélène Alarie	Science, Research and Development	(613) 995-4995	(613) 996-8292
BQ	Antoine Dubé	Economic Development Agency of Canada for the Regions of Quebec	(613) 992-7434	(613) 995-6856
BQ	Yvan Loubier	Western Economic Diversification	(613) 996-4585	(613) 992-1815
NDP	John Solomon	Cooperatives; Small Business; Western Economic Diversification	(613) 992-4573	(613) 996-6885

▶

Party Affiliation	Cabinet Critic	Specific Area of Expertise	Telephone	Fax Number
▶ PC	Rick Borotsik	Western Economic Diversification	(613) 995-9372	(613) 992-1265
PC	André Harvey	Economic Development Agency of Canada for the Regions of Quebec	(613) 992-7207	(613) 992-0431
PC	John Herron	Small Business	(613) 996-2332	(613) 995-4286
PC	Jim Jones	Science, Research and Development	(613) 996-3374	(613) 992-3921
PC	Mark Muise	Atlantic Canada Opportunities Agency	(613) 995-5711	(613) 996-9857
Infrastructure				
Ref.	John Williams	. . . .	(613) 996-4722	(613) 995-8880
BQ	Pierrette Venne	. . . .	(613) 996-2416	(613) 995-6973
NDP	Bev Desjarlais	. . . .	(613) 992-3018	(613) 996-5817
PC	Scott Brison	. . . .	(613) 995-8231	(613) 996-9349
Intergovernmental Affairs				
Ref.	Val Meredith	. . . .	(613) 947-4497	(613) 947-4500
BQ	Pierre Brien	. . . .	(613) 996-3250	(613) 992-3672
BQ	Gilles-A. Perron	Public Service Renewal	(613) 992-7330	(613) 992-2602
NDP	William Blaikie	. . . .	(613) 995-6339	(613) 995-6688
PC	André Bachand	. . . .	(613) 992-4473	(613) 995-2026
International Cooperation				
BQ	Monique Guay	. . . .	(613) 992-3257	(613) 992-2156
PC	Diane St-Jacques	. . . .	(613) 992-5279	(613) 992-7871
International Trade				
Ref.	Charlie Penson	. . . .	(613) 992-5685	(613) 947-4782
BQ	Benoît Sauvageau	. . . .	(613) 992-5257	(613) 996-4338
NDP	William Blaikie	. . . .	(613) 995-6339	(613) 995-6688
PC	André Bachand	. . . .	(613) 992-4473	(613) 995-2026
Justice and Attorney General of Canada				
Ref	John Reynolds	. . . .	(613) 947-4617	(613) 947-4620
BQ	Michel Bellehumeur	. . . .	(613) 992-0164	(613) 992-5341
BQ	Madeleine Dalphond-Guiral	Human Rights	(613) 995-7398	(613) 996-1195
NDP	Peter Mancini	. . . .	(613) 995-6459	(613) 995-2963
NDP	Louise Hardy	Human Rights	(613) 995-9368	(613) 995-0945
PC	Peter Mackay	. . . .	(613) 992-6022	(613) 992-2337
Labour				
Ref.	Dale Johnston	. . . .	(613) 995-8886	(613) 996-9860
BQ	Yves Rocheleau	. . . .	(613) 992-2349	(613) 995-9498
NDP	Pat Martin	. . . .	(613) 992-5308	(613) 992-2890
PC	Jean Dubé	. . . .	(613) 995-0581	(613) 996-9736
Leader of the Government in the House of Commons				
Ref.	Randy White	. . . .	(613) 995-0183	(613) 996-9795
BQ	Michel Gauthier	. . . .	(613) 992-2244	(613) 992-9954
BQ	Stéphane Bergeron	Parliamentary Affairs	(613) 996-2998	(613) 995-1062
NDP	William Blaikie	. . . .	(613) 995-6339	(613) 995-6688
PC	Peter Mackay	. . . .	(613) 992-6022	(613) 992-2337
National Defence				
Ref.	Art Hanger	. . . .	(613) 947-4487	(613) 947-4490
BQ	René Laurin	. . . .	(613) 996-6910	(613) 995-2818
NDP	Gordon Earle	. . . .	(613) 996-3085	(613) 996-6988
PC	David Price	. . . .	(613) 995-2024	(613) 992-1696
National Revenue				
Ref.	Jason Kenney	. . . .	(613) 992-2235	(613) 992-1920
BQ	Gilles-A. Perron	. . . .	(613) 992-7330	(613) 992-2602 ▶

Party Affiliation	Cabinet Critic	Specific Area of Expertise	Telephone	Fax Number
▶ NDP	Lorne Nystrom	....	(613) 992-4593	(613) 996-3120
PC	Scott Brison	....	(613) 995-8231	(613) 996-9349
Natural Resources				
Ref.	David Chatters	....	(613) 996-1783	(613) 995-1415
BQ	René Canuel	....	(613) 995-1013	(613) 995-5184
BQ	Pierre de Savoye	....	(613) 992-2798	(613) 995-1637
BQ	Ghislain Fournier	Mines	(613) 992-5681	(613) 992-7276
NDP	Yvon Godin	....	(613) 992-2165	(613) 992-4558
NDP	Dick Proctor	Canadian Wheat Board	(613) 992-9115	(613) 992-0131
PC	Gerald Keddy	....	(613) 996-0877	(613) 996-0878
PC	Rick Borotsik	Canadian Wheat Board	(613) 995-9372	(613) 992-1265
Privy Council				
Ref.	Val Meredith	....	(613) 947-4497	(613) 947-4500
BQ	Pierre Brien	....	(613) 996-3250	(613) 992-3672
NDP	William Blaikie	....	(613) 995-6339	(613) 995-6688
PC	André Bachand	....	(613) 992-4473	(613) 995-2026
Public Works and Government Services				
Ref.	Werner Schmidt	....	(613) 992-7006	(613) 992-7636
BQ	Ghislain Lebel	....	(613) 992-6035	(613) 995-6223
BQ	Réal Ménard	Housing	(613) 947-4576	(613) 947-4579
NDP	Bev Desjarlais	Housing	(613) 992-3018	(613) 996-5817
PC	Gilles Bernier	....	(613) 947-4431	(613) 947-4434
PO	Jean Dubé	Housing	(613) 995-0581	(613) 996-9736
Ind.	Réjean Lefebvre	Canada Post Corporation	(613) 996-1806	(613) 996-6883
Solicitor General				
Ref.	Jim Abbott	....	(613) 995-7246	(613) 996-9923
BQ	Richard Marceau	....	(613) 995-8857	(613) 995-1625
NDP	Peter Mancini	....	(613) 995-6459	(613) 995-2963
PC	Peter Mackay	....	(613) 992-6022	(613) 992-2337
Speaker of the House of Commons				
BQ	Louis Plamondon	Library of Parliament	(613) 995-9241	(613) 995-6784
State				
Ref.	Randy White	....	(613) 995-0183	(613) 996-0706
BQ	Michel Gauthier	....	(613) 992-2244	(613) 992-9954
NDP	William Blaikie	....	(613) 995-6339	(613) 995-6688
PC	Peter Mackay	....	(613) 992-6022	(613) 992-2337
Transport				
Ref.	Lee Morrison	....	(613) 992-0657	(613) 992-5508
BQ	Michel Guimond	....	(613) 995-9732	(613) 996-2656
BQ	Paul Mercier	Railway Transportation	(613) 947-4788	(613) 947-4879
NDP	Bev Desjarlais	....	(613) 992-3018	(613) 996-5817
PC	William Casey	....	(613) 992-3366	(613) 992-7220
Treasury Board				
Ref.	John Williams	....	(613) 996-4722	(613) 995-8880
BQ	Pierrette Venne	....	(613) 996-2416	(613) 995-6973
NDP	Bev Desjarlais	....	(613) 992-3018	(613) 996-5817
PC	Scott Brison	....	(613) 995-8231	(613) 996-9349
Veterans Affairs				
Ref.	Peter Goldring	....	(613) 992-3821	(613) 992-6898
BQ	Maurice Godin	....	(613) 996-7265	(613) 996-9287
NDP	Gordon Earle	....	(613) 996-3085	(613) 996-6988
PC	Elsie Wayne	....	(613) 947-4571	(613) 947-4574

Members of Canada's Senate

(3 vacancies as of Oct. 5, 1999)

The Governor General appoints senators under the Great Seal of Canada on the prime minister's advice.

To be eligible for the Senate, a candidate must be a Canadian citizen and at least 30 years old. A candidate must also live in the region the appointment represents—either Ontario, Quebec, the West, the Maritimes or a territory. He or she must own land in that region with an unencumbered value of at least $4,000 and have a net estate worth at least $4,000. A senator from Quebec must either live in or have land in Quebec. A senator must retire at age 75.

Senator	Birthdate	Date Appointed	Appointed by	Province
Willie Adams	June 22, 1934	Apr. 5, 1977	Trudeau	Nunavut
Raynell Andreychuk	Aug. 14, 1944	Mar. 11, 1993	Mulroney	Sask.
W. David Angus	July 21, 1937	June 10, 1993	Mulroney	Que.
Norm Atkins	June 27, 1934	July 2, 1986	Mulroney	Ont.
Jack Austin	Mar. 2, 1932	Aug. 19, 1975	Trudeau	BC
Lise Bacon	Aug. 25, 1934	Sept. 15, 1994	Chrétien	Que.
James Balfour	May 22, 1928	Sept. 13, 1979	Clark	Sask.
Gérald Beaudoin	Apr. 15, 1929	Sept. 26, 1988	Mulroney	Que.
Eric Arthur Berntson	May 16, 1941	Sept. 27, 1990	Mulroney	Sask.
Roch Bolduc	Sept. 10, 1928	Sept. 26, 1988	Mulroney	Que.
J. Bernard Boudreau	1944	Oct. 4, 1999	Chrétien	NS
John G. Bryden	Aug. 25, 1937	Nov. 23, 1994	Chrétien	NB
John Buchanan	Apr. 22, 1931	Sept. 12, 1990	Mulroney	NS
Catherine Callbeck	July 25, 1939	Sept. 23, 1997	Chrétien	PEI
Pat Carney	May 26, 1935	Aug. 30, 1990	Mulroney	BC
Sharon Carstairs	Apr. 26, 1942	Sept. 15, 1994	Chrétien	Man.
Thelma Chalifoux	Feb. 8, 1929	Nov. 26, 1997	Chrétien	Alta
Ione Christensen	Oct. 10, 1933	Sept. 2, 1999	Chrétien	YT
Ethel Cochrane	Sept. 23, 1937	Nov. 17, 1986	Mulroney	Nfld
Michel Cogger	Mar. 21, 1939	May 2, 1986	Mulroney	Que.
Erminie J. Cohen	July 23, 1926	June 4, 1993	Mulroney	NB
Gérald J. Comeau	Feb. 1, 1946	Aug. 30, 1990	Mulroney	NS
Joan Cook	Oct. 6, 1934	Mar. 6, 1998	Chrétien	Nfld
Anne C. Cools	Aug. 12, 1943	Jan. 13, 1984	Trudeau	Ont.
Eymard Corbin	Aug. 2, 1934	July 9, 1984	Turner	NB
Pierre De Bané	Aug. 2, 1938	June 29, 1984	Trudeau	Que.
Mabel Margaret DeWare	Aug. 9, 1926	Sept. 23, 1990	Mulroney	NB
Consiglio Di Nino	Jan. 24, 1938	Aug. 30, 1990	Mulroney	Ont.
C. William Doody	Feb. 26, 1931	Oct. 3, 1979	Clark	Nfld
John Trevor Eyton	July 12, 1934	Sept. 23, 1990	Mulroney	Ont.
Joyce Fairbairn	Nov. 6, 1939	June 29, 1984	Trudeau	Alta
Marisa Ferratti Barth	Apr. 28, 1931	Sept. 23, 1997	Chrétien	Que.
Sheila Finestone	Jan. 28, 1927	Aug. 11, 1999	Chrétien	Que.
Isobel Finnerty	July 15, 1930	Sept. 2, 1999	Chrétien	Ont.
D. Ross Fitzpatrick	Feb. 4, 1933	Mar. 6, 1998	Chrétien	BC
John Michael Forrestall	Sept. 23, 1932	Sept. 27, 1990	Mulroney	Maritime[1]
Joan Fraser	1945	Sept. 17, 1998	Chrétien	Que.
George Furey	May 12, 1948	Aug.11, 1999	Chrétien	Nfld
Jean-Robert Gauthier	Oct. 22, 1929	Nov. 23, 1994	Chrétien	Ont.
Ronald D. Ghitter	Aug. 22, 1935	Mar. 25, 1993	Mulroney	Alta
Aurélien Gill	1933	Sept. 17, 1998	Chrétien	Que.
Jerahmiel S. Grafstein	Jan. 2, 1935	Jan. 13, 1984	Trudeau	Ont.
B. Alasdair Graham	May 21, 1929	Apr. 27, 1972	Trudeau	NS
Normand Grimard	June 16, 1925	Sept. 27, 1990	Mulroney	Que.[1]
Leonard J. Gustafson	Nov. 10, 1933	May 26, 1993	Mulroney	Sask.
Daniel Hays	Apr. 24, 1939	June 29, 1984	Trudeau	Alta
Céline Hervieux-Payette	Apr. 22, 1941	Mar. 21, 1995	Chrétien	Que.
Janis Johnson	Apr. 27, 1946	Sept. 27, 1990	Mulroney	Man.
Serge Joyal	Feb. 1, 1945	Nov. 26, 1997	Chrétien	Que.
James Francis Kelleher	Oct. 2, 1930	Sept. 23, 1990	Mulroney	Ont.
William M. Kelly	July 21, 1925	Dec. 23, 1982	Trudeau	Ont.
Colin Kenny	Dec. 10, 1943	June 29, 1984	Trudeau	Ont.
Wilbert Joseph Keon	May 17, 1935	Sept. 27, 1990	Mulroney	Ont.[1]
Noel A. Kinsella	Nov. 28, 1939	Sept. 12, 1990	Mulroney	NB
Michael Kirby	Aug. 5, 1941	Jan. 13, 1984	Trudeau	NS
E. Leo Kolber	Jan. 18, 1929	Dec. 23, 1983	Trudeau	Que.

▶

Senator	Birthdate	Date Appointed	Appointed by	Province
▶ Richard H. Kroft	May 22, 1938	June 11, 1998	Chrétien	Man.
Thérèse Lavoie-Roux	Mar. 12, 1928	Sept. 27, 1990	Mulroney	Que.[1]
Edward M. Lawson	Sept. 24. 1929	Oct. 7, 1970	Trudeau	BC
Marjory LeBreton	July 4, 1940	June 18, 1993	Mulroney	Ont.
P. Derek Lewis	Nov 28, 1924	Mar. 23, 1978	Trudeau	Nfld
Rose-Marie Losier-Cool	June 18, 1937	Mar. 21. 1995	Chrétien	NB
John Lynch-Staunton	June 19, 1930	Sept. 23, 1990	Mulroney	Que.
Shirley Maheu	Oct. 7, 1931	Feb. 1, 1996	Chrétien	Que.
Frank Mahovlich	Jan. 10, 1938	June 11, 1998	Chrétien	Ont.
Michael Arthur Meighen	Mar. 25, 1939	Sept. 27, 1990	Mulroney	Ont.[1]
Léonce Mercier	Aug. 11, 1926	Aug. 9, 1996	Chrétien	Que.
Lorna Milne	Dec. 13, 1934	Sept. 22, 1995	Chrétien	Ont.
Gildas L. Molgat	Jan. 25, 1927	Oct. 7, 1970	Trudeau	Man.
Wilfred P. Moore	Jan. 14, 1942	Sept. 26, 1996	Chrétien	NS
Lowell Murray	Sept. 26, 1936	Sept. 13, 1979	Clark	Ont.
Pierre Claude Nolin	Oct. 30, 1950	June 18, 1993	Mulroney	Que.
Donald H. Oliver	Nov. 16, 1938	Sept. 7, 1990	Mulroney	NS
Landon Pearson	Nov. 16, 1930	Sept. 15, 1994	Chrétien	Ont.
Lucie Pépin	Sept. 7, 1936	Apr. 8, 1997	Chrétien	Que.
Raymond J. Perrault	Feb. 6, 1926	Oct. 5, 1973	Trudeau	BC
Melvin Perry	August 23, 1925	Aug. 11, 1999	Chrétien	PEI
P. Michael Pitfield	June 18, 1937	Dec. 22, 1982	Trudeau	Ont.
Marie-Paul Poulin	June 21, 1945	Sept. 21, 1995	Chrétien	Ont.
Vivienne Poy	1941	Sept. 17, 1998	Chrétien	Ont.
Marcel Prud'homme	Nov. 30, 1934	May 26, 1993	Mulroney	Que.
Jean-Claude Rivest	Jan. 27, 1943	Mar. 1, 1993	Mulroney	Que.
Fernand Roberge	July 19, 1940	May 26, 1993	Mulroney	Que.
Brenda Mary Robertson	May 23, 1929	Dec. 21, 1984	Mulroney	NB
Fernand Robichaud	Dec. 2, 1939	Sept. 23, 1997	Chrétien	NB
Louis J. Robichaud	Oct. 21, 1925	Dec. 21, 1973	Trudeau	NB
Douglas Roche	1929	Sept. 17, 1998	Chrétien	Alta.
William Rompkey	May 13, 1936	Sept. 22, 1995	Chrétien	Nfld
Eileen Rossiter	July 14, 1929	Nov. 17, 1986	Mulroney	PEI
Calvin Ruck	Sept. 4, 1925	June 11, 1998	Chrétien	NS
Gerry St. Germain	Nov. 6, 1937	June 23, 1993	Mulroney	BC
Nick G. Sibbeston	Nov 21, 1943	Sept 2, 1999	Chrétien	NWT
Jean-Maurice Simard	June 21, 1931	June 26, 1985	Mulroney	NB
Herbert O. Sparrow	Jan. 4, 1930	Feb. 9, 1968	Pearson	Sask.
Mira Spivak	July 12, 1934	Nov. 17, 1986	Mulroney	Man.
John B. Stewart	Nov. 19, 1924	Jan. 13, 1984	Trudeau	NS
Peter A. Stollery	Nov. 29, 1935	July 2, 1981	Trudeau	Ont.
Terrance R. Stratton	Mar. 16, 1938	Mar. 25, 1993	Mulroney	Man.
Nicholas W. Taylor	Nov. 17, 1927	Mar. 7, 1996	Chrétien	Alta.
David Tkachuk	Feb. 18, 1945	June 8, 1993	Mulroney	Sask.
Charlie Watt	June 29, 1944	Jan. 16, 1984	Trudeau	Que.
The Very Rev. Lois Wilson	Apr. 8, 1927	June 11, 1998	Chrétien	Ont.

(1) Represents region rather than a province

Senate Changes

*A*s of Oct. 1, 1999, two senators are slated to retire in 1999: John B. Stewart on Nov. 19 and P. Derek Lewis on Nov. 28. In the year 2000, five senators are slated to retire: Normand Grimard on June 16, William M. Kelly on July 21, Melvin Perry (who was appointed in 1999) on Aug. 23, Calvin Woodrow Ruck on Sept. 4 and Louis J. Robichaud on Oct. 21. All were Liberal appointments.

Members of Parliament

(as of Oct. 1999)

Correspondence to Members of Parliament should be addressed individually and may be sent postage free to the following address: (Name of MP), House of Commons, Ottawa, Ontario, K1A 0A6. For general information, call (613) 992-4793.

To contact a government department or minister's office via the Internet, go to http://canada.gc.ca/main_e.html (the website for the Government of Canada) and access "Directories."

■ Newfoundland

Riding	Member (year of birth)	Party	Occupation	First Elected[1]
Bonavista/Trinity/Conception	Fred Mifflin (1938)	Lib.	Politician	1988
Burin/St. George's	Bill Matthews (1947)	Lib.	Politician	1997
Gander/Grand Falls	George S. Baker (1942)	Lib.	M.P.	1974
Humber/St. Barbe/Baie Verte	Gerry Byrne (1966)	Lib.	Civil Servant	1996*
Labrador	Lawrence O'Brien (1951)	Lib.	Civil Servant	1996*
St. John's East	Norman Doyle (1945)	PC	Politician	1997
St. John's West	Charlie Power (1948)	PC	Politician	1997

■ Prince Edward Island

Riding	Member (year of birth)	Party	Occupation	First Elected[1]
Cardigan	Lawrence MacAulay (1946)	Lib.	M.P.	1988
Egmont	Joe McGuire (1944)	Lib.	M.P.	1988
Hillsborough	George Proud (1939)	Lib.	Property Sup.	1988
Malpeque	Wayne Easter (1949)	Lib.	Farmer	1993

■ Nova Scotia

Riding	Member (year of birth)	Party	Occupation	First Elected[1]
Bras d'Or/Cape Breton	Michelle Dockrill (1960)	NDP	Health-care	1997
Cumberland/Colchester	Bill Casey (1945)	PC	Financial advisor	1997
Dartmouth	Wendy Lill (1950)	NDP	Writer/Soc. worker	1997
Halifax	Alexa McDonough (1945)	NDP	Social worker	1997
Halifax West	Gordon Earle (1943)	NDP	Civil servant	1997
Kings/Hants	Scott Brison (1967)	PC	Small business	1997
Pictou/Antigonish/Guysborough	Peter Mackay (1965)	PC	Crown attorney	1997
Sackville/Musquodoboit Valley/ Eastern Shore	Peter Stoffer (1956)	NDP	Customer Serv.	1997
South Shore	Gerald Keddy (1953)	PC	Businessman	1997
Sydney/Victoria	Peter Mancini (1956)	NDP	Legal Aid Lawyer	1997
West Nova	Mark Muise (1957)	PC	Insurance Agent	1997

■ New Brunswick

Riding	Member (year of birth)	Party	Occupation	First Elected[1]
Acadie/Bathurst	Yvon Godin (1955)	NDP	Staff Reprsntative	1997
Beauséjour/Petitcodiac	Angela Vautour (1960)	PC	Parks Canada	1997
Fredericton	Andy Scott (1955)	Lib.	Public Servant	1993
Fundy/Royal	John Herron (1967)	PC	Manager	1997
Madawaska/Restigouche	Jean Dubé (1962)	PC	Businessman	1997
Miramichi	Charles Hubbard (1940)	Lib.	School Principal	1993
Moncton/Riverview/Dieppe	Claudette Bradshaw (1949)	Lib.	Public servant	1997
New Brunswick Southwest	Greg Thompson (1947)	PC	Educator	1997
Saint John	Elsie Wayne (1932)	PC	Retired	1993
Tobique/Mactoguac	Gilles Bernier (1955)	PC	Businessman	1997

▶

▶ ■ **Quebec**

Riding	Member (year of birth)	Party	Occupation	First Elected[1]
Abitibi/Baie-James/Nunavik	Guy St-Julien (1940)	Lib.	Lawyer	1997
Ahuntsic	Eleni Bakopanos (1954)	Lib.	Political admin.	1993
Anjou/Rivière-des-Prairies	Yvon Charbonneau (1940)	Lib.	Politician	1997
Argenteuil/Papineau/Mirabel	Maurice Dumas (1927)	BQ	Professor	1993
Bas-Richelieu/Nicolet/Bécancour	Louis Plamondon (1943)	BQ	Businessman	1984
Beauce	Claude Drouin (1956)	Lib.	Civil servant	1997
Beauharnois/Salaberry	Daniel Turp (1955)	BQ	Professor	1997
Beauport/Montmorency/ Côte-de-Beaupré/Île-d'Orléans	Michel Guimond (1953)	Lib.	Lawyer	1993
Bellechasse/Etchemins/Montmagny/L'Islet	Gilbert Normand (1943)	Lib.	Doctor	1997
Berthier/Montcalm	Michel Bellehumeur (1963)	BQ	Lawyer	1993
Bonaventure/Gaspé/ Îes-de-la-Madeleine/Pabok	Yvan Bernier (1960)	BQ	Administrator	1993
Bourassa	Denis Coderre (1963)	Lib.	Editor	1997
Brome/Missisquoi	Denis Paradis (1949)	Lib.	Lawyer	1995
Brossard/La Prairie	Jacques Saada (1947)	Lib.	Teacher	1997
Chambly	Ghislain Lebel (1946)	BQ	Notary Public	1993
Champlain	Réjean Lefebvre (1943)	Ind.	Forestry	1993
Charlesbourg	Richard Marceau (1970)	BQ	Lawyer	1997
Charlevoix	Gérard Asselin (1950)	BQ	Foreman	1993
Châteauguay	Maurice Godin (1932)	BQ	Retired	1993
Chicoutimi	André Harvey (1941)	PC	School Com.	1997
Compton/Stanstead	David Price (1945)	PC	Mayor	1997
Drummond	Pauline Picard (1947)	BQ	Admin. Assistant	1993
Frontenac/Mégantic	Jean-Guy Chrétien (1946)	BQ	Professor	1993
Gatineau	Mark Assad (1940)	Lib.	Professor	1988
Hochelaga/Maisonneuve	Réal Ménard (1962)	BQ	Political Attaché	1993
Hull/Aylmer	Marcel Massé (1940)	Lib.	Economist	1993
Joliette	René Laurin (1940)	BQ	Director General	1993
Jonquière	Jocelyne Girard-Bujold (1943)	BQ	Businesswoman	1997
Kamouraska/Rivière-du-Loup/ Témiscouata/Les Basques	Paul Crête (1943)	BQ	Personnel Dir.	1993
Lac-Saint-Jean	Stéphan Tremblay (1973)	BQ	Bush Pilot	1996*
Lac-Saint-Louis	Clifford Lincoln (1928)	Lib.	Consultant	1993
LaSalle/Émard	Paul Martin (1938)	Lib.	M.P.	1988
Laurentides	Monique Guay (1959)	BQ	Businesswoman	1993
Laurier/Sainte-Marie	Gilles Duceppe (1947)	BQ	M.P.	1990*
Laval Centre	Madeleine Dalphond-Guiral (1938)	BQ	Professor	1993
Laval-Est	Maud Debien (1938)	BQ	Retired	1993
Laval-Ouest	Raymonde Folco (1940)	Lib.	Commissioner	1997
Lévis-et-Chutes-de-la-Chaudière	Antoine Dubé (1947)	BQ	Administrator	1993
Longueuil	Caroline St. Hilaire (1969)	BQ	Author agent	1997
Lotbinière	Odina Desrochers (1951)	BQ	Civil servant	1997
Louis-Hébert	Helene Alarie (1941)	BQ	Civil servant	1997
Manicouagan	Ghislain Fournier (1938)	BQ	Businessman	1997
Matapédia/Matane	René Canuel (1936)	BQ	Teacher	1993
Mercier	Francine Lalonde (1940)	BQ	Lecturer	1993
Mont-Royal	Vacant			
Notre-Dame-de-Grâce/Lachine	Marlene Jennings (1951)	Lib.	Public servant	1965
Outremont	Martin Cauchon (1962)	Lib.	Lawyer	1993
Papineau/Saint-Denis	Pierre Pettigrew (1951)	Lib.	Businessman	1996*
Pierrefonds/Dollard	Bernard Patry (1943)	Lib.	Doctor	1993
Pontiac/Gatineau/Labelle	Robert Bertrand (1953)	Lib.	Insurance Agent	1993
Portneuf	Pierre de Savoye (1942)	BQ	Professor	1993
Québec	Christiane Gagnon (1948)	BQ	Real Estate Agent	1993
Québec-Est	Jean-Paul Marchand (1944)	BQ	Writer	1993
Repentigny	Benoît Sauvageau (1963)	BQ	Teacher	1997
Richmond/Arthabaska	André Bachand (1951)	PC	Educator	1997

▶

▶ Rimouski/Mitis.....................................Suzanne Tremblay (1937)......................BQ   Professor   1993
Rivière-des-Mille-Îles......................Gilles–A. Perron (1940)........................BQ   Pol. Advisor   1997
Roberval..Michel Gauthier (1950)........................BQ   Administrator   1993
Rosemont...Bernard Bigras (1970)..........................BQ   Civil servant   1997
Saint-Hyacinthe/Bagot ....Yvan Loubier (1959)............................BQ   Economist   1993
Saint-Léonard/Saint-Michel ....Alfonso Gagliano (1942).......................Lib.   CGA   1984
Saint-Bruno/Saint-Hubert..................Pierrette Venne (1945).........................BQ   Notary Public   1988
Saint-Jean.......................................Claude Bachand (1951)........................BQ   Educator   1993
Saint-Lambert..................................Yolande Thibeault (1939)......................Lib.   Director (DRO)   1997
Saint-Laurent/Cartierville ....Stéphane Dion (1955)...........................Lib.   Professor   1996*
Saint-Maurice...................................Jean Chrétien (1934)...........................Lib.   Lawyer   1963
Shefford...Diane St-Jacques (1953) ....PC   P.R.   1997
Sherbrooke......................................Serge Cardin (n.a.) ....BQ   Accountant   1998*
Témiscamingue.................................Pierre Brien (1970)..............................BQ   Economist   1993
Terrebonne/Blainville ....Paul Mercier (1924)............................BQ   Mayor   1997
Trois-Rivières...................................Yves Rocheleau (1944)........................BQ   Dev. Consultant   1993
Vaudreuil/Solanges...........................Nunzio Discepola (1949)......................Lib.   Mayor   1993
Verchères/Les-Patriotes....................Stéphane Bergeron (1965)....................BQ   Political Attaché   1993
Verdun/Saint-Henri ....Raymond Lavigne (1945) ....Lib.   Consultant   1993
Westmount/Ville-Marie ....Lucienne Robillard (1945) ....Lib.   Politician   1995

■ Ontario

Riding	Member (year of birth)	Party	Occupation	First Elected[1]
Algoma/Manitoulin	Brent St. Denis (1950)	Lib.	Parl. Assistant	1993
Barrie/Simcoe/Bradford	Aileen Carroll (1944)	Lib.	Businesswoman	1997
Beaches/East York	Maria Minna (1948)	Lib.	Consultant	1993
Bramalea/Gore/Malton/Springdale	Gurbax Singh Malhi (1949)	Lib.	Real Estate Agent	1993
Brampton Centre	Sarkis Assadourian (1948)	Lib.	Businessman	1993
Brampton West/Missisauga	Colleen Beaumier (1944)	Lib.	Businesswoman	1993
Brant	Jane Stewart (1955)	Lib.	Human Resources	1993
Broadview/Greenwood	Dennis Mills (1946)	Lib.	Businessman	1988
Bruce/Grey	Ovid L. Jackson (1939)	Lib.	Teacher	1993
Burlington	Paddy Torsney (1962)	Lib.	Consultant	1993
Cambridge	Janko Peric (1949)	Lib.	Welder	1993
Carleton/Gloucester	Eugène Bellemare (1932)	Lib.	M.P.	1988
Chatham/Kent/Essex	Jerry Pickard (1940)	Lib.	Teacher	1997
Davenport	Charles Caccia (1930)	Lib.	Economist	1968
Don Valley East	David Collenette (1946)	Lib.	Mgmt. Consultant	1993
Don Valley West	John Godfrey (1942)	Lib.	Journalist	1993
Dufferin/Peel/Wellington/Grey	Murray Calder (1951)	Lib.	Poultry Producer	1993
Durham	Alex Shepherd (1946)	Lib.	C.A.	1993
Eglinton/Lawrence	Joseph Volpe (1947)	Lib.	Educator	1988
Elgin/Middlesex/London	Gar Knutson (1956)	Lib.	Manager	1993
Erie/Lincoln	John Maloney (1945)	Lib.	Lawyer	1993
Essex	Susan Whelan (1963)	Lib.	Lawyer	1993
Etobicoke Centre	Allan Rock (1947)	Lib.	Lawyer	1993
Etobicoke North	Roy Cullen (1944)	Lib.	Accountant	1996*
Etobicoke/Lakeshore	Jean Augustine (1937)	Lib.	School Principal	1993
Glengarry/Prescott/Russell	Don Boudria (1949)	Lib.	Civil Servant	1984
Guelph/Wellington	Brenda Chamberlain (1952)	Lib.	Exec. Director	1993
Haldimand/Norfolk/Brant	Bob Speller (1956)	Lib.	M.P.	1988
Haliburton/Victoria/Brock	John O'Reilly (1940)	Lib.	Real Estate Broker	1993
Halton	Julian Reed (1936)	Lib.	Farmer	1993
Hamilton East	Sheila Copps (1952)	Lib.	M.P.	1984
Hamilton Mountain	Beth Phinney (1938)	Lib.	M.P.	1988
Hamilton West	Stan Keyes (1953)	Lib.	M.P.	1988
Hastings/Frontenac/Lennox & Addington	Larry McCormick (1940)	Lib.	Consultant	1993
Huron/Bruce	Paul Steckle (1942)	Lib.	Businessman	1993
Kenora/Rainy River	Robert D. Nault (1955)	Lib.	M.P.	1988
Kingston & the Islands	Peter Milliken (1946)	Lib.	Lawyer	1988
Kitchener Centre	Karen Redman (1953)	Lib.	Councillor	1997
Kitchener/Waterloo	Andrew Telegdi (1946)	Lib.	Mun. Politician	1993
Lambton/Kent/Middlesex	Rose-Marie Ur (1946)	Lib.	Sr. Const. Asst.	1993

▶

▶	Lanark/Carleton	Ian Murray (1951)	Lib.	Govt. Relations	1993
	Leeds/Grenville	Joe Jordan (1958)	Lib.	Professor	1997
	London North Centre	Joe Fontana (1950)	Lib.	Businessman	1988
	London West	Sue Barnes (1952)	Lib.	Lawyer	1993
	London/Fanshawe	Pat O'Brien (1948)	Lib.	Teacher	1993
	Markham	Jim Jones (1945)	PC	Marketing Mgr	1997
	Mississauga Centre	Carolyn Parrish (1946)	Lib.	Public servant	1993
	Mississauga East	Albina Guarnieri (1953)	Lib.	M.P.	1988
	Mississauga South	Paul Szabo (1948)	Lib.	Chartered Acct.	1993
	Mississauga West	Steve Mahoney (1947)	Lib.	Bus./Politician	1997
	Nepean/Carleton	David Pratt (1955)	Lib.	Mun. Politician	1997
	Niagara Centre	Gilbert Parent (1935)	Lib.	Teacher	1997
	Niagara Falls	Gary Pillitteri (1936)	Lib.	Farmer	1993
	Nickel Belt	Raymond Bonin (1942)	Lib.	Professor	1993
	Nipissing	Bob Wood (1940)	Lib.	M.P.	1988
	Northumberland	Christine Stewart (1941)	Lib.	M.P.	1988
	Oak Ridges	Bryon Wilfert (1952)	Lib.	Ed/Mun. Politics	1997
	Oakville	Bonnie Brown (1941)	Lib.	Social Worker	1993
	Oshawa	Ivan Grose (1928)	Lib.	Businessman	1993
	Ottawa Centre	Mac Harb (1953)	Lib.	M.P.	1988
	Ottawa South	John Manley (1950)	Lib.	Lawyer	1988
	Ottawa West/Nepean	Marlene Catterall (1939)	Lib.	M.P.	1988
	Ottawa/Vanier	Mauril Bélanger (1955)	Lib.	M.P.	1995
	Oxford	John Finlay (1929)	Lib.	Retired	1993
	Parkdale/High Park	Sarmite Bulte (1953)	Lib.	Lawyer	1997
	Parry Sound/Muskoka	Andy Mitchell (1953)	Lib.	Bank Manager	1993
	Perth/Middlesex	John Richardson (1932)	Lib.	Self-employed	1993
	Peterborough	Peter Adams (1936)	Lib.	Professor	1993
	Pickering/Ajax/Uxbridge	Dan McTeague (1962)	Lib.	Media Relations	1993
	Prince Edward/Hastings	Lyle Vanclief (1943)	Lib.	Agrologist	1988
	Renfrew/Nipissing/Pembroke	Hec Clouthier (1949)	Lib.	Businessman	1997
	Sarnia/Lambton	Roger Gallaway (1948)	Lib.	Lawyer	1993
	Sault Ste. Marie	Carmen Provenzano (1942)	Lib.	Lawyer	1997
	Scarborough Centre	John Cannis (1951)	Lib.	HR Consultant	1993
	Scarborough East	John McKay (1948)	Lib.	Lawyer	1997
	Scarborough Southwest	Tom Wappel (1950)	Lib.	M.P.	1988
	Scarborough/Agincourt	Jim Karygiannis (1955)	Lib.	Ind. Engineer	1988
	Scarborough/Rouge River	Derek Lee (1948)	Lib.	Lawyer	1988
	Simcoe North	Paul DeVillers (1946)	Lib.	Lawyer	1993
	Simcoe/Grey	Paul Bonwick (1964)	Lib.	Businessman	1997
	St. Catharines	Walt Lastewka (1940)	Lib.	Plant Manager	1993
	St. Paul's	Carolyn Bennett (1950)	Lib.	Doctor	1997
	Stoney Creek	Tony Valeri (1957)	Lib.	Insurance	1993
	Stormont/Dundas/Charlottenburgh	Bob Kilger (1944)	Lib.	Businessman	1988
	Sudbury	Diane Marleau (1943)	Lib.	M.P.	1988
	Thornhill	Elinor Caplan (1944)	Lib.	Provincial Politician	1997
	Thunder Bay/Atikokan	Stan Dromisky (1931)	Lib.	Retired	1993
	Thunder Bay/Superior North	Joe Comuzzi (1933)	Lib.	M.P.	1988
	Timiskaming/Cochrane	Benoît Serré (1951)	Lib.	Businessman	1993
	Timmins/James Bay	Réginald Bélair (1949)	Lib.	M.P.	1997
	Toronto Centre/Rosedale	Bill Graham (1939)	Lib.	Lawyer	1993
	Trinity/Spadina	Tony Ianno (1957)	Lib.	Businessman	1993
	Vaughan/King/Aurora	Maurizio Bevilacqua (1960)	Lib.	Consultant	1988
	Waterloo/Wellington	Lynn Myers (1951)	Lib.	Mayor	1997
	Wentworth/Burlington	John Bryden (1943)	Lib.	Journalist	1993
	Whitby/Ajax	Judi Longfield (1947)	Lib.	Exec. Assistant	1997
	Willowdale	Jim Peterson (1941)	Lib.	Lawyer	1988
	Windsor West	Herb Gray (1931)	Lib.	Lawyer	1962
	Windsor/St. Clair	Richard Limoges	Lib.	Bank Manager	1999*
	York Centre	Arthur C. Eggleton (1943)	Lib.	Consultant	1993
	York North	Karen Kraft Sloan (1952)	Lib.	Consultant	1993
	York South/Weston	John Nunziata (1955)	Ind.	Lawyer	1984
	York West	vacant			▶

▶ ■ **Manitoba**

Riding	Member (year of birth)	Party	Occupation	First Elected[1]
Brandon/Souris	Rick Borotsik (1950)	PC	Mayor	1997
Charleswood St. James/Assiniboia	John Harvard (1938)	Lib.	Broadcaster	1988
Churchill	Bev Desjarlais (1955)	NDP	School trustee	1997
Dauphin/Swan River	Inky Mark (1947)	Ref.	Mayor	1997
Portage/Lisgar	Jake E. Hoeppner (1936)	Ind.-Ref.	Farmer	1993
Provencher	David Iftody (1956)	Lib.	Business Adv.	1993
Saint Boniface	Ronald J. Duhamel (n.a.)	Lib.	M.P.	1988
Selkirk/Interlake	Howard Hilstrom (1947)	Ref.	RCMP Officer	1997
Winnipeg Centre	Pat Martin (1955)	NDP	Union Official	1997
Winnipeg North-St. Paul	Rey Pagtakhan (1935)	Lib.	Physician	1988
Winnipeg North	Judy Wasylycia-Leis (1951)	NDP	Provincial Politician	1997
Winnipeg South	Reg Alcock (1948)	Lib.	Politician	1993
Winnipeg South Centre	Lloyd Axworthy (1939)	Lib.	M.P.	1979
Winnipeg/Transcona	Bill Blaikie (1951)	NDP	Clergyman	1979

■ **Saskatchewan**

Riding	Member (year of birth)	Party	Occupation	First Elected[1]
Battlefords/Lloydminster	Gerry Ritz (1951)	Ref.	Rancher	1997
Blackstrap	Allan Kerpan (1954)	Ref.	Farmer	1997
Churchill River	Rick Laliberte (1958)	NDP	Education	1997
Cypress Hills/Grasslands	Lee Morrison (1932)	Ref.	Farmer	1993
Palliser	Dick Proctor (1941)	NDP	Journalist	1997
Prince Albert	Derrek Konrad (1943)	Ref.	Surveyor	1997
Regina/Lumsden/Lake Centre	John Solomon (1950)	NDP	Businessman	1993
Regina/Qu'Appelle	Lorne Nystrom (1947)	NDP	Politician	1968
Saskatoon/Humboldt	Jim Pankiw (1966)	Ref.	Chiropractor	1997
Saskatoon/Rosetown/Biggar	vacant			
Souris/Moose Mountain	Roy Bailey (1928)	Ref.	School Supt.	1997
Wanuskewin	Maurice Vellacott (1955)	Ref.	Minister	1997
Wascana	Ralph E. Goodale (1949)	Lib.	Business Exec.	1993
Yorkton-Melville	Garry Breitkreuz (1945)	Ref.	Teacher	1993

■ **Alberta**

Riding	Member (year of birth)	Party	Occupation	First Elected[1]
Athabasca	David Chatters (1946)	Ref.	Farmer	1993
Calgary Centre	Eric Lowther (1954)	Ref.	Mgt. Consultant	1997
Calgary East	Deepak Obhrai (1950)	Ref.	Entrepreneur	1997
Calgary Northeast	Art Hanger (1943)	Ref.	Police Officer	1993
Calgary/Nose Hill	Diane Ablonczy (1949)	Ref.	Lawyer	1993
Calgary Southeast	Jason Kenney (1968)	Ref.	CEO-Taxpyrs.' org.	1997
Calgary Southwest	Preston Manning (1942)	Ref.	Consultant	1993
Calgary West	Rob Anders (1972)	Ref.	Lobbyist	1997
Crowfoot	Jack Ramsay (1937)	Ref.	Bus. Consultant	1993
Edmonton East	Peter Goldring (1944)	Ref.	Businessman	1997
Edmonton North	Deborah Grey (1952)	Ref.	Teacher	1989*
Edmonton Southeast	David Kilgour (1941)	Lib.	M.P.	1979
Edmonton/Strathcona	Rahim Jaffer (1971)	Ref.	Entrepreneur	1997
Edmonton Southwest	Ian McClelland (1942)	Ref.	Businessman	1993
Edmonton West	Anne McLellan (1950)	Lib.	Professor	1993
Elk Island	Ken Epp (1939)	Ref.	Instructor	1993
Lakeland	Leon E. Benoit (1950)	Ref.	Civ.servant/ Farmer	1993
Lethbridge	Rick Casson (1943)	Ref.	Manager/Printer	1997
Macleod	Grant Hill (1943)	Ref.	Physician	1993
Medicine Hat	Monte Solberg (1958)	Ref.	Businessman	1993 ▶

▶ Peace River..Charlie Penson (1942) ....Ref.   Farmer   1993
Red Deer...Bob Mills (1941) ....Ref.   Businessman   1993
St Albert..John Williams (1946) ....Ref.   Accountant   1993
Wetaskiwin..Dale Johnston (1941) ....Ref.   Farmer   1993
Wild Rose ....Myron Thompson (1936)............................Ref.   Retired   1993
Yellowhead...Cliff Breitkreuz (1940)..............................Ref.   Farmer   1993

■ British Columbia

Riding	Member (year of birth)	Party	Occupation	First Elected[1]
Burnaby/Douglas	Svend J. Robinson (1952)	NDP	M.P.	1979
Cariboo/Chilcotin	Philip Mayfield (1937)	Ref.	Ord. Minister	1993
Delta/South Richmond	John Cummins (1942)	Ref.	Teacher	1993
Dewdney/Alouette	Grant McNally (1962)	Ref.	Teacher	1997
Esquimalt/Juan de Fuca	Keith Martin (1960)	Ref.	Physician	1993
Fraser Valley	Chuck Strahl (1957)	Ref.	Logging Cont.	1993
Kamloops/Thompson/Highland Valleys	Nelson Riis (1942)	NDP	M.P.	1980
Kelowna	Werner Schmidt (1932)	Ref.	Businessman	1993
Kootenay/Boundary/Okanagan	Jim Gouk (1946)	Ref.	Real Estate Agt.	1993
Kootenay/Columbia	Jim Abbott (1942)	Ref.	Businessman	1993
Langley/Abbotsford	Randy White (1948)	Ref.	CMA	1993
Nanaimo/Alberni	Bill Gilmour (1942)	Ref.	Forester	1993
Nanaimo/Cowichan	Reed Elley (1945)	Ref.	Minister	1997
New Westminster/Coquitlam/Burnaby	Paul E. Forseth (1946)	Ref.	Probation Officer	1993
North Vancouver	Ted White (1949)	Ref.	Company Pres.	1993
Okanagan/Coquihalla	Jim Hart (1955)	Ref.	Account Exec.	1993
Okanagan/Shuswap	Darrel Stinson (1945)	Ref.	Mining	1993
Port Moody/Coquitlam/Port Coquitlam	Lou Sekora (1931)	Lib.	Politician	1998*
Prince George/Bulkley Valley	Richard M. Harris (1944)	Ref.	Retired	1993
Prince George/Peace River	Jay Hill (1952)	Ref.	Farmer	1993
Richmond	Raymond Chan (1951)	Lib.	Research Eng.	1993
Saanich/Gulf Islands	Gary Lunn (1957)	Ref.	Lawyer	1997
Skeena	Mike Scott (1954)	Ref.	Businessman	1993
South Surrey/White Rock/Langley	Val Meredith (1949)	Ref.	Businesswoman	1993
Surrey Central	Gurmant Grewal (1957)	Ref.	Real Estate Agt.	1997
Surrey North	Chuck Cadman (1948)	Ref.	Elec. Eng. Tech.	1997
Vancouver Centre	Hedy Fry (1941)	Lib.	Physician	1993
Vancouver East	Elizabeth Davies (1953)	NDP	Councillor	1997
Vancouver Island North	John Duncan (1948)	Ref.	Forester	1993
Vancouver Kingsway	Sophia Leung (1934)	Lib.	Social Worker	1997
Vancouver Quadra	Ted McWhinney (1924)	Lib.	Professor	1993
Vancouver South/Burnaby	Harbance Singh Dhaliwal (1952)	Lib.	Businessman	1993
Victoria	David Anderson (1937)	Lib.	Env. Consultant	1968
West Vancouver/Sunshine Coast	John Reynolds (1942)	Ref.	Businessman	1997

■ Yukon

Riding	Member (year of birth)	Party	Occupation	First Elected[1]
Yukon	Louise Hardy (1959)	NDP	Social worker	1997

■ Northwest Territiories

Riding	Member (year of birth)	Party	Occupation	First Elected[1]
Western Arctic	Ethel Blondin-Andrew (1951)	Lib.	Politician	1988

■ Nunavut

Riding	Member (year of birth)	Party	Occupation	First Elected[1]
Nunavut	Nancy Karetak-Lindell (1957)	Lib.	Businessperson	1997

(1) General election unless * indicating by-election. (n.a.) not available. PC—Progressive Conservative; Lib.—Liberal; NDP—New Democratic Party; Ref.—Reform Party; Ind.—Independent; Ind. Lib.—Independent Liberal; Ind. Ref.—Independent Reform.

Salaries of Federal Political Figures

(as of October 1999)

The **GOVERNOR GENERAL** receives $102 700 per year.
All **LIEUTENANT–GOVERNORS** receive $97 200 per year (taxable).
SENATORS.................$66 900 plus $10 500 tax-free expense allowance and 64 travel points[2] per year.

The following senators receive as *extra* salary on top of their Senate salaries:

Leader of the Government	$48 400 plus $2 080 car allowance.
Leader of the Opposition	$24 600
Speaker of the Senate	$37 400 plus $3 000 residence allowance and $1 040 car allowance.
Deputy Leader of the Government	$15 400
Deputy Leader of the Opposition	$9 600
Government Whip	$7 700
Opposition Whip	$4 800

MEMBERS OF PARLIAMENT—$66 900 plus $22 100 tax-free expense allowance[1] and 64 travel points[2] per year.[3]

The following members of Parliament receive as *extra* salary on top of their MP salaries:

Prime Minister	$72 700
Cabinet Ministers	$48 400
Speaker of the House	$51 000
Secretaries of State	$36 300
Deputy Speaker	$26 700
Official Opposition Leader	$51 000
Other Opposition Party Leaders	$30 600
Official Opposition House Leader	$24 600
Other House Leaders	$10 500
Government and Official Opposition Whips	$13 600
Other Party Whips	$7 700
Government and Opposition Deputy Whips	$7 700
Deputy Chairman, Committees of the Whole House	$10 900
Assistant Deputy Chairman, Committees of the Whole House	$10 900
Parliamentary Secretaries	$10 900

(1) MPs representing large rural districts listed in Schedule III of the Canada Elections Act receive an annual tax-free expense allowance of $27,200; MPs from Nunavut and the Western Arctic receive annual tax-free expense allowances of $29,200 each. (2) One travel point represents a first-class return air trip anywhere in Canada and can be used by representatives or their spouses or a designated family member. (3) Members who travel in Canada on official business and are at least 100 km from their principal residences may claim up to $6,000 in food, accomodation, and incidental expenses.

■ OFFICE BUDGET

Each of the 301 elected members has an office in both Ottawa and their riding, with staff to assist constituents with problems they may encounter when dealing with federal government departments and agencies. Each member's office budget covers staff salaries in Ottawa and constituency offices, as well as individuals or firms hired under contract. The budget is also intended to cover the costs of renting, equipping and maintaining constituency offices, as well as covering the costs of travel within the constituency and within the member's province.

A Member's office budget is set at $190,000; $193,300 or $196,500 according to the size of the constituency and its number of urban and/or rural polling divisions.

Geographic and Electoral Supplement: Members receive supplements to the main office budget if they represent large constituencies with over 70,000 voters (e.g. the riding of York North) and/or geographic boundaries over 8,000 sq. km (e.g. the riding of Nunavut). These annual budgetary supplements cover the additional staff, operating and travel expenses required to serve the riding. Based on constituency characteristics, these supplements range from $5,920 to $35,440 and may change after each general election as the riding demographics change. A member may have more than one constituency office should he or she so desire, and many do.

Other Services: To help meet the needs and requests of their constituents, members are also given access to printing, translation, mail and other support services that help them respond to the thousands of letters and requests they receive. (Canadians may write to members of Parliament free of charge from anywhere in Canada.) The services also allow members to keep the public up-to-date on the events in Ottawa through a parliamentary report generally known as a "householder." Finally, members are provided with desks, computers, typewriters, photocopiers and other office supplies and equipment required to run an efficient office in Ottawa.

■ PARLIAMENTARY PENSION PLAN

Members' pensions are provided for by law under the "Members of Parliament Retiring Allowances Act" and, like many pension plans, members must make a financial contribution. Specifically, members must contribute 9% of their annual sessional allowance (salary) of $66,900. For members who are receiving additional salaries for extra duties such as ministers, whips or parliamentary secretaries, they have the option to contribute up to 9% of these salaries as well. The Act also provides that, upon ceasing to be a member of the House of Commons, a former member who retired prior to 1995 is immediately entitled to an annual pension after a minimum of six years of service. This pension is payable at the rate of 4% per year of service (i.e., a minimum of 24%: 6 x 4%) up to a maximum of 75% (18.75 years of service) of the average of the best consecutive six years of earnings. Members who serve less than six years must withdraw their contributions.

Indexing of a former member of the House of Commons' pension begins only when he or she reaches the age of 60, except for extraordinary situations such as disability. Survivors' benefits are payable to spouses and dependent children. If a former member in receipt of a pension is re-elected to the House of Commons or becomes a senator, the pension allowance is suspended for the period in office. In 1995 the pension plan was amended to allow members to opt out; eliminate "double dipping" (drawing more than one pension after holding several positions); and provide that a former member cannot receive a pension until they are at least 55 years old.

Source: *Public Information Office, House of Commons*

Supreme Court Justices of Canada

(as of October 1999)

For information, recent judgements, and research information, visit the Supreme Court of Canada's website at www.scc-csc.gc.ca

Name	Date of Birth	Date Appointed	Appointed from
The Right Hon. Mr. Justice Antonio Lamer	July 8, 1933	Mar. 28, 1980[1,2]	Quebec Court of Appeal
The Hon. Madam Justice Beverley McLachlin	Sept. 7, 1943	Mar. 30, 1989	Supreme Court of BC
The Hon. Madam Justice Claire L'Heureux-Dubé	Sept. 7, 1927	Apr. 15, 1987	Quebec Court of Appeal
The Hon. Madam Justice Louise Arbour	Feb. 10, 1947	June 10, 1999	Ontario Court of Appeal
The Hon. Mr. Justice Charles Doherty Gonthier	Aug. 1, 1928	Feb. 1, 1989	Quebec Court of Appeal
The Hon. Mr. Justice Frank Iacobucci	June 29, 1937	Jan. 7, 1991	Federal Court of Canada
The Hon. Mr. Justice Ian Binnie	Apr. 14, 1939	Jan. 8, 1998	private law practice
The Hon. Mr. Justice John Charles Major	Feb. 20, 1931	Nov. 13, 1992	Alberta Court of Appeal
The Hon. Mr. Justice Michel Bastarache	June 10, 1947	Oct. 1, 1997	NB Court of Appeal

(1) Appointed Chief Justice July 1, 1990. (2) Stepping down January 7, 2000.

Lieutenant-Governors and Commissioners

(as of October 1999)

On the advice of the prime minister, the governor general of Canada appoints 10 provincial lieutenant-governors and three territorial commissioners. Lieutenant-governors and commissioners represent the monarch and perform the same duties at the provincial and territorial levels that the governor general performs at the federal level. They open, prorogue and dissolve legislatures and give royal assent to legislation and orders-in-council.

Lieutenant-governors and commissioners are paid by the federal government and usually serve terms of five years.

Province	Lieutenant-Governor	Birthdate	Date Sworn in
Newfoundland	Hon. A.M. House	Aug. 10, 1926	Feb. 5, 1997
Prince Edward Island	Hon. Gilbert R. Clements	Sept. 11, 1928	Aug. 30, 1995
Nova Scotia	Hon. J. James Kinley	Sept. 23, 1925	June 23, 1994
New Brunswick	Hon. Marilyn T. Counsell	Oct. 22, 1933	Apr. 18, 1997
Quebec	Hon. Lise Thibault	Apr. 2, 1939	Jan. 30, 1997
Ontario	Hon. Hilary Weston	Jan. 12, 1942	Jan. 24, 1997
Manitoba	Hon. Peter M. Liba	May 10, 1940	Mar. 2, 1999
Saskatchewan	Hon. John E.N. Wiebe	May 31, 1936	May 31, 1994
Alberta	Hon. H. (Bud) Olson	Oct. 6, 1925	Apr. 17, 1996
British Columbia	Hon. Garde B. Gardom	July 17, 1924	Apr. 21, 1995
Nunavut	Hon. Helen Maksagak	1931	Apr. 1, 1999
Northwest Territories	Hon. Daniel J. Marion	Dec. 6, 1945	Apr. 20, 1999
Yukon	Hon. Judy Gingell	Nov. 26, 1946	June 12, 1995

n.a. not available

Provincial Premiers: A Historical Listing

(as of October 1999)

■ Newfoundland

Premier	Term	Party	Elected or sworn in
Joseph R. Smallwood	1949–1972	Liberal	Apr. 1, 1949
Frank D. Moores	1972–1979	Conservative	Jan. 18, 1972
A. Brian Peckford	1979–1989	Conservative	Mar. 26, 1979
Tom Rideout	1989	Conservative	Mar. 22, 1989
Clyde Wells	1989–1996	Liberal	May 5, 1989
Brian Tobin	1996—	Liberal	Jan. 26, 1996

■ Prince Edward Island

Premier	Term	Party	Elected or sworn in
C. Pope	1873	Conservative	Apr., 1873
L. C. Owen	1873–76	Conservative	Sept., 1873
L. H. Davies	1876–79	Liberal (Coalition)	Aug.,1876
W. W. Sullivan	1879–89	Conservative	Apr. 25, 1879
N. McLeod	1889–91	Conservative	Nov., 1889
F. Peters	1891–97	Liberal	Apr. 27, 1891
A. B. Warburton	1897–98	Liberal	Oct., 1897
D. Farquharson	1898–1901	Liberal	Aug., 1898
A. Peters	1901–08	Liberal	Dec. 29, 1901
F. L. Haszard	1908–11	Liberal	Feb. 1, 1908
H. James Palmer	1911	Liberal	May 16, 1911
John A. Mathieson	1911–17	Conservative	Dec. 2, 1911
Aubin Arsenault	1917–19	Conservative	June, 21, 1917
J. H. Bell	1919–23	Liberal	Sept. 9, 1919
James D. Stewart	1923–27	Conservative	Sept. 5, 1923
Albert C. Saunders	1927–30	Liberal	Aug. 12, 1927
Walter M. Lea	1930–31	Liberal	May 20, 1930
James D. Stewart	1931–33	Conservative	Aug. 29, 1931
William J. P. MacMillan	1933–35	Conservative	Oct. 14, 1933

Walter M. Lea	1935–36	Liberal	Aug. 15, 1935
Thane A. Campbell	1936–43	Liberal	Jan. 14, 1936
J. Walter Jones	1943–53	Liberal	May 11, 1943
Alexander W. Matheson	1953–59	Liberal	May 25, 1953
Walter Shaw	1959–66	Prog. Conservative	Sept. 16, 1959
Alexander B. Campbell	1966–78	Liberal	July 28, 1966
William Bennett Campbell	1978–79	Liberal	Sept. 18, 1978
J. Angus MacLean	1979–81	Prog. Conservative	May 3, 1979
James M. Lee	1981–86	Prog. Conservative	Nov. 17, 1981
Joseph A. Ghiz	1986–93	Liberal	May 2, 1986
Catherine Callbeck	1993–96	Liberal	Jan. 25, 1993
Keith Milligan	1996	Liberal	Oct. 10, 1996
Pat Binns	1996—	Prog. Conservative	Nov. 27, 1996

■ Nova Scotia

Premier	Term	Party	Elected or sworn in
H. Blanchard	1867	Conservative	July 4, 1867
William Annand	1867–75	Liberal	Nov. 7, 1867
P. C. Hill	1875–78	Liberal	May 11, 1875
S. H. Holmes	1878–82	Conservative	Oct. 22, 1878
John S. D. Thompson	1882	Conservative	May 25, 1882
W. T. Pipes	1882–84	Liberal	Aug. 3, 1882
W. S. Fielding	1884–96	Liberal	July 28, 1884
George H. Murray	1896–1923	Liberal	July 20, 1896
E. H. Armstrong	1923–25	Liberal	Jan. 24, 1923
E. N. Rhodes	1925–30	Conservative	July 16, 1925
Col. Gordon S. Harrington	1930–33	Conservative	Aug. 11, 1930
Angus L. Macdonald	1933–40	Liberal	Sept. 5, 1933
A. S. MacMillan	1940–45	Liberal	July 10, 1940
Angus L. Macdonald	1945–54	Liberal	Sept. 8, 1945
Harold Connolly	1954	Liberal	Apr. 13, 1954
Henry D. Hicks	1954–56	Liberal	Sept. 30, 1954
Robert L. Stanfield	1956–67	Prog. Conservative	Nov. 20, 1956
George Smith	1967–70	Prog. Conservative	Sept. 13, 1967
Gerald A. Regan	1970–78	Liberal	Oct. 28, 1970
John Buchanan	1978–90	Prog. Conservative	Oct. 5, 1978
Roger Bacon	1990–91	Prog. Conservative	Sept. 12, 1990
Donald Cameron	1991–93	Prog. Conservative	Feb. 9, 1991
John Savage	1993–97	Liberal	June 11, 1993
Russell MacLellan	1997–99	Liberal	July 18, 1997
John Hamm	1999–	Prog. Conservative	July 27, 1999

■ New Brunswick

Premier	Term	Party	Elected or sworn in
Andrew Wetmore	1867–70	Confederation Party	1867
G.E. King	1870–71	Conservative	1870
George Hatheway	1871–72	Conservative	1871
G.E. King	1872–78	Conservative	1872
James Fraser	1878–82	Conservative	1878
D. L. Hanington	1882–83	Conservative	1882
Andrew Blair	1883–96	Liberal	1883
James Mitchell	1896–97	Liberal	July, 1896
Henry Emmerson	1897–1900	Liberal	Oct. 29, 1897
L. J. Tweedie	1900–07	Liberal	Aug. 31, 1900
William Pugsley	1907	Liberal	Mar. 6, 1907
Clifford Robinson	1907–08	Liberal	May 31, 1907
John Douglas Hazen	1908–11	Conservative	Mar. 24, 1908
James K. Flemming	1911–14	Conservative	Oct. 16, 1911
George J. Clark	1914–17	Conservative	Dec. 17, 1914
James Murray	1917	Conservative	Feb. 1, 1917
Walter E. Foster	1917–23	Liberal	Apr. 4, 1917
Peter Veniot	1923–25	Liberal	Feb. 28, 1923
John B. M. Baxter	1925–31	Conservative	Sept. 14, 1925
Charles D. Richards	1931–33	Conservative	May 19, 1931

Leonard Tilley	1933–35	Conservative	June 1, 1933
Allison Dysart	1935–40	Liberal	July 16, 1935
John McNair	1940–52	Liberal	Mar. 13, 1940
Hugh J. Flemming	1952–60	Prog. Conservative	Oct. 8, 1952
Louis J. Robichaud	1960–70	Liberal	July 12, 1960
Richard Hatfield	1970–87	Prog. Conservative	Nov. 12, 1970
Frank McKenna	1987–97	Liberal	Oct. 27, 1987
Ray Frenette (interim)	1997–98	Liberal	Oct 14, 1997
Camille Thériault	1998–99	Liberal	May 14, 1998
Bernard Lord	1999—	Prog. Conservative	June 21, 1999

■ Quebec

Premier	Term	Party	Elected or sworn in
Pierre-Joseph-Olivier Chauveau	1867–73	Conservative	July 15, 1867
Gédéon Ouimet	1873–74	Conservative	Feb. 26, 1873
Charles E. Boucher deBoucherville	1874–78	Conservative	Sept. 22, 1874
Henri Joly	1878–79	Liberal	Mar. 8, 1878
J. Adolphe Chapleau	1879–82	Conservative	Oct. 31, 1879
J. Alfred Mousseau	1882–84	Conservative	July 31, 1882
John J. Ross	1884–87	Conservative	Jan. 23, 1884
L. Olivier Taillon	1887	Conservative	Jan. 25, 1887
Honoré Mercier	1887–91	Liberal	Jan. 27, 1887
Charles E. Boucher deBoucherville	1891–92	Conservative	Dec. 21, 1891
L. Olivier Taillon	1892–96	Conservative	Dec. 16, 1892
Edmund J. Flynn	1896–97	Conservative	May 11, 1896
F. Gabriel Marchand	1897–1900	Liberal	May 24, 1897
S. Napoléon Parent	1900–05	Liberal	Oct. 3, 1900
Lomer Gouin	1905–20	Liberal	Mar. 23, 1905
L. Alexandre Taschereau	1920–36	Liberal	July 9, 1920
Adélard Godbout	1936	Liberal	June 11, 1936
Maurice Duplessis	1936–39	Union Nationale	Aug. 26, 1936
Adélard Godbout	1939–44	Liberal	Nov. 8, 1939
Maurice Duplessis	1944–59	Union Nationale	Aug. 30, 1944
Paul Sauvé	1959–60	Union Nationale	Sept. 11, 1959
Antonio Barrette	1960	Union Nationale	Jan. 8, 1960
Jean Lesage	1960–66	Liberal	July 5, 1960
Daniel Johnson	1966–68	Union Nationale	June 16, 1966
Jean-Jacques Bertrand	1968–70	Union Nationale	Oct. 2, 1968
Robert Bourassa	1970–76	Liberal	May 12, 1970
René Lévesque	1976–85	Parti Québécois	Nov. 25, 1976
Pierre-Marc Johnson	1985	Parti Québécois	Oct. 3, 1985
Robert Bourassa	1985–94	Liberal	Dec. 12, 1985
Daniel Johnson	1994–94	Liberal	Jan. 11, 1994
Jacques Parizeau	1994–96	Parti Québécois	Sept. 26, 1994
Lucien Bouchard	1996—	Parti Québécois	Jan. 29, 1996

■ Ontario

Premier	Term	Party	Elected or sworn in
J.S. Macdonald	1867–71	Coalition	July 16, 1867
Edward Blake	1871–72	Liberal	Dec. 20, 1871
Oliver Mowat	1872–96	Liberal	Oct. 25, 1872
Arthur S. Hardy	1896–99	Liberal	July 25, 1896
George William Ross	1899–1905	Liberal	Oct. 21, 1899
Sir James P. Whitney	1905–14	Conservative	Feb. 8, 1905
Sir William Hearst	1914–19	Conservative	Oct. 2, 1914
Ernest C. Drury	1919–23	United Farmers of Ontario	Nov. 14, 1919
George Howard Ferguson	1923–30	Conservative	July 16, 1923
George Stewart Henry	1930–34	Conservative	Dec. 15, 1930
Mitchell F. Hepburn	1934–42	Liberal	July 10, 1934
Gordon Daniel Conant	1942–43	Liberal	Oct. 21, 1942
Harry C. Nixon	1943	Liberal	May 18, 1943
George Drew	1943–48	Prog. Conservative	Aug. 17, 1943
Thomas L. Kennedy	1948–49	Prog. Conservative	Oct. 19, 1948
Leslie M. Frost	1949–61	Prog. Conservative	May 4, 1949

John P. Robarts	1961–71	Prog. Conservative	Nov. 8, 1961
William G. Davis	1971–85	Prog. Conservative	Mar. 1, 1971
Frank Miller	1985	Prog. Conservative	Feb. 8, 1985
David Peterson	1985–90	Liberal	June 26, 1985
Bob Rae	1990–95	New Democratic	Oct. 1, 1990
Mike Harris	1995—	Prog. Conservative	June 28, 1995

■ Manitoba

Premier	Term	Party	Elected or sworn in
A. Boyd	1870–71	n.a.	Sept. 16, 1870
M. A. Girard	1871–72	Conservative	Dec. 14, 1871
H. H. Clarke	1872–74	n.a.	Mar. 14, 1872
M. A. Girard	1874	Conservative	July 8, 1874
R. A. Davis	1874–78	n.a.	Dec. 3, 1874
John Norquay	1878–87	Conservative	Oct. 16, 1878
D. H. Harrison	1887–88	Conservative	Dec. 26, 1887
T. Greenway	1888–1900	Liberal	Jan. 19, 1888
H. J. Macdonald	1900	Conservative	Jan. 8, 1900
Sir R. P. Roblin	1900–15	Conservative	Oct. 29, 1900
T. C. Norris	1915–22	Liberal	May 12, 1915
John Bracken	1922–43	Coalition[1]	Aug. 8, 1922
S. S. Garson	1943–48	Coalition	Jan. 8, 1943
D. L. Campbell	1948–58	Conservative	Nov. 11, 1948
Duff Roblin	1958–67	Prog. Conservative	June 16, 1958
Walter Weir	1967–69	Prog. Conservative	Nov. 25, 1967
Edward Schreyer	1969–77	New Democratic	July 15, 1969
Sterling Lyon	1977–81	Prog. Conservative	Nov. 24, 1977
Howard Pawley	1981–88	New Democratic	Nov. 30, 1981
Gary Filmon	1988–99	Prog. Conservative	Apr. 26, 1988
Gary Doerr	1999—	New Democratic	Oct. 5, 1999

■ Saskatchewan

Premier	Term	Party	Elected or sworn in
Walter Scott	1905–16	Liberal	Sept. 5, 1905
W. M. Martin	1916–22	Liberal	Oct. 20, 1916
C. A. Dunning	1922–26	Liberal	Apr. 5, 1922
J. G. Gardiner	1926–29	Liberal	Feb. 26, 1926
J. T. M. Anderson	1929–34	Conservative	Sept. 9, 1929
J. G. Gardiner	1934–35	Liberal	July 19, 1934
W. J. Patterson	1935–44	Liberal	Nov. 1, 1935
Tommy Douglas	1944–61	C.C.F.[2]	July 10, 1944
W. S. Lloyd	1961–64	C.C.F.—N.D.P.	Nov. 7, 1961
W. Ross Thatcher	1964–71	Liberal	May 22, 1964
Allan E. Blakeney	1971–82	New Democratic	June 30, 1971
Grant Devine	1982–91	Prog. Conservative	May 8, 1982
Roy Romanow	1991—	New Democratic	Nov. 1, 1991

■ Alberta

Premier	Term	Party	Elected or sworn in
Alex Rutherford	1905–10	Liberal	Sept. 2, 1905
A. L. Sifton	1910–17	Liberal	May 26, 1910
Charles Stewart	1917–21	Liberal	Oct. 30, 1917
Herbert Greenfield	1921–25	United Farmers of Alberta	Aug. 13, 1921
John E. Brownlee	1925–34	United Farmers of Alberta	Nov. 23, 1925
Richard G. Reid	1934–35	United Farmers of Alberta	July 10, 1934
William Aberhart	1935–43	Social Credit	Sept. 3, 1935
E. C. Manning	1943–68	Social Credit	May 31, 1943
Harry Strom	1968–71	Social Credit	Dec. 12, 1968
Peter Lougheed	1971–85	Prog. Conservative	Sept. 10, 1971
Don Getty	1985–92	Prog. Conservative	Nov. 1, 1985
Ralph P. Klein	1992—	Prog. Conservative	Dec. 14, 1992

■ **British Columbia**

Premier	Term	Party	Elected or sworn in
J. F. McCreight	1871–72	n.a.	Nov. 13, 1871
Amor De Cosmos	1872–74	n.a.	Dec. 23, 1872
G. A. Walkem	1874–76	n.a.	Feb. 11, 1874
A. C. Elliott	1876–78	n.a.	Feb. 1, 1876
G. A. Walkem	1878–82	n.a.	June 25, 1878
Robert Beaven	1882–83	n.a.	June 13, 1882
William Smithe	1883–87	n.a.	Jan. 29, 1883
A. E. B. Davie	1887–89	n.a.	May 1, 1887
John Robson	1889–92	n.a.	Aug. 2, 1889
Theodore Davie	1892–95	n.a.	July 2, 1892
J. H. Turner	1895–98	n.a.	Mar. 4, 1895
C. A. Semlin	1898–1900	n.a.	Aug. 15, 1898
Joseph Martin	1900	n.a.	Feb. 28, 1900
James Dunsmuir	1900–02	n.a.	June 15, 1900
E. G. Prior	1902–03	n.a.	Nov. 21, 1902
Richard McBride	1903–15	Conservative	June 1, 1903
William J. Bowser	1915–16	Conservative	Dec. 15, 1915
Harlan C. Brewster	1916–18	Liberal	Nov. 23, 1916
John Oliver	1918–27	Liberal	Mar. 6, 1918
John D. MacLean	1927–28	Liberal	Aug. 20, 1927
Simon F. Tolmie	1928–33	Conservative	Aug. 21, 1928
T. D. Pattullo	1933–41	Liberal	Nov. 15, 1933
John Hart	1941–47	Liberal[3]	Dec. 9, 1941
Byron Johnson	1947–52	Liberal[3]	Dec. 29, 1947
W. A. C. Bennett	1952–72	Social Credit	Aug. 1, 1952
David Barrett	1972–75	New Democratic	Sept. 15, 1972
William R. Bennett	1975–86	Social Credit	Dec. 22, 1975
Bill Vander Zalm	1986–91	Social Credit	Aug. 6, 1986
Rita Johnston	1991–91	Social Credit	Apr. 2, 1991
Michael Harcourt	1991–96	New Democratic	Nov. 5, 1991
Glen Clark	1996–99	New Democratic	Feb. 22, 1996
Dan Miller	1999—	New Democratic	Aug. 25, 1999

■ **Nunavut**

Premier	Term	Party	Elected or sworn in
Paul Okalik	1999—	n.a.	Apr. 1, 1999

■ **Northwest Territories**

Premier	Term	Party	Elected or sworn in
George Braden	1980–83	n.a.	July 25, 1980
Richard Nerysoo	1984–85	n.a.	Jan. 12, 1984
Nick Sibbeston	1985–87	n.a.	Nov. 5, 1985
Dennis Patterson	1987–91	n.a.	Nov. 12, 1987
Nellie Cournoyea	1991–95	n.a.	Nov. 13, 1991
Don Morin	1995–98	n.a.	Nov. 20, 1995
James L. Antoine	1998—	n.a.	Dec. 10, 1998

■ **Yukon**

Government Leader	Term	Party	Elected or sworn in
Chris Pearson	1978–85	Yukon Progressive Conservative	
Willard Phelps	1985	Yukon Progressive Conservative	
Tony Penikett	1985–92[4]	New Democratic	
John Ostashek	1992–96	Yukon Party	
Piers McDonald	1996—	New Democratic	

Source: *Historical Statistics of Canada; Provincial Archives*

(1) United Farmer/Progressive, 1922–27; Coalition, 1927–37; Liberal—Progressive, 1937–43. (2) Co-operative Commonwealth Federation. (3) Coalition. (4) From 1989–92, Government Leader was designated Premier. (n.a.) not available.

Cabinets of the Provinces and Territories

(as of October 1999)

■ Newfoundland

Ministry or Portfolio	Minister
Premier	Brian Tobin
Development and Rural Renewal	Beaton Tulk
Education	Judy Foote
Environment and Labour	Oliver Langdon
Finance; Justice	Paul Dicks
Fisheries and Aquaculture	John Efford
Forest Resources and Agrifoods	Kevin Aylward
Government Services and Lands	Ernest McLean
Health and Community Services	Joan-Marie Aylward
Human Resources and Employment	Julie Bettney
Industry, Trade and Technology	Sandra Kelly
Intergovernmental Affairs	Walter Noel
Mines and Energy	Roger Grimes
Municipal and Provincial Affairs	Lloyd Matthews
President of Treasury Board	Anna Thistle
Tourism, Culture and Recreation	Chuck Furey
Works, Services and Transportation	Rick Woodford

■ New Brunswick

Ministry or Portfolio	Minister
Premier; Intergovernmental and Aboriginal Affairs	Bernard Lord
Deputy Premier; Supply and Services	Dale Graham
Agriculture and Rural Development	Milton Shorwood
Attorney General and Justice	Bradley Green
Economic Development, Tourism and Culture	Peter Mesheau
Education	Elvy Robichaud
Environment	Kim Jardine
Finance	Norman Betts
Fisheries and Aquaculture	Paul Robichaud
Health and Community Services	Dennis Furlong
Labour	Norman McFarlane
Municipalities and Housing	Joan MacAlpine
Natural Resources and Energy	Jeannot Volpé
Solicitor General; Human Resources Development	Percy Mockler
Transportation	Margaret-Ann Blaney

■ Nova Scotia

Ministry or Portfolio	Minister
Premier; President of Executive Council; Intergovernmental Affairs	John Hamm
Community Services	Peter G. Christie
Economic Development; Transportation and Public Works	Gordon D. Balser
Education; Technology and Science Secretariat	Jane S. Purves
Finance; Business and Consumer Services	Neil J. LeBlanc
Health	Jamie A. Muir
Housing and Municipal Affairs	Angus MacIsaac
Human Resources	John E. Chataway
Justice	Michael G. Baker
Labour; Environment	Ronald S. Russell
Natural Resources; Agriculture and Marketing; Fisheries and Aquaculture	Ernie Fage
Tourism and Culture	Rodney J. MacDonald

■ Prince Edward Island

Ministry or Portfolio	Minister
Premier; Intergovernmental Affairs	Patrick G. Binns
Agriculture and Forestry	J. Eric Hammill
Attorney General; Community Affairs	J. Weston MacAleer
Development	Don MacKinnon

▶

▶ Education	J. Chester Gillan
Fisheries and Tourism	Kevin J. MacAdam
Health and Social Services	Mildred A. Dover
Provincial Treasurer	Patricia J. Mella
Technology and Environment	P. Mitchell Murphy
Transportation and Public Works	Michael F. Currie

■ Quebec

Ministry or Portfolio	Minister
Premier	Lucien Bouchard
Deputy Premier; Finance; Industry and Trade; Revenue	Bernard Landry
Administration and Public Service; Treasury Board	Jacques Léonard
Agriculture, Fisheries and Food	Rémy Trudel
Canadian Intergovernmental Affairs	Joseph Facal
Charter of the French Language; International Relations; Relations with French-speaking Communities	Louise Beaudoin
Child and Family Welfare; Health and Social Services	Pauline Marois
Child and Family Welfare	Nicole Léger
Culture and Communications	Agnés Maltais
Education; Education and Youth	François Legault
Electoral Reform; Native Affairs; Transport; Wildlife	Guy Chevrette
Employment; Labour	Diane Lemieux
Environment	Paul Bégin
Government House Leader; Natural Resources; Parliamentary Reform	Jacques Brassard
Health, Social and Youth Protection	Gilles Baril
Industry and Trade	Guy Julien
Information Highway and Government Services	David Cliché
Justice; Status of Women	Linda Goupil
Municipal Affairs and Greater Montreal; Seniors	Louise Harel
Public Security	Serge Ménard
Regions	Jean-Pierre Jolivet
Relations with Citizens and Immigration	Robert Perreault
Research, Science and Technology	Jean Rochon
Social Solidarity	André Boisclair
Tourism	André Arseneau
Transport	Jacques Baril

■ Ontario

Ministry or Portfolio	Minister
Premier	Michael D. Harris
Deputy Premier; Finance	Ernie Eves
Agriculture, Food and Rural Affairs	Ernie Hardeman
Attorney General; Native Affairs	James M. Flaherty
Citizenship, Culture and Recreation; Seniors and Women	Helen Joanne Johns
Community and Social Services; Francophone Affairs	John R. Baird
Consumer and Commercial Relations	Robert Runciman
Correctional Services	Rob Sampson
Economic Development and Trade	Al Palladini
Education	Janet Lynne-Ecker
Energy, Science and Technology	Jim Wilson
Environment	Tony Clement
Government House Leader; Intergovernmental Affairs	Norman W. Sterling
Health and Long-Term Care	Elizabeth Witmer
Labour	Chris Stockwell
Management Board of Cabinet	Chris Hodgson
Municipal Affairs and Housing	James Stevenson Gilchrist
Natural Resources	John C. Snobelen
Northern Development and Mines	Timothy Patrick Hudak
Solicitor General	David H. Tsubouchi
Tourism	Cameron D. Jackson
Transportation	David Turnbull
Min. without Portfolio; Children	Margaret Marland
Min. without Porfolio; Chief Government Whip and Deputy House Leader	Frank F. Klees

▶ ■ Manitoba

Ministry or Portfolio	Minister
Premier; Pres. of Exec. Council; Federal-Provincial Relations	Gary Doer
Aboriginal and Northern Affairs	Eric Robinson
Agriculture and Food	Rosann Wowchuk
Conservation	Oscar Lathlin
Consumer and Corporate Affairs	Ron Lemieux
Culture and Tourism; Status of Women; Seniors	Diane McGifford
Education and Training	Drew Caldwell
Family Services and Housing	Tim Sale
Finance; French Language Services	Gregory F. Selinger
Health; Sport	David Chomiak
Highways and Government Services	Steve Ashton
Industry and Trade	MaryAnn Mihychuk
Intergovernmental Affairs	Jean Friesen
Justic and Attorney General; Constitutional Affairs	Gord Mackintosh
Labour; Multiculturalism; Civil Service	Becky Barrett

■ Saskatchewan

Ministry or Portfolio	Minister
Premier	Roy Romanow
Deputy Premier; Agriculture and Food	Dwain Lingenfelter
Crown Investments Corporation	John Nilson
Economic and Co-operative Development	Janice MacKinnon
Education	Jim Melanchuk
Energy and Mines	Eldon Lautermilch
Environment and Resource Management	Buckley Belanger
Finance	Eric Cline
Health	Patricia Atkinson
Health, Associate Minister; Seniors	Judy Junor
Highways & Transportation	Maynard Sonntag
Intergovernmental and Aboriginal Affairs	Jack Hillson
Justice and Attorney General	Chris Axworthy
Labour	Joanne Crofford
Municipal Affairs, Culture and Housing	Clay Serby
Northern Affairs	Keith Goulet
Post-Secondary Education and Skills Training	Glenn Hagel
Saskatchewan Property Management Corporation; Gaming	Doreen Hamilton
Social Services	Harry Van Mulligan

■ Alberta

Ministry or Portfolio	Minister
Premier	Ralph Klein
Aboriginal Affairs (Assoc. Min.)	Pearl Calahasen
Agriculture, Food and Rural Development	Ty Lund
Children's Services	Iris Evans
Community Development; Seniors' Housing	Stan Woloshyn
Economic Development	Jon Havelock
Environment	Gary Mar
Forestry (Assoc. Min.)	Mike Cardinal
Gaming	Murray D. Smith
Government Services; Consumer Affairs	Pat L. Nelson
Health and Wellness	Halvar C. Jonson
Health and Wellness (Assoc. Min.)	Gene Zwozdesky
Human Resources and Employment	Clint Dunford
Infrastructure; Transportation; Utilities	Ed Stelmach
Innovation and Science	Lorne Taylor
International and Intergovernmental Relations	Shirley McClellan
Justice and Attorney General	Dave Hancock
Learning	Lyle Oberg

▶

▶ Municipal Affairs .... Walter Paszkowski
Resource Development; Energy .... Stephen C. West
Treasury .... Stockwell B. Day

■ British Columbia

Ministry or Portfolio	Minister
Premier; Energy and Mines; Northern Development	Dan Miller
Deputy Premier; Children and Families	Lois Boone
Aboriginal Affairs; Insurance Corporation of British Columbia	Dale Lovick
Advanced Education, Training and Technology; Intergovernmental Relations; Youth	Andrew Petter
Agriculture and Food	Corky Evans
Attorney General; Multiculturism, Human Rights and Immigration	Ujjal Dosanjh
Community Development, Cooperatives and Volunteers	Jan Pullinger
Education; BC Ferries	Gordon Wilson
Employment and Investment	Michael Farnworth
Environment, Lands and Parks	Joan Sawicki
Finance and Corporate Relations	Paul Ramsay
Fisheries	Dennis Streifel
Forests	David G. Zirnhelt
Health; Seniors	Penny Priddy
Labour	Joan Smallwood
Municipal Affairs	Jim Doyle
Public Service	Helmut Giesbrecht
Small Business, Tourism and Culture	Ian Waddell
Social Development and Economic Security	Moe Sihota
Transportation and Highways	Harry Lali
Women's Equality	Jenny Kwan

■ Nunavut

Ministry or Portfolio	Minister
Premier; Executive and Intergovernmental Affairs	Paul Okalik
Community Government, Housing and Transportation; Justice	Jack Anawak
Culture, Language, Elders and Youth; Status of Women	Donald Havioyak
Education	James Arvaluk
Finance and Administration; Human Resources; Workers Compensation Board	Kelvin Ng
Health and Social Services; Northwest Territories Power Corporation	Edward Picco
Public Works, Telecommunications and Technical Services	Manitok Thompson
Sustainable Development	Peter Kilabuk

■ Northwest Territories

Ministry or Portfolio	Minister
Premier; Aboriginal Affairs; Intergovernmental Affairs	James L. Antoine
Deputy Premier; Health and Social Services; Northwest Territories Housing Corporation; Seniors	Floyd Roland
Education, Culture and Employment; Workers' Compensation Board; Public Utilities Board; Youth	Michael Miltenberger
Finance; Financial Management Board; Northwest Territories Power Corporartion; Women's Directorate	Charles Dent
Justice; National Constitutional Affairs; Resources, Wildlife and Economic Development	Stephen Kakfwi
Municipal and Community Affairs; Public Works and Services; Transportation	Vince Steen

■ Yukon Territory

Ministry or Portfolio	Minister
Government Leader; Finance	Piers McDonald
Education; Justice; Women's Directorate	Lois Moorcroft
Government House Leader; Economic Development; Public Service Commission; Yukon Development Corporation and Energy Corporation; Workers' Compensation, Health and Safety Board	Trevor Harding
Health and Social Services; Government Services	David Sloan
Renewable Resources; Yukon Housing Corporation	Eric Fairclough
Tourism; Community and Transportation Services	Dave Keenan

Provinces on the Internet

The federal government (see page 141) is not the only one with a home page. All of the provinces and territories offer a variety of information and services on-line, as do many cities and municipalities. Anyone searching for tourist or business information should start by checking the province's website to find out what's available. These websites can be accessed through the federal government's site (Other Governments) or directly.

Alberta: http://www.gov.ab.ca
British Columbia: http://www.gov.bc.ca
Manitoba: http://www.gov.mb.ca
New Brunswick: http://www.gov.nb.ca
Newfoundland: http://www.nf.ca
Northwest Territories: http://www.gov.nt.ca
Nova Scotia: http://www.gov.ns.ca

Nunavut: http://www.gov.nu.ca
Ontario: http://www.gov.on.ca
Prince Edward Island: http://www2.gov.pe.ca
Quebec: http://www.gouv.qc.ca
Saskatchewan: http://www.gov.sk.ca
Yukon Territory: http://www.gov.yk.ca

POLITICS AND ELECTIONS

Registered Federal Political Parties

(as of October 1999)

Federal political parties can only be registered at election time, when they qualify for registration by fielding at least 50 candidates by the nomination deadline in a forthcoming election. In between elections, parties can be founded and organized and apply for registration to the chief electoral officer.

Bloc Québécois—Rm 055, 1200 Papineau Ave, Montréal, QC H2K 4R5; Tel: (514) 526-3000; Fax: (514) 526-2868; leader: Gilles Duceppe. Web site: http://www.blocquebecois.parl.gc.ca

Canadian Action Party—Ste 302, 99 Atlantic Ave, Toronto, ON M6K 3J8; Tel: (416) 535-4144; Fax: (416) 535-6325; leader: The Hon. Paul Hellyer.

Christian Heritage Party of Canada—Ste 200, Heritage Pl, 155 Queen St, Ottawa, ON K1P 6L1; Tel: (613) 788-3716; Fax: (819) 457-9242; leader: Ronald O. Gray.

Liberal Party of Canada—Ste 400, 81 Metcalfe St, Ottawa, ON K1P 6M8; Tel: (613) 237-0740; Fax: (613) 235-7208; leader: The Right Hon. Jean Chrétien. Web site: http://www.liberal.ca

Marxist-Leninist Party of Canada—Ste 405, 396 Cooper St, Ottawa, ON K2P 2H7; Tel: (613) 565-6446; Fax: (613) 565-8787; leader: Sandra Smith.

Natural Law Party of Canada—500 Wilbrod St, Ottawa, ON K1N 6N2; Tel: (613) 565-8517; Fax: (613) 565-1596; leader: Dr. Neil Paterson. Web site: http://www.natural-law.ca

New Democratic Party—Ste 900, 81 Metcalfe St, Ottawa, ON K1P 6K7; Tel: (613) 236-3613; Fax: (613) 230-9050; leader: Alexa McDonough. Web site: http://www.ndp.ca

Progressive Conservative Party of Canada—5th Flr, Ste 501, 275 Slater St, Ottawa, ON K1P 5H9; Tel: (613) 238-6111; Fax: (613) 238-7429; leader: The Right Hon. Joe Clark. Web site: http://www.pcparty.ca

Reform Party of Canada—Ste 600, 833–4th Ave SW, Calgary, AB T2P 0K5; Tel: (403) 269-1990; Fax: (403) 269-4077; leader: E. Preston Manning. Web site: http://www.reform.ca

The Green Party of Canada—244 Gerrard St E, Toronto, ON M5A 2G2; Tel: (416) 647-3366; leader: Dr Joan Russow. Web site: http://green.ca

---

Accepted for registration: **Communist Party of Canada**—290A Danforth Ave, Toronto, ON M4K 1N6 Tel: (416) 469-2446; Fax: (416) 469-4063; leader: Miguel Figueroa. Web site: http://www.communist-party.ca

---

Source: *Elections Canada*

Federal Election Results, 1867–1997

🍁 1867–1904

	1867	1872	1874	1878	1882	1887	1891	1896	1900	1904
Canada										
Conservative	101	103	73	137	139	123	123	89	80	75
Liberal	80	97	133	69	71	92	92	117	133	139
Other	—	—	—	—	—	—	—	7	—	—
Prince Edward Island[1]										
Conservative	—	—	—	5	4	—	2	3	2	3
Liberal	—	—	6	1	2	6	4	2	3	1
Nova Scotia										
Conservative	3	11	4	14	15	14	16	10	5	—
Liberal	16	10	17	7	6	7	5	10	15	18
New Brunswick										
Conservative	7	7	5	5	10	10	13	9	5	6
Liberal	8	9	11	11	6	6	3	5	9	7
Quebec										
Conservative	45	38	32	45	48	33	30	16	7	11
Liberal	20	27	33	20	17	32	35	49	58	54
Other	—	—	—	—	—	—	—	5	—	—
Ontario										
Conservative	46	38	24	59	54	52	48	44	55	48
Liberal	36	50	64	29	37	40	44	43	37	38
Other	—	—	—	—	—	—	—	5	—	—
Manitoba[2]										
Conservative	—	3	2	3	2	4	4	4	4	3
Liberal	—	1	2	1	3	1	1	2	3	7
Other	—	—	—	—	—	—	—	1	—	—
British Columbia[3]										
Conservative	—	6	6	6	6	6	6	2	2	—
Liberal	—	—	—	—	—	—	—	4	4	7
Yukon[4]										
Conservative	—	—	—	—	—	—	—	—	—	1
Northwest Territories[2]										
Conservative	—	—	—	—	—	4	4	1	—	3
Liberal	—	—	—	—	—	—	—	2	4	7
Other	—	—	—	—	—	—	—	1	—	—

🍁 1908–1940

	1908	1911	1917[7]	1921	1925	1926	1930	1935	1940
Canada									
Conservative	85	133	153	50	116	91	137	39	39
Liberal	133	86	82	117	101	116	88	171	178
Progressive	—	—	—	64	25	—	2	—	—
CCF	—	—	—	—	—	—	—	7	8
Social Credit	—	—	—	—	—	—	—	17	10
Other	3	2	—	4	3	38	18	11	10
Prince Edward Island									
Conservative	1	2	2	—	2	1	3	—	—
Liberal	3	2	2	4	2	3	1	4	4
Nova Scotia									
Conservative	6	9	12	—	11	12	10	—	1
Liberal	12	9	4	16	3	2	4	12	10
CCF	—	—	—	—	—	—	—	—	1

(1) Entered Confederation July 1, 1873. (2) Entered Confederation July 15, 1870. (3) Entered Confederation July 20, 1871. (4) Entered Confederation June 13, 1898. (5) Entered Confederation Mar. 31, 1949. (6) Entered Confederation Sept. 1, 1905. (7) For the 1917 election, Conservative refers to "Unionists," a coalition of Conservatives and pro-conscription Liberals; Liberals, for the 1917 election, are sometimes called "Laurier Liberals" because of their support for Laurier's anti-conscription stand. (8) The New Democratic Party (NDP) replaced the Co-operative Commonwealth Federation (CCF) in Aug. 1961. (9) From 1908-1957 shared one representative.

🍁 1908–1940	1908	1911	1917[7]	1921	1925	1926	1930	1935	1940
New Brunswick									
Conservative	2	5	7	5	10	7	10	1	5
Liberal	11	8	4	5	1	4	1	9	5
Other	—	—	—	1	—	—	—	—	—
Quebec									
Conservative	11	27	3	—	4	4	24	5	—
Liberal	53	37	62	65	60	60	40	55	61
Other	1	1	—	—	1	1	1	5	4
Ontario									
Conservative	48	72	74	37	68	53	59	25	25
Liberal	36	36	8	21	12	23	22	56	55
Progressive	—	—	—	24	2	4	—	—	—
Other	2	1	—	—	—	2	1	1	2
Manitoba									
Conservative	8	8	14	—	7	—	11	1	1
Liberal	2	2	1	2	1	4	1	12	14
CCF	—	—	—	—	—	—	—	2	1
Progressive	—	—	—	12	7	4	—	—	—
Other	—	—	—	1	2	9	5	2	1
Saskatchewan[6]									
Conservative	1	1	16	—	—	—	8	1	2
Liberal	9	9	—	1	15	16	11	16	12
CCF	—	—	—	—	—	—	—	2	5
Progressive	—	—	—	15	6	5	2	—	—
Social Credit	—	—	—	—	—	—	—	2	—
Other	—	—	—	—	—	—	—	—	2
Alberta[6]									
Conservative	3	1	11	—	3	1	4	1	—
Liberal	4	6	1	—	4	3	3	1	7
Progressive	—	—	—	10	9	—	—	—	—
Social Credit	—	—	—	—	—	—	—	15	10
United Farmers of Alta	—	—	—	—	—	11	9	—	—
Other	—	—	—	2	—	1	—	—	—
British Columbia									
Conservative	5	7	13	7	10	12	7	5	4
Liberal	2	—	—	3	3	1	5	6	10
CCF	—	—	—	—	—	—	—	3	1
Progressive	—	—	—	2	1	—	—	—	—
Social Credit	—	—	—	—	—	—	—	—	—
Other	—	—	—	1	—	1	2	2	1
Yukon and Northwest Territories[9]									
Conservative	—	1	—	1	1	1	1	—	1
Liberal	1	—	—	—	—	—	—	—	—
Other	—	—	—	—	—	—	—	1	—

🍁 1945–1968	1945	1949	1953	1957	1958	1962	1963	1965	1968
Canada									
Conservative	67	41	51	112	208	116	95	97	72
Liberal	125	190	170	105	48	99	129	131	155
NDP (CCF)[8]	28	13	23	25	8	19	17	21	22
Social Credit	13	10	15	19	—	30	24	5	—
Other	12	8	6	4	1	1	—	11	15
Newfoundland[5]									
Conservative	—	2	—	2	2	1	—	—	6
Liberal	—	5	7	5	5	6	7	7	1
NDP (CCF)	—	—	—	—	—	—			
Prince Edward Island									
Conservative	1	1	1	4	4	4	2	4	4
Liberal	3	3	3	—	—	—	2	—	—

❖ 1945–1968

	1945	1949	1953	1957	1958	1962	1963	1965	1968
Nova Scotia									
Conservative	3	2	1	10	12	9	7	10	10
Liberal	8	10	10	2	—	2	5	2	1
NDP (CCF)	1	1	1	—	—	1	—	—	—
New Brunswick									
Conservative	3	2	3	5	7	4	4	4	5
Liberal	7	7	7	5	3	6	6	6	5
Other	—	1	—	—	—	—	—	—	—
Quebec									
Conservative	1	2	4	9	50	14	8	8	4
Liberal	54	66	66	63	25	35	47	56	56
NDP (CCF)	—	—	—	—	—	—	—	—	—
Social Credit	—	—	—	—	—	26	20	—	—
Other	10	5	5	3	—	—	—	11	14
Ontario									
Conservative	48	25	33	61	67	35	27	25	17
Liberal	34	56	50	20	14	43	52	51	64
NDP (CCF)	—	—	—	3	3	6	6	9	6
Other	—	2	2	1	1	1	—	—	1
Manitoba									
Conservative	2	1	3	8	14	11	10	10	5
Liberal	10	12	8	1	—	1	2	1	5
NDP (CCF)	5	3	3	5	—	2	2	3	3
Saskatchewan									
Conservative	1	1	1	3	16	16	17	17	5
Liberal	2	14	5	4	—	1	—	—	2
NDP (CCF)	18	5	11	10	1	—	—	—	6
Alberta									
Conservative	2	2	2	3	17	15	14	15	15
Liberal	2	5	4	1	—	—	1	—	4
NDP (CCF)	—	—	—	—	—	—	—	—	—
Social Credit	13	10	11	13	—	2	2	2	—
British Columbia									
Conservative	5	3	3	7	18	6	4	3	—
Liberal	5	11	8	2	—	4	7	7	16
NDP (CCF)	4	3	7	7	4	10	9	9	7
Social Credit	—	—	4	6	—	2	2	3	—
Other	2	1	—						
Yukon[9]									
Conservative	1	—	—	—	1	1	1	1	1
Liberal	—	1	2	1	—	—	—	—	—
NDP (CCF)	—	—	—	—	—	—	—	—	—
Northwest Territories[9]									
Conservative	n.a.	n.a.	n.a.	—	—	—	1	—	—
Liberal	n.a.	n.a.	n.a.	1	1	1	—	1	1
NDP (CCF)	n.a.	n.a.	n.a.	—	—	—	—	—	—

❖ 1972–1997

	1972	1974	1979	1980	1984	1988	1993	1997
Canada								
Bloc Québécois	—	—	—	—	—	—	54	44
Conservative	107	95	136	103	211	169	2	20
Liberal	109	141	114	147	40	83	177	155
NDP (CCF)[8]	31	16	26	32	30	43	9	21
Reform	—	—	—	—	—	—	52	60
Social Credit	15	11	6	—	—	—	—	—
Other	2	1	—	—	1	—	1	1
Newfoundland								
Conservative	4	3	2	2	4	2	—	3
Liberal	3	4	4	5	3	5	7	4
NDP (CCF)	—	—	1	—	—	—	—	—
Prince Edward Island								
Conservative	3	3	4	2	3	—	—	—
Liberal	1	1	—	2	1	4	4	4
Nova Scotia								
Conservative	10	8	8	6	9	5	—	5
Liberal	1	2	2	5	2	6	11	—
NDP (CCF)	—	1	1	—	—	—	—	6

🍁1972–1997	1972	1974	1979	1980	1984	1988	1993	1997
New Brunswick								
Conservative	5	3	4	3	9	5	1	5
Liberal	5	6	6	7	1	5	9	3
NDP	—	—	—	—	—	—	—	2
Other	—	1	—	—	—	—	—	—
Quebec								
Bloc Québécois	—	—	—	—	—	—	54	44
Conservative	2	3	2	1	58	63	1	5
Liberal	56	60	67	74	17	12	19	26
NDP (CCF)	—	—	—	—	—	—	—	—
Social Credit	15	11	6	—	—	—	—	—
Other	1	—	—	—	—	—	1	—
Ontario								
Conservative	40	25	57	38	67	46	—	1
Liberal	36	55	32	52	14	43	98	101
NDP (CCF)	11	8	6	5	13	10	—	—
Reform	—	—	—	—	—	—	1	—
Other	1	—	—	—	1	—	—	1
Manitoba								
Conservative	8	9	7	5	9	7	—	1
Liberal	2	2	2	2	1	5	12	6
NDP (CCF)	3	2	5	7	4	2	1	4
Reform	—	—	—	—	—	—	1	3
Saskatchewan								
Conservative	7	8	10	7	9	4	—	—
Liberal	1	3	—	—	—	—	5	1
NDP (CCF)	5	2	4	7	5	10	5	5
Reform	—	—	—	—	—	—	4	8
Alberta								
Conservative	19	19	21	21	21	25	—	—
Liberal	—	—	—	—	—	—	4	2
NDP (CCF)	—	—	—	—	—	i	—	—
Reform	—	—	—	—	—	—	22	24
British Columbia								
Conservative	8	13	19	16	19	12	—	—
Liberal	4	8	1	—	1	1	6	6
NDP (CCF)	11	2	8	12	8	19	2	3
Reform	—	—	—	—	—	—	24	25
Yukon								
Conservative	1	1	1	1	1	—	—	—
Liberal	—	—	—	—	—	—	—	—
NDP (CCF)	—	—	—	—	—	1	1	1
Northwest Territories								
Conservative	—	—	1	1	2	—	—	—
Liberal	—	—	—	—	—	2	2	2
NDP (CCF)	1	1	1	1	—	—	—	—

Voter Turnout at Canada's Federal Elections, 1867–1997

(percentage of eligible voters casting votes)

Year	Voter turnout[1]	Year	Voter turnout[1]	Year	Voter turnout[1]	Year	Voter turnout[1]
1867	73%	1904	84%	1940	71%	1968	76%
1872	70	1908	79	1945	76	1972	77
1874	75	1911	72	1949	75	1974	71
1878	71	1917	90	1953	68	1979	76
1882	72	1921	71	1957	75	1980	69
1887	70	1925	69	1958	81	1984	75
1891	65	1926	70	1962	80	1988	76
1896	61	1930	76	1963	80	1993	70
1900	79	1935	75	1965	76	1997	67

Source: *Elections Canada*

(1) Percentage of actual votes to eligible voters. In many early general elections, several electoral districts were won by acclamation; hence, no eligible voters nor actual votes were recorded. Furthermore, in some of the more remote districts, votes were cast but no voters' lists had been prepared.

Federal Political Party Leaders

■ Progressive Conservative[1] Party

Leader	Term
Sir John A. Macdonald	1854–July 6, 1891
Sir J.J.C. Abbott	June 16, 1891–Dec. 5, 1892
Sir John Thompson	Dec. 5, 1892–Dec. 12, 1894
Sir Mackenzie Bowell	Dec. 21, 1894–Apr. 27, 1896
Sir Charles Tupper	May 1, 1896–Feb. 5, 1901
Sir Robert Borden	Feb. 6, 1901–July 10, 1920
Arthur Meighen	July 10, 1920–Oct. 11, 1926
Hugh Guthrie[2]	Oct. 11, 1926–Oct. 12, 1927
R.B. Bennett	Oct. 12, 1927–July 7, 1938
R.J. Manion	July 7, 1938–May 13, 1940
R.B. Hanson[2]	May 13, 1940–Nov. 12, 1941
Arthur Meighen	Nov. 12, 1941–Dec. 11, 1942
John Bracken	Dec. 11, 1942–Oct. 2, 1948
George A. Drew	Oct. 2, 1948–Dec. 14, 1956
John G. Diefenbaker	Dec. 14, 1956–Sept. 9, 1967
Robert L. Stanfield	Sept. 9, 1967–Feb. 22, 1976
Joe Clark	Feb. 22, 1976–Feb. 8, 1983
Erik Nielsen[2]	Feb. 9, 1983–June 11, 1983
Brian Mulroney	Jun. 11, 1983–Jun. 13, 1993
Kim Campbell	June 13, 1993–Dec. 13, 1993
Jean Charest	Dec. 14, 1993–Apr. 3, 1998
Elsie Wayne	Apr. 6, 1998–Nov. 13, 1998
Joe Clark	Nov. 14, 1998–

■ Liberal Party

Leader	Term
Robert Baldwin	1804–1858
Louis-H. Lafontaine	1807–1864
George Brown	1867–1872
Alexander Mackenzie	Mar. 6, 1873–Apr. 27, 1880
Edward Blake	May 4, 1880–June 2, 1887
Sir Wilfrid Laurier	June 1887–Feb. 17, 1919
Daniel D. McKenzie[2]	Feb. 1919–Aug. 1919
W.L. Mackenzie King	Aug. 7, 1919–Aug. 7, 1948
Louis St. Laurent	Aug. 7, 1948–Jan. 16, 1958
Lester B. Pearson	Jan. 16, 1958–Apr. 2, 1968
Pierre E. Trudeau	Apr. 6, 1968–June 16, 1984
John N. Turner	June 16, 1984–June 23, 1990
Jean Chrétien	June 23, 1990–

■ New Democratic Party[3]

Leader	Term
James S. Woodsworth	Aug. 1932–July 1942
M.J. Coldwell	July 1942–Aug. 1960
Hazen Argue	Aug. 1960–Aug. 1961
Tommy Douglas	Aug. 1961–Apr. 1971
David Lewis	Apr. 24, 1971–July 7, 1975
Ed Broadbent	July 7, 1975–Dec. 2, 1989
Audrey McLaughlin	Dec. 2, 1989–Oct. 1995
Alexa McDonough	Oct. 14, 1995–

■ Bloc Québecois

Leader	Term
Lucien Bouchard	June 15, 1991–Jan. 18, 1996
Michel Gauthier	Feb. 17, 1996–Mar. 15, 1997
Gilles Duceppe	Mar. 16, 1997–

■ The Reform Party of Canada

Leader	Term
E. Preston Manning	Nov. 1, 1987–

(1) Name changed from Conservative to Progressive Conservative Dec. 1942. (2) Interim leader appointed to fill a vacancy until a party leadership convention could be held. (3) Prior to Aug. 1961 was called the Co-operative Commonwealth Federation (CCF).

Provincial Election Results

■ Newfoundland

	1971	1972	1975	1979	1982	1985	1989	1993	1996	1999
Liberal	20	9	16	19	8	15	31	35	37	32
Progressive Conservative	21	33	30	33	44	36	21	16	9	14
New Democratic	—	—	—	—	—	1	—	1	1	2
Other	1	—	5	—	—	—	—	—	1	—
Size of legislature	42	42	51	52	52	52	52	52	48	48

■ Prince Edward Island

	1966	1970	1974	1978	1979	1982	1985	1989	1993	1996
Liberal	17	27	26	17	11	14	21	30	31	8
Progressive Conservative	15	5	6	15	21	18	11	2	1	18
New Democratic	—	—	—	—	—	—	—	—	—	1
Size of legislature	32	32	32	32	32	32	32	32	32	27

■ Nova Scotia

	1967	1970	1974	1978	1981	1984	1988	1993	1998	1999
Liberal	6	23	31	17	13	6	21	40	19	11
New Democratic[1]	—	2	3	4	1	3	2	3	19	30
Progressive Conservative[2]	40	21	12	31	37	42	28	9	14	11
Other	—	—	—	—	1	1	1	—	—	—
Size of legislature	46	46	46	52	52	52	52	52	52	52

■ New Brunswick

	1963	1967	1970	1974	1978	1982	1987	1991	1995	1999
Liberal	332	32	26	25	28	18	58	46	48	10
Progressive Conservative[3]	20	26	32	33	30	39	—	3	6	44
New Democratic	—	—	—	—	—	1	—	1	1	1
Confederation of Regions	—	—	—	—	—	—	—	8	—	—
Size of legislature	52	58	58	58	58	58	58	58	55	55

■ Quebec

	1962	1966	1970	1973	1976	1981	1985	1989	1994	1998
Crédit Social	—	—	12	2	1	—	—	—	—	—
Equality	—	—	—	—	—	—	—	4	—	—
Liberal	63	50	72	102	26	42	99	92	47	48
Parti Québécois[4]	—	—	7	6	71	80	23	29	77	76
Union Nationale	31	56	17	—	11	—	—	—	—	—
Other	1	2	—	—	1	—	—	—	1	1
Size of legislature	95	108	108	110	110	122	122	125	125	125

■ Ontario

	1967	1971	1975	1977	1981	1985	1987	1990	1995	1999
Liberal	28	20	36	34	34	48	95	36	30	35
New Democratic[5]	20	19	38	33	21	25	19	74	17	9
Progressive Conservative[3]	69	78	51	58	70	52	16	20	82	59
Independent	—	—	—	—	—	—	—	—	1	—
Size of legislature	117	117	125	125	125	125	130	130	130	103

■ Manitoba

	1966	1969	1973	1977	1981	1986	1988	1990	1995	1999
Liberal	14	4	5	1	—	1	20	7	3	1
New Democratic[5]	11	28	31	23	34	30	12	20	23	32
Progressive Conservative[6]	31	22	21	33	23	26	25	30	31	24
Other	1	3	—	—	—	—	—	—	—	—
Size of legislature	57	57	57	57	57	57	57	57	57	57

■ Saskatchewan

	1964	1967	1971	1975	1978	1982	1986	1991	1995	1999
Liberal	33	35	15	15	—	—	1	1	11	4
New Democratic[7]	25	24	45	39	44	8	25	55	42	29
Progressive Conservative[8]	1	—	—	7	17	56	38	10	5	—
Saskatchewan Party	—	—	—	—	—	—	—	—	—	25
Size of legislature	59	59	60	61	61	64	64	66	58	58

■ Alberta

	1963	1967	1971	1975	1979	1982	1986	1989	1993	1997
Liberal	2	3	—	—	—	—	4	8	32[9]	18
New Democratic[1]	—	—	1	1	1	2	16	16	—	2
Progressive Conservative[6]	—	6	49	69	74	75	61	59	51	63
Social Credit	60	55	24	4	4	—	—	—	—	—
Other	1	1	1	1	—	2	2	—	—	—
Size of legislature	63	65	75	75	79	79	83	83	83	83

■ British Columbia

	1963	1966	1969	1972	1975	1979	1983	1986	1991	1996
Liberal	5	6	5	5	1	—	—	—	17	33
New Democratic[5]	14	16	12	38	18	26	21	22	51	39
Progressive Conservative[6]	—	—	—	2	1	—	—	—	—	—
Social Credit	33	33	38	10	35	31	35	47	7	—
Other	—	—	—	—	—	—	—	1	—	3
Size of legislature	52	55	55	55	55	57	57	69	75	75

(1) Known as the Co-operative Commonwealth Federation until 1962. (2) Known as the Conservative Party until 1946. (3) Known as the Conservative Party until 1943. (4) Formed in 1968. (5) Known as the Co-operative Commonwealth Federation until 1961. (6) Known as the Conservative Party until 1944. (7) Known as the Co-operative Commonwealth Federation until 1967. (8) Known as the Conservative Party until 1945. (9) One Alberta Liberal now sits as an independent.

Provincial Party Leaders[1]

(as of October 1999)

■ Newfoundland

Progressive Conservative Party	Liberal Party	New Democratic Party
A. Brian Peckford 1979–89	Len Sterling 1982–84	Peter Fenwick 1981–89
Tom Rideout 1989–91	Stephen Neary 1984–85	Cle Newhook 1989–92
Len Simms 1991–95	Leo Barry 1985–87	Jack Harris .... 1992—
Lynn Verge............. 1995–96	Clyde Wells 1987–96	
Loyola Sullivan.......... 1996–98	Brian Tobin............. 1996—	
Ed Byrne............... 1998—		

■ Prince Edward Island

Progressive Conservative Party	Liberal Party	New Democratic Party
James M. Lee 1981–87	Alex Campbell 1965–78	Douglas Murray 1979–81
Leone Bagnall 1987–88	Bennett Campbell 1978–81	David Burke 1982–83
Melbourne Gass 1988–90	Joseph Ghiz 1981–93	Jim Mayne 1983–89
Pat Mella 1990–96	Catherine Callbeck 1993–96	Larry Duchesne 1991–95
P. Binns .... 1996—	Keith Milligan 1996–99	Herb Dickieson .... 1995—
	Wayne Carew .... 1999—	

■ Nova Scotia

Progressive Conservative Party[2]	Liberal Party	New Democratic Party[3]
George I. Smith 1967–71	Vincent J. MacLean 1985	James Aitchison 1966–68
John M. Buchanan 1971–90	J. William Gillis 1985–86	Jeremy Akerman 1968–80
Donald Cameron 1991–93	Vincent J. MacLean 1986–92	Alexa McDonough 1980–94
Terence R.B. Donahoe 1993–95	John Savage 1992–97	John Holme............ 1994–96
Dr. John Hamm 1995	Russell MacLellan ...... 1997—	Robert Chisholm .... 1996—

■ New Brunswick

Progressive Conservative Party	Liberal Party	New Democratic Party
Richard B. Hatfield 1969–87	Robert Higgins 1971–78	Elizabeth Weir .... 1988—
Malcolm MacLeod 1987–89	Joe Daigle 1978–8	
Barbara Baird Filliter....... 1989–91	Doug Young 1982–83	
Dennis Cochrane 1991–95	Frank McKenna 1985–97	
Bernard Valcourt*........ 1995–97	Ray Frenette (interim)..... 1997–98	
Bernard Lord .... 1997—	Camille Theriault .... 1998—	

■ Quebec

Parti Québécois	Parti Libéral	Action démocratique
René Lévesque 1968–85	Robert Bourassa 1970–77	Mario Dumont.......... 1994—
Pierre-Marc Johnson 1985–88	Claude Ryan 1978–82	
Jacques Parizeau 1988–96	Robert Bourassa 1983–94	
Lucien Bouchard .... 1996—	Daniel Johnson 1994–98	
	Jean Charest............ 1998—	

■ Ontario

Progressive Conservative Party	Liberal Party	New Democratic Party[4]
William G. Davis 1971–85	Robert Nixon 1967–76	Donald C. MacDonald .. 1953–70
Frank Miller 1985	Stuart Smith 1977–81	Stephen H. Lewis 1970–78
Larry Grossman 1985–87	David Peterson 1982–90	Michael Cassidy 1978–82
Andrew Brandt 1987–90	Lyn McLeod 1992–96	Bob Rae 1982–96
Mike Harris .... 1990—	Dalton McGinty .... 1996—	Howard Hampton ..... 1996—

■ Manitoba

Progressive Conservative Party	Liberal Party	New Democratic Party[4]
Duff Roblin 1954–67	Sharon Carstairs 1984–93	Lloyd Stinson 1952–60
Walter C. Weir 1967–70	Paul Edwards 1993–96	A. Russell Paulley 1960–69
Sidney Spivak 1971–75	Ginny Hasselfield 1996–98	Edward R. Schreyer 1969–79
Sterling Lyon 1975–83	Neil Gaudry 1998	Howard R. Pawley 1979–88
Gary Filmon .... 1983—	Jon Gerrard 1998–	Gary Doer .... 1988—

■ Saskatchewan

Progressive Conservative Party	Liberal Party	New Democratic Party[4]
Party inactive as of Nov. 9, 1997	Ron Osika (interim) 1996	John H. Brockelbank ... 1941–44
Saskatchewan Party	Jim Melenchuk........... 1996—	Tommy Douglas 1944–61
		Woodrow Lloyd 1961–70
Ken Karwetz 1997–98		Allan Blakeney 1970–87
Elwin Hermanson .... 1998—		Roy Romanow .... 1987—

■ Alberta

Progressive Conservative Party	Liberal Party	New Democratic Party[4]
Ernest Watkins 1960–62	Nick Taylor 1974–88	Neil Reimer 1955–67
Milt Harradance 1962–64	Laurence Decore 1988–94	W. Grant Notley 1968–84
Peter Lougheed 1965–85	Betty Hewes (interim) 1994	Ray Martin 1984–94
Donald R. Getty 1985–92	Grant Mitchell 1994–98	Ross Harvey........... 1994–96
Ralph P. Klein .... 1992—	Nancy MacBeth .... 1998—	Pam Barrett .... 1996—

■ British Columbia

Reform Party of British Columbia	New Democratic Party	Liberal
Ron Gamble 1993–95	Dave Barrett 1969–84	Jevington Blair Tothill .. 1979–81
Jack Weisgerber 1995–97	Bob Skelly 1984–87	Shirley McLoughlin 1981–83
Wilf Hanni 1997-98	Michael Harcourt 1987–96	Arthur Lee 1984–87
Bill Vander Zalm .... 1998—	Glen Clark 1996–99	Gordon Wilson 1987–93
	Dan Miller.............. 1999—	Gordon Campbell ..... 1993—

(1) Includes up to 5 most recent leaders of the major parties; for years no leader is listed, the leadership was vacant or there was an interim leader. (2) Known as the Conservative Party until 1946. (3) Known as the Co-operative Commonwealth Federation until 1962. (4) Known as the Co-operative Commonwealth Federation until 1961.

DEFENCE

Canadian security policy is based on three elements: defence and collective security, arms control and disarmament, and the peaceful resolution of disputes. The Department of National Defence and the Canadian Forces support this policy by their contributions to strategic deterrence, conventional defence, sovereignty, peacekeeping and arms control.

In addition, the Department of National Defence provides special support to other government departments in areas such as search and rescue, fisheries patrols, enforcement of drug prohibitions, disaster relief, and aid to civil powers in law enforcement. These tasks are carried out both in emergencies and where it complements military surveillance and control responsibilities.

The Defence Department's website can be found at http://www.dnd.ca

Canadian Regular Armed Forces Strength

Canada has an all-volunteer Armed Forces which, since 1968, has been a single body composed of what had been a separate army, navy and air force.

	Navy	Army	Air Force	Total Armed Forces		Navy	Army	Air Force	Total Armed Forces
1914	379	3 000	—	3 379	**1951**	11 082	34 986	22 359	68 427
1915	1 255	81 195	—	82 450	**1952**	13 505	49 278	32 611	95 394
1916	1 557	274 194	—	275 751	**1953**	15 546	48 458	40 423	104 427
1917	2 220	304 585	—	306 805	**1955**	19 207	49 409	49 461	118 077
1918	4 792	326 258	—	331 050	**1960**	20 675	47 185	51 737	119 597
1919	5 495	228 292	—	233 787	**1965**	19 756	46 264	48 144	114 164
1920	1 040	1 681	—	5 732	**1970**	—	—	—	93 353
1925	496	3 410	384	4 290	**1975**	—	—	—	79 817
1930	783	3 510	844	5 137	**1980**	—	—	—	80 166
1935	860	3 509	794	5 163	**1985**	—	—	—	83 740
1939	1 585	4 169	2 191	7 945	**1990**	—	—	—	87 976
1940	6 135	76 678	9 483	92 296	**1991**	—	—	—	87 319
1941	17 036	194 774	48 743	260 553	**1992**	—	—	—	84 792
1942	32 067	311 118	111 223	454 408	**1993**	—	—	—	78 376
1943	56 259	460 387	176 307	692 953	**1994**	—	—	—	75 949
1944	81 582	495 804	210 089	787 475	**1995**	—	—	—	72 079
1945	92 520	494 258	174 254	761 041	**1996**	—	—	—	61 336
1950	9 259	20 652	17 274	47 185	**1997**	—	—	—	60 320
					1998	—	—	—	60 942

Source: *Department of National Defence*

Senior Canadian Military Personnel

(as of Oct. 1, 1999)

Chief of the Defence Staff . . . . General Maurice Baril

Vice-Chief of the Defence Staff . . . . Vice-Admiral Gary L. Garnett

Deputy Chief of the Defence Staff . . . . Lt.-General Raymond R. Henault

Chief of the Land Staff . . . . Lt.-General Bill Leach

Chief of the Maritime Staff . . . . Vice-Admiral Greg R. Maddison

Chief of the Air Staff . . . . Lt.-General David N. Kinsman

Canadian Military Representative, North Atlantic Treaty Organization . . . . Vice-Admiral J.A. King

Deputy Commander-in-Chief, North American Aerospace Defence . . . . Lt.-Gen. G.E.C. Macdonald

Commander, Canadian Defence Liaison Staff (London) . . . . Brig.-Gen. J.S.R. Bastien

Commander, Canadian Defence Liaison Staff (Washington) . . . . Rear-Admiral F.W. Gibson

Source: *Department of National Defence*

Canadian Military Ranks

Army/Air Force

General Officers: General, Lieutenant-General, Major-General, Brigadier-General

Senior Officers: Colonel, Lieutenant-Colonel, Major

Junior Officers: Captain, Lieutenant, Second-Lieutenant, Officer Cadet

Non-commissioned Members: Chief Warrant Officer, Master Warrant Officer, Warrant Officer, Sergeant, Master Corporal, Corporal, Private

Navy

General Officers: Admiral, Vice-Admiral, Rear-Admiral, Commodore

Senior Officers: Captain (N), Commander, Lieutenant-Commander

Junior Officers: Lieutenant (N), Sub-Lieutenant, Acting Sub-Lieutenant

Non-commissioned Members: Chief Petty Officer 1st class, Chief Petty Officer 2nd class, Petty Officer 1st class, Petty Officer 2nd class, Master Seaman, Leading Seaman, Able Seaman

Source: *Department of National Defence*

Canadian Participation in UN Peacekeeping Missions 1947-1999

Location	Year	Mission (Canadian participation)
Korea	1947-8	Supervision of elections (2)
India-Pakistan	1949-96	Supervision of ceasefire between India and Pakistan (39)
Korea	1950-53	Supervision of Armistice Agreement (6 146)
Korea	1953—	Supervise armistice agreement between North and South Korea (1)
Cambodia, Laos, Vietnam	1954-74	Supervision of withdrawal of French forces (133)
Middle East	1954—	UN Truce Supervision of 1949 armistice between Israel and Egypt, Lebanon, Jordan and Syria (11)
Egypt (Sinai)	1956-67	Supervision of French, British and Israeli forces (1 007)
Lebanon	1958	Ensure no infiltration across Lebanese borders (77)
Congo	1960-4	Assist in maintaining law and order (421)
West New Guinea (now West Irian)	1962-3	Maintain peace and security (13)
Yemen	1963-4	Observe withdrawal of Egyptian troops (36)
Cyprus	1964, 1974—	Maintain 1974 ceasefire, preserve peace (2).
Dominican Republic	1965-6	Observe withdrawal of OAS forces (1)
India-Pakistan border	1965-6	Supervise ceasefire (112)
Nigeria	1968-70	Observation of ceasefire (2)
Egypt (Sinai)	1973-9	Supervise redeployment of Israeli and Egyptian forces (1 145)
South Vietnam	1973	Truce supervision (248)
Syria, Israel	1974—	Supervise ceasefire on Golan Heights (185)
Southern Lebanon	1978	Confirm withdrawal of Israeli forces (117)
Sinai, Egypt	1986—	Supervise 1979 peace treaty between Israel, Egypt and US (Camp David Accord) (25)
Afghanistan	1988-90	Confirm withdrawal of Soviet forces (5)
Iran/Iraq	1988-91	Supervise ceasefire and withdrawal of forces (525)
Namibia	1989-90	Assist in transition to independence (301)
Central America	1989-92	Verify compliance with Esquipulas Agreement (174)
Afghanistan, Pakistan	1990-92	Military advisory unit (1)
Haiti	1990-91	Observe 1990 elections (11)
Persian Gulf	1990-91	Air, naval, infantry units to help secure liberation of Kuwait
Iraq-Kuwait	1991	Monitor demilitarized pre-war boundary at end of Persian Gulf War (5)
Iraq	1991—	Supervision of destruction of Iraq's nuclear, biological and chemical weapons (12); periodic enforcement of UN restrictions on Iraq's oil trade; periodic monitoring of no-fly zones over Iraq.
Western Sahara	1991-94	Monitor ceasefire; supervise referendum (34)
Angola	1991-93	Monitor ceasefire (15)
El Salvador	1991-94	Investigate human rights violations and monitor progress leading to military reform (55)
Former Yugoslavia and neighbouring states	1991-4	Monitor and report on the implementation of ceasefire (15); report on breaches of Geneva Convention (7)
Red Sea	1992	Naval participation in post Gulf War embargo of Iraq (250)
Cambodia	1992-93	Monitor ceasefire, establish mine awareness and monitor disarmament (240)
Yugoslavia	1992-95	Observation patrols, mine clearance, construction and maintenance of shelters (2 400)
El Salvador	1992-95	Investigate human rights violations; develop process for military reform and elections (55)

Somalia	1992-93	Headquarters personnel (12)
Somalia, Kenya	1992-3	Distribution of relief supplies (1 250)
Mozambique	1993-95	Security, monitor de-mining operations, ceasefire verification (4)
Cambodia	1993—	Assist the Cambodian Mine Action Centre in de-mining the country (7)
Somalia	1993-5	Assist in provision of relief, economic rehabilitation and political reconciliation (9)
Uganda, Rwanda	1993-94	Monitor border to enforce military embargo (3)
Haiti	1993-94	Embargo Enforcement (250)
Rwanda	1993-96	Provide security and protection for refugees and civilians, distribution of relief supplies (112)
Yugoslavia	1993-95	Enforcing no-fly zone (13)
Dominican Republic	1994	Monitor DR-Haitian border, provide technical advice to UN re: enforcement of Haitian trade embargo (15)
Haiti	1994-96	Provide secure and stable environment for training of Haitian armed forces and police and for legislative elections (500)
Haiti	1996, 1997—	Assist government of Haiti in professionalizing the Haitian National Police Force (5)
Bosnia-Herzegovina	1995—	Participate in stabilization force to allow for consolidation of peace as set out in Dayton peace agreement (1, 350)
Guatemala	1997—	Verify implementation of Comprehensive Agreement on Human Rights and strengthen institutions for the protection of human rights (1)
Central African Republic	1998—	Maintain and improve security and stability following a series of mutinies, disarmament, police training, advice and technical support (55)
Central Europe	1998–99	Participate in Organization for Security and Cooperation in Europe military inspections in Macedonia and Slovakia and military evaluations in Estonia and Moldova.
Kosovo	1999	Support CF-18 fighter jets in Italy (260); support NATO land forces in Macedonia (800); coordinate humanitarian aid in Albania (10)
Mozambique	1999	Assist UN in demining the country (3)

Source: *Department of National Defence*

Canadian Forces Units in Canada

A Canadian Forces Base (CFB) is designated by the minister of national defence. It provides accomodation and support to assigned units. (BFC is the French acronym for CFB.) A Canadian Forces Station (CFS) is much smaller than a base. Stations have fewer resources and personnel; they are organized for operations and lack support capability. An Area Support Unit (ASU) provides food, fuel, maintenance and transportation for nearby operational units.

Maritime Region:

☐ **CFB Gagetown**:
P.O. Box 17000, Station Forces, Oromocto, New Brunswick, E2V 4J5.

☐ **CFB Gander**:
P.O. Box 6000, Gander, Newfoundland, A1V 1X1

☐ **CFB Goose Bay**:
Postal Station A, Happy Valley Goose Bay, Newfoundland, A0P 1S0

☐ **CFB Greenwood**:
Greenwood, Nova Scotia, B0P 1N0

☐ **CFB Halifax**:
P.O. Box 99000, Station Forces, Halifax, Nova Scotia, B3K 5X5

☐ **CFB Shearwater**:
Shearwater, Nova Scotia, B0J 3A0

Central Canada:

☐ **CFS Alert**:
Belleville, Ontario, K0K 3S0

☐ **BFC Bagotville**:
Alouette, Quebec, G0V 1A0

☐ **CFB Borden**:
Borden, Ontario, L0M 1C0

☐ **CFB Kingston**:
P.O. Box 17000, Station Forces, Kingston, Ontario, K7K 7B4

☐ **ASU Longue-Pointe**:
P.O. Box 4000 Station K, Montreal, Quebec, H1N 3R9

☐ **BFC Montreal**:
St-Hubert, Quebec, J3Y 5T4

☐ **CFB North Bay**:
Hornell Heights, Ontario, P0H 1P0

Source: *Department of National Defence*

as of Oct. 1999

☐ **CFB Petawawa**: Petawawa, Ontario, K8H 2X3	☐ **CFB Edmonton**: P.O. Box 10500, Station Forces, Alberta, T5J 4J5
☐ **ASU Saint-Jean**: P.O. Box 100 Station Main, Richelain, Quebec, J0J 1R0	☐ **CFB Esquimalt**: P.O. Box 17000, Station Forces, Victoria, British Columbia, V9A 7N2
☐ **CFB Trenton**: P.O. Box 1000, Station Forces, Astra, Ontario, KOK 3W0	☐ **CFB Moose Jaw**: P.O. Box 5000, Moose Jaw, Saskatchewan, S6H 7Z8
☐ **ASU Valcartier**: P.O. Box 1000, Station Forces, Courcelette, Quebec, GOA 4Z0	☐ **CFB Shilo**: Shilo, Manitoba, ROK 2A0
Western Canada:	☐ **CFB Suffield**: P.O. Box 6000, Medicine Hat, Alberta, T1A 8K8
☐ **CFB Cold Lake**: Medley, Alberta, TOA 2M0	☐ **CFB Winnipeg**: P.O. Box 17000, Station Forces, Winnipeg, Manitoba, R3J 3Y5
☐ **CFB Comox**: Lazo, British Columbia, VOR 2K0	

Source: *Department of National Defence*   as of Oct.. 1999

Humanitarian Missions

Canadian Forces have taken part in numerous humanitarian missions since 1947. Recent efforts have included hurricane disaster relief in Florida and the Caribbean; relief after the 1998 mudslides in Sarno, Italy; and aid to Turkish residents following the August 1999 earthquake.

The delivery of such aid has changed since 1947. After the 1994 medical relief mission in Rwanda, it became clear that humanitarian efforts now require a rapid-response capability in order to be most effective. Canada's Disaster Assistance Response Team (DART) was created to serve as the primary component of such operations.

The four critical needs in most emergencies have been identified as medical care, clean drinking water, engineering assistance, and communications. DART was designed to include all these components and to deploy them rapidly during crisis situations that could include natural disasters as well as humanitarian emergencies.

The team consists of 180 highly trained Canadian Forces personnel, mostly from the Land Force Command units, ready to move quickly to conduct up to 40 days of emergency relief while longer term assistance is organized. The medical platoon can set up a field hospital with 45 staff and care for up to 500 outpatients and 30 inpatients daily. The 40-staff engineer troop provides water purification, fresh water distribution, power generation, explosives disposal and mine-awareness training. Approximately 35 more personnel provide liaison and communications support; the remainder supply support services, security and general labour operations for the whole unit.

Year	Aid was brought to:	Year	Aid was brought to:
1947	Japan	1989	Monserrat
1948	British Columbia	1989/90/91	Northern Ontario
1960	Congo, Chile	1991	Iraq
1965	Zambia	1992	Bahamas, Florida
1967	India	1992-3	Somalia, CIS
1970	Peru	1992-6	Sarajevo
1971	Pakistan	1993-5	Somalia
1973	West Africa, Newfoundland	1994, 1996	Rwanda
1973/9	Nicaragua	1996	Haiti
1974/89	Manitoba	1996	Quebec (Saguenay floods)
1974	Saskatchewan	1997	Manitoba
1979	St. Vincent	1998	Quebec, Ont., NB, Italy, Carribbean
1983	Grenada		
1988/91	Ethiopia	1999	Turkey

Source: *Department of National Defence*

CRIME AND JUSTICE

Rates[1] of Criminal Code Incidents in Canada, 1987-98

	1987	1988	1989	1990	1991	1992
Population[2](000)	26 549.7	2 6798.3	27 286.2	27 700.6	28 030.9	28 376.6
Violent crime rate	829	868	911	973	1 059	1 084
Annual % change	5.6	4.6	5.0	6.8	8.9	2.3
Property crime rate	5 552	5 438	5 289	5 611	6 160	5 902
Annual % change	0.0	–2.1	–2.8	6.1	9.8	–4.2
Other criminal code rate	2 575	2 612	2 691	2 900	3 122	3 051
Annual % change	7.6	1.5	3.0	7.8	7.7	–2.3
Total[3] criminal code rate	8 956	8 919	8 891	9 484	10 342	10 036
Annual % change	2.6	–0.4	–0.3	6.7	9.0	–3.0

	1993	1994	1995	1996	1997	1998
Population[2](000)	28 703.1	29 036.0	29 353.9	29 671.9	30 004.0	30 300.4
Violent crime rate	1 081	1 046	1007	1000	990	975
Annual % change	–0.3	–3.2	–3.7	–0.7	–1.1	–1.5
Property crime rate	5 571	5 250	5 283	5 264	4 864	4 541
Annual % change	–5.6	–5.8	0.6	–0.4	–7.6	–6.7
Other criminal code rate	2 879	2 817	2 702	2 650	2 594	5 586
Annual % change	–5.6	–2.2	–4.1	–1.9	–2.1	–0.3
Total[3] criminal code rate	9 531	9 114	8 993	8 914	8 448	8 102
Annual % change	–5.0	–4.4	–1.3	–0.9	–5.2	–4.1

Source: *Uniform Crime Reporting Survey, Canadian Centre for Justice Statistics,* © *Statistics Canada*
(1) Rates are calculated per 100000 people. (2) Population estimates as of July 1. (3) Does not include traffic violations.

Percentage of Persons Charged, by Gender and Age, 1998

	Age Group by Gender				Total by Age Group	
	Adults		Youth[1]			
	Male	Female	Male	Female	Adults	Youth
Homicides	87%	13%	96%	4%	88%	12%
Attempted murder	88	12	96	4	88	12
Assaults	85	15	70	30	85	15
Sexual assaults	98	2	97	3	85	15
Other sexual offences	97	3	97	3	86	14
Abduction	55	45	100	0	96	4
Robbery	91	9	85	15	64	36
Total violent crime	**86**	**14**	**74**	**26**	**84**	**16**
Break and enter	94	6	90	10	60	40
Motor vehicle theft	93	7	86	14	58	42
Fraud	70	30	67	33	93	7
Theft over $5 000	79	21	83	17	81	19
Theft $5 000 and under	70	30	67	33	73	27
Total property crime	**77**	**23**	**78**	**22**	**72**	**28**
Mischief	88	12	89	11	66	34
Arson	81	19	87	13	59	41
Prostitution	46	54	10	90	97	3
Offensive weapons	92	8	92	8	79	21
Total Criminal Code	**82**	**18**	**77**	**23**	**78**	**22**
Impaired driving[2]	90	10	88	12	99	1
Cocaine – possession	82	18	68	32	95	5
Cocaine – trafficking	84	16	72	23	95	5
Cannabis – possession	90	10	89	11	83	17
Cannabis – trafficking	84	16	89	11	85	15

Source: *Uniform Crime Reporting Survey, Canadian Centre for Justice statistics,* © *Statistics Canada*
(1) Canadians between the ages of 12 and 17. (2) Includes impaired operation of a vehicle causing death, causing bodily harm, alcohol rate over 80 mg, failure or refusal to provide a breath or blood sample.

Selected Criminal Code Incidents by Province, 1998

	Canada	Nfld	PEI	NS	NB	Que	Ont
Population[2] 1998	30 300 422	544 400	136 388	934 587	752 999	7 333 283	11 411 547
Homicides							
- number	555	7	—	24	5	137	155
- rate[1]	1.8	1.3	—	2.6	0.7	1.9	1.4
Sexual assault							
- number	25 493	610	156	951	866	3 236	9 012
- rate	84	112	144	102	115	44	79
Assault							
- number	223 260	3 934	755	7 269	5 161	31 706	78 021
- rate	737	723	554	778	685	432	684
Robbery							
- number	28 952	74	24	458	145	8 010	9 152
- rate	96	14	18	49	19	109	80
TOTAL VIOLENT CRIME							
- number	**295 369**	**4 864**	**994**	**9 155**	**6 632**	**47 146**	**101 959**
- rate	**1 156**	**893**	**729**	**980**	**881**	**643**	**893**
Break & enter							
- number	350 176	4 479	700	9 118	5 574	97 774	101 126
- rate	1 156	823	513	976	740	1 333	886
Motor vehicle theft							
- number	165 799	644	181	2 816	1 299	47 244	50 372
- rate	547	118	133	301	173	644	441
Other theft							
- number	736 598	7 563	2 322	22 221	11 185	133 909	224 920
- rate	2 431	1 389	1 702	2 376	1 485	1 826	2 146
TOTAL PROPERTY CRIME							
- number	**1 375 881**	**14 512**	**3 747**	**37 964**	**21 181**	**298 821**	**440 912**
- rate	**4 541**	**2 666**	**2 747**	**4 062**	**2 813**	**4 075**	**3 864**
Offensive weapons							
- number	16 735	126	37	489	221	997	7 112
- rate	55	23	27	52	29	14	62
Mischief							
- number	325 884	4 723	1 414	11 942	6 561	54 649	106 538
- rate	1 076	868	1 037	1 278	871	745	934
Other criminal code							
- number	783 631	12 218	3 820	28 956	18 845	125 095	258 252
- rate	2 586	2 244	2 801	3 098	2 503	1 706	2 263
TOTAL CRIMINAL CODE OFFENSES[3]							
- number	**2 454 881**	**31 594**	**8 561**	**76 075**	**46 658**	**471 062**	**801 123**
- rate	**8 102**	**5 803**	**6 277**	**8 140**	**6 196**	**6 424**	**7 020**
% change in rate from 1997	−4.1	2.7	−7.9	−3.6	−1.3	−4.8	−5.8

	Man	Sask	Alta	BC	Yukon	NWT
Population 1998[2]	1 138 872	1 024 387	2 914 918	4 009 922	31 651	67 468
Homicides						
- number	33	32	64	90	3	5
- rate[1]	2.9	3.1	2.2	2.2	9.5	7.4
Sexual assault						
- number	1 287	1 505	2 911	4 391	107	461
- rate	113	147	100	110	338	683
Assault						
- number	14 084	12 499	24 214	42 013	737	2 867
- rate	1 237	1 220	831	1 048	2 329	4 249
Robbery						
- number	1 821	990	2 560	5 699	12	37
- rate	160	97	88	141	38	55
TOTAL VIOLENT CRIME						
- number	**18 295**	**16 265**	**31 605**	**53 901**	**919**	**3 634**
- rate	**1 606**	**1 588**	**1 084**	**1 344**	**2 904**	**5 386**
Break & enter						
- number	16 023	17 813	29 861	65 457	608	1 643
- rate	1 407	1 739	1 024	1 632	1 921	2 435
Motor vehicle theft						
- number	10 539	7 263	15 519	29 318	213	391
- rate	925	709	532	731	673	580
Other theft						
- number	27 616	30 090	80 124	173 499	1 224	1 925
- rate	2 425	2 937	2 749	4 327	3 867	2 853
TOTAL PROPERTY CRIME						
- number	**58 762**	**62 287**	**143 471**	**287 816**	**2 210**	**4 198**
- rate	**5 160**	**6 080**	**4 922**	**7 178**	**6 982**	**6 222**
Offensive weapons						
- number	1 070	860	1 945	3 697	41	140
- rate	94	84	67	92	130	208
Mischief						
- number	21 339	17 255	38 601	58 378	785	3 699
- rate	1 874	1 684	1 324	1 456	2 480	5 483
Other criminal code						
- number	43 828	48 504	88 528	145 144	2 576	7 865
- rate	3 848	4 735	3 037	3 620	8 139	11 657
TOTAL CRIMINAL CODE OFFENSES[3]						
- number	**120 885**	**127 056**	**263 604**	**486 861**	**5 705**	**15 697**
- rate	**10 614**	**12 403**	**9 043**	**12 141**	**18 025**	**23 266**
% change in rate from 1997	−3.5	2.2	−1.6	−4.8	−13.3	4.9

Source: *Uniform Crime Reporting Survey, Canadian Centre for Justice Statistics, © Statistics Canada*

(1) Rates are calculated per 100 000 people. (2) Population estimates at July 1. (3) Does not include traffic offences. (—) Nil or zero.

Change in Rates of Violent Crime for Major CMAs, 1992-8

A CMA is a Census Metropolitan Area defined by Statistics Canada as a very large urban centre, together with neighbouring urban/rural areas that are integrated economically and socially. (For population and size of CMAs, see p. 55; complete profiles can be found on pp. 31-37.)

	1992	1993	1994	1995	1996	1997	1998	% Change 1992-1998
Toronto	996	1 010	962	909	873	852	836	
% change	-7.9	1.4	-4.7	-5.5	-4.0	-1.4	-2.2	-16.7
Montreal	1 043	965	960	858	839	782	827	
% change	2.5	-7.5	-0.5	-10.7	-2.2	-7.0	4.9	-20.2
Vancouver	1 425	1 397	1 319	1 297	1 325	1 258	1 170	
% change	5.5	-2.0	-5.6	-1.7	2.2	-4.7	-5.2	-16.9
Edmonton	1 283	1 184	961	924	922	960	996	
% change	-1.7	-7.7	-18.8	-3.9	-0.2	4.0	2.0	-21.5
Calgary	880	823	832	739	769	833	849	
% change	-19.7	-6.5	1.2	-11.2	4.1	8.0	0.4	-5.8
Ottawa	1 122	1 179	1 019	988	911	795	879	
% change	5.8	5.1	-13.6	-3.0	-7.8	-2.3	-2.6	-15.6
Quebec	574	564	601	579	539	504	456	
% change	-0.5	-1.7	6.6	-3.7	-6.9	-6.1	-11.4	-23.6
Winnipeg	1 128	1 270	1 289	1 196	1 304	1 456	1 299	
% change	18.9	12.6	1.5	-7.2	9.0	11.0	-10.8	18.3
Hamilton	1 163	1 125	1 112	1 139	1 131	1 122	1 025	
% change	9.7	-3.3	-1.2	2.3	-0.7	-1.8	-7.3	10.8

Source: *Uniform Crime Reporting Survey, Canadian Centre for Justice Statistics,* © *Statistics Canada*
Rates are calculated per 100 000 people.. Population estimates at July 1.

Change in Rates of Property Crime for Major CMAs, 1992-8

	1992	1993	1994	1995	1996	1997	1998	% Change 1992-1998
Toronto	5 118	4 839	4 495	4 494	4 314	3 932	3 354	
% change	-8.8	-5.4	-7.1	0.0	-4.0	-9.1	-14.8	-38.0
Montreal	6 416	5 884	5 326	5 144	5 351	5 126	4 922	
% change	-5.8	-8.3	-9.5	-3.5	4.0	-4.3	-6.8	-26.9
Vancouver	10 008	9 575	9 477	10 050	10 494	9 080	8 239	
% change	-2.2	-4.3	-1.0	6.0	4.4	-13.1	-7.4	-16.7
Edmonton	8 075	6 701	5 589	5 277	5 219	5 198	4 984	
% change	-9.6	-17.0	-16.6	-5.6	-1.1	-0.5	-5.5	-38.2
Calgary	7 689	6 930	5 841	5 376	5 384	5 221	5 254	
% change	-4.2	-9.9	-15.7	-8.0	0.1	-3.3	-1.7	-33.8
Ottawa	6 620	6 756	6 813	7 072	5 940	4 648	4 593	
% change	-1.6	2.1	0.8	3.8	-16.0	-12.25	-11.0	-33.0
Quebec	5 234	4 671	4 042	4 129	4 380	3 765	3 511	
% change	-6.5	-10.8	-13.5	2.1	6.1	-14.2	-8.3	-36.4
Winnipeg	6 810	7 103	7 383	6 656	6 456	5 972	5 717	
% change	-5.9	4.3	3.9	-9.9	-3.0	-9.0	-4.3	-16.6
Hamilton	5 256	5 644	5 078	5 060	4 770	4 406	3 958	
% change	-5.0	7.4	-10.0	-0.4	-5.7	-8.6	-7.5	-23.7

Source: *Uniform Crime Reporting Survey, Canadian Centre for Justice Statistics,* © *Statistics Canada*
Rates are calculated per 100 000 people.. Population estimates at July 1.

Youth Crime in Canada, 1990-98

	1991	1992	1993	1994	1995	1996	1997	1998
Population[1]								
(12-17)	2 273 918	2 305 122	2 330 863	2 359 075	2 386 304	2 417 604	2 439 839	2 451 946
Homicide								
- number ...	49	53	36	52	68	49	54	56
- rate	2.2	2.3	1.5	2.2	2.8	2.0	2.2	2.3
Assaults								
- number ...	12 815	13 584	14 981	15 363	15 898	15 945	15 612	15 830
- rate	564	589	643	651	666	660	640	646
Sexual assaults								
- number ...	1 906	2 074	2 132	1 896	1 586	1 581	1 494	1 438
- rate	84	90	91	80	66	65	61	59
Robbery								
- number ...	2 746	2 966	2 996	3 006	3 535	3 741	3 792	3 569
- rate	121	129	129	127	148	155	155	146
Total violent crime								
- number ...	18 919	20 028	21 477	21 629	22 441	22 521	22 172	22 145
- rate	832	869	921	917	940	932	909	903
Break and enter								
- number ...	26 901	24 747	21 947	19 992	18 654	18 532	17 092	15 961
- rate	1 183	1 074	942	847	782	767	701	651
Motor vehicle theft								
- number ...	8 768	8 122	8 211	7 476	6 875	7 011	6 468	6 172
- rate	386	352	352	317	288	290	265	252
Theft								
- number ...	45 221	39 648	35 301	32 228	33 762	32 473	27 060	24 778
- rate	1 989	1 720	1 515	1 366	1 415	1 343	1 109	1 011
Total property crime								
- number ...	91 656	83 603	74 981	68 907	68 105	66 702	58 340	54 047
- rate	4 031	3 627	3 217	2 921	2 854	2 759	2 391	2 204
Mischief								
- number ...	9 725	9 066	8 214	7 687	7 745	7 695	7 005	6 868
- rate	428	393	352	326	325	318	287	280
Offensive weapons								
- number ...	2 020	1 906	1 932	1 963	1 693	1 551	1 478	1 459
- rate	89	83	83	83	71	64	61	60
Total other criminal code								
- number ...	31 741	31 651	30 429	29 089	30 117	30 187	30 329	30 792
- rate	1 396	1 373	1 305	1 233	1 262	1 249	1 243	1 256
Total criminal code								
- number ...	142 316	135 282	126 887	119 625	120 663	119 410	110 841	106 984
- rate	6 259	5 869	5 444	5 071	5 056	4 939	4 543	4 363

Source: *Uniform Crime Reporting Survey, Canadian Centre for Justice Statistics,* © *Statistics Canada*

(1) Population estimates at July 1. Rates are calculated per 100000 people.

THE ECONOMY

Understanding the Economy: A Glossary of Terms

Appreciation: the increase in the value of a currency relative to other currencies under free market conditions.

Balanced budget: when a government's budget is balanced, all revenues equal expenditures in a budget year. There is no surplus or deficit, but a national debt may still exist.

Balance of payments: a measure of all yearly business transactions between one country and the rest of the world. It is the difference between the value of exports and imports, as well as the difference between investment money coming into and leaving the country.

Bank of Canada: the sole money-issuing bank in Canada, acting as banker to all other financial institutions and the government. It is responsible for Canada's banking system, sets interest rates and regulates the money supply.

Bank rate: the interest rate at which the Bank of Canada lends money to the chartered banks.

Cartel: a group of companies in a specific industry that band together to restrict output and increase prices to get higher profits. In Canada, cartels are illegal. The best known international cartel is the Organization of Petroleum Exporting Countries (OPEC).

Constant dollars: dollars as if in some base year used to adjust for the effects of inflation.

Consumer price index: an indexed measure of the average prices of household goods to show inflationary trends; compiled monthly by Statistics Canada.

Cost of living: the cost of maintaining a particular standard of living measured in terms of purchased goods and services. The rise in the cost of living is the same as the rate of inflation.

Current dollars: cost of an asset in today's prices.

Deficit spending: the practice whereby a government goes into debt to finance some expenditures.

Deflation: a decline in general price levels, often caused by a reduction in the supply of money or credit.

Depreciation: the decrease in the value of a currency relative to other currencies under free market conditions. This differs from a devaluation.

Depression: a long period of little business activity when prices are low, unemployment is high, and purchasing power decreases sharply.

Devaluation: the official lowering of the value of a nation's currency relative to foreign currencies.

Disposable income: income after taxes available to persons for spending and saving.

Equalization payments: transfers of tax revenues from the Canadian government to provinces with a high proportion of lower-income earners as compensation for their lower per capita tax revenues.

Exchange rate: the price of one country's currency relative to another country's currency.

Fiscal policy: the deliberate use of government budget measures (i.e., tax and spending policies) to alleviate economic problems such as low GNP, high unemployment and inflation.

Free trade: a system whereby the free movement of all goods and services, investment money and workers between countries is neither restricted nor encouraged by governments.

Gross domestic product (GDP): the value of all goods and services produced in a country.

Gross national product (GNP): the value of all goods and services produced by citizens of a country both inside and outside the country.

Inflation: a steady rise in the average level of prices in an economy.

Less developed countries (LDCs): also known as Third World countries, these are countries considered economically underdeveloped relative to the western industrialized nations.

Minimum wage: a minimum hourly wage as set by federal or provincial legislation.

Monetary policy: the government's manipulation of interest rates and the money supply to achieve economic growth, employment and price stability.

Money supply: the amount of money in an economy, with money defined as all currency in circulation and in chequing accounts.

National debt: the debt of the central government; in Canada's case, the federal government.

Per capita GNP: also known as per capita income, it is the nation's gross national product divided by its population.

Prime interest rate: the rate charged by chartered banks on short-term loans to large commercial customers with the best credit rating.

Protectionism: government policies designed to restrict imports to protect domestic industries. These policies include customs duties (tariffs) and restrictions on the quantity of imports (quotas). ▶

▶ **Real GNP:** gross national product adjusted for inflation.

Recession: not as severe or as long-lasting as a depression but with the same general characteristics: a decline in real GNP for two consecutive quarters, with consequent unemployment and widespread softening in many sectors of the economy.

Stagflation: a high inflation rate combined with a high unemployment rate.

Supply-side economics: a school of thinking that states that an economy can prosper through policies affecting costs of production—that is, by giving production incentives to labour and greater financial rewards to investors.

Trade balance: the difference between the value of exports and imports.

Transfer payments: government payments to the provinces where no productive return is provided, such as old age pensions, unemployment insurance and welfare.

Wage-price controls: legislation whereby the government sets wage, salary and price increases to curb inflation.

Wage-price spiral: inflation brought about by increased wages that increase costs to the producers, who in turn increase prices. The increase in prices would cause labour to bargain for higher wages, resulting in a spiralling inflation.

ECONOMIC INDICATORS

Canadian Gross Domestic Product

(millions of dollars)

The gross domestic product (GDP) measures the value of all goods and services produced in Canada. The real (adjusted for inflation) change in the GDP shows year-to-year changes in economic activity and is considered a prime indicator of how well the nation's economy is performing.

	Current Dollars		Constant (1986) Dollars	
	GDP	Annual % Change	Real GDP	Annual % Change
1926	5 354	n.a.	43 986	n.a.
1927	5 777	7.9	48 108	9.4
1928	6 279	8.7	52 527	9.2
1929	6 400	1.9	52 997	0.9
1930	6 009	-6.1	51 262	-3.3
1931	4 975	-17.2	45 521	-11.2
1932	4 079	-18.0	41 302	-9.3
1933	3 723	-8.7	38 331	-7.2
1934	4 186	12.4	42 318	10.4
1935	4 514	7.8	45 357	7.2
1936	4 879	8.1	47 437	4.6
1937	5 477	12.3	51 635	8.9
1938	5 523	0.8	52 354	1.4
1939	5 880	6.5	56 265	7.5
1940	6 987	18.8	63 722	13.3
1941	8 532	22.1	72 214	13.3
1942	10 497	23.0	84 925	17.6
1943	11 282	7.5	88 164	3.8
1944	12 068	7.0	91 385	3.7
1945	12 063	0.0	89 170	-2.4
1946	12 167	0.9	87 177	-2.2
1947	13 940	14.6	91 665	5.1
1948	15 969	14.6	93 056	1.5
1949	17 347	8.6	97 234	4.5
1950	19 125	10.3	104 821	7.8
1951	22 280	16.5	109 492	4.5
1952	25 170	13.0	118 627	8.3
1953	26 395	4.9	124 526	5.0
1954	26 531	0.5	123 163	-1.1
1955	29 250	10.2	134 889	9.5
1956	32 902	12.5	146 523	8.6
1957	34 467	4.8	150 179	2.5
1958	35 689	3.5	153 439	2.2
1959	37 877	6.1	159 484	3.9
1960	39 448	4.1	164 126	2.9
1961	41 253	n.a.	220 816	n.a

	Current Dollars		Constant (1992) Dollars[1]	
	GDP	Annual % Change	Real GDP	Annual % Change
1962	44 755	8.5	235 900	6.8
1963	48 059	7.4	247 944	5.1
1964	52 527	9.6	264 174	6.5
1965	58 050	10.3	281 249	6.5
1966	64 943	11.9	299 689	6.6
1967	69 834	7.5	308 639	3.0
1968	76 285	9.2	325 147	5.3
1969	84 006	10.1	342 468	5.3
1970	90 367	7.6	351 434	2.6
1971	98 630	9.1	370 859	5.5
1972	110 124	11.7	390 702	5.4
1973	129 196	17.3	418 797	7.2
1974	154 290	19.4	436 151	4.1
1975	173 893	12.7	445 813	2.2
1976	200 296	15.2	470 291	5.5
1977	221 358	10.5	486 562	3.5
1978	245 526	10.9	506 413	4.1
1979	280 309	14.2	527 703	4.2
1980	315 245	12.5	535 007	1.4
1981	360 494	14.4	551 305	3.0
1982	379 734	5.3	535 113	-2.9
1983	411 160	8.3	549 843	2.8
1984	449 249	9.3	581 038	5.7
1985	485 139	8.0	612 416	5.4
1986	511 796	5.5	628 575	2.6
1987	558 106	9.0	654 360	4.1
1988	611 785	9.6	686 176	4.9
1989	656 190	7.3	703 577	2.5
1990	678 135	3.3	705 464	0.3
1991	683 239	0.8	692 247	-1.9
1992	698 544	2.2	698 544	0.9
1993	724 960	3.8	714 583	2.3
1994	767 506	5.9	748 350	4.7
1995	807 088	5.2	769 082	2.8
1996	833 921	3.3	782 130	1.7
1997	873 947	4.8	813 031	3.9
1998	895 704	2.5	838 265	3.1

Source: © *Statistics Canada*

(n.a.) Not available. (1) New base for constant dollars.

Canadian Consumer Price Index by Year

1992 = 100

1915	.7.3	1958	.18.0	1973	.28.1	1988	.84.8
1920	.13.5	1959	.18.3	1974	.31.1	1989	.89.0
1925	.10.9	1960	.18.5	1975	.34.5	1990	.93.3
1930	.10.9	1961	.18.7	1976	.37.1	1991	.98.5
1935	.8.7	1962	.18.9	1977	.40.0	1992	.100.0
1940	.9.5	1963	.19.2	1978	.43.6	1993	.101.8
1945	.10.9	1964	.19.6	1979	.47.6	1994	.102.0
1950	.14.9	1965	.20.0	1980	.52.4	1995	.104.2
1951	.16.4	1966	.20.8	1981	.58.9	1996	.105.9
1952	.16.9	1967	.21.5	1982	.65.3	1997	.107.6
1953	.16.7	1968	.22.4	1983	.69.1	1998	.108.6
1954	.16.8	1969	.23.4	1984	.72.1	1999[1]	.110.5
1955	.16.8	1970	.24.2	1985	.75.0		
1956	.17.1	1971	.24.9	1986	.78.1		
1957	.17.6	1972	.26.1	1987	.81.5		

Source: © *Statistics Canada*   (1) As of June 1999.

Canadian Consumer Price Index by Item

1992 = 100

This table shows the relative costs, as far back as 1950, of categories of purchases made by Canadian consumers. To compare 1997 costs with those of another year, divide the 1997 index by the index for the year you wish to compare it with; then multiply that by your actual cost in the year for which you are making the comparison.

Example: you spent $65 per week on family food purchases in 1985. To calculate what that would be in today's dollars, divide the 1998 food index (110.2) by the 1985 food index (78.8). Now multiply the result by $65. The answer, $90.90, is what you now must spend to buy the same package of groceries that cost $65 in 1985.

	All Items	Food	Housing	Clothing	Trans-portation	Health and Personal Care	Recreation and Education	Tobacco and Alcohol
1950	14.9	14.2	n.a.	n.a.	14.8	12.0	15.7	11.3
1955	16.8	15.5	n.a.	n.a.	16.6	14.9	18.9	11.8
1960	18.5	16.9	n.a.	n.a.	19.7	18.2	22.3	12.7
1965	20.0	18.8	n.a.	n.a.	20.7	20.6	23.8	13.4
1970	24.2	22.3	n.a.	n.a.	24.6	25.5	29.6	16.2
1975	34.5	36.4	n.a.	n.a.	33.1	34.6	39.3	20.6
1980	52.4	58.6	50.2	n.a.	51.4	51.8	53.0	30.4
1981	58.9	65.3	56.9	n.a.	60.8	57.5	58.4	34.4
1982	65.3	70.0	64.6	n.a.	69.4	63.5	63.4	39.7
1983	69.1	72.6	69.3	70.4	72.8	67.9	67.5	44.7
1984	72.1	76.6	72.1	72.4	75.9	70.6	69.8	48.3
1985	75.0	78.8	74.7	74.8	79.6	73.1	72.9	52.9
1986	78.1	82.8	76.8	76.8	82.1	76.1	76.6	59.2
1987	81.5	86.4	80.3	79.8	85.1	80.0	80.4	63.1
1988	84.8	88.7	84.0	84.2	86.7	83.5	84.9	67.8
1989	89.0	92.0	88.9	87.6	91.2	87.1	88.8	74.1
1990	93.3	95.8	93.9	90.0	96.3	91.4	92.5	80.6
1991	98.5	100.4	98.2	99.0	98.0	97.8	98.9	94.4
1992	100.0	100.0	100.0	100.0	100.0	100.0	100.0	100.0
1993	101.8	101.7	101.4	101.0	103.2	102.7	102.4	101.6
1994	102.0	102.1	101.8	101.6	107.8	103.6	105.5	85.0
1995	104.2	104.5	102.9	101.6	113.4	103.5	109.5	84.9
1996	105.9	105.9	103.1	101.3	117.8	104.1	112.1	86.6
1997	107.6	107.6	103.3	103.0	121.5	105.9	114.9	89.3
1998	108.6	109.3	103.7	104.1	120.5	108.1	117.5	92.6

Source: © *Statistics Canada*

Canadian Inflation Rate by Year

This table shows annual inflation rates, as measured by the percentage change in the Consumer Price Index (CPI) from one year to the next. The CPI, determined monthly by Statistics Canada, is a "weighted" average of the cost of a package of goods and services—such as food, clothing, housing and health care—normally purchased by Canadian households. Weighted average means that some items are given more importance according to the proportion of household income spent on them.

Prices increase for several reasons: rising production costs, limited availability of the commodity, unfavourable exchange rates pushing up import prices, excessive consumer demand and too much currency in the economy.

1915	1.4	1958	2.3	1973	7.7	1988	4.0
1920	16.4	1959	1.7	1974	10.7	1989	5.0
1925	1.9	1960	1.1	1975	10.9	1990	4.8
1930	-0.9	1961	1.1	1976	7.5	1991	5.6
1935	1.2	1962	1.1	1977	7.8	1992	1.5
1940	3.3	1963	1.6	1978	9.0	1993	1.8
1945	0.9	1964	2.1	1979	9.2	1994	0.2
1950	2.8	1965	2.0	1980	10.1	1995	2.2
1951	10.1	1966	4.0	1981	12.4	1996	1.6
1952	3.0	1967	3.4	1982	10.9	1997	1.6
1953	-1.2	1968	4.2	1983	5.8	1998	1.0
1954	0.6	1969	4.5	1984	4.3	1999[1]	1.0
1955	0.0	1970	3.4	1985	4.0		
1956	1.8	1971	2.9	1986	4.1		
1957	2.9	1972	4.8	1987	4.4		

Source: © *Statistics Canada*   (1) As of June 1999.

Canadian Interest Rates

(average annual)

	Bank Rate	Prime Rate	Savings Rate[1]	Conventional 5 Year Mortgage	Govt. of Canada Average Bond Yield (10 yrs. and over)
1981	17.93	19.29	15.42	18.15	15.22
1982	13.96	15.81	11.50	17.89	14.26
1983	9.55	11.17	6.85	13.29	11.79
1984	11.31	12.06	7.69	13.59	12.75
1985	9.65	10.58	6.08	12.13	11.04
1986	9.21	10.52	6.02	11.21	9.52
1987	8.40	9.52	4.81	11.17	9.95
1988	9.69	10.83	5.69	11.65	10.22
1989	12.29	13.33	8.08	12.06	9.92
1990	13.05	14.06	8.77	13.35	10.85
1991	9.03	9.94	4.48	11.13	9.76
1992	6.78	7.48	2.27	9.51	8.77
1993	5.09	6.10	0.77	8.78	7.85
1994	5.79	7.25	0.50	9.53	8.63
1995	7.31	8.65	0.50	9.16	8.28
1996	4.53	6.06	0.50	7.93	7.50
1997	3.52	4.96	0.50	7.07	6.42
1998	5.10	6.60	0.24	5.47	5.45
1999[2]	5.00	6.54	n.a.	5.37	5.36

Source: *Bank of Canada*   (n.a.) Not available. (1) Non-chequable savings deposit. (2) As of June 1999.

1992 = 100

*A*ll indexes measuring changes over time must have a specified time base. The time base is the reference point against which all levels are compared. Without a common time base, the indexes are meaningless.

The official time base for the indexes has been 1986 since 1990. As of January, 1998, the time base became 1992. All constant dollar series were converted to 1992 dollars during the process, including historical tables for CPI. When quoting an index figure, the time base should always be included [e.g., all-items CPI in 1983 was 69.1 (1992 = 100)].

Foreign Currency Exchange Rates

	Canadian Dollars in US Dollars			Foreign Currency Units Per Canadian Dollar (annual averages)				
	High	Low	Average	British Pound	French Franc	German Mark	Swiss Franc	Japanese Yen
1975	1.0095	0.9615	0.9830	0.4426	4.2070	2.4131	2.53 68	291.5452
1976	1.0389	0.9588	1.0141	0.5615	4.8379	2.5510	2.53 36	300.5711
1977	0.9985	0.8963	0.9403	0.5385	4.6189	2.1805	2.25 02	251.2563
1978	0.9170	0.8363	0.8770	0.4568	3.9448	1.7572	1.55 47	182.4818
1979	0.8778	0.8320	0.8536	0.4023	3.6311	1.5640	1.41 92	186.0465
1980	0.8767	0.8249	0.8554	0.3677	3.6088	1.5518	1.43 14	192.9385
1981	0.8506	0.8031	0.8340	0.4117	4.3346	1.8804	1.63 35	183.4862
1982	0.8446	0.7680	0.8103	0.4634	5.3050	1.9662	1.64 18	201.3693
1983	0.8208	0.7990	0.8114	0.5352	6.1576	2.0687	1.70 27	192.6782
1984	0.8038	0.7486	0.7723	0.5780	6.7250	2.1911	1.80 93	183.2509
1985	0.7587	0.7107	0.7325	0.5649	6.5232	2.1381	1.78 09	173.4004
1986	0.7332	0.6913	0.7197	0.4905	4.9751	1.5564	1.28 72	120.5400
1987	0.7721	0.7248	0.7541	0.4603	4.5290	1.3543	1.12 30	108.8376
1988	0.8444	0.7688	0.8124	0.4560	4.8263	1.4229	1.18 44	104.0150
1989	0.8652	0.8254	0.8445	0.5151	5.3821	1.5863	1.38 01	116.1980
1990	0.8859	0.8275	0.8570	0.4806	4.6577	1.3824	1.18 62	123.6094
1991	0.8934	0.8573	0.8728	0.4932	4.9044	1.4422	1.24 58	117.3709
1992	0.8771	0.7729	0.8276	0.4694	4.3706	1.2892	1.1592	104.7120
1993	0.8065	0.7416	0.7753	0.5162	4.3879	1.2814	1.1449	85.8369
1994	0.7642	0.7097	0.7321	0.4778	4.0502	1.1843	0.9976	74.6826
1995	0.7533	0.7009	0.7285	0.4614	3.6311	1.0426	0.8596	68.0272
1996	0.7474	0.7267	0.7331	0.4701	3.7453	1.0250	0.9049	79.7448
1997	0.7413	0.7008	0.7220	0.4409	4.2194	1.2516	0.9548	87.3362
1998	0.7061	0.6472	0.6767	0.4073	3.9833	1.1882	0.9790	88.3411

Source: *Bank of Canada*

Construction in Canada—Building Permits

(millions of dollars)

	Canada Total	Annual Percent Change	Residential	Non-Residential Total	Industrial	Commercial	Institutional and Government
1950	958	28.6	531	427	64	241	110
1955	1 805	18.6	1 031	774	196	254	311
1960	2 025	(14.9)	944	1 080	184	433	460
1965	3 810	16.6	1 757	2 053	430	783	840
1970	4 700	(4.0)	2 312	2 389	498	807	1 084
1975	10 598	14.2	6 129	4 469	876	2 251	1 342
1980	15 452	9.2	7 468	7 984	1 911	4 322	1 751
1981	18 735	21.2	9 815	8 921	1 731	5 230	1 960
1982	12 789	(31.7)	6 133	6 656	1 096	3 485	2 074
1983	14 571	13.9	8 859	5 712	940	2 761	2 012
1984	15 502	6.4	8 513	6 988	1 367	3 715	1 906
1985	19 524	25.9	10 883	8 641	1 885	4 640	2 116
1986	24 690	26.5	14 219	10 471	1 899	6 152	2 420
1987	30 981	25.5	18 832	12 148	2 806	7 039	2 303
1988	34 829	12.4	20 119	14 710	3 046	8 756	2 908
1989	39 318	12.9	21 268	18 050	5 492	9 666	2 892
1990	32 131	(18.3)	17 424	14 706	3 393	7 975	3 338
1991	28 468	(11.4)	16 632	11 836	2 120	5 906	3 811
1992	26 995	(5.2)	17 161	9 834	1 643	4 918	3 273
1993	25 586	(5.2)	16 433	9 154	1 756	4 268	3 130
1994	27 637	8.0	17 590	10 047	2 250	4 993	2 803
1995	24 595	(11.0)	13 242	11 353	2 823	5 441	3 089
1996	26 155	6.3	15 718	10 437	2 643	5 567	2 227
1997	31 249	19.5	18 317	12 931	3 455	6 520	2 956
1998	33 199	6.2	17 953	15 246	3 951	8 100	3 195

Source: © *Statistics Canada*

Annual Bankruptcies in Canada 1966-

	Personal	Business	Total		Personal		Total
1966	1 903	2 774	4 677	1982	30 643		41 408
1967	1 549	2 474	4 023	1983	26 822	10 260	37 082
1968	1 308	2 481	3 789	1984	22 022	9 578	31 600
1969	1 725	2 354	4 079	1985	19 752	8 663	28 415
1970	2 732	2 927	5 659	1986	21 765	8 502	30 267
1971	3 107	3 045	6 152	1987	24 384	7 659	32 043
1972	3 647	3 081	6 728	1988	25 817	8 031	33 848
1973	6 271	2 934	9 205	1989	29 202	8 664	37 866
1974	6 992	2 790	9 782	1990	42 782	11 642	54 424
1975	8 335	2 958	11 293	1991	62 277	13 496	75 773
1976	10 049	3 136	13 185	1992	61 822	14 317	76 139
1977	12 772	3 905	16 677	1993	54 456	12 527	66 983
1978	15 938	5 546	21 484	1994	53 802	11 810	65 612
1979	17 876	5 694	23 570	1995	65 432	13 258	78 690
1980	21 025	6 595	27 620	1996	79 631	14 229	93 860
1981	23 036	8 055	31 091	1997	85 297	12 200	97 497
				1998	75 465	10 791	86 256

Source: Bankruptcy Branch, Industry Canada

Business Bankruptcies by Province[1] 1998

	Total Bankruptcies	Total Assets	Total Liabilities	Total Deficiency
Canada	10 791	17 11 750 691	4 281 055 895	2 569 305 215
Newfoundland	119	24 272 677	61 892 100	37 619 423
Prince Edward Island	32	4 178 012	8 040 781	3 862 769
Nova Scotia	343	18 126 415	270 232 089	252 105 674
New Brunswick	239	14 584 524	38 995 692	24 411 168
Quebec	3 825	371 132 145	982 210 971	611 078 826
Ontario	3 139	249 035 516	996 175 713	747 140 197
Manitoba	266	37 099 994	137 960 621	100 860 627
Saskatchewan	438	32 849 112	72 178 841	39 329 728
Alberta	1 351	115 673 001	247 073 461	131 400 460
British Columbia	10 311	844 408 910	1 465 162 408	620 753 498
Yukon	6	5 150	107 454	102 304
Northwest Territories	2	385 224	1 025 765	640 541

Source: Bankruptcy Branch, Industry Canada   (1) Totals include all reported bankruptcies.

Don't Wait to File a Proposal

*E*ven if a company is insolvent, it can often be saved by filing a proposal with a trustee to the business's creditors. The creditors are asked to accept an offer from the company to pay only so many cents on each dollar owed (maybe 20 or 50 cents) over time. The company wins because it gets a chance to survive. The creditors win because they receive more than they would from a bankruptcy.

Filing a proposal places the fate of the company in the hands of the creditors. At a meeting held three weeks after the company files the proposal documents, the creditors vote on whether or not to accept the proposal. If the proposal is accepted by the creditors and approved by the court, all the unsecured creditors(not just the creditors who vote in favor of the proposal—will be bound by its terms. If the proposal is rejected, the business is placed in bankruptcy.

New Vehicle Sales in Canada 1953–98

(thousands of units)

	Total units sold	Total commercial vehicles	Total passenger cars	Passenger cars manufactured in North America	% of total passenger cars	Passenger cars manufactured overseas	% of total passenger cars
1953	466	103	363	337	93	26	7
1954	384	72	312	292	94	20	6
1955	463	78	385	363	94	23	6
1956	495	91	404	370	92	34	8
1957	460	76	384	333	87	50	13
1958	450	69	381	302	79	78	21
1959	500	78	423	310	73	113	27
1960	522	75	446	321	72	126	28
1961	515	75	440	339	77	102	23
1962	577	82	495	420	85	74	15
1963	648	98	550	499	91	51	9
1964	723	108	614	549	89	65	11
1965	828	122	706	631	89	75	11
1966	831	133	698	630	90	68	10
1967	812	136	677	603	89	74	11
1968	887	148	739	636	86	104	14
1969	920	157	763	641	84	122	16
1970	773	134	640	496	78	144	22
1971	935	159	776	588	76	187	24
1972	1 062	207	855	651	76	204	24
1973	1 230	256	973	784	81	190	19
1974	1 249	306	943	796	84	147	16
1975	1 328	328	1 000	844	84	156	16
1976	1 281	343	939	785	84	153	16
1977	1 349	355	994	802	81	192	19
1978	1 365	377	987	816	83	171	17
1979	1 396	393	1 003	862	86	141	14
1980	1 268	332	936	742	79	194	21
1981	1 191	286	906	649	72	256	28
1982	925	207	718	494	69	224	31
1983	1 079	238	841	623	74	218	26
1984	1 283	312	971	724	75	247	25
1985	1 528	393	1 135	795	70	340	30
1986	1 523	422	1 102	765	69	337	31
1987	1 530	469	1 061	698	66	364	34
1988	1 564	508	1 056	724	69	332	31
1989	1 481	496	985	671	68	313	32
1990	1 318	433	885	579	65	306	35
1991	1 288	415	873	573	66	300	34
1992	1 227	429	798	503	63	295	37
1993	1 193	454	739	494	67	245	33
1994	1 260	511	749	573	77	175	23
1995	1 167	496	670	553	83	117	17
1996	1 205	544	661	573	87	88	13
1997	1 424	685	739	629	85	110	15
1998	1 428	688	741	591	80	150	20

Source: © *Statistics Canada*

Cars Still Expensive in Canada

*A*utomobile prices declined in January 1999, mainly due to the fall in the value of the U.S. dollar. About 90 percent of vehicles manufactured in Canada are exported, mostly to the United States. Export prices were down for both automobiles (–0.8 percent) and trucks (–0.7 percent). Domestic automobile prices, however, were up 1.8 percent and domestic truck prices were up 0.1 percent.

Canadian Unemployment Rates[1]

	1970	1975	1980	1985	1990	1993	1994	1995	1996	1997	1998
Canada	**5.7**	**6.9**	**7.5**	**10.5**	**8.1**	**11.2**	**10.4**	**9.5**	**9.7**	**9.2**	**8.3**
Newfoundland	7.3	14.0	13.2	20.8	17.0	20.1	20.4	18.3	19.4	18.8	17.9
Prince Edward Island	n.a.	8.0	10.8	13.4	14.9	18.1	17.1	14.7	14.5	14.9	13.9
Nova Scotia	5.3	7.7	9.7	13.6	10.5	14.7	13.3	12.1	12.6	12.2	10.7
New Brunswick	6.3	9.8	11.1	15.2	12.1	12.6	12.4	11.5	11.7	12.8	12.1
Quebec	7.0	8.1	9.9	11.9	10.2	13.2	12.2	11.3	11.8	11.4	10.4
Ontario	4.4	6.3	6.9	8.1	6.3	10.6	9.6	8.7	9.1	8.5	7.2
Manitoba	5.3	4.5	5.5	8.2	7.3	9.3	9.2	7.5	7.5	6.6	5.7
Saskatchewan	4.2	2.9	4.4	8.2	7.0	8.0	7.0	6.9	6.6	6.0	5.9
Alberta	5.1	4.1	3.8	10.1	7.0	9.7	8.6	7.8	7.0	6.0	5.7
British Columbia	7.7	8.5	6.8	14.2	8.4	9.7	9.4	9.0	8.9	8.7	8.9

Source: © *Statistics Canada*   (1) Percentage of labour force.

FEDERAL GOVERNMENT SPENDING

Statement of Assets and Liabilities

as at March 31, 1998

(in millions of dollars)

	1998	1997
FINANCIAL ASSETS		
CURRENT ASSETS		
CASH	10 379	9 300
CASH IN TRANSIT	4 530	4 062
Less outstanding cheques and warrants	(3 218)	(3 253)
ACCOUNTS RECEIVABLE[1]	4 122	4 416
FOREIGN EXCHANGE ACCOUNTS	28 968	26 813
LOANS, INVESTMENTS AND ADVANCES		
Enterprise Crown corporations	12 601	13 842
National governments incl. developing countries and international organizations	6 869	8 691
Provincial and territorial governments and other loans, investments and advances	2 591	2 788
Portfolio investments	1 241	1 300
Less allowance for valuation	(9 266)	(10 554)
TOTAL ASSETS	**58 817**	**57 471**
ACCUMULATED DEFICIT	**579 708**	**583 186**
LIABILITIES		
CURRENT LIABILITIES AND ALLOWANCES		
Accounts payable and accrued liabilities	22 364	19 265
Interest and matured debt	10 419	10 402
Allowance for employee benefits	6 729	5 180
Allowance for loan guarantees and borrowings of Crown corporations	4 188	5 253
INTEREST-BEARING DEBT		
Unmatured debt payable in Canadian currency		
Marketable bonds	294 583	282 498
Treasury bills	112 300	135 400
Canada savings bonds	29 769	32 470
Bonds for Canada Pension Plan	3 456	3 468
Unmatured debt payable in foreign currencies	27 183	23 016
Public sector pensions	117 457	114 205
Canada Pension Plan (net of securities)	4 205	3 718
Other pension and other accounts	5 872	5 782
TOTAL LIABILITIES	**638 525**	**640 657**

Source: *Finance Canada, Auditor General*   (1) Net of allowance for doubtful accounts of $2 462 million in 1998 and $2 246 million in 1997.

Statement of Revenue and Expenditure

for the Year Ended March 31, 1998

(net, in millions of dollars)

	1998	1997
REVENUE		
Tax revenue		
Income tax		
Personal	70 787	63 282
Corporation	22 496	17 020
Other income tax revenues	96 257	2 847
Employment insurance premiums	18 802	19 816
Excise tax and duties		
Goods and services tax	19 461	18 079
Energy taxes	4 638	4 467
Customs import duties	2 766	2 676
Other excise taxes and duties	3 995	3 876
Non-tax Revenue		
Return on investments	4 427	4 210
Other non-tax revenue	2 816	4 623
TOTAL REVENUE	**153 162**	**140 896**
EXPENSES		
Transfer payments		
Old age security benefits, guaranteed income supplements and spouses' allowances	22 225	21 606
Other levels of government	20 054	22 564
Employment insurance benefits	11 842	12 380
Other transfer payments	20 664	17 460
Crown Corporation expenditures	2 548	3 578
Other program expenditures		
National Defence	8 879	8 541
All other departments and agencies	20 068	18 691
Public debt charges	43 620	44 973
TOTAL EXPENDITURE	**150 350**	**149 793**
SURPLUS OR DEFICIT FOR THE YEAR	**2 812**	**−8 897**

Source: *Finance Canada, Auditor General*

Federal Ministry Spending[1], 1977–98

(millions of dollars)

Department	1977-78	1987-88	1996-97	1997-98
Agriculture and Agri-Food	958.6	3.386.6	2 591.4	1 911.7
Agriculture and Agri-Food	958.6	3.386.6	2 591.4	1 911.7
Canadian Heritage (Communications)	89.5	1 706.5	2 803.0	2 619.6
Citizenship and Immigration	—	—	759.0	748.8
Consumer and Corporate Affairs	71.8	533.7	—[2]	—[2]
Energy, Mines & Resources	1 566.4	1 335.8	—[3]	—[3]
Environment	547.3	784.9	591.3	557.9
Finance	9 298.6	35 973.6	69 306.2	64 439.9
Fisheries and Oceans	—	608.5	1 323.9	1 151.5
Foreign Affairs and International Trade (External Affairs)	1 125.6	3 172.8	3 313.2	3 363.8
Governor General (and Lieutenant-Governors	3.0	8.1	10.7	11.2
Health	—	—	1 758.5	1 884.3
Human Resources Dev.	—	—	24 351.9	24 943.5
Indian Aff. & Northern Dev.	1 169.6	2 824.1	4 272.6	4 555.9
Industry, Trade and Commerce	542.7	—	3 765.0	4 523.2
Justice	101.2	567.9	776.2	828.1
Labour	40.7	222.7	—[5]	—[5]
Manpower/Employment and Immigration	2 638.5	4 622.5	—[5]	—[5]
National Defence	3 771.0	10 650.4	10 573.3	10 187.3
National Health and Welfare	11 172.6	28 973.6	—[6]	—[6]
National Revenue	522.3	1 328.5	2 236.2	2 441.9
Natural Resources	—	—	861.3	753.3
Parliament	88.6	225.2	272.8	296.5
Post Office	1 237.2	—	—	—
Privy Council	43.7	88.2	185.9	339.4
Public Works	808.4	2 925.1	4 102.9	3 757.0
Regional Economic (Industrial) Expansion	562.2	1 425.7	—[2]	—[2]
Science and Technology	273.6	799.2	—[2]	—[2]
Secretary of State	2 193.5	3 382.7	—[7]	—[7]
Solicitor General	807.3	1 905.3	2 631.9	2 738.0
Supply & Services	127.3	768.8	—[8]	—[8]
Transport	1 470.8	4 758.6	1 942.6	2 256.4
Treasury Board	180.1	417.8	978.9	1 150.6
Urban Affairs and Housing	629.4	—	—	—
Veterans Affairs	840.9	1 611.7	1 890.4	1 934.7
Western Economic Div	—	—	—[2]	
TOTAL	**42 882.3**	**115 110.5**	**141 298.8**	**137 394.2**

Source: *Public Accounts of Canada*
(1) See Manpower/Employment & Immigration. (2) See Industry. (3) See Natural Resources. (4) See Environment.
(5) Responsibilities moved to Human Resources development. (6) See Health. (7) Split between Canadian Heritage and Human Resources Development. (8) See Public Works.

Federal Government Annual Surplus or Deficit[1]

(Fiscal Year Ending Mar. 31; millions of dollars)

	Surplus or Deficit	% of GDP[2]		Surplus or Deficit	% of GDP[2]		Surplus or Deficit	% of GDP[2]
1958	-196	0.6[3]	1972	-1 542	1.6	1986	-34 404	7.2
1959	-877	2.5[3]	1973	-1 675	1.5	1987	-30 733	6.0
1960	-600	1.7[3]	1974	-1 999	1.6	1988	-28 201	5.1
1961	-529	1.4[3]	1975	-2 009	1.3	1989	-28 951	4.8
1962	-948	2.3	1976	-5 737	3.3	1990	-28 996	4.4
1963	-833	1.9	1977	-6 297	3.2	1991	-30 618	4.7
1964	-1 169	2.5	1978	-10 426	4.8	1992	-34 643	5.1
1965	-315	0.6	1979	-12 617	5.2	1993	-41 021	5.8
1966	-303	0.5	1980	-11 501	4.2	1994	-42 012	5.6
1967	-187	0.3	1981	-13 522	4.4	1995	-37 462	4.8
1968	-711	1.0	1982	-14 872	4.2	1996	-28 617	3.6
1969	-400	0.5	1983	-27 816	7.4	1997	-8 897	1.0
1970	332	0.4	1984	-32 399	8.0	1998	3 478	0.4
1971	-780	0.9	1985	-38 324	8.7			

Source: *Finance Canada*

(1) A minus (-) sign indicates a deficit. (2) GDP (Gross Domestic Product) represents the value (in current dollars) of all goods and services produced in Canada. (3) Represents percentage of GNP.

Per Capita Accumulated Federal Debt, 1940–98

	(millions of dollars)		(dollars)	
Year[1]	Net Debt[2]	Interest on Debt	Net Debt Per Capita	Interest Per Capita
1940	3 271	139	288	12
1945	11 298	409	936	34
1950	11 645	440	849	32
1955	11 263	478	718	30
1960	12 089	736	677	41
1965	15 504	1 012	789	52
1970	16 943	1 676	796	79
1975	19 276	3 164	849	139
1980	72 159	8 494	2 853	353
1981	85 681	10 658	3 520	438
1982	100 553	15 114	4 090	615
1983	128 369	16 903	5 179	682
1984	160 768	18 077	6 436	724
1985	199 092	22 445	7 911	892
1986	233 496	25 441	9 210	1 003
1987	264 101	26 658	10 306	1 040
1988	292 184	29 028	11 276	1 120
1989	320 918	33 183	12 240	1 266
1990	357 811	38 820	13 484	1 472
1991	388 429	42 537	14 424	1 590
1992	423 072	41 020	15 469	1 499
1993	466 198	38 825	16 301	1 356
1994	508 210	37 982	17 381	1 299
1995	545 672	42 046	18 435	1 420
1996	574 289	46 905	19 908	1 626
1997	583 186	44 973	19 247	1 484
1998	579 708	43 620	19 132	1 440

Source: *Finance Canada*

(1) As of Mar. 31, on a public accounts basis. (2) Accumulated budgetary deficit (net recorded assets minus gross liabilities) since Confederation.

Annual Federal Government Expenditure

(millions of dollars)[1]

Year	Total Expenditure	Expenditure on Goods & Services	Transfer Payments[2]	Interest on Public Debt
1965	8 684	3 093	4 389	1 052
1970	15 294	4 922	8 215	1 862
1975	35 778	9 369	22 038	3 705
1980	61 969	15 335	35 666	9 897
1981	73 030	18 219	39 936	13 739
1982	85 126	20 608	46 477	16 675
1983	92 688	21 769	51 992	17 463
1984	104 088	23 819	57 437	21 006
1985	114 367	26 701	61 043	24 738
1986	116 693	27 335	60 959	26 216
1987	123 120	28 434	64 248	27 883
1988	131 691	29 950	67 216	31 711
1989	141 462	31 904	69 419	37 424
1990	154 648	35 067	74 814	41 880
1991	164 771	35 910	84 722	41 053
1992	168 275	36 498	89 128	39 558
1993	172 146	37 318	92 667	39 276
1994	169 293	36 833	89 523	40 155
1995	177 142	37 887	93 001	46 254
1996	171 456	37 418	86 686	45 352
1997	166 377	36 500	90 150	43 727
1998	170 726	38 112	88 029	44 515

Source: © *Statistics Canada*

(1) Expressed in constant dollars, 1992 = 100. (2) Includes payments to persons, businesses, non-residents, and provinces and local administrations.

Interest on Public Debt

(millions of dollars[1])

Year	Mun.	Prov.	Fed.	Total	Year	Mun.	Prov.	Fed.	Total
1961	222	182	786	1 190	1980	1 986	5 150	9 897	17 033
1962	249	207	865	1 321	1981	2 257	6 534	13 739	22 530
1963	264	238	935	1 437	1982	2 544	8 200	16 675	27 419
1964	290	267	995	1 552	1983	2 837	9 558	17 463	29 858
1965	330	306	1 052	1 688	1984	3 015	11 126	21 006	35 147
1966	373	359	1 151	1 883	1985	3 298	12 549	24 738	40 585
1967	430	435	1 245	2 110	1986	3 313	13 693	26 216	43 222
1968	476	548	1 409	2 433	1987	3 340	15 056	27 883	46 279
1969	517	710	1 589	2 816	1988	3 365	15 730	31 711	50 806
1970	591	856	1 862	3 309	1989	3 495	17 366	37 424	58 285
1971	728	1 049	1 974	3 751	1990	3 722	18 684	41 880	64 286
1972	748	1 243	2 253	4 244	1991	3 886	19 587	41 053	64 526
1973	858	1 534	2 518	4 910	1992	4 089	21 594	39 558	65 241
1974	846	1 681	2 961	5 488	1993	4 140	23 097	39 276	66 513
1975	942	1 992	3 705	6 639	1994	4 224	24 929	40 155	69 308
1976	1 220	2 503	4 519	8 242	1995	4 292	28 957	46 254	79 503
1977	1 443	2 888	5 101	9 432	1996	4 171	26 715	45 352	76 238
1978	1 638	3 693	6 410	11 741	1997	4 334	27 204	43 727	75 265
1979	1 781	4 196	8 080	14 057	1998	4 218	27 670	44 515	76 403

Source: © *Statistics Canada*

(1) Expressed in constant dollars, 1992 = 100.

Major Federal Transfer Payments to Provinces and Territories

1997–98 to 1999–2000

(millions of dollars)

	Newfoundland	Prince Edward Island	Nova Scotia	New Brunswick	Quebec	Ontario
1997–98						
Canada Health and Social Transfer[1]	510	117	816	647	6 895	9 253
Equalization	1 088	223	1 301	1 093	4 820	–
TOTAL [2]	**1 495**	**328**	**2 003**	**1 633**	**11 233**	**9 253**
1998–99						
Canada Health and Social Transfer[1]	499	117	819	648	6 882	9 453
Equalization	1 040	222	1 255	1 077	4 618	–
TOTAL [2]	**1 440**	**317**	**1 960**	**1 619**	**11 018**	**9453**
1999–2000						
Canada Health and Social Transfer[1]	511	127	877	700	7 035	5 664
Equalization	1 003	222	1 239	1 054	4 464	–
TOTAL [2]	**1 416**	**327**	**2 002**	**1 648**	**11 020**	**5 664**
1999–2000 Per Capita Transfer Payment	*2 625*	*2 385*	*2 130*	*2 185*	*1 495*	*918*
% of 1999–2000 Revenue	43	42	41	35	26	20

	Manitoba	Saskatchewan	Alberta	British Columbia	Yukon Territory[3]	Northwest Territories[3]	Nunavut[3]
1997–98							
Canada Health and Social Transfer[1]	975	850	2 236	3 275	30	70	–
Equalization	1 016	117	–	–	298	892	–
TOTAL [2]	**1 919**	**854**	**2 324**	**3 275**	**328**	**962**	**–**
1998–99							
Canada Health and Social Transfer[1]	980	858	2 324	3 343	29	68	–
Equalization	960	407	–	–	296	886	–
TOTAL [2]	**1 870**	**1 151**	**2 324**	**3 343**	**326**	**954**	**–**
1999–2000							
Canada Health and Social Transfer[1]	1 063	946	2 669	3 765	31	40	27
Equalization	929	377	–	–	301	493	505
TOTAL [2]	**1 924**	**1 210**		**3 765**	**332**	**532**	**533**
1999–2000 Per Capita Transfer Payment	*1 675*	*1 175*	*908*	*919*	*10 203*	*12 737*	*19 885*
% of 1999–2000 Revenue	34	23	17	19	n.a.	n.a.	n.a.

Source: *Finance Canada*

(1) CHST is a combination of cash and tax transfers. (2) Equalization associated with CHST tax transfer is included in both CHST and Equalization. Totals have been adjusted to avoid double counting. (3) Non CHST payment is in the form of formula financing rather than equalization.

Employment Insurance

On July 1, 1996, the Employment Insurance (EI) Act replaced the Unemployment Insurance and the National Training Act. The EI program consists of two parts—Income Benefits (Part 1) and Active Re-employment Benefits (Part 2).

EI Income Benefits provide temporary income support for claimants while they look for work. Under the EI program every hour of work, including part-time, counts toward determining eligibility. There is also a Family Income Supplement that increases benefits of low-income claimants with children.

Active Re-employment Benefits provide assistance to unemployed workers returning to work through a set of active re-employment benefits and support measures. Targeted wage subsidies, self-employment assistance and job creation partnerships are available in all provinces and territories. Skills loans and grants are being implemented with the agreement of provinces and territories.

Eligibility

Most claimants require 420 to 700 insured hours of employment within the last 52 weeks, depending on the local unemployment rate. The higher the rate, the fewer hours of work required. Claimants who are entering the workforce for the first time or re-entering after a two-year absence will require 910 hours of work. To qualify for special benefits (sickness, maternity, parental), all claimants require 700 hours regardless of where they live.

Source: *Human Resources Development Canada*

Income Benefits

Claimants will receive 55 percent of their average weekly insured earnings to a maximum of $413 per week. Claimants who have previously collected EI benefits have their basic rate (55 percent) reduced by 1 percent for every 20 weeks of benefits collected after the first 20 weeks in the last five years, to a maximum reduction of 5 percent. Claimants in receipt of the Family Income Supplement are exempt from the reduction of the benefit rate.

Claim Period

A claim for benefits last a maximum of one year or until all benefits have been collected, whichever occurs first. The number of weeks of benefits a claimant is entitled to is determined by the unemployment rate in the claimant's region and the number of insured hours used to establish the claim. The more insured hours used, the more weeks of benefits; the higher the unemployment rate, the more weeks of benefits.

Special Benefits

Claimants who are unable to work due to illness or injury are also entitled to benefits. A maximum of 15 weeks of sick benefits can be paid per claim. Claimants who are on maternity leave are entitled to a maximum of 15 weeks of benefits. A claimant off work caring for a newly born or adopted child can collect 10 weeks of parental benefits. A claimant can not collect more than a total of 30 weeks of special benefits (sick, maternity, parental) per claim.

Employment Insurance Program Payments

Year	Claims[1,2] (000s)	Benefit payments ($000)	Weeks paid (000s)	Maximum weekly payment	Average weekly payment
1945	296.4	$ 14 576	1 224	$ 14.40	$ 11.91
1950	1 150.2	98 994	6 980	21.00	14.18
1955	1 929.8	228 860	12 375	30.00	18.49
1960	2 700.4	481 836	21 592	36.00	22.32
1965	1 628.2	312 110	12 718	36.00	24.54
1970	2 260.8	695 222	19 817	53.00	35.08
1975	2 857.2	3 146 497	37 327	123.00	84.64
1980	2 762.2	4 393 308	36 333	174.00	120.92
1985	3 312.4	10 266 888	59 788	276.00	171.05
1990	3 259.0	13 189 000	57 052	384.00	231.18
1995	3 095.8	13 748 243	50 462	448.00	260.14
1996	2 972.5	13 069 982	47 932	413.00	259.26
1997	2 766.7	12 018 601	40 933	413.00	254.13
1998	2 842.2	11 995 880	39 102	413.00	258.60

Source: *Human Resources Development Canada*

(1) Refers to the program in place prior to July 1, 1996. (2) Initial and renewal. (3) Prior to April 1, 1993, the maximum weekly payment for 1993 was $447.00. The figure listed above was the maximum weekly payment which came into effect as a result of an amendment to the Unemployment Insurance Act that took effect on that date.

Canada and Quebec Pension Plans

The Canada and Quebec Pension Plans were instituted in 1966 to provide benefits to Canadians who have contributed to the plan during their working lives. Both plans pay a monthly retirement benefit in addition to a one-time death benefit, survivor benefits for the spouse and dependent children of a deceased contributor and benefits to the severely disabled and their families.

Payments to the plan are made by all workers between the ages of 18 and the time they claim retirement (between the ages of 60 and 70). Payments are based on a contribution rate which in 1999 was 7.0 percent of "pensionable earnings." This payment is shared equally by employers and employees; self-employed persons must pay the entire amount themselves. The contribution rate is scheduled to increase steadily, reaching 9.1 percent in 2011. Contributions are not paid if income falls below an annual minimum ($3 500 in 1999) or on income above an annual maximum ($37 400 in 1999).

Retirement benefits from the plan are based on lifetime earnings and generally amount to 25 percent of average annual income, adjusted for inflation. The maximum monthly benefit at age 65 in 1999 was $751.67.

Source: *Human Resources Development Canada*

Spouses in a continuing marriage and partners in a common-law relationship may apply to receive an equal share of the retirement pension earned by both parties during their life together.

A provision that allows divorced couples to divide CPP credits earned during marriage was introduced in 1978. On Jan. 1, 1987, the provision was expanded to include legally-separated married spouses and those living in a common- law union. In March 1991 a further amendment allowed those previously denied a division due to a property waiver to have their situation remedied.

Since Jan. 1987, Canadians eligible for CPP benefits who retire before age 65 can receive partial pensions beginning as early as age 60. Those who begin collecting at 60 receive 70 percent of the amount they would be entitled to at age 65. For each month past age 60 that a person delays retirement, an additional half a percentage point is added—so that someone retiring at age 61 would receive 76 of their full (age 65) pension while someone postponing retirement to age 70 would receive 130 percent.

The Canada Pension Plan is administered by the federal government while the Quebec Pension Plan is administered by the Government of Quebec's Pension Board. Essentially the same rules and benefits apply to each.

Canada and Quebec Pension Plans Payments

	Canada Pension			Quebec Pension Plan			
	Benefi-ciaries[1]	Benefits paid[2] ($000)	Contrib-utors[4] (000s)	Avg. monthly retirement payments[1]	Benefi-ciaries[1]	Benefits paid[2] ($000s)	Contrib-utors[4] (000s)	Avg. monthly retirement payments[1]
1971	251 853	$ 89 236	6 755	$ 23	79 649	$ 47 576	2 234	$ 25
1976	774 890	587 834	7 561	67	232 815	266 181	2 726	66
1981	1 274 306	2 010 924	8 626	144	406 069	704 798	2 909	148
1986	1 764 604	4 887 134	8 932	247	627 317	1 899 730	2 932	243
1988	2 173 225	7 329 222	9 530	289	702 141	2 406 453	3 132	276
1989	2 335 711	8 445 044	9 600	306	736 176	2 663 521	3 176	292
1990	2 463 222	9 472 955	9 603	324	771 838	2 946 125	3 167	307
1991	2 584 986	10 541 912	9 630	342	809 409	3 182 379	3 149	323
1992	2 713 692	11 792 756	9 429	363	845 846	3 605 378	3 107	341
1993	2 845 059	13 199 084	9 399	370	883 610	3 860 717	3 039	349
1994	2 988 911	14 402 175	9 595	380	919 866	4 217 524	3 019	357
1995	3 116 453	15 256 542	9 726	384	964 116	4 505 435	3 055	354
1996	3 212 847	15 969 269	9 800	393	1 015 819	4 815 659	3 089	359
1997	3 281 603	16 675 314	10 051	400	1 061 569	5 055 947	3 094	360
1998	3 365 808	17 536 907	n.a.	409	1 095 971	5 333 715	n.a.	366
1999	3 437 649	18 184 939	n.a.	412	1 127 050	5 575 730	n.a.	368

Source: *Human Resources Development Canada; Régie des Rentes du Québec; Statistics Canada*

(n.a.) Not available. (1) As of March. (2) For fiscal years ending Mar. 31. (3) From 1971 to 1978, data is for calendar years; Jan. 1979 to Mar. 1980, data is for 15 months; from 1981 to 1988, data is for fiscal years ending Mar. 31. (4) Calendar years.

Old Age Security, Guaranteed Income Supplement and Spouse's Allowance

The Old Age Security (OAS) program, introduced in 1952, provides pensions to persons 65 years and older who meet Canadian residence requirements. Full monthly pensions ($411.23 per month as of April 1, 1999) are given to persons who have lived in Canada for 40 years since the age of 18; some persons who have lived in Canada for 10 consecutive years are also eligible for full pensions. Partial pensions, introduced in 1977, are based on the number of years a pensioner has lived in Canada.

The Guaranteed Income Supplement (GIS) was introduced in 1966 to assist those with little or no income other than their OAS pension. The amount of income supplement depends upon the pensioner's income, marital status and spouse's income. Generally, the maximum GIS payment is reduced by $1 for every $2 of income a pensioner has above his/her old age security pension. For example, in April 1999 a single pensioner with no personal income received OAS benefits of $411.23 per month and an income supplement of $488.72 per month. If this person had a private pension of $400 per month, the GIS would be reduced $200 to $288.72 per month.

Spouse's Allowance (SPA) benefits are payable to persons aged 60 to 64 whose spouses have died or those with low income whose spouse receives an Old Age Security pension. Like Guaranteed Income Supplement benefits, the amount of the SPA benefit is dependent on income and marital status. The maximum SPA benefit payable in April 1999 was $797.45 for widows and widowers and $729.56 for spouses of OAS pensioners.

Source: *Human Resources Development Canada*

Old Age Security Program Payments

	Number of Recipients[1] (000s)			Net Payments[2] ($000 000)			Average Yearly[3] payment per pensioner		
	OAS	GIS	SPA	OAS	GIS	SPA	OAS	GIS	SPA
1952......	643	n.a.	n.a.	$76	$n.a.	$n.a.	$n.a.	$n.a.	$n.a.
1961	905	n.a.	n.a.	592	n.a.	n.a.	n.a.	n.a.	n.a.
1966	1 106	n.a.	n.a	927	n.a.	n.a.	n.a.	n.a.	n.a.
1971	1 720	860	n.a.	1 627	280	n.a.	956	340	n.a.
1976	1 957	1 087	54	2 976	923	35	1 537	863	1 788
1981	2 303	1 245	85	5 322	1 918	178	2 338	1 592	2 168
1986	2 652	1 330	142	8 858	3 319	348	3 385	2 555	3 105
1987	2 749	1 345	144	9 520	3 451	473	3 517	2 615	3 375
1988	2 835	1 357	140	10 248	3 618	483	3 659	2 702	3 474
1989	2 919	1 364	134	10 963	3 766	473	3 803	2 803	3 538
1990	3 006	1 359	127	11 804	3 888	461	3 974	2 907	3 652
1991	3 099	1 346	121	12 705	3 976	450	4 153	3 009	3 759
1992	3 180	1 329	116	13 808	4 139	446	4 386	3 171	3 927
1993	3 264	1 331	113	14 421	4 250	435	4 464	3 268	3 964
1994	3 341	1 355	112	15 027	4 446	429	4 542	3 372	3 984
1995	3 420	1 377	112	15 478	4 604	429	4 570	3 422	3 942
1996	3 500	1 368	106	15 999	4 628	408	4 615	3 464	3 980
1997	3 564	1 376	103	16 576	4 639	396	4 678	3 452	3 951
1998	3 635	1 376	100	17 114	4 729	389	4 745	3 466	3 934
1999	3 694	1 382	99	17 564	4 805	383	4 785	3 532	3 944

Source: *Human Resources Development Canada*

(n.a.) Not available or not applicable. (1) As of March. (2) For fiscal years ending Mar. 31. (3) For fiscal years ending Mar. 31 using annual average number of recipients. OAS = Old Age Security; GIS = Guaranteed Income Supplement; SPA = Spouse's Allowance.

Health Care

Total Health Care Spending[1] by Use of Funds

(millions of dollars)[2]

	Hospitals	Other Institutions	Physicians	Other Professionals[3]	Drugs[4]	Capital	Other[5]	Total	% Change
1975......	5514.3	1124.3	1 839.9	1 098.4	1 076.2	536.1	1 074.6	12 260.1	n.a.
1980......	9 399.2	2 644.9	3 287.5	2 260.0	1 881.5	960.7	1 989.4	22 383.4	16.2
1985......	16 386.3	4 069.1	6 045.7	4 131.9	3 793.4	1 657.7	3 784.4	39 889.5	8.5
1990......	24 058.4	5 757.5	9 258.1	6 415.4	6 906.3	2 162.5	6 671.2	61 229.5	8.7
1995......	25 917.0	7 355.4	10 597.6	8 454.5	9 925.0	2 295.8	9 678.2	74 223.3	1.2
1996......	25 861.3	7 528.2	10 650.5	8 827.0	10 207.0	2 221.0	9 914.2	75 210.2	1.3
1997[6]	25 696.3	7 654.7	10 946.5	9 277.0	10 581.2	2 131.4	10 386.7	78 946.9	2.3
1998[6]	26 750.1	7 973.9	11 374.9	9 712.3	11 205.4	2 096.0	10 767.2	79 879.8	3.8

Source: *Canadian Institute for Health Information*

(n.a.) Not available. (1) Public and private sector. (2) Current dollars. (3) Includes dental services, vision-care services, and other. (4) Includes prescription and nonprescription drugs. (5) Includes pre-payment administration, public health, health research and other. (6) Preliminary figures.

Total Health Care Spending[1] Per Capita by Use of Funds

(dollars)[2]

	Hospitals	Other Institutions	Physicians	Other Professionals[3]	Drugs[4]	Capital	Other[4]	Total	% Change
1975......	237.59	46.44	75.28	47.16	46.37	23.10	46.30	526.24	n.a.
1980......	382.19	103.48	133.67	91.90	78.51	40.28	80.89	908.92	14.7
1985......	531.66	157.63	233.09	159.28	145.23	63.90	145.88	1 537.66	7.5
1990......	865.70	207.18	333.14	230.85	248.51	77.81	240.05	2 203.25	7.1
1995......	875.70	248.35	357.82	285.48	335.11	77.51	326.78	2 506.07	-0.1
1996......	862.83	251.23	355.38	294.54	340.56	74.11	320.81	2 509.58	0.1
1997[6]	857.45	252.74	361.43	306.31	349.37	70.38	342.95	2 540.82	1.2
1998[6]	873.65	260.42	371.50	317.20	365.96	68.45	351.85	2 608.84	2.7

Source: *Canadian Institute for Health Information*

(n.a.) Not available. (1) Public and private sector. (2) Current dollars. (3) Includes dental services, vision-care services, and other. (4) Includes prescription and nonprescription drugs. (5) Includes pre-payment administration, public health, health research and other. (6) Preliminary figures.

Percentage Distribution of Health Care Spending[1] by Use of Funds

(of millions of dollars)[2]

	Hospitals	Other Institutions	Physicians	Other Professionals[3]	Drugs[4]	Capital	Other[5]
1975	45.0	9.2	15.0	8.9	8.8	4.4	8.8
1980	42.0	11.4	14.7	10.1	8.4	4.4	8.9
1985	41.1	10.3	15.2	10.4	9.8	4.2	9.5
1990	39.3	9.4	15.1	10.5	11.3	3.5	10.8
1995	34.9	9.9	14.3	11.4	13.4	3.1	13.0
1996	34.4	10.0	14.2	11.7	13.6	3.0	13.2
1997[6]	33.7	9.9	14.2	12.1	13.8	2.8	13.5
1998[6]	33.5	10.0	14.2	12.2	14.0	2.6	13.5

Source: *Canadian Institute for Health Information*

(n.a.) Not available. (1) Public and private sector. (2) Current dollars. (3) Includes dental services, vision-care services, and other. (4) Includes prescription and nonprescription drugs. (5) Includes pre-payment administration, public health, health research and other. (6) Preliminary figures.

FOREIGN TRADE

Canadian Balance of International Payments

(millions of dollars)

The Canadian balance of payments is a measure of all yearly business transactions between Canada and the world. These transactions are in two accounts: current account and capital account. The current account notes all Canadian payments for imported goods and services and all money received for Canadian exports of goods and services. The capital account records all investment transactions (stocks, bonds, real estate, new companies, loans, foreign currency trading, interest payments) between Canada and other countries.

Year	Current Account			Capital Account		
	Receipts[1]	Payments	Balance[2]	Investment Inflow[3]	Investment Outflow[4]	Total Investment Balance[5]
1970	22 436	21 944	494	3 944	4 448	-504
1971	23 167	24 211	-1 042	3 993	1 888	2 105
1972	25 428	27 810	-2 383	5 770	2 216	3 554
1973	32 999	35 036	-2 037	8 447	5 988	2 459
1974	42 098	46 554	-4 454	8 017	3 209	4 808
1975	43 038	51 347	-8 310	10 355	1 954	8 401
1976	48 068	55 609	-7 542	16 311	6 303	10 008
1977	56 058	63 474	-7 415	12 841	4 356	8 485
1978	66 872	76 199	-9 328	21 604	10 020	11 584
1979	84 919	94 729	-9 810	22 698	12 064	10 634
1980	98 418	105 548	-7 128	27 894	21 411	6 483
1981	108 933	123 873	-14 941	41 249	22 459	18 790
1982	112 361	109 990	2 365	8 070	9 656	-1 586
1983	115 409	118 519	-3 111	15 141	9 973	5 160
1984	143 435	145 030	-1 596	20 228	12 634	7 594
1985	151 338	159 047	-7 709	19 555	7 351	12 204
1986	155 322	170 682	-15 359	35 746	20 152	15 594
1987	162 736	180 375	-17 639	34 869	17 715	17 154
1988	181 790	199 926	-18 136	30 599	17 602	12 997
1989	186 280	211 916	-25 636	41 882	19 746	22 136
1990	194 972	217 920	-22 948	38 664	19 699	18 965
1991	188 719	214 151	-25 432	34 511	15 128	19 383
1992	205 455	230 639	-25 184	27 726	14 411	13 315
1993	236 016	264 033	-28 017	51 313	27 275	24 038
1994	284 517	304 741	-20 224	57 272	48 907	8 365
1995	330 618	337 065	-6 447	31 665	38 701	-7 036
1996	350 433	345 903	4 530	51 104	72 127	-21 023
1997	377 223	390 038	-12 815	63 966	51 706	12 260
1998[6]	402 493	420 915	-18 423	49 533	43 536	5 997

Source: © *Statistics Canada*

(1) Money received for Canadian exports of goods and services. (2) Receipts minus payments. (3) Represents net foreign investment to Canada. (4) Represents net Canadian investment to other countries. (5) Investment inflow minus investment outflow. (6) Preliminary figures

Canadian Imports by Country

(millions of dollars)

	1994	%	1995	%	1996	%	1997	%	1998	%
Total Imports[1]	202 736	100.0	225 553	100.0	232 557	100.0	272 856	100.0	298 545	100.0
Australia	1 121	0.6	1 283	0.6	1 291	0.6	1 182	0.4	1 282	0.4
Belgium	606	0.3	723	0.3	817	0.4	845	0.3	1 071	0.4
Brazil	961	0.5	1 038	0.5	1 134	0.5	1 320	0.5	1 377	0.5
Chile	238	0.1	279	0.1	342	0.2	326	0.1	360	0.1
China	3 856	1.9	4 639	2.1	4 931	2.1	6 341	2.3	7 653	2.6
Colombia	257	0.1	372	0.2	297	0.1	302	0.1	340	0.1
Cuba	194	0.1	321	0.1	401	0.2	353	0.1	334	0.1
Egypt	15	...	19	...	20	...	29	...	35	...
El Salvador	40	...	44	...	28	...	45	...	32	...
France	2 513	1.2	3 124	1.4	3 402	1.5	5 137	1.9	4 941	1.7
Germany	4 384	2.2	4 799	2.1	4 824	2.1	5 410	2.0	6 120	2.1
Hong Kong	1 190	0.6	1 305	0.6	1 142	0.5	1 266	0.5	1 256	0.4
Hungary	47	...	45	...	48	...	75	...	95	...
India	459	0.2	541	0.2	604	0.3	743	0.3	899	0.3
Iran	117	0.1	122	0.1	238	0.1	506	0.2	154	0.1
Israel	183	0.1	241	0.1	267	0.1	315	0.1	417	0.1
Italy	2 588	1.3	3 271	1.5	2 719	1.2	3 069	1.1	3 436	1.2
Jamaica	211	0.1	200	0.1	239	0.1	258	0.1	256	0.1
Japan	11 367	5.6	12 094	5.4	10 439	4.5	12 555	4.6	13 991	4.7
Kenya	19	...	19	...	19	...	18	...	19	...
Malaysia	1 214	0.6	1 550	0.7	1 579	0.7	1 991	0.7	1 997	0.7
Mexico	4 525	2.2	5 353	2.4	6 035	2.6	7 019	2.6	7 671	2.6
Morocco	50	...	70	...	82	...	66	...	88	...
Netherlands	858	0.4	999	0.4	927	0.4	1 174	0.4	1 181	0.4
New Zealand	321	0.2	298	0.1	322	0.1	369	0.1	383	0.1
Nigeria	632	0.3	585	0.3	311	0.1	521	0.2	301	0.1
Peru	96	0.1	96	...	126	0.1	135	0.1	171	0.1
Philippines	469	0.2	498	0.2	553	0.2	726	0.3	958	0.3
Poland	102	0.1	121	0.1	144	0.1	147	0.1	171	0.1
Romania	73	...	60	...	50	...	69	...	121	...
Russia	362	0.2	498	0.2	449	0.2	621	0.2	732	0.3
Saudi Arabia	541	0.3	502	0.2	267	0.3	315	0.2	417	0.1
Singapore	1 152	0.6	1 311	0.6	1 192	0.5	1 174	0.4	1 181	0.4
South Africa	306	0.2	419	0.2	439	0.2	497	0.2	514	0.2
South Korea	2 504	1.2	3 204	1.4	2 729	1.2	2 838	1.0	3 315	1.1
Spain	637	0.3	706	0.3	687	0.3	786	0.3	834	0.3
Sweden	1 128	0.6	1 303	0.6	1 201	0.5	1 316	0.5	1 368	0.5
Switzerland	763	0.4	902	0.4	938	0.4	932	0.3	1 124	0.4
Taiwan	2 780	1.4	2 791	1.2	2 852	1.2	3 475	1.3	4 030	1.4
Turkey	120	0.1	150	0.1	152	0.1	194	0.1	250	0.1
United Kingdom	5 033	2.5	5 476	2.4	5 908	2.5	6 502	2.4	6 233	2.1
United States[2]	137 335	67.8	150 682	66.8	156 944	67.5	184 344	67.6	205 561	68.2
Venezuela....................	508	0.3	669	0.3	726	0.3	972	0.4	841	0.3
Yugoslavia[3]	79	...	0.3	...	3	...	10	...	6	...

Source: © *Statistics Canada*

(…) = Too small to be included. (1) Total includes countries not shown. (2) Includes Puerto Rico and the U.S. Virgin Islands. (3) Denotes former Yugoslavia.

Canadian Exports by Country

(millions of dollars)

	1994	%	1995	%	1996	%	1997	%	1998	%
Total Imports[1]	212 493	100.0	246 390	100.0	259 295	100.0	281 226	100.0	297 590	100.0
Australia	861	0.4	1 152	0.5	974	0.4	950	0.3	945	0.3
Belgium	1 344	0.6	1 854	0.8	1 497	0.6	1 463	0.5	1 464	0.5
Brazil	953	0.5	1 281	0.5	1 336	0.5	1 555	0.6	1 254	0.5
Chile	230	0.1	369	0.2	396	0.2	379	0.1	327	0.1
China	2 128	1.0	3 294	1.3	2 871	1.1	2 355	0.8	2 475	0.8
Colombia	407	0.2	350	0.1	459	0.2	431	0.2	436	0.2
Cuba	117	0.1	259	0.1	263	0.1	323	0.1	419	0.1
Egypt	96	0.1	131	0.1	127	0.1	176	0.1	153	0.1
El Salvador	18	...	23	...	11	...	21	...	33	...
France	1 335	0.6	1 914	0.8	1 684	0.7	1 608	0.6	1 597	0.5
Germany	2 210	1.0	3 172	1.3	3 167	1.2	2 625	1.0	2 543	0.9
Hong Kong	908	0.4	1 381	0.6	1 188	0.5	1 663	0.6	1 255	0.4
Hungary	29	...	41	...	42	...	89	...	94	...
India	282	0.1	434	0.2	347	0.1	482	0.2	384	0.1
Iran	447	0.2	429	0.2	561	0.2	723	0.3	263	0.1
Israel	153	0.1	218	0.1	217	0.1	227	0.1	214	0.1
Italy	1 185	0.6	1 778	0.7	1 323	0.5	1 497	0.5	1 494	0.5
Jamaica	90	...	97	...	83	...	84	...	96	
Japan	9 648	4.5	11 906	4.9	11 072	4.3	11 043	3.9	8 515	2.9
Kenya	19	...	17	...	33	...	38	...	24	...
Malaysia	272	0.1	536	0.2	517	0.2	686	0.2	453	0.2
Mexico	1 055	0.5	1 124	0.5	1 218	0.5	1 219	0.4	1 388	0.5
Morocco	74	...	189	0.1	194	0.1	200	0.1	189	0.1
Netherlands	1 214	0.6	1 615	0.7	1 594	0.6	1 635	0.6	1 779	0.6
New Zealand	139	0.1	182	0.1	221	0.1	294	0.1	206	0.1
Nigeria	15	...	26	...	42	...	104	...	200	...
Peru	84	...	137	0.1	168	0.1	309	0.1	185	0.1
Philippines	196	0.1	326	0.1	287	0.1	418	0.2	248	0.1
Poland	55	...	116	0.1	161	0.1	142	0.1	184	0.1
Romania	120	0.1	21	...	97	...	64	...	54	...
Russia	184	0.1	190	0.1	312	0.1	361	0.1	276	0.1
Saudi Arabia	285	0.3	324	0.2	225	0.2	361	0.2	309	0.1
Singapore	367	0.2	484	0.2	536	0.2	515	0.2	376	0.1
South Africa	285	0.1	324	0.1	225	0.1	361	0.1	309	0.1
South Korea	2 216	1.0	2 703	1.1	2 776	1.1	2 985	1.1	1 787	0.6
Spain	383	0.2	613	0.3	512	0.2	588	0.2	564	0.2
Sweden	236	0.1	326	0.1	259	0.1	375	0.1	341	0.1
Switzerland	891	0.4	534	0.2	910	0.4	414	0.2	901	0.3
Taiwan	1 203	0.6	1 706	0.7	1 369	0.5	1 576	0.6	1 126	0.4
Turkey	140	0.1	281	0.1	257	0.1	330	0.1	212	0.1
United Kingdom	3 180	1.5	3 755	1.5	3 838	1.5	3 641	1.3	4 156	1.4
United States[2]	172 182	81.0	184 350	78.9	208 806	80.5	229 279	81.5	251 114	84.4
Venezuela	303	0.1	378	0.2	461	0.2	508	0.2	433	0.2
Yugoslavia[3]	31	...	2	...	6	...	17	...	9	...

Source: © *Statistics Canada*

(...) = Too small to be included. (1) Total includes countries not shown. (2) Includes Puerto Rico and the U.S. Virgin Islands. (3) Denotes former Yugoslavia.

Foreign Investment in Canada

(millions of dollars)

	Total	United States	United Kingdom	Other EU[1]	Japan	Other OECD[2]	All Other
1926	1 782	1 403	336	—	—	—	43
1930	2 427	1 993	392	—	—	—	42
1935	2 284	1 870	373	—	—	—	41
1940	2 477	2 064	362	—	—	—	51
1945	2 831	2 422	348	—	—	—	61
1950	4 098	3 549	468	—	—	—	81
1951	4 642	4 014	497	—	—	—	131
1952	5 358	4 661	553	—	—	—	144
1953	6 177	5 368	622	—	—	—	187
1954	6 960	5 969	772	—	—	—	219
1955	8 010	6 778	905	—	—	—	327
1956	9 314	7 798	1 068	—	—	—	448
1957	10 538	8 844	1 184	—	—	—	510
1958	11 371	9 504	1 321	346	—	—	200
1959	12 464	10 432	1 411	396	—	—	225
1960	13 583	11 210	1 550	553	—	—	270
1961	14 391	11 892	1 627	608	1	178	85
1962	15 380	12 661	1 723	728	1	196	71
1963	16 276	13 514	1 788	698	7	195	74
1964	16 473	13 308	2 007	829	8	226	95
1965	17 864	14 408	2 107	968	10	240	131
1966	19 550	15 942	2 125	1 054	17	255	157
1967	21 287	17 395	2 236	1 160	34	273	189
1968	23 234	18 975	2 409	1 222	62	321	245
1969	25 241	20 493	2 540	1 429	70	435	274
1970	27 374	22 054	2 641	1 617	103	580	379
1971	28 989	23 117	2 858	1 724	187	699	404
1972	30 563	24 304	2 960	1 914	194	779	412
1973	33 977	26 919	3 310	2 287	250	806	405
1974	37 557	29 870	3 681	2 380	258	902	466
1975	38 728	30 506	3 830	2 520	257	987	628
1976	41 623	32 726	4 165	2 799	293	1 003	637
1977	45 132	35 595	4 348	3 081	336	1 026	746
1978	50 089	39 352	4 770	3 473	402	1 213	879
1979	56 785	44 006	5 543	4 315	485	1 382	1 054
1980	64 708	50 368	5 773	5 168	605	1 524	1 270
1981	70 327	53 777	6 635	5 861	1 000	1 677	1 377
1982	72 814	54 457	7 149	6 476	1 341	1 760	1 631
1983	79 669	59 706	7 949	6 110	1 772	2 087	2 045
1984	85 984	64 762	8 358	6 470	2 074	2 338	1 983
1985	90 358	67 874	8 643	6 774	2 250	2 562	2 255
1986	96 054	69 241	11 317	7 526	2 679	2 709	2 582
1987	105 937	74 022	12 401	8 907	3 045	4 680	2 882
1988	114 175	76 049	15 696	9 747	3 568	5 180	3 935
1989	122 664	80 427	15 556	12 342	4 769	5 547	4 022
1990	130 932	84 089	17 185	14 339	5 222	5 871	4 227
1991	135 234	86 396	16 224	14 908	5 596	6 803	5 308
1992	137 918	88 161	16 799	15 056	5 962	6 913	5 027
1993	141 493	90 600	15 872	15 732	6 249	7 312	5 727
1994	154 594	102 629	14 693	16 824	6 587	7 989	5 873
1995	168 352	113 206	14 095	21 857	6 952	5 888	6 354
1996	179 515	120 370	14 200	23 844	7 828	6 578	6 697
1997	196 713	131 917	15 102	25 196	8 087	9 347	7 064
1998	217 053	147 345	17 720	27 278	8 058	8 890	7 762

Source: © *Statistics Canada*

(1) Other European Union countries (EU) include Belgium, Denmark, Germany, France, Greece, Ireland, Italy, Luxembourg, Netherlands, Portugal, Spain; from Jan. 1995, Austria, Finland and Sweden. (2) Other OECD countries include Australia, Iceland, New Zealand, Norway, Switzerland and Turkey; from July 1994, Mexico; from Dec. 1995, Czech Republic; from May 1996, Hungary; from Nov. 1996 Poland; and up to Dec. 1994, Austria, Finland and Sweden.

Canadian Investment Abroad

(millions of dollars)

	Total	United States	United Kingdom	Other EU[1]	Japan	Other OECD[2]	All Other
1920	212	132	1	—	1	—	78
1925	246	144	1	—	1	—	100
1930	443	260	14	—	1	—	168
1935	485	266	46	—	—	—	173
1940	681	412	58	—	1	—	210
1945	720	455	54	—	2	—	209
1950	1 043	814	73	—	—	—	156
1951	1 228	958	84	—	—	—	187
1952	1 333	1 012	91	—	3	—	226
1953	1 556	1 177	116	—	4	—	259
1954	1 706	1 295	132	—	5	—	274
1955	1 835	1 362	145	—	6	—	322
1956	1 992	1 469	154	—	8	—	361
1957	2 184	1 533	189	—	7	—	455
1958	2 264	1 525	218	31	12	—	479
1959	2 409	1 579	254	41	13	—	521
1960	2 600	1 716	277	46	15	—	546
1961	2 735	1 827	309	56	21	25	497
1962	2 933	1 896	367	64	22	39	545
1963	3 247	2 044	417	84	23	55	624
1964	3 447	2 097	458	112	24	51	706
1965	3 655	2 178	510	125	28	44	769
1966	3 910	2 247	571	143	29	47	873
1967	4 010	2 360	548	191	36	88	1 034
1968	4 865	2 729	608	228	38	92	1 170
1969	5 490	3 185	638	290	47	131	1 200
1970	6 520	3 518	636	304	48	142	1 871
1971	6 889	3 658	643	289	58	466	1 775
1972	7 075	3 698	685	304	72	531	1 785
1973	8 255	4 236	862	457	72	627	2 000
1974	9 704	5 134	979	549	77	654	2 310
1975	11 091	5 975	1 105	633	74	699	2 605
1976	12 107	6 547	1 131	712	67	797	2 853
1977	14 233	7 651	1 533	829	61	899	3 260
1978	17 303	9 613	1 658	962	65	928	4 076
1979	21 595	12 976	2 355	1 269	82	1 111	3 802
1980	28 413	17 849	3 080	1 377	109	1 370	4 628
1981	35 662	23 695	3 252	1 660	99	1 710	5 246
1982	37 464	25 189	3 069	1 615	110	1 917	5 565
1983	44 587	30 262	3 459	1 901	184	2 021	6 760
1984	52 778	36 683	3 896	2 078	312	1 968	7 841
1985	60 292	41 851	4 865	2 868	276	2 293	8 139
1986	64 794	44 461	5 206	3 155	461	2 116	9 395
1987	74 137	48 876	7 341	4 213	363	2 449	10 896
1988	79 763	51 025	8 812	5 291	481	3 152	11 002
1989	89 851	56 578	11 085	6 247	507	3 730	11 704
1990	98 402	60 049	13 527	7 098	917	3 996	12 815
1991	109 068	63 379	15 262	8 505	2 182	3 548	16 192
1992	111 691	64 502	12 271	9 071	2 521	3 957	19 370
1993	122 427	67 677	12 907	11 478	2 845	4 355	23 165
1994	146 315	77 987	15 038	15 620	3 485	6 635	27 551
1995	164 205	87 596	16 455	18 108	2 735	7 168	32 143
1996	181 357	95 006	17 809	19 264	2 676	8 319	38 285
1997	205 701	102 815	21 827	22 268	3 002	9 214	46 576
1998	239 754	126 005	22 716	23 594	3 150	9 759	54 529

Source: © *Statistics Canada*

(1) Other European Union countries (EU) include Belgium, Denmark, Germany, France, Greece, Ireland, Italy, Luxembourg, Netherlands, Portugal, Spain; from Jan. 1995, Austria, Finland and Sweden. (2) Other OECD countries include Australia, Iceland, New Zealand, Norway, Switzerland and Turkey; from July 1994, Mexico; from Dec. 1995, Czech Republic; from May 1996, Hungary; from Nov. 1996 Poland; and up to Dec. 1994, Austria, Finland and Sweden.

Canadian Trade Balance[1]

(millions of dollars)

	1993	1994	1995	1996	1997	1998
All Countries	-12 465	9 757	20 837	26 738	8 370	-955
Australia	357	-260	-131	-317	-232	-337
Belgium[3]	-521	738	1 131	680	618	393
Brazil	36	-8	243	202	235	-123
Chile	15	-8	90	54	53	-33
China	1 574	-1 728	-1 345	-2 060	-3 986	-5 178
Colombia	-50	150	-22	162	129	96
Cuba	32	-77	-62	-138	-30	85
Egypt	21	81	112	107	147	118
El Salvador	-3	-22	-21	-17	-24	1
France	1 024	-1 178	-1 210	-1 718	-3 529	-3 344
Germany	1 088	-2 178	-1 627	-1 657	-2 785	-3 577
Hong Kong	583	-282	76	46	397	-1
Hungary	8	-18	-4	-6	14	-1
India	79	-177	-107	-257	-261	-515
Iran	-45	330	307	323	217	109
Israel	15	-30	-23	-50	-88	-203
Italy	1 048	-1 403	-1 493	-1 396	-1 572	-1 942
Jamaica	96	-121	-103	-156	-174	-162
Japan	2 288	-1 719	-188	633	-1 512	-5 476
Kenya	5	0	-2	14	20	5
Malaysia	670	-942	-1 014	-4 817	-1 305	-1 544
Mexico	2 911	-3 470	-4 229	-4 817	-5 800	-6 283
Morocco	-25	24	119	112	134	101
Netherlands	-664	356	616	667	461	598
New Zealand	135	-182	-116	-101	-75	-177
Nigeria	631	-617	-559	-269	-417	-101
Peru	-19	-12	41	42	174	14
Philippines	193	-273	-172	-266	-308	-710
Poland	-18	-47	-5	17	-5	13
Romania	-3	47	-39	47	-5	-67
Russia	-6	-178	-308	-137	-260	-456
Saudi Arabia	-7	-256	-178	-42	46	-108
Singapore	476	-785	-827	-656	-659	-805
South Africa	-19	-21	-95	-214	-136	-205
South Korea	493	-288	-501	47	147	-1 528
Spain	134	-254	-93	-175	-198	-270
Sweden	680	-892	-977	-942	-941	-1 027
Switzerland	-266	128	-368	-28	-518	-223
Taiwan	1 622	-1 577	-1 085	-1 483	-1 899	-2 904
Turkey	-69	20	131	105	136	-38
United Kingdom	1 630	-1 858	-1 721	-2 070	-2 861	-2 077
United States[2]	-28 664	34 847	33 668	51 862	44 935	45 553
Venezuela	39	-205	-291	-265	-464	-408
Yugoslavia[3]	31	-48	1.7	3	7	3

Source: © *Statistics Canada*

(1) The trade balance is the value of merchandise exports minus the value of merchandise imports; it does not include services. (2) Total includes countries not shown. (3) Includes Luxembourg. (4) Includes Puerto Rico and the U.S. Virgin Islands. (5) Serbia and Montenegro.

BUSINESS

Mining in Canada

(millions of dollars)

	1950	1960	1970	1980	1990	1996	1997
Total Value.................	1 045.5	2 492.5	5 722.1	31 841.8	40 778.4	49 171.8	49 843.2
METALS:							
Cadmium...........................	1.9	3.3	15.3	7.6	11.6	5.9	2.1
Cobalt..............................	1.0	6.7	10.2	134.7	49.6	168.4	150.8
Copper.............................	123.2	264.8	779.2	1 859.6	2 428.9	2 037.2	2 065.5
Gold................................	168.9	157.2	88.1	1 165.4	2 407.6	2 803.0	2 510.4
Iron Ore...........................	23.4	175.1	588.6	1 700.9	1 258.8	1 310.5	1 431.2
Lead	47.9	43.9	123.1	273.7	279.3	261.6	148.4
Nickel..............................	112.1	295.6	830.2	1 497.4	2 027.9	1 958.2	1 777.1
Platinum metals................	10.3	28.9	43.6	159.1	189.4	146.2	152.3
Silver...............................	18.8	30.2	81.9	828.8	249.7	280.5	259.1
Uranium	n.a.	269.9	n.a.	702.0	887.9	645.8	559.2
Zinc	98.0	108.6	398.9	858.2	2 272.6	1 652.3	1 875.5
NON-METALS:							
Asbestos...........................	65.9	121.4	208.1	618.5	272.1	238.1	224.0
Gypsum............................	6.7	9.5	14.2	39.5	80.1	93.1	91.7
Potash	—	178.7	108.7	1 020.7	964.9	1 263.8	1 465.6
Salt..................................	7.1	19.4	36.1	122.8	240.9	316.2	380.7
Sulphur (elemental)..........	2.2	4.3	28.4	444.1	368.9	95.6	86.6
STRUCTURAL MATERIALS:							
Cement.............................	35.9	93.3	155.7	581.4	991.4	931.5	1 022.3
Sand and gravel................	36.4	111.2	133.6	508.4	817.3	778.3	800.5
Stone...............................	25.9	60.6	87.9	341.2	663.4	552.6	617.7

Source: © *Statistics Canada*

Mining by Province, 1997

(millions of dollars)

	Nfld	PEI	NS	NB	Que	Ont	Man	Sask	Alta	BC	Yuk	NWT
METALS												
Copper..................	1.0	—	—	42.1	402.6	752.4	165.4	—	—	702.0	—	—
Gold.....................	43.3	—	—	3.4	555.8	1 170.6	119.6	60.8		255.7	101.3	200.0
Iron Ore	883.4	—	—	—	...	...	—	—	—	2.3	—	—
Lead.....................	—	—	—	63.1	—	—	—	—	—	40.1	23.4	21.8
Nickel...................	—	—	—	—	—	1 334.7	442.4	—	—	—	—	—
Zinc......................	—	—	—	497.8	335.4	213.3	149.0	—	—	299.0	71.4	309.7
NON-METALS												
Asbestos...............	—	—	—	—	224.0	—	—	—	—	—	—	—
STRUCTURAL MATERIALS												
Cement	...	—	...	—	219.8	407.7	—	—	...	187.2	—	—
Sand & Gravel.......	10.5	1.4	16.1	...	72.0	329.3	...	...	134.5	151.5	3.0	6.2
Stone	22.1	—	35.5	17.9	182.0	288.3	17.4	—	6.8	46.7	—	.9

Source: © *Statistics Canada*   (···) Sample too small for release.

FOCUS ON...

The Canadian Wheat Board

The Canadian Wheat Board (CWB) was established in 1935 and works in partnership with the Canadian Grain Industry for Prairie farmers of wheat and barley. The CWB's purpose is to market these grains at the best possible price. The proceeds from sales, less marketing costs, are returned to the farmers.

Around 80 percent of Canada's agricultural land is in Manitoba, Saskatchewan, Alberta, and part of British Columbia. The Prairies produce approximately 25 million tonnes of wheat and about 11 million tonnes of barley annually. While Canada produces only about 5 percent of the world's wheat and 7 percent of the world's barley, it has a 21 percent share of the world wheat market, and a 22 percent share of the world barley market. The CWB exports wheat to more than 60 countries and barley to more than 14 countries.

To give wheat and barley growers a measure of power and security in the marketplace, the Canadian government granted the CWB monopoly status, meaning that the CWB is the only exporter of these western Canadian grains. Canada's 110000 farmers sell as one entity, keeping prices high, rather than competing against each other and driving prices lower.

All grain sales are pooled by type, meaning the grains are deposited into pool accounts. This price pooling system ensures that the farmers benefit equally, no matter when their crop is sold. Price pooling also helps to smooth out price movements through the year. Farmers who deliver the same grade of grain receive the same return at the end of the crop year. The crop year runs from August 1 to July 31.

Of course, the farmers don't wait until the end of the crop year to receive their total payment. An initial amount is paid on delivery and guaranteed by the Canadian government. If the total sales in the crop year exceed the total amount of these initial payments less expenses, the farmers get a final payment. If sales fall short, which has rarely happened, the federal government makes up the difference. The federal government also guarantees the CWB's borrowing, giving CWB a lower interest rate than comparable private sector companies. This arrangement results in savings to farmers.

The CWB is, legally, a Crown agency accountable to Parliament, but the CWB is also accountable to the farmers. The company is the farmers' marketing agency and the farmers pay the cost of running it. While it is a Crown agency, the CWB does not fall under the authority of the auditor general because of its independence from Parliament and its commercial nature. The amended Canadian Wheat Board Act provided for a one-time audit of the CWB's books by the auditor general.

Annual sales by the CWB top $6 billion, and operating costs are less than 1 percent at around $48 million. The company has about 500 employees, most of whom work at the head office in Winnipeg. The CWB also has offices in Vancouver, Tokyo and Beijing.

For more information, you can visit the Canadian Wheat Board on the Web www.cwb.ca or you can call 1-800-ASK-4-CWB (275-4292).

Agriculture in Canada

(millions of dollars)[1]

	1950	1960	1970	1980	1990[2]	1997[2]	1998[2]
Total value of							
agricultural products ...	**2 135.8**	**2 811.7**	**4 250.9**	**15 958.8**	**21 997.9**	**29 848.9**	**29 344.3**
Barley	45.8	69.4	144.7	553.6	545.2	733.0	534.0
Canola	n.a	14.8	96.7	673.6	789.6	2 042.4	2 793.9
Cattle	421.8	469.7	858.9	3 221.4	3 627.1	4 732.0	4 964.2
Corn	7.2	10.1	49.4	467.5	521.5	695.6	640.5
Dairy products	328.2	486.5	678.9	2 015.5	3 154.8	3 709.3	3 833.9
Eggs	86.9	137.8	172.8	407.0	482.3	486.3	476.0
Fruits	33.6	52.1	91.8	137.3	348.1	480.5	466.5
Ginseng	n.a.	n.a.	n.a.	n.a.	30.5	63.5	59.2
Honey	n.a	n.a.	n.a.	44.8	45.0	77.6	77.6
Maple products	8.9	9.5	8.1	34.1	88.1	131.1	145.4
Nurseries	n.a.	n.a.	n.a.	276.2	913.6	1 088.7	1 198.4
Oats	42.6	23.9	20.9	53.5	81.0	273.3	214.6
Pigs	286.9	266.8	484.5	1 404.2	2 021.2	2 989.1	2 216.7
Potatoes	29.9	67.4	90.1	211.9	399.0	512.6	616.9
Poultry	80.1	135.5	262.7	670.2	4 356.3	1 587.2	1 627.6
Sheep	1.3	0.4	0.3	2.9	2.3	3.5	3.9
Soybeans	n.a.	10.0	20.7	183.3	256.6	813.1	796.6
Sugar Beets	13.5	12.8	15.1	73.5	42.9	34.5	39.8
Tobacco	56.7	96.4	154.8	212.5	281.1	359.3	357.5
Vegetables	43.8	68.1	125.1	360.1	706.5	1032.7	1 028.5
Wheat	377.5	442.7	570.1	2 774.5	2 351.5	2 932.9	1 745.3

Source: © *Statistics Canada*   (1) Not adjusted for inflation. (2) Based on intercensal counts (1991–96).

Canadian Agriculture by Province, 1998

(thousands of dollars)

	Nfld	PEI	NS	NB	Que	Ont	Man	Sask	Alta	BC
Barley	...	2 537	301	656	17 952	10 148	48 714	255 963	194 901	2 824
Canola	...	...	...	...	4 172	17 870	649 750	1 240 973	859 527	21 618
Cattle	1 596	28 315	27 224	21 032	206 116	784 356	315 109	320 034	2 745 912	214 482
Dairy Products	23 928	48 316	90 716	64 980	1 436 505	1 267 756	145 626	105 301	314 527	336 212
Eggs	9 659	2 925	19 690	12 037	78 602	184 158	47 457	20 577	36 464	64 412
Fruit	1 102	2 373	33798	11 936	64 038	186 930	2 218	763	3 228	159 963
Nurseries	6 153	1 536	30 518	18 996	155 874	577 397	27 319	15 119	64 608	300 841
Pigs	674	20584	26 227	21 857	679 828	589 665	394 867	131 506	313 876	37 618
Poultry	21725	5 102	54 923	44 585	444 215	559 579	75 997	12 729	136 983	240 194
Vegetables	3 970	7 552	21 020	7 578	238 107	481 848	22 603	2 866	56 831	186 141
Wheat		2 133	828	241	9 186	99 692	321 438	805 421	500 509	5812

Source: © *Statistics Canada*

Energy Consumption by OECD Countries

	Coal (million short tons)		Natural Gas (billion cubic feet)		Petroleum (thousand barrels per day)		Hydroelectric Power (billion kilowatt hours)	
	198	1997	1988	1997	1988	1997	1988	1997
Australia	95.83	135.39	555	704	652	819	13.4	16.5
Austria	7.56	5.94	183	273	212	243	35.2	35.9
Belgium	13.96	13.21	337	468	469	591	0.4	0.3
Canada	60.19	61.75	2 331	2 959	1 693	1 857	303.5	348.4
Czech Republic	0.00	67.19	0	330	0	177	0.0	1.4
Denmark	12.43	17.29	56	154	205	235	n.a.	n.a.
Finland	7.28	8.77	58	127	228	221	13.2	11.7
France	24.95	22.71	961	1 287	1 797	1 955	74.0	61.3
Germany	0.00	277.33	0	3 388	0	1 955	0.0	19.6
Greece	56.22	68.98	4	6	285	347	2.4	3.8
Hungary	26.98	19.08	407	431	193	155	0.2	0.2
Iceland	0.10	0.09	n.a.	n.a.	n.a.	n.a.	4.2	5.1
Ireland	3.63	3.10	71	118	78	133	0.9	0.7
Italy	23.37	16.88	1 460	2 044	1 836	2 045	40.2	41.7
Japan	122.58	122.69	1 618	2 340	4 752	5 711	89.9	85.9
Korea	120.14	134.63	94	525	769	2295	34.7	27.7
Luxembourg	1.76	0.49	15	25	28	40	0.1	0.1
Mexico	8.09	12.00	926	1 198	1 550	1 860	21.0	26.2
Netherlands	12.77	20.15	1 513	1 763	716	808	n.a	n.a
New Zealand	2.42	2.65	166	199	95	128	23.1	22.6
Norway	1.61	1.61	71	108	187	227	107.9	108.7
Poland	253.41	194.88	447	438	350	380	4.2	3.6
Portugal	3.71	5.59	0	3	206	299	12.0	13.0
Spain	52.25	38.62	129	428	980	1295	34.8	24.2
Sweden	4.94	4.34	13	33	359	328	69.0	67.9
Switzerland	0.55	0.80	63	93	261	284	35.4	33.3
Turkey	50.82	69.80	43	346	447	634	28.4	39.4
United Kingdom	122.84	77.83	1 972	3 216	1 697	1 799	4.9	4.1
United States	885.24	890.92	18 030	21 972	17 283	18 620	257.8	377.3

	Nuclear Power (billion kilowatt hours)		Total Net Electricity (billion kilowatt hours)		Other[1] (billion kilowatt hours)	
	1988	1997	1988	1997	1988	1997
Australia	n.a.	n.a.	121.4	161.3	0.0	0.0
Austria	n.a.	n.a.	40.8	49.7	n.a.	n.a.
Belgium	40.9	45.0	54.7	71.8	n.a.	n.a.
Canada	78.2	77.9	242.8	475.1	0.0	0.1
Czech Republic	0.0	12.5	0.0	55.3	n.a.	n.a.
Denmark	n.a.	n.a.	28.2	29.2	0.3	1.8
Finland	18.4	19.0	48.3	66.0	n.a.	n.a.
France	260.3	374.3	307.9	375.5	0.6	0.5
Germany	0.0	161.9	0.0	477.3	0.0	2.9
Greece	n.a.	n.a.	28.0	40.2	0.0	0.0
Hungary	12.7	13.3	36.9	33.2	n.a.	n.a.
Iceland	n.a.	n.a.	4.1	5.1	0.2	0.4
Ireland	n.a.	n.a.	11.1	17.4	0.0	0.0
Italy	n.a.	n.a.	193.0	257.0	2.9	4.5
Japan	173.9	306.1	664.2	904.6	1.3	3.7
Korea	37.8	73.2	122.8	228.50	n.a.	n.a.
Luxembourg	n.a.	n.a.	4.3	5.6	n.a.	n.a.
Mexico	0.0	9.9	100.3	154.3	4.7	5.2
Netherlands	3.5	2.3	66.7	88.1	0.0	0.6
New Zealand	n.a.	n.a.	27.2	32.4	1.2	1.8
Norway	n.a.	n.a.	95.2	105.5	0.0	0.0
Poland	n.a.	n.a.	130.9	122.9	0.0	0.0
Portugal	n.a.	n.a.	21.3	33.3	0.0	0.1
Spain	48.3	52.5	119.3	149.4	0.0	0.4
Sweden	65.6	66.7	128.2	131.3	0.0	0.2
Switzerland	21.5	24.0	43.7	48.3	n.a.	n.a.
Turkey	n.a.	n.a.	43.4	94.3	0.1	0.1
United Kingdom	55.6	89.3	280.5	309.6	0.0	0.5
United States	527.0	529.4	2 578.1	3 278.5	12.0	86.8

Source: National Energy Information Center, Energy Information Administration, *International Energy Annual*

(n.a.) Not available. (1) Includes geothermal, solar and wind electric power.

Fuel Production in Canada

(millions of dollars)

	1950	1960	1970	1980	1990	1996	1997
Total Fuels	**201.2**	**565.9**	**1 717.7**	**17 943.9**	**22 989.9**	**32 127.1**	**32 721.1**
Coal....................	110.1	74.7	86.1	932.0	1 823.7	1 943.1	1 929.5
Natural gas.............	6.4	52.2	315.1	6 148.8	5 692.0	8 718.9	10 109.5
Natural gas by-products[1] .	n.a.	16.1	160.1	1 825.1	2 370.8	2 456.5	2 552.0
Petroleum, crude	84.6	422.9	1 156.5	9 037.9	13 103.4	19 008.5`	18 130.2

Source: © *Statistics Canada*

(1) Incl. butane, propane and pentane plus.

Primary Energy Supply

(annual petajoules[1])

	Natural[2] Gas	Coal	Hydro-electricity	Nuclear[3] Energy	Petroleum	Steam and Biomass	Total
1971	2 185	405	580	14	3 461	404	7 049
1972	2 491	461	648	24	4 006	329	7 959
1973	2 577	495	694	51	4 596	345	8 758
1974	2 552	526	760	50	4 361	345	8 594
1975	2 580	635	729	43	3 775	257	8 019
1976	2 593	620	766	59	3 478	263	7 779
1977	2 733	686	791	89	3 486	264	8 049
1978	2 530	744	842	106	3 438	305	7 965
1979	2 800	811	875	120	3 911	324	8 842
1980	2 560	891	902	130	3 760	348	8 590
1981	2 526	970	948	130	3 410	336	8 326
1982	2 580	1 028	919	130	3 360	351	8 368
1983	2 476	1 066	948	165	3 537	381	8 574
1984	2 695	1 396	1 022	177	3 757	378	9 426
1985	2 927	1 487	1 085	205	3 834	391	9 928
1986	2 716	1 382	1 111	242	3 837	413	9 702
1987	2 932	1 394	1 131	262	4 038	430	10 188
1988	3 445	1 614	1 097	281	4 249	416	11 101
1989	3 631	1 718	1 039	271	4 147	413	11 220
1990	3 732	1 669	1 058	248	4 140	388	11 234
1991	3 980	1 748	1 100	288	4 146	404	11 666
1992	4 419	1 546	1 128	274	4 320	502	12 188
1993	4 901	1 651	1 154	319	4 556	500	13 081
1994	5 353	1 735	1 176	366	4 829	541	14 000
1995	5 648	1 799	1 196	332	4 451	589	14 598
1996	5 846	1 833	1 269	315	4 592	548	15 016
1997	5 950	1 898	1 252	280	4 820	588	15 384

Source: © *Statistics Canada*

(1) A petajoule is one quadrillion joules (10^{15}) (2) Incl. butane, propane and pentane plus. (3) 3.6 MJ/kwh.

Television Operating Revenues and Expenses[1], 1994-97

	1994		1995		1996		1997	
	Private Broadcasters[2]	Cable[3]	Private Broadcasters[2]	Cable[3]	Private Broadcasters[2]	Cable[3]	Private Broadcasters[2]	Public[3]
REVENUES.....................	1 490 061	1 759 126	1 530 515	1 846 052	1 581 024	1 903 556	1 703 298	1 967 920
EXPENSES								
- program	820 885	80 197	825 206	85 384	861 944	85 541	1 524 015	2 041 315
- technical services...........................	71 520	415 714	75 486	605 668	75 946	643 080	917 540	85 236
- sales and promotion...	154 202	49 650	168 201	59 512	172 057	69 815	73 837	641 833
- administration and general...............	220 629	355 609	210 069	409 864	199 434	409 864	187 962	61 869
- depreciation	56 066	275 369	55 674	297 280	58 835	324 139	200 014	394 190
- interest exp...................	89 930	207 859	103 893	337 638	102 126	409 366	59 716	368 866
NET PROFIT AFTER INCOME TAX.....	38 399	184 349	44 272	226 221	30 168	132 396	85 340	151 682
TOTAL SUBSCRIBERS.............		7 833		7 791		7 867		7 957

Source: © *Statistics Canada*

(1) Figures in thousands. (2) Excludes cable TV, pay TV and non-commercial broadcasting stations operated by religious groups, educational institutions and provincial governments. (3) Includes all cable TV systems licensed to operate in Canada by the CRTC. Master antenna TV and pay TV (such as First Choice or Superchannel) are not included.

Communications—Telephones

	Revenue (millions of dollars)			Lines in service (thousands)		
	Total	Local	Long Distance	Total	Residential	Business
1975	2 788	1 307	1 407	12 328	8 620	3 709
1976	3 296	1 537	1 664	12 975	9 067	3 908
1977	3 766	1 756	1 892	13 695	9 599	4 095
1978	4 391	2 010	2 239	14 337	10 053	4 284
1979	5 080	2 246	2 636	15 071	10 534	4 538
1980	5 775	2 512	3 053	15 844	11 054	4 790
1981	6 828	2 948	3 625	16 375	11 366	5 008
1982	7 708	3 360	4 058	16 503	11 499	5 004
1983	8 363	3 524	4 404	16 296	11 467	4 829
1984	9 099	3 666	4 842	16 174	11 480	4 693
1985	9 814	3 798	5 333	15 555	11 126	4 429
1986	10 455	3 896	5 817	15 524	11 086	4 438
1987	10 954	4 044	6 055	15 383	10 991	4 392
1988	11 704	4 237	6 319	15 392	10 915	4 476
1989	12 659	4 593	6 791	15 497	10 949	4 548
1990	13 251	4 906	7 143	15 472	10 888	4 585
1991	13 267	5 137	7 006	15 187	10 671	4 515
1992	13 536	5 430	6 915	14 690	10 314	4 376
1993	13 838	5 827	6 795	14 182	9 985	4 196
1994	13 988	6 216	6 475	13 696	9 624	4 072
1995	14 106	6 647	5 983	n.a.	n.a.	n.a.
1996	15 889	6 391	5 483	17 781	11 910	5 871
1997	16 845	7 080	5 391	18 101	12 084	6 017
1998	17 367	8 118	4 793	18 688	12 295	6 392

Source: © *Statistics Canada*

Transportation and Storage Industries

(Gross Domestic Product, $millions)

	1994	1995	1996	1997	1998
Transportation and Storage Industries Total	30 815	31 282	31 246	32 648	32 382
Transportation	25 322	25 665	25 883	27 358	27 796
Air	3 335	3 442	3 687	4 096	4 239
Railway	4 288	3 904	3 826	4 148	4 039
Water	2 089	1 924	1 910	1 954	1 981
Truck	8 617	9 345	9 854	10 564	10 975
Public passenger transit systems	3 245	3 286	3 123	3 236	3 254
Other transport and services . . .	3 748	3 764	3 483	3 360	3 308
Pipeline transport	4 721	4 810	4 519	4 395	4 340
Storage and warehousing industries	772	807	844	895	898

Source: © *Statistics Canada*

Transportation—Railways

	Total Railway Operating Revenue ($millions)	Freight Revenues ($millions)	Passenger Revenues ($millions)	Passenger (thousands)	Passenger Kilometres (thousands)
1991.	$7 156 652	$6 184 085	$154 985	4 256	1 425 619
1992.	6 909 544	5 930 457	158 639	4 241	1 439 122
1993.	6 992 827	5 959 792	168 592	4 112	1 412 752
1994.	7 510 192	6 584 631	180 033	4 184	1 439 932
1995.	7 206 586	6 370 251	179 470	4 082	1 472 620
1996.	7 180 061	6 386 604	185 738	4 060	1 518 969
1997.	7 887 807	7 067 550	820 257	4 104	1 514 593

Source: © *Statistics Canada*

Major Canadian Airlines

	Total Operating Revenues ($thousands)	Total Operating Expenses ($thousands)	Total Passengers (thousands)	Total Passenger Kilometres (thousands)	Total Goods Transported (thousands of kilograms)	Total Goods Tonne-kilometres (thousands)
1984	4 169 498	4 089 755	22 628	44 665 698	396 632	1 120 391
1985	4 653 924	4 564 665	23 281	47 169 986	403 403	1 169 013
1986	4 889 763	4 599 049	23 188	49 124 261	379 238	1 155 488
1987	4 980 699	4 796 049	23 799	48 628 014	380 907	1 210 285
1988	5 453 507	5 262 624	24 097	54 279 293	403 806	1 323 315
1989	5 608 588	5 535 479	22 482	53 178 429	442 675	1 445 191
1990	5 660 477	5 765 017	21 236	50 091 785	435 224	1 487 833
1991	5 514 264	5 845 917	21 000	43 626 433	390 819	1 315 448
1992	5 498 189	5 820 218	21 261	45 414 285	392 514	1 331 586
1993	5 601 108	5 739 512	21 947	44 806 137	419 838	1 463 995
1994	5 529 198	5 356 713	19 126	45 281 336	395 674	1 537 977
1995	6 114 883	5 932 592	21 428	51 798 045	386 560	1 728 762
1996	6 322 113	6 369 399	23 164	57 016 000	405 975	1 882 803
1997	7 128 654	6 694 766	24 363	62 479 000	449 828	2 058 953
1997	7 463 998	7 382 909	24 571	64 426 065	431 150	2 340 594

Source: © *Statistics Canada*

Manufacturing in Canada

(millions of dollars)[1]

	1985		1990	
	Value of Shipments of Goods Manufactured	**Value Added**	**Value of Shipments of Goods Manufactured**	**Value Added**
All Industries	**248 492.6**	**95 875.3**	**298 918.5**	**122 972.5**
Food	32 792.9	9 737.6	38 582.5	13 126.3
Beverage	4 863.7	2 735.9	5 620.6	3 331.0
Tobacco products	1 640.9	808.6	1 883.3	1 123.6
Rubber products	2 554.2	1 268.4	2 557.9	1 310.6
Plastic products	3 860.9	1 749.0	5 996.8	2 760.3
Leather and allied products	1 308.2	634.0	1 162.3	548.5
Primary textile	2 669.7	1 156.7	2 779.6	1 259.8
Textile products	2 650.1	1 145.8	3 363.6	1 418.6
Clothing	5 543.2	2 807.9	6 831.3	3 438.4
Wood	11 121.6	4 623.8	14 805.9	5 648.3
Furniture and fixtures	3 398.6	1 797.1	4 661.9	2 430.4
Paper and allied products	18 074.6	7 555.2	24 026.3	10 474.6
Printing, publishing and allied products	9 534.8	5 982.6	13 703.9	8 729.4
Primary metal	16 971.0	7 006.3	19 243.8	7 461.6
Fabricated metal products	13 971.0	6 638.1	17 876.9	8 678.1
Machinery	7 450.8	3 634.9	10 396.1	5 049.1
Transportation equipment	43 182.3	14 089.5	51 654.9	15 906.2
Electrical and electronic products	13 270.3	6 677.0	18 474.8	9 119.6
Non-metallic mineral products	5 879.1	3 047.1	7 391.6	3 836.1
Refined petroleum and coal products	24 420.8	2 614.2	18 569.5	2 703.9
Chemical and chemical products	18 268.6	7 625.3	23 117.9	11 330.3
Other manufacturing	5 065.4	2 540.6	6 217.2	3 287.8

	1995		1996	
	Value of Shipments of Goods Manufactured	**Value Added**	**Value of Shipments of Goods Manufactured**	**Value Added**
All Industries	**396 384.3**	**161 793.0**	**406 486.9**	**164 940.1**
Food	44 956.6	14 721.4	47 987.1	15 774.8
Beverage	6 808.5	3 893.1	6 856.2	4 061.6
Tobacco products	2 505.0	1 651.2	2 561.4	1 727.7
Rubber products	3 887.7	1 703.5	4 093	1 895.6
Plastic products	8 243.1	3 742.5	9 120.5	4 459.9
Leather and allied products	958.9	445.8	922.1	425.3
Primary textile	3 401.0	1 525.1	3 480.0	1 657.3
Textile products	3 286.7	1 480.0	3 258.4	1 489.9
Clothing	6 497.9	3 298.2	6 608.2	3 338.0
Wood	23 257.1	8 865.1	24 766.1	10 025.6
Furniture and fixtures	5 000.1	2 651.7	5 583.6	2 994.7
Paper and allied products	36 393.1	18 032.8	31 155.9	13 593.4
Printing, publishing and allied products	14 637.4	9 109.5	15 339.8	9 709.3
Primary metal	25 861.8	10 926.0	25 949.7	10 146.2
Fabricated metal products	20 226.6	10 319.4	22 045.9	11 536.3
Machinery	14 989.0	7 545.7	15 933.4	8 101.2
Transportation equipment	85 546.3	25 423.6	87 180.8	27 995.4
Electrical and electronic products	28 827.0	11 080.8	28 066.4	10 925.2
Non-metallic mineral products	7 137.2	3 842.6	7 764.1	4 287.9
Refined petroleum and coal products	18 066.7	2 848.2	20 976.9	2 040.0
Chemical and chemical products	28 553.8	14 490.9	28 689.1	14 052.4
Other manufacturing	7 342.7	4 196.0	8 148.0	4 702.2

Source: © *Statistics Canada*   (1) Not adjusted for inflation.

Value of Manufacturing[1] by Province, 1996

(millions of dollars)

	Newfoundland	Prince Edward Island	Nova Scotia	New Brunswick	Quebec
All Industries	**1 615.5**	**690.0**	**6 308.1**	**8 366.4**	**97 383.1**
Food	595.5	444.1	1 593.6	1 509.9	10 994.4
Beverage	101.3	n.a.	n.a.	221.3	1 884.9
Rubber products	n.a.	n.a.	n.a.	1.4	1 177.9
Plastic products	n.a.	n.a.	n.a.	n.a.	2 293.6
Leather and allied products	n.a.	n.a.	n.a.	4.5	
Primary textile	n.a.	n.a.	n.a.	n.a.	1 804.6
Textile products	0.6	n.a.	n.a.	n.a.	1 635.5
Clothing	n.a.	n.a.	n.a.	n.a.	4 105.5
Wood	39.6	17.0	222.4	897.3	5 916.8
Furniture and fixtures	n.a.	n.a.	n.a.	n.a.	1 527.7
Paper and allied products	n.a.	6.7	n.a.	1 924.1	10 108.9
Printing, publishing and allied products	53.9	22.2	175.3	122.7	4 169.9
Primary metal	n.a.	n.a.	n.a.	n.a.	8 694.9
Fabricated metal products	n.a.	n.a.	157.6	214.7	4 762.8
Machinery	3.6	n.a.	n.a.	n.a.	2 913.2
Transportation equipment	29.8	67.1	922.0	313.8	10 370.5
Electrical and electronic products	n.a.	n.a.	n.a.	n.a.	3 511.1
Non-metallic mineral products	38.4	27.9	116.3	161.4	1 702.6
Refined petroleum and coal products	n.a.	n.a.	n.a.	n.a.	4 090.9
Chemical and chemical products	n.a.	41.1	97.0	n.a.	6 731.5
Other manufacturing	n.a.	n.a.	n.a.	n.a.	2 436.7

	Ontario	Manitoba	Saskatchewan	Alberta	British Columbia
All Industries	**212 685.2**	**8 951.5**	**5 282.5**	**31 062.4**	**34 083.7**
Food	19 759.3	1 899.0	1 255.9	6 269.8	3 665.6
Beverage	3 079.4	159.6	80.1	550.3	665.6
Rubber products	2 113.7				
Plastic products	5 132.7	282.0	51.5	524.7	595.7
Leather and allied products	n.a.	58.1	4.7	31.2	12.5
Primary textile	1 399.8	n.a.	n.a.	n.a.	8.5
Textile products	1 272.7	n.a.	n.a.	n.a.	n.a.
Clothing	1 644.2	325.3	35.0	171.2	245.9
Wood	3 835.6	365.9	258.1	1 935.4	11 278
Furniture and fixtures	3 049.5	295.6	12.2	388.4	237.6
Paper and allied products	9 465.8	396.4	345.2	1 637.4	5 913.4
Printing, publishing and allied products	7 740.4	568.3	242.3	949.0	1 295.7
Primary metal	13 733.9			1 000.9	
Fabricated metal products	12 651.7	506.1	278.7	1 694.4	1 727.5
Machinery	8 588.3	1 170.3	464.9	1 612.6	1 026.1
Transportation equipment	72 353.5	1 212.7	160.8	501.9	1 248.7
Electrical and electronic products	15 824.0	361.1	323.9	1 886.8	1 031.2
Non-metallic mineral products	3 653.0	162.9	73.7	913.6	914.3
Refined petroleum and coal products	6 661.7	n.a.	n.a.	n.a.	n.a.
Chemical and chemical products	14 430.6	406.6	482.9	5 424.3	n.a.
Other manufacturing	4 546.8	117.7	43.5	353.3	n.a.

Source: © *Statistics Canada*

(n.a.) Not reported. (1) Value of shipments of goods of own manufacture only (i.e.) does not include value added.

Employment in Manufacturing, by Sector

1989	Number of Manufacturing Establishments	Number of Production and Related Workers	Person Hours Paid
All Industries	**39 150**	**1 495 937**	**3 124 874**
Food	3 385	145 804	296 875
Beverage	274	15 828	33 136
Tobacco products	19	2 874	5 050
Rubber products	193	18 793	39 463
Plastic products	1 257	43 556	90 919
Leather and allied products	353	16 353	33 368
Primary textile	221	18 428	40 097
Textile products	915	30 170	64 574
Clothing	2 686	97 276	194 245
Wood	3 380	106 682	223 850
Furniture and fixtures	1 845	55 784	116 937
Paper and allied products	746	90 781	195 159
Printing, publishing and allied products	5 207	87 002	173 098
Primary metal	523	82 110	173 558
Fabricated metal products	5 926	153 392	319 939
Machinery	2 173	72 519	153 113
Transportation equipment	1 699	188 887	411 579
Electrical and electronic products	1 627	104 259	215 776
Non-metallic mineral products	1 688	46 019	98 861
Refined petroleum and coal products	163	6 973	14 482
Chemical and chemical products	1 443	51 955	110 458
Other manufacturing	3 427	60 492	120 336

1996	Number of Manufacturing Establishments	Number of Production and Related Workers	Person Hours Paid
All Industries	**36 239**	**1 279 030**	**2 693 882**
Food	3 317	142 229	289 508
Beverage	220	12 189	25 142
Tobacco products	15	2 340	4 699
Rubber products	213	18 047	38 587
Plastic products	1 322	46 708	98 538
Leather and allied products	221	6 169	18 195
Primary textile	176	15 462	33 501
Textile products	787	21 445	45 148
Clothing	1 756	68 241	141 491
Wood	3 162	100 456	210 975
Furniture and fixtures	1 406	41 179	86 911
Paper and allied products	706	78 238	168 346
Printing, publishing and allied products	5 037	68 241	141 067
Primary metal	452	68 962	149 936
Fabricated metal products	6 009	121 479	257 712
Machinery	2 118	65 133	136 714
Transportation equipment	1 526	184 526	393 580
Electrical and electronic products	1 565	77 308	164 158
Non-metallic mineral products	1 661	33 604	71 086
Refined petroleum and coal products	178	6 263	13 338
Chemical and chemical products	1 385	47 259	102 099
Other manufacturing	3 187	50 552	103 148

Source: © *Statistics Canada*

Retail Merchandising in Canada

(millions of dollars[1])

	1993	1994	1995	1996	1997	1998
TOTAL	194 325	207 841	213 774	220 870	237 597	246 161
Total excl. motor vehicles	152 112	159 096	161 714	165 367	174 829	181 703
Supermarkets and grocery stores	47 182	48 793	49 162	48 918	51 655	53 346
All other food stores	3 445	3 831	4 332	4 417	4 294	4 318
General merchandise stores	20 582	21 679	22 805	24 009	26 183	27 956
Other semi-durable goods stores	6 711	7 266	7 222	7 519	8 188	8 218
Other durable goods stores	5 198	5 596	5 475	5 551	6 008	6 750
Rec. & motor vehicles	42 213	48 745	52 060	55 503	62 768	54 458
Gasoline service stations	14 280	14 256	14 766	16 774	16 668	15 707
Automotive parts	10 860	11 840	11 321	12 133	13 628	14 336
Clothing stores - men's	1 730	1 687	1 623	1 516	1 570	1 582
Clothing stores - women's	3 872	4 127	4 229	4 203	4 335	4 406
Other clothing stores	4 303	4 812	5 377	5 522	5 830	6 259
Shoe stores	1 605	1 751	1 682	1 683	1 650	1 671
Furniture and appliance stores	8 429	8 749	8 657	8 469	9 305	10 107
Other household furnishings stores	2 153	2 126	2 067	2 079	2 300	2 429
Drug stores	11 796	11 870	11 705	12 107	12 298	12 944
All other retail stores	9 966	10 714	11 293	10 469	10 897	11 675

Source: © *Statistics Canada*

(1) Current dollars. (2) Data does not include the Goods and Services Tax (GST).

Retail Merchandising by Province, 1998

(millions of dollars)

	Nfld	PEI	NS	NB	Que	Ont
Supermarkets, grocery and other food stores[1]	1 083.3	255.3	1 916.9	1 515.7	13 664.2	17 175.0
Drugs and patent medicine stores	236.4	72.9	527.6	333.6	2 907.8	5 264.1
Clothing stores	140.8	37.0[1]	294.6	231.6	3 182.3	4 779.7
Shoe stores	14.5	n.a.	26.7	22.8	565.2	634.9
Household goods	126.4	41.8	249.0	219.3	3 147.3	4 625.3
Motor vehicle, recreational vehicle, gas stations and automotive parts stores	1 325.4	388.2	2 853.5	2 041.0	21 859.2	36 598.2
General merchandise and all other stores	854.3	270.8	1 640.3	1 211.8	10 401.6	22 424.4

	Man	Sask	Alta	BC	Yuk/NWT
Supermarkets, grocery and other food stores[1]	2 095.5	1 8616	6 076.7	7 751.9	198.3
Drugs and patent medicine stores	285.4	396.7	1 243.2	1708.7	n.a
Clothing stores	351.5	303.5	1 420.6	1 514.3	204.3[1]
Shoe stores	49.7	25.0	136.8	191.2	n.a.
Household goods	375.1	328.7	1 598.8	1 864.2	20.7
Motor vehicle, recreational vehicle, gas stations and automotive parts stores	3 678.5	3 000.2	11 130.3	11 880.9	133.70[1]
General merchandise and all other stores	1 886.6	1 649.4	6 393.2	7 774.2	315.7

Source: © *Statistics Canada*

(n.a.) Indicates data could not be made available without breaching confidentiality (1) Data incomplete due to n.a. in this category.

Canada's Largest Corporations, 1998[1]

(ranked by revenue)

Company (Head office)	Revenues ($millions)	Assets ($millions)	Profit or Loss (−) ($millions)	Employees	% Foreign Owned
General Motors of Canada Ltd. (Oshawa, ON)	31 764.6	n.a.		26.000	100
BCE Inc. (Montreal)	27 454.0	32 072.0	4 598.0	58 000	11
Ford Motor Co. of Canada, Ltd. (Oakville, ON)......	26 469.2	8 651.9	n.a.	21700	100
Nortel Networks Corp. (Brampton, ON)......	26 072.5	30 255.1	(796.6)	75052	41
Chrysler Canada Ltd. (Windsor, ON)...........	20 712.0	n.a.	n.a.	16000	100
TransCanada PipeLines Ltd. (Calgary)........	17 288.0	25 561.0	432.0	4700	−
Power Corp of Canada (Montreal)..............	15 055.0	58 925.0	420.0	23000	−
George Weston Ltd. (Toronto)	14 726.0	9 036.0	773.0	107000	−
The Seagram Co. Ltd. (Montreal)	13 431.3	32 554.3	1 341.0	25000	n.a.
Alcan Aluminium Ltd. (Montreal)	11 555.0	15 181.2	591.9	40000	40
Bombardier Inc. (Montreal).........................	11 500.1	14 272.2	554.0	53000	n.a.
Canadian Pacific Ltd. (Calgary).................	10 151.0	19 669.4	801.3	30000	50
The Thomson Corp. (Toronto).....................	9 300.1	19 085.0	2 738.5	39000	−
Magna International Inc. (Markham, ON) ...	9 190.8	8 620.7	506.2	49000	−
Onex Corp. (Toronto)	8 812.7	6 820.2	176.7	53000	−
IBM Canada Ltd. (Markham, ON)	8 700.0	n.a.	n.a.	17122	100
Imasco Ltd. (Montreal)................................	8 584.0	51 522.0	759.0	20500	48
Quebecor Inc. (Montreal)	8 425.2	9 841.4	172.7	43000	−
Imperial Oil Ltd. (Toronto).........................	7 812.0	9 429.0	554.0	6689	82
Westcoast Energy Inc. (Vancouver)	7 376.0	10 820.0	198.0	6300	24
Hudson's Bay Co. (Toronto).......................	7 075.0	4 604.6	39.7	64000	n.a.
Noranda Inc. (Toronto)...............................	6 013.0	11 175.0	658.0	18394	−
Air Canada (St. Laurent, QC)	5 932.0	6 422.0	(16.0)	22836	12
BCT.TELUS Communications Inc. (Edmonton and Burnaby, BC).................	5 772.0	7 923.2	603.0	25000	33
EdperBrascan Corp. Toronto	5 766.0	10 942.0	415.0	55000	−

Source: © *The Financial Post 500 Magazine, 1999*   (1) Figures represent fiscal year ending Dec. 1998 unless otherwise stated.

Largest Foreign-Owned Companies in Canada, 1998

(ranked by revenues)

Company	Revenues ($thousands)	% Foreign Ownership	Parent
General Motors of Canada Ltd......................	31 784.6	100	General Motors (US)
Ford Motor Co. Of Canada., Ltd....................	26 469.2	100	Ford Motor (US)
Chrysler Canada Ltd.	20 172.0	100	DaimlerChrysler (US)
IBM Canada Ltd.	8 700.0	100	IBM (US)
Imperial Oil Ltd.	7 812.0	82	Exxon 70% (US)
Sears Canada Inc.	4 966.6	55	Sears Roebuck (US)
Honda Canada...	4 813.8	100	Honda (Japan)
Canada Safeway Ltd.	4808.4	100	Safeway (US)
Shell Canada Ltd.	4 506.0	80	Shell 78% (Netherlands)
Cargill Ltd...	3 818.1	100	Cargill (US)

Source: © *The Financial Post 500 Magazine, 1999*

Operating Profits by Major Industry, 1998

(millions of dollars)[1]

Some industries have fared better than others when it comes to making profits in the last fifteen years—or perhaps just not quite as badly. While businesses in industries such as food, computers and electronics, and communications have experienced a measure of stability when it comes to making profits, others—such as wood and paper, construction, metals, motor vehicles and transportation—have come through much more volatile times.

Nineteen ninety-eight saw some growth in profits for most industries, but there were some glaring exceptions. Oil and gas and metals both saw sharp declines in profits of 39 percent and 44 percent respectively, while machinery, real estate, construction, insurance, communications and transportation experienced some decline in profits. Bank profits rose only 6 percent from 1997.

Year	Food	Wood and Paper	Oil and Gas	Metals	Machinery	Motor Vehicles	Banks	Consumer Services
1980	2 255	3 080	10 064	3 357	1 769	1 755	1 917	4 005
1981	2 385	2 434	9 691	1 986	1 582	2 058	2 650	4 014
1982	2 449	880	10 986	184	888	1 473	1 394	3 578
1983	2 660	1 413	12 136	625	616	3 744	2 395	3 849
1984	2 852	2 152	14 250	1 584	1 217	5 568	2 243	4 218
1985	2 899	2 549	14 487	1 144	1 419	5 236	2 403	4 715
1986	3 329	3 829	7 533	1 200	1 213	4 180	2 953	4 993
1987	3 641	5 963	8 854	2 302	1 529	2 872	2 674	5 434
1988	3 608	6 097	6 803	4 225	1 947	3 881	4 416	6 037
1989	3 438	4 911	6 649	3 877	2 058	3 306	3 991	6 693
1990	3 835	1 825	7 656	1 748	1 464	2 308	4 670	5 547
1991	3 735	-1 033	4 609	14	1 060	2 014	5 704	4 263
1992	3 244	-124	5 467	526	1 058	1 350	1 505	3 386
1993	3 508	1 849	7 788	-253	1 173	2 870	3 869	3 997
1994	4 318	5 790	9 525	1 702	1 963	5 088	5 798	5 682
1995	4 765	10 611	10 413	2 923	2 533	6 027	9 000	5 627
1996	4 565	4 296	13 468	2 147	2 170	6 145	11 799	4 892
1997	4 642	3 420	14 075	2 529	2 709	8 852	15 568	6 875
1998[2]	5 035	4 625	8 573	1 417	2 591	9 270	16 517	7 295

Year	Real Estate	Business Services	Computers and Electronics	Construction	Insurance	Communications	Transportation
1980	4 593	1 223	575	1 926	620	1 276	1 497
1981	5 275	1 319	688	2 211	614	1 514	1 397
1982	4 216	1 331	561	1 768	580	1 626	1 199
1983	4 377	1 362	579	1 834	860	1 889	1 433
1984	5 091	1 686	683	2 134	722	2 075	1 794
1985	5 934	1 631	651	2 488	1 027	2 239	1 489
1986	6 087	1 428	705	2 552	1 083	2 419	1 613
1987	6 766	1 680	804	2 836	1 183	2 547	1 892
1988	7 171	1 554	965	3 005	1 341	2 627	1 793
1989	7 602	1 654	1 662	3 360	1 421	2 769	1 663
1990	6 684	1 271	1 515	2 439	1 381	2 937	1 346
1991	5 973	795	671	1 494	1 056	3 438	843
1992	4 157	621	1 036	367	859	3 561	171
1993	4 480	1 046	974	309	1 541	3 306	1 460
1994	5 344	1 496	2 063	1 245	1 748	3 355	2 419
1995	5 886	2 197	1 935	1 156	2 078	3 076	2 131
1996	4 949	1 257	2 581	1 616	2 345	3 804	2 266
1997	4 604	1 765	3 676	1 864	2 604	4 319	3 488
1998[2]	4 512	2 288	4 406	1 162	2 560	4 297	2 454

Source: © *Statistics Canada*

(1) Not adjusted for inflation. (2) Preliminary figures.

LABOUR

Provincial Labour Force by Industry, 1988

(thousands)

	Canada	Nfld	PEI	NS	NB	Que	Ont	Man	Sask	Alta	BC
All Industries	13 900.5	237.3	62.4	419.6	331.2	3 445.3	45 407.7	551.3	502.3	1 333.0	1 610.5
Agriculture	464.3	1.9	6.1	9.3	6.4	74.8	112.4	38.6	82.8	91.7	40.3
Primary Industries[1].	354.3	20.1	3.5	23.3	15.0	53.2	66.7	10.1	14.2	83.8	64.5
Utilities..................	121.9	2.6	0.2	3.6	3.7	29.8	52.9	5.5	4.4	10.3	8.9
Construction............	881.3	17.7	5.2	31.2	25.2	213.3	327.8	30.2	31.4	88.9	110.3
Manufacturing........	2 262.8	30.2	5.3	49.9	44.8	663.9	1 090.2	64.5	27.7	102.2	184.2
Trade[2].....................	2 236.4	39.7	8.9	70.8	54.7	537.7	877.6	88.1	79.8	210.9	268.2
Transportation & Warehousing.......	659.5	10.7	2.5	19.6	19.1	165.1	226.6	37.5	21.6	69.4	87.5
Finance, Insurance, Real Estate & Leasing .	823.0	7.3	2.0	20.4	13.8	185.2	366.3	27.9	24.1	70.1	106.1
Services[3]	550.6	4.7	1.1	12.6	6.5	119.1	242.7	15.5	12.5	60.4	75.4
Management, admin. & Other Support	334.4	4.8	1.1	8.2	4.8	81.3	141.2	11.1	8.4	32.5	41.1
Educational Serv.	845.9	17.4	3.9	27.3	21.8	214.1	320.4	34.6	31.1	86.5	88.7
Health Care & Social Assist.......	1 249.8	22.8	5.9	41.4	34.2	326.7	458.9	57.5	48.6	111.0	142.8
Information, Culture & Rec.	543.9	5.9	2.4	14.2	10.1	121.8	229.9	20.8	19.2	53.5	64.3
Accommodation & Food Serv............	831.5	12.0	4.4	25.3	20.0	201.8	302.5	35.0	30.2	80.8	119.7
Other Services.........	669.2	12.8	3.5	21.3	19.3	176.4	236.0	26.8	26.5	67.6	79.1
Public Administration[4]	838.1	19.4	5.5	33.2	24.4	200.6	308.7	38.7	30.3	88.4	88.8
Unclassified.............	233.6	7.3	0.9	8.0	7.3	80.4	47.0	9.0	9.6	23.3	40.8

Source: © *Statistics Canada*

(1) Primary industries include fishing, trapping, forestry, mining, oil and gas extractions. (2) Trade is the sales and distribution network of merchandise. Includes wholesale and retail. (3) Services refers to professional, scientific and technical occupations in which a service is provided but no goods are produced. (4) Includes municipal, provincial and federal levels.

Provincial Employment by Industry, 1988

(thousands)

	Canada	Nfld	PEI	NS	NB	Que	Ont	Man	Sask	Alta	BC
All Industries	12 818.9	198.4	54.3	376.7	291.5	3 120.7	5 136.0	507.8	464.8	1 224.4	1 444.3
Agriculture	437.8	1.4	5.4	8.0	5.4	68.3	106.8	37.5	81.1	89.9	34.0
Primary Industries[1]...	317.4	17.9	2.7	20.7	12.6	45.4	62.7	9.5	13.1	78.0	54.8
Utilities....................	118.6	2.5	0.2	3.4	3.6	29.0	51.7	5.4	4.3	9.8	8.7
Construction............	778.3	14.4	4.1	25.8	19.5	186.3	305.9	24.9	27.0	77.3	95.1
Manufacturing........	2 120.3	24.4	4.4	45.5	39.8	612.1	1 042.3	60.8	25.8	94.7	170.6
Trade[2].....................	2 102.5	35.6	8.3	65.4	50.5	497.1	842.2	82.4	75.0	197.5	248.4
Transportation & Warehousing.......	621.5	9.7	2.3	18.2	17.5	154.8	215.9	35.5	20.5	65.3	81.8
Finance, Insurance, Real Estate & Leasing .	796.1	6.8	1.8	19.5	13.2	177.1	358.7	27.0	23.3	66.7	102.0
Services[3]	526.4	4.4	1.1	11.9	5.9	113.7	234.1	15.0	11.8	56.8	71.8
Management, admin. & Other Support..	301.3	3.6	0.9	7.0	3.9	73.3	131.4	9.6	7.3	28.5	35.7
Educational Serv.	814.8	16.5	3.7	26.3	20.7	204.4	311.5	33.0	30.1	83.6	84.9
Health Care & Social Assist.......	1 202.1	20.6	5.5	39.3	32.5	313.6	446.3	55.3	46.8	106.5	135.6
Information, Culture & Rec.	507.0	5.3	2.1	12.9	9.3	111.1	218.0	19.2	18.0	51.6	59.4
Accommodation & Food Serv...........	750.9	10.2	3.6	22.2	17.4	179.7	282.1	31.3	27.0	71.3	106.0
Other Services.........	628.0	10.5	3.1	6.2	17.6	165.0	226.5	25.2	25.1	62.5	72.9
Public Administration[4] ...	796.0	16.8	5.1	n.a.	22.2	189.8	229.8	36.2	28.6	84.2	82.7

Source: © *Statistics Canada*

(1) Primary industries include fishing, trapping, forestry, mining, oil and gas extractions. (2) Trade is the sales and distribution network of merchandise. Includes wholesale and retail. (3) Services refers to professional, scientific and technical occupations in which a service is provided but no goods are produced. (4) Includes municipal, provincial and federal levels.

Provincial Labour Force by Industry, 1998

(thousands)

	Canada	Nfld	PEI	NS	NB	Que	Ont	Man	Sask	Alta	BC
All Industries	15 631.5	241.1	70.7	452.1	368.9	3 713.3	6 49.7	578.9	508.6	1 605.6	2042.6
Agriculture	44.7	1.8	5.2	8.8	7.5	82.6	114.9	35.8	72.7	83.9	31.3
Primary Industries[1].	33.0	20.1	4.5	19.3	15.9	53.0	42.4	10.3	17.1	95.9	59.4
Utilities	120.9	2.1	0.0	2.2	3.6	30.9	49.6	6.3	3.5	9.6	13.2
Construction...........	862.0	15.9	5.3	27.1	26.7	156.1	316.1	31.8	26.6	120.3	135.9
Manufacturing........	2 282.6	21.6	6.2	48.2	44.0	658.2	1 064.4	66.8	33.2	131.4	208.6
Trade[2].....................	2 301.6	34.9	10.3	74.7	56.4	538.2	874.2	87.3	72.4	237.6	315.6
Transportation & Warehousing......	735.6	10.8	2.2	20.0	18.8	158.2	273.9	32.5	23.1	88.9	107.1
Finance, Insurance, Real Estate & Leasing...	868.6	7.6	2.3	22.8	14.8	185.8	393.4	28.7	25.2	74.4	113.5
Services[3]	931.2	7.5	2.1	18.8	11.9	214.1	395.7	25.5	17.7	101.4	136.5
Management, admin. & Other Support..	541.2	5.3	1.6	13.9	12.3	116.1	233.9	18.3	13.2	52.6	74.0
Educational Serv.	978.3	18.6	4.6	29.8	22.8	233.6	357.9	41.5	36.8	106.1	126.6
Health Care & Social Assist......	1 059.4	30.2	7.5	50.5	43.2	348.6	556.5	68.6	54.0	144.9	205.4
Information, Culture & Rec.	669.7	7.6	2.1	17.7	13.1	155.9	261.6	19.3	21.5	73.7	97.1
Accommodation & Food Serv...........	995.7	13.7	5.7	29.6	23.8	228.2	356.7	34.6	31.5	111.5	160.5
Other Services........	761.9	12.7	3.6	24.2	19.2	179.2	288.9	27.2	24.0	85.1	97.9
Public Administration[4]	822.5	16.4	6.1	29.9	23.9	217.8	299.9	34.8	28.4	69.4	95.9
Unclassified.............	467.6	14.4	1.1	14.5	11.0	156.8	169.7	9.5	7.7	18.9	64.2

Source: © *Statistics Canada*

(1) Primary industries include fishing, trapping, forestry, mining, oil and gas extractions. (2) Trade is the sales and distribution network of merchandise. Includes wholesale and retail. (3) Services refers to professional, scientific and technical occupations in which a service is provided but no goods are produced. (4) Includes municipal, provincial and federal levels.

Provincial Employment by Industry, 1998

(thousands)

	Canada	Nfld	PEI	NS	NB	Que	Ont	Man	Sask	Alta	BC
All Industries	14 326 4	197.9	60.9	403.7	324.2	3327.5	5 612.9	546.1	478.6	1 514.0	1 860.4
Agriculture	418.7	1.2	4.3	7.3	6.3	75.7	108.2	34.9	71.4	82.2	27.3
Primary Industries[1]...	297.0	16.9	3.4	16.3	13.0	44.6	39.0	9.7	15.7	88.5	50.1
Utilities	117.4	2.0	0.0	2.1	3.5	29.6	48.5	6.3	3.5	9.0	12.8
Construction...........	762.0	10.7	4.1	22.6	20.6	131.5	289.3	28.8	23.6	110.3	120.5
Manufacturing........	2 146.6	16.4	5.3	43.5	39.2	612.8	1 016.8	64.0	31.3	12.8	193.6
Trade[2].....................	2 182.9	31.8	9.7	70.3	52.5	503.9	833.9	84.3	69.2	228.2	299.1
Transportation & Warehousing......	701.3	9.7	1.9	18.8	17.1	148.9	263.4	31.4	22.2	85.5	102.4
Finance, Insurance, Real Estate & Leasing...	846.0	7.2	2.1	22.1	14.3	179.2	384.4	28.1	24.8	72.4	111.4
Services[3]	896.8	6.8	2.0	17.8	11.0	203.5	383.8	24.9	17.1	98.9	131.0
Management, Admin. & Other Support..	491.6	4.5	1.4	12.2	10.5	105.1	213.1	16.9	12.3	48.6	67.1
Educational Serv.	942.7	17.4	4.2	28.7	21.4	223.5	348.5	39.9	35.6	102.2	121.2
Health Care & Social Assist........	1 465.3	28.3	7.2	48.4	41.4	337.0	541.9	67.4	52.6	140.7	200.3
Information, Culture & Rec.	632.6	6.8	1.8	16.5	11.9	145.6	248.8	18.4	20.3	71.2	91.1
Accommodation & Food Serv...........	916.4	12.0	4.8	26.8	21.7	208.8	329.2	32.2	29.1	103.9	147.9
Other Services........	719.2	11.2	3.2	22.6	17.6	168.9	272.9	26.0	23.1	81.7	92.2
Public Administration[4]	790.1	15.0	5.4	27.9	22.3	208.8	291.3	33.1	27.0	66.8	92.6

Source: © *Statistics Canada*

(1) Primary industries include fishing, trapping, forestry, mining, oil and gas extractions. (2) Trade is the sales and distribution network of merchandise. Includes wholesale and retail. (3) Services refers to professional, scientific and technical occupations in which a service is provided but no goods are produced. (4) Includes municipal, provincial and federal levels.

Canadian Labour Force by Province, 1998

(thousands)

	Population 15 Years and Over	Labour Force[1]	Participation Rate[2]	Employed	Employment Population Ratio[3]	Un-employed	% Un-employed[4]
Canada.........................	23 993.9	15 631.5	65.1	14 326.4	59.7	1 305.1	8.3
Newfoundland	446.0	241.0	54.1	197.9	44.4	43.1	17.9
Prince Edward Island..........	107.1	70.7	66.0	60.9	56.9	9.8	13.9
Nova Scotia	746.3	452.1	60.6	403.7	54.1	48.4	10.7
New Brunswick...................	605.6	368.9	60.9	324.2	53.5	44.7	12.1
Quebec	5 968.2	3 713.3	62.2	3 327.5	55.8	385.8	10.4
Ontario...............................	9 118.8	6 049.7	66.3	5 612.9	61.6	436.8	7.2
Manitoba	862.6	578.9	67.1	546.1	63.3	32.8	5.7
Saskatchewan....................	763.8	508.6	66.6	478.6	62.7	30.0	5.9
Alberta	2 225.1	1 605.6	72.2	1 514.0	68.0	91.6	5.7
British Columbia	3 150.4	2 042.6	64.8	1 860.4	59.1	182.1	8.9

Source: © *Statistics Canada*

(1) The labour force consists of employed workers and those who are unemployed but actively seeking work. (2) Participation rate is the percent of the total population aged 15 and over that makes up the labour force. (3) The percent of the total population aged 15 and over that is employed. (4) The percent of the labour force that is unemployed.

Labour Force by Age, 1998

(thousands)

	Population 15 Years and Over	Labour Force[1]	Participation Rate[2]	Employed	Employment Population Ratio[3]	Un-employed	% Un-employed[4]
MALES	**11 779.9**	**8 530.0**	**72.4**	**7 802.6**	**66.2**	**727.4**	**8.5**
15-19.................................	1 025.4	495.7	48.3	389.3	38.0	106.4	21.5
20-24.................................	1 008.8	797.2	79.0	688.7	68.3	108.5	13.6
25-34.................................	2 281.3	2 102.9	92.2	1 928.9	86.2	17.4	8.3
35-44.................................	2 592.6	2 400.0	92.6	2 233.6	86.2	166.5	6.9
45-54.................................	2 031.3	1 798.8	88.6	1 684.7	82.9	114.1	6.3
55-59.................................	709.2	505.6	71.3	741.0	66.4	34.5	6.8
60-64.................................	585.8	266.5	45.5	247.5	42.2	19.0	7.1
65-69.................................	537.8	98.7	18.4	95.7	17.8	3.0	3.0
70 and over	1 007.6	64.5	6.4	63.1	6.3	0.0	0.0
FEMALES	**12 214.0**	**7 101.5**	**58.1**	**6 523.8**	**53.4**	**577.7**	**8.1**
15-19.................................	978.7	468.4	47.9	382.3	39.1	86.0	18.4
20-24.................................	986.5	718.7	72.9	641.6	65.0	77.2	10.7
25-34.................................	2 273.8	1 785.1	75.5	1 643.6	72.3	141.6	6.2
35-44.................................	2 593.8	2 051.1	79.1	1 907.9	73.6	143.2	1.0
45-54.................................	2 034.8	1 500.0	73.7	1 407.4	69.2	92.6	6.2
55-59.................................	719.8	357.5	49.7	331.8	46.1	25.7	7.2
60-64.................................	2 015.9	151.3	24.8	141.9	23.2	9.3	6.1
65-69.................................	585.8	42.9	7.3	42.9	7.1	1.6	3.7
70 and over	1 430.1	26.5	1.9	26.5	1.8	0.0	0.0

Source: © *Statistics Canada*

(1) The labour force consists of employed workers and those who are unemployed but actively seeking work. (2) Participation rate is the percent of the total population aged 15 and over that makes up the labour force. (3) The percent of the total population aged 15 and over that is employed. (4) The percent of the labour force that is unemployed.

Average Weekly Earnings

	1995	1996	1997	1998
Goods Producing (all)	721.81	742.16	762.22	776.46
Forestry	735.30	768.63	793.12	767.91
Mines, quarries, oil wells	991.43	1 039.08	1 057.61	1 111.62
Manufacturing (all)	694.58	718.62	736.69	755.92
Non-durable goods	650.98	666.23	680.89	693.92
Durable goods	730.44	757.17	780.95	804.30
Construction	680.59	695.67	711.35	697.57
Services Producing	529.62	539.29	548.56	533.87
Transportation, communication, utilities	729.16	735.32	754.55	786.68
Trade	431.35	439.72	451.89	467.77
Finance, insurance, real estate	658.48	704.59	742.17	754.62
Services	490.73	501.18	506.58	507.09
Public administration	750.65	740.05	739.57	737.53

Source: *Statistics Canada*

Labour Income[1]

(millions of dollars)

	1970	1975	1980	1985	1990
Total labour income[2]	**215 562**	**299 915**	**351 781**	**368 916**	**428 291**
Agriculture, fishing and trapping . . .	1 809	2 345	2 746	3 115	3 081
Forestry	2 356	2 890	3 333	2 669	2 913
Mines, quarries and oil wells	4 788	6 296	9 206	9 635	8 638
Manufacturing.	52 797	63 076	71 172	69 459	71 550
Construction	14 024	24 279	23 009	19 076	26 504
Transportation, communication and utilities	22 492	28 897	34 427	34 962	36 738
Trade.	28 537	39 722	44 190	44 403	55 094
Finance, insurance and real estate ...	11 093	17 304	22 972	25 476	32 272
Services	49 162	70 146	85 129	95 690	116 982
Public Administration	15 258	2 2677	25 751	28 403	31 202

	1995	1996	1997	1998
Total labour income[2]	**435 528**	**442 600**	**457 797**	**471 975**
Agriculture, fishing and trapping . . .	3 164	3 624	3 606	3 627
Forestry	3 202	3 108	3 150	3 036
Mines, quarries and oil wells	7 881	8 621	8 304	9 645
Manufacturing.	68 729	69 892	73 253	77 623
Construction	20 876	20 857	22 218	22 918
Transportation, communication and utilities	35 864	35 565	36 738	38 105
Trade.	54 089	55 039	58 502	61 114
Finance, insurance and real estate. .	31 460	33 314	36 339	37 767
Services	124 562	126 539	128 692	131 587
Public Administration	29 650	31 195	29 987	29 462

Source: © *Statistics Canada*   (1) Figures adjusted for inflation. (2) Total includes income categories not shown.

PERSONAL FINANCE

What's a Dollar Worth?[1]

This table shows how many current (1999) dollars it would take to equal the purchasing power of a single dollar in earlier years. For example, if you spent $30 a week on groceries in 1985 and want to know what that would be by today's standards, multiply $30 times the relative value of a 1985 dollar ($1.47) and you have your answer: $44.10. The relative value of a dollar for the years listed was calculated according to changes in the cost of living in Canada as measured by the Consumer Price Index.

CPI by Year	Rate	1999		CPI by Year	Rate	1999		CPI by Year	Rate	1999		CPI by Year	Rate	1999
1915	7.3	$15.14		**1957**	17.6	6.28		**1970**	24.2	4.57		**1985**	75.0	1.47
1920	13.5	8.19		**1958**	18.0	6.14		**1971**	24.9	4.44		**1986**	78.1	1.41
1925	10.9	10.14		**1959**	18.3	6.04		**1972**	26.1	4.23		**1987**	81.5	1.36
1930	10.9	10.14		**1960**	18.5	5.97		**1973**	28.1	3.93		**1988**	84.8	1.30
1935	8.7	12.70		**1961**	18.7	5.91		**1974**	31.1	3.55		**1989**	89.0	1.24
1940	9.5	11.63		**1962**	18.9	5.85		**1975**	34.5	3.20		**1990**	93.3	1.18
1945	10.9	10.14		**1963**	19.2	5.76		**1976**	37.1	2.98		**1991**	98.5	1.12
1950	14.9	7.42		**1964**	19.6	5.64		**1977**	40.0	2.76		**1992**	100.0	1.11
1951	16.4	6.74		**1965**	20.0	5.53		**1978**	43.6	2.53		**1993**	101.8	1.09
1952	16.9	6.54		**1966**	20.8	5.31		**1979**	47.6	2.32		**1994**	102.0	1.08
1953	16.7	6.62		**1967**	21.5	5.14		**1980**	52.4	2.11		**1995**	104.2	1.06
1954	16.8	6.58		**1968**	22.4	4.93		**1981**	58.9	1.88		**1996**	105.9	1.04
1955	16.8	6.58		**1969**	23.4	4.72		**1982**	65.3	1.69		**1997**	107.6	1.03
1956	17.1	6.46						**1983**	69.1	1.60		**1998**	108.6	1.02
								1984	72.1	1.53		**1999**	110.5	1.00

(1) Based on Consumer Price Index as of June 30, 1999.

Credit Summary, 1971–98

(millions of dollars)[1]

	Household Credit			Business Credit
Year	**Consumer**	**Mortgage**	**Total**	
1971	11 441	19 520	30 961	58 927
1972	13 334	23 214	36 548	63 890
1973	16 091	28 138	44 229	69 995
1974	18 966	34 269	53 236	80 039
1975	21 746	40 269	62 014	90 701
1976	25 234	48 067	73 302	100 988
1977	29 039	58 538	87 577	113 709
1978	33 362	69 767	103 129	128 428
1979	38 465	81 333	119 798	151 813
1980	42 738	90 543	133 261	180 134
1981	47 464	96 475	143 939	221 514
1982	47 168	97 668	144 836	252 247
1983	47 285	101 932	149 217	257 244
1984	50 191	110 383	160 574	269 788
1985	55 729	117 945	173 673	291 701
1986	62 433	132 801	195 233	317 735
1987	69 929	155 329	225 258	346 821
1988	79 768	181 274	261 042	382 601
1989	89 668	209 143	298 812	425 081
1990	98 432	238 961	337 392	466 070
1991	101 027	258 568	359 595	482 163
1992	101 331	281 655	382 986	491 735
1993	104 233	303 936	408 169	493 627
1994	111 483	324 036	435 519	518 038
1995	118 544	336 126	454 670	543 816
1996	127 148	349 862	477 010	571 917
1997	139 565	368 707	508 272	624 583
1998	152 970	386 941	539 911	687 186

Source: *Bank of Canada*   (1) Not adjusted for inflation.

Total Provincial Wages and Salaries[1]

(millions of dollars)

	Nfld	PEI	NS	NB	Que	Ont	Man	Sask	Alta	BC
1965	401	79	805	606	8 015	12 459	1 262	865	1 915	3 052
1970	667	133	1 296	973	12 520	21 164	2 012	1 239	3 417	5 143
1975	1 415	281	2 607	2 018	24 307	39 861	3 819	2 605	7 499	11 375
1980	2 353	499	4 244	3 313	43 074	66 735	6 258	4 910	16 931	21 486
1985	3 560	788	7 074	5 158	59 759	104 715	9 457	7 773	26 621	29 102
1990	5 074	1 182	9 757	7 445	84 208	157 425	12 392	9 330	35 341	44 223
1991	5 254	1 218	10 047	7 712	86 177	160 189	12 692	9 795	37 120	46 304
1992	5 179	1 234	10 179	7 984	88 060	162 815	12 996	10 003	37 760	48 933
1993	5 219	1 275	10 273	8 142	89 052	164 383	13 183	10 133	39 502	51 355
1994	5 479	1 316	10 306	8 301	91 094	167 173	13 447	10 502	40 876	54 018
1995	5 573	1 431	10 508	8 611	93 535	173 228	13 921	10 942	41 853	56 795
1996	5 506	1 526	10 569	8 709	94 911	177 889	14 336	11 244	43 564	58 577
1997	5 375	1 430	10 767	8 964	98 104	187 161	14 789	11 902	47 473	60 607
1998[2]	5 509	1 479	11 118	9 218	100 944	195 397	15 561	12 522	50 444	61 609

Source: © *Statistics Canada*   (1) Exclusive of supplementary labour income. (2) Preliminary numbers.

Minimum Hourly Wage by Province

On December 18, 1996, the minimum hourly wage provisions of the Canada Labour Code were amended to align the federal minimum wage with the provincial and territorial general adult minimum wage rates. Minimum wage rates may not apply to registered apprentices who are paid according to a provincial apprenticeship act, to certain employees who are being trained on the job or special types of employees in some provinces (see table).

If an employees is paid through a system based on something besides hours (such as mileage), the employee's pay, if divided by the hours worked, must be equivalent to the appropriate provincial or territorial minimum wage.

	Adult Minimum Wage Rate	Date Effective	Other Categories of Workers	Minimum Wage Rates
Newfoundland	$5.25	April 1997	–	–
Prince Edward Island	5.40	September 1997	–	–
Nova Scotia	5.50	February 1997	inexperienced employees	5.05
New Brunswick	5.50	July 1996	employees whose hours aren't verifiable and counsellors and program staff at residential summer camps	242/week
Quebec	6.90	October 1998	–	–
Ontario	6.85	January 1995	–	–
Manitoba	6.00	April 1999	–	–
Saskatchewan	6.00	January 1999	–	–
Alberta	5.65	April 1999	under 18 attending school	4.50
British Columbia	7.15	April 1998	crop harvesters	rates based on gross volume or weight packed
Yukon	7.20	October 1998		
Northwest Territories	6.50	April 1998	under age 16	6.00
Remote Regions	7.00			6.50
Nunavut	6.50	April 1999	–	–

Source: *Human Resources Development Canada*

(–) Not applicable.

Canadian Income Tax

Income tax was introduced in 1917 as a temporary measure to finance Canada's participation in World War I. The law introducing the tax (the Income War Tax Act) was shorter and much simpler than our current legislation. It imposed tax at graduated rates, ranging from 4 percent on the first $1 500 to 25 percent for income over $100 000.

This "temporary" tax was not repealed when the war ended. But on Jan. 1, 1949, the federal government removed "war" from the title and gave the statute the name it has today—the Income Tax Act. This act has been amended many times—most notably in 1972 when a major overhaul of the tax system broadened the tax base and introduced a tax on capital gains. This is still the basis of our federal income tax laws today.

In 1988, all personal exemptions and many deductions were changed to non-refundable tax credits. Unlike deductions, which reduce taxable income, credits are used to reduce the amount of tax payable. The term "non-refundable" refers to the fact that, although you can use these credits to reduce or eliminate your federal tax payable, any unused portion is not refundable to you. In some cases, however, you may be able to transfer the unused portion of the credits to someone else.

Because the credits are calculated by multiplying eligible amounts by 17 percent—the same as the lowest personal tax rate—the change makes no difference to those whose income falls within the lowest tax bracket. But it increases taxes for most of those with higher incomes.

Source: *Revenue Canada*

For 1999, the federal income tax rates for individuals were: 17 percent on income up to $29 590; $5 030 plus 26 percent on the next $29 590 up to $59 180; and $12 724 plus 29 percent on income in excess of $59 180.

Provincial Income Tax

Every province except Quebec collects income tax from its residents by "piggy-backing" on the federal tax. Each province imposes taxes of a fixed percentage based on the amount of income tax an individual must pay to the federal government. The federal government collects the tax, then remits the appropriate amounts to the provincial governments.

Quebec, however, chooses to collect its own provincial income tax, so Quebec residents must file both the federal return filed by all Canadian taxpayers, and the Quebec provincial income tax return.

Filing Tax Returns

Though corporations must file tax returns each year, individuals need only file if they owe taxes or if they are eligible to claim tax credits such as the Child Tax Credit or the Goods and Services Tax Credit. Persons owing money must file a return by Apr. 30 of the year following the taxation year. Failure to do so makes the taxpayer liable to a late-filing penalty of 5 percent of unpaid tax plus an additional penalty of 1 percent per month on the amount outstanding, to a maximum of 12 months, plus interest on amounts owing.

Taxes Paid by Province, 1996

	Taxable Returns Filed	Total Income Assessed ($thousands)	Net Federal Tax Payable ($thousands)	Net Provincial Tax Payable ($thousands)
Canada	**14 172 530**	**549 101 590**	**68 505 363**	**30 339 212**
Newfoundland	227 360	7 538 319	788 182	532 211
Prince Edward Island	65 690	2 046 272	207 669	122 011
Nova Scotia	421 870	14 667 355	1 628 269	927 776
New Brunswick	340 850	11 504 243	1 253 377	782 515
Quebec	3 444 050	124 000 654	14 559 970	16 619
Ontario	5 386 750	222 904 379	29 258 012	16 755 402
Manitoba	530 860	18 564 125	2 093 465	1 333 780
Saskatchewan	469 920	16 177 392	1 777 761	1 197 845
Alberta	1 350 380	54 477 707	7 122 767	3 360 147
British Columbia	1 878 640	74 703 704	9 430 060	5 151 417
Yukon	14 710	634 977	75 408	36 642
Northwest Territories	24 730	1 211 019	156 987	68 102
Outside Canada	16 710	671 444	153 435	54 745

Source: *Taxation Statistics, Revenue Canada*

Individual Income Tax Rates, 1999

Federal Components

The federal components of personal income tax rates apply to all taxpayers except in Quebec.

Before Surtaxes and Basic Credit						After Surtaxes and Basic Credit	
Basic Federal Brackets	Marginal Rate	Tax at Bottom of Bracket	Effect of Basic Credit[1]	Brackets After Basic Credit and Surtaxes	Effect of Federal Surtaxes[2]	Total Marginal Rate	Tax at Bottom of Bracket
$59 180	29%	$12 724	0%	$62 391	+1.89%	30.89%	$12 668
				59 180	+1.31	30.31	11 714
$29 590	26%			46 735	+1.17	27.17	8 333
				29 590	0	26.00	3 875
$0	17%			19 794		17.00	2 210
			+0.34%	7 294		17.34	43
			−17%	7 044		17.00	0
				0		0	

(1) The basic personal credit eliminates tax for taxable income below $7044. An additional $250 disappears as income increases and is eliminated for taxable incomes over $19 794. This adds 0.34 percent to the federal tax rate for taxable incomes between $7294 and $19 794. (2) The former general federal surtax of 3 percent of basic federal tax was eliminated effective July 1, 1999. The 5 percent high-earner surtax, which applies to basic federal tax over $12 500, remains.

Provincial Components (Except Quebec)

All provinces and territories except Quebec compute provincial tax as a percentage of basic federal tax. Most have surtaxes, calculated as a percentage of provincial tax. Three are two-tiered, three provinces have flat taxes and five have tax reductions for low incomes. The Northwest Territories and Nunavut have a cost of living tax that reduces territorial tax payable for incomes up to $66,000.

	% of Federal Tax	Provincial Surtax		Provincial Flat Tax		Provincial Tax Reduction for Low Incomes[1]	
		% of Prov. Tax	On Prov. Tax Above	% of Income[2]	On Income Above		
Nfld	69	10	$7 900				
PEI	58.5	10	5 200				
NS	57.5	10	10 000				
NB	60	8	13 500				
Ont.	39.5	20	3 750	n.a.	n.a.	8 662	10 618
	+36	4 681	n.a.	n.a.	n.a.	n.a.	
Man.	48.5	n.a.	n.a.	2	7 794[3]	7 965	21 500
			4	30 000[2]			
Sask.	48	10	1 500[4]	2	7 040[3]	7 334	14 000
	+15	4 000[4]					
Alta.	44	8	3 500	0.5	9 545[3]	9 820	16 872
BC	49.5	30	5 300				
	+19						
NWT & Nun	45						
YT	50	5	6 000				
Nonresidents	52						

Source: *PricewaterhouseCoopers*

(1) Provincial tax reductions eliminate provincial income tax up to the first taxable income figure shown and reduce provincial income tax up to the second figure shown. (2) Provincial flat taxes are calculated as the given percentage of taxable income in Alberta. In Manitoba and Saskatchewan, the percentage applies to net income. Manitoba's 2 percent second-tier flat tax applies to net income over a threshold of $30 000 (or higher, if certain credits apply). (3) Provincial flat taxes in Alberta, Manitoba and Saskatchewan would apply to income even smaller than those noted, except for the effect of the provincial tax reduction. (4) Saskatchewan's surtax applies to the flat tax as well as the provincial tax.

Personal Tax Credits, 1999

	Basic Amount	Federal Credit	Quebec Credit
Basic	$6 794	$1 155	$1 357
Age 65[1]	3 482	592	506
Disability	4 233	720	506
Married[2]	5 718	972	n.a.
Dependants[3] — 1st	—	—	598
— Other	—	—	552
Disabled dependant[4]	2 353	400	1 357
Single parent	—	—	299
Charitable donations:			
First $200	—	17%	23%
Remainder	—	29%	23%
Medical expenses[5]	—	17%	23%
Education credit	—	17%[6]	23%
CPP/QPP/EI	—	17%	23%
Tuition	—	17%	23%
Pension income	1 000	170	$230
Union, Professional Dues	—	—[7]	23%
Dividends[8]	—	13.33%	9.85%

Source: *PricewaterhouseCoopers*

(1) Federal Credit reduced where net income exceeds $25 921; Quebec credit reduced where net income exceeds $26 000. (2) The credit is reduced where the spouse or qualifying dependant has income in excess of $538. (3) Under 19 years of age at the end of the year or full-time student. (4) Those over 18 years of age at the end of the year. Dependant's income over $4103 reduces the Federal credit and any income reduces the Quebec credit. (5) Based upon the amount by which qualifying expenses exceed the lesser of $1614 or 3% of net income. (6) The credit is $34 per month for federal purposes and $380 per term (maximum 2) for supporting Quebec parent. (7) For federal purposes, a deduction is available for union and professional dues, not a credit. (8) The credit for taxable Canadian dividends is applied at the specified percentages to the grossed-up amount (125%) of dividends.

Individual Tax Tables, 1999

This table shows the combined federal and provincial income taxes, including surtaxes and flat taxes, payable on the assumption that only the basic personal tax credit is available. The political contribution tax credit and provincial credits for homeowners, renters, sales tax, cost of living and children have not been taken into account.

Taxable Income

	$20 000	$30 000	$40 000	$50 000	$60 000	$70 000	$80 000	$90 000	$100 000
Newfoundland	3 794	6 729	11 123	15 56	20 134	25 410	30 699	35 989	41 279
Prince Edward Island	3 558	6 311	10 432	14 609	19 040	23 981	28 936	33 890	38 845
Nova Scotia	3 486	6 272	10 367	14 500	18 752	23 494	28 262	33 185	38 108
New Brunswick	3 592	6 371	10 531	14 729	19 047	23 861	28 690	33 518	38 390
Quebec[1]	4 526	8 132	12 610	17 126	22 044	27 248	32 465	37 683	42 901
Ontario	3 132	5 555	9 182	12 847	16 809	21 664	26 540	31 415	36 291
Manitoba[2]	3 704	6 513	10 774	15 073	19 489	24 370	29 265	34 160	39 055
Saskatchewan[2]	3 723	6 594	10 787	15 229	19 797	24 861	29 940	35 018	40 097
Alberta	3 333	5 884	9 678	13 553	17 593	22 096	26 613	31 129	35 646
British Columbia	3 356	5 953	9 840	13 765	17 970	22 911	27 876	33 104	38 331
Yukon Territory	3 368	5 973	9 873	13 811	17 866	22 458	27 069	31 680	36 291
Northwest Territory & Nunavut[3]	3 025	5 444	9 114	12 827	16 676	21 010	25 404	29 797	34 191

Source: *PricewaterhouseCoopers*

(1) In some situations, the calculation of taxable income for federal and Quebec purposes may be different, and the amounts shown may require adjustments. (2) Flat taxes in Manitoba and Saskatchewan are based on net income rather than taxable income. In those provinces, when net income exceeds taxable income, tax payable increases by 2% of the excess. (3) Amounts shown include NWT's and Nunavut's cost of living tax credit, which affects taxable incomes up to $66,000.

Taxable Income by Age and Gender, 1996

	Number of Tax Returns Filed		Total Income Assessed ($millions)		Average Income Assessed	
	Male	Female	Male	Female	Male	Female
under 20	121 090	70 530	2 580	2 063	21 306	29 250
20-24	524 890	403 080	11 704	9 007	22 298	22 345
25-29	745 090	609 390	22 971	16 638	30 830	27 303
30-34	932 440	765 280	36 673	23 842	39 330	31 155
35-39	1 019 740	818 980	46 934	27 027	46 025	33 001
40-44	932 100	790 320	47 190	27 089	50 628	34 276
45-49	819 400	723 290	44 304	24 896	54 069	34 420
50-54	680 220	540 990	37 744	18 179	55 488	33 603
55-59	501 530	380 490	26 517	12 420	52 872	32 642
60-64	453 860	312 910	20 992	9 455	46 252	30 216
65-69	397 640	281 390	17 431	9 765	43 836	34 703
70-74	310 990	262 490	12 645	9 128	40 660	34 775
75 and over	364 130	409 160	15 193	16 682	41 724	40 771
Total	**7 804 020**	**6 368 510**	**342 902**	**206 199**	**43 939**	**32 378**

Source: *Revenue Canada*

Income Taxes Collected from Individuals and Corporations

(millions of dollars)[1]

Year[2]	Total Net Collected[3]	Total Net Collections from Individuals[4]	% of Total	Total Net Collections from Corporations[5]	% of Total
1950	6 846.3	3 273.7	47.8	3 174.7	46.4
1955	11 427.9	5 974.0	52.3	4 960.5	43.4
1960	13 283.5	7 393.2	55.7	5 207.6	39.2
1965	19 239.1	11 308.0	58.8	7 026.5	36.5
1970	35 480.8	24 739.7	69.7	9 945.1	28.0
1975	52 657.9	39 450.0	74.9	12 186.4	23.1
1980	55 548.7	41 570.1	74.8	12 666.1	22.8
1985	69 670.8	55 362.4	79.5	10 465.3	15.0
1986	72 857.1	59 658.8	81.9	9 983.0	13.7
1987	77 298.4	65 268.6	84.4	10 142.1	13.1
1988	86 477.7	74 207.5	85.8	11 082.1	12.8
1989	86 138.8	73 008.2	84.8	11 517.5	13.4
1990	91 168.8	77 595.0	85.1	12 247.3	13.4
1991	93 490.0	82 891.2	88.7	9 291.8	9.9
1992	94 806.5	86 301.6	91.0	7 306.4	7.7
1993	91 285.9	83 860.8	91.9	6 318.1	6.9
1994	86 955.2	78 366.4	90.1	7 419.1	8.5
1995	96 698.9	84 503.4	87.4	10 867.2	11.2
1996	102 068.0	87 930.2	86.1	12 581.4	12.3

Source: *Revenue Canada.*

(1) All money figures in millions of dollars are in constant dollars where 1986 Base Year = 100. (2) For fiscal year ending Mar. 31. (3) Also includes non-resident tax, miscellaneous tax revenue. (4) Includes federal and provincial income tax, CPP contributions, UI premiums and OAS tax. (5) Includes federal and provincial income tax and OAS tax.

Mortgage Rates by Year[1]

	One-Year	Three-Year	Five-Year		One-Year	Three-Year	Five-Year
1980	13.98	n.a.	14.52	**1990**	13.40	13.38	13.35
1981	1812	18.33	18.38	**1991**	10.08	10.90	11.13
1982	16.85	17.83	18.04	**1992**	7.87	8.95	9.51
1983	10.98	12.52	13.23	**1993**	6.91	8.10	8.78
1984	12.00	13.21	13.58	**1994**	7.74	8.99	9.42
1985	10.31	11.54	12.12	**1995**	8.44	8.82	9.19
1986	10.15	10.88	11.21	**1996**	6.25	7.37	7.95
1987	9.85	10.69	11.17	**1997**	5.54	n.a.	7.07
1988	10.83	11.42	11.65	**1998**	6.50	n.a.	6.93
1989	12.85	12.15	12.06	**1999**	n.a.	n.a.	7.12[2]

Source: *Bank of Canada, CMHC*

(1) Average typical mortgage rates. (2) Preliminary figure.

Average Resale Value of Canadian Homes[1]

The average value of resale homes in Canada decreased by more than $2000 between 1997 and 1998. Calgary, Alberta, had the largest increase at 9.8 percent, with Mississauga, Ontario, running a distant second at 3.9 percent. Greater Vancouver, while still ranking as the most expensive place to buy a resale home, saw its prices fall for the second consecutive year.

	1980	1985	1990	1995	1996	1997	1998
Canada	**66 951**	**80 122**	**139 922**	**150 321**	**150 812**	**154 630**	**152 361**
Calgary............................	93 977	80 462	128 484	132 114	134 643	143 305	157 353
Edmonton	84 623	74 309	101 040	110 329	109 042	111 587	114 527
Halifax-Dartmouth............	53 161	79 350	97 238	103 011	105 869	109 827	114 025
Metropolitan Hamilton	54 835	72 973	165 742	141 109	142 267	151 538	153 628
Mississauga......................	80 341	99 675	224 449	180 295	180 485	194 582	202 194
Montreal............................	49 419	70 564	111 956	109 929	108 020	112 362	115 573
Ottawa-Carleton	63 177	107 640	141 562	143 127	140 513	143 866	143 914
Regina...............................	48 628	61 403	71 054	76 629	76 781	82 643	85 425
Saint John........................	45 170	57 088	78 041	83 498	82 066	86 171	87 087
St. John's.........................	53 247	66 642	88 939	89 655	94 142	92 797	92 500
Toronto	75 621	109 094	254 890	203 028	198 150	211 307	216 815
Greater Vancouver	100 065	112 852	226 385	307 747	288 268	287 094	278 659
Victoria..............................	85 066	88 451	160 743	210 669	211 602	218 398	217 886
Winnipeg...........................	50 491	62 478	81 740	82 994	86 142	86 040	85 932[2]

Source: *The Canadian Real Estate Association*

(1) Average price of all homes sold on the Multiple Listing Service in constant dollars. (2) Information from the Winnipeg Real Estate Board.

The Effect of Interest Rate Changes on Mortgage Payments

The table below shows the monthly mortgage payment (principal and interest) for each $1000 of mortgage debt. To calculate your payment at a given interest rate, choose the corresponding amount in the amortization column you select and multiply the amount by the number of thousands of dollars of debt. For example, if you want to know the cost per month to carry an $85000 mortgage amortized over 25 years at 7.00 percent, multiply 7 by 85 and the result, $595, is your monthly payment. If the same mortgage was coming up for renewal at 8.00 percent, the new payment amount would be $648.66 (7.63 x 85) or $53.56 more each month.

Monthly Payments for Each $1 000 of Mortgage

Interest Rate (%)	Amortization Period							
	1 Year	2 Years	3 Years	5 Years	10 Years	15 Years	20 Years	25 Years
4.00	$85.13	$43.41	$29.51	$18.40	$10.11	$7.38	$6.04	$5.26
4.25	85.25	43.52	29.62	18.51	10.23	7.50	6.17	5.40
4.50	85.36	43.63	29.73	18.62	10.34	7.63	6.30	5.53
4.75	85.47	43.74	29.84	18.74	10.46	7.75	6.44	5.67
5.00	85.58	43.85	29.95	18.85	10.58	7.88	6.57	5.82
5.25	85.70	43.96	30.06	18.96	10.70	8.01	6.71	5.95
5.50	85.81	44.07	30.17	19.07	10.82	8.14	6.84	6.10
5.75	85.92	44.18	30.28	19.19	10.94	8.27	6.98	6.25
6.00	86.03	44.29	30.39	19.30	11.07	8.40	7.12	6.40
6.25	86.14	44.40	30.50	19.41	11.19	8.53	7.26	6.55
6.50	86.26	44.51	30.61	19.53	11.31	8.66	7.41	6.70
6.75	86.37	44.62	30.72	19.64	11.43	8.80	7.55	6.85
7.00	86.48	44.73	30.83	19.75	11.56	8.93	7.69	7.00
7.25	86.59	44.84	30.94	19.87	11.68	9.07	7.84	7.16
7.50	86.70	44.95	31.05	19.98	11.81	9.21	7.99	7.32
7.75	86.82	45.06	31.16	20.10	11.94	9.34	8.13	7.47
8.00	86.93	45.17	31.28	20.21	12.06	9.48	8.28	7.63
8.25	87.04	45.28	31.39	20.33	12.19	9.62	8.43	7.79
8.50	87.15	45.39	31.50	20.45	12.32	9.76	8.59	7.95
8.75	87.26	45.50	31.61	20.56	12.45	9.90	8.74	8.12
9.00	87.38	45.61	31.72	20.68	12.58	10.05	8.89	8.28
9.25	87.49	45.72	31.84	20.80	12.71	10.19	9.05	8.44
9.50	87.60	45.83	31.95	20.91	12.84	10.33	9.20	8.61
9.75	87.71	45.94	32.06	21.03	12.97	10.48	9.36	8.78
10.00	87.82	46.05	32.17	21.15	13.10	10.62	9.52	8.94
10.25	87.93	46.16	32.28	21.27	13.24	10.77	9.68	9.11
10.50	88.04	46.27	32.40	21.38	13.37	10.92	9.83	9.28
10.75	88.16	46.38	32.51	21.50	13.50	11.06	10.00	9.45
11.00	88.27	46.49	32.62	21.62	13.64	11.21	10.16	9.63
11.25	88.38	46.61	32.74	21.74	13.77	11.36	10.32	9.80
11.50	88.49	46.72	32.85	21.86	13.91	11.51	10.48	9.97
11.75	88.60	46.83	32.96	21.98	14.04	11.66	10.65	10.14
12.00	88.71	46.94	33.08	22.10	14.18	11.82	10.81	10.32
12.25	88.82	47.05	33.19	22.22	14.32	11.97	10.98	10.49
12.50	88.94	47.16	33.30	22.34	14.46	12.12	11.14	10.67
12.75	89.05	47.27	33.42	22.46	14.59	12.28	11.31	10.85
13.00	89.18	47.38	33.53	22.58	14.73	12.43	11.48	11.02

Source: *The Royal Bank of Canada*

Housing Affordability Table

The table below shows how expensive a home an individual or family could likely afford, using various income levels and mortgage interest rates(assuming a down-payment of 25 percent of the purchase price. As income rises, housing becomes more affordable, but it becomes less affordable as interest rates increase.

For example, most couples with a combined annual income of $60,000 would qualify for a mortgage on a home costing $152,375 at an 11 percent interest rate(provided they had a downpayment of $38,094 (25 percent of the purchase price). But at a 13 percent interest rate, the same couple earning the same income could only afford a $133,042 home.

The table assumes that mortgage payments, property taxes, heating costs and 50 percent of condominium fees should not exceed 32 percent of gross income (net income if self-employed). Most lending institutions use this percentage when calculating how large a mortgage you can afford. For this table, we have established annual costs of $2400 for taxes and $2400 for taxes and $2400 for heating. Most lenders will also require that you total debt service ratio (mortgage payments, property taxes, heating cots 50 percent of condo fees and any other liabilities such as car loans or other debts) does not exceed 40 percent of gross income.

Mortgage Interest Rate (%)[1]	Annual Income							
	$30 000	**$40 000**	**$50 000**	**$60 000**	**$70 000**	**$80 000**	**$90 000**	**$100 000**
4.00	$25 348	109 838	194 332	278 823	363 314	439 357	506 951	574 546
4.25	24 707	107 062	189 420	271 776	354 132	428 252	494 138	560 024
4.50	24 090	104 391	184 693	264 993	345 294	417 564	481 806	546 048
4.75	23 497	101 818	180 142	258 464	336 785	407 275	469 934	532 593
5.00	22 925	99 341	175 760	252 176	328 592	397 367	458 501	519 636
5.25	22 374	96 955	171 538	246 119	320 700	387 823	447 489	507 155
5.50	21 844	94 658	167 471	240 283	313 095	378 627	436 878	495 129
5.75	21 333	92 440	163 550	234 658	305 766	369 764	426 652	483 539
6.00	20 840	90 3.4	159 771	229 236	298 701	361 220	416 793	472 386
6.25	20 364	88 244	156 127	224 007	291 887	352 980	407 285	461 591
6.50	19 906	86 257	152 611	218 863	185 315	345 032	398 115	451 197
6.75	19 463	84 340	149 219	214 096	278 973	337 363	389 265	441 169
7.00	19 036	82 490	145 946	209 399	272 853	329 962	380 726	431 490
7.25	18 624	80 704	142 785	204 865	256 945	322 817	372 482	422 147
7.50	18 226	78 979	139 733	200 486	261 239	315 917	364 520	413 124
7.75	17 842	77 313	136 785	196 257	255 728	309 252	356 830	404 408
8.00	17 470	75 703	133 937	192 170	250 403	302 813	349 400	395 987
8.25	17 111	74 147	131 184	188 220	245 256	296 589	342 219	387 848
8.50	16 764	72 643	128 523	184 402	240 281	290 572	335 276	379 981
8.75	16 428	71 188	125 950	180 170	235 470	284 754	328 583	372 372
9.00	16 103	69 781	123 461	177 138	230 816	279 127	322 070	365 013
9.25	15 789	68 420	121 052	173 683	226 314	273 682	315 787	357 893
9.50	15 485	67 103	118 722	170 339	221 958	268 413	309 707	351 002
9.75	15 191	65 827	116 465	167 102	217 738	263 312	303 822	344 332
10.00	14 906	64 593	114 281	163 967	213 654	258 372	296 122	337 873
10.25	14 630	63 397	112 165	160 932	209 698	253 588	292 602	331 616
10.50	14 363	62 238	110 115	157 990	205 865	248 953	287 254	325 555
10.75	14 104	61 115	108 128	155159	202 151	244 462	282 072	319 682
11.00	13 852	60 027	106 202	152 376	198 550	240 108	277 048	313 988
11.25	13 609	58 971	104 335	149 697	195 060	235 886	272 177	308 468
11.50	13 373	57 948	102 524	147 099	191674	231 792	267 453	303 114
11.75	13 144	56 955	100 767	144 579	188 390	227 820	262 870	297 920
12.00	12 921	55 991	99 063	142 133	185 203	223 966	258 423	292 880
12.25	12 705	55 058	97 408	139 759	182 110	220 225	254 107	287 988
12.50	14 496	54 148	95 802	137 454	179 196	216 594	249 917	283 239
12.75	12 292	53 267	94 242	135 216	176 190	213 067	245 847	278 627
13.00	12 095	52 410	92 727	133 042	173 358	209 642	241 895	274 148

Source: *The Royal Bank of Canada*

(1) Compounded semi-annually. Mortgage payments based on a 25-year amortization.

Personal Income and Savings

	Total Personal Income ($millions)	Annual % Change in Personal Income	Total Personal Disposable Income ($millions)	Total Personal Saving ($millions)	Personal Saving Rate
1965	41 881	9.8	37 113	2 306	6.2
1970	67 840	8.3	55 295	3 537	6.4
1971	74 531	9.9	60 462	4 222	7.0
1972	84 423	13.3	68 838	5 902	8.6
1973	98 528	16.7	80 373	8 324	10.4
1974	117 905	19.7	95 304	11 166	11.7
1975	136 921	16.1	111 258	14 052	12.6
1976	156 372	14.2	126 157	15 543	12.3
1977	173 286	10.8	139 752	16 536	11.8
1978	193 519	11.7	158 055	20 292	12.8
1979	217 974	12.6	178 544	23 792	13.3
1980	248 188	13.9	203 161	28 960	14.3
1981	289 797	16.8	235 056	37 349	15.9
1982	320 241	10.5	259 065	48 039	18.5
1983	337 138	5.3	270 794	40 963	15.1
1984	365 056	8.3	294 145	44 020	15.0
1985	395 166	8.2	317 392	44 390	14.0
1986	423 088	7.1	334 854	39 244	11.7
1987	454 736	7.5	356 134	35 928	10.1
1988	499 206	9.8	388 639	40 903	10.5
1989	542 295	8.6	425 566	47 744	11.2
1990	581 741	7.3	449 644	50 030	11.1
1991	600 658	3.3	464 289	52 832	11.4
1992	616 055	2.6	475 645	53 381	11.2
1993	627 885	1.9	486 641	48 618	10.0
1994	640 275	2.0	493 625	39 345	8.0
1995	666 390	4.0	511 378	37 608	7.4
1996	681 509	2.3	519 105	27 924	5.4
1997	701 049	2.9	529 082	11 353	2.1
1998[1]	727 444	3.8	545 585	6 573	1.2

Source: © *Statistics Canada*

(1) As of June 1999.

Tax Reductions

*S*ince Finance Minister Paul Martin forecast a balanced-or-better budget for 1998–99 and the following two years, he introduced some tax reductions in the 1999 federal budget. The budget increased the base for the personal tax credit, effective July 1, 1999. It also eliminated the 3 percent federal surtax on higher incomes, extending the process begun in the 1998 budget. There is no change to the 5 percent surtax on high-income individuals. The budget also commits $300 million to increase Canada Child Tax Benefit payments to modest- and lower-income families.

These measures will provide Canadians with a cumulative total of $7.7 billion in income-tax relief over the next three fiscal years, says Mr. Martin. When measures from the 1998 budget are added in, he adds, tax relief from the two budgets combined amounts to $16.5 billion over three years.

Source: *1999 Federal Budget Commentary*

INVESTMENT

Investment: A Glossary of Terms

Annual report: A report issued by a company to its shareholders at the end of the fiscal year. It contains a report on company operations and formal financial statements.

Bankers' acceptance: A commercial draft backed by the guarantee of a bank. The bankers' acceptance promises repayment on a certain date, usually not more than 90 days ahead, and bears a rate of return competitive with other chartered bank securities.

Bear market: A market in which prices are falling.

Bid and ask: The bid price is the highest price anyone is willing to pay to buy a stock; the ask is the lowest price anyone will accept to sell a stock. Together, the bid and ask prices are a quote.

Blue chip stocks: Stocks with good investment qualities, usually common shares of well-established companies with good earnings records and long-time dividend payments.

Board lot: A unit of trading. Board lots on the Toronto Stock Exchange are: under 10 cents each—1000 shares; between 10 cents and 99 cents each—500 shares; at and above $1 each—100 shares.

Bond: A written promise or IOU by the issuer to repay a fixed amount of borrowed money on a specified date, and to pay a set annual rate of interest in the meantime, generally at semi-annual intervals. Bonds are usually considered a safe investment because the borrower (whether a company or the government) must make interest payments before its money is spent on anything else.

Bull market: A market in which prices are rising.

Call: An option to buy a fixed amount of a certain stock at a specified price within a specified time.

Canada Savings Bonds: These are issued each fall, and are popular with small investors because they come in denominations starting at $100. They are not traded. They have a term of several years and a minimum guaranteed rate of interest. However, the government sets an effective rate during the issuing period each year, and adjusts it when necessary to conform with interest rate trends. Interest can be awarded yearly or compounded, depending upon the type of bond.

Capital gain or loss: Profit or loss resulting from the sale of an asset, such as a security. The gain or loss is the difference between the buying and selling price of the security with commissions figured in.

Commercial paper: Short-term negotiable securities issued by corporations that call for the payment of a specific amount of money at a given time.

Common shares: Securities issued by the company that represent part-ownership in the company. Common shares sometimes carry a voting privilege and entitle the holder to a share in the company's profits, usually issued in the form of dividends.

Convertible bond: A corporate bond (see below) that may be converted into a stated number of shares of the corporation's common stock. Its price tends to fluctuate with the price of the stock, as well as with changes in interest rates.

Corporate bonds: Evidence of debt by a corporation. The bond bears interest much like a government bond, and matures at a certain date in the future. Considered safer than the common or preferred stock of the same company.

Day order: An order to buy or sell a security valid only for the day the order is given.

Dividend: A portion of a company's profit paid to the common and preferred shareholders. The amount is decided upon by the company's board of directors, and may be paid in cash or stock.

Equities: Common and preferred stocks that represent a share in the ownership of a company.

Ex-dividend: Without dividend. The buyer of shares quoted ex-dividend is not entitled to receive an already declared dividend. When shares are un-dividend, the purchaser will receive the declared dividend.

Floor trader: A brokerage-firm employee who works on the stock exchange trading floor, and is responsible for executing buy and sell orders on behalf of the firm and its clients.

Futures: Contracts to buy or sell specific quantities of a commodity or financial instrument with delivery delayed until some agreed-upon time in the future.

Government of Canada bonds: These bear a fixed rate of interest and a maturation date in the future, and are traded on the market, with the price rising and falling in response to interest rate trends. ▶

▶ Long-term government bonds are considered a safe investment. Provinces and municipalities may also issue long-term bonds.

Index: Statistical measure of the state of the stock market or economy, based on the performance of stocks or other components. Examples are the TSE 300 Composite Index and the Toronto 35 Index.

Limit order: An order to buy or sell securities in which the client has specified the price. The order can be executed only at the specified price or a better one.

Liquidity: The measure of how quickly an investor can turn securities into cash. A security is liquid if it can be bought and sold quickly with small price changes between transactions.

Long: A term signifying ownership of securities. "I am long 100 XYZ" means that the speaker owns 100 shares of XYZ.

Margin: The amount paid by clients when they use credit to buy a security, the balance being loaned by their brokers.

Market order: An order to buy a security immediately at the best possible price.

Money market: Part of the capital market established for short-term borrowing and lending of funds. Money market dealers conduct business over the telephone, and trade securities such as short-term (three years and less) government bonds, government treasury bills and commercial paper.

Mutual fund: A portfolio, or selection, of professionally bought and managed stocks in which the investor pools money with thousands of others. A share price is based on net asset value, or the value of all the investments owned by the fund, less any debt, divided by the total number of shares. The major advantage is less risk—an investment is spread out over many stocks, and if one or two do badly, the remainder may shield the investor from the losses. Bond funds are mutual funds that deal in the bond market exclusively. Money market mutual funds concentrate on debt instruments sold on the money market. Equity mutual funds place their investments in the common shares of companies.

Odd lot: A number of shares less than a board lot.

Open order: An order to buy or sell a security at a specified price, valid until executed or cancelled.

Over-the-counter: The over-the-counter (OTC) or unlisted market is the market maintained by securities dealers for issues not listed on a stock exchange.

Penny stock: Low-priced, often speculative issues selling at less than $1 a share.

Preferred shares: Shares that carry dividends at fixed rates that must be paid before any dividends are paid to common shareholders.

Price/earnings ratio: A common stock's current market price divided by the company's annual per share earnings.

Prospectus: A legal document describing securities being offered for sale to the public. It must be prepared in accordance with provincial securities commission regulations.

Put: An option to sell a fixed amount of a certain stock at a specified price within a specified time.

Registered representative: A salesperson or broker employed by an investment firm. Salespersons must be registered with the provincial securities commission.

Right: A temporary privilege granted to existing common shareholders to purchase additional shares directly from the company at a stated price.

Settlement date: The date on which a securities buyer must pay for a purchase or a seller must deliver the securities sold. In general, settlement must be made on or before the third business day following the transaction date.

Short sale: The sale of shares that the seller does not own. The seller is speculating that the stock price will fall, in the hope of later purchasing the same number of securities at a lower price, thereby making a profit. Sellers must advise their brokers when they are selling short.

Stock yield: The percentage of the dividend paid in relation to the price of the stock. For example, a stock selling at $40 a share with an annual dividend of $2 a share yields 5 percent.

Transfer agent: A trust company appointed by a company to keep a record of the names, addresses and numbers of shares held by its shareholders. Transfer agents are often responsible for distributing dividend cheques.

Underwriting: The purchase for resale of a new issue of securities by an investment dealer or group of dealers.

Warrant: A certificate giving the holder the right to purchase securities at a stipulated price within a specified period of time. They are often detachable and may be traded separately.

Government of Canada Average Bond Yields, 1981–98

Year	1 to 3 Years	3 to 5 Years	5 to 10 Years	10 Years and Over
1981	15.97	15.68	15.29	15.22
1982	13.95	14.00	14.03	14.26
1983	10.18	10.61	11.11	11.79
1984	11.67	11.91	12.42	12.75
1985	10.12	10.39	10.78	11.04
1986	9.09	9.21	9.37	9.52
1987	9.19	9.42	9.55	9.95
1988	9.67	9.77	9.76	10.22
1989	10.71	10.20	9.83	9.92
1990	11.65	11.19	10.82	10.85
1991	8.99	9.16	9.36	9.76
1992	7.03	7.43	8.16	8.77
1993	5.89	6.46	7.24	7.85
1994	7.14	7.79	9.01	8.63
1995	7.26	7.63	7.93	9.49
1996	5.35	5.80	6.88	7.75
1997	4.53	4.98	5.80	6.66
1998	5.05	5.13	5.21	5.45

Source: *Bank of Canada*

Value of RRSP Holdings by Canadians

(millions of dollars)

Year	Value	Year	Value	Year	Value
1961	2 812	1974	20 092	1987	102 660
1962	2 968	1975	24 592	1988	115 884
1963	3 120	1976	29 992	1989	116 356
1964	3 328	1977	33 184	1990	132 316
1965	3 648	1978	36 416	1991	143 704
1966	6 912	1979	39 372	1992	158 212
1967	7 804	1980	43 912	1993	162 548
1968	8 572	1981	55 940	1994	171 468
1969	9 616	1982	61 732	1995	179 032
1970	10 152	1983	70 736	1996	177 220
1971	10 760	1984	76 292	1997	183 832
1972	12 344	1985	85 084	1998	191 072
1973	14 512	1986	92 916		

Source: *© Statistics Canada*   (1) Not adjusted for inflation.

Toronto and Montreal Stock Exchange Activity

Year	Montreal Stock Exchange		Toronto Stock Exchange	
	Combined volume (millions)	Value of shares traded ($millions)	Combined volume (millions)	Value of shares traded ($millions)
1960	77	481	470	1 223
1965	428	1 251	934	3 199
1970	268	1 205	523	3 654
1975	135	1 385	470	4 089
1980	299	3 857	2 009	29 514
1985	643	10 553	3 298	44 196
1990	1 365	15 405	5 660	64 009
1991	1 350	18 333	5 838	67 749
1992	1 683	21 064	7 326	76 161
1993	2 706	30 330	14 882	147 057
1994	2 482	32 443	15 460	182 202
1995	2 881	38 834	15 758	207 665
1996	4 302	50 167	22 341	301 299
1997	4 321	61 912	25 670	423 170
1998	3 532	55 647	26 800	493 212

Source: *Monthly Review, Montreal and Canadian Stock Exchanges; Toronto Stock Exchange*

Global Superlatives

Largest continent	Asia	44 485 900 sq. km
Smallest continent	Australia	7 682 300 sq. km
Largest ocean	Pacific	166 241 000 sq. km
Smallest ocean	Arctic	9 485 000 sq. km
Deepest point of any ocean	Mariana Trench, Pacific Ocean	10 924 m
Largest sea	South China Sea	2 974 600 sq. km
Largest lake	Caspian Sea, Russian Fed., Kazakhstan, Turkmenistan, Iran, Azerbaijan	371 000 sq. km
Deepest lake	Lake Baykal, Russia	1 620 m
Largest freshwater lake	Lake Superior, North America	82 100 sq. km
Highest major lake	Lake Titicaca, Bolivia-Peru, South America	3 809 m
Lowest major lake	Caspian Sea, Russian Fed., Kazakhstan, Turkmenistan, Iran, Azerbaijan	-28 m
Largest island	Greenland, Denmark	2 175 600 sq. km
Longest reef	Great Barrier Reef, Australia-Papua New Guinea	2 027 km
Longest river	Nile, Africa	6 671 km
Largest nation	Russia	17 075 272 sq. km
Smallest nation	Vatican City	.44 ha. km
Most populous nation	People's Republic of China (July 1998 est)	pop. 1 236 914 658
Oldest city	Damascus, Syria	continuously inhabited since c. 2500 B.C.
Highest point	Mount Everest, Nepal-Tibet	8 848 m
Lowest point	Dead Sea, Israel-Jordan	-400 m
Highest city	La Paz, Bolivia	3 636 m
Coldest city	Norilsk, Russia	average temp. -10.9°C
Hottest city	Djibouti, Djibouti	average temp. 30°C
Coldest place	Plateau Station, Antarctica	-56.7°C
Hottest place	Dalol, Danakil Depression, Ethiopia	35°C avg.
Coldest recorded temperature	Vostok, Antarctica (Australian territory), July 21, 1983	-89.2°C
Hottest recorded temperature (shade)	Al-Aziziyah, Libya, Sept. 13, 1922	58°C
Wettest spot	Mount Waialeale, Kauai, Hawaii	avg. ann. rainfall of 16 800 mm
Driest spot	Atacama Desert, Chile	avg. ann. precipitation barely measurable
Greatest snowfall in 24 hrs	Silver Lake, Colorado, U.S., Apr. 14–15, 1921	193 cm
Greatest rainfall in 24 hrs	Cilaos, Reunion Island, Indian Ocean, Mar. 15–16, 1952	1 870 cm
Largest desert	Sahara, Africa	9 million sq. km
Largest waterfall (by volume)	Khone, Kampuchea-Laos	11 610 cu. m/sec.
Tallest waterfall	Angel Falls, Venezuela	807 m
Largest gorge	Grand Canyon, Colorado River, Arizona	349 km long; 6–20 km wide; 1.6 km deep
Deepest gorge	Colca River Canyon, Peru	3 223 m
Oldest tree	a bristlecone pine, Wheeler's Peak, Nevada	approx. age of 5 100 yrs.
Greatest tides	Bay of Fundy, Nova Scotia	14.5 m
Most devastating volcanic eruption	Tambora, Sumbawa, Indonesia, Apr. 5–7, 1815	92 000 deaths
Longest covered bridge	Hartland, New Brunswick	390.8 m
Longest bridge	Confederation, linking New Brunswick and Prince Edward Island (main span 11 km); bridge between the tip of Florida and Key West is also 11 km.	12.9 km
Largest man-made lake	Owen Falls, Uganda	2 700 000 cu. m
Longest street	Yonge Street, from Toronto, Ont. to Rainy River (at. Man. border)	1 896.2 km
Tallest building	Sears Tower, Chicago, Illinois	110 storeys, 443 m
Tallest free-standing structure	CN Tower, Toronto, Ont.	553.34 m
Most common language	Mandarin	approx. 750 million speakers
Most common religion	Christianity	(approx. ⅓ of world's pop.) 1 949 566 000

GEOGRAPHY

The Continents

Continent	Total Area (sq. km)	% of Earth's Land	Population	% of World Total
Asia	44 485 900	30.0	3 292 337 000	62.4
Africa	30 269 680	20.4	702 013 000	13.2
North and Central America	24 235 280	16.3	441 826 000	8.4
South America	17 820 770	12.0	309 634 000	5.9
Antarctica	13 209 000	8.9	uninhabited	
Europe	10 530 750	7.1	504 925 000	9.6
Oceania	7 830 682	5.3	27 752 000	.5

Source: *National Geographic Atlas of the World (1990), FAO Production Yearbook (1993)*

Highest and Lowest Points on Each Continent

Continent	Highest Point (metres)		Lowest Point (metres)	
Asia	Everest	8 848	Dead Sea	-400
South America	Aconcagua	6 960	Valdés Peninsula	-40
North America	McKinley (Denali)	6 194	Death Valley	-86
Africa	Kilimanjaro	5 895	Lake Assal	-156
Europe	El'brus	5 642	Caspian Sea	-28
Antarctica	Vinson Massif	4 897	—	-2 538
Australia	Kosciusko	2 228	Lake Eyre	-16

Source: *National Geographic Atlas of the World (1990)*

World's Highest Cities

City	Altitude	City	Altitude
La Paz, Bolivia	3 636 m	Mexico City, Mexico	2 309 m
Quito, Ecuador	2 850 m	Nairobi, Kenya	1 820 m
Sucre, Bolivia	2 790 m	Johannesburg, South Africa	1 734 m
Bogotá, Colombia	2 639 m	**Calgary, Alta.**	**1 045 m**
Addis Ababa, Ethiopia	2 450 m	Sao Paulo, Brazil	776 m

Source: *Global Atlas, Gage Educational Publishing Co., South American Handbook.*

Oceans' Area and Depth

Ocean	Area (sq. km)	% of Earth's Water Area	Deepest Point	Depth (metres)
Pacific	166 241 000	46.0	Mariana Trench	10 924
Atlantic	86 557 000	23.9	Puerto Rico Trench	8 605
Indian	73 427 000	20.3	Java Trench	7 258
Arctic	9 485 000	2.6	Eurasia Basin	5 122

Source: *National Geographic Atlas of the World (1990)*

Major Seas of the World

Sea	Area (sq. km)	Average Depth (metres)	Sea	Area (sq. km)	Average Depth (metres)
South China	2 974 600	1 464	Sea of Japan	1 012 900	1 667
Caribbean	2 515 900	2 575	Hudson Bay	730 100	93
Mediterranean	2 510 000	1 501	East China	664 600	189
Bering	2 261 100	1 491	Andaman	564 900	1 118
Gulf of Mexico	1 507 600	1 615	Black	507 900	1 191
Sea of Okhotsk	1 392 100	973	Red	453 000	538

Source: *National Geographic Atlas of the World (1990)*

Largest Lakes of the World

Lake	Location	Area sq. mi.	Area sq. km
Caspian (Sea)	Iran/Caspian Sea, Russian Fed., Kazakhstan, Turkmenistan, Iran, Azerbaijan	146 100	378 400
Superior	Canada/U.S.	31 760	82 260
Aral (Sea)	Kazakhstan-Uzbekistan	24 750	64 100
Victoria	Kenya/Tanzania/Uganda	24 300	62 940
Huron	Canada/U.S.	23 000	59 580
Michigan	U.S.	22 400	58 020
20 Tanganyika	Burundi/Tanzania/Zaire/Zambia	12 350	32 000
Baykal	Russia	12 160	31 500
Great Bear	**NWT, Canada**	**12 030**	**31 150**
Great Slave	**NWT, Canada**	**11 030**	**28 570**

Source: *World Facts and Figures, 1989; Victor Showers; John Wiley & Sons, Inc.*

Major Islands of the World

Island	Area (sq. km)	Island	Area (sq. km)
Greenland (Denmark)	2 175 600	Sumatra (Indonesia)	427 300
New Guinea (independent)	792 500	Honshu (Japan)	227 400
Borneo (Indonesia)	725 500	Great Britain (independent)	218 100
Madagascar (independent)	587 000	**Victoria (Canada)**	**217 300**
Baffin (Canada)	**507 500**	**Ellesmere (Canada)**	**196 200**

Source: *National Geographic Atlas of the World (1990)*

Highest Waterfalls in the World

Fall/Country	Height[1] (m)	Fall/Country	Height[1] (m)
Angel, Venezuela	807	Pilao, Brazil	524
Monge, Norway	774	Montoya, Venezuela	505
Itatinga, Brazil	628	Ribbon, United States	491
Ormeli, Norway	563	Great, Guyana	488
Tusse, Norway	533	Vestre Mardals, Norway	468

Source: *World Facts and Figures, 1989; Victor Showers; John Wiley & Sons Inc.*

(1) Height of the greatest individual leap.

Highest Mountains by Continent

Peak	Mountain Range or System	Location	Elevation[1] ft	Elevation[1] m	First Ascent
■ Africa					
Kibo	n.a.	Tanganyika, Tanzania	19 340	5 890	1889
Mawensi	n.a.	Tanganyika, Tanzania	17 100	5 210	1912
Batian	n.a.	Kenya	17 050	5 200	1899
Nelion	n.a.	Kenya	17 020	5 190	1929
Margherita	Ruwenzori	Uganda/D. Rep. of Congo	16 760	5 110	1906
Alexandra	Ruwenzori	Uganda/D. Rep. of Congo	16 700	5 090	1906
Albert	Ruwenzori	Dem. Rep. of Congo	16 690	5 090	1932
Savoia	Ruwenzori	Uganda	16 330	4 980	1906
Elena	Ruwenzori	Uganda	16 300	4 970	1906
Elizabeth	Ruwenzori	Uganda	16 170	4 930	1953
■ Antarctica					
—	Sentinel	Antarctica	16 860	5140	1966
Tyree	Sentinel	Antarctica	16 290	4970	1967
Shinn	Sentinel	Antarctica	15 750	4800	1966
Gardner	Sentinel	Antarctica	15 370	4690	1966
Epperly	Sentinel	Antarctica	15 100	4600	n.a.
Kirkpatrick	Queen Alexandra	Antarctica	14 850	4530	n.a.
Elizabeth	Queen Alexandra	Antarctica	14 700	4480	n.a.
Markham	Queen Elizabeth	Antarctica	14 290	4360	n.a.
Bell	Queen Alexandra	Antarctica	14 120	4300	n.a.
Mackellar	Queen Alexandra	Antarctica	14 100	4300	n.a.
■ Asia					
Everest (alt Qomolangma, Chumulangma)	Nepal Himalaya	China/Nepal	29 030	8 850	1953
K2 (alt Chogori, Dapsang, Godwin Austen)	Karakoram	Pakistan-held Kashmir	28 250	8 610	1954
Kangchenjunga (alt Kanchenjunga): highest peak	Nepal Himalaya	India/Nepal	28 170	8 590	1955
Lhotse (alt E1, Luozi, Lotzu)	Nepal Himalaya	China/Nepal	27 890	8 500	1956
Kangchenjunga: S peak	Nepal Himalaya	India/Nepal	27 800	8 470	n.a.
Makalu I	Nepal Himalaya	China/Nepal	27 790	8 470	1955
Kangchenjunga: W peak	Nepal Himalaya	India/Nepal	27 620	8 420	1973
Lhotse Shar (alt Lhotse: E peak) .	Nepal Himalaya	China/Nepal	27 500	8 380	1970
Dhaulagiri I (alt Daulagiri I)	Nepal Himalaya	Nepal	26 810	8 170	1960
Cho Oyu (alt Zhuoaoyu, Choaoyu): highest peak	Nepal Himalaya	China/Nepal	26 750	8 150	1954
■ Europe					
Elbrus (for Elborus): W peak	Caucasus (off Kavkaz)	Russia	18 480	5630	1874
Elbrus: E peak	Caucasus	Russia	18 360	5 590	1829
Shkhara: E peak	Caucasus	Georgia/Russia	17 060	5 200	1888
Dykh(-Tau): W peak	Caucasus	Russia	17 050	5 200	1888
Dykh(-Tau): E peak	Caucasus	Russia	16 900	5 150	1938
Koshtan(-Tau)	Caucasus	Russia	16 880	5 140	1888
Shkhara: W peak	Caucasus	Georgia/Russia	16 880	5 140	n.a.
Pushkina	Caucasus	Russia	16 730	5 100	1938
Dzhangi(-Tau): NW peak	Caucasus	Georgia	16 570	5 050	1903
Kazbek: E peak	Caucasus	Georgia	16 560	5 050	1868 ▶

► ■ **North America**

McKinley: S peak	Alaska	Alaska, U.S.	20 320	6 190	1913
Logan: central peak	Saint Elias	Yukon, Canada	19 520	5 959	1925
Logan: W peak	Saint Elias	Yukon, Canada	19 470	5 930	1925
McKinley: N peak	Alaska	Alaska, U.S.	19 470	5 930	1910
Logan: E peak	Saint Elias	Yukon, Canada	19 420	5 920	1957
Citlaltepetl (alt Orizaba)	Neovolcanica	Puebla-Veracruz, Mexico	18 410	5 610	1848
Logan: N peak	Saint Elias	Yukon, Canada	18 270	5 570	1959
Saint Elias	Saint Elias	Canada/U.S.	18 010	5 490	1897
Popocatepetl	Neovolcanica	Puebla, Mexico	17 930	5 460	1520
Foraker	Alaska	Alaska, U.S.	17 400	5 300	1934

■ **Oceania**

Jaya (for Carstensz, Djaja, Sukarno)	Sudirman (for Nassau)	Irian Jaya, Indonesia	16 500	5 030	1936
Daam	Jayawijaya (for Djajawidjaja, Orange)	Irian Jaya, Indonesia	16 150	4 920	n.a.
Pilimsit (for Idenburg)	Sudirman	Irian Jaya, Indonesia	15 750	4 800	1962
Trikora (for Wilhelmina)	Jayawijaya	Irian Jaya, Indonesia	15 580	4 750	1913
Mandala (for Juliana)	Jayawijaya	Irian Jaya, Indonesia	15 420	4 700	1959
Wilhelm	Bismarck	Papua New Guinea	15 400	4 690	n.a.
Wisnumurti (for Jan Pieterszoon Coen)	Jayawijaya	Irian Jaya, Indonesia	15 080	4 590	n.a.
Yamin (for Prins Hendrik)	Jayawijaya	Irian Jaya, Indonesia	14 860	4 530	n.a.
Kubor	Kubor	Papua New Guinea	14 300	4 360	n.a.
Herbert	Bismarck	Papua New Guinea	14 000	4 270	n.a.

■ **South America**

Aconcagua	Andes	Mendoza, Argentina	22 840	6 960	1897
Ojos del Salado: SE peak	Andes	Argentina/Chile	22 560	6 870	1937
Bonete	Andes	La Rioja, Argentina	22 550	6 870	1913
Pissis	Andes	Catamarca, La Rioja, Argentina	22 240	6 780	1937
Huascaran: S peak	Blanca (Andes)	Peru	22 210	6 770	1932
Mercedario	Andes	San Juan, Argentina	22 210	6 770	1934
Llullaillaco	Andes	Argentina/Chile	22 100[1]	6 730	bef 1550
Libertador (for Cachi: N peak)	Andes	Salta, Argentina	22 050	6 720	1950
Ojos del Salado: NW peak	Andes	Argentina/Chile	22 050	6 720	1937
Tupungato	Andes	Argentina/Chile	21 900	6 670	1897

Source: *World Facts and Figures, 1989; Victor Showers; John Wiley & Sons, Inc.*

(1) Rounded figures except from some Canadian peaks from Energy, Mines and Resources Canada. n.a. not available or not applicable.

Longest Rivers in the World

River	Outflow and Location	Length	
		mi.	km
Nile-Kagera-Ruvuvu-Luvironza	Mediterranean Sea, Egypt	4 140	6 670
Amazon-Ucayali-Tambo-Ene-Apurimac	Atlantic Ocean, Amapa-Para, Brazil	4 080	6 570
Yangtze	East China Sea, Jiangsu, China	3 720	5 980
Mississippi-Missouri-Jefferson-Beaverhead-Red Rock	Gulf of Mexico, Louisiana, U.S.	3 710	5 970
Yenisey-Angara-Selenga-Ider	Yenisey Gulf of Kara Sea, Russia	3 650	5 870
Amur-Argun-Kerulen	Tatar Strait, Russia	3 590	5 780
Ob-Irtysh	Gulf of Ob of Kara Sea, Russia	3 360	5 410
Plata-Parana-Grande	Atlantic Ocean, Argentina-Uruguay	3 030	4 880
Huang	Gulf of Chihli of Yellow Sea, Shandong, China	3 010	4 840
Congo-Lualaba	Atlantic Ocean, Angola-Dem. Rep. of Congo	2 880	4 630

Source: *World Facts and Figures, 1989; Victor Showers; John Wiley & Sons, Inc.*

POPULATION

The World's 20 Most Populous Nations, 1997

(millions)

China	1 243.7	Mexico	94.3
India	960.2	Germany	82.2
United States	271.6	Vietnam	76.5
Indonesia	203.5	Iran	71.5
Brazil	163.1	Philippines	70.7
Russian Federation	147.7	Egypt	64.5
Pakistan	143.8	Turkey	62.8
Japan	125.6	Ethiopia	60.1
Bangladesh	122.0	Thailand	59.2
Nigeria	118.4	France	58.5

Source: *The State of the World Population, 1997,* UN Population Fund

The World's 20 Most Populous Nations by 2025

(millions)

China	1 480.4	Mexico	130.2
India	1 330.2	Iran	128.3
United States	332.5	Japan	121.3
Indonesia	275.2	Vietnam	110.1
Pakistan	268.9	Democratic Republic of the Congo	105.9
Nigeria	238.4	Philippines	105.2
Brazil	216.6	Egypt	95.8
Bangladesh	180.0	Turkey	85.8
Ethiopia	136.3	Germany	80.9
Russian Federation	131.4	South Africa	71.6

Source: *The State of the World Population, 1997,* UN Population Fund

The World's 20 Least Populous Nations, 1997

(millions)

Jamaica	2.5	Botswana	1.5
Latvia	2.5	Estonia	1.5
Mauritania	2.4	Trinidad and Tobago	1.3
Oman	2.4	Mauritius	1.1
United Arab Emirates	2.3	Gabon	1.1
Macedonia	2.2	Guinea-Bissau	1.1
Lesotho	2.1	Belize	0.2
Slovenia	1.9	New Caledonia	0.2
Kuwait	1.7	Vanautu	0.2
Namibia	1.6	Bhutan	0.1

Source: *The State of the World Population, 1997,* UN Population Fund

The World's 20 Least Populous Nations by 2025

(millions)

Uruguay	3.7	Gabon	2.1
Ireland	3.7	Latvia	2.1
Bhutan	3.6	Guinea-Bissau	1.9
Lithuania	3.5	Trinidad and Tobago	1.7
Jamaica	3.4	Slovenia	1.7
United Arab Emirates	3.3	Mauritius	1.5
Namibia	3.0	Estonia	1.3
Kuwait	2.9	Belize	0.4
Botswana	2.6	New Caledonia	0.3
Macedonia	2.5	Vanautu	0.3

Source: *The State of the World Population, 1997,* UN Population Fund

Population Projections, by Region and for Selected Countries: 2000 to 2030

(in thousands)

Region and Country	2000	2030
World total	**6 091 351**	**8 371 602**
More developed[1]	1 186 990	1 212 147
Less developed[1]	4 904 360	7 159 455
Least developed	660 347	1 267 203
Africa	819 910	1 588 909
Eastern Africa[2]	255 500	529 882
Burundi	6 974	13 428
Eritrea	3 809	7 019
Ethiopia	66 175	153 598
Kenya	30 340	53 632
Madagascar	17 395	38 179
Malawi	10 984	22 601
Mauritius	1 179	1 529
Mozambique	19 563	39 139
Rwanda	7 674	13 807
Somalia	11 530	26 548
Uganda	22 459	50 053
United Republic of Tanzania	33 687	68 571
Zambia	9 133	17 491
Zimbabwe	12 423	20 567
Middle Africa	95 385	209 289
Angola	12 781	28 558
Cameroon	15189	31 538
Cen. African Rep.	3 640	6 514
Chad	7 270	13 866
Congo	2 982	6 415
Democratic Republic of the Congo 118 985		51 749
Gabon	1 235	2 308
Northern Africa[2]	175 037	27 1243
Algeria	31 599	50 212
Egypt	68 119	100 616
Libya	6 387	14 301
Morocco	28 984	41 857
Sudan	29 823	49 619
Tunisia	9 837	14 167
Southern Africa	52 887	87 942
Botswana	1 619	2 728
Lesotho	2 294	4 396
Namibia	1 733	3 266
South Africa	46 257	75 765
Western Africa[2]	241 102	490 554
Benin	6 222	13 598
Burkina Faso[3]	12 057	26 157
Côte d'Ivoire	15 144	25 873
Ghana	19928	39 640
Guinea	7 861	17 017
Guinea-Bissau	1 180	2 090
Liberia	3 256	7 363
Mali	12 559	27 362
Mauritania	2 580	4 819
Niger	10 805	25 158
Nigeria	128 786	261 588
Senegal	9 495	18 419
Sierra Leone	4 866	8 944
Togo	4 676	9 664
Latin America & the Caribbean	514 688	719 858
Caribbean[2]	37 757	50 311
Cuba	11 201	11 791
Dominican Rep.	8 495	11 663
Haiti	7 817	13 707
Jamaica	2 587	3 515
Puerto Rico	3 877	4 778
Trinidad and Tobago	1 341	1 746
Central America	135 497	199 203
Belize	242	400
Costa Rica	3 798	5 923
El Salvador	6 319	9 722
Guatemala	12 222	23 425
Honduras	6 485	11 392
Mexico	98 881	136 240
Nicaragua	4 694	8 168
Panama	2 856	3 933
South America[2]	341 434	470 344
Argentina	37 032	48 896
Bolivia	8 329	13 999
Brazil	169 202	223 801
Chile	15 211	20 240
Colombia	38 905	55 044
Ecuador	12 646	18 641
Paraguay	5 496	10 104
Peru	25 662	37 201
Uruguay	3 274	3 768
Venezuela	24 170	36 548
Northern America[2]	308 636	374 063
Canada	**30 679**	**36 633**
United States	277 825	337 277
Asia	3 688 535	4 956 764
Eastern Asia[2]	1 483 111	1 713 775
China	1 270 301	1 409 782
Japan	126 428	118 640
North Korea	23 913	31 098
South Korea	46 883	53 007
Mongolia	2 736	4 284
South-Eastern Asia[2]	521 983	722 807
Cambodia	11 207	17 870
Indonesia	212 565	286 441
Lao People's Democratic Republic 10 875		5 693
Malaysia	22 299	33 231
Myanmar	49 342	70 943
Philippines	75 037	111 266
Singapore	3 587	4 276
Thailand	60 495	70 735
Viet Nam	80 549	115 459
Southern Central Asia	1 495 977	2 201 533
Afghanistan	25 592	49 414
Bangladesh	128 310	189 056
Bhutan	2 032	4 003
India	1 006 770	1 384 188
Iran	76 429	137 089
Nepal	24 347	43 120
Pakistan	156 007	286 736
Sri Lanka	18 821	24 704 ▶

▶ Western Asia[2]	187 463	318 648	Greece	10 597	9 885
Iraq	23 109	44 847	Italy	57 194	50 109
Israel	6 077	8 277	Macedonia	2 233	2 573
Jordan	6 330	12 976	Portugal	9 788	9 321
Kuwait	1 966	3 032	Slovenia	1 914	1 687
Lebanon	3 289	4 635	Spain	39 801	36 612
Oman	2 717	7 502	Yugoslavia	10 502	10 709
Saudi Arabia	21 661	46 455	**Western Europe**	184 077	181 713
Syria	16 126	28 089	Austria	8 292	8 180
Turkey	65 732	89 085	Belgium	10 257	10 203
United Arab Emirates	2 444	3 388	France	59 061	60 174
Yemen	18 118	44 691	Germany	82 688	79 105
Europe	729 328	690 090	The Netherlands	15 871	16 001
Eastern Europe	306 654	278 448	Switzerland	7 412	7 497
Bulgaria	8 306	7 282	**Oceania[2]**	30 253	41 918
Czech Republic	10 195	9 412	Australia	18 838	24 364
Hungary	9 811	8 448	Melanesia	6 489	10 739
Poland	38 727	39 939	New Caledonia	195	265
Romania	22 505	20 732	New Zealand	3 760	4 989
Slovakia	5 372	5 441	Papua New Guinea	4 811	7 966
Northern Europe[2]	93 736	95 530	Vanuatu	192	361
Denmark	5 274	5 316	**Former Soviet Union**		
Estonia	1 418	1 220	Armenia	3 662	4 252
Finland	5 179	5 275	Azerbaijan	7 828	10 034
Ireland	3 574	3 741	Belarus	10 284	9 468
Latvia	2 397	2 060	Georgia	5 418	5 836
Lithuania	3 690	3 474	Kazakhstan	16 928	20 596
Norway	4 407	4 684	Kyrgyzstan	4 543	6 255
Sweden	8 898	9 539	Republic of Moldova	4 458	4 932
United Kingdom	58 336	59 547	Russian Federation	146 196	127 874
Southern Europe[2]	144 861	134 399	Tajikistan	6 398	10 335
Albania	3 493	4 435	Turkmenistan	4 479	6 824
Bosnia & Herzegovina	4 338	4 229	Ukraine	50 801	44 920
Croatia	4 485	4 181	Uzbekistan	25 018	38 580

Source: *World Population Prospects: The 1996 Revision, Population Division of the United Nations*

(1) Region. (2) Includes areas not shown separately. (3) Formerly Upper Volta.

Beyond 6 Billion

*T*he United Nations Population Fund predicted that the 6 billionth baby would be born October 12, 1999. This represents a doubling of the world's estimated population since 1960. (Global population has quadrupled in the last century). The UNPFA also predicted that the world's population will continue to increase by 77 million a year, and could be 9 billion or more by 2050. The bulk of the increase is expected in the least developed countries, highlighting a trend that has seen population growth decrease as economic development increases.

Population statistics have also been affected by an increase in average life expectancy throughout the world. In 1950 the global death rate was 20 per year per thousand; in 1999, the rate was less than 10. Average global life expectancy is now 66 years, up from 46 five decades ago.

One of the most significant factors in both decreasing fertility and increased life expectancy is women's education—children of better-educated women are more likely to survive, and the women themselves are more likely to delay childbearing and be able to space the births of their children.

Threats to the people of the globe include climate change, environmental damage, new diseases and large scale social and economic instability. Each spreads more widely and more quickly in the "global village" than ever before. However, solutions based on social progress, technology and opportunities can also spread more quickly than ever before.

For more information about the state of the world's population, refer to UNFPA publications, or visit their web site at http:/www.unfpa.org

The World's Largest Corporations, 1998

Rank in 1998	Rank in 1997	Company (Ranked by 1998 Sales)	Country	Sales (millions)	Profits (millions)	Employees
1	1	General Motors	US	$161 315.0	$2 956.0	594 000
2	17	DaimlerChrysler	Germany	154 615.0	5 656.0	441 502
3	2	Ford Motor	US	144 416.0	22 071.0	345 175
4	8	Wal-Mart Stores	US	139 208.0	4 430.0	910 000
5	3	Mitsui	Japan	109 372.9	233.0	32 961
6	6	Itochu	Japan	108 749.1	(266.7)	5 775
7	4	Mitsubishi	Japan	107 184.4	244.0	36 000
8	7	Exxon	US	100 697.0	6 370.0	79 000
9	12	General Electric	US	100 469.0	9 296.0	293 000
10	11	Toyota Motor	Japan	99 740.1	2 786.5	183 879
11	5	Royal Dutch/Shell Group	Brit./Neth.	93 692.0	350.0	102 000
12	9	Marubeni	Japan	93 568.6	(921.0)	65 000
13	10	Sumitomo	Japan	89 020.7	(102.3)	30 700
14	14	Intl. Business Machines	US	81 667.0	6 328.0	291 067
15	16	AXA	France	78 729.3	1 702.4	87 896
16	58	Citigroup	US	76 431.0	5 807.0	170 100
17	22	Volkswagen	Germany	76 306.6	1 261.3	297 916
18	15	Nippon Telegraph & Telephone	Japan	76 118.7	4 715.1	224 400
19	20	BP Amoco	Britain	68 304.0	3 260.0	96 650
20	13	Nissho Iwai	Japan	67 741.7	(770.9)	19 461
21	19	Nippon Life Insurance	Japan	66 299.6	827.6	71 015
22	24	Siemens	Germany	66 037.8	370.3	416 000
23	28	Allianz	Germany	64 874.7	2 021.9	105 676
24	21	Hitachi	Japan	62 409.9	(2 650.5)	328 351
25	27	U.S. Postal Service	US	60 072.0	550.0	904 636

Top 25 Industry Totals, Ranked by Sales, 1998

Rank (by 1998 Sales)	Sales (millions)	Profits (millions)	Employees
Banks, Commercial and Savings	$1 291 120	$51 149	3 521 262
Motor Vehicles and Parts	1 109 949	44 772	3 577 247
Trading	848 061	274	515 009
Electronics, Electrical Equipment	778 602	28 253	3 649 669
Petroleum Refining	748 439	26 883	2 198 434
Food and Drug Stores	561 980	10 726	3 109 232
Telecommunications	520 961	49 704	2 090 024
Insurance: P&C (Stock)	425 722	20 614	640 544
Insurance: Life, Health (Mutual)	416 966	8 986	467 798
General Merchandisers	394 913	9 819	2 552 963
Insurance: Life, Health (Stock)	379 561	12 296	439 648
Utilities, Gas and Electric	337 707	12 126	696 684
Computers, Office Equipment	281 740	10 119	972 766
Chemicals	257 477	13 886	897 695
Food	217 739	7 829	993 394
Pharmaceuticals	204 400	35 402	729 649
Aerospace	184 426	7 716	952 547
Specialty Retailer	177 554	7 863	897 989
Mail, Package, Freight Delivery	175 673	4 095	2 257 636
Industrial and Farm Equipment	169 512	5 938	853 764
Wholesalers	158 310	977	214 234
Engineering, Construction	153 831	(726)	595 648
Diversified Financials	145 110	13 066	261 832
Miscellaneous	120 394	2 580	608 764
Airlines	119 800	5 038	597 957

World Agricultural Production, 1997

(thousands of metric tons)

	1992 Total	1997 Total		1992 Total	1997 Total
■ Total Cereals			**■ Corn**		
World production	1 970 920	2 096 430	World production	531 913	585 828
North and Central America	435 358	427 210	North and Central America	265 971	266 635
Europe	254 722	304 658	Europe	52 692	71 600
Oceania	26 027	29 534	Oceania	437	576
Africa	90 644	109 242	Africa	28 376	37 891
Asia	890 254	971 956	Asia	131 262	143 082
South America	85 045	100 751	South America	46 115	56 459
■ Wheat			**■ Barley**		
World production	565 126	609 566	World production	165 788	156 617
North and Central America	100 659	96 700	North and Central America	21 570	22 320
Europe	114 989	130 561	Europe	59 575	65 790
Oceania	14 930	18 810	Oceania	5 716	6 034
Africa	13 330	15 700	Africa	4 598	3 854
Asia	216 182	249 630	Asia	20 642	20 856
South America	15 154	19 683	South America	1 343	1 512
■ Rice (paddy)			**■ Root Crops**		
World production	526 032	573 263	World production	599 787	639 896
North and Central America	10 281	10 376	North and Central America	27 557	29 733
Europe	2 277	2 669	Europe	85 293	80 235
Oceania	1 145	1 371	Oceania	3 120	3 283
Africa	13 761	16 552	Africa	126 848	135 553
Asia	480 142	523 243	Asia	242 523	266 182
South America	16 486	17 994	South America	39 441	47 069
■ Coarse Grains			**■ Potatoes**		
World production	879 762	913 596	World production	277 687	295 407
North and Central America	324 418	320 134	North and Central America	24 597	26 794
Europe	137 455	171 428	Europe	85 217	80168
Oceania	9 952	9 352	Oceania	1 417	1 592
Africa	63 552	76 991	Africa	7 677	9 275
Asia	193 930	199 083	Asia	73 882	86 310
South America	53 405	63 074	South America	9 893	13 429

NOTES: The country categories are as follows: **North and Central America:** Anguilla, Antigua and Barbuda, Aruba, Bahamas, Barbados, Belize, Bermuda, British Virgin Islands, Canada, Cayman Islands, Costa Rica, Cuba, Dominica, Dominican Republic, El Salvador, Greenland, Grenada, Guadeloupe, Guatemala, Haiti, Honduras, Jamaica, Martinique, Mexico, Montserrat, Netherlands Antilles, Nicaragua, Panama, Puerto Rico, Saint Kitts and Nevis, Saint Lucia, Saint Pierre and Miquelon, Saint Vincent and the Grenadines, Trinidad and Tobago, Turks and Caicos Islands, United States, United States Virgin Islands; **Europe:** Albania, Andorra, Austria, Belarus, Belgium-Luxembourg, Bosnia and Herzegovina, Bulgaria, Croatia, former Czechoslovakia, Czech Republic, Denmark, Estonia, Faeroe Islands, Finland, France, Germany, Gibraltar, Greece, Holy See, Hungary, Iceland, Ireland, Italy, Latvia, Liechtenstein, Lithuania, the former Yugoslav Republic of Macedonia, Malta, Moldova, Monaco, Netherlands, Norway, Poland, Portugal, Romania, Russian Federation, San Marino, Slovakia, Slovenia, Spain, Sweden, Switzerland, Ukraine, United Kingdom, Federal Republic of Yugoslavia (Serbia and Montenegro), former Socialist Federal Republic of Yugoslavia; **Oceania:** American Samoa, Australia, Caton and Enderbury Islands, Christmas Island, Cocos (Keeling) Islands, Cook Islands, Fiji, French Polynesia, ▶

	1992 Total	1997 Total		1992 Total	1997 Total
■ Total Pulses			**■ Cocoa Beans**		
World production	51 021	57 651	World production	2 490	2 918
North and Central America	3 726	5 873	North and Central America	114	123
Europe..	6 711	6 198	Europe..	–	–
Oceania	2 100	2 294	Oceania	44	34
Africa	6 500	7 389	Africa	1 405	1 815
Asia..	21 767	27 853	Asia..	415	470
South America............................	3 699	3 938	South America............................	513	475
■ Vegetables and Melons			**■ Green Coffee**		
World production	478 575	595 565	World production	5 989	5 555
North and Central America	41 677	46 477	North and Central America	1 182	1 203
Europe..	67 850	68 745	Europe..	–	–
Oceania	2 445	2 928	Oceania	51	58
Africa	33 488	38 047	Africa	1 048	1 090
Asia..	290 966	395 227	Asia..	1 016	1 079
South America............................	14 590	17 346	South America............................	2 692	2 125
■ Fruit			**■ Tea**		
World production	379 026	429 447	World production	2 451	2 734
North and Central America	49 587	57 409	North and Central America	1	1
Europe..	77 430	63 956	Europe..	–	–
Oceania	4 953	4 938	Oceania	9	9
Africa	50 541	54 831	Africa	302	356
Asia..	124 931	168 103	Asia..	2 028	2 262
South America............................	59 200	68 741	South America............................	54	69
■ Apples			**■ Total Meat**		
World production	56 987	56 087	World production	186 403	221 025
North and Central America	5 986	5 846	North and Central America	38 361	43 474
Europe..	16 552	12 153	Europe..	43 105	42 757
Oceania	804	826	Oceania	4 651	4 676
Africa	1 203	1 492	Africa	8 968	9 462
Asia..	14 670	27 593	Asia..	58 581	90 268
South America............................	2 638	3 192	South America............................	16 644	20 582

▶ Guam, Johnston Island, Kiribati, Midway Islands, Nauru, New Caledonia, New Zealand, Niue, Norfolk Island, Pacific Islands (Marshall Islands, Micronesia, Federated States of Northern Mariana Island, Palau), Papua New Guinea, Pitcairn, Samoa, Solomon Islands, Tokelau, Tonga, Tuvalu, Vanuatu, Wake Island, Wallis and Futuna Islands; **Africa:** Algeria, Angola, Benin, Botswana, British Indian Ocean Territory, Burkina Faso, Burundi, Cameroon, Cape Verde, Central African Republic, Chad, Comoros, Congo, Cote d'Ivoire, Dem. Rep. of Congo, Djibouti, Egypt, Equatorial Guinea, Eritrea, Ethiopia, former People's Democratic Republic of Ethiopia, Gabon, Gambia, Ghana, Guinea, Guinea-Bissau, Kenya, Lesotho, Liberia, Libyan Arab Jamahiriya, Madagascar, Malawi, Mali, Mauritania, Maruitius, Morocco, Mozambique, Namibia, Niger, Nigeria, Réunion, Rwanda, Saint Helena, Sao Tome and principe, Senegal, Seychelles, Sierra Leone, Somalia, South Africa, Sudan, Swaziland, Tanzania, Togo, Tunisia, Uganda, Western Sahara, Zambia, Zimbabwe; **Asia:** Afghanistan, Armenia, Azerbaijan, Bahrain, Bangladesh, Bhutan, Brunei Darussalam, Cambodia, China, Cyprus, East Timor, Gaza Strip, Georgia, Hong Kong, India, Indonesia, Iran, Iraq, Israel, Japan, Jordan, Kazakhstan, North Korea, South Korea, Kuwait, Kyrgyzstan, Laos, Lebanon, Macau, Malaysia, Maldives, Mongolia, Myanmar, Nepal, Oman, Pakistan, Philippines, Quatar, Saudi Arabia, Singapore, Sri Lanka, Syria, Tajikistan, Thailand, Turkey, Turkmenistan, United Arab Emirates, Uzbekistan, Viet Nam, Yemen; **South America:** Argentina, Bolivia, Brazil, Chile, Colombia, Ecuador, Falkland Islands, French Guiana, Guyana, Paraguay, Peru, Suriname, Uruguay, Venzuela. **Total meat** incl. beef and veal, lamb and mutton, pork, poultry, goat, buffalo. **Total cereals** include dry grain only, including mixed grains and buckwheat. Not including hay, feed, silage, grazing grain. **Wheat** includes spelt. **Root crops** does not incl. crops grown for feed such as turnips, mangels and swedes. **Pulses** incl. the edible seeds of peas, beans, lentils. **Vegetables and Melons** incl. crops grown for human consumption, and excl. crops grown in kitchen gardens or small family gardens.

Source: Food and Agriculture Organization of the UN, *FAO Production Yearbook , 1998*

	1992 Total	1997 Total		1992 Total	1997 Total
■ Total Milk			**■ Sugar (raw)**		
World production	528 699	547 935	World production	117 105	123 947
North and Central America	86 853	91 093	North and Central America	21 255	20 180
Europe	162 665	169 558	Europe	21 413	22 257
Oceania	15 064	20 511	Oceania	4 718	6 363
Africa	20 950	23 173	Africa	6 851	8 627
Asia	117 479	141 159	Asia	40 180	39 493
South America	34 744	42 734	South America	15 781	22 023
■ Hen Eggs			**■ Tobacco**		
World production	37 143	46 926	World production	8 329	8 238
North and Central America	6 095	6 604	North and Central America	964	932
Europe	6 714	6 616	Europe	632	551
Oceania	217	217	Oceania	13	9
Africa	1 601	1 737	Africa	486	515
Asia	16 240	26 356	Asia	5 264	5 485
South America	2 352	2 683	South America	765	652
■ Total Nuts			**■ Natural Rubber**		
World production	5 044	5 230	World production	5 526	6 766
North and Central America	880	1 054	North and Central America	22	31
Europe	1 001	1 024	Europe	–	–
Oceania	26	38	Oceania	4	7
Africa	420	471	Africa	299	308
Asia	2 368	2 255	Asia	5 159	6 355
South America	194	217	South America	43	65
■ Total Oil Crops			**■ Vegetable Fibres**		
World production	232 890	290 581	World production	23 880	25 471
North and Central America	72 104	91 733	North and Central America	3 780	4 512
Europe	17 665	20 548	Europe	448	609
Oceania	1 595	2 336	Oceania	471	610
Africa	10 301	13 903	Africa	1 471	1 867
Asia	83 624	102 574	Asia	13 765	15 022
South America	38 804	52 181	South America	1 644	1 124

NOTES: The country categories are as follows: **North and Central America:** Anguilla, Antigua and Barbuda, Aruba, Bahamas, Barbados, Belize, Bermuda, British Virgin Islands, Canada, Cayman Islands, Costa Rica, Cuba, Dominica, Dominican Republic, El Salvador, Greenland, Grenada, Guadeloupe, Guatemala, Haiti, Honduras, Jamaica, Martinique, Mexico, Montserrat, Netherlands Antilles, Nicaragua, Panama, Puerto Rico, Saint Kitts and Nevis, Saint Lucia, Saint Pierre and Miquelon, Saint Vincent and the Grenadines, Trinidad and Tobago, Turks and Caicos Islands, United States, United States Virgin Islands; **Europe:** Albania, Andorra, Austria, Belarus, Belgium-Luxembourg, Bosnia and Herzegovina, Bulgaria, Croatia, former Czechoslovakia, Czech Republic, Denmark, Estonia, Faeroe Islands, Finland, France, Germany, Gibraltar, Greece, Holy See, Hungary, Iceland, Ireland, Italy, Latvia, Liechtenstein, Lithuania, the former Yugoslav Republic of Macedonia, Malta, Moldova, Monaco, Netherlands, Norway, Poland, Portugal, Romania, Russian Federation, San Marino, Slovakia, Slovenia, Spain, Sweden, Switzerland, Ukraine, United Kingdom, Federal Republic of Yugoslavia (Serbia and Montenegro), former Socialist Federal Republic of Yugoslavia; **Oceania:** American Samoa, Australia, Caton and Enderbury Islands, Christmas Island, Cocos (Keeling) Islands, Cook Islands, Fiji, French Polynesia, Guam, Johnston Island, Kiribati, Midway Islands, Nauru, New Caledonia, New Zealand, Niue, Norfolk Island, Pacific Islands (Marshall Islands, Micronesia, Federated States of Northern Mariana Island, Palau), Papua New Guinea, Pitcairn, Samoa, Solomon Islands, Tokelau, Tonga, Tuvalu, Vanuatu, Wake Island, Wallis and Futuna Islands; **Africa:** Algeria, Angola, Benin, Botswana, British Indian Ocean Territory, Burkina Faso, Burundi, Cameroon, Cape Verde, Central African Republic, Chad, Comoros, Congo, Cote d'Ivoire, Dem. Rep. of Congo, Djibouti, Egypt, Equatorial Guinea, Eritrea, Ethiopia, former People's Democratic Republic of Ethiopia, Gabon, Gambia, Ghana, Guinea, Guinea-Bissau, Kenya, Lesotho, Liberia, Libyan Arab Jamahiriya, Madagascar, Malawi, Mali, Mauritania, Maruitius, Morocco, Mozambique, Namibia, Niger, Nigeria, Réunion, Rwanda, Saint Helena, Sao Tome and principe, Senegal, Seychelles, Sierra Leone, Somalia, South Africa, Sudan, Swaziland, Tanzania, Togo, Tunisia, Uganda, Western Sahara, Zambia, Zimbabwe; **Asia:** Afghanistan, Armenia, Azerbaijan, Bahrain, Bangladesh, Bhutan, Brunei Darussalam, Cambodia, China, Cyprus, East Timor, Gaza Strip, Georgia, Hong Kong, India, Indonesia, Iran, Iraq, Israel, Japan, Jordan, Kazakhstan, North Korea, South Korea, Kuwait, Kyrgyzstan, Laos, Lebanon, Macau, Malaysia, Maldives, Mongolia, Myanmar, Nepal, Oman, Pakistan, Philippines, Quatar, Saudi Arabia, Singapore, Sri Lanka, Syria, Tajikistan, Thailand, Turkey, Turkmenistan, United Arab Emirates, Uzbekistan, Viet Nam, Yemen; **South America:** Argentina, Bolivia, Brazil, Chile, Colombia, Ecuador, Falkland Islands, French Guiana, Guyana, Paraguay, Peru, Suriname, Uruguay, Venzuela. **Oil crops** incl. canola, linseed, cottonseed, olive oil, palm kernels and coconuts.

Source: Food and Agriculture Organization of the UN, *FAO Production Yearbook*, 1998

INTERNATIONAL ORGANIZATIONS

United Nations

The first United Nations declaration was signed by 22 Allied governments on January 1, 1942, and was an alliance against Germany, Italy and Japan. This anti-Axis coalition was converted into an international body in 1945 when 51 nations signed a United Nations Charter to form an organization that would "save succeeding generations from the scourge of war." The Charter was drawn up at the Conference on International Organization held in San Francisco from Apr. 25 to June 26, 1945, and took effect Oct. 24, 1945. UN membership has since grown to 187.

The UN has six parts, with the General Assembly—the central organ—acting as the main deliberative body. General Assembly meetings have been held at UN Headquarters in New York since 1946. The International Court of Justice in The Hague, Netherlands, is the only major UN organ not based in New York. Specialized agencies are located throughout the world.

General Information on the UN may be requested from the Public Inquiries Unit, Dept. of Public Information, Room GA-057A, United Nations, New York, NY 10017; or the United Nations Association in Canada, 900-130 Slater St., Ottawa, Ont., K1P 6E2, or obtained from the UN website at http://www.un.org

■ Structure of the United Nations

General Assembly The General Assembly is the UN's forum for discussing issues, reviewing UN activities and setting the agenda for initiatives. All member states are represented, and each is entitled to one vote. Resolutions require a majority vote before adoption. A president, 21 vice-presidents and six committee chairs head the Assembly, which sits from mid-September to mid-December. The six committees study issues relating to: disarmament and security; economy and finance; social, humanitarian and cultural issues; UN administrative and budgetary matters; legal issues; and political and security issues and report back to a plenary session of the Assembly.

The General Assembly sets UN policies, admits new members on recommendation of the Security Council, approves the budget and receives reports from all other UN bodies.

Security Council The Security Council has the power to act for the maintenance of peace and security. It can enforce military action or economic sanctions, and it can send peace-keeping units (the Blue Berets) to troubled areas. The Security Council may also try to negotiate a ceasefire in the case of conflicts.

The Council has 15 members, five permanent and 10 elected by the General Assembly for two-year terms. Decisions require nine affirmative votes, but all permanent members have the right to veto. The permanent members are: China, France, the United Kingdom, the United States and the Russian Federation. Canada is serving its sixth term as a non-permanent member of the Council (January 1, 1999 to December 31, 2000). The Security Council is permanently in session and representatives are on call 24 hours a day.

Economic and Social Council The Economic and Social Council co-ordinates the economic and social work of the UN and its related agencies. The Council's 54 members hold two month-long sessions each year: one in New York, the other in Geneva. Each member is elected by the General Assembly for a three-year term.

Trusteeship Council The council, created to oversee the independence of trust territories, is now in abeyance.

International Court of Justice (World Court) The Security Council elects 15 judges to the Court for nine-year terms. No two members may be from the same nation. The Court, located in The Hague, only sits in judgement on disputes between states. Both member and non-member states may submit grievances (border disputes, resource access, breach of treaty, etc.).

Countries can opt out of any proceeding, unless required to participate by treaty provisions. But after agreeing to become a party in a case, a nation must comply with the Court's decision, enforced by the Security Council.

Secretariat The Secretariat administers the programs and policies laid out by other UN bodies. The Secretary General is the Chief Administrative Officer of the Secretariat, which administers the work of the UN as directed by the General Assembly, Security Council and other organs.

Glossary of United Nations Acronyms

FAO: Food and Agriculture Organization
IAEA: International Atomic Energy Agency
IBRD: International Bank for Reconstruction and Development
ICAO: International Civil Aviation Organization
IDA: International Development Association
IFAD: International Fund for Agricultural Development
IFC: International Finance Corporation
ILO: International Labour Organization
IMF: International Monetary Fund
INSTRAW: International Research and Training Institute for the Advancement of Women
ITU: International Telecommunications Union
MINUCRA: United Nations Mission in the Central African Republic
MINURSO: United Nations Mission for the Referendum in Western Sahara
MIPONUH: United Nations Civilian Police Mission in Haiti
MONUA: United Nations Ovserver Mission in Angola
UNCHS/HABITAT: United Nations Centre for Human Settlements
UNCTAD: United Nations Conference on Trade and Development
UNDOF: United Nations Disengagement Observer Force
UNDHA: United Nations Department of Humanitarian Affairs
UNDP: United Nations Development Programme
UNEP: United Nations Environment Programme
UNESCO: United Nations Educational, Scientific and Cultural Organization
UNFICYP: United Nations Peacekeeping Force in Cyprus
UNFPA: United Nations Population Fund
UNHCR: Office of the United Nations High Commissioner for Refugees
UNICEF: United Nations Children's Fund
UNIDO: United Nations Industrial Development Organization
UNIFIL: United Nations Interim Force in Lebanon
UNIKOM: United Nations Iraq-Kuwait Observation Mission
UNITAR: United Nations Institute for Training and Research

UNMIBH: United Nations Mission in Bosnia and Herzegovina
UNMIK: United Nations Interim Administration Mission in Kosovo
UNMOGIP: United Nations Military Observer Group in India and Pakistan
UNMOP: United Nations Mission of Observers in Prevlaka
UNMOT: United Nations Mission of Observers in Tajikstan
UNOMIG: United Nations Mission of Observers in Georgia
UNOMSIL: United Nations Mission of Observers in Sierra Leone
UNRWA: United Nations Relief and Works Agency for Palestine Refugees in the Near East
UNSMIH: United Nations Support Mission in Haiti
UNTSO: United Nations Truce Supervision Organization
UNU: United Nations University
UNV: United Nations Volunteers
UPU: Universal Postal Union
WFP: World Food Programme
WHO: World Health Organization
WIPO: World Intellectual Property Organization
WMO: World Meteorological Organization
WTO: World Trade Organization (formerly General Agreement on Tariffs and Trade)

■ Functional Commissions

Commission for Social Development
Commission of Sustainable Development
Commission on Human Rights
Commission on Narcotic Drugs
Commission on the Status of Women
Population Commission
Statistical Commission

■ Regional Commissions

ESCAP: Economic and Social Commission for Asia and the Pacific
ESCWA: Economic and Social Commission for Western Asia
ECA: Economic Commission for Africa
ECE: Economic Commission for Europe
ECLAC: Economic Commission for Latin America and the Caribbean

The United Nations System

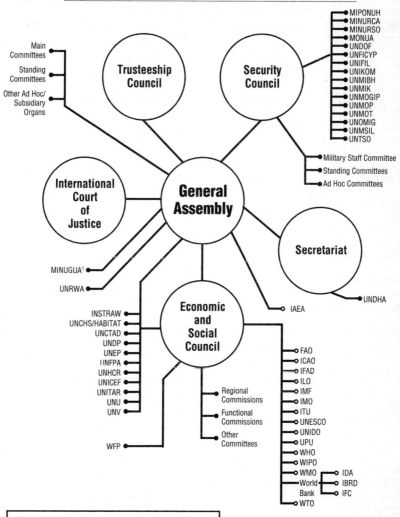

○ Principal organs of the United Nations

● United Nations programmes and organs

○ Specialized agencies and other autonomous organizations within the system

[1]The United Nations Mission for the Verification of Human Rights in Guatemala was established by the General Assembly in September 1994, on the recommendation of the Secretary-General, to monitor on-going human rights abuses.

N.B. The establishment of an International Criminal Court was approved in July 1998 at a UN conference but has yet to be ratified and therefore is not included on this chart.

United Nations Association in Canada – August 1999

Roster of the United Nations

(As of October 1999)

The 188 members of the United Nations, with the years in which they became members.

Member	Year
Afghanistan	1946
Albania	1955
Algeria	1962
Andorra	1993
Angola	1976
Antigua and Barbuda	1981
Argentina	1945
Armenia	1992
Australia	1945
Austria	1955
Azerbaijan	1992
Bahamas	1973
Bahrain	1971
Bangladesh	1974
Barbados	1966
Belarus	1945
Belgium	1945
Belize	1981
Benin	1960
Bhutan	1971
Bolivia	1945
Bosnia and Hercegovina	1992
Botswana	1966
Brazil	1945
Brunei Darussalam	1984
Bulgaria	1955
Burkina Faso	1960
Burundi	1962
Cambodia	1955
Cameroon	1960
Canada	1945
Cape Verde	1975
Central Afr. Rep.	1960
Chad	1960
Chile	1945
China	1945
Colombia	1945
Comoros	1975
Congo	1960
Costa Rica	1945
Côte d'Ivoire	1960
Croatia	1992
Cuba	1945
Cyprus	1960
Czech Republic	1993
Democratic Republic of the Congo (formerly Zaïre)	1960
Denmark	1945
Djibouti	1977
Dominica	1978
Dominican Rep.	1945
Ecuador	1945
Egypt	1945
El Salvador	1945
Equatorial Guinea	1968
Eritrea	1993
Estonia	1991

Member	Year
Ethiopia	1945
Fiji	1970
Finland	1955
France	1945
Gabon	1960
Gambia	1965
Georgia	1992
Germany	1973
Ghana	1957
Greece	1945
Grenada	1974
Guatemala	1945
Guinea	1958
Guinea-Bissau	1974
Guyana	1966
Haiti	1945
Honduras	1945
Hungary	1955
Iceland	1946
India	1945
Indonesia	1950
Iran	1945
Iraq	1945
Ireland	1955
Israel	1949
Italy	1955
Jamaica	1962
Japan	1956
Jordan	1955
Kazakhstan	1992
Kenya	1963
Kiribati	1999
Korea, Democratic People's Republic of	1991
Korea, Republic of	1991
Kuwait	1963
Kyrgyzstan	1992
Lao People's Democratic Republic	1955
Latvia	1991
Lebanon	1945
Lesotho	1966
Liberia	1945
Libya	1955
Liechtenstein	1990
Lithuania	1991
Luxembourg	1945
Macedonia, Former Yugoslav Republic of	1993
Madagascar	1960
Malawi	1964
Malaysia	1957
Maldives	1965
Mali	1960
Malta	1964
Marshall Islands	1991
Mauritania	1961
Mauritius	1968

Member	Year
Mexico	1945
Micronesia, Federated States of	1991
Moldova	1992
Monaco	1993
Mongolia	1961
Morocco	1956
Mozambique	1975
Myanmar (Burma)	1948
Namibia	1990
Nauru	1999
Nepal	1955
Netherlands	1945
New Zealand	1945
Nicaragua	1945
Niger	1960
Nigeria	1960
Norway	1945
Oman	1971
Pakistan	1947
Palau	1995
Panama	1945
Papua New Guinea	1975
Paraguay	1945
Peru	1945
Philippines	1945
Poland	1945
Portugal	1955
Qatar	1971
Romania	1955
Russian Federation	1945
Rwanda	1962
Saint Kitts & Nevis	1983
Saint Lucia	1979
Saint Vincent and the Grenadines	1980
Samoa	1976
San Marino	1992
Sao Tome and Principe	1975
Saudi Arabia	1945
Senegal	1960
Seychelles	1976
Sierra Leone	1961
Singapore	1965
Slovak Republic	1993
Slovenia	1992
Solomon Islands	1978
Somalia	1960
South Africa	1945
Spain	1955
Sri Lanka	1955
Sudan	1956
Suriname	1975
Swaziland	1968
Sweden	1946
Syria	1945
Tajikistan	1992
Tanzania, United Rep. of	1961
Thailand	1946

Member	Year	Member	Year	Member	Year
Togo	1960	Ukraine	1945	Venezuela	1945
Tonga	1999	United Arab Emirates	1971	Vietnam	1977
Trinidad & Tobago	1962	United Kingdom	1945	Yemen	1947
Tunisia	1956	United States of America	1945	Yugoslavia, Federal Republic of,	
Turkey	1945	Uruguay	1945	(Serbia and Montenegro)	1945
Turkmenistan	1992	Uzbekistan	1992	Zambia	1964
Uganda	1962	Vanuatu	1981	Zimbabwe	1980

Source: *United Nations Association   http://www.un.org*

United Nations Secretaries-General

The Secretary-General, heading the Secretariat, is responsible for the UN's administration and for alerting the Security Council to any threats to international peace and security, and acts as spokesperson for the UN. The Secretary-General is elected by the General Assembly on the recommendation of the Security Council and cannot be from one of the five permanent members of the Security Council.

Secretary, Nation	Date Installed	Secretary, Nation	Date Installed
Trygve Lie, Norway	Feb. 1946	Javier Perez de Cuellar, Peru	Dec. 1981
Dag Hammarskjold, Sweden	Apr. 1953	Boutros Boutros-Ghali, Egypt	Jan. 1992
U Thant, Burma	Nov. 1961	Kofi Annan, Ghana	Jan. 1997
Kurt Waldheim, Austria	Dec. 1971		(to Dec. 31, 2001)

Source: *United Nations Association*

Canadian Ambassadors to the United Nations

Ambassador	Date Appointed	Ambassador	Date Appointed
Andrew McNaughton	Jan. 1948	Saul Forbes Rae	June 1972
John Holmes	Jan. 1950	William Barton	May 1976
Gerald Riddell	June 1950	Michel Dupuy	Mar. 1980
David Johnson	Oct. 1951	Gérard Pelletier	Aug. 1981
Robert MacKay	June 1955	Stephen H. Lewis	Oct. 1984
Charles Ritchie	Nov. 1957	Yves Fortier	July 1988
Paul Tremblay	May 1962	Louise Fréchette	Jan. 1992
George Ignatieff	Mar. 1966	Robert K. Fowler	Jan. 1995
Yvon Beaulne	Jan. 1969		

Source: *Dept. of Foreign Affairs*

Other International Organizations in the News

Arab League
(also known as League of Arab States)
Midan Attahrir, Tahrir Square, P.O. Box 11642, Cairo, Egypt
Established: 22 March 1945
Aim: to promote economic, social, political, and military cooperation among member states
Members: (21 plus the Palestine Liberation Organization) Algeria, Bahrain, Comoros, Djibouti, Egypt, Iraq, Jordan, Kuwait, Lebanon, Libya, Mauritania, Morocco, Oman, Qatar, Saudi Arabia, Somalia, Sudan, Syria, Tunisia, UAE, Yemen

Arctic Council
Ambassador for Circumpolar Affairs, Dept. of Foreign Affairs and International Trade, 125 Sussex Dr., Ottawa, ON K1A 0G2
Website: http://www.dfait-maeci.gc.ca/arctic/menu-e.htm
Established: 19 September 1996
Aim: to promote sustainable development and environmental protection through circumpolar cooperation
Members: (8) Canada, Denmark/Greenland, Finland, Iceland, Norway, Russia, Sweden and the USA; plus 4 international aboriginal organizations with permanent participant status

Association of Southeast Asian Nations (ASEAN)
Jalan Sisingamangaraja 70A, Kebayoran Baru, P.O. Box 2072, Jakarta 12110, Indonesia

Website: http://www.aseansec.org
Established: 9 August 1967
Aim: to encourage regional economic, social and cultural cooperation among member states
Members: (10) Brunei Darussalam, Cambodia, Indonesia, Laos, Malaysia, Myanmar, Philippines, Singapore, Thailand, Vietnam

Commonwealth

Commonwealth Secretariat, Marlborough House, Pall Mall, London SWIY 5HX
Website: http://www.tcol.co.uk/index.htm
Established: 11 December 1931
Aim: to promote democracy and co-operation among former members of the British Empire.
Members: 54 including Canada

International Civil Aviation Organization (ICAO)

999 University St., Montreal PQ H3C 5H7, Canada
Website: http://www.icao.int
Established: 7 December 1944
Aim: to promote international cooperation in civil aviation; a UN specialized agency
Members: 185 including Canada

International Criminal Police Organization (Interpol)

BP 6041, F-69411 Lyon CEDEX 06, France
Website: http://www.interpol.com
Established: 13 June 1956
Aim: to promote international cooperation among police authorities in fighting crime
Members: 177 including Canada and 11 Territories

International Monetary Fund (IMF)

700 19th Street NW, Washington, DC 20431, USA
Website: http://www.imf.org/external/index.htm
Established: 22 July 1944
Aim: to promote world monetary stability and economic development; a UN specialized agency
Members: 182 including Canada

International Olympic Committee (IOC)

Chateau de Vidy, CH-1007 Lausanne, Switzerland
Website: http://www.olympic.org
Established: 23 June 1894
Aim: to promote the Olympic ideals and administer the Olympic games: 2000 Summer Olympics in Sydney, Australia ; 2002 Winter Olympics in Salt Lake City, United States
Members: 197 National Olympic Committees - including Canada recognized by the International Olympic Committee

International Organization for Standardization (ISO)

CP 56, 1 rue de Varembe, CH-1211 Geneva 20, Switzerland
Website: http://www.iso.ch
Established: February 1947
Aim: to promote the development of international standards to aid the international exchange of goods and services and to develop cooperation in intellectual, scientific, technological and economic activity
Members: 130 national standards organizations including Canada

International Organization of Francophones (also known as La Francophonie)

Website: http://www.francophonie.org
Established: 20 March 1970
Aim: to promote peace, democracy and French culture throughout the French-speaking world
Members: 52 including Canada; plus 3 observers

Organization of American States (OAS)

corner of 17th St. and Constitution Ave. NW, Washington, DC 20006, USA
Website: http://www.oas.org
Established: 30 April 1948
Aim: to promote regional peace and security as well as economic and social development
Members: 35 including Canada; plus 45 observers including the European Union

Organization of Petroleum Exporting Countries (OPEC)

Obere Donaustrasse 93, A-1020 Vienna, Austria
Website: http://www.opec.org
Established: 14 September 1960
Aim: to coordinate petroleum policies
Members: (11) Algeria, Indonesia, Iran, Iraq, Kuwait, Libya, Nigeria, Qatar, Saudi Arabia, UAE, Venezuela

The European Union (EU)

The European Union (EU) represents a unique relationship among 15 democratic nations, with the aim of constructing a united Europe. The EU is more than an international organization, but not a full-blown federation. The European Union is the world's largest trading entity, accounting for well over 20% of world trade. Its population totals nearly 375 million people.

The European Union originated as the European Coal and Steel Community (ECSC), formed in 1951 by France, West Germany, Italy, the Netherlands, Belgium and Luxembourg and became operational in 1952.

The ECSC boosted internal trade in coal and steel by 129% in five years. Its success spurred the Six to apply the same approach to the entire economy. In 1957, the same six countries formed the European Economic Community (EEC), creating a common market for all sectors of the economy. The EEC committed the Six to dismantle trade barriers and to allow the free movement of goods, services, capital and people between member countries. At the same time the Six formed the European Atomic Energy Community (Euratom) to further the use of nuclear energy for peaceful purposes.

In 1967, the institutions of the ECSC, Euratom and the EEC were merged. In 1973, Denmark, Ireland and the United Kingdom became members, as did Greece in 1981, Spain and Portugal in 1986 and Austria, Finland and Sweden in 1995.

From its inception, the EC has been dedicated to reducing the gap in living standards between the various Member States and supporting the development of the poorer regions. To that end, the EC uses four main sources of funding, known as the Structural Funds: The European Regional Development Fund, the European Social Fund, the European Agricultural Guidance and Guarantee Fund, and the Cohesion Fund. Greece, Portugal, Ireland and parts of Spain and Italy have been targeted for aid to bring their standards of living closer to that of the other Member States.

The Europe 1992 project to complete the common market and create one single internal market by dismantling the remaining physical, technical and fiscal barriers among the Member States was part of the Single European Act, which came into force in 1987.

The Maastricht Treaty on European Union was signed in 1992 and came into effect in November 1993. It was one further step on the road to a European constitution and integrated the previous EC structures.

The European Union consists of three pillars. The first pillar is the European Community with its joint supranational institutions. The two new pillars are intergovernmental cooperation in foreign and security policy as well as intergovernmental cooperation in justice and home affairs. While this cooperation is intergovernmental, the European Commission is fully associated with all activities.

The Maastricht Treaty committed the Member States to create an economic and monetary Union. In January 1999, the EURO was introduced as the new single European currency. The Treaty also committed the 15 to political union, by developing a common foreign and security policy, which might lead to a common defence policy.

The Maastricht Treaty committed the Member States to:
- establish a European Central Bank and introduce a common currency;
- develop a common foreign and security policy, notably through joint actions;
- increase the power for the European Parliament; by involvement in the enactment of legislation: in the appointment of the Commission; and assent for major international agreements;
- establish closer cooperation on justice and home affairs, including visa policy and immigration;
- introduce new responsibilities to the European Community in the area of social policy, public health, education, culture, environment and research and development;
- strengthen the Cohesion Fund to increase aid to the Union's less favoured regions;
- give the regions a part to play in the Community, through a Committee of the Regions; and
- introduce the principle of subsidiarity, according to which the EC should deal only with the enactment of matters it is better equipped to deal with, than the Member States.

In 1997, the 15 agreed to revise the Maastricht Treaty by drawing up a new Treaty of Amsterdam. Coming into force in May 1999, the Treaty of Amsterdam contains four major objectives. They are to:
- put employment and citizens' rights at the heart of the Union;
- ensure that citizens can move freely within the Union and live in a secure environment;

- strengthen the Union's objectives in foreign policy, thereby giving the EU a single voice in foreign affairs; and
- make the Union's institutions and decision-making process more effective.

In 1998, the process of accession to the EU of 11 applicant countries was launched. Negotiations are currently being held with Estonia, Hungary, Poland, the Czech Republic, Slovenia and Cyprus. The basic principle of the negotiations is that all the applicants must accept existing EU law. Negotiations have not yet started with Bulgaria, Latvia, Lithuania, Romania and the Slovak Republic.

■ INSTITUTIONS OF THE EU

The European Union creates its own laws and policies through the following institutions:

The European Commission proposes legislation, implements policy and enforces the treaties. It has investigative powers and can take legal action. It also represents the EU in trade negotiations. The Commission is headed by 20 Commissioners: France, Germany, Italy, Spain and the UK each appoint two Commissioners while the other Member States appoint one Commissioner each. The Commissioners are appointed for five years.

The European Parliament is directly elected by the citizens of the Union. Its 626 members debate issues, question the Commission and Council, and scrutinize proposed legislation. It can dismiss the Commission and has final approval over the EC budget. Elections take place every five years. The number of MPs from each country are: Germany 99, UK 87, France 87, Italy 87, Spain 64, Netherlands 31, Belgium 25, Portugal 25, Greece 25, Sweden 22, Austria 21, Denmark 16, Finland 16, Ireland 15 and Luxembourg 6. MPs sit according to political affiliation and not nationality.

The Council of the European Union is composed of ministers from the 15 member countries. The Council acts on Commission proposals and is the final decision-making body. Participation in the meetings changes according to the agenda. Agricultural ministers, for instance, decide on agricultural matters and economic and finance ministers on economic and monetary matters. Ministers represent and defend the interest of their countries, while seeking agreements that promote the Union's goals. The presidency of the Council rotates among the Member States every six months. In one of the EC's most important reforms, the Single European Act provided for majority voting in the Council in certain areas that previously required unanimity. Areas for majority voting were extended again in the Maastricht and Amsterdam Treaties.

The European Council is comprised of the heads of state or government of the EU Member States and the Commission president. The group meets at least twice a year to define major internal and foreign policy orientations. The European Council does not legislate, but its written conclusions provide guidance.

The Court of Justice is the EC's supreme court. It interprets EC law and its rulings are binding—also on Member States. The court comprises 15 judges, assisted by 9 advocates-general. Both groups are appointed for six years by mutual consent of the Member States.

The Court of Auditors audits the accounts of the EC and EC bodies.

The Committee of the Regions and the **Economic and Social Committee** must be consulted by the Commission and the Council on policies and proposals for legislation.

The European Central Bank governs monetary policy.

Members of the European Union as of October 1999

(As of October 1998)

Member	Year Joined	Member	Year Joined
Austria	1995	Luxembourg	1952
Belgium	1952	Netherlands	1952
Denmark	1973	Portugal	1986
France	1952	Spain	1986
Germany	1952	Suomi-Finland	1995
Greece	1981	Sweden	1995
Ireland	1973	United Kingdom	1973
Italy	1952		

Source: *Commission of the European Communities   For internet information, visit: http://europa.eu.int*

Asia-Pacific Economic Cooperation (APEC)

APEC is an association of 21 Asia-Pacific countries. It promotes economic cooperation, freer trade and greater prosperity throughout the Pacific basin. APEC's members include wealthy countries (e.g., the United States) and poor countries (e.g., Vietnam). Members include capitalist and socialist economies. From 1989 to late 1997, APEC helped turn the Asia-Pacific region into the fastest growing economic region in the world.

APEC was established in 1989 at a conference of trade and foreign ministers in Canberra, Australia. The 12 founding states included Canada. APEC's members agreed to meet annually for informal talks in different member countries. They also agreed to hold alternate ministerial meetings in APEC countries that belonged to the Association of Southeast Asian Nations (ASEAN).

In the first years, talks were held at the ministerial level. In 1990, Singapore hosted the second meeting of ministers which created seven working groups. These groups focussed on trade and investment data, trade promotion, investment and technology transfer, human resource development, regional energy cooperation, marine resource conservation and telecommunications.

In 1991, APEC's members met in Seoul, Korea. They committed themselves to private enterprise and "open regionalism." China, Hong Kong and Taiwan participated for the first time. Three new working groups were created: fisheries, tourism and transportation. In 1992 in Bangkok, Thailand, the ministers decided to create a permanent Secretariat in Singapore and a central fund to cover APEC's administration.

In 1993, the United States hosted ministerial talks in Seattle and, for the first time, the political leaders of APEC's member states met for separate talks on Blake Island. The resulting "Economic Vision Statement" recognized the interdependence of Asia-Pacific economies and the need for freer trade. The talks also produced a Committee on Trade and Investment to increase cooperation in the exchange of goods, services and investment according to the principles of the World Trade Organization.

Separate meetings of APEC's political leaders became annual events. In 1994, after a ministerial meeting in Jakarta, Indonesia,

APEC's leaders issued the "Bogor Declaration of Common Resolve." This statement set the goals of total free trade and investment within the region by 2010 for APEC's industrialized economies and by 2020 for its developing economies. The 1995 meetings in Osaka, Japan, and the 1996 meetings in the Philippines discussed how to accomplish these goals. At Osaka, APEC created a Business Advisory Council (ABAC) to enlist more support from private businesses.

The 1997 conferences took place in Vancouver amidst a financial crisis in Southeast Asia. APEC conferees identified 15 economic sectors for early trade liberalization: environmental goods and services, fish, toys, forest products, gems and jewellery, medical equipment, chemicals, energy, food, natural and synthetic rubber, telecommunications, fertilizers, automobiles, oilseeds and civil aircraft. APEC also aimed at streamlining customs procedures by 2002.

In 1998, APEC participants met in Kuala Lumpur, Malaysia. The United States and Japan proposed a US$10 billion aid package to ease the financial crisis which, APEC leaders acknowledged, had spread beyond the Asia-Pacific region. The leaders recommitted themselves to international cooperation, open markets and the timetable of the Bogor Declaration. The 1999 summit was in Auckland, New Zealand; the ministerial summit in 2000 will be held in November in Brunei Darussalem.

Member Economies (date of membership)

Australia (1989)	Peoples Republic of China (1991)
Brunei Darussalam (1989)	Peru (1998)
Canada (1989)	Republic of Korea (1989)
Chile (1994)	
Chinese Taipei (1991)	Republic of the Philippines (1989)
Hong Kong (1991)	Russia (1998)
Indonesia (1989)	Singapore (1989)
Japan (1989)	Thailand (1989)
Malaysia (1989)	United States (1989)
Mexico (1993)	Vietnam (1998)
New Zealand (1989)	
Papua New Guinea (1993)	

For more information about APEC, visit the website at http://www.apecsec.org or the Dept. of Foreign Affairs at http://www.DFAIT-maeci.gc.ca/~apec

Organization for Economic Co-operation and Development (OECD)

The Organization for Economic Co-operation and Development was inaugurated in 1961 with a mandate to foster economic growth among industrialized nations, and to contribute to the development of the world economy. Its origins are in the post-World War II years, when European countries were struggling to rebuild their economies. The organization established to administer the Marshall Plan was known as the Organization for European Economic Co-operation (OEEC) and was the root of the OECD.

The organization offers, through its many committees and working groups, an opportunity for members of various governments to talk to each other about economic and social policy. The groups meet between two and four times a year and are composed of senior policy-makers. The goal of these groups is to assist member countries in formulating domestic policies that minimize conflict with those of other countries where these policies affect other countries (particularly in the areas of trade and investment.)

The OECD has been variously described as a think tank, a monitoring agency and a rich man's club. The organization acknowledges that it is a club of rich countries in that the OECD member countries produce two-thirds of the world's goods and services. However, it also characterizes itself as an organization that brings together those who share "the principles of the market economy, pluralist democracy and respect for human rights." New countries have joined since the organization's inception with 20 members—there are now 29, and more countries participate in some OECD activities. (Often this participation is a precursor to full membership.)

OECD headquarters are located on the western edge of Paris at the Château de la Muette, and the Secretariat there facilitates the flow of information and analysis among member countries. Parts of the OECD Secretariat collect data, monitor trends, analyse and forecast economic developments, while other divisions study social changes, trade patterns, agriculture, taxation, technology or the environment. The work is done in consultation with policy-makers from the member governments which use the data, and it also supports international discussion at committee level.

Among the numerous divisions (directorates), the most well-known is the Economics Department which publishes the *Economic Outlook* twice a year, in June and December. That publication evaluates trends in the recent past and forecasts economic conditions for the coming 12 months. The economy of each member country (and many non-members) is monitored by the Country Studies Branch and that data is published annually in an *Economic Survey*.

The Statistics Directorate collects economic statistics from across the OECD. The figures are made internationally comparable and are published in electronic and printed form in the monthly *Main Economic Indicators*, as well as other specialized publications.

Other directorates focus on environmental issues, aid to developing countries, public management (how governments go about their business), trade, market development, science and technology as it relates to industry, social policy (including education, unemployment and migration), agriculture, energy (including nuclear), and how cities and regions grow and develop.

For more information about the OECD, visit the website at http://www.oecd.org/

Members (date of membership)

Australia (1971)	Korea, South (1996)
Austria (1961)	Luxembourg (1961)
Belgium (1961)	Mexico (1994)
Canada (1961)	Netherlands (1961)
Czech Republic (1995)	New Zealand (1973)
Denmark (1961)	Norway (1961)
Finland (1969)	Poland (1996)
France (1961)	Portugal (1961)
Germany (1961)	Spain (1961)
Greece (1961)	Sweden (1961)
Hungary (1996)	Switzerland (1961)
Iceland (1961)	Turkey (1961)
Ireland (1961)	United Kingdom (1961)
Italy (1961)	United States (1961)
Japan (1964)	

The World Trade Organization (WTO)

The World Trade Organization (WTO) was established on January 1, 1995. It was the result of eight years of global trade negotiations, collectively known as the Uruguay Round, among 125 nations. The result of those negotiations–a 22,000-page 385-pound agreement–was signed in Marrakech, Morocco, on April 15, 1994. It created the WTO and established the framework for global commerce.

The WTO is now the only international body dealing with the rules of trade among nations. It succeeds the General Agreement on Tariffs and Trade (GATT) which was established provisionally after the Second World War in the wake of other new institutions dedicated to international economic cooperation–including the forerunners to the World Bank and the International Montary Fund.

■ Promoting fair competition

The WTO is not a true "free trade" institution because it permits tariffs and, in limited circumstances, other forms of economic protection. But the WTO does oversee a system of rules dedicated to open, fair and undistorted competition. All WTO agreements are founded on the basic principles of non-discrimination, freer trade, predictable policy-making, encouragement of competition and providing for less developed countries.

The rules on non-discrimination are designed to secure fair trade conditions; so too are the rules on dumping and subsidies. Previous GATT rules established which governments could impose compensating duties on these two forms of "unfair" competition, but GATT's rules only dealt with goods. WTO agreements have extended and clarified GATT's rules to include services and intellectual property.

At the close of the 20th century, the WTO focuses on five policies that support the organization's main tasks: assisting developing and transitional economies, providing specialized help for export promotion, arranging regional trade, cooperating in global economic policy-making and notifying members when trade measures are introduced or changed.

■ The structure of the WTO

The WTO has 134 member countries, 37 observer countries and seven observer organizations to the General Council. As of February 10, 1999, Latvia was the last country to join; most observer nations are waiting for full membership.

The WTO's highest authority is the Ministerial Conference. It consists of representatives of all WTO members, and it must meet at least once every two years. It decides on all matters that affect any of the trade agreements.

The General Council directs the daily work of the WTO. It consists of all WTO members and reports to the Ministerial Conference. The General Council works regularly for the Conference and convenes two more bodies: the Dispute Settlement Body and the Trade Policy Review Body. The latter regularly reviews the trade policies of individual WTO members. Numerous other councils, committees, working parties and negotiating groups are responsible for specific areas or agreements.

Mike Moore, a New Zealander, is the Director-General of the WTO. His three-year term began on September 1, 1999. He will be succeeded by Dr. Supachai Panitchpakdi of Thailand in 2002.

For more information on the WTO, visit the website at http://www.wto.org or write to the World Trade Organization at 154 Rue de Lausanne, 1211 Geneva 21, Switzerland.

Source: *Information and Media Relations Division, WTO 1997; http://www.DFAIT-maeci.gc.ca*

North Atlantic Treaty Organization (NATO)

The North Atlantic Treaty Organization (NATO) is a political and military alliance, created in Washington on April 4, 1949, when 12 states in Europe and North America signed the North Atlantic Treaty. NATO defends the peace and freedom of its members through collective security without sacrificing members' sovereignty. Headquarters is in Brussels, Belgium.

NATO was created to defend Western and Southern Europe from a perceived threat of invasion by the Soviet Union following World War II. Western leaders began negotiating in 1948, after a Soviet attempt to deny Western access to West Berlin.

Today 19 countries belong, including the original 12: Belgium, Canada, Denmark, France, Iceland, Italy, Luxembourg, the Netherlands, Norway, Portugal, the United Kingdom and the United States, plus Greece and Turkey (1952), Germany (joined as West Germany, 1955) and Spain (1982). On March 12, 1999, NATO admitted its newest members—former members of the Soviet-led Warsaw Pact—Hungary, Poland and the Czech Republic.

The highest authority within NATO is the North Atlantic Council (NAC). It consists of Permanent Representatives, who act as ambassadors for their respective countries, and is directed by a Secretary General. Meetings are weekly; the NAC also convenes less frequent meetings of Foreign or Defence Ministers or Heads of State. Discussions cover political, economic, military and scientific issues. The NAC reaches decisions only after all member states have been consulted. It cannot impose decisions on any of its members, although members can block the wishes of others by withholding consent.

The NAC can create subordinate committees and planning groups. The most important are the Defence Planning Committee and the Nuclear Planning Group. The Defence Planning Committee, which consists of Permanent Representatives and Defence Ministers, deals with collective defence planning. The Nuclear Planning Group, which consists of Defence Ministers, deals with nuclear weapons issues. Both are chaired by the NAC's Secretary General. This post is currently held by Dr. Javier Solana (appointed in 1995); his designated successor is Lord George Richardson, who has served as UK Secretary of State for Defence.

At the Rome Summit in 1991, NATO outlined a new strategy for Europe in response to the collapse of the Soviet Union: cooperation with the ex-Warsaw Pact states, reduced dependence on nuclear weapons, reductions in the size and readiness of military forces, improvements in military flexibility, greater use of multinational military units and a new focus on peacekeeping.

Also concurrent with the disintegration of the Soviet Union, NATO created a number of mechanism for consultation and co-operation with former Warsaw Pact states, including the North Atlantic Cooperation Council (NACC) (1991), the Partnership for Peace program (1994) and the Euro-Atlantic Partnership Council (1997). The goal of these organisations was peaceful progress toward a new security environment in Europe. Despite these efforts, the political and economic transformation of many of the former Soviet republics destabilized the area as regional ethnic and political rivalries emerged.

In 1995, NATO first sent land troops outside NATO territory when 60 000 personnel went into Bosnia and Herzegovina under United Nations' authority to enforce the Dayton Peace Accord, negotiated to end armed conflict in the former Yugoslavia. NATO forces and troops from 19 non-NATO countries, including Russia, worked together during the mission, first as part of the Implementation Force (IFOR) and then as the Stabilisation Force (SFOR), which is ongoing.

On March 23, 1999, the NAC authorised air strikes by NATO forces against targets in the Federal Republic of Yugoslavia in an effort to end that country's campaign against ethnic Albanians in Kosovo. The air strike campaign continued until June 10, when the withdrawal of Yugoslav forces from the Kosovo region began. As of June 12, NATO forces joined a UN-mandated peacekeeping force (Kosovo Force or KFOR), to enforce the withdrawal agreement.

For more information about NATO, visit the websites at http://www.nato.int

HISTORY IN HEADLINES

■ Ancient History 5000 BC to AD 476

5000–3501: The earliest known cities are in Mesopotamia—in southwest Asia between the Tigris and Euphrates Rivers—a plain rendered fertile by canals; the Egyptian calendar is regulated by the sun and moon; Sumerian writing exists, in southern Mesopotamia on clay tablets, consisting of 2,000 pictograph signs; the Neolithic period in western Europe is characterized by polished stone weapons and tools and agriculturally-based settlements; Cretan ships appear in the Mediter-ranean Sea; copper alloys are used, and there is smelting of gold and silver in Sumer and Egypt; harps and flutes are played in Egypt; painted pottery appears along the Mediter-ranean; coloured ceramic ware from Russia reaches China.

3500–2001: The Middle Eastern Bronze Age begins (c. 3500 BC); the height of Sumerian civilization (in the region of the Euphrates River valley) is noted for having a numerical system, irrigated agriculture, poetry, potters' wheels, linen, wheeled vehicles, wedge-shaped (cuneiform) script, barley, bread, beer, use of metal coins as legal tender, oil-burning lamps, brick temples and medicine; the dynasty of Pharoahs as god-kings in Egypt begins (2200–525 BC); the Great Sphinx of Gizeh is built; wrestling is the first highly developed sport; glass beads are worn in Egypt; the bow and arrow is first used in warfare; the Yao dynasty is the first recorded in China (2500–2300); the Indus civilization begins in India; the earliest Egyptian mummies are made; equinoxes and solstices are calculated in China; the first library is in Egypt.

2000–1501: The Egyptian height of power and achievement (18th dynasty) features an irrigation system, contraceptives, bathrooms with a water supply, an alphabet of 24 signs, and the oldest form of a novel (*Story of Sinuhe*); the Persian empire begins (1750–1550); the first legal system and laws of a kingdom are set up by Hammurabi, king of Babylonia; the first of seven periods of Chinese literature begins; Stonehenge is built; Abraham, the patriarch of the Jewish religion, lives (c. 1800); Babylonia uses geometry as the basis for astronomical measurements, and describes the signs of the Zodiac; religious dances are performed in Crete.

1500–1001: The Israelites, led by Moses, leave bondage in Egypt (eventually settling in Canaan in 1250), and receive the Ten Commandments and the world's first monotheistic belief at Mt Sinai; the decline of Egyptian power begins (1200–1090); Troy is destroyed during the Trojan War (1193–83) over Helen of Sparta (Greek legend); the Iron Age begins in the Mediterranean area (1000); obelisk structures are used as sundials in Egypt; the first Chinese dictionary is written; silk fabrics appear in China; leprosy spreads in India and Egypt; Phoenicia is the dominant trading power in the Mediterranean; the Mexican Sun Pyramid is built in Teotihuacan.

1000–901: Asiatic and Greek civilizations are linked by Phoenician trading; David is the king of the united kingdom of Judah and Israel (1000–960) with Jerusalem as its capital; David is succeeded by his son Solomon who presides over the height of Israel's ancient civilization (960–25); classical paganism reigns in Greece; pantheistic belief reigns in India (teaching reincarnation and the caste system); the Chou dynasty's rational philosophy reigns in China; Pinto Indians build huts in southwest North America; brush and ink painting appears in China; gold vessels and jewellery are made in northern Europe; the Hebrew alphabet and literature are developed; the Germanic peoples begin to migrate en masse.

900–601: Carthage is founded as a trading centre (813); *Iliad* and *Odyssey* are written and credited to the poet Homer (c. 800); according to legend, Rome is founded by the twins Romulus and Remus (753); the first recorded Olympic Games are held in Greece (776), and every four years thereafter during ancient times; the earliest record of music is a hymn on a Sumerian tablet; arts and crafts flourish in Asia Minor and Greece; a canal between the Nile River and the Red Sea is started under Pharoah Nechos; Etruscan art forms emerge in Tuscany; the Assyrians destroy Babylon and divert the Euphrates River to cover the site of the city; the Babylonians and their allies later destroy the Assyrian empire, which is then divided among the conquerors; the Acropolis, a fortified hill and religious centre, is built in Athens; limestone and marble are used in the construction of Greek temples; flutes and lyres accompany song; Greek choral and lyric poetry use strophe and antistrophe; Zoroaster, a religious teacher and prophet of ancient Persia, lives (c. 628–c. 551).

600–451: The Mayan civilization flourishes in Mexico; Nebuchadnezzer builds what may be the terraced Hanging Gardens of Babylon (600); Babylonian troops destroy the Jewish Temple at Jerusalem and take many Jews as slaves; Jews write the early books of the Bible during the Babylonian Captivity; Siddhartha Gautama, who becomes Buddha, the "enlightened" Indian philosopher and religious teacher, is born (563): at age 29 he renounces world luxuries and searches for enlightenment, which he attains at age 35 while meditating under a pipal tree at Bodh Gaya, and he teaches monks to continue his work; Confucius, the Chinese philosopher and teacher, is born (551); his moral and religious system governs China and is contained in the sayings of *Analects*; Cyrus II the Great of Persia conquers Babylon and surrounding areas and transforms Persia into a vast empire (c. 540): he frees the Jews from Babylon (536) and aids their return to Israel; Darius I divides the Persian empire into 20 provinces and introduces reforms including a common currency, regular taxes and a standing army; Solon's laws are adopted in Athens; Milo of Crotona, a legendary athlete, is crowned six times at the Olympic Games (536); Chinese feudal structure begins to weaken during Chou dynasty (c. 500–451); Greek cities are freed from Persian domination when the Greeks in Cyprus win the Persian Wars (490–49); the marble temple of Apollo is built at Delphi (478); the statue of Zeus, the centrepiece of the temple of Olympia, is built (460); Aeschylus writes *Prometheus Bound* (460); the *Fables of Aesop* is written by a former Phrygian slave.

450–301: The Greek Periclean Age unfolds with the philosophers Socrates and (his pupil) Plato, the dramatists Sophocles and Euripides and historians Thucydides and Herodotus; the beginning of the Indian empire is centred at Magadha (the "cradle of Buddhism"); the Torah becomes the moral code of the Jewish people; Celtic settlements begin in the British Isles; the Spartans use chemicals in warfare (charcoal, sulphur and pitch); the Parthenon, the masterpiece of Greek architecture, is built (447–32); the population of Greece reaches two million citizens and one million slaves; indigenous Indian civilization ends in Mexico; the Peloponnesian Wars between Athens and

Sparta (431–04) end when the Spartan navy destroys the Athenian navy at Aegospotami: this leads to the decline of Athens as a great power; the first horoscopes are developed in Mesopotamia (c. 410); Socrates is put to death for state offences (399); Brennus leads the Gauls from northern Italy to sack Rome (390); Rome is rebuilt (387) and city walls are built around it (377); Plato, a Greek philosopher, founds the most influential school in the world, the Academy (c. 387); the use of catapults as weapons of war begins; Aristotle, the Greek philosopher, is born (384); Alexander the Great, son of Philip II of Macedon, is born (356); Shung-tse founds Chinese monist philosophy (the doctrine that the universe can be explained by one principle) (350); Corinth becomes a trading centre (338); Philip II is assassinated (336); Alexander succeeds his father and conquers Persia, Jerusalem and Tyre, extending his empire to the Indus River in India where his generals force him to turn back; Alexander dies in Babylon (323) and his empire is divided among his generals who fight civil wars for a time (beginning in 321); the Hellenistic period of Greek arts begins (330–20) and the leading Greek schools of thought are: Stoics, Epicureans and Cynics; Euclid writes *Elements*, a standard work on geometry (323); Alexandria is the centre of Greek learning.

300–151: The Mexican sun temple Atetello is built at Teotihuacan (300); accurate star maps are compiled by Chinese astronomers (c. 300); full equality between patricians and plebeians is mandated in Rome (287); Archi-medes, the Greek mathematician, is born (287); the practical end of the history of Babylon coincides with Babylonian re-establishment in the new city of Seleucia (275); Manetho, the high priest of Egypt, writes a history of Egypt in Greek (275); the Colossus at Rhodes is completed (275); the Lighthouse of Pharos is completed at Alexandria (275); the First Punic War between the Cartha-ginians and the Romans (264–41) arises out of a dispute involving the Sicilian cities of Messana and Syracuse: the Romans win naval battles at Mylae (260) and Cape Ecnomus (256) but lose in Africa (255); a Roman victory of the Aegadian Isles (241) brings a peace treaty that gives Sicily to Rome, but Rome reneges on the treaty and invades Sardinia and Corsica; the leap year is introduced into the Egyptian calendar (239); the Greeks and Romans play ball games, roll dice and play board games; the death of Sun-tsi marks the end of Chinese classical philosophy; the Great Wall of China (2,400 km long) is built to keep out invaders (215); the Second Punic War (218–01) opens when Hannibal and the Carthaginians conquer the Spanish city Saguntum, a Roman ally, and Rome declares war: Hannibal successfully invades Italy from the north (217) and makes an alliance with Philip V of Macedon (216), but is later defeated by the Romans at Zama (202) in Africa; Carthage surrenders its war fleet to Rome as well as its Spanish province; the Second Macedonian War (200–197) ends with the Romans under Flamius defeating Philip V of Macedon; the use of gears leads to the invention of the ox-driven water wheel for irrigation (200); an inscription is engraved on the Rosetta Stone (c. 200); Antiochus IV of Syria persecutes the Jews in Israel and desecrates their Temple of Jerusalem (168); the Jews revolt under Judas Maccabeus and repel the Syrians, then rededicate (Chanukah) the Temple (165); the inventor of trigonometry, Hipparchus of Nicaea, is born (160).

150–1 BC: During the Third Punic War (149–46) the Romans destroy Corinth and massacre the inhabitants of Carthage (due to alleged breach of treaty); the Roman Empire now consists of seven provinces; the Venus of Milo is sculpted (140); Cicero, the greatest Roman orator, is born (106); the first Chinese ships reach the east coast of India (100); the greatest of Roman poets, Virgil, is born (70); he pens the epic *Aeneid*; Horace, the lyric poet, is born (65); Julius Caesar, Roman military commander, organizes the First Trium-virate (60) with Pompey, commander-in-chief of the army, and Marcus Crassus; Caesar conquers the northern Gauls (55) and the Britons; Caesar and Pompey battle for control of Rome after Caesar crosses the Rubicon River and provokes a civil war; Caesar emerges victorious (48); the Julian calendar and leap year are adopted in Rome (46); Cleopatra, the last queen of Egypt, orders the death of Pompey; Caesar, now the dictator of Rome, is murdered by a group headed by Brutus and Cassius Longinus (44); Mark Antony, Octavian and Lepidus form the Second Triumvirate and defeat Brutus and Cassius at Phillipi (42); Mark Antony returns to Egypt (38) where he and Cleopatra commit suicide after being defeated by Octavian at Actium (31); Octavian, retitled Augustus, is a virtual emperor of Rome

(30–AD 14); Herod the Great is appointed king of Judea by the Romans (c. 40); the probable date of the birth of Jesus, the Jewish son of Mary, in Bethlehem (AD 4).

AD 1–150: Jesus, who is revered as the Son of God by his followers, the Christians, preaches for three years in Galilee (c. 30); in the third year of his preaching, Jesus is crucified in Jerusalem by Roman authorities at the request of local political and religious leaders; Caligula becomes emperor of Rome (37) and is known for his ruthlessness and insanity: he is assassinated by the Praetorian Guard (42) and is succeeded by Claudius I, who consolidates and reinvigorates the empire despite a paralysis (dies in 54); the apostle Paul sets out on his missionary travels (45) and spreads Christianity; Nero, emperor of Rome, is the first to persecute the Christians, for allegedly burning half of Rome (64); the Gospels according to Matthew, Mark and John are written; Jews revolt against Rome and the Romans destroy the second Temple at Jerusalem and enslave many inhabitants (70); 1,000 Jewish Zealots hold off the 15,000-member Roman legion for three years on the mountaintop fortress of Masada, and the Zealots commit suicide to escape capture (73); under Emperor Trajan, the Roman Empire reaches its greatest geographical extent when he conquers Dacia and much of Parthia (98–116); paper is made by the Chinese, though not for writing (by 100); Hadrian's Wall is built as the northern boundary and defence line of the Roman Empire (122–26); the medical authority up to the 16th century, Greek physician and writer Galen, (c. 130–200) demonstrates that arteries carry blood (not air) and establishes the importance of the spinal cord by correlating earlier medical knowledge with his discoveries based on experiments and animal dissection; the earliest known Sanskrit inscriptions are made in India (150).

151–300: Ptolemy, a Greco-Egyptian thinker, compiles *Almagest*, the 13-volume work on ancient astronomy (earth-centred universe), mathematics, geography and science, which is influential to the 16th century; the oldest known Maya monuments are built (c. 164); the period of Neo-Platonism, the last of the Greek philosophies, begins (c. 200); silkworms are exported from Korea to China and then to Japan (c. 200); citizenship is granted to every freeborn subject in the Roman Empire (212); Afghanistan is invaded by the Huns (200); the

Goths invade Asia Minor and the Balkan Peninsula (220); the end of the Han dynasty in China is followed by four centuries of division (220); the southern part of India breaks into several kingdoms; Rome celebrates its 1,000th anniversary (248); persecution of Christians increases and martyrs are revered as saints (c. 250); the first book of algebra is written by Diophantus of Alexandria (c. 250); the Goths attack the Black Sea area (257) as well as Athens, Sparta and Corinth (268); Pappus of Alex-andria documents use of cogwheel, lever, pulley, screw and wedge (c. 285); Rome is partitioned into a western and an eastern empire; five distinct German dukedoms emerge (Saxons, Franks, Alemanni, Thuringians and Goths) (c. 300).

301–400: Constantine the Great reunites the western and eastern Roman Empires and becomes sole emperor (310–37); Constantine establishes toleration of Christianity with the Edict of Milan (313); the seat of the Roman Empire is moved to Constantinople (c. 331); the Basilican Church of St Peter is erected (330); Emperor Constantine is baptized on his deathbed (337) and is succeeded by his three sons, who again split Rome into two empires; the Huns invade Europe (360) and Russia (376); books begin to replace scrolls (360); Lo-Tsun, a Chinese monk, founds the Caves of the Thousand Buddhas in Kansu (360); Theodosius the Great becomes the last emperor of a united Roman Empire (392); Alaric, king of the Visigoths, invades Greece (396) and plunders Athens and the Balkans (398); the first definite records of Japanese history appear (400), although legend claims Japan was founded in 660 BC.

401–76: The Visigoths invade Italy (401); Alaric sacks Rome (410); Roman legions withdraw from Britain to defend Italy from the Visigoths (410); barbarians settle in Roman provinces (425); Attila becomes ruler of the Huns (433); St Augustine, Christian theologian, writes *The City of God* (411); alchemy begins with the search for the Philosopher's Stone and the Elixir of Life as chief objects; pre-Inca culture develops in Peru; Venice is founded by refugees from Attila's Huns (452); the Vandals sack Rome (455) and destroy the Roman fleet at Cartegena (460); the Huns leave Europe (470); the Mayan civilization flourishes in southern Mexico (c. 470); the first Shinto religious shrines are built in Japan (478): they deal primarily with nature and ancestor worship; the German barbarian Odoacer takes Ravenna and deposes Emperor Romulus Augustulus, thereby ending the Western Roman Empire (476); Aryabhata, Hindu astronomer and mathematician, studies powers and roots of numbers (b. 476).

■ Middle or Dark Ages: 477–1450

477–529: Chi dynasty in southern China (479–502); Clovis, leader of the Franks (since 481), converts to Christianity (496); the first schism between the Western and Eastern Churches occurs when Pope Felix III excommunicates Patriarch Acacius of Constantinople (484–519); Armenian Church separates from Byzantium and Rome (491); the Moshica culture of the Chimic Indians flowers in Peru with agriculture, pottery and textiles; the Vatican Palace in Rome is first planned (500); Tamo carries tea from India to China (c. 500); Clovis kills Alaric II and annexes the Visigoth kingdom of Toulouse (507), and Clovis's realm is divided among his four sons upon his death (511); Emperor Wu-Ti converts to Buddhism and encourages the new religion in central China (517); Justinian I becomes the Byzantine Emperor (527): he is known for heavy taxes, public works and codifying Roman law; the Saxon kingdoms of Essex and Middlesex appear; Chosroes I is king of Persia (531–79) and encourages culture and art.

530–99: Arthur, the semi-legendary king of the Britons, is first mentioned at the Battle of Mt Badon (c. 540); the earliest Chinese roll paintings appear in Tun-huang (landscapes); war breaks out between Persia and the Byzantine Empire (539–62); St Gildas writes the first important source of early British history, *De excido et conquestu Brittaniae* (542); disastrous earthquakes occur around the world (543); the plague of Constantinople, imported by rats from Egypt and Syria, spreads throughout Europe and reaches Britain (547); the Golden Era of Byzantine art begins (550); Poles settle in western Galicia, Ukrainians in eastern Galicia (550); chess begins in India (c. 550); Buddhism is introduced into Japan by Emperor Shotoko Taishi (c.552–621), and the first Buddhist monastery in Japan is founded (587); Japanese prehistory ends and the Asuka period begins; Justinian sends missionaries to China and Ceylon to smuggle out silkworms and the European silk industry becomes a Byzantine state monopoly (553); Mohammed, the founder of Islam, is born (570); war is renewed between Persia and the Byzantine Empire (572–91), and again when Chosroes II ascends the throne of Persia (590–628); the plague ends after killing half the population of Europe (542–94); first verified account of decimal number system in India (595); probably the first English school is established at Canterbury (598); the authoritative Talmud Babli, a compilation of Jewish Oral Law with rabbinical interpretations, is compiled (c. 6th century).

600–749: Books printed in China (600); Czechs and Slovaks take up land in Bohemia and Moravia, Yugoslavs in Serbia (c. 600); smallpox spreads from India, via China and Asia Minor, to southern Europe; the oldest surviving wooden building in the world, the Horyuji temple and hospital, is completed in Japan (607); Mohammed experiences a religious vision on Mt Hira (610); "burning water" (petroleum) is used in Japan (615); orchestras are formed in China (619); porcelain is produced in China (620); the Hegira is named after Mohammed's flight from hostile Mecca to Yathrib (later renamed Medina), and is year one in the Muslim calendar (622); an encyclopedia of arts and sciences is written by Isidore of Seville (622); Shaka Trinity, the famous altarpiece of the Kondo in Japan, is built by Tori (623); Mohammed begins to dictate the Koran (the sacred book of Islam) in Arabic (625); the Byzantines decisively defeat the Persians at Nineveh (627); Mohammed captures Mecca and writes letters to world leaders explaining the Muslim faith (628); cotton is introduced in Arab countries (630); Buddhism becomes the state religion in Tibet (632); Medina is the seat of the first caliph (religious and political leader of Muslims) who is Abu Bekr, Mohammed's father-in-law; the Arabs attack Persia (633); Damascus is the new capital of the caliphs (635–70); Jerusalem is conquered by the Arabs (637); the book-copying industry of the west is destroyed by the Arabs and the Alexandrian school ceases to be the centre of Western culture (641); the Arabs under Omar destroy the Persian Empire: the caliphs rule the area (until 1258), and Islam replaces the religion of Zoroaster; the Eastern Roman Empire is weakened by the Arab conquest of Egypt, Mesopotamia and Syria (642); the Dome of the Rock, a Muslim mosque, is begun in Jerusalem (643); the Muslim fleet destroys the Byzantine fleet at Lycia (655);

Croats and Serbs settle in Bosnia (650); Chinese artists invent lamp-black ink and wood block printing (c. 650); Caliphs organize first news service (650); Japanese Buddhism and Shintoism are reconciled by the Korean-born priest Gyogi (c. 668–749); the Byzantines use "Greek Fire," a missile weapon of sulphur, rock, salt, resin and petroleum, against the Arabs at the siege of Constantinople (671–78); glass windows appear in English churches (674); the first Arab coinage is introduced (695); the Arabs destroy Carthage (697); Greek, instead of Latin, becomes the official language of the Eastern Roman Empire (700); the Arabs conquer Algiers (700) and virtually eliminate Christianity in northern Africa; mass migration of European peoples is followed by their subjection at the hands of property owners; China's population grows rapidly (700) and the first large urban developments appear there; the Great Mosque of Damascus is built (705); Buddhist monasteries in Japan become centres of civilization (710); the first written history of Japan, *Kojiki*, is compiled (712); the Lombard kingdom in northern Italy reaches its height (c. 600–c. 799); the Muslim empire now extends from the Pyrenees to China, with Damascus as its capital (715); the earliest Islamic paintings appear (715); Caliph Omar II grants tax exemption to all Muslim believers (717); the Chinese capital Ch'ang-an is the largest city in the world and Constantinople is the second largest (725); Casa Grande, a North American Indian fort and large irrigation works, is built in Arizona (725); Charles Martel (mayor of the Frankish court) wins victory over the Arabs in the battle of Tours and halts their westward advance (732); first printed newspaper published in Beijing (748).

750–849: Pueblos are built in southwest North America (750–900); Spain, under Arab influence, excels in mathematics, optics and chemistry (c. 750); Kiev, Russia, becomes known as a trading centre (750); the Turkish Empire is founded by a Tartar tribe in Armenia (760); Charlemagne becomes ruler of the Franks after the death of his father (Pepin the Short, son of Charles Martel) (768) and brother Carloman (771); Arabic learning flourishes under Harun-al-Rashid (790), peaks during reign of Caliph Mamun (813–33); the Byzantine Empress Irene overthrows her son Constantine (797), an act heralded by the Greek Church; Charlemagne is crowned Holy Roman Emperor (Western Empire) at Rome (800); the earliest records of Persian poetry and literature appear (800); the Vikings dominate Ireland (802); Arabic numerals are created under Indian influence (814); the Arabs conquer Crete, proceed as far as the Greek isles (826) and begin their conquest of Italy and Sardinia (827); Prince Mimir founds the Great Moravian Empire (830) from a confederation of Slavs in Bohemia, Moravia, Slovakia, Hungary and Transylvania; the Treaty of Verdun divides the Frankish Empire into France, Germany and Italy (843); paper currency in China creates inflation and state bankruptcy (845); Abu Tamman writes *Hamasa*, a collection of Arabian legends, proverbs and heroic stories (845); the Arabs sack Rome (846), damage the Vatican and destroy the Venetian fleet.

850–99: Salerno University is founded (850); the discovery of coffee is credited to Arabia (850); Jews settling in Germany develop the Yiddish language (c. 850); the first important Japanese painter, Kudara Kuwanari, dies (853); Norse pirates enter the Mediterranean and sack the coast up to Asia Minor (859); Iceland is discovered by the Northmen (861); Russian Northmen sack parts of France (861) and attack Constantinople (865); Basil I, the Byzantine Emperor, compiles the Basilican code (reforming finance and law and restoring the prestige of the military), and begins the Macedonian dynasty (867); Alfred the Great, king of England, recaptures London from the Danes (878); Emperor Charles III becomes king of France and once more unites the empire of Charlemagne (884), he is deposed (887) and there is a final separation of Germany and France; England's King Alfred establishes a regular militia and navy, extends the power of the king's courts and institutes fairs and markets (890).

900–99: The Vikings discover Greenland (900); the Mayans relinquish their settlements in the lowlands of Mexico and emigrate to the Yucatan peninsula (900); England is divided into shires with county courts in order to safeguard the civil rights of the inhabitants (900); the Arabian tales *A Thousand and One Nights* is begun (900); castles become the seats of the European nobility (900); Cordoba, Spain, is the seat of Arab learning, science, commerce and industry (930); Yenching becomes new capital city of China, later known as Beijing (938); revolts against imperial rule in Japan set off a period of civil war (939–1185); the Arab

empire creates advanced postal and news services (942); the earliest record of the existence of a London bridge (963); a Chinese encyclopedia of 1,000 volumes is begun (978–84); the rule of nobles in Rome ends (980); Venice and Genoa carry on a flourishing trade between Asia and Western Europe (983); systematic musical notation develops (990); canonization of Christian saints begins.

1000–99: The heroic poem *Beowulf* is written in Old English by an unknown author (1000); Leif Ericsson, son of Eric the Red, sails to North America (1000); the Chinese invent gunpowder (1000); Mayan culture on the Yucatan peninsula achieves its zenith (1000); Sridhara, Indian mathematician, describes the importance of zero (1000); the Holy Sepulchre in Jerusalem is sacked by Muslims (1009); Danes under Canute control England (1016); Canute conquers Norway (1028); Jaroslav the Wise, Prince of Kiev (1020–54), codifies Russian law and builds cities, schools and churches; Byzantine power begins to decline (1025); Canute dies (1035) and his kingdom of England, Norway and Denmark is divided among his three sons; after murdering Duncan of Scotland, Macbeth becomes king (1040) and is later murdered by Malcolm (1057); time values are given to musical notes (1050); the separation of the Roman and Eastern Churches becomes permanent (1054); Westminster Abbey is consecrated (1065); William of Normandy is crowned William the Conqueror, of England (1066); the comet, later known as Halley's comet, appears (1066); She-tsung, Emperor of China, nationalizes agricultural production and distribution (1068); Constantine the African brings Greek medicine to the Western world (1071); the original Tower of London is built (1078); the Domesday Book, a survey of assessment for tax purposes, is compiled (1086); the start of the First Crusade (1096) is proclaimed by Pope Urban II to recapture the Holy Land from the Turks; Crusaders take Jerusalem (1099).

1100–99: Middle English supercedes Old English (1100); Islamic science begins to decline; secular music first appears; Robert of Normandy is appeased after invading England in the Treaty of Alton (1101); colonization of eastern Germany begins (1105); the earliest record of a miracle play is from Dunstable, England (1110): based on Scriptures and the lives of saints, they are widely performed until the 16th century; Bologna University founded

(1119); the earliest account of a mariner's compass is by Alexander Neckham (1125); the Second Crusade begins (1146) and fails one year later; Paris University is founded (1150); Bologna Medical School is founded (1150); the first recorded fire and plague insurance is in Iceland (1151); the Japanese clans Taira and Minamoto fight each other (1156); Eric of Sweden conquers Finland (1157); Thomas à Becket is elected Archbishop of Canterbury (1162) in an effort to curb church power, but he later quarrels with King Henry II over growing royal power; Becket is murdered by Norman knights (1170) and buried at Canterbury; jails are ordered erected in all English counties and boroughs (1166); Oxford University is founded (1167); rules for the canonization of saints are established by Pope Alexander III (1170); first authenticated influenza epidemics occur (1173); the Campanile ("Leaning Tower") of Pisa is built (1174); Walter Map organizes the Arthurian legends in their present form (1176); all Jews are banished from France (1182); the Third Crusade (1189–93) fails to recapture Jerusalem from the Muslims; Moses Maimonides, Jewish philosopher, introduces Aristotle to modern western philosophy when he attempts to reconcile Aristotle's theories with those of Jewish philosophy in *Guide to the Perplexed* (1190), and he is also credited with organizing all Jewish law for the layman as well as religious educators.

1200–49: Cambridge University founded (1200); Islam takes root in India; the Fourth Crusade begins with crusaders from Venice fighting Constantinople and establishing a Latin Kingdom of Jerusalem (1204); St Francis of Assisi issues the first rules of his brotherhood of educators and missionaries, the Franciscans (1209); in the Children's Crusade (1212), thousands of children from Europe leave for the Holy Land, but most are either sold as slaves or die of hunger or disease; Genghis Khan becomes chief prince of the Mongols (1206) and conquers most of the Chinese empire of north China (1213–15) as well as Turkistan, Afghanistan and Trans-oxania (1218–24), and he raids Persia and Eastern Europe; Genghis Khan's empire is divided among his descendants upon his death (1227); the Council of St Albans is the precursor to the British Parliament (1213); King John puts his seal on England's Magna Carta at Runnymede under compulsion by the barons (1215): it

defines the limitations of royal power and sets out basic civil rights; the Fifth Crusade fails in Egypt (1217–21); the oldest national flag in the world, Danneborg, is adopted by Denmark (1218); the form of the sonnet develops in Italian poetry (1221); Thomas Aquinas (1225–74) theorizes philosophical proofs for the existence of God and reconciles Greek ideas with Christian theology; the Sixth Crusade is led by Emperor Frederick II (1228); crusaders bring back leprosy to Europe (1230), and they secure a temporary truce with the Muslims; three later crusades against Muslims in the 13th century fail; coal is mined for the first time in Newcastle, England (1233); the Inquisition begins as the pope makes Dominicans responsible for putting an end to heresy (1233); Alexander Nevski made Grand Duke of Novgorod (1236).

1250–99: Kublai Khan becomes governor of China (1251) and ruler of the Mongol peoples (1259–94); he fails to conquer Japan (1274), southeast Asia and Indonesia, but he defeats the Sung dynasty of China (1279); instruments of torture are first used in the Inquisition (1252); the Sorbonne is founded by Robert de Sorbon as the Paris School of Theology (1254); the House of Commons is established in England (1258); Mongols control Baghdad, end caliphate (1258); Roger Bacon writes *"De computo naturali"* (1264); the glass mirror is invented (1278); Marco Polo, the Venetian explorer, journeys to China (1271–95) and is in the diplomatic service of Kublai Khan (1275–92); Florence, Italy, is the leading European city in commerce and finance (c. 1282); the Teutonic Order, a German military and religious order, conquers Prussia (1283) after killing the native "heathens" and replacing them with Germans; spectacles (eyeglasses) are invented (1290); the crusades end and the Knights of St John of Jerusalem settle in Cyprus (1291).

1300–99: Trade fairs at Bruges, Antwerp, Lyons and Geneva (c. 1300); Edward I of England standardizes the yard and the acre (1305); Dante composes his *Divina Commedia* (1307–21); mechanical clocks are driven by weights in Europe; Salic Law, excluding women from succession to the throne, is adopted in France (1317); No plays originate in Japan (1325); the Aztecs establish Mexico City (1327); the sawmill is invented (1328); weaving at York first documented (1331); the Hundred Years War between

France and England begins (1337) as a dispute over lands held by the English crown in France: it later becomes a dispute over the French crown itself; the first scientific weather forecasts are attempted by William Merlee of Oxford (1337); the Black Death (bubonic plague) devastates Europe, killing about 75 million people, more than one-third of the population (1347–51); Boccaccio writes *Decameron* (1348–53), which is intended to be a diversion from the horrors of the plague; Timur the Lame (Tamerlaine) begins his conquest of Asia (1363); the Aztecs of Mexico build their capital, Tenochtitlan (1364); the Mongol Yüan dynasty in China is overthrown by the national Ming dynasty (1368–1644); the building of the Bastille begins in Paris (1369); "Robin Hood," the legendary hero who robbed the rich to help the poor, appears in English ballads and literature; The Great Schism in the Catholic Church begins (1378–1417) when, after the death of Pope Gregory XI, two popes are elected, one each at Rome and Avignon; Venice wins its Hundred Years War against Genoa (1256–1381); Briton John Wyclif calls for the reform of church practices (1379); he is condemned as a heretic (1380, 1382) and inspires the first English translation of the Latin Bible, the Wyclif Bible; Chaucer writes *The Canterbury Tales*; the rival southern and northern courts of Japan's divided imperial family reunite after 50 years of strife; Denmark, Sweden and Norway unite under Queen Margaret of Denmark (1397) in the Union of Kalmar.

1400–39: Russia's greatest icon painter, Andrei Rublex, creates *Trinity* (1411); England and France sign a perpetual peace treaty upon the marriage of Henry V and Catherine of Valois (1420); Joan of Arc and her French followers defeat the British at Orleans (1429) and march triumphantly to Paris: she is then taken prisoner by the Burgundians (1430) and condemned and executed (1431) in a political inquisition and trial; complete suits of metal armor plate replace chain mail in Europe (1430); China shuts out the western world and bans voyages there (1433) because Confucian doctrine sees little merit in trade; the Portugese find the way round Cape Bojador (on the west coast of Africa) under Henry the Navigator (1434); the Greek (Eastern or Byzantine) Church unites with the Roman church (1439) in order to save itself from the Turkish threat; Montezuma becomes ruler of the Aztecs in

Mexico (1440) and begins to conquer surrounding tribes.

■ Renaissance: 1440–1650

1440–69: The rise of the Italian city-states heralds the Renaissance (1440–50), and the richest families (such as the Medici) vie with each other as patrons of art and learning (mainly in Florence); the first oil painter, Jan van Eyck, dies in Flanders (1441); France defeats England at Castillion, ending the Hundred Years War (1453), and the English give up everything except Calais, thus ending English rule in France; Zimbabwe, the great African kingdom, declines after 200 years of expansion (1450) because of food shortages; Constantinople, the old capital of the Byzantine empire, falls to the Ottomans (1453); a treaty unites rival Italian city-states (1454), requiring them to protect each other from outside aggression; Ming porcelain pottery appears in Europe (1460); the Bible is printed mechanically with metal type faces and oil-based ink by Johann Gutenberg (1455); the Wars of the Roses begin in England (1455) as a struggle for the throne between the houses of York and Lancaster, and end (1485) when Henry VII of the house of Lancaster prevails over Richard III; Plato's writings are translated into Latin at the Platonic Academy in Florence (1469).

1470–99: Music sheets, maps and posters are mechanically printed (1470s); Vlad the Impaler dies in Transylvania (1477) and the mass murderer becomes the source for Dracula legends; Peruvian-centred Inca rule expands to include the entire Andean region (3,200 sq. km) under Pachacuti, and his son Topa Inca (1470), and it is characterized by terracing, irrigation, pantheistic religion with human sacrifice, advanced metalwork, tapestry making and construction; the Spanish Catholic Inquisition begins (1478); King Ferdinand V of Aragón and Queen Isabella I of Castile unite their crowns in Spain to ward off Alfonso V of Portugal (1479); Ivan the Great declares Russian independence (1480) from the Mongols when he refuses to continue paying them tribute; the first European manual of navigation and nautical almanac is prepared in Portugal by mathematical experts (1484) who calculate the latitude of the sun, based on the work of the Jewish astronomer Abraham Zacuto; the spread of witchcraft and heresy in Germany is attacked by Pope Innocent VIII (1484) and he authorizes Dominican inquisitors to torture and burn witches; the publication of an encyclopedia of witchcraft, *Malleus Maleficarum* (1486), adds to witch hunt hysteria; the Genoese seaman Christopher Columbus secures the sponsorship of Queen Isabella of Spain (1486) for his expedition to discover a western route to Asia (he sets sail with his three ships: Santa María, Pinta and Niña in 1492); the Aztecs of Mexico inaugurate the Great Temple of Tenochtitlan (1487) when they ritually sacrifice the hearts of 20,000 people; the Portugese explorer Bartholomew Dias rounds the Cape of Good Hope off South Africa (1488); Leonardo da Vinci is in his prime in Italy (1488) as an artist, scientist, inventor and philosopher, with inventions centuries ahead of their time (e.g., he conceives of flying machines and an apparatus to enable humans to breathe under water); the Great Wall of China is rebuilt by Ming emperors as a defence against attacks by northern Barbarians (1488); the first terrestrial globe is made by Martin Behaim, a German (1492); Jews are ordered by Spain's Catholic rulers to choose between expulsion or forced conversion (1492), and the rulers change the options to conversion or death (1498); Spain conquers Granada (1492), the last Muslim kingdom in Spain; Spain and Portugal sign a treaty dividing lands discovered in the new world, but Spain benefits the most from the treaty (1494); French armies in Italy bring a virus later identified as syphilis to Naples and the epidemic spreads through Europe (1495); Columbus brings tobacco back from the new world (1496); the Chinese invent a toothbrush (1498); Vasco da Gama discovers a sea route round the Cape of Good Hope to India via the Indian Ocean (1498); the Italian navigator Amerigo Vespucci explores the northeast coast of South America (1499) and reports cannibals (1502); Portugal's Pedro Cabral discovers the east coast of Brazil and observes natives using stone to cut wood (1499).

1500–25: The discovery of plays and poems by Hroswitha of Gandersheim, a 10th-century saxoness, makes her the first European playwright since the Classical Age (1500); King Ferdinand of Spain sanctions a system of levying tribute payments from Indians in the new world and using Indians as forced labour (1501); Shi'ism becomes the state religion in Persia (1502) and Sunni Muslim dissenters are executed there; a hand-held timepiece, made

possible by the invention of the coiled mainspring, is constructed by German locksmith Peter Henlein (1502); *David*, a 13-foot statue, is completed by Michelangelo Buon-arrotti (1504) in Florence, Italy; Leonardo da Vinci paints the *Mona Lisa* (1505); Venice dominates Mediterranean trade (c. 1507); a map calls the new world "America" after Amerigo Vespucci (1507) and shows it as a distinct continent; the first great German artist, Albrecht Dürer (painter/engraver), creates his *Adam and Eve* oil painting (1507); Michelangelo paints the ceiling of the Sistine Chapel (1508–12); Sebastion Cabot sails around Cuba, proving it is an island (1508) and later reaches Hudson Bay in search of a northwest passage; the first African slaves are brought to the Americas (Cuba) (1510); Erasmus, the Dutch humanist, writes the satirical *In Praise of Folly* (1511); Juan Ponce de Léon claims Florida for Spain (1513) while searching for the Fountain of Youth; Niccolo Machiavelli writes *The Prince* (1513) which discusses the uses and abuses of power; Vasco Núñez de Balboa discovers the "South Sea," or Pacific Ocean, for Spain (1513); Spain orders new world natives to convert to Christianity under threat of enslavement or death (1514); Henry VIII of England puts forth measures to protect peasants from enclosure—the dividing and closing off of common land (1515); Sir Thomas More writes *Utopia*, which depicts an ideal state (1516); Martin Luther, a German Augustinian monk, writes his *95 Theses*, attacking the Catholic church's sale of indulgences granting the forgiveness of sins (1517) and nails it to the door of the Wittenberg church; English sailors complain to King Henry VIII about the growing number of French cod fishermen in Newfoundland (1517); the rule of Suleiman I the Magnificent sees the Ottoman Turks reach the zenith of their empire with the conquest of Egypt, Syria and Hungary (1520); Ferdinand Magellan begins a three-year voyage to circumnavigate the globe (1519); Hernando Cortes lands at Vera Cruz, Mexico, where Montezuma II and the Aztecs surrender (1519); chocolate is introduced to Europe from Mexico (1520); Nicholas Copernicus publishes his "Commentariolus" stating his theory that the earth revolves around the sun (1521); Martin Luther translates the Bible into German (1522).

1526–49: Lutheran German troops sack and burn Rome (1527); Hippocrates' ancient idea of the four humours governing bodily health is first disputed (1528); Henry VIII separates from the Church of Rome and becomes head of the English Church (1534) after he is refused an annulment of his first marriage; the Jesuit order of missionaries is founded by Ignatius Loyola (1534); Jacques Cartier searches for riches in North America along the St Lawrence River (1535); John Calvin, the French leader of the Protestant Refor-mation in Geneva, theorizes the concepts of predestina-tion and God's omniscience (1536); the first mechanical artificial limbs appear for crippled war veterans (1539); the founder of the Sikh religion, Guru Nanak, dies in India (1539); Henry VIII becomes King of Ireland and Head of the Irish Church (1541); John Knox leads the Calvinist Reformation in Scotland (1541); oil is discovered in North America by the Spaniards (1543); Portugese traders are the first to sell guns to Japan (1543); Nostradamus, the French astrologer, begins making predictions (1547); Ivan IV (the Terrible) is crowned the first czar of Russia (1547): he calls the first national assembly (1549).

1550–99: Jesuit missionaries protect natives in the new world from slavery (1551); Ivan the Terrible defeats the Mongols (1552), and con-quers as far as the Caspian Sea (1556); Lady Jane Grey is executed for treason in England by Queen Mary Tudor (1554), who becomes known as "Bloody Mary" after persecuting Protestants (1555); Mary restores papal author-ity in England and Wales (1554); Charles V relinquishes the Holy Roman Empire and Spain to his brother and son, and goes to a monastery (1556); an influenza epidemic hits Europe (1557); Elizabeth I becomes Queen of England (1558) and rejects papal power in England (1559); the Huguenot (Calvinist French Protestant) conspiracy occurs at Amboise: liberty of worship is promised in France (1560); the Edict of Orleans suspends persecution of Huguenots (1561); the Peace of Amboise ends the first War of Religion in France and the Huguenots are granted limited toleration (1563); Andreas Vesalius, the Flemish founder of modern anatomy, dies (1564); Nobunaga deposes the Japanese shogu-nate and centralizes the government (1567); the Iroquois Confederacy of five North American nations (Mohawk, Oneida, Onondaga, Cayuga, Seneca) is founded (c. 1570); Huguenots are massacred on St Bartholomew's Day in Paris (1572); the Dutch War of Independence begins (1572); the Union

of Utrecht is the foundation of the Dutch Republic (1579); William of Orange accepts the sovereignty of northern Nether-lands and is assassinated (1584); the first English colony in Newfoundland is founded (1582); Elizabeth of England orders Mary Queen of Scots beheaded for treason (1587); Christopher Marlowe com-pletes *Dr. Faustus* (1588); the first Spanish Armada leaves for England and is defeated by the English under Charles Howard (1588); Sir Francis Drake, with 18,000 men, fails to take Lisbon for England (1589); William Shakespeare completes the play *Romeo and Juliet* (1594); the Second Spanish Armada leaves for England but is scattered by storms (1597); an English Act of Parliament calls for convicted criminals to serve their terms in the colonies (1597).

1600–49: France boasts the largest population in central Europe, with 16 million persons (1600); William Shakespeare completes *Hamlet* (1600); Dutch opticians invent the tele-scope (1600); the first modern public company is founded, the Dutch East India Company (1602); Guy Fawkes is arrested and accused of trying to blow up the House of Lords during James I's state opening of Parliament (The Gunpowder Plot, 1605); Fawkes is sentenced to death (1606); the first English settlement on the American mainland is founded at Jamestown, Virginia (1607); Shakespeare writes his *Sonnets* (1609); the first cheques appear in Netherlands as "cash letters" (1608); the *King James Bible* is published (1611); Peter Paul Rubens paints *Descent from the Cross* (1611); the North American Indian princess Pocahantas marries English colonist John Rolfe (1614); Galileo Galilei, Italian astronomer, faces the Inquisition for the first time for renouncing the Ptolemaic system of the earth-centred universe and embracing the Copernican sun-centred system (1615); the Thirty Years War begins in Prague as Protestants rebel against Catholic oppression (1618); slavery in North America begins when the first Africans are brought to Virginia (1619) and the triangular slave trade starts (British goods are sent to west Africa and are traded for slaves, who are traded for agricul-tural staples in the new world, which are sent back to Britain); pilgrims arriving on the *Mayflower* found Plymouth Colony, Massachusetts (1620); patent law is created in England to protect inventors (1623); construc-tion begins on the Taj Mahal mausoleum in

Agra, North India (1628); Charles I dissolves the English Parliament for 11 years (1629); Cardinal Richelieu, chief minister of Louis XIII of France, rules France (1630–42); Galileo is forced by the Inquisition to cease promulgating the theories of Copernicus (1633); Japan forbids foreign books, Christianity and any European contacts (1637); René Descartes, called the father of modern philosophy, writes *Discourse on Method* (1637); the Ming dynasty in China ends and the Manchu dynasty takes power (1644–1912); Charles I of England, after a long struggle for power with Parliament (English Civil War 1642–48), is beheaded by Oliver Cromwell for treason (1649).

1650–99: Bishop James Ussher dates the creation of the world at Oct. 23, 4004 BC (1650); the wholesale massacre of North American Indians by European settlers begins (1650); Thomas Hobbes writes *Leviathan*, a defence of absolute monarchy in England (1651); Oliver Cromwell becomes Lord Protector in England, dissolves Parliament, divides England into 11 districts, prohibits Anglican services (1653) and readmits Jews to England after 365 years (1655); Blaise Pascal (French) develops the basic laws of probability (1654); the Portugese drive the Dutch out of Brazil (1654); the first London opera house opens (1656); Dutch peasants (Boers) first settle in South Africa (1660); the Royal Society is founded in London to promote scientific discussion among great thinkers (1660); the earliest condemnation of industrial pollution, *The Inconvenience of the Air and Smoke of London Dissipated*, is written by John Evelyn (1661); Louis XIV (the Sun King) begins to build the palace at Versailles (1662); Jean Baptiste Colbert forms the North American colony of New France with Quebec as its capital (1663); the British annex New Netherlands from the Dutch and rename the main city New York (1664); Isaac Newton begins to experiment with gravity and develops calculus (1664–66); the cell is named and described by Briton Robert Hooke (1665); the French army uses the first hand grenades (1667); Portugal gains independence from Spain through the Treaty of Lisbon (1668); microorganisms are discovered by Anton van Leeuwenhoek (Dutch, 1669) who later observes bacteria (1683) for the first time; the Hudson's Bay Company is incorporated by a British royal charter to trade in the region of North America defined by those rivers which

drain into Hudson Bay (1670); Dutch philosopher Baruch Spinoza writes *Ethics* (1675); the poems of Bashu (a pseudonym) popularize Japanese haiku poetry (1675); the *Declaration of the People of Virgina* by Nathaniel Bacon lends support to rebellion against authorities in the colonies (1676); Roman Catholics are excluded from both houses of Parliament in England (1678); the Habeas Corpus Amendment Act in England protects citizens from unjust imprisonment (1679); the French colonial empire of North America, reaching from Quebec to the mouth of the Mississippi River, is organized (1680); the large dodo bird with small, flightless wings becomes extinct (1680); Sir Isaac Newton writes *Principles of Natural Philo-sophy* (1687), which discusses universal gravitation; the Glorious Revolution establishes the constitutional monarchy in England (1688–89) and William of Orange III and Mary II ascend the throne; Peter the Great becomes Czar of Russia (1689); John Locke writes *Essay Concerning Human Understanding* and *Two Treatises on Civil Government* (1690).

1700–49: The War of the Spanish Succession to the childless Charles II, Hapsburg king of Spain, is fought (1701–14) between the French Bourbons and Austrian Hapsburgs; rebellion occurs in Astrakhan against Czar Peter's westernization of Russia (1705); England and Scotland form Great Britain (1707); the Peace of Utrecht is signed between Spain and England: Spain cedes Gibraltar and Minorca to England (1713) and Philip of France retains the Spanish crown; D.G. Fahrenheit constructs a mercury thermometer with a temperature scale (1714); George F. Handel writes *Water Music* for King George I (1717); Daniel Defoe writes *The Life and Strange Surprising Adventures of Robinson Crusoe* (1719); the German composer and virtuoso organist J.S. Bach composes *The Brandenburg Concertos* (1721); Johnathan Swift writes *Gulliver's Travels* (1726); Benjamin Franklin, American statesman, scientist, printer and writer, writes *Poor Richard's Almanack* (1732); John Kay patents the fly shuttle loom, which revolutionizes weaving (1733); Alexander Pope, poet and English verse satirist, writes *Essay on Man* (1733); the modern classification system of plants and animals is introduced by Carolus Linnaeus (Swedish, 1735); Alaska is discovered by Victor Behring (1740); Frederick the Great introduces freedom of the press and freedom of worship in Prussia (1740); sign language for the deaf is created by Rodriguez Pereire (1749).

■ Industrial Revolution: 1750–1850

1750–99: Benjamin Franklin experimented with static electricity and invented the lightning conductor (1752); in the Seven Years War (1756–63) Britain declares war on France and, in the North American colonies, the French drive the British from the Great Lakes area (1756); the French lose Quebec to the British (1759) during the battle on the Plains of Abraham; Voltaire writes the philosophical novel *Candide* (1759); Catherine II (the Great) becomes czarina of Russia (1762); Swiss-French philosopher Jean Jacques Rousseau writes *Social Contract* (1762) which discusses his theory of "natural man"; the Peace of Paris (1763) ends the war between England and France and gives Canada to England; eight-year-old Mozart writes his first symphony (1764); the spinning jenny, which spins up to 120 threads at once is invented by Briton James Hargreaves (1764); the British Parliament passes the Stamp Act for taxing American colonies: Virginia and New York challenge the right of Britain to taxation without representation (1766); the Mason-Dixon Line is drawn by English surveyors between Pennsylvania and Maryland (1767) and is later the boundary between "slave" and "free" states; Daniel Rutherford and Joseph Priestley independently discover nitrogen (1772); the Bolshoi Ballet is founded in Russia (1773); during the Boston Tea Party American colonists protesting British taxes dress as Indians and dump the cargo of three tea ships in the Boston, Mass., harbor (1773); James Watt, Scottish inventor, perfects the steam engine (1775); the American Revolution begins (1775); the Second Continental Congress assembles at Philadelphia and appoints George Washington commander-in-chief of the American forces; the Americans proclaim the *Declara-tion of Independence* (July 4, 1776); Edward Gibbon writes *Decline and Fall of the Roman Empire* (1776); Adam Smith completes *Wealth of Nations* (1776); after the American victory in the Saratoga Campaign (1777) France entered into an alliance with the Americans (1778); Washington's army suffers at Valley Forge (1778); Hawaii is discovered by James Cook (1778); Franz Mesmer practices mesmerism (hypnotism) (1778); Spain joins the American War of Indepen-dence against Britain (1779); the Dutch support the American side (1780); Sir William Herschel discovers Uranus (1781); British General Cornwallis surrenders to the Ameri-cans (Oct. 1781) at the end of the Yorktown Campaign, and the Treaty of Paris recognizes American independence (1783); John Wesley writes the *Deed of Declaration*, the charter of Wesleyan Methodism (1784); the British colony of Australia is founded (1788); the French Revolution begins (1789); a Paris mob opposing the monarchy storms the Bastille jail; French royalists begin to emigrate; the French revolutionaries proclaim the Decrees of Aug. 4 and the *Declaration of the Rights of Man and of the Citizen;* the government limits the monarchy's power, abolishes the French feudal system, extends religious tolerance to Jews and protestants and reorganizes the Catholic Church; A.L. Lavoisier completes the *Table of Thirty-One Chemical Elements* (1790); the Constitutional Act divides Britain's Canadian colony into Upper Can-ada (English-speaking) and Lower Canada (French-speaking) (1791); Thomas Paine writes *The Rights of Man* in defence of the French Revolution (1791); the French King Louis XIV and Queen Marie Antoinette are beheaded for treason (Jan., 1793); the Reign of Terror (guillotine executions of prisoners) under the Jacobin government ends with the execution of Maximilien Robespierre; Robert Burns' *Auld Lang Syne* is published (1794); Edward Jenner discovers a smallpox vaccine (1796).

1800–09: Ottawa is founded (1800); Eli Whitney makes muskets with interchangeable parts (1800); the Library of Congress is established in Washington, DC by Thomas Jefferson (1800); the first battery is produced from zinc and copper plates by Alessandro Volto (1800); William Herschel discovers the existence of infrared solar rays (1800); the first submarine *Nautilus* is made by American civil engineer Robert Fulton (1801); the atomic theory of chemistry is put forth by John Dalton (1802); the US buys land from France in the Louisiana Purchase (1803); Henry Shrapnel invents the shell used in warfare (1803); Napoleon crowns himself emperor of the French empire (1804) and king of Italy (1805); modern Egypt is established when Mehemet Ali becomes Pasha (1805); morphine is isolated by F.W.A. Satürner (1805); Napoleon wins his greatest victory, at Austerlitz, over the Austrians and Russians allied against him (1805); the American frigate *Chesapeake* is stopped and boarded by British naval officers looking for deserters, almost causing a war (1807); Ludwig van Beethoven, the great German composer who brought together Classical and Romantic styles, performs his *Fifth Symphony* (written for Napoleon) and *Sixth Symphony* (1808); the first part of J.W. von Goethe's *Faust* is published (1808); Washington Irving writes *Rip van Winkle* (1809).

1810–19: Simón Bolívar becomes a leading figure in South American politics (1810) and liberates Greater Colombia (Panama, Venezuela, Ecuador and Colombia) (1819) and Peru (1824) from Spanish rule; a machine for spinning flax is invented by Philippe Girard (1812); German folklorist Jakob Grimm completes *Grimm's Fairy Tales* (1812–15); Napoleon Bonaparte's first military setback is in the Peninsular War (1808–14); and he later retreats from an unsuccessful invasion of Russia; the War of 1812 (1812–14) between Britain and the United States is foreshadowed by the battle at Tippecanoe (1811); Jane Austen writes *Pride and Prejudice* (1813), depicting English country life and mores; Austria, Russia and Prussia form an alliance against Napoleon and defeat him at Leipzig (1813) and recapture Paris (1814); Napoleon abdicates and is exiled to Elba Island; the War of 1812 continues in North America as the British capture Washington, DC (1814) but the Americans win battles at Fort McHenry, Thames (killing Tecumseh, an Indian ally of the British) and at Plattsburgh (1814); the British initiate peace in the Treaty of Ghent (1814) but this news travels too slowly to stop the Battle of New Orleans (1815), won by the Americans; Napoleon escapes from exile and returns to march on Paris; he is defeated at Waterloo (1815), abdicates again and is banished to St Helena Island; the German Confederation, dominated by Austria and Prussia, is created to replace the Holy Roman Empire (1815); Argentina declares its independence from Spain (1816); the classical economist David Ricardo (British) writes *The Principles of Political Economy and Taxation* (1817), discussing the determination of wage and value; Georg Hegel writes his all-embracing *Encyclopedia of the Philosophical Sciences* (1817); Mary Wollstonecraft Shelley writes

Frankenstein (1818); Lord Byron begins *Don Juan* (1818–23); Chile proclaims its independence from Spain (1818); electromagnetism is discovered by Danish physicist Hans C. Oersted (1819); Greater Colombia (including Panama, Venezuela, Ecuador and Colombia) declares independence from Spain (1819).

1820–29: Andre Ampere (French) writes *Laws of Electrodynamic Action* (1820); Liberia is founded by the Washington Colonization Society, for the repatriation of black slaves (1820); Sir Walter Scott writes *Ivanhoe* (1820); John Keats writes *Ode to a Nightingale* (1820); an electric recording device for sound reproduction is invented by Sir Charles Wheatstone (1821); Peru and Guatemala declare their independence from Spain (1821); the Reign of Terror begins between the Greeks and the Turks (1821); Franz Liszt, the Hungarian pianist who revolutionizes Romantic music and invents the symphonic poem, makes his debut at age 11 in Vienna (1822); Brazil declares itself independent from Portugal (1822); the Monroe Doctrine closes the American continent to colonial settlement by European powers (1823); Spanish are defeated and Paris independence recognized (1824); Simón Bolívar creates his namesake, Bolivia (1825); the first steam-powered railroads carrying freight and passengers, operated by the the Stockton and Darlington Railway, run in England (1825); the Erie Canal opens, linking the Hudson River and the Great Lakes (1825); the first major American author, James Fenimore Cooper, writes *The Last of the Mohicans* (1826); Felix Mendelssohn composes the Overture to *A Midsummer Night's Dream* (1826); the great cholera epidemic begins in India (1826) and spreads from Russia into Central Europe; J. J. Audubon writes *Birds of North America* (1827); Noah Webster writes the *American Dictionary of the English Language* (1828); Uruguay declares independence from Brazil (1828); the Peace of Adrianople ends the Russo-Turkish war and Turkey acknowledges the independence of Greece (1829); Frederic Chopin, the Polish pianist, debuts in Vienna (1829); Venezuela withdraws from Greater Colombia and becomes independent (1829).

1830–39: Charles Lyell of Scotland divides the geological system into three groups: Eocene, Miocene and Pliocene (1830); Ecuador declares independence (1830); mass demonstrations in Swiss cities lead to liberal reforms

(1831); Charles Darwin sails on the HMS *Beagle* as a naturalist, surveying South America, New Zealand and Australia (1831–36); the leading anti-slavery leader in the United States, W. L. Garrison, begins publishing *The Liberator* in Boston (1831); the wealthy middle classes emerging from the Industrial Revolution are enfranchised in Britain, doubling the number of voters (1832); the New England anti-slavery society is founded in Boston (1832); slavery is abolished in the British Empire (1833); the Spanish Inquisition, begun during the 13th century, is finally abolished (1834); France's leading writer, Victor Hugo, writes *The Hunchback of Notre Dame* (1834); the Poor Law Amendment Act decrees that no able-bodied person (displaced by the Industrial Revolution) in Great Britain shall receive assistance unless he or she enters a workhouse (1834); Hans Christian Anderson writes his first stories for children (1835); the American writer Ralph Waldo Emerson writes *Nature* (1836); the People's Charter initiates Britain's first national working-class movement, calling for universal suffrage for men and voting by ballot (1836); the Dutch (Afrikaner) farmers begin "The Great Trek" of emigration across the Orange and Vaal Rivers, South Africa (1836); the first botanical textbook, *The Elements of Botany*, is written by American Asa Gray (1836); Victoria becomes Queen of Great Britain (1837); citizens stage unsuccessful rebellions in Lower and Upper Canada (1837); Louis Braille invents his reading system for the blind (1837); Charles Dickens's *Oliver Twist,* a critique of British industrial society, is a bestseller (1838); the first bicycle is invented by a Scot, Kirkpatrick Macmillan (1839); the cell-growth theory is put forth by Theodor Schwann (1839); ozone is discovered by Christian Schönbein, a German-Swiss chemist (1839); American Charles Goodyear develops the process of vulcanization, making the commercial use of rubber possible (1839); a photograph produced on a silver-coated copperplate treated with iodine vapor, the daguerreotype, is invented by Louis Daguerre and J. Niepce (French) (1839); the First Opium War between Britain and China begins (1839).

1840–49: New Zealand becomes a British colony (1840); philosopher Thomas Carlyle writes *On Heroes, Hero-Worship and the Heroic in History* in support of strong government (1841); the father of the guided tour,

Thomas Cook (British), arranges his first trip (1841); showman P.T. Barnum gains fame after opening his American Museum of freak exhibitions (1841); the Webster-Ashburton Treaty between Britain and the US settles American border disputes with Canada (1842); the Treaty of Nanking ends the Opium War between Britain and China and confirms the cession of Hong Kong to Great Britain (1842); riots and strikes erupt in northern England's industrial areas (1842); Richard Wagner (German) finishes the opera *The Flying Dutchman* (1843); the amount of work required to produce a unit of heat, the joule, is determined by English physicist James P. Joule (1843); American social reformer Dorothea Dix reports on the shocking conditions in prisons and asylums, influencing the establishment of state hospitals for the insane in Europe and North America (1843); Samuel Morse's telegraph is used for the first time between Baltimore and Washington (1844); US troops are victorious over the Mexicans at Palo Alto (1846), Congress formally declares war, US forces take Santa Fe and annex New Mexico; the Smithsonian Institution, a research and educational centre, is founded in Washington, DC (1846); ether is first used as an anaesthetic by dentist W.T. Morton (1846); sisters Charlotte and Emily Brontë publish *Jane Eyre* and *Wuthering Heights* respectively (1847); US forces capture Mexico City (1847) and the Treaty of Guadalupe Hidalgo ends the Mexican-US war (1848), the US acquires Texas and much of the surrounding territory in return for $15 million; gold discoveries in California lead to the first gold rush (1848); a revolt in Paris causes Louis Philippe to abdicate (1848); a revolution in Vienna brings Metternich's resignation (1848); revolutions in Venice, Berlin, Milan, Rome and Parma (1848); the first Public Health Act is introduced in Britain (1848); the first women's rights convention, organized by Elizabeth Stanton and Lucretia Mott, is held in Seneca Falls, New York (1848); the *Communist Manifesto* is issued by Germans Karl Marx and Friedrich Engels (1848), championing the working class and establishing socialist theory.

1850–59: Harriet Beecher Stowe writes her anti-slavery novel *Uncle Tom's Cabin* (1852); the Transvaal is granted self-government (1852); the Crimean War (1853–56) begins when Russia occupies Moldavia and Walachia and Turkey declares war, the Russians destroy the Turkish fleet off Sinope, and England, France and Sardinia join Turkey's fight; after a long siege the Russian base Sevastopol falls to the allied forces (1855), and after the allied victory at Balaklava, Russia recognizes the integrity of Turkey (1856); English nurse Florence Nightingale founds modern nursing while tending soldiers during the Crimean War (1853–56); the first hypodermic syringe is used by Alexander Wood (1853); Samuel Colt revolutionizes the manufacture of small arms (1853); Commander Matthew Perry negotiates the first American-Japanese treaty, permitting US ships to use two Japanese ports (1854); the Elgin Reciprocity Treaty between Great Britain and the US implements free trade between Canada and the US (1854); steel making becomes inexpensive when Henry Bessemer introduces a converter into his process for making steel (1855); pure cocaine is extracted from coca leaves (1856); Gustave Flaubert, the French master of realistic novels, writes *Madame Bovary* (1856); Louis Pasteur discovers that fermentation is caused by micro-organisms (1857), and later invents pasteurization and discovers a vaccine for rabies; the first Neanderthal skeleton is found in a cave in Neander Valley (near Düsseldorf, Germany); the Indian Mutiny against British rule (1857) causes the British siege and capture of Delhi; the British Royal Navy destroys the Chinese fleet, and Britain and France take Canton (1857); Guiseppe Garibaldi forms the Italian National Association for the unification of Italy (1857); the Treaty of Tientsin ends the Anglo-Chinese war (1858); Charles Darwin writes *On the Origin of Species by Natural Selection*, explaining his theory of evolution (1859); the German National Association is formed to unite Germany under Prussia (1859); John Stuart Mill (British) writes his essay *On Liberty* (1859).

■ Modern Era

1860–64: Garibaldi and his redshirts sail from Genoa to take Palermo and Naples; Victor Emmanuel II (King of Sardinia) invades the Papal States and defeats the Papal troops, Garibaldi proclaims Emmanuel II king of Italy (1860); Anglo-French troops defeat the Chinese at Pa-li-Chau (1860) and sign the Treaty of Peking; the first Food and Drugs Act is enacted in Britain (1860); Lenoir constructs the first internal-combustion engine (1860); a

primitive form of typewriter is created by American Christopher L. Sholes (1860); hundreds of thousands of Irish and British citizens flee their homelands following the potato famine (by 1860); Russian troops fire at anti-Russian demonstrators in Poland during the Warsaw Massacre (1861); the first machine-chilled cold storage unit is built by T. S. Mort (1861); Krupp begins arms production in Essen, Germany (1861); the Archaeopteryx, the skeleton linking reptiles and birds, is discovered at Solnhofen, Germany (1861); the American Civil War (1861–65) begins after Abraham Lincoln, who views slavery as evil, is elected president; South Carolina secedes in protest, followed by 10 other southern states, to form the Confederacy fighting for states' rights and opposing the abolition of slavery; Lincoln issues the Emancipation Proclamation (1862) calling for the freeing of black slaves in Confederate territory; the Red Cross voluntary relief organization is proposed by Jean Henri Dunant, a Swiss humanist (1862); the first form of a machine gun is invented by the American Richard Gatling (1862); Otto von Bismarck becomes the prime minister of Prussia (1862) and begins his system of alliances and alignments that result in German preeminence in Europe; Victor Hugo writes *Les Miserables* (1862); Leo Tolstoy writes *War and Peace* (1864); the Geneva Convention establishes the neutrality of battlefield medical facilities (1864); liberalism, socialism and rationalism are condemned in *Syllabus Errorum*, issued by Pope Pius IX (1864); Cheyenne and Arapahoe Indians are massacred at Sand Creek, Colorado (1864); the First International Workingmen's Association is founded by Karl Marx in London and New York (1864); Confederate forces surrender finally at Appomattox, Virginia (1865) marking the end of the war and victory for the Union; slavery in the US is abolished by the Thirteenth Amendment; US Pres. Lincoln is assassinated by the actor John Wilkes Booth (1865).

1865–69: Lewis Carroll (British) writes *Alice's Adventures in Wonderland* (1865); Joseph Lister initiates antiseptic surgery by using carbolic acid on a compound wound (1865); line geometry is invented by German mathematician Julius Plücker (1865); Gregor Mendel, an Austrian monk, describes his Law of Heredity (1865); Bismarck, the Prussian foreign minister, provoked the brief Austro-Prussian War by invading the duchies of Schleswig-Holstein and overrunning the German states allied with Austria; after seven weeks a peace settlement gave Schleswig-Holstein, Hanover, Hesse, Nasau and Frankfurt to Prussia and excluded Austria from influence in German affairs (1866); *Crime and Punishment* by Feodor Dosto-evsky is published (1866); Alfred Nobel invents dynamite (1866); Johann Strauss popularizes the Viennese waltz with Blue Danube (1866); the underwater torpedo is invented by Robert Whitehead, an English engineer (1866); the fundamental law of biogenetics, *General Morphology,* is published by Ernst Haeckel (1866); Claude Monet, a French founder of Impressionism, paints *Camille* (1866); Russia sells Alaska to the US for $7.2 million (1867); Karl Marx writes *Das Kapital,* volume I (1867); the British North America Act establishes the Dominion of Canada and John A. Macdonald becomes prime minister (1867); Louisa May Alcott describes Victorian American life in *Little Women* (1868); a skeleton of Cro Magnon man from the Upper Paleolithic age (the first Homo sapiens in Europe, successor to the Neanderthal man) is found in France by Louis Lartet (1868); the first regular Trades Union Congress is held at Manchester, England (1868); Dmitri Mendeleyev formulates his periodic law for the classification of the elements (1869); John Stuart Mill writes *On the Subjection of Women* (1869); the major early treatise on eugenics, *Hereditary Genius,* is published by Francis Galton (1869); J.W. Hyatt invents celluloid (plastic) (1869); the First Nihilist Congress is held at Basel, Switzerland (1869); the strategically important Suez Canal opens (1869); the doctrine of papal infallibility is established by Pope Pius IX during Vatican Council I (1869–79).

1870–79: US industrialist John D. Rockefeller founds the Standard Oil Company (1870); T.H. Huxley, English biologist and educator, writes the *Theory of Biogenesis* (1870); the Franco-Prussian War begins (1870) and France under Napoleon III capitulates; William I, king of Prussia, is proclaimed the German Emperor at Versailles, and in the Peace of Frankfurt France cedes Alsace-Lorraine to Germany (1871); the Italian Law of Guarantees allows the Pope possession of the Vatican (1871); labour unions become legal in Britain (1871); Charles Darwin writes *The Descent of Man* (1871); the Great Fire ravages Chicago (1871);

explorer Sir Henry M. Stanley is sent to find David Livingstone in Africa (1871); the first modern luxury liner, SS *Oceanic,* is launched (1871); Civil War in Spain ends with the Carlists' defeat (1872); the Three Emperors League is established in Berlin as an alliance between Germany, Russia and Austria-Hungary (1872); colour photographs are first developed (1873); James C. Maxwell writes *Electricity and Magnetism* (1873); Willhelm Wundt, known for the experimental method, writes *Physiological Psychology* (1873); under the direction of Benjamin Disraeli as prime minister, Britain expands its imperial power by annexing the Fiji islands (1874); Johannes Brahms composes the *Hungarian Dances* (1874); Johann Strauss II performs the operetta *Die Fledermaus* in Vienna (1874); Bosnia and Herzegovina rebel against Turkish rule (1875): Turkish sultan promises reforms (1875); Mary Baker Eddy writes *Science and Health* (1875) and she founds the Christian Science movement (1879); Georges Bizet performs *Carmen* in Paris (1875); British Queen Victoria is crowned empress of India (1876); Britain annexes the Transvaal (1877); US General George Custer is killed along with his cavalry by Cheyenne Indians in the Battle of the Little Bighorn (1876); Alexander Graham Bell constructs a telephone (1876); first national lawn tennis championship played at Wimbledon (1877); German historian Heinrich Treitschke begins a racial anti-semite movement (1878); Gilbert and Sullivan write *HMS Pinafore* (1878); British troops are massacred by Zulus in Isand-hlwana, Africa (1879); the British occupy the Khyber Pass near Afghanistan and are massacred in Kabul (1879); Norwegian Henrik Ibsen completes the play *A Doll's House* (1879); Chile invades Bolivia and its ally Peru after Bolivia cancels a Chilean company's contract to exploit Bolivia's nitrate deposits (1879).

1880–84: Auguste Rodin sculpts *The Thinker* (1880); France annexes Tahiti (1880); Transvaal declares its independence from Britain and the Boers establish a republic after a brief war with Britain (1880–81); the first practical electrical lights are independently made by Thomas Edison and J.W. Swan (1880); the malaria parasite is discovered by Charles Laveran (1880); the first large steel furnace is developed by American steel baron Andrew Carnegie (1880); the Vatican opens its archives to scholars (1881); the first Japanese political parties are founded (1881); violent government-condoned attacks (po-groms) are carried out against Russian Jews (1881–1917) causing large-scale Jewish emigration to North America; the Federation of Organized Trades and Labor Unions of the US and Canada is formed (1881); Germany, Austria and Italy form an alliance (1882); the three-mile limit for territorial waters is agreed upon at the Hague Convention (1882); Peter I. Tchaikovsky composes the *1812 Overture* (1882); psychoanalysis begins when Joseph Breuer (Austrian) uses hypnosis to treat hysteria (1882); Thomas Edison designs the first hydroelectric plant in Wisconsin (1882); the Orient Express train between Paris and Istanbul makes its first run (1883); *On the Size of Atoms* is published by British scientist William Thomson, later Lord Kelvin (1883); peace is restored between Peru and Chile (1883); Friedrich Nietzsche (German philosopher) begins *Thus Spake Zarathustra* (1884–91); gold is discovered in the Transvaal (1884) and this leads to the rise of Johannesburg; a truce is signed between Bolivia and Chile, with Bolivia forced to cede its only coastal territory to Chile (1884); the *Oxford English Dictionary* begins publication (1884–1928); the Berlin Conference of 14 nations on African affairs is held (1884).

1885–89: Karl Benz builds the single-cylinder engine for motor cars (1885); the individuality of fingerprints is proved by Sir Francis Galton (1885); the first Indian National Congress meets (1886); the Statue of Liberty is presented to the US by France (1886); steam is first used to sterilize surgical instruments by Ernst von Bergmann (1886); Irish politician Charles Parnell, the Fenians, and British Prime Min. William Gladstone try unsuccessfully to pass the first Irish Home Rule Bill to give Ireland control over domestic affairs (1886); Sir Arthur Conan Doyle writes the first Sherlock Holmes story, *A Study in Scarlet* (1887); William II (the Kaiser) becomes emperor of Germany (1888); Vincent Van Gogh paints the series of sunflowers (1888) and later, *Starry Night*; the electric motor is first constructed by Nikola A. Tesla and manufactured by George Westinghouse (1888); radio waves are discovered to be of the same family as light waves by the independently working Heinrich Hertz and Oliver Lodge (1888); Kodak box camera produced by George Eastman (1888); "Jack the Ripper" murders six women in London (1888);

Alexander G. Eiffel designs the Eiffel Tower for the Paris World Exhibition (1889).

1890–94: The first Japanese general election is held (1890); German Chancellor Bismarck dismissed by Emperor William II (1890); the first moving picture shows appear in New York (1890); Oscar Wilde writes *The Picture of Dorian Gray* (1890); antitoxins are discovered by Emil von Behring (1890); the first entirely steel-framed building is erected in Chicago (1890); the Triple Alliance between Austria, Germany and Italy is renewed for 12 years (1891); Briton Thomas Hardy writes *Tess of the D'Ubervilles* (1891); Henri Toulouse-Lautrec produces his first music hall posters (1891); *Experiments in Aero-dynamics* is published by Samuel P. Langley (1891); the All-Deutschland Verband (Pan-Germany League) is founded (1891); Russia experiences widespread famine (1891); an earthquake in Japan kills ten thousand people (1891); the Java Man (*Pithecanthropus homo erectus*) is discovered by Dutch anthropologist Eugène Dubois, in Java (1891); Paul Gauguin (French) paints *By the Sea* in Tahiti (1892); Rudolph Diesel (German) patents his internal-combustion engine (1892); Tchai-kovsky performs his *The Nutcracker* ballet score in St Petersburg (1892); Karl Benz constructs his four-wheel car (1893); Jewish French army captain Alfred Dreyfus is arrested under controversy and convicted of spying for Germany (1894); Rudyard Kipling writes *The Jungle Book* (1894); after Japan sends troops to Seoul, Korea, Japan declares war on China and defeats the Chinese at Port Arthur (1894); Emil Berliner develops a horizontal gramophone disc, replacing the record cylinder for sound reproduction (1894).

1895–99: The Chinese-Japanese war ends with Japan victorious: Formosa and Port Arthur are first ceded to Japan and later returned to China for payment (1895); H.G. Wells writes *The Time Machine* (1895); William B. Yeats writes *Poems* (1895); x-rays are discovered by William Röntgen (1895); Marchese Marconi invents radio telegraphy (1895); the principle of rocket reaction propulsion is developed by Konstantin Isiolkovski (1895); the first modern Olympics is held in Athens, Greece (1896); Anton Chekhov (Russian) writes *The Sea Gull* (1896); five annual Nobel prizes are established by Alfred Nobel for persons who have contributed the most in the fields of physics, physiology and medicine, chemistry, literature and peace (1896); Wilfrid Laurier becomes the first French Canadian prime minister of Canada (1896–1911); the Klondike gold rush in Bonanza Creek, Canada, begins (1896); Edmond Rostand writes *Cyrano de Bergerac* (1897); Queen Victoria celebrates her Diamond Jubilee (1897); French writer Emile Zola writes an open letter, *J'accuse*, condemning the Dreyfus espionage trial and he is imprisoned (1898), Col. Henry admits forging documents in the case (1898), and Captain Dreyfus is pardoned after a retrial (1899)—the case polarized French politics for a decade; the US declares war on Spain over Cuba and destroys the Spanish fleet at Manila (1898); Spain cedes Cuba, Puerto Rico, Guam and the Philippines to the US for $20 million at the Treaty of Paris; Chinese Boxers, an anti-Western organization, is formed (1898); the Boer War begins as the South African Republic (Transvaal) and the Orange Free State unite against the British (1898); Marie and Pierre Curie discover radium and polonium (1898); German Count Ferdinand von Zeppelin builds his airship (1898); photographs using artificial light are first taken (1898); Marchese Marconi invents the radio (1899).

1900: The Boer War continues and Canadian troops set sail for South Africa to fight for England in their first foreign war; Boxer rebellion against Western influence, supported by the Dowager Empress Tzu-hsi, continues in China against Christian missionaries and foreigners; Sigmund Freud, the founder of psychoanalysis (Austrian), completes *The Interpretation of Dreams*; Wilhelm Wundt writes *Comparative Psychology*; Shintoism is reinstated in Japan to counter Buddhist influence; Commonwealth of Australia is created; Max Planck formulates the quantum theory; human speech is first transmitted via radio waves by the Canadian-born scientist R.A. Fessenden; Holland's senate creates an international arbitration court at The Hague; millions are reported starving in India; botanist Hugo de Vries rediscovers Gregor Mendel's laws of heredity after 30 years; 10,000 Ashanti natives attack a British force of 400 at Cape Coast, Ghana, and are defeated.

1901: Queen Victoria dies and is succeeded by her son Edward VII; the Dutch Boers begin organized guerrilla warfare against the British; the Cuba Convention makes Cuba a US protectorate; US Pres. William McKinley is assassinated and is succeeded by Theodore Roosevelt; a treaty is signed to build the Panama Canal

under US supervision; the hormone adrenaline is first isolated; Walter Nernst postulates the "third law of thermodynamics"; John Pierpont Morgan organizes the US Steel Corp., the first billion-dollar corporation; the Peace of Peking ends the Boxer uprising and China is forced to pay an indemnity of $333 million to the Allies to amend commercial treaties in favor of foreign nationals and to allow foreign troops to be posted in Peking; French physicist Henri Becquerel determines that atoms have internal structure; there are racial riots in New Orleans when American black leader Booker T. Washington is invited to the White House; the Trans-Siberian railroad reaches Port Arthur on the east coast of Russia; oil drilling begins in Persia (Iran).

1902: An Anglo-Japanese treaty recognizes the independence of China and Korea; the Treaty of Vereeniging ends the Boer War and the Orange Free State becomes a British colony; the Triple Alliance between Ger-many, Austria and Italy is renewed for another six years; the US acquires perpetual control over the Panama Canal; the Colonial Conference meets in London; the Committee of Imperial Defence meets in London for the first time; Jean Sibelius, Finnish composer and conductor, completes *Symphony No. 2*; Egypt's Aswan Dam is opened.

1903: The "Entente Cordiale" between England and France is established to counter German imperialism; the Russian Social Democratic Party splits into Mensheviks (led by Plechanoff) and Bolsheviks (led by Vladimir Lenin and Leon Trotsky); *The Conduction of Electricity through Gases* is published by Joseph John Thomson; Briton George Bernard Shaw writes *Man and Superman*; Orville and Wilbur Wright successfully fly a powered airplane near Kitty Hawk, North Carolina; the electrocardiograph, which records heart action, is invented by William Einthoven; Briton Emmeline Pankhurst founds the National Women's Social and Political Union and campaigns for women's right to vote; Albert I, Prince of Monaco, founds the International Peace Institute; Henry Ford founds the Ford Motor Company.

1904: The Russo-Japanese War breaks out over Korea and Manchuria; the Japanese besiege Port Arthur and occupy Seoul; the Russian fleet is partially destroyed off Port Arthur; the Russians are defeated at Mukden and Toushima Straits; Max Weber writes *The Protestant Ethic and the Birth of Capitalism*; the first performance of Giacomo Puccini's opera *Madame Butterfly* in Milan; the first radio transmission of music is at Graz, Austria; the general theory of radioactivity is postulated by Ernest Rutherford and Frederick Soddy; W.C. Gorgas eradicates yellow fever in the Panama Canal Zone; silicones are discovered by F.S. Kipping.

1905: Albert Einstein publishes four papers detailing his special theory of relativity, the relationship between mass and energy, the Brownian theory of motion and another formulating the photon theory of light; the Russian city of Port Arthur surrenders to the Japanese; in Russia troops fire at peaceful protest marchers heading for the czar's Winter Palace in St Petersburg, and the event becomes known as "Bloody Sunday"; Wil-liam II of Germany and Nicholas II of Russia sign the Treaty of Bjorko for mutual help in Europe; the Treaty of Portsmouth ends the Russo-Japanese War; a general strike in Russia in response to Bloody Sunday includes a sailors' mutiny on the battleship *Potemkin* and the creation of the first workers soviet in St Petersburg; Czar Nicholas establishes a constitutional government (the Imperial Duma); the Norwegian Parliament decides to separate from Sweden; the Anglo-Japanese alliance is renewed for 10 years; the Sinn Fein nationalist party is formed in Ireland; George Santayana writes his philosophical work *The Life of Reason*.

1906: Reform laws are proposed in Russia and the Imperial Duma is dissolved by the czar to end the radical change; the All India Muslim League is founded by Aga Khan; the term "allergy" is introduced by Clemens von Pirquet; the position of the magnetic North Pole is determined by Norwegian explorer Roald Amundsen; night-shift work for women is forbidden in many countries; the San Francisco earthquake kills 700 people and causes $400 million in property loss; Transvaal and Orange River colonies are granted self-government.

1907: The second Russian Duma meets in March; its radical proposals lead to its dissolution five months later; the US prohibits Japanese immigration; Lenin leaves Russia and founds the newspaper *The Proletarian*; Grigori Rasputin, a Russian mystic, gains influence with the royal family when he treats the hemo-philiac son of Nicholas II; New Zealand becomes a dominion within the British Empire; Baden-Powell forms the Boy Scout movement; Korea becomes a Japanese protectorate; Russian artist Marc Chagall paints *Peasant Women*; Gustav Mahler (Austrian) composes *Symphony No. 8*; Ivan Pavlov (Russian) studies conditioned reflexes in dogs; the SS *Lusitania* beats the SS *Mauritania* in a race from Ireland to New York.

1908: Austria occupies Bosnia and Herzegovina; Bulgaria declares independence from Turkey; Isadora Duncan emerges as a popular modern dancer; the Zeppelin airship crashes near Echterdingen; General Motors Corporation is formed in the US; Henry Ford designs the inexpensive, standardized Model T automobile while pioneering assembly line techniques for autos; an earthquake in Sicily and Calabria kills 150,000; American Gertrude Stein writes *Three Lives*; French writer Anatole France completes the political satire *Penguin Island*; Canadian Lucy Maud Montgomery writes *Anne of Green Gables*.

1909: Turkey and Serbia acknowledge Austrian control of Bosnia and Herzegovina; sultan of Turkey is deposed and replaced by his brother; Ezra Pound writes *Exultations*; the first newsreels appear and director D.W. Griffith features Canadian-born Mary Pickford, who becomes the first film star; Sergei Diaghilev presents his *Ballets Russes*, revolutionizing dance, in Paris; Blériot flies from Calais to Dover in 37 minutes, Farman makes the first 100-mile flight; W.E. Du Bois cofounds the National Negro Committee which becomes the National Association for the Advancement of Colored People in 1910; Girl Guides organized in Britain; Thomas Hunt Morgan begins research in genetics; US explorer Robert E. Peary reaches the North Pole.

1910: The Union of South Africa becomes a dominion within the British Empire with Louis Botha as premier; China abolishes slavery; Japan takes over Korea; Montenegro becomes an independent kingdom; Portugal becomes a republic after a revolution ends the monarchy; Albania rebels against Turkish rule; Roger Fry arranges the Post-Impressionist Exhibition in London with works by Cezanne, van Gogh and Matisse; Igor Stravinsky performs his ballet score *The Firebird* in Paris; the South American tango is the dance craze in Europe and North America; the first deep-sea research expedition is undertaken by Murray and Hjort; the five-day work week is instituted in the US, making the "week-end" possible.

1911: US-Japanese and Anglo-Japanese commercial treaties are signed; Diaz surrenders power in Mexico but revolutions continue; the Kaiser's Hamburg speech promises Germany's "Place in the Sun"; war erupts between Turkey and Italy and aircraft are first used for offensive measures; a revolution in Central China is followed by the fall of the Manchu dynasty (in power since 1644) and the proclamation of a Chinese Republic; Sun Yat-sen is elected president and he appoints Chiang Kai-shek as his military adviser; Russian premier, Peter Stolypin, is assassinated; Roald Amundsen reaches the South Pole; Marie Curie is the first person to win a second Noble Prize, in chemistry; Rutherford formulates his theory of atomic structure.

1912: British dock workers, coal miners and transport workers strike; the German-Austro-Italian alliance is renewed again; Lenin becomes editor of *Pravda*; Sun Yat-sen founds Kuomintang (Chinese National Party); Montenegro declares war against Turkey and Bulgaria, Greece and Serbia mobilize; Carl Jung writes *The Theory of Psychoanalysis*; the term "vitamin" is coined by Polish chemist Kasimir Funk; Stefansson and Anderson explore Arctic Canada; Wilson's cloud chamber (particle detector) photographs lead to the detection of protons and electrons; the Royal Flying Corps (later RAF) is established in Britain; SS *Titanic* sinks on its first voyage after colliding with an iceberg: 1,513 people drown.

1913: The London Peace Treaty ending the First Balkan War is signed and Turkey loses all possessions in Europe except E. Thrace; the Second Balkan War breaks out as Bulgaria attacks Serbia and Greece; Russia declares war on Bulgaria, Bulgaria and Turkey settle a peace treaty and Turkey regains Thrace, Serbia invades Albania; Greece and Turkey make peace; police crack down on suffragette demonstrations led by Emmeline Pankhurst in London; Maxim Gorki, the father of Soviet literature, writes *My Childhood*; Charlie Chaplin first stars in movies; Niels Bohr formulates his theory of atomic structure; Albert Schweitzer, medical missionary, opens his famous hospital in Lambaréné, French Congo.

1914: Archduke Francis Ferdinand, heir to the Austrian throne, is assassinated in Sarajevo (capital of the Austro-Hungarian province of Bosnia) by a Serbian nationalist (June 28); Austria-Hungary challenges Serbia and declares war (July 28); Russia and France support Serbia and mobilize troops; Austria's ally Germany declares war on Russia and France in response; the members of the Triple Entente (Britain, France, Russia) declare war on Turkey after Turks attack Russia; Germany, Austria-Hungary and the Ottoman Empire (Turkey) form alliance of Central Powers, they are opposed by UK, members of British Empire, France, Russia, Belgium, Japan and Serbia (Allied Powers); Germany invades Belgium, attacks France, and establishes the Eastern Front against the Russians at Tannenberg and the Masurian Lakes; on the Western Front the Germans are held in check after battles at Marne River, France (Sept. 6); the First Battle of Ypres, Belgium, is waged to prevent the Germans from cutting British supply lines to France; Austria-Hungary fails in three attacks on Serbia and, after the Russians capture the province of Galicia, retreats to its own territory; by Nov. 14, 1914 there is a deadlock along the Western Front (stretching 720 km across Belgium and northeast France to the Swiss border) that remains throughout the war; Irish writer James Joyce writes *Dubliners* (1914); John B. Watson writes *Behavior: an Introduction to Comparative Psychology* (1914); the first successful heart surgery is performed on a dog by Dr. Alexis Carrel (1914); the Panama Canal opens (1914); millions of immigrants leave southern and eastern Europe between 1905 and 1914.

1915: The Allied Gallipoli Campaign to neutralize Turkey fails and Australian and New Zealand troops suffer heavy losses; the first German submarine (U-boat) attack is at Le Havre; the German blockade of England begins; at the Second Battle of Ypres, Canadian forces hold off the German advance while under heavy fire and attacks from chlorine gas and newly-introduced flame throwers; Italy joins the Allied Powers, declares war on Austria-Hungary (May 23) and an Italian Front soon opens; a German submarine sinks the *Lusitania* (May 7); the first Zeppelin air attack takes place on London; Ottoman-controlled Mesopotamia (now Iraq) surrenders to Britain; Italians fight Austria-Hungary in continuous battles at Isonzo (1915–17); Germans invade

Warsaw and Brest-Litovsk; Allied troops land at Salonika; the first fighter airplane is constructed by Hugo Junkers; Henry Ford develops a farm tractor; the dysentery bacillus is isolated by British chemist James Kendall; the first book advocating birth control, by American Margaret Sanger, is published, and the author is sent to jail.

1916: Germany stages a Zeppelin raid on Paris and declares war on Portugal; Portugal and Rumania later join the Allied Powers; in the Middle East, T.E. Lawrence leads an Arab revolt against Turkey; heavy casualties occur at Verdun (Feb. 21); British and German fleets clash at the Battle of Jutland (May 31–June 1); the 1st Newfoundland Regiment is annihilated along with 624,000 Allied troops during the offensive at the Somme (launched July 1); HMS *Hampshire* is sunk; Italy declares war on Germany; the Germans first use gas masks and steel helmets; peace notes are exchanged between Germany and the Allies; Lloyd George becomes British prime minister; blood for transfusion is first refrigerated; the theory of shell shock is put forth by F.W. Mott; an underwater ultrasonic source for submarine detection is built by Paul Langevin; Britain initiates daylight-saving time; US purchases the Virgin Islands for $25 million.

1917: The United States enters the war on the Allied side (Apr. 6); Germans withdraw on the Western Front; the Russian Black Sea fleet mutinies at Sebastopol; there is revolution in Russia in Feb. and the Czar abdicates (Mar. 16); Kerensky becomes Russian premier and continues the war effort; Canadian forces seize Vimy Ridge in northern France; Germany stages air attacks on England; Greece joins the Allies (July); China declares war on Germany and Austria; the British-led offensive at the Third Battle of Ypres (Passchendaele) fails (July 31); the Italian army is defeated at Caporetto by Austria-Hungary; Kerensky's government is overthrown in Petrograd in Oct. and Lenin is appointed Chief Commissar, Trotsky becomes Commissar for Foreign Affairs and Russia seeks peace with Germany; the first tank battle is at Cambrai; starvation sweeps Germany; Finland declares independence from Russia; the Allies execute dancer Mata Hari as a spy; Lord Arthur Balfour, the British Foreign Secretary, issues the Balfour Declaration stating British support for a Jewish national homeland in Palestine; women are arrested for suffrage activities in the US.

1918: Russia, the Ukraine and the Central Powers conclude the Treaties of Brest-Litovsk: the first one establishes the independence of the Ukraine, the second strips Russia of its Baltic and Polish possessions; Turks surrender to British at Jerusalem; US Pres. Wilson puts forth Fourteen Points for world peace (including a proposal for a League of Nations); Rumania signs a peace treaty with the Central Powers; Germany launches three final offensives on the Western Front (Mar. 21); Germans bomb Paris; the Second Battle of the Marne (July 15–Aug. 6) is won by the Allies; the Allies win victories on all fronts in the fall; the Japanese push into Siberia; Germany and Austria agree to retreat to their own territory before an armistice is signed; the Hungarian premier is assassinated; the Turkish and Austro-Hungarian empires and Bulgaria surrender to the Allies (Nov. 3); the German fleet mutinies at Kiel and the emperor flees; an armistice between the Allies and Germany is signed (Nov. 11); Germany agrees to the provisions of the Treaty of Versailles after the Allies threaten to invade; Emperor Charles of Austria loses the throne; the map of Europe is reshaped: Austria becomes a republic and the Serbo-Croatian-Slovene Kingdom of Yugoslavia is proclaimed, Poland and Czechoslovakia are created; Iceland becomes independent state; the Russian Revolution continues as Bolshevik workers take over government buildings, the Winter Palace and later Moscow and other cities; civil war between the Bolshevik (Red) and anti-Bolshevik (White) continues (until 1920); British, French and American troops intervene against the Reds; the British government abandons Home Rule for Ireland; ex-Czar Nicholas II and family are executed by Russian revolutionaries; Hsu-Shih-Chang becomes president of the Chinese Republic; women over 30 get the vote in Britain; controversy rages over the psychology of Freud and Jung; the true dimensions of the Milky Way are discovered by Harlow Shapley, an American astronomer.

1919: US Pres. Woodrow Wilson heads the first League of Nations meeting in Paris; the Peace Conference opens at Versailles; Benito Mussolini founds the Fasci del Combattimento in Italy; socialist governments are founded in Austria and Budapest, Hungary; the Treaty of Versailles is signed with Germany; the final treaty exacts heavy financial penalties on Germany, restricts the German army and navy, blames Germany for provoking the war and establishes the League of Nations; US refusal to ratify the treaty excludes it from League membership; the Allied peace treaty with Austria is signed at St Germain; the Treaty of Neuilly with Bulgaria is signed; the International Labor Congress in Washington endorses the eight-hour workday; the Red (Soviet) forces win successive battles in the Russian civil war; Soviets attack Finland; the first nonstop flight across the Atlantic is made from Newfound-land to Ireland by J.W. Alcock and A. Whitten Brown; Lady Astor is elected to Britain's Parliament, becoming the first female MP.

1920: The League of Nations is founded in Paris and establishes headquarters in Geneva; Russian civil war ends with Soviet victory; Great Britain gains control of Palestine from the Turks; The Hague becomes the International Court of Justice; the Little Entente between Czechoslovakia, Yugoslavia and Rumania is formed; the Treaty of Trianon is signed with Hungary; the Treaty of Sevres is signed with the Ottoman Empire; the 19th Amendment gives American women the vote; 200,000 Chinese die in an earthquake in Kansu province; the world population is 1.8 billion; Britain establishes separate parliaments for Northern and Southern Ireland; Adolph Hitler founds the Nazi party in Munich, Germany, and announces his 25-point program, blaming Germany's war defeat on Jews and Communists; Mohandas (Mahatma) Ghandi becomes India's leader in its struggle for independence from Britain; Prohibition goes into effect in the US, banning the sale and consumption of alcoholic beverages; a worldwide influenza epidemic, which began in 1918, leaves 22 million dead.

1921: The first Indian Parliament meets; German reparations payments totalling $33.3 million are fixed by the Allies at a Paris conference; Hitler's storm troopers (SA) begin to terrorize ideological opponents; Mackenzie King is elected prime minister of Canada; British Broadcasting Company is founded (changed to the British Broadcasting Corporation in 1927); the Spanish prime minister and Japanese premier are assassinated; founder of Portuguese republic is murdered; ex-emperor Charles stages two failed coup attempts to regain Hungarian throne; Britain and Ireland sign a peace treaty; German mark falls and rapid inflation plagues the economy;

coal is successfully hydrogenated into oil by Friedrich Bergius; the tuberculosis vaccine (B-C-G) is developed by Albert Calmette and Camille Guerin; the chromosome theory of heredity is put forth by American biologist Thomas Morgan; Albert Einstein wins Nobel Prize for Physics; Ku Klux Klan members terrorize blacks and black sympathizers in the southern US; one of the founders of modern aeronautics, Hermann J. Oberth, writes *The Rocket into Interplanetary Space*.

1922: Gandhi is sentenced to six years imprisonment for civil disobedience; German reconstruction minister Walter Rathenau is assassinated by German nationalists; the Arab Congress at Nablus rejects the British control of Palestine; Austria denounces "Anschluss" (union with Germany); Mussolini stages the March on Rome and forms a Fascist government; Irish Free State is proclaimed; the tomb of Tutankhamen is discovered by Lord Carnarvaron and Howard Carter; a self-winding wristwatch is invented by John Harwood (patented in 1924); a stock market "boom" begins in the US; Soviet states form the USSR; insulin, prepared by Canadian physicians Frederick Banting, Charles Best and John Macleod, is first given to diabetic patients.

1923: An earthquake kills 120,000 people in Tokyo and Yokohama; Adolph Hitler tries (and fails) to overthrow the German government ("Beer Hall Putsch"); Greek army overthrows monarch; Jewish philosopher Martin Buber writes the theological *I and Thou*; the theory of acids and bases is postulated by J.N. Brönsted; Lee de Forest demonstrates the process for motion pictures with sound; the first commercial airline, Aeroflot, is founded in the USSR.

1924: Ramsay MacDonald forms the first Labour government in Britain; Adolph Hitler writes *Mein Kampf* during an eight-month jail term; R.C. Andrews discovers skulls and skeletons of Mesozoic dinosaurs in the Gobi desert; Winston Churchill, having switched from the Liberals to the Conservatives, is named Chancellor of the Exchequer in Britain; in Russia, Lenin dies and Stalin, Zinoviev and Kamenev ally against Trotsky; the "Zinoviev letter," purported to be calling for a communist revolution in Britain, is published by the British Foreign Office; Greece becomes a republic; elections are held in Italy and Mussolini wins support of 65% of the electorate; leader of Italian socialists is murdered; Albanian Republic is founded; Sigmund Freud begins *Collected Writings* (12 vols. 1924–39); Ghandi fasts for 21 days, protesting feuding between Hindus and Muslims in India; British astronomer Arthur Eddington discovers that the luminosity of a star is approximately related to its mass; insecticides are used for the first time; a patent application for iconoscope (television) is filed by Russian-American inventor V.K. Zworkin; Danish polar explorer Knud Ras-mussen completes the longest dog-sled journey ever made across the North American Arctic; British Imperial Airways begins commercial air flights.

1925: Locarno Conference creates a series of treaties between Germany, France, Belgium, Poland, UK, Italy and Czechoslovakia that set up a demilitarized zone in the Rhineland and confirmed borders between Belgium, France and Germany; Mrs Nellie Tayloe Ross of Wyoming becomes the first woman governor in the US; the United Church of Canada is founded; recognizable human features are transmitted by television by Scottish inventor John Logie Baird; Walter P. Chrysler founds the Chrysler Corporation; the (Franz) Fischer and (Hans) Tropsch synthesis leads to the industrial development of synthetic oil; Heisenberg, Bohr and Jordan develop quantum mechanics for atoms; the presence of cosmic rays in the upper atmosphere is discovered by US physicist Robert Andrews Millikan; the "flapper" era takes hold; an international convention condemns the illegal narcotics trade.

1926: Fascist youth organizations appear: "Balilla" in Italy and "Hitlerjugend" in Germany; Josef Pilsudski successfully stages a coup d'état in Poland and begins a military dictatorship; commerce in Britain is stopped by a general strike; Trotsky is expelled from Moscow; Hirohito succeeds his father Taisho as Emperor of Japan; Robert H. Goddard fires the first liquid fuel rocket; vitamin B is isolated by B. Jansen and W. Donath; Kodak produces the first 16mm movie film; British Imperial Chemical Industries (ICI) begins operations; H.L. Mencken writes *Notes on Democracy*; Turkish reforms include the abolition of polygamy, modernization of female attire and adoption of Latin alphabet (1926–28).

1927: The Allied military control of Germany ends; an economic conference in Geneva is attended by 52 nations; the economic system in Germany collapses ("Black Friday"); Trotsky expelled from the Communist Party in the USSR; Nazis on trial in Austria for political murder are acquitted and socialists riot in Venice to protest; the first film with sound, a "talkie," *The Jazz Singer*, stars Al Jolson; Lev Theremin invents the earliest electronic musical instrument; Charles Lindbergh flies the monoplane *Spirit of St Louis* in the first solo transatlantic flight, nonstop from New York to Paris in 33.5 hours; Canadian forests are the first sprayed with insecticides by airplanes; the first vehicular tunnel, the Holland Tunnel, links New York and New Jersey.

1928: The Supreme Court of Canada rules that women may not hold public office because they are not "persons" as defined by the British North America Act, but the British Privy Council overturns the decision in a landmark Commonwealth case in 1929; the Kellogg-Briand Pact outlawing war is signed by 65 states; Josef Stalin emerges as leader of Soviet Union; the first economic five-year plan begins in the USSR; Chiang Kai-Shek is elected president of China; over-production of coffee leads to the collapse of Brazil's economy; penicillin is discovered by Alexander Fleming (Scottish); American anthropologist Margaret Mead writes *Coming of Age in Samoa;* the first colour motion pictures are exhibited by George Eastman in Rochester, New York; J.L. Baird presents colour television; Mickey Mouse makes his Disney debut.

1929: The US Stock Exchange collapses on Oct. 28, Black Friday; the Great Depression, a world economic crisis, begins and is primarily caused by easy credit and stock market over-speculation, overproduction of goods and tariff and war-debt policies; six Chicago-area gangsters are machine-gunned to death in the St Valentine's Day Massacre; a dictatorship is established in Serbo-Croat-Slovene kingdom by the monarch and the country's name is changed to Yugoslavia; Trotsky is exiled from USSR; talks on Indian sovereignty begin betweeen Indian leaders and the Viceroy; the Lateran Treaty establishes the independence of Vatican City; precise timekeeping is made possible with the quartz-crystal clocks by W.A. Morrison; the airship *Graf Zeppelin* flies around the world in 21 days.

1930: Austria and Italy sign a treaty of friendship; Britain, the US, Japan, France and Italy sign a treaty on naval disarmament; right-wing coalition comes to power in Germany, Nazis later capture 107 more seats in an election; right-wing government is formed in Poland; Catholic-Fascist units are established in Austria; revolution in Argentina brings new military dictatorship to power; the planet Pluto is discovered by C.W. Tombaugh at Lowell Observatory; a yellow fever vaccine is developed by South African microbiologist Max Theiler; photoflash bulb is introduced; the word "technocracy," meaning the domination of technology, comes into use.

1931: A financial crisis in central Europe is caused by the collapse of Austria's Credit-Anstalt; all German banks close following the bankruptcy of the German Danatbank; Britain abandons the gold standard; Fascist party is formed in Britain; the Statute of Westminster established the British Commonwealth of Nations as a free association of autonomous nations sharing a common allegiance to the British crown, and declared that British Parliament could no longer legislate for any member states unless requested to do so; US Pres. Hoover proposes a one-year moratorium for reparations and war debts; the first trans-African railroad line is completed, Benguella-Katanga; the northern face of the Matterhorn is climbed for the first time by Franz and Toni Schmid.

1932: The Indian National Congress, a nationalist party dedicated to home rule, is declared illegal and its leader, Mahatma Gandhi, is arrested; the US criticizes Japanese aggression in Manchuria; the Nazis sweep the German Reichstag (Parliament) elections while WWI hero Hindenburg wins the Presidential election; Hitler refuses Hinden-burg's offer to become Vice Chancellor, and the Austrian-born Hitler receives German citizenship; Franklin D. Roosevelt wins the US presidential election and proposes domestic reform programs to provide recovery and relief from the Great Depression ("New Deal"); the USSR suffers famine; Zuider Zee, a huge dam and drainage project in Holland, is completed; Amelia Earheart is the first woman to fly solo across the Atlantic; Japan conquers world markets by undercutting prices; about 30 million people are unemployed worldwide; the neutron is discovered by James Chadwick; vitamin D is discovered.

1933: Reichstag building is burned in Berlin and Hitler uses the event to justify banning opposition parties and labour unions; Hitler is appointed German Chancellor and granted dictatorial powers with the Enabling Law; Nazi Hermann Goering is named Prussian prime minister; Parliamentary government is suspended in Austria; starvation spreads in USSR; Paul Joseph Goebbels is named Hitler's Minister of Propaganda; Japan withdraws from the League of Nations; the first concentration camps are built by the Nazis in Germany to hold Jews and ideological opponents; books by non-Nazi and Jewish authors are burned in Germany; Germans begin to boycott and restrict Jewish services; an anti-Nazi treatise, *Judaism-Christendom-Germanism*, is published by Cardinal von Faulhaber in Munich; Assyrian Christians are massacred in Iraq; US goes off the gold standard and tries to stimulate its economy by creating The Tennessee Valley Authority to construct dams and generate electricity.

1934: A revolution in Austria overturns the Social Democrats and Austrian Chancellor is assassinated by the Nazis; a general strike takes place in France; the USSR is admitted to the League of Nations; Winston Churchill warns the British Parliament of the German air menace; Hitler oversees purge of his associates and many are executed; a national vote grants him the title Führer (leader); Stalin's purge of the Soviet Communist party begins and he reportedly oversees the murder of millions of people; German scientist Albert Einstein is persecuted by the Nazis for being Jewish and he flees, settling in the US; Japan renounces the Washington treaties of 1922 and 1930; Mao Tse-tung, leader of the Chinese Communists, heads the Long March.

1935: Nazis repudiate the Treaty of Versailles and reintroduce compulsory military service; the autonomous territory of Saarland votes for reunion with Germany; an Anglo-German Naval Agreement is concluded; Nazis implement the Nuremburg Laws against Jews, stripping them of civic rights and forbidding intermarriage with non-Jews; Mussolini invades Ethiopia, and the League of Nations retaliates by imposing sanctions; the Chaco War, a bitter conflict between Paraguay and Bolivia begun in 1932 and fought over oil-rich but otherwise barren territory, ended after 100,000 lives were lost and both sides were exhausted (treaty not concluded until 1938); radar equipment to detect aircraft is built by Robert Watson Watt; oil pipelines between Iraq, Haifa and Tripoli open; Persia changes its name to Iran.

1936: King George V of England dies and is succeeded by Edward VIII; German troops occupy the Rhineland and Hitler wins the German elections with 99 percent of the vote; Italy, Austria and Hungary sign the Rome Pact; Britain, France and the US sign the London Naval Convention; an Austro-German convention acknowledges Austrian independence; the Spanish Civil War begins and Francisco Franco is appointed Chief of State by the Nationalist insurgents against the government's Loyalist republicans; Franco begins the siege of Madrid, rebels take Malaga and destroy Guernica and Gijon and Franco begins a naval blockade (1937); Heinrich Himmler is appointed head of the Gestapo, responsible for Nazi concentration camps (1936–45); King Edward VIII abdicates in order to marry American divorcee Wallis Simpson; Mussolini and Hitler proclaim the Rome-Berlin Axis; the Anti-Comintern Pact is signed by Germany and Japan; Chiang Kai-shek declares war on Japan; Dr Alexis Carrel develops an artificial heart; the airship *Hindenburg* burns at Lakehurst New Jersey, after a transatlantic flight; black American athlete Jesse Owens upsets the Nazis when he wins four gold medals at the Olympic Games in Berlin.

1937: Poland refuses to return Danzig to Germany; the first worldwide radio broadcast is heard when George VI is crowned King of Great Britain; Roosevelt signs a US Neutrality Act, intended to keep the US out of a possible European war; Trotsky, exiled from Russia in 1929, is forced to leave Norway and settles in Mexico; aggressive Japanese war policy begins when Prince Konoye is named the Japanese premier, and the Japanese seize major Chinese cities (Beijing, Tianjin, Shanghai, Nanjing and Hangzhou), forcing Chiang Kai-shek and the Communists, under Mao Tse-tung and Chou En-lai, to unite; the Chinese government makes Chungking its capital; the Royal Commission on Palestine recommends the establishment of Arab and Jewish states; Stalin initiates a purge of Soviet generals and show trials of political leaders; Britain signs naval agreements with Germany and the USSR; Germany guarantees Belgian sovereignty; Italy joins the Anti-Comintern Pact and withdraws from the League of Nations; Japanese planes sink US gunboat in Chinese waters; Amelia Earheart disappears during a Pacific flight.

1938: Germany annexes Austria, "Anschluss" (Mar.); France calls up reservists; Great Britain, France and Italy agree to let Germany absorb the Sudetenland, Czechoslovakia, in a policy of appeasement (Munich Pact, Sept.) and Germany promises to cease its aggressive expansion; British foreign minister Anthony Eden resigns in protest against the appeasement policy and Winston Churchill also voices opposition; Franco begins an offensive against the Spanish Loyalists in Catalonia; anti-Jewish legislation is enacted in Italy; Kristallnacht, or "Night of Broken Glass," is a large-scale pogrom by the Nazis against German Jews; the US and Germany recall their respective ambassadors; Japan withdraws from the League of Nations and sets up a puppet Chinese government in Nanking; Howard Hughes flies around the world in less than four days.

1939: US Pres. Roosevelt demands assurances from Hitler and Mussolini that they have no plans to attack other states; Germany breaks the Munich Pact and occupies Bohemia and Moravia; Slovakia is placed under "protection"; Italy invades Albania; Germany renounces the nonaggression pact with Poland and naval agreement with England, and concludes a 10-year alliance with Italy and a nonaggression pact with the USSR, secretly dividing Poland; Germany stages a surprise (blitzkrieg) invasion of Poland, and annexes Danzig (Sept. 1); Britain and France declare war on Germany (Sept. 3); the Allied powers are Britain and France and the Axis powers are led by Germany; Canada declares war (Sept. 10); US Pres. Roosevelt announces US neutrality; Soviets invade Poland from the east (Sept. 17), Germans overrun western Poland and reach Brest-Litovsk and Warsaw; France masses troops along the Maginot Line on the eastern frontier of France and Germany sends troops to its parallel Siegfried Line; the British Expeditionary Force is sent to France; the USSR invades Finland and is expelled from the League of Nations; Japan occupies Hainan and blockades the British at Tientsin; the US renounces the Japanese trade agreement of 1911; the Spanish Civil War ends with Franco's Nationalists (supported by Hitler and Mussolini) victorious over the Loyalists (supported by the USSR); Spain joins the Anti-Comintern Pact and leaves the League of Nations; England and Poland sign a treaty of mutual assistance; women and children are first evacuated from London; the first helicopter is built by Russian-American Igor Sikorsky; the US economy booms from arms sales to Europe.

1940: Food rationing begins in Britain; Finland surrenders (Mar.) and signs a peace treaty with the USSR; Germany invades Norway and Denmark (Apr. 9); Winston Churchill becomes British prime minister (May 10); Norway falls (June); Germany invades Belgium, Luxembourg and the Netherlands (May 10); Holland and Belgium surrender to Germany and 340,000 Allied forces are trapped in Belgium, but most are evacuated from Dunkirk, a French seaport on the English channel (May 29 to June 3); Italy declares war on France and Britain; Germans attack France from the north and enter Paris (June 14); France concludes an armistice with Germany; southern France remains unoccupied until 1942 and is ruled by the Vichy government; USSR seizes Estonia, Latvia and Lithuania (summer); the Royal Navy sinks the French fleet in Oran; the Royal Air Force begins night bombing of Germany; the Battle of Britain in Aug. is the first battle fought completely in the air; Hitler begins bombing England (all-night blitzes) throughout fall and winter; Japan, Germany and Italy sign a military and economic pact; US destroyers are sold to Britain; Germany intensifies U-boat warfare; Italian forces attempt to take Egypt and Libya in order to cut off British access to Middle East oil and the Suez Canal; the British Eighth Army opens an offensive in North Africa and defeats the Italian forces; Trotsky is murdered in Mexico; Batista becomes president of Cuba; wall paintings dating to about 20,000 BC are discovered in France, the Lascaux caves; a giant cyclotron is built at the University of California for producing mesotrons from atomic nuclei.

1941: The British invade Ethiopia and defeat the Italians (by May); Germany opens a counter-offensive in North Africa to aid Italy; German General Rommel regains Libya and Egypt; Germans launch an airborne invasion against Crete, thereby securing an important base in the Mediterranean (by the end of May); England sinks the German battleship *Bismarck* in an effort to protect vital US shipments to Great Britain; Allies develop radar and sonar to track U-boats; German air raids over London continue; US freezes German and Italian assets in that country; Germans invade Russia (Operation Barbarossa, June 22); Churchill and Roosevelt sign the Atlantic charter (Aug. 14); German troops surround Leningrad and Moscow (Nov.), but an early, harsh winter saves the USSR; Marshal Timoshenko

launches the Russian counter-offensive; the US ambassador to Japan warns Pres. Roosevelt of possible Japanese attack; Japanese bomb Pearl Harbor (Dec. 7) and the US and Britain declare war on Japan (Dec. 8); China declares war on the Axis (Dec. 9); Japan invades the Philippines; Germany and Italy declare war on the US; the US declares war on Germany and Italy; British Hong Kong surrenders to the Japanese; Henry Moore draws refugees in London air raid shelters while an official war artist; Dmitri Shostakovich writes *Symphony No. 7* during the German siege of Leningrad; German dramatist Bertolt Brecht writes *Mother Courage and Her Children* while in exile from the Nazis.

1942: Hitler's Final Solution, the systematic murder of Jews in the Nazi gas chambers (Holocaust) is in full force at death camps such as Auschwitz and Dachau; the 26 Allied nations agree not to make separate treaties with the Axis powers; Rommel breaks through British lines and reaches El Alamein (320 km from the Suez Canal); Montgomery (British Eighth Army) scores the first decisive defeat of Rommel at El Alamein; Germans reach Stalingrad, Russia; 400,000 American troops land in French North Africa; Rommel, in full retreat, loses Tobruk and Benghazi; Japan invades Burma, the Dutch East Indies, and captures Singapore; the British bomb Cologne and Lübeck; the US and Canada intern residents of Japanese heritage in camps; many American and Philippine prisoners die in the Japanese-forced Bataan Death March; Americans bomb Tokyo; Americans begin successful island-hopping strategy against Japan and win the battles of the Coral Sea and Midway; French navy loses in Toulon; British and Indian troops advance in Burma; Fermi achieves the first controlled nuclear chain reaction when he splits the atom; the Manhattan Project of intensive US atomic research begins; the first electronic brain or automatic computer is developed in the US; a recorder using plastic magnetic recording tape is invented by German engineers; Gandhi demands independence from Britain and is arrested.

1943: German troops surrender at Stalingrad (Feb. 2) and begin to withdraw from the Caucasus; Churchill and Roosevelt meet in Casablanca; the Japanese are driven from Guadalcanal by US troops; the British Eighth Army reaches Tripoli; Axis powers surrender in North Africa (Tunisia, May 13); Russians destroy the German army southwest of Stalingrad; Russians recapture Rostov and Kharkov; the Royal Air Force raids Berlin; US planes sink the 22-ship Japanese convoy in the Battle of the Bismarck Sea; British and US armies in Africa link up and Rommel retreats; an armed Jewish uprising begins in the overcrowded Warsaw ghetto, but it is crushed by German troops (1943–44) who massacre Jewish inhabitants; the RAF bombs Ruhr dams; US forces land in New Guinea; US recaptures Aleutians; Allies land in Sicily (July 10); Churchill, Roosevelt and Mackenzie King meet in Quebec; US troops bomb Ploesti oil fields in Rumania and enter Messina; Allies land in Salerno Bay and invade Italy, which surrenders unconditionally (Sept. 8); Russians take Kiev; Chinese Gen. and Mme Chiang Kai-shek meet with Roosevelt and Churchill in Cairo and pledge to liberate Korea after Japan is defeated; Churchill, Stalin and Roosevelt hold the Teheran Conference; Allied round-the-clock bombing of Germany begins; the first fully electronic computer is used by the British government to crack German military codes; penicillin is used to treat chronic diseases; Bengal is swept by famine; rationing of selected foods begins in the US; major US cities are troubled by race riots.

1944: Germany continues air raids on London; Russian offensives continue in the Ukraine and Crimea; Allies bomb Berlin; Monte Cassino and Rome are liberated by the Allies June 4; D-day landings in Normandy (France, June 6): over 700 ships and 4,000 landing craft are involved and Canadian troops lead the trek from the Normandy beaches; Germans drop first flying bomb (V-1) on London; southern Japan is bombed by the US; US troops take Saipan; Russians capture 100,000 Germans at Minsk; German officers unsuccessfully attempt to assassinate Hitler; Russians reach Brest-Litovsk; Amer-icans capture Guam from the Japanese; the British Eighth Army takes Florence; creation of a United Nations is discussed at the Dunbarton Oaks conference in Washington; Charles De Gaulle leads the Free French into Paris (Aug. 25); Allies liberate Belgium; the first V-2 rockets land in Britain; Churchill and Roosevelt meet in Quebec; Americans cross the German frontier near Trier; British airborne forces land at Eindhoven and Arnheim but have to withdraw; US troops land in the Philippines; Russians and Yugoslavs enter Belgrade; Russian Army

occupies Hungary; Japanese suffer heavy losses in Battle of Leyte Gulf; Battle of the Bulge (Ardennes Forest) results in Allied victory; France regains Lorraine; Rommel commits suicide; Vietnam, under Ho Chi Minh, declares independence from France; American playwright Tennessee Williams completes *The Glass Menagerie*; quinine is synthesized; Richard Strauss completes the opera *Die Liebe der Danae* in Austria but its performance is cancelled when the Nazis shut down the theatres; French playwright Jean-Paul Sartre writes the existentialist work *Being and Nothingness*.

1945: Britain begins major offensive in Burma; Russians take Warsaw, Cracow and reach Oder River; Churchill, Roosevelt and Stalin meet at the Yalta Conference; Americans enter Manila; Russians take Budapest; British troops reach the Rhine; US air raids on Tokyo, Cologne and Danzig; Okinawa is captured; the British Second Army crosses the Rhine; the last German V-2 rocket falls on Britain; Franklin D. Roosevelt dies and is succeeded by Harry S. Truman; Russians reach Berlin; Bologna is captured; US and Soviet troops meet at Torgau and both liberate Nazi death camps, finding gas chambers and crematoriums; anti-Axis coalition agrees to set up new international body to replace ineffective League of Nations; new United Nations charter drawn up at conference in San Francisco (Apr.–June); Bremen, Genoa, Verona and Venice are captured by the Allies; the Allies cross the Elbe; Mussolini is killed by Italian partisans; Hitler commits suicide (Apr. 30); the German army on the Italian front surrenders; Berlin surrenders to the Russians (May 2) and Germany capitulates to the Allies (May 7); V-E Day (Victory in Europe) ends the war in Europe (May 8); Germany is divided into four zones by the Allies and the three-power occupation of Berlin begins; Churchill, Truman and Stalin meet at Potsdam; Clement Attlee replaces Churchill as prime minister of Great Britain in a Labour landslide; the first atomic bomb is detonated near Alamogordo, New Mexico after being developed by J. Robert Oppenheimer, Enrico Fermi and others (July 16); the Soviet Union declares war on Japan and occupied Manchuria; the US drops atomic bombs on Hiroshima (Aug. 6) and Nagasaki (Aug. 9); Japan surrenders and World War II ends; war dead are estimated at 35 million plus victims of Nazi concentration camps; the Nuremburg trials of Nazi war criminals begin; the League of Nations holds its final meeting in Geneva and turns over its assets to the UN (Oct.); Charles De Gaulle is elected president of the French provisional government; Tito is chief of state of the newly created Federal People's Republic of Yugoslavia; Nationalists and Communists resume civil war in north China; the Arab League is founded to oppose the creation of a Jewish state; Shintoism is abolished in Japan; vitamin A is synthesized; black markets for food, clothing and cigarettes develop in Europe; the UN World Bank (International Bank for Reconstruction and Development) is founded with authorized share capital of $27 billion.

1946: Albania, Bulgaria, Hungary and Transjordan become sovereign states; the UN General Assembly holds its first session in London (Jan. 7), electing Trygve Lie of Norway as its first Secretary-General, and its permanent headquarters is made in New York; Juan Perón is elected president of Argentina; a Peace Conference of 21 nations is held in Paris; 12 leading Nazis are sentenced to death following the Nuremburg trials and others get life imprisonment; power in Japan is transferred from the Emperor to an elected assembly; the UN Atomic Energy Commission is formed to monitor member nations; after a referendum in Italy, the king abdicates, Italy becomes a republic and de Gasperi becomes head of state; xerography (photocopying) is invented by Chester Carl-son; Dr Benjamin Spock writes *Baby and Child Care*, the "baby boom" reference book.

1947: British coal industry is nationalized; *The Diary of Anne Frank* is published by Anne's father, the only member of the German-Jewish Frank family to survive the Holocaust; Burma proclaims its independence; Paris Peace treaties signed; the Dead Sea Scrolls, dating from about 22 BC to AD 100, are discovered in Wadi Qumran, Palestine; American Chuck Yeager flies the first airplane at supersonic speeds; the transistor is invented by Bell Telephone Laboratory scientists; the UN divides Palestine, which is under British mandate, into a Jewish and an Arab state (Nov. 1947) and the British withdraw six months later; India gains independence from Great Britain and is partitioned into India and East and West Pakistan.

1948: Gandhi is assassinated by a Hindu opposing his tolerance of Muslims; a Communist coup d'état takes place in Czechoslovakia (Feb. 25); the Marshall Plan providing $17 billion in aid for Europe is passed by the US Congress; Winston Churchill chairs the Hague Congress for European unity; the Jewish state of Israel is proclaimed with Chaim Weizmann as president and David Ben-Gurion as premier (May 14); neighbouring Arab states declare war (1948–49) on Israel but by the end of the conflict Israel succeeds in increasing its territory; the Berlin airlift by the west begins after the USSR imposes a land and water blockade (1948–Sept. 1949); bread rationing ends in Britain; the World Council of Churches is organized in Amsterdam; American biologist Alfred C. Kinsey writes *Sexual Behavior in the Human Male*; the first World Health Assembly meets in Geneva; the first port radar system is installed in Liverpool, England.

1949: Tianjin, China, falls to the Communists, Chiang Kai-shek resigns as president of China, and removes his Nationalist forces to Formosa; the Communist People's Republic is proclaimed under Mao Tse-tung, with Chou En-lai as premier; the North Atlantic Treaty establishing a defence alliance (NATO) is signed by all parties (Belgium, Canada, Denmark, France, Iceland, Italy, Luxembourg, the Netherlands, Norway, Portugal, UK and US) in Washington; the Berlin blockade by the Soviet Union is lifted; the German Federal Republic (West Ger-many) comes into being with Bonn as its capital and Konrad Adenauer as Chancellor; republic of Eire is proclaimed with its capital in Dublin; Transjordan is renamed the Hashemite Kingdom of Jordan; the state of Vietnam, under Ho Chi Minh, is established at Saigon; civil war looms in Korea; the apartheid program of official racial discrimination is established in South Africa; the Democratic Republic is established in East Germany with Pieck as president; India becomes a federal republic with Pandit Nehru as prime minister; Indonesia gains sovereignty from Holland; the USSR tests its first atomic bomb; the US launches a guided missile to a height of 400 km, the highest altitude yet; George Orwell publishes *Nineteen Eighty-Four*.

1950: Communist China and Russia sign a treaty of friendship and mutual assistance, Britain also recognizes Communist China; 18 protesters are killed in anti-apartheid riots in South Africa; Vietnam, Laos and Cambodia gain independence from France; North Korea invades South Korea, capturing Seoul and forcing Pres. Syngman Rhee to flee; US Atomic Energy Commission begins work on hydrogen bomb; UN forces under Gen. Douglas MacArthur land in South Korea and push north of the 38th parallel, prompting Communist China to enter the war; US recognizes Vietnam, sends military supplies and instructors and signs pact for military assistance with Vietnam, Laos, Cambodia and France.

1951: North Korean forces reach the 38th parallel and capture Seoul: attempts to negotiate peace fail; Gen. MacArthur is replaced as commander in Korea for threatening massive retaliation against China; Winston Churchill forms the government in Britain; Remington Rand produces UNIVAC, the first large-scale, general-purpose computer; electricity is produced from atomic energy in the US; heart-lung machine devised by J. Andre-Thomas; penicillin and streptomycin available in US.

1952: Dwight D. Eisenhower is elected US president; Britain produces an atomic bomb; Elizabeth II becomes Queen of England; Egypt rocked by anti-British riots: premier resigns and the army seizes power; Mau-maus rebel in Kenya and government declares a state of emergency; first hydrogen bomb at Eniwetok Atoll in the Pacific; British Overseas Airways introduces the world's first jet passenger service from London to Rome; the first pocket-sized transistor radio is marketed by Sony in Japan.

1953: An armistice ending the Korean War is signed at Panmunjom; Soviet leader Joseph Stalin dies and is replaced by Malenkov; Sweden's Dag Hammarskjöld is elected UN secretary-general; the Soviet Union explodes a hydrogen bomb; Yugoslavia proclaims a new constitution and Marshall Tito becomes president; Egyptian generals establish a dictatorship and proclaim a republic; rebels from Vietnam attack Laos; Fidel Castro begins a campaign to overthrow Cuban dictator Fulgencio Batista; Ethel and Julius Rosenberg are executed after being convicted of passing American atomic secrets to the Soviet Union; Edmund Hillary and Tenzing Norgay become the first to scale Mt Everest; the first successful open heart surgery is performed in the US; researchers associate lung cancer with cigarette smoking.

1954: Vietnamese Communists defeat the French at Dien Bien Phu; racial segregation in public schools is banned by the US Supreme Court; Gammal Abdel Nasser becomes leader in Egypt; the US Senate censures Sen. Joseph McCarthy for launching a Communist witch-hunt; Canada and the US plan a joint radar defence system in the north (Distant Early Warning, DEW Line); the US *Nautilus* becomes the first nuclear-powered submarine; Dr Jonas Salk begins inoculating children against polio; the oral contraceptive pill is introduced in the US; the first successful kidney transplant is performed in the US; Roger Bannister becomes the first to run a mile in less than four minutes.

1955: Churchill resigns in Britain and is succeeded by Anthony Eden; Bulganin succeeds Malenkov as Soviet premier; eight east-European Communist bloc countries adopt the Warsaw Pact mutual defence treaty; West Germany joins NATO; border clashes between Israel and Jordan increase; Juan Perón is ousted by a military coup in Argentina; the first optical fibres are produced in Britain.

1956: Nasser elected Egyptian president; Egypt seizes control of the Suez Canal; Israeli troops invade Egypt and push towards the canal; British and French forces invade Egypt; a United Nations force arrives in Egypt, prompting a cease-fire; UN truce proposals for dispute between Jordan and Israel accepted; Soviet Communist leader Nikita Khrushchev denounces Joseph Stalin's "cult of personality"; Soviet tanks and troops crush an anti-Communist rebellion in Hungary; Sudan becomes a democratic republic; Pakistan becomes an Islamic republic; Martin Luther King, Jr, leads the campaign against racial segregation in the US South; trans-atlantic telephone service begins; the first computer programming language (FORTRAN) is developed in the US.

1957: Israeli troops withdraw from Egypt and the Gaza Strip comes under UN jurisdiction; UN reopens the Suez Canal; the space race begins as the USSR launches the first earth-orbiting satellite *Sputnik 1*; Belgium, France, Italy, Luxembourg, the Netherlands and West Germany sign the Rome Treaty to extend the common market established for the steel industry to all sectors of the economy; Pres. Eisenhower warns that the US will oppose Communist takeovers in the Middle East; Harold Macmillan leads the new Conserva-tive government in Britain; John Diefenbaker becomes Canada's prime minister.

1958: Nikita Khrushchev becomes Soviet premier; Charles De Gaulle is elected president of France; Pope Pius XII dies and is succeeded by John XXIII; the first US space satellite, *Explorer I*, is launched; scientists in the USSR send two dogs into space and return them safely; Egypt and Syria form the United Arab Republic; Iraq's King Faisal is assassinated in a military coup; Alaska becomes the 49th US state.

1959: Fidel Castro overthrows Fulgencio Batista and establishes a Communist government in Cuba, expropriating sugar mills owned by the US; Soviet Prem. Khrushchev visits the US; American Vice-Pres. Richard Nixon visits the Soviet Union and has the "kitchen debate" with Khrushchev; the USSR sends a space probe to the moon and photographs its hidden side; the St Lawrence Seaway opens; the first commercial photocopier is introduced; the Dalai Lama flees Tibet; Hawaii becomes the 50th state of the US.

1960: An American U-2 spy plane is shot down over the USSR, prompting Soviet Prem. Nikita Khrushchev to cancel a Soviet-American summit meeting; 50 South African black protesters are massacred at Sharpeville; the Congo (Zaïre) gains independence from Belgium, sparking political instability and UN intervention; Cyprus becomes independent and Archbishop Makarios wins the first presidential election; Israeli agents capture former Gestapo chief Adolf Eichmann in Argentina and smuggle him to Israel for trial; Germany bans Neo-Nazi political groups; John F. Kennedy is elected US president; the first weather and communications satellites are launched in the US; the first heart pacemaker is developed.

1961: Soviet Major Yuri Gagarin becomes the first man in space; US breaks off diplomatic ties with Cuba; the US-backed Bay of Pigs invasion by Cuban exiles fails to topple Cuba's Fidel Castro; astronaut Alan Shepard becomes the first American in space with a sub-orbital flight; East Germany builds the Berlin Wall to stop its citizens from moving to the West; Kuwait becomes independent from Britain, which sends troops to counter Iraqi annexation threats; UN Sec.-Gen. Dag Hammarskjöld dies in a plane crash over Northern Rhodesia; UK applies for membership in the Common Market; the silicon chip is patented by Texas Instruments in the US.

1962: Fearing nuclear war, many North Americans build fallout shelters; John Glenn becomes the first American to orbit the earth; US establishes a military council in South Vietnam; the discovery of Soviet missile bases in Cuba leads to a US naval blockade; the Cuban Missile Crisis ends when Soviet leader Khrushchev agrees to dismantle the bases; UN troops quell rebellion in the Congo's Katanga province; Algeria, Uganda and Jamaica gain independence; the UN votes in favor of economic sanctions against South Africa; Pope John XXIII opens the Second Vatican Council which will modernize the Catholic church; the TV satellite *Telstar* is launched in the US.

1963: US Pres. John Kennedy is assassinated in Dallas and Lyndon Johnson succeeds him; the US, Soviet Union and Britain ban nuclear tests in the atmosphere; South Vietnamese leader Ngo Dinh Diem is assassinated following a military coup; US sends financial aid to South Vietnam; Zanzibar and Kenya gain independence; Dr. Martin Luther King leads the March on Washington seeking equality for US blacks; the "hot line" emergency communications link is established between the White House and the Kremlin; UK application to Common Market rejected after French opposition; British government rocked by the Profumo affair and the scandal forces the resignation of a senior minister; Pope John XXIII dies and is succeeded by Paul VI; archaeologists find the remains of a thousand-year-old Viking settlement in Newfoundland; the first liver and lung transplants are performed; Valentina Tereshkova becomes the first female astronaut.

1964: Harold Wilson becomes prime minister in Britain; Communist China announces it has developed an atomic bomb; the US escalates its military involvement in Vietnam following a reported North Vietnamese attack on US destroyers in the Gulf of Tonkin; the Palestine Liberation Organization (PLO) is formed; Zambia, Malta and Malawi become independent; the sultan of Zanzibar is banished and the country is declared a republic; Zanzibar unites with Tanganyika to form Tanzania; Northern Rhodesia declares independence and adopts the name Zambia; Leonid Brezhnev and Alexei Kosygin become Soviet leaders after Khrushchev is deposed; the first word processor is developed by IBM; the Beatles appear on the Ed Sullivan Show as "Beatlemania" sweeps North America.

1965: Ferdinand Marcos is elected president of the Philippines; Gambia and Rhodesia declare independence from Britain; Rhodesia's declaration is met by an oil embargo; a massive power failure blacks out most of the northeast US and eastern Canada; Pope Paul VI reaffirms the Catholic Church's opposition to birth control; a Soviet cosmonaut is the first to leave a spacecraft and "float" in space; two US Gemini capsules rendezvous in space.

1966: China's Red Guards demonstrate against western influences as Mao launches the Cultural Revolution; Indira Gandhi becomes India's prime minister; floods destroy art treasures in Florence, Italy; De Gaulle asks that NATO forces leave France; South African Pres. Hendrik Verwoerd is stabbed to death during a Parliamentary session; Lesotho and Guyana become independent; civilian protests against the Vietnam War escalate in the US; government in Ghana overthrown by military coup; an artificial heart is successfully implanted for the first time by Dr Michael De Bakey in Houston; the Soviet Union lands an unmanned spacecraft on the moon.

1967: Israel defeats Egypt, Syria and Jordan in the Six Day War and occupies the Sinai Peninsula, Golan Heights, Gaza Strip and the east bank of the Suez Canal; Expo 67 world fair opens in Montreal; a Soviet cosmonaut becomes the first reported casualty of the space race; US manned space flights are suspended after astronauts Grissom, White and Chaffee die in Apollo capsule fire; race riots erupt in US cities during the "long hot summer"; Canada celebrates its centennial; Dr Christiaan Barnard of South Africa performs the world's first successful human heart transplant: the patient survives for 18 days.

1968: The US intelligence ship *Pueblo* is captured by North Korea; US civil rights leader Martin Luther King is assassinated in Memphis; presidential candidate Robert Kennedy is assassinated in Los Angeles; Soviet troops crush liberal reform in Czechoslovakia; a treaty limiting military use of outer space is signed by 62 nations; university student protest movement spreads worldwide; Richard Nixon is elected US president; Pierre Trudeau becomes prime minister in Canada; peace talks between the US and North Vietnam begin in Paris; British colony of Mauritius becomes independent; Pope Paul

VI issues an encyclical banning artificial birth control; three US astronauts circle the moon and return to Earth; *Surveyor 7*, uncrewed, lands on moon.

1969: US astronaut Neil Armstrong becomes the first man to walk on the moon as *Apollo 11* lands on the lunar surface; Yasir Arafat becomes PLO chairman; North Vietnamese leader Ho Chi Minh dies at age 79; the International Red Cross estimates that 1.5 million Biafrans have died, mostly by starvation, in the civil war with Nigeria; the US begins withdrawal of troops from Vietnam; Golda Meir becomes Israeli prime minister; the Concorde supersonic airliner makes its first flight; *Mariner* space probes transmit pictures of Mars back to earth.

1970: An earthquake kills about 30,000 people in Peru; US National Guardsmen kill four Kent State University students during anti-war protests at the campus and two students are killed at Jackson State following similar demonstrations; the first complete synthesis of a gene is announced by University of Wisconsin scientists; Arab commandos hijack three jets bound for New York from Europe; the civil wars in Nigeria end when Biafra capitulates to the federal government; the Front de Libération du Québec (FLQ) kidnaps British trade commissioner James Cross, and kidnaps and murders Quebec cabinet minister Pierre Laporte; the Canadian federal government responds to this "October Crisis" by invoking the War Measures Act, temporarily suspending civil liberties in Canada; Israel and United Arab Republic declare a 99-day truce in latest conflict; Gambia becomes a republic; a cyclone and tidal wave hit the offshore islands in the Ganges Delta of East Pakistan, leaving at least 168,000 people dead and about 1 million homeless.

1971: US planes bomb Cambodia, attacking Vietcong supply routes; fighting in Indochina spreads to Laos and Cambodia; the US conducts large-scale bombing raids against North Vietnam; mainland China is admitted to the United Nations; women are granted the right to vote in Switzerland; violence in Northern Ireland escalates after Britain introduces policies of internment without trial; India fights with the Bengali rebels against Pakistan; the US and USSR sign a treaty banning nuclear weapons on the ocean floor; Algeria seizes majority control of all French oil and gas interests within its borders but promises resti- tution; Idi Amin takes control over Uganda; Mao Zedong's heir-apparent, Lin Piao, dies in a mysterious air crash; the USSR soft-lands a space capsule on Mars; a Los Angeles earth- quake kills 60 people and causes $1 billion in damage; the hormone that controls human growth is synthesized by Dr. Choh Hao Li at the University of California.

1972: The world's largest diamond (969.8 carats) is unearthed in Sierra Leone; US Pres. Richard Nixon meets Mao Zedong in China; Britain imposes direct rule on Northern Ireland and 467 people are killed in violence between Catholics and Protestants; Ceylon becomes a republic and changes its name to Sri Lanka; Philippine Pres. Ferdinand Marcos assumes near-dictatorial powers; a Soviet spacecraft soft-lands on Venus; more than 70 nations sign a treaty prohibiting the stockpil- ing of biological weapons; the US conducts its heaviest B-52 bombing raids of the war against North Vietnam but continues to with- draw troops, despite lack of progress at Paris peace talks; Arab terrorists massacre 11 Israeli Olympic athletes in a stand-off with West German police at the summer Olympic games in Munich; Richard Leakey and Glynn Isaac discover a 2.5-million-year-old human skull in northern Kenya; a US federal grand jury indicts seven persons, including two former White House aids, on charges of conspiracy to break into the Democratic national headquar- ters (in the Watergate building) in Washington, DC; Richard Nixon is reelected as US president.

1973: A cease-fire agreement, intended to end the Vietnam war, is signed in Paris; fighting in the Middle East between Israeli and Arab forces (Yom Kippur War) is resolved by a shaky ceasefire; Arab oil-producing states cut petroleum exports to the US, western Europe and Japan because of their support of Israel; the US Senate begins televised hearings on the Watergate scandal and it is revealed that Pres. Nixon had secretly taped all conversations in his White House office; US vice-president resigns in an unrelated scandal; US combat involvement in Indochina officially ends as American planes halt their bombing of Cambodia; typhoon "Nora" leaves 800,000 Filipinos homeless on the island of Luzon; Great Britain, Ireland and Denmark formally join the Common Market; the Bahamas are granted independence from Britain after three

centuries of colonial rule; Chilean Marxist Pres. Salvadore Allende is overthrown by a CIA-backed military junta which claims Allende commits suicide; Shah of Iran nation- alizes foreign-owned oil companies.

1974: Oil-producing nations boost their prices and worldwide inflation accelerates as eco- nomic growth slows to near zero in most industrialized nations; the government of China launches a new "Cultural Revolution" program aimed at condemning both the Chinese philosopher Confucius and former Defence Minister Lin Piao; West German Chancellor Willy Brandt resigns after a scan- dal involving an East German spy; the Tower of London and the British Houses of Parliament are bombed by the Irish Republican Army; Soviet Nobel prize-winning author Aleksandr Solzhenitsyn is stripped of his citizenship and exiled; Portuguese dictator- ship ended by military coup and democratic reforms are initiated; rebels supported by Greece overthrow government in Cyprus: Turkish forces invade and take over much of the island; India explodes a nuclear device; Syria and Israel agree to the boundaries of a demilitarized zone in the Golan Heights and they begin troop withdrawals from the region; US Pres. Richard Nixon resigns to avoid impeachment by Congress for his coverup of the Watergate scandal; Gerald Ford is sworn in to replace Nixon; the US and Soviet Union reach a tentative agreement to limit the num- bers of strategic offensive nuclear weapons and delivery vehicles; severe drought threatens millions in Africa; scientists warn of the effects of chloroflourocarbons (CFCs) on the ozone layer.

1975: Portugal's new constitution grants most power to the military; Angola, Cape Verde, São Tomé and Principe and Mozambique gain independence from Portugal; Turkish Cypriots declare the establishment of a separate state in the northern half of the island; US evacuates as North Vietnam seizes Saigon; Egypt reopens the Suez Canal, which had been closed since the 1967 Arab-Israeli war; a UN Security Council resolution calling for the imposition of an arms embargo against South Africa is vetoed by the US, Great Britain and France; Generalissimo Franco, Spain's chief of state, dies and is replaced by King Juan Carlos I; Peru's president is ousted in a mili- tary coup and replaced by a general; a democ- ratic republic is proclaimed in Laos; Papua

New Guinea and Surinam become independent; civil war breaks out in Beirut between Christians and Muslims; rebels in Eritrea provoke battles with Ethiopian government.

1976: Chinese Prem. Chou En-lai and Communist Chinese leader Mao Zedong die within months of each other; riots against apartheid take place in the all-black township of Soweto outside of Johannesburg and spread to Cape Town in black townships and white areas; first reports surface that Libyan leader Col. Moammar Qaddafi is financing, training and arming a widespread terrorist network; the Parti Québécois wins power in Quebec's provincial election, raising the possibility of Quebec's secession from Canada; worldwide earthquakes kill an estimated 780,000 people; the Gang of Four (Mao Zedong's widow and three others) unsuccessfully attempt a coup in China; Venezuela nationalizes petroleum industry; president of Argentina overthrown by military junta; Spanish Sahara released from Spain's jurisdiction and divided between Morocco and Mauritania; North and South Vietnam reunited under Communist government; a military coup in Thailand topples the government; 9,000 refugees flee Angolan civil war.

1977: Cambodian refugees report economic and social disaster following the Communists' capture of Phnom Penh; Egypt severs diplomatic relations with Syria, Iraq, Libya, Algeria and South Yemen for attempting to disrupt its peace overtures to Israel; over 570 die in the world's worst aviation disaster when two Boeing 747s collide on the runway on the Canary Island of Tenerife; black South African leader Steven Biko dies in jail; French territories of Afars and Issa unite to form independent Republic of Djibouti; government of Pakistan is overthrown and martial law is imposed; Leonid Brezhnev becomes USSR president and Communist Party chief; Somalia-backed Eritrean guerrillas are stopped by Ethiopian army; Thailand government seized by military junta; Rhodesia's white government announces it will begin negotiations with black majority; cyclone in India leaves 20,000 dead and 2 million homeless; US unmanned spacecrafts *Voyager I* and *II* begin journeys to explore the outer solar system; the neutron bomb, which causes great loss of life but little property damage, is developed in the US.

1978: A Soviet-supported military junta takes power in Afghanistan and Soviet troops occupy the country; Lebanon is torn by Christian and Muslim militia activity as well as Palestinian guerrilla activity, and Arab League intervenes to restore peace; Israeli forces withdraw; Syria declares a unilateral cease-fire in and around Beirut, Lebanon; Egyptian Pres. Anwar Sadat and Israeli Prem. Menachem Begin sign peace accords, mediated by US Pres. Jimmy Carter; Shah Mohammed Riza Pahlevi of Iran imposes martial law to suppress anti-government demonstrations; leftist Sandinista guerrillas attempt to overthrow the government of Nicaraguan Pres. Anastasio Somoza; US establishes full diplomatic relations with Communist China; the first peaceful transfer of power takes place in Dominican Republic; Zaïre invaded by secessionist rebels: defence aid comes from other African nations, and France and Belgium after the massacre of Europeans; military junta seizes power in Honduras; army seizes government power in Bolivia; former Italian Prem. Aldo Moro is kidnapped and murdered by the Red Brigades, a revolutionary terrorist group; John Paul II (Karol Wojtyla) of Poland becomes the first non-Italian Pope in four centuries; the first "test-tube baby" (human baby conceived outside the womb) is born in England.

1979: Armed Islamic revolutionary followers of Ayatollah Khomeini overthrow the government of Iran and the Shah flees; students demanding the Shah's return to stand trial seize hostages at US embassy; a malfunction in the cooling system of a nuclear reactor at Three Mile Island in Pennsylvania, US, closes down the reactor and radiation escapes into the air; Conservative Margaret Thatcher becomes Britain's first female prime minister; a black government is formally installed in Rhodesia and its name is changed to Zimbabwe; China and the US establish formal commercial relations for the first time since 1949; Vietnamese army invades Cambodia and installs new government; St Lucia, St Vincent and the Grenadines become independent; coup in Grenada replaces government leader; president of Uganda, Idi Amin, overthrown; Egypt is expelled from Arab League after signing Camp David peace treaty; first elections for European Parliament held; the US-USSR SALT (Strategic Arms Limitation Treaty) Agreement is signed in Vienna; Iran nationalizes remaining privately-owned industries without compensation; sharp oil price increases contribute to high inflation worldwide; South Korean Pres. Park Chung Hee and his chief body guard are assassinated by a government official; emperor of Central African Empire overthrown; president of El Salvador is ousted by military coup.

1980: Soviet dissident Andrei Sakharov, a Nobel prize-winning physicist, is arrested in Moscow; human interferon, a promising natural disease-fighting substance, is made by gene splicing; Mt St Helens erupts in Washington, in a blast that sends debris 20 km up into the atmosphere and is heard over 300 km away; in a political comeback, Indira Gandhi wins a landslide victory in India's parliamentary elections; Soviet war in Afghanistan escalates as the US imposes an embargo on the sale of grain and high technology to the Soviet Union in response to the continued occupation of Afghanistan, and 50 nations boycott the Moscow Olympics in protest; Roman Catholic Archbishop Oscar Arnulfo Romero, an El Salvadoran reformer, is assassinated while saying mass; some 10,800 Cubans seek asylum in Peru's Cuban embassy and more than 125,000 Cubans escape by boat to the US; Liberian Pres. William Tolbert, Jr, is killed in a coup; military coup in Turkey unseats government; Zimbabwe gains independence from Britain; 350 Bengalis are massacred by native tribal people in India; black guerrillas successfully bomb two South African petroleum plants and a refinery; mass labour strikes in Poland force the government to allow independent trade unions, including Solidarity, led by Lech Walesa; 20 terrorist bomb attacks take place in France; the Iran-Iraq war begins when Iraqi fighter-bombers attack Iranian airfields and lay siege to its southwestern cities; 3,000 are killed in earthquakes centred in southern Italy; 20,000 die in two strong earthquakes in Algeria; *Voyager I* sends back the first pictures of Saturn; wreck of the *Titanic* found in North Atlantic.

1981: Aquired Immune Deficiency Syndrome (AIDS) is first recognized, in the US; in El Salvador, heavy fighting occurs between the government and leftist insurgents; the world's first reusable spacecraft, the Space Shuttle *Columbia*, is sent into space; clashes between Syrian troops and Christian militiamen in Lebanon are followed by Israeli bombing in support of Christian forces; artificial bone and skin are developed in the US; Pope John Paul II is shot and seriously wounded outside the Vatican by a Turkish terrorist; Israel is condemned worldwide after Israeli warplanes destroy an Iraqi atomic reactor near Baghdad; Irish prisoners in Belfast stage hunger strikes to force the British government to grant political prisoner status to Irish nationalist inmates, and some die; South African troops invade Angola in pursuit of guerrillas; Belize, formerly British Honduras, becomes independent from Britain; Pres. Anwar el-Sadat of Egypt is assassinated by Muslim extremists during a military parade; Israel formally annexes the Golan Heights; a five-day war between Ecuador and Peru erupts over a border dispute; Greece joins the European Community; Italian government rocked by revelation that nearly 1,000 key government, army and business leaders support a secret outlawed Masonic lodge; president of Bangladesh assassinated; Iranian president, prime minister and 29 others killed in bomb attack; 5,000 die when Indonesian ferry sinks in Java Sea; martial law is instituted in Poland in the face of continued labour unrest; the personal computer is introduced by IBM in the US.

1982: Argentina moves to reclaim Malvinas (the Falkland Islands) from UK by invading the territory; Britain defeats Argentina in the subsequent war; Canada gains the power to amend its own constitution from Britain; Israel withdraws from the Sinai and turns it over to Egypt, fulfilling their 1979 peace treaty; Israel invades Lebanon and the PLO leadership leaves Lebanon under UN protection; Lebanese Christian militiamen massacre Palestinians in refugee camps and Israel is accused of indirectly aiding the attack; Iran invades Iraq, but Iraq claims to have killed 27,000 Iranians in 18 days of battle; a series of IRA bombs explode in London, killing nine and wounding 51; western nations debate a proposed Soviet oil pipeline to western Europe; Lech Walesa, former leader of Solidarity, the outlawed Polish labour union, is freed after 11 months of imprisonment; military coups in Bangladesh and Guatemala force changes in government; Soviet leader Leonid Brezhnev dies and Yuri Andropov succeeds him; in Cambodia, support for Khmer Rouge grows as coalition against Vietnamese-backed government joined by Prince Sihanouk; up to 1,200 Afghan civilians and

Soviet soldiers die in a tunnel explosion caused by the collision of two trucks; the first permanent artificial heart is transplanted into Dr Barney B. Clark, 61, in Utah; Mexican volcano, El Chichón, erupts, blasting debris into the stratosphere.

1983: Klaus Barbie, former chief of the German Gestapo in Lyons, France, during WW II is deported to France from Bolivia to face charges of "crimes against humanity"; Soviet citizens and diplomats accused of espionage are expelled from France, Spain, the US and Britain; the US government is accused of having illegally aided Nicaraguan rebels; anti-government protests increase in Chile, governed by Gen. Pinochet; Ethiopia appeals for aid to 4 million victims of drought and famine; Sri Lankan Sinhalese and Tamil forces clash, killing hundreds and destroying the homes of thousands of others; 1,200 die in an earthquake in Turkey; martial law is formally lifted in Poland; the Organization of Petroleum Exporting Countries (OPEC) agrees to cut crude oil prices for the first time in its 23-year history; all 269 people aboard are killed when the Soviet Union shoots down a South Korean airliner, claiming that the plane had been on a spying mission and strayed into Soviet airspace; Benigno Aquino, opponent of Philippine Pres. Marcos, returns to Manila and is assassinated; 241 US Marines and sailors and 40 French paratroopers, members of a multinational peacekeeping force in Lebanon, are killed by suicide terrorists; the US and France support Chad's government against Libyan-supported guerrillas; Israeli withdrawal from Lebanon is followed by full-scale fighting between Lebanese ethnic and religious groups; US-led forces invade the small island of Grenada; US Cruise missiles in Europe are deployed in Britain despite Soviet and civilian opposition; white South Africans approve a new constitution granting limited political participation for persons of mixed race and Asians, but not for blacks, in a new tricameral legislature; Yasir Arafat and PLO guerrillas are evacuated from Lebanon to Tunis, under UN sponsorship; riots in Assam, India claim 5,000 lives and 300,000 refugees flee; the compact disc is introduced; after an 11-year journey, the *Pioneer 10* spacecraft leaves the solar system.

1984: Cholesterol is linked to heart disease following a 10-year study by US researchers; the Apple Macintosh with mouse enters the personal computer market; Konstantin Chernenko becomes Soviet leader following the death of Yuri Andropov; US astronauts fly free of the space shuttle *Challenger*, the first humans to do so without a tether; US and UN forces are withdrawn from Lebanon; French and American researchers, working separately, report that they have identified viruses which appear to be the cause of AIDS; Saudi, Greek and Swiss tankers are attacked by both Iran and Iraq in the Persian Gulf and Saudi Arabia shoots down two Iranian jets; hundreds die during a battle for the Golden Temple in Amritsar between Sikh militants and police in India; Indian Prime Min. Indira Gandhi is slain by two of her Sikh bodyguards in New Delhi and widespread violence follows; Daniel Ortega, Sandinista leader, wins in Nicaraguan elections; the international community sends aid to starving Ethiopians; in a secret operation, Israel airlifts 25,000 Ethiopian Jews (Falashas) out of the Sudan; Britain and China finalize an agreement on Hong Kong's future, guaranteeing its capitalist system for 50 years after it is turned over to China in 1997; a Union Carbide chemical plant leak kills 2,500 in Bhopal, India; the European Space Agency launches the largest telecommunications satellite in the world.

1985: South African police kill 18 blacks commemorating the Sharpville massacre in 1960, 19 more are killed while participating in a funeral procession and later the government declares a state of emergency; Daniel Ortega becomes president of Nicaragua; US president urges military aid to Nicaraguan opposition forces but only humanitarian aid is approved; Mikhail Gorbachev succeeds Konstantin Chernenko as Soviet leader and he opens disarmament talks with the US; Iraq turns back an Iranian offensive, allegedly killing 30,000 to 50,000 Iranians; Shiite Muslim hijackers release hostages after 17 days of captivity in Beirut, having demanded the release of hundreds of Shiites detained by Israeli forces; Argentine president imposes drastic economic measures to cut 1,010 percent inflation rate; top French officials are linked to the bombing of a ship owned by Greenpeace; two leading Soviet KGB officials defect to Britain and the US, where both name Soviet spies in the two countries; a cyclone and tidal waves hit Bangladesh, killing 10,000; a Mexican earthquake kills more than 7,000 and causes widespread destruction, leaving thousands homeless; border dispute between Mali and Burkina Faso leads to war but is eventually referred to International Court of Justice; Nicaragua suspends civil rights; four Palestinians seize the Italian cruise ship *Achille Lauro* off the coast of Egypt, murdering a wheelchair-bound American; Reagan and Gorbachev meet at the first superpower summit in six years; 95 Colombians die when 60 rebels seize the Palace of Justice in Bogotá and take more than 300 persons hostage; 60 die when Arab gunmen hijack an Egyptian jetliner, in an act allegedly backed by Libya's leader Col. Muammar Qaddafi; a Colombian volcanic eruption kills 20,000 people; Guatemala elects its first civilian president following three decades of military rule; Uruguay's military government replaced by civilian government; Sudanese and Ugandan presidents ousted by military coups; terrorists kill 20 people at two airports (in Rome and Vienna), both at the ticket counters of El Al, Israel's national airline; Live Aid rock concert in London, UK and Philadelphia, US raises over $60 million for African famine relief.

1986: Portugal and Spain join the European Community; Jean-Claude Duvalier, Haiti's "president for life," flees to France in the face of nationwide protest; Portugal elects its first civilian president in 60 years; Gorbachev calls for "radical reform" of Soviet economy and reshapes the leadership of the Communist party; Philippine Pres. Ferdinand Marcos flees to the US after allegations of electoral fraud; his opponent, Corazon Aquino, succeeds Marcos as president; Swedish Prime Min. Olof Palme is assassinated; former UN secretary general Kurt Waldheim is elected president of Austria; US planes bomb Libya citing retaliatory measures after missile attacks; radiation is spread following the meltdown of the Chernobyl nuclear power plant in the USSR; South African forces attack alleged African National Congress (ANC) bases in neighbouring Botswana, Zambia and Zim-babwe; the *New York Times* first links Panama's General Manuel Noriega with drug and arms trafficking; US president acknowledges a secret and illegal arms deal with Iran: the "Iran-Contra Affair" involving the US sale of arms in exchange for hostages is first reported in a Lebanese newspaper; The US space shuttle *Challenger* explodes one minute after liftoff and all seven crew members die instantly; *Voyager 2* spacecraft passes Uranus.

1987: Soviet leader Mikhail Gorbachev begins a campaign for openness (glasnost) and reconstruction (perestroika); Tamil separatists kill hundreds of Sri Lankans, mostly Sinhalese, and clash with government forces; German pilot Mathias Rust, 19, embarrasses Soviets when he lands his single-engine Cessna in Red Square, Moscow; Moscow's Communist Party chief, Boris Yeltsin, is dismissed after criticizing Soviet leader Gorbachev; South Africa withdraws its troops from Angola; an Iraqi warplane's missile kills 37 US sailors in the Persian Gulf, and the US escorts Kuwaiti oil tankers despite danger posed by the Iran-Iraq war; 402 Iranian pilgrims to Mecca die in battles with Saudi police; 24 nations sign a treaty to protect the ozone layer; Portugal and China agree that the Portuguese colony of Macao will be returned to China in 1999; stock market prices plunge worldwide; the Palestinian intifadah (uprising) begins against Israeli authorities in the Gaza Strip and West Bank, and thousands of protesters are imprisoned; Syrian troops enter Beirut in an attempt to bring a cease-fire; Lebanese prime minister dies in a bomb attack; a military coup ousts coalition government in Chad; 2,000 die in the Philippines when a ferry sinks.

1988: Nicaraguan contras and the Sandinista government reach a cease-fire agreement; the US and Soviet Union sign a treaty on intermediate-range nuclear forces (INF); Soviet troops begin to pull out of Afghanistan after a nine-year occupation; nationalist groups in Soviet-controlled Azerbaijan and Armenia clash; Colombian drug cartels defy government attempts to bring them to justice, and fight among themselves; a US navy warship accidentally shoots down a commercial Iranian airliner over the Persian Gulf, killing all 290 persons aboard; the Soviet communist party backs Gorbachev's plan for perestroika; Canadian and US governments ratify a free trade agreement, to take effect Jan. 1, 1989; Iran and Iraq agree on a cease-fire to end their eight-year war; Iraq uses poison gas on its Kurdish minority and razes Kurdish villages; Libya and Chad formally end their war; Thailand and Laos do battle in a brief border dispute; Ethiopia and Somalia end 11 years of disputes over borders with a peace treaty; Solidarity supporters stage widespread strikes in Poland; Vietnamese troops leave Kampuchea; a military coup in Burma causes a change in leadership; Yugoslavia's inflation rate tops 250%, ethnic Albanians in Kosovo province demand freedom from Serbian rule; Benazir Bhutto, daughter of a former Pakistani president, becomes prime minister of Pakistan; 270 people die when a bomb blows up a Pan Am jetliner over Lockerbie, Scotland; 25,000 Armenians die during an earthquake.

1989: Iran's Ayatollah Khomeini calls for the execution of UK author Salman Rushdie for blaspheming the prophet Mohammed; the Soviet Union holds historic multicandidate parliamentary elections and Boris Yeltsin emerges as Russian leader; Japanese Prime Min. Noboru Takeshita is toppled by financial scandal, Emperor Hirohito dies and is succeeded by his son; Chinese students lead more than one million in demonstrations for democratic reforms, but spreading unrest is checked by a government crackdown in Tiananmen Square that is suspected to have killed thousands; Hungary opens its border with Austria and moves toward political and economic reform; anti-Communist forces continue to battle the government in Afghanistan; fighting between Christians and Muslims in Beirut intensifies; 90 people die in ethnic violence in Soviet Uzbekistan; Poles participate in their first open election in 40 years and Solidarity wins a solid victory; the three Baltic states (Estonia, Latvia and Lithuania) protest Soviet domination; a Colombian presidential candidate is slain, prompting a renewed crackdown on illegal drug traffickers; thousands of East Germans flee to West Germany and the East German government proposes political reforms; Vietnamese forces withdraw from Cambodia; East German communist leader Erich Honecker is removed from power, he is later charged with corruption; thousands demonstrate in Czechoslovakia and force the communist government to resign, Vaclav Havel is elected president; the spaceship *Atlantis* is launched on a journey to Jupiter; East Germany opens the Berlin wall after 28 years and lifts visa and emigration restrictions; Panama's General Noriega annuls presidential elections after an opposition party victory, the US invades Panama and Noriega goes into hiding; Romanian Pres. Nicolae Ceausescu is overthrown and executed with his wife for genocide, abuse of power and theft; 80 nations sign an agreement to limit production of chorofluorocarbons (CFCs) to protect the ozone layer; Paraguay's president is toppled by a military coup; the Exxon *Valdez* runs aground in Alaska and spills thousands of litres of oil; *Voyager 2* spacecraft reaches Neptune.

1990: Panama's Manuel Noriega surrenders to US authorities; violence erupts in Soviet Azerbaijan as Azerbaijanis attack Armenians; Bulgaria and Yugoslavia switch to multiparty systems; Violeta Chamorro defeats Sandinista leader Daniel Ortega to become the Nicaraguan president; South African government lifts restrictions on opposition organizations and declares amnesty for political prisoners, black leader Nelson Mandela is freed after 27 years in prison; the US, France, Great Britain and the Soviet Union reach agreement on a reunited Germany; Lithuania proclaims its sovereignty and Soviet troops move in; Namibia gains independence from South Africa; newly-released Soviet documents prove Soviet secret police killed 15,000 Polish military officers in the Katyn forest massacre of 1940; the $1.5-billion Hubble Space Tele-scope is sent into space, but flawed light-gathering mirrors distort transmissions; Iran's worst earthquake kills 40,000; more than 1,400 Muslim pilgrims to Mecca suffocate in a stampede in an overcrowded tunnel; the Ukraine declares its sovereignty within the Soviet Union; the two Germanys reunite, merging their economic, legal and political systems; Czechoslovakia and Romania hold their first free elections in the postwar era (Aug. 2); Iraq invades Kuwait over disagreements regarding oil production levels and appears ready to invade Saudi Arabia; the UN passes sweeping trade and financial sanctions against Iraq, and aid and troops pour into Saudi Arabia; civil war in black South African townships kills hundreds; the first human gene therapy for disease is done by blood transfusion; South Africa bans racial discrimination in public places; following a political challenge from within her own party, British Prime Min. Margaret Thatcher resigns and is succeeded by John Major; Mozambique adopts a constitution allowing for a multiparty democracy; civil war in Chad ends with overthrow of president; a military coup in Bangladesh unseats the president; Soviet Pres. Mikhail Gorbachev proposes Union Treaty to restructure Soviet Union; Helmut Kohl elected Chancellor of Unified Germany; Lech Walesa elected president of Poland; African National Congress (ANC) holds first conference in South Africa in 31 years; Rev. Jean-Bertrand Aristide elected president of Haiti; Edward Shevardnadze resigns as Soviet foreign minister; Slovenia and Croatia initiate secession from Yugoslavian republic.

1991: Iraq ignores Jan. 15 deadline for withdrawal from Kuwait and Allied forces (including the US, Canada, Britain, France, Italy, Japan, Pakistan and members of the Arab League) launch a six-week air attack; Soviets suppress independence movements in Baltic republics; US and Italy begin rescue of foreigners trapped in Somalian civil war; limited integration of schools begins in South Africa and sweeping reforms of apartheid law are proposed; Allies launch ground assault on Iraqi forces and informal cease-fire follows; 1,200 killed in major earthquake in Pakistan and Afghanistan; Lithuanians vote to secede from Soviet Union; Estonia and Latvia vote for independence from the Soviet Union; violent protests held in Belgrade to topple Yugoslavian government; Kuwaiti government forced to resign in wake of failure to establish post-war order; UN cease-fire formally ends Gulf War (Apr.) and Kurds flee from Iraq; Soviet republic of Georgia votes for independence; cease-fire declared in Angola's 16-year civil war; Rajiv Ghandi assassinated during Indian national election campaign; Boris Yeltsin elected president of Russia; Mt Pinatubo volcano erupts in Philippines; Population Registration Act repealed in South Africa; fighting between Yugoslav military and Slovenian nationalists escalates; Soviet hardliners attempt a coup against Mikhail Gorbachev: its failure results in the dissolution of the Communist party; rebels oust Haitian Pres. Jean-Bertrand Aristide; Serbia and Croatia reach political settlement but civil war continues; peace accord signed in El Salvador, paving the way to end of 11-year civil war; failed coup in Soviet Union speeds disintegration of the country as Lithuania, Estonia and Latvia act to enforce their independence; civil war in Croatia escalates; warring factions in Cambodia sign peace accord; talks on new constitution begin in South Africa; rebels fighting in Somalia claim to have taken over Mogadishu and deposed the president; Gorbachev resigns as USSR formally dissolved and Commonwealth of Independent States (CIS) created; fighting escalates in Somalia; Slovenia and Croatia recognized as independent states by Germany; Islamic Salvation Front leads in Algerian elections; by year-end, cholera epidemic has killed 3,500 in Latin America and 12,500 in Africa.

1992: A Jan. military coup in Algeria gives power to a committee which cancels elections in progress; in June the Algerian president is assassinated and the defense minister assumes power. Brazil is the site of the Earth Summit (June), which sees 100 world leaders and 30,000 participants gather in Rio de Janeiro to discuss worldwide environmental protection; the country is rocked by political unrest in Aug., which results in the end of the presidency of President Fernando Collor de Mello over an influence-peddling and bribery scandal. The European Community's Maastricht Treaty is first rejected by Denmark (June), then ratified by Irish (June) and French (Sept.) voters, and the Italian senate (Sept.). Czechoslovakia's president, Vaclav Havel, resigns on July 20 and the Parliament of Slovakia declares its sovereignty. An earthquake on Oct. 12 leaves 300 dead and thousands injured in Egypt. The Uruguay round of the GATT (General Agreement on Tariffs and Trade) negotiations remains stalled over the issue of farm subsidies. Germany is plagued by riots and firebombings staged by right-wing extremists attacking foreign-born workers and refugees. Israel's national election results in a victory for the Labour Party and its leader, Yitzhak Rabin; in Aug., Rabin begins to hint that compromise in the area of peace and territorial disputes might be possible. Italy continues an anti-Mafia crackdown despite the assassination of two prominent judges and a police investigator. A ruptured petrol pipeline in Mexico's working-class district of Guadalajara is blamed for an explosion that kills 200 and injures nearly 1,500 in Apr. Peru's president, Alberto Fujimori, suspends sections of the country's constitution in Apr. and seizes power, citing a need to root out corruption and combat the combined forces of the Shining Path guerrillas and various drug barons. Russia's first experiments with free markets trigger soaring inflation and shortages. Civil war in Somalia brings 4.5 million of its people to the brink of starvation; by Aug. the UN brings in forces to ensure that food is distributed to the hungry, but is unable to restore order. The government in South Africa continues to work towards a power-sharing agreement with the black majority after receiving nearly 70% support in a Mar. whites-only referendum; in Sept. troops from the Ciskei homeland open fire on ANC supporters massed at the border and talks on democratic reform are again delayed. Citizens in Thailand take to the streets in a series of demonstrations that eventually force constitutional reforms and democratic elections. In the United Kingdom, the scandals of the royal family threaten the credibility of the monarchy; uncertainty over the fate of the Maastricht Treaty and pressure on UK currency force a withdrawal from the European Monetary System in Sept. and a devaluation of the UK pound. In the United States, riots in Los Angeles in late Apr./early May leave 42 dead; the US state of Florida is devastated by Hurricane Andrew (Aug.) which does an estimated $15 billion damage; on Oct. 12, the *Pioneer* spacecraft plunges into the scorching atmosphere surrounding the planet Venus and ends a 14-year space mission; in Nov., the Democrats, under Bill Clinton and Al Gore, are elected to a four-year term. Yugoslavia continues to disintegrate: the UN Security Council deploys peacekeepers in Jan.; Croatia and Slovenia are given diplomatic recognition by the European community as well as 20 other countries (including Canada); by Feb., Serbia and Montenegro reach agreement on a common state retaining the Yugoslav flag, anthem and joint parliament; in Mar., citizens of the republic of Bosnia-Hercegovina vote for independence; however, ethnic fighting over Bosnian territory escalates throughout the year amid charges of ethnic cleansing and atrocities, and a series of cease-fires that rarely hold for more than a few days; on Sept. 22, Yugoslavia (Serbia and Montenegro) is expelled from the UN General Assembly.

1993: Both sides in the Bosnia-Hercegovina conflict reject peace plans to settle the conflict. In Burundi an abortive Oct. coup leaves the President and 6 ministers dead before the army decides to back the existing government and order is restored. Despite opposition and active interference by the Khmer Rouge, 90% of registered voters cast their ballots in Cambodia's national election in May. One of the longest civil wars in Africa ends when the separation of Eritrea from Ethiopia is approved in a referendum. After 7 years of negotiation, the latest version of the GATT agreement is approved by 117

countries in late Dec. German military forces took part in missions outside its borders for the first time since WWII; the German parliament bows to right-wing pressures and places limits on their liberal immigration laws. Neither the OAS nor the UN is able to restore Haiti's deposed president Jean-Bertrand Aristide to power despite intense negotiations and increased blockades. On Sept 13, PLO leader Yasser Arafat and Israeli Prime Min. Yitzak Rabin meet in Washington to sign a peace agreement secretly negotiated in Norway; the agreement grants Palestinian autonomy over certain lands and recognized Israel's right to exist. The results of the June election in Nigeria are nullified by the long-time dictator, despite protests which include a 3-day general strike. A battle for power in the Russian parliament sees Pres. Boris Yeltsin strip Vice-Pres. Rutskoi of his powers and dissolve parliament to call Dec. elections; parliamentarians respond by barricading themselves in the building which is then surrounded by government troops; the seige is lifted when the insurgents surrender on Oct. 4; a new parliament is elected in Dec. and a new constitution is approved. Slovakia and the Czech republic declare independence on Jan 1. UK Prime Min. John Major and his Irish counterpart announce a tentative peace plan for Northern Ireland that would allow the people to decide their own fate. US troops in Somalia hands the mission to re-establish order over to a UN force made up of personnel from 20 countries and announces they will pull out at the end of Mar. 1994. In Sept. an agreement is reached in South Africa that paves the way for a multi-party transitional council that includes blacks; in Oct. the United Nations lifts economic sanctions; in Nov. a new constitution is approved and national all-race elections are scheduled; white rule ends officially in Dec. In the United States, a standoff outside the compound of a religious group in Waco Texas ends in tragedy when authorities stormed the area and the buildings erupt in flames. (Apr.); a rainy summer leads to record-breaking floods in nine states along the Mississippi River and in Oct. brush fires devaste six counties in California; in Nov. Pres. Clinton secures approval for NAFTA in the House of Representatives.

1994: Islamic fundamentalists in Algeria continue their fight to oust the government, targetting foreigners, journalists, and intellectuals. In Nov., government and rebel negotiators sign a truce and power sharing arrangement to end the civil war in Angola. In Feb. a Bosnian Serb mortar attack on a Sarajevo marketplace kills 66, injures 200 and prompts NATO to threaten punitive bombing if Serb guns are not pulled back from the city; in Aug. the Bosnian Serb rejection of a peace plan moves the government of Serbia to sever relations; in Dec. Bosnian Serbs kidnap UN peace keepers and use them as human shields to halt NATO airstrikes. In Brazil, radical steps are taken to curb inflation; the currency (cruzeiro) is scrapped and replaced by the real, and severe budget cuts are instituted. Increasing numbers of Cuban citizens flee the country in the face of the effects of the trade embargo. Cairo is the site of a UN-sponsored conference on population in September; in Nov., floods trigger the rupture of two oil storage tanks that unleash a wave of burning oil killing 500 and leaving thousands homeless in the town of Durunka (west of Cairo). A car ferry enroute from Estonia to Finland sinks, killing over 900 passengers and crew. In Dec. Algerian highjackers bring an Air France jet to Marseilles, intending to blow the plane up over Paris, commandos storm the plane, killing the highjackers and freeing the passengers. Throughout the year German officials seize illegal shipments of plutonium apparently smuggled out of the former Soviet Union. A US-led force lands in Haiti on Sept. 19, and president-in-exile Jean Bertrand Aristide returns to Haiti in Oct.. In Sept., an outbreak of pneumonic plague in the city of Surat, India sparks panic among local residents, as well as concern among national and international medical authorities. In Jan. a heavily-armed Jewish settler enters a mosque in Hebron on the West Bank and opens fire on Muslim worshippers; 40 Palestinians die and more than 250 are wounded in the riots that follow; throughout the year Islamic fundamentalists use suicide bombing in an effort to derail the peace talks. In May, Yasser Arafat and Israeli Prime Min. Rabin sign the peace accord that inaugurates Palestinian self-rule on the Gaza Strip and in Jericho; the PLO begins to create a government structure for the areas; in July, Jordan and Israel sign an agreement to normalize relations. Japan suffers a year of political uncertainty as a series of prime ministers are unable to maintain a coalition government. A string of comet fragments known as Shoemaker-Levy 9 collide with Jupiter between July 16-22, causing massive explosions in the planet's atmosphere. The government of North Korea reluctantly agrees to allows nuclear inspectors to visit the majority of their nuclear sites. Ruler Kim Il Sung dies as negotiations end; his son and successor Kim Jong Il appears to have a tenuous grip on power. A New Year's dayrebellion in Mexico sets the stage for a turbulent year—Zapatista rebels in the southern state of Chiapas demand land reforms; in Mar. Luis Colosio, the leading candidate in the national election, was gunned down at an outdoor rally; in Dec., the peso loses 40% of its value over 8 days and trade allies move to prop up the economy. Workers try to bring down the military government in Nigeria by staging a general strike that drags on for six weeks. In Northern Ireland, the political wing of the IRA announces a "complete cessation of military operations" in Sept., paving the way for peace talks. In Oct., economic reforms lead to a steep plunge in the value of the ruble and widespread protests over unemployment; a leaky pipeline spills a massive quantity of oil onto the fragile permafrost and into surrounding rivers; in Dec., 40,000 Russian troops invade the rebel area of Chechnya to end the region's drive for independence. Plagued by racially motivated skirmishes at the beginning of the year, Rwanda dissolves into an ethnic blood bath after the death of the president in a plane crash; tens of thousands of Rwandans, mostly Tutsi, die at the hands of the rival Hutus in a killing spree that lasts for months; Tutsi-led forces eventually regain control of the country and thousands more flee to refugee camps in neighbouring countries to escape feared reprisals. In Somalia, factional fighting reignites as both the US and the UN withdraw the forces policing the area. All race elections are held for the first time in Apr. 26-28, and Nelson Mandela is elected president; South Africa is given full membership to the United Nations in June. In the US, California is rocked by a major earthquake in Jan., in Feb., Aldrich Ames, a mid-level officer in the CIA, is exposed as a spy operating for Moscow since the mid-1980s. By June, the US dollar was in a record-breaking dive. North and South Yemen erupt in civil war as the conservative north and formerly Marxist areas of the south try to gain supremacy; by July, the southern separatists are routed.

1995: The Algerian civil war continued, with Muslim extremists stepping up attacks on foreigners, collaborators, journalists, women who adopted modern ways of life and the families of government officials. In the Atlantic region, a particularly harsh hurricane season brought death and destruction to the Caribbean area in the latter part of the year. In the Bosnian war, the blockade of Sarajevo continued for much of the year as truces failed to hold. In May NATO launched two days of airstrikes to break the impasse and Bosnian Serbs seized nearly 400 UN peace keepers and chained them to possible bombing targets to forestall further attacks. The hostages were slowly freed throughout May and June. In July Bosnian Serbs overran the UN safe areas of Srebrenica and Zepa and carried out a plan to clear the territory of Muslims. By August, NATO had resumed airstrikes in response to the shelling of a marketplace in Sarajevo. The bombing missions continued in Sept. in an effort to force the Bosnian Serbs to withdraw from positions around Sarajevo; a ceasefire was finally inaugurated in October. In November, negotiators for all sides in the Bosnian conflict met at the Wright-Patterson Air Force Base outside Dayton, Ohio for a three-week effort to hammer out a workable peace plan. By Dec. US and British military personnel were arriving in Bosnia to assist in the implementation of the agreement. Burmese officials freed political dissident and activist Aung San Suu Kyi from house arrest in July In Burundi, murders by members of rival factions raised fears of Rwandan-style massacres; thousands of Rwandan refugees fled to Tanzania in an attempt to escape the violence. Canada ignited a worldwide protest against EU overfishing when it seized a Spanish fishing vessel at gunpoint on the Grand Banks. In October, the country stepped back from brink as the referendum on separation held in Quebec resulted in a very narrow victory for the federalists. The UN's Fourth World Conference on Women was held in China in September, despite widespread controversy. In Croatia, Pres. Tudjman allowed the UN peacekeeping mandate to lapse; in August, Croatian troops regained the territory in Krajina that had been lost to Croatian Serbs in 1991. France conducted three nuclear tests around the Muroroa Atoll in the South Pacific during the year, despite international protests and local demonstrations. Haitians went to the polls on December 17 in the first election since exiled Pres. Jean-Bertrand Aristide was returned to power. In Ireland, a bitter campaign over the issue of lifting the ban on divorce ended in narrow approval for liberalizing the laws in November. Israel and the Palestinians struggled with the peace process throughout the year, postponing deadlines as suicide bomb attacks in Israel threatened to derail the process altogether. In October, Israeli forces began to withdraw from parts of the West Bank in accordance with an agreement on Palestinian self rule. On November 4, a 25-year-old militant Jewish law student shot and killed Israeli Prime Min. Yitzak Rabin. On Jan. 17, the port of Kobe in Japan was struck by an earthquake measuring 7.2 on the Richter scale; 5,000 residents were killed, 25,000 were injured and 300,000 were left homeless. Also, in Japan a March nerve-gas attack during Monday morning rush hour in a Tokyo subway left 10 dead and 5 500 injured; two more incidents took place in April in Yokohama; police traced the attacks to a religious cult known as Aum Shinrikyo and arrested its leader Shoko Asahara. The Galileo space probe arrived at Jupiter in December after a 3.7 billion km trip that took six years. Mexico spent the early part of the year grappling with a financial crisis that saw the peso fall to record lows; the US engineered a financial bail-out that was conditional upon stringent austerity measures and the reform of the country's electoral process; loan repayments began in October, ahead of schedule. In November, the military government in Nigeria condemned environmentalist and activist Ken Saro-Wiwa and eight others to death; the sentence was carried out on Nov. 10. Nigeria was suspended from the Commonwealth and several countries withdrew their ambassadors in protest. Peru and Ecuador engaged in a month-long border war in the early part of the year. In Poland, long-time president Lech Walesa was defeated by a former communist who promised to continue western-style reforms in November. Throughout the year Russia was unable to subdue guerrillas in the breakaway republic of Chechnya; bombing raids on the capital of Grozny reduced the city to rubble. A 7.5 (Richter scale) earthquake struck the Sakhalin Island in Russia's far east in May, killing nearly 2,000. UN forces pulled out of Somalia after a two-year attempt to restore order amid pervasive drought, starvation and continuous clan warfare. Sri Lanka's civil war with Tamil rebels continued as the Tamils declined to consider peace proposals. The United Kingdom's financial district was rocked when a rogue trader operating out of Singapore for the 232-year-old Barings Bank engaged in disastrous speculation on the currency market that left the bank with more than $1 billion in losses; unable to cover such losses the bank collapsed. The United Nations marked its 50 anniversary in October, amid calls for reform of the world body. In the US, on the anniversary of the government attack on the Branch Davidian compound in Waco, Texas a massive bomb was detonated outside a government building in Oklahoma City, killing more than 100 and injuring over 400; a suspect with links to American right wing militia groups was arrested. On Oct. 16, Nation of Islam minister Louis Farrakhan rallied nearly a million black men in a march to Washington that he characterised as a day of "atonement." The Venezuelan government was forced to take over two insolvent banks in that country, covering more than $330 million in bad debts; 16 banks had failed in the past 18 months and the accumulated debts of $7 billion virtually paralysed the national economy. In Zaire, the city of Kikwit was the site of an outbreak of a deadly virus known as Ebola in May; over 100 people died of the fever that has no cure.

1996: The Algerian civil war continued throughout the year, as Islamic militants targeted various parts of the population for assassination. In Bangladesh, Premier Zia stepped down in Mar. after repeated protests and non-co-operation campaigns after a controversial Feb. election. In Bosnia, prisoners were exchanged, residents evacuated and Sarajevo was handed over to the Muslim-Croat federation; public pressure forced Radovan Karadzic to withdraw from his public role in Serbian affairs in July; in Sept. a gen.election was held for a three-member presidencey and 42-member national parliament and two subordinate legislatures for the Serb Republic and the Muslim-Croat Federation. Bulgaria was plunged into a crisis when the national currency collapsed in May; the government tried to enact reforms as hyperinflation paralysed the economy. In Burundi, the Red Cross withdrew its staff

after 3 workers were killed on June 4; Rwandan refugees were forcibly repatriated in mid-July; at the end of the month the Tutsi-dominated army seized power in a coup; borders were closed as neighbouring states proclaimed sanctions; the new president announced the government pledged a return to democracy after 3 years and the end of ethnic strife. In Aug. 3 top generals with the Khmer Rouge opened amnesty negotiations with the Cambodian government to end the decades of bloodshed. Hurricane Bertha hit the Caribbean islands and eastern US in July, doing major damage in St. Thomas, US Virgin Islands, Puerto Rico and coastal N. Carolina. In May, unrest in Tibet increased as Chinese authorities forbade demonstrations supporting the Dalai Lama; on June 25 the Chinese government had their choice as Panchem Lama initiated as a monk. On July 29, the Chinese conducted an underground nuclear test, then announced that it was their last and declared a moratorium on future testing. On Feb. 24 Cuban fighter planes shot down two civilian aircraft from the US, claiming that they had violated Cuban air space. Feb. saw renewed violence in Egypt and 24 deaths in strongholds of Islamic fundamentalism; an Arab summit held in Cairo in June called for Israeli withdrawal from Palestinian territory, including Arab Jerusalem. France's former Pres. Francois Mitterand died Jan. 8; the country conducted a 6th nuclear test Jan. 27; Jan. 29, Pres. Chirac announced a permanent end to the nuclear tests, cancelling the last two. On Feb. 19 the World Health Organization confirmed that 13 had died of the Ebola virus in Gabon. Greece's Prime Min. Papandreou resigned in Jan.; he died June 23. Haiti had a new president, René Préval, on Feb. 7; the UN extended the mandate of its mission at the end of Feb. and Canada took command as the US prepared to pull out. In India general elections in Apr. and May failed to produce a clear winner; a ruling coalition finally won a vote of confidence on June 12. In Israel, Yassir Arafat was sworn in as president of the Palestinian Council's executive in Feb.; on Apr. 24 the PLO revoked the charter clauses that called for the destruction of Israel and the waging of war against the Jewish state; a May gen. election resulted in victory for Benjamin Netanyahu and the right-wing Likud party; in Sept. an archaeological tunnel bordering Islam's third-holiest site, the Al Aqsa Mosque was opened, touching off a wave of violent protest. The Bank of Tokyo and Mitsubishi Bank merged on April 1 to create the world's largest bank. In May 13 the World Food Programme and the FAO issued a joint special alert over food shortages in N. Korea. In S. Korea, two former presidents were convicted on charges of accepting bribes during their tenure as dictator; in Sept., a N. Korean submarine ran aground in S. Korea, most crew members died on S. Korean soil. On Apr. 6 the Liberian capital city of Monrovia was torn by factional fighting; hundreds of foreign nationals were evacuated; UN troops arrived and took control of Monrovia on Apr. 21. A military coup in Niger on Jan. 27 saw the Chief of Gen. Staff seize power and suspend the constitution. In Nov. Pakistan Prime Min. Benazir Bhutto was dismissed by the president, who also dismissed her government and called for new elections in wake of allegations of corruption. A Christmas party at the Japanese ambassador's residence in Lima, Peru was invaded by Tupac Amaru guerillas who held a number of high-level diplomats hostage for several months. In Russia, skirmishes with Chechen rebels continued until May when a ceasefire was brokered; July saw some bombing on both sides; a definitive ceasefire was put in place in Sept. In June Russian Pres. Yeltsin narrowly won elections and a run-off in July confirmed the victory; in Sept. he acknowledged that he would require extensive heart surgery, which was performed in Nov. Clashes between Hutu and Tutsi military personnel again had Rwandans on the run in Jan.; by July. thousands of displaced Hutus (many who had been away since 1994) were returning home from Zaire. Serbian Pres. Milosevic ordered results of local elections annulled in Nov. when opposition parties won; outraged citizens took to the streets in nightly protests that continued well into 1997. On Mar. 29 leaders of Sierra Leone's military government transferred power to a democratically elected government. South Africa's new constitution was agreed upon by the main political parties on May 8; on May 9, F.W. de Klerk took his National Party out of the government coalition. In Spain, Basque separatists detonated four bombs during July, killing at least 35 and prompting public demonstrations against the ETA. In the UK, the IRA ended a 17-month cease-fire in Feb. with 3 bombings;

attacks continued through June; on Mar. 13 a gunman killed 16 kindergarten children and their teacher in Dunblane, Scotland before killing himself; also in Mar. a "mad-cow disease" scare prompted the banning of British beef by on domestic markets and by the EC, and the eventual slaughter of thousands of cattle and the destruction of embryos in an effort to contain the problem; Northern Ireland's July marching season was marked by renewed violence. In the US, outrage over the Feb. downing of two US civilian aircraft by Cuba cleared the way for the controversial Helms-Burton law; on Apr. 3 an arrest was made in the 17-year-long Unabomber case; the Summer Olympic Games opened in Atlanta on Jul. 19; in Sept. Hurricane Fran battered the US east coast; US Pres. Clinton was re-elected in November.

1997: In Afghanistan, the Taliban gained the upper hand in the 4 1/2 year civil war, taking control of Kabul and other key cities; by year-end they had imposed strict Islamic rule on many areas, severely restricting the lives of both men and women, with all females largely confined to their homes. Albania experienced a financial crisis in Jan. The crash triggered civil unrest and an all-out rebellion that saw nearly 1/3 of the country, primarily in the south, in the hands of rebels. An election in June led to the defeat of the government and order was gradually restored. Algeria was rocked by terrorist violence which increased in viciousness throughout the year; over 2,000 were killed in nearly 50 massacres as suspected Islamic terrorists continued their 5-year war against the Algerian government; a June election gave the military-backed regime a clear majority. The worst flooding of the century hit several countries in eastern Europe in July, incl. Austria, Czech Republic, Germany, Poland, and Slovakia, leaving hundreds dead and dozens missing as dams broke and power failed in many communities. In Bulgaria, anti-government strikes, demonstrations and a stand-off between the two main political parties in Jan. led to a general economic collapse. In Cambodia, in July, Second Prime Minister Hun Sen seized control of Phnom Penh while his co-prime minister was out of the country. 2nd Prime Min. Hun Sen later used force to crush forces loyal to his former co-prime minister and drive them out of the country. Chinese premier Deng Xiaoping died on Feb. 19. On

July 1, the British colony of Hong Kong was returned to China, ending a 99-year lease agreement. Indonesia's traditional slash-and-burn farming technique combined with a delayed rainy season to blanket much of the country as well as neighbouring Singapore and Malaysia with a thick blanket of smoke that threatened the health of nearly 20 million people in Indonesia alone. Iraqi leader Saddam Hussein provoked a confrontation with the U.S. in November by barring American members of the UN weapons inspection team; the battle of wills escalated into an allied mobilization before Hussein allowed inspectors to continue their duties. Liberia's former rebel Charles Taylor, a key figure in the country's 7-year civil war, won 75% of the presidential vote and a legislative majority in the country's general election on July 24. A major volcanic eruption on Montserrat killed 19 on June 25. The island's Soufriege Hill volcano erupted in Aug., forcing residents to flee to the northern part of the island. The Muslim League easily defeated Pakistan's former Prime Min. Bhutto's party in national elections on Feb. 3, despite a low turnout. In Russia, Pres. Boris Yeltsin was hospitalized on Jan. 8 with double pneumonia; the Duma began to discuss the possibility of impeaching the ailing president. On Apr. 14 the World Bank agreed to a loan of US$6 billion over two years, if Russia's economic reforms continued. Serbian protesters continued to demand that the results of a Nov. election be respected and by Feb., parliament had voted to recognize the results of those elections and allow the victors to take office. In Sierra Leone, in June, the third military coup in six years brought an end to the fledgling civilian government. Delegates from Somalia's 26 factions met on Jan. 3 in an attempt to form a national unity government that could stabilize the region. Known as the National Salvation Council, the group's first task was to establish a provisional central government. In Mar., Thailand's largest finance company nearly collapsed and on Mar. 2 the government halted trading in all bank and general financial sector stocks. The crisis continued as the government was forced to prop up the *baht* and Asian neighbours offered loans to help maintain foreign currency reserves. The crisis eventually forced the Philippines, Malaysia and Indonesia to devalue their currency and the IMF stepped in to offer aid throughout the

region, in exchange for economic reforms. The Turkish army launched an offensive in May that wiped out Kurdish party camps in Northern Iraq. Embryologist Ian Wilmut and four colleagues at Roslin Institute near Edinburgh, Scotland, revealed that they had successfully cloned a sheep. On May 1, 18 years of Conservative government came to an end as Tony Blair and the Labour Party took 418 of the 659 seats in the British House of Commons. Viewers in the US and around the world watched pictures sent back from Mars by the Pathfinder mission in July. In Zaire, rebels took control of the country during Mar. and Apr., Pres. Mobutu left on May 16; on May 17 troops entered Kinshasa and Laurent Kabila took control. Kabila renamed the country the Democratic Republic of the Congo. In Oct., fires burned out of control in Indonesia, blanketing the country and its neighbours with dense smoke. On Oct. 6, the space shuttle *Atlantis* docked with the *Mir* space station. On Mars, *Pathfinder* fell silent. Historic peace talks in Northern Ireland began on Oct. 7 as all parties, including Sinn Fein, tried to end violence. In Nevada, British pilot Andy Green broke the sound barrier on Oct. 13 by driving a jet-propelled automobile at 1,229.775 kph. On Oct. 15, the space probe *Cassini* was launched, headed for Saturn. In late Oct., Hong Kong's stock market dropped over 10% in four days; global markets followed suit. In Iraq, Americans working for UN arms inspection teams were ordered to leave the country on Oct. 29. In Nov., 30,000 protesters demonstrated against the government in Algiers. In Egypt, terrorists killed 68 people in Luxor. On Nov. 20, weapons inspectors were allowed to resume duties in Iraq, ending a three-week standoff with the US. In India, the Congress Party withdrew from the government coalition on Nov. 23, forcing the resignation of Prime Min. Kuman Gujral. In Japan, Yamichi Securities, one of the largest brokerages in the country, shut down on Nov. 24 amid the collapse of stock prices and a payoff scandal; the closure left US$24 billion in debts. US military forces went on high alert as Iraq's Saddam Hussein blocked the work of UN weapons inspectors. In Dec., representatives from 150 nations met in Japan to devise controls on greenhouse gases to slow ozone damage and global warming. The leaders of 26 Somalian factions met in Cairo for a national reconciliation conference and to create an interim government–the first since the collapse of the central government in 1991. British Prime Min. Tony Blair and Sinn Fein leader Gerry Adams met at Downing Street on Dec. 11 to discuss Northern Ireland's peace–the first such meeting since the 1920s.

1998: In Jan., China ordered the slaughter of over one million poultry in Hong Kong to end the threat of the chicken flu discovered in Dec. In Iran, Pres. Khatami called for dialogue with the US on Jan. 7 to resume formal relations for the first time since 1979. An earthquake measuring 6.2 on the Richter scale killed 50 and left 540,000 homeless in China's Hebei province. The last US shuttle to *Mir* was launched Jan. 22 to aid the aging space station. Pope John Paul II visited Catholics and Fidel Castro in Cuba from Jan. 21-25. US Pres. Clinton gave a deposition in the Paula Jones case (Jan. 17) and denied his sexual relationship with former intern Monica Lewinsky (Jan. 26). On Jan. 29, tobacco executives acknowledged that smoking endangered health and agreed to a US$368.5 billion settlement in exchange for immunity from further lawsuits. In Feb., an earthquake in Afghanistan brought hillsides crashing down, destroyed 15,000 homes and killed an estimated 5,000 people. The first tremor, 6.1 on the Richter scale, was followed by five days of aftershocks. In Bangladesh, a 22-year-old war in the southeastern part of the country ended when tribal fighters surrendered their weapons for more autonomy for their Buddhist culture. In China, Zhu Rongji was elected premier in Mar., taking over from Premier Li Peng. In his farewell speech, Li Peng called for measures such as cutting four million bureaucrats from government. In India, the BJP built a coalition of over 20 parties to form a government in the 545-seat parliament (Mar. 11). On Mar. 19 A.B. Vijpayee was sworn in as prime min. On Mar. 23, Russian Pres.Yeltsin fired his prime min., Viktor Chernomyrdin, and his entire cabinet; Yeltsin then appointed Sergei Kiriyenko as acting prime min. In Sri Lanka, suicide bombers using boats packed with explosives rammed a navy convoy transporting troops to the Jaffna peninsula; two vessels went down and at least 40 soldiers were killed. Mid-month, two bombs exploded in Colombo, killing 32 people. On Mar. 24, two boys, aged 11 and 13, gunned down four classmates and a teacher in a shooting incident that wounded 10 others in Jonesboro, Arkansas. The drug company Pfizer released Viagra in the US, a pill effective in treating male impotence. On Mar. 24, fighting erupted again between ethnic Albanians in Kosovo and Serbian police. Earlier in the month a 10-day police action against the Kosovar Liberation Front caused 100 deaths of mostly elderly people, women and children. On Apr. 6, Pakistan announced the firing of a medium-range test missile. On Apr. 10, after 22 months of negotiating, the governments of Ireland and Britain and representatives of the warring factions agreed to permit a referendum on the future of Northern Ireland and the creation of an assembly elected by Northern Ireland voters to govern themselves and to replace rule from London. While the IRA retained its initial ceasefire, dissident groups began a campaign of violence. On Apr. 15, Pol Pot, the Khmer Rouge leader responsible for killing more than a million Cambodians in the 1970s, died unpunished. On Apr. 19, 34 leaders from the Western Hemisphere met in Santiago, Chile, to begin talks for a free-trade zone that would include all countries in the hemisphere except Cuba. On Apr. 24, after two unsuccessful attempts, Russian president Yeltsin's choice of PM was finally confirmed, averting the dissolution of the Duma and an election call. On May 10, Sinn Fein members voted to support the Easter peace agreement and allow its members to sit in Northern Ireland's new assembly. By the end of the month, most Irish in the north and south supported the Easter pact. On May 12, Suharto's troops fired on student protesters in Indonesia; on May 18, a few hundred students occupied the parliament buildings and thousands of others massed outside. On May 21, Suharto resigned; V. Pres. B.J. Habibie was sworn in as his successor. On May 22, the military peacefully cleared the parliament buildings of 2,000 student occupiers. In May, India and Pakistan exchanged artillery fire along the Kashmiri border. On May 11, India exploded three nuclear devices in underground tests. Two more were detonated on May 13. On May 28, Pakistan announced the successful underground test of five nuclear devices. Ethnic turmoil exploded in Kosovo, an Albanian-dominated province in Yugoslavia. As Serb police and military forces moved to quell the violence, it spilled over into Albania. In June, Ethiopia and

Eritrea fought a border war. On June 9, a cyclone hit India's west coast and killed at least 950 people. Muslim separatists in Kashmir killed 25 Hindus. NATO warplanes flew over Kosovo to end Serbia's four-month battle with insurgents that had created 65,000 refugees. In July, monsoons in Bangladesh stranded eight million people near the country's capital. Against a backdrop of sectarian violence, David Trimble, leader of the Ulster Unionist Party, was selected to be the First Minister of the new Northern Ireland assembly. Former Italian prime min. Silvio Berlusconi was sentenced for bribing tax inspectors. In Nigeria, Gen. Abubakar released hundreds of prisoners and abolished three discredited electoral bodies. On July 17, Papua New Guinea was devastated by tidal waves that killed at least 3,000 people; another 3,000 were unaccounted for; an undersea earthquake measuring 7 on the Richter scale triggered the killer waves. In Russia, as economic woes mounted, the IMF and other foreign lenders offered a US$22.6 billion rescue package on July 13; the remains of Tsar Nicholas and his family were interred in St. Petersburg on July 17. By mid-July, UN officials said 2.4 million Sudanese faced starvation because of a two-year-drought and a 15-year civil war. In Florida more than 120,000 people were evacuated from the paths of wildfires. In mid-July, 110 were killed in Kosovo as supporters of Kosovar separatists tried to enter the territory from Albania and clashed with the Yugoslav army. Yugoslavia's army launched an offensive to recapture the southern territory from rebels on July 24; it ended in early Aug. In the United States, the Dow Jones started a nosedive in late July; by Aug. 7, it had lost 10% of its value. Stock markets around the world followed suit. On Aug. 7, a car bomb exploded outside the US embassy in Kenya; 263 were killed and over 4,500 were injured. A second car bomb exploded outside the US embassy in Tanzania. On Aug. 12, a US$300 million rocket carrying a spy satellite valued at US$1 billion exploded 42 seconds after take-off. Monica Lewinsky, a former White House intern, testified before a grand jury that she had sex with US Pres. Clinton between Nov. 1995 and May 1997–a relationship he had denied in Jan. On Aug. 15, an IRA splinter group that refused to support the ceasefire in Northern Ireland detonated a car bomb in Omagh that killed 29 and injured over 220; all supporters of peace condemned the bombing. On Aug. 15, the Iraqi national assembly voted to suspend co-operation with the UN weapons inspectors to protest over eight years of economic sanctions. On Aug. 20, the US military fired missiles at the camp and operations of suspected terrorist Osama bin Laden in retaliation for the bombing of its embassies in Africa. China suffered its worst flood season in 50 years; 3,600 were killed and over 1.4 million were displaced. By Aug. 27, massive flooding in northern and eastern India stranded some 1.5 million people. Homes and crops were submerged and up to 20 isolated hamlets disappeared completely. As food prices hit record highs, Indonesian students took to the streets in August to demand the resignation of B.J. Habibie. In Russia, the ruble fell on Aug. 17 and the government suspended debt repayments. Pres. Yeltsin fired his entire cabinet and reappointed Viktor Chernomyrdin as acting prime min. On Aug. 23, the Duma refused to confirm the appointment. On Aug. 29, Yeltsin agreed to give up some powers for the confirmation. In North Korea, a multi-stage missile, which the government later insisted was a satellite launch, was fired Aug. 31. In Sept. Hurricane Georges hit the Dominican Republic, Haiti and other islands killing over 200 people and leaving hundreds of thousands homeless. On Sept. 7, tens of thousands of people in Côte d'Ivoire demonstrated against Pres. Bedie who had changed the constitution to lengthen his term. In Liberia, civil war flared up in the capital; thousands fled during the fighting. Floods in the southern part of Mexico left 1.2 million without homes or food. In Russia, Pres. Yeltsin proposed and the Duma confirmed Yevgeni Primakov for prime min. On Sept. 11, US Pres. Clinton admitted his affair with Lewinsky; the admission prompted calls for his resignation or impeachment because he had lied to the public. Special Prosecutor Kenneth Starr delivered his report on Clinton to the US Congress on the same day; his report was posted on the Internet. On Sept. 27, one of Europe's longest serving leaders, German Pres. Helmut Kohl, was defeated at the polls by Social Democrat Gerhard Schroeder.

1999: See "News Events of the Year

NATIONS OF THE WORLD

THE STATISTICS SHOWN ARE INTENDED TO PRESENT an informative and comparative picture of the various nations of the world and their dependent territories. All data, including the geographic, population and government data, are taken from the latest available sources. The economic and finance/trade data indicate the size of the national economies and the amount of economic activity in the respective countries; the population, health and education data, and communications and transportation data give some evidence of the quality of life and the state of the infrastructure in each nation.

All dollar amounts are in US dollars. In GDP figures (and where indicated as "purchasing power parity") international dollar price weights have been used instead of an official currency exchange rate in an attempt to make a more equitable comparison of GDPs. Other figures expressed as a percentage of GDP were calculated using official currency exchange rates.

The figures for "Number of Physicians" under "Population" have been dropped due to the age of the data available. Instead we have substituted "Total Fertility Rate." This figure represents the number of children born per woman, and indicates the potential for population growth. A high total fertility rate will have an impact on a nation's workforce—women's participation may be limited; it may also have an impact on the amount of education available and the level of education achieved in the general population.

The information contained in this section reflects data available up to and including October 1, 1999. Sources used for information include:

CIA World Fact Book 1998 • "Compendium of Statistics: Illiteracy" (UNESCO) • "Facts on File" • Demographic Yearbook (UN) • "Digest of Statistics: Traffic" (International Civil Aviation Organization) • Encyclopedia Britannica • Direction of Trade Statistics (International Monetary Fund) • Foreign Affairs Canada • Government Finance Statistics Yearbook (International Monetary Fund) • "Human Development Report" (UN Development Programme) • International Financial Statistics Yearbook (International Monetary Fund) • International Financial Statistics (monthly IMF update) • "Keesing's Record of World Events" • Monthly Bulletin of Statistics (UN Statistical Division) • "Population and Vital Statistics Report" (UN Dept. of International Economic and Social Affairs) • Statesman's Yearbook (Macmillan) • UNESCO Statistical Yearbook • World Bank Atlas (World Bank) • World Book Encyclopedia • World Debt Tables • "World Development Report" (World Bank) • "World Motor Vehicle Data" (Motor Vehicle Manufactures Assoc. of the US Inc.) • "World Population" (UNESCO) • "World Population Data Sheet" (Population Reference Bureau Inc.) • World Resources (World Resources Institute) • World Statistics Pocketbook • "World Tables" (Johns Hopkins UP) • Worldwide Government Directory with International Organizations (Belmont Publications) • Year Book of Labour Statistics (International Labour Office, Geneva).

Afghanistan

Long-Form Name: Islamic State of Afghanistan
Capital: Kabul

■ GEOGRAPHY

Area: 647,500 sq. km
Coastline: none: landlocked
Climate: arid to semi-arid; cold winters and hot summers, considerable snowfall
Environment: damaging earthquakes occur in Hindu Kush mountains; poor soil, flooding, desertification (largely due to logging for building materials and fuel), overgrazing, deforestation, pollution

Terrain: mostly rugged mountains; plains in north and southwest
Land Use: 12% arable land; no permanent crops; 46% meadows and pastures; 3% forest and woodland; 39% other, includes about 26,600 sq. km of irrigated farmland
Location: SW Asia (Middle East)

■ PEOPLE

Population: 24,792,375 (July 1998 est.)
Nationality: Afghan
Age Structure: 0-14 yrs: 43%; 15-64: 54%; 65+: 3% (1998 est.)
Population Growth Rate: 4.21% (1998 est.)
Net Migration: 17.14 migrants/1,000 population (1998 est.)

Ethnic Groups: 38% Pathan, 25% Tajik, 6% Uzbek, 19% Hazara; minor ethnic groups include Charar Aimaks, Turkoman, Baloch and others

Languages: 35% Pushtu (official), 50% Afghan Persian (Dari), 11% Turkic languages (primarily Uzbek and Turmen), 4% thirty minor languages (primarily Balochi and Pahai); much bilingualism

Religions: Islam (84% Sunni Muslim, 15% Shi'a Muslim), 1% other

Birth Rate: 42.37/1,000 population (1998 est.)

Death Rate: 17.4/1000 population (1998 est.)

Infant Mortality: 143.63 deaths/1,000 live births (1998 est.)

Life Expectancy at Birth: 46.83 years male, 46.29 years female (1998 est.)

Total Fertility Rate: 6.01 children born/woman (1998 est.)

Literacy: 31.5% (1997 est.)

■ GOVERNMENT

Leader(s): Due to a coup by the Taliban movement of Muslim fundamentalists, there is currently no functioning national government; Taliban Supreme Leader is Mullah Mohammad Omar Mujahid.

Government Type: transitional government: a six-member council appointed by the Taliban movement of Muslim fundamentalists

Administrative Divisions: 30 provinces

Nationhood: Aug. 19, 1919 (from UK)

National Holiday: Victory of the Muslim Nation, Apr. 28; Remembrance Day for Martyrs and the Disabled, May 4; Independence Day, August 19

■ ECONOMY

Overview: a poor country, largely dependent on farming (wheat) and livestock (sheep and goats). The economy is adversely affected by political and military disruptions

GDP: $19.3 billion, per capita $800; real growth rate n.a. (1997 est.)

Inflation: n.a.

Industries: accounts for 15% of GDP; small-scale production of textiles, soap, furniture, shoes, fertilizer and cement; handwoven carpets; natural gas, oil, coal, copper

Labour Force: 6,403,000 (1995); 68% agriculture and animal husbandry, 10% industry, 22% services and other

Unemployment: 8% (1995 est.)

Agriculture: largely subsistence farming and nomadic animal husbandry; cash products–wheat, fruit, nuts, karakul pelts, wool, mutton, barley, corn; production is limited due to the shortage of modern machinery, high-grade seed, and fertilizer. Accounts for 56% of GDP.

Natural Resources: natural gas, crude oil, copper, coal, salt, talc, barites, sulphur, lead, zinc, iron ore, slate, precious and semi-precious stones, especially lapis lazuli, amethysts, rubies

■ FINANCE/TRADE

Currency: afghani (Af) = 100 puls

International Reserves Excluding Gold: n.a.

Gold Reserves: n.a.

Budget: n.a.

Defence Expenditures: n.a.

Education Expenditures: n.a.

External Debt: n.a.

Exports: $80 million (1996 est.); commodities: natural gas 55%, fruit and nuts 24%, handwoven carpets, wool, cotton, hides; partners: FSU, Pakistan, Iran, Germany, India, UK, Belgium, Luxembourg, Czechoslovakia

Imports: $150 million (1996 est.); commodities: food and petroleum products, most consumer goods; partners: FSU, Pakistan, Iran, Japan, Singapore, India, South Korea, Germany

■ COMMUNICATIONS

Daily Newspapers: 12 (1996 est.)

Televisions: 12/1,000 inhabitants (1996 est.)

Radios: 122/1,000 inhabitants (1996 est.)

Telephones: 0.1/100 inhabitants (1996 est.)

■ TRANSPORTATION

Motor Vehicles: 67,000; 35,000 passenger cars (1997 est.)

Roads: 21,000 km; 2,793 km paved

Railway: 9.6 km from Kushka (Turkmenistan) to Towraghondi and 15.0 km from Termez (Uzbekistan) to Kheyrabad

Air Traffic: 256,000 passengers carried (1996)

Airports: 44; 11 have paved runways (1997 est.)

Canadian Embassy: c/o Canadian High Commission, Diplomatic Sector G-5, Islamabad; mailing address: GPO Box 1042, Islamabad, Pakistan. Tel: (011-92-51) 27-91-00. Fax (011-92-51) 27-91-10.

Embassy in Canada: c/o High Commission for the Islamic Republic of Pakistan, Burnside Building, 151 Slater St, Ste 608, Ottawa ON K1P 5H3. Tel: (613) 238-7881. Fax: (613) 238-7296.

Albania

Long-Form Name: Republic of Albania

Capital: Tirana

■ GEOGRAPHY

Area: 28,750 sq. km
Coastline: 362 km
Climate: mild temperate; cool, cloudy, wet winters; hot, clear, dry summers; interior is cooler and wetter, with severe winters
Environment: subject to destructive earthquakes; soil erosion; water pollution; tsunami occur along southwestern coast; deforestation and water pollution are still current issues
Terrain: mostly mountains and hills; small plains along coast
Land Use: 21% arable land; 5% permanent crops; 15% meadows and pastures; 38% forest and woodland, including 30% scrub forest; 21% other, includes 1.5% irrigated
Location: SE Europe, bordering on Adriatic Sea

■ PEOPLE

Population: 3,330,754 (July 1998 est.)
Nationality: Albanian
Age Structure: 0-14 yrs: 33%; 15-64: 61%; 65+: 6% (1998 est.)
Population Growth Rate: 0.97% (1998 est.)
Net Migration: -4.16 migrants/1,000 population (1998 est.)
Ethnic Groups: 95% Albanian, 3% Greek, 2% others (Vlachs, Gypsies, Serbs and Bulgarians)
Languages: Albanian (Tosk is official dialect, also Gheg dialect), Greek
Religions: 70% Muslim, 20% Albanian Orthodox, 10% Roman Catholic
Birth Rate: 21.35/1,000 population (1998 est.)
Death Rate: 7.45/1,000 population (1998 est.)
Infant Mortality: 45.01 deaths/1,000 live births (1998 est.)
Life Expectancy at Birth: 65.58 male, 71.94 years female (1998 est.)
Total Fertility Rate: 2.57 children born/woman (1998 est.)
Literacy: 72% (1997 est.)

■ GOVERNMENT

Leader(s): Pres. Rexhep Mejdani, Prime Min. Pandeli Majko
Government Type: in transition to democracy
Administrative Divisions: 36 districts
Nationhood: Nov. 28, 1912 (from Ottoman Empire); People's Socialist Republic of Albania declared Jan. 11, 1946
National Holiday: Independence Day, Nov. 28

■ ECONOMY

Overview: the poorest country in Europe, it is a Stalinist-type economy (central planning and state ownership of the means of production). Though largely self-sufficient in food until 1990, the recent break-up of cooperative farms and the general economic decline has forced Albania to rely increasingly on foreign aid. Unemployment remains a severe problem, affecting almost one-fifth of the work force
GDP: $4.5 billion, per capita $1,370; real growth rate -8% (1997 est.)
Inflation: 16.9% (as of July 1998)
Industries: accounts for 21% of GDP; food processing, textiles and clothing, lumber, oil, cement, chemicals, basic metals, hydroelectricity; most industries produce at only fraction of past levels
Labour Force: 2 million (1997 est.); 24.1% agriculture, 35.3% industry, 15.9% service
Unemployment: officially 14% (Oct. 1997), but likely to be as high as 28%
Agriculture: accounts for 56% of GDP; arable land per capita among lowest in Europe; one-half of workforce engaged in farming; produces wide range of temperate-zone crops and livestock; claims self-sufficiency in grain output; 80% of all arable land is now in private ownership
Natural Resources: crude oil, natural gas, coal, chromium, copper, timber, nickel, petroleum

■ FINANCE/TRADE

Currency: lek (L) = 100 quintars
International Reserves Excluding Gold: $443 million (Nov. 1998)
Gold Reserves: 0.117 million fine troy ounces (Dec. 1998)
Budget: revenues $624 million; expenditures $996 million, including capital expenditures n.a. (1995)
Defence Expenditures: 1.5 to 2% of GDP (1996)
Education Expenditures: 1.5 to 2.0% of GDP (1996)
External Debt: $781 million (1996)
Exports: $205 million (1998); commodities: asphalt, bitumen, petroleum products, metals and metallic ores, electricity, oil, vegetables, fruit, tobacco; partners: Italy, Yugoslavia, Germany, Greece, Czech and Slovak Republics, Poland, Romania, Bulgaria, Hungary
Imports: $788 million (1998); commodities: machinery, machine tools, iron and steel products, textiles, chemicals, pharmaceuticals; partners: Italy, Yugoslavia, Germany, Czech and Slovak Republics, Romania, Poland, Hungary, Bulgaria

■ COMMUNICATIONS

Daily Newspapers: 5 (1996)
Televisions: 118/1,000 inhabitants (1996)
Radios: 235/1,000 inhabitants (1996)
Telephones: 1.2/100 persons (1996 est.)

■ TRANSPORTATION

Motor Vehicles: n.a.
Roads: 18,000 km; 5,400 km paved (1996)
Railway: 670 km (1996)
Air Traffic: 14,000 passengers carried (1996)
Airports: 9; 5 have paved runways (1997 est.)

Canadian Embassy: The Canadian Embassy to Albania, c/o The Canadian Embassy, Via Zara 30, 00198 Rome, Italy. Tel: (011-39-06) 445981. Fax: (011-39-06) 445 98912.
Embassy in Canada: c/o Embassy of the People's Republic of Albania, 1511 K St NW, Ste 1000, Washington DC 20005, USA. Tel: (202) 223-4942. Fax: (202) 628-7342.

Algeria

Long-Form Name: Democratic and Popular Republic of Algeria
Capital: Algiers

■ GEOGRAPHY

Area: 2,381,740 sq. km
Coastline: 998 km
Climate: arid to semi-arid; mild, wet winters with hot, dry summers along coast; drier with cold winters and hot summers on high plateau; sirocco is a hot, dust/sand-laden wind especially common in summer
Environment: mountainous areas subject to severe earthquakes; desertification; industrial and domestic pollution and soil erosion contribute to environmental problems
Terrain: mostly high plateau and desert; some mountains; narrow, discontinuous coastal plain
Land Use: 3% arable land; 0% permanent crops; 13% meadows and pastures; 2% forest and woodland; 82% other; cattle, sheep and goat grazing on grassland and shrub regions, includes negligible irrigated
Location: N Africa, bordering on Mediterranean Sea

■ PEOPLE

Population: 30,480,793 (July 1998 est.)
Nationality: Algerian
Age Structure: 0-14 yrs: 38%; 15-64: 58%; 65+: 4% (1998 est.)
Population Growth Rate: 2.14% (1998 est.)
Net Migration: -0.49 migrants/1,000 population (1998 est.)
Ethnic Groups: 99% Arab-Berber, less than 1% European
Languages: Arabic (official), French, Berber dialects

Religions: 99% Sunni Muslim (state religion); 1% Christian and Jewish
Birth Rate: 27.51/1,000 population (1998 est.)
Death Rate: 5.63/1,000 population (1998 est.)
Infant Mortality: 45.44 deaths/1,000 live births (1998 est.)
Life Expectancy at Birth: 67.78 male, 70.12 years female (1998 est.)
Total Fertility Rate: 3.38 children born/woman (1998 est.)
Literacy: 61.6% (1997 est.)

■ GOVERNMENT

Leader(s): Pres. Abdelaziz Bouteflika, Prem. Smail Hamdani
Government Type: republic
Administrative Divisions: 48 "wilaya" (provinces)
Nationhood: July 5, 1962 (from France)
National Holiday: Anniversary of the Revolution, Nov. 1

■ ECONOMY

Overview: the economy is largely based on the exploitation of oil and natural gas products. Dropping oil and gas prices have contributed to Algeria's most serious social and economic crisis since independence. Recently, reforms have been implemented to combat social and economic problems
GDP: $120.4 billion, per capita $4,000; real growth rate 2.5% (1997 est.)
Inflation: 3.6% (as of June 1997)
Industries: petroleum, light industries, natural gas, mining, electrical, petrochemical, food processing. Accounts for 50% of GDP
Labour Force: 9.3 million (1997 est.); 11% industry, 14% agriculture, 75% services
Unemployment: 28% (1997 estimate)
Agriculture: accounts for 12% of GDP and employs 22% of labour force; products include wheat, barley, grapes, oats, olives, fruit, livestock; must import more than one-third of its food
Natural Resources: crude oil, natural gas, iron ore, phosphates, uranium, lead, zinc, mercury

■ FINANCE/TRADE

Currency: dinar (DA) = 100 centimes
International Reserves Excluding Gold: $6.846 billion (Jan. 1999)
Gold Reserves: 5.583 million fine troy ounces (Jan. 1999)
Budget: revenues $13.7 billion; expenditures $13.1 billion, including capital expenditures $5.1 million (1996 est.)
Defence Expenditures: 4% of GDP (1996)
Education Expenditures: n.a.

External Debt: $33 billion (1997 est.)
Exports: $12.621 billion (1996); commodities: petroleum and natural gas 98%; partners: Netherlands, Czech and Slovak Republics, Romania, Italy, France, US
Imports: $8.690 billion (1996); commodities: capital goods 35%, consumer goods 36%, food 20%; partners: France 25%, Italy 8%, Germany 8%, US 6–7%

■ COMMUNICATIONS

Daily Newspapers: 5 (1996)
Televisions: 104/1,000 inhabitants (1996)
Radios: 239/1,000 inhabitants (1996)
Telephones: 4.3/100 inhabitants (1996 est.)

■ TRANSPORTATION

Motor Vehicles: 930,000; 500,000 passenger cars (1997 est.)
Roads: 102,424 km; 70,570 km paved (1996)
Railway: 4,772 km (1996)
Air Traffic: 3,494,057 passengers carried (1996)
Airports: 136; 66 have paved runways (1997 est.)

Canadian Embassy: The Canadian Embassy, 18 Mustapha Khalef Street, Ben Aknoun, Algiers, Algeria; mailing address: P.O. Box 48, Alger-Gare, 1600 Alger, Algeria. Tel: (011-213-2) 914951. Fax: (011-213-2) 914973.
Embassy in Canada: Embassy of the People's Democratic Republic of Algeria, 435 Daly Ave, Ottawa ON K1N 6H3. Tel: (613) 789-8505. Fax: (613) 789-1406.

American Samoa

Long-Form Name: Territory of American Samoa
Capital: Pago Pago (on Tutuila Island)

■ GEOGRAPHY

Area: 199 sq. km
Climate: tropical maritime, plentiful rainfall, temperatures consistent throughout the year
Land Use: 5% arable land, 10% permanent crops, 0% meadows and pastures, 70% forest and woodland, 15% other
Location: S Pacific Ocean, NW of Australia and New Zealand

■ PEOPLE

Population: 62,093 (July 1998 est.)
Nationality: American Samoan; nationals of the United States
Ethnic Groups: Samoan (Polynesian) 89%, Caucasian 2%, Tongan 4%, other 5%
Languages: Samoan (a Polynesian dialect), English

■ GOVERNMENT

Colony Territory of: Dependent Territory of the United States
Leader(s): Pres. W.J. Clinton; Gov. Tavese P. Sunia
Government Type: US dependency with democratically elected governor: unorganized unincorporated territory
National Holiday: Territorial Flag Day, Apr. 17

■ ECONOMY

Overview: agriculture: taro, bread-fruit, yams, bananas, coconuts; livestock includes pigs, goats, poultry; industries: fish (tuna) canning; economic activity is closely tied to US; tourism is slowly developing

■ FINANCE/TRADE

Currency: American dollar (US$) = 100 cents

Canadian Embassy: n.a.
Representative to Canada: c/o Embassy of the United States of America, 100 Wellington St., Ottawa ON K1P 5A1. Tel: (613) 238-5335. Fax: (613) 238-5720.

Andorra

Long-Form Name: Principality of Andorra
Capital: Andorra-la-Vella

■ GEOGRAPHY

Area: 450 sq. km
Coastline: none: landlocked
Climate: temperate; snowy, cold winters and warm, dry summers
Environment: deforestation, overgrazing, soil erosion; avalanches are a natural hazard
Terrain: rugged mountains separated by narrow valleys
Land Use: 2% arable land; 0% permanent crops; 56% meadows and pastures; 22% forest and woodland; 20% other
Location: SW Europe

■ PEOPLE

Population: 64,716 (July 1998 est.)
Nationality: Andorran
Age Structure: 0-14 yrs: 14%; 15-64: 73%; 65+: 13% (1998 est.)
Population Growth Rate: 1.5% (1998 est.)
Net Migration: 19.84 migrants/1,000 population (1998 est.)
Ethnic Groups: Catalan stock; 61% Spanish, 30% Andorran, 6% French, 3% other
Languages: Catalan (official); many also speak some French and Spanish

Religions: predominantly Roman Catholic
Birth Rate: 10.48/1,000 population (1998 est.)
Death Rate: 5.35/1,000 population (1998 est.)
Infant Mortality: 4.09 deaths/1,000 live births (1998 est.)
Life Expectancy at Birth: 80.54 years male, 86.54 years female (1998 est.)
Total Fertility Rate: 1.23 children born/woman (1998 est.)
Literacy: n.a.

■ GOVERNMENT

Leader(s): Co-Chiefs of State Jacques Chirac (France) and Jose Maria Aznar (Spain), Prem. Marc Forné Molné
Government Type: parliamentary democracy; retains as its heads of state a co-principality of president of France and Spanish bishop of Seo de Urgel, who are represented locally by officials called veguers
Administrative Divisions: 7 parishes
Nationhood: 1278 (from France and Spain)
National Holiday: Mare de Deu de Meritxell, Sept. 8

■ ECONOMY

Overview: tourism is the backbone of the economy, due to its duty-free status and year-round resorts. Most food is imported due to a scarcity of arable land
GDP: $1.2 billion, per capita $18,000, real growth rate n.a. (1995 est.)
Inflation: n.a.
Industries: tourism (particularly skiing), sheep, timber, tobacco, banking
Labour Force: n.a.
Unemployment: 0%
Agriculture: sheep raising, small quantities of tobacco, rye, wheat, barley, buckwheat, maize, oats and some vegetables, especially potatoes
Natural Resources: hydroelectricity, mineral water, timber, iron ore, lead

■ FINANCE/TRADE

Currency: French Franc, Spanish peseta (F Ptas)
International Reserves Excluding Gold: n.a.
Gold Reserves: n.a.
Budget: n.a.
Defence Expenditures: defence is the responsibility of Spain and France
Education Expenditures: n.a.
External Debt: n.a.
Exports: $47 million (1995); commodities: electricity, tobacco products, furniture; partners: France, Spain
Imports: $1 billion (1995); commodities: consumer goods, food; partners: France, Spain, US

■ COMMUNICATIONS

Daily Newspapers: 3 (1996)
Televisions: 370/1,000 inhabitants (1996)
Radios: 217/1,000 inhabitants (1996)
Telephones: 43.7/100 inhabitants (1996 est.)

■ TRANSPORTATION

Motor Vehicles: 36,000; 35,500 passenger cars (1997 est.)
Roads: 269 km; 198 km paved
Railway: none
Air Traffic: n.a.
Airports: none

Canadian Embassy: The Canadian Embassy to Andorra, Apartado 587, 28080, Madrid, Spain. Tel: (011-34) 91-423-3250. Fax: (011-34) 91-423-3251, or (011-34) 91-423-3252.
Embassy in Canada: c/o Permanent Mission of the Principality of Andorra to the United Nations, 2 United Nations Plaza, 25th Floor, New York NY 10017, USA. Tel: (212) 750-8064. Fax: (212) 750-6630.

Angola

Long-Form Name: Republic of Angola
Capital: Luanda

■ GEOGRAPHY

Area: 1,246,700 sq. km
Coastline: 1,600 km
Climate: semi-arid in south and along coast to Luanda; north has cool, dry season (May to October) and hot, rainy season (Nov. to Apr.)
Environment: locally heavy rainfall causes periodic flooding on plateau; desertification, especially on coastal plain, soil erosion and water pollution; deforestation
Terrain: narrow coastal plain rises abruptly to vast interior plain
Land Use: 2% arable land; 0% permanent crops; 23% meadows and pastures; 43% forest and woodland; 32% other
Location: SW Africa

■ PEOPLE

Population: 10,864,512 (July 1998 est.)
Nationality: Angolan
Age Structure: 0-14 yrs: 45%; 15-64: 52%; 65+: 3% (1998 est.)
Population Growth Rate: 2.84% (1998 est.)
Net Migration: 1.65% migrants/1,000 population (1998 est.)
Ethnic Groups: 37% Ovimbundu, 25% Kimbundu, 13% Bakongo, 2% Mestiço, 1% European, 22% other

Languages: Portuguese (official); Bantu dialects spoken include Ovimbundu, Kimbundu, Bakongo and Chokwe
Religions: 38% Roman Catholic, 15% Protestant, 47% Animist (indigenous beliefs)
Birth Rate: 43.58/1,000 population (1998 est.)
Death Rate: 16.79/1,000 population (1998 est.)
Infant Mortality: 132.44 deaths/1,000 live births (1998 est.)
Life Expectancy at Birth: 45.6 years male, 50.23 years female (1998 est.)
Total Fertility Rate: 6.2 children born/woman (1998 est.)
Literacy: 42% (1997 est.)

■ GOVERNMENT

Leader(s): Pres. José Eduardo dos Santos
Government Type: transitional government, nominally a democracy with strong presidential system
Administrative Divisions: 18 provinces
Nationhood: Nov. 11, 1975 (from Portugal)
National Holiday: Independence Day, Nov. 11

■ ECONOMY

Overview: subsistence agriculture is the main livelihood of the population, but oil production is the most lucrative activity. Recent internal war has weakened the economy, and food must be imported
GDP: $8.3 billion, per capita $800; real growth rate 9% (1996 est.)
Inflation: n.a.
Industries: accounts for 56% of GDP; petroleum, mining (phosphate rock, uranium, gold, iron ore, bauxite, feldspar, diamonds), fish processing, brewing, tobacco, sugar, textiles, cement, food processing, building construction
Labour Force: 5.1 million economically active (1997 est.); 74% agriculture, 10% industry, 16% services
Unemployment: extensive unemployment and underemployment affects more than half the population (1997 est.)
Agriculture: accounts for 12% of GDP; cash crops—coffee, sisal, corn, cotton, sugar, manioc, tobacco; food crops—cassava, corn, vegetables, plantains, bananas and other local foodstuffs
Natural Resources: petroleum, diamonds, iron ore, phosphates, copper, feldspar, gold, bauxite, uranium

■ FINANCE/TRADE

Currency: new kwanza (Kz) = 100 lwei
International Reserves Excluding Gold: n.a.
Gold Reserves: n.a.

Budget: n.a.
Defence Expenditures: 6.4% of GDP (1996)
Education Expenditures: n.a.
External Debt: $10.612 billion (1996 est.)
Exports: n.a.; commodities: oil, coffee, diamonds, sisal, fish and fish products, timber, cotton; partners: US, former USSR countries, Cuba, Portugal, Brazil
Imports: n.a.; commodities: capital equipment (machinery and electrical equipment), food, vehicles and spare parts, textiles and clothing, medicines, substantial military deliveries; partners: US, former USSR countries, Cuba, Portugal, Brazil

■ COMMUNICATIONS

Daily Newspapers: 5 (1996)
Televisions: 27/1,000 inhabitants (1996)
Radios: 54/1,000 inhabitants (1996)
Telephones: 0.7/100 inhabitants (1996 est.)

■ TRANSPORTATION

Motor Vehicles: 225,000; 200,000 passenger cars (1997 est.)
Roads: 72,626 km; 18,157 km paved
Railway: 2,952 km (1997 est.)
Air Traffic: 585,000 passengers carried (1996)
Airports: 252; n.a. have paved runways (1997 est.)

Canadian Embassy: Consulate of Canada, Rua Rei Katyavala 113, Luanda, Angola. Tel: (011-244-2) 348-371. Fax: (011-244-2) 34-94-94.
Embassy in Canada: Embassy of the Republic of Angola, 75 Albert St, Ste 900, Ottawa ON K1P 5E7. Tel: (613) 234-1152. Fax: (613) 234-1179.

Anguilla

Long-Form Name: Anguilla
Capital: The Valley

■ GEOGRAPHY

Area: 91 sq. km
Climate: dry and sunny, tropical with moderating northeast trade winds
Land Use: mostly rock, with sparse scrub, few trees, some commercial salt ponds; low rainfall limits agricultural potential
Location: West Indies

■ PEOPLE

Population: 11,147 (July 1998 est.)
Nationality: Anguillan
Ethnic Groups: of English ancestry, black/mixed-black African
Languages: English (official)

■ GOVERNMENT

Colony Territory of: Dependent Territory of the United Kingdom
Leader(s): Gov. Robert M. Harris
Government Type: dependent territory of the U.K.
National Holiday: Anguilla Day, May 30

■ ECONOMY

Overview: agriculture: pigeon peas, corn, sweet potatoes; fishing; livestock includes sheep, goats, cattle, poultry; main trading partner: U.K. There are few natural resources and the economy depends heavily on tourism

■ FINANCE/TRADE

Currency: Eastern Caribbean dollar (EC$) = 100 cents

Canadian Embassy: c/o The Canadian High Commission, Macdonald House 1, Grosvenor Square, London W1X 0AB, England, UK. Tel: (011-44-171) 258-6600. Fax: (011-44-171) 258-6333.
Representative to Canada: c/o British High Commission, 80 Elgin St, Ottawa ON K1P 5K7. Tel: (613) 237-1530. Fax: (613) 237-7980.

Antigua and Barbuda

Long-Form Name: Antigua and Barbuda
Capital: Saint John's (on Antigua)

■ GEOGRAPHY

Area: 440 sq. km; includes Redonda (1.3 sq. km)
Coastline: 153 km
Climate: tropical marine; little seasonal temperature variation
Environment: subject to hurricanes and tropical storms (July to Oct.); insufficient freshwater resources are decreased further by clear-cutting of trees, which promotes rain run-off; occasional long periods of drought; deeply indented coastline provides many natural harbours
Terrain: mostly low-lying limestone and coral islands with some higher volcanic areas
Land Use: 18% arable land; 0% permanent crops; 9% meadows and pastures; 11% forest and woodland; 62% other
Location: Caribbean islands

■ PEOPLE

Population: 64,006 (July 1998 est.)
Nationality: Antiguan, Barbudan
Age Structure: 0-14 yrs: 26%; 15-64: 68%; 65+: 6% (1998 est.)

Population Growth Rate: 0.39% (1998 est.)
Net Migration: -6.92 migrants/1,000 population (1998 est.)
Ethnic Groups: almost entirely of black African origin; some of British, Portuguese, Lebanese and Syrian origin
Languages: English (official), local dialects
Religions: Anglican (predominant), other Protestant sects, some Roman Catholic
Birth Rate: 16.72/1,000 population (1998 est.)
Death Rate: 5.87/1,000 population (1998 est.)
Infant Mortality: 21.35 deaths/1,000 live births (1998 est.)
Life Expectancy at Birth: 68.82 years male, 73.69 years female (1998 est.)
Total Fertility Rate: 1.74 children born/woman (1998 est.)
Literacy: 89% (1997 est.)

■ GOVERNMENT

Leader(s): Queen Elizabeth II/Gov. Gen. James B. Carlisle, Prime Min. Lester Bird
Government Type: parliamentary democracy
Administrative Divisions: 6 parishes, 2 dependencies
Nationhood: Nov. 1, 1981 (from UK)
National Holiday: Independence Day, Nov. 1

■ ECONOMY

Overview: tourism is the backbone of this service-oriented economy, therefore economic downturns, particularly in the US, can have adverse effects. A labour shortage is plaguing some sectors of the economy; agriculture is a minor but growing sector of the economy
GDP: $470 million, per capita $7,400; real growth rate 3.3% (1997 est.)
Inflation: n.a.
Industries: accounts for 18.9% of GDP; tourism, construction, light manufacturing (clothing, alcohol, household appliances)
Labour Force: n.a.
Unemployment: 5–10% (1995 est.)
Agriculture: accounts for 3.8% of GDP; expanding output of cotton, fruit, vegetables and livestock; other crops—bananas, coconuts, sugar cane, cucumbers, mangoes; not self-sufficient in food
Natural Resources: negligible; pleasant climate and beautiful beaches foster tourism

■ FINANCE/TRADE

Currency: East Caribbean dollar ($EC) = 100 cents
International Reserves Excluding Gold: $59 million (Dec. 1998)
Gold Reserves: n.a.

Budget: revenues $134 million; expenditures $135.4 million, including capital expenditures n.a. (1995)
Defence Expenditures: 0.8% of GDP (1996)
Education Expenditures: n.a.
External Debt: $435 million (1996 est.)
Exports: n.a.; commodities: petroleum products 46%, manufactures 23%, food and live animals 4%, machinery and transport equipment 17%; partners: Trinidad and Tobago 2%, Barbados 15%, US 0.3%, others 26%
Imports: n.a.; commodities: food and live animals, machinery and transport equipment, manufactures, chemicals, oil; partners: US 27%, UK 16%, OECS 3%, Canada 4%, other 50%

■ COMMUNICATIONS

Daily Newspapers: 1 (1996)
Televisions: 457/1,000 inhabitants (1996)
Radios: 522/1,000 inhabitants (1996)
Telephones: 33.2/100 inhabitants (1996 est.)

■ TRANSPORTATION

Motor Vehicles: 14,800; 13,400 passenger cars (1997 est.)
Roads: 250 km (1996 est.)
Railway: 77 km
Air Traffic: 1,098,000 passengers carried (1996)
Airports: 3, 2 have paved runways (1997 est.)

Canadian Embassy: c/o The Canadian High Commission, Bishop's Court Hill, St. Michael; mailing address: P.O. Box 404, Bridgetown, Barbados.
Embassy in Canada: High Commission for Antigua and Barbuda, 112 Kent St, Ste 1610, Place de Ville, Tower B, Ottawa ON K1P 5P2. Tel: (613) 236-8952. Fax: (613) 236-3042.

Argentina

Long-Form Name: Argentine Republic
Capital: Buenos Aires

■ GEOGRAPHY

Area: 2,766,890 sq. km
Coastline: 4,989 km
Climate: mostly temperate; arid in southeast; subantarctic in southwest
Environment: Tucamán and Mendoza areas in Andes subject to earthquakes; pamperos are violent windstorms that can strike the Pampas and northeast; irrigated soil degradation; desertification; air and water pollution in Buenos Aires; erosion is a current problem
Terrain: rich plains of the Pampas in northern half, flat to rolling plateau of Patagonia in south, rugged Andes along western border
Land Use: 9% arable land; 1% permanent crops; 52% meadows and pastures; 19% forest and woodland; 19% other, includes less than 1% irrigated
Location: SE South America

■ PEOPLE

Population: 36,265,463 (July 1998 est.)
Nationality: Argentine or Argentinian
Age Structure: 0-14 yrs: 27%; 15-64: 62%; 65+: 11% (1998 est.)
Population Growth Rate: 1.3% (1998 est.)
Net Migration: 0.66 migrants/1,000 population (1998 est.)
Ethnic Groups: 85% white, 15% mestizo, Indian, or other nonwhite groups
Languages: Spanish (official), English, Italian, German, French
Religions: 90% nominally Roman Catholic (less than 20% practising), 2% Protestant, 2% Jewish, 6% other
Birth Rate: 19.96/1,000 population (1998 est.)
Death Rate: 7.67/1,000 population (1998 est.)
Infant Mortality: 19.03 deaths/1,000 live births (1998 est.)
Life Expectancy at Birth: 70.9 years male, 78.31 years female (1998 est.)
Total Fertility Rate: 2.68 children born/woman (1998 est.)
Literacy: 96.2% (1997 est.)

■ GOVERNMENT

Leader(s): Pres. Carlos Saùl Menem, V. Pres. Carlos Ruckauf
Government Type: republic
Administrative Divisions: 23 provinces and 1 federal district
Nationhood: July 9, 1816 (from Spain)
National Holiday: Revolution Day, May 25

■ ECONOMY

Overview: though the country possesses abundant natural resources and a diversified industrial base, burgeoning debt is weakening the economy
GDP: $348.2 billion, per capita $9,700; real growth rate +8.4% (1997 est.)
Inflation: 1.2% (July 1998)
Industries: accounts for 36% of GDP; food processing (especially meat packing), motor vehicles, consumer durables, textiles, chemicals and petrochemicals, printing, metallurgy, steel
Labour Force: 14.2 million (1997 est.); 13% agriculture, 34% industry, 53% services
Unemployment: 13.7% (Oct. 1997)
Agriculture: accounts for 7% of GNP (including

fishing); produces abundant food for both domestic consumption and exports; among world's top five exporters of grain and beef; principal crops—wheat, corn, sorghum, soybeans, sugar beets

Natural Resources: fertile plains of the Pampas, lead, zinc, tin, copper, iron ore, manganese, crude oil, uranium

■ FINANCE/TRADE

Currency: nuevo peso argentino = 100 centavos
International Reserves Excluding Gold: $23.863 billion (Jan. 1999)
Gold Reserves: 0.356 million fine troy ounces (Jan. 1999)
Budget: revenues $55 billion; expenditures $59 billion, including capital expenditures of $ n.a. (1997 est.)
Defence Expenditures: 1.5% of GDP (1997)
Education Expenditures: 5.74% of total govt. expenditure (1996)
External Debt: $115 billion (1997 est.)
Exports: $25.227 billion (1998); commodities: meat, wheat, corn, oil seed, hides, wool; partners: US 14%, former USSR countries, Italy, Brazil, Japan, Netherlands
Imports: $31.402 billion (1998); commodities: machinery and equipment, metals, chemicals, fuels and lubricants, agricultural products; partners: US 25%, Brazil, Germany, Bolivia, Japan, Italy, Netherlands

■ COMMUNICATIONS

Daily Newspapers: 181 (1996)
Televisions: 221/1,000 inhabitants (1996)
Radios: 677/1,000 inhabitants (1996)
Telephones: 17.3/100 inhabitants (1996)

■ TRANSPORTATION

Motor Vehicles: 6,100,000; 4,800,000 passenger cars (1997 est.)
Roads: 218,276 km; 63,518 km paved (1996)
Railway: 37,910 km
Air Traffic: 7,913,000 passengers carried (1996)
Airports: 1,411; 598 have paved runways (1997 est.)

Canadian Embassy: The Canadian Embassy, 2828 Tagle, 1425 Buenos Aires; mailing address: Casilla de Correo 1598, Buenos Aires, Argentina. Tel: (011-54-1) 4805-3032. Fax: (011-54-1) 4806-1209.
Embassy in Canada: Embassy of the Argentine Republic, Royal Bank Centre, 90 Sparks St, Ste 910, Ottawa ON K1P 5B4. Tel: (613) 236-2351. Fax: (613) 235-2659.

■ Armenia

Long-Form Name: Republic of Armenia
Capital: Yerevan

■ GEOGRAPHY

Area: 29,800 sq. km
Coastline: none: landlocked
Climate: severe winters; hot summers; dry year-round
Environment: prone to earthquakes; little land suitable for cultivation; air and water pollution; deforestation and drought; soil pollution is a current problem
Terrain: rugged highlands; 70% is mountains; little forest land; fast-flowing rivers; Aras River valley has good soil
Land Use: 17% arable, 3% permanent crops, 24% meadows and pasture, 15% forests and woodland, 41% other, includes 10% irrigated; most farmland lies in the Aras Valley; animal herding predominant in the highlands
Location: SW Asia

■ PEOPLE

Population: 3,421,775 (July 1998 est.)
Nationality: Armenian
Age Structure: 0-14 yrs: 26%; 15-64: 65%; 65+: 9% (1998 est.)
Population Growth Rate: -0.36% (1998 est.)
Net Migration: -8.29 migrants/1,000 population (1998 est.)
Ethnic Groups: 93% Armenians, 2% Russians, 3% Azerbaijanis, 2% other, predominantly Kurds
Languages: Armenian (official), Azerbaijan, Russian
Religions: predominantly Armenian Orthodox
Birth Rate: 13.52/1,000 population (1998 est.)
Death Rate: 8.82/1,000 population (1998 est.)
Infant Mortality: 40.77 deaths/1,000 live births (1998 est.)
Life Expectancy at Birth: 62.45 years male, 71.23 years female (1998 est.)
Total Fertility Rate: 1.69 children born/woman (1998 est.)
Literacy: 99% (1997 est.)

■ GOVERNMENT

Leader(s): Prime Min. Robert Kocharian, Prem. Armen Darbinyan
Government Type: republic
Administrative Divisions: 10 provinces ("marzer") and 1 city
Nationhood: Sept. 23, 1991 (from Soviet Union)
National Holiday: Referendum Day, Sept. 21

■ ECONOMY

Overview: predominantly manufacturing and agriculture; production has dropped sharply since 1991, due largely to ongoing armed conflict; high inflation weakens the economy
GDP: $9.5 billion, per capita $2,750; real growth rate 2.7% (1997 est.)
Inflation: 22.2% per month (Dec. 1997)
Industries: accounts for 32% of GDP; electrical equipment and machinery, chemicals, machine tools, vehicles, textiles
Labour Force: 2 million; 42% industry and construction, 18% agriculture and forestry, 40% other (1997 est.)
Unemployment: 10.6%, but large numbers of underemployed (June 1997)
Agriculture: accounts for approximately 38% of GDP; only 17% of land is arable; fruit, grapes, vegetables, tobacco, grains, beetroot, potatoes, geranium oil, cattle and sheep herding
Natural Resources: marble, precious metals, iron, tufa, small deposits of gold, copper, molybdenum, zinc, alumina

■ FINANCE/TRADE

Currency: dram = 100 luma
International Reserves Excluding Gold: $309 million (Jan. 1999)
Gold Reserves: 0.043 million fine troy ounces (Jan. 1999)
Budget: revenues $322 million; expenditures $424 million, including capital expenditures of $80 million (1998 est.)
Defence Expenditures: n.a.
Education Expenditures: n.a.
External Debt: $820 million (1997 est.)
Exports: $233 million (1997); commodities include cotton, fruit, olives, pomegranates, machine tools, instruments, shoes
Imports: $892 million (1997); commodities include machinery, energy, consumer goods

■ COMMUNICATIONS

Daily Newspapers: 11 (1996)
Televisions: 225/1,000 inhabitants (1996)
Radios: n.a.
Telephones: 15.5/100 persons (1996 est.)

■ TRANSPORTATION

Motor Vehicles: n.a.
Roads: 8,580 km; 8,580 km paved
Railway: 825 km (does not include industrial lines)
Air Traffic: 358,000 passengers carried (1996)
Airports: 11; 5 have paved runways (1997 est.)

Canadian Embassy: The Consulate of Canada, #21, 25 Demirjian St, Yerevan, Armenia. Tel: (011-3741) 401-238. Fax: (011-3742) 56-79-03; mailing address: c/o Starokonyushenny Per 23, Moscow 121002, Russian Federation.
Embassy in Canada: Embassy of the Republic of Armenia, 7 Delaware Ave, Ottawa ON K2P 0Z2. Tel: (613) 234-3710. Fax: (613) 234-3444.

Aruba

Long-Form Name: Aruba
Capital: Oranjestad

■ GEOGRAPHY

Area: 193 sq. km
Climate: tropical marine; little seasonal temperature variation
Land Use: 11% arable land; 0% permanent crops; 0% meadows and pastures; 0% forest and woodland; 89% other
Location: Caribbean island, off N coast of South America

■ PEOPLE

Population: 68,325 (July 1998 est.)
Nationality: Aruban
Ethnic Groups: 80% mixed European/Caribbean Indian
Languages: Dutch (official), Papiamento (a Spanish, Portuguese, Dutch, English dialect), English (widely spoken), Spanish

■ GOVERNMENT

Colony Territory of: Dependent Territory of the Netherlands
Leader(s): Chief of State: Queen Beatrix (Netherlands); Gov. Gen. Olindo Koolman; Prime Min. Hendrik Eman
Government Type: part of the Dutch realm; autonomy in internal affairs obtained in 1986
National Holiday: Flag Day, Mar. 18

■ ECONOMY

Overview: tourism is the mainstay; banking and oil refinery are also important

■ FINANCE/TRADE

Currency: Aruban florin (Af)

Canadian Embassy: c/o The Canadian Embassy, Sophialaan 7, 2514JP, The Hague, Netherlands. Tel.: (011-31-70) 311-1600. Fax: (011-31-70) 311-1620.
Representative to Canada: c/o Embassy of the Kingdom of the Netherlands, 350 Albert St, Ste 2020, Ottawa ON K1R 1A4. Tel: (613) 237-5030. Fax: (613) 237-6471.

Australia

Long-Form Name: Commonwealth of Australia
Capital: Canberra

■ GEOGRAPHY

Area: 7,686,850 sq. km; includes Macquarie Island
Coastline: 25,760 km
Climate: generally arid to semi-arid; temperate in south and east; tropical in north
Environment: subject to severe droughts and floods; cyclones along coast; limited freshwater availability; soil degradation; regular, tropical, invigorating, sea breeze known as "the Doctor" occurs along west coast in summer; desertification. Shipping activities and tourism are threatening the Great Barrier Reef
Terrain: mostly low plateau with deserts; fertile plain in southeast
Land Use: 6% arable land; negligible permanent crops; 54% meadows and pastures; 19% forest and woodland; 21% other, includes negligible irrigated
Location: divides Indian and Pacific Oceans

■ PEOPLE

Population: 18,613,087 (July 1998 est.)
Nationality: Australian
Age Structure: 0-14 yrs: 21%; 15-64: 66%; 65+: 13% (1998 est.)
Population Growth Rate: 0.93% (1998 est.)
Net Migration: 2.69 migrants/1,000 population (1998 est.)
Ethnic Groups: 95% Caucasian, 4% Asian, 1% Aboriginal and other
Languages: English, native languages
Religions: 26.1% Anglican, 26% Roman Catholic, 24.3% other Christian; most of the rest do not profess a religion
Birth Rate: 13.47/1,000 population (1998 est.)
Death Rate: 6.89/1,000 population (1998 est.)
Infant Mortality: 5.26 deaths/1,000 live births (1998 est.)
Life Expectancy at Birth: 76.95 years male, 82.98 years female (1998 est.)
Total Fertility Rate: 1.82 children born/woman (1998 est.)
Literacy: 100% (1997)

■ GOVERNMENT

Leader(s): Queen Elizabeth II/Gov. Gen. William Deane, Prime Min. John Howard
Government Type: federal parliamentary state
Administrative Divisions: 6 states, 2 territories; dependent areas inc.: Ashmore and Cartier Islands (uninhabited), Australian Antarctic Territory (uninhabited except for scientific staff), Cocos (Keeling) Islands, Coral Sea Islands Territory (uninhabited), Christmas Island, Heard and McDonald Islands (uninhabited), Norfolk Island
Nationhood: Jan. 1, 1901 (federation of UK colonies)
National Holiday: Australia Day, Jan. 26

■ ECONOMY

Overview: successful Western-style capitalist economy and a major exporter of natural resources and agricultural products. Is looking to increase exports of manufactured goods
GDP: $394 billion, per capita $21,400; real growth rate 3.3% (1997 est.)
Inflation: 0.7 (June 1998)
Industries: accounts for 31% of GDP; mining, industrial and transportation equipment, food processing, chemicals, steel, motor vehicles
Labour Force: 8,526,400 (1997); 27.5% community, social and business services, 25.5% trade and tourism, 14.2% manufacturing
Unemployment: 8.1% (Jan. 1999)
Agriculture: accounts for 4% of GDP and 30% of export revenues; world's largest exporter of beef and wool, second largest for mutton, and among top wheat exporters; major crops—wheat, barley, sugar cane, fruit; livestock—cattle, sheep, poultry
Natural Resources: bauxite, coal, iron ore, copper, tin, silver, uranium, nickel, tungsten, mineral sands, lead, zinc, diamonds, natural gas, crude oil

■ FINANCE/TRADE

Currency: dollar ($A) = 100 cents
International Reserves Excluding Gold: $15.360 billion (Jan. 1999)
Gold Reserves: 2.561 million fine troy ounces (Jan. 1999)
Budget: revenues $89.35 billion; expenditures $91.92 billion, including capital expenditures $n.a. (1997–98 est.)
Defence Expenditures: 1.9% of GDP (1997-98)
Education Expenditures: 7.53% of govt. expenditure (1997)
External Debt: $134 billion (1996)
Exports: $55.895 billion (1998); commodities: wheat, barley, beef, lamb, dairy products, wool, coal, iron ore; partners: Japan 26%, US 11%, New Zealand 6%, S Korea 4%, Singapore 4%, former USSR countries 3%
Imports: $64.679 billion (1998); commodities: manufactured raw materials, capital equipment, consumer goods; partners: US 22%, Japan 22%, UK 7%, Germany 6%, New Zealand 4%

■ COMMUNICATIONS

Daily Newspapers: 65 (1996)
Televisions: 554/1,000 inhabitants (1996)
Radios: 1,385/1,000 inhabitants (1996)
Telephones: 52.1/100 inhabitants (1996 est.)

■ TRANSPORTATION

Motor Vehicles: 10,900,000; 9,000,000 passenger cars (1997 est.)
Roads: 913,000 km; 353,331 km paved (1996)
Railway: 38,563 km
Air Traffic: 30,075,000 passengers carried (1996)
Airports: 419; 259 have paved runways (1997 est.)

Canadian Embassy: The Canadian High Commission, Commonwealth Ave, Canberra A.C.T. 2600, Australia. Tel: (011-61-2) 6273-3844. Fax: (011-61-2) 6273-3285.
Embassy in Canada: Australian High Commission, 50 O'Connor St, Ste 710, Ottawa ON K1P 6L2. Tel: (613) 236-0841. Fax: (613) 236-4376.

Austria

Long-Form Name: Republic of Austria
Capital: Vienna

■ GEOGRAPHY

Area: 83,850 sq. km
Coastline: none: landlocked
Climate: temperate; continental, cloudy; cold winter with frequent rain in lowlands and snow in mountains; cool summers with occasional showers
Environment: because of steep slopes, poor soils and cold temperatures, population is concentrated on eastern lowlands; air and soil pollution
Terrain: mostly mountains with Alps in west and south; flat, with gentle slopes along eastern and northern margins
Land Use: 17% arable land; 1% permanent crops; 23% meadows and pastures; 39% forest and woodland; 20% other, includes negligible irrigated
Location: SC Europe

■ PEOPLE

Population: 8,133,611 (July 1998 est.)
Nationality: Austrian
Age Structure: 0-14 yrs: 17%; 15-64: 68%; 65+: 15% (1998 est.)
Population Growth Rate: -0.05% (1998 est.)
Net Migration: -0.65 migrants/1,000 population (1998 est.)

Ethnic Groups: 99.4% German, 0.3 % Croatian, 0.2% Slovene, 0.1% others
Languages: German (official); Slovene, Hungarian, and a Croatian dialect also spoken
Religions: 85% Roman Catholic, 6% Protestant, 9% other
Birth Rate: 9.89/1,000 population (1998 est.)
Death Rate: 10.05/1,000 population (1998 est.)
Infant Mortality: 5.16 deaths/1,000 live births (1998 est.)
Life Expectancy at Birth: 74.13 years male, 80.67 years female (1998 est.)
Total Fertility Rate: 1.37 children born/woman (1998 est.)
Literacy: 99% (1997 est.)

■ GOVERNMENT

Leader(s): Chanc. Viktor Klima, Pres. Thomas Klestil
Government Type: federal republic
Administrative Divisions: 9 states
Nationhood: Nov. 12, 1918 (from Austro-Hungarian Empire)
National Holiday: National Day, Oct. 26

■ ECONOMY

Overview: prosperous, Western capitalist economy, as well as substantial welfare benefits and extensive nationalized industry. Unemployment is a growing problem
GDP: $174.1 billion, per capita $21,400; real growth rate 2.1% (1997 est.)
Inflation: 0.9% (June 1998)
Industries: accounts for 31.6% of GDP; foods, iron and steel, machines, textiles, chemicals, electrical, paper and pulp, tourism, mining
Labour Force: 3,048,500 (1997 est.); 25.1% manufacture, 24.5% community, social and business services, 19.5% trade and tourism; an estimated 200,000 Austrians are employed in other European countries; foreign labourers in Austria number 177,840, about 6% of labour force
Unemployment: 9.1% (Jan. 1999)
Agriculture: accounts for 1.5% of GDP (including forestry); principal crops and animals—grains, fruit, potatoes, sugar beets, sawn wood, cattle, pigs, poultry; 80–90% self-sufficient in food
Natural Resources: iron ore, crude oil, timber, magnesite, aluminum, lead, coal, lignite, copper, hydroelectricity

■ FINANCE/TRADE

Currency: schilling (S) = 100 groschen [As of Jan. 1, 1999, Government securities are issued in Euros (EUR)]

International Reserves Excluding Gold: $15.881 billion (Jan. 1999)

Gold Reserves: 13.00 million fine troy ounces (Jan. 1999)

Budget: revenues $61.2 billion; expenditures $71 billion, capital expenditures n.a. (1996 est.)

Defence Expenditures: 0.83% of GDP (1998 est.)

Education Expenditures: 9.19% of total govt. expenditure (1996)

External Debt: $30.2 billion (1996 est.)

Exports: $58.497 billion (1997); commodities: machinery and equipment, iron and steel, lumber, textiles, paper products, chemicals; partners: Germany 35%, Italy 10%, Eastern Europe 9%, Switzerland 7%, US 4%, OPEC 3%

Imports: $64.928 billion (1997); commodities: petroleum, foodstuffs, machinery and equipment, vehicles, chemicals, textiles and clothing, pharmaceuticals; partners: Germany 44%, Italy 9%, Eastern Europe 6%, Switzerland 5%, US 4%, USSR 2%

■ COMMUNICATIONS

Daily Newspapers: 17 (1996)

Televisions: 518/1,000 inhabitants (1996)

Radios: 740/1,000 inhabitants (1996)

Telephones: 46.7/100 inhabitants (1996 est.)

■ TRANSPORTATION

Motor Vehicles: 5,000,000; 4,000,000 passenger cars (1997 est.)

Roads: 200,000 km

Railway: 5,636 km

Air Traffic: 4,719,000 passengers carried (1996)

Airports: 55; n.a. have paved runways (1997 est.)

Canadian Embassy: The Canadian Embassy, Laurenzerberg 2 A-1010 Vienna, Austria. Tel: (011-43-1) 531-38-3000. Fax: (011-43-1) 531-38-3321.

Embassy in Canada: Embassy of the Republic of Austria, 445 Wilbrod St, Ottawa ON K1N 6M7. Tel: (613) 789-1444. Fax: (613) 789-3431.

Azerbaijan

Long-Form Name: Azerbaijani Republic

Capital: Baku

■ GEOGRAPHY

Area: 86,600 sq. km

Coastline: none; landlocked. Inland coastline (Caspian Sea) approximately 800 km.

Climate: Alpine to subtropical; dry, semi-arid steppe subject to drought

Environment: severe air and water pollution render Aspheron Peninsula, including Baku and Sumgait, the "most ecologically devastated area in the world," according to local scientists

Terrain: fertile central lowlands; large flat Kura-Aras Lowland; Caucasus Mountains in north; western uplands

Land Use: 18% arable, 5% permanent crops, 11% forests and woodland, 25% meadows and pastures, 41% other (includes 16% irrigated); grazing land in the Caucasus mountains; farming in lowlands

Location: SW Asia, bordering on Caspian Sea

■ PEOPLE

Population: 7,855,576 (July 1998 est.)

Nationality: Azerbaijani

Age Structure: 0-14 yrs: 32%; 15-64: 61%; 65+: 7% (1998 est.)

Population Growth Rate: 0.7% (1998 est.)

Net Migration: -5.75 migrants/1,000 population (1998 est.)

Ethnic Groups: 90% Azerbaijani, 2.5% Russians, 2.3% Armenians, 3.2% Daghestanis, 2% other

Languages: Azerbaijani (official), Armenian, Russian, 6% other

Religions: Muslim 93.4%, Russian Orthodox 2.3%, Armenian Orthodox 2.3%, other 1.8%

Birth Rate: 22.2/1,000 population (1998 est.)

Death Rate: 9.41/1,000 population (1998 est.)

Infant Mortality: 81.64 deaths/1,000 live births (1998 est.)

Life Expectancy at Birth: 59.01 years male, 67.81 years female (1998 est.)

Total Fertility Rate: 2.72 children born/woman (1998 est.)

Literacy: 97% (1997 est.)

■ GOVERNMENT

Leader(s): Pres. Haydar Aliyev, Prem. Artur Rasizade

Government Type: republic

Administrative Divisions: 59 rayons, 11 cities, 1 autonomous republic

Nationhood: Aug. 30, 1991 (from Soviet Union)

National Holiday: Independence Day, May 28

■ ECONOMY

Overview: cotton and refining industries are most prominent; Azerbaijan is least industrially developed of the Transcaucasian States, and its economy, weakened by massive inflation, continues to fall

GDP: $11.9 billion, per capita $1,460; real growth rate 5.8% (1997 est.)

Inflation: 411.8% per month (end of 1995)

Industries: accounts for 23% of GDP; oil extraction and refining, steel, cement, textiles, chemicals, petrochemicals

Labour Force: 3 million (1997 est.); 32% agriculture and forestry, 26% industry and construction, 42% other
Unemployment: 20% (1996)
Agriculture: accounts for 30% of GDP; cotton, grain, grapes, tea, citrus fruit, vegetables, sheep and horse breeding
Natural Resources: oil reserves, minerals, iron, aluminum

■ FINANCE/TRADE

Currency: manat = 100 gopik
International Reserves Excluding Gold: $516 million (Jan. 1999)
Gold Reserves: none (Dec. 1996)
Budget: revenues $565 million; expenditures $682 million, including capital expenditures n.a. (1996 est.)
Defence Expenditures: n.a.
Education Expenditures: 3.0 % of GNP (1995)
External Debt: $435 million (1996 est.)
Exports: $781 million (1997) to outside the successor states of the former USSR; oil and gas and related equipment, textiles, cotton. Partners: European and successor states of the former USSR
Imports: $794 million (1997) from outside the successor states of the former USSR; machinery and parts, foodstuffs, textiles, consumer durables

■ COMMUNICATIONS

Daily Newspapers: 6 (1996)
Televisions: 22/1,000 inhabitants (1996)
Radios: 20/1,000 inhabitants (1996)
Telephones: 8.5/100 persons (1996 est.)

■ TRANSPORTATION

Motor Vehicles: n.a.
Roads: 57,770 km; 54,188 km hard-surfaced
Railway: 2,125 km (does not include industrial lines)
Air Traffic: 1,251,200 passengers carried (1996)
Airports: 69; 29 have paved runways (1997 est.)

Canadian Embassy: c/o The Canadian Embassy, Nenehatun Caddesi No. 75, Gaziosmanpasa 06700, Ankara, Turkey. Tel: (011-90-312) 436-1275. Fax: (011-90-312) 446-4437.
Embassy in Canada: Embassy of the Republic of Azerbaijan, 927 15th St NW, Ste 700, Washington DC 20005, USA. Tel: (202) 842-0001. Fax: (202) 842-0004.

Bahamas

Long-Form Name: Commonwealth of The Bahamas
Capital: Nassau

■ GEOGRAPHY

Area: 13,940 sq. km
Coastline: 3,542 km
Climate: tropical marine; moderated by warm waters of Gulf Stream
Environment: subject to hurricanes and other tropical storms that cause extensive flood and wind damage; coral reef decay is a current issue
Terrain: long, flat coral islands with some low, rounded hills
Land Use: 1% arable land; 0% permanent crops; 0% meadows and pastures; 32% forest and woodland; 67% other
Location: Caribbean islands

■ PEOPLE

Population: 279,833 (July 1998 est.)
Nationality: Bahamian
Age Structure: 0-14 yrs: 28%; 15-64: 67%; 65+: 5% (1998 est.)
Population Growth Rate: 1.39% (1998 est.)
Net Migration: -1.72 migrants/1,000 population (1998 est.)
Ethnic Groups: 85% black, 15% white
Languages: English; some Creole among Haitian immigrants
Religions: 32% Baptist, 20% Anglican, 19% Roman Catholic, smaller groups of other Protestants, Greek Orthodox and Jews
Birth Rate: 21.03/1,000 population (1998 est.)
Death Rate: 5.44/1,000 population (1998 est.)
Infant Mortality: 18.97 deaths/1,000 live births (1998 est.)
Life Expectancy at Birth: 70.65 years male, 77.42 years female (1998 est.)
Total Fertility Rate: 2.33 children born/woman (1998 est.)
Literacy: 98.2% (1997 est.)

■ GOVERNMENT

Leader(s): Queen Elizabeth II/Gov. Gen. Orville Turnquest, Prime Min. Hubert Alexander Ingraham
Government Type: commonwealth
Administrative Divisions: 21 districts
Nationhood: July 10, 1973 (from UK)
National Holiday: National Day, July 10

■ ECONOMY

Overview: tourism and offshore banking are features of this stable, middle-income developing nation
GDP: $5.36 billion, per capita $19,400; real growth rate 3.5% (1997 est.)
Inflation: 1.2% (May 1998)
Industries: accounts for 5% of GDP; banking, tourism, cement, oil refining and transshipment,

salt production, rum, aragonite, pharmaceuticals, spiral welded steel pipe
Labour Force: 150,000 (1995 est.); 30% government, 40% hotels and restaurants, 10% business services, 5% agriculture
Unemployment: 10% (1997 est.)
Agriculture: accounts for 3% of GDP; dominated by small-scale producers; principal products— citrus fruit, vegetables, poultry; large net importer of food
Natural Resources: salt, aragonite, timber

■ FINANCE/TRADE

Currency: Bahamian dollar ($B) = 100 cents
International Reserves Excluding Gold: $352 million (Jan. 1999)
Gold Reserves: none (Jan. 1999)
Budget: revenues $687.5 million; expenditures $827 million, including capital expenditures $112 million (1996–97 est.)
Defence Expenditures: 0.6% of GDP (1996)
Education Expenditures: n.a.
External Debt: $381.7 million (1997)
Exports: $253 million (1997 est.); commodities: pharmaceuticals, cement, rum, crawfish; partners: US 90%, UK 10%
Imports: $1.263 billion (1997 est.); commodities: foodstuffs, manufactured goods, mineral fuels; partners: Nigeria 21%, US 35%, Japan 13%, Angola 11%

■ COMMUNICATIONS

Daily Newspapers: 3 (1996)
Televisions: 232/1,000 inhabitants (1996)
Radios: 739/1,000 inhabitants (1996)
Telephones: 28.3/100 inhabitants (1996 est.)

■ TRANSPORTATION

Motor Vehicles: 59,000; 47,000 passenger cars (1996 est.)
Roads: 2,693 km; 1,546 km paved
Railway: none
Air Traffic: 978,000 passengers carried (1996)
Airports: 62; 32 have paved runways (1997 est.)

Canadian Embassy: Consulate of Canada, Shirley Street Plaza, Nassau; mailing address: Consulate of Canada, P.O. Box SS-6371, Nassau, Bahamas. Tel: (1-242) 393-2123. Fax: (1-242) 393-1305.
Embassy in Canada: High Commission for the Commonwealth of the Bahamas, 50 O'Connor St, Ste 1313, Ottawa ON K1P 6L2. Tel: (613) 232-1724. Fax: (613) 232-0097.

Bahrain

Long-Form Name: State of Bahrain
Capital: Manama

■ GEOGRAPHY

Area: 620 sq. km
Coastline: 161 km
Climate: arid; mild, pleasant winters; very hot, humid summers
Environment: subsurface water sources being rapidly depleted (requires development of desalination facilities); dust storms; desertification; drought; coastal degradation resulting from oil industry
Terrain: mostly low desert plain rising gently to low central escarpment
Land Use: 1% arable land; 1% permanent crops; 6% meadows and pastures; 0% forest and woodland; 92% other; includes negligible irrigated
Location: Persian Gulf

■ PEOPLE

Population: 616,342 (July 1998 est.)
Nationality: Bahraini
Age Structure: 0-14 yrs: 31%; 15-64: 67%; 65+: 2% (1998 est.)
Population Growth Rate: 2.09% (1998 est.)
Net Migration: 1.73 migrants/1,000 population (1998 est.)
Ethnic Groups: 63% Bahraini, 13% Asian, 10% other Arab, 8% Iranian, 6% other
Languages: Arabic (official); English also widely spoken; Farsi, Urdu
Religions: Muslim (70% Shi'a, 30% Sunni)
Birth Rate: 22.43/1,000 population (1998 est.)
Death Rate: 3.25/1,000 population (1998 est.)
Infant Mortality: 15.54 deaths/1,000 live births (1998 est.)
Life Expectancy at Birth: 72.42 years male, 77.57 years female (1998 est.)
Total Fertility Rate: 3.01 children born/woman (1998 est.)
Literacy: 85.2% (1997 est.)

■ GOVERNMENT

Leader(s): Prime Min. Khalifa bin Salman Al Khalifa, Amir Hamad bin Isa al-Khalifa
Government Type: traditional monarchy
Administrative Divisions: 12 municipalities
Nationhood: Aug. 15, 1971 (from UK)
National Holiday: Independence Day, Dec. 16

■ ECONOMY

Overview: petroleum production and processing are the backbone of the economy and any change in the world oil market affects the economy
GDP: $8.2 billion, per capita $13,700; real growth rate 2.7% (1997 est.)
Inflation: -0.2% (1996)

Industries: accounts for 38% of GDP; petroleum processing and refining, aluminum smelting, offshore banking, ship repairing

Labour Force: 125,000 (1995 est.); 42% of labour force is Bahraini; 78% industry, commerce and services, 21% government, 1% agriculture

Unemployment: 15% (1996 est.)

Agriculture: including fishing, accounts for 1% of GDP; not self-sufficient in food production; heavily subsidized sector produces fruit, vegetables, poultry, dairy products, shrimp and fish

Natural Resources: oil, associated and nonassociated natural gas, fish

■ FINANCE/TRADE

Currency: Bahraini dinar (BD) = 1,000 fils

International Reserves Excluding Gold: $1.059 billion (Jan. 1999)

Gold Reserves: 0.15 million fine troy ounces (Jan. 1999)

Budget: revenues $1.7 billion; expenditures $1.9 billion, capital expenditures $400 million (1998 est.)

Defence Expenditures: 17.58% of total govt. expenditures (1997)

Education Expenditures: 13.68% of govt. expenditure (1997)

External Debt: $3.2 billion (1995)

Exports: $4.346 billion (1997); commodities: petroleum 80%, aluminum 7%, other 13%; partners: US, United Arab Emirates, Japan, Singapore, Saudi Arabia

Imports: $3.924 billion (1997); commodities: non oil 59%, crude oil 41%; partners: UK, Saudi Arabia, US, Japan

■ COMMUNICATIONS

Daily Newspapers: 4 (1996)

Televisions: 470/1,000 inhabitants (1996)

Radios: 579/1,000 inhabitants (1996)

Telephones: 24.0/100 inhabitants (1996 est.)

■ TRANSPORTATION

Motor Vehicles: 178,000; 143,000 passenger cars (1997 est.)

Roads: 3,013 km; 2,284 km paved

Railway: none

Air Traffic: 1,200,000 passengers carried (1996)

Airports: 3; 2 have paved runways (1997 est.)

Canadian Embassy: The Canadian Embassy to Bahrain, c/o The Canadian Embassy, P.O. Box 94321, Riyadh 11693, Saudi Arabia. Tel: (011-966-1) 488-2288. Fax: (011-966-1) 488-1997.

Embassy in Canada: The Embassy of the State of Bahrain, 3502 International Dr NW, Washington DC 20008, USA. Tel: (202) 342-0741. Fax: (202) 362-2192.

Bangladesh

Long-Form Name: People's Republic of Bangladesh

Capital: Dhaka

■ GEOGRAPHY

Area: 144,000 sq. km

Coastline: 580 km

Climate: tropical; cool, dry winter (Oct. to Mar.); hot, humid summer (Mar. to June)

Environment: vulnerable to droughts; much of country routinely flooded during summer monsoon season (June to Oct.); overpopulation; deforestation; cyclones

Terrain: mostly flat alluvial plain; hilly in southeast

Land Use: 73% arable land; 2% permanent crops; 5% meadows and pastures; 15% forest and woodland; 5% other, includes 19% irrigated

Location: S Asia, bordering on Bay of Bengal

■ PEOPLE

Population: 127,567,002 (July 1998 est.)

Nationality: Bangladeshi

Age Structure: 0-14 yrs: 38%; 15-64: 59%; 65+: 3% (1998 est.)

Population Growth Rate: 1.76% (1998 est.)

Net Migration: -0.69 migrants/1,000 population (1998 est.)

Ethnic Groups: 98% Bengali, 250,000 Biharis, less than 1 million tribals

Languages: Bangla (official), English widely used, 5% tribal dialects

Religions: 83% Muslim, 16% Hindu, less than 1% Buddhist, Christian and other

Birth Rate: 28.89/1,000 population (1998 est.)

Death Rate: 10.6/1,000 population (1998 est.)

Infant Mortality: 97.67 deaths/1,000 live births (1998 est.)

Life Expectancy at Birth: 56.69 years male, 56.63 years female (1998 est.)

Total Fertility Rate: 3.32 children born/woman (1998 est.)

Literacy: 38.1% (1997 est.)

■ GOVERNMENT

Leader(s): Pres. Mustafizur Rahman, Prime Min. Sheikh Hasina Wajed

Government Type: republic

Administrative Divisions: 4 divisions

Nationhood: Dec. 16, 1971 (from Pakistan; Bangladesh formerly known as East Pakistan)

National Holiday: Independence Day, Mar. 26

■ ECONOMY

Overview: one of the poorest nations in the world; the economy is based on a small number of agricultural exports, which are vulnerable to natural disasters. Few natural resources. Frequent cyclones and floods, a rapidly growing labour force that cannot be absorbed by agriculture, a low level of industrialization, government interference with the economy, failure to exploit energy reserves, and inadequate power supplies all contribute to stifling economic growth. In 1992 and 1993, excellent rice crops and an expansion of the clothing industry boosted the economy

GDP: $167 billion, per capita $1,330; real growth rate 5.5% (1997 est.)

Inflation: 6.9% (Apr. 1998)

Industries: accounts for 18% of GDP, jute manufacturing, food processing, cotton textiles, petroleum, urea fertilizer

Labour Force: 62.5 million (1997 est.); 56.5% agriculture, 33.7% services, 9.8% industry; extensive export of labour to Saudi Arabia, United Arab Emirates, Oman and Kuwait

Unemployment: 35.2% (1996)

Agriculture: accounts for about 30% of GDP, 65% of employment and 20% of exports; imports 10% of food grain requirements; world's largest exporter of jute; commercial products—jute, rice, wheat, tea, sugar cane, potatoes, beef, milk, poultry

Natural Resources: natural gas, arable land, timber

■ FINANCE/TRADE

Currency: taka (Tk) = 100 poisha

International Reserves Excluding Gold: $1.725 billion (Jan. 1999)

Gold Reserves: 0.105 million fine troy ounces (Jan. 1999)

Budget: revenues $3.6 billion; expenditures $5.3 billion, including capital expenditures of $3 billion (1996-97 est.)

Defence Expenditures: 1.7% of GDP (1996)

Education Expenditures: 2.3% of GNP (1995)

External Debt: $17.1 billion (1996)

Exports: $3.778 billion (1997); commodities: jute, tea, leather, shrimp, manufacturing; partners: US 25%, Western Europe 22%, Middle East 9%, Japan 8%, Eastern Europe 7%

Imports: $6.896 billion (1997); commodities: food, petroleum and other energy, nonfood consumer goods, semiprocessed goods and capital equipment; partners: Western Europe 18%, Japan 14%, Middle East 9%, US 8%

■ COMMUNICATIONS

Daily Newspapers: 37 (1996)

Televisions: 6.2/1,000 inhabitants (1996)

Radios: 50/1,000 inhabitants (1996)

Telephones: 0.2/100 inhabitants (1996 est.)

■ TRANSPORTATION

Motor Vehicles: 225,000; 152,000 passenger cars (1997 est.)

Roads: 223,391 km; 16,084 km paved

Railway: 2,892 km

Air Traffic: 1,252,000 passengers carried (1996)

Airports: 16; 15 have paved runways (1997 est.)

Canadian Embassy: The Canadian High Commission, House CWN 16/A, Rd. 48, Gulshan; mailing address: G.P.O. Box 569, Dhaka, Bangladesh. Tel: (011-880-2) 988-7091. Fax: (011-880-2) 88-30-43.

Embassy in Canada: High Commission for the People's Republic of Bangladesh, 275 Bank St, Ste 302, Ottawa ON K2P 2L6. Tel: (613) 236-0138. Fax: (613) 567-3213.

Barbados

Long-Form Name: Barbados

Capital: Bridgetown

■ GEOGRAPHY

Area: 430 sq. km

Coastline: 97 km

Climate: tropical; rainy season (June to Oct.)

Environment: subject to hurricanes, especially June to Oct.; water pollution and soil erosion; landslides

Terrain: relatively flat; rises gently to a central highland region

Land Use: 37% arable land; 0% permanent crops; 5% meadows and pastures; 12% forest and woodland; 46% other

Location: Caribbean islands

■ PEOPLE

Population: 259,025 (July 1998 est.)

Nationality: Barbadian

Age Structure: 0-14 yrs: 23%; 15-64: 67%; 65+: 10% (1998 est.)

Population Growth Rate: 0.09% (1998 est.)

Net Migration: -5.86 migrants/1,000 population (1998 est.)

Ethnic Groups: 80% African, 16% mixed, 4% European

Languages: English

Religions: 67% Protestant, 9% Methodist, 4% Roman Catholic, 9% other, including Moravian

Birth Rate: 14.92/1,000 population (1998 est.)
Death Rate: 8.21/1,000 population (1998 est.)
Infant Mortality: 17.25 deaths/1,000 live births (1998 est.)
Life Expectancy at Birth: 72.03 years male, 77.62 years female (1998 est.)
Total Fertility Rate: 1.85 children born/woman (1998 est.)
Literacy: 97.4% (1997 est.)

■ GOVERNMENT

Leader(s): Queen Elizabeth II/Gov. Gen. Sir Clifford Husbands, Prime Min. Owen Seymour Arthur
Government Type: parliamentary democracy
Administrative Divisions: 11 parishes
Nationhood: Nov. 30, 1966 (from UK)
National Holiday: Independence Day, Nov. 30

■ ECONOMY

Overview: has one of the highest standards of living of islands in the region; the tourist industry and traditional sugar cane cultivation are main parts of the economy; manufacturing and tourism have become increasingly important in recent years
GDP: $2.8 billion, per capita $10,900; real growth rate 3% (1997 est.)
Inflation: -1.3% (May 1998)
Industries: accounts for 17% of GDP; tourism, sugar, light manufacturing, component assembly for export
Labour Force: 135,000 (1997 est.); 39.9% community, social and business services, 15.2% trade and tourism, 10.5% manufacturing
Unemployment: 11.8% (Nov. 1998)
Agriculture: accounts for 7% of GDP; major cash crop is sugar cane; other crops—vegetables and cotton; not self-sufficient in food
Natural Resources: crude oil, fishing, natural gas

■ FINANCE/TRADE

Currency: Barbadian dollar ($BDS) = 100 cents
International Reserves Excluding Gold: $302 million (Jan. 1999)
Gold Reserves: none (Jan. 1999)
Budget: revenues $600 million; expenditures $645 million, including capital expenditures of $80 million (1996–97 est.)
Defence Expenditures: 0.7% of GDP (1996)
Education Expenditures: n.a.
External Debt: $359 million (1996)
Exports: $283 million (1997); commodities: sugar and molasses, electrical components, clothing, rum, machinery and transport equipment; partners: US 30%, CARICOM, UK, Puerto Rico, Canada

Imports: $996 million (1997); commodities: foodstuffs, consumer durables, raw materials, crude oil; partners: US 34%, CARICOM, Japan, UK, Canada

■ COMMUNICATIONS

Daily Newspapers: 2 (1996)
Televisions: 287/1,000 inhabitants (1996)
Radios: 904/1,000 inhabitants (1996)
Telephones: 36.0/100 inhabitants (1996 est.)

■ TRANSPORTATION

Motor Vehicles: 48,500; 45,000 passenger cars (1997 est.)
Roads: 1,640 km; 1,573 km paved
Railway: none
Air Traffic: n.a.
Airports: 1, usable and with a paved runway (1997 est.)

Canadian Embassy: The Canadian High Commission, Bishop's Court Hill, St. Michael, Barbados; mailing address: P.O. Box 404, Bridgetown, Barbados. Tel: (246) 429-3550. Fax: (246) 429-3780.
Embassy in Canada: High Commission for Barbados, 130 Albert St, Ste 302, Ottawa ON K1P 5G4. Tel: (613) 236-9517. Fax: (613) 230-4362.

Belarus

Long-Form Name: Republic of Belarus
Capital: Minsk

■ GEOGRAPHY

Area: 207,600 sq. km
Coastline: none; landlocked
Climate: mild and moist, transitional between continental and maritime
Environment: southern region is badly contaminated with nuclear fallout from 1986 Chernobyl reactor accident; pesticide use results in extensive soil pollution
Terrain: land of forests, lakes, rivers, and marshes; soil poor, sandy, marshy
Land Use: 29% arable, 1% permanent crops and forest, 34% forests and woodland, 15% meadows and pastures, 21% other
Location: E Europe

■ PEOPLE

Population: 10,409,050 (July 1998 est.)
Nationality: Belarusian
Age Structure: 0-14 yrs: 20%; 15-64: 67%; 65+: 13% (1998 est.)
Population Growth Rate: -0.05% (1998 est.)

Net Migration: 3.25 migrants/1,000 population (1998 est.)
Ethnic Groups: 77.9% Byelorussian, 13.2% Russian, 4.1% Polish, 2.9% Ukrainian, 1.9% other
Languages: Byelorussian, Russian
Religions: predominantly Roman Catholic and Eastern Orthodox
Birth Rate: 9.71/1,000 population (1998 est.)
Death Rate: 13.47/1,000 population (1998 est.)
Infant Mortality: 14.16 deaths/1,000 live births (1998 est.)
Life Expectancy at Birth: 62.26 years male, 74.56 years female (1998 est.)
Total Fertility Rate: 1.34 children born/woman (1998 est.)
Literacy: 98% (1997 est.)

▓ GOVERNMENT

Leader(s): Pres. Aleksandr Lukashenko, Prem. Sergei Ling
Government Type: republic
Administrative Divisions: 6 regions ("voblastsi"), 1 municipality ("harady")
Nationhood: Aug. 25, 1991 (from Soviet Union)
National Holiday: Independence Day, July 3

▓ ECONOMY

Overview: strong emphasis on mining and agriculture, with growing manufacturing (heavy machinery, chemicals, fertilizer) and services sector; Belarus is an important transport link for the former Soviet states
GDP: $50.4 billion; per capita $4,800; real growth rate 8.5% (1997 est.)
Inflation: 42.7% (July 1998)
Industries: accounts for 43% of GDP; machinery, tools, refineries, fertilizer production; about 50% of labour force is employed in industry
Labour Force: 5 million (1997 est.); 27.4% manufacturing, 22.4% community, social and business services, 21.9% agriculture
Unemployment: 3.3%, but large numbers of underemployed (Jul. 1997)
Agriculture: accounts for almost 21% of GDP; potatoes, flax, rye, oats, barley, wheat, cattle breeding, milk, vegetables, pigs, potatoes, peat, forest resources
Natural Resources: oil, potassium, forest land, peat deposits

▓ FINANCE/TRADE

Currency: Belarusian ruble
International Reserves Excluding Gold: $696 million (Dec. 1998)
Gold Reserves: n.a.

Budget: revenues $4 billion; expenditures $4.1 billion, including capital expenditures $180 million (1997 est.)
Defence Expenditures: 3.59% of total govt. expenditures (1996)
Education Expenditures: 5.20% of total govt. expenditures (1996)
External Debt: $970 million (1997 est.)
Exports: $7.301 billion (1997); agricultural and transport machinery, computers, refrigerators, foodstuffs; partners: Russia, Ukraine, Poland, Germany
Imports: $8.689 billion (1997); commodities: fuels, raw materials, textiles, sugar; partners: Russia, Ukraine, Poland, Germany

▓ COMMUNICATIONS

Daily Newspapers: 8 (1996)
Televisions: 242/1,000 inhabitants (1996)
Radios: 290/1,000 inhabitants (1996)
Telephones: 19.2/100 inhabitants (1996 est.)

▓ TRANSPORTATION

Motor Vehicles: n.a.
Roads: 52,131 km; 36,544 km hard-surfaced
Railway: 5,488 km (does not include industrial lines)
Air Traffic: 843,000 passengers carried (1996)
Airports: 118; 36 have paved runways (1997 est.)

Canadian Embassy: c/o Starokonyushenny Per 23, Moscow 121002, Russian Federation. Tel: (011-7-095) 956-6666. Fax: (011-7-095) 232-9948.

Embassy in Canada: Embassy of the Republic of Belarus, 130 Albert St, Ste 600, Ottawa ON K1P 5G4. Tel: (613) 233-9994, Fax: (613) 233-8500.

Belgium

Long-Form Name: Kingdom of Belgium
Capital: Brussels

▓ GEOGRAPHY

Area: 30,510 sq. km
Coastline: 64 km
Climate: temperate; mild winters, cool summers; rainy, humid, cloudy
Environment: air and water pollution; acid rain
Terrain: flat coastal plains in northwest central rolling hills, rugged mountains of Ardennes Forest in southeast
Land Use: 24% arable land; 1% permanent crops; 20% meadows and pastures; 21% forest and woodland; 34% other; includes negligible irrigated

Location: NW Europe, bordering on North Sea

■ PEOPLE

Population: 10,174,922 (July 1998 est.)
Nationality: Belgian
Age Structure: 0-14 yrs: 17%; 15-64: 66%; 65+: 17% (1998 est.)
Population Growth Rate: 0.09% (1998 est.)
Net Migration: 1.05 migrants/1,000 population (1998 est.)
Ethnic Groups: 55% Flemish, 33% Walloon, 12% mixed or other
Languages: Dutch or Flemish spoken in north (Flanders), French in south (Wallonia), both languages official; small English-speaking minority in east, German 1%
Religions: 75% Roman Catholic, remainder Protestant or other
Birth Rate: 10.21/1,000 population (1998 est.)
Death Rate: 10.41/1,000 population (1998 est.)
Infant Mortality: 6.27 deaths/1,000 live births (1998 est.)
Life Expectancy at Birth: 74.13 years male, 80.74 years female (1998 est.)
Total Fertility Rate: 1.49 children born/woman (1998 est.)
Literacy: 99% (1997 est.)

■ GOVERNMENT

Leader(s): King Albert II, Prime Min. Guy Verhofstadt
Government Type: constitutional monarchy
Administrative Divisions: 9 provinces
Nationhood: Oct. 4, 1830 (from the Netherlands)
National Holiday: National Day, July 21

■ ECONOMY

Overview: a small, private-enterprise-based economy possessing few natural resources, it is therefore highly vulnerable to the state of world markets. Burgeoning public debt offsets economic growth
GDP: $236.3 billion, per capita $23,200; real growth rate 2.3% (1997 est.)
Inflation: 1.0% (July 1998)
Industries: accounts for 28% of GDP; engineering and metal products, processed food and beverages, chemicals, basic metals, textiles, glass, petroleum, coal
Labour Force: 4 million (1997 est.); 32.9% community, social and business services, 23.1% manufacturing, 17.5% trade and tourism
Unemployment: 12.2% (Jan. 1999)
Agriculture: accounts for 2.0% of GDP; emphasis on livestock production—beef, veal, pork, milk; major crops are sugar beets, fresh vegetables, fruit, grain and tobacco; net importer of farm products
Natural Resources: coal, natural gas

■ FINANCE/TRADE

Currency: Belgian franc (BF) = 100 centimes [As of Jan. 1, 1999, Government securities are issued in Euros (EUR)]
International Reserves Excluding Gold: $11.867 billion (Jan. 1999)
Gold Reserves: 8.652 million fine troy ounces (Jan. 1999)
Budget: n.a.
Defence Expenditures: 1.7% of GDP (1995)
Education Expenditures: 5.7% of GNP (1995)
External Debt: n.a.
Exports: $165.58 billion (1997) Belgium-Luxembourg Economic Union; commodities: iron and steel, transportation equipment, tractors, diamonds, petroleum products; partners: European Community 74%, US 5%, Communist countries 2%
Imports: $155.49 billion (1997) Belgium-Luxembourg Economic Union; commodities: fuels, grains, chemicals, foodstuffs; partners: European Community 72%, US 5%, oil-exporting, less-developed countries 4%, Communist countries 3%

■ COMMUNICATIONS

Daily Newspapers: 30 (1996)
Televisions: 463/1,000 inhabitants (1996)
Radios: 792/1,000 inhabitants (1996)
Telephones: 46.2/100 inhabitants (1996 est.)

■ TRANSPORTATION

Motor Vehicles: 5,000,000; 4,450,000 passenger cars (1997 est.)
Roads: 143,175 km, all paved
Railway: 3,368 km
Air Traffic: 5,174,000 passengers carried (1996)
Airports: 42; 24 have paved runways (1997 est.)

Canadian Embassy: The Canadian Embassy, 2, Avenue de Tervuren, 1040 Brussels, Belgium. Tel: (011-32-2) 741-0611. Fax: (011-32-2) 741-0643.
Embassy in Canada: Embassy of the Kingdom of Belgium, 80 Elgin St, 4th Fl, Ottawa ON K1P 1B7. Tel: (613) 236-7267. Fax: (613) 236-7882.

Belize

Long-Form Name: Belize
Capital: Belmopan

■ GEOGRAPHY

Area: 22,960 sq. km

Coastline: 386 km
Climate: tropical; very hot and humid; rainy season (May to Feb.)
Environment: frequent devastating hurricanes (Sept. to Dec.) and coastal flooding, especially in south; deforestation; industrial and agricultural water pollution
Terrain: flat, swampy coastal plain; low mountains in south
Land Use: 2% arable land; 1% permanent crops; 2% meadows and pastures; 92% forest and woodland; 3% other, includes negligible irrigated
Location: Central (Latin) America, bordering on Caribbean Sea

■ PEOPLE

Population: 230,160 (July 1998 est.)
Nationality: Belizean
Age Structure: 0-14 yrs: 42%; 15-64: 54%; 65+: 4% (1998 est.)
Population Growth Rate: 2.42% (1998 est.)
Net Migration: -1.38 migrants/1,000 population (1998 est.)
Ethnic Groups: 30% Creole, 44% Mestizo, 11% Maya, 7% Garifuna, 8% other
Languages: English (official), Spanish, Maya, Garifuna (Carib)
Religions: 62% Roman Catholic, 30% Protestant sects, 2% none, 6% other
Birth Rate: 31.05/1,000 population (1998 est.)
Death Rate: 5.5/1,000 population (1998 est.)
Infant Mortality: 32.36 deaths/1,000 live births (1998 est.)
Life Expectancy at Birth: 67.01 years male, 71.03 years female (1998 est.)
Total Fertility Rate: 3.87 children born/woman (1998 est.)
Literacy: 70.3% (1997 est.)

■ GOVERNMENT

Leader(s): Queen Elizabeth II/Gov. Gen. Colville Young, Prime Min. Said Musa
Government Type: parliamentary democracy
Administrative Divisions: 6 districts
Nationhood: Sept. 21, 1981 (from UK; Belize formerly known as British Honduras)
National Holiday: Independence Day, Sept. 21

■ ECONOMY

Overview: economy primarily based on agriculture and merchandising; sugar is the main crop; tourism and construction are becoming increasingly important
GDP: $680 million, per capita $3,000; real growth rate 2.9% (1997 est.)
Inflation: -0.5% (Mar. 98)

Industries: accounts for 27% of GDP; sugar refining, clothing, timber and forest products, furniture, rum, soap, beverages, cigarettes, tourism, garment production, citrus concentrates
Labour Force: 71,000 (1997 est.); 30% agriculture, 16% services, 15.4% government, 11.2% commerce, 27.4% other
Unemployment: 13% (1997 est.)
Agriculture: accounts for 20% of GDP (including fish and forestry) and 75% of export earnings; commercial crops include sugar cane, bananas, cocoa, citrus fruit; expanding output of lumber and cultured shrimp; net importer of basic foods
Natural Resources: arable land potential, timber, fish

■ FINANCE/TRADE

Currency: Belizean dollar ($BZ) = 100 cents
International Reserves Excluding Gold: $48 million (Jan. 1999)
Gold Reserves: n.a.
Budget: revenues $140 million; expenditures $142 million, including capital expenditures of n.a. (1997-98 est.)
Defence Expenditures: 5.02% of total govt. expenditure (1996)
Education Expenditures: 20.39% of govt. expenditures (1996)
External Debt: $192 million (1996)
Exports: $177 million (1998 est.); commodities: sugar, clothing, seafood, molasses, citrus, wood and wood products; partners: US 47%, UK, Trinidad and Tobago, Canada
Imports: $295 million (1998 est.); commodities: machinery and transportation equipment, food, manufactured goods, fuels, chemicals, pharmaceuticals; partners: US 55%, UK, Netherlands Antilles, Mexico

■ COMMUNICATIONS

Daily Newspapers: 0 (1996)
Televisions: 183/1,000 inhabitants (1996)
Radios: 589/1,000 inhabitants (1996)
Telephones: 13.3/100 inhabitants (1996 est.)

■ TRANSPORTATION

Motor Vehicles: 5,600; 2,400 passenger cars (1997 est.)
Roads: 2,248 km; 427 km paved
Railway: none
Air Traffic: n.a.
Airports: 44; 3 have paved runways (1997 est.)

Canadian Embassy: Consulate of Canada, 85 North Front St, P.O. Box 610, Belize City, Belize. Tel: (011-501-2) 33-722. Fax: (011-501-2) 30-060.

Embassy in Canada: c/o High Commission for Belize, 2535 Massachusetts Ave NW, Washington DC, USA. 20008. Tel: (202) 332-9636. Fax: (202) 332-6888.

Benin

Long-Form Name: Republic of Benin
Capital: Porto Novo (official); Cotonou (de facto)

■ GEOGRAPHY

Area: 112,620 sq. km
Coastline: 121 km
Climate: tropical; hot, humid in south; semi-arid in north
Environment: hot, dry, dusty harmattan wind may affect north in winter; deforestation; desertification; recent droughts have severely affected marginal agriculture in north; insufficient safe drinking water
Terrain: mostly flat to undulating plain; some hills and low mountains
Land Use: 13% arable land; 4% permanent crops; 4% meadows and pastures; 31% forest and woodland; 48% other, includes negligible irrigated
Location: WC Africa, bordering on South Atlantic Ocean

■ PEOPLE

Population: 6,100,799 (July 1998 est.)
Nationality: Beninese
Age Structure: 0-14 yrs: 48%; 15-64: 50%; 65+: 2% (1998 est.)
Population Growth Rate: 3.31% (1998 est.)
Net Migration: 0 migrants/1,000 population (1998 est.)
Ethnic Groups: 99% African (42 ethnic groups, most important being Fon, Adja, Yoruba, Bariba); 5,500 Europeans
Languages: French (official); also Fon, Yoruba, Fulami, Bariba
Religions: majority Animist, 15% Islam, 15% Christian
Birth Rate: 45.82/1,000 population (1998 est.)
Death Rate: 12.77/1,000 population (1998 est.)
Infant Mortality: 100.22 deaths/1,000 live births (1998 est.)
Life Expectancy at Birth: 51.56 years male, 55.72 years female (1998 est.)
Total Fertility Rate: 6.48 children born/woman (1998 est.)
Literacy: 37% (1997 est.)

■ GOVERNMENT

Leader(s): Pres. Mathieu Kerekov, Prime Min. Pierre Osho

Government Type: republic under multi-party democratic rule
Administrative Divisions: 6 provinces
Nationhood: Aug. 1, 1960 (from France; Benin formerly Dahomey)
National Holiday: National Day, Aug. 1

■ ECONOMY

Overview: one of the least developed countries in the world; limited natural resources and an underdeveloped infrastructure characterize the economy; agricultural products are a major export
GDP: $11.3 billion, per capita $1,900; real growth rate 5.8% (1997 est.)
Inflation: 3.4% (1997)
Industries: accounts for 14% of GDP; palm oil and palm kernel oil processing, textiles, beverages, petroleum, cigarettes, construction materials, foodstuffs
Labour Force: 3.1 million (1997 est.); 70.2% agriculture, 23.1% services, 6.6% industry
Unemployment: n.a.
Agriculture: accounts for 34% of GDP; small farms produce 90% of agricultural output; production is dominated by food crops—corn, sorghum, cassava, beans and rice; cash crops include cotton, palm oil and peanuts; poultry and livestock output has not kept up with consumption
Natural Resources: small offshore oil deposits, limestone, marble, timber

■ FINANCE/TRADE

Currency: Communauté financière africaine franc (CFAF) = 100 centimes
International Reserves Excluding Gold: $223 million (Nov. 1998)
Gold Reserves: 0.011 million fine troy ounces (July 1998)
Budget: revenues $299 million; expenditures $445 million, including capital expenditures of $14 million (1995 est.)
Defence Expenditures: 1.4% of GDP (1996)
Education Expenditures: n.a.
External Debt: $1.594 billion (1996)
Exports: $400 million (1997)
Imports: $614 million (1997)

■ COMMUNICATIONS

Daily Newspapers: 1 (1996)
Televisions: 18/1,000 inhabitants (1996)
Radios: 108/1,000 inhabitants (1996)
Telephones: 0.5/100 inhabitants (1996 est.)

■ TRANSPORTATION

Motor Vehicles: 56,000; 36,400 passenger cars (1997 est.)

Roads: 8,460 km; 2,656 km paved
Railway: 578 km
Air Traffic: 75,000 passengers carried (1996)
Airports: 6; 2 have paved runways (1997 est.)

Canadian Embassy: c/o The Canadian Embassy, P.O. Box 4104, Abidjan 01, Cote d'Ivoire. Tel: (011-225) 21-20-09. Fax: (011-225) 21-77-28.
Embassy in Canada: Embassy of the Republic of Benin, 58 Glebe Ave, Ottawa ON K1S 2C3. Tel: (613) 233-4429. Fax: (613) 233-8952.

Bermuda

Long-Form Name: Commonwealth of Bermuda
Capital: Hamilton

■ GEOGRAPHY

Area: 50 sq. km
Climate: subtropical; mild, humid; gales, strong winds common in winter
Land Use: 6% arable land; 0% permanent crops; 0% meadows and pastures; 20% forest and woodland; 74% other
Location: North Atlantic Ocean

■ PEOPLE

Population: 62,009 (July 1998 est.)
Nationality: Bermudian
Ethnic Groups: 61% black, 39% white and other
Languages: English

■ GOVERNMENT

Colony Territory of: Dependent Territory of the United Kingdom
Leader(s): Chief of State: Queen Elizabeth II, Gov. Thorold Masefield, Prem. Jennifer Smith
Government Type: dependent territory of the UK
National Holiday: Bermuda Day, May 24

■ ECONOMY

Overview: a successful tourist industry accounts for its high per capita income; the industrial sector is small, and agriculture is limited by the lack of suitable land; 80% of food must be imported

■ FINANCE/TRADE

Currency: Bermudian dollar ($Ber) = 100 cents

Canadian Embassy: The Canadian Commission to Bermuda, c/o The Canadian Consulate General, 1251 Avenue of the Americas, New York NY, 10020-1175, USA. Tel: (212) 768-2400. Fax: (212) 596-1790.
Representative to Canada: c/o High Commission

for the United Kingdom of Great Britain and Northern Ireland, 80 Elgin St, Ottawa ON K1P 5K7. Tel: (613) 237-1530. Fax: (613) 237-7980.

Bhutan

Long-Form Name: Kingdom of Bhutan
Capital: Thimphu

■ GEOGRAPHY

Area: 47,000 sq. km
Coastline: none: landlocked
Climate: varies; tropical in southern plains; cool winters and hot summers in central valleys; severe winters and cool summers in Himalayas
Environment: violent storms coming from the Himalayas were the source of the country's name, which means Land of the Thunder Dragon; soil erosion and limited access to water are ongoing problems
Terrain: mostly mountainous with some fertile valleys and savanna
Land Use: 2% arable land; negligible permanent crops; 6% meadows and pastures; 66% forest and woodland; 26% other
Location: S Asia

■ PEOPLE

Population: 1,908,307 (July 1998 est.)
Nationality: Bhutanese
Age Structure: 0-14 yrs: 40%; 15-64: 56%; 65+: 4% (1998 est.)
Population Growth Rate: 2.27% (1998 est.)
Net Migration: 0 migrants/1,000 population (1998 est.)
Ethnic Groups: 50% Bhote, 35% ethnic Nepalese, 15% indigenous or migrant tribes
Languages: Bhotes speak various Tibetan dialects—the most widely spoken dialect is Dzongkha (official); Nepalese speak various Nepalese dialects
Religions: 75% Mahayana Buddhism (state religion), Hinduism (25%, mainly ethnic Nepalese)
Birth Rate: 37.33/1,000 population (1998 est.)
Death Rate: 14.6/1,000 population (1998 est.)
Infant Mortality: 111.66 deaths/1,000 live births (1998 est.)
Life Expectancy at Birth: 52.77 years male, 51.83 years female (1998 est.)
Total Fertility Rate: 5.22 children born/woman (1998 est.)
Literacy: 42.2% (1997 est.)

■ GOVERNMENT

Leader(s): King Jigme Singye Wangchuk

Government Type: monarchy; special treaty relationship with India
Administrative Divisions: 18 districts
Nationhood: Aug. 8, 1949 (from India)
National Holiday: National Day, Dec. 17

■ ECONOMY

Overview: agriculture and forestry are the bedrock of the economy; it is poorly developed due to omnipresent rugged topography
GDP: adjusted for purchasing power parity: $1.3 billion, per capita $730; real growth rate 6.9% (1995 est.)
Inflation: 7.4% (June 1997)
Industries: accounts for 32% of GDP; cement, chemical products, mining, distilling, food processing, handicrafts, wood products, calcium carbide. Industries are small and technologically underdeveloped
Labour Force: 675,000 (1995); 93% agriculture, 2% industry; 5% services
Unemployment: n.a.
Agriculture: accounts for 42% of GDP and provides a living for 90% of the population; based on subsistence farming and animal husbandry; self-sufficient in food except for foodgrains; other production—rice, corn, root crops, citrus fruit, dairy and eggs
Natural Resources: timber, hydroelectricity, gypsum, calcium carbide, tourism potential

■ FINANCE/TRADE

Currency: ngultrum (Nu) = 100 chetrum
International Reserves Excluding Gold: $221 million (Sep. 1998)
Gold Reserves: n.a.
Budget: revenues $146 million; expenditures $152 million, including capital expenditures of $94 million (1995-96 est.); the government of India finances almost 60% of Bhutan's expenditures
Defence Expenditures: negligible
Education Expenditures: 11.18% of govt. expenditure (1997)
External Debt: $87 million (1996)
Exports: $77.4 million (1996 est.) commodities: cardamom, gypsum, timber, handicrafts, cement, fruit, electricity, precious stones, spices; partners: India, Bangladesh
Imports: $104.1 million (1996 est.) commodities: fuel and lubricants, grain, machinery and parts, vehicles, fabrics, rice; partners: India, Japan, UK, Germany, US

■ COMMUNICATIONS

Daily Newspapers: 0 (1996)
Televisions: 5.7/1,000 inhabitants (1996)

Radios: 19/1,000 inhabitants (1996)
Telephones: 1.0/100 inhabitants (1996 est.)

■ TRANSPORTATION

Motor Vehicles: n.a.
Roads: 3,285 km; 1,994 surfaced
Railway: none
Air Traffic: 35,000 passengers carried (1996)
Airports: 2; 1 has paved runway (1997 est.)

Canadian Embassy: The Canadian High Commission, 7/8 Shantipath, Chanakyapuri, New Delhi 110021; mailing address: P.O. Box 5207, New Delhi, India. Tel: (011-91-11) 687-6500. Fax: (011-91-11) 379-3170.
Embassy in Canada: c/o High Commission for the Republic of India, 10 Springfield Road, Ottawa ON K1M 1C9. Tel: (613) 744-3751. Fax: (613) 744-0913.

Bolivia

Long-Form Name: Republic of Bolivia
Capital: La Paz (seat of government); Sucre (legal capital and seat of judiciary)

■ GEOGRAPHY

Area: 1,098,580 sq. km
Coastline: none: landlocked
Climate: varies with altitude; humid and tropical to cold and semi-arid
Environment: cold, thin air of high plateau is obstacle to efficient fuel combustion; overgrazing, soil erosion, desertification; deforestation, pollution of drinking water
Terrain: Andes Mountains, high plateau, hills, lowland plains in Amazon basin
Land Use: 2% arable land; negligible permanent crops; 24% meadows and pastures; 53% forest and woodland; 21% other; includes negligible irrigated
Location: C South America

■ PEOPLE

Population: 7,826,352 July 1998 est.)
Nationality: Bolivian
Age Structure: 0-14 yrs: 39%; 15-64: 56%; 65+: 5% (1998 est.)
Population Growth Rate: 2.0% (1998 est.)
Net Migration: -1.53 migrants/1,000 population (1998 est.)
Ethnic Groups: 30% Quechua, 25% Aymara, 25–30% mixed, 5–15% European
Languages: Spanish, Quechua and Aymara (all official)
Religions: 95% Roman Catholic; 5% Protestant, especially Methodist

Birth Rate: 31.43/1,000 population (1998 est.)
Death Rate: 9.89/1,000 population (1998 est.)
Infant Mortality: 63.86 deaths/1,000 live births (1998 est.)
Life Expectancy at Birth: 57.98 years male, 63.94 years female (1998 est.)
Total Fertility Rate: 4.05 children born/woman (1998 est.)
Literacy: 83.1% (1997 est.)

■ GOVERNMENT

Leader(s): Pres. Hugo Banzer Suarez
Government Type: republic
Administrative Divisions: 9 departments
Nationhood: Aug. 6, 1825 (from Spain)
National Holiday: Independence Day, Aug. 6

■ ECONOMY

Overview: a poor economy vulnerable to price fluctuations for its small number of exports; a major step towards the privatization of the economy was taken in early 1994; market-oriented economic reforms and tighter fiscal discipline are leading to generally improving economic conditions
GDP: $23.1 billion, per capita $3,000; real growth rate 4.4% (1997 est.)
Inflation: 6.8% (July 1998)
Industries: accounts for 26% of GDP; mining, smelting, petroleum, food and beverage, tobacco, handicrafts, clothing; illicit drug industry reportedly produces the largest revenues
Labour Force: 3.1 million (1997 est.); 29.1% trade and tourism, 26.2% community, social and business services, 19.4% manufacturing
Unemployment: 10%
Agriculture: accounts for about 17% of GDP (including forestry and fisheries); principal commodities—coffee, coca, cotton, corn, sugar cane, rice, potatoes, timber; self-sufficient in food
Natural Resources: tin, natural gas, crude oil, zinc, tungsten, antimony, silver, iron ore, lead, gold, timber

■ FINANCE/TRADE

Currency: Boliviano ($b) = 100 centavos
International Reserves Excluding Gold: $830 million (Jan. 1999)
Gold Reserves: 0.939 million fine troy ounces (Jan. 1999)
Budget: revenues $3.75 billion; expenditures $3.75 billion, including capital expenditures of $556.2 million (1995 est.)
Defence Expenditures: 8.26% of total govt. expenditure (1997)

Education Expenditures: 19.29% of govt. expenditure (1997)
External Debt: $4.2 billion (1997)
Exports: $1.103 billion (1998); commodities: metals 45%, natural gas 32%, coffee, soyabeans, sugar, cotton, timber; partners: Argentina, UK, US
Imports: $1.983 billion (1998); commodities: food, petroleum, consumer goods, capital goods; partners: US, Brazil, Japan, Argentina

■ COMMUNICATIONS

Daily Newspapers: 18 (1996)
Televisions: 115/1,000 inhabitants (1996)
Radios: 672/1,000 inhabitants (1996)
Telephones: 5.1/100 inhabitants (1996 est.)

■ TRANSPORTATION

Motor Vehicles: 433,000; 200,000 passenger cars (1997 est.)
Roads: 52,216 km; 2,872 km paved
Railway: 3,691 km
Air Traffic: 1,783,000 passengers carried (1996)
Airports: 1,153 airfields; 11 have paved runways (1997 est.)

Canadian Embassy: The Office of Canadian Cooperation, Avenida 20 de Octubre, 2475 Plaza Avaroa Sopocachi, La Paz; mailing address: Casilla Postal 13032, La Paz, Bolivia. Tel: (011-591-2) 432-838. Fax: (011-591-2) 430-250.
Embassy in Canada: Embassy of the Republic of Bolivia, 130 Albert St, Ste 416, Ottawa ON K1P 5G4. Tel: (613) 236-5730. Fax: (613) 236-8237.

Bosnia and Herzegovina

Long-Form Name: Republic of Bosnia and Herzegovina
Capital: Sarajevo

■ GEOGRAPHY

Area: 51,233 sq. km
Coastline: 20 km
Climate: hot summers and cold winters; regions with high elevation have short, cool summers and long, severe winters; mild, rainy winters along the coast
Environment: air pollution; scarce water; waste disposal sites limited; subject to frequent destructive earthquakes
Terrain: mountains and valleys
Land Use: 14% arable, 5% permanent crops, 20% meadows and pastures, 39% forests, 22% other
Location: SE Europe

■ PEOPLE

Population: 3,365,727 (July 1998 est.)
Nationality: Bosnian, Herzegovinian
Age Structure: 0-14 yrs: 18%; 15-64: 71%; 65+: 11% (1998 est.)
Population Growth Rate: 3.63% (1998 est.)
Net Migration: 36.91 migrants/1,000 population (1998 est.)
Ethnic Groups: 38% Muslim, 40% Serb, 22% Croat
Languages: 99% Serbo-Croatian (often called Bosnian)
Religions: 40% Muslim, 31% Orthodox, 15% Catholic, 4% Protestant, 10% other
Birth Rate: 8.72/1,000 population (1998 est.)
Death Rate: 12.32/1,000 population (1998 est.)
Infant Mortality: 30.8 deaths/1,000 live births (1998 est.)
Life Expectancy at Birth: 58.35 years male, 68.02 years female (1998 est.)
Total Fertility Rate: 1.14 children born/woman (1998 est.)
Literacy: n.a.

■ GOVERNMENT

Leader(s): Chief of State: President Alija Izetbegovic; head of govt. Prime Min. Milorad Dodik. There is a collective (six-member) presidency
Government Type: in transition to democracy
Administrative Divisions: reportedly 10 cantons
Nationhood: Apr. 1992 (from Yugoslavia)
National Holiday: Republic Day, January 9; Independence Day, March 1; Republic Day, November 25

■ ECONOMY

Overview: though farms are almost entirely privately owned, they are small and inefficient, and food must be imported; inter-ethnic warfare has caused sharp decreases in industrial output and soaring unemployment
GDP: $4.41 billion, per capita $1,690; real growth rate 35% (1997 est.)
Inflation: n.a.
Industries: accounts for 23% of GDP; steel production, mining (esp. coal, iron ore, lead, zinc), manufacturing (esp. vehicle assembly, textiles, tobacco products, wood furniture), oil refining
Labour Force: 1,900,000 (1995); 2% agriculture, 45% industry and mining
Unemployment: 40-50% (1996 est.)
Agriculture: accounts for 19% of GDP; regularly produces less than half the region's food needs; foothills of northern Bosnia support orchards, vineyards, livestock and some wheat and corn; long winters and heavy precipitation reduce agricultural output in mountains; farms are generally not very productive
Natural Resources: coal, iron, bauxite, manganese, timber, copper, lead, zinc

■ FINANCE/TRADE

Currency: convertible marka = 100 convertible pfenniga
International Reserves Excluding Gold: n.a.
Gold Reserves: n.a.
Budget: n.a.
Defence Expenditures: n.a.
Education Expenditures: n.a.
External Debt: $3.5 billion (year-end 1995 est.)
Exports: $152 million (1997 est.)
Imports: $1.1 billion (1997 est.)

■ COMMUNICATIONS

Daily Newspapers: 3 (1996)
Televisions: 0.3/1,000 inhabitants (1996)
Radios: 248/1,000 inhabitants (1996)
Telephones: 5.0/100 inhabitants (1996 est.)

■ TRANSPORTATION

Motor Vehicles: n.a.
Roads: 21,846 km; 11,436 km paved
Railway: 1,021 km
Air Traffic: n.a.
Airports: 26; 9 have paved runways (1997 est.)

Canadian Embassy: The Canadian Embassy, Logavina 7, 71000 Sarajevo. Tel: (011-387-71) 447-900. Fax: (011-387-71) 447-901.
Embassy in Canada: Embassy of Bosnia and Herzogovina, 130 Albert St., Ste 805, Ottawa, ON K1P 5G4. Tel: (613) 236-0028. Fax: (613) 236-1139.

Botswana

Long-Form Name: Republic of Botswana
Capital: Gaborone

■ GEOGRAPHY

Area: 600,370 sq. km
Coastline: none: landlocked
Climate: subtropical to semi-arid; warm winters and hot summers
Environment: overgrazing; desertification; limited resources of fresh water, periodic droughts, sand and dust storms
Terrain: predominantly flat to gently rolling tableland; Kalahari Desert in southwest
Land Use: 1% arable land; 0% permanent crops; 46% meadows and pastures; 47% forest and woodland; 6% other; includes negligible irrigated
Location: SC Africa

■ PEOPLE

Population: 1,448,454 (July 1998 est.)
Nationality: Motswana (sing.), Batswana (pl.)
Age Structure: 0-14 yrs: 42%; 15-64: 54%; 65+: 4% (1998 est.)
Population Growth Rate: 1.11% (1998 est.)
Net Migration: 0 migrants/1,000 population (1998 est.)
Ethnic Groups: 95% Batswana; about 4% Kalanga, Basarwa and Kgalagadi; about 1% white
Languages: English (official), Setswana
Religions: 50% indigenous beliefs, 50% Christian
Birth Rate: 32.02/1,000 population (1998 est.)
Death Rate: 20.89/1,000 population (1998 est.)
Infant Mortality: 59.29 deaths/1,000 live births (1998 est.)
Life Expectancy at Birth: 39.46 years male, 40.75 years female (1998 est.)
Total Fertility Rate: 4.03 children born/woman (1998 est.)
Literacy: 69.8% (1997 est.)

■ GOVERNMENT

Leader(s): Pres. Festus Mogae
Government Type: parliamentary republic
Administrative Divisions: 10 districts and 4 town councils
Nationhood: Sept. 30, 1966 (from UK; Botswana formerly known as Bechuanaland)
National Holiday: Independence Day, Sept. 30

■ ECONOMY

Overview: economy based on mining (diamonds) and traditionally, cattle raising and crops; exhibits high unemployment
GDP: $5 billion, per capita $3,300; real growth rate 6% (1997 est.)
Inflation: 6.6% (May 1998)
Industries: accounts for 45% of GDP; livestock processing; mining of diamonds, copper, nickel, coal, salt, soda ash, potash; tourism
Labour Force: 1 million (1997 est.); 36.6% community, social and business services; 18% trade and tourism, 11.2% manufacturing; 19,000 are employed in various mines in South Africa
Unemployment: 20-40% (1997 est.)
Agriculture: plagued by erratic rainfall and poor soil; accounts for only 4% of GDP; subsistence farming predominates; cattle raising supports 50% of the population; must import large share of food needs
Natural Resources: diamonds, copper, nickel, salt, soda ash, potash, coal, iron ore, silver, natural gas

■ FINANCE/TRADE

Currency: pula (P) = 100 thebe
International Reserves Excluding Gold: $6.044 billion (Nov. 1998)
Gold Reserves: n.a.
Budget: revenues $1.6 billion; expenditures $1.8 billion, including capital expenditures of $560 million (1996-97 est.)
Defence Expenditures: 8.13% of total govt. expenditure (1996)
Education Expenditures: 26.34% of total govt. expenditure (1996)
External Debt: $613 million (1996)
Exports: $2.942 billion (1997); commodities: diamonds 88%, copper and nickel 5%, meat 4%, cattle, animal products; partners: Switzerland, US, UK, other European Community-associated members of Southern African Customs Union
Imports: $2.262 billion (1997); commodities: foodstuffs, vehicles, textiles, petroleum products; partners: Switzerland

■ COMMUNICATIONS

Daily Newspapers: 1 (1996)
Televisions: 20/1,000 inhabitants (1996)
Radios: 155/1,000 inhabitants (1996)
Telephones: 4.7/100 inhabitants (1996 est.)

■ TRANSPORTATION

Motor Vehicles: 100,000; 83,000 passenger cars (1997 est.)
Roads: 18,482 km; 4,343 km paved
Railway: 971 km
Air Traffic: 104,000 passengers carried (1996)
Airports: 92; 12 have paved runways (1997 est.)

Canadian Embassy: c/o The Canadian High Commission, P.O. Box 1430, Harare, Zimbabwe. Tel: (011-267) 30-44-11. Fax: (011-267) 30-44-11.
Embassy in Canada: c/o High Commission for the Republic of Botswana, 1531-1533 New Hampshire Ave. NW, Washington DC 20036, USA. Tel: (202) 244-4990. Fax: (202) 244-4164.

Brazil

Long-Form Name: Federative Republic of Brazil
Capital: Brasilia

■ GEOGRAPHY

Area: 8,511,965 sq. km; includes Arquipélago de Fernando de Noronha, Atol das Rocas, Ilha da Trindade, Ilhas Martin Vaz and Penedos de São Pedro e São Paulo

Coastline: 7,491 km

Climate: mostly tropical, but temperate in south

Environment: recurrent droughts in northeast; floods and frost in south; deforestation in Amazon basin; air and water pollution in Rio de Janeiro and São Paulo and several other large cities

Terrain: mostly flat to rolling lowlands in north; some plains, hills, mountains and narrow coastal belt

Land Use: 5% arable land; 1% permanent crops; 22% meadows and pastures; 58% forest and woodland; 14% other; includes negligible irrigated

Location: E South America

■ PEOPLE

Population: 169,806,557 (July 1998 est.)

Nationality: Brazilian

Age Structure: 0-14 yrs: 30%; 15-64: 65%; 65+: 5% (1998 est.)

Population Growth Rate: 1.24% (1998 est.)

Net Migration: -0.03 migrants/1,000 population (1998 est.)

Ethnic Groups: Portuguese, Italian, German, Japanese, black, Amerindian; 55% white, 38% mixed, 6% black, 1% other

Languages: Portuguese (official), Spanish, English, French

Religions: 70% Roman Catholic (nominal)

Birth Rate: 20.92/1,000 population (1998 est.)

Death Rate: 8.53/1,000 population (1998 est.)

Infant Mortality: 36.96 deaths/1,000 live births (1998 est.)

Life Expectancy at Birth: 59.39 years male, 69.59 years female (1998 est.)

Total Fertility Rate: 2.33 children born/woman (1998 est.)

Literacy: 83.3% (1997 est.)

■ GOVERNMENT

Leader(s): Pres. Fernando Henrique Cardoso, V. Pres. Marco Maciel

Government Type: federal republic

Administrative Divisions: 26 states and 1 federal district

Nationhood: Sept. 7, 1822 (from Portugal)

National Holiday: Independence Day, Sept. 7

■ ECONOMY

Overview: inflation has dropped sharply and sweeping reforms have boosted the economy, but the domestic debt remains burdensome. Brazil's natural resources remain a major, long-term economic strength

GDP: $1.04 trillion, per capita $6,300; real growth rate 3% (1997 est.)

Inflation: 3.9% (May 1998)

Industries: accounts for 38% of GDP; textiles and other consumer goods, shoes, chemicals, cement, lumber, iron ore, steel, motor vehicles and auto parts, metalworking, capital goods, tin

Labour Force: 73.7 million (1997 est.); 34.9% community, social and business services, 22.8% agriculture, 15.2% industry

Unemployment: 7% (1997 est.)

Agriculture: accounts for 13% of GDP; world's largest producer and exporter of coffee and orange juice concentrate and second-largest exporter of soybeans; self-sufficient in food, except for wheat

Natural Resources: iron ore, manganese, bauxite, nickel, uranium, phosphates, tin, hydroelectricity, gold, platinum, crude oil, timber

■ FINANCE/TRADE

Currency: real (CR$) = 100 centavos

International Reserves Excluding Gold: $34.177 billion (Jan. 1999)

Gold Reserves: 1.492 million fine troy ounces (Jan. 1999)

Budget: revenues $87.5 billion; expenditures $96 billion, including capital expenditures of n.a. (1996)

Defence Expenditures: 1.9% of GDP (1997)

Education Expenditures: n.a.

External Debt: $192.9 billion (1997)

Exports: $50.992 billion (1998); commodities: coffee, metallurgical products, foodstuffs, iron ore, automobiles and parts; partners: US 28%, European Community 26%, Latin America 11%, Japan 6%

Imports: $65.007 billion (1997); commodities: crude oil, capital goods, chemical products, foodstuffs, coal; partners: Middle East and Africa 24%, European Community 22%, US 21%, Latin America 12%, Japan 6%

■ COMMUNICATIONS

Daily Newspapers: 380 (1996)

Televisions: 223/1,000 inhabitants (1996)

Radios: 435/1,000 inhabitants (1996)

Telephones: 7.7/100 inhabitants (1996 est.)

■ TRANSPORTATION

Motor Vehicles: 16,700,000; 13,100,000 passenger cars (1997 est.)

Roads: 1.98 million km; 184.140 km paved

Railway: 26,895 km

Air Traffic: 22,011,000 passengers carried (1996)

Airports: 3,291 airfields; n.a. have paved runways (1997 est.)

Canadian Embassy: Setor de Embaixadas Sul, Avenida das Nacoes, Quadra 803, Lote 16, Brasilia DF, 70410-900; mailing address: Caixa Postal 00961, 70359-900 Brasilia DF, Brazil. Tel: (011-55-61) 321-2171. Fax: (011-55-61) 321-4529.
Embassy in Canada: Embassy of the Federative Republic of Brazil, 450 Wilbrod St, Ottawa ON K1N 6M8. Tel: (613) 237-1090. Fax: (613) 237-6144.

British Indian Ocean Territory

Long-Form Name: British Indian Ocean Territory
Capital: None; Victoria (Seychelles) is administrative headquarters

■ GEOGRAPHY

Area: 60 sq. km
Climate: tropical maritime, hot and humid, moderated by trade winds
Land Use: no arable land; 0% permanent crops, meadows or pastures, 100% other
Location: Indian Ocean, the Chagos Archipelago island group NE of Madagascar

■ PEOPLE

Population: no indigenous inhabitants; US and UK military personnel
Nationality: n.a.
Ethnic Groups: n.a.
Languages: n.a.

■ GOVERNMENT

Colony Territory of: Dependent Territory of the United Kingdom
Leader(s): Chief of State: Queen Elizabeth II, Comm. Anthony Lonrigg, Administrator M.G. Richardson; all reside in the UK
Government Type: dependency of Great Britain
National Holiday: n.a.

■ ECONOMY

Overview: fishing, coconuts, guano fertilizer; all economic activity takes place on the largest island, Diego Garcia, where joint US–UK defence facilities are located; there are no industrial or agricultural activities on the islands

■ FINANCE/TRADE

Currency: pound sterling (£ or £ stg)

Canadian Embassy: c/o of the Canadian High Commission, Macdonald House, 1 Grosvenor Square, London W1X 0AB, England, UK. Tel: (011-44-171) 258-6600. Fax: (011-44-171) 258-6333.

Representative to Canada: c/o British High Commission, 80 Elgin St, Ottawa ON K1P 5K7. Tel: (613) 237-1530. Fax: (613) 237-7980.

British Virgin Islands

Long-Form Name: British Virgin Islands
Capital: Road Town

■ GEOGRAPHY

Area: 150 sq. km; includes the island of Anegada
Climate: subtropical and humid; moderated by trade winds; hurricanes and tropical storms occur from July to Oct.
Land Use: 15% arable; 6% permanent crops; 26% permanent pastures; 6% forests; 47% other
Location: Caribbean islands

■ PEOPLE

Population: 18,705 (July 1998 est.)
Nationality: British Virgin Islander
Ethnic Groups: 90% black, 10% white, Asian, and other
Languages: English (official)

■ GOVERNMENT

Colony Territory of: Dependent territory of the UK
Leader(s): Chief of State: Queen Elizabeth II; Governor Peter Alfred Penfold; Chief Minister Ralph Telford O'Neal
Government Type: dependency
National Holiday: Territory Day, July 1

■ ECONOMY

Overview: one of the most prosperous economies in the Caribbean; highly dependent on tourism

■ FINANCE/TRADE

Currency: US dollar ($) = 100 cents

Canadian Embassy: c/o The Canadian High Commission, Macdonald House, 1 Grosvenor Square, London, W1X OAB, England, UK. Tel: (011-44-171) 258-6600. Fax: (011-44-171) 258-6333.
Representative to Canada: c/o British High Commission, 80 Elgin St, Ottawa ON K1P 5K7. Tel: (613) 237-1530. Fax: (613) 237-7980.

Brunei Darussalam

Long-Form Name: Negara Brunei Darussalam
Capital: Bandar Seri Begawan

■ GEOGRAPHY

Area: 5,770 sq. km
Coastline: 161 km
Climate: tropical; hot, humid, rainy
Environment: typhoons, earthquakes and severe floods occasionally occur
Terrain: flat coastal plain rises to mountainous east; hilly lowland in west
Land Use: 1% arable land; 1% permanent crops; 1% meadows and pastures; 85% forest and woodland; 12% other, includes negligible irrigated
Location: Indonesia (island of Borneo), bordering on South China Sea and Malaysia

■ PEOPLE

Population: 315,292 (July 1998 est.)
Nationality: Bruneian
Age Structure: 0-14 yrs: 33%; 15-64: 63%; 65+: 4% (1998 est.)
Population Growth Rate: 2.44% (1998 est.)
Net Migration: 4.61 migrants/1,000 population (1998 est.)
Ethnic Groups: 64% Malay, 20% Chinese, 16% other
Languages: Malay (official), English and Chinese
Religions: Islam (official, mainly Sunni Muslims); majority of Chinese are Buddhist, Confucian or Taoist
Birth Rate: 24.92/1,000 population (1998 est.)
Death Rate: 5.17/1,000 population (1998 est.)
Infant Mortality: 23.3 deaths/1,000 live births (1998 est.)
Life Expectancy at Birth: 70.17 years male, 73.29 years female (1998 est.)
Total Fertility Rate: 3.35 children born/woman (1998 est.)
Literacy: 88.2% (1997 est.)

■ GOVERNMENT

Leader(s): Sultan, Prime Min. and Minister of Defence Sir Hassanal Bolkiah
Government Type: constitutional sultanate
Administrative Divisions: 4 districts
Nationhood: Jan. 1, 1984 (from UK)
National Holiday: National Day, Feb. 23

■ ECONOMY

Overview: economy is based on crude oil and natural gas exports and the per capita GDP is one of the highest for underdeveloped nations; almost totally supported by exports of crude oil and natural gas
GDP: $5.4 billion, per capita $18,000; real growth rate 3.5% (1997 est.)
Inflation: n.a.

Industries: accounts for 46% of GDP; petroleum, liquefied natural gas, construction
Labour Force: 144,000 (1995 est.) (includes members of the army) ; 42% production of oil, natural gas and construction; 48% trade, services and other; 4% agriculture, forestry and fishing; 6% other
Unemployment: 4.6% (1995)
Agriculture: accounts for 5% of GDP; imports about 80% of its food needs; principal crops and livestock include rice, cassava, bananas, buffalo and pigs
Natural Resources: crude oil, natural gas, timber

■ FINANCE/TRADE

Currency: Bruneian dollar ($B) = 100 cents
International Reserves Excluding Gold: n.a.
Gold Reserves: n.a.
Budget: revenues $2.5 billion; expenditures $2.6 billion, including capital expenditures of $768 million (1995 est.)
Defence Expenditures: 6.5% of GDP (1996)
Education Expenditures: n.a.
External Debt: none (1997)
Exports: $2.273 billion (1995); commodities: crude oil, liquefied natural gas, petroleum products; partners: Japan 55%
Imports: $1.915 billion (1995); commodities: machinery and transport equipment, manufactured goods, food, beverages, tobacco, consumer goods; partners: Singapore 31%, US 20%, Japan 6%

■ COMMUNICATIONS

Daily Newspapers: 1 (1996)
Televisions: 250/1,000 inhabitants (1996)
Radios: 300/1,000 inhabitants (1996)
Telephones: 25.8/100 inhabitants (1996 est.)

■ TRANSPORTATION

Motor Vehicles: 166,000; 148,000 passenger cars (1997 est.)
Roads: 1,150 km; 399 km paved
Railway: 13 km private line
Air Traffic: 857,000 passengers carried (1996)
Airports: 2; 1 has paved runway (1997 est.)

Canadian Embassy: The High Commission of Canada, Suite 51, Britannia House, Jalan Cator, Bandar Seri Begawan; mailing address: P.O. Box 2808, Bandar Seri, Begawan 1928, Brunei Darussalam. Tel: (011-673-2) 22-00-43. Fax (011-673-2) 22-00-40.
Embassy in Canada: High Commission for Brunei, 395 Laurier Ave E, Ottawa ON K1N 6R4. Tel: (613)234-5656. Fax: (613) 234-4397.

Bulgaria

Long-Form Name: Republic of Bulgaria
Capital: Sofia

■ GEOGRAPHY

Area: 110,910 sq. km
Coastline: 354 km
Climate: temperate; cold, damp winters; hot, dry summers
Environment: subject to earthquakes, landslides, deforestation, air and water pollution
Terrain: mostly mountains with lowlands in north and south
Land Use: 37% arable land; 2% permanent crops; 16% meadows and pastures; 35% forest and woodland; 10% other, includes 10 sq. km irrigated
Location: SE Europe, bordering on Black Sea

■ PEOPLE

Population: 8,240,426 (July 1998 est.)
Nationality: Bulgarian
Age Structure: 0-14 yrs: 16%; 15-64: 68%; 65+: 16% (1998 est.)
Population Growth Rate: -0.6% (1998 est.)
Net Migration: -0.8 migrants/1,000 population (1998 est.)
Ethnic Groups: 85.3% Bulgarian, 8.5% Turk, 2.6% Gypsy, 2.5% Macedonian, 0.3% Armenian, 0.2% Russian, 0.6% other
Languages: Bulgarian (official), Turkish; secondary languages closely correspond to ethnic breakdown
Religions: 85% Bulgarian Orthodox, 13% Muslim (practised by Turkish and Pomak minorities), 0.8% Jewish, 0.7% Roman Catholic, 0.5% Protestant, Gregorian-Armenian and other
Birth Rate: 8.08/1,000 population (1998 est.)
Death Rate: 13.24/1,000 population (1998 est.)
Infant Mortality: 12.78 deaths/1,000 live births (1998 est.)
Life Expectancy at Birth: 68.39 years male, 75.74 years female (1998 est.)
Total Fertility Rate: 1.14 children born/woman (1998 est.)
Literacy: 98% (1997 est.)

■ GOVERNMENT

Leader(s): Pres. Petar Stoyanov, Prime Min. Ivan Kostov
Government Type: emerging democracy
Administrative Divisions: 9 provinces
Nationhood: Sept. 22, 1908 (from Turkey)
National Holiday: Independence Day, Mar. 3

■ ECONOMY

Overview: heavily in debt with low growth, the economy is also hindered by antiquated industrial plants; continues to adjust to a market economy
GDP: $35.6 billion, per capita $4,100; real growth rate -7.4% (1997 est.)
Inflation: 77.8% (Feb. 1998)
Industries: accounts for 31% of GDP; food processing, machine building and metal working, electronics, chemicals
Labour Force: 4 million (1997 est.); 33.9% industry, 18% agriculture, 21.9% community, social and business services
Unemployment: 14% (1997 est.)
Agriculture: accounts for 12% of GNP; climate and soil conditions support livestock raising and the growing of various grain crops, oilseeds, vegetables, fruit and tobacco; more than one-third of the arable land devoted to grain; world's fourth largest tobacco exporter; surplus food producer
Natural Resources: bauxite, copper, lead, zinc, coal, timber, arable land

■ FINANCE/TRADE

Currency: lev (pl. leva) (Lv) = 100 stotinki
International Reserves Excluding Gold: $2.623 billion (Jan. 1999)
Gold Reserves: 1.031 million fine troy ounces (Jan. 1999)
Budget: revenues $2.7 billion; expenditures $3.2 billion, capital expenditures n.a. (1997 est.)
Defence Expenditures: 8.03% of total govt. expenditure (1997)
Education Expenditures: 5.65% of total govt. expenditure (1997)
External Debt: $10 billion (1997 est.)
Exports: $4.377 billion (1998 est.); commodities: machinery and equipment 60.5%, agricultural products 14.7%, manufactured consumer goods 10.6%, fuels, minerals, raw materials and metals 8.5%, other 5.7%; partners: socialist countries 82.5%, developed countries 6.8%, less developed countries 10.7%
Imports: $4.847 billion (1998 est.); commodities: fuels, minerals, raw materials 45.2%, machinery and equipment 39.8%, manufactured consumer goods 4.6%, agricultural products 3.8%, other 6.6%; partners: socialist countries 80.5%, developed countries 15.1%, less developed countries 4.4%

■ COMMUNICATIONS

Daily Newspapers: 17 (1996)
Televisions: 390/1,000 inhabitants (1996)
Radios: 531/1,000 inhabitants (1996)
Telephones: 31.4/100 inhabitants (1996 est.)

■ TRANSPORTATION

Motor Vehicles: 1,990,000; 1,680,000 passenger cars (1997 est.)
Roads: 36,720 km; 33,746 km hard-surfaced
Railway: 4,294 km
Air Traffic: 718,000 passengers carried (1996)
Airports: 355; 116 have paved runways (1995)

Canadian Embassy: The Canadian Embassy to Bulgaria, Price Waterhouse (Sofia), 2 Serdika St, 1000 Sofia, Bulgaria; postal address: P.O. Box 117, Post Office No. 22, Bucharest, Romania. Tel: (011-3592) 980-8884. Fax: (011-3592) 980-0404.
Embassy in Canada: Embassy of the Republic of Bulgaria, 325 Stewart St, Ottawa ON K1N 6K5. Tel: (613) 789-3215. Fax: (613) 789-3524.

Burkina Faso

Long-Form Name: Burkina Faso
Capital: Ouagadougou

■ GEOGRAPHY

Area: 274,200 sq. km
Coastline: none. landlocked
Climate: tropical; warm, dry winters; hot, wet summers
Environment: recent droughts and desertification severely affecting marginal agricultural activities, population distribution, economy; overgrazing; desertification
Terrain: mostly flat to dissected, undulating plains; hills in west and southeast
Land Use: 13% arable land; 0% permanent crops; 22% meadows and pastures; 50% forest and woodland; 15% other, includes negligible irrigated
Location: WC Africa

■ PEOPLE

Population: 11,266,393 (July 1998 est.)
Nationality: Burkinabe
Age Structure: 0-14 yrs: 48%; 15-64: 49%; 65+: 3% (1997 est.)
Population Growth Rate: 2.72% (1998 est.)
Net Migration: -1.41 migrants/1,000 population (1998 est.)
Ethnic Groups: more than 50 tribes; principal tribe is Mossi (about 24% of pop.); other important groups are Gurunsi, Senufo, Lobi, Bobo, Mande and Fulani
Languages: French (official); tribal languages belong to Sudanic family, spoken by 90% of population
Religions: 40% indigenous beliefs, about 50% Muslim, 10% Christian (mainly Roman Catholic)
Birth Rate: 46.24/1,000 population (1998 est.)
Death Rate: 17.65/1,000 population (1998 est.)
Infant Mortality: 109.15 deaths/1,000 live births (1998 est.)
Life Expectancy at Birth: 45.38 years male, 46.85 years female (1998 est.)
Total Fertility Rate: 6.64 children born/woman (1998 est.)
Literacy: 19.2% (1997 est.)

■ GOVERNMENT

Leader(s): Head of State, Head of Government & Chairman, Capt. Blaise Compaoré, Prime Min. Kadre Desire Oudraogo
Government Type: parliamentary democracy
Administrative Divisions: 30 provinces
Nationhood: Aug. 5, 1960 (from France; Burkina Faso formerly known as Upper Volta)
National Holiday: Anniversary of the Revolution, Aug. 4

■ ECONOMY

Overview: a poor economy with high population density and few natural resources, it relies heavily on subsistence agriculture, economic development is hindered by a poor communication network; agriculture provides approximately 30% of national income
GDP: $10.3 billion, per capita $950; real growth rate 6% (1997 est.)
Inflation: -0.3% (1997)
Industries: accounts for 26% of GDP; agricultural processing plants; brewery, cement and brick plants; soap, cigarettes, textiles, gold mining and extraction; a few other small consumer goods enterprises
Labour Force: 6.1 million (1997 est.); 86.6% agriculture, 4.3% industry, 9.1% services; 20% of male labour force migrates annually to neighbouring countries for seasonal employment
Unemployment: n.a.
Agriculture: accounts for 32% of GDP; cash crops—peanuts, shea nuts, sesame, cotton; food crops—sorghum, millet, corn, rice; livestock; not self-sufficient in food grains
Natural Resources: manganese, limestone, marble; small deposits of gold, antimony, copper, nickel, bauxite, lead, phosphates, zinc, silver

■ FINANCE/TRADE

Currency: Communauté financière africaine franc (CFAF) = 100 centimes
International Reserves Excluding Gold: $338

million (Nov. 1998)
Gold Reserves: 0.011 million fine troy ounces (June 1998)
Budget: revenues $277 million; expenditures $492 million, including capital expenditures of $233 million (1995 est.)
Defence Expenditures: 2.4% of GDP (1996)
Education Expenditures: 3.6% of GNP (1995)
External Debt: $1.294 billion (1996)
Exports: $205 million (1997); commodities: oilseeds, cotton, live animals, gold; partners: European Community 42%, Taiwan 17%, Ivory Coast 15%
Imports: $530 million (1997); commodities: grain, dairy products, petroleum, machinery; partners: European Community 37%, Africa 31%, US 15%

■ COMMUNICATIONS

Daily Newspapers: 4 (1996)
Televisions: 8.3/1,000 inhabitants (1996)
Radios: 32/1,000 inhabitants (1996)
Telephones: 0.3/100 inhabitants (1996 est.)

■ TRANSPORTATION

Motor Vehicles: 55,000; 35,600 passenger cars (1997 est.)
Roads: 12,506 km; 2,001 km paved
Railway: 622 km
Air Traffic: 138,000 passengers carried (1996)
Airports: 33; 2 have paved runways (1997 est.)

Canadian Embassy: The Canadian Embassy, rue Agostino Neto, Ouagadougou; mailing address: Office of the Canadian Embassy, P.O. Box 548, Ouagadougou 01, Province du Kadiogo, Burkina Faso. Tel: (011-226) 31-18-95. Fax (011-226) 31-19-00.
Embassy in Canada: Embassy of Burkina Faso, 48 Range Rd, Ottawa ON K1N 8J4. Tel: (613) 238-4796. Fax: (613) 238-3812.

Burundi

Long-Form Name: Republic of Burundi
Capital: Bujumbura

■ GEOGRAPHY

Area: 27,830 sq. km
Coastline: none: landlocked
Climate: temperate; warm; occasional frost in uplands
Environment: soil exhaustion; soil erosion; deforestation; flooding and landslides are natural hazards
Terrain: mostly rolling to hilly highland; some plains

Land Use: 44% arable land; 9% permanent crops; 36% meadows and pastures; 3% forest and woodland; 8% other, includes negligible irrigated
Location: EC Africa

■ PEOPLE

Population: 5,537,387 (July 1998 est.)
Nationality: Burundian
Age Structure: 0-14 yrs: 47%; 15-64: 50%; 65+: 3% (1998 est.)
Population Growth Rate: 3.51% (1998 est.)
Net Migration: 10.84 migrants/1,000 population (1998 est.)
Ethnic Groups: Africans: 85% Hutu (Bantu), 14% Tutsi (Hamitic), 1% Twa (Pygmy); non-Africans: 3,000 Europeans, 2,000 South Asians
Languages: Kirundi and French (official); Swahili used commercially
Religions: about 67% Christian (62% Roman Catholic, 5% Protestant), 32% indigenous beliefs, 1% Moslem
Birth Rate: 41.61/1,000 population (1998 est.)
Death Rate: 17.38/1,000 population (1998 est.)
Infant Mortality: 101.19 deaths/1,000 live births (1998 est.)
Life Expectancy at Birth: 43.79 years male, 47.38 years female (1998 est.)
Total Fertility Rate: 6.4 children born/woman (1998 est.)
Literacy: 35.3$ (1997 est.)

■ GOVERNMENT

Leader(s): Pres. Maj. Pierre Buyoya (ret.); First V.Pres. Frederic Bamvuginyumvira
Government Type: republic
Administrative Divisions: 15 provinces
Nationhood: July 1, 1962 (from UN trusteeship under Belgian administration)
National Holiday: Independence Day, July 1

■ ECONOMY

Overview: economy is heavily dependent on the coffee crop and therefore vulnerable to market conditions; there are only a few basic industries. Massive ethnic-based violence has also interfered with economic activity
GDP: $4 billion, per capita $660; real growth rate 4.4% (1997 est.)
Inflation: 9.2% (May 1998)
Industries: accounts for 18% of GDP; light consumer goods such as blankets, shoes, soap; assembly of imports; public works construction; food processing
Labour Force: 3.1 million (1997 est.); 39.6% community, social and business services, 14.8% manufacturing

Unemployment: n.a.

Agriculture: accounts for 56% of GDP; 90% of population dependent on subsistence farming; marginally self-sufficient in food production; cash crops—coffee, cotton, tea; food crops—corn, sorghum, sweet potatoes, bananas, manioc; livestock—meat, milk, hides and skins

Natural Resources: nickel, uranium, rare earth oxide, peat, cobalt, copper, platinum (not yet exploited), vanadium

■ FINANCE/TRADE

Currency: Burundi franc (FBu) = 100 centimes

International Reserves Excluding Gold: $66 million (Dec. 1998)

Gold Reserves: 0.017 million fine troy ounces (Dec. 1998)

Budget: revenues $222 million, expenditures $258 million, including capital expenditures of $92 million (1995 est.)

Defence Expenditures: 26.11% of total govt. expenditure (1997)

Education Expenditures: 13.87% of total govt. expenditure (1997)

External Debt: $1.127 billion (1996)

Exports: $62.7 million (1998 est.); commodities: coffee 88%, tea, hides and skins; partners: European Community 83%, US 5%, Asia 2%

Imports: $164 million (1998 est.); commodities: capital goods 31%, petroleum products 15%, foodstuffs, consumer goods; partners: European Community 57%, Asia 23%, US 3%

■ COMMUNICATIONS

Daily Newspapers: 1 (1996)

Televisions: 3.2/1,000 inhabitants (1996)

Radios: 68/1,000 inhabitants (1996)

Telephones: 0.3/100 inhabitants (1996 est.)

■ TRANSPORTATION

Motor Vehicles: 20,000; 8,200 passenger cars (1997 est.)

Roads: 14,480 km; 1,028 km paved

Railway: none

Air Traffic: 9,000 passengers carried (1996)

Airports: 4; 1 has paved runways (1997 est.)

Canadian Embassy: c/o The Canadian High Commission, P.O. Box 30481, Nairobi, Kenya. Tel: (011-254-2) 21-48-04. Fax: (011-254-2) 22-69-87.

Embassy in Canada: Embassy of the Republic of Burundi, 50 Kaymar St, Rothwell Heights, Gloucester ON K1J 7C7. Tel: (613) 741-8828. Fax: (613) 741-2424.

Cambodia

Long-Form Name: Kingdom of Cambodia

Capital: Phnom Penh

■ GEOGRAPHY

Area: 181,040 sq. km

Coastline: 443 km

Climate: tropical; rainy, monsoon season (May to Oct.); dry season (Dec. to Mar.); little seasonal temperature variation

Environment: a land of paddies and forests dominated by Mekong River and Tonle Sap; deforestation, monsoons; logging and strip mining are resulting in environmental degradation

Terrain: mostly low, flat plains; mountains in southwest and north

Land Use: 13% arable land; 0% permanent crops; 11% meadows and pastures; 66% forest and woodland; 10% other

Location: SE Asia, bordering on the Gulf of Siam

■ PEOPLE

Population: 11,339,562 (July 1998 est.)

Nationality: Cambodian

Age Structure: 0-14 yrs: 45%; 15-64: 52%; 65+: 3% (1998 est.)

Population Growth Rate: 2.51% (1998 est.)

Net Migration: 0 migrants/1,000 population (1998 est.)

Ethnic Groups: 90% Khmer (Cambodian), 5% Vietnamese, 1% Chinese, 4% other minorities

Languages: Khmer (official), French

Religions: 95% Theravada Buddhism, 5% Christianity

Birth Rate: 41.63/1,000 population (1998 est.)

Death Rate: 16.49/1,000 population (1998 est.)

Infant Mortality: 106.76 deaths/1,000 live births (1998 est.)

Life Expectancy at Birth: 46.64 years male, 49.41 years female (1998 est.)

Total Fertility Rate: 5.81 children born/woman (1998 est.)

Literacy: 35% (1997 est.)

■ GOVERNMENT

Leader(s): King Norodom Sihanouk, First Prem. Hun Sen

Government Type: liberal democracy under constitutional monarchy

Administrative Divisions: 20 provinces and 3 municipalities

Nationhood: Nov. 9, 1949 (from France)

National Holiday: Independence Day, Nov. 9

■ ECONOMY

Overview: a desperately poor country; the economy has suffered badly due to internal war; the country has not been able to feed its people; economy remains essentially rural, with 90% of the population dependent mainly on subsistence agriculture

GDP: $7.7 billion, per capita $715; real growth rate 1.5% (1997 est.)

Inflation: 14.8% (July 1998)

Industries: accounts for 15.4% of GDP; rice milling, fishing, wood and wood products, rubber, cement, gem mining

Labour Force: 5.1 million (1997 est.); 74.4% agriculture, 6.7% industry, 18.9% services

Unemployment: n.a.

Agriculture: accounts for 47.3% of GDP, mainly subsistence farming except for rubber plantations; main crops—rice, rubber, corn; food shortages—rice, meat, vegetables, dairy products, sugar, flour

Natural Resources: timber, gemstones, some iron ore, manganese, phosphates, hydroelectricity potential

■ FINANCE/TRADE

Currency: new riel (KR) = 100 sen

International Reserves Excluding Gold: $347 million (Jan. 1999)

Gold Reserves: n.a.

Budget: revenues $261 million; expenditures $496 million, capital expenditures n.a. (1995 est.)

Defence Expenditures: 5.7% of GDP (1996)

Education Expenditures: n.a.

External Debt: $2.111 billion total (1996)

Exports: $615 million (1996 est.); commodities: timber, garments, rubber, soybeans, sesame; partners: Singapore, Japan, Thailand, Hong Kong, Indonesia, Malaysia, US

Imports: $1 billion (1996 est.); commodities: cigarettes, construction matierals, petroleum products, machinery, motor vehicles; partners: Singapore, Vietnam, Japan, Australia, Hong Kong, Indonesia

■ COMMUNICATIONS

Daily Newspapers: 0 (1996)

Televisions: 8.8/1,000 inhabitants (1996)

Radios: 127/1,000 inhabitants (1996)

Telephones: 0.1/100 inhabitants (1996 est.)

■ TRANSPORTATION

Motor Vehicles: n.a.

Roads: 35,769 km, but some roads are in serious disrepair; 4,165 km paved

Railway: 603 km, much inoperational since 1973

Air Traffic: n.a.

Airports: 20; 7 have paved runways (1997 est.)

Canadian Embassy: The Canadian Embassy, Villa 9, Senei Vinnavaut Oum, Chaktamouk, Daun Penh District, Phnom Penh. Tel: (011-855-23) 426-000. Fax: (011-855-23) 211-389.

Embassy in Canada: n.a.

Cameroon

Long-Form Name: Republic of Cameroon

Capital: Yaoundé

■ GEOGRAPHY

Area: 475,440 sq. km

Coastline: 402 km

Climate: varies with terrain from tropical along coast to semi-arid and hot in north

Environment: recent volcanic activity with release of poisonous gases; deforestation; overgrazing; desertification; diseases transmitted through the water supply are common

Terrain: coastal plain in southwest, dissected plateau in centre, mountains in west, plains in north

Land Use: 13% arable land; 2% permanent crops; 4% meadows and pastures; 78% forest and woodland; 3% other, includes negligible irrigated

Location: WC Africa, bordering on South Atlantic Ocean

■ PEOPLE

Population: 15,029,433 (July 1998 est.)

Nationality: Cameroonian

Age Structure: 0-14 yrs: 46%; 15-64: 51%; 65+: 3% (1998 est.)

Population Growth Rate: 2.81% (1998 est.)

Net Migration: 0 migrants/1,000 population (1998 est.)

Ethnic Groups: over 200 tribes of widely differing background; 31% Cameroon Highlanders, 19% Equatorial Bantu, 11% Kirdi, 10% Fulani, 8% Northwestern Bantu, 7% Eastern Nigritic, 13% other African, less than 1% non-African

Languages: English and French (official), 24 major African language groups, including Fang, Bamileke, Duala

Religions: 51% indigenous beliefs, 33% Christian, 16% Muslim

Birth Rate: 42.06/1,000 population (1998 est.)

Death Rate: 13.98/1,000 population (1998 est.)

Infant Mortality: 76.88 deaths/1,000 live births (1998 est.)

Life Expectancy at Birth: 49.9 years male, 53.03 years female (1998 est.)
Total Fertility Rate: 5.86 children born/woman (1998 est.)
Literacy: 63.4% (1997 est.)

■ GOVERNMENT

Leader(s): Pres. Paul Biya, Prime Min. Peter Mafany Musonge
Government Type: unitary republic; multi-party presidential regime (opposition parties legalized in 1990)
Administrative Divisions: 10 provinces
Nationhood: Jan. 1, 1960 (from UN trusteeship under French administration; Cameroon formerly known as French Cameroon)
National Holiday: National Day, May 20

■ ECONOMY

Overview: an offshore oil industry has boosted the economy but the government is now emphasizing diversification, particularly in agriculture
GDP: $30.9 billion, per capita $2,100; real growth rate 5% (1997 est.)
Inflation: -1.2% (Mar. 1998)
Industries: accounts for 27% of GDP; crude oil products, small aluminum plant, food processing, light consumer goods industries, textiles, sawmills
Labour Force: 6.1 million (1997 est.); 74% agriculture, 4.5% industry, 21.5% services
Unemployment: n.a.
Agriculture: the agriculture and forestry sectors provide employment for the majority of the population, contributing 32% to GDP and providing a high degree of self-sufficiency in staple foods
Natural Resources: crude oil, bauxite, iron ore, timber, hydroelectricity potential

■ FINANCE/TRADE

Currency: Communauté financière africaine franc (CFAF) = 100 centimes
International Reserves Excluding Gold: $1 million (May 1998)
Gold Reserves: 0.03 million fine troy ounces (June 1998)
Budget: revenues $2.23 billion; expenditures $2.23 billion, including capital expenditures of n.a. (1997 est.)
Defence Expenditures: 12.24% of total govt. expenditure (1995)
Education Expenditures: 14.62% of govt. expenditure (1995)
External Debt: $9.515 billion (1996)
Exports: $1.861 billion (1997); commodities: petroleum products 56%, coffee, cocoa, timber, manufacturing; partners: European Community 50%, US 3%
Imports: $1.359 million (1997); commodities: machines and electrical equipment, transport equipment, chemical products, consumer goods; partners: France 42%, Japan 7%, US 4%

■ COMMUNICATIONS

Daily Newspapers: 2 (1996)
Televisions: 29/1,000 inhabitants (1996)
Radios: 162/1,000 inhabitants (1996)
Telephones: 0.4/100 inhabitants (1996 est.)

■ TRANSPORTATION

Motor Vehicles: 153,000; 92,000 passenger cars (1997 est.)
Roads: 34,300 km; 4,288 km paved
Railway: 1,104 km (1995 est.)
Air Traffic: 362,000 passengers carried (1996)
Airports: 52; 11 have paved runways (1997 est.)

Canadian Embassy: The Consulate of Canada, c/o PRO-PME, 1726 avenue de Gaulle, Bonanjo, Douala. mailing address: P.O. Box 2373, Douala, Cameroon. Tel: (011-237) 22-19-36. Гах. (011-237) 22 10 90.
Embassy in Canada: High Commission for the Republic of Cameroon, 170 Clemow Ave, Ottawa ON K1S 2B4. Tel: (613) 236-1522. Fax: (613) 236-3385.

Canada

Long-Form Name: Canada
Capital: Ottawa

■ GEOGRAPHY

Area: 9,976,140 sq. km
Coastline: 243,791 km
Climate: varies from temperate in south to subarctic and arctic in north
Environment: 80% of population concentrated within 160 km of US border; permafrost in north a serious obstacle to development; acid rain and ocean-water pollution resulting from industrial and agricultural activities are an increasing problem
Terrain: mostly plains with mountains in west and lowlands in southeast
Land Use: 5% arable land; negligible permanent crops; 3% meadows and pastures; 54% forest and woodland; 38% other, includes negligible irrigated
Location: N North America, bordering on North Atlantic Ocean, Arctic Ocean, North Pacific Ocean

■ PEOPLE

Population: 30,675,398 (July 1998 est.)
Nationality: Canadian
Age Structure: 0-14 yrs: 20%; 15-64: 68%; 65+: 12% (1998 est.)
Population Growth Rate: 1.09% (1998 est.)
Net Migration: 6.03 migrants/1,000 population (1998 est.)
Ethnic Groups: 40% British, 27% French, 20% other European, 11.5% other, 1.5% Aboriginal
Languages: English and French (both official)
Religions: 45% Roman Catholic, 12% United Church, 8% Anglican, 35% other
Birth Rate: 12.12/1,000 population (1998 est.)
Death Rate: 7.25/1,000 population (1998 est.)
Infant Mortality: 5.59 deaths/1,000 live births (1998 est.)
Life Expectancy at Birth: 75.86 years male, 82.63 years female (1998 est.)
Total Fertility Rate: 1.65 children born/woman (1998 est.)
Literacy: 97% (1997 est.)

■ GOVERNMENT

Leader(s): Queen Elizabeth II/Gov. Gen. Adrienne Clarkson, Prime Min. Jean Chrétien
Government Type: confederation with parliamentary democracy
Administrative Divisions: 10 provinces, 3 territories
Nationhood: July 1, 1867 (from UK)
National Holiday: Canada Day, July 1

■ ECONOMY

Overview: abundant natural resources, skilled labour force, and high-tech industrialization characterize a market-oriented economy. Slower economic growth has been emphasized by high unemployment and a large public sector debt in the 1990s
GDP: $658 billion, per capita $21,700; real growth rate 3.5% (1997 est.)
Inflation: 1.1% (June 1998)
Industries: accounts for 31% of GDP; processsed and unprocessed minerals, food products, wood and paper products, transportation equipment, chemicals, fish products, petroleum, natural gas
Labour Force: 16.2 million (1997 est.); 31.8% community, social and business services, 23.5% trade and tourism, 14.5% manufacturing
Unemployment: 8.6% (Dec. 1997)
Agriculture: accounts for 3% of GDP; one of the world's major producers and exporters of grain (wheat and barley); key source of US agricultural imports; large forest resources cover 35% of total land area

Natural Resources: nickel, zinc, copper, gold, lead, molybdenum, potash, silver, fish, timber, wildlife, coal, crude oil, natural gas

■ FINANCE/TRADE

Currency: dollar ($ or $Can) = 100 cents
International Reserves Excluding Gold: $23.324 billion (Jan. 1999)
Gold Reserves: 2.487 million fine troy ounces (Jan. 1999)
Budget: revenues $106.5 billion; expenditures $117.2 billion, capital expenditures $1.7 billion (1996)
Defence Expenditures: 1.2% of GDP (1997-98)
Education Expenditures: 7.3% of GNP (1995)
External Debt: $253 billion (1996)
Exports: $211.396 billion (1998 est.); commodities: newsprint, wood pulp, timber, grain, crude petroleum, natural gas, ferrous and nonferrous ores, motor vehicles; partners: US, Japan, UK, Germany, other European Community, former USSR countries
Imports: $198.444 billion (1998 est.); commodities: processed foods, beverages, crude petroleum, chemicals, industrial machinery, motor vehicles, durable consumer goods, electronic computers; partners: US, Japan, UK, Germany, other European Community, Taiwan, S Korea, Mexico

■ COMMUNICATIONS

Daily Newspapers: 107 (1996)
Televisions: 714/1,000 inhabitants (1996)
Radios: 1,078/1,000 inhabitants (1996)
Telephones: 60.2/100 inhabitants (1996 est.)

■ TRANSPORTATION

Motor Vehicles: 17,200,000; 13,600,000 passenger cars (1997 est.)
Roads: 1,021,000 km; 358,371 km paved
Railway: 72,963 km
Air Traffic: 22,856,000 passengers carried (1996)
Airports: 1,393; 515 have paved runways (1997 est.)

Canadian Embassy: n.a.
Embassy in Canada: n.a.

Cape Verde

Long-Form Name: Republic of Cape Verde
Capital: Praia

■ GEOGRAPHY

Area: 4,030 sq. km
Coastline: 965 km
Climate: temperate; warm, dry, very erratic summer precipitation

Environment: subject to prolonged droughts; harmattan wind can obscure visibility; volcanically and seismically active; deforestation; desertification; overgrazing and overfishing
Terrain: steep, rugged, rocky, volcanic
Land Use: 11% arable land; negligible permanent crops; 6% meadows and pastures; negligible forest and woodland; 83% other, includes negligible irrigated
Location: Atlantic Ocean W of Africa

■ PEOPLE

Population: 399,857 (July 1998 est.)
Nationality: Cape Verdean
Age Structure: 0-14 yrs: 46%; 15-64: 48%; 65+: 6% (1998 est.)
Population Growth Rate: 1.49% (1998 est.)
Net Migration: -12.54 migrants/1,000 population (1998 est.)
Ethnic Groups: approx. 71% Creole (mulatto), 28% African, 1% European
Languages: Portuguese and Crioulo, a blend of Portuguese and West African tongues
Religions: Roman Catholicism fused with indigenous beliefs
Birth Rate: 34.47/1,000 population (1998 est.)
Death Rate: 7.04/1,000 population (1998 est.)
Infant Mortality: 47.53 deaths/1,000 live births (1998 est.)
Life Expectancy at Birth: 67.21 years male, 73.89 years female (1998 est.)
Total Fertility Rate: 5.08 children born/woman (1998 est.)
Literacy: 71.6% (1997 est.)

■ GOVERNMENT

Leader(s): Pres. Antonio Mascarenhas Monteiro, Prime Min. Carlos Alberto Wahnon de Carvalho Veiga
Government Type: republic
Administrative Divisions: 14 districts
Nationhood: July 5, 1975 (from Portugal)
National Holiday: Independence Day, July 5

■ ECONOMY

Overview: a service-oriented economy, which suffers from a poor natural resource base, a high birth rate and a long-term drought
GDP: $538 million, per capita $1,370; real growth rate 4.5% (1997 est.)
Inflation: 6.5% (1996)
Industries: accounts for 18% of GDP, fish processing, salt mining, clothing factories, ship repair, construction materials, food and beverage production
Labour Force: n.a.; 52% agriculture (mostly subsistence), 25% services, 23% industry

Unemployment: n.a.
Agriculture: accounts for 8% of GDP; largely subsistence farming; bananas are the only export crop; annual food imports required; growth potential limited by poor soils and limited rainfall. Approximately 90% of food needs must be imported
Natural Resources: salt, basalt rock, pozzolana, limestone, kaolin, fish

■ FINANCE/TRADE

Currency: Cape Verdean escudo (C.V. Esc.) = 100 centavos
International Reserves Excluding Gold: $33 million (June 1998)
Gold Reserves: n.a.
Budget: revenues $253.7 million; expenditures $276 million, including capital expenditures of n.a. (1997 est.)
Defence Expenditures: 2.2% of GDP (1997 est.)
Education Expenditures: n.a.
External Debt: $211 million (1996)
Exports: $8.4 million (1995); commodities: fish, bananas, salt; partners: Portugal, Angola, Algeria, Belgium/Luxembourg, Italy
Imports: $238 million (1995); commodities: petroleum, foodstuffs, consumer goods, industrial products; partners: Portugal, Netherlands, Spain, France, US, Germany

■ COMMUNICATIONS

Daily Newspapers: 0 (1996)
Televisions: 3.7/1,000 inhabitants (1996)
Radios: 179/1,000 inhabitants (1996)
Telephones: 6.1/100 inhabitants (1996 est.)

■ TRANSPORTATION

Motor Vehicles: 18,000; 11,000 passenger cars (1997 est.)
Roads: 1,100 km; 858 km paved
Railway: none
Air Traffic: 129,000 passengers carried (1996)
Airports: 6; all have paved runways (1997 est.)

Canadian Embassy: c/o The Canadian Embassy, P.O. Box 3373, Dakar, Senegal. Tel: (011-221) 823-92-90. Fax: (011-221) 823-87-49.
Embassy in Canada: c/o Embassy of the Republic of Cape Verde, 3415 Massachusetts Ave NW, Washington DC 20007, USA. Tel: (202) 965-6820. Fax: (202) 965-1207.

Cayman Islands

Long-Form Name: Cayman Islands
Capital: George Town (on Grand Cayman Island)

■ GEOGRAPHY

Area: 260 sq. km (three islands: Grand Cayman, Little Cayman, Cayman Brac)
Climate: tropical maritime; warm, rainy summers (May to Oct.); cool season: Nov. to March, hurricane-prone July to Nov.
Land Use: 0% arable, 0% permanent crops; 8% meadows and pastures; 23% forest and woodland; 69% other
Location: Caribbean Sea, S of Cuba

■ PEOPLE

Population: 37,716 (July 1998 est.)
Nationality: Caymanian
Ethnic Groups: 40% mixed, 20% white, 20% black, 20% expatriates of various ethnic groups, various Hispanic strains, descendants of European settlers
Languages: English (official)

■ GOVERNMENT

Colony Territory of: United Kingdom Crown Colony
Leader(s): Chief of State: Queen Elizabeth II, Gov. Peter John Smith; Chief Sec. James Ryan
Government Type: United Kingdom Crown Colony
National Holiday: Constitution Day (first Monday in July)

■ ECONOMY

Overview: chiefly tourism (70% of GDP and 75% of export earnings) and financial services; main export turtle products; imports: foodstuffs, (about 90% of food and consumer goods must be imported), manufactured items, textiles, building materials, cars, petroleum products

■ FINANCE/TRADE

Currency: Caymanian dollar (CI$)

Canadian Embassy: c/o The Canadian High Commission, Macdonald House, 1 Grosvenor Square, London W1X 0AB, England, UK. Tel: (011-44-171) 258-6600. Fax: (011-44-171) 258-6333.
Representative to Canada: British High Commission, 80 Elgin St, Ottawa ON K1P 5K7. Tel: (613) 237-1530. Fax: (613) 237-7980.

Central African Republic

Long-Form Name: Central African Republic
Capital: Bangui

■ GEOGRAPHY

Area: 622,980 sq. km
Coastline: none: landlocked
Climate: tropical; hot, dry winters; mild to hot, wet summers
Environment: hot, dry, dusty harmattan winds affect northern areas; poaching has diminished reputation as one of last great wildlife refuges; desertification and flooding; tap water is not safe to drink
Terrain: vast, flat to rolling, monotonous plateau; scattered hills in northeast and southwest
Land Use: 3% arable land; negligible permanent crops; 5% meadows and pastures; 75% forest and woodland; 17% other
Location: C Africa

■ PEOPLE

Population: 3,375,771 (July 1998 est.)
Nationality: Central African
Age Structure: 0-14 yrs: 44%; 15-64: 52%; 65+: 4% (1998 est.)
Population Growth Rate: 2.02% (1998 est.)
Net Migration: -1.78 migrants/1,000 population (1998 est.)
Ethnic Groups: about 80 ethnic groups, the majority of which have related ethnic and linguistic characteristics; 34% Baya, 27% Banda, 10% Sara, 21% Mandjia, 4% Mboum, 4% m'Baka; 6,500 Europeans, of whom 3,600 are French
Languages: French (official); Sangho (lingua franca and national language); Arabic, Hunsa, Swahili
Religions: 25% indigenous beliefs, 25% Protestant, 25% Roman Catholic, 15% Muslim, 10% other; animistic beliefs and practices strongly influence the Christian majority
Birth Rate: 38.72/1,000 population (1998 est.)
Death Rate: 16.75/1,000 population (1998 est.)
Infant Mortality: 105.73 deaths/1,000 live births (1998 est.)
Life Expectancy at Birth: 45.02 years male, 48.68 years female (1998 est.)
Total Fertility Rate: 5.12 children born/woman (1998 est.)
Literacy: 60% (1997 est.)

■ GOVERNMENT

Leader(s): Pres. Ange Felix Patassé, Prime Min. Michel Gbezzera-Bria
Government Type: republic
Administrative Divisions: 14 prefectures, 2 economic prefectures, 1 capital commune
Nationhood: Aug. 13, 1960 (from France; formerly known as Central African Empire)
National Holiday: National Day (proclamation of the republic), Dec. 1

■ ECONOMY

Overview: subsistence agriculture and forestry are the backbone of the economy. It suffers from a poor transportation infrastructure and a weak human resource base; diamond industry accounts for 54% of export earnings

GDP: $3.3 billion, per capita $1,000; real growth rate n.a. (1997 est.)

Inflation: 0.5% (Feb. 1998)

Industries: accounts for 13% of GDP; sawmills, breweries, diamond mining, textiles, footwear, assembly of bicycles and motorcycles

Labour Force: 2 million (1997 est.); 32.6% construction industries, 30.5% manufacturing, 17.6% agriculture

Unemployment: n.a.

Agriculture: accounts for 44% of GDP; self-sufficient in food production except for grain; commercial crops—cotton, coffee, tobacco, timber; food crops—manioc, yams, millet, corn, bananas

Natural Resources: diamonds, uranium, timber, gold, oil

■ FINANCE/TRADE

Currency: Communauté financière africaine franc (CFAF) = 100 centimes

International Reserves Excluding Gold: $146 million (Dec. 1998)

Gold Reserves: 0.011 million fine troy ounces (June 1998)

Budget: n.a.

Defence Expenditures: 2.4% of GDP (1996)

Education Expenditures: n.a.

External Debt: $928 million (1996)

Exports: $235 million (1997 est.); commodities: diamonds, cotton, coffee, timber, tobacco; partners: France, Belgium, Italy, Japan, US

Imports: $291 million (1997 est.); commodities: food, textiles, petroleum products, machinery, electrical equipment, motor vehicles, chemicals, pharmaceuticals, consumer goods, industrial products; partners: France, other European Community, Japan, Algeria, former Yugoslavia

■ COMMUNICATIONS

Daily Newspapers: 3 (1996)

Televisions: 4.5/1,000 inhabitants (1996)

Radios: 84/1,000 inhabitants (1996)

Telephones: 0.2/100 inhabitants (1996 est.)

■ TRANSPORTATION

Motor Vehicles: 20,000; 11,000 passenger cars (1997 est.)

Roads: 23,810 km; 429 km paved

Railway: none

Air Traffic: 75,000 passengers carried (1996)

Airports: 52; 3 have paved runways (1997 est.)

Canadian Embassy: The Canadian High Commission, P.O. Box 572, Yaounde, Cameroon. Tel: (011-236) 61-09-73. Fax: (011-236) 61-40-74.

Embassy in Canada: c/o Embassy of the Central African Republic, 1618-22nd St NW, Washington DC 20008, USA. Tel: (202) 483-7800.

Chad

Long-Form Name: Republic of Chad

Capital: N'Djamena

■ GEOGRAPHY

Area: 1,284,000 sq. km

Coastline: none: landlocked

Climate: tropical in south, desert in north

Environment: hot, dry, dusty harmattan winds occur in north; drought and desertification adversely affecting south; subject to plagues of locusts; unsafe water supply

Terrain: broad, arid plains in centre, desert in north, mountains in northwest, lowlands in south

Land Use: 3% arable land; negligible permanent crops; 36% meadows and pastures; 26% forest and woodland; 35% others, includes negligible irrigated

Location: NC Africa

■ PEOPLE

Population: 7,359,512 (July 1998 est.)

Nationality: Chadian

Age Structure: 0-14 yrs: 44%; 15-64: 53%; 65+: 3% (1998 est.)

Population Growth Rate: 2.66% (1998 est.)

Net Migration: 0 migrants/1,000 population (1998 est.)

Ethnic Groups: some 200 distinct ethnic groups, most of whom are Muslims in the north and centre, and non-Muslims in the south; some 150,000 non-indigenous, of whom 1,000 are French

Languages: French and Arabic (official); Sara and Sango in south; more than 100 different languages and dialects are spoken

Religions: 50% Muslim, 25% Christian, 25% animism

Birth Rate: 43.45/1,000 population (1998 est.)

Death Rate: 16.86/1,000 population (1998 est.)

Infant Mortality: 116.97 deaths/1,000 live births (1998 est.)

Life Expectancy at Birth: 45.81 years male, 50.73 years female (1998 est.)
Total Fertility Rate: 5.74 children born/woman (1998 est.)
Literacy: 48.1% (1997 est.)

■ GOVERNMENT

Leader(s): Pres. Col. Idriss Deby, Prime Min. Nassour Guelengdouksia Ouaidou
Government Type: republic
Administrative Divisions: 14 prefectures
Nationhood: Aug. 11, 1960 (from France)
National Holiday: Independence Day, Aug. 11

■ ECONOMY

Overview: Chad is one of the world's most underdeveloped countries; civil war, drought and food shortages have adversely affected the economy, which is based on subsistence farming and fishing
GDP: $4.3 billion, per capita $600; real growth rate 5.5% (1997 est.)
Inflation: 1.7% (1997)
Industries: accounts for 18% of GDP, cotton textile mills, slaughterhouses, soap, cigarettes, brewery, natron (sodium carbonate), construction materials
Labour Force: 3.1 million (1997 est.); 42.3% manufacturing, 19.1% community, social and business services, 8.0% transportation and communication
Unemployment: n.a.
Agriculture: accounts for 48% of GDP; largely subsistence farming; cotton most important cash crop; food crops include sorghum, millet, peanuts, rice, potatoes, manioc; livestock— cattle, sheep, goats, camels; self-sufficient in food in years of adequate rainfall
Natural Resources: small quantities of crude oil (unexploited but exploration beginning), uranium, natron, kaolin, fish (Lake Chad)

■ FINANCE/TRADE

Currency: Communauté financière africaine franc (CFAF) = 100 centimes
International Reserves Excluding Gold: $97 million (May 1998)
Gold Reserves: 0.011 million fine troy ounces (June 1998)
Budget: revenues $198 million; expenditures $218 million, including capital expenditures of $146 million (1998 est.)
Defence Expenditures: 2.7% of GDP (1996)
Education Expenditures: 2.2% of GNP (1995)
External Debt: $997 million (1996)
Exports: $252 million (1995); commodities: cotton 43%, cattle 35%, textiles 5%, fish; partners: France, Nigeria, Cameroon

Imports: $220 million (1995); commodities: machinery and transportation equipment 39%, industrial goods 20%, petroleum products 13%, foodstuffs 9%; partners: US, France

■ COMMUNICATIONS

Daily Newspapers: 1 (1996)
Televisions: 1.4/1,000 inhabitants (1996)
Radios: 249/1,000 inhabitants (1996)
Telephones: 0.1/100 inhabitants (1996 est.)

■ TRANSPORTATION

Motor Vehicles: 24,600; 10,000 passenger cars (1997 est.)
Roads: 32,700 km; 262 km paved
Railway: none
Air Traffic: 93,000 passengers carried (1996)
Airports: 53; 6 have paved runways (1997 est.)

Canadian Embassy: c/o The Canadian Embassy, Édifice Stamatiades, Place de l'Hôtel de Ville, Yaoundé; mailing address: CP 572, Yaoundé, Cameroon. Tel: (011-237) 22-19-36. Fax: (011-237) 22-10-90.
Embassy in Canada: c/o Embassy of the Republic of Chad, 2002 R St NW, Washington DC 20009, USA. Tel: (202) 462-4009. Fax: (202) 265-1937.

Channel Islands

Long-Form Name: Channel Islands; Guernsey: Bailiwick of Guernsey; Jersey: Bailiwick of Jersey
Capital: St. Helier (Jersey), St. Peter Port (Guernsey)

■ GEOGRAPHY

Area: Jersey: 117 sq. km; Guernsey: 194 sq. km
Climate: temperate, with mild winters and cool summers
Land Use: Jersey: 57% arable, remainder n.a.; Guernsey: n.a.
Location: English Channel, off the coast of France

■ PEOPLE

Population: Jersey: 89,136; Guernsey: 64,555 (July 1998 est.)
Nationality: Channel Islander
Ethnic Groups: English, French
Languages: English (official), French (official only on Jersey), Norman-French dialect

■ GOVERNMENT

Colony Territory of: Dependent Territory of the United Kingdom

Leader(s): Head of State: Queen Elizabeth II; Jersey: Lt. Gov. and Commander-in-Chief Air Marshal Sir Michael Wilkes, Guernsey: Lt. Gov. and Commander-in-Chief Sir John Coward
Government Type: largely self-governing British Crown dependency
National Holiday: Liberation Day, May 9

■ ECONOMY

Overview: Jersey: economy is based chiefly on financial services, agriculture and tourism, vegetable and flower exports, Jersey cattle; Guernsey: tourism, financial services, Guernsey cattle, and tomato and flower exports make up backbone of the economy

■ FINANCE/TRADE

Currency: Jersey pound, Guernsey pound, both = 100 pence; both are at par with the British pound

Canadian Embassy: c/o The Canadian High Commission, Macdonald House, 1 Grosvenor Square, London W1X 0AB, England, UK. Tel: (011-44-171) 258-6600. Fax: (011-44-171) 258-6333.
Representative to Canada: c/o British High Commission, 80 Elgin St, Ottawa ON K1P 5K7. Tel: (613) 237-1530. Fax: (613) 237-7980.

Chile

Long-Form Name: Republic of Chile
Capital: Santiago

■ GEOGRAPHY

Area: 756,950 sq. km
Coastline: 6,435 km
Climate: temperate; desert in north; cool and damp in south
Environment: subject to severe earthquakes, active volcanism, tsunami; Atacama Desert one of world's driest regions; desertification; deforestation; air and water pollution
Terrain: low coastal mountains; fertile central valley; rugged Andes in east
Land Use: 5% arable land; negligible permanent crops; 18% meadows and pastures; 22% forest and woodland; 55% other, includes 1.5% irrigated
Location: SW South America

■ PEOPLE

Population: 14,787,781 (July 1998 est.)
Nationality: Chilean
Age Structure: 0-14 yrs: 28%; 15-64: 65%; 65+: 7% (1998 est.)

Population Growth Rate: 1.27% (1998 est.)
Net Migration: 0 migrants/1,000 population (1998 est.)
Ethnic Groups: 95% European and European-Indian, 3% Indian, 2% other
Languages: Spanish
Religions: 89% Roman Catholic, 11% Protestant and small Jewish population
Birth Rate: 18.28/1,000 population (1998 est.)
Death Rate: 5.55/1,000 population (1998 est.)
Infant Mortality: 10.39 deaths/1,000 live births (1998 est.)
Life Expectancy at Birth: 72.01 years male, 78.48 years female (1998 est.)
Total Fertility Rate: 2.3 children born/woman (1998 est.)
Literacy: 95.2% (1997 est.)

■ GOVERNMENT

Leader(s): Pres. Eduardo Frei Ruiz-Tagle
Government Type: republic
Administrative Divisions: 13 regions
Nationhood: Sept. 18, 1810 (from Spain)
National Holiday: Independence Day, Sept. 18

■ ECONOMY

Overview: copper is the single largest export in this economy, which has benefited from growth in industry, agriculture and construction
GDP: $168.5 billion, per capita $11,600; real growth rate 7.1% (1997 est.)
Inflation: 5.3% (July 1998)
Industries: accounts for 33% of GDP; copper (Chile is the world's largest producer and exporter of copper), other minerals, foodstuffs, fish processing, iron and steel, wood and wood products, transport equipment, textiles, cement
Labour Force: 6.1 million (1997); 24.79 community, social and business services, 18.6% trade and tourism, 16.6% agriculture
Unemployment: 6.8% (Aug. 1998)
Agriculture: accounts for about 8% of GDP (including fishing and forestry); major exporter of fruit, fish and timber products; major crops—wheat, corn, grapes, beans, sugar beets, potatoes, fruit; net agricultural importer
Natural Resources: copper, timber, iron ore, nitrates, precious metals, molybdenum

■ FINANCE/TRADE

Currency: peso ($CH) = 100 centavos
International Reserves Excluding Gold: $15.119 billion (Jan. 1999)
Gold Reserves: 1.222 million fine troy ounces (Jan. 1999)
Budget: revenues $17 billion; expenditures $17 billion, including capital expenditures n.a. (1996 est.)

Defence Expenditures: 3.5% of GDP (1997)
Education Expenditures: 15.98% of govt. expenditure (1997)
External Debt: $26.7 billion (1997 est.)
Exports: $14.895 billion (1998); commodities: copper 48%, industrial products 33%, molybdenum, iron ore, wood pulp, fishmeal, fruit; partners: European Community 34%, US 22%, Japan 10%, Brazil 7%
Imports: $18.828 billion (1998); commodities: petroleum, wheat, capital goods, spare parts, raw materials; partners: European Community 23%, US 20%, Japan 10%, Brazil 9%

■ COMMUNICATIONS

Daily Newspapers: 52 (1996)
Televisions: 215/1,000 inhabitants (1996)
Radios: 354/1,000 inhabitants (1996)
Telephones: 14.9/100 inhabitants (1996 est.)

■ TRANSPORTATION

Motor Vehicles: 1,375,000; 900,000 passenger cars (1997 est.)
Roads: 79,800 km; 11,012 km paved
Railway: 6,782 km
Air Traffic: 3,621,900 passengers carried (1996)
Airports: 380; 52 have paved runways (1997 est.)

Canadian Embassy: The Canadian Embassy, 12th Fl., Nueva Tajamar 481, Santiago, Chile; mailing address: Casilla 139-10, Santiago, Chile. Tel: (011-56-2) 362-9660. Fax: (011-56-2) 362-9661.
Embassy in Canada: Embassy of the Republic of Chile, 50 O'Connor St, Ste 1413, Ottawa ON K1P 6L2. Tel: (613) 235-9940. Fax: (613) 235-1176.

China

Long-Form Name: People's Republic of China
Capital: Beijing

■ GEOGRAPHY

Area: 9,596,960 sq. km
Coastline: 14,500 km
Climate: extremely diverse; tropical in south to subarctic in north
Environment: frequent typhoons (about five times per year along southern and eastern coasts), damaging floods, tsunamis, earthquakes; deforestation; soil erosion; industrial pollution; water and air pollution; desertification; lack of safe drinking water
Terrain: mostly mountains, high plateaus, deserts in west; plains, deltas and hills in east
Land Use: 10% arable land; negligible permanent crops; 43% meadows and pastures; 14% forest and woodland; 33% other; includes 5% irrigated
Location: SE Asia, bordering on South China Sea, Yellow Sea

■ PEOPLE

Population: 1,236,914,658 (July 1998 est.)
Nationality: Chinese
Age Structure: 0-14 yrs: 26%; 15-64: 68%; 65+: 6% (1998 est.)
Population Growth Rate: 0.83% (1998 est.)
Net Migration: -0.41 migrants/1,000 population (1998 est.)
Ethnic Groups: 91.9% Han Chinese; 8.1% Zhuang, Uigur, Hui, Yi, Tibetan, Miao, Manchu, Mongol, Buyi, Korean and other nationalities
Languages: Standard Chinese (Putonghua) or Mandarin (based on the Beijing dialect), Yue (Cantonese), Wu (Shanghainese), Minbei (Fuzhou), Minnan. The Tibetans, Uigurs, Mongols, and others have their own languages
Religions: officially atheist, but traditionally pragmatic and eclectic; Confucianism, Taoism and Buddhism; approx. 2–3% Muslim, 1% Christian
Birth Rate: 15.73/1,000 population (1998 est.)
Death Rate: 6.99/1,000 population (1998 est.)
Infant Mortality: 45.46 deaths/1,000 live births (1998 est.)
Life Expectancy at Birth: 68.32 years male, 71.06 years female (1998 est.)
Total Fertility Rate: 1.8 children born/woman (1998 est.)
Literacy: 81.5% (1997 est.)

■ GOVERNMENT

Leader(s): Pres. Jiang Zemin, Prem. Zhu Rongji
Government Type: Communist Party-led state
Administrative Divisions: 23 provinces, 5 autonomous regions, 4 government-controlled municipalities
Nationhood: People's Republic established Oct. 1, 1949
National Holiday: National Day, Oct. 1

■ ECONOMY

Overview: the Soviet-style, centrally planned economy has been recently altered to include increased local authority which has led to greater production; population control is vital but has been weakened by popular resistance and loss of authority by rural cadres. Decentralization of the economic system is slowly progressing
GDP: $4.25 trillion, per capita $3,460; real growth rate 8.8% (1997 est.)

Inflation: -1.3% (June 1998)
Industries: accounts for 49% of GDP; iron, steel, coal, machine building, armaments, textiles, petroleum, chemical fertilizer, cement, consumer durables, food processing
Labour Force: 730 million (1997 est.); 60% agriculture, 17.1% industry, 6.9% community, social and business services
Unemployment: 4.3% (May 1998)
Agriculture: accounts for almost 20% of GDP; among the world's largest producers of rice, potatoes, sorghum, peanuts, tea, millet, barley and pork; commercial crops include cotton, other fibres and oilseeds; produces variety of livestock products; self-sufficient in food
Natural Resources: coal, iron ore, crude oil, mercury, tin, tungsten, antimony, manganese, molybdenum, vanadium, magnetite, aluminum, lead, zinc, uranium, world's greatest hydroelectricity potential

■ FINANCE/TRADE

Currency: yuan (¥), pl. yen; = 10 jiao
International Reserves Excluding Gold: $149.208 billion (Jan. 1999)
Gold Reserves: 12.7 million fine troy ounces (Jan. 1999)
Budget: n.a.
Defence Expenditures: 13.23% of total govt. expenditure (1996)
Education Expenditures: 2.08% of govt. expenditure (1996)
External Debt: $131 billion (1997 est.)
Exports: $22.062 billion (1997); commodities: manufactured goods, agricultural products, oilseeds, grain (rice and corn), oil, minerals; partners: US, Japan, former USSR countries, Singapore, Germany
Imports: $17.154 billion (1997); commodities: grain (mostly wheat), chemical fertilizer, steel, industrial raw materials, machinery, equipment; partners: Japan, US, Germany, former USSR countries

■ COMMUNICATIONS

Daily Newspapers: 39 (1996)
Televisions: 319/1,000 inhabitants (1996)
Radios: 195/1,000 inhabitants (1996)
Telephones: 4.4/100 inhabitants (1996 est.)

■ TRANSPORTATION

Motor Vehicles: 11,450,000; 4,700,000 passenger cars (1997 est.)
Roads: 1,180,000 km; 241,300 km paved
Railway: 64,900 km
Air Traffic: 45,465,000 passengers carried (1996)
Airports: 206; 192 have paved runways (1996)

Canadian Embassy: The Canadian Embassy, 19 Dong Zhi Men Wai St, Chao Yang District, Beijing 100600, People's Republic of China. Tel: (011-86-10) 6532-3536. Fax (011-86-10) 6532-4311.
Embassy in Canada: Embassy of the People's Republic of China, 515 St. Patrick St, Ottawa ON K1N 5H3. Tel: (613) 789-3434. Fax: (613) 789-1911.

Christmas Island

Long-Form Name: Territory of Christmas Island
Capital: The Settlement

■ GEOGRAPHY

Area: 135 sq. km (land area); includes one of the largest coral islands in the Pacific
Climate: tropical, with little seasonal variation; heat and humidity moderated by trade winds
Land Use: dry sandy soil does not permit much cultivation
Location: SE Asia, between Australia and Indonesia

■ PEOPLE

Population: 2,195 (July 1998 est.)
Nationality: Christmas Islander
Ethnic Groups: 61% Chinese, 25% Malay, 11% European, 3% other. There is no indigenous population
Languages: English, Chinese, Oriental and European-speaking minorities

■ GOVERNMENT

Colony Territory of: Dependent Territory of Australia
Leader(s): Chief of State: Queen Elizabeth II; Administrator Bill Taylor appointed byAustralian Commonwealth govt.
Government Type: dependency of Australia
National Holiday: n.a.

■ ECONOMY

Overview: extraction and export of rock phosphate dust was the only significant economic activity until 1987, when the mine was closed. It was reopened in 1990.

■ FINANCE/TRADE

Currency: Australian dollar = 100 cents

Canadian Embassy: c/o The Canadian High Commission, Commonwealth Ave, Canberra A.C.T. 2600, Australia. Tel: (011-61-2) 6273-3844. Fax: (011-61-2) 6273-3285

Representative to Canada: c/o Australian High Commission, 50 O'Connor St, Ste 710, Ottawa ON K1P 6L2. Tel: (613) 236-0841. Fax: (613) 236-4376.

Cocos (Keeling) Islands

Long-Form Name: Territory of Cocos (Keeling) Islands
Capital: West Island

■ GEOGRAPHY

Area: 14.2 sq. km
Climate: tropical maritime modified by southeast trade wind for 9 months of the year; moderate rainfall
Land Use: primarily subsistence agriculture
Location: Indian Ocean, SW of Sumatra

■ PEOPLE

Population: 637 (July 1998 est.)
Nationality: Cocos Islander
Ethnic Groups: West Island: Europeans; Home Island: Cocos Malays
Languages: English, Malay

■ GOVERNMENT

Colony Territory of: Dependent Territory of Australia
Leader(s): Chief of State: Queen Elizabeth II; Administrator Bill Taylor (appointed by Gov. Gen. of Australia)
Government Type: territory of Australia; dependency placed under Australian govt. authority by Cocos (Keeling) Islands Act of 1955
National Holiday: n.a.

■ ECONOMY

Overview: little industrial activity; agriculture limited to copra and coconut cultivation

■ FINANCE/TRADE

Currency: Australian dollar = 100 cents

Canadian Embassy: c/o The Canadian High Commission, Commonwealth Ave, Canberra A.C.T. 2600, Australia. Tel: (011-61-2) 6273-3844. Fax: (011-61-2) 6273-3285
Representative to Canada: c/o Australian High Commission, 50 O'Connor St, Ste 710, Ottawa ON K1P 6L2. Tel: (613) 236-0841. Fax: (613) 236-4376.

Colombia

Long-Form Name: Republic of Colombia
Capital: Bogotá

■ GEOGRAPHY

Area: 1,138,910 sq. km; includes Isla de Malpelo, Roncador Cay, Serrana Bank, and Serranilla Bank
Coastline: 3,208 km total (1,448 km North Pacific Ocean; 1,760 Caribbean Sea)
Climate: tropical along coast and eastern plains; cooler in highlands
Environment: highlands subject to volcanic eruptions; deforestation; soil damage from overuse of pesticides; periodic droughts; air pollution
Terrain: mixture of flat coastal lowlands, plains in east, central highlands, some high mountains (Andes)
Land Use: 4% arable land; 1% permanent crops; 39% meadows and pastures; 48% forest and woodland; 8% other, includes negligible irrigated
Location: NW South America, bordering on Caribbean Sea, Pacific Ocean

■ PEOPLE

Population: 38,580,949 (July 1998 est.)
Nationality: Colombian
Age Structure: 0-14 yrs: 33%; 15-64: 62%; 65+: 5% (1998 est.)
Population Growth Rate: 1.89% (1998 est.)
Net Migration: -0.34 migrants/1,000 population (1998 est.)
Ethnic Groups: 58% mestizo, 20% white, 14% mulatto, 4% black, 4% Indian
Languages: Spanish
Religions: 95% Roman Catholic
Birth Rate: 24.93/1,000 population (1998 est.)
Death Rate: 5.69/1,000 population (1998 est.)
Infant Mortality: 25.44 deaths/1,000 live births (1998 est.)
Life Expectancy at Birth: 66.15 years male, 74.11 years female (1998 est.)
Total Fertility Rate: 2.9 children born/woman (1998 est.)
Literacy: 91.3% (1997 est.)

■ GOVERNMENT

Leader(s): Pres. Andrés Pastrana Arango; V.Pres. Lemas Gustavo Bell
Government Type: republic; executive branch dominates government structure
Administrative Divisions: 32 departments, 1 capital district
Nationhood: July 20, 1810 (from Spain)
National Holiday: Independence Day, July 20

■ ECONOMY

Overview: traditionally coffee has been the main export though other industries such as oil and coal are developing; drug-related violence is an increasing threat to economic growth

GDP: $231.1 billion, per capita $6,200; real growth rate 3.1% (1997 est.)

Inflation: 24.3% (June 1998)

Industries: accounts for 26% of GDP; textiles, food processing, oil, clothing and footwear, beverages, chemicals, metal products, cement; mining—gold, coal, emeralds, iron, nickel, silver, salt

Labour Force: 16.5 million (1997 est.); 28.6% community, social and business services, 23.5% industry, 7.1% finance

Unemployment: 14.5% (Mar. 1998)

Agriculture: accounts for 19% of GDP; crops make up two-thirds and livestock one-third of agricultural output; climate and soils permit a wide variety of crops, such as coffee, rice, tobacco, corn, sugar cane, cocoa beans, oilseeds, vegetables; forest products and shrimp farming are increasing in importance

Natural Resources: crude oil, natural gas, coal, iron ore, nickel, gold, copper, emeralds

■ FINANCE/TRADE

Currency: peso ($Col) = 100 centavos

International Reserves Excluding Gold: $8.294 billion (Dec. 1998)

Gold Reserves: 0.358 million fine troy ounces (Dec. 1998)

Budget: revenues $27 billion; expenditures $30 billion, including capital expenditures n.a. (1997 est.)

Defence Expenditures: 2.6% of GDP (1996)

Education Expenditures: 3.5 % of GNP (1995)

External Debt: $17.1 billion (1997 est.)

Exports: $8.086 billion (1998 est.); commodities: coffee 30%, petroleum 24%, coal, bananas, fresh cut flowers; partners: US 36%, European Community 21%, Japan 5%, Netherlands 4%, Sweden 3%

Imports: $15.463 billion (1998 est.); commodities: industrial equipment, transportation equipment, foodstuffs, chemicals, paper products; partners: US 34%, European Community 16%, Brazil 4%, Venezuela 3%, Japan 3%

■ COMMUNICATIONS

Daily Newspapers: 37 (1996)

Televisions: 123/1,000 inhabitants (1996)

Radios: 565/1,000 inhabitants (1996)

Telephones: 10.6/100 inhabitants (1996 est.)

■ TRANSPORTATION

Motor Vehicles: 1,700,000; 1,150,000 passenger cars (1997 est.)

Roads: 107,000 km; 12,733 km paved

Railway: 3,386 km

Air Traffic: 8,342,000 passengers carried (1996)

Airports: 1,136; 86 have paved runways (1997 est.)

Canadian Embassy: The Canadian Embassy, Calle 76, No. 11-52, Bogotá, Colombia; mailing address: Apartado Aereo 53531, Bogotá 2, Colombia. Tel: (011-57-1) 657-9800. Fax (011-57-1) 657-9912.

Embassy in Canada: Embassy of the Republic of Colombia, 360 Albert St, Ste 1002, Ottawa ON K1R 7X7. Tel: (613) 230-3760. Fax: (613) 230-4416.

Comoros

Long-Form Name: Federal Islamic Republic of the Comoros

Capital: Moroni

■ GEOGRAPHY

Area: 2,170 sq. km

Coastline: 340 km

Climate: tropical marine; rainy season (Nov. to May)

Environment: soil degradation and erosion; deforestation; cyclones possible during rainy season

Terrain: volcanic islands, interiors vary from steep mountains to low hills

Land Use: 35% arable; 10% permanent; 7% meadows; 18% forest; 30% other

Location: Indian Ocean E of Africa

■ PEOPLE

Population: 545,528 (July 1998 est.)

Nationality: Comoran

Age Structure: 0-14 yrs: 43%; 15-64: 54%; 65+: 3% (1998 est.)

Population Growth Rate: 3.1% (1998 est.)

Net Migration: 0 migrants/1,000 population (1998 est.)

Ethnic Groups: Antalote, Cafre, Makoa, Oimatsaha, Sakalava

Languages: French and Arabic (both official), Shaafi Islam (a Swahili dialect), Malagasy; majority speaks Comoran

Religions: 86% Sunni Muslim, 14% Roman Catholic

Birth Rate: 40.52/1,000 population (1998 est.)

Death Rate: 9.52/1,000 population (1998 est.)

Infant Mortality: 84.54 deaths/1,000 live births (1998 est.)

Life Expectancy at Birth: 57.95 years male, 62.84 years female (1998 est.)

Total Fertility Rate: 5.48 children born/woman (1998 est.)
Literacy: 57.3% (1997 est.)

■ GOVERNMENT

Leader(s): Col. Assumani Azzali
Government Type: independent republic
Administrative Divisions: 3 islands and 4 municipalities
Nationhood: July 6, 1975 (from France)
National Holiday: Independence Day, July 6

■ ECONOMY

Overview: agriculture is the main sector of the economy though it does not feed citizens adequately; lack of natural resources makes Comoros one of the world's poorest countries
GDP: $400 million, per capita $685; real growth rate 3.5% (1997 est.)
Inflation: 9.7% (Nov. 1996)
Industries: accounts for 14% of GDP; perfume distillation, textiles, furniture, jewelry, soft drinks, construction materials
Labour Force: 144,500 (1996 est.); 80% agriculture, 6% industry, 14% services
Unemployment: 20% (1996 est.)
Agriculture: accounts for 40% of GDP; most of population works in subsistence agriculture and fishing; plantations produce cash crops for export—vanilla, cloves, perfume essences and copra; principal food crops—coconuts, bananas, cassava; large net food importer
Natural Resources: negligible

■ FINANCE/TRADE

Currency: Comoran franc (CFAF) = 100 centimes
International Reserves Excluding Gold: $39 million (Dec. 1998)
Gold Reserves: 0.001 million fine troy ounces (June 1998)
Budget: revenues $55 million; expenditures $71 million, including capital expenditures of $15 million (1995 est.)
Defence Expenditures: n.a.
Education Expenditures: n.a.
External Debt: $206 million (1996)
Exports: $11 million (1995); commodities: vanilla, cloves, perfume oil, copra; partners: US 53%, France 41%, Africa 4%, Germany 2%
Imports: $63 million (1995); commodities: rice and other foodstuffs, cement, petroleum products, consumer goods; partners: Europe 62% (France 22%, other 40%), Africa 5%, Pakistan, China

■ COMMUNICATIONS

Daily Newspapers: 0 (1996)

Televisions: 1.6/1,000 inhabitants (1996)
Radios: 138/1,000 inhabitants (1996)
Telephones: 0.9/100 inhabitants (1996 est.)

■ TRANSPORTATION

Motor Vehicles: n.a.
Roads: 880 km; 673 km paved
Railway: none
Air Traffic: 27,000 passengers carried (1996)
Airports: 4; all have paved runways (1997 est.)

Canadian Embassy: Canadian Embassy to the Comoros, c/o The Canadian High Commission, P.O. Box 1022, Dar-es-Salaam, Tanzania. Tel: (011-255-51) 112-832. Fax: (011-255-51) 116-896.
Embassy in Canada: Embassy of the Islamic Federal Republic of Comoros, 90 John St, Ste 501, New York NY 10038, USA. Tel: (212) 349-2030. Fax: (212) 619-5832.

Congo

Long-Form Name: People's Republic of the Congo
Capital: Brazzaville

■ GEOGRAPHY

Area: 342,000 sq. km
Coastline: 169 km
Climate: tropical; rainy season (Mar. to June); dry season (June to Oct.); constant high temperatures and humidity; particularly enervating climate astride the Equator
Environment: deforestation; air and water pollution; unsafe water supply; about 70% of the population lives in Brazzaville, Pointe Noire or along the railroad between them
Terrain: coastal plain, southern basin, central plateau, northern basin
Land Use: 0% arable land; negligible permanent; 29% meadows; 62% forest; 9% other
Location: WC Africa, bordering on South Atlantic Ocean

■ PEOPLE

Population: 2,658,123 (July 1998 est.)
Nationality: Congolese
Age Structure: 0-14 yrs: 43%; 15-64: 54%; 65+: 3% (1998 est.)
Population Growth Rate: 2.21% (1998 est.)
Net Migration: 0 migrants/1,000 population (1998 est.)
Ethnic Groups: about 15 ethnic groups divided into some 75 tribes, almost all Bantu; most important ethnic groups are Kongo (48%) in south, Sangha (20%) and M'Bochi (12%) in the

north, Teke (17%) in the centre; about 8,500
Europeans, mostly French
Languages: French (official); many African
languages with Lingala and Kikongo most
widely used
Religions: 50% Christian, 48% animist, 2%
Muslim
Birth Rate: 38.5/1,000 population (1998 est.)
Death Rate: 16.45/1,000 population (1998 est.)
Infant Mortality: 102.69 deaths/1,000 live births
(1998 est.)
Life Expectancy at Birth: 47.07 years male, 48.89
years female (1998 est.)
Total Fertility Rate: 4.98 children born/woman
(1998 est.)
Literacy: 74.9% (1997 est.)

■ GOVERNMENT

Leader(s): Pres. Denis Sassou-Nguesso
Government Type: republic
Administrative Divisions: 9 regions, 1 commune
Nationhood: Aug. 15, 1960 (from France;
formerly known as Congo/Brazzaville)
National Holiday: Congolese National Day, Aug.
15

■ ECONOMY

Overview: oil revenues are responsible for one of
the highest growth rates in Africa, though the
country faces increasing foreign debt and is
vulnerable to the oil market. Recent efforts at
economic reform are beginning to show results
GDP: purchasing power parity: $5.25 billion, per
capita $2,000; real growth rate 4% (1997 est.)
Inflation: -9.2% (Mar. 1997)
Industries: accounts for 35% of GDP; petroleum,
lumbering, cement, sawmills, brewery, sugar
mills, palm oil, soap, cigarettes
Labour Force: 1 million (1997 est.); 62.4%
agriculture, 25.6% services, 11.9% industry
Unemployment: n.a.
Agriculture: accounts for 11% of GDP (including
fishing and forestry); cassava accounts for 90%
of food output; other crops—rice, corn, peanuts,
vegetables; cash crops include coffee and cocoa;
forest products important export earner; imports
over 90% of food needs
Natural Resources: petroleum, timber, potash,
lead, zinc, uranium, copper, phosphate, natural
gas

■ FINANCE/TRADE

Currency: Communauté financière africaine
franc (CFAF) = 100 centimes
International Reserves Excluding Gold: $26
million (Dec. 1998)
Gold Reserves: 0.011 million fine troy ounces
(June 1998)

Budget: revenues $870 million; expenditures
$970 million including capital expenditures of
n.a. (1997 est.)
Defence Expenditures: 1.9% of GDP (1996)
Education Expenditures: 5.9% of GNP (1995)
External Debt: $5.3 billion (1996)
Exports: $1.345 billion (1996); commodities:
crude petroleum 72%, lumber, plywood, coffee,
cocoa, sugar, diamonds; partners: US, France,
other European Community
Imports: $1.551 billion (1996); commodities:
foodstuffs, consumer goods, intermediate
manufactures, capital equipment; partners:
France, Italy, other European community
members, U.S., Germany, Spain, Japan, Brazil

■ COMMUNICATIONS

Daily Newspapers: 6 (1996)
Televisions: 11.2/1,000 inhabitants (1996)
Radios: 124/1,000 inhabitants (1996)
Telephones: 0.8/100 inhabitants (1996 est.)

■ TRANSPORTATION

Motor Vehicles: 47,000; 30,000 passenger cars
(1997 est.)
Roads: 12,800 km; 1,242 km paved
Railway: 795 km
Air Traffic: 253,000 passengers carried (1996)
Airports: 37; 4 have paved runways (1997 est.)

Canadian Embassy: The Canadian Embassy to
the Republic of the Congo, P.O. Box 4037,
Libreville, Gabon. Tel: (011-241) 74-34-64.
Fax: (011-241) 74-34-66.
Embassy in Canada: c/o Embassy of the Republic
of the Congo, 4891 Colorado Ave NW,
Washington DC 20011, USA. Tel: (202) 726-
5500. Fax: (202) 726-1860.

Cook Islands

Long-Form Name: Cook Islands
Capital: Avarua (on Rarotonga Island)

■ GEOGRAPHY

Area: 240 sq. km
Climate: mild year-round, moderated by trade
winds
Land Use: 9% arable, 13% permanent crops,
negligible meadows and pastures, negligible
forest and woodland, 78% other
Location: S Pacific Ocean, NE of New Zealand

■ PEOPLE

Population: 19,989 (July 1998 est.)
Nationality: Cook Islander
Ethnic Groups: Polynesian 81.3%, Polynesian-

European mixture 7.7%, Polynesian-other mixture 7.7%, European 2.4%, other 0.9%
Languages: English (official), Cook Islands Maori

■ GOVERNMENT

Colony Territory of: Territory in free association with New Zealand
Leader(s): Chief of State: Queen Elizabeth II, Prime Min. Joe Williams
Government Type: self-governing territory in free association with New Zealand; Cook Island is fully responsible for internal affairs; New Zealand retains responsibility for external affairs, in consultation with the Cook Islands
National Holiday: Constitution Day, Aug. 4

■ ECONOMY

Overview: agriculture provides the backbone of the economy: copra, fruits, tomatoes; livestock: pigs, goats; fishing; manufacturing is limited

■ FINANCE/TRADE

Currency: New Zealand dollar (NZ$) = 100 cents

Canadian Embassy: c/o The Canadian High Commission, 3rd Fl, 61 Molesworth St, Thorndon, Wellington, New Zealand; postal address: c/o Box 12-049, Thorndon, Wellington, New Zealand. Tel: (011-64-4) 473-9577. Fax: (011-64-4)471-2082
Representative to Canada: c/o New Zealand High Commission, Metropolitan House, 99 Bank St, Ste 727, Ottawa ON K1P 6G3. Tel: (613) 238-5991. Fax: (613) 238-5707.

Costa Rica

Long-Form Name: Republic of Costa Rica
Capital: San José

■ GEOGRAPHY

Area: 51,100 sq. km; includes Isla del Coco
Coastline: 1,290 km
Climate: tropical; dry season (Dec. to Apr.); rainy season (May to Nov.)
Environment: subject to occasional earthquakes, hurricanes along Atlantic coast; frequent flooding of lowlands at onset of rainy season; active volcanoes; deforestation; soil erosion
Terrain: coastal plains separated by rugged mountains
Land Use: 6% arable; 5% permanent; 46% meadows; 31% forest; 12% other, includes 2% irrigated
Location: Central (Latin) America, bordering on Caribbean Sea, Pacific Ocean

■ PEOPLE

Population: 3,604,642 (July 1998 est.)
Nationality: Costa Rican
Age Structure: 0-14 yrs: 34%; 15-64: 61%; 65+: 5% (1998 est.)
Population Growth Rate: 1.95% (1998 est.)
Net Migration: 0.72 migrants/1,000 population (1998 est.)
Ethnic Groups: 96% white (including mestizo), 2% black, 1% Indian, 1% Chinese
Languages: Spanish (official), English is spoken around Puerto Limon
Religions: 95% Roman Catholic
Birth Rate: 22.89/1,000 population (1998 est.)
Death Rate: 4.15/1,000 population (1998 est.)
Infant Mortality: 13.1 deaths/1,000 live births (1998 est.)
Life Expectancy at Birth: 73.5 years male, 78.48 years female (1998 est.)
Total Fertility Rate: 2.81 children born/woman (1998 est.)
Literacy: 94.8% (1997 est.)

■ GOVERNMENT

Leader(s): Pres. Miguel Angel Rodríquez Echeverría; First V.Pres. Astrid Fischel Volio
Government Type: democratic republic
Administrative Divisions: 7 provinces
Nationhood: Sept. 15, 1821 (from Spain)
National Holiday: Independence Day, Sept. 15

■ ECONOMY

Overview: inflation and external debt are high, many people are underemployed; coffee and banana crops are vital
GDP: $19.6 billion, per capita $5,500; real growth rate 3% (1997 est.)
Inflation: 11.7% (July 1998)
Industries: accounts for 24% of GDP; food processing, textiles and clothing, plastics products, construction materials, fertilizer, tourism
Labour Force: 1 million (1997 est.); 24.1% community, social and business services, 24.1% agriculture, 18.9% industry
Unemployment: 5.7% (1997 est.), but there is much underemployment
Agriculture: accounts for 18% of GDP and 70% of exports; cash commodities—coffee, beef, bananas, sugar; normally self-sufficient in food except for grain; depletion of forest resources resulting in lower timber output
Natural Resources: hydroelectricity potential

■ FINANCE/TRADE

Currency: colón (pl. colones) (C/) = 100 centimes

International Reserves Excluding Gold: $1.395 billion (Jan. 1999)
Gold Reserves: 0.002 million fine troy ounces (Jan. 1999)
Budget: n.a.
Defence Expenditures: 0.6% of GDP (1996)
Education Expenditures: 4.5% of GNP (1996)
External Debt: $3.454 billion (1996 est.)
Exports: $5.315 billion (1998 est.); commodities: coffee, bananas, textiles, sugar; partners: US 75%, Germany, Guatemala, Netherlands, UK, Japan
Imports: $6.005 billion (1998 est.); commodities: petroleum, machinery, consumer durables, chemicals, fertilizer, foodstuffs; partners: US 35%, Japan, Guatemala, Germany

■ COMMUNICATIONS

Daily Newspapers: 6 (1996)
Televisions: 143/1,000 inhabitants (1996)
Radios: 271/1,000 inhabitants (1996)
Telephones: 19.6/100 inhabitants (1996 est.)

■ TRANSPORTATION

Motor Vehicles: 121,000; 49,600 passenger cars (1997 est.)
Roads: 35,600 km; 6,051 km paved
Railway: 950 km
Air Traffic: 869,400 passengers carried (1996)
Airports: 158; 27 have paved runways (1997 est.)

Canadian Embassy: The Canadian Embassy, Oficentro Ejecutivo La Sabana-detrás de la Contraloría, Sabana Sur, San José; mailing address: Canadian Embassy, P.O. Box 351-1007, Centro Colon, San José, Costa Rica. Tel: (011-506) 296-4149. Fax: (011-506) 296-4270.
Embassy in Canada: Embassy of the Republic of Costa Rica, 135 York St, Ste 208, Ottawa ON K1N 5T4. Tel: (613) 562-2855. Fax: (613) 562-2582.

Côte d'Ivoire (Ivory Coast)

Long-Form Name: Republic of Côte d'Ivoire
Capital: Yamoussoukro

■ GEOGRAPHY

Area: 322,460 sq. km
Coastline: 515 km
Climate: tropical along coast, semi-arid in far north; three seasons: warm and dry (Nov. to Mar.), hot and dry (Mar. to May), hot and wet (June to Oct.)
Environment: coast has heavy surf and no natural harbours; severe deforestation; water pollution; heavy flooding is possible during rainy season

Terrain: mostly flat to undulating plains; mountains in northwest
Land Use: 8% arable; 4% permanent; 41% permanent pastures; 22% forest; 25% other
Location: WC Africa, bordering on South Atlantic Ocean

■ PEOPLE

Population: 15,446,231 (July 1998 est.)
Nationality: Ivorian
Age Structure: 0-14 yrs: 47%; 15-64: 51%; 65+: 2% (1998 est.)
Population Growth Rate: 2.41% (1998 est.)
Net Migration: -1.96 migrants/1,000 population (1998 est.)
Ethnic Groups: over 60 ethnic groups; most important are the Baoule 23%, Bete 18%, Senoufou 15%, Malinke 11% and Agni; about 2 million foreign Africans mostly Burkinabe; about 130,000 to 330,000 non-Africans (30,000 French and 100,000-300,000 Lebanese)
Languages: French (official), 60 native dialects, of which Dioula is the most widely spoken
Religions: 28% indigenous, 60% Muslim, 12% Christian
Birth Rate: 42.15/1,000 population (1998 est.)
Death Rate: 16.12/1,000 population (1998 est.)
Infant Mortality: 95.95 deaths/1,000 live births (1998 est.)
Life Expectancy at Birth: 44.73 years male, 47.8 years female (1998 est.)
Total Fertility Rate: 5.97 children born/woman (1998 est.)
Literacy: 40.1% (1997 est.)

■ GOVERNMENT

Leader(s): Pres. Henri Konan Bedie, Prime Min. Kablan Daniel Duncan
Government Type: republic; multi-party presidential regime
Administrative Divisions: 50 departments
Nationhood: Aug. 7, 1960 (from France)
National Holiday: National Day, Aug. 7

■ ECONOMY

Overview: despite attempts to diversify, the economy is largely dependent on agriculture and related industries; highly sensitive to fluctuations in world prices for coffee and cocoa and to weather conditions
GDP: $25.8 billion, per capita $1,700; real growth rate 6.5% (1997 est.)
Inflation: 5.1% (1997)
Industries: accounts for 20% of GDP; foodstuffs, wood processing, oil refinery, automobile assembly, textiles, fertilizer, beverages
Labour Force: 5.1 million (1997 est.); 45.4%

community, social and business services, 15.6% industry, 13.8% agriculture

Unemployment: n.a.

Agriculture: most important sector, contributing 31% to GDP and 80% to exports; cash crops include coffee, cocoa beans, timber, bananas, palm kernels, rubber; food crops; not self-sufficient in bread grain and dairy products

Natural Resources: crude oil, diamonds, manganese, iron ore, cobalt, bauxite, copper

■ FINANCE/TRADE

Currency: Communauté financière africaine franc (CFAF) = 100 centimes

International Reserves Excluding Gold: $554 million (Nov. 1998)

Gold Reserves: 0.045 million fine troy ounces (July 1998)

Budget: revenues $2.4 billion; expenditures $2.7 billion, including capital expenditures of $600 million (1996 est.)

Defence Expenditures: 0.9% of GDP (1996)

Education Expenditures: n.a.

External Debt: $19.713 billion (1996)

Exports: $29.624 million (1998) adjusted for purchasing power parity; commodities: cocoa 30%, coffee 20%, tropical woods 11%, cotton, bananas, pineapples, palm oil; partners: France, Germany, Netherlands, US, Belgium, Spain

Imports: $20.208 million (1998) adjusted for purchasing power parity; commodities: manufactured goods and semifinished products 50%, consumer goods 40%, raw materials and fuels 10%; partners: France, other European Community, Nigeria, US, Japan

■ COMMUNICATIONS

Daily Newspapers: 12 (1996)

Televisions: 62/1,000 inhabitants (1996)

Radios: 157/1,000 inhabitants (1996)

Telephones: 0.8/100 inhabitants (1996 est.)

■ TRANSPORTATION

Motor Vehicles: 255,000; 160,000 passenger cars (1997 est.)

Roads: 50,400 km; 4,889 km paved

Railway: 660 km

Air Traffic: 179,000 passengers carried (1996)

Airports: 36; 7 have paved runways (1997 est.)

Canadian Embassy: The Canadian Embassy, Immeuble Trade-Center, 23 rue Nogues, Le Plateau, Abidjan; mailing address: BP 4104, Abidjan 01, Côte d'Ivoire. Tel: (011-225) 21-20-09. Fax: (011-225) 21-77-28.

Embassy in Canada: Embassy of the Republic of Côte d'Ivoire, 9 Marlborough Ave, Ottawa ON K1N 8E6. Tel: (613) 236-9919. Fax: (613) 563-8287.

Croatia

Long-Form Name: Republic of Croatia

Capital: Zagreb

■ GEOGRAPHY

Area: 56,538 sq. km

Coastline: 5,790 km

Climate: hot summers and cold winters; along coast, mild winters and dry summers

Environment: air pollution (including acid rain), damaged forests, coastal pollution; subject to frequent and destructive earthquakes

Terrain: flat plains along Hungarian border, low mountains and highlands along Adriatic coast, coastline, and islands

Land Use: 21% arable, 2% permanent crops, 20% meadows and pastures, 38% forest and woodland, 19% other

Location: S Europe, bordering on Adriatic Sea

■ PEOPLE

Population: 4,671,584 (July 1998 est.)

Nationality: Croat

Age Structure: 0-14 yrs: 17%; 15-64: 68%; 65+: 15% (1998 est.)

Population Growth Rate: 0.13% (1998 est.)

Net Migration: 1.94 migrants/1,000 population (1998 est.)

Ethnic Groups: 78% Croat, 12% Serb, 0.9% Muslim, 0.5% Hungarian, 0.5% Slovenian, 8.1% other

Languages: Serbo-Croatian 96%, other 4%

Religions: 76.5% Catholic, 11.1% Orthodox, 1.2% Slavic Muslim, 0.4% Protestant, 10.8% others and unknown

Birth Rate: 10.45/1,000 population (1998 est.)

Death Rate: 11.14/1,000 population (1998 est.)

Infant Mortality: 8.0 deaths/1,000 live births (1998 est.)

Life Expectancy at Birth: 70.43 years male, 77.28 years female (1998 est.)

Total Fertility Rate: 1.54 children born/woman (1998 est.)

Literacy: 97% (1997 est.)

■ GOVERNMENT

Leader(s): Pres. Franjo Tudjman, Prime Min. Zlatko Matesa

Government Type: parliamentary democracy

Administrative Divisions: 21 counties

Nationhood: June 25, 1991, secession from federal Yugoslavia

National Holiday: Statehood Day, May 30

■ ECONOMY

Overview: tourism, manufacturing including chemicals, food products, petroleum, ships and textiles. War and internal strife have severely disrupted economy

GDP: $22.7 billion, per capita $4,500; real growth rate 4.4% (1997 est.)

Inflation: 7.1% (Mar. 1998)

Industries: accounts for 24% of GDP; mining, fertilizers, plastics, chemicals, fabricated metal, pig iron and rolled steel products, paper, wood products, shipbuilding, food processing, beverages, sugar, cotton fabrics, machinery

Labour Force: 2 million (1997 est.); 33.6% industry, 22.7% community, social and business services, 15.8% trade and tourism

Unemployment: 9.8% (Apr. 1998)

Agriculture: accounts for 12% of GDP; Croatia normally produces a food surplus, but much land has been put out of production by fighting; products include wheat, maize, potatoes, plums, fish, livestock, esp. cattle, sheep, pigs, poultry, cereal grains, citrus fruit, vegetables

Natural Resources: oil, salt, coal, bauxite, brown coal and lignite, iron ore, china clay

■ FINANCE/TRADE

Currency: Croatian kuna = 100 lipas

International Reserves Excluding Gold: $2.612 billion (Jan. 1999)

Gold Reserves: none (Jan. 1999)

Budget: revenues $5.3 billion, expenditures $6.3 billion, including capital expenditures of $78.5 million (1997 est.)

Defence Expenditures: 11.83% of total govt. expenditure (1997)

Education Expenditures: 6.55% of total govt. expenditure (1997)

External Debt: $5.904 billion (Oct. 1997)

Exports: $4.464 billion (1998 est.); machinery and transportation equipment and other manufactured goods; partners: mostly Italy, Germany, United States, successor states of the former USSR

Imports: $8.327 billion (1998 est.); machinery and transportation equipment, chemicals, raw materials

■ COMMUNICATIONS

Daily Newspapers: 10 (1996)

Televisions: 267/1,000 inhabitants (1996)

Radios: 333/1,000 inhabitants (1996)

Telephones: 28.0/100 inhabitants (1996 est.)

■ TRANSPORTATION

Motor Vehicles: n.a.

Roads: 27,247 km; 22,206 km paved

Railway: 1,907 km; railway service disrupted due to territorial dispute (1997)

Air Traffic: 823,010 passengers carried (1996)

Airports: 71; 20 have paved runways (1997 est.)

Canadian Embassy: The Canadian Embassy, Hotel Esplanade, Mihanoviceva 1, 10000 Zagreb. Tel: (011-385-1) 457-3223. Fax: (011-385-1) 457-7913.

Embassy in Canada: Embassy of the Republic of Croatia, 130 Albert St, Ste 1700, Ottawa ON K1P 5G4. Tel: (613) 230-7351. Fax: (613) 230-7388.

Cuba

Long-Form Name: Republic of Cuba

Capital: Havana

■ GEOGRAPHY

Area: 110,860 sq. km

Coastline: 3,735 km

Climate: tropical; moderated by trade winds; dry season (Nov. to Apr.); rainy season (May to Oct.)

Environment: averages one hurricane every two years; water pollution and deforestation

Terrain: mostly flat to rolling plains with rugged hills and mountains in the southeast

Land Use: 24% arable; 7% permanent; 27% pasture; 24% forest; 18% other, including 8% irrigated

Location: West Indies, bordering on Caribbean Sea, Atlantic Ocean

■ PEOPLE

Population: 11,050,729 (July 1998 est.)

Nationality: Cuban

Age Structure: 0-14 yrs: 22%; 15-64: 69%; 65+: 9% (1998 est.)

Population Growth Rate: 0.42% (1998 est.)

Net Migration: -1.53 migrants/1,000 population (1998 est.)

Ethnic Groups: 51% mulatto, 37% white, 11% black, 1% Chinese

Languages: Spanish

Religions: Christianity (majority Roman Catholic)

Birth Rate: 13.13/1,000 population (1998 est.)

Death Rate: 7.35/1,000 population (1998 est.)

Infant Mortality: 7.89 deaths/1,000 live births (1998 est.)

Life Expectancy at Birth: 73.29 years male, 78.13 years female (1998 est.)

Total Fertility Rate: 1.57 children born/woman (1998 est.)

Literacy: 95.7% (1997 est.)

■ GOVERNMENT

Leader(s): Pres. of the Council of State Fidel Castro Ruz

Government Type: communist state
Administrative Divisions: 14 provinces and 1 special municipality
Nationhood: May 20, 1902 (from Spain Dec. 10, 1898; administered by the US from 1898 to 1902)
National Holiday: Rebellion Day, July 26; Liberation Day, Jan. 1

■ ECONOMY

Overview: The state plays the primary role in the economy and controls practically all foreign trade. Recent government reforms aim at alleviating serious shortages of food, consumer goods, and services. Tourism plays a key role in foreign currency earnings.
GDP: $16.9 billion, per capita $1,540; real growth rate 2.5% (1997 est.)
Inflation: n.a.
Industries: accounts for 35% of GDP; sugar milling, petroleum refining, food and tobacco processing, textiles, chemicals, paper and wood products, metals (particularly nickel), cement, fertilizers, consumer goods, agricultural machinery
Labour Force: 5.1 million (1997 est.); 47.7% services, 28.5% industry, 23.8% agriculture
Unemployment: 8% (1996 est.)
Agriculture: accounts for 7.6% of GDP (including fishing and forestry); key commercial crops—sugar cane, tobacco and citrus fruit; other products—coffee, rice, potatoes, meat, beans; world's largest sugar exporter; not self-sufficient in food
Natural Resources: cobalt, nickel, iron ore, copper, manganese, salt, timber, silica, petroleum

■ FINANCE/TRADE

Currency: peso ($) = 100 centavos
International Reserves Excluding Gold: n.a.
Gold Reserves: n.a.
Budget: n.a.
Defence Expenditures: 5.4% of GDP (1996)
Education Expenditures: n.a.
External Debt: $10.5 billion (1996)
Exports: $2.015 billion (1996); commodities: sugar, nickel, shellfish, citrus, tobacco, coffee; partners: Russia 30%, China 9%, Canada 10%, Japan 6%, Spain 4%
Imports: $3.205 billion (1996); commodities: capital goods, industrial raw materials, food, petroleum; partners: Russia 10%, China 9%, Spain 9%, Mexico 5%, Italy 5%, Canada 4%, France 4%

■ COMMUNICATIONS

Daily Newspapers: 17 (1996)
Televisions: 236/1,000 inhabitants (1996)
Radios: 351/1,000 inhabitants (1996)
Telephones: 3.2/100 inhabitants (1996 est.)

■ TRANSPORTATION

Motor Vehicles: n.a.
Roads: 27,700 km; 15,484 km paved
Railway: 4,677 km
Air Traffic: 929,000 passengers carried (1996)
Airports: 171; 77 have paved runways (1997 est.)

Canadian Embassy: The Canadian Embassy, Calle 30, No. 518 Esquina 7a, Avenida Miramar, Havana, Cuba. Tel: (011-53-7) 24-25-16. Fax: (011-53-7) 24-20-44.
Embassy in Canada: Embassy of the Republic of Cuba, 388 Main St, Ottawa ON K1S 1E3. Tel: (613) 563-0141. Fax: (613) 563-0068.

Cyprus

Long-Form Name: Republic of Cyprus
Capital: Nicosia

■ GEOGRAPHY

Area: 9,250 sq. km
Coastline: 648 km
Climate: temperate, Mediterranean with hot, dry summers and cool, wet winters
Environment: moderate earthquake activity; water resource problems (no natural reservoir catchments, seasonal disparity in rainfall and most potable resources concentrated in the Turkish-Cypriot area)
Terrain: central plain with mountains to north and south, plain along south coast
Land Use: 12% arable; 5% permanent; negligible permanent pastures; 13% forest; 70% other, including 4% irrigated
Location: Middle East, in the Mediterranean Sea

■ PEOPLE

Population: 748,982 (July 1998 est.)
Nationality: Cypriot
Age Structure: 0-14 yrs: 25%; 15-64: 65%; 65+: 10% (1998 est.)
Population Growth Rate: 0.69% (1998 est.)
Net Migration: 0.44 migrants/1,000 population (1998 est.)
Ethnic Groups: 78% Greek; 18% Turkish; 4% other
Languages: 80% Greek, Turkish, English
Religions: 78% Greek Orthodox; 18% Muslim; 4% Maronite, Armenian, Apostolic and other

Birth Rate: 13.93/1,000 population (1998 est.)
Death Rate: 7.51/1,000 population (1998 est.)
Infant Mortality: 7.97 deaths/1,000 live births (1998 est.)
Life Expectancy at Birth: 74.62 years male, 79.07 years female (1998 est.)
Total Fertility Rate: 2.03 children born/woman (1998 est.)
Literacy: 94% (1997 est.)

■ GOVERNMENT

Leader(s): Pres. Glafcos Clerides
Government Type: republic; Greek Cypriots control the only internationally recognized government
Administrative Divisions: 6 districts
Nationhood: Aug. 16, 1960 (from UK)
National Holiday: Independence Day, Oct. 1 (Nov. 15 is celebrated as Independence Day in the Turkish area)

■ ECONOMY

Overview: the severe economic crisis affecting the Turkish mainland has devastated economic growth, and inflation is soaring especially in the Turkish area
GDP: $11.19 billion, per capita $13,500; real growth rate 2.4% (1997 est.)
Inflation: 2.5% (May 1998)
Industries: accounts for 23% of GDP; mining (iron pyrites, gypsum, asbestos); manufactured products—beverages, footwear, clothing and cement—are principally for local consumption, tourism
Labour Force: 287,700 (1996); 67.4% services, 18.9% industry, 13.7% agriculture
Unemployment: 9.8% (Apr. 1998)
Agriculture: accounts for 5 to 11% of GDP; employs 25% of labour force; major crops—potatoes, vegetables, barley, grapes, olives and citrus fruit; vegetables and fruit provide 25% of export revenues
Natural Resources: copper, pyrites, asbestos, gypsum, timber, salt, marble, clay earth pigment

■ FINANCE/TRADE

Currency: Cypriot pound (£ or £C) and Turkish lira (TL)
International Reserves Excluding Gold: $1.459 billion (Oct. 1998)
Gold Reserves: 0.462 million fine troy ounces (Nov. 1998)
Budget: Greek area: revenues $2.9 billion; expenditures $3.4 billion, including capital expenditures of $345 million; Turkish area: revenues $171 million; expenditures $306 million, including capital expenditures of $56.8 million (1997 est.)

Defence Expenditures: 5.4% of GDP (1996)
Education Expenditures: 11.54% of govt. expenditures (1995)
External Debt: $1.8 billion (1996)
Exports: $1.063 billion (1998); commodities: citrus, potatoes, grapes, wine, cement, clothing and shoes; partners: Middle East and North Africa 37%, UK 27%, other European Community 11%, US 2%
Imports: $3.680 billion (1998); commodities: consumer goods 23%, petroleum and lubricants 12%, food and feed grains, machinery; partners: European Community 60%, Middle East and North Africa 7%, US 4%

■ COMMUNICATIONS

Daily Newspapers: 9 (1996)
Televisions: 323/1,000 inhabitants (1996)
Radios: 397/1,000 inhabitants (1996)
Telephones: 47.2/100 inhabitants (1996 est.)

■ TRANSPORTATION

Motor Vehicles: 340,000; 230,000 passenger cars (1997 est.)
Roads: 12,765 km; 7,317 km paved
Railway: none
Air Traffic: 1,225,063 passengers carried (1996)
Airports: 15; 12 have paved runways (1997 est.)

Canadian Embassy: The High Commission for Canada to Cyprus, c/o the Canadian Embassy, P.O. Box 3394, Damascus, Syria. Tel and fax c/o the Consulate of Canada in Nicosia: Tel (011-357-2) 775-508. Fax: (011-357-2) 779-939.

Embassy in Canada: c/o Embassy of the Republic of Cyprus, 2211 R St NW, Washington DC 20008, USA. Tel: (202) 462-5772. Fax: (202) 483-6710.

Czech Republic

Long-Form Name: Czech Republic
Capital: Prague

■ GEOGRAPHY

Area: 78,703 sq. km
Coastline: none: landlocked
Climate: temperate; cool summers; cold, cloudy, humid winters
Environment: air and water pollution and acid rain; recently there has been severe flooding
Terrain: Bohemia in the west consists of rolling plains, hills and plateaus surrounded by low mountains; Moravia in east consists of very hilly country
Land Use: 41% arable; 2% permanent crops;

11% permanent pastures; 34% forests and woodland; 12% other
Location: C Europe

■ PEOPLE

Population: 10,286,470 (July 1998 est.)
Nationality: Czech
Age Structure: 0-14 yrs: 17%; 15-64: 69%; 65+: 14% (1998 est.)
Population Growth Rate: -0.11% (1998 est.)
Net Migration: 0.92 migrants/1,000 population (1998 est.)
Ethnic Groups: 94% Czech, 3% Slovak, 0.2% Hungarian, 0.5% German, 0.6% Polish, 0.3% Ukrainian, 0.1% Russian, 0.3% Gypsy, 1% other
Languages: Czech and Slovak
Religions: 39.8% atheist, 39.2% Roman Catholic, 4.6% Protestant, 3% Orthodox, 13.4% other
Birth Rate: 8.96/1,000 population (1998 est.)
Death Rate: 10.92/1,000 population (1998 est.)
Infant Mortality: 6.79 deaths/1,000 live births (1998 est.)
Life Expectancy at Birth: 70.75 years male, 77.65 years female (1998 est.)
Total Fertility Rate: 1.17 children born/woman (1998 est.)
Literacy: 99% (1997 est.)

■ GOVERNMENT

Leader(s): Pres. Vaclav Havel, Prem. Milos Zeman
Government Type: parliamentary democracy
Administrative Divisions: 8 regions
Nationhood: Jan. 1, 1993 (from Czechoslovakia)
National Holiday: National Liberation Day, May 8; Founding of the Republic, Oct. 28

■ ECONOMY

Overview: economy is beginning the transition from a command to a market economy; economic growth is less important at this point than economic restructuring
GDP: $111.9 billion, per capita $10,800; real growth rate 0.7% (1997 est.)
Inflation: 12.0% (June 1998)
Industries: accounts for 40.6% of GDP; fuels, ferrous metallurgy, machinery and equipment, coal, motor vehicles, glass, armaments
Labour Force: 6 million (1997 est.); 37.9% industry, 8.1% agriculture, 8.8% construction, 45.2% communications and other
Unemployment: 7% (Nov. 1998)
Agriculture: accounts for 5% of GDP; largely self-sufficient in food production; diversified crop and livestock production, including grains,

sugar beets, potatoes, hops, fruit, hogs, cattle and poultry
Natural Resources: hard coal, kaolin, clay, graphite

■ FINANCE/TRADE

Currency: koruna (pl. koruny) (Kcs) = 100 halerv
International Reserves Excluding Gold: $12.354 billion (Nov. 1998)
Gold Reserves: 0.288 million fine troy ounces (Dec. 1998)
Budget: revenues $14.2 billion; expenditures $14.6 billion, including capital expenditures n.a. (1997)
Defence Expenditures: 4.66% of total govt. expenditure (1997)
Education Expenditures: 11.34% of total govt. expenditure (1997)
External Debt: $20.094 billion (1996)
Exports: $25.888 billion (1998 est.); commodities: machinery and equipment 58.5%, industrial consumer goods 15.2%, fuels, minerals and metals 10.6%, agricultural and forestry products 6.1%, other products 15.2%; partners: former USSR countries, Germany, Poland, Hungary, former Yugoslavia, Austria, Bulgaria, Romania, US
Imports: $27.808 billion (1998 est.); commodities: machinery and equipment 41.6%, fuels, minerals, metals 32.2%, agricultural and forestry products 11.5%, industrial consumer goods 6.7%, other products 8%; partners: former USSR countries, Germany, Poland, Hungary, former Yugoslavia, Austria, Bulgaria, Romania, US

■ COMMUNICATIONS

Daily Newspapers: 21 (1996)
Televisions: 534/1,000 inhabitants (1996)
Radios: 806/1,000 inhabitants (1996)
Telephones: 25.7/100 inhabitants (1996 est.)

■ TRANSPORTATION

Motor Vehicles: 5,000,000; 4,600,000 passenger cars (1997 est.) (includes data for Slovakia)
Roads: n.a.
Railway: 9,441 km
Air Traffic: 1,612,100 passengers carried (1996)
Airports: 66; 33 have paved runways (1997 est.)

Canadian Embassy: The Canadian Embassy, Mickiewiczova 6, 125 33 Prague 6, Czech Republic. Tel: (011-420-2) 7210-1800. Fax: (011-420-2) 7210-1890.
Embassy in Canada: Embassy of the Czech Republic, 541 Sussex Dr, Ottawa ON K1N 6Z6. Tel: (613) 562-3875. Fax: (613) 562-3878.

Democratic Republic of the Congo

Long-Form Name: Democratic Republic of the Congo
Capital: Kinshasa

■ GEOGRAPHY

Area: 2,345,410 sq. km
Coastline: 37 km along South Atlantic Ocean
Climate: tropical; hot and humid in equatorial river basin; cooler and drier in southern highlands; cooler and wetter in eastern highlands
Environment: dense tropical rainforest in central river basin and eastern highlands; periodic droughts in south; water pollution, deforestation; poaching negatively affects wildlife populations
Terrain: vast central basin is a low-lying plateau; mountains in east
Land Use: 3% arable; negligible permanent; 7% meadows; 77% forest; 13% other
Location: C Africa, just barely bordering on South Atlantic Ocean

■ PEOPLE

Population: 49,000,511 (July 1998 est.)
Nationality: Congolese
Age Structure: 0-14 yrs: 48%; 15-64: 49%; 65+: 3% (1998 est.)
Population Growth Rate: 2.99% (1998 est.)
Net Migration: -1.63 migrants/1,000 population (1998 est.)
Ethnic Groups: over 200 African ethnic groups, the majority are Bantu; four largest tribes— Mongo, Luba, Kongo (all Bantu) and the Mangbetu-Azande (Hamitic)—make up 45% of the population
Languages: French (official), Lingala, Swahili, Kinggwana, Kikongo, Tshiluba
Religions: 50% Roman Catholic, 20% Protestant, 10% Kimbanguist, 10% Muslim, 10% other syncretic sects and traditional beliefs
Birth Rate: 46.77/1,000 population (1998 est.)
Death Rate: 15.2/1,000 population (1998 est.)
Infant Mortality: 101.6 deaths/1,000 live births (1998 est.)
Life Expectancy at Birth: 47.27 years male, 51.4 years female (1998 est.)
Total Fertility Rate: 6.51 children born/woman (1998 est.)
Literacy: 77.3% (1997 est.)

■ GOVERNMENT

Leader(s): Pres. Laurent Kabila
Government Type: dictatorship; presumably undergoing a transition to representative government

Administrative Divisions: 10 regions and 1 town
Nationhood: June 30, 1960 (from Belgium; formerly known as Belgian Congo, then Congo/Leopoldville, then Congo/Kinshasa)
National Holiday: Anniversary of independence from Belgium, June 30

■ ECONOMY

Overview: Despite its vast potential wealth, the Democratic Republic of the Congo continues to suffer from a decline in the national economy. Tight fiscal policies have curbed inflation and currency depreciation. A barter economy flourishes in all but the largest cities.
GDP: $18 billion, per capita $400; real growth rate 1.5% (1997 est.)
Inflation: -10% (Feb. 1998)
Industries: accounts for 15% of GDP; mining, mineral processing, consumer products (including textiles, footwear and cigarettes), processed foods and beverages, cement, diamonds
Labour Force: 19.5 million (1997 est.); 71.5% agriculture, 12.9% industry, 15.6% services
Unemployment: n.a.
Agriculture: accounts for 59% of GDP; cash crops: coffee, palm oil, rubber, quinine; food crops: cassava, bananas, root crops, corn
Natural Resources: cobalt, copper, cadmium, crude oil, industrial and gem diamonds, gold, silver, zinc, manganese, tin, germanium, uranium, radium, bauxite, iron ore, coal, hydroelectric potential

■ FINANCE/TRADE

Currency: zaire (Z) = 100 makuta
International Reserves Excluding Gold: $83 million (Dec. 1996)
Gold Reserves: 0.05 million fine troy ounces (Dec. 1997)
Budget: revenues $479 million; expenditures $479 million; capital expenditures n.a. (1996 est.)
Defence Expenditures: 2.8% of GDP (1996)
Education Expenditures: 0.82% of total govt. expenditure (1995)
External Debt: $12.826 billion (1996)
Exports: $269 million (1997 est.); commodities: copper 37%, coffee 24%, diamonds 12%, cobalt, crude oil; partners: US, Belgium, France, Germany, Italy, UK, Japan
Imports: $220 million, adjusted for purchasing power parity (1997 est.); commodities: consumer goods, foodstuffs, mining and other machinery, transport equipment, fuels; partners: US, Belgium, France, Germany, Italy, Japan, UK

■ COMMUNICATIONS

Daily Newspapers: 9 (1996)
Televisions: 3.2/1,000 inhabitants (1996)
Radios: 98/1,000 inhabitants (1996)
Telephones: 0.1/100 inhabitants (1996 est.)

■ TRANSPORTATION

Motor Vehicles: 530,000; 330,000 passenger cars (1997 est.)
Roads: 146,500 km; 2,800 km paved
Railway: 5,138 km
Air Traffic: 184,000 passengers carried (1995)
Airports: 234; 24 have paved runways (1997 est.)

Canadian Embassy: The Canadian Embassy to the Democratic Republic of Congo, 17 avenue Pumbu, Commune de Gombe, Democratic Republic of Congo; mailing address: P.O. Box 8431, Kinshasa 1, Democratic Republic of Congo. Tel: (011-243) 884-1276. Fax: (011-243) 884-1277.
Embassy in Canada: Embassy of the Democratic Republic of Congo, 18 Range Rd, Ottawa ON K1N 8J3. Tel: (613) 230-6391. Fax: (613) 230-1945.

Denmark

Long-Form Name: Kingdom of Denmark
Capital: Copenhagen

■ GEOGRAPHY

Area: 43,094 sq. km; includes the island of Bornholm in the Baltic Sea and the rest of metropolitan Denmark, but excludes the Faroe Islands and Greenland
Coastline: 3,379 km
Climate: temperate; humid and overcast; mild, windy winters and cool summers
Environment: air and water pollution; pollution of drinking water
Terrain: low and flat to gently rolling plains
Land Use: 60% arable land; negligible permanent; 5% meadows; 10% forest; 25% other, includes 10% irrigated
Location: N Europe, bordering on North Sea, Baltic Sea

■ PEOPLE

Population: 5,333,617 (July 1998 est.)
Nationality: Dane
Age Structure: 0-14 yrs: 18%; 15-64: 67%; 65+: 15% (1998 est.)
Population Growth Rate: 0.49% (1998 est.)
Net Migration: 3.77 migrants/1,000 population (1998 est.)

Ethnic Groups: Scandinavian, Eskimo, Faroese, German
Languages: Danish, Faroese, Greenlandic (an Eskimo dialect); small German-speaking minority
Religions: 91% Evangelical Lutheran, 2% other Protestant and Roman Catholic, 7% other
Birth Rate: 12.18/1,000 population (1998 est.)
Death Rate: 11.08/1,000 population (1998 est.)
Infant Mortality: 5.17 deaths/1,000 live births (1998 est.)
Life Expectancy at Birth: 73.64 years male, 79.12 years female (1998 est.)
Total Fertility Rate: 1.68 children born/woman (1998 est.)
Literacy: 99% (1997 est.)

■ GOVERNMENT

Leader(s): Queen Margrethe II, Prime Min. Poul Nyrup Rasmussen
Government Type: constitutional monarchy
Administrative Divisions: 14 counties and 2 kommunes; dependent areas inc.: Faroe Islands, Greenland (see Greenland entry for details)
Nationhood: became a constitutional monarchy in 1849
National Holiday: Birthday of the Queen, Apr. 16

■ ECONOMY

Overview: advanced agriculture and industry; extensive government welfare measures; highly dependent on foreign trade
GDP: $122.5 billion, per capita $23,200; real growth rate 3% (1997 est.)
Inflation: 1.8% (June 1998)
Industries: accounts for 27% of GDP; food processing, machinery and equipment, textiles and clothing, chemical products, electronics, construction, furniture and other wood products
Labour Force: 3 million (1997 est.); 36% community, social and business services, 20.2% industry, 14.4% trade and tourism
Unemployment: 5.6% (Dec. 1998)
Agriculture: accounts for 4% of GNP and employs 5.6% of labour force (includes fishing); farm products account for nearly 15% of export revenues; principal products—meat, dairy, grain, potatoes, rape, sugar beets, fish; self-sufficient in food production
Natural Resources: crude oil, natural gas, fish, salt, limestone

■ FINANCE/TRADE

Currency: krone (pl. kroner) (DKr) = 100 oere
International Reserves Excluding Gold: $15.264 billion (Dec. 1998)
Gold Reserves: 2.143 million fine troy ounces (Jan. 1999)

Budget: revenues $62.1 billion; expenditures $66.4 billion, including capital expenditures n.a. (1996 est.)
Defence Expenditures: 1.6% of GDP (1997 est.)
Education Expenditures: 8.3% of GNP (1996 est.)
External Debt: $44 billion (1996)
Exports: $45.448 billion (1998 est.); commodities: meat and meat products, dairy products, transport equipment, fish, chemicals, industrial machinery; partners: US 6%, Germany, Norway, Sweden, UK, other European Community, Japan
Imports: $43.759 billion (1998 est.); commodities: petroleum, machinery and equipment, chemicals, grain and foodstuffs, textiles, paper; partners: US 7%, Germany, Netherlands, Sweden, UK, other European Community

■ COMMUNICATIONS

Daily Newspapers: 37 (1996)
Televisions: 592/1,000 inhabitants (1996)
Radios: 1,146/1,000 inhabitants (1996)
Telephones: 62.4/100 inhabitants (1996 est.)

■ TRANSPORTATION

Motor Vehicles: 2,200,000; 1,830,000 passenger cars (1997 est.)
Roads: 71,600 km; all paved
Railway: 3,358 km
Air Traffic: 4,595,800 passengers carried (1996)
Airports: 118; 28 have paved runways (1997 est.)

Canadian Embassy: The Canadian Embassy, Kr. Bernikowsgade 1, 1105 Copenhagen K, Denmark. Tel: (011-45) 33-48-32-00. Fax: (011-45) 33-48-32-20.
Embassy in Canada: Embassy of the Kingdom of Denmark, 47 Clarence St, Ste 450, Ottawa ON K1N 9K1. Tel: (613) 562-1811. Fax: (613) 562-1812.

Djibouti

Long-Form Name: Republic of Djibouti
Capital: Djibouti

■ GEOGRAPHY

Area: 22,000 sq. km
Coastline: 314 km
Climate: desert; torrid, dry
Environment: vast wasteland; desertification; droughts and earthquakes; occasional cyclones; inadequate safe drinking water
Terrain: coastal plain and plateau separated by central mountains
Land Use: 0% arable; 0% permanent; 9% permanent pastures; negligible forest; 91% other
Location: E Africa, bordering on Gulf of Aden

■ PEOPLE

Population: 440,727 (July 1998 est.)
Nationality: Djiboutian
Age Structure: 0-14 yrs: 43%; 15-64: 55%; 65+: 2% (1998 est.)
Population Growth Rate: 1.51% (1998 est.)
Net Migration: -11.91 migrants/1,000 population (1998 est.)
Ethnic Groups: 60% Somali (Issa), 35% Afar, 5% French, Arab, Ethiopian and Italian
Languages: French and Arabic (both official); Somali and Afar widely used
Religions: 94% Muslim, 6% Christian
Birth Rate: 41.75/1,000 population (1998 est.)
Death Rate: 14.69/1,000 population (1998 est.)
Infant Mortality: 102.4 deaths/1,000 live births (1998 est.)
Life Expectancy at Birth: 49.06 years male, 53.15 years female (1998 est.)
Total Fertility Rate: 5.94 children born/woman (1998 est.)
Literacy: 46.2% (1997 est.)

■ GOVERNMENT

Leader(s): Pres. Ismail Omar Guelleh, Prime Min. Barkat Gourad Hamadou
Government Type: republic
Administrative Divisions: 5 districts
Nationhood: June 27, 1977 (from France; formerly known as French Territory of the Afars and Issas)
National Holiday: Independence Day, June 27

■ ECONOMY

Overview: based on service activities related to country's strategic location and status as a free trade zone; Djibouti is heavily dependent on foreign aid
GDP: $520 million, per capita $1,200; real growth rate 0.5% (1997 est.)
Inflation: 6.7% (Feb. 1997)
Industries: accounts for 20% of GDP; limited to a few small-scale enterprises, such as dairy products and mineral-water bottling
Labour Force: n.a.; 75% agriculture, 11% industry, 14% services
Unemployment: 40–50% (1996 est.)
Agriculture: accounts for only 3% of GDP; scanty rainfall limits crop production to mostly fruit and vegetables; half of population pastoral nomads herding goats, sheep and camels; imports bulk of food needs
Natural Resources: geothermal areas

■ **FINANCE/TRADE**

Currency: Djiboutian franc (DF) = 100 centimes
International Reserves Excluding Gold: $65 million (Jan. 1999)
Gold Reserves: n.a.
Budget: revenues $156 million; expenditures $175 million, including capital expenditures of n.a. (1997 est.)
Defence Expenditures: 5.2% of GDP (1996)
Education Expenditures: n.a.
External Debt: $241 million (1996)
Exports: n.a.; commodities: hides and skins, coffee (in transit); partners: Middle East 50%, Africa 43%, Western Europe 7%
Imports: n.a.; commodities: foods, beverages, transport equipment, chemicals, petroleum products; partners: European Community 36%, Africa 21%, Bahrain 14%, Asia 12%, US 2%

■ **COMMUNICATIONS**

Daily Newspapers: 0 (1996)
Televisions: 44/1,000 inhabitants (1996)
Radios: 81/1,000 inhabitants (1996)
Telephones: 1.3/100 inhabitants (1996 est.)

■ **TRANSPORTATION**

Motor Vehicles: 16,500; 13,500 passenger cars (1997 est.)
Roads: 2,890 km; 364 km paved
Railway: 97 km
Air Traffic: n.a.
Airports: 11; 2 have paved runways (1997 est.)

Canadian Embassy: The Canadian Embassy to Djibouti, c/o The Canadian Embassy, P.O. Box 1130, Addis Ababa, Ethiopia. Tel: (011-251-1) 71-30-22. Fax: (011-251-1) 71-30-33.
Embassy in Canada: Embassy of the Republic of Djibouti, 1156 15th St. NW, Ste 515, Washington DC 20005, USA. Tel: (202) 331-0270. Fax: (202) 331-0302.

Dominica

Long-Form Name: Commonwealth of Dominica
Capital: Roseau

■ **GEOGRAPHY**

Area: 750 sq. km
Coastline: 148 km
Climate: tropical; moderated by northeast trade winds; heavy rainfall
Environment: flash floods a constant hazard; occasional hurricanes
Terrain: rugged mountains of volcanic origin
Land Use: 9% arable; 13% permanent; 3% meadows; 67% forest and woodland; 8% other
Location: Caribbean islands

■ **PEOPLE**

Population: 65,777 (July 1998 est.)
Nationality: Dominican
Age Structure: 0-14 yrs: 27%; 15-64: 63%; 65+: 10% (1998 est.)
Population Growth Rate: -1.33% (1998 est.)
Net Migration: -24.36 migrants/1,000 population (1998 est.)
Ethnic Groups: mostly black; some Carib Indians
Languages: English (official); French patois widely spoken
Religions: 77% Roman Catholic; 15% Protestant, 2% none, 1% unknown, 5% other
Birth Rate: 17.35/1,000 population (1998 est.)
Death Rate: 6.29/1,000 population (1998 est.)
Infant Mortality: 9.04 deaths/1,000 live births (1998 est.)
Life Expectancy at Birth: 74.94 years male, 80.8 years female (1998 est.)
Total Fertility Rate: 1.9 children born/woman (1998 est.)
Literacy: 94% (1997 est.)

■ **GOVERNMENT**

Leader(s): Pres. Crispin Anselm Sorhaindo, Prime Min. Edison James
Government Type: parliamentary democracy
Administrative Divisions: 10 parishes
Nationhood: Nov. 3, 1978 (from UK)
National Holiday: Independence Day, Nov. 3

■ **ECONOMY**

Overview: dependent on agriculture and vulnerable to climatic conditions; tourist potential (undeveloped)
GDP: $208 million, per capita $2,500; real growth rate 3.7% (1996)
Inflation: 0.6% (June 1998)
Industries: agricultural processing, tourism, soap and other coconut-based products, cigars, pumice mining, cement blocks, shoes
Labour Force: n.a.; agriculture 40%, industry and commerce 32%, services 28%
Unemployment: n.a.
Agriculture: accounts for 26% of GDP; principal crops—bananas, citrus fruit, coconuts, root crops; bananas provide the bulk of export earnings; forestry and fisheries potential not exploited
Natural Resources: timber

■ **FINANCE/TRADE**

Currency: East Caribbean dollar ($EC) = 100 cents

International Reserves Excluding Gold: $19 million (Mar. 1998)

Gold Reserves: n.a.

Budget: revenues $80 million; expenditures $95.8 million, including capital expenditures of n.a. (1995–96)

Defence Expenditures: n.a.

Education Expenditures: n.a.

External Debt: $111 million (1996 est.)

Exports: $53 million (1997); commodities: bananas, coconuts, grapefruit, soap, galvanized sheets; partners: UK 72%, Jamaica 10%, OECS 6%, US 3%, other 9%

Imports: $125 million (1997); commodities: food, oils and fats, chemicals, fuels and lubricants, manufactured goods, machinery and equipment; partners: US 23%, UK 18%, CARICOM 15%, OECS 15%, Japan 5%, Canada 3%, other 21%

■ COMMUNICATIONS

Daily Newspapers: 0 (1996)

Televisions: 77/1,000 inhabitants (1996)

Radios: 634/1,000 inhabitants (1996)

Telephones: 26.4/100 inhabitants (1996 est.)

■ TRANSPORTATION

Motor Vehicles: 5,700; 2,800 passenger cars (1997 est.)

Roads: 780 km; 393 km paved

Railway: none

Air Traffic: n.a.

Airports: 2; both have paved runways (1997 est.)

Canadian Embassy: c/o The Canadian High Commission, Bishop's Court Hill, St. Michael, Barbados; mailing address: P.O. Box 404, Bridgetown, Barbados. Tel: (246) 429-3550. Fax: (246) 429-3780.

Embassy in Canada: c/o High Commission for the Countries of the Organization of Eastern Caribbean States, 112 Kent St, Ste 1610, Place de Ville, Tower B, Ottawa ON K1P 5P2. Tel: (613) 236-8952. Fax: (613) 236-3042.

Dominican Republic

Long-Form Name: Dominican Republic

Capital: Santo Domingo

■ GEOGRAPHY

Area: 48,730 sq. km

Coastline: 1,288 km

Climate: tropical maritime; little seasonal temperature variation

Environment: subject to occasional hurricanes (July to Oct.); deforestation; erosion and water shortage

Terrain: rugged highlands and mountains interspersed with fertile valleys

Land Use: 21% arable; 9% permanent; 43% meadows; 12% forest; 15% other, includes 5% irrigated

Location: West Indies, bordering on Caribbean Sea, Atlantic Ocean

■ PEOPLE

Population: 7,998,766 (July 1998 est.)

Nationality: Dominican

Age Structure: 0-14 yrs: 35%; 15-64: 60%; 65+: 5% (1998 est.)

Population Growth Rate: 1.63% (1998 est.)

Net Migration: -4.37 migrants/1,000 population (1998 est.)

Ethnic Groups: 73% mixed, 16% white, 11% black

Languages: Spanish

Religions: 95% Roman Catholic

Birth Rate: 26.42/1,000 population (1998 est.)

Death Rate: 5.73/1,000 population (1998 est.)

Infant Mortality: 44.26 deaths/1,000 live births (1998 est.)

Life Expectancy at Birth: 67.53 years male, 72.04 years female (1998 est.)

Total Fertility Rate: 3.06 children born/woman (1998 est.)

Literacy: 82.1% (1997 est.)

■ GOVERNMENT

Leader(s): Pres. Leonel Fernandez Reyna, V.Pres. Jaime David Fernandez Mirabal

Government Type: republic

Administrative Divisions: 29 provinces and 1 district

Nationhood: Feb. 27, 1844 (from Haiti)

National Holiday: Independence Day, Feb. 27

■ ECONOMY

Overview: agriculture is the backbone of the economy (sugar cane) and has been adversely affected by drought in the mid-1990s; tourism and a free trade zone help

GDP: $38.3 billion, per capita $4,700; real growth rate 7% (1997 est.)

Inflation: 5.2% (Mar. 1998)

Industries: accounts for 22% of GDP; tourism, sugar processing, ferronickel and gold mining, textiles, cement, tobacco

Labour Force: 3.1 million (1997 est.); 45.7% agriculture, 38.8% services, 15.5% industry

Unemployment: 16.7% (1996)

Agriculture: accounts for 15% of GDP and employs almost half of labour force; sugar cane most important commercial crop, followed by coffee, cotton and cocoa; food crops; animal

output; not self-sufficient in food
Natural Resources: nickel, bauxite, gold, silver

■ FINANCE/TRADE

Currency: Dominican peso ($RD) = 100 centavos
International Reserves Excluding Gold: $496 million (Jan. 1999)
Gold Reserves: 0.018 million fine troy ounces (Jan. 1999)
Budget: revenues $2 billion; expenditures $2 billion, including capital expenditures of $994 million (1996 est.)
Defence Expenditures: 4.01% of total govt. expenditure (1996)
Education Expenditures: 12.60% of govt. expenditure (1996)
External Debt: $3.6 billion (1997)
Exports: $882 million (1997); commodities: sugar, coffee, cocoa, gold, ferronickel; partners: US (including Puerto Rico) 74%
Imports: $4.120 billion (1997); commodities: foodstuffs, petroleum, cotton and fabrics, chemicals and pharmaceuticals; partners: US (including Puerto Rico) 36%

■ COMMUNICATIONS

Daily Newspapers: 12 (1996)
Televisions: 94/1,000 inhabitants (1996)
Radios: 177/1,000 inhabitants (1996)
Telephones: 7.4/100 inhabitants (1996 est.)

■ TRANSPORTATION

Motor Vehicles: 209,000; 114,200 passenger cars (1997 est.)
Roads: 12,600 km; 6,224 km paved
Railway: 757 km
Air Traffic: n.a.
Airports: 36; 14 have paved runways (1997 est.)

Canadian Embassy: The Canadian Embassy, Maximo Gomez 30, Santo Domingo; mailing address: Apartado 2054, Santo Domingo 1, Dominican Republic. Tel: (809) 689-0002. Fax: (809) 682-2691.
Embassy in Canada: c/o Consulate General, 1470 Peel St, Ste 263, Tower A, Montreal PQ H3A 1T1. Tel: (514) 284-5455. Fax: (514) 284-5511.

Ecuador

Long-Form Name: Republic of Ecuador
Capital: Quito

■ GEOGRAPHY

Area: 283,560 sq. km
Coastline: 2,237 km

Climate: tropical along coast becoming cooler inland
Environment: subject to frequent earthquakes, landslides, volcanic activity; deforestation; desertification; soil erosion; periodic droughts
Terrain: coastal plain, inter-Andean central highlands and flat to rolling eastern jungle
Land Use: 6% arable; 5% permanent; 18% meadows; 56% forest; 15% other, includes 2% irrigated
Location: NW South America, bordering on Pacific Ocean

■ PEOPLE

Population: 12,336,572 (July 1998 est.)
Nationality: Ecuadorian
Age Structure: 0-14 yrs: 36%; 15-64: 60%; 65+: 4% (1998 est.)
Population Growth Rate: 1.86% (1998 est.)
Net Migration: 0.56 migrants/1,000 population (1998 est.)
Ethnic Groups: 55% mestizo (mixed Indian and Spanish), 25% Indian, 10% Spanish, 10% black
Languages: Spanish (official), Indian languages, especially Quechua
Religions: 95% Roman Catholic
Birth Rate: 23.16/1,000 population (1998 est.)
Death Rate: 5.17/1,000 population (1998 est.)
Infant Mortality: 32.07 deaths/1,000 live births (1998 est.)
Life Expectancy at Birth: 69.19 years male, 74.54 years female (1998 est.)
Total Fertility Rate: 2.75 children born/woman (1998 est.)
Literacy: 90.1% (1997 est.)

■ GOVERNMENT

Leader(s): Pres. Jamil Mahuad, V.Pres. Gustavo Noboa
Government Type: republic
Administrative Divisions: 21 provinces
Nationhood: May 24, 1822 (from Spain; Battle of Pichincha)
National Holiday: Independence Day, Aug. 10

■ ECONOMY

Overview: vulnerable to international oil prices; the banana crop, second in importance only to oil, has been hurt by EC import quotas and banana blight; strict austerity program has resulted in economic stabilization
GDP: $53.4 billion, per capita $4,400; real growth rate 3.4% (1997 est.)
Inflation: 34.2% (June 1998)
Industries: accounts for 37% of GDP; food processing, textiles, metal works, paper products, chemicals, fishing, timber, petroleum

Labour Force: 4.1 million (1997 est.); 29.7% trade and tourism, 27.7% community, social and business services, 17.5% industry
Unemployment: 6.9%, with widespread underemployment (Aug. 1997 est.)
Agriculture: accounts for 12% of GDP and 35% of labour force (including fishing and forestry); leading producer and exporter of bananas and balsawood; crop and livestock sector; net importer of food-grain, dairy products and sugar
Natural Resources: petroleum, fish, timber

■ **FINANCE/TRADE**

Currency: sucre (S/) = 100 centavos
International Reserves Excluding Gold: $1.724 billion (Jan. 1999)
Gold Reserves: 0.414 million fine troy ounces (Jan. 1999)
Budget: revenues $3.6 billion; expenditures $3.6 billion, including capital expenditures (1997 est.)
Defence Expenditures: 2.1% of GDP (1997)
Education Expenditures: 3.4% of GNP (1995)
External Debt: $12.5 billion (1997)
Exports: $4.133 billion (1998); commodities: petroleum 47%, coffee, bananas, cocoa products, shrimp, fish products; partners: US 38%, Latin America, Caribbean, European Community countries
Imports: $5.496 billion (1998); commodities: transport equipment, vehicles, machinery, chemicals, petroleum; partners: US 28%, Latin America, Caribbean, European Community, Japan

■ **COMMUNICATIONS**

Daily Newspapers: 29 (1996)
Televisions: 128/1,000 inhabitants (1996)
Radios: 342/1,000 inhabitants (1996)
Telephones: 6.9/100 inhabitants (1996 est.)

■ **TRANSPORTATION**

Motor Vehicles: 684,000; 258,000 passenger cars (1997 est.)
Roads: 43,249 km; 5,752 km paved
Railway: 965 km
Air Traffic: 1,925,000 passengers carried (1996)
Airports: 183; 52 have paved runways (1997 est.)

Canadian Embassy: The Canadian Embassy, Avenida 6 de Diciembre, 2816 y James Orton, Edificio Josueth Gonzalez, 4th Fl., Quito, Ecuador; mailing address: P.O. Box 17-11-8512, Quito, Ecuador. Tel: (011-593-2) 564-795. Fax: (011-593-2) 503-108.
Embassy in Canada: Embassy of the Republic of Ecuador, 50 O'Connor St, Ste 1311, Ottawa ON K1P 6L2. Tel: (613) 563-8206. Fax: (613) 235-5776.

Egypt

Long-Form Name: Arab Republic of Egypt
Capital: Cairo

■ **GEOGRAPHY**

Area: 1,001,450 sq. km
Coastline: 2,450 km
Climate: desert; hot, dry summers with moderate winters
Environment: Nile is only perennial water source; increasing soil salinization below Aswan High Dam; hot, driving windstorm called khamsin occurs in spring; water pollution; desertification; urbanization and erosion are decreasing the arable land available
Terrain: vast desert plateau interrupted by Nile valley and delta
Land Use: 2% arable; 0% permanent; 0% meadows; negligible forest; 98% other, includes 3% irrigated
Location: NE Africa, bordering on Mediterranean Sea, Red Sea

■ **PEOPLE**

Population: 66,050,004 (July 1998 est.)
Nationality: Egyptian
Age Structure: 0-14 yrs: 36%; 15-64: 60%; 65+: 4% (1998 est.)
Population Growth Rate: 1.86% (1998 est.)
Net Migration: -0.35 migrants/1,000 population (1998 est.)
Ethnic Groups: 99% Eastern Hamitic stock; 1% Greek, Italian, Syro-Lebanese, Armenian
Languages: Arabic (official); English and French
Religions: 94% Muslim (mostly Sunni), 6% Coptic Christian and other
Birth Rate: 27.31/1,000 population (1998 est.)
Death Rate: 8.41/1,000 population (1998 est.)
Infant Mortality: 69.23 deaths/1,000 live births (1998 est.)
Life Expectancy at Birth: 60.09 years male, 64.14 years female (1998 est.)
Total Fertility Rate: 3.41 children born/woman (1998 est.)
Literacy: 51.4% (1997 est.)

■ **GOVERNMENT**

Leader(s): Pres. Mohammad Hosni Mubarak, Prime Min. Kamal Ahmed al-Ganzouri
Government Type: republic
Administrative Divisions: 26 governorates
Nationhood: Feb. 28, 1922 (from UK; formerly known as United Arab Republic)
National Holiday: Anniversary of the Revolution, July 23

■ ECONOMY

Overview: urban population growth puts pressure on the agricultural sector; having difficulty with its debt servicing; vulnerable to oil prices; unemployment has become a growing problem
GDP: $267.1 billion, per capita $4,400; real growth rate 5.2% (1997 est.)
Inflation: 3.6% (June 1998)
Industries: accounts for 32% of GDP, textiles, food processing, tourism, chemicals, petroleum, construction, cement, metals
Labour Force: 22.5 million (1997 est.); 31.3% agriculture, 22.2% community, social and business services, 15.4% industry
Unemployment: 9.4% (1997 est.)
Agriculture: accounts for 17% of GDP and employs more than one-third of labour force; dependent on irrigation water from the Nile; world's fifth largest cotton exporter; other crops include rice, corn, wheat, beans, fruit, vegetables; not self-sufficient in food
Natural Resources: crude oil, natural gas, iron ore, phosphates, manganese, limestone, gypsum, talc, asbestos, lead, zinc

■ FINANCE/TRADE

Currency: Egyptian pound (LE) = 100 piasters
International Reserves Excluding Gold: $18.124 billion (Dec. 1998)
Gold Reserves: 2.432 million fine troy ounces (Dec. 1998)
Budget: revenues $19.2 billion; expenditures $19.8 billion, including capital expenditures of $4 billion (1996-97 est.)
Defence Expenditures: 8.2% of GDP (1996)
Education Expenditures: 5.6% of GNP (1995)
External Debt: $30.5 billion (1996-97 est.)
Exports: $3.921 billion (1997); commodities: raw cotton, crude and refined petroleum, cotton yarn, textiles; partners: US, European Community, Japan, Eastern Europe
Imports: $13.211 billion (1997); commodities: foods, machinery and equipment, fertilizers, wood products, durable consumer goods, capital goods; partners: US, European Community, Japan, Eastern Europe

■ COMMUNICATIONS

Daily Newspapers: 17 (1996)
Televisions: 119/1,000 inhabitants (1996)
Radios: 316/1,000 inhabitants (1996)
Telephones: 4.8/100 inhabitants (1996 est.)

■ TRANSPORTATION

Motor Vehicles: 1,711,000; 1,300,000 passenger cars (1997 est.)
Roads: 64,000 km; 49,984 km paved

Railway: 4,751 km
Air Traffic: 5,281,500 passengers carried (1996)
Airports: 89; 70 have paved runways (1997 est.)

Canadian Embassy: The Canadian Embassy, Arab International Bank Building, 5 Midan El Saraya el Kobra, Garden City, Cairo, Egypt; mailing address: P.O. Box 1667, Cairo, Egypt. Tel: (011-20-2) 354-3110. Fax: (011-20-2) 356-3548.
Embassy in Canada: Embassy of the Arab Republic of Egypt, 454 Laurier Ave E, Ottawa ON K1N 6R3. Tel: (613) 234-4931. Fax: (613) 234-9347.

El Salvador

Long-Form Name: Republic of El Salvador
Capital: San Salvador

■ GEOGRAPHY

Area: 21,040 sq. km
Coastline: 307 km
Climate: tropical; rainy season (May to Oct.), dry season (Nov. to Apr.)
Environment: the Land of Volcanoes; subject to frequent and sometimes very destructive earthquakes; deforestation; soil erosion and pollution; water pollution
Terrain: mostly mountains with narrow coastal belt and central plateau
Land Use: 27% arable; 8% permanent; 29% meadows; 5% forest; 31% other, includes 6% irrigated
Location: Central (Latin) America, bordering on Pacific Ocean

■ PEOPLE

Population: 5,752,067 (July 1998 est.)
Nationality: Salvadoran
Age Structure: 0-14 yrs: 37%; 15-64: 58%; 65+: 5% (1998 est.)
Population Growth Rate: 1.57% (1998 est.)
Net Migration: -4.73 migrants/1,000 population (1998 est.)
Ethnic Groups: 94% mestizo, 5% Indian, 1% white
Languages: Spanish, Nahua spoken among some Indians
Religions: approx. 75% Roman Catholic, with activity by Protestant groups throughout the country
Birth Rate: 26.71/1,000 population (1998 est.)
Death Rate: 6.32/1,000 population (1998 est.)
Infant Mortality: 29.07 deaths/1,000 live births (1998 est.)
Life Expectancy at Birth: 66.31 years male, 73.17 years female (1998 est.)

Total Fertility Rate: 3.06 children born/woman (1998 est.)
Literacy: 71.5% (1997 est.)

■ GOVERNMENT

Leader(s): Pres. Francisco Flores Perez, V.Pres. Carlos Quintanilla
Government Type: republic
Administrative Divisions: 14 departments
Nationhood: Sept. 15, 1821 (from Spain)
National Holiday: Independence Day, Sept. 15

■ ECONOMY

Overview: agricultural sector accounts for one-quarter of GDP and employs majority of labour force; major crop is coffee; economic losses due to guerrilla sabotage are extensive
GDP: $17.8 billion, per capita $3,000; real growth rate 4% (1997 est.)
Inflation: 2.8% (July 1998)
Industries: accounts for 24% of GDP; food processing, textiles, non-metallic products, tobacco, beverages, clothing, petroleum products, cement
Labour Force: 2.1 million (1997 est.); 35.8% agriculture, 19.6% community, social and business services, 17.4% trade and tourism
Unemployment: 7.7% (1997 est.)
Agriculture: accounts for 15% of GDP and 40% of labour force (including fishing and forestry); coffee most important commercial crop; other products—sugar cane, corn, rice, beans, oilseeds, beef, dairy products, shrimp; not self-sufficient in food
Natural Resources: hydroelectricity and geothermal power, crude oil

■ FINANCE/TRADE

Currency: colón (pl. colones) (C/) = 100 centavos
International Reserves Excluding Gold: $1.757 billion (Oct. 1998)
Gold Reserves: 0.469 million fine troy ounces (Oct. 1998)
Budget: revenues $1.75 billion, expenditures $1.82 billion, including capital expenditures of $317 million (1997 est.)
Defence Expenditures: 7.09% of total govt. expenditure (1997)
Education Expenditures: 19.64% of govt. expenditure (1997)
External Debt: $2.6 billion (1997)
Exports: $1.263 billion (1998); commodities: coffee 60%, sugar, cotton, shrimp; partners: US 49%, Germany 24%, Guatemala 7%, Costa Rica 4%, Japan 4%
Imports: $3.112 billion (1998); commodities:

petroleum products, consumer goods, foodstuffs, machinery, construction materials, fertilizer; partners: US 40%, Guatemala 12%, Venezuela 7%, Mexico 7%, Germany 5%, Japan 4%

■ COMMUNICATIONS

Daily Newspapers: 5 (1996)
Televisions: 675/1,000 inhabitants (1996)
Radios: 461/1,000 inhabitants (1996)
Telephones: 6.1/100 inhabitants (1996 est.)

■ TRANSPORTATION

Motor Vehicles: 80,100; 35,300 passenger cars (1997 est.)
Roads: 9,977 km; 1,985 km paved
Railway: 602 km
Air Traffic: 1,800,000 passengers carried (1996)
Airports: 88; 4 have paved runways (1997 est.)

Canadian Embassy: Office of the Canadian Embassy, 111 Avenida Las Palmas, Colonia San Benito, San Salvador, El Salvador. Tel: (011-503) 279-4655. Fax: (011-503) 279-0765.
Embassy in Canada: Embassy of the Republic of El Salvador, 209 Kent St, Ottawa ON K2P 1Z8. Tel: (613) 238-2939. Fax: (613) 238-6940.

Equatorial Guinea

Long-Form Name: Republic of Equatorial Guinea
Capital: Malabo

■ GEOGRAPHY

Area: 28,050 sq. km
Coastline: 296 km
Climate: tropical; always hot, humid
Environment: subject to violent windstorms; desertification; unsafe drinking water
Terrain: coastal plains rise to interior hills; islands are volcanic
Land Use: 5% arable; 4% permanent; 4% meadows; 46% forest; 41% other
Location: WC Africa, bordering on South Atlantic Ocean

■ PEOPLE

Population: 454,001 (July 1998 est.)
Nationality: Equatorial Guinean or Equatoguinean
Age Structure: 0-14 yrs: 43%; 15-64: 53%; 65+: 4% (1998 est.)
Population Growth Rate: 2.56 (1998 est.)
Net Migration: 0 migrants/1,000 population (1998 est.)
Ethnic Groups: indigenous population of Bioko, primarily Bubi, some Fernandinos; Rio Muni,

primarily–Fang; less than 1,000 Europeans, mostly Spanish
Languages: Spanish (official), pidgin English, Fang, Bubi, Ndowe, Bujeba, Anobones and Corisqueño
Religions: natives all nominally Christian and predominantly Roman Catholic; some pagan practices retained (5%)
Birth Rate: 38.9/1,000 population (1998 est.)
Death Rate: 13.32/1,000 population (1998 est.)
Infant Mortality: 93.45 deaths/1,000 live births (1998 est.)
Life Expectancy at Birth: 51.61 years male, 56.31 years female (1998 est.)
Total Fertility Rate: 5.06 children born/woman (1998 est.)
Literacy: 78.5% (1997 est.)

■ GOVERNMENT

Leader(s): Pres. Teodoro Obiang Nguema Mbasogo, Prime Min. Serafin Seriche Dougan
Government Type: republic in transition to multi-party democracy
Administrative Divisions: 7 provinces
Nationhood: Oct. 12, 1968 (from Spain; formerly Spanish Guinea)
National Holiday: Independence Day, Oct. 12

■ ECONOMY

Overview: the economy is recovering from destruction by a past regime; subsistence agriculture, forestry and fishing predominate; little industry; many undeveloped natural resources, but increased exploitation of recently discovered natural gas resources is boosting the economy
GDP: $660 million, per capita $1,500; real growth rate n.a. (1997 est.)
Inflation: 7.3% (Nov. 1996)
Industries: accounts for 33% of GDP; fishing, sawmilling
Labour Force: n.a.; 66% agriculture, 23% services, 11% industry
Unemployment: n.a.
Agriculture: accounts for 46% of GDP; cash crops—timber and coffee from Rio Muni, cocoa from Bioko; food crops—rice, yams, cassava, bananas, oil, palm nuts, manioc, livestock
Natural Resources: timber, crude oil, small unexploited deposits of gold, manganese, uranium

■ FINANCE/TRADE

Currency: Communauté financière africaine franc (CFAF) = 100 centimes
International Reserves Excluding Gold: $14 million (May 1998)

Gold Reserves: n.a.
Budget: revenues $47 million, expenditures $43 million, including capital expenditures of $7 million (1996 est.)
Defence Expenditures: 1.0% of GDP (1996)
Education Expenditures: n.a.
External Debt: $282 million (1996)
Exports: $175 million (1996); commodities: coffee, timber, cocoa beans; partners: Spain 44%, Germany 19%, Italy 12%, Netherlands 11%
Imports: $292 million (1996); commodities: petroleum, food, beverages, clothing, machinery; partners: Spain 34%, Italy 16%, France 14%, Netherlands 8%

■ COMMUNICATIONS

Daily Newspapers: 1 (1996)
Televisions: 9.6/1,000 inhabitants (1996)
Radios: 427/1,000 inhabitants (1996)
Telephones: 0.6/100 persons (1996 est.)

■ TRANSPORTATION

Motor Vehicles: 10,500; 6,500 passenger cars (1997 est.)
Roads: 2,820 km, none paved
Railway: none
Air Traffic: 15,000 passengers carried (1996)
Airports: 3; 2 have paved runways (1997 est.)

Canadian Embassy: The Canadian Embassy to Equatorial Guinea, c/o P.O. Box 4037, Libreville, Gabon. Tel: (011-241) 74-34-64. Fax (011-241) 74-34-66.
Embassy in Canada: Embassy of Equatorial Guinea, 1511 K St NW, Washington DC 20005, USA. Tel: (202) 393-0525. Fax: (202) 393-0348.

Eritrea

Long-Form Name: State of Eritrea
Capital: Asmara (formerly Asmera)

■ GEOGRAPHY

Area: 121,320 sq. km
Coastline: 1,151 km mainland coast; 2,234 km including island coastlines
Climate: hot, dry desert along Red Sea coast, cooler and wetter in central highlands, semi-arid in west
Environment: frequent droughts, famine, deforestation, soil erosion, overgrazing
Terrain: highlands descending to coastal desert in east, hilly in northwest, flat to rolling plains in southwest
Land Use: 12% arable, 1% permanent crops,

48% meadows and pastures, 20% forests and woodland, 19% other
Location: E Africa

■ PEOPLE

Population: 3,842,436 (July 1998 est.)
Nationality: Eritrean
Age Structure: 0-14 yrs: 43%; 15-64: 54%; 65+: 3% (1998 est.)
Population Growth Rate: 3.39% (1998 est.)
Net Migration: 3.9 migrants/1,000 population (1998 est.)
Ethnic Groups: 50% ethnic Tigrinya, 40% Tigre and Kunama, 4% Afar, 3% Saho, 3% other
Languages: Afar, Amharic, Tigre and Kunama, Cushitic dialects, Tigrinya, Nora Bana, Arabic
Religions: Muslim, Coptic Christian, Roman Catholic, Protestant
Birth Rate: 42.52/1,000 population (1998 est.)
Death Rate: 12.57/1,000 population (1998 est.)
Infant Mortality: 78.51 deaths/1,000 live births (1998 est.)
Life Expectancy at Birth: 53.19 years male, 57.51 years female (1998 est.)
Total Fertility Rate: 5.99 children born/woman (1998 est.)
Literacy: n.a.

■ GOVERNMENT

Leader(s): Pres. Isaias Afewerki, V.Pres. Mahmud Ahmed Sherifo
Government Type: transitional govt.
Administrative Divisions: 8 provinces
Nationhood: May 27, 1993 (from Ethiopia)
National Holiday: National Day (independence from Ethiopia), May 24

■ ECONOMY

Overview: with independence from Ethiopia, Eritrea faces the bitter economic problems of a small and desperately poor nation; subsistence farming will continue to be the people's economic mainstay; production is augmented by remittances from abroad, and there are long-term prospects for revenue from offshore oil development, offshore fishing, and tourism; Ethiopia is largely dependent on Eritrean ports for foreign trade
GDP: $2.2 billion, per capita $600; real growth rate 6.8% (1997 est.)
Inflation: 10% (1995 est.)
Industries: accounts for 20% of GDP; food processing, beverages, textiles, clothing manufacture
Labour Force: 2.1 million (1997 est.)
Unemployment: n.a.
Agriculture: accounts for 18% of GDP; livestock,

fish, vegetables, sorghum, cotton, coffee and tobacco
Natural Resources: gold, potash, copper, zinc, salt, fish

■ FINANCE/TRADE

Currency: nafka = 100 cents
International Reserves Excluding Gold: n.a.
Gold Reserves: n.a.
Budget: revenues $226 million; expenditures $453 million, including capital expenditures of $88 million (1996)
Defence Expenditures: 7.5% of GDP (1996)
Education Expenditures: n.a.
External Debt: $46 million (1996 est.)
Exports: $71 million (1996 est.); commodities: livestock, sorghum, textiles, food, small manufactures; partners: Ethiopia, Sudan, Saudi Arabia, US, Italy, Yemen
Imports: $499 million (1996 est.); commodities: processed goods, machinery, petroleum products; partners: Ethiopia, Saudi Arabia, Italy, United Arab Emirates

■ COMMUNICATIONS

Daily Newspapers: 0 (1996)
Televisions: 0.3/1,000 inhabitants (1996)
Radios: 101/1,000 inhabitants (1996)
Telephones: 0.5/100 inhabitants (1996 est.)

■ TRANSPORTATION

Motor Vehicles: n.a.
Roads: 4,010 km, 874 km paved
Railway: 307 km; not operational
Air Traffic: n.a.
Airports: 20; 2 have paved runways (1997 est.)

Canadian Embassy: The Canadian Embassy to Eritrea, c/o P.O. Box 1130, Addis Ababa, Ethiopia. Tel: (011-251-1) 71-30-22. Fax: (011-251-1) 71-30-33.
Embassy in Canada: Embassy of the State of Eritrea, 75 Albert St., Suite 610, Ottawa, ON K1P 5E7. Tel: (613) 234-3989. Fax: (613) 234-6213

Estonia

Long-Form Name: Republic of Estonia
Capital: Tallinn

■ GEOGRAPHY

Area: 45,226 sq. km
Coastline: 1,393 km
Climate: wet, moderate winter; long windy autumn; warm sunny summer; late and short spring

Environment: severe air pollution, soil and ground water contamination (chemicals and petroleum products), radioactive waste; frequent spring floods are a natural hazard
Terrain: marshy, lowlands, sloping coastal plain; islands account for 10% of the region
Land Use: 22% arable, negligible permanent crops; 11% meadows and pastures; 31% forest and woodland; 36% other
Location: NE Europe, bordering on Baltic Sea

■ PEOPLE

Population: 1,421,335 (July 1998 est.)
Nationality: Estonian
Age Structure: 0-14 yrs: 19%; 15-64: 67%; 65+: 14% (1998 est.)
Population Growth Rate: -0.99% (1998 est.)
Net Migration: -4.76 migrants/1,000 population (1998 est.)
Ethnic Groups: 64.2% Estonian, 28.7% Russian, 2.7% Ukrainian, 1.5% Byelorussian, 1.9% other
Languages: Estonian (official), Russian, Latvian, Lithuanian, English and German also spoken
Religions: Lutheran, Orthodox Christian
Birth Rate: 9.04/1,000 population (1998 est.)
Death Rate: 14.15/1,000 population (1998 est.)
Infant Mortality: 13.98 deaths/1,000 live births (1998 est.)
Life Expectancy at Birth: 62.5 years male, 74.83 years female (1998 est.)
Total Fertility Rate: 1.29 children born/woman (1998 est.)
Literacy: 100% (1997 est.)

■ GOVERNMENT

Leader(s): Pres. Lennart Meri, Prme Min. Mart Laar
Government Type: parliamentary democracy
Administrative Divisions: 15 counties
Nationhood: Sept. 6, 1991 (from Soviet Union)
National Holiday: Independence Day, Feb. 24

■ ECONOMY

Overview: market reforms and stabilizing measures are rapidly transforming the economy; living standards and incomes are rising, but so are unemployment and inflation
GDP: $9.38 billion, per capita $6,450; real growth rate 10% (1997 est.)
Inflation: 12.6% (Apr. 1998)
Industries: accounts for approximately 25% of GDP; electronics, electrical engineering, textiles, clothing, footwear, shipbuilding
Labour Force: 1 million (1997 est.); 24.6% industry, 25.1% community, social and business services, 12.9% trade and tourism
Unemployment: 3.6% (1997 est.); large numbers of underemployed

Agriculture: contributes 7% to GDP, and employs 20% of labour force; dairy products, pork, poultry, eggs, fruit, vegetables; net exports of meat, fish, dairy products, potatoes
Natural Resources: fish, shale, phosphorites, amber, limestone, peat, dolomite

■ FINANCE/TRADE

Currency: kroon (pl. kroons) = 100 cents
International Reserves Excluding Gold: $759 million (Dec. 1998)
Gold Reserves: 0.010 million fine troy ounces (Jan. 1999)
Budget: revenues $1.7 billion; expenditures $1.8 billion, including capital expenditures of $214 million (1996 est.)
Defence Expenditures: 4.6% of govt. expenditure (1997)
Education Expenditures: 10.16% of govt. expenditure (1997)
External Debt: $405 million (1996)
Exports: $3.130 billion (1998); dairy products, fish, furniture, electrical power, meat; partners: Russia and other former Soviet republics 50%, West 50%
Imports: $4.612 billion (1998); machinery 45%, oil 13%, chemicals 12%; partners: Finland, Russia

■ COMMUNICATIONS

Daily Newspapers: 15 (1996)
Televisions: 408/1,000 inhabitants (1996)
Radios: 680/1,000 inhabitants (1996)
Telephones: 30.2/100 inhabitants (1996 est.)

■ TRANSPORTATION

Motor Vehicles: n.a.
Roads: 15,304 km; 8,142 km paved
Railway: 1,018 km (does not include industrial lines)
Air Traffic: 165,600 passengers carried (1996)
Airports: 5; all have paved runways (1997 est.)

Canadian Embassy: Office of the Canadian Embassy, Toom Kooli 13, 2nd Fl, 0100 Tallinn, Estonia. Tel: (011-372) 631-3570. Fax: (011-372) 631-3573.
Embassy in Canada: c/o Embassy of the Republic of Estonia, 2131 Massachusetts Ave NW, Washington DC 20008, USA. Tel: (202) 588-0101. Fax: (202) 588-0108.

Ethiopia

Long-Form Name: Federal Democratic Republic of Ethiopia
Capital: Addis Ababa

■ GEOGRAPHY

Area: 1,127,127 sq. km
Coastline: none; landlocked
Climate: tropical with wide topographic-induced variation; prone to extended droughts
Environment: geologically active Great Rift Valley susceptible to earthquakes, volcanic eruptions; deforestation; overgrazing; soil erosion; desertification; frequent droughts; famine
Terrain: high plateau with central mountain range divided by Great Rift Valley
Land Use: 12% arable; 1% permanent; 40% meadows; 25% forest; 22% other
Location: E Africa, between Somalia and Sudan

■ PEOPLE

Population: 58,390,351 (July 1998 est.)
Nationality: Ethiopian
Age Structure: 0-14 yrs: 46%; 15-64: 51%; 65+: 3% (1998 est.)
Population Growth Rate: 2.21% (1998 est.)
Net Migration: -1.33 migrants/1,000 population (1998 est.)
Ethnic Groups: 40% Oromo, 32% Amhara and Tigrean, 9% Sidamo, 6% Shankella, 6% Somali, 4% Afar, 2% Gurage, 1% other
Languages: Amharic (official), Tigrinya, Orominga, Guaraginga, Somali, Arabic, English (major foreign language taught in schools)
Religions: 45–50% Muslim, 35–40% Ethiopian Orthodox, 12% animist, 5% other
Birth Rate: 44.69/1,000 population (1998 est.)
Death Rate: 21.25/1,000 population (1998 est.)
Infant Mortality: 125.65 deaths/1,000 live births (1998 est.)
Life Expectancy at Birth: 39.76 years male, 41.97 years female (1998 est.)
Total Fertility Rate: 6.88 children born/woman (1998 est.)
Literacy: 35.5% (1997 est.)

■ GOVERNMENT

Leader(s): Pres. Negasso Ghidada, Prem. Meles Zenawi
Government Type: federal republic
Administrative Divisions: 9 administrative regions and 1 federal capital
Nationhood: oldest (at least 2,000 years) independent country in Africa and one of the oldest in the world
National Holiday: National Day, May 28

■ ECONOMY

Overview: Ethiopia remains one of the poorest and least developed countries in the world. Its economy is based on agriculture and suffers from recent periods of drought, poor cultivation practices, and the deterioration of internal security conditions.
GDP: $29 billion, per capita $530; real growth rate 5% (1997 est.)
Inflation: 0.1% (1997)
Industries: accounts for 12% of GDP, cement, textiles, food processing, beverages, chemicals, metals processing, oil refinery
Labour Force: 26.7 million (1997 est.); 80% agriculture, 12% services, 8% industry
Unemployment: n.a.
Agriculture: accounts for 55% of GDP even though frequent droughts, poor cultivation practices and state economic policies keep farm output low; famines not uncommon; estimated 50% of agricultural production at subsistence level
Natural Resources: small reserves of gold, platinum, copper, potash

■ FINANCE/TRADE

Currency: birr (Br) = 100 cents
International Reserves Excluding Gold: $483 million (Jan. 1999)
Gold Reserves: 0.030 million fine troy ounces (Jan. 1999)
Budget: revenues $1 billion; expenditures $1.48 billion, including capital expenditures of $415 million (1997 est.)
Defence Expenditures: 2.0% of GDP (1996)
Education Expenditures: 4.7% of GNP (1995)
External Debt: $10.077 billion (1996)
Exports: $587 million (1997); commodities: coffee 60%, hides; partners: US, Germany, Djibouti, Japan, Yemen, France, Italy
Imports: $1.142 billion (1995); commodities: food, fuels, capital goods; partners: former USSR countries, Italy, Germany, Japan, UK, US, France

■ COMMUNICATIONS

Daily Newspapers: 4 (1996)
Televisions: 5.2/1,000 inhabitants (1996)
Radios: 194/1,000 inhabitants (1996)
Telephones: 0.2/100 inhabitants (1996 est.)

■ TRANSPORTATION

Motor Vehicles: 69,000; 46,400 passenger cars (1997 est.)
Roads: 28,500 km; 4,275 km paved
Railway: 681 km
Air Traffic: 743,000 passengers carried (1996)
Airports: 86; 10 have paved runways (1997 est.)

Canadian Embassy: The Canadian Embassy, Old Airport Area, Higher 23, Kebele 12, House

Number 122, Addis Ababa; mailing address: P.O. Box 1130, Addis Ababa, Ethiopia. Tel: (011-251-1) 71-30-22. Fax: (011-251-1) 71-30-33.
Embassy in Canada: Embassy of the Federal Democratic Republic of Ethiopia, 151 Slater St, Ste 210, Ottawa ON K1P 5H3. Tel: (613) 235-6637. Fax: (613) 235-4638.

Falkland Islands

Long-Form Name: Colony of the Falkland Islands
Capital: Stanley (on East Falkland)

■ GEOGRAPHY

Area: numerous islands covering 12,170 sq. km
Climate: damp, cool, temperate; strong winds, esp. in spring; occasional snow all year
Land Use: 99% pastureland
Location: S South America, in the South Atlantic Ocean

■ PEOPLE

Population: 2,805 (July 1998 est.)
Nationality: Falkland Islander
Ethnic Groups: almost 100% British descent
Languages: English

■ GOVERNMENT

Colony Territory of: Dependent Territory of the United Kingdom
Leader(s): Chief of State: Queen Elizabeth II; Governor Donald Lamont, Chief Executive Andrew Gurr
Government Type: dependent territory of the UK, although in 1990 Argentina declared the Falklands and other British-held South Atlantic Islands part of new Argentine province Tierra del Fuego
National Holiday: Liberation Day, June 14

■ ECONOMY

Overview: heavily agricultural, esp. sheep farming, with wool main product; fishing: illex squid; exports tend to outweigh imports in value; chief trading partner: United Kingdom

■ FINANCE/TRADE

Currency: Falkland Islands pound (FKP) = 100 pence, at parity with the British pound sterling

Canadian Embassy: c/o The Canadian High Commission, Macdonald House, 1 Grosvenor Square, London W1X 0AB, England, UK. Tel: (011-44-171) 258-6600. Fax: (011-44-171) 445-3302.

Representative to Canada: c/o British High Commission, 80 Elgin St, Ottawa ON K1P 5K7. Tel: (613) 237-1530. Fax: (613) 237-7980.

Faroe Islands

Long-Form Name: Faroe Islands
Capital: Tórshavn (island of Stremoy)

■ GEOGRAPHY

Area: 1,399 sq. km (total of 18 islands and some reefs)
Climate: cold and windy; mild winters, cool summers; foggy
Land Use: 6% arable; 94% other
Location: Norwegian Sea (N Atlantic Ocean), N of Scotland

■ PEOPLE

Population: 41,834 (July 1998 est.)
Nationality: Faroese
Ethnic Groups: Scandinavian
Languages: Faroese (derived from Old Norse), Danish

■ GOVERNMENT

Colony Territory of: Dependent Territory of Denmark
Leader(s): Queen Margrethe II of Denmark, represented by High Comm. Vibeke Larsen
Government Type: dependency with some degree of self-rule
National Holiday: Birthday of the Queen, Apr. 16

■ ECONOMY

Overview: fishing main industry, now in decline, which poses great danger to the economy; steep coastline and treacherous currents make trading by sea difficult; exports: fish and fish products; partners: Denmark, Norway, Sweden, Germany, United States

■ FINANCE/TRADE

Currency: Danish krone (kr) = 100 oere

Canadian Embassy: c/o The Canadian Embassy, Kr. Bernikowsgade 1, 1105 Copenhagen K, Denmark. Tel: (011-45) 33-48-32-00. Fax: (011-45) 33-48-32-20.
Representative to Canada: c/o Embassy of the Kingdom of Denmark, 47 Clarence St, Ste 450, Ottawa ON K1N 9K1. Tel: (613) 562-1811. Fax: (613) 562-1812.

Fiji

Long-Form Name: Republic of Fiji
Capital: Suva

■ GEOGRAPHY

Area: 18,270 sq. km; includes 332 islands of which approx. 110 are inhabited
Coastline: 1,129 km
Climate: tropical marine; only slight seasonal temperature variation
Environment: subject to hurricanes from Nov. to Jan.; deforestation and soil erosion
Terrain: mostly mountains of volcanic origin
Land Use: 10% arable; 4% permanent; 10% meadows; 65% forest; 11% other
Location: Pacific Ocean, N of New Zealand

■ PEOPLE

Population: 802,611 (July 1998 est.)
Nationality: Fijian
Age Structure: 0-14 yrs: 34%; 15-64: 63%; 65+: 3% (1998 est.)
Population Growth Rate: 1.28% (1998 est.)
Net Migration: -3.92 migrants/1,000 population (1998 est.)
Ethnic Groups: 46% Indian, 49% Fijian, 5% European, other Pacific Islanders, overseas Chinese and others
Languages: English (official); Fijian; Hindi
Religions: Christianity 52%, Hinduism 38%, Muslim 8%, other 2%
Birth Rate: 22.92/1,000 population (1998 est.)
Death Rate: 6.25/1,000 population (1998 est.)
Infant Mortality: 16.65 deaths/1,000 live births (1998 est.)
Life Expectancy at Birth: 63.92 years male, 68.78 years female (1998 est.)
Total Fertility Rate: 2.74 children born/woman (1998 est.)
Literacy: 91.6% (1997 est.)

■ GOVERNMENT

Leader(s): Pres. Ratu Kamisese Mara, Prime Min. Mahendra Pal Chaudhry
Government Type: republic
Administrative Divisions: 4 divisions and 1 dependency
Nationhood: Oct. 10, 1970 (from UK)
National Holiday: Independence Day, Oct. 10

■ ECONOMY

Overview: the economy, based on agriculture, has recovered from military coups, droughts and a drop in tourism; sugar exports are a major source of income
GDP: $5.1 billion, per capita $6,500; real growth rate 5% (1996 est.)
Inflation: 6.8% (July 1998)
Industries: accounts for 18% of GDP; sugar, copra, tourism, gold, silver, fishing, clothing, lumber, small cottage industries

Labour Force: 97,280 (1995); 29.3% community, social and business services, 24.9% industry, 14.5% trade and tourism
Unemployment: 6% (1997 est.)
Agriculture: accounts for 21% of GDP; principal cash crop is sugar cane; coconuts, cassava, rice, sweet potatoes and bananas; small livestock sector includes cattle, pigs, horses and goats; annual fish catch is significant
Natural Resources: timber, fish, gold, copper, offshore oil potential

■ FINANCE/TRADE

Currency: Fijian dollar ($F) = 100 cents
International Reserves Excluding Gold: $383 million (Nov. 1998)
Gold Reserves: 0.001 million fine troy ounces (Jan. 1999)
Budget: revenues $540.65 million; expenditures $742.65 million, including capital expenditures n.a. (1997 est.)
Defence Expenditures: 5.0% of GDP (1997)
Education Expenditures: 18.19% of govt. expenditure (1996)
External Debt: $333.8 million (1996 est.)
Exports: $589 million (1997); commodities: sugar 49%, copra, processed fish, lumber; partners: UK 45%, Australia 21%, US 4.7%
Imports: $965 million (1997); commodities: food 15%, petroleum products, machinery, consumer goods; partners: US 48%, New Zealand, Australia, Japan

■ COMMUNICATIONS

Daily Newspapers: 1 (1996)
Televisions: 25/1,000 inhabitants (1996)
Radios: 615/1,000 inhabitants (1996)
Telephones: 8.8/100 inhabitants (1996 est.)

■ TRANSPORTATION

Motor Vehicles: 59,000; 30,000 passenger cars (1997 est.)
Roads: 3,440 km; 1,692 km paved
Railway: 597 km
Air Traffic: 480,000 passengers carried (1996)
Airports: 24; 3 have paved runways (1997 est.)

Canadian Embassy: The Canadian Embassy to Fiji, c/o The Canadian High Commission, P.O. Box 12-049, Thorndon, Wellington, New Zealand. Tel: (011-679) 721-936. Fax: (011-679) 750-666.
Embassy in Canada: Embassy of the Republic of Fiji, 630 Third Ave, 7th Fl, New York NY 10017, USA. Tel: (212) 687-4130. Fax: (212) 687-3963.

Finland

Long-Form Name: Republic of Finland
Capital: Helsinki

■ GEOGRAPHY

Area: 337,030 sq. km
Coastline: 1,126 km excluding islands and coastal indentations
Climate: cold temperate; potentially subarctic, but comparatively mild because of moderating influence of the North Atlantic Current, Baltic Sea and more than 60,000 lakes
Environment: permanently wet ground covers approx. 30% of land; air and water pollution
Terrain: mostly low, flat to rolling plains interspersed with lakes and low hills
Land Use: 8% arable; 0% permanent; 0% meadows; 76% forest; 16% other
Location: N Europe, bordering on Baltic Sea

■ PEOPLE

Population: 5,149,242 (July 1998 est.)
Nationality: Finn
Age Structure: 0-14 yrs: 19%; 15-64: 67%; 65+: 14% (1998 est.)
Population Growth Rate: 0.2% (1998 est.)
Net Migration: 0.45 migrants/1,000 population (1998 est.)
Ethnic Groups: 93% Finn, 6% Swede, 0.11% Lapp, 0.12% Gypsy, 0.02% Tatar
Languages: 93.5% Finnish, 6.3% Swedish (both official); small Lapp-and Russian-speaking minorities; business language is English
Religions: 89% Evangelical Lutheran, 9% atheist, 1% Eastern Orthodox, 1% other
Birth Rate: 11.24/1,000 population (1998 est.)
Death Rate: 9.65/1,000 population (1998 est.)
Infant Mortality: 3.82 deaths/1,000 live births (1998 est.)
Life Expectancy at Birth: 73.61 years male, 80.83 years female (1998 est.)
Total Fertility Rate: 1.73 children born/woman (1998 est.)
Literacy: 100% (1997 est.)

■ GOVERNMENT

Leader(s): Pres. Martti Ahtisaari, Prime Min. Paavo Lipponen
Government Type: republic
Administrative Divisions: 6 provinces
Nationhood: Dec. 6, 1917 (from Soviet Union)
National Holiday: Independence Day, Dec. 6

■ ECONOMY

Overview: the manufacturing sector and trade are vital to this highly industrialized, largely free market economy; because of the climate, agricultural development is limited to maintaining self-sufficiency in basic products. Unemployment is a continuing problem
GDP: $102.1 billion, per capita $20,000; real growth rate 4.6% (1997 est.)
Inflation: 1.6% (June 98)
Industries: accounts for 37% of GDP; metal manufacturing and shipbuilding, forestry and wood processing (pulp, paper), copper refining, foodstuffs, textiles, clothing
Labour Force: 2,210,000 (1997); 33.9% community, social and business services, 19.2% industry, 14.6% trade and tourism
Unemployment: 11% (Jan. 1999)
Agriculture: accounts for 7% of GDP (including forestry); livestock production, especially dairy cattle, predominates; forestry is an important export earner; main crops—cereals, sugar beets, potatoes; 85% self-sufficient, but short of food and fodder grains
Natural Resources: timber, copper, zinc, iron ore, silver

■ FINANCE/TRADE

Currency: markkaa, or Finmark = 100 pennia [As of Jan. 1, 1999, Government securities are issued in Euros (EUR)]
International Reserves Excluding Gold: $8.498 billion (Jan. 1999)
Gold Reserves: 1.577 million fine troy ounces (Jan. 1999)
Budget: revenues $33 billion; expenditures $40 billion, including capital expenditures of n.a. (1996 est.)
Defence Expenditures: 3.85% of total govt. expenditure (1996)
Education Expenditures: 10.13% of total govt. expenditure (1996)
External Debt: n.a.
Exports: $42.973 billion (1998); commodities: timber, paper and pulp, ships, machinery, clothing and footwear; partners: European Community 44.2% (UK 13%, Germany 10.8%), former USSR countries 14.9%, Sweden 14.1%, US 5.8%
Imports: $32.339 billion (1998); commodities: foodstuffs, petroleum and petroleum products, chemicals, transport equipment, iron and steel, machinery, textile yarn and fabrics, fodder grains; partners: European Community 43.5% (Germany 16.9%, UK 6.8%), Sweden 13.3%, former USSR countries 12.1%, US 6.3%

■ COMMUNICATIONS

Daily Newspapers: 56 (1996)
Televisions: 605/1,000 inhabitants (1996)

Radios: 1,385/1,000 inhabitants (1996)
Telephones: 55.0/100 inhabitants (1996 est.)

■ TRANSPORTATION

Motor Vehicles: 2,270,000; 2,000,000 passenger cars (1997 est.)
Roads: 77,782 km; 49,780 km paved
Railway: 5,895 km
Air Traffic: 6,313,000 passengers carried (1996)
Airports: 158; 69 have paved runways (1997 est.)

Canadian Embassy: The Canadian Embassy, Pohjois Esplanadi 25B, 00100 Helsinki; mailing address: Box 779, 00101 Helsinki, Finland. Tel: (011-358-9) 17-11-41. Fax (011-358-9) 60-10-60.
Embassy in Canada: Embassy of Finland, 55 Metcalfe St, Ste 850, Ottawa ON K1P 6L5. Tel: (613) 236-2389. Fax: (613) 238-1474.

France

Long-Form Name: French Republic
Capital: Paris

■ GEOGRAPHY

Area: 547,030 sq. km; includes Corsica and the rest of metropolitan France, but excludes the overseas administrative divisions
Coastline: 3,427 km (includes Corsica, 644 km)
Climate: generally cool winters and mild summers, but mild winters and hot summers along the Mediterranean
Environment: most of large urban areas and industrial centres in Rhône, Garonne, Seine or Loire River basins; occasional warm, tropical winds known as mistrals are in central south; air and water pollution; acid rain
Terrain: mostly flat plains or gently rolling hills in north and west; remainder is mountainous, especially Pyrenees in south and Alps in east
Land Use: 33% arable; 2% permanent; 20% meadows; 27% forest; 18% other, includes 3% irrigated
Location: W Europe, bordering on Atlantic Ocean, Mediterranean Sea

■ PEOPLE

Population: 58,804,944 (July 1998 est.)
Nationality: French
Age Structure: 0-14 yrs: 19%; 15-64: 65%; 65+: 16% (1998 est.)
Population Growth Rate: 0.31% (1998 est.)
Net Migration: 0.58 migrants/1,000 population (1998 est.)
Ethnic Groups: Celtic and Latin with Teutonic, Slavic, North African, Indochinese and Basque minorities

Languages: French (100% of population); rapidly declining regional dialects (Provençal, Breton, Alsatian, Corsican, Catalan, Basque, Flemish)
Religions: 90% Roman Catholic, 2% Protestant, 1% Jewish, 1% Muslim (North African workers), 6% unaffiliated
Birth Rate: 11.68/1,000 population (1998 est.)
Death Rate: 9.12/1,000 population (1998 est.)
Infant Mortality: 5.69 deaths/1,000 live births (1998 est.)
Life Expectancy at Birth: 74.6 years male, 82.62 years female (1998 est.)
Total Fertility Rate: 1.63 children born/woman (1998 est.)
Literacy: 99% (1997 est.)

■ GOVERNMENT

Leader(s): Pres. Jacques Chirac, Prime Min. Lionel Jospin
Government Type: republic
Administrative Divisions: 22 regions; dependent areas inc.: French Polynesia, Guadeloupe, Guiana (French Guiana), Martinique, Mayotte, New Caledonia, Réunion, St. Pierre and Miquelon, Southern and Antarctic Territories, Wallis and Futuna Islands
Nationhood: unified by Clovis in 486, First Republic proclaimed in 1792
National Holiday: Taking of the Bastille, July 14

■ ECONOMY

Overview: one of the world's most developed economies; largely self-sufficient in agricultural products; the leading agricultural producer in Western Europe; highly diversified industrial sector; economic integration into the European Community has unknown consequences; unemployment is rising rapidly
GDP: $1.32 trillion, per capita $22,700; real growth rate 2.3% (1997 est.)
Inflation: 0.8% (July 1998)
Industries: accounts for 27% of GDP; steel, machinery, chemicals, automobiles, metallurgy, aircraft, electronics, mining, textiles, food processing, tourism
Labour Force: 26.1 million (1997 est.); 34.3% community, social and business services, 16.6% trade and tourism, 10.1% finance
Unemployment: 12.4% (1997)
Agriculture: accounts for 2.4% of GNP (including fishing and forestry); one of the world's top five wheat producers; self-sufficient for most temperate-zone foods; shortages include fats and oils and tropical produce, but overall net exporter of farm products
Natural Resources: coal, iron ore, bauxite, fish, timber, zinc, potash

■ FINANCE/TRADE

Currency: franc (F or FF) = 100 centimes [As of Jan. 1, 1999, Government securities are issued in Euros (EUR)]
International Reserves Excluding Gold: $35.353 billion (Jan. 1999)
Gold Reserves: 97.243 million fine troy ounces (Jan. 1999)
Budget: revenues $222 billion; expenditures $265 billion, including capital expenditures of n.a. (1998 est.)
Defence Expenditures: 3.1% of GDP (1995)
Education Expenditures: 5.9% of GNP (1995)
External Debt: $117.6 billion (1996 est.)
Exports: $296.061 billion (1998 est.); commodities: machinery and transportation equipment, chemicals, foodstuffs, agricultural products, iron and steel products, textiles and clothing; partners: Germany 15.8%, Italy 12.2%, UK 9.8%, Belgium/Luxembourg 8.9%, Netherlands 8.7%, US 6.7%, Spain 5.6%, Japan 1.8%, former USSR countries 1.3%
Imports: $278.476 billion (1998 est.); commodities: crude oil, machinery and equipment, agricultural products, chemicals, iron and steel products; partners: Germany 19.4%, Italy 11.5%, Belgium/ Luxembourg 9.2%, US 7.7%, UK 7.2%, Netherlands 5.2%, Spain 4.4%, Japan 4.1%, former USSR countries 2.1%

■ COMMUNICATIONS

Daily Newspapers: 117 (1996)
Televisions: 591/1,000 inhabitants (1996)
Radios: 943/1,000 inhabitants (1996)
Telephones: 56.7/100 inhabitants (1996 est.)

■ TRANSPORTATION

Motor Vehicles: 30,755,000; 25,500,000 passenger cars (1997 est.)
Roads: 892,500 km; all paved
Railway: 32,027 km
Air Traffic: 41,300,000 passengers carried (1997 est)
Airports: 473; 266 have paved runways (1997 est.)

Canadian Embassy: The Canadian Embassy, 35-37 avenue Montaigne, 75008, Paris, France. Tel: (011-33-1) 44-43-29-00. Fax: (011-33-1) 44-43-29-99.
Embassy in Canada: Embassy of France, 42 Sussex Dr, Ottawa ON K1M 2C9. Tel: (613) 789-1795. Fax: (613) 562-3735.

French Guiana

Long-Form Name: Department of Guiana
Capital: Cayenne

■ GEOGRAPHY

Area: 91,000 sq. km
Climate: tropical, warm and humid, little seasonal temperature variation
Land Use: 83% forest and woodland; interior is uncultivated wilderness, with mineral and forest resources that have not been tapped; 31,000 acres under cultivation
Location: N South America, bordering on Atlantic Ocean

■ PEOPLE

Population: 162,547 (July 1998 est.)
Nationality: French Guianese
Ethnic Groups: 66% black or mulatto, 12% Caucasian, 12% East Indian, Chinese, Amerindian, 10% other
Languages: French (official), Creole patois

■ GOVERNMENT

Colony Territory of: Overseas Department of France
Leader(s): Prefect of French Govt. Henri Masse, Pres. of General Council André Lecante
Government Type: overseas department of France
National Holiday: Taking of the Bastille, July 14

■ ECONOMY

Overview: economy is closely tied to that of France through subsidies and imports; agriculture: rice, manioc, sugar cane, livestock; forestry, fisheries, food processing industry; chief trading partners: France, EC countries, Japan, US. Unemployment is particularly serious among younger workers

■ FINANCE/TRADE

Currency: French franc = 100 centimes

Canadian Embassy: c/o The Canadian Embassy, 35-57 avenue Montaigne, Paris 75008, France. Tel: (011-33-1) 44-43-29-00. Fax: (011-3-1) 44-43-29-99.
Representative to Canada: c/o Embassy of France, 42 Sussex Dr, Ottawa ON K1M 2C9. Tel: (613) 789-1795. Fax: (613) 562-3735.

French Polynesia

Long-Form Name: Territory of French Polynesia
Capital: Papeete (Windward Islands)

■ GEOGRAPHY

Area: 4,167 sq. km, consisting of five island archipelagoes scattered widely over Eastern Pacific; uninhabited Clipperton Territory is a dependency of French Polynesia but does not form part of the territory
Climate: warm and humid; tropical but moderate
Land Use: 1% arable, 6% permanent crops, 5% meadows and pastures, 31% forest and woodland, 57% other
Location: eastern Pacific Ocean

■ PEOPLE

Population: 237,844 (July 1998 est.)
Nationality: French Polynesian
Ethnic Groups: 78% Polynesian, 12% Chinese, 6% local French, 4% metropolitan French
Languages: French and Tahitian (both official)

■ GOVERNMENT

Colony Territory of: Overseas Territory of France
Leader(s): Head of State: Jacques Chirac (France), Prefect Jean Aribaud; Prime. Min. Gaston Flosse
Government Type: French overseas territory
National Holiday: Taking of the Bastille, July 14

■ ECONOMY

Overview: agriculture: copra, tropical fruits grown for local consumption; tourism accounts for approximately 20% of GDP and is primary source of revenue; trading partners: France, UK, US

■ FINANCE/TRADE

Currency: CFP franc = 100 centimes

Canadian Embassy: c/o The Canadian Embassy, 35-37 avenue Montaigne, Paris 75008, France. Tel: (011-33-1) 44-43-29-00. Fax: (011-33-1) 44-43-29-99.
Representative to Canada: c/o Embassy of France, 42 Sussex Dr, Ottawa ON K1M 2C9. Tel: (613) 789-1795. Fax: (613) 562-3735.

Gabon

Long-Form Name: Gabonese Republic
Capital: Libreville

■ GEOGRAPHY

Area: 267,670 sq. km
Coastline: 885 km
Climate: tropical; always hot, humid
Environment: deforestation and poaching

Terrain: narrow coastal plain; hilly interior; savanna in east and south
Land Use: 1% arable; 1% permanent; 18% meadows; 77% forest; 3% other
Location: WC Africa, bordering on South Atlantic Ocean

■ PEOPLE

Population: 1,207,844 (July 1998 est.)
Nationality: Gabonese
Age Structure: 0-14 yrs: 33%; 15-64: 61%; 65+: 6% (1998 est.)
Population Growth Rate: 1.48% (1998 est.)
Net Migration: 0 migrants/1,000 population (1998 est.)
Ethnic Groups: about 40 Bantu tribes, including four major tribal groupings (Fang, Eshira, Bapounou, Bateke); approx. 100,000 expatriate Africans and Europeans, including 27,000 French
Languages: French (official), Fang, Myene, Bateke, Bapounou/Eschira, Bandjabi
Religions: 55–75% Roman Catholic, 1% Muslim, remainder animist
Birth Rate: 28.0/1,000 population (1998 est.)
Death Rate: 13.23/1,000 population (1998 est.)
Infant Mortality: 85.43 deaths/1,000 live births (1998 est.)
Life Expectancy at Birth: 53.55 years male, 59.56 years female (1998 est.)
Total Fertility Rate: 3.81 children born/woman (1998 est.)
Literacy: 63.2% (1997 est.)

■ GOVERNMENT

Leader(s): Pres. El Hadj Omar Bongo, Prem. Jean-François Ntoutoumc-Emane
Government Type: republic; multi-party presidential regime (opposition parties legalized in 1990)
Administrative Divisions: 9 provinces
Nationhood: Aug. 17, 1960 (from France)
National Holiday: Independence Day, Aug. 17

■ ECONOMY

Overview: economy is dependent on oil, which has contributed to an increase in per capita income; agricultural and industrial sectors are relatively underdeveloped
GDP: $6.3 billion, per capita $5,400; real growth rate 2.6% (1996 est.)
Inflation: 4.4% (Mar. 1997)
Industries: accounts for 55% of GDP; sawmills, cement, petroleum, food and beverages; mining of increasing importance (especially manganese and uranium)
Labour Force: 1 million (1997 est.); 75.5% agriculture, 10.8% industry, 13.7% services

Unemployment: n.a.
Agriculture: accounts for 7.1% of GDP (including fishing and forestry); cash crops—cocoa, coffee, palm oil; livestock not developed; importer of food; okoume (a tropical softwood) is the most important timber product
Natural Resources: crude oil, manganese, uranium, gold, timber, iron ore

■ FINANCE/TRADE

Currency: Communauté financière africaine franc (CFAF) = 100 centimes
International Reserves Excluding Gold: $129 million (May 1998)
Gold Reserves: 0.013 million fine troy ounces (June 1998)
Budget: revenues $1.5 billion; expenditures $1.3 billion, including capital expenditures of $302 million (1996 est.)
Defence Expenditures: 2.0% of GDP (1996)
Education Expenditures: n.a.
External Debt: $3.9 billion (1996)
Exports: $2.714 billion (1995); commodities: crude oil 70%, manganese 11%, wood 12%, uranium 6%; partners: France 53%, US 22%, Germany, Japan
Imports: $883 million (1995); commodities: foodstuffs, chemical products, petroleum products, construction materials, manufacturers, machinery; partners: France 48%, US 2.6%, Germany, Japan, UK

■ COMMUNICATIONS

Daily Newspapers: 2 (1996)
Televisions: 54/1,000 inhabitants (1996)
Radios: 182/1,000 inhabitants (1996)
Telephones: 2.2/100 inhabitants (1996 est.)

■ TRANSPORTATION

Motor Vehicles: 39,500; 23,800 passenger cars (1997 est.)
Roads: 7,670 km; 629 km paved
Railway: 649 km
Air Traffic: 431,000 passengers carried (1996)
Airports: 64; 10 have paved runways (1997 est.)

Canadian Embassy: The Canadian Embassy, P.O. Box 4037 Libreville, Gabon. Tel: (011-241) 74-34-64. Fax: (011-241) 74-34-66.
Embassy in Canada: Embassy of the Gabonese Republic, 4 Range Rd, Ottawa ON K1N 8J5. Tel: (613) 232-5301. Fax: (613) 232-2916.

Gambia

Long-Form Name: Republic of the Gambia
Capital: Banjul

■ GEOGRAPHY

Area: 11,300 sq. km
Coastline: 80 km
Climate: tropical; hot, rainy season (June to Nov.); cooler, dry season (Nov. to May)
Environment: deforestation and desertification; diseases spread through the water supply are common
Terrain: flood plain of the Gambia River flanked by some low hills
Land Use: 18% arable; 0% permanent; 9% meadows; 28% forest; 45% other
Location: W Africa, bordering on Atlantic Ocean

■ PEOPLE

Population: 1,291,858 (July 1998 est.)
Nationality: Gambian
Age Structure: 0-14 yrs: 46%; 15-64: 52%; 65+: 2% (1998 est.)
Population Growth Rate: 3.42% (1998 est.)
Net Migration: 3.77 migrants/1,000 population (1998 est.)
Ethnic Groups: 99% African (42% Mandinka, 18% Fula, 16% Wolof, 10% Jola, 9% Serahuli, 4% other); 1% non-Gambian
Languages: English (official); Mandinka, Wolof, Fula, other indigenous vernaculars
Religions: 90% Moslem, 9% Christian, 1% indigenous beliefs
Birth Rate: 43.3/1,000 population (1998 est.)
Death Rate: 12.93/1,000 population (1998 est.)
Infant Mortality: 77.07 deaths/1,000 live births (1998 est.)
Life Expectancy at Birth: 51.59 years male, 56.29 years female (1998 est.)
Total Fertility Rate: 5.91 children born/woman (1998 est.)
Literacy: 38.6% (1997 est.)

■ GOVERNMENT

Leader(s): Pres. Yahya Jammeh; V.Pres. Isatou Nijie Saidy
Government Type: republic
Administrative Divisions: 5 divisions and 1 city (Banjul)
Nationhood: Feb. 18, 1965 (from UK)
National Holiday: Independence Day, Feb. 18

■ ECONOMY

Overview: a poor country, lacking in natural resources and possessing a limited agricultural base of peanut products; small-scale manufacturing activity accounts for only 15% of GDP
GDP: adjusted for purchasing power parity: $1.23 billion, per capita $1,000; real growth rate 2.1% (1997 est.)

Inflation: -2.0% (May 1998)
Industries: accounts for 15% of GDP; peanut processing, tourism, beverages, agricultural machinery assembly, woodworking, metalworking, clothing
Labour Force: 1 million (1997 est.); 35.4% community, social and business services, 17% trade and tourism, 11.7% transportation and communication
Unemployment: n.a.
Agriculture: accounts for 27% of GDP and employs about 75% of the population; imports one-third of food requirements; major export crop is peanuts; forestry and fishing resources not fully exploited
Natural Resources: fish

■ FINANCE/TRADE

Currency: dalasi (D) = 100 butut
International Reserves Excluding Gold: $106 million (Jan. 1999)
Gold Reserves: n.a.
Budget: revenues $88.6 million; expenditures $98.2 million, including capital expenditures n.a. (1997 est.)
Defence Expenditures: 3.9% of GDP (1996)
Education Expenditures: 5.5% of GNP (1995)
External Debt: $452 million (1996)
Exports: $14 million (1997); commodities: peanuts and peanut products, fish, cotton lint, palm kernels; partners: Ghana 49%, Europe 27%, Japan 12%, US 1%
Imports: $278 million (1997); commodities: foodstuffs, manufacturers, raw materials, fuel, machinery and transport equipment; partners: Europe 55%, (European Community 39%, other 16%), Asia 20%, US 11%, Senegal 4%

■ COMMUNICATIONS

Daily Newspapers: 1 (1996)
Televisions: 3.5/1,000 inhabitants (1996)
Radios: 164/1,000 inhabitants (1996)
Telephones: 1.7/100 inhabitants (1996 est.)

■ TRANSPORTATION

Motor Vehicles: 9,000; 8,000 passenger cars (1997 est.)
Roads: 2,700 km; 956 km paved
Railway: none
Air Traffic: 20,000 passengers carried (1995 est.)
Airports: 1, with paved runway (1997 est.)

Canadian Embassy: The Canadian High Commission to the Gambia, c/o The Canadian Embassy, P.O. Box 3373, Dakar, Senegal. Tel: (011-221) 823-92-90. Fax: (011-221) 823-87-49.

Embassy in Canada: High Commission for the Republic of the Gambia, 1155 15th St NW, Ste 1000, Washington DC, 20005-2 USA. Tel: (202) 785-1399. Fax: (202) 785-1430.

Georgia

Long-Form Name: Republic of Georgia
Capital: T'bilisi

■ GEOGRAPHY

Area: 69,700 sq. km
Coastline: 310 km
Climate: Alpine to subtropical with warm, humid coastlands
Environment: soil, air and water pollution
Terrain: largely mountainous in north and south; lowlands open to Black Sea in west; Kura River Basin in east; good soils in river valley, flood plains and lowlands
Land Use: 34% forests and woodlands; 9% arable; 4% permanent crops; 25% meadows and pastures; 28% other, includes 6.5% irrigated
Location: SW Asia, bordering on Black Sea

■ PEOPLE

Population: 5,108,527 (July 1998 est.)
Nationality: Georgian
Age Structure: 0-14 yrs: 22%; 15-64: 66%; 65+: 12% (1998 est.)
Population Growth Rate: -0.92% (1998 est.)
Net Migration: -6.79 migrants/1,000 population (1998 est.)
Ethnic Groups: 70.1% Georgian, 8.1% Armenian, 6.3% Russian, 5.7% Azerbaijani, 3% Ossetian, 1.9% Greek, 1.8% Abkhazian, 1% Ukrainian, 2.1% other
Languages: Armenian 7%, Azeri 6%, Georgian 71% (official), Russian 9%, other 7%
Religions: Christian Orthodox 75%, Muslim 11%, Armenian Apostolic 8%, unknown 6%
Birth Rate: 11.72/1,000 population (1998 est.)
Death Rate: 14.1/1,000 population (1998 est.)
Infant Mortality: 51.07 deaths/1,000 live births (1998 est.)
Life Expectancy at Birth: 61.36 years male, 68.4 years female (1998 est.)
Total Fertility Rate: 1.54 children born/woman (1998 est.)
Literacy: 99% (1997 est.)

■ GOVERNMENT

Leader(s): Chairman of Parliament Eduard A. Shevardnadze
Government Type: republic
Administrative Divisions: 53 rayons, 9 cities and 2 autonomous regions

Nationhood: April 9, 1991 (from Soviet Union)
National Holiday: Independence Day, May 26

■ ECONOMY

Overview: steel processing and light industry predominate; agriculture hindered by extensive wooded areas; international transportation services through key ports are Georgia's main hope for the future
GDP: $8.1 billion, per capita $1,570; real growth rate 11.8% (1997 est.)
Inflation: 7.1% (1997 est.)
Industries: accounts for 16% of GDP; coal and non-ferrous metals refining, machinery and instruments, electrical engineering, chemical production, food processing, cloth, hosiery, shoes, vehicles, mining, esp. manganese, coal, baryta
Labour Force: 3 million (1997 est.); 31% industry and construction, 25% agriculture and forestry, 44% other
Unemployment: 16% (1996 est.)
Agriculture: accounts for 29% of GDP; grapes, tobacco, bay leaves, tea, citrus fruit, sugar, vegetables, grains, tobacco, tung, silk, orchard fruit
Natural Resources: manganese deposits; sulphur and other medicinal springs, forest resources, hydropower, coal and oil

■ FINANCE/TRADE

Currency: lari
International Reserves Excluding Gold: n.a.
Gold Reserves: n.a.
Budget: revenues $441 million; expenditures $606 million, including capital expenditures of $54 million (1996 est.)
Defence Expenditures: 10.19% of total govt. expenditure (1997)
Education Expenditures: 5.78% of total govt. expenditure (1997)
External Debt: $1.6 billion (1996 est.)
Exports: $140 million, adjusted for purchasing power parity (1995); grain, fruit, vegetables, tea, electric mine cars, seamless pipes
Imports: $250 million, adjusted for purchasing power parity (1995); fuel, foodstuffs, machinery, equipment

■ COMMUNICATIONS

Daily Newspapers: n.a.
Televisions: 470/1,000 inhabitants (1996)
Radios: 553/1,000 inhabitants (1996)
Telephones: 10.8/100 inhabitants (1996 est.)

■ TRANSPORTATION

Motor Vehicles: n.a.

Roads: 20,700 km; 19,354 km hard-surfaced
Railway: 1,583 km
Air Traffic: 152,000 passengers carried (1996)
Airports: 28; 14 have paved runways (1997 est.)

Canadian Embassy: The Canadian Embassy to Georgia, c/o The Canadian Embassy, Nenehatun Caddesi No. 75, Gaziosmanpasa 06700, Ankara, Turkey. Tel: (011-90-312) 436-1275. Fax: (011-90-312) 446-4437.
Embassy in Canada: Embassy of the Republic of Georgia, 1511 K St NW, Ste 424, Washington DC 20005, USA. Tel: (202) 393-5959. Fax: (202) 393-4537.

Germany

Long-Form Name: Federal Republic of Germany
Capital: Berlin

■ GEOGRAPHY

Area: 356,910 sq. km
Coastline: 2,389 km
Climate: temperate; cool, wet summers; cool to cold, cloudy winters with frequent rain and snow; occasional warm, tropical föhn wind; high relative humidity
Environment: air and water pollution; significant deforestation in mountain regions due to environmental pollution
Terrain: flat plains; lowlands in north; central uplands; Bavarian Alps in southwest
Land Use: 33% arable land; 1% permanent crops; 15% meadows and pastures; 31% forest and woodland; 20% other, includes 1.3% irrigated
Location: NC Europe, bordering on North Sea, Baltic Sea

■ PEOPLE

Population: 82,079,454 (July 1998 est.)
Nationality: German
Age Structure: 0-14 yrs: 16%; 15-64: 68%; 65+: 16% (1998 est.)
Population Growth Rate: 0.02% (1998 est.)
Net Migration: 2.08 migrants/1,000 population (1998 est.)
Ethnic Groups: German 91.5%, Turkish 2.4%, Italian 0.7%, Greek 0.4%. Polish 0.4%, other 4.6%
Languages: German (official)
Religions: 45% Protestant, 37% Roman Catholic, 18% unaffiliated
Birth Rate: 8.84/1,000 population (1998 est.)
Death Rate: 10.77/1,000 population (1998 est.)
Infant Mortality: 5.2 deaths/1,000 live births (1998 est.)

Life Expectancy at Birth: 73.83 years male, 80.33 years female (1998 est.)
Total Fertility Rate: 1.25 children born/woman (1998 est.)
Literacy: 99% (1997 est.)

■ GOVERNMENT

Leader(s): Chancellor Gerhard Schroeder, Pres. Johannes Rau
Government Type: federal republic
Administrative Divisions: 16 states
Nationhood: January 18, 1871 (unification of German Empire); West Germany and East Germany were unified on Oct. 3, 1990
National Holiday: German Unity Day, Oct. 3

■ ECONOMY

Overview: Former W Germany: highly urbanized with advanced market economy and strong exports; manufacturing and service industries dominate with imported raw materials and semimanufactured products. As the world's third-most powerful economy, the former W Germany faces unique problems in bringing the eastern areas up to standard after 45 years of Communist rule. Former E Germany: outmoded economy, slow pace of economic reform deters outside investors; former W Germany's legal, social welfare and economic systems have been extended to the east. Unified Germany: slight nation-wide post-reunification recession.
GDP: $1.74 trillion, per capita $20,800; real growth rate 2.4% (1997 est.)
Inflation: 0.9% (July 1998)
Industries: accounts for 35% of GDP; iron, steel, coal, chemicals, vehicles, ships, machinery, food and beverages, electronics, brown coal, shipbuilding, textiles, petroleum refining
Labour Force: 34,008,000 (1997); 30.8% industry, 28.2% community, social and business services, 14.9% trade and tourism
Unemployment: 12.8% (Jan. 1999)
Agriculture: agriculture, including fishing and forestry, accounts for about 1% of GDP in west, 10% in east; diversified crop and livestock farming, including wheat, potatoes, barley, sugar beets, fruit, livestock products; net importer of food
Natural Resources: iron ore, coal, potash, natural gas, salt, nickel, timber

■ FINANCE/TRADE

Currency: Deutsche Mark (DM) = 100 pfennige [As of Jan. 1, 1999, Government securities are issued in Euros (EUR)]
International Reserves Excluding Gold: $62.752 billion (Jan. 1999)

Gold Reserves: 111.519 million fine troy ounces (Jan. 1999)
Budget: revenues $755 billion; expenditures $832.1 billion, including capital expenditures n.a. (1995)
Defence Expenditures: 1.5% of GDP (1995)
Education Expenditures: 4.7% of GNP (1995)
External Debt: exact figures n.a., but very high (1998)
Exports: $540.591 billion (1998); manufactured goods 88%, agricultural products 5%, raw materials 2.3%, other 4.7%; partners: EU 58%, Eastern Europe 8%, other West European countries 7.5%, US 7%, Japan 2.5%, other 17%
Imports: $467.347 billion (1998); manufactured goods 74%, agricultural products 10%, fuels 6.4%, raw materials 6%, other 3.6%; partners: EU 56%, Eastern Europe 9%, other West European countries 7%, US 7%, Japan 5%, China 2.5%, other 13.5%

■ COMMUNICATIONS

Daily Newspapers: 375 (1996)
Televisions: 564/1,000 inhabitants (1996)
Radios: 964/1,000 inhabitants (1996)
Telephones: 50.8/100 inhabitants (1996 est.)

■ TRANSPORTATION

Motor Vehicles: 47,000,000; 42,800,000 passenger cars (1997 est.)
Roads: 633,000 km; 627,303 km paved
Railway: 43,966 km
Air Traffic: 41,000,000 passengers carried (1997 est.)
Airports: 620; 321 have paved runways (1997 est.)

Canadian Embassy: The Canadian Embassy, Friedrich-Wilhelm-Strasse 18, 53113 Bonn, Germany. Tel. (011-49-228) 968 0. Fax: (011-49-228) 968-3904.
Embassy in Canada: Embassy of the Federal Republic of Germany, 1 Waverley St, Ottawa ON K2P 0T8. Tel: (613) 232-1101. Fax: (613) 594-9330.

Ghana

Long-Form Name: Republic of Ghana
Capital: Accra

■ GEOGRAPHY

Area: 238,540 sq. km
Coastline: 539 km
Climate: tropical; warm and comparatively dry along southeast coast; hot and humid in southwest; hot and dry in north

Environment: recent drought in north severely affecting marginal agricultural activities; deforestation; overgrazing; soil erosion; dry, northeasterly harmattan wind (Jan. to Mar.); water pollution and insufficient safe drinking water

Terrain: mostly low plains with dissected plateau in south-central area

Land Use: 12% arable; 7% permanent crops; 22% meadows; 35% forest; 24% other

Location: WC Africa, bordering on South Atlantic Ocean

■ PEOPLE

Population: 18,497,206 (July 1998 est.)

Nationality: Ghanaian

Age Structure: 0-14 yrs: 43%; 15-64: 54%; 65+: 3% (1998 est.)

Population Growth Rate: 2.13% (1998 est.)

Net Migration: -0.9% migrants/1,000 population (1998 est.)

Ethnic Groups: 99.8% black African (major tribes—44% Akan, 16% Moshi-Dagomba, 13% Ewe, 8% Ga, 18.8% other), 0.2% European and other

Languages: English (official); African languages include Akan, Moshi-Dagomba, Ewe and Ga

Religions: 38% indigenous beliefs, 30% Muslim, 24% Christian, 8% other

Birth Rate: 32.81/1,000 population (1998 est.)

Death Rate: 10.63/1,000 population (1998 est.)

Infant Mortality: 77.53 deaths/1,000 live births (1998 est.)

Life Expectancy at Birth: 54.77 years male, 58.92 years female (1998 est.)

Total Fertility Rate: 4.27 children born/woman (1998 est.)

Literacy: 64.5% (1997 est.)

■ GOVERNMENT

Leader(s): Pres. Flt. Lt. (Ret.) Jerry John Rawlings; V. Pres. John Evans Atta Mills

Government Type: constitutional democracy

Administrative Divisions: 10 regions

Nationhood: Mar. 6, 1957 (from UK, formerly known as Gold Coast)

National Holiday: Independence Day, Mar. 6

■ ECONOMY

Overview: heavily dependent on cocoa, gold and timber exports; international assistance boosts this economy, which depends on good harvests; population growth is a burden

GDP: adjusted for purchasing power parity: $36.2 billion, per capita $2,000; real growth rate 3% (1997 est.)

Inflation: 24.1% (1997)

Industries: accounts for 14% of GDP; mining, lumbering, light manufacturing, fishing, aluminum, food processing

Labour Force: 8.2 million (1997 est.); 59.3% agriculture, 11.1% industry, 29.6% services

Unemployment: 20% (1997 est.)

Agriculture: accounts for almost 41% of GDP; major cash crop is cocoa; other crops: rice, coffee, cassava, peanuts, corn; normally self-sufficient in food

Natural Resources: gold, timber, industrial diamonds, bauxite, manganese, fish, rubber

■ FINANCE/TRADE

Currency: cedi (C/) = 100 pesewas

International Reserves Excluding Gold: $328 million (Oct. 1998)

Gold Reserves: 0.277 million fine troy ounces (Nov. 1998)

Budget: revenues $1.39 billion; expenditures $1.47 billion, including capital expenditures of $370 million (1996 est.)

Defence Expenditures: 1.4% of GDP (1996)

Education Expenditures: n.a.

External Debt: $5.2 billion (1996)

Exports: $2.27 billion (1995); commodities: cocoa 60%, timber, gold, tuna, bauxite, and aluminum; partners: US 23%, UK, other European Community

Imports: n.a.; commodities: petroleum 16%, consumer goods, foods, intermediate goods, capital equipment; partners: US 10%, UK, Germany, France, Japan, S Korea

■ COMMUNICATIONS

Daily Newspapers: 4 (1996)

Televisions: 93/1,000 inhabitants (1996)

Radios: 238/1,000 inhabitants (1996)

Telephones: 0.4/100 inhabitants (1996 est.)

■ TRANSPORTATION

Motor Vehicles: 135,000; 90,000 passenger cars (1997 est.)

Roads: 39,409 km; 11,653 km hard-surfaced

Railway: 953 km

Air Traffic: 197,000 passengers carried (1996)

Airports: 12; 6 have paved runways (1997 est.)

Canadian Embassy: Canadian High Commission, 42 Independence Ave, Accra, Ghana; P.O. Box 1639, Accra, Ghana. Tel: (011-233-21) 77-37-91. Fax: (011-233-21) 77-37-92.

Embassy in Canada: High Commission for the Republic of Ghana, 1 Clemow Ave, Ottawa ON K1S 2A9. Tel: (613) 236-0871. Fax: (613) 236-0874.

Gibraltar

Long-Form Name: Gibraltar
Capital: Gibraltar

■ GEOGRAPHY

Area: 6.5 sq. km
Climate: warm, temperate, low precipitation, mild winters, warm summers
Land Use: almost 100% bare limestone (Rock of Gibraltar) and/or built up; no farmland
Location: Iberian Peninsula of S Spain, bordering on Mediterranean Sea

■ PEOPLE

Population: 29,045 (July 1998 est.)
Nationality: Gibraltarian
Ethnic Groups: Portuguese, Maltese, Spanish, Italian, English
Languages: English (used in schools and for official purposes), Spanish, Italian, Portuguese, Russian

■ GOVERNMENT

Colony Territory of: Dependent Territory of United Kingdom
Leader(s): Chief of State: Queen Elizabeth II, Gov. Sir Richard Luce; Chief Min. Peter Caruana
Government Type: dependent territory of the UK
National Holiday: Commonwealth Day (second Monday in March)

■ ECONOMY

Overview: tourism most important; industries: construction materials, beverage bottling; re-exports: tobacco, petroleum, wine; exports of local products negligible; must import all food; more than 70% of the economy is in the public sector

■ FINANCE/TRADE

Currency: Gibraltar pound = 100 pence

Canadian Embassy: c/o The Canadian High Commission, Macdonald House, 1 Grosvenor Square, London W1X 0AB, England, UK. Tel: (011-44-171) 258-6600. Fax: (011-44-171) 258-6333.
Representative to Canada: c/o British High Commission, 80 Elgin St, Ottawa ON K1P 5K7. Tel: (613) 237-1530. Fax: (613) 237-7980.

Greece

Long-Form Name: Hellenic Republic
Capital: Athens

■ GEOGRAPHY

Area: 131,940 sq. km
Coastline: 13,676 km
Climate: temperate; mild, wet winter; hot, dry summer
Environment: subject to severe earthquakes; air pollution; archipelago of 2,000 islands; water pollution
Terrain: mostly mountainous with ranges extending into sea as peninsulas or chains of islands
Land Use: 19% arable; 8% permanent crops; 41% meadows; 20% forest; 12% other, includes 9% irrigated
Location: S Europe, bordering on Adriatic Sea

■ PEOPLE

Population: 10,662,138 (July 1998 est.)
Nationality: Greek
Age Structure: 0-14 yrs: 16%; 15-64: 67%; 65+: 17% (1998 est.)
Population Growth Rate: 0.43% (1998 est.)
Net Migration: 4.0 migrants/1,000 population (1998 est.)
Ethnic Groups: 98% Greek, 2% others
Languages: Greek (official); English, German and French widely understood
Religions: 98% Greek Orthodox, 1.3% Muslim, 0.7% other
Birth Rate: 9.65/1,000 population (1998 est.)
Death Rate: 9.37/1,000 population (1998 est.)
Infant Mortality: 7.26 deaths/1,000 live births (1998 est.)
Life Expectancy at Birth: 75.76 years male, 81.04 years female (1998 est.)
Total Fertility Rate: 1.31 children born/woman (1998 est.)
Literacy: 95% (1997 est.)

■ GOVERNMENT

Leader(s): Pres. Costis Stefanopoulos, Prime Min. Costas Simitis
Government Type: presidential parliamentary government
Administrative Divisions: 51 prefectures (nomoi, singular–nomós) and 1 autonomous region
Nationhood: 1829 (from the Ottoman Empire)
National Holiday: Independence Day (proclamation of the war of independence), Mar. 25

■ ECONOMY

Overview: a large commodity trade deficit is offset by the successful tourism industry; economy is characterized by low GDP growth, and high inflation and national debt
GDP: $137.4 billion, per capita $13,000; real

growth rate 3.7% (1997 est.)
Inflation: 5.2% (June 1998)
Industries: accounts for 25% of GDP; food and tobacco processing, textiles, chemicals, metal products, tourism, mining, petroleum
Labour Force: 4 million (1997 est.); 21.9% agriculture, 20.1% community, social and business services, 19% industry
Unemployment: 10% (1997 est.)
Agriculture: accounts for 11% of GDP (including fishing and forestry); self-sufficient in food; principal products—wheat, corn, barley, sugar beets, olives, tomatoes, wine, tobacco, potatoes, beef, mutton, pork, dairy products
Natural Resources: bauxite, lignite, magnesite, crude oil, marble

■ FINANCE/TRADE

Currency: drachma (Dr) = 100 lepta
International Reserves Excluding Gold: $20.709 billion (Jan. 1999)
Gold Reserves: 4.529 million fine troy ounces (Jan. 1999)
Budget: revenues $37 billion; expenditures $45 billion, capital expenditures n.a. (1998 est.)
Defence Expenditures: 7.33% of total govt. expenditure (1996)
Education Expenditures: 9.58% of total govt. expenditure (1996)
External Debt: $33 billion (1997 est.)
Exports: $8.603 billion (1997); commodities: manufactured goods, food and live animals, fuels and lubricants, raw materials; partners: Germany 24%, Italy 14%, non-oil-developing countries 11.8%, France 9.5%, US 7.1%, UK 6.8%
Imports: $27.717 billion (1997); commodities: machinery and transport equipment, light manufactures, fuels and lubricants, foodstuffs, chemicals; partners: Germany 22%, non-oil-developing countries 14%, oil-exporting countries 13%, Italy 12%, France 8%, US 3.2%

■ COMMUNICATIONS

Daily Newspapers: 156 (1996)
Televisions: 238/1,000 inhabitants (1996)
Radios: 477/1,000 inhabitants (1996)
Telephones: 50.6/100 inhabitants (1996 est.)

■ TRANSPORTATION

Motor Vehicles: 3,500,000; 2,440,000 passenger cars (1997 est.)
Roads: 117,000 km; 107,406 km paved
Railway: 2,474 km
Air Traffic: 5,939,000 passengers carried (1996)
Airports: 78; 63 have paved runways (1997 est.)

Canadian Embassy: The Canadian Embassy, 4 Ioannou Gennadiou St, Athens 115 21, Greece. Tel: (011-30-1) 727-3400. Fax: (011-30-1) 685-9622.
Embassy in Canada: Embassy of the Hellenic Republic, 76-80 MacLaren St, Ottawa ON K2P 0K6. Tel: (613) 238-6271. Fax: (613) 238-5676.

Greenland

Long-Form Name: Grønland
Capital: Nuuk (Godthab)

■ GEOGRAPHY

Area: 2,175,600 sq. km
Climate: arctic to subarctic; cool summers, cold winters
Land Use: 1% meadow and pastures; negligible forest and woodland; 99% other
Location: N North America, bordering on Atlantic Ocean, Greenland Sea, Arctic Ocean, Baffin Bay

■ PEOPLE

Population: 59,309 (July 1998 est.)
Nationality: Greenlander
Ethnic Groups: 87% Greenlander (Inuit and Greenland-born Caucasians), 13% Danish
Languages: Inuit dialects, Danish

■ GOVERNMENT

Colony Territory of: Dependent Territory of Denmark
Leader(s): Queen Margrethe II of Denmark, represented by High Commissioner Gunnar Martens; Prem. Jonathan Motzfeldt
Government Type: part of the Danish realm; self-governing overseas administrative division
National Holiday: Birthday of the Queen, Apr. 16

■ ECONOMY

Overview: dependent on annual subsidy from the Danish government; unemployment is on the increase; fishing is the most important industry; mineral resource exploitation is limited to lead and zinc

■ FINANCE/TRADE

Currency: Danish krone (DKr) = 100 oere

Canadian Embassy: c/o Kr. Bernikowsgade 1, 1105 Copenhagen K, Denmark. Tel: (011-45) 33-48-32-00. Fax: (011-45) 33-48-32-20.
Representative to Canada: c/o Royal Danish Embassy, 47 Clarence St., Ste. 450, Ottawa ON K1N 9K1. Tel: (613) 562-1811. Fax: (613) 562-1812.

Grenada

Long-Form Name: Grenada
Capital: Saint George's

■ GEOGRAPHY

Area: 340 sq. km
Coastline: 121 km
Climate: tropical; tempered by northeast trade winds
Environment: lies on edge of hurricane belt; hurricane season lasts from June to Nov.
Terrain: volcanic in origin with central mountains
Land Use: 15% arable; 18% permanent crops; 3% meadows; 9% forest; 55% other
Location: Caribbean islands

■ PEOPLE

Population: 96,217 (July 1998 est.)
Nationality: Grenadian
Age Structure: 0-14 yrs: 43%; 15-64: 52%; 65+: 5% (1998 est.)
Population Growth Rate: 0.77% (1998 est.)
Net Migration: -15.11 migrants/1,000 population (1998 est.)
Ethnic Groups: mainly of black African descent
Languages: English (official); some French patois
Religions: largely Roman Catholic; Anglican; other Protestant sects
Birth Rate: 28.1/1,000 population (1998 est.)
Death Rate: 5.33/1,000 population (1998 est.)
Infant Mortality: 11.37 deaths/1,000 live births (1998 est.)
Life Expectancy at Birth: 68.77 years male, 74.0 years female (1998 est.)
Total Fertility Rate: 3.64 children born/woman (1998 est.)
Literacy: 98% (1997 est.)

■ GOVERNMENT

Leader(s): Queen Elizabeth II/Gov. Gen. Daniel Williams, Prime Min. Keith Mitchell
Government Type: parliamentary democracy
Administrative Divisions: 6 parishes and 1 dependency
Nationhood: Feb. 7, 1974 (from UK)
National Holiday: Independence Day, Feb. 7

■ ECONOMY

Overview: the economy is based on agriculture (spices, tropical plants) and tourism; unemployment is high
GDP: $300 million, per capita $3,160; real growth rate 3% (1996 est.)
Inflation: 1.0% (Jan. 1998)
Industries: accounts for 40% of GDP; food and beverage, textiles, light assembly operations, tourism, construction
Labour Force: n.a.; services 31%, agriculture 24%, construction 8%, manufacturing 5%, other 32%
Unemployment: 20% (Oct. 1996)
Agriculture: accounts for 10% of GDP, 80% of exports and employs 24% of the labour force; bananas, cocoa, nutmeg and mace are major crops; small-scale farms predominate
Natural Resources: timber, tropical fruit, deepwater harbours

■ FINANCE/TRADE

Currency: East Caribbean dollar ($EC) = 100 cents
International Reserves Excluding Gold: $31 million (Mar. 1998)
Gold Reserves: n.a.
Budget: revenues $75.7 million; expenditures $126.7 million, including capital expenditures of $51 million (1996 est.)
Defence Expenditures: n.a.
Education Expenditures: 16.85% of govt. expenditure (1995)
External Debt: $120 million (1996)
Exports: $23 million (1997); commodities: nutmeg 35%, cocoa beans 15%, bananas 13%, mace 7%, textiles; partners: US 4%, UK, Germany, Netherlands, Trinidad and Tobago
Imports: $171 million (1997); commodities: machinery 24%, food 22%, manufactured goods 19%, petroleum 8%; partners: US 32%, UK, Trinidad and Tobago, Japan, Canada

■ COMMUNICATIONS

Daily Newspapers: n.a.
Televisions: 351/1,000 inhabitants (1996)
Radios: 652/1,000 inhabitants (1996)
Telephones: 27.8/100 inhabitants (1996 est.)

■ TRANSPORTATION

Motor Vehicles: n.a.
Roads: 1,040 km; 638 km paved
Railway: none
Air Traffic: n.a.
Airports: 3; 2 have paved runways (1997 est.)

Canadian Embassy: The Canadian High Commission to Grenada, c/o The Canadian High Commission, P.O. Box 404, Bridgetown, Barbados. Tel: (246) 429-3550. Fax: (246) 429-3780.
Embassy in Canada: c/o High Commission for the Countries of the Organization of Eastern Caribbean States, 112 Kent St, Ste 1610, Place de Ville, Tower B, Ottawa ON K1P 5P2. Tel: (613) 236-8952. Fax: (613) 236-3042.

Guadeloupe

Long-Form Name: Department of Guadeloupe
Capital: Basse-Terre (seat of govt.); each of the 7 inhabited islands has its own chief town

■ GEOGRAPHY

Area: 1,779 sq. km (2 main islands, 5 small islands, one small island group called Iles des Saintes)
Climate: subtropical tempered by trade winds; hot and humid May–Dec., cool and dry Dec.–April
Land Use: 14% arable, 4% permanent crops, 14% meadows and pastures, 39% forest and woodland, 29% other
Location: Caribbean, among the Lesser Antilles

■ PEOPLE

Population: 416,439 (July 1998 est.)
Nationality: Guadeloupian
Ethnic Groups: 90% black or mulatto, 5% white, less than 5% East Indian, Lebanese, Chinese
Languages: French, Creole dialect

■ GOVERNMENT

Colony Territory of: Dependency of France
Leader(s): Chief of State: Jacques Chirac (France), Prefect Jean-Francois Carenco, Pres. General Council Marcellin Lubeth
Government Type: overseas department of France
National Holiday: Taking of the Bastille, July 14

■ ECONOMY

Overview: economy depends on agriculture, tourism, light industry and services; unemployment is especially high among youth; agriculture: includes bananas, sugar cane, rum, flowers, livestock; vegetables and tobacco grown for local consumption; forestry, fisheries, tourism, food processing; partners: France, Martinique

■ FINANCE/TRADE

Currency: French franc = 100 centimes

Canadian Embassy: c/o The Canadian Embassy, 35-37 avenue Montaigne, Paris, 75008, France. Tel: (011-331) 44-43-29-00. Fax: (011-331) 44-43-29-99.
Representative to Canada: c/o Embassy of France, 42 Sussex Dr, Ottawa ON K1M 2C9. Tel: (613) 789-1795. Fax: (613) 562-3735.

Guam

Long-Form Name: Territory of Guam
Capital: Agana

■ GEOGRAPHY

Area: 541.3 sq. km
Climate: tropical maritime, with little seasonal variation, but typhoon-prone and suffers from earthquakes; wet all year
Land Use: 11% arable, 11% permanent crops, 15% meadows and pastures, 18% forest and woodland, 45% other; interior is mountainous and volcanic hills dominate the south, but many forests in northern Guam have been cleared for farming and the construction of airfields; coconut trees grow throughout the island
Location: N Pacific Ocean, E of the Philippines

■ PEOPLE

Population: 148,060 (July 1998 est.)
Nationality: Guamanian
Ethnic Groups: 47% Chamorro, 25% Filipino, 10% Caucasian, 18% Chinese, Japanese, Korean and other
Languages: English (official), Chamorro, Japanese

■ GOVERNMENT

Colony Territory of: Unincorporated Outlying Territory of the United States
Leader(s): Chief of State: William Clinton (US); Gov. Carl T.C. Gutierrez
Government Type: unincorporated outlying territory of the US; executive powers of the legislature similar to those of an American state legislature
National Holiday: Guam Discovery Day (first Monday in March); also Liberation Day, July 21

■ ECONOMY

Overview: economy depends mainly on US military spending and on tourism; agriculture: corn, coconuts, sweet potatoes, cucumbers, watermelons, beans, livestock, esp. cattle and pigs, fruit, vegetables, fish; industry: textile manufacture, cement, petroleum, printing, plastics, ship repair; tourism of growing importance

■ FINANCE/TRADE

Currency: American dollar = 100 cents

Canadian Embassy: c/o The Canadian Embassy, 501 Pennsylvania Avenue NW, Washington DC 20001, USA. Tel: (202) 682-1740. Fax: (202) 682-7726.
Representative to Canada: c/o Embassy of the United States of America, 100 Wellington St., Ottawa ON K1P 5A1. Tel: (613) 238-5335. Fax: (613) 238-5720.

Guatemala

Long-Form Name: Republic of Guatemala
Capital: Guatemala

■ GEOGRAPHY

Area: 108,890 sq. km
Coastline: 400 km
Climate: tropical; hot, humid in lowlands; cooler in highlands
Environment: numerous volcanoes in mountains, with frequent violent earthquakes; Caribbean coast subject to hurricanes and other tropical storms; deforestation; soil erosion; water pollution
Terrain: mostly mountainous with narrow coastal plains and rolling limestone plateau (Petén)
Land Use: 12% arable; 5% permanent; 24% permanent pastures; 54% forest; 5% other
Location: Central (Latin) America, bordering on Caribbean Sea, Pacific Ocean

■ PEOPLE

Population: 12,007,580 (July 1998 est.)
Nationality: Guatemalan
Age Structure: 0-14 yrs: 43%; 15-64: 54%; 65+: 3% (1998 est.)
Population Growth Rate: 2.71% (1998 est.)
Net Migration: -1.99 migrants/1,000 population (1998 est.)
Ethnic Groups: 56% Ladino (mestizo-mixed Indian and European ancestry), 44% Indian
Languages: 60% Spanish, but 40% of the population speaks an Indian language as a primary tongue (23 Indian dialects, including Quiche, Cakchiquel, Kekchi)
Religions: predominantly Roman Catholic; also Protestant, traditional Mayan
Birth Rate: 36.02/1,000 population (1998 est.)
Death Rate: 6.96/1,000 population (1998 est.)
Infant Mortality: 47.68 deaths/1,000 live births (1998 est.)
Life Expectancy at Birth: 63.4 years male, 68.81 years female (1998 est.)
Total Fertility Rate: 4.81 children born/woman (1998 est.)
Literacy: 55.6% (1997 est.)

■ GOVERNMENT

Leader(s): Pres. Alvaro Arzu Irigoyen; V.Pres. Luis Alberto Flores Asturias
Government Type: republic
Administrative Divisions: 22 departments (departamento, pl. departamentos)
Nationhood: Sept. 15, 1821 (from Spain)
National Holiday: Independence Day, Sept. 15

■ ECONOMY

Overview: the inflation rate has dropped significantly as a result of government economic reforms, but political uncertainty casts a shadow over the agriculturally based economy
GDP: $45.8 billion, per capita $4,000; real growth rate 4.1% (1997 est.)
Inflation: 7.3% (May 1998)
Industries: accounts for 21% of GDP; sugar, textiles and clothing, furniture, chemicals, petroleum, metals, rubber, tourism
Labour Force: 4.1 million (1997); 36.9% community, social and business services, 26.1% agriculture, 16.6% industry
Unemployment: 5.2% (1997 est.)
Agriculture: accounts for 24% of GDP and employs 60% of the labour force; principal crops—sugar cane, corn, bananas, coffee, beans, cardamom; livestock—cattle, sheep, pigs, chickens; food importer
Natural Resources: crude oil, nickel, rare woods, fish, chicle

■ FINANCE/TRADE

Currency: quetzal (pl. quetzalas) (Q) = 100 centavos
International Reserves Excluding Gold: $1.194 billion (Jan. 1999)
Gold Reserves: 0.215 million fine troy ounces (Jan. 1999)
Budget: revenues $1.6 billion; expenditures $1.88 billion, including capital expenditures of $570 million (1996 est.)
Defence Expenditures: 0.66% (1998 est.)
Education Expenditures: 16.77% of total govt. expenditure (1995)
External Debt: $3.785 billion (1996)
Exports: $2.344 billion (1997); commodities: coffee 38%, bananas 7%, sugar 7%, cardamon 4%; partners: US 29%, El Salvador, Germany, Costa Rica, Italy
Imports: $3.852 billion (1997); commodities: fuel and petroleum products, machinery, grain, fertilizers, motor vehicles; partners: US 38%, Mexico, Germany, Japan, El Salvador

■ COMMUNICATIONS

Daily Newspapers: 7 (1996)
Televisions: 57/1,000 inhabitants (1996)
Radios: 73/1,000 inhabitants (1996)
Telephones: 3.0/100 inhabitants (1996 est.)

■ TRANSPORTATION

Motor Vehicles: 199,000; 102,000 passenger cars (1997 est.)
Roads: 13,100 km; 3,616 km paved
Railway: 884 km

Air Traffic: 300,000 passengers carried (1996)
Airports: 479; 12 have paved runways (1997 est.)

Canadian Embassy: The Canadian Embassy, 13 Calle 8-44, Zone 10, Guatemala City; mailing address: P.O. Box 400, Guatemala City, Guatemala, C.A. Tel: (011-502) 333-61-04. Fax: (011-502) 333-61-61.
Embassy in Canada: Embassy of the Republic of Guatemala, 130 Albert St, Ste 1010, Ottawa ON K1P 5G4. Tel: (613) 233-7237. Fax: (613) 233-0135.

Guinea

Long-Form Name: Republic of Guinea
Capital: Conakry

■ GEOGRAPHY

Area: 245,860 sq. km
Coastline: 320 km
Climate: generally hot and humid; monsoonal-type rainy season (June to Nov.) with southwesterly winds; dry season (Dec. to May) with northeasterly harmattan winds
Environment: hot, dry, dusty harmattan haze may reduce visibility during dry season; deforestation; insufficient safe drinking water
Terrain: generally flat coastal plain, hilly to mountainous interior
Land Use: 2% arable; negligible permanent; 22% permanent pastures; 59% forest; 17% other
Location: W Africa, bordering on Atlantic Ocean

■ PEOPLE

Population: 7,477,110 (July 1998 est.)
Nationality: Guinean
Age Structure: 0-14 yrs: 44%; 15-64: 53%; 65+: 3% (1998 est.)
Population Growth Rate: 0.83% (1998 est.)
Net Migration: -15.25 migrants/1,000 population (1998 est.)
Ethnic Groups: 40% Peuhl, 30% Malinke, 20% Sousou, 10% smaller tribes
Languages: French (official); each tribe has its own language; 8 official languages are taught in schools, including Fulani, Malinke, Soussou
Religions: 85% Muslim, 7% indigenous beliefs, 8% Christian
Birth Rate: 41.28/1,000 population (1998 est.)
Death Rate: 17.76/1,000 population (1998 est.)
Infant Mortality: 128.92 deaths/1,000 live births (1998 est.)
Life Expectancy at Birth: 43.58 years male, 48.52 years female (1998 est.)
Total Fertility Rate: 5.59 children born/woman (1998 est.)

Literacy: 35.9% (1997 est.)

■ GOVERNMENT

Leader(s): Pres. Gen. Lansana Conté, Premier Lamine Sidime
Government Type: republic
Administrative Divisions: 33 administrative regions and 1 national capital
Nationhood: Oct. 2, 1958 (from France; formerly known as French Guinea)
National Holiday: Anniversary of the Second Republic, Apr. 3

■ ECONOMY

Overview: although possessing numerous natural resources and potential for agricultural development, it is one of the poorest countries in the world; mining accounts for the bulk of Guinea's exports and apart from the bauxite industry, foreign investment remains low
GDP: adjusted for purchasing power parity: $8.3 billion, per capita $1,100; real growth rate 4.8% (1997 est.)
Inflation: 3.0% (Nov. 1996)
Industries: accounts for 31% of GDP; bauxite mining, alumina, diamond mining, light manufacturing and agricultural processing industries
Labour Force: 3.1 million (1997 est.); 78.1% agriculture, 1.3% industry, 20.6% services
Unemployment: n.a.
Agriculture: accounts for 24% of GDP and employs 80% of the workforce, (including fishing and forestry); mostly subsistence farming; principal products—rice, coffee, pineapples, palm kernels, cassava, sweet potatoes, timber; livestock—cattle, sheep and goats
Natural Resources: bauxite, iron ore, diamonds, gold, uranium, hydroelectricity, fish

■ FINANCE/TRADE

Currency: Guinean franc = 100 centimes
International Reserves Excluding Gold: $192 million (July 1998)
Gold Reserves: n.a.
Budget: revenues $519 million; expenditures $947 million, including capital expenditures of n.a. (1995 est.)
Defence Expenditures: 1.9% of GDP (1996)
Education Expenditures: n.a.
External Debt: $3 billion (1997 est.)
Exports: n.a.; commodities: alumina, bauxite, diamonds, coffee, pineapples, bananas, palm kernels; partners: US 33%, European Community 33%, Eastern Europe 20%, Canada
Imports: n.a.; commodities: petroleum products,

metals, machinery, transport equipment, foodstuffs, textiles and grain; partners: US 16%, France, Brazil

■ COMMUNICATIONS

Daily Newspapers: 0 (1996)
Televisions: 10/1,000 inhabitants (1996)
Radios: 47/1,000 inhabitants (1996)
Telephones: 0.2/100 inhabitants (1996 est.)

■ TRANSPORTATION

Motor Vehicles: 33,000; 13,700 passenger cars (1997 est.)
Roads: 30,500 km; 5,033 km paved
Railway: 1,086 km
Air Traffic: 36,000 passengers carried (1996)
Airports: 15; 5 have paved runways (1997 est.)

Canadian Embassy: The Canadian Embassy, P.O. Box 99, Conakry, Guinea. Tel: (011-224) 46-23-95. Fax: (011-224) 46-42-35.
Embassy in Canada: Embassy of the Republic of Guinea, 483 Wilbrod St, Ottawa ON K1N 6N1. Tel: (613) 789-8444. Fax: (613) 789-7560.

Guinea-Bissau

Long-Form Name: Republic of Guinea-Bissau
Capital: Bissau

■ GEOGRAPHY

Area: 36,120 sq. km
Coastline: 350 km
Climate: tropical; generally hot and humid; monsoon-type rainy season (June to Nov.) with southwesterly winds; dry season (Dec. to May) with northeasterly harmattan winds
Environment: hot, dry, dusty harmattan haze may reduce visibility during dry season; deforestation, soil erosion
Terrain: mostly low coastal plain rising to savanna in east
Land Use: 11% arable; 1% permanent; 38% meadows; 38% forest; 12% other
Location: W Africa, bordering on Atlantic Ocean

■ PEOPLE

Population: 1,206,311 (July 1998 est.)
Nationality: Guinean
Age Structure: 0-14 yrs: 42%; 15-64: 55%; 65+: 3% (1998 est.)
Population Growth Rate: 2.32% (1998 est.)
Net Migration: 0 migrants/1,000 population (1998 est.)
Ethnic Groups: approx. 99% African (including 30% Balanta, 20% Fula, 14% Manjaca, 13% Mandinga, 7% Papel); less than 1% European and mulatto

Languages: Portuguese (official); Crioulo (a Portuguese-based Creole), Balante and numerous African languages
Religions: 65% indigenous beliefs, 30% Muslim, 5% Christian
Birth Rate: 38.67/1,000 population (1998 est.)
Death Rate: 15.48/1,000 population (1998 est.)
Infant Mortality: 111.61 deaths/1,000 live births (1998 est.)
Life Expectancy at Birth: 47.47 years male, 50.85 years female (1998 est.)
Total Fertility Rate: 5.17 children born/woman (1998 est.)
Literacy: 53.9% (1997 est.)

■ GOVERNMENT

Leader(s): Pres. Malan Bacai Sanha, Prem. Francisco Fadul
Government Type: republic; multi-party since 1991
Administrative Divisions: 9 regions (regiões, singular–região)
Nationhood: Sept. 10, 1974 (from Portugal; formerly known as Portuguese Guinea)
National Holiday: Independence Day, Sept. 24

■ ECONOMY

Overview: this poor country is focusing on agricultural development; exploitation of mineral deposits is hampered by a weak infrastructure and high costs. The heavy foreign debt is a burden
GDP: $1.15 billion, per capita $975; real growth rate 5% (1997 est.)
Inflation: 13.4% (Mar. 1998)
Industries: accounts for 18% of GDP, agricultural processing, beer, soft drinks
Labour Force: 1 million (1997 est.); 82% agriculture, 4% industry, 14% services
Unemployment: n.a.
Agriculture: accounts for 45% of GDP; nearly 100% of exports and 90% of employment; rice is the staple; not self-sufficient in food; fishing and forestry not fully exploited; crops include corn, beans, cassava, cashew nuts, peanuts, palm kernels and cotton
Natural Resources: unexploited deposits of petroleum, bauxite, phosphates; fish, timber

■ FINANCE/TRADE

Currency: Communauté financière africaine (CFAF) franc = 100 centimes
International Reserves Excluding Gold: $16 million (Mar. 1997)
Gold Reserves: n.a.
Budget: n.a.
Defence Expenditures: 2.9% (1996)

Education Expenditures: n.a.
External Debt: $937 million (1996)
Exports: $31 million (1996); commodities: cashews, fish, peanuts, palm kernels; partners: Portugal, Spain, Switzerland, Cape Verde, China
Imports: $93 million (1996); commodities: capital equipment, consumer goods, semiprocessed goods, foods, petroleum; partners: Portugal, former USSR countries, European Community, other European, Senegal, US

■ COMMUNICATIONS

Daily Newspapers: 1 (1996)
Televisions: n.a.
Radios: 43/1,000 inhabitants (1996)
Telephones: 0.9/100 inhabitants (1996 est.)

■ TRANSPORTATION

Motor Vehicles: 6,900; 4,000 passenger cars (1997 est.)
Roads: 4,400 km; 453 km paved
Railway: none
Air Traffic: 21,000 passengers carried (1996)
Airports: 30; 3 have paved runways (1997 est.)

Canadian Embassy: The Canadian Embassy to Guinea-Bissau, c/o The Canadian Embassy, P.O. Box 3373, Dakar, Senegal. Tel: (011-221) 823-92-90. Fax: (011-221) 823-87-49.
Embassy in Canada: Embassy of the Republic of Guinea-Bissau, 1511 K St NW, Ste 519, Washington DC 20005, USA. Tel: (202) 347-3950. Fax: (202) 347-3954.

Guyana

Long-Form Name: Co-operative Republic of Guyana
Capital: Georgetown

■ GEOGRAPHY

Area: 214,970 sq. km
Coastline: 459 km
Climate: tropical; hot, humid, moderated by northeast trade winds; two rainy seasons (May to mid-Aug., mid-Nov. to mid-Jan.)
Environment: flash floods a constant threat during rainy seasons; water pollution; deforestation
Terrain: mostly rolling highlands; low coastal plain; savanna in south
Land Use: 2% arable; negligible permanent; 6% meadows; 84% forest; 8% other
Location: N South America, bordering on Atlantic Ocean

■ PEOPLE

Population: 707,954 (July 1998 est.)
Nationality: Guyanese
Age Structure: 0-14 yrs: 31%; 15-64: 64%; 65+: 5% (1998 est.)
Population Growth Rate: -0.47% (1998 est.)
Net Migration: -14.45 migrants/1,000 population (1998 est.)
Ethnic Groups: 51% East Indian, 43% black and mixed, 4% Amerindian, 2% European and Chinese
Languages: English, Hindi, Urdu, Amerindian dialects
Religions: 57% Christian, 33% Hindu, 9% Muslim, 1% other
Birth Rate: 18.49/1,000 population (1998 est.)
Death Rate: 8.72/1,000 population (1998 est.)
Infant Mortality: 48.67 deaths/1,000 live births (1998 est.)
Life Expectancy at Birth: 59.5 years male, 63.32 years female (1998 est.)
Total Fertility Rate: 2.12 children born/woman (1998 est.)
Literacy: 98.1% (1997 est.)

■ GOVERNMENT

Leader(s): Head of State and Government Bharrat Jagdeo, Prime Min. Samuel Hinds
Government Type: republic
Administrative Divisions: 10 regions
Nationhood: May 26, 1966 (from UK; formerly known as British Guyana)
National Holiday: Republic Day, Feb. 23

■ ECONOMY

Overview: Guyana is one of the world's poorest countries, with a per capita income less than one-fifth the South American average; however, the economy is on an upswing and inflation is decreasing
GDP: $1.8 billion, per capita $2,500; real growth rate 5% (1997 est.)
Inflation: 4.5% (1997 est.)
Industries: accounts for 28% of GDP; bauxite mining, sugar, rice milling, timber, fishing (shrimp), textiles, gold mining
Labour Force: n.a.; 26% industry, 27% agriculture, 47% services
Unemployment: n.a.
Agriculture: most important sector, accounting for 39% of GDP; sugar and rice are main crops; not self-sufficient in food; development potential exists for fishing and forestry
Natural Resources: bauxite, gold, diamonds, hardwood timber, shrimp, fish

■ FINANCE/TRADE

Currency: Guyanese dollar ($G) = 100 cents
International Reserves Excluding Gold: $277 million (Dec. 1998)
Gold Reserves: n.a.
Budget: revenues $278 million; expenditures $299 million, including capital expenditures of $133 million (1996 est.)
Defence Expenditures: 1.0% of GDP (1996)
Education Expenditures: n.a.
External Debt: $1.631 billion (1996)
Exports: $643 million (1997); commodities: bauxite, sugar, rice, shrimp, gold, molasses, timber, rum; partners: UK 37%, US 12%, Canada 10.6%, CARICOM 4.8%
Imports: $629 million (1997); commodities: manufactures, machinery, food, petroleum; partners: CARICOM 41%, US 18%, UK 9%, Canada 3%

■ COMMUNICATIONS

Daily Newspapers: 2 (1996)
Televisions: 54/1,000 inhabitants (1996)
Radios: 495/1,000 inhabitants (1996)
Telephones: 5.3/100 inhabitants (1996 est.)

■ TRANSPORTATION

Motor Vehicles: 33,000; 24,000 passenger cars (1997 est.)
Roads: 7,970 km; 590 km paved
Railway: 88 km; no public railroads
Air Traffic: 126,000 passengers carried (1996)
Airports: 50; 5 have paved runways (1997 est.)

Canadian Embassy: Canadian High Commission, High and Young Streets, Georgetown; mailing address: P.O. Box 10880, Georgetown, Guyana. Tel: (011-592-2) 72081. Fax: (011-592-2) 58380.
Embassy in Canada: High Commission for the Co-operative Republic of Guyana, Burnside Bldg, 151 Slater St, Ste 309, Ottawa ON K1P 5H3. Tel: (613) 235-7249. Fax: (613) 235-1447.

Haiti

Long-Form Name: Republic of Haiti
Capital: Port-au-Prince

■ GEOGRAPHY

Area: 27,750 sq. km
Coastline: 1,771 km
Climate: tropical; semi-arid where mountains in east cut off trade winds
Environment: lies in the middle of the hurricane belt and subject to severe storms from June to Oct.; occasional flooding and earthquakes; deforestation; soil erosion, insufficient safe drinking water

Terrain: mostly rough and mountainous
Land Use: 20% arable; 13% permanent; 18% meadows; 5% forest; 44% other
Location: West Indies, bordering on Caribbean Sea, Atlantic Ocean

■ PEOPLE

Population: 6,780,501 (July 1998 est.)
Nationality: Haitian
Age Structure: 0-14 yrs: 43%; 15-64: 53%; 65+: 4% (1998 est.)
Population Growth Rate: 1.51% (1998 est.)
Net Migration: -3.61 migrants/1,000 population (1998 est.)
Ethnic Groups: 95% black, 5% mulatto and European
Languages: French (official) spoken by only 10% of population; all speak Creole
Religions: 80% Roman Catholic (of which an overwhelming majority also practice Voodoo), 16% Protestant, 4% other
Birth Rate: 32.84/1,000 population (1998 est.)
Death Rate: 14.17/1,000 population (1998 est.)
Infant Mortality: 98.98 deaths/1,000 live births (1998 est.)
Life Expectancy at Birth: 49.33 years male, 53.58 years female (1998 est.)
Total Fertility Rate: 4.67 children born/woman (1998 est.)
Literacy: 45% (1997 est.)

■ GOVERNMENT

Leader(s): Pres. Rene Préval, Prem. Jacques-Edouard Alexis
Government Type: republic
Administrative Divisions: 9 departments (départements)
Nationhood: Jan. 1, 1804 (from France)
National Holiday: Independence Day, Jan. 1

■ ECONOMY

Overview: about 75% of the population live in absolute poverty, and do not have access to safe drinking water, medical care or sufficient food; agriculture based on small-scale subsistence farming; trade sanctions have further damaged the economy
GDP: $7.1 billion, per capita $1,070; real growth rate 1.1% (1997 est.)
Inflation: 10.9% (June 1998)
Industries: accounts for 13% of GDP; sugar refining, textiles, flour milling, cement manufacturing, bauxite mining, tourism, light assembly industries based on imported parts
Labour Force: 3 million (1997 est.); 50.4% agriculture, 43.9% services, 5.7% industry
Unemployment: 60% (1996 est.)

Agriculture: accounts for 44% of GDP and employs 70% of workforce; mostly small-size subsistence farms; commercial crops include coffee and sugar cane; staple crops include rice, corn, sorghum and mangoes
Natural Resources: bauxite

■ FINANCE/TRADE

Currency: gourde (G) = 100 centimes
International Reserves Excluding Gold: $81 million (Aug. 1998)
Gold Reserves: 0.020 million fine troy ounces (Jan. 1999)
Budget: adjusted for purchasing power parity: revenues $284 million; expenditures $308 million, including capital expenditures n.a. (1996-97 est.)
Defence Expenditures: 3.5%s of GDP (1996)
Education Expenditures: n.a.
External Debt: $897 million (1996)
Exports: $179 million (1998 est.); commodities: light manufactures 65%, coffee 17%, other agriculture 8%, other products 10%; partners: US 77%, France 5%, Italy 4%, Germany 3%, other industrial 9%, less developed countries 2%
Imports: $636 million (1998 est.); commodities: machines and manufactures 36%, food and beverages 21%, petroleum products 11%, fats and oils 12%, chemicals 12%; partners: US 65%, Netherlands Antilles 6%, Japan 5%, France 4%, Canada 2%, Asia 2%

■ COMMUNICATIONS

Daily Newspapers: 4 (1996)
Televisions: 5.0/1,000 inhabitants (1996)
Radios: 55/1,000 inhabitants (1996)
Telephones: 0.8/100 inhabitants (1996 est.)

■ TRANSPORTATION

Motor Vehicles: 53,000; 32,000 passenger cars (1997 est.)
Roads: 4,160 km; 1,011 km paved
Railway: 40 km
Air Traffic: n.a.
Airports: 14; 3 have paved runways (1997 est.)

Canadian Embassy: The Canadian Embassy, Édifice Banque de Nova Scotia, route de Delmas, Port-au-Prince, Haiti; mailing address: C.P. 826, Port-au-Prince, Haiti. Tel: (011-509) 23-2358. Fax: (011-509) 23-8720.
Embassy in Canada: Embassy of the Republic of Haiti, 112 Kent St, Ste 205, Place de Ville, Tower B, Ottawa ON K1P 5P2. Tel: (613) 238-1628. Fax (613) 238-2986.

Honduras

Long-Form Name: Republic of Honduras
Capital: Tegucigalpa

■ GEOGRAPHY

Area: 112,090 sq. km
Coastline: 820 km
Climate: subtropical in lowlands, temperate in mountains
Environment: subject to frequent, but generally mild, earthquakes; damaging hurricanes along Caribbean coast; deforestation; soil erosion; mining pollution of freshwater resources
Terrain: mostly mountainous in interior, narrow coastal plains
Land Use: 15% arable; 3% permanent; 14% permanent pastures; 54% forest and woodlands; 14% other
Location: Central (Latin) America, bordering on Caribbean Sea, Pacific Ocean

■ PEOPLE

Population: 5,861,955 (July 1998 est.)
Nationality: Honduran
Age Structure: 0-14 yrs: 42%; 15-64: 55%; 65+: 3% (1998 est.)
Population Growth Rate: 2.33% (1998 est.)
Net Migration: -1.48 migrants/1,000 population (1998 est.)
Ethnic Groups: 90% mestizo (mixed Indian and European), 7% Indian, 2% black, 1% white
Languages: Spanish, Indian dialects
Religions: about 97% Roman Catholic; small Protestant minority
Birth Rate: 31.79/1,000 population (1998 est.)
Death Rate: 7.02/1,000 population (1998 est.)
Infant Mortality: 41.88 deaths/1,000 live births (1998 est.)
Life Expectancy at Birth: 63.31 years male, 66.8 years female (1998 est.)
Total Fertility Rate: 4.12 children born/woman (1998 est.)
Literacy: 72.7% (1997 est.)

■ GOVERNMENT

Leader(s): Pres. Carlos Roberto Flores Facusse; First V.Pres. William Handal
Government Type: republic
Administrative Divisions: 18 departments (departamentos)
Nationhood: Sept. 15, 1821 (from Spain)
National Holiday: Independence Day, Sept. 15

■ ECONOMY

Overview: one of the poorest countries in the Western hemisphere, with a high population growth rate, a high unemployment rate, a lack of basic services, and an export sector vulnerable to world prices (coffee, bananas)

GDP: $12.7 billion, per capita $2,200; real growth rate 4.5% (1997 est.)

Inflation: 14.8% (July 1998)

Industries: accounts for 19% of GDP; agricultural processing (sugar and coffee), textiles, clothing, wood products

Labour Force: 2.1 million (1997 est.); 38.2% agriculture, 19.9% community, social and business services, 37.4% undefined

Unemployment: 6.3%, with 30% underemployment (1997 est.)

Agriculture: accounts for 20% of GDP, over 60% of the labour force and 20% of exports; main products include bananas, coffee, timber, beef, citrus fruit, shrimp; importer of wheat

Natural Resources: timber, gold, silver, copper, lead, zinc, iron ore, antimony, coal, fish

■ FINANCE/TRADE

Currency: lempira (L) = 100 centavos

International Reserves Excluding Gold: $818 million (Dec. 1998)

Gold Reserves: 0.021 million fine troy ounces (Dec. 1998)

Budget: revenues $655 million; expenditures $850 million, including capital expenditures of $150 million (1997 est.)

Defence Expenditures: 1.5% of GDP (1997)

Education Expenditures: 3.9% of GNP (1995)

External Debt: $4.453 billion (1996)

Exports: $1.447 billion (1997); commodities: bananas, coffee, shrimp, lobster, minerals, lumber; partners: US 52%, Germany 11%, Japan, Italy, Belgium

Imports: $2.048 billion (1997); commodities: machinery and transport equipment, chemical products, manufactured goods, fuel and oil, foodstuffs; partners: US 39%, Japan 9%, CACM, Venezuela, Mexico

■ COMMUNICATIONS

Daily Newspapers: 7 (1996)

Televisions: 95/1,000 inhabitants (1996)

Radios: 409/1,000 inhabitants (1996)

Telephones: 3.4/100 inhabitants (1996 est.)

■ TRANSPORTATION

Motor Vehicles: 185,000; 80,000 passenger cars (1997 est.)

Roads: 15,400 km; 3,126 km paved

Railway: 595 km

Air Traffic: 474,000 passengers carried (1996 est.)

Airports: 122; 12 have paved runways (1997 est.)

Canadian Embassy: Office of the Canadian Embassy, Edificio Comercial Los Castanos, 6th Fl., Boulevard Morazan, Tegucigalpa. Tel: (011-504) 232-6787.

Embassy in Canada: Embassy of the Republic of Honduras, 151 Slater St, Ste 805, Ottawa ON K1P 5H3. Tel: (613) 233-8900. Fax: (613) 232-0193.

Hong Kong

Long-Form Name: Hong Kong

Capital: Victoria

■ GEOGRAPHY

Area: 1,092 sq. km

Climate: tropical monsoon; cool and humid in winter, hot and rainy from spring through summer, warm and sunny in fall

Land Use: 6% arable land; 1% permanent; 1% meadows; 22% forest; 70% other, includes 2% irrigated

Location: SE Asia, bordering on South China Sea

■ PEOPLE

Population: 6,706,965 (July 1998 est.)

Nationality: Chinese

Ethnic Groups: 95% Chinese, 5% other

Languages: Chinese (Cantonese), English

■ GOVERNMENT

Colony Territory of: Special Administrative Region (SAR) of the People's Republic of China

Leader(s): Chief of State: Pres. of China, Jiang Zemin; Chief Exec. Tung Che Wah

Government Type: reverted to China July 1, 1997

National Holiday: National Day, Oct. 1-2

■ ECONOMY

Overview: manufacturing and services (finance, business and professional) are the basis of the economy; natural resources are limited and food and raw materials must be imported

■ FINANCE/TRADE

Currency: Hong Kong dollar (HK$) = 100 cents

Canadian Embassy: c/o The Canadian Embassy, 19 Dong Zhi Men Wai, Chao Yang District, Beijing, PDR China. Tel: (011-86-10) 6532-3536. Fax: (011-86-10) 6532-4311.

Representative to Canada: c/o Embassy of the People's Republic of China, 515 St. Patrick St, Ottawa ON K1N 5H3. Tel: (613) 789-3434. Fax: (613) 789-1911.

Hungary

Long-Form Name: Republic of Hungary
Capital: Budapest

■ GEOGRAPHY

Area: 93,030 sq. km
Coastline: none: landlocked
Climate: temperate; cold, cloudy, humid winter; warm summer
Environment: levees are common along many streams, but flooding occurs almost every year; pollution of air, soil and underground water resources
Terrain: mostly flat to rolling plains
Land Use: 51% arable; 2% permanent crops; 13% permanent pastures; 19% forest; 15% other, includes 2% irrigated
Location: C Europe

■ PEOPLE

Population: 10,208,128 (July 1998 est.)
Nationality: Hungarian
Age Structure: 0-14 yrs: 18%; 15-64: 68%; 65+: 14% (1998 est.)
Population Growth Rate: -0.23% (1998 est.)
Net Migration: 0.49 migrants/1,000 population (1998 est.)
Ethnic Groups: 89.9% Hungarian, 4% Gypsy, 2% Serb, 2.6% German, 0.8% Slovak, 0.7% Romanian
Languages: Hungarian (Magyar, official), 1.8% other
Religions: 67.5% Roman Catholic, 20% Calvinist, 5% Lutheran, 7.5% atheist and other
Birth Rate: 10.69/1,000 population (1998 est.)
Death Rate: 13.46/1,000 population (1998 est.)
Infant Mortality: 9.7 deaths/1,000 live births (1998 est.)
Life Expectancy at Birth: 66.46 years male, 75.44 years female (1998 est.)
Total Fertility Rate: 1.45 children born/woman (1998 est.)
Literacy: 99% (1997 est.)

■ GOVERNMENT

Leader(s): Pres. Arpad Goncz; Prime Min. Victor Orban
Government Type: republic
Administrative Divisions: 39 counties and 1 capital city (Budapest)
Nationhood: 1001 (unification by King Stephen I)
National Holiday: St. Stephen's Day, Aug. 20 (National Day)

■ ECONOMY

Overview: Hungary has consolidated its stabilization program and undergone enough restructuring to become an established market economy. It appears to have entered a period of sustainable growth, gradually falling inflation, and stable external balances. The government's main economic priorities are to complete structural reforms, particularly in pension, taxation, and healthcare reforms.
GDP: $73.2 billion, per capita $7,400; real growth rate 4.4% (1997 est.)
Inflation: 14.2% (June 1998)
Industries: accounts for 32% of GDP; mining, metallurgy, engineering industries, processed foods, textiles, chemicals (especially pharmaceuticals)
Labour Force: 4.9 million (1997 est.); 29.1% industry, 28.4% community, social and business services, 13.2% agriculture
Unemployment: 9% (1997 est.)
Agriculture: accounts for about 7% of GDP (including forestry) and 16% of employment; highly diversified crop-livestock farming; main crops—wheat, corn, sunflowers, potatoes, sugar beets; livestock—hogs, cattle, poultry and dairy products; self-sufficient in food
Natural Resources: bauxite, coal, natural gas, fertile soils

■ FINANCE/TRADE

Currency: forint (Ft) = 100 filler
International Reserves Excluding Gold: $9.319 billion (Dec. 1998)
Gold Reserves: 0.101 million fine troy ounces (Jan. 1999)
Budget: revenues $12.1 billion; expenditures $13.8 billion, including capital expenditures of n.a. (1997 est.)
Defence Expenditures: 1.81% of total govt. expenditure (1997)
Education Expenditures: 2.45% of total govt. expenditure (1997)
External Debt: $27.5 billion (1996 est.)
Exports: $21.785 billion (1998 est.); commodities: capital goods 36%, foods 24%, consumer goods 18%, fuels and minerals 11%, other 11%; partners: EU nations 65%, former USSR and Eastern Europe 35%
Imports: $24.413 billion (1998 est.); commodities: machinery and transport 28%, fuels 20%, chemical products 14%, manufactured consumer goods 16%, agriculture 6%, other 16%; partners: former USSR countries 43%, Eastern Europe 28%, less developed countries 23%, US 3%

■ COMMUNICATIONS

Daily Newspapers: 40 (1996)
Televisions: 438/1,000 inhabitants (1996)
Radios: 697/1,000 inhabitants (1996)
Telephones: 20.0/100 inhabitants (1996 est.)

■ TRANSPORTATION

Motor Vehicles: 2,810,000; 2,310,000 passenger cars (1997 est.)
Roads: 158,633 km; 69,957 km paved
Railway: 7,606 km
Air Traffic: 1,563,000 passengers carried (1996)
Airports: 25; 15 have paved runways (1997 est.)

Canadian Embassy: The Canadian Embassy, Budakeszi ut 32, 1121 Budapest, Hungary. Tel.: (011-36-1) 275-1200. Fax: (011-36-1) 275-1210.
Embassy in Canada: Embassy of the Republic of Hungary, 299 Waverley St, Ottawa ON K2P 0V9. Tel: (613) 230-2717. Fax: (613) 230-7560.

Iceland

Long-Form Name: Republic of Iceland
Capital: Reykjavik

■ GEOGRAPHY

Area: 103,000 sq. km
Coastline: 4,988 km
Climate: temperate; moderated by North Atlantic Current; mild, windy winters; damp, cool summers
Environment: subject to earthquakes and volcanic activity; water pollution
Terrain: mostly plateau interspersed with mountain peaks, ice fields; coast deeply indented by bays and fjords
Land Use: 0% arable; 0% permanent; 23% meadows; 1% forest; 76% other
Location: NW Europe, bordering on Norwegian Sea, Atlantic Ocean

■ PEOPLE

Population: 271,033 (July 1998 est.)
Nationality: Icelander
Age Structure: 0-14 yrs: 24%; 15-64: 65%; 65+: 11% (1998 est.)
Population Growth Rate: 0.52% (1998 est.)
Net Migration: -2.94 migrants/1,000 population (1998 est.)
Ethnic Groups: homogeneous mixture of descendants of Norwegians and Celts
Languages: Icelandic
Religions: Christianity (predominantly Protestant)

Birth Rate: 15.11/1,000 population (1998 est.)
Death Rate: 6.97/1,000 population (1998 est.)
Infant Mortality: 5.27 deaths/1,000 live births (1998 est.)
Life Expectancy at Birth: 76.76 years male, 81.05 years female (1998 est.)
Total Fertility Rate: 2.04 children born/woman (1998 est.)
Literacy: 100% (1997 est.)

■ GOVERNMENT

Leader(s): Pres. Olafur Ragnar Grimsson, Prime Min. David Oddsson
Government Type: constitutional republic
Administrative Divisions: 23 counties and 14 independent towns
Nationhood: June 17, 1944 (from Denmark)
National Holiday: Anniversary of the Establishment of the Republic, June 17

■ ECONOMY

Overview: Iceland's economy is basically capitalistic, but it has an extensive welfare system, low unemployment, and an unusually even distribution of income. The economy depends heavily on the fishing industry and is vulnerable to changing world fish prices.
GDP: $5.71 billion; per capita $21,000; real growth rate 4.9% (1997 est.)
Inflation: 2.3% (June 1998)
Industries: accounts for 22% of GDP; fish processing, aluminum smelting, ferro-silicon production, hydroelectricity
Labour Force: 139,500 (1997); 55% commerce, finance and services, 14% other manufacturing, 6% agriculture, 8% fish processing, 5% fishing
Unemployment: 2.1% (Oct. 1998)
Agriculture: accounts for about 10% of GDP (including fishing); fishing is the most important economic activity, contributing nearly 75% to export earnings; principal crops include potatoes and turnips; livestock—cattle, sheep; self-sufficient in crops
Natural Resources: fish, hydroelectric and geothermal power, diatomite

■ FINANCE/TRADE

Currency: króna (pl. krónur) (ISK) = 100 aurar
International Reserves Excluding Gold: $441 million (Dec. 1998)
Gold Reserves: 0.056 million fine troy ounces (Jan. 1999)
Budget: revenues $1.9 billion; expenditures $2.1 billion, including capital expenditures of $146 million (1996 est.)
Defence Expenditures: none
Education Expenditures: 12.83% of govt. expenditure (1996)

External Debt: $2.2 billion (1996 est.)
Exports: $2.050 billion (1998); commodities: fish and fish products, animal products, aluminum, diatomite; partners: European Community 58.9% (UK 23.3%, Germany 10.3%), US 13.6%, former USSR countries 3.6%
Imports: $2.489 billion (1998); commodities: machinery and transportation equipment, petroleum, foodstuffs, textiles; partners: European Community 58% (Germany 16%, Denmark 10.4%, UK 9.2%), US 8.5%, former USSR countries 3.9%

■ COMMUNICATIONS

Daily Newspapers: 5 (1996)
Televisions: 354/1,000 inhabitants (1996)
Radios: 923/1,000 inhabitants (1996)
Telephones: 55.5/100 inhabitants (1996 est.)

■ TRANSPORTATION

Motor Vehicles: 144,000; 125,300 passenger cars (1997 est.)
Roads: 12,341 km; 3,196 km paved
Railway: none
Air Traffic: 1,275,300 passengers carried (1996)
Airports: 90; 11 have paved runways (1997 est.)

Canadian Embassy: c/o The Canadian Embassy, Wergelandsveien 7, 0244 Oslo, Norway. Tel. in Reykjavik, Iceland: (011-354-5) 680-820; fax: (011-354-5) 680-899.
Embassy in Canada: Embassy of the Republic of Iceland, 1156 15th St NW, Ste 1200, Washington DC 20005-1, USA. Tel: (202) 265-6653. Fax: (202) 265-6656.

India

Long-Form Name: Republic of India
Capital: New Delhi

■ GEOGRAPHY

Area: 3,287,590 sq. km
Coastline: 7,000 km
Climate: varies from tropical monsoon in south to temperate in north
Environment: deforestation; soil erosion; overgrazing; air and water pollution; desertification, droughts, flash floods, severe thunderstorms common; earthquakes are a hazard
Terrain: upland plain (Deccan Plateau) in south, flat to rolling plain along the Ganges, deserts in west, Himalayas in north
Land Use: 56% arable; 1% permanent; 4% meadows; 23% forest; 16% other, includes 13% irrigated

Location: S Asia, bordering on Arabian Sea, Indian Ocean, Bay of Bengal

■ PEOPLE

Population: 984,003,683 (July 1998 est.)
Nationality: Indian
Age Structure: 0-14 yrs: 34%; 15-64: 61%; 65+: 5% (1998 est.)
Population Growth Rate: 1.71% (1998 est.)
Net Migration: -0.08 migrants/1,000 population (1998 est.)
Ethnic Groups: 72% Indo-Aryan, 25% Dravidian, 3% Mongoloid and other
Languages: Hindi (official, spoken by 30%); English; 19 regional languages, including Bengali, Tlegu, Marathi, Tamil, Urdu, Gujarati, Malayalam, Kannada, Oriya, Punjabi, Assamese, Kashmiri, Sindhi and Sanskrit; 24 languages spoken by a million or more persons each; numerous other languages
Religions: 80% Hindu, 14% Muslim, 2.4% Christian, 2% Sikh, 0.7% Buddhist, 0.5% Jains, 0.4% other
Birth Rate: 25.91/1,000 population (1998 est.)
Death Rate: 8.69/1,000 population (1998 est.)
Infant Mortality: 63.14 deaths/1,000 live births (1998 est.)
Life Expectancy at Birth: 62.11 years male, 63.73 years female (1998 est.)
Total Fertility Rate: 3.24 children born/woman (1998 est.)
Literacy: 52% (1997 est.)

■ GOVERNMENT

Leader(s): Pres. Kocheril Raman Narayanan, Prime Min. Atal Behari Vajpayee
Government Type: federal republic
Administrative Divisions: 25 states and 7 union territories
Nationhood: Aug. 15, 1947 (from UK)
National Holiday: Anniversary of the Proclamation of the Republic, Jan. 26

■ ECONOMY

Overview: a mixture of traditional village farming and handicrafts, modern agriculture, old and new branches of industry and a multitude of support services; millions still live in poverty, hoping to benefit from modern farming techniques
GDP: $1.534 trillion, per capita $1,600; real growth rate 5% (1997 est.)
Inflation: 8.3% (Mar. 1998)
Industries: accounts for 28% of GDP, textiles, food processing, steel, machinery, transportation equipment, cement, jute manufactures, mining, petroleum, power, chemicals, pharmaceuticals, electronics

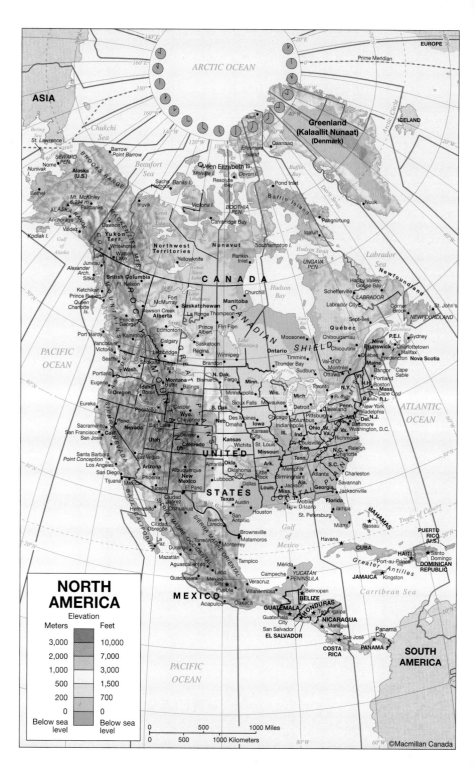

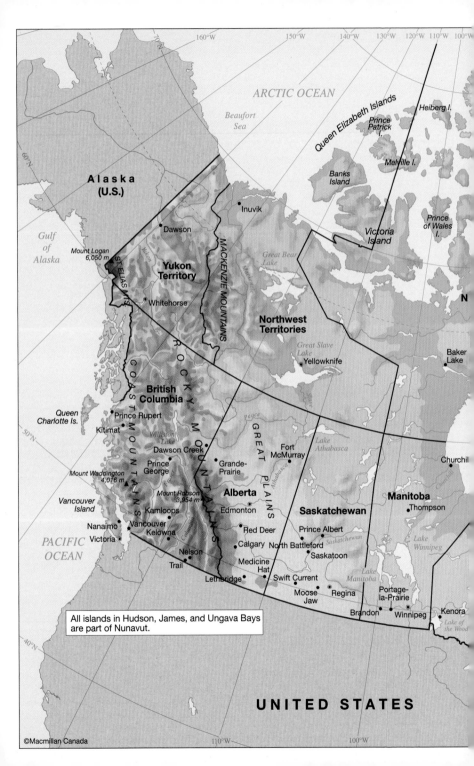

ARCTIC OCEAN

Beaufort Sea

Queen Elizabeth Islands

Heiberg I.

Prince Patrick I.

Melville I.

Banks Island

Prince of Wales I.

Alaska (U.S.)

Inuvik

Victoria Island

Dawson

Gulf of Alaska

Mount Logan 6,050 m

ST. ELIAS MTS.

Yukon Territory

MACKENZIE MOUNTAINS

Whitehorse

Great Bear Lake

Northwest Territories

N

Great Slave Lake

Yellowknife

Baker Lake

ROCKY

COAST MOUNTAINS

British Columbia

Queen Charlotte Is.

Prince Rupert

Kitimat

Williston Lake

Dawson Creek

Prince George

MOUNTAINS

Peace

GREAT

Fort McMurray

Lake Athabasca

Churchill

Grande-Prairie

Mount Waddington 4,016 m

Vancouver Island

Mount Robson 3,954 m

PLAINS

Alberta

Edmonton

Kamloops

Vancouver

Kelowna

Red Deer

Saskatchewan

Manitoba

Thompson

Nanaimo

Victoria

Nelson

Trail

Medicine Hat

Calgary

North Battleford

Prince Albert

Saskatoon

Saskatchewan

Lake Winnipeg

PACIFIC OCEAN

Lethbridge

Swift Current

Moose Jaw

Regina

Lake Manitoba

Portage-la-Prairie

Kenora

Brandon

Winnipeg

Lake of the Wood

All islands in Hudson, James, and Ungava Bays are part of Nunavut.

UNITED STATES

©Macmillan Canada

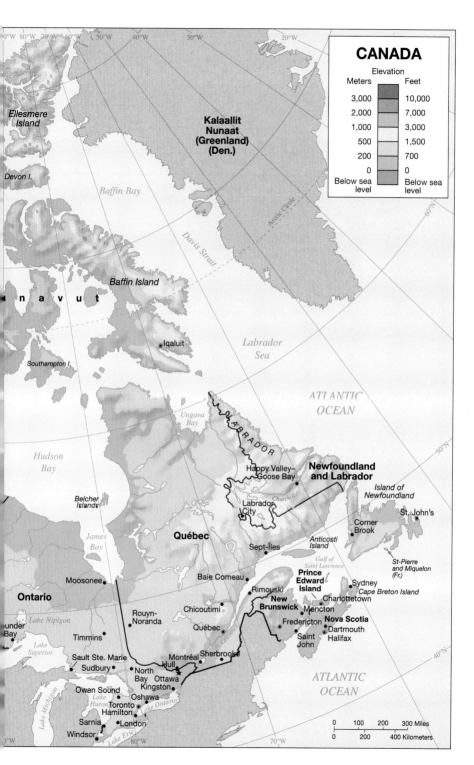

CANADA

Elevation

Meters	Feet
3,000	10,000
2,000	7,000
1,000	3,000
500	1,500
200	700
0	0
Below sea level	Below sea level

Ellesmere Island

Devon I.

Kalaallit Nunaat (Greenland) (Den.)

Baffin Bay

Arctic Circle

Davis Strait

Baffin Island

n a v u t

Iqaluit

Southampton I.

Labrador Sea

ATLANTIC OCEAN

Ungava Bay

LABRADOR

Hudson Bay

Happy Valley–Goose Bay

Newfoundland and Labrador

Island of Newfoundland

Belcher Islands

Church

Labrador City

Corner Brook

St. John's

James Bay

Québec

Sept-Îles

Anticosti Island

St-Pierre and Miquelon (Fr.)

Gulf of Saint Lawrence

Moosonee

Baie Comeau

Prince Edward Island

Sydney

Cape Breton Island

Ontario

Rouyn-Noranda

Chicoutimi

Rimouski

New Brunswick

Charlottetown

Moncton

Lake Nipigon

Québec

Fredericton

Nova Scotia

under Bay

Timmins

St. Lawrence

Saint John

Dartmouth

Halifax

Lake Superior

Sault Ste. Marie

Sherbrooke

Sudbury

Montréal

North Bay

Hull

Owen Sound

Kingston

Ottawa

Lake Huron

Oshawa

ATLANTIC OCEAN

Toronto

Lake Ontario

Hamilton

Sarnia

London

Lake Erie

Windsor

0	100	200	300 Miles
0	200		400 Kilometers

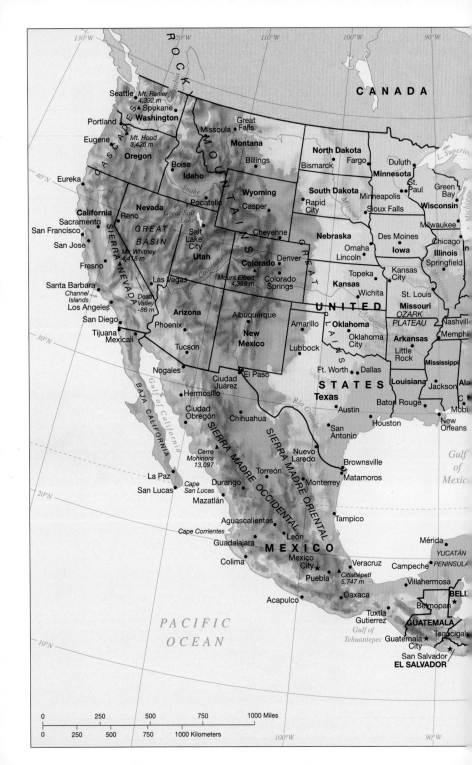

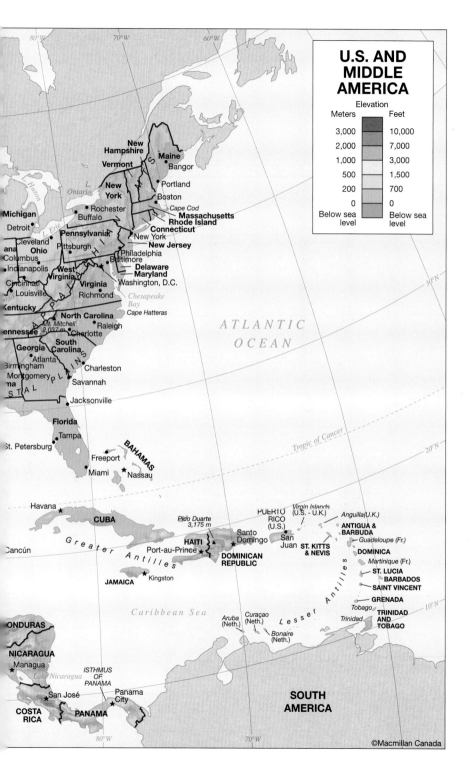

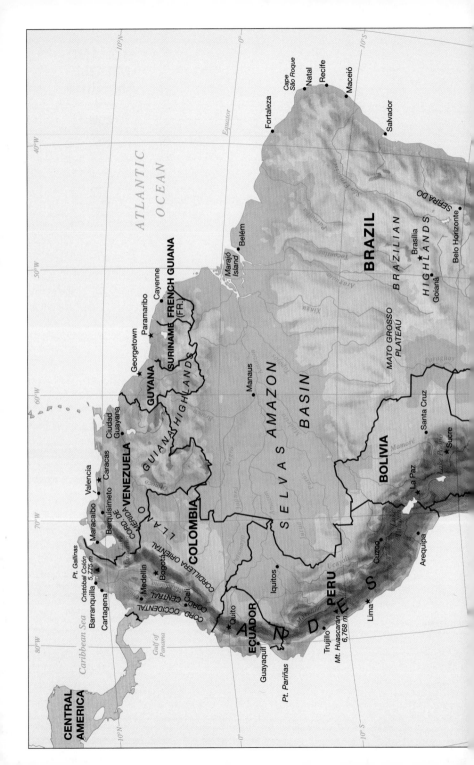

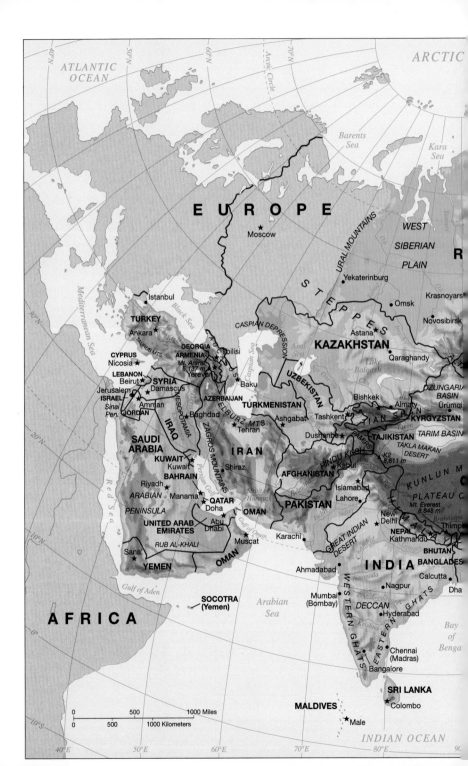

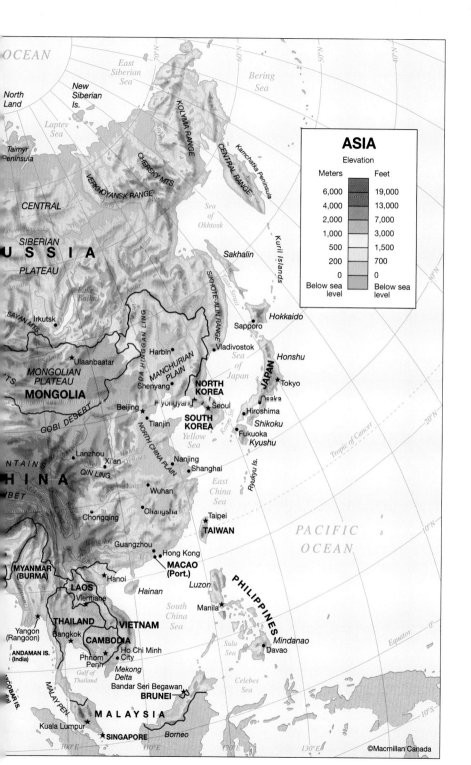

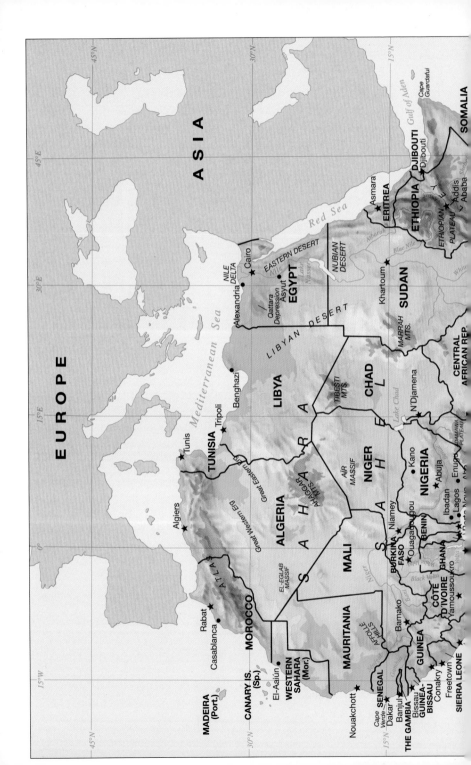

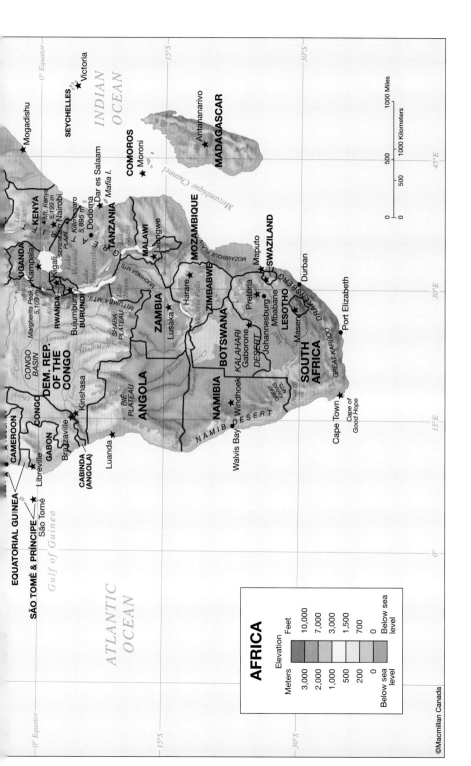

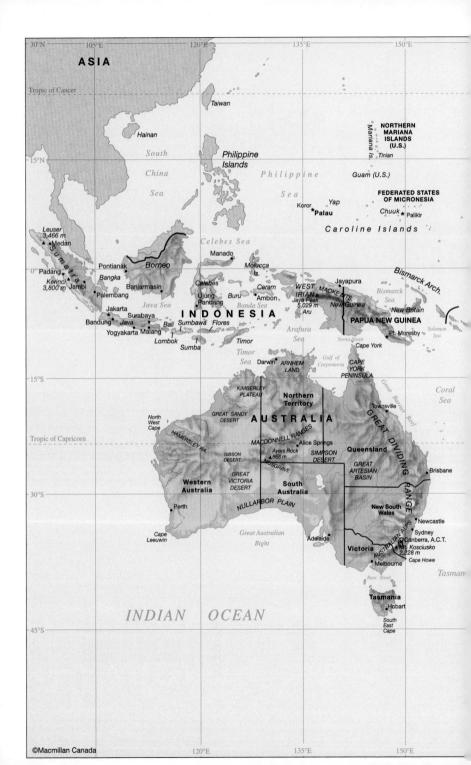

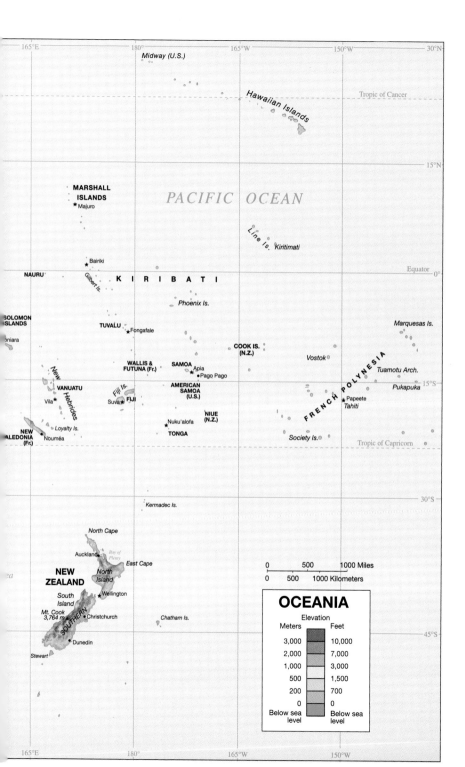

Midway (U.S.)

Tropic of Cancer

Hawaiian Islands

165°E 180° 165°W 150°W 30°N

15°N

MARSHALL
ISLANDS
★ Majuro

PACIFIC OCEAN

Line Is. Kiritimati

NAURU

Bairiki ★

Gilbert Is.

Equator 0°

K I R I B A T I

SOLOMON
ISLANDS

niara

Phoenix Is.

Marquesas Is.

TUVALU Fongafale

COOK IS.
(N.Z.)

Vostok

FRENCH POLYNESIA

Tuamotu Arch.

WALLIS &
FUTUNA (Fr.)

SAMOA Apia
● Pago Pago

Pukapuka

New Hebrides

VANUATU

Fiji Is.

AMERICAN
SAMOA
(U.S.)

15°S

Vila ★

Suva ★ FIJI

NIUE
(N.Z.)

★ Papeete
Tahiti

NEW
CALEDONIA
(Fr.)

Loyalty Is.

Nouméa

Nuku'alofa

TONGA

Society Is.

Tropic of Capricorn

30°S

Kermadec Is.

North Cape

Auckland

Bay of
Plenty

East Cape

0 500 1000 Miles

0 500 1000 Kilometers

NEW
ZEALAND

North
Island

Wellington ★

South
Island

Mt. Cook
3,764 m

● Christchurch

SOUTHERN

Chatham Is.

OCEANIA

Elevation

Meters Feet

Dunedin

45°S

Stewart

3,000 10,000

2,000 7,000

1,000 3,000

500 1,500

200 700

0 0

Below sea
level

Below sea
level

165°E 180° 165°W 150°W

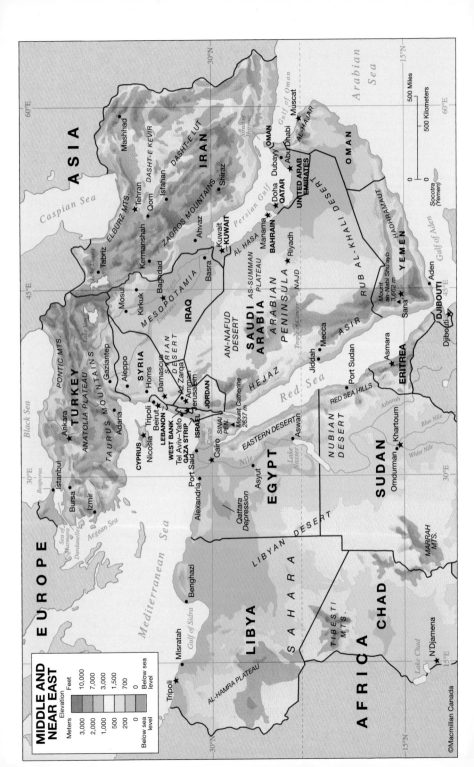

Labour Force: 415.3 million (1997 est.); 62.6% agriculture, 10.8% industry, 26.6% services
Unemployment: 10.9% (1996)
Agriculture: accounts for 30% of GDP and employs 65% of labour force; self-sufficient in food grains; main crops—rice, wheat, oilseeds, cotton, jute, tea, sugar cane, potatoes; livestock— cattle, buffalo, sheep, goats and poultry; in top 10 of fishing nations
Natural Resources: coal, iron ore, manganese, mica, bauxite, titanium ore, chromite, natural gas, diamonds, crude oil, limestone

■ FINANCE/TRADE

Currency: rupee (Rs) = 100 paise
International Reserves Excluding Gold: $27.772 billion (Jan. 1999)
Gold Reserves: 11.487 million fine troy ounces (Jan. 1999)
Budget: revenues $39 billion; expenditures $61 billion, including capital expenditures of $10 billion (1997-98 est.)
Defence Expenditures: 15.21% of govt. expenditure (1997)
Education Expenditures: 2.49% of govt. expenditure (1997)
External Debt: $90.7 billion (1997)
Exports: $33.185 billion (1998 est.); commodities: tea, coffee, iron ore, fish products, manufactures; partners: European Community 25%, former USSR countries and Eastern Europe 17%, US 19%, Japan 10%
Imports: $42.567 billion (1998 est.); commodities: petroleum, edible oils, textiles, clothing, capital goods; partners: European Community 33%, Middle East 19%, Japan 10%, US 9%, former USSR countries and Eastern Europe 8%

■ COMMUNICATIONS

Daily Newspapers: n.a.
Televisions: 61/1,000 inhabitants (1996)
Radios: 105/1,000 inhabitants (1996)
Telephones: 1.4/100 inhabitants (1996 est.)

■ TRANSPORTATION

Motor Vehicles: 6,990,000; 4,300,000 passenger cars (1997 est.)
Roads: 2,060,000 km; 1,034,120 km hard-surfaced
Railway: 62,660 km
Air Traffic: 14,000,000 passengers carried (1997 est.)
Airports: 343; 237 have paved runways (1997 est.)

Canadian Embassy: The Canadian High Commission, 7/8 Shantipath, Chanakyapuri, New Delhi 110021; mailing address: The Canadian High Commission, P.O. Box 5207, New Delhi 110021, India. Tel: (011-91-11) 687-6500. Fax: (011-91-11) 687-6579.
Embassy in Canada: High Commission for the Republic of India, 10 Springfield Rd, Ottawa ON K1M 1C9. Tel: (613) 744-3751. Fax: (613) 744-0913.

Indonesia

Long-Form Name: Republic of Indonesia
Capital: Jakarta

■ GEOGRAPHY

Area: 1,919,440 sq. km (13,677 islands)
Coastline: 54,716 km
Climate: tropical; hot, humid; more moderate in highlands
Environment: archipelago of more than 13,500 islands (6,000 inhabited); occasional floods, severe droughts and tsunamis; deforestation; environmental pollution
Terrain: mostly coastal lowlands; larger islands have interior mountains
Land Use: 10% arable; 7% permanent crops; 7% meadows; 62% forest; 14% other, includes 4% irrigated
Location: SE Asia, bordering on Indian Ocean

■ PEOPLE

Population: 212,941,810 (July 1998 est.)
Nationality: Indonesian
Age Structure: 0-14 yrs: 31%; 15-64: 65%; 65+: 4% (1998 est.)
Population Growth Rate: 1.49% (1998 est.)
Net Migration: 0 migrants/1,000 population (1998 est.)
Ethnic Groups: majority of Malay stock comprising 45% Javanese, 14% Sundanese, 7.5% Madurese, 7.5% coastal Malays, 26% other
Languages: Bahasa Indonesia (modified form of Malay; official); English and Dutch leading foreign languages; 25 local dialects, the most widely spoken of which is Javanese
Religions: 87% Muslim, 6% Protestant, 3% Roman Catholic, 2% Hindu, 1% Buddhist, 1% other
Birth Rate: 23.1/1,000 population (1998 est.)
Death Rate: 8.22/1,000 population (1998 est.)
Infant Mortality: 59.23 deaths/1,000 live births (1998 est.)
Life Expectancy at Birth: 60.28 years male, 64.81 years female (1998 est.)
Total Fertility Rate: 2.61 children born/woman (1998 est.)
Literacy: 83.8% (1997 est.)

■ GOVERNMENT

Leader(s): Pres. Megawhati
Government Type: republic
Administrative Divisions: 24 provinces, 2 special regions and 1 special capital city district. Note: On Aug. 30, 78.5% of residents of East Timor voted for independence from Indonesia.
Nationhood: Aug. 17, 1945 (from Netherlands; formerly known as Netherlands or Dutch East Indies)
National Holiday: Independence Day, Aug. 17

■ ECONOMY

Overview: a mixed economy with many socialist institutions and central planning but with a recent emphasis on deregulation and private enterprise; hampered by large population growth; possesses abundant natural wealth
GDP: $960 billion, per capita $4,600; real growth rate 4% (1997 est.)
Inflation: 39.1% (Mar. 1998)
Industries: accounts for 43% of GDP; petroleum, textiles, mining, cement, chemical fertilizer production, timber, food, rubber
Labour Force: 93.4 million (1997 est.); 54.1% agriculture, 10.3% industry, 37.6% services
Unemployment: 15%; 50% underemployment (1998 est.)
Agriculture: accounts for 16% of GDP; subsistence food production; small-holder and plantation production for export; rice, cassava, peanuts, rubber, cocoa, coffee, copra, other tropical products; the staple crop is rice; once the world's largest rice importer, Indonesia is now nearly self-sufficient
Natural Resources: crude oil, tin, natural gas, nickel, timber, bauxite, copper, fertile soils, coal, gold, silver

■ FINANCE/TRADE

Currency: rupiah (Rp)
International Reserves Excluding Gold: $23.751 billion (Jan. 1999)
Gold Reserves: 3.101 million fine troy ounces (Jan. 1999)
Budget: revenues $41.5 billion; expenditures $41.5 billion, including capital expenditures of $16 billion (1998 est.)
Defence Expenditures: 1.3% of GNP (1997–98)
Education Expenditures: 9.03% of govt. expenditure (1996)
External Debt: $136 billion (1997 est.)
Exports: $38.864 billion (1998 est.); commodities: petroleum and liquefied natural gas 40%, timber 15%, textiles 7%, rubber 5%, coffee 3%; partners: Japan 42%, US 16%, Singapore 9%, European Community 11%
Imports: $20.997 billion (1998 est.); commodities: machinery 39%, chemical products 19%, manufactured goods 16%; partners: Japan 26%, European Community 19%, US 13%, Singapore 7%,

■ COMMUNICATIONS

Daily Newspapers: 69 (1996)
Televisions: 67/1,000 inhabitants (1996)
Radios: 155/1,000 inhabitants (1996)
Telephones: 2.1/100 inhabitants (1996 est.)

■ TRANSPORTATION

Motor Vehicles: 4,600,000; 2,500,000 passenger cars (1997 est.)
Roads: 393,000 km; 178,815 km paved
Railway: 6,458 km
Air Traffic: 17,600,000 passengers carried (1997 est.)
Airports: 442; 124 have paved runways (1997 est.)

Canadian Embassy: The Canadian Embassy, Flr 5 Wisma Metropolitan, Jalan Jendral Sudirman, Jakarta 12920; mailing address: P.O. Box 8324/JKS.MP, Jakarta 12084, Indonesia. Tel: (011-62-21) 525-0709. Fax: (011-62-21) 571-2251.
Embassy in Canada: Embassy of the Republic of Indonesia, 55 Parkdale Ave, Ottawa ON K1Y 1E5. Tel: (613) 724-1100. Fax: (613) 724-1105.

Iran

Long-Form Name: Islamic Republic of Iran
Capital: Tehran

■ GEOGRAPHY

Area: 1,648,000 sq. km
Coastline: 2,440 km
Climate: mostly arid or semi-arid, subtropical along Caspian coast
Environment: deforestation; overgrazing; desertification; air and water pollution; periodic droughts and floods
Terrain: rugged mountainous rim; high, central basin with deserts, mountains; small, discontinuous plains along both coasts
Land Use: 10% arable; 1% permanent crops; 27% meadows; 7% forest; 55% other, includes 3.5% irrigated
Location: SW Asia (Middle East), bordering on Persian Gulf

■ PEOPLE

Population: 68,959,931 (July 1998 est.)
Nationality: Iranian
Age Structure: 0-14 yrs: 43%; 15-64: 53%; 65+: 4% (1998 est.)

Population Growth Rate: 2.04% (1998 est.)
Net Migration: -4.79 migrants/1,000 population (1998 est.)
Ethnic Groups: 51% Persian, 24% Azerbaijani, 7% Kurd, 8% Gilaki and Mazandarani, 2% Lur, 2% Baloch, 3% Arab, 2% Turkmen, 1% other
Languages: Farsi (Persian) (official) 58%, Turkic and Turkic dialects 26%, Kurdish 9%, Luri 2%, Balochi 1%, Turkish 1%, Arabic 1%, 2% other
Religions: Muslim (89% Shia, 10% Sunni), Christianity, Judaism, Zoroastrianism 1%
Birth Rate: 31.37/1,000 population (1998 est.)
Death Rate: 6.19/1,000 population (1998 est.)
Infant Mortality: 48.95 deaths/1,000 live births (1998 est.)
Life Expectancy at Birth: 66.83 years male, 69.74 years female (1998 est.)
Total Fertility Rate: 4.31 children born/woman (1998 est.)
Literacy: 72.1% (1997 est.)

■ GOVERNMENT

Leader(s): Pres. Mohammed Khatami, Supreme Religious Leader Ayatollah Mohammed Ali Hoseini Khamenei
Government Type: theocratic republic
Administrative Divisions: 25 provinces
Nationhood: Apr. 1, 1979, Islamic Republic of Iran proclaimed
National Holiday: Islamic Republic Day, Apr. 1

■ ECONOMY

Overview: Iran's economy is a mixture of central planning, state ownership of oil and other large enterprises, village agriculture, and small-scale private trading and service ventures. Soaring external debt and high unemployment impede progress towards recovery from the economic devastation of the war with Iraq
GDP: $371.2 billion, per capita $5,500; real growth rate 3.2% (1997 est.)
Inflation: 20.5% (Apr. 1998)
Industries: accounts for 37% of GDP; petroleum, petrochemicals, textiles, cement and other building materials, food processing (particularly sugar refining and vegetable oil production), metal fabricating (steel and copper)
Labour Force: 19.5 million (1997 est.); 36.4% agriculture, 32.8% industry, 30.8% services
Unemployment: over 30% (1998 est.)
Agriculture: accounts for 21% of GDP; principal products—rice, other grains, sugar beets, fruits, nuts, cotton, dairy products, wool, caviar; not self-sufficient in food
Natural Resources: petroleum, natural gas, coal, chromium, copper, iron ore, lead, manganese, zinc, sulphur

■ FINANCE/TRADE

Currency: 10 rials (RIs) = 1 toman
International Reserves Excluding Gold: n.a.
Gold Reserves: 5.42 million fine troy ounces (Mar. 1996)
Budget: revenues $34.6 billion; expenditures $34.9 billion, including capital expenditures of $11.8 billion (1996-97)
Defence Expenditures: 7.69% of govt. expenditure (1997)
Education Expenditures: 14.55% of govt. expenditure (1997)
External Debt: $30 billion (1996 est.)
Exports: $22.391 billion (1996); commodities: petroleum 90%, carpets, fruit, nuts, hides; partners: Japan, Turkey, Italy, Netherlands, Spain, France, Germany
Imports: $16.274 billion (1996); commodities: machinery, military supplies, metal works, foodstuffs, pharmaceuticals, technical services, refined oil products; partners: Germany, Japan, Turkey, UK, Italy

■ COMMUNICATIONS

Daily Newspapers: 32 (1996)
Televisions: 64/1,000 inhabitants (1996)
Radios: 237/1,000 inhabitants (1996)
Telephones: 8.5/100 inhabitants (1996 est.)

■ TRANSPORTATION

Motor Vehicles: 2,239,000; 1,630,000 passenger cars (1997 est.)
Roads: 162,000 km; 93,378 km paved
Railway: 7,286 km
Air Traffic: 7,392,400 passengers carried (1996)
Airports: 280; 103 have paved runways (1997 est.)

Canadian Embassy: The Canadian Embassy to the Islamic Republic of Iran, 57 Shahid Javad-e-Sarafraz, Ostad-Motahari Ave, 15868 Tehran; mailing address: P.O. Box 11365-4647, Tehran, Iran. Tel: (011-98-21) 873-2623. Fax: (011-98-21) 873-3202.
Embassy in Canada: Embassy of the Islamic Republic of Iran, 245 Metcalfe St, Ottawa ON K2P 2K2. Tel: (613) 235-4726. Fax: (613) 232-5712.

Iraq

Long-Form Name: Republic of Iraq
Capital: Baghdad

■ GEOGRAPHY

Area: 437,072 sq. km

Coastline: 58 km
Climate: desert; mild to cool winters with dry, hot, cloudless summers
Environment: development of Tigris-Euphrates river systems contingent upon agreements with upstream riparians (Syria and Turkey); air and water pollution; soil degradation (salinization) and erosion; desertification
Terrain: mostly broad plains; reedy marshes in southeast; mountains along borders with Iran and Turkey
Land Use: 12% arable; 0% permanent; 9% meadows; 0% forest; 79% other, includes 6% irrigated
Location: SW Asia (Middle East), bordering on Persian Gulf

■ **PEOPLE**

Population: 21,722,287 (July 1998 est.)
Nationality: Iraqi
Age Structure: 0-14 yrs: 44%; 15-64: 53%; 65+: 3% (1998 est.)
Population Growth Rate: 3.2% (1998 est.)
Net Migration: 0 migrants/1,000 population (1998 est.)
Ethnic Groups: 75–80% Arab, 15–20% Kurdish, 5% Turkoman and other
Languages: Arabic (official), Kurdish (official in Kurdish region), Assyrian, Armenian
Religions: 97% Muslim (60–65% Shi'a, 32–37% Sunni), 3% Christian or other
Birth Rate: 38.58/1,000 population (1998 est.)
Death Rate: 6.57/1,000 population (1998 est.)
Infant Mortality: 62.41 deaths/1,000 live births (1998 est.)
Life Expectancy at Birth: 65.54 years male, 67.56 years female (1998 est.)
Total Fertility Rate: 5.23 children born/woman (1998 est.)
Literacy: 58% (1997 est.)

■ **GOVERNMENT**

Leader(s): Pres. and Prem. Saddam Hussein at-Takriti; Deputy Premiers Tariq Aziz, Mohammed Hamsa al-Zubaydi
Government Type: republic
Administrative Divisions: 18 provinces
Nationhood: Oct. 3, 1932 (from League of Nations mandate under British administration)
National Holiday: Anniversary of the Revolution, July 17

■ **ECONOMY**

Overview: industrial production and foreign trade is centrally planned and managed while some small-scale industry and services and most agriculture is left to private enterprise

GDP: $42.8 billion, per capita $2,000; real growth rate 0% (1997 est.)
Inflation: n.a.
Industries: petroleum, chemicals, textiles, construction materials, food processing
Labour Force: 6.2 million (1997 est.); 79.7% services, 12.5% agriculture, 7.8% industry
Unemployment: n.a.
Agriculture: accounted for 11% of GNP and 30% of labour force before the Gulf War; principal products— wheat, barley, rice, vegetables, dates, other fruit, cotton, wool; livestock— cattle, sheep; not self-sufficient in food output
Natural Resources: crude oil, natural gas, phosphates, sulphur

■ **FINANCE/TRADE**

Currency: dinar = 1,000 fils
International Reserves Excluding Gold: n.a.
Gold Reserves: n.a.
Budget: n.a.
Defence Expenditures: 8.3% of GDP (1996)
Education Expenditures: n.a.
External Debt: precise figures n.a., but a considerable portion of the GDP (1996)
Exports: n.a.; commodities: crude oil and refined products, machinery, chemicals, dates; partners: US, Brazil, former USSR countries, Italy, Turkey, France, Japan, former Yugoslavia
Imports: n.a.; commodities: manufactures, food; partners: Turkey, US, Germany, UK, France, Japan, Romania, former Yugoslavia, Brazil

■ **COMMUNICATIONS**

Daily Newspapers: 4 (1996)
Televisions: 82/1,000 inhabitants (1996)
Radios: 228/1,000 inhabitants (1996)
Telephones: 3.2/100 inhabitants (1996 est.)

■ **TRANSPORTATION**

Motor Vehicles: 1,040,000; 672,000 passenger cars (1997 est.)
Roads: 47,400 km; 40,764 km paved
Railway: 2,032 km
Air Traffic: 33,000 passengers carried (1995 est.)
Airports: 111; 76 have paved runways (1997 est.)

Canadian Embassy: The Canadian Embassy to Iraq, c/o The Canadian Embassy, P.O. Box 815403, Amman, Jordan. 11180. Tel: (011-962-6) 566-61-24. Fax: (011-962-6) 568-92-27.
Embassy in Canada: Embassy of the Republic of Iraq, 215 McLeod St, Ottawa ON K2P 0Z8. Tel: (613) 236-9177. Fax: (613) 567-1101.

Ireland

Long-Form Name: Ireland
Capital: Dublin

■ GEOGRAPHY

Area: 70,280 sq. km
Coastline: 1,448 km
Climate: temperate maritime; modified by North Atlantic Current; mild winters, cool summers; consistently humid; overcast about half the time
Environment: deforestation and water pollution
Terrain: mostly level to rolling interior plains surrounded by rugged hills and low mountains; sea cliffs on west coast
Land Use: 13% arable; negligible permanent; 68% meadows; 5% forest; 14% other
Location: NW Europe, bordering on Atlantic Ocean

■ PEOPLE

Population: 3,619,480 (July 1998 est.)
Nationality: Irish
Age Structure: 0-14 yrs: 22%; 15-64: 67%; 65+: 11% (1998 est.)
Population Growth Rate: 0.36% (1998 est.)
Net Migration: -1.39 migrants/1,000 population (1998 est.)
Ethnic Groups: Celtic, with English minority
Languages: Irish (official first language, but use is limited) and English; English is the language generally used, with Gaelic spoken in a few areas, mostly along the western seaboard
Religions: 93% Roman Catholic, 3% Anglican, 1% atheist, 3% other
Birth Rate: 13.49/1,000 population (1998 est.)
Death Rate: 8.51/1,000 population (1998 est.)
Infant Mortality: 6.04 deaths/1,000 live births (1998 est.)
Life Expectancy at Birth: 73.44 years male, 79.11 years female (1998 est.)
Total Fertility Rate: 1.82 children born/woman (1998 est.)
Literacy: 98% (1997 est.)

■ GOVERNMENT

Leader(s): Pres. Mary McAleese, Prime Min. Bertie Ahern
Government Type: republic
Administrative Divisions: 26 counties
Nationhood: Dec. 6, 1921 (from UK)
National Holiday: St. Patrick's Day, Mar. 17

■ ECONOMY

Overview: a small, open economy that is trade dependent; unemployment is high but inflation has been considerably lowered and the deficit burden relieved
GDP: $59.9 billion, per capita $18,600; real growth rate 6% (1997 est.)
Inflation: 2.7% (July 1998)
Industries: account for 38% of GDP, 80% of exports and employs almost 30% of the workforce; food products, brewing, textiles, clothing, chemicals, pharmaceuticals, machinery, transportation equipment, glass and crystal
Labour Force: 1 million (1997 est.); 25.4% community, social and business services, 19.7% industry, 17.7% trade and tourism
Unemployment: 11.8% (1997)
Agriculture: accounts for 9% of GDP and 13% of the labour force; principal crops include turnips, barley, potatoes, sugar, beets, wheat; livestock— meat and dairy products; 85% self-sufficient in food; food shortages include bread grain, fruits, vegetables
Natural Resources: zinc, lead, natural gas, crude oil, barite, copper, gypsum, limestone, dolomite, peat, silver

■ FINANCE/TRADE

Currency: Irish pound (£ or £Ir) = 100 pence [As of Jan. 1, 1999, Government securities are issued in Euros (EUR)]
International Reserves Excluding Gold: $6.474 billion (Jan. 1999)
Gold Reserves: 0.193 million fine troy ounces (Jan. 1999)
Budget: revenues $20.6 billion; expenditures $20.3 billion, including capital expenditures of $5.2 billion (1997)
Defence Expenditures: 2.84% of total govt. expenditure (1995)
Education Expenditures: 13.17% of total govt. expenditure (1995)
External Debt: $14 billion (1996)
Exports: $61.548 billion (1998 est.); commodities: live animals, animal products, chemicals, data processing equipment, industrial machinery; partners: European Community 74% (U.K. 35%, Germany 11%, France 9%), US 8%
Imports: $42.631 billion (1998 est.); commodities: food, animal feed, chemicals, petroleum and petroleum products, machinery, textiles, clothing; partners: European Community 66% (U.K. 42%, Germany 9%, France 4%), US 16%

■ COMMUNICATIONS

Daily Newspapers: 6 (1996)
Televisions: 411/1,000 inhabitants (1996)
Radios: 703/1,000 inhabitants (1996)
Telephones: 37.7/100 inhabitants (1996 est.)

■ TRANSPORTATION

Motor Vehicles: 1,320,000; 1,100,00 passenger cars (1997 est.)
Roads: 92,500 km; 87,042 km paved

Railway: 1,947 km
Air Traffic: 7,677,000 passengers carried (1996)
Airports: 44; 15 have paved runways (1997 est.)

Canadian Embassy: The Canadian Embassy, 65 St Stephen's Green, Dublin, Ireland. Tel: (011-353-1) 478-1988. Fax: (011-353-1) 478-1285.
Embassy in Canada: Embassy of Ireland, 130 Albert St, Ste 1105, Ottawa ON K1P 5G4. Tel: (613) 233-6281. Fax: (613) 233-5835.

Isle of Man

Long-Form Name: Isle of Man
Capital: Douglas

■ GEOGRAPHY

Area: 588 sq. km
Climate: temperate maritime, cool summers and mild winters, humid, overcast about half the time
Land Use: most of island covered by farmland and moors; low mountain chain extends through island; 85% of cultivated land area used for farming, 68,000 acres farmland, 37,000 acres grazing
Location: Irish Sea, between Great Britain and Northern Ireland

■ PEOPLE

Population: 75,121 (July 1998 est.)
Nationality: Manxman, Manxwoman
Ethnic Groups: Manx (Norse-Celtic descent), Briton
Languages: English, Manx, Gaelic

■ GOVERNMENT

Colony Territory of: Dependency of United Kingdom
Leader(s): Chief of State Queen Elizabeth II, represented by Sir Timothy Daunt; head of govt., Pres. Sir Charles Kerruish
Government Type: Crown dependency administered in accordance with its own laws
National Holiday: Tynwald Day, July 5

■ ECONOMY

Overview: Offshore banking, manufacturing, and tourism are key sectors of the economy. The government's policy of offering incentives to high-technology companies and financial institutions to locate on the island has paid off in expanding employment opportunities in high-income industries.

■ FINANCE/TRADE

Currency: Manx pound = 100 pence; on a par with British pound sterling

Canadian Embassy: c/o The Canadian High Commission, Macdonald House, 1 Grosvenor Square, London W1X 0AB, England, UK. Tel: (011-44-171) 258-6600. Fax: (011-44-171) 258-6333.
Representative to Canada: c/o British High Commission, 80 Elgin St, Ottawa ON K1P 5K7. Tel: (613) 237-1530. Fax: (613) 237-7980.

Israel

Long-Form Name: State of Israel
Capital: Jerusalem

■ GEOGRAPHY

Area: 20,770 sq. km
Coastline: 273 km
Climate: temperate; hot and dry in desert areas
Environment: sandstorms may occur during spring and summer; limited arable land and natural water resources pose serious constraints; deforestation
Terrain: Negev desert in the south; low coastal plain; central mountains; Jordan Rift Valley
Land Use: 17% arable; 4% permanent; 7% permanent pastures; 6% forest; 66% other, includes 10% irrigated
Location: SW Asia (Middle East), bordering on Mediterranean Sea

■ PEOPLE

Population: 5,643,966 (July 1998 est.)
Nationality: Israeli
Age Structure: 0-14 yrs: 28%; 15-64: 62%; 65+: 10% (1998 est.)
Population Growth Rate: 1.91% (1998 est.)
Net Migration: 5.25 migrants/1,000 population (1998 est.)
Ethnic Groups: 82% Jewish, 18% non-Jewish (mostly Arab)
Languages: Hebrew (official); Arabic used officially for Arab minority; European languages (mostly English)
Religions: 82% Judaism, 14% Islam (mostly Sunni Muslim), 2% Christian and Druze, 2% other
Birth Rate: 19.99/1,000 population (1998 est.)
Death Rate: 6.19/1,000 population (1998 est.)
Infant Mortality: 8.02 deaths/1,000 live births (1998 est.)
Life Expectancy at Birth: 76.52 years male, 80.39 years female (1998 est.)

Total Fertility Rate: 2.71 children born/woman (1998 est.)
Literacy: 95% (1997 est.)

■ GOVERNMENT

Leader(s): Prime Min. Ehud Barak, Pres. Ezer Weizman
Government Type: republic
Administrative Divisions: 6 districts
Nationhood: May 14, 1948 (from League of Nations mandate under British administration)
National Holiday: Independence Day, May 14; the Jewish calendar is lunar and the holiday may occur in Apr. or May

■ ECONOMY

Overview: a market economy with government participation; despite limited natural resources, this country has strong agriculture and industry sectors; transfer payments and foreign loans offset the deficit; the Palestinian uprising and Russian immigration stifle growth; high Jewish immigration from the former Soviet states has created massive housing problems
GDP: $96.7 billion, per capita $17,500; real growth rate 1.9% (1997 est.)
Inflation: 4.9% (May 1998)
Industries: accounts for 17% of GDP; food processing, diamond cutting and polishing, textiles, clothing, chemicals, metal products, military equipment, transport equipment, electrical equipment, miscellaneous machinery, potash mining, high-technology electronics, tourism
Labour Force: 2.1 million (1997 est.); 36.1% community, social and business services, 14.3% trade and tourism, 20.9% industry
Unemployment: 8.2% (Nov. 1998)
Agriculture: accounts for 2% of GDP; largely self-sufficient in food production, except for bread grains; principal products—citrus and other fruit, vegetables, cotton; livestock products—beef, dairy and poultry
Natural Resources: copper, phosphates, bromide, potash, clay, sand, sulphur, asphalt, manganese, small amounts of natural gas and crude oil

■ FINANCE/TRADE

Currency: new Israeli shekel (NIS) = 100 new agorot
International Reserves Excluding Gold: $22.636 billion (Jan. 1999)
Gold Reserves: none (Jan. 1999)
Budget: revenues $55 billion; expenditures $58 billion, capital expenditures n.a. (1998 est.)
Defence Expenditures: 17.89% (1997)
Education Expenditures: 14.02% (1997)

External Debt: $18.7 billion (1997)
Exports: $22.502 billion (1997); commodities: polished diamonds, citrus and other fruit, textiles and clothing, processed foods, fertilizer and chemical products, military hardware, electronics; partners: US, UK, Germany, France, Belgium, Luxembourg, Italy
Imports: $30.783 billion (1997); commodities: military equipment, rough diamonds, oil, chemicals, machinery, iron and steel, cereals, textiles, vehicles, ships, aircraft; partners: US, Germany, UK, Switzerland, Italy, Belgium, Luxembourg

■ COMMUNICATIONS

Daily Newspapers: 34 (1996)
Televisions: 291/1,000 inhabitants (1996)
Radios: 530/1,000 inhabitants (1996)
Telephones: 43.1/100 inhabitants (1996 est.)

■ TRANSPORTATION

Motor Vehicles: 1,600,000; 1,220,000 passenger cars (1997 est.)
Roads: 15,065 km, all paved
Railway: 610 km
Air Traffic: 3,800,000 passengers carried (1997 est.)
Airports: 54; 31 have paved runways (1997 est.)

Canadian Embassy: The Canadian Embassy, 3 Nirim St., 4th Fl, Tel Aviv, 67060; mailing address: P.O. Box 9442, Tel Aviv, Israel. Tel: (011-972-3) 636-3300.
Embassy in Canada: Embassy of Israel, 50 O'Connor St, Ste 1005, Ottawa ON K1P 6L2. Tel: (613) 567-6450. Fax: (613) 237-8865.

Italy

Long-Form Name: Italian Republic
Capital: Rome

■ GEOGRAPHY

Area: 301,230 sq. km; includes Sardinia and Sicily
Coastline: 7,600 km
Climate: predominantly Mediterranean; Alpine in far north; hot, dry in south
Environment: regional risks include landslides, mudflows, snowslides, earthquakes, volcanic eruptions, flooding; land sinkage in Venice; serious air and water pollution
Terrain: mostly rugged and mountainous; some plains, coastal lowlands
Land Use: 31% arable; 10% permanent; 15% meadows; 23% forest; 21% other, includes 10% irrigated

Location: S Europe, bordering on Adriatic Sea, Mediterranean Sea

■ PEOPLE

Population: 56,782,748 (July 1998 est.)
Nationality: Italian
Age Structure: 0-14 yrs: 14%; 15-64: 68%; 65+: 18% (1998 est.)
Population Growth Rate: -0.08% (1998 est.)
Net Migration: 0.21 migrants/1,000 population (1998 est.)
Ethnic Groups: primarily Italian but population includes small clusters of German-, French- and Slovene-Italians in the north and Albanian-Italians in the south; Sicilians; Sardinians
Languages: Italian; parts of Trentino-Alto Adige region are predominantly German-speaking; significant French-speaking minority in Valle d'Aosta region; Slovene-speaking minority in the Trieste-Gorizia area
Religions: almost 100% nominally Roman Catholic
Birth Rate: 9.13/1,000 population (1998 est.)
Death Rate: 10.18/1,000 population (1998 est.)
Infant Mortality: 6.4 deaths/1,000 live births (1998 est.)
Life Expectancy at Birth: 75.26 years male, 81.7 years female (1998 est.)
Total Fertility Rate: 1.19 children born/woman (1998 est.)
Literacy: 97% (1997 est.)

■ GOVERNMENT

Leader(s): Pres. Carlo Azeglio Ciampi, Prem. Massimo D'Alema
Government Type: republic
Administrative Divisions: 20 regions
Nationhood: Mar. 17, 1861, Kingdom of Italy proclaimed
National Holiday: Anniversary of the Republic, June 2

■ ECONOMY

Overview: country is divided into a developed industrial north, and an undeveloped agricultural south; an inadequate communications system, high pollution and economic integration into the European Union pose continuing challenges
GDP: $1.24 trillion, per capita $21,500; real growth rate 1.5% (1997 est.)
Inflation: 2.1% (June 1998)
Industries: accounts for 33% of GDP; machinery and transportation equipment, iron and steel, chemicals, food processing, textiles, motor vehicles
Labour Force: 25.2 million (1997 est.); 21.7% industry, 21.4% trade and tourism, 28.5% community, social and business services

Unemployment: 12.2% (Dec. 1997 est.)
Agriculture: accounts for about 3% of GDP and 10% of the workforce; self-sufficient in foods other than meat and dairy products; principal crops—fruit, vegetables, grapes, potatoes, sugar beets, soybeans, grain, olives
Natural Resources: mercury, potash, marble, sulphur, dwindling natural gas and crude oil reserves, fish, coal

■ FINANCE/TRADE

Currency: lira (Lit) = 100 centesimi [As of Jan. 1, 1999, Government securities are issued in Euros (EUR)]
International Reserves Excluding Gold: $23.028 billion (Jan. 1999)
Gold Reserves: 78.829 million fine troy ounces (Jan. 1999)
Budget: revenues $416 billion; expenditures $506 billion, including capital expenditures n.a. (1996 est.)
Defence Expenditures: 1.9% of GDP (1995)
Education Expenditures: 4.9% of GNP (1995)
External Debt: $45 billion (1996 est.)
Exports: $239.440 billion (1998 est.); commodities: textiles, wearing apparel, metals, transportation equipment, chemicals; partners: European Community 57%, US 9%, OPEC 4%
Imports: $212.448 billion (1998 est.); commodities: petroleum, industrial machinery, chemicals, metals, foods, agricultural products; partners: European Community 57%, OPEC 6%, US 6%

■ COMMUNICATIONS

Daily Newspapers: 78 (1996)
Televisions: 524/1,000 inhabitants (1996)
Radios: 874/1,000 inhabitants (1996)
Telephones: 44.7/100 inhabitants (1996 est.)

■ TRANSPORTATION

Motor Vehicles: 34,000,000; 31,000,000 passenger cars (1997 est.)
Roads: 317,000 km; all paved
Railway: 19,437 km
Air Traffic: 25,900,000 passengers carried (1997 est.)
Airports: 136; 96 have paved runways (1997 est.)

Canadian Embassy: The Canadian Embassy, Via Zara 30, 00198 Rome, Italy. Tel: (011-39-06) 445981. Fax: (011-39-06) 445 98912.
Embassy in Canada: Embassy of the Italian Republic, 275 Slater St, 21st Fl, Ottawa ON K1P 5H9. Tel: (613) 232-2401. Fax: (613) 233-1484.

Jamaica

Long-Form Name: Jamaica
Capital: Kingston

■ GEOGRAPHY

Area: 10,990 sq. km
Coastline: 1,022 km
Climate: tropical; hot, humid; temperate interior
Environment: subject to hurricanes (especially July to Nov.); deforestation; water pollution
Terrain: mostly mountainous with narrow, discontinuous coastal plain
Land Use: 14% arable; 6% permanent; 24% meadows; 17% forest; 39% other, includes 3% irrigated
Location: West Indies, bordering on Caribbean Sea

■ PEOPLE

Population: 2,634,678 (July 1998 est.)
Nationality: Jamaican
Age Structure: 0-14 yrs: 32%; 15-64: 62%; 65+: 6% (1998 est.)
Population Growth Rate: 0.07% (1998 est.)
Net Migration: -8.45 migrants/1,000 population (1998 est.)
Ethnic Groups: 76.3% African, 15.1% Afro-European, 3% East Indian and Afro-East Indian, 3.2% white, 1.2% Chinese and Afro-Chinese, 1.2% other
Languages: English (official), Creole
Religions: 55.9% Protestant, 5% Roman Catholic, 39.1% other
Birth Rate: 20.91/1,000 population (1998 est.)
Death Rate: 5.45/1,000 population (1998 est.)
Infant Mortality: 14.47 deaths/1,000 live births (1998 est.)
Life Expectancy at Birth: 73.01 years male, 77.84 years female (1998 est.)
Total Fertility Rate: 2.33 children born/woman (1998 est.)
Literacy: 85% (1997 est.)

■ GOVERNMENT

Leader(s): Queen Elizabeth II/Gov. Gen. Howard Cooke, Prime Min. Percival J. Patterson
Government Type: parliamentary democracy
Administrative Divisions: 14 parishes
Nationhood: Aug. 6, 1962 (from UK)
National Holiday: Independence Day, first Monday in Aug.

■ ECONOMY

Overview: Key sectors in this island economy are bauxite and tourism. Continued tight fiscal policies have helped slow inflation and stabilize the exchange rate, but have resulted in the slowdown of economic growth.
GDP: $9.5 billion, per capita $3,660; real growth rate -1.4% (1997 est.)
Inflation: 8.5% (Apr. 1998)
Industries: accounts for 37% of GDP; tourism, bauxite mining, textiles, food processing, light manufactures
Labour Force: 1 million (1997 est.); 26.1% agriculture, 29.9% community, social and business services, 16.2% finance
Unemployment: 16% (1996 est.)
Agriculture: accounts for about 8% of GDP, 22% of workforce and 17% of exports; principal crops–sugar cane, bananas, coffee, citrus, potatoes and vegetables; not self-sufficient in grain, meat and dairy products
Natural Resources: bauxite, gypsum, limestone

■ FINANCE/TRADE

Currency: Jamaican dollar ($J) = 100 cents
International Reserves Excluding Gold: $743 million (Aug. 1998)
Gold Reserves: n.a.
Budget: revenues $3 billion; expenditures $3 billion, including capital expenditures of $1.163 billion (1997-98 est.)
Defence Expenditures: 0.6% of GDP (1996)
Education Expenditures: 8.2% of GNP (1995)
External Debt: $3.2 billion (1997 est.)
Exports: $1.356 billion (1998 est.); commodities: bauxite, alumina, sugar, bananas; partners: US 40%, UK, Canada, Trinidad and Tobago, Norway
Imports: $2.887 billion (1998 est.); commodities: petroleum, machinery, food, consumer goods, construction goods; partners: US 46%, UK, Venezuela, Canada, Japan, Trinidad and Tobago

■ COMMUNICATIONS

Daily Newspapers: 3 (1996)
Televisions: 181/1,000 inhabitants (1996)
Radios: 482/1,000 inhabitants (1996)
Telephones: 12.8/100 inhabitants (1996 est.)

■ TRANSPORTATION

Motor Vehicles: 58,900; 43,500 passenger cars (1997 est.)
Roads: 18,700; 13,100 km paved
Railway: 370 km
Air Traffic: 1,218,100 passengers carried (1996)
Airports: 36; 11 have paved runways (1997 est.)

Canadian Embassy: The Canadian High Commission, Mutual Security Bank Bldg, 30-36

Knutsford Blvd, Kingston 5; mailing address: The Canadian High Commission, P.O. Box 1500, Kingston 10, Jamaica. Tel: (876) 926-1500. Fax: (876) 926-1702.
Embassy in Canada: Jamaican High Commission, 275 Slater St, Ste 800, Ottawa ON K1P 5H9. Tel: (613) 233-9311. Fax: (613) 233-0611.

Japan

Long-Form Name: Japan
Capital: Tokyo

■ GEOGRAPHY

Area: 377,835 sq. km; includes Bonin Islands (Ogasawara-gunto), Daito-shoto, Minamijima, Okinotori-shima, Ryukyu Islands (Nansei-shoto) and Volcano Islands (Kazan-retto)
Coastline: 29,751 km
Climate: varies from tropical in south to cool temperate in north
Environment: many dormant and some active volcanoes; about 1,500 seismic occurrences (mostly tremors) every year; subject to tsunamis; acid rain caused by industrial emissions
Terrain: mostly rugged and mountainous
Land Use: 11% arable; 1% permanent crops; 2% permanent pastures; 67% forest and woodland; 19% other, includes 8% irrigated
Location: E Asia, bordering on Sea of Japan, North Pacific Ocean

■ PEOPLE

Population: 125,931,533 (July 1998 est.)
Nationality: Japanese
Age Structure: 0-14 yrs: 15%; 15-64: 69%; 65+: 16% (1998 est.)
Population Growth Rate: 0.2% (1998 est.)
Net Migration: -0.36 migrants/1,000 population (1998 est.)
Ethnic Groups: 99.4% Japanese, 0.6% other (mostly Korean)
Languages: Japanese
Religions: most Japanese observe both Shinto and Buddhist rites; about 16% belong to other faiths, including 0.8% Christian
Birth Rate: 10.26/1,000 population (1998 est.)
Death Rate: 7.94/1,000 population (1998 est.)
Infant Mortality: 4.1 deaths/1,000 live births (1998 est.)
Life Expectancy at Birth: 76.91 years male, 83.25 years female (1998 est.)
Total Fertility Rate: 1.46 children born/woman (1998 est.)
Literacy: 99% (1997 est.)

■ GOVERNMENT

Leader(s): Emperor Tsegu no Miya Akihito; Prime Min. Keizo Obuchi
Government Type: constitutional monarchy
Administrative Divisions: 47 prefectures
Nationhood: 660 BC, traditional founding by Emperor Jimmu; May 3, 1947 constitutional monarchy established
National Holiday: Birthday of the Emperor, Dec. 23

■ ECONOMY

Overview: impressive economic growth and status as the second largest industrial economy in the world is due to government-industry cooperation and a strong work ethic; known for high-tech industry
GDP: $3.08 trillion, per capita $24,500; real growth rate 0.9% (1997 est.)
Inflation: 0.1% (June 1998)
Industries: accounts for 42% of GDP, metallurgy, engineering, electrical and electronic, textiles, chemicals, automobiles, fishing
Labour Force: 65.9 million (1997); 22.3% community, social and business services, 23.7% industry; 7.1% agriculture
Unemployment: 4.5% (Jan. 1999)
Agriculture: accounts for 2% of GDP; highly subsidized and protected sector, with crop yields among highest in the world; main crops—rice, sugar beets, vegetables, fruit; animal products include pork, poultry, dairy and eggs; about 50% self-sufficient in food
Natural Resources: negligible mineral resources, fish

■ FINANCE/TRADE

Currency: yen (pl. yen) (¥)
International Reserves Excluding Gold: $221.738 billion (Jan. 1999)
Gold Reserves: 24.227 million fine troy ounces (Jan. 1999)
Budget: revenues $528 billion; expenditures $673 billion, including capital expenditures of $75 billion (1998 est.)
Defence Expenditures: 1.0% of GDP (1996–97)
Education Expenditures: 3.8% of GNP (1995)
External Debt: n.a.
Exports: $388.167 billion (1998); commodities: manufactures 97% (including machinery 38%, motor vehicles 17%, consumer electronics 10%); partners: US 34%, Southeast Asia 22%, Western Europe 21%, Communist countries 5%, Middle East 5%
Imports: $280.674 billion (1998); commodities: manufactures 42%, fossil fuels 30%, foodstuffs

15%, nonfuel raw materials 13%; partners: Southeast Asia 23%, US 23%, Middle East 15%, Western Europe 16%, communist countries 7%

■ COMMUNICATIONS

Daily Newspapers: 122 (1996)
Televisions: 684/1,000 inhabitants (1996)
Radios: 957/1,000 inhabitants (1996)
Telephones: 50.1/100 inhabitants (1996 est.)

■ TRANSPORTATION

Motor Vehicles: 69,700,000; 47,000,000 passenger cars (1997 est.)
Roads: 1,160,000 km; 859,560 km paved
Railway: 23,671 km
Air Traffic: 96,021,100 passengers carried (1996)
Airports: 167; 137 have paved runways (1997 est.)

Canadian Embassy: The Canadian Embassy, 3-38 Akasaka 7-chome, Minato-ku, Tokyo 107, Japan. Tel: (011-81-3) 5412-6200. Fax: (011-81-3) 5412-6303.
Embassy in Canada: Embassy of Japan, 255 Sussex Dr, Ottawa ON K1N 9E6. Tel: (613) 241-8541. Fax: (613) 241-2232.

Jordan

Long-Form Name: Hashemite Kingdom of Jordan
Capital: Amman

■ GEOGRAPHY

Area: 89,213 sq. km
Coastline: 26 km
Climate: mostly arid desert; rainy season in west (Nov. to Apr.)
Environment: lack of natural water resources; deforestation; overgrazing; soil erosion; desertification
Terrain: mostly desert plateau in east, highland area in west; Great Rift Valley separates East and West Banks of the Jordan River
Land Use: 4% arable land; 1% permanent; 9% permanent pastures; 1% forest; 85% other
Location: SW Asia (Middle East)

■ PEOPLE

Population: 4,434,978 (July 1998 est.)
Nationality: Jordanian
Age Structure: 0-14 yrs: 43%; 15-64: 54%; 65+: 3% (1998 est.)
Population Growth Rate: 2.54% (1998 est.)
Net Migration: -5.92 migrants/1,000 population (1998 est.)
Ethnic Groups: 98% Arab, 1% Circassian, 1% Armenian

Languages: Arabic (official); English widely understood among upper and middle classes
Religions: Islam (92% Sunni Muslim, Shia minority), 8% Christianity
Birth Rate: 35.18/1,000 population (1998 est.)
Death Rate: 3.91/1,000 population (1998 est.)
Infant Mortality: 33.29 deaths/1,000 live births (1998 est.)
Life Expectancy at Birth: 70.96 years male, 74.84 years female (1998 est.)
Total Fertility Rate: 4.79 children born/woman (1998 est.)
Literacy: 86.6% (1997 est.)

■ GOVERNMENT

Leader(s): King Abdullah II, Prem. Abdul Raouf al-Rawebdeh
Government Type: constitutional monarchy
Administrative Divisions: 12 governorates
Nationhood: May 25, 1946 (from League of Nations mandate under British administration; formerly known as Trans-Jordan)
National Holiday: Independence Day, May 25

■ ECONOMY

Overview: imports are outweighing exports and foreign aid makes up the difference; droughts are a potential threat; debt, poverty and unemployment remain problems; economic recovery is unlikely without substantial foreign aid, debt relief and economic reform
GDP: $20.7 billion, per capita $4,800; real growth rate 5.3% (1997 est.)
Inflation: 6.5% (Mar. 1998)
Industries: accounts for 30% of GDP; phosphate mining, petroleum refining, cement, potash, light manufacturing
Labour Force: 1.1 million (1997 est.); 9.1% transportation and communication industries, 57.7% services, 16.1% industry
Unemployment: official rate 15%, but actually 20-25% (1997 est.)
Agriculture: accounts for 6% of GDP; principal products are wheat, barley, citrus fruit, tomatoes, melons, olives; livestock—sheep, goats, poultry; large net importer of food
Natural Resources: phosphates, potash, shale oil

■ FINANCE/TRADE

Currency: Jordanian dinar (JD) = 1,000 fils
International Reserves Excluding Gold: $1.754 billion (Jan. 1999)
Gold Reserves: 0.828 million fine troy ounces (Jan. 1998)
Budget: revenues $2.7 billion; expenditures $2.8 billion, including capital expenditures of $630 million (1997 est.)

Defence Expenditures: 8.2% of GDP (1996)
Education Expenditures: 6.3% of GNP (1995)
External Debt: $7.3 billion (1997 est.)
Exports: $1.836 billion (1997); commodities: fruit and vegetables, phosphates, fertilizers; partners: Iraq, Saudi Arabia, India, Kuwait, Japan, China, former Yugoslavia, Indonesia
Imports: $4.102 billion (1997); commodities: crude oil, textiles, capital goods, motor vehicles, foodstuffs; partners: European Community, US, Saudi Arabia, Japan, Turkey, Romania, China, Taiwan

■ COMMUNICATIONS

Daily Newspapers: 4 (1996)
Televisions: 86/1,000 inhabitants (1996)
Radios: 287/1,000 inhabitants (1996)
Telephones: 7.4/100 inhabitants (1996 est.)

■ TRANSPORTATION

Motor Vehicles: 265,000; 175,000 passenger cars (1997 est.)
Roads: 6,750 km, all paved
Railway: 676 km
Air Traffic: 1,299,000 passengers carried (1996)
Airports: 17; 14 have paved runways (1997 est.)

Canadian Embassy: The Canadian Embassy, Pearl of Shmeisani Bldg, Shmeisani, Amman, Jordan; mailing address: P.O. Box 815403, Amman, Jordan 11180. Tel: (011-962-6) 566-61-24. Fax: (011-962-6) 568-92-27.
Embassy in Canada: Embassy of the Hashemite Kingdom of Jordan, 100 Bronson Ave, Ste 701, Ottawa ON K1R 6G8. Tel: (613) 238-8090. Fax: (613) 232-3341.

Kazakhstan

Long-Form Name: Republic of Kazakhstan
Capital: Aqmola

■ GEOGRAPHY

Area: 2,717,300 sq. km
Coastline: none; landlocked; Kazakhstan borders the Aral Sea (1,015 km) and the Caspian Sea (1,894 km)
Climate: dry desert climate; arid and semi-arid; hot summers and cold winters
Environment: drought and desertification; lack of fresh water; drying up of Aral Sea is causing increased concentrations of chemical pesticides and natural salts; industrial pollution, including radioactive or toxic chemical sites
Terrain: desert and steppe; plains in western Siberia to oasis and desert in Central Asia
Land Use: 12% arable; 11% permanent crops; 57% meadows and pastures; 4% forests; 16% other

Location: C Asia, bordering on Caspian Sea

■ PEOPLE

Population: 16,846,808 (July 1998 est.)
Nationality: Kazakhstani
Age Structure: 0-14 yrs: 29%; 15-64: 64%; 65+: 7% (1998 est.)
Population Growth Rate: -0.17% (1998 est.)
Net Migration: -8.79 migrants/1,000 population (1998 est.)
Ethnic Groups: 46% Kazakh, 34.7% Russian, 4.9% Ukrainian, 3.1% German, 2.3% Uzbek, 1.9% Tatar, 7.1% other
Languages: Kazakh (official, spoken by over 40% of population), Russian (official, spoken by two-thirds of population), German, Ukrainian
Religions: primarily Sunni Muslim (47%) and Eastern Orthodox (44%), Protestant (2%), other 7%
Birth Rate: 17.24/1,000 population (1998 est.)
Death Rate: 10.15/1,000 population (1998 est.)
Infant Mortality: 58.25 deaths/1,000 live births (1998 est.)
Life Expectancy at Birth: 58.12 years male, 69.33 years female (1998 est.)
Total Fertility Rate: 2.12 children born/woman (1998 est.)
Literacy: 98% (1997 est.)

■ GOVERNMENT

Leader(s): Pres. Nursultan A. Nazarbayev, Prem. Nurlan Balgimbayev
Government Type: republic
Administrative Divisions: 14 oblasts and 1 city
Nationhood: Dec. 16, 1991 (from Soviet Union)
National Holiday: Independence Day, Oct. 25; Republic Day, Dec. 16

■ ECONOMY

Overview: predominantly mining and manufacturing; agriculture possible only with irrigation; serious pollution problems, lack of modern technology, and little experience in foreign markets hamper economic progress
GDP: $50 billion, per capita $3,000; real growth rate 2.1% (1997 est.)
Inflation: 7.9% (June 1998)
Industries: accounts for 25% of GDP; coal refining, oil and natural gas extraction, mining, agricultural machinery, electric motors, construction materials
Labour Force: 8.1 million (1997 est.); 25.9% community, social and business services, 23.9% agriculture, 15.8% industry
Unemployment: 2.6%; large numbers of underemployed (Dec. 1996 est.)
Agriculture: accounts for 12% of GDP, and

employs one quarter of labour force; wheat, cotton, rice, vineyard and orchard crops, sheep, cattle

Natural Resources: fish, oil, natural gas, zinc, coal, lead, iron ore, rare metals, tungsten, copper, zinc, manganese

■ FINANCE/TRADE

Currency: tenge = 100 tiyn
International Reserves Excluding Gold: $1.010 billion (Nov. 1998)
Gold Reserves: 1.675 million fine troy ounces (Nov. 1998)
Budget: revenues $3 billion; expenditures $4.6 billion, including capital expenditures of $40 million (1996 est.)
Defence Expenditures: n.a.
Education Expenditures: 4.5% of GNP (1995)
External Debt: $3.5 billion (1996)
Exports: $5.623 billion (1998 est.): fuels, karakul fleece, wool, industrial products
Imports: $4.177 billion (1998 est.): fuel, industrial products; partners: mostly Asian countries

■ COMMUNICATIONS

Daily Newspapers: 3 (1996)
Televisions: 230/1,000 inhabitants (1996)
Radios: 384/1,000 inhabitants (1996)
Telephones: 11.8/100 inhabitants (1996 est.)

■ TRANSPORTATION

Motor Vehicles: n.a.
Roads: 141,076 km; 113,566 km hard-surfaced
Railway: 13,841 km
Air Traffic: 568,000 passengers carried (1996)
Airports: 10; 9 have paved runways (1997 est.)

Canadian Embassy: The Canadian Embassy, 34 Karasai Batir, St, Almaty 480100, Kazakhstan. Tel: (011-7-327) 50-11-51. Fax: (011-7-327) 581 1493.
Embassy in Canada: c/o The Embassy of the Republic of Kazhakstan, 1401 16th Street NW, Washington, DC 20036, USA. Tel: (202) 232-5488. Fax: (202) 232-5845.

Kenya

Long-Form Name: Republic of Kenya
Capital: Nairobi

■ GEOGRAPHY

Area: 582,650 sq. km
Coastline: 536 km
Climate: varies from tropical along coast to arid in interior

Environment: unique physiography supports abundant and varied wildlife of scientific and economic value, but poaching is a continuing problem; deforestation; soil erosion; desertification; glaciers on Mt. Kenya; deteriorating water quality
Terrain: low plains rise to central highlands bisected by Great Rift Valley; fertile plateau in west
Land Use: 7% arable; 1% permanent; 37% permanent pastures; 30% forest; 25% other
Location: E Africa, bordering on Indian Ocean

■ PEOPLE

Population: 28,337,071 (July 1998 est.)
Nationality: Kenyan
Age Structure: 0-14 yrs: 44%; 15-64: 54%; 65+: 2% (1998 est.)
Population Growth Rate: 1.71% (1998 est.)
Net Migration: -0.35 migrants/1,000 population (1998 est.)
Ethnic Groups: 22% Kikuyu, 14% Luhya, 13% Luo, 12% Kalenjin, 11% Kamba, 6% Kisii, 6% Meru, 1% Asian, European and Arab, 15% other
Languages: English and Swahili (official); Kikuyu and Luo are widely spoken; numerous indigenous languages
Religions. 28% Roman Catholic, 26% indigenous beliefs, 38% Protestant, 8% other
Birth Rate: 31.68/1,000 population (1998 est.)
Death Rate: 14.19/1,000 population (1998 est.)
Infant Mortality: 59.38 deaths/1,000 live births (1998 est.)
Life Expectancy at Birth: 47.02 years male, 48.13 years female (1998 est.)
Total Fertility Rate: 4.07 children born/woman (1998 est.)
Literacy: 78.1% (1997 est.)

■ GOVERNMENT

Leader(s): Pres. Daniel T. arap Moi; Pres. George Saitoti
Government Type: republic
Administrative Divisions: 7 provinces and 1 area
Nationhood: Dec. 12, 1963 (from UK; formerly known as British East Africa)
National Holiday: Independence Day, Dec. 12

■ ECONOMY

Overview: a large annual population growth, a deteriorating infrastructure and a shortage of arable land threaten economic growth; vulnerable to weather conditions
GDP: $45.3 billion, per capita $1,600; real growth rate 2.9% (1997 est.)
Inflation: 5.9% (Apr. 1998)

Industries: accounts for 20% of GDP; small-scale consumer goods (plastic, furniture, batteries, textiles, soap, cigarettes, flour), agricultural processing, oil refining, cement, tourism

Labour Force: 13.4 million (1997 est.); 43.2% community, social and business services, 18.9% agriculture, 13.1% industry

Unemployment: 30% in urban areas (1995)

Agriculture: accounts for 27% of GDP and 65% of exports; cash crops include coffee, tea, sisal, pineapple; food products—corn, wheat, sugar cane, fruit, vegetables, dairy products; food output not sufficient for existing population

Natural Resources: gold, limestone, diatomite, salt barytes, magnesite, feldspar, sapphires, fluorspar, garnets, wildlife

■ FINANCE/TRADE

Currency: Kenya shilling (KSh) = 100 cents

International Reserves Excluding Gold: $743 million (Jan. 1999)

Gold Reserves: none (Jan. 1999)

Budget: revenues $2.7 billion; expenditures $2.7 billion, including capital expenditures of $620 million (1996)

Defence Expenditures: 5.91% of total govt. expenditure (1996)

Education Expenditures: 20.24% of total govt. expenditure (1996)

External Debt: $6.893 billion (1996)

Exports: $2.062 billion (1997); commodities: coffee 20%, tea 18%, manufactures 15%, petroleum products 10%; partners: Western Europe 45%, Africa 22%, Far East 10%, US 4%, Middle East 3%

Imports: $3.296 billion (1997); commodities: machinery and transportation equipment 36%, raw materials 33%, fuels and lubricants 20%, food and consumer goods 11%; partners: Western Europe 49%, Far East 20%, Middle East 19%, US 7%

■ COMMUNICATIONS

Daily Newspapers: 4 (1996)

Televisions: 25/1,000 inhabitants (1996)

Radios: 108/1,000 inhabitants (1996)

Telephones: 1.0/100 inhabitants (1996 est.)

■ TRANSPORTATION

Motor Vehicles: 364,900; 271,000 passenger cars (1997 est.)

Roads: 63,800 km; 8,868 km paved

Railway: 2,652 km

Air Traffic: 779,000 passengers carried (1996)

Airports: 240; 29 have paved runways (1997 est.)

Canadian Embassy: The Canadian High Commission, Comcraft House, Hailé Sélassie Ave, Nairobi; mailing address: The Canadian High Commission, P.O. Box 30481, Nairobi, Kenya. Tel: (011-254-2) 21-48-04. Fax: (011-254-2) 22-69-87.

Embassy in Canada: High Commission for the Republic of Kenya, 415 Laurier Ave E, Ottawa ON K1N 6R4. Tel: (613) 563-1773. Fax: (613) 233-6599.

Kiribati

Long-Form Name: Republic of Kiribati
Capital: Tarawa

■ GEOGRAPHY

Area: 717 sq. km

Coastline: 1,143 km

Climate: tropical; marine, hot and humid, moderated by trade winds

Environment: typhoons can occur anytime, but usually Nov. to Mar.

Terrain: mostly low-lying coral atolls surrounded by extensive reefs

Land Use: negligible arable; 51% permanent; 0% meadows; 3% forest; 46% other

Location: SW Pacific Ocean

■ PEOPLE

Population: 83,976 (July 1998 est.); 20 of Kiribati's 33 islands are inhabited

Nationality: I-Kiribati

Age Structure: n.a.

Population Growth Rate: 1.82% (1998 est.)

Net Migration: -0.66 migrants/1,000 population (1998 est.)

Ethnic Groups: Micronesian

Languages: English (official), Gilbertese

Religions: 52.6% Roman Catholic, 40.9% Protestant (Congregational), some Seventh-Day Adventist and Baha'i

Birth Rate: 26.46/1,000 population (1998 est.)

Death Rate: 7.62/1,000 population (1998 est.)

Infant Mortality: 49.69 deaths/1,000 live births (1998 est.)

Life Expectancy at Birth: 60.79 years male, 64.68 years female (1998 est.)

Total Fertility Rate: 3.13 children born/woman (1998 est.)

Literacy: 90.6% (1997 est.)

■ GOVERNMENT

Leader(s): Pres. Teburoro Tito, V. Pres. Tewareka Tentoa

Government Type: republic

Administrative Divisions: 3 units

Nationhood: July 12, 1979 (from UK; formerly known as Gilbert Islands)
National Holiday: Independence Day, July 12

ECONOMY

Overview: the economy has fluctuated widely in recent years and copra production and a good fish catch have provided a boost; at present there is a moderate but steady growth trend
GDP: $62 million, per capita $800; real growth rate 1.9% (1996 est.)
Inflation: n.a.
Industries: accounts for 7% of GDP; fishing, handicrafts
Labour Force: n.a.
Unemployment: n.a., but massive underemployment
Agriculture: accounts for 14% of GDP (including fishing); copra and fish contribute 65% to exports; subsistence farming predominates; food crops—taro, breadfruit, sweet potatoes, vegetables; not self-sufficient in food
Natural Resources: tuna fishing, phosphates

FINANCE/TRADE

Currency: Australian dollar ($A) = 100 cents
International Reserves Excluding Gold: n.a.
Gold Reserves: n.a.
Budget: revenues $33.3 million; expenditures $47.7 million, including capital expenditures n.a. (1996 est.)
Defence Expenditures: n.a.
Education Expenditures: n.a.
External Debt: $7.2 million (1996 est.)
Exports: $10 million (1995); commodities: fish 55%, copra 42%; partners: European Community 20%, Marshall Islands 12%, US 8%, American Samoa 4%
Imports: $47 million (1995); commodities: foodstuffs, fuel, transportation equipment; partners: Australia 39%, Japan 21%, New Zealand 6%, UK 6%, US 3%

COMMUNICATIONS

Daily Newspapers: 0 (1996)
Televisions: 13/1,000 inhabitants (1996)
Radios: 213/1,000 inhabitants (1996)
Telephones: 2.8/100 inhabitants (1996 est.)

TRANSPORTATION

Motor Vehicles: n.a.
Roads: 670 km; n.a. km paved
Railway: none
Air Traffic: 28,000 passengers carried (1996)
Airports: 21; 4 have paved runways (1997 est.)

Canadian Embassy: The Canadian High Commission to Kiribati, c/o The Canadian High Commission, P.O. Box 12-049, Thorndon, Wellington, New Zealand. Tel: (011-64-4) 473-9577. Fax: (011-64-4) 471-2082.
Embassy in Canada: c/o New Zealand High Commission, Metropolitan House, 99 Bank St, Ste 727, Ottawa, ON K1P 6G3. Tel: (613) 238-5991. Fax: (613) 238-5707.

Korea (North)

Long-Form Name: Democratic People's Republic of Korea
Capital: Pyongyang

GEOGRAPHY

Area: 120,540 sq. km
Coastline: 2,495 km
Climate: temperate with rainfall concentrated in summer
Environment: isolated mountainous interior, nearly inaccessible and sparsely populated; late spring droughts often followed by severe flooding
Terrain: mostly hills and mountains separated by deep, narrow valleys; coastal plains wide in west, discontinuous in east
Land Use: 14% arable; 2% permanent; negligible meadows; 61% forest; 23% other, includes 12% irrigated
Location: E Asia, bordering on Yellow Sea, Sea of Japan

PEOPLE

Population: 21,234,387 (July 1998 est.)
Nationality: Korean
Age Structure: 0-14 yrs: 26%; 15-64: 68%; 65+: 6% (1998 est.)
Population Growth Rate: -0.03% (1998 est.)
Net Migration: 0 migrants/1,000 population (1998 est.)
Ethnic Groups: Korean (racially homogeneous)
Languages: Korean
Religions: Buddhism and Confucianism; Taoism, Shamanism, Chonodogyu; autonomous religious activities are now almost nonexistent; government-sponsored religious groups exist to provide an illusion of religious freedom
Birth Rate: 15.3/1,000 population (1998 est.)
Death Rate: 5.57/1,000 population (1998 est.)
Infant Mortality: 87.83 deaths/1,000 live births (1998 est.)
Life Expectancy at Birth: 48.88 years male, 53.88 years female (1998 est.)
Total Fertility Rate: 1.6 children born/woman (1998 est.)
Literacy: 99% (1997 est.)

■ GOVERNMENT

Leader(s): Chairman and Pres. Kim Jong Il, Prem. Hong Song-nam
Government Type: communist state; one-person dictatorship
Administrative Divisions: 9 provinces and 3 special cities
Nationhood: Sept. 9, 1948
National Holiday: Independence Day (DPRK Foundation Day), Sept. 9

■ ECONOMY

Overview: a command economy that is almost completely socialized, with state-owned industry, and collectivization of agriculture; state control over economic affairs is unusually tight even for a communist country; six consecutive years of crop failure and severe summer floods in 1995 have resulted in severe food shortages
GDP: $21.8 billion, per capita $900; real growth rate -3.7% (1997 est.)
Inflation: n.a.
Industries: accounts for 60% of GDP; machine building, military products, electric power, chemicals, mining, metallurgy, textiles, food processing
Labour Force: 11.3 million (1997 est.); 42.8% agricultural, 26.9% services, 30.3% industry
Unemployment: n.a.
Agriculture: accounts for about 25% of GNP and 36% of workforce; principal crops—rice, corn, potatoes, soybeans, pulses; fish; livestock and livestock products—cattle, hogs, pork, eggs; not self-sufficient in grain
Natural Resources: coal, lead, tungsten, zinc, graphite, magnesite, iron ore, copper, gold, pyrites, salt, fluorspar, hydroelectricity

■ FINANCE/TRADE

Currency: North Korean won (Wn) = 100 chon
International Reserves Excluding Gold: n.a.
Gold Reserves: n.a.
Budget: n.a.
Defence Expenditures: 25% to 33% of GDP (1995 est.)
Education Expenditures: n.a.
External Debt: $12 billion (1996 est.)
Exports: n.a.; commodities: minerals, metallurgical products, agricultural products, manufactures; partners: former USSR countries, China, Japan, Germany, Hong Kong, Singapore
Imports: n.a.; commodities: petroleum, machinery and equipment, coking coal, grain; partners: former USSR countries, Japan, China, Germany, Hong Kong, Singapore

■ COMMUNICATIONS

Daily Newspapers: 3 (1996)
Televisions: 48/1,000 inhabitants (1996)
Radios: 147/1,000 inhabitants (1996)
Telephones: 4.6/100 inhabitants (1996 est.)

■ TRANSPORTATION

Motor Vehicles: n.a.
Roads: 31,200 km; 1,997 km paved
Railway: 5,000 km
Air Traffic: 254,000 passengers carried (1996)
Airports: 49; 22 have paved runways (1997 est.)

Canadian Embassy: none
Embassy in Canada: none

Korea (South)

Long-Form Name: Republic of Korea
Capital: Seoul

■ GEOGRAPHY

Area: 98,480 sq. km
Coastline: 2,413 km
Climate: temperate, with rainfall heavier in summer than winter
Environment: occasional typhoons bring high winds and floods; earthquakes in southwest; air and water pollution in large cities
Terrain: mostly hilly and mountainous; wide coastal plains in west and south
Land Use: 19% arable; 2% permanent; 1% meadows; 65% forest; 13% other, includes 14% irrigated
Location: E Asia, bordering on Yellow Sea, Sea of Japan

■ PEOPLE

Population: 46,416,796 (July 1998 est.)
Nationality: Korean
Age Structure: 0-14 yrs: 22%; 15-64: 71%; 65+: 7% (1998 est.)
Population Growth Rate: 1.01% (1998 est.)
Net Migration: -0.31 migrants/1,000 population (1998 est.)
Ethnic Groups: homogeneous; small Chinese minority (about 20,000)
Languages: Korean; English widely taught in high school
Religions: 48.6% Christianity, 47.4% Buddhism, 3% Confucianism, 1% other
Birth Rate: 16.08/1,000 population (1998 est.)
Death Rate: 5.67/1,000 population (1998 est.)
Infant Mortality: 7.79 deaths/1,000 live births (1998 est.)
Life Expectancy at Birth: 70.37 years male, 78.0 years female (1998 est.)

Total Fertility Rate: 1.79 children born/woman (1998 est.)
Literacy: 98% (1997 est.)

■ GOVERNMENT

Leader(s): Pres. Kim Dae Jung, Prime Min. Kim Jong Pil
Government Type: republic
Administrative Divisions: 9 provinces and 6 special cities
Nationhood: Aug. 15, 1948
National Holiday: Independence Day, Aug. 15

■ ECONOMY

Overview: dynamic growth is attributed to the planned development of an export-oriented economy in a strongly entrepreneurial society; labour unrest has hurt its record of noninflationary growth; economic growth has slowed somewhat in recent years
GDP: $631.2 billion, per capita $13,700; real growth rate 6% (1997 est.)
Inflation: 7.5% (June 1998)
Industries: accounts for 43% of GDP; textiles, clothing, footwear, food processing, chemicals, steel, electronics, automobile production, ship building
Labour Force: 22.5 million (1997 est.); 25.1% trade and tourism, 23.9% industry, 14.8% agriculture
Unemployment: 8.5% (Jan. 1999)
Agriculture: accounts for 7% of GDP and 21% of workforce (including fishing and forestry); main crops—rice, root crops, barley, vegetables, fruit; livestock and livestock products—cattle, hogs, chickens, milk, eggs; self-sufficient in food, except for wheat; fish catch is seventh largest in the world
Natural Resources: coal, tungsten, graphite, molybdenum, lead, hydroelectricity

■ FINANCE/TRADE

Currency: South Korean won (W) = 100 chun
International Reserves Excluding Gold: 53.531 billion (Jan. 1999)
Gold Reserves: 0.435 million fine troy ounces (Jan. 1999)
Budget: revenues $101 billion; expenditures $101 billion, including capital expenditures of $20 billion (1996 est.)
Defence Expenditures: 16.29% of govt. expenditure (1997)
Education Expenditures: 19.56% of govt. expenditure (1997)
External Debt: $154 billion (1998 est.)
Exports: $135.94 billion (1998 est.); commodities: textiles, clothing, electronic and electrical equipment, footwear, machinery, steel, automobiles, ships, fish; partners: US 33%, Japan 21%
Imports: $95.226 billion (1998 est.); commodities: machinery, electronics and electronic equipment, oil, steel, transport equipment, textiles, organic chemicals, grains; partners: Japan 28%, US 25%

■ COMMUNICATIONS

Daily Newspapers: 60 (1996)
Televisions: 337/1,000 inhabitants (1996)
Radios: 1,037/1,000 inhabitants (1996)
Telephones: 43.2/100 inhabitants (1996 est.)

■ TRANSPORTATION

Motor Vehicles: 10,000,000; 7,000,000 passenger cars (1997 est.)
Roads: 83,400 km; 63,467 km paved
Railway: 3,081 km
Air Traffic: 23,998,000 passengers carried (1996)
Airports: 103; 67 have paved runways (1997 est.)

Canadian Embassy: The Canadian Embassy, Fl. 10 & 11, Kolon Building, 45 Mugyo-Dong, Jung-Ku, Seoul 100-170; mailing address: P.O. Box 6299, Seoul 100-662 Korea. Tel: (011-82-2) 3455-6000. Fax: (011-82-2) 755-0686.
Embassy in Canada: Embassy of the Republic of Korea, 150 Boteler St, Ottawa ON K1A 5A6. Tel: (613) 244-5010. Fax: (613) 244-5043.

Kuwait

Long-Form Name: State of Kuwait
Capital: Kuwait

■ GEOGRAPHY

Area: 17,820 sq. km
Coastline: 499 km
Climate: dry desert; intensely hot summers; short, cool winters
Environment: large and sophisticated desalination plants are required for adequate drinking water supply; air and water pollution; desertification
Terrain: flat to slightly undulating desert plain
Land Use: negligible arable; 0% permanent; 8% meadows; negligible forest; 92% other
Location: SW Asia (Middle East), bordering on Persian Gulf

■ PEOPLE

Population: 1,913,285 (July 1998 est.)
Nationality: Kuwaiti
Age Structure: 0-14 yrs: 32%; 15-64: 66%; 65+: 2% (1998 est.)

Population Growth Rate: 4.1% (1998 est.)
Net Migration: 22.31 migrants/1,000 population (1998 est.)
Ethnic Groups: 45% Kuwaiti, 35% other Arab, 9% South Asian, 4% Iranian, 7% other
Languages: Arabic (official); Kurdish, Farsi, English (commercial) widely spoken
Religions: 85% Muslim (30% Shi'a, 45% Sunni, 10% other), 15% Christian, Hindu, Parsi and other
Birth Rate: 20.97/1,000 population (1998 est.)
Death Rate: 2.29/1,000 population (1998 est.)
Infant Mortality: 10.74 deaths/1,000 live births (1998 est.)
Life Expectancy at Birth: 74.76 years male, 78.91 years female (1998 est.)
Total Fertility Rate: 3.44 children born/woman (1998 est.)
Literacy: 78.6% (1997 est.)

■ GOVERNMENT

Leader(s): Prime Min. Shaikh Saad al-Abdullah al-Salim al-Sabah; Emir: Shaikh Jabir al-Ahmad al-Jabir al-Sabah
Government Type: nominal constitutional monarchy
Administrative Divisions: 5 governorates
Nationhood: June 19, 1961 (from UK)
National Holiday: National Day, Feb. 25

■ ECONOMY

Overview: Kuwait is a small and relatively open economy with crude oil reserves of about 10% of world reserves. Kuwait lacks water and has practically no arable land, thus preventing development of agriculture. With the exception of fish, it depends almost wholly on food imports.
GDP: $46.3 billion, per capita $22,300; real growth rate 1% (1997 est.)
Inflation: 0.7% (June 1997)
Industries: petroleum (accounts for 53% of GDP and 90% of export revenues), petrochemicals, desalination, food processing, salt, construction
Labour Force: 1 million (1997 est.); 45% services, 20% construction, 12% trade, 9% manufacturing, 3% finance and real estate, 2% agriculture, 2% power and water, 1% mining and quarrying
Unemployment: 1.8% (1996 est.)
Agriculture: virtually none; dependent on imports for food; about 75% of potable water (adversely affected by the Gulf War) must be distilled or imported
Natural Resources: petroleum, fish, shrimp, natural gas

■ FINANCE/TRADE

Currency: dinar (KD) = 1,000 fils
International Reserves Excluding Gold: 4.018 billion (Jan. 1999)
Gold Reserves: 2.539 million fine troy ounces (Jan. 1999)
Budget: revenues $10.3 billion; expenditures $14.5 billion, including capital expenditures n.a. (1997-98 est.)
Defence Expenditures: 22.53% of govt. expenditure (1997)
Education Expenditures: 10.86% of govt. expenditure (1997)
External Debt: $8 billion (1995 est.)
Exports: $14.225 billion (1997); commodities: oil 90%; partners: Japan, Italy, Germany, US
Imports: $8.246 billion (1997); commodities: food, construction material, vehicles and parts, clothing; partners: Japan, US, Germany, UK

■ COMMUNICATIONS

Daily Newspapers: 8 (1996)
Televisions: 510/1,000 inhabitants (1996)
Radios: 688/1,000 inhabitants (1996)
Telephones: 22.7/100 inhabitants (1996 est.)

■ TRANSPORTATION

Motor Vehicles: 693,000; 538,000 passenger cars (1997 est.)
Roads: 4,450 km; 3,587 km paved
Railway: none
Air Traffic: 2,133,000 passengers carried (1996)
Airports: 8; 4 have paved runways (1997 est.)

Canadian Embassy: The Canadian Embassy, Villa 24, Area 4, 24 Mutawakel St, Da Aiyah, Kuwait; mailing address: P.O. Box 25281, 13113, Safat, Kuwait City, Kuwait. Tel: (011-965) 256-3025. Fax: (011-965) 256-0173.
Embassy in Canada: Embassy of the State of Kuwait, 80 Elgin St, Ottawa, ON K1P 1C6. Tel: (613) 780-9999. Fax: (613) 780-9905.

Kyrgyzstan

Long-Form Name: Kyrgyz Republic
Capital: Bishkek

■ GEOGRAPHY

Area: 198,500 sq. km
Coastline: none: landlocked
Climate: dry continental to polar in high Tien Shan; subtropical in south; glacial Alpine; moderate in valley regions
Environment: frequent severe earthquakes; water pollution and water-borne diseases are widespread

Terrain: mountainous; 75% of land covered by snow and glaciers; peaks of Tien Shan rise to 7,000 meters, and associated valleys and basins encompass the entire nation

Land Use: land is cultivated mainly in valleys; 7% arable; negligible permanent crops, 44% meadows and pastures; 4% forest and woodland; 45% other; includes 5% irrigated

Location: C Asia

■ PEOPLE

Population: 4,522,281 (July 1998 est.)

Nationality: Kyrgyzstani

Age Structure: 0-14 yrs: 36%; 15-64: 58%; 65+: 6% (1998 est.)

Population Growth Rate: 0.37% (1998 est.)

Net Migration: -9.72 migrants/1,000 population (1998 est.)

Ethnic Groups: 52.4% Kirghiz, 18% Russian, 12.9% Uzbeks, 2.5% Ukrainian, 2.4% German, 1.6% Tatars, 10.2% other

Languages: Kirghiz and Russian (both official) and Dungan

Religions: 75% Muslim, 20% Eastern Orthodox, 5% other

Birth Rate: 22.03/1,000 population (1998 est.)

Death Rate: 8.65/1,000 population (1998 est.)

Infant Mortality: 74.76 deaths/1,000 live births (1998 est.)

Life Expectancy at Birth: 59.45 years male, 68.3 years female (1998 est.)

Total Fertility Rate: 2.68 children born/woman (1998 est.)

Literacy: 97% (1997 est.)

■ GOVERNMENT

Leader(s): Pres. Askar Akayev; Prime Min. Amangeldy Muraliyev

Government Type: republic

Administrative Divisions: 6 oblasttar and 1 city

Nationhood: August 31, 1991 (from Soviet Union)

National Holiday: National Day, Dec. 2; also Independence Day, Aug. 31

■ ECONOMY

Overview: Kyrgyzstan is a small, poor, mountainous country with a predominantly agricultural economy. Kyrgyzstan has been one of the most progressive countries of the former Soviet Union in carrying out market reforms. Foreign assistance played a substantial role in the country's recent economic turnaround.

GDP: $9.7 billion, per capita $2,100; real growth rate 10% (1997 est.)

Inflation: 10.7% (May 1998)

Industries: accounts for 12% of GDP; small machinery, cement, shoes, furniture and appliances, electronics, electrical engineering, silk making

Labour Force: 2 million (1997 est.); 33% agriculture and forestry, 28% industry and construction, 39% other

Unemployment: 8%; large numbers of underemployed (1996 est.)

Agriculture: accounts for 47% of GDP; wheat, barley, beets, cotton, fruit, vegetables, yaks, potatoes, cotton, grain, tobacco, livestock (mainly sheep); irrigation required;

Natural Resources: mercury, antimony, zinc, tungsten deposits, coal, natural gas, oil, nepheline, bismuth

■ FINANCE/TRADE

Currency: som was introduced as national currency on May 10, 1993

International Reserves Excluding Gold: $156 million (Jan. 1999)

Gold Reserves: 0.083 million fine troy ounces (Jan. 1999)

Budget: revenues $225 million; expenditures $308 million, including capital expenditures of $11 million (1996 est.)

Defence Expenditures: n.a.

Education Expenditures: 6.8% of GNP (1995)

External Debt: $789 million (1996)

Exports: $611 million (1997); agricultural products, antimony, silk, carpets, nonferrous metals, electrical equipment, cotton, wool, meat, tobacco, gold, mercury, hydropower, machinery, consumer goods; partners: China, UK

Imports: $694 million (1997); grain, lumber, industrial products, metals, fuel, machinery, consumer goods; partners: Turkey, Cuba, US, Germany

■ COMMUNICATIONS

Daily Newspapers: 3 (1996)

Televisions: 45/1,000 inhabitants (1996)

Radios: 115/1,000 inhabitants (1996)

Telephones: 7.8/100 inhabitants (1996 est.)

■ TRANSPORTATION

Motor Vehicles: n.a.

Roads: 18,560 km; 16,890 km paved or graveled

Railway: 370 km, plus industrial lines

Air Traffic: 559,000 passengers carried (1996)

Airports: 54; 14 have paved runways (1997 est.)

Canadian Embassy: The Canadian Embassy, 34 Kasarai Batir St, Almaty 480100, Kazakhstan. Tel: (011-7-3272) 50-11-51. Fax: (011-7-327) 581-14-93.

Embassy in Canada: c/o Embassy of the Kyrgyz Republic, 1732 Wisconsin Ave NW, Washington DC 20007, USA. Tel: (202) 338-5141. Fax: (202) 338-5139.

Laos

Long-Form Name: Lao People's Democratic Republic
Capital: Vientiane

■ GEOGRAPHY

Area: 236,800 sq. km
Coastline: none: landlocked
Climate: tropical monsoon; rainy season (May to Nov.); dry season (Dec. to Apr.)
Environment: deforestation; soil erosion; subject to floods; limited safe drinking water
Terrain: mostly rugged mountains; some plains and plateaus
Land Use: 3% arable land; negligible permanent crops; 3% meadows; 54% forest; 40% other
Location: SE Asia

■ PEOPLE

Population: 5,260,842 (July 1998 est.)
Nationality: Laotian or Lao
Age Structure: 0-14 yrs: 45%; 15-64: 52%; 65+: 3% (1998 est.)
Population Growth Rate: 2.76% (1998 est.)
Net Migration: 0 migrants/1,000 population (1998 est.)
Ethnic Groups: mostly Laotian; Vietnamese, Kha, Thai, Meo, Hmong, Yao, Chinese, European, Indian and Pakistani minorities
Languages: Lao (official), French, English, tribal languages
Religions: 60% Buddhist, 40% animist and other
Birth Rate: 40.58/1,000 population (1998 est.)
Death Rate: 12.97/1,000 population (1998 est.)
Infant Mortality: 91.81 deaths/1,000 live births (1998 est.)
Life Expectancy at Birth: 52.13 years male, 55.34 years female (1998 est.)
Total Fertility Rate: 5.66 children born/woman (1998 est.)
Literacy: 56.6% (1997 est.)

■ GOVERNMENT

Leader(s): Pres. Khamtai Siphandon, Prime Min. Gen. Sisavat Keobounphan
Government Type: communist state
Administrative Divisions: 16 provinces and 1 municipality and 1 special zone
Nationhood: July 19, 1949 (from France)
National Holiday: National Day (proclamation of the Lao People's Democratic Republic), Dec. 2

■ ECONOMY

Overview: one of the world's poorest nations, landlocked with a primitive infrastructure; while traditionally a communist centrally planned economy with government ownership and control of productive enterprises, the government is now decentralizing control and encouraging some private enterprise; heavily dependent on foreign aid
GDP: $5.9 billion, per capita $1,150; real growth rate 1.5% (1997 est.)
Inflation: 13% (year-end 1996)
Industries: accounts for 19% of GDP; tin mining, timber, electric power, agricultural processing
Labour Force: 2 million (1997 est.); 75.7% agriculture, 7.1% industry, 17.2% services
Unemployment: 1.7%; 4.5% in urban areas (1995)
Agriculture: accounts for 56% of GDP and employs most of the labour force; subsistence farming predominates; normally self-sufficient; principal crops—rice (80% of cultivated land), potatoes, vegetables, coffee, sugar cane, cotton
Natural Resources: timber, hydroelectricity, gypsum, tin, gold, gemstones

■ FINANCE/TRADE

Currency: new kip (NK) = 100 at
International Reserves Excluding Gold: $117 million (Dec. 1998)
Gold Reserves: 0.017 million fine troy ounces (Dec. 1998)
Budget: revenues $218 million; expenditures $379 million, capital expenditures n.a. (1996 est.)
Defence Expenditures: n.a.
Education Expenditures: 2.4% of GNP (1995)
External Debt: $2.263 billion (1996)
Exports: $400 million (1998 est.); wood products, electricity, tin, consumer goods; partners: Vietnam, Thailand, Germany, France
Imports: $594.7 million (1998 est.); machinery and equipment, fuel, vehicles; partners: Thailand, Japan, Vietnam, China, Singapore

■ COMMUNICATIONS

Daily Newspapers: 3 (1996)
Televisions: 9.9/1,000 inhabitants (1996)
Radios: 139/1,000 inhabitants (1996)
Telephones: 0.4/100 inhabitants (1996 est.)

■ TRANSPORTATION

Motor Vehicles: 21,000; 10,000 passenger cars (1997 est.)
Roads: 22,321 km; 3,502 km paved
Railway: none

Air Traffic: 125,000 passengers carried (1996)
Airports: 52; 9 have paved runways (1997 est.)

Canadian Embassy: The Canadian Embassy to Laos, c/o P.O. Box 2090, Bangkok 10500, Thailand. Tel: (011-66-2) 636-0540. Fax: (011-66-2) 636-0565.
Embassy in Canada: Embassy of the Lao People's Democratic Republic, 2222 S St NW, Washington DC 20008, USA. Tel: (202) 332-6416. Fax: (202) 332-4923.

Latvia

Long-Form Name: Republic of Latvia
Capital: Riga

■ GEOGRAPHY

Area: 64,100 sq. km
Coastline: 531 km
Climate: maritime, wet, moderate winters
Environment: air and water pollution, soil and groundwater contaminated with chemicals and petroleum products at military bases
Terrain: hilly, forested land with many lakes and shallow valleys
Land Use: 27% arable, negligible permanent crops, 13% meadows and pastures, 46% forest, 14% other
Location: NE Europe, bordering on Baltic Sea

■ PEOPLE

Population: 2,385,396 (July 1998 est.)
Nationality: Latvian
Age Structure: 0-14 yrs: 19%; 15-64: 66 %; 65+: 15% (1998 est.)
Population Growth Rate: -1.41% (1998 est.)
Net Migration: -6.47 migrants/1,000 population (1998 est.)
Ethnic Groups: 51.8% Latvian, 33.8% Russian, 4.5% Belorussian, 3.4% Ukrainian, 2.3% Polish, 4.2% other
Languages: Lettish (official), Lithuanian, Russian, some others
Religions: Lutheran, Catholic, Russian Orthodox
Birth Rate: 8.14/1,000 population (1998 est.)
Death Rate: 15.78/1,000 population (1998 est.)
Infant Mortality: 17.44 deaths/1,000 live births (1998 est.)
Life Expectancy at Birth: 61.02 years male, 73.5 years female (1998 est.)
Total Fertility Rate: 1.2 children born/woman (1998 est.)
Literacy: 100% (1997 est.)

■ GOVERNMENT

Leader(s): Pres. Vaira Vike-Freiberga, Prime Min. Andris Skele

Government Type: parliamentary democracy
Administrative Divisions: 26 counties and 7 municipalities
Nationhood: Sept. 6, 1991 (from Soviet Union)
National Holiday: Independence Day, Nov. 18

■ ECONOMY

Overview: Latvia lacks natural resources, aside from its arable land and small forests; its most valuable economic asset is its workforce, which is better educated and disciplined than in most of the former Soviet republics. Latvia is rapidly moving towards a dynamic market economy, but the transition has seen dramatic declines in both GDP and industrial production
GDP: $10.4 billion, per capita $4,260; real growth rate 6% (1997 est.)
Inflation: 5.9% (June 1998)
Industries: accounts for 34% of GDP and 31% of labour force; manufacturing of railroad cars, paper, woolen goods, electronics and engineering, food processing
Labour Force: 1.4 million (1997); 41% industry, 16% forestry and agriculture, 43% services
Unemployment: 7% (May 1998), but large numbers of underemployed
Agriculture: accounts for 9% of GDP, employs 9% of labour force and has become largely privatized; poor soil hinders agriculture products including grain, beets, potatoes, cattle and dairy farming, poultry, fishing
Natural Resources: forests, peat deposits, amber, dolomite

■ FINANCE/TRADE

Currency: lat = 100 santims
International Reserves Excluding Gold: $724 million (Jan. 1999)
Gold Reserves: 0.249 milllion fine troy ounces (Jan. 1999)
Budget: n.a.
Defence Expenditures: 2.21% of total govt. expenditure (1997)
Education Expenditures: 5.50% of govt. expenditure (1997)
External Debt: $472 million (1996)
Exports: $1.811 billion (1998.); vehicles, household appliances, electric power
Imports: $3.191 billion (1998): fuels, cars, chemicals and metal products

■ COMMUNICATIONS

Daily Newspapers: 24 (1996)
Televisions: 485/1,000 inhabitants (1996)
Radios: 699/1,000 inhabitants (1996)
Telephones: 30.2/100 inhabitants (1996 est.)

■ TRANSPORTATION

Motor Vehicles: n.a.
Roads: 60,046 km; 22,998 km paved
Railway: 2,412 km
Air Traffic: 285,000 passengers carried (1997 est.)
Airports: 50; 36 have paved runways (1997 est.)

Canadian Embassy: The Canadian Embassy, Doma laukums 4, 4th Fl, Riga LV-1977. Tel. (011-371) 783-0141. Fax: (011-371) 783-1040.
Embassy in Canada: Embassy of Latvia, 112 Kent St, Ste 208, Place de Ville, Tower B, Ottawa ON K1P 5P2. Tel: (613) 238-6014. Fax: (613) 238-7044.

Lebanon

Long-Form Name: Republic of Lebanon
Capital: Beirut

■ GEOGRAPHY

Area: 10,400 sq. km
Coastline: 225 km
Climate: Mediterranean; mild to cool, wet winters with hot, dry summers
Environment: rugged terrain historically helped isolate, protect and develop numerous factional groups based on religion, clan, and ethnicity; deforestation; soil erosion; air and water pollution; desertification
Terrain: narrow coastal plain; al Biqa' separates Lebanon and Anti-Lebanon Mountains
Land Use: 21% arable; 9% permanent; 1% meadow; 8% forest; 61% other, includes 8% irrigated
Location: SW Asia (Middle East), bordering on Mediterranean Sea

■ PEOPLE

Population: 3,505,794 (July 1998 est.)
Nationality: Lebanese
Age Structure: 0-14 yrs: 30%; 15-64: 64%; 65+: 6% (1998 est.)
Population Growth Rate: 1.62% (1998 est.)
Net Migration: 0 migrants/1,000 population (1998 est.)
Ethnic Groups: 95% Arab, 4% Armenian, 1% other
Languages: Arabic and French (both official); Armenian, English, Kurdish
Religions: Muslim 70% (Sunni, Shia and Druse), Christian 30% (mainly Maronite; also, Armenian, Greek and Syrian sects and Protestants)
Birth Rate: 22.66/1,000 population (1998 est.)

Death Rate: 6.51/1,000 population (1998 est.)
Infant Mortality: 31.64 deaths/1,000 live births (1998 est.)
Life Expectancy at Birth: 68.08 years male, 73.33 years female (1998 est.)
Total Fertility Rate: 2.28 children born/woman (1998 est.)
Literacy: 86.4% (1997 est.)

■ GOVERNMENT

Leader(s): Pres. Emile Lahoud; Prime Min. Selim al-Hoss
Government Type: republic
Administrative Divisions: 5 governorates
Nationhood: Nov. 22, 1943 (from League of Nations mandate under French administration)
National Holiday: Independence Day, Nov. 22

■ ECONOMY

Overview: factional infighting has led to deterioration of the infrastructure and disrupted normal economic activity in what used to be the centre for Middle Eastern banking; high unemployment; growing shortages; international aid is vital
GDP: $15.2 billion, per capita $4,400; real growth rate 4% (1997 est.)
Inflation: 13.8% (Feb. 1997)
Industries: accounts for 23% of GDP; banking, food processing, textiles, cement, oil refining, chemicals, jewelry, some metal fabricating
Labour Force: 1 million (1997 est.); 27.4% industry, 58.4% services, 14.3% agriculture
Unemployment: 18% (1997 est.)
Agriculture: accounts for about 4% of GDP; principal products—citrus fruit, vegetables, potatoes, olives, tobacco, hemp (hashish), sheep and goats; not self-sufficient in grain
Natural Resources: limestone, iron ore, salt; water-surplus state in a water-deficit region

■ FINANCE/TRADE

Currency: Lebanese pound (£L) = 100 piasters
International Reserves Excluding Gold: $6.469 billion (Jan. 1999)
Gold Reserves: 9.222 milllion fine troy ounces (Jan. 1999)
Budget: revenues $2.4 billion; expenditures $5.9 billion, including capital expenditures of n.a. (1997 est.)
Defence Expenditures: 10.31% of total govt. expenditure (1996)
Education Expenditures: 6.17% of total govt. expenditure (1996)
External Debt: $2.3 billion (1997 est.)
Exports: $657.3 million (1998 est.); commodities: agricultural products, chemicals,

textiles, metals and jewelry; partners: 21% Saudi Arabia, 9.5% Switzerland, 6% Jordan, 12% Kuwait, 5% US

Imports: $6.996 billion (1998 est.); commodities: consumer goods, machinery and transport equipment, petroleum products; partners: 14% Italy, 12% France, 6% US, 5% Turkey, 3% Saudi Arabia

■ COMMUNICATIONS

Daily Newspapers: 15 (1996)
Televisions: 373/1,000 inhabitants (1996)
Radios: 892/1,000 inhabitants (1996)
Telephones: 7.9/100 inhabitants (1996 est.)

■ TRANSPORTATION

Motor Vehicles: n.a.
Roads: 6,359 km; 6,041 km paved
Railway: 222 km; railroad system in disrepair, considered inoperable
Air Traffic: 775,000 passengers carried (1996)
Airports: 9; 7 have paved runways (1997 est.)

Canadian Embassy: The Canadian Embassy, Coolrite Building, 434 Autostrade, Jal-ed-Dib, Lebanon; mailing address: P.O. Box 60163, Jal-el-Dib, Beirut, Lebanon. Tel: (011-961-4) 521-163. Fax: (011-961-4) 521-167.
Embassy in Canada: Embassy of the Lebanese Republic, 640 Lyon St, Ottawa ON K1S 3Z5. Tel: (613) 236-5825. Fax: (613) 232-1609.

Lesotho

Long-Form Name: Kingdom of Lesotho
Capital: Maseru

■ GEOGRAPHY

Area: 30,350 sq. km
Coastline: none: landlocked
Climate: temperate; cool to cold, dry winters; hot, wet summers
Environment: population pressure forcing settlement in marginal agricultural areas results in overgrazing, severe soil erosion, soil exhaustion; desertification
Terrain: mostly highland with some plateaus, hills and mountains
Land Use: 11% arable; 0% permanent; 66% meadows; 0% forest; 23% other
Location: S Africa

■ PEOPLE

Population: 2,089,829 (July 1998 est.)
Nationality: Mosotho/Basotho (pl.)
Age Structure: 0-14 yrs: 40%; 15-64: 55%; 65+: 5% (1998 est.)

Population Growth Rate: 1.91% (1998 est.)
Net Migration: 0 migrants/1,000 population (1998 est.)
Ethnic Groups: 99.7% Sotho; 1,600 Europeans, 800 Asians
Languages: Sesotho (southern Sotho) and English (official); also Zulu and Xhosa
Religions: 80% Christian, indigenous beliefs
Birth Rate: 31.84/1,000 population (1998 est.)
Death Rate: 12.76/1,000 population (1998 est.)
Infant Mortality: 78.3 deaths/1,000 live births (1998 est.)
Life Expectancy at Birth: 52.18 years male, 55.81 years female (1998 est.)
Total Fertility Rate: 4.13 children born/woman (1998 est.)
Literacy: 71.3% (1997 est.)

■ GOVERNMENT

Leader(s): King Letsie III, Prime Min. Pakalitha Mosisili
Government Type: parliamentary constitutional monarchy
Administrative Divisions: 10 districts
Nationhood: Oct. 4, 1966 (from UK: formerly known as Basutoland)
National Holiday: Independence Day, Oct. 4

■ ECONOMY

Overview. the economy is hampered by the geography of the country (small, landlocked and mountainous) and the lack of natural resources other than water; subsistence farming is the main occupation; labourers in South Africa make remittances; industry is growing in importance
GDP: $5.1 billion, per capita $2,500; real growth rate 9% (1997 est.)
Inflation: 8.8% (June 1997)
Industries: accounts for 53% of GDP; light manufacturing, milling, canning, leather, jute production, textiles, clothing, light engineering, food, beverages, handicrafts, tourism
Labour Force: 1 million (1997 est.); 23.3% agriculture, 33.1% industry, 43.6% services
Unemployment: substantial unemployment and underemployment (1996)
Agriculture: accounts for 10% of GDP; very primitive, mostly subsistence farming and livestock; principal crops are corn, wheat, pulses, sorghum and barley
Natural Resources: some diamonds and other minerals, water, agricultural and grazing land

■ FINANCE/TRADE

Currency: loti, maloti (pl.) = 100 lisente
International Reserves Excluding Gold: $575 million (Dec. 1998)

Gold Reserves: n.a.
Budget: revenues $507 million; expenditures $487 million, including capital expenditures of $170 million (1996-97 est.)
Defence Expenditures: 5.0% of GDP (1996)
Education Expenditures: 5.9% of GNP (1995)
External Debt: $654 million (1996)
Exports: n.a.; commodities: wool, mohair, wheat, cattle, peas, beans, corn, hides, skins, baskets; partners: South Africa 53%, European Community 30%, North and South America 13%
Imports: n.a.; commodities: corn, building materials, clothing, vehicles, machinery, medicines, petroleum, oil and lubricants; partners: South Africa 95%, European Community 2%

■ **COMMUNICATIONS**

Daily Newspapers: 2 (1996)
Televisions: 24/1,000 inhabitants (1996)
Radios: 48/1,000 inhabitants (1996)
Telephones: 0.9/100 inhabitants (1996 est.)

■ **TRANSPORTATION**

Motor Vehicles: n.a.
Roads: 4,955 km; 887 km paved
Railway: 2.6 km, owned, operated by, and included in the statistics for South Africa
Air Traffic: 17,100 passengers carried (1996)
Airports: 29; 3 have paved runways (1997 est.)

Canadian Embassy: The Canadian High Commission to Lesotho, c/o Canadian Embassy, Private Bag X13, Hatfield 0028, Pretoria, South Africa. Also, consulate in Maseru: Canadian Consulate, 1st Floor, Maseru Book Centre, Kingsway, Box 1165, Maseru, Lesotho. Tel: (011-27-12) 422-3000. Fax: (011-27-12) 422-3052.
Embassy in Canada: c/o High Commission for the Kingdom of Lesotho, 2511 Massachusetts Ave NW, Washington DC 20008, USA. Tel: (202) 797-5533. Fax: (202) 234-6815.

Liberia

Long-Form Name: Republic of Liberia
Capital: Monrovia

■ **GEOGRAPHY**

Area: 111,370 sq. km
Coastline: 579 km
Climate: tropical; hot, humid; dry winters with hot days and cool to cold nights; wet, cloudy summers with frequent heavy showers
Environment: West Africa's largest tropical rain forest, subject to deforestation; soil erosion is increasingly a problem; river pollution
Terrain: mostly flat to rolling coastal plains rising to rolling plateau and low mountains in northeast
Land Use: 1% arable; 3% permanent; 59% permanent pastures; 18% forest; 19% other
Location: W Africa, bordering on South Atlantic Ocean

■ **PEOPLE**

Population: 2,771,901 (July 1998 est.)
Nationality: Liberian
Age Structure: 0-14 yrs: 45%; 15-64: 52%; 65+: 3% (1998 est.)
Population Growth Rate: 5.76% (1998 est.)
Net Migration: 27.02 migrants/1,000 population (1998 est.)
Ethnic Groups: 95% indigenous African tribes, including Kpelle, Bassa, Gio, Kru, Grego, Mano, Krahn, Gola, Gbandi, Lom, Kissi, Vai and Bella; 5% descendants of repatriated slaves known as Americo-Liberians
Languages: English (official); 20 local languages of the Niger-Congo language group; English used by approx. 20%
Religions: 70% traditional, 20% Muslim, 10% Christian
Birth Rate: 41.88/1,000 population (1998 est.)
Death Rate: 11.28/1,000 population (1998 est.)
Infant Mortality: 103.13 deaths/1,000 live births (1998 est.)
Life Expectancy at Birth: 56.81 years male, 62.16 years female (1998 est.)
Total Fertility Rate: 6.09 children born/woman (1998 est.)
Literacy: 38.3% (1997 est.)

■ **GOVERNMENT**

Leader(s): Pres. Charles Taylor
Government Type: republic
Administrative Divisions: 13 counties
Nationhood: July 26, 1847
National Holiday: Independence Day, July 26

■ **ECONOMY**

Overview: Civil war since 1990 has destroyed much of Liberia's economy, especially the infrastructure in and around Monrovia. Many business people have fled the country, taking capital and expertise with them.
GDP: $2.6 billion, per capita $1,000; real growth rate n.a. (1997 est.)
Inflation: n.a.
Industries: accounts for 36% of GDP; rubber processing, food processing, construction materials, furniture, palm oil processing, mining (iron ore, diamonds)

Labour Force: 933,000 (1995); 74.2% agriculture, 16.4% services, 9.4% industry
Unemployment: n.a.
Agriculture: accounts for 30% of GDP (including fishing and forestry); principal products—rubber, timber, coffee, cocoa, rice, cassava, palm oil, sugar cane, bananas, sheep and goats; not self-sufficient in food, imports 25% of rice consumption
Natural Resources: iron ore, timber, diamonds, gold

■ FINANCE/TRADE

Currency: Liberian dollar ($L) = 100 cents
International Reserves Excluding Gold: $28 million (Dec. 1995)
Gold Reserves: n.a.
Budget: n.a.
Defence Expenditures: n.a.
Education Expenditures: n.a.
External Debt: $2 billion (1997 est.)
Exports: n.a.; commodities: diamonds, iron ore, rubber, timber, coffee; partners: US, EU, Netherlands, Singapore
Imports: n.a.; commodities: mineral fuels, chemicals, machinery, foodstuffs; partners: EU, US, Japan, China, Netherlands

■ COMMUNICATIONS

Daily Newspapers: 6 (1996)
Televisions: 27/1,000 inhabitants (1996)
Radios: 318/1,000 inhabitants (1996)
Telephones: 0.2/100 inhabitants (1996 est.)

■ TRANSPORTATION

Motor Vehicles: 28,700; 17,800 passenger cars (1997 est.)
Roads: 10,600 km; 657 km paved
Railway: 490 km
Air Traffic: n.a.
Airports: 46; 2 have paved runways (1997 est.)

Canadian Embassy: The Canadian Embassy to Liberia, c/o Canadian Embassy, P O Box 4104, Abidjan 01, Cote d'Ivoire. Tel: (011-225) 21-20-09. Fax: (011-225) 21-77-28.
Embassy in Canada: consular address: Consulate of Liberia, 1080 Beaver Hall Hill, Ste 1720, Montreal PQ H2Z 1S8. Tel: (514) 871-4741. Fax: (514) 397-0816.

Libya

Long-Form Name: Socialist People's Libyan Arab Jamahiriya
Capital: Tripoli

■ GEOGRAPHY

Area: 1,759,540 sq. km
Coastline: 1,770 km
Climate: Mediterranean along coast; dry, extreme desert interior
Environment: hot, dry, dust-laden ghibli is a southern wind lasting one to four days in spring and fall; desertification; dust storms; sparse natural surface-water resources
Terrain: mostly barren, flat to undulating plains, plateaus, depressions
Land Use: 1% arable; 0% permanent; 8% meadows; 0% forest; 91% other
Location: N Africa, bordering on Mediterranean Sea

■ PEOPLE

Population: 5,690,727 (July 1998 est.)
Nationality: Libyan
Age Structure: 0-14 yrs: 48%; 15-64: 49%; 65+: 3% (1998 est.)
Population Growth Rate: 3.68% (1998 est.)
Net Migration: 0 migrants/1,000 population (1998 est.)
Ethnic Groups: 97% Berber and Arab; some Greeks, Maltese, Italians, Egyptians, Pakistanis, Turks, Indians and Tunisians
Languages: Arabic (official); Italian and English widely understood in major cities, Berber
Religions: 97% Sunni Muslim, 3% Christian and other
Birth Rate: 43.95/1,000 population (1998 est.)
Death Rate: 7.15/1,000 population (1998 est.)
Infant Mortality: 55.81 deaths/1,000 live births (1998 est.)
Life Expectancy at Birth: 63.21 years male, 67.78 years female (1998 est.)
Total Fertility Rate: 6.18 children born/woman (1998 est.)
Literacy: 76.2% (1997 est.)

■ GOVERNMENT

Leader(s): Leader Col. Mu'ammar Abu Minyar al-Qadhafi; Sec. of Gen. People's Committee Muhammad Ahmad al-Manqush
Government Type: Jamahiriya (a state of the masses); in theory, governed by the populace through local councils; in fact, a military dictatorship
Administrative Divisions: 25 municipalities
Nationhood: Dec. 24, 1951 (from Italy)
National Holiday: Revolution Day, Sept. 1

■ ECONOMY

Overview: a socialist-oriented economy that depends largely on revenues from the oil sector; cutbacks on imports due to declining oil

revenues have led to shortages of foodstuffs and basic goods; must import 75% of its food needs, as poor soil and climate limit agricultural production
GDP: $38 billion, per capita $6,700; real growth rate 0.5% (1997 est.)
Inflation: n.a.
Industries: accounts for 55% of GDP; petroleum, food processing, textiles, handicrafts, cement
Labour Force: 1.0 million (1997 est.); 28.9% industry, 53% services, 18.1% agriculture
Unemployment: 25% (1997 est.)
Agriculture: accounts for 5% of GDP; cash crops— wheat, barley, olives, dates, citrus fruit, peanuts; 75% of food is imported
Natural Resources: crude oil, natural gas, gypsum

■ FINANCE/TRADE

Currency: Libyan dinar (LD) = 1,000 dirhams
International Reserves Excluding Gold: n.a.
Gold Reserves: n.a.
Budget: revenues $13 billion; expenditures $14.9 billion, including capital expenditures of n.a. (1995 est.)
Defence Expenditures: 5.1% of GDP (1996)
Education Expenditures: n.a.
External Debt: n.a.
Exports: $4.43 billion (1995); commodities: petroleum, peanuts, hides; partners: Italy, former USSR countries, Germany, Spain, France, Belgium/Luxembourg, Turkey
Imports: $9.6 billion (1995); commodities: machinery, transport equipment, food, manufactured goods; partners: Italy, former USSR countries, Germany, UK, Japan

■ COMMUNICATIONS

Daily Newspapers: 4 (1996)
Televisions: 122/1,000 inhabitants (1995 est.)
Radios: 232/1,000 inhabitants (1996)
Telephones: 6.6/100 inhabitants (1996 est.)

■ TRANSPORTATION

Motor Vehicles: 904,000; 592,000 passenger cars (1997 est.)
Roads: n.a.
Railway: no railroads in operation since 1965
Air Traffic: 639,000 passengers carried (1996)
Airports: 145; 60 have paved runways (1997 est.)

Canadian Embassy: The Canadian Embassy to Libya, c/o Canadian Embassy, CP 31, Belvédère, 1002, Tunis-Belvedere, Tunisia. Tel: (011-216-1) 796-577. Fax: (011-216-1) 792-371.
Embassy in Canada: Embassy of the Socialist People's Libyan Arab Jamahiriya, 309–315 East 48th St, New York NY 10017, USA. Tel: (212) 752-5775. Fax: (212) 593-4787.

Liechtenstein

Long-Form Name: Principality of Liechtenstein
Capital: Vaduz

■ GEOGRAPHY

Area: 160 sq. km
Coastline: none: landlocked
Climate: continental; cold, cloudy winters with frequent snow or rain; cool to moderately warm, cloudy, humid summers
Environment: variety of microclimatic variations based on elevation
Terrain: mostly mountainous (Alps) with Rhine Valley in western third
Land Use: 24% arable; 0% permanent; 16% meadows; 35% forest; 25% other
Location: C Europe

■ PEOPLE

Population: 31,717 (July 1998 est.)
Nationality: Liechtensteiner
Age Structure: 0-14 yrs: 19%; 15-64: 70%; 65+: 11% (1998 est.)
Population Growth Rate: 1.05% (1998 est.)
Net Migration: 5.2 migrants/1,000 population (1998 est.)
Ethnic Groups: 95% Alemannic, 5% Italian and other
Languages: German (official), also Alemannic dialect
Religions: 87.3% Roman Catholic, 8.3% Protestant, 2.8% other, 1.6% unknown
Birth Rate: 12.64/1,000 population (1998 est.)
Death Rate: 7.31/1,000 population (1998 est.)
Infant Mortality: 5.28 deaths/1,000 live births (1998 est.)
Life Expectancy at Birth: 75.51 years male, 80.52 years female (1998 est.)
Total Fertility Rate: 1.61 children born/woman (1998 est.)
Literacy: 100% (1997 est.)

■ GOVERNMENT

Leader(s): Head of State: Prince Hans Adam von und zu Liechtenstein II, Prime Min. Mario Frick
Government Type: hereditary constitutional monarchy
Administrative Divisions: 11 communes
Nationhood: Jan. 23, 1719, Imperial Principality of Liechtenstein established
National Holiday: Assumption Day, Aug. 15

■ ECONOMY

Overview: a prosperous economy based mainly on small-scale light industry and some farming; economy closely tied to that of Switzerland in a customs union; known for low business taxes and easy incorporation rules
GDP: $713 million, per capita $23,000; real growth rate n.a. (1996 est.)
Inflation: n.a.
Industries: electronics, metal manufacturing, textiles, ceramics, pharmaceuticals, food products, precision instruments, tourism
Labour Force: 22,891 (1996 est.), of which 13,847 are foreigners; 46% industry, trade and building, 52% services, 2% agriculture, fishing, forestry and horticulture
Unemployment: 1.6% (1997 est.)
Agriculture: livestock, vegetables, corn, wheat, potatoes, grapes
Natural Resources: hydroelectric potential

■ FINANCE/TRADE

Currency: Swiss franc, franken, or franco (SwF) = 100 centimes, rappen, or centesimi
International Reserves Excluding Gold: n.a.
Gold Reserves: n.a.
Budget: revenues $455 million; expenditures $435 million, including capital expenditures n.a. (1996 est.)
Defence Expenditures: defence is the responsibility of Switzerland
Education Expenditures: n.a.
External Debt: none (1996)
Exports: $2.47 billion (1996); small speciality machinery, dental products, stamps, hardware, pottery; partners: EU and EFTA countries, especially Switzerland
Imports: $917.3 million (1996); commodities: machinery, metal goods, textiles, foodstuffs, motor vehicles; partners: EU countries, Switzerland

■ COMMUNICATIONS

Daily Newspapers: 2 (1996)
Televisions: 342/1,000 inhabitants (1996)
Radios: 668/1,000 inhabitants (1996)
Telephones: 65.1/100 inhabitants (1996 est.)

■ TRANSPORTATION

Motor Vehicles: n.a.
Roads: 250 km; all paved
Railway: 18.5 km, owned, operated, and included in statistics for Austria
Air Traffic: n.a.
Airports: none

Canadian Embassy: The Canadian Embassy to Liechtenstein, c/o the Canadian Embassy, P.O.

Box 3000, Berne 6, Switzerland. Tel: (011-41-31) 357-32-00. Fax: (011-41-31) 357-32-10.
Embassy in Canada: Embassy of Liechtenstein, c/o Embassy of Switzerland, 5 Marlborough Ave, Ottawa ON K1N 8E6. Tel: (613) 235-1837. Fax: (613) 563-1394.

Lithuania

Long-Form Name: Republic of Lithuania
Capital: Vilnius

■ GEOGRAPHY

Area: 65,200 sq. km
Coastline: 99 km
Climate: mild, with moderate precipitation
Environment: risk of accidents from the two Chernobyl-type reactors; at military bases, contamination of soil and groundwater with chemicals and petroleum products
Terrain: undulating glacial terrain; rivers, lakes, and swamps predominate
Land Use: 35% arable; 12% permanent crops; 7% permanent pastures; 31% forest; 15% other
Location: NE Europe, bordering on Baltic Sea

■ PEOPLE

Population: 3,600,158 (July 1998 est.)
Nationality: Lithuanian
Age Structure: 0-14 yrs: 20%; 15-64: 67%; 65+: 13% (1998 est.)
Population Growth Rate: -0.45% (1998 est.)
Net Migration: -2.09 migrants/1,000 population (1998 est.)
Ethnic Groups: 80.1% Lithuanian, 8.6% Russian, 7.7% Polish, 1.5% Byelorussian, 2.1% other
Languages: Lithuanian (official), Russian, Polish
Religions: predominantly Protestant, Roman Catholic, Russian Orthodox
Birth Rate: 10.57/1,000 population (1998 est.)
Death Rate: 12.94/1,000 population (1998 est.)
Infant Mortality: 14.75 deaths/1,000 live births (1998 est.)
Life Expectancy at Birth: 62.76 years male, 75.21 years female (1998 est.)
Total Fertility Rate: 1.46 children born/woman (1998 est.)
Literacy: 98% (1997 est.)

■ GOVERNMENT

Leader(s): Pres. Valdas Adamkus, Prime Min. Rolandas Paksas
Government Type: parliamentary democracy
Administrative Divisions: 44 regions and 11 municipalities
Nationhood: Sept. 6, 1991 (from Soviet Union)
National Holiday: Statehood Day, Feb. 16

■ ECONOMY

Overview: arable land and strategic location are Lithuania's only important natural resources; Lithuania remains highly dependent on Russia for energy, raw materials, grains and markets for its products
GDP: $15.4 billion, per capita $4,230; real growth rate 6% (1997 est.)
Inflation: 6.7% (May 1998)
Industries: accounts for 28% of GDP and employs 42% of labour force; heavy engineering, shipbuilding, production of building materials, nuclear and electric power production; electric motors, television sets, appliances, refining, fertilizer
Labour Force: 2 million (1997 est.); 26.9% industry, 22% community, social and business services, 19% agriculture
Unemployment: 6.0% (Oct. 1998); large numbers of underemployed
Agriculture: accounts for 9% of GDP and employs approximately 18% of labour force; beef and dairy cattle and related products, pigs, poultry, grains, flax, potatoes and other vegetables, eggs, fish, dairy products; net exporter of meat, milk and eggs
Natural Resources: amber, oil reserves, peat

■ FINANCE/TRADE

Currency: litas (pl. litai) = 100 centas
International Reserves Excluding Gold: $1.310 billion (Jan. 1999)
Gold Reserves: 0.186 million fine troy ounces (Jan. 1999)
Budget: revenues $1.5 billion; expenditures $1.7 billion, including capital expenditures of n.a. (1997 est.)
Defence Expenditures: 2.85% of govt. expenditure (1997)
Education Expenditures: 6.63% of govt. expenditure (1997)
External Debt: $1.286 billion (1996)
Exports: $3.860 billion (1997); 18% electronics, 5% petroleum products, 10% food, 6% chemicals; partners: 40% Russia, 16% Ukraine, 32% other former Soviet republics, 12% West
Imports: $5.644 billion (1997); 24% oil, 14% machinery, 8% chemicals, grain; partners: 62% Russia, 18% Belarus, 10% other former Soviet republics, 10% West (1989)

■ COMMUNICATIONS

Daily Newspapers: 19 (1996)
Televisions: 451/1,000 inhabitants (1995 est.)
Radios: 292/1,000 inhabitants (1996)
Telephones: 26.5/100 inhabitants (1996 est.)

■ TRANSPORTATION

Motor Vehicles: n.a.
Roads: 65,135 km; 57,058 km paved
Railway: 2,002 km
Air Traffic: 237,200 passengers carried (1996)
Airports: 96; 25 have paved runways (1997 est.)

Canadian Embassy: Office of the Canadian Embassy, Gedimino pr. 64, 2001 Vilnius, Lithuania. Tel: (011-370-2) 220-898. Fax: (011-370-2) 220-884.
Embassy in Canada: Embassy of the Republic of Lithuania, 130 Albert St, Ste 204, Ottawa, ON K1P 5G4. Tel: (613) 567-5458. Fax: (613) 567-5315.

Luxembourg

Long-Form Name: Grand Duchy of Luxembourg
Capital: Luxembourg

■ GEOGRAPHY

Area: 2,586 sq. km
Coastline: none: landlocked
Climate: modified continental with mild winters, cool summers
Environment: deforestation; pollution in urban areas
Terrain: mostly gently rolling uplands with broad, shallow valleys; uplands to slightly mountainous in the north; steep slope down to Moselle floodplain in the southeast
Land Use: 24% arable; 1% permanent; 20% meadows; 21% forest; 34% other
Location: NW Europe

■ PEOPLE

Population: 425,017 (July 1998 est.)
Nationality: Luxembourger
Age Structure: 0-14 yrs: 18%; 15-64: 67%; 65+: 15% (1998 est.)
Population Growth Rate: 1.02% (1998 est.)
Net Migration: 8.4 migrants/1,000 population (1998 est.)
Ethnic Groups: Celtic base, with French and German blend; also guest and worker residents
Languages: Luxembourgisch (official), German (written language of commerce and press), French (administrative), English
Religions: 97% Roman Catholic, 3% Protestant and Jewish
Birth Rate: 11.12/1,000 population (1998 est.)
Death Rate: 9.29/1,000 population (1998 est.)
Infant Mortality: 5.04 deaths/1,000 live births (1998 est.)
Life Expectancy at Birth: 74.41 years male, 80.68 years female (1998 est.)

Total Fertility Rate: 1.63 children born/woman (1998 est.)
Literacy: 100% (1997 est.)

■ GOVERNMENT

Leader(s): Prime Min. Jean-Claude Juncker; Head of State, Jean, Grand Duke of Luxembourg
Government Type: constitutional monarchy
Administrative Divisions: 3 districts
Nationhood: 1839 (Grand Duchy)
National Holiday: National Day (public celebration of the Grand Duke's birthday), June 23

■ ECONOMY

Overview: a stable economy featuring moderate growth, low inflation and negligible unemployment; is in an economic union with Belgium for trade and most financial matters and is also closely connected economically with the Netherlands; financial sector is strong; industrial sector is becoming increasingly diversified
GDP: $13.48 billion, per capita $33,700; real growth rate 3.6% (1997 est.)
Inflation: 1.2% (June 1998)
Industries: accounts for 21% of GDP; banking, iron and steel, food processing, chemicals, metal products, engineering, tires, glass, aluminum
Labour Force: 171,600 (1996); 14% community, social and business services, 20% trade and tourism, mining and manufacturing 16%, construction 11%, transportation and communication 8%, other 42%
Unemployment: 3.4% (Jan. 1999)
Agriculture: accounts for 5% of GDP (including forestry); principal products—barley, oats, potatoes, wheat, fruits, wine grapes; cattle-raising widespread
Natural Resources: iron ore (no longer exploited)

■ FINANCE/TRADE

Currency: Luxembourg franc (LuxF) = 100 centimes [As of Jan. 1, 1999, Government securities are issued in Euros (EUR)]
International Reserves Excluding Gold: $112 million (Jan. 1999)
Gold Reserves: 0.076 million fine troy ounces (Jan. 1999)
Budget: revenues $5.46 billion; expenditures $5.44 billion, including capital expenditures n.a. (1997 est.)
Defence Expenditures: 0.8% of GDP (1995)
Education Expenditures: 10.29% of govt. expenditure (1995)
External Debt: $800 million (1995 est.)

Exports: $165.58 billion (Belgium-Luxembourg Economic Union, 1997); commodities: finished steel products, chemicals, rubber products, glass, aluminum, other industrial products; partners: European Community 75%, US 6%
Imports: $155.488 billion (Belgium-Luxembourg Economic Union, 1997); commodities: minerals, metals, foodstuffs, quality consumer goods; partners: Germany 40%, Belgium 35%, France 15%, US 3%

■ COMMUNICATIONS

Daily Newspapers: 5 (1996)
Televisions: 387/1,000 inhabitants (1996)
Radios: 678/1,000 inhabitants (1996)
Telephones: 57.7/100 inhabitants (1996 est.)

■ TRANSPORTATION

Motor Vehicles: 251,000; 233,000 passenger cars (1997 est.)
Roads: 5,160 km; all paved
Railway: 275 km
Air Traffic: 639,000 passengers carried (1996)
Airports: 2; 1 has paved runways (1997 est.)

Canadian Embassy: The Canadian Embassy to Luxembourg, c/o 2, Avenue de Tervuren, 1040 Brussels, Belgium. Tel: (011-32-2) 741-0611. Fax: (011-32-2) 741-0643. Office. The Consulate of Canada, c/o Price Waterhouse and Co., 16 rue Eugène Ruppert, Box 1443, Luxembourg L-1014. Tel: (011-35-2) 40-24-20. Fax: (011-35-2) 40-24-55.
Embassy in Canada: Embassy of the Grand Duchy of Luxembourg, 2200 Massachusetts Ave NW, Washington DC 20008, USA. Tel: (202) 265-4171. Fax: (202) 328-8270.

Macau

Long-Form Name: Macau
Capital: Macau

■ GEOGRAPHY

Area: 16 sq. km (a peninsula and three small islands)
Climate: subtropical maritime; marine with cool winters, warm summers
Land Use: almost 100% built-up; almost no agricultural lands or fresh water resources
Location: SE coast of China, bordering on South China Sea

■ PEOPLE

Population: 429,152 (July 1998 est.)
Nationality: Macanese
Ethnic Groups: Chinese 95%, Portuguese 3%, other 2%

Languages: Portuguese (official), Cantonese, English widely spoken

■ GOVERNMENT

Colony Territory of: Dependent Territory of Portugal, scheduled to revert to China December 20, 1999
Leader(s): Head of State Jorge Sampaio (Pres. of Portugal), Gov. Gen. Vasco Rocha Vieira; Chief Executive, as of December 20, 1999 when Macau reverts to Chinese control: Edmund Ho Hau Wah
Government Type: overseas territory of Portugal scheduled to revert to China in 1999
National Holiday: Day of Portugal, June 10

■ ECONOMY

Overview: gambling and tourism; industry confined to textiles, fireworks, toy-making, plastics; imports almost all energy, food and water from China

■ FINANCE/TRADE

Currency: pataca (pl. patacas) = 100 avos

Canadian Embassy: The Canadian Consulate General, c/o The Office of the Consulate General for Canada, P.O. Box 11142, Hong Kong Special Administrative Region, PR China. Tel: (011-86-10) 6532-3536. Fax: (011-86-10) 6532-4311.
Representative to Canada: none

Macedonia

Long-Form Name: The Former Yugoslav Republic Macedonia
Capital: Skopje

■ GEOGRAPHY

Area: 25,333 sq. km
Coastline: none: landlocked
Climate: hot, dry summers and autumns; winters relatively cold with heavy snowfall
Environment: high earthquake hazard; air pollution
Terrain: mountainous, with deep valleys and basins; three large lakes
Land Use: 24% arable land, 2% permanent crops, 25% permanent pastures, 39% forests, 10% other
Location: SE Europe

■ PEOPLE

Population: 2,009,387 (July 1998 est.)
Nationality: Macedonian
Age Structure: 0-14 yrs: 24%; 15-64: 67%; 65+: 9% (1998 est.)

Population Growth Rate: 0.68% (1998 est.)
Net Migration: -.0.88 migrants/1,000 population (1998 est.)
Ethnic Groups: 65% Macedonian, 22% Albanian, 4% Turkish, 2% Serb, 3% Gypsies, 4% other
Languages: 70% Macedonian, 21% Albanian, 3% Turkish, 3% Serbo-Croatian, 3% other
Religions: 67% Eastern Orthodox, 30% Muslim, 3% other
Birth Rate: 15.71/1,000 population (1998 est.)
Death Rate: 8.08/1,000 population (1998 est.)
Infant Mortality: 19.49 deaths/1,000 live births (1998 est.)
Life Expectancy at Birth: 70.67 years male, 75.03 years female (1998 est.)
Total Fertility Rate: 2.06 children born/woman (1998 est.)
Literacy: n.a.

■ GOVERNMENT

Leader(s): Pres. Kiro Gligorov, Prime Min. Ljupco Georgievski
Government Type: emerging democracy
Administrative Divisions: 34 counties
Nationhood: Sept. 17, 1991 (from Yugoslavia)
National Holiday: Sept. 8

■ ECONOMY

Overview: although it is the poorest of the six republics of the dissolved Yugoslav federation, Macedonia can meet its basic food requirements; new economic ties are necessary, however, to keep living standards from falling to a bare subsistence level; all oil, gas, modern machinery and parts must be imported; continued political upheaval prevents return to settled economic conditions. An important supplement to GDP is the remittances from thousands of Macedonians working in Germany and other West European countries.
GDP: $2 billion, per capita $960; real growth rate 1.5% (1997 est.)
Inflation: 1.0% (June 1997)
Industries: accounts for 39% of GDP; level of technology is generally low; basic liquid fuels, coal, metallic chromium, lead, zinc; Macedonia is one of the seven legal cultivators of the opium poppy for the world pharmaceutical industry
Labour Force: 1 million (1997 est.); 35.2% industry, 20.2% community, social and business services, 11.6% trade and tourism
Unemployment: 30% (1997 est.)
Agriculture: highly labour-intensive; accounts for 20% of GDP. Rice, tobacco, corn, millet and wheat are the chief crops
Natural Resources: chromium, lead, zinc, manganese, tungsten, nickel, timber

■ FINANCE/TRADE

Currency: denar = 100 deni
International Reserves Excluding Gold: $291 million (Jan. 1999)
Gold Reserves: 0.100 million fine troy ounces (Jan. 1999)
Budget: revenues $1.06 billion; expenditures $1.06 billion, including capital expenditures of n.a. (1996 est.)
Defence Expenditures: n.a.
Education Expenditures: 5.5% of GNP (1995)
External Debt: $1.06 billion (Jun. 1997)
Exports: $1.147 billion (1996); manufactured goods, machinery and transportation equipment, raw materials, food and livestock, tobacco and beverages, chemicals; partners: mostly the former Yugoslav republics, Germany, Albania, Greece
Imports: $1.627 billion (1996); fuel and lubricants, machinery and transport equipment, food and livestock, chemicals, raw materials, manufactures; partners: other former Yugoslav republics, Germany, Albania, Greece, Bulgaria

■ COMMUNICATIONS

Daily Newspapers: 3 (1996)
Televisions: 230/1,000 inhabitants (1996)
Radios: 184/1,000 inhabitants (1996)
Telephones: 16.8/100 inhabitants (1996 est.)

■ TRANSPORTATION

Motor Vehicles: n.a.
Roads: 10,591 km; 5,500 km paved
Railway: 922 km
Air Traffic: 287,000 passengers carried (1996)
Airports: 16; 10 have paved runways (1997 est.)

Canadian Embassy: The Canadian Embassy to the Former Yugoslav Republic of Macedonia, Kneza Milosa 75, 11000 Belgrade, Yugoslavia. Tel: (011-381-11) 64-46-66. Fax: (011-381-11) 64-14-80.
Embassy in Canada: Embassy of the Former Yugoslav Republic of Macedonia, 130 Albert St., Ste. 1006, Ottawa, ON, K1P 5G4. Tel: (613) 234-3882. Fax: (613) 233-1852.

Madagascar

Long-Form Name: Republic of Madagascar
Capital: Antananarivo

■ GEOGRAPHY

Area: 587,040 sq. km
Coastline: 4,828 km
Climate: tropical along coast, temperate inland, arid in south

Environment: subject to periodic cyclones; deforestation; overgrazing; soil erosion; desertification; water pollution
Terrain: narrow coastal plain; high plateau and mountains in centre
Land Use: 4% arable; 1% permanent crops; 41% permanent pastures; 40% forest; 14% other, includes 1.5% irrigated
Location: Indian Ocean, E of Africa

■ PEOPLE

Population: 14,462,509 (July 1998 est.)
Nationality: Malagasy
Age Structure: 0-14 yrs: 45%; 15-64: 52%; 65+: 3% (1998 est.)
Population Growth Rate: 2.81% (1998 est.)
Net Migration: 0 migrants/1,000 population (1998 est.)
Ethnic Groups: basic split between highlanders of predominantly Malayo-Indonesian origin (Merina and Betsileo) and coastal tribes, collectively termed the Côtiers, with mixed African, Malayo-Indonesian and Arab ancestry (Betsimisaraka, Tsimihety, Antaiska, Sakalava)
Languages: French and Malagasy (both official)
Religions: 52% indigenous beliefs; approx. 41% Christian, 7% Muslim
Birth Rate: 41.89/1,000 population (1998 est.)
Death Rate: 13.83/1,000 population (1998 est.)
Infant Mortality: 90.57 deaths/1,000 live births (1998 est.)
Life Expectancy at Birth: 51.7 years male, 54.1 years female (1998 est.)
Total Fertility Rate: 5.76 children born/woman (1998 est.)
Literacy: 80% (1997 est.)

■ GOVERNMENT

Leader(s): Pres. Didier Ratsiraka, Prime Min. Tantley Andrianarivo
Government Type: republic
Administrative Divisions: 6 provinces
Nationhood: June 26, 1960 (from France; formerly known as Malagasy Republic)
National Holiday: Independence Day, June 26

■ ECONOMY

Overview: a poor country, hampered by high population growth and a GDP growth rate that is not keeping pace; agriculture is the basis of the economy; industrial development is hurt by government policies restricting imports of equipment and spare parts
GDP: $10.3 billion, per capita $730; real growth rate 3% (1997 est.)
Inflation: 7.8% (May 1998)
Industries: accounts for 15% of GDP;

agricultural processing (meat canneries, soap factories, breweries, tanneries, sugar refining), light consumer goods industries (textiles, glassware), cement, automobile assembly plant, paper, petroleum
Labour Force: 7.2 million (1997 est.); 59.2% community, social and business services, 26.7% agriculture
Unemployment: n.a.
Agriculture: accounts for 33% of GDP; cash crops–coffee, vanilla, sugar cane, cloves, cocoa; food crops—rice, cassava, beans, bananas, peanuts; almost self-sufficient in rice
Natural Resources: graphite, chromite, coal, bauxite, salt, quartz, tar sands, semi-precious stones, mica, fish

■ FINANCE/TRADE

Currency: Malagasy franc (FMG) = 100 centimes
International Reserves Excluding Gold: $179 million (Jan. 1999)
Gold Reserves: n.a.
Budget: revenues $477 million; expenditures $706 million, including capital expenditures of $264 million (1996 est.)
Defence Expenditures: 5.40% of govt. expenditure (1996)
Education Expenditures: 9.13% of govt. expenditure (1996)
External Debt: $4.4 billion (1996 est.)
Exports: $170 million (1997); commodities: coffee 45%, vanilla 15%, cloves 11%, sugar, petroleum products; partners: France, Japan, Italy, Germany, US
Imports: $327 million (1997); commodities: intermediate manufactures 30%, capital goods 28%, petroleum 15%, consumer goods 14%, food 13%; partners: France, Germany, UK, other European Community, US

■ COMMUNICATIONS

Daily Newspapers: 5 (1996)
Televisions: 20/1,000 inhabitants (1996)
Radios: 192/1,000 inhabitants (1996)
Telephones: 0.2/100 inhabitants (1996 est.)

■ TRANSPORTATION

Motor Vehicles: 74,700; 58,900 passenger cars (1997 est.)
Roads: 49,837 km; 5,781 km paved
Railway: 883 km
Air Traffic: 524,300 passengers carried (1996)
Airports: 136; 30 have paved runways (1997 est.)

Canadian Embassy: The Canadian Embassy to Madagascar, P.O. Box 1022, Dar-es-Salaam, Tanzania. Tel: (011-255-51) 112-831. Fax: (011-255-51) 116-896.
Embassy in Canada: Embassy of the Republic of Madagascar, 649 Blair Rd, Gloucester, ON K1J 7M4. Tel: (613) 744-7995. Fax: (613) 744-2530.

Malawi

Long-Form Name: Republic of Malawi
Capital: Lilongwe

■ GEOGRAPHY

Area: 118,480 sq. km
Coastline: none: landlocked
Climate: tropical; rainy season (Nov. to May); dry season (May to Nov.)
Environment: deforestation; water pollution; soil degradation
Terrain: narrow elongated plateau with rolling plains, rounded hills, some mountains
Land Use: 18% arable; 0% permanent; 20% meadows; 39% forest; 23% other
Location: SE Africa

■ PEOPLE

Population: 9,840,474 (July 1998 est.)
Nationality: Malawian
Age Structure: 0-14 yrs: 46%; 15-64: 52%; 65+: 2% (1998 est.)
Population Growth Rate: 1.66% (1998 est.)
Net Migration: 0 migrants/1,000 population (1998 est.)
Ethnic Groups: Chewa, Nyanja, Tumbuko, Yao, Lomwe, Sena, Tonga, Ngoni, Ngonde, Asian, European
Languages: English and Chichewa (both official); other languages important regionally
Religions: 55% Protestant, 20% Roman Catholic, 25% Muslim, traditional indigenous beliefs
Birth Rate: 40.22/1,000 population (1998 est.)
Death Rate: 23.68/1,000 population (1998 est.)
Infant Mortality: 133.77 deaths/1,000 live births (1998 est.)
Life Expectancy at Birth: 36.64 years male, 36.54 years female (1998 est.)
Total Fertility Rate: 5.62 children born/woman (1998 est.)
Literacy: 56.4% (1997 est.)

■ GOVERNMENT

Leader(s): Pres. Bakili Muluzi; Prime Min. Justin Malewezi
Government Type: multi-party democracy
Administrative Divisions: 24 districts
Nationhood: July 6, 1964 (from UK; formerly known as Nyasaland)

National Holiday: Independence Day, July 6; Republic Day, July 6

■ ECONOMY

Overview: one of the world's least developed countries; the economy is predominantly agricultural, with about 90% of the population living in rural areas; economy depends heavily on foreign aid

GDP: $8.6 billion, per capita $900; real growth rate 6% (1997 est.)

Inflation: 6.8% (June 1997)

Industries: accounts for 30% of GDP; agricultural processing (tea, tobacco, sugar), sawmilling, cement, consumer goods

Labour Force: 5.1 million (1997 est.); 54% agriculture, 12.9% industry, 12.7% services

Unemployment: n.a.

Agriculture: 45% of GDP; crops: tobacco, sugar cane, cotton, tea, corn; subsistence crops: cattle and goats

Natural Resources: limestone; unexploited deposits of uranium, coal and bauxite

■ FINANCE/TRADE

Currency: kwacha (K) = 100 tambala

International Reserves Excluding Gold: $264 million (Jan. 1999)

Gold Reserves: 0.013 million fine troy ounces (Jan. 1999)

Budget: n.a.

Defence Expenditures: 1.2% of GDP (1996)

Education Expenditures: 5.7% of GNP (1995)

External Debt: $2.312 billion (1996)

Exports: $481.19 million (1996); commodities: tobacco, tea, sugar, coffee, peanuts; partners: US, UK, Zambia, South Africa, Germany

Imports: $699.95 million (1996); commodities: food, petroleum, semimanufactures, consumer goods, transportation equipment; partners: South Africa, Japan, US, UK, Zimbabwe

■ COMMUNICATIONS

Daily Newspapers: 5 (1996)

Televisions: n.a.; no TV stations

Radios: 256/1,000 inhabitants (1996)

Telephones: 0.4/100 inhabitants (1996 est.)

■ TRANSPORTATION

Motor Vehicles: 54,300; 25,400 passenger cars (1997 est.)

Roads: 28,400 km; 5,254 km paved

Railway: 789 km

Air Traffic: 153,000 passengers carried (1996)

Airports: 45; 6 have paved runways (1997 est.)

Canadian Embassy: The Canadian High Commission to Malawi, c/o The Canadian High Commission, 5199 United Nations Ave, Lusaka; mailing address: P.O. Box 31313 Lusaka, Zambia. Tel: (011-260-1) 25-08-33. Fax: (011-260-1) 25-41-76.

Embassy in Canada: High Commission for the Republic of Malawi, 7 Clemow Ave, Ottawa ON K1S 2A9. Tel: (613) 236-8931. Fax: (613) 236-1054.

Malaysia

Long-Form Name: Malaysia

Capital: Kuala Lumpur

■ GEOGRAPHY

Area: 329,750 sq. km; includes Sabah and Sarawak

Coastline: 4,675 km total (2,068 km Peninsular Malaysia, 2,607 km East Malaysia)

Climate: tropical; annual southwest (Apr. to Oct.) and northeast (Oct. to Feb.) monsoons

Environment: subject to flooding; air and water pollution; deforestation

Terrain: coastal plains rising to hills and mountains

Land Use: 3% arable; 12% permanent crops; negligible meadows; 68% forest; 17% other, includes 1% irrigated

Location: SE Asia, bordering on South China Sea

■ PEOPLE

Population: 20,932,901 (July 1998 est.)

Nationality: Malaysian

Age Structure: 0-14 yrs: 36%; 15-64: 60%; 65+: 4% (1998 est.)

Population Growth Rate: 2.11% (1998 est.)

Net Migration: 0 migrants/1,000 population (1998 est.)

Ethnic Groups: 59% Malay and other indigenous, 32% Chinese, 9% Indian

Languages: Peninsular Malaysia: Malay (official), English, Chinese dialects, Tamil; State of Sabah: English, Malay, numerous tribal dialects; Chinese State of Sarawak: English, Malay, Mandarin, numerous tribal languages

Religions: Peninsular Malaysia: Muslim (Malays), Buddhist (Chinese), Hindu (Indians); State of Sabah: 38% Muslim, 17% Christian, 45% other; Chinese State of Sarawak: 35% tribal religions, 24% Buddhist and Confucianist, 20% Muslim, 16% Christian, 5% other

Birth Rate: 26.5/1,000 population (1998 est.)

Death Rate: 5.36/1,000 population (1998 est.)

Infant Mortality: 22.45 deaths/1,000 live births (1998 est.)

Life Expectancy at Birth: 67.35 years male, 73.56 years female (1998 est.)

Total Fertility Rate: 3.37 children born/woman (1998 est.)
Literacy: 83.5% (1997 est.)

■ GOVERNMENT

Leader(s): Paramount Ruler (King) Tuanku Jaafar ibni Marhum Abdul Rahman, Prime Min. Mahathir Sultan bin Mohamad
Government Type: constitutional monarchy nominally headed by the paramount ruler (king) and a bicameral parliament
Administrative Divisions: 13 states and 2 federal territories
Nationhood: Aug. 31, 1957 (from UK)
National Holiday: National Day, Aug. 31

■ ECONOMY

Overview: the economy is vulnerable to recession or a fall in world commodity prices because of its high export dependence; the world's largest producer of semiconductor devices; the majority of the rural population subsists at the poverty level but recent increases in economic output have improved living standards and real income. Foreign investment has increased significantly in recent years
GDP: $227 billion, per capita $11,100; real growth rate 7.4% (1997 est.)
Inflation: 5.4% (May 1998)
Industries: accounts for 45% of GDP; rubber and oil palm processing and manufacturing, light manufacturing industries, electronics, tin mining and smelting, logging and processing timber, logging, petroleum production, agriculture processing, petroleum production and refining, logging`
Labour Force: 8.2 million (1997 est.); 26% agriculture, 19.9% industry, 19.9% services
Unemployment: 2.6% (1996 est.)
Agriculture: accounts for 14% of GDP; Peninsular Malaysia—natural rubber, palm oil, rice; Sabah—mainly subsistence; main crops—rubber, timber, coconut, rice; Sarawak—main crops—rubber, timber, pepper; there is a deficit of rice in all areas
Natural Resources: tin, crude oil, timber, copper, iron ore, natural gas, bauxite

■ FINANCE/TRADE

Currency: ringgit ($M) = 100 sen
International Reserves Excluding Gold: $25.559 billion (Dec. 1998)
Gold Reserves: 2.35 million fine troy ounces (Dec. 1998)
Budget: revenues $22.6 billion; expenditures $22 billion, including capital expenditures of $5.3 billion (1996 est.)

Defence Expenditures: 2.6% of GDP (1997)
Education Expenditures: 22.80% of govt. expenditure (1997)
External Debt: $39.777 billion (1996)
Exports: $71.545 billion (1998 est.); commodities: natural rubber, palm oil, tin, timber, petroleum, electronics, light manufactures; partners: Singapore, Japan, former USSR countries, European Community, Australia, US
Imports: $58.537 billion (1998 est.); commodities: food, crude oil, consumer goods, intermediate goods, capital equipment, chemicals; partners: Japan, Singapore, Germany, UK, Thailand, China, Australia, US

■ COMMUNICATIONS

Daily Newspapers: 42 (1996)
Televisions: 170/1,000 inhabitants (1996)
Radios: 432/1,000 inhabitants (1996)
Telephones: 18.3/100 inhabitants (1996 est.)

■ TRANSPORTATION

Motor Vehicles: 3,100,000; 3,050,000 passenger cars (1997 est.)
Roads: 94,500 km; 70,970 km paved
Railway: Peninsular Malaysia: 1,672 km; Sabah: 134 km; Sarawak: none
Air Traffic: 14,284,300 passengers carried (1996)
Airports: 114; 33 have paved runways (1997 est.)

Canadian Embassy: The Canadian High Commission, Flr 7, Plaza OSK, 172 Jalan Ampang, 50450 Kuala Lumpur, Malaysia; mailing address: P.O. Box 10990, 50732 Kuala Lumpur, Malaysia. Tel: (011-60-3) 261-2000. Fax: (011-60-3) 261-3428.
Embassy in Canada: High Commission for Malaysia, 60 Boteler St, Ottawa ON K1N 8Y7. Tel: (613) 241-5182. Fax: (613) 241-5214.

Maldives

Long-Form Name: Republic of Maldives
Capital: Malé

■ GEOGRAPHY

Area: 300 sq. km; 1,190 coral islands grouped in 26 atolls
Coastline: 644 km
Climate: tropical; hot, humid; dry, northeast monsoon (Nov. to Mar.); rainy, southwest monsoon (June to Aug.)
Environment: future rise in ocean level could obliterate large parts of the country; freshwater supplies are limited
Terrain: flat with elevations of only 2.5 metres

Land Use: 10% arable; 0% permanent; 3% meadows; 3% forest; 84% other
Location: Indian Ocean, S of India

■ PEOPLE

Population: 290,211 (July 1998 est.)
Nationality: Maldivian
Age Structure: 0-14 yrs: 47%; 15-64: 50%; 65+: 3% (1998 est.)
Population Growth Rate: 3.42% (1998 est.)
Net Migration: 0 migrants/1,000 population (1998 est.)
Ethnic Groups: mixtures of Sinhalese, Dravidian, Arab and African
Languages: Dhivehi (Maldivian dialect of Sinhara; script derived from Arabic); English spoken by most government officials
Religions: Sunni Muslim
Birth Rate: 40.12/1,000 population (1998 est.)
Death Rate: 5.96/1,000 population (1998 est.)
Infant Mortality: 41.12 deaths/1,000 live births (1998 est.)
Life Expectancy at Birth: 65.87 years male, 69.35 years female (1998 est.)
Total Fertility Rate: 5.84 children born/woman (1998 est.)
Literacy: 93.2% (1997 est.)

■ GOVERNMENT

Leader(s): Pres. Maumoun Abdul Gayoom
Government Type: republic
Administrative Divisions: 19 atolls and 1 other first-order administrative division
Nationhood: July 26, 1965 (from UK)
National Holiday: Independence Day, July 26

■ ECONOMY

Overview: based on fishing, tourism and shipping; fishing is the largest industry; tourism has become one of the largest and most important sources of revenue
GDP: adjusted for purchasing power parity: $500 million, per capita $1,800; real growth rate 6.2% (1997 est.)
Inflation: 3.3% (June 1998)
Industries: accounts for 15% of GDP; fishing and fish processing, tourism, shipping, boat building, some coconut processing, garments, woven mats, coir (rope), handicrafts
Labour Force: n.a.; 25% agriculture, 21% industry, 21% services, transportation and communication 10%, other 23%
Unemployment: negligible
Agriculture: accounts for almost 22% of GDP (including fishing); fishing more important than farming; limited production of coconuts, corn, sweet potatoes; most staple foods must be imported

Natural Resources: fish

■ FINANCE/TRADE

Currency: rufiyaa (Rf) = 100 laari
International Reserves Excluding Gold: $123 million (Jan. 1999)
Gold Reserves: 0.002 million fine troy ounces (Jan. 1999)
Budget: revenues $88 million; expenditures $141 million, including capital expenditures n.a. (1995 est.)
Defence Expenditures: 18.33% of govt. expenditure (1997)
Education Expenditures: 16.50% of govt. expenditure (1997)
External Debt: $167 million (1996)
Exports: $70.67 million (1998 est.); commodities: fish 57%, clothing 39%; partners: Thailand, Western Europe, Sri Lanka
Imports: $346.7 million (1998 est.); commodities: intermediate and capital goods 47%, consumer goods 42%, petroleum products 11%; partners: Japan, Western Europe, Thailand

■ COMMUNICATIONS

Daily Newspapers: 2 (1996)
Televisions: 27/1,000 inhabitants (1996)
Radios: 122/1,000 inhabitants (1996)
Telephones: 6.4/100 inhabitants (1996 est.)

■ TRANSPORTATION

Motor Vehicles: n.a.
Roads: Malé has 9.6 km of coral highways within the city
Railway: none
Air Traffic: 232,800 passengers carried (1996)
Airports: 2; both have paved runways (1997 est.)

Canadian Embassy: The Canadian High Commission to Maldives, c/o The Canadian High Commission, P.O. Box 1006, Colombo 7, Sri Lanka. Tel: (011-94-1) 69-58-41. Fax: (011-94-1) 68-70-49.
Embassy in Canada: Embassy of the Maldives, c/o High Commission for the Democratic Socialist Republic of Sri Lanka, 333 Laurier Ave W, Ste 1204, Ottawa ON K1P 1C1. Tel: (613) 233-8449. Fax: (613) 238-8448.

Mali

Long-Form Name: Republic of Mali
Capital: Bamako

■ GEOGRAPHY

Area: 1,240,000 sq. km
Coastline: none: landlocked

Climate: subtropical to arid; hot and dry Feb. to June; rainy, humid and mild June to Nov.; cool and dry Nov. to Feb.

Environment: hot, dust-laden harmattan haze common during dry seasons; soil erosion; desertification; deforestation

Terrain: mostly flat to rolling northern plains covered by sand; savanna in south, rugged hills in northeast

Land Use: 2% arable; 0% permanent; 25% meadows; 6% forest; 67% other

Location: NW Africa

■ PEOPLE

Population: 10,108,569 (July 1998 est.)

Nationality: Malian

Age Structure: 0-14 yrs: 47%; 15-64: 49%; 65+: 4% (1998 est.)

Population Growth Rate: 3.24% (1998 est.)

Net Migration: 1.57 migrants/1,000 population (1998 est.)

Ethnic Groups: 50% Mande (Bambara, Malinke, Sarakole), 17% Peul, 12% Voltaic, 6% Songhai, 10% Tuareg and Moor, 5% other

Languages: French (official); Bambara spoken by about 80% of the population; numerous African languages

Religions: 90% Muslim, 9% indigenous beliefs, 1% Christian

Birth Rate: 49.88/1,000 population (1998 est.)

Death Rate: 19.04/1,000 population (1998 est.)

Infant Mortality: 121.72 deaths/1,000 live births (1998 est.)

Life Expectancy at Birth: 45.67 years male, 48.43 years female (1998 est.)

Total Fertility Rate: 7.02 children born/woman (1998 est.)

Literacy: 31.0% (1997 est.)

■ GOVERNMENT

Leader(s): Pres. Alpha Oumar Konare, Prime Min. Ibrahim Boubakar Keita

Government Type: republic

Administrative Divisions: 8 regions

Nationhood: Sept. 22, 1960 (from France; formerly French Sudan)

National Holiday: Anniversary of the Proclamation of the Republic, Sept. 22

■ ECONOMY

Overview: Mali is among the poorest countries in the world, with 65% of its land area desert or semidesert. Economic activity is largely confined to the area irrigated by the Niger. Industrial activity is concentrated on processing farm commodities.

GDP: $6 billion, per capita $600; real growth rate 6% (1997 est.)

Inflation: -0.7% (year-end 1997)

Industries: accounts for 17% of GDP; small local consumer goods and processing, construction, phosphate, gold, fishing

Labour Force: 5.1 million (1997 est.); 85.5% agriculture, 12.5% services, 2% industry

Unemployment: n.a.

Agriculture: accounts for 49% of GDP; most production based on small subsistence farms; cotton and livestock products account for over 70% of exports; other crops—millet, rice, corn, vegetables, peanuts; livestock—cattle, sheep and goats

Natural Resources: gold, phosphates, kaolin, salt, limestone, uranium; bauxite, iron ore, manganese, tin and copper deposits are known but not exploited

■ FINANCE/TRADE

Currency: Communauté financière africaine franc (CFAF) = 100 centimes

International Reserves Excluding Gold: $399 million (Nov. 1998)

Gold Reserves: 0.19 million fine troy ounces (July 1998)

Budget: revenues $730 million; expenditures $770 million, including capital expenditures of n.a. (1997 est.)

Defence Expenditures: 2.7% of GDP (1996)

Education Expenditures: 2.2% of GNP (1995)

External Debt: $3.02 billion (1996)

Exports: $563 million (1997); commodities: livestock, peanuts, dried fish, cotton, skins; partners: mostly franc zone and Western Europe

Imports: $691 million (1997); commodities: textiles, vehicles, petroleum products, machinery, sugar, cereals; partners: mostly franc zone and Western Europe

■ COMMUNICATIONS

Daily Newspapers: 3 (1996)

Televisions: 3.6/1,000 inhabitants (1996)

Radios: 49/1,000 inhabitants (1996)

Telephones: 0.2/100 inhabitants (1996 est.)

■ TRANSPORTATION

Motor Vehicles: 41,800; 24,700 passenger cars (1997 est.)

Roads: 15,100 km; 1,827 km paved

Railway: 641 km

Air Traffic: 75,000 passengers carried (1996)

Airports: 28; 6 have paved runways (1997 est.)

Canadian Embassy: The Canadian Embassy, P.O. Box 198, Bamako, Mali. Tel: (011-223) 21-30-96. Fax: (011-223) 21-43-62.

Embassy in Canada: Embassy of the Republic of Mali, 50 Goulburn Ave, Ottawa ON K1N 8C8. Tel: (613) 232-1501. Fax: (613) 232-7429.

Malta

Long-Form Name: Republic of Malta
Capital: Valletta

■ GEOGRAPHY

Area: 320 sq. km
Coastline: 140 km
Climate: Mediterranean with mild, rainy winters and hot, dry summers
Environment: numerous bays provide good harbours; fresh water very scarce, increasing reliance on desalination
Terrain: mostly low, rocky, flat to dissected plains; many coastal cliffs
Land Use: 38% arable; 3% permanent; 0% meadows; 0% forest; 59% other, includes 3% irrigated
Location: Mediterranean Sea, S of Sicily

■ PEOPLE

Population: 379,563 (July 1998 est.)
Nationality: Maltese
Age Structure: 0-14 yrs: 21%; 15-64: 68%; 65+: 11% (1998 est.)
Population Growth Rate: 0.58% (1998 est.)
Net Migration: 1.45 migrants/1,000 population (1998)
Ethnic Groups: mixture of Arab, Sicilian, Norman, Spanish, Italian, English
Languages: Maltese and English (both official), Italian widely spoken
Religions: 98% Roman Catholic
Birth Rate: 11.73/1,000 population (1998 est.)
Death Rate: 7.35/1,000 population (1998 est.)
Infant Mortality: 7.57 deaths/1,000 live births (1998 est.)
Life Expectancy at Birth: 75.3 years male, 80.05 years female (1998 est.)
Total Fertility Rate: 1.73 children born/woman (1998 est.)
Literacy: 88% (1997 est.)

■ GOVERNMENT

Leader(s): Pres. Guido De Marco, Prime Min. Eddie Feneck Adami
Government Type: parliamentary democracy
Administrative Divisions: none
Nationhood: Sept. 21, 1964 (from UK)
National Holiday: Independence Day, Sept. 21

■ ECONOMY

Overview: manufacturing and tourism are important; economy is dependent on foreign trade and services (food, water and energy); Malta produces only 20% of its food needs, has a limited supply of fresh water and lacks domestic energy sources

GDP: $4.9 billion, per capita $12,900; real growth rate 2.8% (1997 est.)
Inflation: 3.6% (Apr. 1998)
Industries: accounts for 34% of GDP; tourism, ship repair yard, clothing, construction, food manufacturing, textiles, footwear, clothing, beverages, tobacco
Labour Force: 147,300 (1996); 22% industry, 66% services, other 12%
Unemployment: 3.7% (year-end 1996)
Agriculture: accounts for 5% of GDP; 20% self-sufficient overall; main products—potatoes, cauliflower, grapes, wheat, barley, tomatoes, citrus, cut flowers, green peppers, hogs, poultry, eggs; adequate supplies of vegetables, poultry, milk, pork products; seasonal or periodic shortages
Natural Resources: limestone, salt

■ FINANCE/TRADE

Currency: Maltese lira (LM) = 100 cents
International Reserves Excluding Gold: $1,429 million (Aug. 1997)
Gold Reserves: 0.014 million fine troy ounces (Nov. 1998)
Budget: revenues $1.3 billion; expenditures $1.5 billion, including capital expenditures of $219 million (1997 est.)
Defence Expenditures: 2.7% of GDP (1996-97)
Education Expenditures: 11.49% of govt. expenditure (1996)
External Debt: $953 million (1996)
Exports: $1.807 million (1998 est.); commodities: clothing, textiles, footwear, ships; partners: Germany 31%, UK 14%, Italy 14%
Imports: $2.605 billion (1998 est.); commodities: food, petroleum, nonfood raw materials; partners: Germany 19%, UK 17%, Italy 17%, US 11%

■ COMMUNICATIONS

Daily Newspapers: 2 (1996)
Televisions: 751/1,000 inhabitants (1996)
Radios: 678/1,000 inhabitants (1996)
Telephones: 46.8/100 inhabitants (1996 est.)

■ TRANSPORTATION

Motor Vehicles: 141,200; 122,100 passenger cars (1997 est.)
Roads: 1,582 km; 1,471 km paved
Railway: none
Air Traffic: 1,077,400 passengers carried (1996)
Airports: 1, with a paved runway (1997 est.)

Canadian Embassy: The Canadian High Commission to Malta, c/o The Canadian Embassy, Via Zara 30, 00198, Rome, Italy. Tel:

(011-39-06) 445981. Fax: (011-39-06) 445 98912.

Embassy in Canada: High Commission for Malta, 2017 Connecticut Ave NW, Washington DC 20008, USA. Tel: (202) 462-3611. Fax: (202) 387-5470.

Marshall Islands

Long-Form Name: Republic of the Marshall Islands
Capital: Majuro

■ GEOGRAPHY

Area: 181.3 sq. km; 2 island chains of 30 atolls and 1,152 islands
Coastline: 370.4 km
Climate: islands border typhoon belt; wet season, May to Nov.; hot and humid
Environment: occasional typhoons; insufficient fresh water
Terrain: low coral limestone and sand islands
Land Use: 0% arable, 60% permanent crops, 0% meadows or forests, 40% other
Location: Oceania, in North Pacific Ocean

■ PEOPLE

Population: 63,031 (July 1998 est.)
Nationality: Marshallese
Age Structure: 0-14 yrs: 50%; 15-64: 48%; 65+: 2% (1998 est.)
Population Growth Rate: 3.85% (1998 est.)
Net Migration: 0 migrants/1,000 population (1998 est.)
Ethnic Groups: Micronesian
Languages: English (official), two major Marshallese dialects, Japanese
Religions: Christian (predominantly Protestant)
Birth Rate: 45.39/1,000 population (1998 est.)
Death Rate: 6.9/1,000 population (1998 est.)
Infant Mortality: 44.54 deaths/1,000 live births (1998 est.)
Life Expectancy at Birth: 62.89 years male, 66.14 years female (1998 est.)
Total Fertility Rate: 6.72 children born/woman (1998 est.)
Literacy: 93% (1997 est.)

■ GOVERNMENT

Leader(s): Pres. Amata Kabua
Government Type: constitutional government in free association with the US
Administrative Divisions: none
Nationhood: Oct. 21, 1986 (from US-administered UN trusteeship)
National Holiday: Proclamation of the Republic of the Marshall Islands, May 1

■ ECONOMY

Overview: agriculture and tourism are the backbone of the economy; industry is on a small scale, limited to handicrafts, copra and fish processing; imports far exceed exports; foreign aid is vital
GDP: adjusted for purchasing power parity: $98 million, per capita $1,680; real growth rate 2% (1997 est.)
Inflation: 4% (1995 est.)
Industries: accounts for 13% of GDP; copra, fish, tourism, crafts; offshore banking is in its infancy
Labour Force: n.a.
Unemployment: n.a.
Agriculture: accounts for 15% of GDP; coconuts, taro, cacao, breadfruit, fruits, poultry, tomatoes, melons, cattle
Natural Resources: phosphate, marine products, minerals

■ FINANCE/TRADE

Currency: US currency is used
International Reserves Excluding Gold: n.a.
Gold Reserves: n.a.
Budget: revenues $80.1 million; expenditures $77.4 million, including capital expenditures of $19.5 million (1995–96 est.)
Defence Expenditures: defence is the responsibility of the US
Education Expenditures: n.a.
External Debt: $128 million (1995-96)
Exports: $17.5 million (1996 est.); fish, coconut oil, trochus shells; partners: US, Japan, Australia
Imports: $71.8 million (1996 est.); foodstuffs, machinery, equipment, fuels, beverages, tobacco; partners: US, Japan, Australia, New Zealand

■ COMMUNICATIONS

Daily Newspapers: n.a.
Televisions: n.a.
Radios: n.a.
Telephones: n.a.

■ TRANSPORTATION

Motor Vehicles: n.a.
Roads: paved roads on major islands only
Railway: none
Air Traffic: 41,000 passengers carried (1996)
Airports: 16; 4 have paved runways (1997 est.)

Canadian Embassy: The Canadian Embassy to the Marshall Islands, c/o The Canadian High Commission, Commonwealth Ave., Canberra A.C.T., Austrailia. Tel: (011-61-2) 6273-3844. Fax: (011-61-2) 6273-3285.

Embassy in Canada: c/o Embassy of the Republic of the Marshall Islands, 2433 Massachusetts Ave NW, Washington DC, USA. Tel: (202) 234-5414. Fax: (202) 232-3236.

Martinique

Long-Form Name: Department of Martinique
Capital: Fort-de-France

■ GEOGRAPHY

Area: 1,100 sq. km
Climate: tropical, moderated by trade winds; rainy season (June to Oct.)
Land Use: 8% arable; 8% permanent crops; 17% permanent pastures; 44% forest; 23% other, includes 5.5% irrigated
Location: Windward Islands, Caribbean

■ PEOPLE

Population: 407,284 (July 1998 est.)
Nationality: Martiniquais
Ethnic Groups: majority black, remainder a mix of black African and Latin ancestry, Caucasian 5%
Languages: French (official), majority speak Creole

■ GOVERNMENT

Colony Territory of: Overseas Department of France
Leader(s): Chief of State: Pres. Jacques Chirac (Pres., France), Prefect Dominique Bellion
Government Type: overseas department of France
National Holiday: Taking of the Bastille, National Day, July 14

■ ECONOMY

Overview: most of the meat, vegetable and grain requirements must be imported; industry: food processing, oil refining, chemical engineering; agriculture: pineapples, tobacco, cotton, bananas, sugar, rum, livestock; forest products; fishing; chief trading partners: France, UK, Guadeloupe

■ FINANCE/TRADE

Currency: French franc (F) = 100 centimes

Canadian Embassy: c/o The Canadian Embassy 35-37 avenue Montaigne, 75008 Paris, France. Tel: (011-33-1) 44-43-29-00. Fax: (011-33-1) 44-43-29-99.
Representative to Canada: c/o Embassy of France, 42 Sussex Dr, Ottawa ON K1M 2C9. Tel: (613) 789-1795. Fax: (613) 562-3735.

Mauritania

Long-Form Name: Islamic Republic of Mauritania
Capital: Nouakchott

■ GEOGRAPHY

Area: 1,030,700 sq. km
Coastline: 754 km
Climate: desert; constantly hot, dry, dusty
Environment: hot, dry, dust/sand-laden sirocco wind blows primarily in Mar. and Apr.; desertification; only perennial river is the Senegal; overgrazing and insufficient fresh water
Terrain: mostly barren, flat plains of the Sahara; some central hills
Land Use: 0% arable; 0% permanent crops; 38% meadows; 4% forest; 58% other
Location: NW Africa, bordering on Atlantic Ocean

■ PEOPLE

Population: 2,511,473 (July 1998 est.)
Nationality: Mauritanian
Age Structure: 0-14 yrs: 46%; 15-64: 51%; 65+: 3% (1998 est.)
Population Growth Rate: 2.52% (1998 est.)
Net Migration: -4.65 migrants/1,000 population (1998 est.)
Ethnic Groups: 30% Maur, 40% mixed Maur-black, 30% black
Languages: Hasaniya Arabic and Wolof (both official), Pular, Soninke
Religions: nearly 100% Muslim
Birth Rate: 44.46/1,000 population (1998 est.)
Death Rate: 14.59/1,000 population (1998 est.)
Infant Mortality: 78.22 deaths/1,000 live births (1998 est.)
Life Expectancy at Birth: 46.95 years male, 53.11 years female (1998 est.)
Total Fertility Rate: 6.41 children born/woman (1998 est.)
Literacy: 37.7% (1997 est.)

■ GOVERNMENT

Leader(s): Pres. Maaouya Ould Taya; Prime Min. Cheikel Afia Ould Mohamed Khouna
Government Type: republic
Administrative Divisions: 12 regions
Nationhood: Nov. 28, 1960 (from France)
National Holiday: Independence Day, Nov. 28

■ ECONOMY

Overview: most of the population is engaged in agricultural and livestock production; substantial iron ores; threatened by foreign

overexploitation of fishing areas; in recent years, droughts, conflicts with Senegal, rising energy costs and economic mismanagement have resulted in a substantial build-up of foreign debt. Short-term growth prospects are dismal
GDP: adjusted for purchasing power parity: $4.1 billion, per capita $1,750; real growth rate 6% (1996 est.)
Inflation: 7.4% (May 1998)
Industries: accounts for 31% of GDP; fishing, fish processing, mining of iron ore and gypsum
Labour Force: 1 million (1997 est.); 69.4% agriculture, 21.7% services, 8.9% industry
Unemployment: n.a.
Agriculture: accounts for 26% of GDP (including fishing); largely subsistence farming, nomadic cattle and sheep herding except in Senegal river valley; crops—dates, millet, sorghum, root crops; fish products number-one export; large food deficit in years of drought
Natural Resources: iron ore, gypsum, fish, copper, phosphate

■ FINANCE/TRADE

Currency: ouguiya (UM) = 5 Khoums
International Reserves Excluding Gold: $192 million (Jan. 1999)
Gold Reserves: 0.012 million fine troy ounces (Jan. 1999)
Budget: revenues $329 million; expenditures $265 million, including capital expenditures of $75 million (1996 est.)
Defence Expenditures: 2.9% of GDP (1996)
Education Expenditures: 5.0% of GNP (1995)
External Debt: $2.363 billion (1996)
Exports: n.a.; commodities: iron ore, processed fish, small amounts of gum arabic and gypsum, unrecorded but numerically significant cattle exports to Senegal; partners: European Community 57%, Japan 39%, Ivory Coast 2%
Imports: n.a.; commodities: foodstuffs, consumer goods, petroleum products, capital goods; partners: European Community 79%, Africa 5%, US 4%, Japan 2%

■ COMMUNICATIONS

Daily Newspapers: 2 (1996)
Televisions: 25/1,000 inhabitants (1996)
Radios: 150/1,000 inhabitants (1996)
Telephones: 0.4/100 inhabitants (1996 est.)

■ TRANSPORTATION

Motor Vehicles: 27,000; 17,800 passenger cars (1997 est.)
Roads: 7,660 km; 866 km paved
Railway: 704 km

Air Traffic: 235,000 passengers carried (1996)
Airports: 26; 8 have paved runways (1997 est.)

Canadian Embassy: The Canadian Embassy to Mauritania, c/o The Canadian Embassy, P.O. Box 3373, Dakar, Senegal. Office: The Consulate of Canada, Plot C Villa No. 455, Nouakchott, Mauritania. Tel: (011-2222) 515-42. Fax: (011-2222) 576-10.
Embassy in Canada: Embassy of the Islamic Republic of Mauritania, 249 McLeod St, Ottawa, ON K2P 1A1. Tel: (613) 237-3283. Fax: (613) 237-3287.

Mauritius

Long-Form Name: Republic of Mauritius
Capital: Port Louis

■ GEOGRAPHY

Area: 1,860 sq. km; includes Agalega Islands, Cargados Carajos Shoals (St. Brandon) and Rodriques
Coastline: 177 km
Climate: tropical modified by southeast trade winds; warm, dry winter (May to Nov.); hot, wet, humid summer (Nov. to May)
Environment: subject to cyclones (Nov. to Apr.); almost completely surrounded by reefs; water pollution is a growing problem
Terrain: small coastal plain rising to discontinuous mountains encircling central plateau
Land Use: 49% arable; 3% permanent crops; 3% meadows; 22% forest; 23% other, includes 9% irrigated
Location: Indian Ocean, E of Africa

■ PEOPLE

Population: 1,168,256 (July 1998 est.)
Nationality: Mauritian
Age Structure: 0-14 yrs: 26%; 15-64: 68%; 65+: 6% (1998 est.)
Population Growth Rate: 1.2% (1998 est.)
Net Migration: 0 migrants/1,000 population (1998 est.)
Ethnic Groups: 68% Indo-Mauritian, 27% Creole, 3% Sino-Mauritian, 2% Franco-Mauritian
Languages: English (official), Creole, French, Hindi, Urdu, Hakka, Bojpoori
Religions: 52% Hindu, 28% Christian (mostly Roman Catholic with a few Anglicans), 17% Muslim, 3% other
Birth Rate: 18.64/1,000 population (1998 est.)
Death Rate: 6.69/1,000 population (1998 est.)
Infant Mortality: 16.54 deaths/1,000 live births (1998 est.)

Life Expectancy at Birth: 67.05 years male, 74.74 years female (1998 est.)
Total Fertility Rate: 2.22 children born/woman (1998 est.)
Literacy: 82.9% (1997 est.)

■ GOVERNMENT

Leader(s): Pres. Cassam Uteem, Prime Min. Sir Navinchandra Ramgoolam
Government Type: parliamentary democracy
Administrative Divisions: 9 administrative districts and 3 dependencies
Nationhood: Mar. 12, 1968 (from UK)
National Holiday: Independence Day, Mar. 12

■ ECONOMY

Overview: based on sugar, manufacturing (textiles) and tourism; features low unemployment and a high real growth rate; industrialization programs stress increasing exports
GDP: adjusted for purchasing power parity: $11.7 billion, per capita $10,300; real growth rate 5% (1996 est.)
Inflation: 6.8% (June 1998)
Industries: accounts for 29% of GDP; food processing (largely sugar milling), textiles, wearing apparel, chemical and chemical products, metal products, transport equipment, nonelectrical machinery, tourism
Labour Force: 500,000 (1996 est.); 14% agriculture, 36% industry, 24% community, social and business services, 26% other
Unemployment: 2.4% (1995 est.)
Agriculture: accounts for 8% of GDP; about 90% of cultivated land in sugar cane (which accounts for 40% of export earnings); other products—tea, corn, potatoes, bananas, pulses, cattle, goats, fish; net food importer, especially rice and fish
Natural Resources: arable land, fish

■ FINANCE/TRADE

Currency: rupee (Mau Rs) = 100 cents
International Reserves Excluding Gold: $619 million (Jan. 1999)
Gold Reserves: 0.062 million fine troy ounces (Jan. 1999)
Budget: revenues $822 million; expenditures $1 billion, including capital expenditures of $198 million (1995-96 est.)
Defence Expenditures: 1.1% of total govt. expenditure (1997)
Education Expenditures: 17.77% of govt. expenditure (1997)
External Debt: $1.818 billion (1996)
Exports: $1.616 billion (1997); commodities: textiles 44%, sugar 40%, light manufactures 10%; partners: European Community 77%, US 15%
Imports: $2.254 billion (1997); commodities: manufactured goods 50%, capital equipment 17%, foodstuffs 13%, petroleum products 8%, chemicals 7%; partners: European Community, US, South Africa, Japan

■ COMMUNICATIONS

Daily Newspapers: 6 (1996)
Televisions: 223/1,000 inhabitants (1996)
Radios: 368/1,000 inhabitants (1996)
Telephones: 14.3/100 inhabitants (1996 est.)

■ TRANSPORTATION

Motor Vehicles: 83,050; 70,000 passenger cars (1997 est.)
Roads: 1,877 km; 1,746 km paved
Railway: none
Air Traffic: 578,800 passengers carried (1996)
Airports: 5; 2 have paved runways (1997 est.)

Canadian Embassy: The Canadian High Commission to Mauritius, c/o The Canadian High Commission, Private Bag X13, Hatfield 0028, Pretoria, South Africa. Office: The Canadian Consulate, P.O. Box 209, Port Louis, Mauritius. Tel: (011-230) 212-5500. Fax: (011-230) 208-3391.
Embassy in Canada: c/o Embassy of Mauritius, 4301 Connecticut Avenue NW, Ste 441, Washington DC 20008, USA. Tel: (202) 244-1491. Fax: (202) 966-0983.

Mayotte

Long-Form Name: Territorial Collectivity of Mayotte
Capital: Mamoutzou

■ GEOGRAPHY

Area: 375 sq. km
Climate: tropical maritime; hot, humid rainy season during northeastern monsoon (Nov. to May), dry season is cooler (May to Nov.)
Land Use: 20,000 acres under agricultural cultivation
Location: Mozambique Channel, off W coast of Africa

■ PEOPLE

Population: 141,944 (July 1998 est.)
Nationality: Mahorais
Ethnic Groups: Antalote, Cafre, Makoa, Oimatsaha, Sakalava
Languages: French (official), Mahorian (a Swahili dialect)

■ GOVERNMENT

Colony Territory of: Territorial Collectivity of France
Leader(s): Chief of State: Jacques Chirac (France), Prefect Pierre Mayle
Government Type: territorial collectivity
National Holiday: Taking of the Bastille, July 14

■ ECONOMY

Overview: industry: lobster, shrimp; agriculture: pineapples, bananas, mangoes, breadfruit, cassava, ylang-ylang, vanilla, coffee, spices; Mayotte must import a large portion of its food requirements, mainly from France; chief trading partners: France, UK, South Africa, Bahrain, Thailand, Réunion

■ FINANCE/TRADE

Currency: French franc (F) = 100 centimes

Canadian Embassy: c/o The Canadian Embassy, 35-37 avenue Montaigne, 75008 Paris, France. Tel: (011-33-1) 44-43-29-00. Fax: (011-33-1) 44-43-29-99.
Representative to Canada: c/o Embassy of France, 42 Sussex Dr, Ottawa ON K1M 2C9. Tel: (613) 789-1795. Fax: (613)562-3735.

Mexico

Long-Form Name: United Mexican States
Capital: Mexico

■ GEOGRAPHY

Area: 1,972,550 sq. km
Coastline: 9,330 km
Climate: varies from tropical to desert
Environment: subject to tsunamis along the Pacific coast and destructive earthquakes in the centre and south; natural water resources scarce and polluted; deforestation; erosion widespread; desertification; serious air pollution
Terrain: high, rugged mountains, low coastal plains, high plateaus and desert
Land Use: 12% arable, 1% permanent; 39% meadows; 26% forest; 22% other, includes 2.5% irrigated
Location: Central (Latin) America, bordering on Gulf of Mexico, Pacific Ocean

■ PEOPLE

Population: 98,552,776 (July 1998 est.)
Nationality: Mexican
Age Structure: 0-14 yrs: 36%; 15-64: 60%; 65+: 4% (1998 est.)
Population Growth Rate: 1.77% (1998 est.)

Net Migration: -2.89 migrants/1,000 population (1998 est.)
Ethnic Groups: 60% mestizo (Indian-Spanish), 30% Amerindian or predominantly Amerindian, 9% white or predominantly white, 1% other
Languages: Spanish, also indigenous (Mayan) languages
Religions: 89% Roman Catholic, 6% Protestant, 5% other
Birth Rate: 25.49/1,000 population (1998 est.)
Death Rate: 4.91/1,000 population (1998 est.)
Infant Mortality: 25.82 deaths/1,000 live births (1998 est.)
Life Expectancy at Birth: 68.62 years male, 74.79 years female (1998 est.)
Total Fertility Rate: 2.91 children born/woman (1998 est.)
Literacy: 89.6% (1997 est.)

■ GOVERNMENT

Leader(s): Pres. Ernesto Zedillo Ponce de Léon
Government Type: federal republic operating under a centralized government
Administrative Divisions: 31 states and 1 federal district
Nationhood: Sept. 16, 1810 (from Spain)
National Holiday: Independence Day, Sept. 16

■ ECONOMY

Overview: The outlook for Mexico remains positive, but this country still needs to overcome many structural problems as it strives to modernize its economy and raise living standards. Income distribution is very unequal, with the top 20% of income earners accounting for 55% of income.
GDP: $694.3 billion, per capita $7,700; real growth rate 7.3% (1997 est.)
Inflation: 15.4% (July 1998)
Industries: accounts for 33% of GDP; food and beverages, tobacco, chemicals, iron and steel, petroleum, mining, textiles, clothing, transportation equipment, tourism
Labour Force: 38.1 million (1997 est.); 57% services, 22.9% agriculture, 20.1% industry
Unemployment: 3.7% (1997 est.); plus considerable underemployment
Agriculture: accounts for 8% of GDP and over 25% of labour force; large number of small farms at subsistence level; major food crops—corn, wheat, rice, beans; cash crops—cotton, coffee, fruit, tomatoes
Natural Resources: crude oil, silver, copper, gold, lead, zinc, natural gas, timber

■ FINANCE/TRADE

Currency: peso ($Mex) = 100 centavos

International Reserves Excluding Gold: $31.681 billion (Jan. 1999)
Gold Reserves: 0.217 million fine troy ounces (Jan. 1999)
Budget: revenues $92 billion; expenditures $94 billion, capital expenditures n.a. (1997 est.)
Defence Expenditures: 1.5% of GDP (1997 est.)
Education Expenditures: 24.5% of total govt. expenditure (1996)
External Debt: $162 billion (1997 est.)
Exports: $64.940 billion (1998 est.); commodities: crude oil, oil products, coffee, shrimp, engines, cotton; partners: US 66%, European Community 16%, Japan 11%
Imports: $81.177 billion (1998 est.); commodities: grain, metal manufactures, agricultural machinery, electrical equipment; partners: US 62%, European Community 18%, Japan 10%

■ **COMMUNICATIONS**

Daily Newspapers: 295 (1996)
Televisions: 270/1,000 inhabitants (1996)
Radios: 324/1,000 inhabitants (1996)
Telephones: 10.1/100 inhabitants (1996 est.)

■ **TRANSPORTATION**

Motor Vehicles: 12,330,000; 8,200,000 passenger cars (1997 est.)
Roads: 252,000 km; 94,248 km paved
Railway: 20,567 km
Air Traffic: 14,862,000 passengers carried (1996)
Airports: 1,810; 231 have paved runways (1997 est.)

Canadian Embassy: The Canadian Embassy, Calle Schiller no. 529, Rincon del Bosque, Colonia Polanco, 11560 Mexico; mailing address· Apartado Postal 105 05, 11580 Mexico, Mexico. Tel: (011-52-5) 724-7900. Fax: (011-52-5) 724-7980.
Embassy in Canada: Embassy of the United Mexican States, 45 O'Connor St, Ste 1500, Ottawa ON K1P 1A4. Tel: (613) 233-8988. Fax: (613) 235-9123.

Micronesia

Long-Form Name: Federated States of Micronesia
Capital: Palikin

■ **GEOGRAPHY**

Area: 702 sq. km.; 4 major island groups totalling 607 islands
Coastline: 6,112 km
Climate: tropical; heavy rainfall all year long, particularly in the eastern islands

Environment: occasional severe typhoons mostly from June to Dec.
Terrain: varies from high, mountainous islands to low coral atolls; volcanic outcroppings
Land Use: n.a.
Location: Oceania, in the N Pacific Ocean

■ **PEOPLE**

Population: 129,658 (July 1998 est.)
Nationality: Micronesian
Age Structure: n.a.
Population Growth Rate: 3.31% (1998 est.)
Net Migration: 11.65 migrants/1,000 population (1998 est.)
Ethnic Groups: 9 Micronesian and Polynesian groups
Languages: English (offical and common), local languages including Pohnpeian, Yapese, Trukese and Kosrean
Religions: Roman Catholic 50%, Protestant 47%, other or none 3%
Birth Rate: 27.55/1,000 population (1998 est.)
Death Rate: 6.07/1,000 population (1998 est.)
Infant Mortality: 34.51 deaths/1,000 live births (1998 est.)
Life Expectancy at Birth: 66.38 years male, 70.34 years female (1998 est.)
Total Fertility Rate: 3.9 children born/woman (1998 est.)
Literacy: 89% (1998 est.)

■ **GOVERNMENT**

Leader(s): Pres. Leo Falcam; V.Pres. Redley Killion
Government Type: constitutional government in free association with the United States
Administrative Divisions: 4 states
Nationhood: Nov. 3, 1986 (from US-administered UN Trusteeship)
National Holiday: Proclamation of the Federated States of Micronesia, May 10

■ **ECONOMY**

Overview: mostly subsistence farming and fishing; few economically viable mineral deposits; region's remote location and lack of adequate facilities hinders development of the tourism potential. The islands are considerably dependant on financial assistance from the US
GDP: $220 million, per capita $1,760; real growth rate 1% (1996 est.)
Inflation: n.a.
Industries: fish processing, crafts, tourism, construction
Labour Force: n.a.; two-thirds are government employees
Unemployment: n.a.

Agriculture: pepper, tropical fruits and vegetables, coconuts, pigs, chickens
Natural Resources: forests, marine products, deep-sea minerals

■ FINANCE/TRADE

Currency: US dollar ($) = 100 cents
International Reserves Excluding Gold: $82 million (Mar. 1998)
Gold Reserves: n.a.
Budget: revenues $45 million; expenditures $32 million, including capital expenditures n.a. (1995 est.)
Defence Expenditures: n.a.
Education Expenditures: n.a.
External Debt: $129 million
Exports: $73 million (1996 est.); commodities: fish, garments, bananas, pepper; partners: Japan, US, Guam
Imports: $168 million (1996 est.); commodities: food, manufactures, machinery and equipment, beverages; partners: US, Japan, Australia

■ COMMUNICATIONS

Daily Newspapers: n.a.
Televisions: n.a.
Radios: n.a.
Telephones: n.a.

■ TRANSPORTATION

Motor Vehicles: n.a.
Roads: 240 km; 42 km paved
Railway: none
Air Traffic: n.a.
Airports: 6.5 paved runways (1997 est.)

Canadian Embassy: The Canadian Embassy to the Federated States of Micronesia, c/o The Canadian Embassy, 9th and 11th Floors, Allied Bank Centre, 6754 Ayala Ave., Makati City, Manila, Philippines. Tel: (011-63-2) 867-0001. Fax: (011-63-2) 810-8839.

Embassy in Canada: c/o The Embassy of the Republic of the Philippines, 130 Albert St, Suite 606, Ottawa, ON K1P 5G4. Tel: (613) 233-1121. Fax: (613) 233-4165.

Moldova

Long-Form Name: Republic of Moldova
Capital: Chisinau

■ GEOGRAPHY

Area: 33,700 sq. km
Coastline: none: landlocked
Climate: mild sunny winters; warm rainy summers; long dry autumns

Environment: heavy use of agricultural chemicals, including banned pesticides such as DDT, has contaminated ground water and soil; erosion severe due to poor farming methods
Terrain: hilly plains in north; southern steppe
Land Use: 53% arable, 14% permanent crops, 13% permanent pastures, 13% forest, 7% other, includes 5% irrigated
Location: E Europe

■ PEOPLE

Population: 4,457,729 (July 1998 est.)
Nationality: Moldovan
Age Structure: 0-14 yrs: 25%; 15-64: 65%; 65+: 10% (1998 est.)
Population Growth Rate: 0.04% (1998 est.)
Net Migration: -1.54 migrants/1,000 population (1998 est.)
Ethnic Groups: 64.5% Moldavian, 13.8% Ukrainian, 13% Russian, 3.5% Gagauz, 1.5% Jews, 3.7% other
Languages: Moldavan (official), Russian, Ukrainian, Gagauz (a Turkish dialect)
Religions: 98.5% Eastern Orthodox, 1.5% Jewish, minority Baptists (note that almost all churchgoers are ethnic Moldovan; the Slavic population are not churchgoers)
Birth Rate: 14.35/1,000 population (1998 est.)
Death Rate: 12.42/1,000 population (1998 est.)
Infant Mortality: 43.72 deaths/1,000 live births (1998 est.)
Life Expectancy at Birth: 59.61 years male, 69.27 years female (1998 est.)
Total Fertility Rate: 1.88 children born/woman (1998 est.)
Literacy: 96% (1997 est.)

■ GOVERNMENT

Leader(s): Pres. Petru Lucinschi, Prem. Ion Sturza
Government Type: republic
Administrative Divisions: previously divided into 40 rayons; to be divided into fewer, larger districts at unspecified future date
Nationhood: Aug. 27, 1991 (from Soviet Union)
National Holiday: Independence Day, Aug. 27

■ ECONOMY

Overview: predominantly agricultural, with important manufacturing sector; Moldova has a climate favourable to agriculture, and this is where the bulk of economic development has taken place
GDP: $10.8 billion, per capita $2,400; real growth rate -2% (1997 est.)
Inflation: 7.6% (May 1998)
Industries: accounts for 36% of GDP; machinery

and appliances, hosiery, refined sugar, vegetable oil, canned food, shoes, textiles
Labour Force: 2 million (1997 est.); 40.5% agriculture, 20.6% services, 19.2% industry
Unemployment: 1.4%; also large numbers of underemployed (Mar. 1997)
Agriculture: accounts for 42% of GDP; grapes and other fruits, vegetables, sugar, wheat and cereal grains, tobacco, oil, essential oil crops
Natural Resources: lignite, phosphorites, gypsum

■ FINANCE/TRADE

Currency: leu (pl. lei)
International Reserves Excluding Gold: $143 million (Dec. 1998)
Gold Reserves: n.a.
Budget: revenues $570 million; expenditures $645 million, including capital expenditures of n.a. (1997 est.)
Defence Expenditures: 2.5% of GDP (1995)
Education Expenditures: 6.1% of GNP (1995)
External Debt: more than 1 billion (1997)
Exports: $650 million (1998); wine, grapes, other agricultural products, machinery, pumps
Imports: $1.081 billion (1998); fuels, metals and metal products, consumer products, foodstuffs

■ COMMUNICATIONS

Daily Newspapers: 4 (1996)
Televisions: 281/1,000 inhabitants (1996)
Radios: 720/1,000 inhabitants (1996)
Telephones: 13.6/1,000 inhabitants (1996 est.)

■ TRANSPORTATION

Motor Vehicles: n.a.
Roads: 12,300 km; 10,738 km hard-surfaced
Railway: 1,328 km, which does not include industrial lines
Air Traffic: 170,000 passengers carried (1996 est.)
Airports: 26; 8 have paved runways (1997 est.)

Canadian Embassy: The Canadian Embassy to Moldova, c/o The Canadian Embassy, P.O. Box 117, Post Office No. 22, 71118 Bucharest, Romania. Tel: (011-40-1) 222-9845. Fax: (011-40-1) 312-9680.
Embassy in Canada: Embassy of the Republic of Moldova, 2101 S. Street NW, Washington DC 20008, USA. Tel: (202) 667-1130. Fax: (202) 667-1204.

Monaco

Long-Form Name: Principality of Monaco
Capital: Monaco

■ GEOGRAPHY

Area: 1.9 sq. km
Coastline: 4.1 km
Climate: Mediterranean with mild, wet winters and hot, dry summers
Environment: almost entirely urban
Terrain: hilly, rugged, rocky
Land Use: almost 100% urban
Location: W Europe, bordering on Mediterranean Sea

■ PEOPLE

Population: 32,035 (July 1998 est.)
Nationality: Monegasque or Monacan
Age Structure: 0-14 yrs: 17%; 15-64: 64%; 65+: 19% (1998 est.)
Population Growth Rate: 0.4% (1998 est.)
Net Migration: 5.18 migrants/1,000 population (1998 est.)
Ethnic Groups: 47% French, 16% Monegasque, 16% Italian, 21% other
Languages: French (official), English, Italian, Monegasque
Religions: 95% Roman Catholic
Birth Rate: 10.71/1,000 population (1998 est.)
Death Rate: 11.86/1,000 population (1998 est.)
Infant Mortality: 6.6 deaths/1,000 live births (1998 est.)
Life Expectancy at Birth: 74.79 years male, 82.21 years female (1998 est.)
Total Fertility Rate: 1.7 children born/woman (1998 est.)
Literacy: 99% (1997 est.)

■ GOVERNMENT

Leader(s): Chief of State Prince Rainier III, Min. of State Michel Leveque
Government Type: constitutional monarchy
Administrative Divisions: 4 districts (quarters)
Nationhood: 1419, rule by the House of Grimaldi
National Holiday: National Day, Nov. 19

■ ECONOMY

Overview: a popular resort, attracting tourists to its casinos and pleasant climate; no income tax and low business taxes make it a tax haven; no data is published on the economy
GDP: adjusted for purchasing power parity: $800 million, per capita $25,000; real growth rate n.a. (1996 est.)
Inflation: n.a.
Industries: pharmaceuticals, food processing, precision instruments, glassmaking, printing, tourism
Labour Force: n.a.
Unemployment: negligible (1996)
Agriculture: none
Natural Resources: none

■ FINANCE/TRADE

Currency: French franc (F) = 100 centimes
International Reserves Excluding Gold: n.a.
Gold Reserves: n.a.
Budget: revenues $623.3 million; expenditures $638.7 million, including capital expenditures n.a. (1995 est.)
Defence Expenditures: defence is the responsibility of France
Education Expenditures: n.a.
External Debt: n.a.
Exports: n.a.
Imports: n.a.

■ COMMUNICATIONS

Daily Newspapers: 1 (1996)
Televisions: 727/1,000 inhabitants (1996)
Radios: 1,021/1,000 inhabitants (1996)
Telephones: n.a.

■ TRANSPORTATION

Motor Vehicles: 21,000; 17,000 passenger cars (1997 est.)
Roads: 50 km paved city streets only
Railway: 1.7 km
Air Traffic: 44,000 passengers carried (1996)
Airports: Monaco is linked to the airport in Nice, France, by helicopter service

Canadian Embassy: The Canadian Consulate General, c/o The Canadian Embassy, 35 av Montaigne, 75008 Paris, France. Tel: (011-33-1) 44-43-22-51. Fax: (011-33-1) 44-43-29-99.
Embassy in Canada: Consulate of Monaco, 1155 Sherbrooke St W, Ste 1500, Montreal PQ H3A 2W1. Tel: (514) 849-0589. Fax: (514) 631-2771.

Mongolia

Long-Form Name: Mongolia
Capital: Ulan Bator

■ GEOGRAPHY

Area: 1,565,000 sq. km
Coastline: none: landlocked
Climate: desert; continental (large daily and seasonal temperature ranges)
Environment: harsh and rugged; water resources are severly limited; deforestation is a problem; spring dust storms are a natural hazard
Terrain: vast semidesert and desert plains; mountains in west and southwest; Gobi desert in southeast
Land Use: 1% arable; 0% permanent; 80% meadows; 9% forest; 10% other
Location: N Asia

■ PEOPLE

Population: 2,578,530 (July 1998 est.)
Nationality: Mongolian
Age Structure: 0-14 yrs: 37%; 15-64: 59%; 65+: 4% (1998 est.)
Population Growth Rate: 1.54% (1998 est.)
Net Migration: 0 migrants/1,000 population (1998 est.)
Ethnic Groups: 90% Mongol, 4% Kazakh, 2% Chinese, 2% Russian, 2% other
Languages: Kazakh and Khalkha Mongol is spoken by over 90% of population; minor languages include Turkic, Russian, Chinese and English
Religions: no state religion; predominantly Buddhist Lamaism and Shamanism, Islam 4%
Birth Rate: 23.56/1,000 population (1998 est.)
Death Rate: 8.19/1,000 population (1998 est.)
Infant Mortality: 66.34 deaths/1,000 live births (1998 est.)
Life Expectancy at Birth: 59.4 years male, 63.61 years female (1998 est.)
Total Fertility Rate: 2.75 children born/woman (1998 est.)
Literacy: 82.9% (1997 est.)

■ GOVERNMENT

Leader(s): Pres. Natsagiin Bagabandi, Prime Min. Rinchinnyamiyn Amarjargal
Government Type: republic
Administrative Divisions: 18 provinces and 3 municipalities
Nationhood: Mar. 13, 1921 (from China; formerly known as Outer Mongolia)
National Holiday: National Day, July 11

■ ECONOMY

Overview: severe climate, widely dispersed population and largely unproductive land have hindered economic development; one-quarter of the population lives below the poverty line; traditionally based on agriculture and the breeding of livestock (has highest number of livestock per person in the world); recently extensive mineral resources have been developed
GDP: $5.6 billion, per capita $2,200; average real growth rate 3.3% (1997 est.)
Inflation: 15.4% (Mar. 1998)
Industries: accounts for 32% of GDP; processing of animal products, building materials, food and beverage, mining (particularly coal), copper
Labour Force: 1.1 million (1997 est.); 39.9% agriculture, 21% industry, 39.2% services
Unemployment: 15% (1997 est.)
Agriculture: accounts for 34% of GDP; 90% of exports, and provides livelihood for about 50%

of the population; livestock raising predominates (sheep, goats, horses); crops—wheat, barley, potatoes, forage

Natural Resources: coal, copper, molybdenum, tungsten, phosphates, tin, nickel, zinc, wolfram, fluorspar, gold

■ FINANCE/TRADE

Currency: tughrik (Tug) = 100 mongos

International Reserves Excluding Gold: $79 million (Jan. 1999)

Gold Reserves: 0.032 million fine troy ounces (Jan. 1999)

Budget: revenues $1.5 billion; expenditures $1.3 billion, including capital expenditures n.a. (1995 est.)

Defence Expenditures: 1.7% of GDP (1997)

Education Expenditures: 5.6% of GNP (1995)

External Debt: $524 million (1996)

Exports: $418 million (1997); commodities: livestock, animal products, wool, hides, fluorspar, nonferrous metals, minerals; partners: former USSR countries 80%

Imports: $443 million (1997); commodities: machinery and equipment, fuels, food products, industrial consumer goods, chemicals, building materials, sugar, tea; partners: former USSR countries 80%

■ COMMUNICATIONS

Daily Newspapers: 4 (1996)

Televisions: 46/1,000 inhabitants (1996)

Radios: 139/1,000 inhabitants (1996)

Telephones: 3.8/100 inhabitants (1996 est.)

■ TRANSPORTATION

Motor Vehicles: n.a.

Roads: 49,200 km; 3,730 km paved

Railway: 1,928 km

Air Traffic: 662,000 passengers carried (1996)

Airports: 34; 8 have paved runways (1997 est.)

Canadian Embassy: The Canadian Embassy to Mongolia, c/o The Canadian Embassy, 19 Dong Zhi Men Wai St, Chao Yang District, Beijing 100600, China. Tel: (011-976-1) 327-586. Fax: (011-976-1) 325-530.

Embassy in Canada: Embassy of Mongolia, 2833 M St NW, Washington DC 20007, USA. Tel: (202) 333-7117. Fax: (202) 298-9227.

Montserrat

Long-Form Name: Montserrat

Capital: Plymouth (abandoned in 1997 due to volcanic activity)

■ GEOGRAPHY

Area: 100 sq. km

Climate: tropical, no well-defined rainy season; June to Nov. hottest; prone to hurricanes

Land Use: 20% arable, 0% permanent crops, 10% meadows and pastures, 40% forests, 30% other

Location: West Indies

■ PEOPLE

Population: 12,828 (July 1998 est.)

Nationality: Montserratian

Ethnic Groups: descendants of British, French, Irish settlers; also black

Languages: English (official)

■ GOVERNMENT

Colony Territory of: Crown Colony of the United Kingdom

Leader(s): Chief of State: Queen Elizabeth II, Gov. John Abbott, Chief Min. Bertrand B. Osborne

Government Type: dependent territory of the UK

National Holiday: Celebration of the Birthday of the Queen, second Saturday in June

■ ECONOMY

Overview: manufacturing accounts for 85% of exports: leather goods, cotton clothing, electronics, plastic bags, herbal teas, ornamental plants, tropical fruit; the economy is heavily dependent on imports, making it vulnerable to fluctuations in world prices. Ongoing major volcanic activity is hindering economic activity

■ FINANCE/TRADE

Currency: Eastern Caribbean dollar = 100 cents

Canadian Embassy: c/o Macdonald House, 1 Grosvenor Square, London WIX OAB, England, UK. Tel: (011-44-171) 258-6600. Fax: (011-44-171) 258-6333.

Representative to Canada: c/o High Commission for the Countries of the Organization of Eastern Caribbean States, 112 Kent St, Ste 1610, Place de Ville, Tower B, Ottawa ON K1P 5P2. Tel: (613) 236-8952. Fax: (613) 236-3042.

Morocco

Long-Form Name: Kingdom of Morocco

Capital: Rabat

■ GEOGRAPHY

Area: 446,550 sq. km

Coastline: 1,835 km
Climate: Mediterranean, becoming more extreme in the interior
Environment: northern mountains geologically unstable and subject to earthquakes; desertification; unsafe water supply; land degradation
Terrain: mostly mountains with rich coastal plains
Land Use: 21% arable; 1% permanent crops; 47% permanent pastures; 20% forest; 11% other, includes 3% irrigated
Location: N Africa, bordering on Atlantic Ocean

■ PEOPLE

Population: 29,114,497 (July 1998 est.)
Nationality: Moroccan
Age Structure: 0-14 yrs: 36%; 15-64: 59%; 65+: 5% (1998 est.)
Population Growth Rate: 1.89% (1998 est.)
Net Migration: -1.28 migrants/1,000 population (1998 est.)
Ethnic Groups: 99.1% Arab-Berber, 0.7% non-Morrocan, 0.2% Jewish
Languages: Arabic (official); several Berber dialects; French is language of business, government, diplomacy and post-primary education
Religions: 98.7% Sunni Muslim, 1.1% Christian, 0.2% Jewish
Birth Rate: 26.37/1,000 population (1998 est.)
Death Rate: 6.24/1,000 population (1998 est.)
Infant Mortality: 52.99 deaths/1,000 live births (1998 est.)
Life Expectancy at Birth: 66.49 years male, 70.64 years female (1997 est.)
Total Fertility Rate: 3.35 children born/woman (1998 est.)
Literacy: 43.7% (1997 est.)

■ GOVERNMENT

Leader(s): Prime Min. Abderrahmane Youssoufi, King Sidi Mohammed VI
Government Type: constitutional monarchy
Administrative Divisions: 37 provinces and 2 municipalities
Nationhood: Mar. 2, 1956 (from France)
National Holiday: National Day (anniversary of King Hassan II's accession to the throne), Mar. 3

■ ECONOMY

Overview: Morocco faces the problems typical of developing countries: restraining government spending, reducing constraints on private activity and foreign trade, and keeping inflation manageable.

GDP: adjusted for purchasing power parity: $107 billion, per capita $3,500; real growth rate - 2.2% (1997 est.)
Inflation: 3.2% (Apr. 1998)
Industries: accounts for 33% of GDP, phosphate rock mining and processing, food processing, leather goods, textiles, construction, tourism
Labour Force: 11.3 million (1997 est.); 45.6% agriculture, 29.4% services, 25% industry
Unemployment: 16% (1997 est.)
Agriculture: accounts for 14% of GDP; 50% of employment and 30% of export value; not self-sufficient in food; cereal farming and livestock raising predominate; barley, wheat, citrus fruit, wine, vegetables, olives
Natural Resources: phosphates, iron ore, manganese, lead, zinc, fish, salt

■ FINANCE/TRADE

Currency: dirham (DH) = 100 centimes
International Reserves Excluding Gold: $4.290 billion (Jan. 1999)
Gold Reserves: 0.704 million fine troy ounces (Jan. 1999)
Budget: revenues $10.4 billion; expenditures $10.75 billion, including capital expenditures n.a. (1996 est.)
Defence Expenditures: 3.7% of GDP (1996)
Education Expenditures: 5.6% of GNP (1995)
External Debt: $21.767 billion (1996)
Exports: $6.832 billion (1998 est.); commodities: food and beverages 30%, semiprocessed goods 23%, consumer goods 21%, phosphates 17%; partners: European Community 58%, India 7%, Japan 5%, former USSR countries 3%, US 2%
Imports: $9.883 billion (1998 est.); commodities: capital goods 24%, semi-processed goods 22%, raw materials 16%, fuel and lubricants 16%, food and beverages 13%, consumer goods 10%; partners: European Community 53%, US 11%, Canada 4%, Iraq 3%, former USSR countries 3%, Japan 2%

■ COMMUNICATIONS

Daily Newspapers: 22 (1996)
Televisions: 111/1,000 inhabitants (1996)
Radios: 241/1,000 inhabitants (1996)
Telephones: 4.8/100 inhabitants (1996 est.)

■ TRANSPORTATION

Motor Vehicles: 1,380,000; 1,040,000 passenger cars (1997 est.)
Roads: 60,626 km; 30,556 km paved
Railway: 1,907 km
Air Traffic: 2,301,000 passengers carried (1996)
Airports: 70; 26 have paved runways (1997 est.)

Canadian Embassy: The Canadian Embassy, 13 bis, rue Jaafar As-Sadik; Rabat-Agdal; mailing address: CP 709, Rabat-Agdal, Morocco. Tel: (011-212-7) 67-28-80. Fax: (011-212-7) 67-21-87.
Embassy in Canada: Embassy of the Kingdom of Morocco, 38 Range Rd, Ottawa ON K1N 8J4. Tel: (613) 236-7391. Fax: (613) 236-6164.

Mozambique

Long-Form Name: Republic of Mozambique
Capital: Maputo

■ GEOGRAPHY

Area: 801,590 sq. km
Coastline: 2,470 km
Climate: tropical to subtropical
Environment: severe drought and floods occur in south; desertification; water pollution; danger of cyclones
Terrain: mostly coastal lowlands, uplands in centre, high plateaus in northwest, mountains in west
Land Use: 4% arable; negligible permanent; 56% meadows; 18% forest; 22% other
Location: SE Africa, bordering on Mozambique Channel

■ PEOPLE

Population: 18,641,469 (July 1998 est.)
Nationality: Mozambican
Age Structure: 0-14 yrs: 45%; 15-64: 53%; 65+: 2% (1998 est.)
Population Growth Rate: 2.57% (1998 est.)
Net Migration: 0 migrants/1,000 population (1998 est.)
Ethnic Groups: majority from indigenous tribal groups; about 0.06% Europeans, 0.2% Euro-Africans, 0.08% Indians
Languages: Portuguese (official); English; many indigenous dialects
Religions: 50% indigenous beliefs, 30% Christian, 20% Muslim
Birth Rate: 43.52/1,000 population (1998 est.)
Death Rate: 17.81/1,000 population (1998 est.)
Infant Mortality: 120.26 deaths/1,000 live births (1998 est.)
Life Expectancy at Birth: 44.22 years male, 46.55 years female (1998 est.)
Total Fertility Rate: 6.0 children born/woman (1998 est.)
Literacy: 40.1% (1997 est.)

■ GOVERNMENT

Leader(s): Pres. Joaquím Alberto Chissano, Prime Min. Pascoal Manuel Mocumbi

Government Type: republic
Administrative Divisions: 10 provinces
Nationhood: June 25, 1975 (from Portugal)
National Holiday: Independence Day, June 25

■ ECONOMY

Overview: internal disorder, lack of government administrative control and a growing foreign debt have contributed to the country's failure to exploit the economic potential of its agricultural, hydropower and transportation resources; depends on much foreign aid; industry operates at only 20–40% of capacity
GDP: $14.6 billion, per capita $800; real growth rate 8% (1997 est.)
Inflation: 1.6% (Mar. 1998)
Industries: accounts for 13% of GDP; food, beverages, chemicals (fertilizer, soap, paints), petroleum products, textiles, nonmetallic mineral products (cement, glass, asbestos), tobacco
Labour Force: 9.2 million (1997 est.); 84.5% agriculture, 7.4% industry, 8.1% services
Unemployment: n.a.
Agriculture: accounts for 35% of GDP, over 90% of labour force and about 90% of exports; cash crops—cotton, cashew nuts, sugar cane, tea, shrimp; other crops—cassava, corn, rice, tropical fruit; not self-sufficient in food
Natural Resources: coal, titanium

■ FINANCE/TRADE

Currency: metical (pl. meticais) (Mt) = 100 centavos
International Reserves Excluding Gold: $608 million (Dec. 1998)
Gold Reserves: n.a.
Budget: revenues $324 million; expenditures $600 million, including capital expenditures $310 million (1996 est.)
Defence Expenditures: 3.7% (1996)
Education Expenditures: n.a.
External Debt: $5.7 billion (1997)
Exports: $169 million (1995); commodities: shrimp 48%, cashews 21%, sugar 10%, copra 3%, citrus 3%; partners: US, Western Europe, Germany, Japan
Imports: $784 million (1995); commodities: food, clothing, farm equipment, petroleum; partners: US, Western Europe, former USSR countries

■ COMMUNICATIONS

Daily Newspapers: 2 (1996)
Televisions: 4.5/1,000 inhabitants (1996)
Radios: 39/1,000 inhabitants (1996)
Telephones: 0.3/100 inhabitants (1996 est.)

■ TRANSPORTATION

Motor Vehicles: 88,800; 67,600 passenger cars (1997 est.)
Roads: 30,400 km; 5,685 km paved
Railway: 3,131 km
Air Traffic: 163,000 passengers carried (1996)
Airports: 174; 22 have paved runways (1997 est.)

Canadian Embassy: The Canadian Embassy, avenida Julius Nyerere, No. 1128, Maputo; mailing address: P.O. Box 1578, Maputo, Mozambique. Tel: (011-258-1) 492-623. Fax: (011-258-1) 492-667.
Embassy in Canada: High Commission for the Republic of Mozambique, 1900 M St NW, Ste 570, Washington DC 20036, USA. Tel: (202) 293-7146. Fax: (202) 835-0245.

Myanmar

Long-Form Name: Union of Myanmar (formerly Burma)
Capital: Rangoon

■ GEOGRAPHY

Area: 678,500 sq. km
Coastline: 1,930 km
Climate: tropical monsoon; cloudy, rainy, hot, humid summers (southwest monsoon, June to Sept.); less cloudy, scant rainfall, mild temperatures, lower humidity during winter (northeast monsoon, Dec. to Apr.)
Environment: subject to destructive earthquakes and cyclones; flooding and landslides common during rainy season (June to Sept.); deforestation
Terrain: central lowlands ringed by steep, rugged highlands
Land Use: 15% arable land; 1% permanent crops; 1% meadows and pastures; 49% forest and woodland; 34% other, includes 2% irrigated
Location: SE Asia, bordering on Bay of Bengal

■ PEOPLE

Population: 47,305,319 (July 1998 est.)
Nationality: Burmese
Age Structure: 0-14 yrs: 36%; 15-64: 59%; 65+: 5% (1998 est.)
Population Growth Rate: 1.65% (1998 est.)
Net Migration: 0 migrants/1,000 population (1998 est.)
Ethnic Groups: 68% Burmese, 9% Shan, 7% Karen, 4% Rakhine, 3% Chinese, 2% Mon, 2% Indian, 5% other
Languages: Myanmar (Burmese); minority ethnic groups have their own languages

Religions: 89% Buddhist, 11% animist beliefs, Muslim, Christian or other
Birth Rate: 28.96/1,000 population (1998 est.)
Death Rate: 12.51/1,000 population (1998 est.)
Infant Mortality: 78.35 deaths/1,000 live births (1998 est.)
Life Expectancy at Birth: 53.03 years male, 56.08 years female (1998 est.)
Total Fertility Rate: 3.7 children born/woman (1998 est.)
Literacy: 83.1% (1997 est.)

■ GOVERNMENT

Leader(s): Chairman and Prime Min. General Than Shwe
Government Type: military regime
Administrative Divisions: 7 divisions, 7 states
Nationhood: Jan. 4, 1948 (from UK)
National Holiday: Independence Day, Jan. 4

■ ECONOMY

Overview: economy is dependent on agriculture and is vulnerable to world market conditions (especially for rice); Myanmar has been unable to achieve much improvement in export earnings due to falling prices for many of its export commodities
GDP: $55.7 billion, per capita $1,190; real growth rate 6% (1997 est.)
Inflation: 50.8% (Apr. 1998)
Industries: accounts for 10% of GDP; agricultural processing; textiles and footwear; wood and wood products; petroleum refining; mining of copper, tin, tungsten, iron; construction materials; pharmaceuticals; fertilizer
Labour Force: 23.4 million (1997 est.); 69.1% agriculture, 8.9% trade and tourism, 7.2% industry
Unemployment: n.a.
Agriculture: accounts for 61% of GDP; self-sufficient in food; principal crops: rice, corn, oilseed, sugar cane, pulses; world's largest stand of hardwood trees; rice and teak account for 55% of exports; world's largest producer of opium poppies
Natural Resources: crude oil, timber, tin, antimony, zinc, copper, tungsten, lead, coal, some marble, limestone, precious stones, natural gas

■ FINANCE/TRADE

Currency: kyat (K) = 100 pyas
International Reserves Excluding Gold: $337 million (Jan. 1999)
Gold Reserves: 0.231 million fine troy ounces (Jan. 1999)

Budget: revenues $7.9 billion; expenditures $12.2 billion, including capital expenditures $5.7 billion (1996-97 est.)
Defence Expenditures: 36.14% of govt. expenditure (1996)
Education Expenditures: 12.45% of govt. expenditure (1996)
External Debt: $5.184 billion (1996)
Exports: $866 million (1997); commodities: teak, rice, oilseed, metals, rubber, gems; partners: Southeast Asia, India, China, European Community, Africa
Imports: $2.037 billion (1997); commodities: machinery, transport equipment, chemicals, food products; partners: Japan, European Community, CEMA, China, Southeast Asia

■ COMMUNICATIONS

Daily Newspapers: 5 (1996)
Televisions: 5.4/1,000 inhabitants (1996)
Radios: 89/1,000 inhabitants (1996)
Telephones: 0.4/100 inhabitants (1996 est.)

■ TRANSPORTATION

Motor Vehicles: 69,000; 35,000 passenger cars (1997 est.)
Roads: 28,200 km; 3,440 km paved
Railway: 3,569 km
Air Traffic: 334,000 passengers carried (1996)
Airports: 80; 24 have paved runways (1997 est.)

Canadian Embassy: The Canadian Embassy to Myanmar, c/o The Canadian Embassy, 11th Floor, Boonmitr Bldg, 138 Silom Rd, Bangkok 10500; mailing address: P.O. Box 2090, Bangkok 10500, Thailand. Tel: (011-66-2) 636-0540. Fax: (011-66-2) 636-0565.
Embassy in Canada: Embassy of the Union of Myanmar, 85 Range Rd, Ste 902, Ottawa ON K1N 8J6. Tel: (613) 232-6434. Fax: (613) 232-6435.

Namibia

Long-Form Name: Republic of Namibia
Capital: Windhoek

■ GEOGRAPHY

Area: 825,418 sq. km
Coastline: 1,572 km
Climate: desert; hot, dry; rainfall sparse and erratic
Environment: inhospitable with very limited natural water resources; drought and desertification
Terrain: mostly high plateau; Namib Desert along coast; Kalahari Desert in east

Land Use: 1% arable; 0% permanent crops; 46% permanent pastures; 22% forest; 31% other
Location: SW Africa, bordering on South Atlantic Ocean

■ PEOPLE

Population: 1,622,328 (July 1998 est.)
Nationality: Namibian
Age Structure: 0-14 yrs: 44%; 15-64: 52%; 65+: 4% (1998 est.)
Population Growth Rate: 1.6% (1998 est.)
Net Migration: 0 migrants/1,000 population (1998 est.)
Ethnic Groups: 86% black, 6.6% white, 7.4% mixed; about 50% of the population belong to the Ovambo tribe and 9% to the Kavangos tribe
Languages: white population: 60% Afrikaans, 33% German, 7% English (all official); several indigenous languages
Religions: 90% Christian, 10% traditional religions
Birth Rate: 35.84/1,000 population (1998 est.)
Death Rate: 19.82/1,000 population (1998 est.)
Infant Mortality: 66.76 deaths/1,000 live births (1998 est.)
Life Expectancy at Birth: 41.73 years male, 41.24 years female (1998 est.)
Total Fertility Rate: 4.99 children born/woman (1998 est.)
Literacy: 38% (1997 est.)

■ GOVERNMENT

Leader(s): Pres. Sam Nujoma, Prime Min. Hage Geingob
Government Type: republic
Administrative Divisions: 13 regions
Nationhood: Mar. 21, 1990 (from South Africa)
National Holiday: Independence Day, Mar. 21

■ ECONOMY

Overview: economy is very dependent on the mining industry to extract and process minerals for export; world's fifth largest producer of uranium; rich diamond deposits; more than 50% of the population depends on subsistence agriculture
GDP: $6.2 billion, per capita $3,700; real growth rate 1.5% (1996 est.)
Inflation: 4.5% (Mar. 1998)
Industries: meat packing, fish processing, dairy products; mining accounts for 20% of GDP (copper, lead, zinc, diamonds, uranium)
Labour Force: 1 million (1997 est.); 43.5% agriculture, 21.9% industry, 34.8% services
Unemployment: 30-40%, including underemployment (1997 est.)
Agriculture: accounts for 15% of GDP (including

fishing); mostly subsistence farming; livestock raising major source of cash income; crops: millet, sorghum, peanuts; large unfulfilled fish catch potential; needs to import food
Natural Resources: diamonds, copper, uranium, gold, lead, tin, zinc, salt, vanadium, natural gas, fish; suspected deposits of coal and iron ore

▣ FINANCE/TRADE

Currency: Namibian dollar = 100 cents
International Reserves Excluding Gold: $321 million (Jan. 1999)
Gold Reserves: none (Jan. 1999)
Budget: revenues $1.1 billion; expenditures $1.2 billion, including capital expenditures of $193 million (1996–97 est.)
Defence Expenditures: 3.0% of GDP (1996)
Education Expenditures: 9.4% of GNP (1995)
External Debt: about $315 million (1996 est.)
Exports: $1.45 billion (1996 est.); commodities: diamonds, uranium, zinc, copper, meat, processed fish, karakul skins; partners: South Africa, UK, Spain, Japan
Imports: $1.55 billion (1996 est.); commodities: foodstuffs, manufactured consumer goods, machinery and equipment; partners: South Africa, Germany, US, Japan

▣ COMMUNICATIONS

Daily Newspapers: 4 (1996)
Televisions: 48/1,000 inhabitants (1996)
Radios: 143/1,000 inhabitants (1996)
Telephones: 5.5/100 inhabitants (1996 est.)

▣ TRANSPORTATION

Motor Vehicles: 129,000; 62,500 passenger cars (1997 est.)
Roads: 64,799 km; 7,841 km paved
Railway: 2,382 km
Air Traffic: 237,000 passengers carried (1996)
Airports: 135; 22 have paved runways (1997 est.)

Canadian Embassy: The Canadian High Commission to Namibia, c/o The Canadian High Commission, 1103 Arcadia St, Hatfield 0083, Pretoria; mailing address: Private Bag X13, Hatfield 0083, Pretoria, South Africa. Tel.: (011-27-12) 422-3000. Fax: (011-27-12) 422-3052.
Embassy in Canada: High Commission for the Republic of Namibia, 1605 New Hampshire Ave NW, Washington DC 20009, USA. Tel: (202) 986-0540. Fax: (202) 986-0443.

Nauru

Long-Form Name: Republic of Nauru
Capital: no capital city as such; government offices in Yaren

▣ GEOGRAPHY

Area: 21 sq. km
Coastline: 30 km
Climate: tropical; monsoonal; rainy season (Nov. to Feb.)
Environment: only 53 km south of equator; periodic droughts; water supply limited and unreliable
Terrain: sandy beach rises to fertile ring around raised coral reefs with phosphate plateau in centre
Land Use: 0% arable; 0% permanent; 0% meadows; 0% forest; 100% other
Location: Melanesia, Pacific Ocean

▣ PEOPLE

Population: 10,501 (July 1998 est.)
Nationality: Nauruan
Age Structure: n.a.
Population Growth Rate: 1.33% (1998)
Net Migration: 0.4 migrants/1,000 population (1998 est.)
Ethnic Groups: 58% Nauruan, 26% other Pacific Islander, 8% Chinese, 8% European
Languages: Nauruan, a distinct Pacific Island language (official); English widely understood, spoken and used for most government and commercial purposes
Religions: Christian (two-thirds Nauruan Protestant, one-third Roman Catholic)
Birth Rate: 18.03/1,000 population (1998 est.)
Death Rate: 5.1/1,000 population (1998 est.)
Infant Mortality: 40.6 deaths/1,000 live births (1998 est.)
Life Expectancy at Birth: 64.3 years male, 69.18 years female (1998 est.)
Total Fertility Rate: 2.08 children born/woman (1998 est.)
Literacy: n.a.

▣ GOVERNMENT

Leader(s): Pres. Rene Harris
Government Type: republic
Administrative Divisions: 14 districts
Nationhood: Jan. 31, 1968 (from UN trusteeship under Australia, New Zealand and UK; formerly known as Pleasant Island)
National Holiday: Independence Day, Jan. 31

▣ ECONOMY

Overview: economy depends on revenues from the export of phosphates, the reserves of which are expected to be exhausted by the year 2000; most other resources are imported; has one of the highest per capita incomes in the Third World; the rehabilitation of mined land and the replacement of income from phosphates are serious long-term considerations

GDP: n.a.
Inflation: n.a.
Industries: phosphate mining, financial services, coconuts
Labour Force: n.a.
Unemployment: 0%
Agriculture: coconuts; other agricultural activities are negligble; almost completely dependent on imports for food and water
Natural Resources: phosphates

■ FINANCE/TRADE

Currency: Australian dollar ($A) = 100 cents
International Reserves Excluding Gold: n.a.
Gold Reserves: n.a.
Budget: revenues $23.4 million; expenditures $64.8 million, capital expenditures n.a. (1996)
Defence Expenditures: no formal defence structure
Education Expenditures: n.a.
External Debt: $33.3 million
Exports: n.a.; commodities: phosphates; partners: Australia, New Zealand
Imports: n.a.; commodities: food, fuel, manufacturers, building materials, machinery; partners: Australia, UK, New Zealand, Japan

■ COMMUNICATIONS

Daily Newspapers: 0 (1996)
Televisions: n.a.
Radios: 582/1,000 inhabitants (1996)
Telephones: n.a.

■ TRANSPORTATION

Motor Vehicles: n.a.
Roads: 30 km; 24 km paved
Railway: 3.9 km
Air Traffic: 137,000 passengers carried (1996)
Airports: 1, with a paved runway (1997 est.)

Canadian Embassy: c/o The Canadian High Commission, Commonwealth Ave, Canberra A.C.T. 2600, Australia. Tel: (011-61-2) 6273-3844. Fax: (011-61-2) 6273-3285.
Embassy in Canada: c/o Australian High Commission, 50 O'Connor St, Ste 710, Ottawa ON K1P 6L2. Tel: (613) 236-0841. Fax: (613) 236-4376.

Nepal

Long-Form Name: Kingdom of Nepal
Capital: Kathmandu

■ GEOGRAPHY

Area: 140,800 sq. km
Coastline: none: landlocked

Climate: varies from cool summers and severe winters in north to subtropical summers and mild winters in south
Environment: contains eight of the world's 10 highest peaks; flooding, drought, landslides; deforestation; soil erosion; water pollution
Terrain: flat river plain of the Ganges in south, central hilly region, rugged Himalayas in north
Land Use: 17% arable; negligible permanent crops; 15% meadows; 42% forest; 26% other, includes 6.5% irrigated
Location: SC Asia

■ PEOPLE

Population: 23,698,421 (July 1998 est.)
Nationality: Nepalese
Age Structure: 0-14 yrs: 42%; 15-64: 55%; 65+: 3% (1998 est.)
Population Growth Rate: 2.52% (1998 est.)
Net Migration: 0 migrants/1,000 population (1998 est.)
Ethnic Groups: Newars, Indians, Tibetans, Gurungs, Magars, Tamangs, Bhotias, Rais, Limbus, Sherpas, as well as many smaller groups
Languages: Nepali (official); 20 languages divided into numerous dialects
Religions: 90% Hindu, 5% Buddhist, 3% Muslim, 2% other; only official Hindu state in the world, although no sharp distinction between many Hindu and Buddhist groups; small groups of Muslims and Christians
Birth Rate: 35.66/1,000 population (1998 est.)
Death Rate: 10.44/1,000 population (1998 est.)
Infant Mortality: 75.98 deaths/1,000 live births (1998 est.)
Life Expectancy at Birth: 58.04 years male, 57.74 years female (1998 est.)
Total Fertility Rate: 4.87 children born/woman (1998 est.)
Literacy: 27.5% (1997 est.)

■ GOVERNMENT

Leader(s): King Birendra Bir Bikram Shah Dev, Prime Min. Krishna Prasad Bhattarai
Government Type: parliamentary democracy as of May 12, 1991
Administrative Divisions: 14 zones
Nationhood: 1768, unified by Prithvi Narayan Shah
National Holiday: Birthday of His Majesty the King, Dec. 28

■ ECONOMY

Overview: one of the poorest and most underdeveloped countries in the world; agriculture provides the backbone of the economy, employing more than 80% of the population. There have been attempts to expand into other economic sectors

GDP: $31.1 billion, per capita $1,370; real growth rate 4.2% (1997 est.)

Inflation: 0.7% (Apr. 1998)

Industries: accounts for 21% of GDP; small rice, jute, sugar and oilseed mills, cigarettes, textiles, cement, brick; tourism, carpet production

Labour Force: 10.2 million (1997 est.); 93% agriculture, 6.5% services, 0.6% industry

Unemployment: n.a., but substantial rate of underemployment (1996)

Agriculture: accounts for 40% of GDP and 80% of workforce; farm products—rice, corn, wheat, sugar cane, root crops, milk, buffalo meat; not self-sufficient in food, particularly in drought years

Natural Resources: quartz, water, timber, hydroelectric potential, scenic beauty; small deposits of lignite, copper, cobalt, iron ore

■ FINANCE/TRADE

Currency: rupee (NRs) = 100 paisa

International Reserves Excluding Gold: $731 million (Nov. 1998)

Gold Reserves: 0.153 million fine troy ounces (Nov. 1998)

Budget: revenues $536 million; expenditures $818 million, including capital expenditures n.a. (1996-97 est.)

Defence Expenditures: 4.53% of govt. expenditure (1998)

Education Expenditures: 13.98% of govt. expenditure (1998)

External Debt: $2.6 billion (1997 est.)

Exports: $402 million (1997); commodities: clothing, carpets, leather goods, grain; partners: India 38%, US 23%, UK 6%, other Europe 9%

Imports: $1.720 billion (1997); commodities: petroleum products 20%, fertilizer 11%, machinery 10%; partners: India 36%, Japan 13%, Europe 4%, US 1%

■ COMMUNICATIONS

Daily Newspapers: 29 (1996)

Televisions: 5.4/1,000 inhabitants (1996)

Radios: 37/1,000 inhabitants (1996)

Telephones: 0.4/100 inhabitants (1996 est.)

■ TRANSPORTATION

Motor Vehicles: n.a.

Roads: 7,700 km; 3,196 km paved

Railway: 101 km

Air Traffic: 755,000 passengers carried (1996)

Airports: 45; 5 have paved runways (1997 est.)

Canadian Embassy: The Canadian Embassy to Nepal, c/o The Canadian High Commission, 7/8 Shantipath, Chanakyapuri, New Delhi 110 021; mailing address: The Canadian High Commission, P.O. Box 5207, New Delhi, India. Tel: (011-9771) 415-193. Fax: (011-9771) 410-422.

Embassy in Canada: Embassy of the Kingdom of Nepal, 2131 Leroy Place NW, Washington DC 20008, USA. Tel: (202) 667-4550. Fax: (202) 667-5534.

Netherlands

Long-Form Name: Kingdom of the Netherlands

Capital: Amsterdam; seat of government: The Hague

■ GEOGRAPHY

Area: 37,330 sq. km

Coastline: 451 km

Climate: temperate; marine; cool summers and mild winters

Environment: nearly half of the land area is below sea level and protected from the North Sea by dikes; water and air pollution

Terrain: mostly coastal lowland and reclaimed land (polders); some hills in southeast

Land Use: 27% arable; 1% permanent; 31% permanent pastures; 10% forest; 31% other, includes 15% irrigated

Location: NW Europe, bordering on North Sea

■ PEOPLE

Population: 15,731,112 (July 1998 est.)

Nationality: Dutch

Age Structure: 0-14 yrs: 18%; 15-64: 68%; 65+: 14% (1998 est.)

Population Growth Rate: 0.50% (1998 est.)

Net Migration: 2.11 migrants/1,000 population (1998 est.)

Ethnic Groups: 96% Dutch, 4% Moroccans, Turks and others

Languages: Dutch, Frisian

Religions: 62% Christianity, of which 34% is Roman Catholic and 25% is Protestant; most of the rest do not profess a religion

Birth Rate: 11.62/1,000 population (1998 est.)

Death Rate: 8.68/1,000 population (1998 est.)

Infant Mortality: 5.17 deaths/1,000 live births (1998 est.)

Life Expectancy at Birth: 75.14 years male, 81.03 years female (1998 est.)

Total Fertility Rate: 2.11 children born/woman (1998 est.)

Literacy: 99% (1997 est.)

■ GOVERNMENT

Leader(s): Queen Beatrix; Prime Min. Wim Kok
Government Type: constitutional monarchy
Administrative Divisions: 12 provinces;
dependent areas: Aruba, Netherland Antilles
Nationhood: 1579 (from Spain)
National Holiday: Queen's Day, Apr. 30

■ ECONOMY

Overview: a highly developed and affluent
economy based on private enterprise; numerous
government-backed welfare programs; trade and
financial sectors are the strongest part of the
economy
GDP: $343.9 billion, per capita $22,00; real
growth rate 3.25% (1997 est.)
Inflation: 2.2% (June 1998)
Industries: contributes 18% to the GDP; agro-
industries, metal and engineering products,
electrical machinery and equipment, chemicals,
petroleum, fishing, construction,
microelectronics
Labour Force: 7.1 million (1997 est.); 35.4%
community, social and business services, 19.2%
trade and tourism, 18% industry
Unemployment: 5.4% (Aug. 1998)
Agriculture: accounts for 4% of GDP and 4% of
labour force; animal production predominates;
crops—grains, potatoes, sugar beets, fruits,
vegetables; shortages of grain, fats and oils
Natural Resources: natural gas, crude oil, fertile
soil

■ FINANCE/TRADE

Currency: guilder, gulden or florin (f.) = 100
cents [As of Jan. 1, 1999, Government securities
are issued in Euros (EUR)]
International Reserves Excluding Gold: $11.459
billion (Jan. 1999)
Gold Reserves: 35.532 million fine troy ounces
(Jan. 1999)
Budget: revenues $107.2 billion; expenditures
$118.9 billion, including capital expenditures of
n.a. (1996 est.)
Defence Expenditures: 3.86% of govt.
expenditures (1997)
Education Expenditures: 9.97% total govt.
expenditures (1997)
External Debt: none
Exports: $196.516 billion (1998 est.);
commodities; agricultural products, processed
foods and tobacco, natural gas, chemicals, metal
products, textiles, clothing; partners: European
community 74.9% (Germany 28.3%, Belgium-
Luxembourg 14.2%, France 10.7, UK 10.2%),
US 4.7%
Imports: $181.754 billion (1998 est.);
commodities: raw materials and semifinished

products, consumer goods, transportation
equipment, crude oil, food products; partners:
European Community 63.8% (Germany 26.5%,
Belgium-Luxembourg 23.1%, UK 8.1%), US
7.9%

■ COMMUNICATIONS

Daily Newspapers: 38 (1996)
Televisions: 514/1,000 inhabitants (1996)
Radios: 963/1,000 inhabitants (1996)
Telephones: 53.8/100 inhabitants (1996 est.)

■ TRANSPORTATION

Motor Vehicles: 6,490,000; 5,750,000 passenger
cars (1997 est.)
Roads: 127,000 km; 114,427 km paved
Railway: 2,739 km
Air Traffic: 17,300,000 passengers carried (1997
est.)
Airports: 28; 19 have paved runways (1997 est.)

Canadian Embassy: The Canadian Embassy,
Sophialaan 7, 2514JP, The Hague, Netherlands.
Tel: (011-31-70) 311-1600. Fax: (011-31-70)
311-1620.
Embassy in Canada: Embassy of the Kingdom of
the Netherlands, 350 Albert St, Ste 2020,
Ottawa ON K1R 1A4. Tel: (613) 237-5030.
Fax: (613) 237-6471.

Netherlands Antilles

Long-Form Name: Netherlands Antilles
Capital: Willemstad

■ GEOGRAPHY

Area: 960 sq. km, 2 island groups
Climate: tropical maritime, moderated by
northeasterly trade winds, short rainy season
Land Use: islands mostly too rocky for
agriculture; only 10% is arable land; 0%
permanent crops, 0% meadows and pastures,
0% forest, 90% other
Location: West Indies

■ PEOPLE

Population: 205,693 (July 1998 est.)
Nationality: Netherlands Antillean
Ethnic Groups: mixed African 85%, Carib Indian,
European, Latin, Oriental
Languages: Dutch (official), Papiamento
(derived from Dutch, Spanish, Portuguese),
English

■ GOVERNMENT

Colony Territory of: Dependent Territory of the
Netherlands

Leader(s): Chief of State: Queen Beatrix, Gov. Jaime M. Saleh; Prime Min. Susanne Camelia-Romer
Government Type: dependency with internal self-government
National Holiday: Queen's Day, Apr. 30

■ ECONOMY

Overview: unlike many Latin American countries, the Netherlands Antilles has avoided crushing external debt; Curaçao has one of the largest ship-repair dry docks in the western hemisphere; almost all consumer goods must be imported; chief trading partner: UK

■ FINANCE/TRADE

Currency: Netherlands Antilles guilder, gulden or florin = 100 cents

Canadian Embassy: c/o The Canadian Embassy, 7, 2514JP The Hague, Netherlands. Tel: (011-31-70) 311-1600. Fax: (011-31-70) 311-1620.
Representative to Canada: c/o Embassy of the Kingdom of the Netherlands, 350 Albert St, Ste 2020, Ottawa ON K1R 1A4. Tel: (613) 237-5030. Fax: (613) 237-6471.

New Caledonia

Long-Form Name: Territory of New Caledonia and Dependencies
Capital: Nouméa

■ GEOGRAPHY

Area: 19,060 sq. km (a peninsula and three small islands)
Climate: humid, subtropical maritime, modified by southeast trade winds
Land Use: 0% arable, 0% permanent crops, 12% meadow and pasture, 39% forest and woodland, 49% other
Location: SW Pacific Ocean (Melanesia)

■ PEOPLE

Population: 194,197 (July 1998 est.)
Nationality: New Caledonian
Ethnic Groups: 42.5% Melanesian, 37.1% European, 8.4% Wallisian, 3.8% Polynesian, 3.6% Indonesian, 1.6% Vietnamese, 3% other
Languages: French (official), 28 Melanesian and Polynesian languages

■ GOVERNMENT

Colony Territory of: Overseas Territory of France
Leader(s): Chief of State: Jacques Chirac (France), High Commissioner Thierry Lataste; Pres. Jean Lèques

Government Type: overseas territory of France since 1956
National Holiday: Taking of the Bastille, July 14

■ ECONOMY

Overview: only a negligible portion of the land is arable, and most food must be imported; the backbone of the economy is nickel export

■ FINANCE/TRADE

Currency: CFP franc = 100 centimes

Canadian Embassy: c/o The Canadian Embassy, 35-37 avenue Montaigne 75008 Paris, France. Tel: (011-33-1) 44-43-29-00. Fax: (011-33-1) 44-43-29-99.
Representative to Canada: c/o Embassy of France, 42 Sussex Dr, Ottawa ON K1M 2C9. Tel: (613) 789-1795. Fax: (613) 562-3735.

New Zealand

Long-Form Name: New Zealand
Capital: Wellington

■ GEOGRAPHY

Area: 268,680 sq. km
Coastline: 15,134 km
Climate: temperate with sharp regional contrasts
Environment: earthquakes are common though usually not severe; deforestation and soil degradation are increasing; occasional volcanic activity
Terrain: predominantly mountainous with some large coastal plains
Land Use: 9% arable; 5% permanent crops; 50% meadows and pastures; 28% forest and woodland; 8% other, includes 1% irrigated
Location: SE of Australia, bordering on Tasman Sea, Pacific Ocean

■ PEOPLE

Population: 3,625,388 (July 1998 est.)
Nationality: New Zealander
Age Structure: 0-14 yrs: 23%; 15-64: 65%; 65+: 12% (1998 est.)
Population Growth Rate: 1.04% (1998 est.)
Net Migration: 3.06 migrants/1,000 population (1998 est.)
Ethnic Groups: 88% European, 8.9% Maori, 2.9% Pacific Islander, 0.2% other
Languages: English (official), Maori
Religions: 75% Christian, 18% unspecified, 7% Hindu, Confucian, other
Birth Rate: 14.89/1,000 population (1998 est.)
Death Rate: 7.6/1,000 population (1998 est.)
Infant Mortality: 6.37 deaths/1,000 live births (1998 est.)

Life Expectancy at Birth: 74.35 years male, 80.19 years female (1998 est.)
Total Fertility Rate: 1.91 children born/woman (1998 est.)
Literacy: 99% (1997 est.)

■ GOVERNMENT

Leader(s): Queen Elizabeth II/Gov. Gen. Sir Michael Hardie-Boyes, Prime Min. Jenny Shipley
Government Type: parliamentary democracy
Administrative Divisions: 93 counties, 9 districts, 3 town districts; dependent areas inc.: the Cook Islands, the Kermadec Islands, Niue, the Ross Dependency (uninhabited except for scientific personnel), Tokelau
Nationhood: Sept. 26, 1907 (from UK)
National Holiday: Waitangi Day, Feb. 6

■ ECONOMY

Overview: government has been reorienting from an agrarian to an open, free-market economy that can compete in the global community; inflation has been reduced; growth has been sluggish, unemployment has been at an all-time high
GDP: $63.4 billion, per capita $17,700; real growth rate 2.5% (1997 est.)
Inflation: 1.7% (June 1998)
Industries: accounts for 26% of GDP; food processing, wool production, wood and paper products, textiles, machinery, transportation equipment, banking and insurance, tourism, mining
Labour Force: 1,688,300 (1997); 28.7% community, social and business services, 21.1% trade and tourism, 17% industry
Unemployment: 7.6% (May 1998)
Agriculture: accounts for 7% of GDP and 11% of workforce; livestock predominates: wool, meat, dairy products; crops: wheat, barley, potatoes, pulses, fruit and vegetables; fish; surplus producer of farm products
Natural Resources: natural gas, iron ore, sand, coal, timber, hydroelectricity, gold, limestone

■ FINANCE/TRADE

Currency: New Zealand dollar (NZ$) = 100 cents
International Reserves Excluding Gold: $4.494 billion (Oct. 1998)
Gold Reserves: none (Oct. 1998)
Budget: revenues $22.18 billion; expenditures $20.28 billion, including capital expenditures n.a. (1995–96 est.)
Defence Expenditures: 2.98% of total govt. expenditure (1997)
Education Expenditures: 15.52% of total govt. expenditure (1997)

External Debt: $28.5 billion (1995-96 est.)
Exports: $12.114 billion (1998); commodities: wool, lamb, mutton, beef, fruit, fish, cheese, manufactures, chemicals, forestry products; partners: European Community 18.3%, Japan 17.9%, Australia 17.5%, US 13.5%
Imports: $12.501 billion (1998); commodities: petroleum, consumer goods, motor vehicles, industrial equipment; partners: Australia 19.7%, Japan 16.9%, European Community 16.9%, US 15.3%, Taiwan 3%

■ COMMUNICATIONS

Daily Newspapers: 23 (1996)
Televisions: 521/1,000 inhabitants (1996)
Radios: 1,027/1,000 inhabitants (1996)
Telephones: 49.1/100 inhabitants (1996 est.)

■ TRANSPORTATION

Motor Vehicles: 2,110,000; 1,770,000 passenger cars (1997 est.)
Roads: 92,306 km; 53,568 km paved
Railway: 3,973 km
Air Traffic: 9,597,000 passengers carried (1996)
Airports: 111; 44 have paved runways (1997)

Canadian Embassy: The Canadian High Commission, 61 Molesworth St, 3rd Floor, Thorndon, Wellington; mailing address: P O Box 12049, Thorndon, Wellington, New Zealand. Tel: (011-64-4) 473-9577. Fax: (011-64-4) 471-2082.
Embassy in Canada: New Zealand High Commission, Metropolitan House, 99 Bank St, Ste 727, Ottawa ON K1P 6G3. Tel: (613) 238-5991. Fax: (613) 238-5707.

Nicaragua

Long-Form Name: Republic of Nicaragua
Capital: Managua

■ GEOGRAPHY

Area: 129,494 sq. km
Coastline: 910 km
Climate: tropical in lowlands, cooler in highlands
Environment: subject to destructive earthquakes, volcanoes, landslides and occasional severe hurricanes; deforestation; soil erosion; water pollution
Terrain: extensive Atlantic coastal plains rising to central interior mountains; narrow Pacific coastal plain interrupted by volcanoes
Land Use: 9% arable; 1% permanent; 46% meadows; 27% forest; 17% other
Location: Central (Latin) America, bordering on Caribbean Sea, Pacific Ocean

■ PEOPLE

Population: 4,583,379 (July 1998 est.)
Nationality: Nicaraguan
Age Structure: 0-14 yrs: 44%; 15-64: 53%; 65+: 3% (1998 est.)
Population Growth Rate: 2.92% (1998 est.)
Net Migration: -1.09 migrants/1,000 population (1998 est.)
Ethnic Groups: 69% mestizo, 17% white, 9% black, 5% Indian
Languages: Spanish (official); English- and Indian-speaking minorities on Atlantic coast
Religions: 95% Roman Catholic, 5% Protestant
Birth Rate: 36.04/1,000 population (1998 est.)
Death Rate: 5.8/1,000 population (1998 est.)
Infant Mortality: 42.26 deaths/1,000 live births (1998 est.)
Life Expectancy at Birth: 64.26 years male, 69.08 years female (1998 est.)
Total Fertility Rate: 4.28 children born/woman (1998 est.)
Literacy: 65.7% (1997 est.)

■ GOVERNMENT

Leader(s): Pres. José Arnoldo Aleman Lacayo, V. Pres. Enriqué Bolanos Geyer
Government Type: republic
Administrative Divisions: 15 departments and 2 autonomous regions
Nationhood: Sept. 15, 1821 (from Spain)
National Holiday: Independence Day, Sept. 15

■ ECONOMY

Overview: the economy is based on the export of coffee and cotton; government control is extensive, including the financial system, wholesale purchasing, production, sales, foreign trade and distribution of goods; many shortages; high inflation
GDP: $9.3 billion, per capita $2,100; real growth rate 6% (1997 est.)
Inflation: 10.2% (Mar. 1997)
Industries: accounts for 21% of GDP; food processing, chemicals, metal products, textiles, clothing, petroleum refining and distribution, beverages, footwear
Labour Force: 2.1 million (1997 est.); 37.7% services, 46.5% agriculture, 15.8% industry
Unemployment: 16%; underemployment approximately 36% (1996 est.)
Agriculture: accounts for 34% of GDP; cash crops—coffee, bananas, sugar cane, cotton; food crops—rice, corn, cassava, citrus fruit, beans; variety of animal products—beef, veal, pork, poultry, dairy; war has lowered self-sufficiency in food
Natural Resources: gold, silver, copper, tungsten, lead, zinc, timber, fish

■ FINANCE/TRADE

Currency: gold córdoba ($C) = 100 centavos
International Reserves Excluding Gold: $350 million (Dec. 1998)
Gold Reserves: n.a.
Budget: revenues $389 million; expenditures $551 million, including capital expenditures n.a. (1996 est.)
Defence Expenditures: 1.35% of GDP (1996)
Education Expenditures: n.a.
External Debt: $5.929 billion (1996)
Exports: $632 million (1998 est.); commodities: coffee, cotton, sugar, bananas, seafood, meat, chemicals; partners: CEMA 15%, OECD 75%, others 10%
Imports: $1.485 billion (1998 est.); commodities: petroleum, food, chemicals, machinery, clothing; partners: CEMA 55%, European Community 20%, Latin America 10%, others 10%

■ COMMUNICATIONS

Daily Newspapers: 4 (1996)
Televisions: 73/1,000 inhabitants (1996)
Radios: 283/1,000 inhabitants (1996)
Telephones: 2.7/100 inhabitants (1996 est.)

■ TRANSPORTATION

Motor Vehicles: 148,000; 73,000 passenger cars (1997 est.)
Roads: 18,000 km; 1,818 km paved
Railway: none
Air Traffic: 51,000 passengers carried (1996)
Airports: 185; 13 have paved runways (1997)

Canadian Embassy: The Office of the Canadian Embassy, Costado Oriental de la Casa Nazareth, Una Quadra Arriba, Calle Noval, Managua. Mailing address: The Office of the Canadian Embassy, Apartado Postal 25, Managua, Nicaragua. Tel: (011-505-2) 68-0433. Fax: (011-505-2) 68-0437.
Embassy in Canada: Embassy of the Republic of Nicaragua, 1627 New Hampshire Ave NW, Washington DC 20009, USA. Tel: (202) 939-6537. Fax: (202) 939-6545.

Niger

Long-Form Name: Republic of Niger
Capital: Niamey

■ GEOGRAPHY

Area: 1,267,000 sq. km
Coastline: none: landlocked
Climate: mostly hot, dry, dusty; tropical in extreme south

Environment: recurrent drought and desertification severely affecting marginal agricultural activities; overgrazing; soil erosion
Terrain: desert and sand dunes; hills in north
Land Use: 3% arable land; 0% permanent; 7% meadows; 2% forest; 88% other
Location: WC Africa

■ PEOPLE

Population: 9,671,848 (July 1998 est.)
Nationality: Nigerien
Age Structure: 0-14 yrs: 48%; 15-64: 50%; 65+: 2% (1998 est.)
Population Growth Rate: 2.96% (1998 est.)
Net Migration: 0 migrants/1,000 population (1998 est.)
Ethnic Groups: 56% Hausa; 22% Djerma; 9% Fula; 8% Tuareg; 4% Beri Beri (Kanouri); 1% Arab, Toubou and Gourmantche; about 4,000 French expatriates
Languages: French (official); Hausa (50%), Djerma, also Tuareg, Fulani
Religions: 80% Muslim, remainder indigenous beliefs and Christians
Birth Rate: 53.01/1,000 population (1998 est.)
Death Rate: 23.38/1,000 population (1998 est.)
Infant Mortality: 114.39 deaths/1,000 live births (1998 est.)
Life Expectancy at Birth: 41.83 years male, 41.21 years female (1998 est.)
Total Fertility Rate: 7.3 children born/woman (1998 est.)
Literacy: 13.6% (1997 est.)

■ GOVERNMENT

Leader(s): Pres. Daouda Malam Wanke, Prem. Ibrahim Hassane Mayaki
Government Type: republic
Administrative Divisions: 7 departments; 1 capital district
Nationhood: Aug. 3, 1960 (from France)
National Holiday: Republic Day, Dec. 18

■ ECONOMY

Overview: about 90% of the population is engaged in livestock rearing and farming; depends heavily on exploitation of uranium deposits, thus vulnerable to demand for uranium; increasing external debt is a problem. GDP growth can barely keep pace with the rapid population growth
GDP: adjusted for purchasing power parity: $6.3 billion, per capita $670; real growth rate 4.5% (1997 est.)
Inflation: 3.8% (year-end 1997)
Industries: accounts for 18% of GDP; cement, brick, rice mills, small cotton gins, textiles, chemicals, oilseed presses, slaughterhouses and a few other small light industries; uranium production began in 1971
Labour Force: 4.1 million (1997 est.); 85% agriculture, 2.7% industry, 12.3% services
Unemployment: n.a.
Agriculture: accounts for 41% of GDP and 90% of labour force; cash crops—cowpeas, cotton, peanuts; food crops—millet, sorghum, cassava, rice; livestock—cattle, sheep, goats; self-sufficient in food except in drought years
Natural Resources: uranium, coal, iron ore, tin, phosphates

■ FINANCE/TRADE

Currency: Communauté financière africaine franc (CFAF) = 100 centimes
International Reserves Excluding Gold: $60 million (Nov. 1998)
Gold Reserves: 0.011 million fine troy ounces (July 1998)
Budget: revenues $370 million; expenditures $370 million, including capital expenditures of $186 million (1998 est.)
Defence Expenditures: 0.9% of GDP (1996)
Education Expenditures: n.a.
External Debt: $1.557 billion (1996)
Exports: $270 million (1997); commodities: uranium 76%, livestock, cowpeas, onions, hides, skins; partners: n.a.
Imports: $363 million (1997); commodities: petroleum products, primary materials, machinery, vehicles and parts, electronic equipment, pharmaceuticals, chemical products, cereals, foodstuffs; partners: n.a.

■ COMMUNICATIONS

Daily Newspapers: 1 (1996)
Televisions: 12/1,000 inhabitants (1996)
Radios: 69/1,000 inhabitants (1996)
Telephones: 0.1/100 inhabitants (1996 est.)

■ TRANSPORTATION

Motor Vehicles: 51,600; 37,500 passenger cars (1997 est.)
Roads: 10,100 km; 798 km paved
Railway: none
Air Traffic: 75,000 passengers carried (1996)
Airports: 27; 9 have paved runways (1997)

Canadian Embassy: Office of the Canadian Embassy, Boulevard Mali Béro, Niamey; mailing address: Box 362, Niamey, Niger. Tel: (011-227) 75-36-86. Fax: (011-227) 75-31-01.
Embassy in Canada: Embassy of the Republic of Niger, 38 Blackburn Ave, Ottawa ON K1N 8A3. Tel: (613) 232-4291. Fax: (613) 230-9808.

Nigeria

Long-Form Name: Federal Republic of Nigeria
Capital: Abuja

■ GEOGRAPHY

Area: 923,770 sq. km
Coastline: 853 km
Climate: varies; equatorial in south, tropical in centre, arid in north
Environment: recent droughts in north severely affecting marginal agricultural activities; desertification; soil degradation, rapid deforestation
Terrain: southern lowlands merge into central hills and plateaus; mountains in southeast, plains in north
Land Use: 33% arable; 3% permanent crops; 44% permanent pastures; 12% forest; 8% other, includes 1% irrigated
Location: WC Africa, bordering on North Atlantic Ocean

■ PEOPLE

Population: 110,532,242 (July 1998 est.)
Nationality: Nigerian
Age Structure: 0-14 yrs: 45%; 15-64: 52%; 65+: 3% (1998 est.)
Population Growth Rate: 2.96% (1998 est.)
Net Migration: 0.32 migrants/1,000 population (1998 est.)
Ethnic Groups: more than 250 tribal groups; Hausa and Fulani of the north, Yoruba of the southwest and Ibos of the southeast make up 65% of the population; about 27,000 non-Africans
Languages: English (official); Hausa, Yoruba, Ibo, Fulani and several other languages also widely used
Religions: 50% Muslim, 40% Christian, 10% indigenous beliefs
Birth Rate: 42.24/1,000 population (1998 est.)
Death Rate: 12.95/1,000 population (1998 est.)
Infant Mortality: 70.74 deaths/1,000 live births (1998 est.)
Life Expectancy at Birth: 52.68 years male, 54.45 years female (1998 est.)
Total Fertility Rate: 6.09 children born/woman (1998 est.)
Literacy: 57.1% (1997 est.)

■ GOVERNMENT

Leader(s): Pres. Olusegun Obasanjo; V.Pres. Atiku Abubakar
Government Type: military government since Dec. 1983; the present regime has announced democratization beginning Oct. 1998

Administrative Divisions: 30 states and 1 territory
Nationhood: Oct. 1, 1960 (from UK)
National Holiday: Independence Day, Oct. 1

■ ECONOMY

Overview: the economy is dependent on oil and vulnerable to oil prices; agricultural production cannot keep pace with rapid population growth and Nigeria, once a large exporter of food, must now import foodstuffs; high inflationary pressures are a concern; government efforts to reduce Nigeria's dependence on oil exports and to sustain noninflationary economic growth have been hampered by inadequate new investment and endemic corruption
GDP: $132.7 billion, per capita $1,300; real growth rate 3.3% (1997 est.)
Inflation: 4.5% (year-end 1997)
Industries: accounts for 31% of GDP; crude oil, natural gas, coal, tin, columbite; palm oil, peanut, cotton, rubber, petroleum, wood, hides and skins; textiles, cement, building materials, food products, footwear, chemicals, printing, ceramics, steel
Labour Force: 46.1 million (1997 est.); 44.6% agriculture, 51.2% services, 4.2% industry
Unemployment: n.a.
Agriculture: accounts for 39% of GDP and half of labour force; inefficient small-scale farming dominates; once a large net exporter of food and now an importer; cash crops—cocoa, peanuts, palm oil, rubber; food crops—corn, rice, sorghum, millet, cassava, yams, fishing and forestry
Natural Resources: crude oil, tin, columbite, iron ore, coal, limestone, lead, zinc, natural gas

■ FINANCE/TRADE

Currency: naira (N) = 100 kobo
International Reserves Excluding Gold: $4,075 million (Dec. 1996)
Gold Reserves: 0.69 million fine troy ounces (Jan. 1997)
Budget: adjusted for purchasing power parity: revenues $13.9 billion; expenditures $13.9 billion, including capital expenditures of n.a. (1998 est.)
Defence Expenditures: 3.5% of GDP (1996)
Education Expenditures: n.a.
External Debt: $34 billion (1997 est.)
Exports: $58.849 billion (1996); commodities: oil 95%, cocoa, palm kernels, rubber; partners: European Community 51%, US 32%
Imports: $25.696 billion (1996); commodities: consumer goods, capital equipment, chemicals, raw materials; partners: European Community, US

■ COMMUNICATIONS

Daily Newspapers: 25 (1996)
Televisions: 57/1,000 inhabitants (1996)
Radios: 197/1,000 inhabitants (1996)
Telephones: 0.4/100 inhabitants (1996 est.)

■ TRANSPORTATION

Motor Vehicles: 970,000; 590,200 passenger cars (1997 est.)
Roads: 32,105 km; 26,005 km paved
Railway: 3,557 km
Air Traffic: 221,000 passengers carried (1996)
Airports: 72; 36 have paved runways (1996)

Canadian Embassy: The Canadian High Commission, 3A Bobo St, Abuja FCT, Nigeria. Tel: (011-234-1) 262-8212. Fax: (011-234-1) 262-8217.
Embassy in Canada: High Commission for the Federal Republic of Nigeria, 295 Metcalfe St, Ottawa, ON K2P 1R9. Tel: (613) 236-0522. Fax: (613) 236-0529.

Niue

Long-Form Name: Niue
Capital: Alofi

■ GEOGRAPHY

Area: 260 sq. km, world's largest uplifted coral island
Climate: tropical maritime, modified by southeasterly trade winds
Land Use: 19% arable, 8% permanent crops, 4% meadows and pastures, 19% forest, 50% other
Location: Pacific Ocean, NE of New Zealand

■ PEOPLE

Population: 1,647 (July 1998 est.)
Nationality: Niuean
Ethnic Groups: Polynesian
Languages: English, Polynesian closely related to Tongan and Samoan

■ GOVERNMENT

Colony Territory of: Territory of New Zealand
Leader(s): Head of State: Queen Elizabeth II, High Commissioner Mike Pointer; Prime Min. Sani Lakatani
Government Type: self-governing territory in free association with New Zealand
National Holiday: Waitangi Day, Feb. 6

■ ECONOMY

Overview: heavily dependent on aid from New Zealand; govt. expenditures regularly exceed

revenues; agriculture includes coconuts, honey, limes, root crops, livestock; chief trading partner: New Zealand

■ FINANCE/TRADE

Currency: New Zealand dollar = 100 cents

Canadian Embassy: c/o The Canadian High Commission, 3rd Fl, 61 Molesworth St, Thorndon, Wellington, New Zealand; Mailing address: c/o P.O. Box 12-049, Thorndon, Wellington, New Zealand. Tel: (011-64-4) 473-9577. Fax: (011-64-4) 471-2082.
Representative to Canada: c/o New Zealand High Commission, Metropolitan House, 99 Bank St, Ste 727, Ottawa ON K1P 6G3. Tel: (613) 238-5991. Fax: (613) 238-5707.

Norfolk Island

Long-Form Name: Territory of Norfolk Island
Capital: Kingston (administrative centre), Burnt Pine (commercial centre)

■ GEOGRAPHY

Area: 34.6 sq. km
Climate: subtropical, mild, little seasonal variation
Land Use: 0% arable, 0% permanent crops, 25% meadows and pastures, 0% forests, 75% other
Location: S Pacific Ocean, NE of Australia

■ PEOPLE

Population: 2,179 (July 1998 est.)
Nationality: Norfolk Islander
Ethnic Groups: majority descendants of Polynesians and British (the latter crew members of the British naval ship Bounty)
Languages: English (official), Norfolk (a mixture of 18th-century English and ancient Tahitian)

■ GOVERNMENT

Colony Territory of: Dependent Territory of Australia
Leader(s): Chief of State: Queen Elizabeth II, represented by Admin. A.J. Messner; Chief Min. George Smith
Government Type: a largely self-governing dependency, territory of Australia
National Holiday: Pitcairners' Arrival Day Anniversary, June 8

■ ECONOMY

Overview: tourism is backbone of economy; revenues from tourism have helped the agricultural sector become self-sufficient in beef, poultry and eggs; export of indigenous fruit and vegetables

■ FINANCE/TRADE

Currency: Australian dollar = 100 cents

Canadian Embassy: c/o The Canadian High Commission, Commonwealth Ave, Canberra, A.C.T. 2600, Australia. Tel: (011-61-2) 6273-3844. Fax: (011-61-2) 6273-3285.
Representative to Canada: c/o Australian High Commission, 50 O'Connor St, Ste 710, Ottawa ON K1P 6L2. Tel: (613) 236-0841. Fax: (613) 236-4376.

Northern Marianas

Long-Form Name: The Commonwealth of the Northern Mariana Islands
Capital: Saipan

■ GEOGRAPHY

Area: 477 sq. km (combined land area of 16 islands)
Climate: tropical maritime, moderated by northeasterly trade winds; little seasonal temperature variation
Land Use: 21% arable on Saipan island; volcanic islands too mountainous for cultivation; chief agricultural use is grazing; 19% meadows and pastures
Location: Pacific Ocean, E of the Philippines

■ PEOPLE

Population: 66,561 (July 1998 est.)
Nationality: no descriptive term; American citizenship
Ethnic Groups: Chamorro, Carolinians and other Micronesians, Caucasian, Japanese, Chinese, Korea
Languages: English (official), Chamorro, Carolinian, Japanese; 86% of the population speaks a language other than English at home

■ GOVERNMENT

Colony Territory of: Outlying Territory of the United States
Leader(s): Chief of State: William Clinton (USA); Head of Government: Pedro P. Tenorio
Government Type: commonwealth in political union with the US; self-governing with locally elected governing body
National Holiday: Commonwealth Day, Jan. 8

■ ECONOMY

Overview: economy benefits from US financial assistance, but the rate of funding has declined as local revenues have increased; tourism is growing in importance and now employs approximately 50% of the workforce; agriculture: cattle, coconuts, breadfruit, vegetables

■ FINANCE/TRADE

Currency: American dollar = 100 cents

Canadian Embassy: c/o The Canadian Embassy, 501 Pennsylvania Ave. NW, Washington DC 20001, USA. Tel: (202) 682-1740. Fax: (202) 456-7726.
Representative to Canada: c/o Embassy of the United States of America, 100 Wellington St, Ottawa ON K1P 5A1. Tel: (613) 238-5335. Fax: (613) 238-5720.

Norway

Long-Form Name: Kingdom of Norway
Capital: Oslo

■ GEOGRAPHY

Area: 324,220 sq. km
Coastline: 21,925 km (3,491 km mainland; 2,413 km large islands; 16,093 km long fjords; numerous small islands and minor indentations); one of the longest and most rugged coastlines in the world
Climate: temperate along coast, modified by North Atlantic Current; colder interior; rainy year-round on west coast
Environment: air and water pollution; acid rain
Terrain: glaciated; mostly high plateaus and rugged mountains broken by fertile valleys; small, scattered plains; coastline deeply indented by fjords; arctic tundra in north
Land Use: 3% arable; 0% permanent crops; negligible meadows, 27% forest; 70% other
Location: N Europe, bordering on Norwegian Sea, North Sea

■ PEOPLE

Population: 4,419,955 (July 1998 est.)
Nationality: Norwegian
Age Structure: 0-14 yrs: 20%; 15-64: 65%; 65+: 15% (1998 est.)
Population Growth Rate: 0.44% (1998 est.)
Net Migration: 1.64 migrants/1,000 population (1998 est.)
Ethnic Groups: Germanic (Nordic, Alpine, Baltic) and racial-cultural minority of 20,000 Lapps

Languages: Norwegian (official); small Lapp- and Finnish-speaking minorities
Religions: Lutheran (88%, state church), other Protestant and Roman Catholic 4%, none 3.2%, other 4.8%
Birth Rate: 12.9/1,000 population (1998 est.)
Death Rate: 10.17/1,000 population (1998 est.)
Infant Mortality: 5.01 deaths/1,000 live births (1998 est.)
Life Expectancy at Birth: 75.42 years male, 81.21 years female (1998 est.)
Total Fertility Rate: 1.8 children born/woman (1998 est.)
Literacy: 99%

■ GOVERNMENT

Leader(s): King Harald V, Prime Min. Kjell Magne Bondevik
Government Type: constitutional monarchy
Administrative Divisions: 19 provinces; dependent areas inc.: Bouvet Island (uninhabited), Jan Mayen (uninhabited), Peter I Island (uninhabited), Queen Maud Land (uninhabited), Svalbard
Nationhood: Oct. 26, 1905 (from Sweden)
National Holiday: Constitution Day, May 17

■ ECONOMY

Overview: a small country with high dependence on international trade; a prosperous capitalist nation which has extensive welfare measures; concerns are the aging population, increased economic integration with Europe and the balance between private and public influence in economic decisions
GDP: $120.5 billion, per capita $27,400; real growth rate 3.5% (1997 est.)
Inflation: 2.4% (July 1998)
Industries: accounts for 35% of GDP; petroleum and gas, food processing, shipbuilding, pulp and paper products, metal, chemicals, timber, mining, textiles, fishing
Labour Force: 2,155,000 (1997); 38.7% community, social and business services, 17.4% trade and tourism, 14.6% industry
Unemployment: 2.3% (Dec. 1998)
Agriculture: accounts for 3% of GDP and 6% of labour force; among world's top 10 fishing nations; livestock output exceeds value of crops; over half of food needs imported
Natural Resources: rich in natural resources: crude oil, copper, natural gas, pyrites, nickel, iron ore, zinc, lead, fish, timber, hydropower

■ FINANCE/TRADE

Currency: krone (pl. kroner) (NKr) = 100 oere
International Reserves Excluding Gold: $18.505 billion (Jan. 1999)

Gold Reserves: 1.184 million fine troy ounces (Jan. 1999)
Budget: n.a.
Defence Expenditures: 6.5% of total govt. expenditure (1996)
Education Expenditures: 6.84% of total govt. expenditure (1996)
External Debt: n.a.
Exports: $39.649 billion (1998); commodities: petroleum and petroleum products 25%, natural gas 11%, fish 7%, aluminum 6%, ships 3.5%, pulp and paper; partners: UK 26%, EFTA 16.3%, less developed countries 14%, Sweden 12%, Germany 12%, US 6%, Denmark 5%
Imports: $36.196 billion (1998); commodities: machinery, fuels and lubricants, transportation equipment, chemicals, foodstuffs, clothing, ships; partners; Sweden 18%, less developed countries 18%, Germany 14%, Denmark 8%, UK 7%, Japan 5%

■ COMMUNICATIONS

Daily Newspapers: 83 (1996)
Televisions: 460/1,000 inhabitants (1996)
Radios: 920/1,000 inhabitants (1996)
Telephones: 56.0/100 inhabitants (1996 est.)

■ TRANSPORTATION

Motor Vehicles: 2,210,000; 1,700,000 passenger cars (1997 est.)
Roads: 91,323 km; 66,342 km paved
Railway: 4,027 km
Air Traffic: 12,760,000 passengers carried (1996)
Airports: 102; 65 have paved runways (1997 est.)

Canadian Embassy: The Canadian Embassy, Wergelandsveien #7, 0244 Oslo, Norway. Tel: (011-47) 22-99-53-00. Fax: (011-47) 22-99-53-01.
Embassy in Canada: Embassy of the Kingdom of Norway, Royal Bank Centre, 90 Sparks St, Ste 532, Ottawa ON K1P 5B4. Tel: (613) 238-6571. Fax: (613) 238-2765.

Oman

Long-Form Name: Sultanate of Oman
Capital: Masqat or Muscat

■ GEOGRAPHY

Area: 212,460 sq. km
Coastline: 2,092 km along the Arabian Sea and Gulf of Oman
Climate: dry desert; hot, humid along coast; hot, dry interior; strong southwest summer monsoon (May to Sept.) in far south
Environment: summer winds often raise large

sandstorms and dust storms in interior; sparse natural freshwater resources are threatened by increasing soil salinity
Terrain: vast central desert plain, rugged mountains in north and south
Land Use: 0% arable; negligible permanent; 5% meadows; 0% forest; 95% other
Location: SW Asia (Middle East), bordering on Arabian Sea

■ PEOPLE

Population: 2,363,591 (July 1998 est.)
Nationality: Omani
Age Structure: 0-14 yrs: 41%; 15-64: 57%; 65+: 2% (1998 est.)
Population Growth Rate: 3.45% (1998 est.)
Net Migration: 1.08 migrants/1,000 population (1998 est.)
Ethnic Groups: almost entirely Arab, with small Balochi, Zanzibari, Pakistani and Indian groups
Languages: Arabic (official); English, Balochi, Urdu, Indian dialects
Religions: 75% Ibadhi Muslim; remainder Sunni Muslim, Shi'a Muslim, Hindu minority
Birth Rate: 37.83/1,000 population (1998 est.)
Death Rate: 4.37/1,000 population (1998 est.)
Infant Mortality: 25.55 deaths/1,000 live births (1998 est.)
Life Expectancy at Birth: 69.04 years male, 73.1 years female (1998 est.)
Total Fertility Rate: 6.13 children born/woman (1998 est.)
Literacy: approaching 80% (1997 est.)

■ GOVERNMENT

Leader(s): Sultan and Prime Min. Qaboos bin Sa'id Al Said
Government Type: absolute monarchy; independent, with residual UK influence
Administrative Divisions: 6 regions and 2 governorates
Nationhood: 1650, expulsion of the Portuguese
National Holiday: National Day, Nov. 18

■ ECONOMY

Overview: economy depends on the success of its oil industry which has 20 years' supply at the current rate of extraction; subsistence agriculture is the major employment, and the general populace relies on imported food
GDP: $17.2 billion, per capita $8,000; real growth rate 3.5% (1997 est.)
Inflation: n.a.
Industries: accounts for 43% of GDP; crude oil production and refining, natural gas production, construction, cement, copper
Labour Force: 1 million (1997 est.); 50%

agriculture, 21.8% industry, 28.6% services; 58% of labour force are non-Omani
Unemployment: n.a.
Agriculture: accounts for 3% of GDP and 40% of labour force (including fishing); less than 2% of land cultivated; largely subsistence farming (dates, limes, bananas, alfalfa, vegetables, camels, cattle); not self-sufficient in food
Natural Resources: crude oil, copper, asbestos, some marble, limestone, chromium, gypsum, natural gas

■ FINANCE/TRADE

Currency: Omani rial (RO) = 1,000 baiza
International Reserves Excluding Gold: $822 million (Jan. 1999)
Gold Reserves: 0.291 million fine troy ounces (Jan. 1999)
Budget: revenues $5.2 billion; expenditures $6 billion, including capital expenditures of $1.3 billion (1998 est.)
Defence Expenditures: 36.2% of govt. expenditure (1997)
Education Expenditures: 14.6% of govt. expenditure (1997)
External Debt: $3 billion (1997 est.)
Exports: $7.630 billion (1997); commodities: petroleum, re-exports, processed copper, dates, nuts, fish; partners: Japan, S Korea, Thailand
Imports: $5.026 billion (1997); commodities: machinery, transportation equipment, manufactured goods, food, livestock, lubricants; partners: Japan, United Arab Emirates, UK, Germany, US

■ COMMUNICATIONS

Daily Newspapers: 4 (1996)
Televisions: 660/1,000 inhabitants (1996)
Radios: 582/1,000 inhabitants (1996)
Telephones: 8.1/100 inhabitants (1996 est.)

■ TRANSPORTATION

Motor Vehicles: 300,000; 209,000 passenger cars (1997 est.)
Roads: 32,800 km; 9,840 km paved
Railway: none
Air Traffic: 1,620,000 passengers carried (1996)
Airports: 138; 6 have paved runways (1997 est.)

Canadian Embassy: The Canadian Embassy to Oman, c/o The Canadian Embassy, P.O. Box 94321, Riyadh 11693, Saudi Arabia. Tel: (011-966-1) 488-2288. Fax: (011-966-1) 488-1997.
Embassy in Canada: c/o Embassy of the Sultanate of Oman, 2535 Belmont Rd. NW, Washington DC 20008, USA. Tel: (202) 387-1980. Fax: (202) 745-4933.

Pakistan

Long-Form Name: Islamic Republic of Pakistan
Capital: Islamabad

■ GEOGRAPHY

Area: 803,940 sq. km
Coastline: 1,046 km along Gulf of Oman and Arabian Sea
Climate: mostly hot, dry desert; temperate in northwest; arctic in north
Environment: frequent earthquakes, occasionally severe especially in north and west; flooding along the Indus after heavy rains (July and Aug.); deforestation; soil erosion; desertification; water pollution from raw sewage
Terrain: flat Indus plain in east; mountains in north and northwest; Balochistan plateau in west
Land Use: 27% arable; 1% permanent crops; 6% meadows; 5% forest; 61% other, includes 21% irrigated
Location: SW Asia (Middle East), bordering on Arabian Sea

■ PEOPLE

Population: 135,135,195 (July 1998 est.)
Nationality: Pakistani
Age Structure: 0-14 yrs: 42%; 15-64: 54%; 65+: 4% (1998 est.)
Population Growth Rate: 2.2% (1998 est.)
Net Migration: -1.71 migrants/1,000 population (1998 est.)
Ethnic Groups: Punjabi, Sindhi, Pashtun (Pathan), Baloch, Muhajir (immigrants from India and their descendents)
Languages: Urdu (official), Punjab (spoken by majority), Sindhi, Pushto, English
Religions: 97% Muslim (77% Sunni, 20% Shi'a), 3% Christian, Hindu and other
Birth Rate: 34.38/1,000 population (1998 est.)
Death Rate: 10.69/1,000 population (1998 est.)
Infant Mortality: 93.48 deaths/1,000 live births (1998 est.)
Life Expectancy at Birth: 58.23 years male, 59.96 years female (1998 est.)
Total Fertility Rate: 4.91 children born/woman (1998 est.)
Literacy: 37.8% (1997 est.)

■ GOVERNMENT

Leader(s): Pres. Rafiq Mohammad Tarar, Prime Min. Nawaz Sharif
Government Type: federal republic
Administrative Divisions: 4 provinces, 1 territory and 1 capital territory
Nationhood: Aug. 14, 1947 (from UK; formerly West Pakistan)

National Holiday: Pakistan Day (proclamation of the republic), Mar. 23

■ ECONOMY

Overview: long-standing economic weaknesses such as indebtedness, a small tax base, large population and dependence on cotton exports hamper the economy
GDP: $344 billion, per capita $2,600; real growth rate 3.1% (1997 est.)
Inflation: 6.5% (June 1998)
Industries: accounts for 26% of GDP; textiles, food processing, beverages, petroleum products, construction materials, clothing, paper products, international finance, shrimp
Labour Force: 49.4 million (1997 est.); 47.4% agriculture, 12.4% industry, 13.3% community, social and business services
Unemployment: n.a.
Agriculture: 24% of GDP; over 50% of labour force; world's largest continuous irrigation system; cotton, wheat, rice, sugar cane, fruits, vegetables, livestock (milk, beef, mutton, eggs); self-sufficient in food grain
Natural Resources: land, extensive natural gas reserves, limited crude oil, poor quality coal, iron ore, copper, salt, limestone

■ FINANCE/TRADE

Currency: Pakistani rupee (PRs) = 100 paisa
International Reserves Excluding Gold: $1.620 billion (Jan. 1999)
Gold Reserves: 2.077 million fine troy ounces (Jan. 1999)
Budget: revenues $9.6 billion; expenditures $13.6 billion, including capital expenditures n.a. (1996-97)
Defence Expenditures: 5.7% of GDP (1997)
Education Expenditures: n.a.
External Debt: $33 billion (1997 est.)
Exports: $8.431 billion (1998 est.); commodities: rice, cotton, textiles, clothing; partners: European Community 31%, US 11%, Japan 11%
Imports: $9.145 billion (1998 est.); commodities: petroleum, petroleum products, machinery, transportation, equipment, vegetable oils, animal fats, chemicals; partners: European Community 26%, Japan 15%, US 11%

■ COMMUNICATIONS

Daily Newspapers: 264 (1996)
Televisions: 21/1,000 inhabitants (1996)
Radios: 92/1,000 inhabitants (1996)
Telephones: 1.7/100 inhabitants (1996 est.)

■ TRANSPORTATION

Motor Vehicles: 1,100,000; 800,000 passenger cars (1997 est.)
Roads: 224,774 km; 128,121 km paved
Railway: 8,163 km
Air Traffic: 5,400,000 passengers carried (1997 est.)
Airports: 115; 80 have paved runways (1997 est.)

Canadian Embassy: The Canadian High Commission, Diplomatic Enclave, Sector G-5, Islamabad; mailing address: The Canadian High Commission, G.P.O. Box 1042, Islamabad, Pakistan. Tel: (011-92-51) 27-91-00. Fax: (011-92-51) 27-91-10.
Embassy in Canada: High Commission for the Islamic Republic of Pakistan, Burnside Bldg, 151 Slater St, Ste 608, Ottawa ON K1P 5H3. Tel: (613) 238-7881. Fax: (613) 238-7296.

Palau

Long-Form Name: Republic of Palau
Capital: Koror (on Koror Island); a new capital is being built 20 km northeast

■ GEOGRAPHY

Area: 458 sq. km (26 islands and 300+ islets)
Coastline: 1,519 km
Climate: tropical, warm year-round; wet season, May to Dec.; dry season, Jan. to April; typhoon-prone with violent winds and heavy rain, esp. in July
Environment: inadequate facilities for waste management; typhoons
Terrain: about 200 islands; topography varies from high and mountainous to low coral reef islands
Land Use: northern islands of volcanic origin, fertile and extensively cultivated; southern islands too rugged for habitation
Location: W Pacific Ocean (Micronesia)

■ PEOPLE

Population: 18,110 (July 1998 est.)
Nationality: Palauan
Age Structure: 0-14 yrs: 27%; 15-64: 68%; 65+: 5% (1998 est.)
Population Growth Rate: 1.96% (1998 est.)
Net Migration: 6.24 migrants/1,000 population (1998 est.)
Ethnic Groups: Polynesian, Malayan, Melanesian, mixtures
Languages: English (official in all states), Sonsorolese, Angaur, Japanese, Tobi, Palauan
Religions: Christian, Modekngei, a religion indigenous to Palau

Birth Rate: 21.26/1,000 population (1998 est.)
Death Rate: 7.9/1,000 population (1998 est.)
Infant Mortality: 18.82 deaths/1,000 live births (1998 est.)
Life Expectancy at Birth: 64.49 years male, 70.78 years female (1998 est.)
Total Fertility Rate: 2.6 children born/woman (1998 est.)
Literacy: 92% (1997 est.)

■ GOVERNMENT

Leader(s): Pres. Kuniwo Nakamura, V. Pres. Tommy Remengesau
Government Type: constitutional government in free association with the US
Administrative Divisions: 16 states
Nationhood: Oct. 1, 1994 (from US-administered UN trusteeship)
National Holiday: Constitution Day, July 9

■ ECONOMY

Overview: subsistence agriculture and fishing; some tourism; government is main employer; phosphate deposits on northern islands; largely dependent on imports from the US
GDP: $160 million, per capita $8,800; real growth rate 10% (1997 est.)
Inflation: n.a.
Industries: some fishing and agriculture, tourism, crafts
Labour Force: n.a.
Unemployment: 7%
Agriculture: subsistence-level cultivation of coconuts, copra, yams, cassava
Natural Resources: marine resources, minerals, forests

■ FINANCE/TRADE

Currency: American dollar (US$) = 100 cents
International Reserves Excluding Gold: n.a.
Gold Reserves: n.a.
Budget: revenues $52.9 million; expenditures $59.9 million, including capital expenditures of n.a. (1997 est.)
Defence Expenditures: defence is the responsibility of the US
Education Expenditures: n.a.
External Debt: n.a.
Exports: $14.3 million (1996 est.); fish, copra, handicrafts; partners: US, Japan
Imports: $72.4 million (1996 est.): partners: US

■ COMMUNICATIONS

Daily Newspapers: n.a.
Televisions: n.a.
Radios: n.a.
Telephones: n.a.

■ TRANSPORTATION

Motor Vehicles: n.a.
Roads: 61 km; 36 km paved
Railway: none
Air Traffic: n.a.
Airports: 3; 1 has a paved runway (1997 est.)

Canadian Embassy: c/o The Canadian Embassy, 501 Pennsylvania Ave NW, Washington DC 20001, USA. Tel: (202) 682-1740. Fax: (202) 456-7726.
Embassy in Canada: c/o Embassy of the United States of America, 100 Wellington St, Ottawa ON K1P 5A1. Tel: (613) 238-5335. Fax: (613) 238-5720.

Panama

Long-Form Name: Republic of Panama
Capital: Panama

■ GEOGRAPHY

Area: 78,200 sq. km
Coastline: 2,490 along Caribbean Sea and North Pacific Ocean (Gulf of Panama)
Climate: tropical; hot, humid, cloudy; prolonged rainy season (May to Jan.); short dry season (Jan. to May)
Environment: dense tropical forest in east and northwest is threatened by deforestation; water pollution and soil degradation
Terrain: interior mostly steep, rugged mountains and dissected, upland plains; coastal areas largely plains and rolling hills
Land Use: 7% arable; 2% permanent crops; 20% meadows; 44% forest; 27% other
Location: Central (Latin) America, bordering on Caribbean Sea, Pacific Ocean

■ PEOPLE

Population: 2,735,943 (July 1998 est.)
Nationality: Panamanian
Age Structure: 0-14 yrs: 32%; 15-64: 62%; 65+: 6% (1998 est.)
Population Growth Rate: 1.56% (1998 est.)
Net Migration: -1.28 migrants/1,000 population (1998 est.)
Ethnic Groups: 70% mestizo (mixed Indian and European ancestry), 14% West Indian, 10% white, 6% Indian
Languages: Spanish (official), 14% English; many Panamanians are bilingual
Religions: 85% Roman Catholic, 15% Protestant
Birth Rate: 21.99/1,000 population (1998 est.)
Death Rate: 5.14/1,000 population (1998 est.)
Infant Mortality: 24.0 deaths/1,000 live births (1998 est.)

Life Expectancy at Birth: 71.73 years male, 77.31 years female (1998 est.)
Total Fertility Rate: 2.57 children born/woman (1998 est.)
Literacy: 90.8% (1997 est.)

■ GOVERNMENT

Leader(s): Pres. Mireya Moscoso, First V. Pres. Arturo Vallarino
Government Type: constitutional republic
Administrative Divisions: 9 provinces and 2 territories
Nationhood: Nov. 3, 1903 (from Colombia; became independent from Spain Nov. 28, 1821)
National Holiday: Independence Day, Nov. 3

■ ECONOMY

Overview: political instability, lack of credit and the erosion of business confidence have drastically hurt the economy; exports are stagnant; unemployment and economic reform are two of the greatest challenges the government must face
GDP: $18 billion, per capita $6,700; real growth rate 3.6% (1997 est.)
Inflation: 0.5% (June 1998)
Industries: accounts for 18% of GDP; manufacturing and construction activities, petroleum refining, brewing, cement and other construction materials, sugar mills
Labour Force: 1 million (1997 est.); 26.9% community, social and business services; 26.3% agriculture, 9.5% industry
Unemployment: 13.1% (1997 est.)
Agriculture: accounts for 8% of GDP and 27% of labour force; bananas, rice, corn, coffee, sugar cane, livestock, fishing, importer of food grain, vegetables, milk products
Natural Resources: copper, mahogany forests, shrimp

■ FINANCE/TRADE

Currency: balboa (B) = 100 centesimos
International Reserves Excluding Gold: $1.0 billion (Jan. 1999)
Gold Reserves: n.a.
Budget: revenues $2.4 billion; expenditures $2.4 billion, including capital expenditures of $341 million (1997 est.)
Defence Expenditures: 4.49% of total govt. expenditure (1996)
Education Expenditures: 16.8% of govt. expenditure (1996)
External Debt: $6.99 billion (1996)
Exports: $723 million (1997); commodities: bananas 40%, shrimp 27%, coffee 4%, sugar, petroleum products; partners: US 90%, Central America and Caribbean, European Community

Imports: $3.002 billion (1997); commodities: foodstuffs 16%, capital goods 9%, crude oil 16%, consumer goods, chemicals; partners: US 35%, Central America and Caribbean, European Community, Mexico, Venezuela

■ COMMUNICATIONS

Daily Newspapers: 7 (1996)
Televisions: 187/1,000 inhabitants (1996)
Radios: 299/1,000 inhabitants (1996)
Telephones: 11.7/100 inhabitants (1996 est.)

■ TRANSPORTATION

Motor Vehicles: 226,800; 144,000 passenger cars (1997 est.)
Roads: 11,100 km; 3,730 km paved
Railway: 335 km
Air Traffic: 700,000 passengers carried (1997 est.)
Airports: 109; 40 have paved runways (1997 est.)

Canadian Embassy: The Canadian Embassy, Avenida Samuel Lewis, Edificio Banco Central Hispano, 4th Fl, Panama City; mailing address: Apartado 3658, Balboa Ancon, Panama City, Panama. Tel: (011-507) 264-9731. Fax: (011-507) 263-8083.
Embassy in Canada: Embassy of the Republic of Panama, 130 Albert St, Ste 300, Ottawa ON K1P 5G4. Tel: (613) 236-7177. Fax: (613) 236-5775.

Papua New Guinea

Long-Form Name: Independent State of Papua New Guinea
Capital: Port Moresby

■ GEOGRAPHY

Area: 462,840 sq. km
Coastline: 5,152 km
Climate: tropical; northwest monsoon (Dec. to Mar.), southeast monsoon (May to Oct.); slight seasonal temperature variation
Environment: one of world's largest swamps along southwest coast; some active volcanos; frequent earthquakes and mudslides; pollution and deforestation
Terrain: mostly mountains with coastal lowlands and rolling foothills
Land Use: negligible arable; 1% permanent crops; negligible meadows; 93% forest; 6% other
Location: Pacific Ocean, Coral Sea N of Australia

■ PEOPLE

Population: 4,599,785 (July 1998 est.)
Nationality: Papua New Guinean

Age Structure: 0-14 yrs: 40%; 15-64: 57%; 65+: 3% (1998 est.)
Population Growth Rate: 2.27% (1998 est.)
Net Migration: 0 migrants/1,000 population (1998 est.)
Ethnic Groups: predominantly Melanesian and Papuan; some Negrito, Micronesian and Polynesian
Languages: pidgin, English, Motu (all official); also 715 local languages
Religions: 22% Roman Catholic, 16% Lutheran, 8% Presbyterian/Methodist/London Missionary Society, 5% Anglican, 4% Evangelical Alliance, 1% Seventh-Day Adventists, 10% other Protestant sects, 34% indigenous beliefs
Birth Rate: 32.37/1,000 population (1998 est.)
Death Rate: 9.65/1,000 population (1998 est.)
Infant Mortality: 57.09 deaths/1,000 live births (1998 est.)
Life Expectancy at Birth: 57.18 years male, 58.98 years female (1998 est.)
Total Fertility Rate: 4.26 children born/woman (1998 est.)
Literacy: 72.2% (1997 est.)

■ GOVERNMENT

Leader(s): Queen Elizabeth II/Gov. Gen. Silas Atopare, Prime Min. Mekere Morauta
Government Type: parliamentary democracy
Administrative Divisions: 20 provinces
Nationhood: Sept. 16, 1975 (from UN trusteeship under Australian administration)
National Holiday: Independence Day, Sept. 16

■ ECONOMY

Overview: country has abundant natural resources but exploitation has been hampered by the rugged terrain and the high cost of developing an infrastructure; subsistence agriculture is the livelihood for 85% of the population; mining accounts for about 60% of export earnings
GDP: $11.6 billion, per capita $2,650; real growth rate 2.3% (1997 est.)
Inflation: 5.3% (Dec. 1997)
Industries: accounts for 41% of GDP; copra crushing, oil palm processing, plywood processing, wood chip production, gold, silver, copper, construction, tourism
Labour Force: 2 million (1997 est.); 85% agriculture, 10.2% industry,
Unemployment: n.a.
Agriculture: 26% of GDP; fertile soils and favourable climate permits cultivating a wide variety of crops; cash crops: coffee, cocoa, coconuts, palm kernels; other products: tea, rubber, sweet potatoes, fruit, vegetables,

poultry, pork; net importer of food for urban centres
Natural Resources: gold, copper, silver, natural gas, timber, oil potential

■ FINANCE/TRADE

Currency: kina (K) = 100 toea
International Reserves Excluding Gold: $210 million (Nov. 1998)
Gold Reserves: 0.063 million fine troy ounces (Nov. 1998)
Budget: revenues $1.5 billion; expenditures $1.35 billion, including capital expenditures (1997 est.)
Defence Expenditures: 1.5% of GDP (1996)
Education Expenditures: n.a.
External Debt: $2.359 billion (1996)
Exports: $1.643 billion (1998 est.); commodities: gold, copper ore, coffee, copra, palm oil, timber, lobster; partners: Germany, Japan, Australia, UK, Spain, US
Imports: $1.828 billion (1998 est.); commodities: machinery and transport equipment, fuels, food, chemicals, consumer goods; partners: Australia, Singapore, Japan, US, New Zealand, UK

■ COMMUNICATION3

Daily Newspapers: 2 (1996)
Televisions: 9.1/1,000 inhabitants (1996)
Radios: 91/1,000 inhabitants (1996)
Telephones: 1.0/100 inhabitants (1996 est.)

■ TRANSPORTATION

Motor Vehicles: 99,300; 21,600 passenger cars (1997 est.)
Roads: 19,600 km; 686 km paved
Railway: none
Air Traffic: 970,000 passengers carried (1996)
Airports: 495; 19 have paved runways (1997 est.)

Canadian Embassy: The Canadian High Commission to Papua New Guinea, c/o The Canadian High Commission, Commonwealth Ave, Canberra A.C.T. 2600, Australia. Office: The Consulate of Canada, P.O. Box 851, Port Moresby, NCD, Papua New Guinea. Tel: (011-675) 322-4800. Fax: (011-675) 322-4824.
Embassy in Canada: c/o High Commission for Papua New Guinea, 1615 New Hampshire Ave, Ste 300, Washington DC 20009, USA. Tel: (202) 745-3680. Fax: (202) 745-3679.

Paraguay

Long-Form Name: Republic of Paraguay
Capital: Asunción

■ GEOGRAPHY

Area: 406,750 sq. km
Coastline: none: landlocked
Climate: subtropical; varies from temperate in east to semi-arid in far west
Environment: local flooding in southeast (early Sept. to June); poorly drained plains may become boggy (early Oct. to June); deforestation and water pollution are increasing
Terrain: grassy plains and wooded hills east of Río Paraguay; Gran Chaco region west of Río Paraguay mostly low, marshy plain near the river and dry forest and thorny scrub elsewhere
Land Use: 6% arable; 0% permanent crops; 55% permanent pastures; 32% forest; 7% other
Location: C South America

■ PEOPLE

Population: 5,291,020 (July 1998 est.)
Nationality: Paraguayan
Age Structure: 0-14 yrs: 39%; 15-64: 56%; 65+: 5% (1998 est.)
Population Growth Rate: 2.68% (1998 est.)
Net Migration: -0.1 migrants/1,000 population (1998 est.)
Ethnic Groups: 95% mestizo (Spanish and Indian), 5% white and Indian
Languages: Spanish (official), Guarani
Religions: 90% Roman Catholic; 10% Mennonite and other Protestant denominations
Birth Rate: 32.21/1,000 population (1998 est.)
Death Rate: 5.29/1,000 population (1998 est.)
Infant Mortality: 37.39 deaths/1,000 live births (1998 est.)
Life Expectancy at Birth: 70.27 years male, 74.29 years female (1998 est.)
Total Fertility Rate: 4.26 children born/woman (1998 est.)
Literacy: 92.1% (1997 est.)

■ GOVERNMENT

Leader(s): Pres. Luis Angel Gonzalez Macchi
Government Type: republic
Administrative Divisions: 18 departments
Nationhood: May 14, 1811 (from Spain)
National Holiday: Independence Days, May 14–15

■ ECONOMY

Overview: in the absence of significant mineral or petroleum resources, the economy is based on agriculture; has a large hydropower potential; is vulnerable to climatic conditions and international commodity prices for agricultural exports. Nontraditional exports are growing rapidly
GDP: $21.9 billion, per capita $3,900; real growth rate 2.6% (1997 est.)

Inflation: 10.8% (June 1998)
Industries: accounts for 25% of GDP; meat packing, oilseed crushing, milling, brewing, textiles, other light consumer goods, cement, construction
Labour Force: 2 million (1997 est.); 26.8% trade and tourism, 17.7% industry, 33.1% services
Unemployment: 8.2% (1996 est.)
Agriculture: accounts for 26% GDP and 45% of labour force; cash crops: cotton, sugar cane; other crops: corn, wheat, tobacco, soybeans, cassava, fruit and vegetables; animal products: beef, pork, eggs, milk; surplus producer of timber; self-sufficient in most foods
Natural Resources: iron ore, manganese, limestone, hydropower, timber

■ FINANCE/TRADE

Currency: guaraní (pl. guaraníes) (G/) = 100 centimos
International Reserves Excluding Gold: $733 million (Jan. 1999)
Gold Reserves: 0.035 million fine troy ounces (Jan. 1999)
Budget: revenues $1.25 billion; expenditures $1.66 billion, including capital expenditures n.a. (1995 est.)
Defence Expenditures: 1.3% of GDP (1996)
Education Expenditures: 2.9% of GNP (1995)
External Debt: $1.3 billion (1996)
Exports: $1.089 billion (1997); commodities: cotton, soybeans, timber, vegetable oils, coffee, tung oil, meat products; partners: European Community 37%, Brazil 25%, Argentina 10%, Chile 6%, US 6%
Imports: $3.403 billion (1997); commodities: capital goods 35%, consumer goods 20%, fuels and lubricants 19%, raw materials 16%, foodstuffs, beverages and tobacco 10%; partners: Brazil 30%, European Community 20%, US 18%, Argentina 8%, Japan 7%

■ COMMUNICATIONS

Daily Newspapers: 5 (1996)
Televisions: 101/1,000 inhabitants (1996)
Radios: 182/1,000 inhabitants (1996)
Telephones: 3.6/100 inhabitants (1996 est.)

■ TRANSPORTATION

Motor Vehicles: 121,000; 71,000 passenger cars (1997 est.)
Roads: 29,500 km; 2,803 km paved
Railway: 971 km
Air Traffic: 260,000 passengers carried (1996)
Airports: 948; 10 have paved runways (1997 est.)

Canadian Embassy: The Canadian Embassy to Paraguay, 1598 Casilla de Correo, 1425 Buenos Aires, Argentina. Office: The Consulate of Canada, Professor Ramirez c/Juan de Salazar, Asunción, Paraguay. Tel: (011-595-21) 227-207. Fax: (011-595-21) 227-208.
Embassy in Canada: Embassy of the Republic of Paraguay, 151 Slater St, Ste 501, Ottawa, ON K1P 5H3. Tel: (613) 567-1283. Fax: (613) 567-1679.

Peru

Long-Form Name: Republic of Peru
Capital: Lima

■ GEOGRAPHY

Area: 1,285,220 sq. km
Coastline: 2,414 km along South Pacific Ocean
Climate: varies from tropical in east to dry desert in west
Environment: subject to earthquakes, tsunamis, landslides, mild volcanic activity; deforestation; overgrazing; soil erosion; desertification; air pollution in Lima; shares control of Lago Titicaca, world's highest navigable lake, with Bolivia
Terrain: western coastal plain (costa), high and rugged Andes in centre (sierra), eastern lowland jungle of Amazon Basin (selva)
Land Use: 3% arable: negligible permanent; 21% meadows; 66% forest; 10% other, includes 1% irrigated
Location: W South America, bordering on Pacific Ocean

■ PEOPLE

Population: 26,111,110 (July 1998 est.)
Nationality: Peruvian
Age Structure: 0-14 yrs: 36%; 15-64: 60%; 65+: 4% (1998 est.)
Population Growth Rate: 1.97% (1998 est.)
Net Migration: -1.15 migrants/1,000 population (1998 est.)
Ethnic Groups: 45% Indian; 37% mestizo (mixed Indian and European ancestry); 15% white; 3% black, Japanese, Chinese and other
Languages: Spanish and Quechua (official), Aymara
Religions: predominantly Roman Catholic
Birth Rate: 26.69/1,000 population (1998 est.)
Death Rate: 5.81/1,000 population (1998 est.)
Infant Mortality: 43.42 deaths/1,000 live births (1998 est.)
Life Expectancy at Birth: 67.78 years male, 72.25 years female (1998 est.)
Total Fertility Rate: 3.31 children born/woman (1998 est.)
Literacy: 88.7% (1997 est.)

■ GOVERNMENT

Leader(s): Pres. Alberto Kenyo Fujimori
Government Type: republic
Administrative Divisions: 24 departments and 1 constitutional province
Nationhood: July 28, 1821 (from Spain)
National Holiday: Independence Day, July 28

■ ECONOMY

Overview: revival of growth in GDP continues to be restricted by the large amount of public and private resources being devoted to strengthening internal security; deficit spending and poor relations with international lenders are problems; labour unrest has cut production; food shortages; world's largest producer of coca (for cocaine)
GDP: $110.2 billion, per capita $4,420; real growth rate 7.3% (1997 est.)
Inflation: 7.4% (July 1998)
Industries: accounts for 41% of GDP, mining of metals, petroleum, fishing, textiles, clothing, food processing, cement, auto assembly, steel, shipbuilding, metal fabrication
Labour Force: 9.3 million (1997 est.); 34.1% trade and tourism, 28.6% community, social and business services, 6% finance
Unemployment: 8.2%, plus extensive underemployment (1996)
Agriculture: accounts for 14% of GDP and 35% of labour force; commercial crops: coffee, cotton, sugar cane; other crops: rice, wheat, potatoes, plantains, coca; animal products: poultry, meats, dairy, wool; not self-sufficient in grain or vegetable oil; fish catch of 6.9 million metric tons
Natural Resources: copper, silver, gold, petroleum, timber, fish, iron ore, coal, phosphate, potash

■ FINANCE/TRADE

Currency: nuevo sol (pl. soles) (S/.) = 100 centimos
International Reserves Excluding Gold: $9.656 billion (Dec. 1998)
Gold Reserves: 1.100 million fine troy ounces (Jan. 1999)
Budget: revenues $8.5 billion; expenditures $9.3 billion, including capital expenditures n.a. (1996 est.)
Defence Expenditures: 1.6% of GDP (1996)
Education Expenditures: n.a.
External Debt: $29.176 billion (1996)
Exports: $6.814 billion (1997); commodities: fishmeal, cotton, sugar, coffee, copper, iron ore, refined silver, lead, zinc, crude petroleum and by products; partners: European Community 22%, US 20%, Japan 11%, Latin America 8%, former USSR countries 4%
Imports: $10.263 billion (1997); commodities: foodstuffs, machinery, transport equipment, iron and steel semimanufactures, chemicals, pharmaceuticals; partners: US 23%, Latin America 16%, European Community 12%, Japan 7%, Switzerland 3%

■ COMMUNICATIONS

Daily Newspapers: 74 (1996)
Televisions: 125/1,000 inhabitants (1996)
Radios: 271/1,000 inhabitants (1996)
Telephones: 6.0/100 inhabitants (1996 est.)

■ TRANSPORTATION

Motor Vehicles: 775,000; 500,000 passenger cars (1997 est.)
Roads: 72,800 km; 7,353 km paved
Railway: 2,041 km
Air Traffic: 2,328,000 passengers carried (1996)
Airports: 244; 43 have paved runways (1997 est.)

Canadian Embassy: The Canadian Embassy, Calle Libertad 130, Miraflores, Lima; mailing address: Casilla 18-1126, Correo Miraflores, Lima, Peru. Tel: (011-51-1) 444-4015. Fax: (011-51-1)242-4050
Embassy in Canada: Embassy of the Republic of Peru, 130 Albert St, Ste 1901, Ottawa ON K1P 5G4. Tel: (613) 238-1777. Fax: (613) 232-3062.

Philippines

Long-Form Name: Republic of the Philippines
Capital: Manila

■ GEOGRAPHY

Area: 300,000 sq. km
Coastline: 36,289 km
Climate: tropical marine; northeast monsoon (Nov. to Apr.); southwest monsoon (May to Oct.)
Environment: astride typhoon belt, usually affected by 15 and struck by five to six cyclonic storms per year; subject to landslides, active volcanoes, destructive earthquakes, tsunami; deforestation; soil erosion; water pollution
Terrain: mostly mountains with narrow to extensive coastal lowlands
Land Use: 19% arable; 12% permanent crops; 4% meadows; 46% forest; 19% other, includes 5.5% irrigated
Location: SE of China, bordering on South China Sea, Pacific Ocean

■ PEOPLE

Population: 77,725,862 (July 1998 est.)
Nationality: Filipino
Age Structure: 0-14 yrs: 38%; 15-64: 59%; 65+: 3% (1998 est.)
Population Growth Rate: 2.09% (1998 est.)
Net Migration: -1.04 migrants/1,000 population (1998 est.)
Ethnic Groups: 91.5% Christian Malay, 4% Muslim Malay, 1.5% Chinese, 3% other
Languages: Pilipino (native national language based on Tagalog) and English (both official); Spanish also spoken, also 76 indigenous languages including Cebuano, Tagalog, Iloco, Ifugao
Religions: 83% Roman Catholic, 9% Protestant, 5% Muslim, 3% Buddhist and other
Birth Rate: 28.43/1,000 population (1998 est.)
Death Rate: 6.52/1,000 population (1998 est.)
Infant Mortality: 34.56 deaths/1,000 live births (1998 est.)
Life Expectancy at Birth: 63.57 years male, 69.28 years female (1998 est.)
Total Fertility Rate: 3.54 children born/woman (1998 est.)
Literacy: 94.6% (1997 est.)

■ GOVERNMENT

Leader(s): Pres. Joseph Estrada, V. Pres. Gloria Macapagal-Arroyo
Government Type: republic
Administrative Divisions: 14 regions, divided into 72 provinces and 61 chartered cities
Nationhood: July 4, 1946 (from US)
National Holiday: Independence Day (from Spain), June 12

■ ECONOMY

Overview: drought and power supply problems have hampered production; world's largest exporter of coconuts and coconut products
GDP: adjusted for purchasing power parity: $244 billion, per capita $3,200; real growth rate 5.1% (1997 est.)
Inflation: 10.1% (July 1998)
Industries: accounts for 32% of GDP; textiles, pharmaceuticals, chemicals, wood products, food processing, electronics assembly, petroleum refining, fishing
Labour Force: 30.8 million (1997 est.); 45.8% agriculture, 17.1% community, social and business services, 9.5% industry
Unemployment: 8.7% (1997)
Agriculture: accounts for about 22% of GDP and 45% of labour force; major crops: rice, coconuts, corn, sugarcane, bananas, pineapples, mangoes; animal products: pork, eggs, beef: net exporter of farm products: fish catch of 2 million metric tons annually
Natural Resources: timber, crude oil, nickel, cobalt, silver, gold, salt, copper

■ FINANCE/TRADE

Currency: peso (P) = 100 centavos
International Reserves Excluding Gold: $9.226 billion (Dec. 1998)
Gold Reserves: 5.432 million fine troy ounces (Dec. 1998)
Budget: revenues $18.4 billion; expenditures $16.5 billion, including capital expenditures n.a. (1996 est.)
Defence Expenditures: 7.98% of total govt. expenditure (1997)
Education Expenditures: 20.41% of total govt. expenditure (1997)
External Debt: $45.4 billion (1997)
Exports: $30.692 billion (1998 est.); commodities: electrical equipment 19%, textiles 16%, minerals and ores 11%, farm products 10%, coconut 10%, chemicals 5%, fish 5%, forest products 4%; partners: US 36%, European Community 19%, Japan 18%, ESCAP 9%, ASEAN 7%
Imports: $55.615 billion (1998 est.); commodities: raw materials 53%, capital goods 17%, petroleum products 17%; partners: US 25%, Japan 17%, ESCAP 13%, European Community 11%, ASEAN 10%, Middle East 10%

■ COMMUNICATIONS

Daily Newspapers: 47 (1996)
Televisions: 51/1,000 inhabitants (1996)
Radios: 159/1,000 inhabitants (1996)
Telephones: 2.4/100 inhabitants (1996 est.)

■ TRANSPORTATION

Motor Vehicles: n.a.
Roads: 182,000 km; 22,489 km paved
Railway: 499 km operational
Air Traffic: 7,400,000 passengers carried (1997 est.)
Airports: 262; 75 have paved runways (1997 est.)

Canadian Embassy: The Canadian Embassy, 9th and 11th Fl, Allied Bank Centre, 6754 Ayala Ave, Makati, Manila, Philippines; mailing address: P.O. Box 2168, Makati CPO 1261 Makati, Metro Manila, Philippines. Tel: (011-63-2) 867-0001. Fax: (011-63-2) 810-8839.
Embassy in Canada: Embassy of the Republic of the Philippines, 130 Albert St, Ste 606, Ottawa ON K1P 5G4. Tel: (613) 233-1121. Fax: (613) 233-4165.

Pitcairn Islands

Long-Form Name: Pitcairn, Henderson, Ducie and Oeno Islands
Capital: Adamstown

■ GEOGRAPHY

Area: 47 sq. km (Pitcairn and 3 small uninhabited islands)
Climate: tropical, hot, humid, modified by southeasterly trade winds; rainy season from Nov. to March
Land Use: rugged but fertile interior
Location: S Pacific Ocean, E of French Polynesia

■ PEOPLE

Population: 50 (July 1998 est.)
Nationality: Pitcairn Islander
Ethnic Groups: descendants of Polynesians and British (the latter crew members of the British naval ship Bounty)
Languages: English (official), Tahitian-English dialect

■ GOVERNMENT

Colony Territory of: Dependent Territory of the United Kingdom
Leader(s): Queen Elizabeth II (UK), Gov. Martin Williams
Government Type: dependency of the UK
National Holiday: Celebration of the Birthday of the Queen, second Saturday in June

■ ECONOMY

Overview: inhabitants subsist on fishing and farming; fertile soil of the valleys produces wide variety of fruit and vegetables; bartering is an important part of the economy; imports: fuel oil, machinery, building materials; no exports other than small tourist trade with passing ships

■ FINANCE/TRADE

Currency: New Zealand dollar = 100 cents

Canadian Embassy: c/o The Canadian High Commission, Macdonald House, 1 Grosvenor Square, London, W1X 0AB. Tel: (011-44-171) 258-6600. Fax: (011-44-171) 258-6333.
Representative to Canada: c/o British High Commission, 80 Elgin St, Ottawa ON K1P 5K7. Tel: (613) 237-1530. Fax: (613) 237-7980.

Poland

Long-Form Name: Republic of Poland
Capital: Warsaw

■ GEOGRAPHY

Area: 312,683 sq. km
Coastline: 491 km along Baltic Sea
Climate: temperate with cold, cloudy, moderately severe winters with frequent precipitation; mild summers with frequent showers and thundershowers
Environment: plain crossed by a few meandering streams; severe air and water pollution in south; flat terrain; lack of natural barriers; recently there has been severe flooding
Terrain: mostly flat plain, mountains along southern border
Land Use: 47% arable; 1% permanent crops; 13% meadows; 29% forest; 10% other
Location: NC Europe, bordering on Baltic Sea

■ PEOPLE

Population: 38,606,922 (July 1998 est.)
Nationality: Polish, Pole
Age Structure: 0-14 yrs: 21%; 15-64: 68%; 65+: 11% (1998 est.)
Population Growth Rate: -0.04% (1998 est.)
Net Migration: -0.4 migrants/1,000 population (1998 est.)
Ethnic Groups: 97.6% Polish, 1.3% German, 0.6% Ukrainian, 0.5% Byelorussian
Languages: Polish
Religions: 95% Roman Catholic (about 75% practising), 5% Russian Orthodox, Protestant and other
Birth Rate: 9.79/1,000 population (1998 est.)
Death Rate: 9.76/1,000 population (1998 est.)
Infant Mortality: 13.18 deaths/1,000 live births (1998 est.)
Life Expectancy at Birth: 68.6 years male, 77.16 years female (1998 est.)
Total Fertility Rate: 1.36 children born/woman (1998 est.)
Literacy: 99% (1997 est.)

■ GOVERNMENT

Leader(s): Pres. Aleksander Kwasniewski, Prem. Jerzy Buzek
Government Type: democratic state
Administrative Divisions: 49 provinces
Nationhood: Nov. 11, 1918, independent republic proclaimed
National Holiday: Constitution Day, May 3; Independence Day, Nov. 11

■ ECONOMY

Overview: Poland continues to make good progress in the difficult transition to a free-market economy. In contrast to the vibrant expansion of private non-farm activity, the large agricultural component remains handicapped by structural problems, surplus labour, inefficient small farms, and lack of investment.

GDP: $280.7 billion, per capita $7,250; real growth rate 6.9% (1997 est.)

Inflation: 12.1% (June 1998)

Industries: accounts for 35% of GDP, machine building, iron and steel, extractive industries, chemicals, shipbuilding, food processing, glass, beverages, textiles

Labour Force: 15,133,000 (1997); 26.7% agriculture, 24.3% industry, 18.7% community, social and business services

Unemployment: 10.4% (Dec. 1998)

Agriculture: accounts for 6.6% GDP and 27% of labour force; 75% of output from private farms, 25% from state farms; low productivity; leading European producer of rye, rapeseed and potatoes; wide variety of other crops and livestock; major exporter of pork products

Natural Resources: coal, sulphur, copper, natural gas, silver, lead, salt

■ FINANCE/TRADE

Currency: zloty (pl. zlotych) (Zl) = 100 groszy

International Reserves Excluding Gold: $26.142 billion (Jan. 1999)

Gold Reserves: 3.305 million fine troy ounces (Jan. 1999)

Budget: revenues $33.8 billion; expenditures $35.5 billion, including capital expenditures n.a. (1997 est.)

Defence Expenditures: 2.3% of GDP or 4.01% of total govt. expenditure (1997)

Education Expenditures: 6.24% of total govt. expenditure (1997)

External Debt: $43 billion (1997 est.)

Exports: $25.751 billion (1997); commodities: machinery and equipment 63%, fuels, minerals and metals 14%, manufactured consumer goods 14%, agricultural and forestry products 5%; partners: former USSR countries 25%, Germany 12%, Czech and Slovak Republics 6%

Imports: $42.308 billion (1997); commodities: machinery and equipment 36%, fuels, minerals and metals 35%, manufactured consumer goods 9%, agricultural and forestry products 12%; partners: former USSR countries 23%, Germany 13%, Czech and Slovak Republics 6%

■ COMMUNICATIONS

Daily Newspapers: 55 (1996)

Televisions: 337/1,000 inhabitants (1996)

Radios: 518/1,000 inhabitants (1996)

Telephones: 16.6/100 inhabitants (1996 est.)

■ TRANSPORTATION

Motor Vehicles: 9,120,000; 7,580,000 passenger cars (1997 est.)

Roads: 374,990 km; 245,243 km paved

Railway: 24,313 km

Air Traffic: 1,485,300 passengers carried (1996)

Airports: 83; 68 have paved runways (1997 est.)

Canadian Embassy: The Canadian Embassy, Ulica Jana Matejki 1/5, 00-481, Warsaw, Poland. Tel: (011-48-22) 629-80-51. Fax: (011-48-22) 629-64-57.

Embassy in Canada: Embassy of the Republic of Poland, 443 Daly Ave, Ottawa ON K1N 6H3. Tel: (613) 789-0468. Fax: (613) 789-1218.

Portugal

Long-Form Name: Portuguese Republic

Capital: Lisbon

■ GEOGRAPHY

Area: 92,391 sq. km; includes Azores and Madeira Islands

Coastline: 1,793 along North Atlantic Ocean

Climate: maritime temperature; cool and rainy in north, warmer and drier in south

Environment: air pollution and soil degradation are accelerating; coastal water pollution; Azores subject to severe earthquakes

Terrain: mountainous north, rolling plains in south

Land Use: 26% arable; 9% permanent crops; 9% meadows; 36% forest; 20% other, includes 7% irrigated

Location: SW Europe, bordering on North Atlantic Ocean

■ PEOPLE

Population: 9,927,556 (July 1998 est.)

Nationality: Portuguese

Age Structure: 0-14 yrs: 17%; 15-64: 68%; 65+: 15% (1998 est.)

Population Growth Rate: -0.07% (1998 est.)

Net Migration: -1.01 migrants/1,000 population (1998 est.)

Ethnic Groups: homogeneous Mediterranean stock in mainland, Azores and Madeira Islands; citizens of black African descent who immigrated to mainland during decolonization number less than 100,000

Languages: Portuguese (official), English, French

Religions: 97% Roman Catholic, 1% Protestant, 2% other

Birth Rate: 10.63/1,000 population (1998 est.)

Death Rate: 10.26/1,000 population (1998 est.)

Infant Mortality: 6.87 deaths/1,000 live births (1998 est.)

Life Expectancy at Birth: 72.27 years male, 79.25 years female (1998 est.)

Total Fertility Rate: 1.35 children born/woman (1998 est.)
Literacy: 85.0% (1997 est.)

■ GOVERNMENT

Leader(s): Pres. Jorge Sampaio, Prem. Antonio Guterres
Government Type: parliamentary democracy
Administrative Divisions: 18 districts and 2 autonomous regions; dependent areas: Macau (scheduled to become a Special Administrative Region of China in 1999)
Nationhood: 1140; independent republic proclaimed Oct. 5, 1910
National Holiday: Day of Portugal, June 10

■ ECONOMY

Overview: the economy has grown recently due to strong domestic consumption and investment spending; government is promoting privatization measures; the global slowdown and tight financial policies to combat inflation have caused economic growth to slow
GDP: $149.5 billion, per capita $15,200; real growth rate 3.3% (1997 est.)
Inflation: 3.1% (July 1998)
Industries: accounts for 36% of GDP; textiles and footwear; wood pulp, paper and cork; metalworking; oil refining; chemicals; fish canning; wine; tourism
Labour Force: 4,335,200 (1997); 24.8% community, social and business services, 23.4% industry, 19.5% trade and tourism
Unemployment: 7% (Jan. 1998)
Agriculture: accounts for 6% of GDP and 20% of labour force; small inefficient farms; imports more than half of food needs; major crops; grain, potatoes, olives, grapes; livestock sector: sheep, cattle, goats, poultry, meat, dairy products
Natural Resources: fish, forests (cork), tungsten, iron ore, uranium ore, marble

■ FINANCE/TRADE

Currency: escudo (Esc) = 100 centavos [As of Jan. 1, 1999, Government securities are issued in Euros (EUR)]
International Reserves Excluding Gold: $14.051 billion (Jan. 1999)
Gold Reserves: 19.504 million fine troy ounces (Jan. 1999)
Budget: revenues $48 billion; expenditures $52 billion, including capital expenditures of $7.4 billion (1996 est.)
Defence Expenditures: 1.9% of GDP (1996)
Education Expenditures: 5.4% of GNP (1995)
External Debt: $13.1 billion (1997 est.)

Exports: $23.523 billion (1998 est.); commodities: cotton textiles, cork and cork products, canned fish, wine, timber and timber products, resin, machinery, appliances; partners: European Community 72%, other developed countries 13%, US 6%
Imports: $34.563 billion (1998 est.); commodities: petroleum, cotton, foodgrains, industrial machinery, iron and steel, chemicals; partners: European Community 67%, other developed countries 13%, less developed countries 15%, US 4%

■ COMMUNICATIONS

Daily Newspapers: 27 (1996)
Televisions: 336/1,000 inhabitants (1996)
Radios: 306/1,000 inhabitants (1996)
Telephones: 37.7/100 inhabitants (1996)

■ TRANSPORTATION

Motor Vehicles: 3,680,700; 2,750,000 passenger cars (1997 est.)
Roads: 68,732 km; 59,110 km surfaced
Railway: 3,072 km
Air Traffic: 5,000,000 passengers carried (1997 est.)
Airports: 69; 41 have paved runways (1997 est.)

Canadian Embassy: The Canadian Embassy, Avenida da Liberdade 144/56, Flr 4, 1269-121 Lisbon, Portugal. Tel: (011-351-1) 347-4892. Fax: (011-351-1) 347-6466.
Embassy in Canada: Embassy of Portugal, 645 Island Park Dr, Ottawa ON K1Y 0B8. Tel: (613) 729-0883. Fax: (613) 729-4236.

Puerto Rico

Long-Form Name: Commonwealth of Puerto Rico
Capital: San Juan

■ GEOGRAPHY

Area: 9,104 sq. km
Climate: tropical marine, mild, little seasonal temperature variation
Land Use: 4% arable; 5% permanent; 26% permanent pastures; 16% forest; 49% other, includes 4% irrigated
Location: West Indies, bordering on Caribbean Sea, Atlantic Ocean

■ PEOPLE

Population: 3,857,070 (July 1998 est.)
Nationality: Puerto Rican
Ethnic Groups: almost entirely Hispanic
Languages: Spanish (official); English is widely understood

■ GOVERNMENT

Colony Territory of: Commonwealth associated with the US
Leader(s): Head of State: William Clinton, Gov. Pedro J. Rossello
Government Type: commonwealth associated with the US
National Holiday: US Independence Day, July 4

■ ECONOMY

Overview: economy (one of the most dynamic in the Caribbean region) has benefited from heavy US investment; new industries include pharmaceuticals and electronics; tourism is important; sugar production has lost out to dairy production and other livestock products as the main facet of the agricultural sector

■ FINANCE/TRADE

Currency: American dollar ($US) = 100 cents

Canadian Embassy: c/o The Canadian Embassy, 501 Pennsylvania Ave NW, Washington DC 20001, USA. Tel: (202) 682-1740. Fax: (202) 456-7726.
Representative to Canada: c/o Embassy of the United States of America, 100 Wellington St, Ottawa ON K1P 5A1. Tel: (613) 238-5335. Fax: (613) 238-5720.

Qatar

Long-Form Name: State of Qatar
Capital: Doha

■ GEOGRAPHY

Area: 11,437 sq. km
Coastline: 563 km
Climate: desert; hot, dry; humid and sultry in summer
Environment: haze, dust storms, sandstorms common; limited freshwater resources mean increasing dependence on large-scale desalination facilities
Terrain: mostly flat and barren desert covered with loose sand and gravel
Land Use: 1% arable; 0% permanent crops; 5% meadows; 0% forest; 94% other
Location: SW Asia (Middle East), bordering on Persian Gulf

■ PEOPLE

Population: 697,126 (July 1998 est.)
Nationality: Qatari
Age Structure: 0-14 yrs: 27%; 15-64: 71%; 65+: 2% (1998 est.)

Population Growth Rate: 3.82% (1998 est.)
Net Migration: 24.76 migrants/1,000 population (1998 est.)
Ethnic Groups: 40% Arab, 18% Pakistani, 18% Indian, 10% Iranian, 14% other
Languages: Arabic (official); English is commonly used as second language
Religions: Islam (native Qataris—less than one-third of the population—principally adhere to orthodox Wahhabi sect of Sunni Muslims)
Birth Rate: 16.97/1,000 population (1998 est.)
Death Rate: 3.53/1,000 population (1998 est.)
Infant Mortality: 18.09 deaths/1,000 live births (1998 est.)
Life Expectancy at Birth: 71.38 years male, 76.54 years female (1998 est.)
Total Fertility Rate: 3.5 children born/woman (1998 est.)
Literacy: 79.4% (1997 est.)

■ GOVERNMENT

Leader(s): Amir and Prime Min. Khalifa ibn Hamad Al Thani; Prime Min. Abdallah bin Khalifa Al Thani
Government Type: traditional monarchy
Administrative Divisions: 9 municipalities
Nationhood: Sept. 3, 1971 (from UK)
National Holiday: Independence Day, Sept. 3

■ ECONOMY

Overview: has one of the highest per capita GDP's in the world, due to oil revenues; reserves should not be completely depleted for about 23 years; production and export of natural gas is becoming increasingly important. Oil has given Qatar a per capita GDP comparable to the leading West European industrial countries.
GDP: $11.2 billion, per capita $16,700; real growth rate 10% (1997 est.)
Inflation: 7.4% (1996)
Industries: accounts for 49% of GDP; crude oil production and refining, fertilizers, petrochemicals, steel, cement
Labour Force: n.a.; 3% agriculture, 28% industry, 69% services; 83% of labour force in private sector is non-Qatari
Unemployment: n.a.
Agriculture: farming and grazing on small scale, less than 1% of GDP; commercial fishing increasing in importance; most food imported
Natural Resources: crude oil, natural gas, fish

■ FINANCE/TRADE

Currency: Qatari riyal (QR) = 100 dirhams
International Reserves Excluding Gold: $694 million (Sep. 1995)
Gold Reserves: 0.054 million fine troy ounces (Nov. 1998)

Budget: revenues $3.7 billion; expenditures $4.5 billion, including capital expenditures of $700 million (1997-98 est.)
Defence Expenditures: 3.5% of GDP (1996 est.)
Education Expenditures: n.a.
External Debt: $11 billion (1997 est.)
Exports: n.a.; commodities: petroleum products 90%, steel, fertilizers; partners: France, Germany, Italy, Japan, Spain
Imports: n.a.; commodities: foodstuffs, beverages, animal and vegetable oils, chemicals, machinery and equipment; partners: European Community, Japan, Arab countries, US, Australia

■ COMMUNICATIONS

Daily Newspapers: 5 (1996)
Televisions: 403/1,000 inhabitants (1996)
Radios: 448/1,000 inhabitants (1996)
Telephones: 24.0/100 inhabitants (1996 est.)

■ TRANSPORTATION

Motor Vehicles: 184,000; 97,000 passenger cars (1997 est.)
Roads: 1,230 km; 1,107 km paved
Railway: none
Air Traffic: 1,200,000 passengers carried (1996)
Airports: 4; 2 have paved runways (1997 est.)

Canadian Embassy: The Canadian Embassy to Qatar, c/o The Canadian Embassy, Villa 24, Area 4, Plot 121, Al-Mutawakel St, Da Aiyah, Kuwait City, Kuwait; mailing address: P.O. Box 25281, 13113, Safat, Kuwait City, Kuwait. Tel: (011-965) 256-3025. Fax: (011-965) 256-0173.
Embassy in Canada: c/o Embassy of the State of Qatar, 747 Third Ave, 22nd Fl, New York NY 10017, USA. Tel: (212) 486-9335. Fax: (212) 758-4952.

Réunion

Long-Form Name: Department of Réunion
Capital: Saint-Denis

■ GEOGRAPHY

Area: 2,512 sq. km; uninhabited islands of Juan de Nova, Europa, Bassas da India, Iles Glorieuses, Tromelin administered by Réunion but do not form part of the territory; Mauritius and the Seychelles claim Tromelin, Madagascar claims all 5 islands
Climate: tropical, but more moderate at higher elevations; May to Nov.: cool and dry; Nov. to April: hot and rainy
Land Use: volcanic island; some cultivation of indigenous plants and cash crops such as corn;

17% arable, 2% permanent crops, 5% meadows and pastures, 35% forest, 41% other
Location: Indian Ocean, E of Africa

■ PEOPLE

Population: 705,053 (July 1998 est.)
Nationality: Réunionese
Ethnic Groups: French Creoles, African, Malagasy, Pakistani, Indian and Chinese minorities
Languages: French (official), Creole vernacular

■ GOVERNMENT

Colony Territory of: Overseas Department of France
Leader(s): Chief of State: Jacques Chirac (France); Prefect Jean Daubigny
Government Type: overseas department of France
National Holiday: Taking of the Bastille, July 14

■ ECONOMY

Overview: agriculture-based economy, of which sugar cane is the backbone; government is promoting the development of the tourist industry; socioeconomic tensions between classes with widely disparate living standards; economy heavily depends on financial assistance from France

■ FINANCE/TRADE

Currency: French franc = 100 centimes

Canadian Embassy: c/o The Canadian Embassy, 35-37 avenue Montaigne, 75008, Paris, France. Tel: (011-33-1) 44-43-29-00. Fax: (011-33-1) 44043-29-99.
Representative to Canada: c/o Embassy of France, 42 Sussex Dr, Ottawa ON K1M 2C9. Tel: (613) 789-1795. Fax: (613) 562-3735.

Romania

Long-Form Name: Romania
Capital: Bucharest

■ GEOGRAPHY

Area: 237,500 sq. km
Coastline: 225 km along Black Sea
Climate: temperate; cold, cloudy winters with frequent snow and fog; sunny summers with frequent showers and thunderstorms
Environment: frequent earthquakes most severe in south and southwest; geologic structure and climate promotes landslides; water pollution; air pollution in south; soil degradation
Terrain: central Transylvanian Basin is separated

from the plain of Moldavia on the east by the Carpathian Mountains and separated from the Walachian Plain on the south by the Transylvanian Alps

Land Use: 41% arable; 3% permanent; 21% meadows; 29% forest; 6% other, includes 14.5% irrigated

Location: SE Europe, bordering on Black Sea

■ PEOPLE

Population: 22,395,848 (July 1998 est.)

Nationality: Romanian

Age Structure: 0-14 yrs: 19%; 15-64: 68%; 65+: 13% (1998 est.)

Population Growth Rate: -0.32% (1998 est.)

Net Migration: -0.88 migrants/1,000 population (1998 est.)

Ethnic Groups: 89.1% Romanian; 8.9% Hungarian; 0.4% German; 1.6% Ukrainian, Serb, Croat, Russian, Turk and Gypsy

Languages: Romanian (official), Hungarian, German; French and English also spoken

Religions: 70% Romanian Orthodox; 6% Roman Catholic; 24% Calvinist, Lutheran, Jewish, Baptist, unaffiliated

Birth Rate: 9.33/1,000 population (1998 est.)

Death Rate: 11.62/1,000 population (1998 est.)

Infant Mortality: 18.83 deaths/1,000 live births (1998 est.)

Life Expectancy at Birth: 66.67 years male, 74.47 years female (1998 est.)

Total Fertility Rate: 1.17 children born/woman (1998 est.)

Literacy: 97% (1997 est.)

■ GOVERNMENT

Leader(s): Pres. Emil Constantinescu, Prem. Radu Vasile

Government Type: republic

Administrative Divisions: 40 counties and 1 municipality

Nationhood: 1881 (from Turkey); republic proclaimed Dec. 30, 1947

National Holiday: National Day of Romania, Dec. 1

■ ECONOMY

Overview: industry suffers from an aging capital plant and shortages of energy; agriculture sector has suffered from drought and mismanagement; private enterprise is increasing in importance. Growing budget deficit, inflation, unemployment and a deteriorating infrastructure hamper economic progress

GDP: $114.2 billion, per capita $5,300; real growth rate -6.6% (1997 est.)

Inflation: 55.09% per month (June 1998)

Industries: accounts for 36% of GDP; mining, timber, construction materials, metallurgy, chemicals, machine building, food processing, petroleum

Labour Force: 11,339,000 (1997); 27.4% industry, 33% agriculture, 10.1% community, social and business services

Unemployment: 11.1% (Jan. 1999)

Agriculture: 19% of GDP and 28% of labour force; major wheat and corn producer, sugar beets, sunflower seeds, potatoes, milk, eggs, meat

Natural Resources: crude oil (reserves being exhausted), timber, natural gas, coal, iron ore, salt

■ FINANCE/TRADE

Currency: leu (pl. lei) = 100 bani

International Reserves Excluding Gold: $2.746 billion (Jan. 1999)

Gold Reserves: 3.228 million fine troy ounces (Jan. 1999)

Budget: revenues $10 billion; expenditures $11.7 billion, including capital expenditures of $1.3 billion (1997 est.)

Defence Expenditures: 2.5% of GDP or 6.05% of total govt. expenditure (1996)

Education Expenditures: 10.10% of total govt. expenditure (1996)

External Debt: 10 billion (1997 est.)

Exports: $8.431 billion (1997); commodities: machinery and equipment 34.7%, fuels, minerals and metals 24.7%, manufactured consumer goods 16.9%, agricultural materials and forestry products 11.9%, other 11.6%; partners: former USSR countries 27%, Eastern Europe 23%, European Community 15%, US 5%, China 4%

Imports: $11.280 billion (1997); commodities: fuels, minerals and metals 51%, machinery and equipment 26.7%, agricultural and forestry products 11%, manufactured consumer goods 4.2%; partners: Communist countries 60%, non-communist countries 40%

■ COMMUNICATIONS

Daily Newspapers: 106 (1996)

Televisions: 231/1,000 inhabitants (1996)

Radios: 317/1,000 inhabitants (1996)

Telephones: 13.9/100 inhabitants (1996 est.)

■ TRANSPORTATION

Motor Vehicles: 3,000,000; 2,460,000 passenger cars (1997 est.)

Roads: 153,170 km; 78,117 km paved

Railway: 11,365 km

Air Traffic: 1,000,000 passengers carried (1997 est.)

Airports: 24; 19 have paved runways (1997 est.)

Canadian Embassy: The Canadian Embassy, 36, Nicolae Iorga, Bucharest 71118; mailing address: P.O. Box 117, Post Office No. 22, Bucharest, Romania. Tel: (011-40-1) 222-9845. Fax: (011-40-1) 312-9680.

Embassy in Canada: Embassy of Romania, 655 Rideau St, Ottawa ON K1N 6A3. Tel: (613) 789-3709. Fax: (613) 789-4365.

Russia

Long-Form Name: Russian Federation
Capital: Moscow

■ GEOGRAPHY

Area: 17,075,200 sq. km
Coastline: 37,653 km
Climate: ranges from steppes in south through humid continental, subarctic in Siberia to tundra in polar north; winters vary—cool along Black Sea, frigid in Siberia; summers—warm in the steppes to cool along Arctic coast
Environment: cold desert in north; volcanic activity; only small percentage of land is arable—much is too far north; permafrost over much of Siberia; severe land, air and water pollution; deforestation and soil erosion
Terrain: rolling western plains, north-south ridge of Ural Mountains, central plateau, rugged eastern uplands
Land Use: 8% arable; 46% forests and woodland; 4% meadows and pastures; remainder steppe and cold desert
Location: E Europe and N Asia, bordering on Barents Sea, Baltic Sea, Black Sea, Caspian Sea

■ PEOPLE

Population: 146,861,022 (July 1998 est.)
Nationality: Russian
Age Structure: 0-14 yrs: 20%; 15-64: 68%; 65+: 12% (1998 est.)
Population Growth Rate: -0.31% (1998 est.)
Net Migration: 2.21 migrants/1,000 population (1998 est.)
Ethnic Groups: 81.5% Russians; 3.8% Tatars, 1.2% Chuvash, 0.9% Bashkir, 0.8% Belorussian, 3% Ukrainian, remainder inc. Chechens, Germans, Udmurts, Mari, Kazakhs, Avars, Jews, Moldavians and Armenians
Languages: Russian (official), Tartar, Ukrainian
Religions: Christianity (Russian Orthodox) with substantial Muslim populations and other religious minorities
Birth Rate: 9.57/1,000 population (1998 est.)
Death Rate: 14.89/1,000 population (1998 est.)

Infant Mortality: 23.26 deaths/1,000 live births (1998 est.)
Life Expectancy at Birth: 58.61 years male, 71.64 years female (1998 est.)
Total Fertility Rate: 1.34 children born/woman (1998 est.)
Literacy: 98% (1997 est.)

■ GOVERNMENT

Leader(s): Pres. Boris N. Yeltsin, Prem. Vladimir Putin
Government Type: federation
Administrative Divisions: 49 oblasts, 21 autonomous republics, 10 autonomous okrugs, 6 krays, 2 federal cities and 1 autonomous oblast
Nationhood: Aug. 24, 1991 (from Soviet Union)
National Holiday: Independence Day, June 12

■ ECONOMY

Overview: a vast country with a great many natural resources, a well-educated population, and a diverse but declining industrial base; foreign trade and exports have dropped sharply since 1992; foreign aid is important as 25% of the population lives below the poverty line and the country continues to experience formidable difficulties in moving from its old centrally planned economy to a modern market economy.
GDP: $692 billion, per capita $4,700; real growth rate 0.4% (1997 est.)
Inflation: 8.0% (Apr. 1998)
Industries: accounts for 39% of GDP; natural gas refining, steel and coal production and processing, all forms of machine building, shipbuilding, transportation equipment, consumer durables, communications and agricultural equipment, medical and scientific instruments
Labour Force: 78.1 million (1997 est.); 25.9% industry, 25.9% community, social and business services, 15.4% agriculture
Unemployment: 0.5% (Sept. 1998); substantial underemployment
Agriculture: accounts for 7% of GDP; grain, sugar beets, sunflower seeds, meat, milk, vegetables, fruit
Natural Resources: iron ore, coal, oil, gold, platinum, copper, zinc, lead, tin, rare metals; climate, terrain and distance hinder exploitation

■ FINANCE/TRADE

Currency: ruble (rbl.) = 100 kopeks
International Reserves Excluding Gold: $7.078 billion (Jan. 1999)
Gold Reserves: 15.143 million fine troy ounces (Jan. 1999)
Budget: revenues $59 billion; expenditures $70

billion, including capital expenditures n.a. (1997 est.)
Defence Expenditures: 12.22% of total govt. expenditure (1995)
Education Expenditures: 2.21% of total govt. expenditure (1995)
External Debt: $124.785 billion (1996)
Exports: $71.960 billion (1998 est.); commodities: fuels, wood products, metals, chemicals, wide range of manufactured products
Imports: $65.860 billion (1998 est.); commodities: machinery, medicine, foodstuffs, consumer products

■ COMMUNICATIONS

Daily Newspapers: 285 (1996)
Televisions: 405/1,000 inhabitants (1996)
Radios: 344/1,000 inhabitants (1996)
Telephones: 17.9/100 inhabitants (1996 est.)

■ TRANSPORTATION

Motor Vehicles: 24,000,000; 14,100,000 passenger cars (1997 est.)
Roads: 948,000 km; 336,000 km paved
Railway: 154,000 km
Air Traffic: 22,117,000 passengers carried (1996)
Airports: 2,517; 630 have paved runways (1997 est.)

Canadian Embassy: The Canadian Embassy, 23 Starokonyushenny Per, Moscow, 121002 Russia. Tel: (011-7-095) 956-6666. Fax: (011-7-095) 232-9948.
Embassy in Canada: Embassy of the Russian Federation, 285 Charlotte St, Ottawa ON K1N 8L5. Tel: (613) 235-4341. Fax: (613) 236-6342.

Rwanda

Long-Form Name: Republic of Rwanda
Capital: Kigali

■ GEOGRAPHY

Area: 26,340 sq. km
Coastline: none: landlocked
Climate: temperate; two rainy seasons (Feb. to Apr., Nov. to Jan.); mild in mountains with frost and snow possible
Environment: deforestation; overgrazing; soil exhaustion; soil erosion; periodic droughts
Terrain: mostly grassy uplands and hills; mountains in west
Land Use: 35% arable; 13% permanent crops; 18% meadows; 22% forest; 12% other
Location: EC Africa

■ PEOPLE

Population: 7,956,172 (July 1998 est.)

Nationality: Rwandan
Age Structure: 0-14 yrs: 45%; 15-64: 53%; 65+: 2% (1998 est.)
Population Growth Rate: 2.5% (1998 est.)
Net Migration: 5.03 migrants/1,000 population (1998 est.)
Ethnic Groups: 80% Hutu, 19% Tutsi, 1% Twa (Pygmoid)
Languages: Kinyarwanda, French, English (all official); Kiswahili used in commercial centres
Religions: 65% Christian (mostly Roman Catholic), 9% Protestant, 1% Muslim, 25% indigenous beliefs and other
Birth Rate: 38.99/1,000 population (1998 est.)
Death Rate: 19.0/1,000 population (1998 est.)
Infant Mortality: 113.31 deaths/1,000 live births (1998 est.)
Life Expectancy at Birth: 41.49 years male, 42.4 years female (1998 est.)
Total Fertility Rate: 5.86 children born/woman (1998 est.)
Literacy: 60.5% (1997 est.)

■ GOVERNMENT

Leader(s): Pres. Pasteur Bizimungu, Prime Min. Celestin Rwigema
Government Type: republic; presidential system in which military leaders hold key offices
Administrative Divisions: 12 prefectures
Nationhood: July 1, 1962 (from UN trusteeship under Belgian administration)
National Holiday: Independence Day, July 1

■ ECONOMY

Overview: a poor nation whose economy is severely hampered by civil war, which has damaged infrastructure and economic prospects; agricultural sector dominates, with coffee and tea making up 80–90% of total exports; manufacturing is largely restricted to the processing of agricultural products
GDP: adjusted for purchasing power parity: $3 billion, per capita $440; real growth rate 13.3% (1996 est.)
Inflation: 10.9% (June 1998)
Industries: accounts for 17% of GDP mining of cassiterite (tin ore) and wolframite (tungsten ore), tin, cement, agricultural processing, small-scale beverage production, soap, furniture, shoes, plastic goods, textiles, cigarettes
Labour Force: 4.1 million (1997 est.); 92.8% agriculture, 4.3% services, 3% industry and commerce
Unemployment: n.a.
Agriculture: accounts for 37% of GDP and about 90% of labour force; cash crops: coffee, tea, pyrethrum (insecticide made from

chrysanthemums); main food crops: bananas, beans, sorghum, potatoes; stock raising; self-sufficiency declining; country imports foodstuffs as farm production fails to keep up with population growth; coffee and tea constitute 80–90% of total exports
Natural Resources: gold, cassiterite (tin ore), wolframite (tungsten ore), natural gas, hydropower

■ FINANCE/TRADE

Currency: Rwandan franc (RF) = 100 centimes
International Reserves Excluding Gold: $151 million (Jan. 1999)
Gold Reserves: none (Jan. 1999)
Budget: revenues $231 million; expenditures $319 million, including capital expenditures of $13 million (1996 est.)
Defence Expenditures: n.a.
Education Expenditures: n.a.
External Debt: $1.034 billion (1996)
Exports: $87 million (1997); commodities: coffee 85%, tea, tin, cassiterite, wolframite, pyrethrum; partners: Germany, Belgium, Italy, Uganda, UK, France, US
Imports: $297 million (1997); commodities: textiles, foodstuffs, machines and equipment, capital goods, steel, petroleum products, cement and construction material; partners: US, Belgium, Germany, Kenya, Japan

■ COMMUNICATIONS

Daily Newspapers: 1 (1996)
Televisions: n.a.
Radios: 102/1,000 inhabitants (1996)
Telephones: 0.2/100 inhabitants (1996 est.)

■ TRANSPORTATION

Motor Vehicles: 27,800; 11,900 passenger cars (1997 est.)
Roads: 12,000 km; 1,000 km paved
Railway: none
Air Traffic: 10,000 passengers carried (1995)
Airports: 7; 4 have paved runways (1997 est.)

Canadian Embassy: Office of the Canadian Embassy, rue Akagera, P.O. Box 1177, Kigali, Rwanda. Tel: (011-250) 73210. Fax: (011-250) 72719.
Embassy in Canada: Embassy of the Republic of Rwanda, 121 Sherwood Dr, Ottawa ON K1Y 3V1. Tel: (613) 722-5835. Fax: (613) 722-4052.

Saint Helena

Long-Form Name: Saint Helena
Capital: Jamestown

■ GEOGRAPHY

Area: 410 sq. km
Climate: tropical marine; little seasonal variation
Land Use: 6% arable, 0% permanent crops, 6% meadows and pastures, 6% forests, 82% other
Location: Atlantic Ocean, SW of Africa

■ PEOPLE

Population: 7,091 (July 1998 est.)
Nationality: Saint Helenian
Ethnic Groups: Europeans, East Indians, Africans
Languages: English (official)

■ GOVERNMENT

Colony Territory of: Dependent Territory of the United Kingdom
Leader(s): Chief of State: Queen Elizabeth II; Gov. and Commander-in-Chief David Hollamby
Government Type: dependent territory of the UK
National Holiday: Celebration of the Birthday of the Queen, second Saturday in June

■ ECONOMY

Overview: depends primarily on financial assistance from UK; fishing, livestock raising and sale of handicrafts provide income for local population, due to the lack of jobs, many inhabitants have emigrated

■ FINANCE/TRADE

Currency: Saint Helenian pound = 100 pence (at par with British pound)

Canadian Embassy: c/o The Canadian High Commission, Macdonald House, 1 Grosvenor Square, London W1X 0AB, England, UK. Tel: (011-44-171) 258-6600. Fax: (011-44-171) 258-6333.
Representative to Canada: c/o British High Commission, 80 Elgin St, Ottawa ON K1P 5K7. Tel: (613) 237-1530. Fax: (613) 237-7980.

Saint Kitts and Nevis

Long-Form Name: Federation of St. Kitts and Nevis
Capital: Basseterre

■ GEOGRAPHY

Area: 269 sq. km
Coastline: 135 km
Climate: subtropical tempered by constant sea breezes; little seasonal temperature variation; rainy season (May to Nov.)
Environment: subject to hurricanes (July to Oct.)

Terrain: volcanic with mountainous interiors
Land Use: 22% arable; 17% permanent; 3% meadows; 17% forest; 41% other
Location: Caribbean islands

■ PEOPLE

Population: 42,291 (July 1998 est.)
Nationality: Kittsian, Nevisian
Age Structure: 0-14 yrs: 33%; 15-64: 61%; 65+: 6% (1998 est.)
Population Growth Rate: 1.23% (1998 est.)
Net Migration: -2.08 migrants/1,000 population (1998 est.)
Ethnic Groups: mainly of black African descent
Languages: English
Religions: Anglican, other Protestant sects, Roman Catholic
Birth Rate: 22.87/1,000 population (1998 est.)
Death Rate: 8.51/1,000 population (1998 est.)
Infant Mortality: 17.89 deaths/1,000 live births (1998 est.)
Life Expectancy at Birth: 64.52 years male, 70.82 years female (1998 est.)
Total Fertility Rate: 2.45 children born/woman (1998 est.)
Literacy: 97% (1997 est.)

■ GOVERNMENT

Leader(s): Queen Elizabeth II/Gov. Gen. Cuthbert Montraville Sebastian, Prime Min. Denzil Douglas
Government Type: constitutional monarchy
Administrative Divisions: 14 parishes
Nationhood: Sept. 19, 1983 (from UK)
National Holiday: Independence Day, Sept. 19

■ ECONOMY

Overview: traditionally dependent on the growing and processing of sugar cane and on remittances from overseas workers; tourism and export-oriented manufacturing are increasing
GDP: $235 million, per capita $5,700; real growth rate 4% (1996 est.)
Inflation: 6.3% (Feb. 1998)
Industries: accounts for 22% of GDP; sugar processing, tourism, cotton, salt, copra, clothing, footwear, beverages
Labour Force: 18,172 (June 1995); 69% services, 31% manufacturing
Unemployment: 4.3% (May 1995)
Agriculture: accounts for 6% of GDP; cash crop: sugar cane; subsistence crops: rice, yams, vegetables, bananas; fishing potential but not fully exploited; most food imported
Natural Resources: negligible

■ FINANCE/TRADE

Currency: East Caribbean dollar ($EC) = 100 cents
International Reserves Excluding Gold: $26 million (Mar. 1998)
Gold Reserves: n.a.
Budget: revenues $100.2 million; expenditures $100.1 million, including capital expenditures of $41.4 million (1996 est.)
Defence Expenditures: n.a.
Education Expenditures: n.a.
External Debt: $58 million (1996)
Exports: $36 million (1997); commodities: sugar, manufactures, postage stamps; partners: US 53%, UK 22%, Trinidad and Tobago 5%, OECS 5%
Imports: $148 million (1997); commodities: foodstuffs, intermediate manufactures, machinery, fuels; partners: US 36%, UK 12%, Trinidad and Tobago 6%, Canada 3%, Japan 3%, OECS 4%

■ COMMUNICATIONS

Daily Newspapers: 0 (1996)
Televisions: 251/1,000 inhabitants (1996)
Radios: 671/1,000 inhabitants (1996)
Telephones: 36.8/100 inhabitants (1996 est.)

■ TRANSPORTATION

Motor Vehicles: n.a.
Roads: 320 km; 136 km paved
Railway: 58 km
Air Traffic: n.a.
Airports: 2, both with paved runways (1997 est.)

Canadian Embassy: The Canadian High Commission to Saint Kitts and Nevis, c/o The Canadian High Commission, Bishop's Court Hill, St. Michael, Barbados; mailing address: P.O. Box 404, Bridgetown, Barbados. Tel: (246) 429-3550. Fax: (246) 429-3780.
Embassy in Canada: c/o High Commission for the Countries of the Organization of Eastern Caribbean States, 112 Kent St, Ste 1610, Place de Ville, Tower B, Ottawa, ON K1P 5P2. Tel: (613) 236-8952. Fax: (613) 236-3042.

Saint Lucia

Long-Form Name: Saint Lucia
Capital: Castries

■ GEOGRAPHY

Area: 620 sq. km
Coastline: 158 km
Climate: tropical, moderated by northeast trade winds; dry season from Jan. to Apr., rainy season from May to Aug.

Environment: subject to hurricanes and volcanic activity; deforestation; soil erosion
Terrain: volcanic and mountainous with some broad, fertile valleys
Land Use: 8% arable; 21% permanent; 5% meadow; 13% forest; 53% other
Location: Caribbean islands

■ PEOPLE

Population: 152,335 (July 1998 est.)
Nationality: Saint Lucian
Age Structure: 0-14 yrs: 34%; 15-64: 60%; 65+: 8% (1998 est.)
Population Growth Rate: 1.11% (1998 est.)
Net Migration: -5.7 migrants/1,000 population (1998 est.)
Ethnic Groups: 90.3% African descent, 5.5% mixed, 3.2% East Indian, 1% Caucasian
Languages: English (official), French patois
Religions: 90% Roman Catholic, 7% Protestant, 3% Anglican
Birth Rate: 22.48/1,000 population (1998 est.)
Death Rate: 5.64/1,000 population (1998 est.)
Infant Mortality: 16.95 deaths/1,000 live births (1998 est.)
Life Expectancy at Birth: 67.94 years male, 75.48 years female (1998 est.)
Total Fertility Rate: 2.35 children born/woman (1998 est.)
Literacy: 67% (1997 est.)

■ GOVERNMENT

Leader(s): Queen Elizabeth II/Gov. Gen. Calliopa Pearlette Louisy, Prime Min. Kenny Anthony
Government Type: parliamentary democracy
Administrative Divisions: 11 quarters
Nationhood: Feb. 22, 1979 (from UK)
National Holiday: Independence Day, Feb. 22

■ ECONOMY

Overview: depends on strong agricultural (bananas) and tourist industry sectors; expanding industrial base supported by foreign investment in manufacturing and activities such as data processing; vulnerable to droughts and tropical storms
GDP: adjusted for purchasing power parity: $695 million, per capita $4,400; real growth rate 4.3% (1996 est.)
Inflation: -1.7% (June 1997)
Industries: accounts for 32% of GDP; clothing, electronic component assembly, beverages, tourism, lime and coconut processing
Labour Force: n.a.
Unemployment: 15% (1996 est.)
Agriculture: accounts for 11% GDP and 43% of labour force; crops: bananas, coconuts, vegetables, citrus fruit, root crops, cocoa; imports food for the tourist industry
Natural Resources: forests, sandy beaches, minerals (pumice), mineral springs, geothermal potential

■ FINANCE/TRADE

Currency: EC dollar (EC$) = 100 cents
International Reserves Excluding Gold: $47 million (Mar. 1998)
Gold Reserves: n.a.
Budget: revenues $155 million expenditures; $169 million, including capital expenditures of $48 million (1996-97 est.)
Defence Expenditures: n.a.
Education Expenditures: n.a.
External Debt: $115 million (1996)
Exports: $61 million (1997); commodities: bananas 67%, cocoa, vegetables, fruit, coconut oil, clothing; partners: UK 55%, CARICOM 21%, US 18%, other 6%
Imports: $332 million (1997); commodities: manufactured goods 22%, machinery and transportation equipment 21%, food and live animals 20%, mineral fuels, foodstuffs, machinery and equipment, fertilizers, petroleum products; partners: US 33%, UK 16%, CARICOM 14.8%, Japan 6.5%, other 29.7%

■ COMMUNICATIONS

Daily Newspapers: 0 (1996)
Televisions: 217/1,000 inhabitants (1996)
Radios: 765/1,000 inhabitants (1996)
Telephones: 19.8/100 inhabitants (1996 est.)

■ TRANSPORTATION

Motor Vehicles: 12,300; 11,400 passenger cars (1997 est.)
Roads: n.a.
Railway: none
Air Traffic: n.a.
Airports: 2, both with paved runways (1997 est.)

Canadian Embassy: The Canadian High Commission to Saint Lucia, c/o The Canadian High Commission, Bishop's Court Hill, St. Michael, Barbados; mailing address: P.O. Box 404, Bridgetown, Barbados. Tel: (246) 429-3550. Fax: (246) 429-3780.
Embassy in Canada: c/o High Commission for the Countries of the Organization of Eastern Caribbean States, 112 Kent St, Ste 1610, Place de Ville, Tower B, Ottawa ON K1P 5P2. Tel: (613) 236-8952. Fax: (613) 236-3042.

Saint Pierre and Miquelon

Long-Form Name: Territorial Collectivity of Saint Pierre and Miquelon
Capital: Saint-Pierre

■ GEOGRAPHY

Area: 242 sq. km, 8 small islands
Climate: cold and wet, misty and foggy, windy spring and autumn, moist, temperate summers, cold and snowy winters
Land Use: 13% arable, 0% permanent crops, 0% meadows and pastures, 4% forest, 83% other
Location: N Atlantic Ocean, S of Newfoundland

■ PEOPLE

Population: 6,914 (July 1998 est.)
Nationality: French
Ethnic Groups: descendants of French settlers, Basques and Bretons (French fishermen)
Languages: French, English

■ GOVERNMENT

Colony Territory of: Territorial Collectivity of France
Leader(s): Chief of State: Jacques Chirac (France); Prefect Rémi Thuau
Government Type: territorial collectivity with internal self-government
National Holiday: Taking of the Bastille, July 14

■ ECONOMY

Overview: fishing, and the servicing of fishing fleets operating off the coast of Newfoundland, have long been an important part of the economy; agriculture: some vegetables and livestock for local consumption; partners: UK, Canada, EEC

■ FINANCE/TRADE

Currency: French franc = 100 centimes

Canadian Embassy: c/o The Canadian Embassy, 35-37 avenue Montaigne, 75008 Paris, France. Tel: (011-33-1) 44-43-29-00. Fax: (011-33-1) 44-43-29-99.
Representative to Canada: c/o Embassy of France, 42 Sussex Dr, Ottawa ON K1M 2C9. Tel: (613) 789-1795. Fax: (613) 562-3735.

Saint Vincent and the Grenadines

Long-Form Name: Saint Vincent and the Grenadines
Capital: Kingstown

■ GEOGRAPHY

Area: 340 sq. km
Coastline: 84 km
Climate: tropical; little seasonal temperature variation; rainy season (May to Nov.)
Environment: subject to hurricanes; Soufrière volcano is a constant threat; water pollution along coasts
Terrain: volcanic, mountainous; Soufrière volcano on the island of Saint Vincent
Land Use: 10% arable; 18% permanent crops; 5% meadows; 36% forest; 31% other
Location: Caribbean islands

■ PEOPLE

Population: 119,818 (July 1998 est.)
Nationality: Saint Vincentian or Vincentian
Age Structure: 0-14 yrs: 31%; 15-64: 64%; 65+: 5% (1998 est.)
Population Growth Rate: 0.6% (1998 est.)
Net Migration: -7.47 migrants/1,000 population (1998 est.)
Ethnic Groups: mainly of black African descent; remainder mixed, with some white, East Indian, Carib Indian
Languages: English (official), some French patois
Religions: Anglican, Methodist, Roman Catholic, Seventh-Day Adventist
Birth Rate: 18.74/1,000 population (1998 est.)
Death Rate: 5.28/1,000 population (1998 est.)
Infant Mortality: 15.69 deaths/1,000 live births (1998 est.)
Life Expectancy at Birth: 72.0 years male, 75.07 years female (1998 est.)
Total Fertility Rate: 1.97 children born/woman (1998 est.)
Literacy: 96% (1997 est.)

■ GOVERNMENT

Leader(s): Queen Elizabeth II/Gov. Gen. David Jack, Prime Min. James F. Mitchell
Government Type: constitutional monarchy
Administrative Divisions: 6 parishes
Nationhood: Oct. 27, 1979 (from UK)
National Holiday: Independence Day, Oct. 27

■ ECONOMY

Overview: overdependence on the weather-plagued banana crop as a major export earner has caused high unemployment; has been unsuccessful in diversifying into new industries
GDP: adjusted for purchasing power parity: $259 million, per capita $2,190; real growth rate 3% (1996 est.)
Inflation: 3.4% (June 1998)
Industries: accounts for 18% of GDP; food

processing (sugar, flour), cement, furniture, rum, starch, sheet metal, beverage
Labour Force: n.a.
Unemployment: 35–40% (1995 est.)
Agriculture: accounts for 11% of GDP and 60% of labour force; provides bulk of exports; products: bananas, arrowroot (world's largest producer), coconuts, sweet potatoes, spices; small numbers of cattle, sheep, hogs, goats; small fish catch used locally
Natural Resources: negligible

■ FINANCE/TRADE

Currency: EC dollar ($EC) = 100 cents
International Reserves Excluding Gold: $23 million (Mar. 1998)
Gold Reserves: n.a.
Budget: revenues $80 million; expenditures $118 million, including capital expenditures of $39 million (1996 est.)
Defence Expenditures: n.a.
Education Expenditures: 13.74% of govt. expenditure (1997)
External Debt: $213 million (1996)
Exports: $46 million (1997); commodities: bananas, eddoes and dasheen (taro), arrowroot starch, copra; partners: CARICOM 37%, UK 43%, US 15%
Imports: $182 million (1997); commodities: foodstuffs, machinery and equipment, chemicals and fertilizers, minerals and fuels; partners: US 42%, CARICOM 19%, UK 15%

■ COMMUNICATIONS

Daily Newspapers: 0 (1996)
Televisions: 159/1,000 inhabitants (1996)
Radios: 673/1,000 inhabitants (1996)
Telephones: 17.3/100 inhabitants (1996 est.)

■ TRANSPORTATION

Motor Vehicles: 8,200; 5,000 passenger cars (1997 est.)
Roads: n.a.
Railway: none
Air Traffic: n.a.
Airports: 6, 5 with paved runways (1997 est.)

Canadian Embassy: The Canadian High Commission to Saint Vincent and the Grenadines, c/o The Canadian High Commission, Bishop's Court Hill, St. Michael, Barbados; mailing address: P.O. Box 404, Bridgetown, Barbados. Tel: (246) 429-3550. Fax: (246) 429-3780.
Embassy in Canada: c/o High Commission for the Countries of the Organization of Eastern Caribbean States, 112 Kent St, Ste 1610, Place de Ville, Tower B, Ottawa, ON K1P 5P2. Tel: (613) 236-8952. Fax: (613) 236-3042.

Samoa

Long-Form Name: Independent State of Western Samoa
Capital: Apia

■ GEOGRAPHY

Area: 2,860 sq. km
Coastline: 403 km
Climate: tropical; rainy season lasts from Oct. to March, dry season from May to Oct.
Environment: volcanism and typhoons are natural hazards; soil erosion
Terrain: interior is rocky, with volcanic mountains; narrow coastal plain
Land Use: 19% arable, 24% permanent crops, 0% meadows and pastures, 47% forest and woodland, 10% other
Location: South Pacific Ocean

■ PEOPLE

Population: 224,713 (July 1998 est.)
Nationality: Samoan
Age Structure: 0-14 yrs: 39%; 15-64: 57%; 65+: 4% (1998 est.)
Population Growth Rate: 2.33% (1998 est.)
Net Migration: -0.8 migrants/1,000 population (1998 est.)
Ethnic Groups: 92.6% Samoan, 7% European-Polynesian; 0.4% Europeans
Languages: Samoan (Polynesian), also English
Religions: almost 100% Christianity
Birth Rate: 29.62/1,000 population (1998 est.)
Death Rate: 5.51/1,000 population (1998 est.)
Infant Mortality: 31.76 deaths/1,000 live births (1998 est.)
Life Expectancy at Birth: 67.07 years male, 71.96 years female (1998 est.)
Total Fertility Rate: 3.72 children born/women (1998 est.)
Literacy: 97% (1997 est.)

■ GOVERNMENT

Leader(s): Head of State Malietoa Tanumafili II, Prime Min. Tuialepa Sailele Malielegaoi
Government Type: constitutional monarchy under a native chief
Administrative Divisions: 11 districts
Nationhood: Jan. 1, 1962
National Holiday: National Day, June 1

■ ECONOMY

Overview: economy is heavily agriculture-oriented, and disease and pests have done much

damage in recent years; tourism has become the most important growth industry
GDP: $450 million; per capita $2,100, real growth rate 5.9% (1996 est.)
Inflation: 2.5% (Feb. 1998)
Industries: accounts for 25% of GDP; fishing, timber, food processing, tourism
Labour Force: n.a.; 65% agriculture, 30% services, 5% industry
Unemployment: n.a.
Agriculture: makes up 40% of GDP; mostly coconuts and fruit
Natural Resources: fish, forest resources

■ FINANCE/TRADE

Currency: tala ($WS) = 100 sene
International Reserves Excluding Gold: $67 million (Jan. 1999)
Gold Reserves: n.a.
Budget: revenues $118 million; expenditures $128 million, including capital expenditures n.a. (1997 est.)
Defence Expenditures: n.a.
Education Expenditures: n.a.
External Debt: $167 million (1996)
Exports: $15 million (1998); commodities: coconut oil and cream, copra, fish, beer; partners: New Zealand, American Samoa, Australia, Germany, US
Imports: $97 million (1998); commodities: intermediate goods, food, capital goods; partners: New Zealand, Australia, Fiji, US

■ COMMUNICATIONS

Daily Newspapers: 0 (1996)
Televisions: 60/1,000 inhabitants (1996)
Radios: 1,054/1,000 inhabitants (1996)
Telephones: 4.9/100 inhabitants (1996 est.)

■ TRANSPORTATION

Motor Vehicles: 2,600; 1,200 passenger cars (1997 est.)
Roads: n.a.
Railway: none
Air Traffic: 270,000 passengers carried (1996)
Airports: 3; 1 has paved runways (1997 est.)

Canadian Embassy: The Canadian High Commission to Western Samoa, c/o The Canadian High Commission, P.O. Box 12049, Thorndon, Wellington, New Zealand. Tel: (011-64-4) 473-9577. Fax: (011-64-4) 471-2082.
Embassy in Canada: c/o Samoa High Commission, 820 Second Ave, Ste 800D, New York NY 10017, USA. Tel: (212) 599-6196. Fax: (613) 599-0797.

San Marino

Long-Form Name: Republic of San Marino
Capital: San Marino

■ GEOGRAPHY

Area: 60 sq. km
Coastline: none: landlocked
Climate: Mediterranean; mild to cool winters; warm, sunny summers
Environment: dominated by the Appenines
Terrain: rugged mountains
Land Use: 17% arable; 0% permanent; 0% meadows; 0% forest; 83% other
Location: S Europe (E Italy)

■ PEOPLE

Population: 24,894 (July 1998 est.)
Nationality: Sammarinese
Age Structure: 0-14 yrs: 16%; 15-64: 67%; 65+: 17% (1998 est.)
Population Growth Rate: 0.7% (1998 est.)
Net Migration: 4.54 migrants/1,000 population (1998 est.)
Ethnic Groups: Sammarinese, Italian
Languages: Italian
Religions: Roman Catholic
Birth Rate: 10.52/1,000 population (1998 est.)
Death Rate: 8.11/1,000 population (1998 est.)
Infant Mortality: 5.44 deaths/1,000 live births (1998 est.)
Life Expectancy at Birth: 77.5 years male, 85.34 years female (1998 est.)
Total Fertility Rate: 1.51 children born/woman (1998 est.)
Literacy: 96% (1997 est.)

■ GOVERNMENT

Leader(s): Captains-Regent: Antonello Baciocchi and Rosa Zafferani
Government Type: republic
Administrative Divisions: 9 municipalities
Nationhood: 301 (by tradition)
National Holiday: Anniversary of the Foundation of the Republic, Sept. 3

■ ECONOMY

Overview: tourism and the sale of postage stamps are vital to the economy; tourism itself contributes more than 50% to the GDP; key industries are clothing, electronics, ceramics, agricultural products, wine and cheese
GDP: $500 million, per capita $20,000; real growth rate 4.8% (1997 est.)
Inflation: n.a.
Industries: wine, olive oil, cement, leather, textiles, tourism

Labour Force: 17,302 (Dec. 1996); 55% community, social and business services, 43% industry, 2% agriculture
Unemployment: 4% (Sept. 1998)
Agriculture: employs 3% of labour force; products: wheat, grapes, corn, olives, meat, cheese, hides; small numbers of cattle, pigs, horses; depends on Italy for food imports
Natural Resources: building stone

■ FINANCE/TRADE

Currency: Italian lire (Lit) = 100 centesimi; San Marino also mints its own coins
International Reserves Excluding Gold: n.a.
Gold Reserves: n.a.
Budget: revenues $320 million; expenditures $320 million, including capital expenditures of $26 million (1995)
Defence Expenditures: 1.0% of GDP (1995)
Education Expenditures: n.a.
External Debt: n.a.
Exports: n.a.; trade data are included in the statistics for Italy
Imports: n.a.; see exports

■ COMMUNICATIONS

Daily Newspapers: 3 (1996)
Televisions: 358/1,000 inhabitants (1996)
Radios: 620/1,000 inhabitants (1996)
Telephones: 47.0/100 inhabitants (1995)

■ TRANSPORTATION

Motor Vehicles: 30,000; 25,000 passenger cars (1997 est.)
Roads: 220 km
Railway: none
Air Traffic: n.a.
Airports: none

Canadian Embassy: The Canadian Consulate to San Marino, c/o The Canadian Embassy, Via Zara, 00198 Rome, Italy. Tel: (011-39-06) 445981. Fax: (011-39-06) 445 98912.
Embassy in Canada: c/o Consulate of San Marino, 15 McMurrich St, Ste 1104, Toronto, ON, M5R 3M6. Tel: (416) 925-7777. Fax: (416) 971-4849.

São Tomé and Príncipe

Long-Form Name: Democratic Republic of São Tomé and Príncipe
Capital: São Tomé

■ GEOGRAPHY

Area: 960 sq. km
Coastline: 209 km

Climate: tropical; hot, humid; one rainy season (Oct. to May)
Environment: deforestation; soil degradation
Terrain: volcanic, mountainous
Land Use: 2% arable; 36% permanent crops; 1% meadows; n.a. forest; 61% other
Location: S Atlantic Ocean, off W African Coast

■ PEOPLE

Population: 150,123 (July 1998 est.)
Nationality: São Toméan
Age Structure: 0-14 yrs: 48%; 15-64: 48%; 65+: 4% (1998 est.)
Population Growth Rate: 3.1% (1998 est.)
Net Migration: -4.15 migrants/1,000 population (1998 est.)
Ethnic Groups: mestiço, angolares (descendents of Angolan slaves), forros (descendents of freed slaves), servicais (contract labourers from Angola, Mozambique and Cape Verde), tongas (children of servicais born on the islands) and European (primarily Portuguese)
Languages: Portuguese (official), Crioulo
Religions: Roman Catholic, Evangelical Protestant, Seventh-Day Adventist
Birth Rate: 43.48/1,000 population (1998 est.)
Death Rate: 8.31/1,000 population (1998 est.)
Infant Mortality: 54.55 deaths/1,000 live births (1998 est.)
Life Expectancy at Birth: 62.87 years male, 65.86 years female (1998 est.)
Total Fertility Rate: 6.19 children born/woman (1998 est.)
Literacy: 73% (1997 est.)

■ GOVERNMENT

Leader(s): Pres. Miguel Trovoada, Prime Min. Guilherme Posser da Costa
Government Type: republic
Administrative Divisions: 2 districts
Nationhood: July 12, 1975 (from Portugal)
National Holiday: Independence Day, July 12

■ ECONOMY

Overview: the economy is hampered by overdependence on cocoa production, which has substantially declined in recent years because of drought and mismanagement; imports 90% of food needs as well as all fuels and most manufactured goods; government is attempting to restructure economy and reduce debt burden
GDP: adjusted for purchasing power parity: $154 million, per capita $1,000; real growth rate 1.5% (1997 est.)
Inflation: n.a.
Industries: accounts for 26% of GDP; light construction, shirts, soap, beer, fisheries, shrimp processing

Labour Force: n.a.; most of population engaged in subsistence agriculture and fishing. There are shortages of skilled workers.
Unemployment: 28% (1996 est.)
Agriculture: 21% of GDP; primary source of exports; cash crops: cocoa (85%), coconuts, palm kernels, coffee; food products: bananas, papayas, beans, poultry, fish; not self-sufficient in food grain and meat
Natural Resources: fish

■ FINANCE/TRADE

Currency: dobra (Db) = 100 centimos
International Reserves Excluding Gold: $6 million (June 1998)
Gold Reserves: n.a.
Budget: n.a.
Defence Expenditures: n.a.
Education Expenditures: n.a.
External Debt: $261 million (1996)
Exports: n.a.; commodities: cocoa 85%, copra, coffee, palm oil; partners: Germany, Netherlands, China
Imports: n.a.; commodities: machinery and electrical equipment 54%, food products 23%, other 23%; partners: Portugal, Germany, Angola, China

■ COMMUNICATIONS

Daily Newspapers: 0 (1996)
Televisions: 166/1,000 inhabitants (1996)
Radios: 272/1,000 inhabitants (1996)
Telephones: 1.9/100 inhabitants (1996 est.)

■ TRANSPORTATION

Motor Vehicles: n.a.
Roads: 320 km; 218 km paved
Railway: none
Air Traffic: 23,000 passengers carried (1996)
Airports: 2, both with paved runways (1997 est.)

Canadian Embassy: The Canadian Embassy to São Tomé and Príncipe, c/o The Canadian Embassy, P.O. Box 4037 Libreville, Gabon. Tel: (011-241) 743464. Fax: (011-241) 743466.
Embassy in Canada: Embassy of São Tomé and Príncipe, 400 Park Ave., 7th Floor, New York, NY 10022. Tel: (212) 317-0533. Fax: (212) 317-0580.

Saudi Arabia

Long-Form Name: Kingdom of Saudi Arabia
Capital: Riyadh (royal); Jeddah (administrative)

■ GEOGRAPHY

Area: 1,960,582 sq. km

Coastline: 2,640 km along Red Sea and Persian Gulf
Climate: harsh, dry desert with great extremes of temperature
Environment: no perennial rivers or permanent water bodies; developing extensive coastal seawater desalination facilities; desertification; coastal pollution; frequent dust and sand storms
Terrain: mostly uninhabited, sandy desert
Land Use: 2% arable; 0% permanent crops; 56% permanent pastures; 1% forest; 41% other
Location: SW Asia (Middle East), bordering on Persian Gulf, Arabian Sea, Red Sea

■ PEOPLE

Population: 20,785,955 (July 1998 est.)
Nationality: Saudi
Age Structure: 0-14 yrs: 43%; 15-64: 55%; 65+: 2% (1998 est.)
Population Growth Rate: 3.41% (1998 est.)
Net Migration: 1.44 migrants/1,000 population (1998 est.)
Ethnic Groups: 90% Arab, 10% Afro-Asian
Languages: Arabic (official); English (business language)
Religions: Muslim (85% Sunni, 15% Shia)
Birth Rate: 37.63/1,000 population (1998 est.)
Death Rate: 5.02/1,000 population (1998 est.)
Infant Mortality: 41.34 deaths/1,000 live births (1998 est.)
Life Expectancy at Birth: 68.19 years male, 71.96 years female (1998 est.)
Total Fertility Rate: 6.38 children born/woman (1998 est.)
Literacy: 62.8% (1997 est.)

■ GOVERNMENT

Leader(s): King and Prime Min. Fahd bin 'Abd al-'Aziz Al Sa'ud
Government Type: monarchy
Administrative Divisions: 13 provinces
Nationhood: Sept. 23, 1932 (unification)
National Holiday: Unification of the Kingdom, Sept. 23

■ ECONOMY

Overview: has the largest reserves of petroleum in the world and is the largest exporter of petroleum; the government is working towards the privatization of the economy; 4 million foreign workers
GDP: $206.5 billion, per capita $10,300; real growth rate 4% (1997 est.)
Inflation: -0.1% (May 1998)
Industries: accounts for 46% of GDP; crude oil production, petroleum refining, basic petrochemicals, cement, small steel-rolling mill, construction, fertilizer, plastic

Labour Force: 6.3 million (1997 est.); 34% government, 28% industry, 22% services, 16% agriculture
Unemployment: n.a.
Agriculture: accounts for 6% of GDP; fastest growing economic sector; subsidized by government; products: wheat, barley, tomatoes, melons, dates, citrus fruit, mutton, chickens, eggs, milk; approaching self-sufficiency in food
Natural Resources: crude oil, natural gas, iron ore, gold, copper

■ **FINANCE/TRADE**

Currency: riyal (SR) = 100 halalah
International Reserves Excluding Gold: $7.239 billion (Jan. 1999)
Gold Reserves: 4.596 million fine troy ounces (Jan. 1999)
Budget: revenues $47.5 billion; expenditures $52.3 billion, including capital expenditures n.a. (1998 est.)
Defence Expenditures: 12% of GDP (1997 est.)
Education Expenditures: 5.5% of GNP (1995)
External Debt: n.a.
Exports: $27.768 billion (1996); commodities: petroleum and petroleum products 89%; partners: Japan 26%, US 26%, France 6%, Bahrain 6%
Imports: $53.82 billion (1996); commodities: manufactured goods, transportation equipment, construction materials, processed food products; partners: US 20%, Japan 18%, UK 16%, Italy 11%

■ **COMMUNICATIONS**

Daily Newspapers: 13 (1996)
Televisions: 260/1,000 inhabitants (1996)
Radios: 319/1,000 inhabitants (1996)
Telephones: 9.7/100 inhabitants (1996 est.)

■ **TRANSPORTATION**

Motor Vehicles: 3,000,000; 1,710,000 passenger cars (1997 est.)
Roads: 162,000 km; 69,174 km paved
Railway: 1,390 km
Air Traffic: 11,706,000 passengers carried (1996)
Airports: 202; 70 have paved runways (1997 est.)

Canadian Embassy: The Canadian Embassy, Diplomatic Quarter, Riyadh; mailing address: P.O. Box 94321, Riyadh 11693, Saudi Arabia. Tel: (011-966-1) 488-2288. Fax: (011-966-1) 488-1997.
Embassy in Canada: Royal Embassy of Saudi Arabia, 99 Bank St, Ste 901, Ottawa ON K1P 6B9. Tel: (613) 237-4100. Fax: (613) 237-0567.

Senegal

Long-Form Name: Republic of Senegal
Capital: Dakar

■ **GEOGRAPHY**

Area: 196,190 sq. km
Coastline: 531 km along the North Atlantic Ocean
Climate: tropical; hot, humid; rainy season (Dec. to Apr.) has strong southeast winds; dry season (May to Nov.) dominated by hot, dry harmattan wind
Environment: lowlands seasonally flooded; deforestation; overgrazing; soil degradation; wildlife populations are endangered by poaching
Terrain: generally low, rolling, plains rising to foothills in southeast
Land Use: 12% arable; 0% permanent; 16% permanent pastures; 54% forest; 18% other, includes 1% irrigated
Location: W Africa, bordering on Atlantic Ocean

■ **PEOPLE**

Population: 9,723,149 (July 1998 est.)
Nationality: Senegalese
Age Structure: 0-14 yrs: 48%; 15-64: 49%; 65+: 3% (1998 est.)
Population Growth Rate: 3.33% (1998 est.)
Net Migration: 0 migrants/1,000 population (1998 est.)
Ethnic Groups: 36% Wolof, 17% Fulani, 17% Serer, 9% Toucouleur, 9% Diola, 9% Mandingo, 1% European and Lebanese, 2% other
Languages: French (official); Wolof, Pulaar, Diola, Mandingo
Religions: 92% Moslem, 6% indigenous beliefs, 2% Christian (mostly Roman Catholic)
Birth Rate: 44.38/1,000 population (1998 est.)
Death Rate: 11.05/1,000 population (1998 est.)
Infant Mortality: 61.2 deaths/1,000 live births (1998 est.)
Life Expectancy at Birth: 54.55 years male, 60.28 years female (1998 est.)
Total Fertility Rate: 6.18 children born/woman (1998 est.)
Literacy: 33.1% (1997 est.)

■ **GOVERNMENT**

Leader(s): Pres. Abdou Diouf, Prime Min. Mamadou Lamine Loum
Government Type: republic under multi-party democratic rule
Administrative Divisions: 10 regions
Nationhood: April 4, 1960 (from France)
National Holiday: Independence Day, Apr. 4

■ ECONOMY

Overview: tourism has emerged as a great boon to the economy; fishing is the main economic resource; mining (phosphate) has been hurt by reduced worldwide demand for fertilizers in recent years. Limited resource base, environmental degradation and very high population growth continue to delay improvements

GDP: adjusted for purchasing power parity: $15.6 billion, per capita $1,850; real growth rate 4.7% (1997 est.)

Inflation: 1.8% (year-end 1997)

Industries: accounts for 17% of GDP; fishing, agricultural processing, phosphate mining, petroleum refining, building materials

Labour Force: 4.1 million (1997 est.); 80.6% agriculture, 6.2% industry, 13.1% services

Unemployment: n.a.

Agriculture: including fishing, accounts for 19% of GDP; major products: peanuts (cash crop), millet, corn, sorghum, rice, cotton, tomatoes, green vegetables; estimated two-thirds self-sufficient in food; fish catch of 354,000 metric tons

Natural Resources: fish, phosphates, iron ore

■ FINANCE/TRADE

Currency: Communauté financière africaine franc (CFAF) = 100 centimes

International Reserves Excluding Gold: $374 million (Nov. 1998)

Gold Reserves: 0.029 million fine troy ounces (July 1998)

Budget: revenues $876 million; expenditures $1.977 billion, including capital expenditures n.a. (1996 est.)

Defence Expenditures: 2.1% of GDP (1996)

Education Expenditures: 3.6% of GNP (1995)

External Debt: $3.663 billion (1996)

Exports: $936 million (1997); commodities: manufactures 30%, fish products 27%, peanuts 11%, petroleum products 11%, phosphates 10%; partners: US, France, other European Community, Ivory Coast, India

Imports: $1.20 billion (1997); commodities: semimanufactures 30%, food 27%, durable consumer goods 17%, petroleum 12%, capital goods 14%; partners: US, France, other European Community, Nigeria, Algeria, China, Japan

■ COMMUNICATIONS

Daily Newspapers: 1 (1996)

Televisions: 41/1,000 inhabitants (1996)

Radios: 141/1,000 inhabitants (1996)

Telephones: 1.0/100 inhabitants (1996 est.)

■ TRANSPORTATION

Motor Vehicles: 160,000; 110,000 passenger cars (1997 est.)

Roads: 14,580 km; 4,271 km paved

Railway: 904 km

Air Traffic: 155,000 passengers carried (1996)

Airports: 20; 10 have paved runways (1997 est.)

Canadian Embassy: The Canadian Embassy, 45 av. de la République; mailing address: P.O. Box 3373, Dakar, Senegal. Tel: (011-221) 823-92-90. Fax: (011-221) 823-87-49.

Embassy in Canada: Embassy of the Republic of Senegal, 57 Marlborough Ave, Ottawa ON K1N 8E8. Tel: (613) 238-6392. Fax: (613) 238-2695.

Serbia and Montenegro

see Yugoslavia

Seychelles

Long-Form Name: Republic of Seychelles

Capital: Victoria

■ GEOGRAPHY

Area: 455 sq. km

Coastline: 491 km

Climate: tropical marine; humid; cooler season during southeast monsoon (late May to Sept.); warmer season during northwest monsoon (Mar. to May)

Environment: lies outside the cyclone belt, so severe storms are rare; short droughts possible; no fresh water, catchments collect rain

Terrain: 40 granitic and about 50 coralline islands; Mahé Group is granitic, narrow coastal strip, rocky, hilly; others are coral, flat, elevated reefs

Land Use: 2% arable; 13% permanent crops; 0% meadows; 11% forest; 74% other

Location: Indian Ocean, NE of Madagascar

■ PEOPLE

Population: 78,641 (July 1998 est.)

Nationality: Seychellois

Age Structure: 0-14 yrs: 30%; 15-64: 64%; 65+: 6% (1998 est.)

Population Growth Rate: 0.67% (1998 est.)

Net Migration: -6.36 migrants/1,000 population (1998 est.)

Ethnic Groups: Seychellois (mixture of Asians, Africans, Europeans)

Languages: English, French (both official), Creole

Religions: 90% Roman Catholic, 8% Anglican, 2% other

Birth Rate: 19.71/1,000 population (1998 est.)
Death Rate: 6.61/1,000 population (1998 est.)
Infant Mortality: 17.0 deaths/1,000 live births (1998 est.)
Life Expectancy at Birth: 66.13 years male, 75.53 years female (1998 est.)
Total Fertility Rate: 1.98 children born/woman (1998 est.)
Literacy: 58% (1997 est.)

■ GOVERNMENT

Leader(s): Pres. France Albert René; V. Pres James Michel
Government Type: republic
Administrative Divisions: 23 administrative districts
Nationhood: June 29, 1976 (from UK)
National Holiday: National Day, June 18 (1993 adoption of a new constitution)

■ ECONOMY

Overview: the government is moving to reduce the high dependence on tourism by promoting the development of farming, fishing and small-scale manufacturing, yet it is also encouraging foreign investment in order to upgrade hotels and other services
GDP: $550 million, per capita $7,000; real growth rate n.a. (1997 est.)
Inflation: 2.1% (Mar. 1998)
Industries: accounts for 15% of GDP; tourism employs 30% of labour force; mostly subsistence farming; cash crops: coconuts, cinnamon, vanilla; other products: sweet potatoes, cassava, bananas; broiler chickens; large share of food needs imported; expansion of tuna fishing under way
Labour Force: 26,000 (1996); 19% industry, 57% services, 14% government, 10% agriculture
Unemployment: n.a.
Agriculture: accounts for 4% of GDP, mostly subsistence farming; cash crops: coconuts, cinnamon, vanilla; large share of food needs imported; tuna fishing is increasing in importance
Natural Resources: fish, copra, cinnamon trees

■ FINANCE/TRADE

Currency: Seychelles rupee (SRe) = 100 cents
International Reserves Excluding Gold: $22 million (Jan. 1999)
Gold Reserves: n.a.
Budget: n.a.
Defence Expenditures: 4.32% of total govt. expenditure (1995)
Education Expenditures: 12.2% of govt. expenditure (1995)

External Debt: $148 million (1996)
Exports: $113 million (1997); commodities: fish, copra, cinnamon bark, petroleum products (re-exports); partners: France 63%, Pakistan 12%, Réunion 10%, UK 7%
Imports: $340 million (1997); commodities: manufactured goods, food, tobacco, beverages, machinery and transportation equipment, petroleum products; partners: UK 20%, France 14%, South Africa 13%, PDRY 13%, Singapore 8%, Japan 6%

■ COMMUNICATIONS

Daily Newspapers: 1 (1996)
Televisions: 145/1,000 inhabitants (1996)
Radios: 541/1,000 inhabitants (1996)
Telephones: 19.0/100 inhabitants (1996 est.)

■ TRANSPORTATION

Motor Vehicles: 8,500; 6,800 passenger cars (1997 est.)
Roads: 280 km; 176 km paved
Railway: none
Air Traffic: 373,000 passengers carried (1996)
Airports: 14; 8 have paved runways (1997 est.)

Canadian Embassy: The Canadian High Commission to Seychelles, c/o The Canadian High Commission, 38 Mirambo St, Dar-es-Salaam; mailing address: P.O. Box 1022, Dar-es-Salaam, Tanzania. Tel: (011-255-51) 112-832. Fax: (011-255-51) 116-896.
Embassy in Canada: High Commission for the Republic of Seychelles, 800 Second Ave, Ste 400C, New York NY 10017, USA. Tel: (212) 972-1785. Fax: (212) 972-1786.

Sierra Leone

Long-Form Name: Republic of Sierra Leone
Capital: Freetown

■ GEOGRAPHY

Area: 71,740 sq. km
Coastline: 402 km
Climate: tropical; hot, humid; summer rainy season (May to Dec.); winter dry season (Dec. to Apr.)
Environment: extensive mangrove swamps hinder access to sea; sand and dust storms; deforestation; soil degradation; population pressure negatively affects land
Terrain: coastal belt of mangrove swamps, wooded hill country, upland plateau, mountains in east
Land Use: 7% arable; 1% permanent crops; 31% meadows; 28% forest; 33% other

Location: WC Africa, bordering on North Atlantic Ocean

■ PEOPLE

Population: 5,080,004 (July 1998 est.)
Nationality: Sierra Leonean
Age Structure: 0-14 yrs: 45%; 15-64: 52%; 65+: 3% (1998 est.)
Population Growth Rate: 4.01% (1998 est.)
Net Migration: 11.18 migrants/1,000 population (1998 est.)
Ethnic Groups: 99% native African (30% Temne, 39% Mende, other 30%); 1% Creole, European, Lebanese and Asian
Languages: English (official); regular use limited to literate minority; principal vernaculars are Mende in south and Temne in north; Krio is the language of the resettled ex-slave population of the Freetown area and is lingua franca
Religions: 60% Muslim, 10% Christian, 30% traditional beliefs
Birth Rate: 46.16/1,000 population (1998 est.)
Death Rate: 17.25/1,000 population (1998 est.)
Infant Mortality: 129.38 deaths/1,000 live births (1998 est.)
Life Expectancy at Birth: 45.56 years male, 51.66 years female (1998 est.)
Total Fertility Rate: 6.23 children born/woman (1998 est.)
Literacy: 31.4% (1997 est.)

■ GOVERNMENT

Leader(s): Pres. Ahmad Tejan Kabbah; V.Pres. Albert Joe Demby
Government Type: constitutional democracy
Administrative Divisions: 3 provinces and 1 area
Nationhood: Apr. 27, 1961 (from UK)
National Holiday: Republic Day, Apr. 27

■ ECONOMY

Overview: the economic and social infrastructure is underdeveloped; subsistence agriculture is the backbone of the economy; problems include unemployment, rising inflation, large trade deficits; diamond mining is an important source of national income
GDP: $2.65 billion, per capita $540; real growth rate -27% (1997 est.)
Inflation: 37.5% (June 1998)
Industries: accounts for 27% of GDP; mining (diamonds, bauxite, rutile), small-scale manufacturing (beverages, textiles, cigarettes, footwear), petroleum refinery
Labour Force: 2 million (1997 est.); 69.6% agriculture, 14.1% industry, 16.4% services
Unemployment: n.a.
Agriculture: accounts for 39% of GDP and two-thirds of the labour force, largely subsistence farming; cash crops: coffee, cocoa, palm kernels; harvest of food staple rice meets 80% of domestic needs; annual fish catch averages 53,000 metric tons
Natural Resources: diamonds, titanium ore, bauxite, iron ore, gold, chromite

■ FINANCE/TRADE

Currency: leone (Le) = 100 cents
International Reserves Excluding Gold: $20 million (Oct. 1998)
Gold Reserves: n.a.
Budget: revenues $96 million; expenditures $150 million, including capital expenditures n.a. (1996 est.)
Defence Expenditures: 5.9% of GDP (1996)
Education Expenditures: n.a.
External Debt: $1.167 billion (1996)
Exports: $17 million (1997); commodities: rutile 50%, bauxite 17%, cocoa 11%, diamonds 3%, coffee 3%; partners: US, UK, Belgium, Germany, (Western Europe)
Imports: $93 million (1997); commodities: capital goods 40%, food 32%, petroleum 12%, consumer goods 7%, light industrial goods; partners: US, European Community, Japan, China, Nigeria

■ COMMUNICATIONS

Daily Newspapers: 1 (1996)
Televisions: 12/1,000 inhabitants (1996)
Radios: 251/1,000 inhabitants (1996)
Telephones: 0.4/100 inhabitants (1996 est.)

■ TRANSPORTATION

Motor Vehicles: 42,500; 21,000 passenger cars (1997 est.)
Roads: 11,700 km; 1,287 km paved
Railway: 84 km
Air Traffic: 15,000 passengers carried (1996)
Airports: 10; 3 have paved runways (1997 est.)

Canadian Embassy: The Canadian High Commission to Sierra Leone, c/o The Canadian Embassy, PO Box 99, Conakry, Guinea. Tel: (011-224) 46-23-95. Fax: (011-224) 46-42-35.
Embassy in Canada: c/o High Commission for the Republic of Sierra Leone, 1701-19th St NW, Washington DC 20009, USA. Tel: (202) 939-9261. Fax: (202) 483-1793.

Singapore

Long-Form Name: Republic of Singapore
Capital: Singapore

■ GEOGRAPHY

Area: 647.5 sq. km
Coastline: 193 km
Climate: tropical; hot, humid, rainy; no pronounced rainy or dry seasons; thunderstorms occur on 40% of all days (67% of days in Apr.)
Environment: mostly urban and industrialized; water supply is limited
Terrain: lowland; gently undulating central plateau contains water catchment area and nature preserve
Land Use: 2% arable; 6% permanent; 0% meadows; 5% forest; 87% other
Location: SE Asia, bordering on South China Sea

■ PEOPLE

Population: 3,490,356 (July 1998 est.)
Nationality: Singaporean
Age Structure: 0-14 yrs: 21%; 15-64: 72%; 65+: 7% (1998 est.)
Population Growth Rate: 1.2% (1998 est.)
Net Migration: 2.87 migrants/1,000 population (1998 est.)
Ethnic Groups: 76.4% Chinese, 14.9% Malay, 6.4% Indian, 2.3% other
Languages: Chinese (Mandarin), Malay, Tamil and English (all official), Malay (national)
Religions: majority of Chinese are Buddhists or atheists; Malays nearly all Muslim (minorities are Christians, Hindus, Sikhs, Taoists, Confucianists)
Birth Rate: 13.79/1,000 population (1998 est.)
Death Rate: 4.68/1,000 population (1998 est.)
Infant Mortality: 3.87 deaths/1,000 live births (1998 est.)
Life Expectancy at Birth: 75.46 years male, 81.77 years female (1998 est.)
Total Fertility Rate: 1.46 children born/woman (1998 est.)
Literacy: 91.1% (1997 est.)

■ GOVERNMENT

Leader(s): Pres. S.R. Nathan, Prime Min. Goh Chok Tong
Government Type: republic within Commonwealth
Administrative Divisions: none
Nationhood: Aug. 9, 1965 (from Malaysia)
National Holiday: National Day, Aug. 9

■ ECONOMY

Overview: has an open entrepreneurial economy with strong service and manufacturing sectors and good international trading links; growth has traditionally run at high rates; per capita GDP is among the highest in Asia; rising labour costs continue to adversely affect Singapore's competitiveness
GDP: $84.6 billion, per capita $24,600; real growth rate 6% (1997 est.)
Inflation: -0.2% (June 1998)
Industries: accounts for 28% of GDP; petroleum refining, electronics, oil drilling equipment, rubber processing and rubber products, processed food and beverages, ship repair, entrepôt trade, financial services, biotechnology
Labour Force: 1.856 million (1997 est.); 27% industry, 22.8% trade and tourism, 21.6% community, social and business services
Unemployment: 2.0% (Jan. 1998)
Agriculture: minor importance in the economy; self-sufficient in poultry and eggs; must import most other food; major crops: rubber, copra, fruit, vegetables
Natural Resources: fish, deepwater ports

■ FINANCE/TRADE

Currency: Singapore dollar ($S) = 100 cents
International Reserves Excluding Gold: $73.995 billion (Jan. 1999)
Gold Reserves: n.a.
Budget: revenues $16.3 billion; expenditures $13.6 billion, including capital expenditures n.a. (1997-98 est.)
Defence Expenditures: 4.3% of GDP (1996–97)
Education Expenditures: 3.0% of GNP (1995)
External Debt: n.a.
Exports: $109.906 billion (1998); commodities (includes transshipments to Malaysia): petroleum products, rubber electronics, manufactured goods; partners: US 24%, Malaysia 14%, Japan 9%, Thailand 6%, Hong Kong 5%, Australia 3%, Germany 3%
Imports: $101.732 billion (1998); commodities (includes transshipments from Malaysia): capital equipment, petroleum, chemicals, manufactured goods, foodstuffs; partners: Japan 22%, US 16%, Malaysia 15%, European Community 12%, Kuwait 1%

■ COMMUNICATIONS

Daily Newspapers: 8 (1996)
Televisions: 384/1,000 inhabitants (1996)
Radios: 739/1,000 inhabitants (1996)
Telephones: 50.2/100 inhabitants (1996 est.)

■ TRANSPORTATION

Motor Vehicles: 545,000; 390,000 passenger cars (1997 est.)
Roads: 3,010 km; 2,932 km paved
Railway: 38.6 km
Air Traffic: 11,857,000 passengers carried (1996)
Airports: 9; all have paved runways (1997 est.)

Canadian Embassy: Canadian High Commission, IBM Towers, 14th & 15th Fls, 80 Anson Rd, Singapore 079907; mailing address: Robinson Rd, P.O. Box 845, Singapore 901645. Tel: (011-65) 325-3200. Fax: (011-65) 325-3297.
Embassy in Canada: c/o High Commission for the Republic of Singapore, 231 East 51st St, New York NY 10022, USA. Tel: (212) 826-0840. Fax: (212) 826-2964.

Slovakia

Long-Form Name: Slovak Republic
Capital: Bratislava

■ GEOGRAPHY

Area: 48,845 sq. km
Coastline: none: landlocked
Climate: temperate: cool summers, cold, cloudy, humid winters
Environment: severe damage to forests from acid rain; industrial air pollution
Terrain: rugged mountains in central region and north, lowlands in south
Land Use: 31% arable; 3% permanent crops; 17% permanent pastures; 41% forests; 8% other
Location: C Europe

■ PEOPLE

Population: 5,392,982 (July 1998 est.)
Nationality: Slovak
Age Structure: 0-14 yrs: 21%; 15-64: 68%; 65+: 11% (1998 est.)
Population Growth Rate: 0.08% (1998 est.)
Net Migration: 0.33 migrants/1,000 population (1998 est.)
Ethnic Groups: 85.7% Slovak, 10.7% Hungarian, 1.5% Gypsy, 2.1% other
Languages: Slovak (official), Hungarian
Religions: 60.3% Roman Catholic, 9.7% atheist, 8.4% Protestant, 4.1% Orthodox, 17.5% other
Birth Rate: 9.96/1,000 population (1998 est.)
Death Rate: 9.48/1,000 population (1998 est.)
Infant Mortality: 9.73 deaths/1,000 live births (1998 est.)
Life Expectancy at Birth: 69.41 years male, 77.15 years female (1998 est.)
Total Fertility Rate: 1.27 children born/woman (1998 est.)
Literacy: n.a.

■ GOVERNMENT

Leader(s): Pres. Rudolf Schuster, Prime Min. Mikulas Dzurinda
Government Type: parliamentary democracy
Administrative Divisions: 8 departments
Nationhood: Jan. 1, 1993 (from Czechoslovakia)

National Holiday: Slovak Constitution Day, Sept. 1; Anniversary of Slovak National Uprising, Aug. 29

■ ECONOMY

Overview: Slovakia continues the difficult transition from a centrally controlled economy to a modern market-oriented economy. Private activity now makes up more than two-thirds of GDP. Slovakia continues to experience difficulty in attracting foreign investment.
GDP: $46.3 billion, per capita $8,600; real growth rate 5.9% (1997 est.)
Inflation: 7.4% (June 1998)
Industries: accounts for 39% of GDP; mining, chemicals, metalworking, consumer appliances, plastics, armaments
Labour Force: 2,197,000 (1997); 29.3% industry, 26.4% community, social and business services, 12.4% agriculture
Unemployment: 12.3% (1997)
Agriculture: accounts for 5% of GDP; very diversified crop and livestock production including grains, livestock, poultry; mostly self-sufficient in food
Natural Resources: brown coal and lignite, iron ore, copper, manganese, salt, gas

■ FINANCE/TRADE

Currency: koruna (pl. koruny) (Kc) = 100 halierov
International Reserves Excluding Gold: $2.869 billion (Dec. 1998)
Gold Reserves: 1.290 million fine troy ounces (Dec. 1998)
Budget: revenues $5.7 billion; expenditures $6.4 billion, including capital expenditures n.a. (1996)
Defence Expenditures: 2.7% of GDP (1996)
Education Expenditures: 4.4% of GNP (1995)
External Debt: $9.5 billion (1997 est.)
Exports: $10.657 billion (1998); machinery and transport equipment, chemicals, fuels, minerals, agricultural products; partners: Czech Republic, successor states of the former USSR, Germany, Poland, Austria, France, US, UK
Imports: $12.952 billion (1998); machinery and transport equipment, fuels, lubricants, manufactured goods, chemicals, agricultural products

■ COMMUNICATIONS

Daily Newspapers: 19 (1996)
Televisions: 486/1,000 inhabitants (1996)
Radios: 580/1,000 inhabitants (1996)
Telephones: 23.6/100 inhabitants (1996 est.)

■ TRANSPORTATION

Motor Vehicles: included in the data for the Czech Republic
Roads: 36,608 km; 36,059 km paved
Railway: 3,665 km
Air Traffic: 65,000 passengers carried (1997 est.)
Airports: 13; 8 have paved runways (1997 est.)

Canadian Embassy: The Canadian Embassy to Slovakia, c/o The Canadian Embassy, Mickiewiczova 6, 125 33 Prague 6, Czech Republic. Tel: (011-420-2) 7210-1800. Fax: (011-420-2) 7210-1890.
Embassy in Canada: Embassy of the Slovak Republic, 50 Rideau Terrace, Ottawa ON K1M 2A1. Tel: (613) 749-4442. Fax: (613) 749-4989.

Slovenia

Long-Form Name: Republic of Slovenia
Capital: Ljubljana

■ GEOGRAPHY

Area: 20,256 sq. km
Coastline: 46.6 km
Climate: Mediterranean climate on the coast, continental climate with mild to hot summers and cold winters in the plateaus and eastern valleys
Environment: pollution of Sava River; heavy metals and toxic chemicals along coast; forest damage from air pollution; subject to flooding and earthquakes
Terrain: short coastal strip, alpine mountain region, mixed mountains and valleys and numerous rivers in east
Land Use: 12% arable; 3% permanent crops; 28% meadows and pastures; 51% forests and woodland; 6% other
Location: southern Europe, bordering on Adriatic Sea

■ PEOPLE

Population: 1,971,739 (July 1998 est.)
Nationality: Slovene
Age Structure: 0-14 yrs: 17%; 15-64: 70%; 65+: 13% (1998 est.)
Population Growth Rate: -0.08% (1998 est.)
Net Migration: 0.21 migrants/1,000 population (1998 est.)
Ethnic Groups: 91% Slovene, 3% Croat, 2% Serb, 1% Muslim, 3% other
Languages: 91% Slovenian, 6% Serbo-Croatian, 3% other
Religions: 71% Roman Catholic, 1% Lutheran, 1% Muslim, 4.3% athiest, 23% other

Birth Rate: 8.58/1,000 population (1998 est.)
Death Rate: 9.56/1,000 population (1998 est.)
Infant Mortality: 5.34 deaths/1,000 live births (1998 est.)
Life Expectancy at Birth: 71.48 years male, 79.02 years female (1998 est.)
Total Fertility Rate: 1.17 children born/woman (1998 est.)
Literacy: 99% (1997 est.)

■ GOVERNMENT

Leader(s): Pres. Milan Kucan, Prime Min. Janez Drnovsek
Government Type: parliamentary democratic republic
Administrative Divisions: 136 municipalities and 11 urban areas
Nationhood: June 25, 1991 (from Yugoslavia)
National Holiday: National Statehood Day, June 25

■ ECONOMY

Overview: tourism has suffered due to internal strife; destruction of trade channels and the influx of tens of thousands of refugees have interfered with economic recovery after secession from Yugoslavia; there are efforts towards the privatization of major industrial firms; inflation and unemployment rates are gradually beginning to drop; chief trading partners: Germany, Italy, former Soviet countries, France, Austria, US
GDP: $19.5 billion, per capita $10,000; real growth rate 3.25% (1997 est.)
Inflation: 8.0% (June 1998)
Industries: accounts for 33% of GDP; metallurgy, furniture, sports equipment, steel, cars, sugar, cement, textiles, machine tools
Labour Force: 1 million (1997 est.); 39.3% industry, 23.1% community, social and business services, 11.1% trade and tourism
Unemployment: 7.1% (1997 est.)
Agriculture: accounts for 5% of GDP; products include wheat, maize, sugar beets, potatoes, cabbages, livestock (esp. cattle, sheep, pigs, poultry); fishing; forestry; many other agricultural products must be imported
Natural Resources: brown coal and lignite deposits, lead, zinc, mercury, uranium

■ FINANCE/TRADE

Currency: Slovenian tolar = 100 stotins (at parity with Yugoslav dinar)
International Reserves Excluding Gold: $3.639 billion (Dec. 1998)
Gold Reserves: none (Jan. 1999)
Budget: revenues $8.48 billion; expenditures

$8.53 billion, including capital expenditures (1996 est.)
Defence Expenditures: 1.5 to 1.7% of GDP (1996)
Education Expenditures: 5.8% of GNP (1995)
External Debt: $4.031 billion (1996)
Exports: $9.041 billion (1998); machinery, semifinished goods, raw materials, electric motors, transportation equipment, clothing, foodstuffs
Imports: $10.083 billion (1998); raw materials, semifinished goods, machinery, foodstuffs

■ COMMUNICATIONS

Daily Newspapers: 7 (1996)
Televisions: 364/1,000 inhabitants (1996)
Radios: 416/1,000 inhabitants (1996)
Telephones: 33.3/100 inhabitants (1996 est.)

■ TRANSPORTATION

Motor Vehicles: n.a.
Roads: 14,910 km; 12,226 km paved
Railway: 1,201 km
Air Traffic: 393,000 passengers carried (1996)
Airports: 14; 6 have paved runways (1997 est.)

Canadian Embassy: The Canadian Embassy to Slovenia, c/o The Canadian Embassy Budakeszi ut 32, 1121 Budapest, Hungary. Tel.: (011-36-1) 275-1200: (011-36-1) 275-1210.
Embassy in Canada: Embassy of the Republic of Slovenia, 150 Metcalfe St, Ste 2101, Ottawa, ON K2P 1P1. Tel: (613) 565-5781. Fax: (613) 565-5783.

Solomon Islands

Long-Form Name: Solomon Islands
Capital: Honiara (on island of Guadalcanal)

■ GEOGRAPHY

Area: 28,450 sq km
Coastline: 5,313 km
Climate: tropical monsoon; few extremes of temperature and weather
Environment: subject to typhoons, which are rarely destructive; geologically active region with frequent earth tremors; soil degradation and deforestation; deterioration of coral reefs
Terrain: mostly rugged mountains with some low coral atolls
Land Use: 1% arable; 1% permanent; 1% meadows; 88% pastures; 9% other
Location: Melanesia, Pacific Ocean

■ PEOPLE

Population: 441,039 (July 1998 est.)

Nationality: Solomon Islander
Age Structure: 0-14 yrs: 45%; 15-64: 52%; 65+: 3% (1998 est.)
Population Growth Rate: 3.24% (1998 est.)
Net Migration: 0 migrants/1,000 population (1998 est.)
Ethnic Groups: 93% Melanesian, 4% Polynesian, 1.5% Micronesian, 0.8% European, 0.3% Chinese, 0.4% other
Languages: English (official), Pidgin, 120 local languages
Religions: 34% Anglican, 19% Roman Catholic, 17% South Seas Evangelical, 25% other Protestant, 5% other
Birth Rate: 36.62/1,000 population (1998 est.)
Death Rate: 4.21/1,000 population (1998 est.)
Infant Mortality: 23.93 deaths/1,000 live births (1998 est.)
Life Expectancy at Birth: 69.26 years male, 74.41 years female (1998 est.)
Total Fertility Rate: 5.12 children born/woman (1998 est.)
Literacy: 60% (1997 est.)

■ GOVERNMENT

Leader(s): Queen Elizabeth II/Gov. Gen. John Lapli, Prime Min. Bartholomew Ulufa'alu
Government Type: parliamentary democracy
Administrative Divisions: 7 provinces and 1 town
Nationhood: July 7, 1978 (from UK; formerly known as British Solomon Islands)
National Holiday: Independence Day, July 7

■ ECONOMY

Overview: about 90% of the population depend on subsistence agriculture, fishing and forestry for at least part of their livelihood; possesses an abundance of undeveloped mineral resources; little manufacturing activity—most manufactured goods must be imported. Uncontrolled government spending is leading to national financial ruin despite a rich natural resource base
GDP: $1.27 billion, per capita $3,000; real growth rate 3.5% (1997 est.)
Inflation: 8.4% (1997)
Industries: copra, fish (tuna)
Labour Force: n.a.; 41.5% community, social and business services, 23.7% agriculture, 11.9% trade and tourism
Unemployment: n.a.
Agriculture: including fishing and forestry, accounts for approx. 31% of GDP; mostly subsistence farming; cash crops: cocoa, beans, coconuts, palm kernels, timber; other products: rice, potatoes, vegetables, fruit, cattle, pigs; not self-sufficient in food grains; 90% of fish catch is exported

Natural Resources: fish, forests, gold, bauxite, phosphates

■ FINANCE/TRADE

Currency: Solomon Islands dollar ($SI) = 100 cents
International Reserves Excluding Gold: $51 million (Jan. 1999)
Gold Reserves: n.a.
Budget: revenues $147 million; expenditures $168 million, including capital expenditures n.a. (1997 est.)
Defence Expenditures: negligible
Education Expenditures: n.a.
External Debt: $145 million (1996)
Exports: $131 million (1995); commodities: fish 46%, timber 31%, copra 5%, palm oil 5%; partners: Japan 51%, UK 12%, Thailand 9%, Netherlands 8%, Australia 2%, US 2%
Imports: $154 million (1995); commodities: plant and machinery 30%, fuel 19%, food 16%; partners: Japan 36%, US 23%, Singapore 9%, UK 9%, New Zealand 9%, Australia 4%, Hong Kong 4%, China 3%

■ COMMUNICATIONS

Daily Newspapers: 0 (1996)
Televisions: 6.1/1,000 inhabitants (1996)
Radios: 141/1,000 inhabitants (1996)
Telephones: 1.7/100 inhabitants (1996 est.)

■ TRANSPORTATION

Motor Vehicles: n.a.
Roads: n.a.; 32 km paved
Railway: none
Air Traffic: 94,000 passengers carried (1996)
Airports: 32; 2 have paved runways (1997 est.)

Canadian Embassy: The Canadian High Commission to Solomon Islands, c/o The Canadian High Commission, Commonwealth Ave, Canberra A.C.T. 2600, Australia. Tel: (011-61-2) 6273-3844. Fax: (011-61-2) 6273-3285.
Embassy in Canada: c/o High Commission for the Solomon Islands, 820-2nd Ave, Ste 800B, New York NY 10017, USA. Tel: (212) 599-6194. Fax: (212) 661-6405.

Somalia

Long-Form Name: Somalia
Capital: Mogadishu

■ GEOGRAPHY

Area: 637,660 sq. km
Coastline: 3,025 km

Climate: desert; northeast monsoon (Dec. to Feb.), cooler southwest monsoon (May to Oct.); irregular rainfall; hot, humid periods (tangambili) between monsoons
Environment: recurring droughts; frequent dust storms over eastern plains in summer; deforestation; overgrazing; soil erosion; desertification
Terrain: mostly flat to undulating plateau rising to hills in north
Land Use: 2% arable; negligible permanent crops; 69% permanent pastures; 26% forest; 3% other
Location: E Africa, bordering on Gulf of Aden, Indian Ocean

■ PEOPLE

Population: 6,841,695 (July 1998 est.)
Nationality: Somali
Age Structure: 0-14 yrs: 44%; 15-64: 53%; 65+: 3% (1998 est.)
Population Growth Rate: 4.43% (1998 est.)
Net Migration: 16.08 migrants/1,000 population (1998 est.)
Ethnic Groups: 85% Somali, rest mainly Bantu; 30,000 Arabs, 3,000 Europeans, 800 Asians
Languages: Somali (official); Arabic, Italian, English
Religions: almost entirely Sunni Muslim, small Christian community
Birth Rate: 46.75/1,000 population (1998 est.)
Death Rate: 18.5/1,000 population (1998 est.)
Infant Mortality: 125.77 deaths/1,000 live births (1998 est.)
Life Expectancy at Birth: 44.66 years male, 47.85 years female (1998 est.)
Total Fertility Rate: 7.01 children born/woman (1998 est.)
Literacy: 24% (1997 est.)

■ GOVERNMENT

Leader(s): interim government has not been recognized internationally; due to political violence throughout the country, no functioning government is in place
Government Type: n.a.
Administrative Divisions: 18 regions
Nationhood: July 1, 1960 (from a merger of British Somaliland, which became independent from the UK on June 26, 1960, and Italian Somaliland, which became independent from the Italian-administered UN trusteeship on July 1, 1960, to form the Somali Republic)
National Holiday: Anniversary of the Revolution, Oct. 21

■ ECONOMY

Overview: nomads or semi-nomads who are dependent upon livestock for their livelihoods make up about 50% of the population; one of the world's least developed countries, possessing few resources; problems include high external debt, double-digit inflation and bitter civil war which has devastated much of the economy

GDP: $8 billion, per capita $600; real growth rate 4% (1996 est.)

Inflation: n.a.

Industries: accounts for 10% of GDP; based on processing of agricultural products; sugar refining, textiles, petroleum refining

Labour Force: 3,709,000 (1995); 75.6% agriculture, 8.4% industry, 16% services

Unemployment: n.a.

Agriculture: livestock accounts for 59% of GDP and 65% of export revenue: cattle, sheep, goats; fishing potential largely unexploited; crops: bananas, sorghum, corn, mangoes, sugar cane; not self-sufficient in food

Natural Resources: uranium and largely unexploited reserves of iron ore, tin, gypsum, bauxite, copper, salt

■ FINANCE/TRADE

Currency: Somali shilling (So.Sh.) = 100 cents

International Reserves Excluding Gold: n.a.

Gold Reserves: n.a.

Budget: n.a.

Defence Expenditures: n.a.

Education Expenditures: n.a.

External Debt: $2.643 billion (1996)

Exports: n.a.; commodities: livestock, hides, skins, bananas, fish; partners: US 0.5%, Saudi Arabia, Italy, Germany

Imports: n.a.; commodities: textiles, petroleum products, foodstuffs, construction materials; partners: US 13%, Italy, Germany, Kenya, UK, Saudi Arabia

■ COMMUNICATIONS

Daily Newspapers: 2 (1996)

Televisions: 13/1,000 inhabitants (1996)

Radios: 46/1,000 inhabitants (1996)

Telephones: 0.2/100 inhabitants (1996 est.)

■ TRANSPORTATION

Motor Vehicles: 20,000; 10,000 passenger cars (1997 est.)

Roads: 22,100 km; 2,700 km paved

Railway: none

Air Traffic: n.a.

Airports: 61; 7 have paved runways (1997 est.)

Canadian Embassy: The Canadian Embassy to Somalia, c/o The Canadian High Commission, Comcraft House, Hailé Sélassie Ave, Nairobi; mailing address: The Canadian High Commission, P.O. Box 30481, Nairobi, Kenya. Tel: (011-254-2) 21-48-04. Fax: (011-254-2) 22-69-87.

Embassy in Canada: c/o The High Commission for the Republic of Kenya, 415 Laurier Ave E, Ottawa ON K1N 6R4. Tel: (613) 563-1773. Fax: (613) 233-6599.

South Africa

Long-Form Name: Republic of South Africa

Capital: Pretoria (administrative), Cape Town (legislative), Bloemfontein (judicial)

■ GEOGRAPHY

Area: 1,219,912 sq. km; includes Walvis Bay, Marion Island, and Prince Edward Island

Coastline: 2,798 km along Indian Ocean and South Atlantic Ocean

Climate: mostly semi-arid; subtropical along coast; sunny days, cool nights

Environment: lack of important arterial rivers or lakes requires extensive water conservation and control measures; prolonged droughts and increasing water pollution exacerbate the problem

Terrain: vast interior plateau rimmed by rugged hills and narrow coastal plain

Land Use: 10% arable; 1% permanent; 67% meadows; 7% forest; 15% other, includes 1% irrigated

Location: S Africa, bordering on Indian Ocean, South Atlantic Ocean

■ PEOPLE

Population: 42,834,520 (July 1998 est.)

Nationality: South African

Age Structure: 0-14 yrs: 35%; 15-64: 61%; 65+: 4% (1998 est.)

Population Growth Rate: 1.42% (1998 est.)

Net Migration: 0.08 migrants/1,000 population (1998 est.)

Ethnic Groups: 75.2% black, 13.6% white, 8.6% coloured, 2.6% Indian

Languages: 11 official languages: Afrikaans, English, Ndebele, Pedi, Sotho, Swazi, Tsonga, Tswana, Venda, Xhosa, Zulu

Religions: most of whites, coloureds and approx. 60% of blacks are Christian; approx. 60% of Indians are Hindu, 20% Muslim

Birth Rate: 26.43/1,000 population (1998 est.)

Death Rate: 12.28/1,000 population (1998 est.)

Infant Mortality: 52.04 deaths/1,000 live births (1998 est.)

Life Expectancy at Birth: 53.56 years male, 57.8 years female (1998 est.)
Total Fertility Rate: 3.16 children born/woman (1998 est.)
Literacy: 81.8% (1997 est.)

■ GOVERNMENT

Leader(s): Pres. Thabo Mvuyelwa Mbeki
Government Type: republic
Administrative Divisions: 9 provinces; after the election bringing Mandela to power, all 10 black homelands and 4 provinces existing earlier were dissolved
Nationhood: May 31, 1910 (from UK)
National Holiday: Freedom Day, April 27

■ ECONOMY

Overview: there is great disparity in living standards between the white minority (favoured) and the black majority; international embargoes against the country (because of its policy of apartheid) hurt the economy; burgeoning unemployment; has rich mineral resources (diamonds)
GDP: $270 billion, per capita $6,200; real growth rate 3% (1997 est.)
Inflation: 5.2% (June 1998)
Industries: accounts for 37% of GDP; mining (world's largest producer of platinum, gold, chrome), automobile assembly, metalworking, machinery, textile, iron and steel, chemical, fertilizer, foodstuffs
Labour Force: 15.3 million (1997 est.); 28.3% industry, 26.5% community, social and business services, 15.4% trade and tourism
Unemployment: 39.2%, with high unemployment (1997 est.)
Agriculture: accounts for 5% of GDP and 30% of labour force; diversified agriculture, with emphasis on livestock; products: cattle, poultry, sheep, wool, milk, beef, corn, wheat; sugar cane, fruit, vegetables; self-sufficient in food
Natural Resources: gold, chromium, antimony, coal, iron ore, manganese, nickel, phosphates, tin, uranium, gem diamonds, platinum, copper, vanadium, salt, natural gas

■ FINANCE/TRADE

Currency: rand (R) = 100 cents
International Reserves Excluding Gold: $4.350 billion (Jan. 1999)
Gold Reserves: 4.020 million fine troy ounces (Jan. 1999)
Budget: revenues $30.5 billion; expenditures $38 billion, including capital expenditures of $2.6 billion (1996 est.)
Defence Expenditures: 2.2% of GDP (1996)

Education Expenditures: 6.8% of GNP (1995)
External Debt: $23.5 billion (1997 est.)
Exports: $25.396 billion (1998); commodities: gold 40%, minerals and metals 23%, food 6%, chemicals 3%; partners: Germany, Japan, UK, US, other European Community, Hong Kong
Imports: $28.277 billion (1998); commodities: machinery 27%, chemicals 11%, vehicles and aircraft 11%, textiles, scientific instruments, base metals; partners: US, Germany, Japan, UK, France, Italy, Switzerland

■ COMMUNICATIONS

Daily Newspapers: 17 (1996)
Televisions: 118/1,000 inhabitants (1996)
Radios: 316/1,000 inhabitants (1996)
Telephones: 9.9/100 inhabitants (1996 est.)

■ TRANSPORTATION

Motor Vehicles: 6,280,000; 4,120,000 passenger cars (1997 est.)
Roads: 331,265 km; 137,475 km paved
Railway: 21,431 km
Air Traffic: 7,183,000 passengers carried (1996)
Airports: 750; 143 have paved runways (1997 est.)

Canadian Embassy: The Canadian High Commission, 1103 Arcadia, Hatfield 0028, Pretoria; mailing address: Private Bag X13, Hatfield 0028, South Africa. Tel: (011-27-12) 422-3000. Fax: (011-27-12) 422-3052.
Embassy in Canada: Embassy of the Republic of South Africa, 15 Sussex Dr, Ottawa ON K1M 1M8. Tel: (613) 744-0330. Fax: (613) 741-1639.

Spain

Long-Form Name: Kingdom of Spain
Capital: Madrid

■ GEOGRAPHY

Area: 504,750 sq. km; includes Balaeric Islands, Canary Islands, Ceuta, Melilla, Islas Chafarinas, Peñón de Vélez de la Gomera
Coastline: 4,964 km along Mediterranean Sea, Balearic Sea, Bay of Biscay, Strait of Gibraltar and North Atlantic Ocean
Climate: temperate; clear, hot summers in interior, more moderate and cloudy along coast; cloudy, cold winters in interior, partly cloudy and cool along coast
Environment: deforestation; air and water pollution; soil degradation; desertification; periodic droughts
Terrain: large, flat to dissected, rugged hills; Pyrenees in north

Land Use: 30% arable; 9% permanent crops; 21% meadows; 32% forest; 8% other, includes 6.5% irrigated

Location: SW Europe, bordering on Mediterranean Sea

■ PEOPLE

Population: 39,133,996 (July 1998 est.)
Nationality: Spanish
Age Structure: 0-14 yrs: 15%; 15-64: 69%; 65+: 16% (1998 est.)
Population Growth Rate: 0.08% (1998 est.)
Net Migration: 0.66 migrants/1,000 population (1998 est.)
Ethnic Groups: composite of Mediterranean and Nordic types
Languages: Castilian Spanish; second languages include 17% Catalan (northeast), 7% Galician (northwest), 2% Basque (north)
Religions: 99% Roman Catholic, 1% other sects
Birth Rate: 9.73/1,000 population (1998 est.)
Death Rate: 9.62/1,000 population (1998 est.)
Infant Mortality: 6.51 deaths/1,000 live births (1998 est.)
Life Expectancy at Birth: 73.78 years male, 81.59 years female (1998 est.)
Total Fertility Rate: 1.21 children born/woman (1998 est.)
Literacy: 96% (1997 est.)

■ GOVERNMENT

Leader(s): King Juan Carlos I, Prime Min. Jose Maria Aznar
Government Type: parliamentary monarchy
Administrative Divisions: 17 autonomous communities
Nationhood: 1492 (expulsion of the Moors and unification)
National Holiday: National Day, Oct. 12

■ ECONOMY

Overview: Spain advocates liberalization, privatization, and deregulation of the economy, and has introduced some tax reforms to that end. Nevertheless, unemployment remains the highest of all the EEU nations.
GDP: $642.4 billion, per capita $16,400; real growth rate 3.3% (1997 est.)
Inflation: 2.1% (June 1998)
Industries: accounts for 34% of GDP; textiles and apparel (including footwear), food and beverages, metals and metal manufacturing, chemicals, shipbuilding, automobiles, machine tools
Labour Force: 16.2 million (1997 est.); 64% services, 28% manufacturing and mining, 8% agriculture

Unemployment: 21% (1997 est.)
Agriculture: accounts for 4% of GDP and 14% of labour force; major products: grain, vegetables, olives, wine grapes, sugar beets, citrus fruit, beef, pork, poultry, dairy; largely self-sufficient in food; fish catch of 1.4 million metric tons
Natural Resources: coal, lignite, iron ore, uranium, mercury, pyrites, fluorspar, gypsum, zinc, lead, tungsten, copper, kaolin, potash, hydropower

■ FINANCE/TRADE

Currency: peseta (Pta) = 100 centimos [As of Jan. 1, 1999, Government securities are issued in Euros (EUR)]
International Reserves Excluding Gold: $53.353 billion (Jan. 1999)
Gold Reserves: 16.800 million fine troy ounces (Jan. 1999)
Budget: revenues $113 billion; expenditures $139 billion, including capital expenditures of $15 billion (1995)
Defence Expenditures: 1.4% of GDP (1995)
Education Expenditures: 5.0% of GNP (1995)
External Debt: n.a.
Exports: $106.281 billion (1998 est.); commodities: foodstuffs, live animals, wood, footwear, machinery, chemicals; partners: European Community 66%, US 8%, other developed countries 9%
Imports: $128.251 billion (1998 est.); commodities: petroleum, footwear, machinery, chemicals, grain, soybeans, coffee, tobacco, iron and steel, timber, cotton, transport equipment; partners: European Community 57%, US 9%, other developed countries 13%, Middle East 3%

■ COMMUNICATIONS

Daily Newspapers: 87 (1996)
Televisions: 406/1,000 inhabitants (1996)
Radios: 328/1,000 inhabitants (1996)
Telephones: 39.6/100 inhabitants (1996 est.)

■ TRANSPORTATION

Motor Vehicles: 18,300,000; 14,900,000 passenger cars (1997 est.)
Roads: 344,847 km; 341,399 km paved
Railway: 15,172 km
Air Traffic: 30,565,600 passengers carried (1996)
Airports: 98; 64 have paved runways (1997 est.)

Canadian Embassy: The Canadian Embassy, Calle Nunez de Balboa, 35, 28001 Madrid; mailing address: Apartado 587, 28080 Madrid, Spain. Tel: (011-34) 91-423-3250. Fax: (011-34) 91-423-3251.

Embassy in Canada: Embassy of the Kingdom of Spain, 74 Stanley Ave, Ottawa ON, K1M IP4. Tel: (613) 747-2252. Fax: (613) 744-1224.

Sri Lanka

Long-Form Name: Democratic Socialist Republic of Sri Lanka
Capital: Colombo

▇ GEOGRAPHY

Area: 65,610 sq. km
Coastline: 1,340 km along Indian Ocean, Bay of Bengal, Gulf of Mannar, Palk Bay
Climate: tropical; monsoonal; northeast monsoon (Dec. to Mar.); southwest monsoon (June to Oct.)
Environment: occasional cyclones, tornados; deforestation; soil erosion; pollution of fresh water resources
Terrain: mostly low, flat to rolling plain; mountains in south-central interior
Land Use: 14% arable; 15% permanent crops; 7% meadows; 32% forest; 32% other, includes 8.5% irrigated
Location: Indian Ocean, S of India

▇ PEOPLE

Population: 18,933,558 (July 1998 est.)
Nationality: Sri Lankan
Age Structure: 0-14 yrs: 28%; 15-64: 66%; 65+: 6% (1998 est.)
Population Growth Rate: 1.12% (1998 est.)
Net Migration: -1.25 migrants/1,000 population (1998 est.)
Ethnic Groups: 74% Sinhalese; 18% Tamil; 7% Moor; 1% Burgher, Malay and Veddha
Languages: Sinhala (official); Sinhala and Tamil are the national languages; Sinhala spoken by about 74% of population, Tamil spoken by about 18%; English commonly used in government and spoken by about 10% of the population
Religions: 69% Buddhist, 15% Hindu (Tamil speakers), 8% Christian, 8% Muslim
Birth Rate: 18.4/1,000 population (1998 est.)
Death Rate: 5.96/1,000 population (1998 est.)
Infant Mortality: 16.33 deaths/1,000 live births (1998 est.)
Life Expectancy at Birth: 69.82 years male, 75.41 years female (1998 est.)
Total Fertility Rate: 2.12 children born/woman (1998 est.)
Literacy: 90.2% (1997 est.)

▇ GOVERNMENT

Leader(s): Pres. Chandrika Bandaranaike Kumaratunga, Prime Min. Sirimavo Bandaranaike
Government Type: republic
Administrative Divisions: 8 provinces
Nationhood: Feb. 4, 1948 (from UK; formerly known as Ceylon)
National Holiday: Independence and National Day, Feb. 4

▇ ECONOMY

Overview: Sustained economic growth, coupled with low population growth, has pushed Sri Lanka from the ranks of the poorest countries in the world up to the threshold of the middle income countries.
GDP: $72.1 billion, per capita $3,800; real growth rate 6% (1997 est.)
Inflation: 10.3% (Apr. 1998)
Industries: accounts for 18% of GDP; processing of rubber, tea, coconuts and other agricultural commodities; cement, petroleum refining, textiles, tobacco. The apparel industry has surpassed all other kinds of manufacturing
Labour Force: 8.2 million (1997 est.); 38.7% agriculture, 18.3% community, social and business services, 12.7% industry
Unemployment: 11% (1997 est.)
Agriculture: accounts for 18.4% of GDP and almost 45% of labour force; most important staple crop is paddy rice; other field crops: sugar cane, grains, pulses, oilseeds, roots; spices; cash crops: tea, rubber, coconuts; animal products: milk, eggs, hides, meat; not self-sufficient in rice production
Natural Resources: limestone, graphite, mineral sands, gems, phosphates, clay

▇ FINANCE/TRADE

Currency: rupee (SL Re) = 100 cents
International Reserves Excluding Gold: $1.898 billion (Jan. 1999)
Gold Reserves: 0.063 million fine troy ounces (Jan. 1999)
Budget: revenues $3 billion; expenditures $4.2 billion, including capital expenditures of $1 billion (1997)
Defence Expenditures: 16.19% of total govt. expenditure (1997)
Education Expenditures: 9.76% of govt. expenditure (1997)
External Debt: $7.995 billion (1996)
Exports: $4.633 billion (1997); commodities: tea, textiles and garments, petroleum products, coconut, rubber, agricultural products, gems and jewelry, marine products; partners: US 26%, Egypt, Iraq, UK, Germany, Singapore, Japan
Imports: $5.851 billion (1997); commodities:

petroleum, machinery and equipment, textiles and textile materials, wheat, transportation equipment, electrical machinery, sugar, rice; partners: Japan, Saudi Arabia, US 5.6%, India, Singapore, Germany, UK, Iran

■ COMMUNICATIONS

Daily Newspapers: 9 (1996)
Televisions: 83/1,000 inhabitants (1996)
Radios: 210/1,000 inhabitants (1996)
Telephones: 1.1/100 inhabitants (1996 est.)

■ TRANSPORTATION

Motor Vehicles: 468,900; 220,000 passenger cars (1997 est.)
Roads: 99,200 km; 39,680 km paved
Railway: 1,501 km
Air Traffic: 1,183,000 passengers carried (1996)
Airports: 13, 12 have paved runways (1997 est.)

Canadian Embassy: The Canadian High Commission, 6 Gregory's Rd, Cinnamon Gardens, Colombo 7; mailing address: P.O. Box 1006, Colombo 7, Sri Lanka. Tel: (011-94-1) 69-58-41. Fax: (011-94-1) 68-70-49.
Embassy in Canada: High Commission for the Democratic Socialist Republic of Sri Lanka, 333 Laurier Ave W, Ste 1204, Ottawa ON K1P 1C1. Tel: (613) 233-8449. Fax: (613) 238-8448.

Sudan

Long-Form Name: Republic of the Sudan
Capital: Khartoum

■ GEOGRAPHY

Area: 2,505,810 sq. km
Coastline: 853 km along Red Sea
Climate: tropical in south; arid desert in north; rainy season (Apr. to Oct.)
Environment: dominated by the Nile and its tributaries; dust storms; desertification; unsafe drinking water resources; overhunting threatens wildlife population
Terrain: generally flat, featureless plain; mountains in east and west
Land Use: 5% arable; negligible permanent; 46% permanent pastures; 19% forest; 30% other
Location: NE Africa, bordering on Red Sea

■ PEOPLE

Population: 33,550,552 (July 1998 est.)
Nationality: Sudanese
Age Structure: 0-14 yrs: 45%; 15-64: 52%; 65+: 3% (1998 est.)
Population Growth Rate: 2.73% (1998 est.)
Net Migration: -1.73 migrants/1,000 population (1998 est.)

Ethnic Groups: 52% black, 39% Arab, 6% Beja, 2% foreigners, 1% other
Languages: Arabic (official), Nubian, Ta Bedawie, diverse dialects of Nilotic, Nilo-Hamatic and Sudanic languages, English; program of Arabization in process
Religions: 70% Sunni Muslim (in north), 25% indigenous beliefs, 5% Christian (mostly in south and Khartoum)
Birth Rate: 39.94/1,000 population (1998 est.)
Death Rate: 10.88/1,000 population (1998 est.)
Infant Mortality: 72.64 deaths/1,000 live births (1998 est.)
Life Expectancy at Birth: 55.0 years male, 56.98 years female (1998 est.)
Total Fertility Rate: 5.68 children born/woman (1998 est.)
Literacy: 46.1% (1997 est.)

■ GOVERNMENT

Leader(s): Pres. Omar Hassan Ahmed al-Bashir; First V.Pres. Ali Osman Mohamed Taha
Government Type: transitional; government was civilianized after the ruling military junta was dissolved on Oct. 16, 1993
Administrative Divisions: 26 states
Nationhood: Jan. 1, 1956 (from Egypt and UK; formerly known as Anglo-Egyptian Sudan)
National Holiday: Independence Day, Jan. 1

■ ECONOMY

Overview: a very poor country, hurt by civil war, chronic political instability, adverse weather and counterproductive governmental economic policies; agriculture is the economic base. It employs 80% of the labour force and focuses chiefly on processing agricultural produce; international aid is helping the country manage a high foreign debt but creditors want economic reform
GDP: $26.6 billion; per capita $875; real growth rate 5% (1997 est.)
Inflation: 66% (June 1995 est.)
Industries: accounts for 17% of GDP; cotton ginning, textiles, cement, edible oils, sugar, soap distilling, shoes, petroleum refining
Labour Force: 10.2 million (1997 est.); 63.4% agriculture, 4.3% industry, 32.3% services
Unemployment: n.a.
Agriculture: accounts for 33% of GDP and 80% of labour force; untapped potential for higher farm production; water shortages; two-thirds of land area suitable for crops and livestock; major products: cotton, oilseeds, sorghum, millet, wheat, gum arabic, sheep; marginally self-sufficient in most foods
Natural Resources: modest reserves of crude oil,

iron ore, copper, chromium ore, zinc, tungsten, mica, silver, crude oil

■ FINANCE/TRADE

Currency: Sudanese pound (LSd) = 100 piastres
International Reserves Excluding Gold: $79 million (June 1998)
Gold Reserves: n.a.
Budget: revenues $482 million; expenditures $1.5 billion, including capital expenditures of $30 million (1996)
Defence Expenditures: 4.3% of GDP (1996)
Education Expenditures: n.a.
External Debt: $16.972 billion (1996)
Exports: $594 million (1997); commodities: cotton 43%, sesame, gum arabic, peanuts; partners: Western Europe 46%, Saudi Arabia 14%, Eastern Europe 9%, Japan 9%, US 3%
Imports: $1.580 billion (1997); commodities: petroleum products, manufactured goods, machinery and equipment, medicines and chemicals; partners: Western Europe 32%, Africa and Asia 15%, US 13%, Eastern Europe 3%

■ COMMUNICATIONS

Daily Newspapers: 5 (1996)
Televisions: 84/1,000 inhabitants (1996)
Radios: 270/1,000 inhabitants (1996)
Telephones: 0.3/100 inhabitants (1996 est.)

■ TRANSPORTATION

Motor Vehicles: 75,000 registered vehicles, including 35,000 passenger cars (1996)
Roads: 11,900 km; 4,320 km paved
Railway: 5,516 km
Air Traffic: 491,000 passengers carried (1996)
Airports: 65; 12 have paved runways (1997 est.)

Canadian Embassy: The Canadian Embassy to the Sudan, c/o The Canadian Embassy, Old Airport Area, Higher 23, Kebele 12, House Number 122, Addis Ababa; mailing address: P.O. Box 1130, Addis Ababa, Ethiopia. Tel: (011-251-1) 71-30-22. Fax: (011-251-1) 71 30 33.
Embassy in Canada: Embassy of the Republic of the Sudan, 85 Range Rd, Ste 507–508, Ottawa ON K1N 8J6. Tel: (613) 235-4000. Fax: (613) 235-6880.

Suriname

Long-Form Name: Republic of Suriname
Capital: Paramaribo

■ GEOGRAPHY

Area: 163,270 sq. km

Coastline: 386 km along Atlantic Ocean
Climate: tropical; moderated by trade winds
Environment: mostly tropical rain forest; deforestation
Terrain: mostly rolling hills; narrow coastal plain with swamps
Land Use: 0% arable; 0% permanent; 0% meadows; 96% forest; 4% other
Location: N South America, bordering on Atlantic Ocean

■ PEOPLE

Population: 427,980 (July 1998 est.)
Nationality: Surinamer
Age Structure: 0-14 yrs: 33%; 15-64: 62%; 65+: 5% (1998 est.)
Population Growth Rate: 0.77% (1998 est.)
Net Migration: -8.99 migrants/1,000 population (1998 est.)
Ethnic Groups: 37% Hindustani (East Indian), 31% Creole (black and mixed), 15% Javanese, 10% Bush black, 3% Amerindian, 2% Chinese, 1% European, 1% other
Languages: Dutch (official), Hindustani 32%, Javanese 15%; the majority can speak the native language Sranang Tongo (Taki-Taki); English is also widely spoken
Religions: 27.4% Hindu, 19.6% Muslim, 22.8% Roman Catholic, 25.2% Protestant (predominantly Moravian), about 5% indigenous beliefs
Birth Rate: 22.48/1,000 population (1998 est.)
Death Rate: 5.79/1,000 population (1998 est.)
Infant Mortality: 27.44 deaths/1,000 live births (1998 est.)
Life Expectancy at Birth: 68.05 years male, 73.29 years female (1998 est.)
Total Fertility Rate: 2.59 children born/woman (1998 est.)
Literacy: 93% (1997 est.)

■ GOVERNMENT

Leader(s): Pres. Jules Wijdenbosch, V. Pres. Pretaapnarian Radhakishun
Government Type: republic
Administrative Divisions: 10 districts
Nationhood: Nov. 25, 1975 (from Netherlands; formerly known as Netherlands Guiana or Dutch Guiana)
National Holiday: Independence Day, Nov. 25

■ ECONOMY

Overview: the economy is vulnerable to world prices for its bauxite, which provides more than 15% of the GDP and 65+% of export earnings. Guerrilla activity has targeted the economic infrastructure; high inflation, high unemployment, widespread black-market activity and hard currency shortfalls continue to characterize the economy

GDP: $1.44 billion, per capita $3,400; real growth rate 4% (1997 est.)

Inflation: 21.0% (June 1998)

Industries: accounts for 33% of GDP; bauxite mining, alumina and aluminum production, lumbering, food processing, fishing

Labour Force: 90,100 (1995); 20% agriculture, 8.9% industry, 49.4% services, 15.2% trade and tourism

Unemployment: 20% (1997)

Agriculture: accounts for 14% of GDP and 25% of export earnings; paddy rice planted on 85% of arable land and represents 60% of total farm output; other products: bananas, palm kernels, coconuts, plantains, peanuts, beef, chicken; shrimp and forestry products of increasing importance

Natural Resources: timber, hydropower potential, fish, shrimp, bauxite, iron ore and modest amounts of nickel, copper, platinum, gold

■ FINANCE/TRADE

Currency: Surinamese guilder, gulden or florin (Sf) = 100 cents

International Reserves Excluding Gold: $100 million (Nov. 1998)

Gold Reserves: 0.212 million fine troy ounces (Nov. 1998)

Budget: adjusted for purchasing power parity: revenues $317 million; expenditures $333 million, including capital expenditures of $52 million (1997 est.)

Defence Expenditures: 1.6% of GDP (1997 est.)

Education Expenditures: n.a.

External Debt: $216 million (1996 est.)

Exports: n.a.; commodities: alumina, bauxite, aluminum, rice, wood and wood products, shrimp and fish, bananas; partners: Netherlands 28%, US 22%, Norway 18%, Japan 11%, Brazil 10%, UK 4%

Imports: n.a.; commodities: capital equipment, petroleum, foodstuffs, cotton, consumer goods; partners: US 34%, Netherlands 20%, Trinidad and Tobago 8%, Brazil 5%, UK 3%

■ COMMUNICATIONS

Daily Newspapers: 2 (1996)

Televisions: 144/1,000 inhabitants (1996)

Radios: 683/1,000 inhabitants (1996)

Telephones: 14.2/100 inhabitants (1996 est.)

■ TRANSPORTATION

Motor Vehicles: 66,000; 46,900 passenger cars (1997 est.)

Roads: 4,530 km; 1,178 km paved

Railway: 166 km

Air Traffic: 195,000 passengers carried (1996)

Airports: 45; 5 have paved runways (1997 est.)

Canadian Embassy: The Canadian Embassy to Suriname, c/o Canadian High Commission, High and Young Streets, Georgetown; mailing address: P.O. Box 10880, Georgetown, Guyana. Office: Canadian Consulate, Wagenwagstraat 50 bov Paramaribo, Suriname. Tel. (011-597) 424-527. Fax: (011-597) 425-962.

Embassy in Canada: c/o Embassy of the Republic of Suriname, Van Ness Center, 4301 Connecticut Ave NW, Ste 108, Washington DC 20008, USA. Tel: (202) 244-7488. Fax: (202) 244-5878.

Svalbard

Long-Form Name: Svalbard

Capital: Longyearbyen

■ GEOGRAPHY

Area: 62,050 sq. km, 5 large islands, many smaller ones

Climate: arctic, tempered by mild Atlantic winds, cool suumers, cold winters

Land Use: undeveloped except for mining establishments; no trees—the only bushes are crowberry and cloudberry

Location: Arctic Ocean, midway between Norway and the North Pole

■ PEOPLE

Population: 2,594 (July 1998 est.)

Nationality: Norwegian

Ethnic Groups: 62% Russian and Ukrainian; 38% Norwegian

Languages: Norwegian, Russian

■ GOVERNMENT

Colony Territory of: Dependent Territory of Norway

Leader(s): Chief of State: King Harald V (Norway); Governor Morten Ruud, Ass't Gov. Odd Reidar Humlegaard

Government Type: Territory of Norway

National Holiday: n.a.

■ ECONOMY

Overview: tourism most important; coal mining only industry (the Norwegian state-owned company employs almost 60% of the population); some trapping of seal, polar bear, fox and walrus

■ FINANCE/TRADE

Currency: Norwegian krone = 100 oere

Canadian Embassy: c/o The Canadian Embassy, Wergelandsveien 7, 0244 Oslo, Norway. Tel: (011-47) 22-99-53-00. Fax: (011-47) 22-99-53-01.

Representative to Canada: c/o Embassy of the Kingdom of Norway, Royal Bank Centre, 90 Sparks St, Ste 532, Ottawa ON K1P 5B4. Tel: (613) 238-6571. Fax: (613) 238-2765.

Swaziland

Long-Form Name: Kingdom of Swaziland
Capital: Mbabane (administrative); Lobamba (legislative)

■ GEOGRAPHY

Area: 17,360 sq. km
Coastline: none: landlocked
Climate: varies from tropical to near temperate
Environment: overhunting and overgrazing; soil degradation; soil erosion; limited safe drinking water
Terrain: mostly mountains and hills; some moderately sloping plains
Land Use: 11% arable; 0% permanent; 62% meadows; 7% forest; 20% other
Location: S Africa

■ PEOPLE

Population: 966,462 (July 1998 est.)
Nationality: Swazi
Age Structure: 0-14 yrs: 46%; 15-64: 51%; 65+: 3% (1998 est.)
Population Growth Rate: 1.96% (1998 est.)
Net Migration: 0 migrants/1,000 population (1998 est.)
Ethnic Groups: 97% African, 3% European
Languages: English and siSwati (official); government business conducted in English
Religions: 60% Christian, 40% indigenous beliefs
Birth Rate: 41.0/1,000 population (1998 est.)
Death Rate: 21.4/1,000 population (1998 est.)
Infant Mortality: 103.37 deaths/1,000 live births (1998 est.)
Life Expectancy at Birth: 37.31 years male, 39.79 years female (1998 est.)
Total Fertility Rate: 5.96 children born/woman (1998 est.)
Literacy: 76.7% (1997 est.)

■ GOVERNMENT

Leader(s): King Mswati III; Premier Barnabas Sibusiso Dlamini

Government Type: monarchy; independent member of Commonwealth
Administrative Divisions: 4 districts
Nationhood: Sept. 6, 1968 (from UK)
National Holiday: Somhlolo (Independence) Day, Sept. 6

■ ECONOMY

Overview: the economy is based on subsistence agriculture and is closely tied to that of its neighbour, South Africa, from which it receives 90% of its imports and to which it sends about half of its exports; manufacturing focuses on the processing of agricultural products; mining is becoming less important. Overgrazing, soil deterioration and recurrent droughts are persistent problems
GDP: adjusted for purchasing power parity: $3.9 billion, per capita $3,800; real growth rate 3% (1997 est.)
Inflation: 21.1% (Mar. 1997)
Industries: accounts for 42% of GDP; mining (coal and asbestos), wood pulp, sugar; asbestos is declining in importance
Labour Force: 135,000 (1996); 74% agriculture, 17% services, 9% industry; 24,000–29,000 employed in South Africa
Unemployment: 22% (1995 est.)
Agriculture: accounts for 10% of GDP and over 60% of labour force; mostly subsistence agriculture; cash crops: sugar cane, citrus fruit, cotton, pineapple; other crops and livestock: corn, sorghum, peanuts, cattle, goats, sheep; not self-sufficient in grain
Natural Resources: asbestos, coal, clay, tin, hydroelectric power, forests and small gold and diamond deposits

■ FINANCE/TRADE

Currency: lilangeni (pl. emalangeni) (E) = 100 cents
International Reserves Excluding Gold: $364 million (Jan. 1999)
Gold Reserves: n.a.
Budget: revenues $400 million; expenditures $450 million, including capital expenditures of $115 million (1996-97)
Defence Expenditures: n.a.
Education Expenditures: n.a.
External Debt: $220 million (1996)
Exports: $893 million (1996); commodities: sugar, asbestos, wood pulp, citrus, canned fruit, soft drink concentrates; partners: South Africa, UK, US
Imports: $1.286 billion (1997); commodities: motor vehicles, machinery, transport equipment, chemicals, petroleum products, foodstuffs; partners: South Africa, US, UK

■ COMMUNICATIONS

Daily Newspapers: 3 (1996)
Televisions: 23/1,000 inhabitants (1996)
Radios: 170/1,000 inhabitants (1996)
Telephones: 2.1/100 inhabitants (1996 est.)

■ TRANSPORTATION

Motor Vehicles: 36,755; 28,523 passenger cars (1997 est.)
Roads: 2,885 km; 814 km paved
Railway: 297 km, including 71 km disused
Air Traffic: 54,000 passengers carried (1996)
Airports: 18; 1 has paved runways (1997 est.)

Canadian Embassy: The Canadian High Commission to Swaziland, c/o The Canadian Embassy, 1103 Arcadia St, Hatfield 0028, Pretoria; mailing address: Private Bag X13, Hatfield 0028, Pretoria, South Africa. Tel: (011-27-12) 422-3000. Fax (011-27-12) 422-3052.
Embassy in Canada: High Commission for the Kingdom of Swaziland, 130 Albert St, Ste 1204, Ottawa ON K1P 5G4. Tel: (613) 567-1480. Fax: (613) 567-1058.

Sweden

Long-Form Name: Kingdom of Sweden
Capital: Stockholm

■ GEOGRAPHY

Area: 449,960 sq. km
Coastline: 3,218 km
Climate: temperate in south with cold, cloudy winters and cool, partly cloudy summers, subarctic in north
Environment: water pollution; acid rain; ice floes in coastal waters hinder navigation
Terrain: mostly flat or gently rolling lowlands; mountains in west
Land Use: 7% arable; 0% permanent crops; 1% meadows; 68% forest; 24% other
Location: N Europe, bordering on Baltic Sea

■ PEOPLE

Population: 8,886,738 (July 1998 est.)
Nationality: Swedish
Age Structure: 0-14 yrs: 19%; 15-64: 64%; 65+: 17% (1998 est.)
Population Growth Rate: 0.26% (1998 est.)
Net Migration: 1.69 migrants/1,000 population (1998 est.)
Ethnic Groups: homogeneous white population; small Lappish minority; about 12% foreign born or first-generation immigrants (Finns, Yugoslavs, Danes, Norwegians, Greeks, Turks)

Languages: Swedish (official), small Lapp- and Finnish-speaking minorities; immigrants speak native languages
Religions: 94% Evangelical Lutheran, 1.5% Roman Catholic, 4.5% other
Birth Rate: 11.7/1,000 population (1998 est.)
Death Rate: 10.77/1,000 population (1998 est.)
Infant Mortality: 3.93 deaths/1,000 live births (1998 est.)
Life Expectancy at Birth: 76.52 years male, 82.0 years female (1998 est.)
Total Fertility Rate: 1.76 children born/woman (1998 est.)
Literacy: 99% (1997 est.)

■ GOVERNMENT

Leader(s): King Carl XVI Gustaf, Prime Min. Goran Persson
Government Type: constitutional monarchy
Administrative Divisions: 24 provinces
Nationhood: June 6, 1809, constitutional monarchy established
National Holiday: Day of the Swedish Flag, June 6

■ ECONOMY

Overview: a mixed system of high-tech capitalism and extensive welfare benefits; has benefited from neutrality in world wars; economy is heavily oriented towards foreign trade; has excellent communications systems but faces loss of competitive edge as inflation and unemployment rates rise
GDP: $176.2 billion, per capita $19,700; real growth rate 2.1% (1997 est.)
Inflation: 0.1% (July 1998)
Industries: accounts for 27% of GDP; iron and steel, precision equipment (bearings, radio and telephone parts, armaments), wood pulp and paper products, processed foods, motor vehicles
Labour Force: 3,982,000 (1997); 40.4% community, social and business services, 18.3 industry, 14.3 % trade and tourism
Unemployment: 6.2% (Jan. 1999)
Agriculture: accounts for 2% of GDP; animal husbandry predominates, with milk and dairy products accounting for 37% of farm income; main crops: grains, sugar beets, potatoes; 100% self-sufficient in grains and potatoes, 85% self-sufficient in sugar beets
Natural Resources: zinc, iron ore, lead, copper, silver, timber, uranium, hydropower potential

■ FINANCE/TRADE

Currency: krona (pl. kronor) (Skr) = 100 oere
International Reserves Excluding Gold: $14.112 billion (Jan. 1999)

Gold Reserves: 5.961 million fine troy ounces (Jan. 1999)
Budget: revenues $109.4 billion; expenditures $146.1 billion, including capital expenditures n.a. (1995–96)
Defence Expenditures: 5.35% of govt. expenditure (1997)
Education Expenditures: 5.66% of govt. expenditure (1997)
External Debt: n.a.
Exports: $82.548 billion (1998 est.); commodities: machinery, motor vehicles, paper products, pulp and wood, iron and steel products, chemicals, petroleum and petroleum products; partners: European Community 52.1%, (Germany 12.1%, UK 11.2%, Denmark 6.8%), US 9.8%, Norway 9.3%
Imports: $65.976 billion (1998 est.); commodities: machinery, petroleum and petroleum products, chemicals, motor vehicles, foodstuffs, iron and steel, clothing; partners: European Community 55.8%, (Germany 21.2%, UK 8.6%, Denmark 6.6%), US 7.5%, Norway 6%

■ **COMMUNICATIONS**

Daily Newspapers: 94 (1996)
Televisions: 499/1,000 inhabitants (1996)
Radios: 907/1,000 inhabitants (1996)
Telephones: 68.2/100 inhabitants (1996 est.)

■ **TRANSPORTATION**

Motor Vehicles: 4,00,000; 3,800,000 passenger cars (1997 est.)
Roads: 138,000 km; 105,018 km paved
Railway: 11,837 km
Air Traffic: 10,000,000 passengers carried (1997 est.)
Airports: 255; 145 have paved runways (1997 est.)

Canadian Embassy: The Canadian Embassy, Tegelbacken 4 (Flr 7), Stockholm; mailing address: P.O. Box 16129; S-10323 Stockholm, Sweden. Tel: (011-46-8) 453-3000. Fax: (011-46-8) 24 24 91.
Embassy in Canada: Embassy of Sweden, Mercury Court, 377 Dalhousie St, Ottawa ON K1N 9N8. Tel: (613) 241-8553. Fax: (613) 241-2277.

Switzerland

Long-Form Name: Swiss Confederation
Capital: Bern

■ **GEOGRAPHY**

Area: 41,290 sq. km

Coastline: none: landlocked
Climate: temperate, but varies with altitude; cold, cloudy, rainy/snowy winters; cool to warm, cloudy, humid summers with occasional showers
Environment: dominated by Alps; air and water pollution; avalanches, flash floods and landslides are natural hazards
Terrain: mostly mountains (Alps in south, Jura in northwest) with a central plateau of rolling hills, plains and large lakes
Land Use: 10% arable; 2% permanent; 28% permanent pastures; 32% forest; 28% other
Location: SC Europe

■ **PEOPLE**

Population: 7,260,357 (July 1998 est.)
Nationality: Swiss
Age Structure: 0-14 yrs: 17%; 15-64: 68%; 65+: 15% (1998 est.)
Population Growth Rate: 0.22% (1998 est.)
Net Migration: 0.42 migrants/1,000 population (1998 est.)
Ethnic Groups: total population: 65% German, 18% French, 10% Italian, 1% Romansch, 6% other; Swiss nationals: 74% German, 20% French, 4% Italian, 1% Romansch, 1% other
Languages: 65% German, 18% French, 12% Italian, 1% Raeto-Romansch (all official), 4% other
Religions: 47.6% Roman Catholic, 44.3% Protestant, 8.1% other
Birth Rate: 10.81/1,000 population (1998 est.)
Death Rate: 9.03/1,000 population (1998 est.)
Infant Mortality: 4.92 deaths/1,000 live births (1998 est.)
Life Expectancy at Birth: 75.71 years male, 82.22 years female (1998 est.)
Total Fertility Rate: 1.46 children born/woman (1998 est.)
Literacy: 99% (1997 est.)

■ **GOVERNMENT**

Leader(s): Pres. Ruth Dreifuss; V.Pres. Adolf Ogi
Government Type: federal republic
Administrative Divisions: 26 cantons
Nationhood: Aug. 1, 1291
National Holiday: Anniversary of the Founding of the Swiss Confederation, Aug. 1

■ **ECONOMY**

Overview: country has the highest per capita output, general living standards, education and science, healthcare and diet standards in Europe; important banking and tourist sectors; low inflation and negligible unemployment is due partly to government policies; has rejected membership in the European Economic Community

GDP: $172.4 billion, per capita $23,800; real growth rate 0.4% (1997 est.)

Inflation: 0.1% (July 1998)

Industries: accounts for 31% of GDP; machinery, chemicals, watches, textiles, precision instruments

Labour Force: 4 million (1997 est.); 24.3% industry, 23.6% community, social and business services, 20.3% trade and tourism

Unemployment: 3.4% (Feb. 1999)

Agriculture: accounts for 3% of GDP; dairy farming predominates; less than 50% self-sufficient; food shortages: fish, refined sugar, fats and oils (other than butter), grains, eggs, fruit, vegetables, meat

Natural Resources: hydropower potential, timber, salt; scenic beauty

■ FINANCE/TRADE

Currency: Swiss franc, franken, or franco (SwF) = 100 centimes, rappen, or centesimi

International Reserves Excluding Gold: $38.695 billion (Jan. 1999)

Gold Reserves: 83.277 million fine troy ounces (Jan. 1999)

Budget: revenues $25.8 billion; expenditures $30.8 billion, including capital expenditures of $2.3 billion (1997)

Defence Expenditures: 5.81% of total govt. expenditure (1996)

Education Expenditures: 2.58% of total govt. expenditure (1996)

External Debt: n.a.

Exports: $75.400 billion (1998); commodities: machinery and equipment, precision instruments, metal products, foodstuffs, textiles and clothing; partners: Europe 64% (European Community 56%, other 8%), US 9%, Japan 4%

Imports: $73.885 billion (1998); commodities: agricultural products, machinery and transportation equipment, chemicals, textiles, construction materials; partners: Europe 79% (European Community 72%, other 7%), US 5%

■ COMMUNICATIONS

Daily Newspapers: 88 (1996)

Televisions: 443/1,000 inhabitants (1996)

Radios: 969/1,000 inhabitants (1996)

Telephones: 62.5/100 inhabitants (1996 est.)

■ TRANSPORTATION

Motor Vehicles: 3,700,000; 3,300,000 passenger cars (1997 est.)

Roads: 71,117 km; all paved

Railway: 5,249 km

Air Traffic: 10,800,000 passengers carried (1997 est.)

Airports: 67; 42 have paved runways (1997 est.)

Canadian Embassy: Canadian Embassy, Kirchenfeldstrasse 88, 3005 Berne, Switzerland; mailing address: Box 3000, Berne 6, Switzerland. Tel: (011-41-31) 357-32-00. Fax: (011-41-31) 357-32-10.

Embassy in Canada: Embassy of Switzerland, 5 Marlborough Ave, Ottawa ON K1N 8E6. Tel: (613) 235-1837. Fax: (613) 563-1394.

Syria

Long-Form Name: Syrian Arab Republic
Capital: Damascus

■ GEOGRAPHY

Area: 185,180 sq. km; including 1,295 sq. km of Israeli-occupied territory

Coastline: 193 km along Mediterranean Sea

Climate: mostly desert; hot, dry, sunny summers (June to Aug.) and mild, rainy winters (Dec. to Feb.) along coast

Environment: deforestation; overgrazing; soil erosion; desertification; unsafe drinking water

Terrain: primarily semi-arid and desert plateau; narrow coastal plain; mountains in west

Land Use: 28% arable; 4% permanent crops; 43% meadows; 3% forest; 22% other; includes 5.5% irrigated

Location: SW Asia (Middle East), bordering on Mediterranean Sea

■ PEOPLE

Population: 16,673,282 (July 1998 est.)

Nationality: Syrian

Age Structure: 0-14 yrs: 46%; 15-64: 51%; 65+: 3% (1998 est.)

Population Growth Rate: 3.23% (1998 est.)

Net Migration: 0 migrants/1,000 population (1998 est.)

Ethnic Groups: 90.3% Arab; 9.7% Kurds, Armenians and other

Languages: Arabic (official), Kurdish, Armenian, Aramaic, Circassian; English and French widely understood

Religions: 74% Sunni, 16% Alawite, Druze and other Muslim sects, 10% Christian

Birth Rate: 37.83/1,000 population (1998 est.)

Death Rate: 5.55/1,000 population (1998 est.)

Infant Mortality: 37.6 deaths/1,000 live births (1998 est.)

Life Expectancy at Birth: 66.48 years male, 69.11 years female (1998 est.)

Total Fertility Rate: 5.55 children born/woman (1998 est.)

Literacy: 70.8% (1997 est.)

■ GOVERNMENT

Leader(s): Pres. Lt.-Gen. Hafez al-Assad, V.Pres. Abd al-Halim ibn Said Khaddam
Government Type: republic under leftwing military regime
Administrative Divisions: 14 provinces
Nationhood: Apr. 17, 1946 (from League of Nations mandate under French administration; formerly known as United Arab Republic)
National Holiday: National Day, Apr. 17

■ ECONOMY

Overview: economic difficulties are due, in part, to severe drought in several recent years, costly but unsuccessful attempts to match Israel's military strength, a fall-off in Arab aid and insufficient foreign exchange earnings to buy needed imports; agricultural output is poor; a major long-term concern is the additional drain of upstream Euphrates water by Turkey once its vast dam and irrigation projects are completed
GDP: $106.1 billion, per capita $6,600; real growth rate 4.6% (1997 est.)
Inflation: -4.8% (June 1998)
Industries: accounts for 14% of GDP, textiles, food processing, beverages, tobacco, phosphate rock mining, petroleum
Labour Force: 4.1 million (1997 est.); 62.9% services, 22% agriculture, 15.1% industry
Unemployment: 12% (1997 est.)
Agriculture: accounts for 28% of GDP; all major crops (wheat, barley, cotton, lentils, chickpeas) grown on rain-fed land causing wide swings in yields; animal products: beef, lamb, eggs, poultry, milk; not self-sufficient in grain or livestock products
Natural Resources: crude oil, phosphates, chrome and manganese ores, asphalt, iron ore, rock salt, marble, gypsum

■ FINANCE/TRADE

Currency: Syrian pound (£S) = 100 piastres
International Reserves Excluding Gold: n.a.
Gold Reserves: 0.833 million fine troy ounces (Jan. 1999)
Budget: revenues $3.9 billion; expenditures $4.3 billion, including capital expenditures of $1.9 billion (1996 est.)
Defence Expenditures: 26.19% of govt. expenditure (1996)
Education Expenditures: 10.39% of govt. expenditure (1996)
External Debt: $20 billion (1997 est.)
Exports: $3.916 billion (1997); commodities: petroleum, textiles, fruit and vegetables, phosphates; partners: Italy, Romania, former USSR countries, US, Iran, France
Imports: $4.028 billion (1997); commodities:

petroleum, machinery, base metals, foodstuffs and beverages; partners: Iran, Germany, former USSR countries, France, Libya, US

■ COMMUNICATIONS

Daily Newspapers: 8 (1996)
Televisions: 69/1,000 inhabitants (1996)
Radios: 274/1,000 inhabitants (1996)
Telephones: 7.7/100 inhabitants (1996 est.)

■ TRANSPORTATION

Motor Vehicles: 352,900; 134,000 passenger cars (1997 est.)
Roads: 40,480 km; n.a. paved
Railway: 1,998 km
Air Traffic: 605,000 passengers carried (1997 est.)
Airports: 104; 24 have paved runways (1997 est.)

Canadian Embassy: The Canadian Embassy, Lot 12, Mezzah Autostrade, Damascus; mailing address: P.O. Box 3394, Damascus, Syria. Tel: (011-963-11) 611-6692. Fax: (011-963-11) 611-4000.
Embassy in Canada: c/o Embassy of the Syrian Arab Republic, 2215 Wyoming Ave NW, Washington DC 20008, USA. Tel: (202) 232-6313. Fax: (202) 234-9548.

Taiwan

Long-Form Name: Taiwan
Capital: Taipei

■ GEOGRAPHY

Area: 35,980 sq. km; includes the Pescadores, Matsu and Quemoy
Coastline: 1,448 km
Climate: tropical; marine; rainy season during southwest monsoon (June to Aug.)
Environment: subject to earthquakes and typhoons; water and air pollution
Terrain: eastern two-thirds mostly rugged mountains; flat to gently rolling plains in west
Land Use: 24% arable; 1% permanent; 5% meadows; 55% forest; 15% other
Location: SE of China, bordering on South and East China Seas, Pacific Ocean

■ PEOPLE

Population: 21,908,135 (July 1998 est.)
Nationality: Chinese
Age Structure: 0-14 yrs: 22%; 15-64: 69%; 65+: 9% (1998 est.)
Population Growth Rate: 0.94% (1998 est.)
Net Migration: -0.02 migrants/1,000 population (1998 est.)

Ethnic Groups: 84% Taiwanese, 14% mainland Chinese, 2% aborigine
Languages: Mandarin Chinese (official); Taiwanese and Hakka dialects also used
Religions: 93% mixture of Buddhist, Islam, Confucian and Taoist, 5% Christian, 3% other
Birth Rate: 14.79/1,000 population (1998 est.)
Death Rate: 5.42/1,000 population (1998 est.)
Infant Mortality: 6.34 deaths/1,000 live births (1998 est.)
Life Expectancy at Birth: 73.82 years male, 80.05 years female (1998 est.)
Total Fertility Rate: 1.77 children born/woman (1998 est.)
Literacy: 86% (1997 est.)

■ GOVERNMENT

Leader(s): Pres. Lee Teng-hui, Prem. Vincent Siew
Government Type: multi-party democratic regime
Administrative Divisions: 16 counties, 5 municipalities, 2 special municipalities
Nationhood: n.a.
National Holiday: National Day (Anniversary of the Revolution), Oct. 10

■ ECONOMY

Overview: Taiwan has a dynamic capitalist economy with gradually decreasing guidance of investment and foreign trade by government authorities and partial government ownership of some large banks and industrial firms.
GDP: $308 billion, per capita $14,200; real growth rate 6.8% (1997 est.)
Inflation: 4% (1995 est.)
Industries: accounts for 36% of GDP, textiles, clothing, chemicals, electronics, food processing, plywood, sugar milling, cement, shipbuilding, petroleum
Labour Force: 9.4 million (1997 est.); 52% services, 38% industry, 10% agriculture
Unemployment: 2.7% (1997)
Agriculture: accounts for 3% of GDP; heavily subsidized sector; major crops: rice sugar cane, sweet potatoes, fruit, vegetables; livestock: hogs, poultry, beef, milk, cattle; not self-sufficient in wheat, soybeans, corn; fish catch expanding, 1.4 million metric tons
Natural Resources: small deposits of coal, natural gas, limestone, marble and asbestos

■ FINANCE/TRADE

Currency: New Taiwan dollar (NT$) = 100 cents
International Reserves Excluding Gold: $61.888 billion (Dec. 1997)
Gold Reserves: n.a.
Budget: revenues $40 billion; expenditures $55 billion, including capital expenditures of n.a. (1998 est.)
Defence Expenditures: 3.6% of GDP (1996–97)
Education Expenditures: n.a.
External Debt: $80 million (1997 est.)
Exports: $121.301 billion (1997); commodities: textiles 16%, electrical machinery 19%, general machinery and equipment 14%, telecommunications equipment 9%, basic metals and metal products 5%, foodstuffs 0.9%, plywood and wood products 1.3%; partners: US 36.2%, Japan 13.7%
Imports: $113.930 billion (1997); commodities: machinery and equipment 15.9%, crude oil 5%, chemical and chemical products 11.1%, basic metals 7.4%, foodstuffs 2%; partners: Japan 31%, US 23%, Saudi Arabia 8.6%

■ COMMUNICATIONS

Daily Newspapers: n.a.
Televisions: n.a.
Radios: n.a.
Telephones: n.a.

■ TRANSPORTATION

Motor Vehicles: 5,225,000; 4,300,000 passenger cars (1997 est.)
Roads: 19,701 km; 17,238
Railway: 4,600 km
Air Traffic: n.a.
Airports: 40; 36 have paved runways (1997 est.)

Canadian Embassy: none
Embassy in Canada: none

Tajikistan

Long-Form Name: Republic of Tajikistan
Capital: Dushanbe

■ GEOGRAPHY

Area: 143,100 sq. km
Coastline: none; landlocked
Climate: continental; severe winters in east; extremely hot summers; wet spring; semi-arid to polar in Pamir mountains
Environment: lack of fresh water; little land suitable for cultivation; industrial pollution
Terrain: mountains and glaciers constitute 93% of land area, predominantly herding and nonagricultural
Land Use: 6% arable, negligible permanent crops, 25% meadows and pastures, 4% forest and woodland, 65% other, includes 5% irrigated
Location: C Asia

■ PEOPLE

Population: 6,020,095 (July 1998 est.)

Nationality: Tajik, Tajikistani
Age Structure: 0-14 yrs: 41%; 15-64: 54%; 65+: 5% (1998 est.)
Population Growth Rate: 1.3% (1998 est.)
Net Migration: -6.87 migrants/1,000 population (1998 est.)
Ethnic Groups: 64.9% Tajik, 25% Uzbek, 3.5% Russian (declining due to emigration), 6.6% other
Languages: Tajik (official), Uzbek, Russian
Religions: 80% Sunni Muslim, 5% Shia Muslim, 15% other
Birth Rate: 27.67/1,000 population (1998 est.)
Death Rate: 7.77/1,000 population (1998 est.)
Infant Mortality: 112.14 deaths/1,000 live births (1998 est.)
Life Expectancy at Birth: 61.35 years male, 67.77 years female (1998 est.)
Total Fertility Rate: 3.53 children born/woman (1998 est.)
Literacy: 98% (1997 est.)

■ GOVERNMENT

Leader(s): Pres. Imamoli Rakhmanov, Prime Min. Yakhyo Azimov
Government Type: republic
Administrative Divisions: 2 oblasts and 1 autonomous oblast
Nationhood: Sept. 9, 1991 (from Soviet Union)
National Holiday: National Day, Sept. 9

■ ECONOMY

Overview: mostly mining and manufacturing with strong agricultural sector; industry and agriculture have been producing at reduced capacity due to civil unrest. Currency incompatibility with neighbouring countries is straining trade relations
GDP: adjusted for purchasing power parity: $4.1 billion, per capita $700; real growth rate -10% (1997 est.)
Inflation: 28% per month (1995 est.)
Industries: accounts for 35% of GDP; aluminum and electrochemical plants, textile machinery, silk and carpet mills; zinc, lead, chemicals and fertilizers, cement, vegetable oil, refrigerators and freezers
Labour Force: 2 million (1997 est.); 43% agriculture and forestry, 22% industry and construction, 35% other
Unemployment: 2.4% (Dec. 1996); also large numbers of underemployed
Agriculture: accounts for 25% of GDP; cotton, grapes, fruit, grains, silkworm farming, cattle breeding, sheep, goats, pigs
Natural Resources: coal, oil, rare metals, rock crystal, mica, gold, hydropower potential, uranium, mercury, zinc

■ FINANCE/TRADE

Currency: Tajik ruble (R) = 100 tanga
International Reserves Excluding Gold: n.a.
Gold Reserves: n.a.
Budget: n.a.
Defence Expenditures: 3.4% of GDP (1995)
Education Expenditures: 8.6% of GNP (1995)
External Debt: $707 million (1996)
Exports: $785 million (1997); commodities: fruit, plant products, aluminum; partners: other Central Asian countries
Imports: $797 million (1997); commodities: fuel, machinery, foodstuffs; partners: other Central Asian countries

■ COMMUNICATIONS

Daily Newspapers: 2 (1996)
Televisions: n.a.
Radios: n.a.
Telephones: 4.4/100 inhabitants (1996 est.)

■ TRANSPORTATION

Motor Vehicles: n.a.
Roads: 32,752 km; 21,119 km paved
Railway: 480 km, not including industrial lines
Air Traffic: 594,000 passengers carried (1996)
Airports: 39, 14 have paved runways (1997 est.)

Canadian Embassy: The Canadian Embassy to Tajikistan, c/o The Canadian Embassy, 34 Kasarai Batir St, Almaty 480100, Kazakhstan. Tel: (011-7-3272) 50-11-51. Fax: (011-7-327) 581-14-93.
Embassy in Canada: n.a.

Tanzania

Long-Form Name: United Republic of Tanzania
Capital: Dar es Salaam

■ GEOGRAPHY

Area: 945,090 sq. km
Coastline: 1,424 km along Indian Ocean, lakes
Climate: varies from tropical along coast to temperate in highlands
Environment: deforestation; lack of water limits agriculture; recent droughts affected marginal agriculture
Terrain: plains along coast; central plateau; highlands in north, south; Kilimanjaro is highest point in Africa
Land Use: 3% arable; 1% permanent; 40% meadows; 38% forest; 18% other
Location: E Africa, bordering on Indian Ocean

■ PEOPLE

Population: 30,608,769 (July 1998 est.)
Nationality: Tanzanian
Age Structure: 0-14 yrs: 45%; 15-64: 53%; 65+: 2% (1998 est.)
Population Growth Rate: 2.14% (1998 est.)
Net Migration: -2.61 migrants/1,000 population (1998 est.)
Ethnic Groups: 99% native African consisting of well over 100 tribes; 1% Asian, European and Arab
Languages: Swahili and English (official); English primarily language of commerce, administration and higher education; Swahili widely understood and generally used for communication between ethnic groups
Religions: mainland: 45% Christian, 35% Muslim, 20% indigenous beliefs; Zanzibar: almost all Muslim
Birth Rate: 40.75/1,000 population (1998 est.)
Death Rate: 16.71/1,000 population (1998 est.)
Infant Mortality: 96.94 deaths/1,000 live births (1998 est.)
Life Expectancy at Birth: 44.22 years male, 48.59 years female (1998 est.)
Total Fertility Rate: 5.49 children born/woman (1998 est.)
Literacy: 67.8% (1997 est.)

■ GOVERNMENT

Leader(s): Pres. Benjamin William Mkapa, Prem. Frederick Sumaye
Government Type: republic
Administrative Divisions: 25 regions
Nationhood: April 26, 1964; Tanganyika became independent on Dec. 9, 1961 (from UN trusteeship under British administration); Zanzibar became independent Dec. 19, 1963 (from UK); Tanganyika united with Zanzibar Apr. 26, 1964 to form the political unit that was renamed Tanzania on Oct. 29, 1964
National Holiday: Union Day, Apr. 26

■ ECONOMY

Overview: world aid is increasing the availability of imports and providing funds to rehabilitate this country's deteriorated economic infrastructure; this poor economy is heavily dependent on agriculture; industry is largely confined to processing agricultural products; mining is increasing in importance
GDP: $21.1 billion, per capita $700; real growth rate 4.3% (1997 est.)
Inflation: 12.6% (May 1998)
Industries: accounts for 17% of GDP; primarily agricultural processing (sugar, beer, cigarettes, sisal twine), diamond mines, oil refineries, shoes, cement, textiles, wood products, fertilizer

Labour Force: 16.5 million (1997 est.); 90% agriculture, 10% industry and commerce
Unemployment: n.a.
Agriculture: accounts for 57% of GDP, 85% of exports and employs 90% of workforce; topography and climatic conditions limit cultivated crops to only 5% of land area; cash crops: coffee, sisal, tea, cotton, pyrethrum (insecticide made from chrysanthemums), cashews, tobacco, cloves (Zanzibar); corn, wheat, beans, fruit and vegetables grown for local consumption
Natural Resources: hydropower potential, tin, phosphates, iron ore, coal, diamonds, gemstones, gold, natural gas, nickel

■ FINANCE/TRADE

Currency: Tanzania shilling (TSh) = 100 cents
International Reserves Excluding Gold: $586 million (Jan. 1999)
Gold Reserves: n.a.
Budget: revenues $959 million; expenditures $1.1 billion, including capital expenditures of $214 million (1996-97 est.)
Defence Expenditures: 2.5 of GDP (1996)
Education Expenditures: n.a.
External Debt: $7.9 billion (1997 est.)
Exports: $676 million (1998.); commodities: coffee, cotton, sisal, cashew nuts, meat, tobacco, tea, diamonds, coconut products, pyrethrum, cloves; partners: Germany, UK, US, Netherlands, Japan
Imports: $1.454 billion (1998); commodities: manufactured goods, machinery and transportation equipment, cotton piece goods, crude oil, foodstuffs; partners: Germany, UK, US, Iran, Japan, Italy

■ COMMUNICATIONS

Daily Newspapers: 3 (1996)
Televisions: 3.2/1,000 inhabitants (1996)
Radios: 278/1,000 inhabitants (1996)
Telephones: 0.3/100 inhabitants (1996 est.)

■ TRANSPORTATION

Motor Vehicles: 133,800; 55,000 passenger cars (1997 est.)
Roads: 88,200 km; 3,704 paved
Railway: 3,569 km
Air Traffic: 225,700 passengers carried (1996)
Airports: 123; 11 have paved runways (1997 est.)

Canadian Embassy: The Canadian High Commission, 38 Mirambo St, Dar-es-Salaam; mailing address: P.O. Box 1022, Dar-es-Salaam, Tanzania. Tel: (011-255-51) 112-832. Fax: (011-255-51) 116-896.

Embassy in Canada: High Commission for the United Republic of Tanzania, 50 Range Rd, Ottawa ON, K1N 8J4. Tel: (613) 232-1500. Fax: (613) 232-5184.

Thailand

Long-Form Name: Kingdom of Thailand
Capital: Bangkok

■ GEOGRAPHY

Area: 514,000 sq. km
Coastline: 3,219 km
Climate: tropical; rainy, warm, cloudy southwest monsoon (mid-May to Sept.); dry, cool, northeast monsoon (Nov. to mid-Mar.); southern isthmus always hot and humid
Environment: air and water pollution; land subsidence in Bangkok area; deforestation; soil erosion; illegal hunting threatens wildlife populations
Terrain: central plain; eastern plateau (Khorat); mountains elsewhere
Land Use: 34% arable; 6% permanent crops; 2% permanent pastures; 26% forest; 32% other, includes 8% irrigated
Location: SE Asia, bordering on Bay of Bengal, South China Sea

■ PEOPLE

Population: 60,037,366 (July 1998 est.)
Nationality: Thai
Age Structure: 0-14 yrs: 24%; 15-64: 70%; 65+: 6% (1998 est.)
Population Growth Rate: 0.97% (1998 est.)
Net Migration: 0 migrants/1,000 population (1998 est.)
Ethnic Groups: 75% Thai, 14% Chinese, 11% other
Languages: Thai; English is the secondary language of the elite; small minorities speak Chinese, Malay, indigenous languages
Religions: 95% Buddhist (Theravada), 3.8% Muslim, 0.5% Christianity, 0.1% Hinduism, 0.6% other
Birth Rate: 16.76/1,000 population (1998 est.)
Death Rate: 7.11/1,000 population (1998 est.)
Infant Mortality: 30.82 deaths/1,000 live births (1998 est.)
Life Expectancy at Birth: 65.35 years male, 72.83 years female (1998 est.)
Total Fertility Rate: 1.84 children born/woman (1998 est.)
Literacy: 93.8% (1997 est.)

■ GOVERNMENT

Leader(s): King Phumiphon Adulyadej (Rama IX), Prem. Chuan Leekpai

Government Type: constitutional monarchy
Administrative Divisions: 76 provinces
Nationhood: 1238 (traditional founding date); never colonized
National Holiday: Birthday of His Majesty the King, Dec. 5

■ ECONOMY

Overview: improved weather, increased tourism, export-oriented investment and sound governmental fiscal and monetary policy have all contributed to impressive growth in this country; the government is refurbishing the infrastructure
GDP: $525 billion, per capita $8,800; real growth rate -0.4% (1997 est.)
Inflation: 10.2% (May 1998)
Industries: accounts for 29% of GDP, tourism is the largest source of foreign exchange; textiles and garments, agricultural processing, beverages, tobacco, cement, other light manufacturing, such as jewelry; electric appliances and components, integrated circuits, furniture, plastics
Labour Force: 35.7 million (1997 est.); 60.3% agriculture, 11.2% trade and tourism, 11.1% industry
Unemployment: 5.3% (May 1998)
Agriculture: accounts for 10% of GDP and 57% of labour force; leading producer and exporter of rice and cassava; other crops: rubber, corn, sugar cane, coconuts, soybeans; self-sufficient in food except for wheat
Natural Resources: tin, rubber, natural gas, tungsten, tantalum, timber, lead, fish, gypsum, lignite, fluorite

■ FINANCE/TRADE

Currency: baht (pl. baht) (B) = 200 satang
International Reserves Excluding Gold: $28.302 billion (Jan. 1999)
Gold Reserves: 2.474 million fine troy ounces (Jan. 1999)
Budget: revenues $24 billion; expenditures $25 billion, including capital expenditures of $8 billion (1996–97)
Defence Expenditures: 11.57% of govt. expenditure (1997)
Education Expenditures: 21.61% of govt. expenditure (1997)
External Debt: $90 billion (1997)
Exports: $57.560 billion (1997); commodities: textiles 12%, fishery products 12%, rice 8%, tapioca 8%, jewelry 6%, manufactured gas, corn, tin; partners: US 18%, Japan 14%, Singapore 9%, Netherlands, Malaysia, Hong Kong, China

Imports: $62.881 billion (1997); commodities: machinery and parts 23%, petroleum products 13%, chemicals 11%, iron and steel, electrical appliances; partners: Japan 26%, US 14%, Singapore 7%, Germany, Malaysia, UK

■ COMMUNICATIONS

Daily Newspapers: 30 (1996)
Televisions: 189/1,000 inhabitants (1996)
Radios: 204/1,000 inhabitants (1996)
Telephones: 7.0/100 inhabitants (1996 est.)

■ TRANSPORTATION

Motor Vehicles: 5,700,000; 1,550,000 passenger cars (1997 est.)
Roads: 64,600 km; 62,985 km paved
Railway: 4,623 km
Air Traffic: 14,153,400 passengers carried (1996)
Airports: 106; 55 have paved runways (1997 est.)

Canadian Embassy: The Canadian Embassy, 11th Fl, Boonmitr Bldg, 138 Silom Rd, Bangkok 10500; mailing address: P.O. Box 2090, Bangkok 10500, Thailand. Tel: (011-66-2) 636-0540. Fax: (011-66-2) 636-0565.
Embassy in Canada: The Royal Thai Embassy, 180 Island Park Dr, Ottawa ON K1Y 0A2. Tel: (613) 722-4444. Fax: (613) 722-6624.

Togo

Long-Form Name: Republic of Togo
Capital: Lomé

■ GEOGRAPHY

Area: 56,790 sq. km
Coastline: 56 km along Bight of Benin
Climate: tropical; hot, humid in south; semi-arid in north
Environment: hot, dry harmattan wind; recent droughts affecting agriculture; deforestation
Terrain: gently rolling savanna in north; low coastal plain with extensive lagoons and marshes
Land Use: 38% arable; 7% permanent crops; 4% meadows; 17% forest; 34% other
Location: WC Africa, bordering on South Atlantic Ocean

■ PEOPLE

Population: 4,905,827 (July 1998 est.)
Nationality: Togolese
Age Structure: 0-14 yrs: 48%; 15-64: 49%; 65+: 3% (1998 est.)
Population Growth Rate: 3.52% (1998 est.)
Net Migration: 0 migrants/1,000 population (1998 est.)

Ethnic Groups: 37 tribes; largest and most important are Ewe, Mina and Kabyè; under 1% European and Syrian-Lebanese
Languages: French, both official and language of commerce; major African languages are Ewe and Mina in the south and Dagomba and Kabyè in the north
Religions: about 70% indigenous beliefs, 20% Christian, 10% Muslim
Birth Rate: 45.23/1,000 population (1998 est.)
Death Rate: 10.0/1,000 population (1998 est.)
Infant Mortality: 79.8 deaths/1,000 live births (1998 est.)
Life Expectancy at Birth: 56.52 years male, 61.12 years female (1998 est.)
Total Fertility Rate: 6.6 children born/woman (1998 est.)
Literacy: 51.7% (1997 est.)

■ GOVERNMENT

Leader(s): Pres. Gen. Gnassingbé Eyadéma, Prime Min. Eugene Koffi Adoboli
Government Type: republic; one-party presidential regime under transition to multiparty democratic rule
Administrative Divisions: 21 circumscriptions
Nationhood: Apr. 27, 1960 (from UN trusteeship under French administration; formerly known as French Togo)
National Holiday: Independence Day, Apr. 27

■ ECONOMY

Overview: an underdeveloped country that is heavily dependent on subsistence agriculture and phosphate mining; self-sufficient in basic foodstuffs when harvests are normal; political unrest and widespread strikes have interfered with economic activity
GDP: $6.2 billion, per capita $1,300; real growth rate 4.8% (1997 est.)
Inflation: 9.4% (June 1997)
Industries: accounts for 23% of GDP; phosphate mining, agricultural processing, cement, handicrafts, textiles, beverages
Labour Force: 2.05 million (1997 est.); 64.3% agriculture, 6.3% industry, 29.4% services
Unemployment: n.a.
Agriculture: accounts for 32% of GDP and 64% of labour force; cash crops: coffee, cocoa, cotton; food crops: yams, cassava, corn, beans, rice, millet, sorghum, fish
Natural Resources: phosphates, limestone, marble

■ FINANCE/TRADE

Currency: Communauté financière africaine franc (CFAF) = 100 centimes

International Reserves Excluding Gold: $112 million (Nov. 1998)
Gold Reserves: 0.013 million fine troy ounces (July 1998)
Budget: revenues $242 million; expenditures $262 million, including capital expenditures n.a. (1997 est.)
Defence Expenditures: 2.5% of GDP (1996)
Education Expenditures: 5.6% of GNP (1995)
External Debt: $1.463 billion (1996)
Exports: $346 million (1997); commodities: phosphates, cocoa, coffee, cotton, manufactures, palm kernels; partners: European Community 70%, Africa 9%, US 2%, other 19%
Imports: $503 million (1997); commodities: food, fuels, durable consumer goods, other intermediate goods, capital goods; partners: European Community 69%, Africa 10%, Japan 7%, US 4%, other 10%

■ COMMUNICATIONS

Daily Newspapers: 1 (1996)
Televisions: 17/1,000 inhabitants (1996)
Radios: 217/1,000 inhabitants (1996)
Telephones: 0.5/100 inhabitants (1996 est.)

■ TRANSPORTATION

Motor Vehicles: 110,000; 75,000 passenger cars (1997 est.)
Roads: 7,520 km; 2,376 km paved
Railway: 525 km
Air Traffic: 75,000 passengers carried (1996)
Airports: 9; 2 have paved runways (1997 est.)

Canadian Embassy: The Canadian Embassy to Togo, c/o Canadian High Commission, 42 Independence Ave, Accra, Ghana; P.O. Box 1639, Accra. Tel: (011-233-21) 77-37-91. Fax: (011-233-21) 77-37-92.
Embassy in Canada: Embassy of the Republic of Togo, 12 Range Rd, Ottawa ON K1N 8J3. Tel: (613) 238-5916. Fax: (613) 235-6425.

Tokelau

Long-Form Name: Tokelau
Capital: none; each atoll has its own administrative centre

■ GEOGRAPHY

Area: 10 sq. km, 3 atolls
Climate: tropical maritime, moderated by trade winds (April–Nov.)
Land Use: 0% arable, permanent crops, meadows/pastures or forests; 100% other
Location: S Pacific Ocean

■ PEOPLE

Population: 1,443 (July 1998 est.)
Nationality: Tokelauan
Ethnic Groups: Polynesian
Languages: Tokelauan, English

■ GOVERNMENT

Colony Territory of: Overseas Territory of New Zealand
Leader(s): Head of State: Queen Elizabeth II, Administrator Lindsay Watt
Government Type: territory of New Zealand
National Holiday: Waitangi Day, Feb. 6

■ ECONOMY

Overview: Tokelau's small size, great distance from markets and lack of resources greatly hinder economic development; copra is only agricultural product of significance; the people rely on aid from New Zealand, supplemented by revenue from postage stamps, souvenir coins, and handicrafts

■ FINANCE/TRADE

Currency: New Zealand dollar = 100 cents

Canadian Embassy: c/o The Canadian High Commission, 3rd Fl, 61 Molesworth St. Thorndon, Wellington, New Zealand. Tel: (011-64-4) 473-9577. Fax: (011-64-4) 471-2082.
Representative to Canada: c/o New Zealand High Commission, Metropolitan House, 99 Bank St, Ste 727, Ottawa ON K1P 6G3. Tel: (613) 238-5991. Fax: (613) 238-5707.

Tonga

Long-Form Name: Kingdom of Tonga
Capital: Nuku'alofa

■ GEOGRAPHY

Area: 748 sq. km; archipelago of 170 islands, of which 36 are inhabited
Coastline: 419 km
Climate: tropical; modified by trade winds; warm season (Dec. to May), cool season (May to Dec.)
Environment: subject to cyclones (Oct. to Apr.); deforestation and overhunting of native animals
Terrain: most islands have limestone base formed from uplifted coral formation; others have limestone overlying volcanic base
Land Use: 24% arable; 43% permanent; 6% meadows; 11% forest; 16% other
Location: Pacific Ocean, NW of New Zealand

■ PEOPLE

Population: 108,207 (July 1998 est.)
Nationality: Tongan
Age Structure: n.a.
Population Growth Rate: 0.81% (1998 est.)
Net Migration: -1.23 migrants/1,000 population (1998 est.)
Ethnic Groups: Polynesian; about 300 Europeans
Languages: Tongan, English
Religions: Christian; Free Wesleyan Church claims over 30,000 adherents
Birth Rate: 26.43/1,000 population (1998 est.)
Death Rate: 6.07/1,000 population (1998 est.)
Infant Mortality: 38.57 deaths/1,000 live births (1998 est.)
Life Expectancy at Birth: 67.51 years male, 71.96 years female (1998 est.)
Total Fertility Rate: 3.63 children born/woman (1998 est.)
Literacy: 57%

■ GOVERNMENT

Leader(s): King Taufa'ahau Tupou IV, Prime Min. Baron Vaea
Government Type: hereditary constitutional monarchy
Administrative Divisions: three island groups
Nationhood: June 4, 1970 (from UK; formerly known as Friendly Islands)
National Holiday: Emancipation Day, June 4

■ ECONOMY

Overview: the economy's base is agriculture though the country must import a high proportion of its food, for the most part from New Zealand; tourism is the main source of hard currency; the country also remains dependent on sizeable external aid and remittances to offset its trade deficit.
GDP: $228 million, per capita $2,140; real growth rate -1.9% (1996 est.)
Inflation: 3.0% (Mar. 1998)
Industries: accounts for 10% of GDP; tourism, fishing
Labour Force: n.a.; 70% agriculture, 30% mining
Unemployment: n.a.
Agriculture: 32% of GDP and 70% of labour force; dominated by coconut, copra and banana production; vanilla beans, cocoa, coffee, ginger, black pepper
Natural Resources: fish, fertile soil

■ FINANCE/TRADE

Currency: pa'anga ($T) = 100 seniti
International Reserves Excluding Gold: $14 million (June 1998)
Gold Reserves: n.a.

Budget: revenues $49 million; expenditures $120 million, including capital expenditures of $75 million (1996-97 est.)
Defence Expenditures: n.a.
Education Expenditures: n.a.
External Debt: $70 million (1996)
Exports: $0.6 million (1997 est.); commodities: coconut oil, desiccated coconut, copra, bananas, taro, vanilla beans, fruit, vegetables, fish; partners: New Zealand 54%, Australia 30%, US 8%, Fiji 5%
Imports: $61 million (1997 est.); commodities: food products, beverages, tobacco, fuels, machinery, transport equipment, chemicals, building materials; partners: New Zealand 39%, Australia 25%, Japan 9%, US 6%, European Community 5%

■ COMMUNICATIONS

Daily Newspapers: 1 (1996)
Televisions: 20/1,000 inhabitants (1996)
Radios: 612/1,000 inhabitants (1996)
Telephones: 6.9/100 inhabitants (1996 est.)

■ TRANSPORTATION

Motor Vehicles: n.a.
Roads: 680 km; 184 km paved
Railway: none
Air Traffic: 56,000 passengers carried (1996)
Airports: 6; 1 have paved runways (1997 est.)

Canadian Embassy: The Canadian High Commission to Tonga, c/o The Canadian High Commission, 61 Molesworth St, 3rd Floor, Thorndon, Wellington; mailing address: P.O. Box 12-049, Thorndon, Wellington, New Zealand. Tel: (011-64-4) 473-9577. Fax: (011-64-4) 471-2082.
Embassy in Canada: c/o New Zealand High Commission, Metropolitan House, 99 Bank St, Ste 727, Ottawa, ON K1P 6G3. Tel: (613) 238-5991. Fax: (613) 238-5707.

Trinidad and Tobago

Long-Form Name: Republic of Trinidad and Tobago
Capital: Port of Spain

■ GEOGRAPHY

Area: 5,130 sq. km
Coastline: 362 km
Climate: tropical; rainy season (June to Dec.)
Environment: outside usual path of hurricanes and other tropical storms; water pollution and soil deterioration; oil pollution of beaches
Terrain: mostly plains with some hills and low mountains

Land Use: 15% arable; 9% permanent crops; 2% meadows; 46% forest; 28% other, includes 4% irrigated
Location: Atlantic Ocean, off N coast of South America

■ PEOPLE

Population: 1,116,595 (July 1998 est.)
Nationality: Trinidadian, Tobagonian
Age Structure: 0-14 yrs: 28%; 15-64: 65%; 65+: 7% (1998 est.)
Population Growth Rate: -1.27% (1998 est.)
Net Migration: -19.55 migrants/1,000 population (1998 est.)
Ethnic Groups: 40% black, 40% East Indian, 14% mixed, 1% white, 1% Chinese, 4% other
Languages: English (official), Hindi, French, Spanish, Chinese
Religions: Christianity 61%, Hinduism 24%, Islam 6%, 9% other
Birth Rate: 14.89/1,000 population (1998 est.)
Death Rate: 8.0/1,000 population (1998 est.)
Infant Mortality: 18.84 deaths/1,000 live births (1998 est.)
Life Expectancy at Birth: 68.06 years male, 73.03 years female (1998 est.)
Total Fertility Rate: 2.09 children born/woman (1998 est.)
Literacy: 97.9% (1997 est.)

■ GOVERNMENT

Leader(s): Pres. Arthur Napoleon Raymond Robinson, Prime Min. Basdeo Panday
Government Type: parliamentary democracy
Administrative Divisions: 8 counties, 3 municipalities and 1 ward
Nationhood: Aug. 31, 1962 (from UK)
National Holiday: Independence Day, Aug. 31

■ ECONOMY

Overview: the economy has suffered in recent years because of the sharp decline in the price of oil; the unemployment rate has risen due to the government's austerity programs; the government is seeking to diversify the country's export base
GDP: $17.1 billion, per capita $13,500; real growth rate 3.1% (1996 est.)
Inflation: 3.6% (Mar. 1998)
Industries: accounts for 45% of GDP; petroleum, chemicals, tourism, food processing, cement, beverage, cotton textiles
Labour Force: 515,000 (1995); 30.4% community, social and business services, 11.3% agriculture, 10.9% construction
Unemployment: 16.1% (Dec. 1996)
Agriculture: accounts for approx. 2% of GDP; highly subsidized sector; major crops: cocoa and sugar cane; sugar cane acreage is being shifted into rice, citrus, coffee, vegetables; must import large share of food needs
Natural Resources: crude oil, natural gas, asphalt

■ FINANCE/TRADE

Currency: Trinidad and Tobago dollar ($TT) = 100 cents
International Reserves Excluding Gold: $767 million (Jan. 1999)
Gold Reserves: 0.058 million fine troy ounces (Jan. 1999)
Budget: revenues $1.7 billion; expenditures $1.6 billion, including capital expenditures of $243 million (1997 est.)
Defence Expenditures: 1.1% of GDP (1996)
Education Expenditures: 4.5% of GNP (1995)
External Debt: $2.242 billion (1996)
Exports: $2.542 billion (1997); commodities (including re-exports): petroleum and petroleum products 70%, fertilizer, chemicals 15%, steel products, sugar, cocoa, coffee, citrus; partners: US 61%, European Community 15%, CARICOM 9%, Latin America 7%, Canada 3%
Imports: $2.990 billion (1997); commodities: raw materials 41%, capital goods 30%, consumer goods 29%; partners: US 42%, European Community 21%, Japan 10%, Canada 6%, Latin America 6%, CARICOM 4%

■ COMMUNICATIONS

Daily Newspapers: 4 (1996)
Televisions: 323/1,000 inhabitants (1996)
Radios: 517/1,000 inhabitants (1996)
Telephones: 16.4/100 inhabitants (1996 est.)

■ TRANSPORTATION

Motor Vehicles: 155,000; 128,000 passenger cars (1997 est.)
Roads: 8,320 km; 4,252 km paved
Railway: minimal agricultural railway system near San Fernando
Air Traffic: 897,000 passengers carried (1996)
Airports: 6; 3 have paved runways (1997 est.)

Canadian Embassy: The Canadian High Commission, Maple House, 3-3A Sweet Briar Road, St. Clair, Port-of-Spain; mailing address: P.O. Box 1246, Port-of-Spain, Trinidad and Tobago. Tel: (868) 622-6232. Fax: (868) 628-1830.
Embassy in Canada: High Commission for the Republic of Trinidad and Tobago, 75 Albert St, Ste 508, Ottawa ON K1P 5E7. Tel: (613) 232-2418. Fax: (613) 232-4349.

Tunisia

Long-Form Name: Republic of Tunisia
Capital: Tunis

■ GEOGRAPHY

Area: 163,610 sq. km
Coastline: 1,148 km along the Mediterranean Sea
Climate: temperate in north with mild, rainy winters and hot, dry summers; desert in south
Environment: deforestation; overgrazing; soil erosion; desertification; ineffective disposal of toxic and hazardous wastes
Terrain: mountains in north; hot, dry central plain; semi-arid south merges into the Sahara
Land Use: 19% arable; 13% permanent; 20% meadows; 4% forest; 44% other, includes 1.5% irrigated
Location: N Africa, bordering on Mediterranean Sea

■ PEOPLE

Population: 9,380,404 (July 1998 est.)
Nationality: Tunisian
Age Structure: 0-14 yrs: 32%; 15-64: 63%; 65+: 5% (1998 est.)
Population Growth Rate: 1.43% (1998 est.)
Net Migration: -0.73 migrants/1,000 population (1998 est.)
Ethnic Groups: 98% Arab-Berber, 1% European, less than 1% Jewish
Languages: Arabic (official); Arabic and French (commerce)
Religions: 98% Muslim, 1% Christian, less than 1% Jewish
Birth Rate: 20.07/1,000 population (1998 est.)
Death Rate: 5.06/1,000 population (1998 est.)
Infant Mortality: 32.64 deaths/1,000 live births (1998 est.)
Life Expectancy at Birth: 71.72 years male, 74.58 years female (1998 est.)
Total Fertility Rate: 2.44 children born/woman (1998 est.)
Literacy: 66.7% (1997 est.)

■ GOVERNMENT

Leader(s): Pres. Gen. Zine El Abidine Ben Ali, Prime Min. Hamed Karoui
Government Type: republic
Administrative Divisions: 23 governorates
Nationhood: Mar. 20, 1956 (from France)
National Holiday: National Day, Mar. 20

■ ECONOMY

Overview: Tunisia has a diverse economy, with important agriculture, mining, energy, tourism, and manufacturing sectors. Governmental control of economic affairs has gradually lessened over the past decade with increasing privatization of trade and commerce, simplification of the tax structure, and a prudent approach to debt.
GDP: $56.5 billion, per capita $6,100; real growth rate 5.6% (1997 est.)
Inflation: 3.3% (June 1998)
Industries: accounts for 28% of GDP; petroleum, mining (particularly phosphate and iron ore), textiles, footwear, food, beverages, tourism
Labour Force: 3.1 million (1997 est.); 21.6% agriculture, 16.3% industry, 62.1% services
Unemployment: 15% (1997 est.)
Agriculture: accounts for 14% of GDP; output subject to severe fluctuations because of frequent droughts; export crops: olives, dates, oranges, almonds; other products: grain, sugar beets, wine grapes, poultry, beef, dairy; not self-sufficient in food
Natural Resources: crude oil, phosphates, iron ore, lead, zinc, salt

■ FINANCE/TRADE

Currency: Tunisian dinar (D) = 1,000 millimes
International Reserves Excluding Gold: $1.691 billion (Jan. 1999)
Gold Reserves: 0.022 million fine troy ounces (Jan. 1999)
Budget: revenues $6.3 billion; expenditures $6.8 billion, including capital expenditures of $1.5 billion (1997 est.)
Defence Expenditures: 6.23% of govt. expenditure (1996)
Education Expenditures: 18.68% of govt. expenditures (1996)
External Debt: $10.6 billion (1997 est.)
Exports: $5.746 billion (1998); commodities: hydrocarbons, agricultural products, phosphates and chemicals; partners: European Community 73%, Middle East 9%, US 1%, Turkey, former USSR countries
Imports: $8.333 billion (1998); commodities: industrial goods and equipment 57%, hydrocarbons 13%, food 12%, consumer goods; partners: European Community 68%, US 7%, Canada, Japan, former USSR countries, China, Saudi Arabia, Algeria

■ COMMUNICATIONS

Daily Newspapers: 8 (1996)
Televisions: 98/1,000 inhabitants (1996)
Radios: 218/1,000 inhabitants (1996)
Telephones: 6.1/100 inhabitants (1996 est.)

■ TRANSPORTATION

Motor Vehicles: 531,000; 248,000 passenger cars (1997 est.)
Roads: 23,100 km; 18,226 km paved
Railway: 2,260 km
Air Traffic: 1,371,000 passengers carried (1996)
Airports: 32; 15 have paved runways (1997 est.)

Canadian Embassy: Canadian Embassy, 3, rue du Sénégal, Place d'Afrique, 1002 Tunis-Belvedere, Tunisia; mailing address: CP 31, Le Belvédère, 1002, Tunis-Belvedere, Tunisia. Tel: (011-216-1) 796-577. Fax: (011-216-1) 792-371.
Embassy in Canada: Embassy of the Republic of Tunisia, 515 O'Connor St, Ottawa ON, K1S 3P8. Tel: (613) 237-0330. Fax: (613) 237-7939.

Turkey

Long-Form Name: Republic of Turkey
Capital: Ankara

■ GEOGRAPHY

Area: 780,580 sq. km
Coastline: 7,200 km along Black Sea and Mediterranean Sea
Climate: temperate; hot, dry summers with mild, wet winters; harsher in interior
Environment: subject to severe earthquakes, especially along major river valleys in west; water and air pollution; desertification
Terrain: mostly mountains; narrow coastal plain; high central plateau (Anatolia)
Land Use: 32% arable; 4% permanent; 16% meadows; 26% forest; 22% other, includes 3% irrigated
Location: SW Asia (Near East), bordering on Mediterranean Sea, Black Sea, Aegean Sea

■ PEOPLE

Population: 64,566,511 (July 1998 est.) Note: Estimates of the number killed in an August 1999 earthquake are as high as 45,000
Nationality: Turk
Age Structure: 0-14 yrs: 31%; 15-64: 63%; 65+: 6% (1998 est.)
Population Growth Rate: 1.6% (1998 est.)
Net Migration: 0 migrants/1,000 population (1998 est.)
Ethnic Groups: 80% Turkish, 20% Kurd
Languages: Turkish (official), Kurdish 7%, Arabic; English (business language)
Religions: 99.8% Muslim (mostly Sunni), 0.2% other (mostly Christian and Jewish)
Birth Rate: 21.38/1,000 population (1998 est.)

Death Rate: 5.35/1,000 population (1998 est.)
Infant Mortality: 38.27 deaths/1,000 live births (1998 est.)
Life Expectancy at Birth: 70.38 years male, 75.39 years female (1998 est.)
Total Fertility Rate: 2.47 children born/woman (1998 est.)
Literacy: 82.3% (1997 est.)

■ GOVERNMENT

Leader(s): Pres. Suleyman Demirel, Prime Min. Bulent Ecevit
Government Type: republican parliamentary democracy
Administrative Divisions: 80 provinces
Nationhood: Oct. 29, 1923 (successor state to the Ottoman Empire)
National Holiday: Anniversary of the Declaration of the Republic, Oct. 29

■ ECONOMY

Overview: Turkey's dynamic economy is a complex mix of modern industry and commerce along with traditional village agriculture and crafts. It has a strong and rapidly growing private sector, yet the state still plays a major role in basic industry, banking, transport, and communication. Note: Major economic disruption in August 1999 due to a massive earthquake.
GDP: $388.3 billion, per capita $6,100; real growth rate 7.1% (1997 est.)
Inflation: 85.3% (July 1998)
Industries: accounts for 28% of GDP; textiles, food processing, mining (coal, chromite, copper, boron minerals), steel, petroleum, construction, lumber, paper
Labour Force: 29.7 million (1997 est.); 43.6% agriculture, 15% industry, 14% community, social and business services; about 1,000,000 Turks work abroad
Unemployment: 5.9%; another 5.1% is officially considered underemployed (Apr. 1997)
Agriculture: accounts for 15% of GDP and 46% the labour force; products: tobacco, cotton, grain, olives, sugar beets, pulses, citrus fruit, variety of animal products; self-sufficient in food most years
Natural Resources: antimony, coal, chromium, mercury, copper, borate, sulphur, iron ore

■ FINANCE/TRADE

Currency: Turkish lira (TL)
International Reserves Excluding Gold: $19.712 billion (Jan. 1999)
Gold Reserves: 3.748 million fine troy ounces (Jan. 1999)

Budget: revenues $38.5 billion; expenditures $52.9 billion, including capital expenditures of $4.2 billion (1997)

Defence Expenditures: 8.42% of govt. expenditure (1996)

Education Expenditures: 11.17% of total govt. expenditure (1996)

External Debt: $84.5 billion (1997)

Exports: $26.245 billion (1997); commodities: industrial products 70%, crops and livestock products 25%; partners: Germany 18.4%, Iraq 8.5%, Italy 8.2%, US 6.5%, UK 4.9%, Iran 4.7%

Imports: $48.585 billion (1997); commodities: crude oil, machinery, transport equipment, metals, pharmaceuticals, dyes, plastics, rubber, mineral fuels, fertilizers, chemicals; partners: Germany 14.3%, US 10.6%, Iraq 10.0%, Italy 7.0%, France 5.8%, UK 5.2%

■ COMMUNICATIONS

Daily Newspapers: 57 (1996)
Televisions: 333/1,000 inhabitants (1996)
Radios: 178/1,000 inhabitants (1996)
Telephones: 22.4/100 inhabitants (1996 est.)

■ TRANSPORTATION

Motor Vehicles: 4,400,000; 3,300,000 passenger cars (1997 est.)
Roads: 381,631; 95,408 km paved
Railway: 10,386 km
Air Traffic: 9,280,800 passengers carried (1996)
Airports: 114; 80 have paved runways (1997 est.)

Canadian Embassy: The Canadian Embassy, Nenehatun Caddesi 75, Gaziosmanpasa, 06700 Ankara, Turkey. Tel: (011-90-312) 436-1275. Fax: (011-90-312) 446-4437.

Embassy in Canada: Embassy of the Republic of Turkey, 197 Wurtemburg St, Ottawa ON K1R 7X7. Tel: (613) 789-4044. Fax: (613) 789-3442.

Turkmenistan

Long-Form Name: Turkmenistan
Capital: Ashkhabad

■ GEOGRAPHY

Area: 488,100 sq. km
Coastline: landlocked; 1,768 km coastline along Caspian Sea
Climate: subtropical desert; long, extremely hot summers; short and cold winters; rainfall occurs only in the mountains
Environment: soil and groundwater contaminated with chemicals and pesticides; salinization and waterlogging of soil due to poor irrigation methods; desertification in some areas; prone to earthquakes
Terrain: flat to rolling sandy desert; Caspian Sea in west
Land Use: 3% arable, 0% permanent crops, 63% pastures and meadows, 8% forests, 26% other, includes 2.5% irrigated
Location: SC Asia, bordering on Caspian Sea

■ PEOPLE

Population: 4,297,629 (July 1998 est.)
Nationality: Turkmen
Age Structure: 0-14 yrs: 39%; 15-64: 57%; 65+: 4% (1998 est.)
Population Growth Rate: 1.6% (1998 est.)
Net Migration: -1.58 migrants/1,000 population (1998 est.)
Ethnic Groups: 77% Turkmen, 6.7% Russian, 9.2% Uzbek, 2% Kazakh, 5.1% other
Languages: 72% Turkmen (official), 12% Russian, 9% Uzbek, 7% other
Religions: 89% Muslim, 9% Eastern Orthodox, 2% unknown
Birth Rate: 26.24/1,000 population (1998 est.)
Death Rate: 8.7/1,000 population (1998 est.)
Infant Mortality: 72.89 deaths/1,000 live births (1998 est.)
Life Expectancy at Birth: 57.68 years male, 65.11 years female (1998 est.)
Total Fertility Rate: 3.26 children born/woman (1998 est.)
Literacy: 98% (1997 est.)

■ GOVERNMENT

Leader(s): Pres. Saparmurad Niyazov
Government Type: republic
Administrative Divisions: 5 regions ("welayatlar")
Nationhood: Oct. 27, 1991 (from Soviet Union)
National Holiday: Independence Day, Oct. 27

■ ECONOMY

Overview: mining produces the greatest part of Turkmenistan's economic production value, but agriculture is the chief occupation; industry leans heavily towards the energy sector (gas, oil), but the lack of pipeline access to hard currency markets limits expansion. Efforts at gas and oil export expansion will take many more years to pay off
GDP: $11.8 billion, per capita $2,840; real growth rate 0.1% (1996 est.)
Inflation: n.a.
Industries: accounts for 50% of GDP; oil production and refining, natural gas extraction, chemicals, electrical engineering, fertilizer, carpets, textiles and clothing, food processing

Labour Force: 2.1 million (1997 est.); 42% agriculture and forestry, 21% industry and construction, 37% other
Unemployment: n.a.
Agriculture: accounts for 18% of GDP; irrigation is mandatory for agriculture; products include cotton, grains, fruit, livestock, fish, vegetables
Natural Resources: extensive mineral deposits, including the world's largest sulfur deposits; oil, natural gas, potassium, salts, sulphur

■ FINANCE/TRADE

Currency: manat = 100 tenesi
International Reserves Excluding Gold: n.a.
Gold Reserves: n.a.
Budget: revenues $521 million; expenditures $548 million, including capital expenditures of $83 million (1996 est.)
Defence Expenditures: 3% of GDP (1995)
Education Expenditures: n.a.
External Debt: $825 million (1996)
Exports: $1.7 billión (1996); oil, natural gas, electric power, clothing and textiles, petroleum products, carpets; partners: Hong Kong, Switzerland, US, FSU, Germany, Turkey
Imports: $1.5 billion (1996); machinery, foodstuffs, consumer products, plastics and rubber, textiles; partners: US, FSU, Turkey, Germany, Cyprus

■ COMMUNICATIONS

Daily Newspapers: n.a.
Televisions: 193/1,000 inhabitants (1996)
Radios: 96/1,000 inhabitants (1996)
Telephones: 7.2/100 inhabitants (1996 est.)

■ TRANSPORTATION

Motor Vehicles: n.a.
Roads: 24,000 km; 19,488 km paved
Railway: 2,187 km
Air Traffic: 523,000 passengers carried (1996)
Airports: 64; 22 have paved runways (1997 est.)

Canadian Embassy: c/o The Canadian Embassy, Nenehatun Caddesi 75, Gaziosmanpasa 06700, Ankara, Turkey. Tel: (011-90-312) 436-1275. Fax: (011-90-312) 446-4437.
Embassy in Canada: c/o Embassy of the Republic of Turkmenistan, 2207 Massachusetts Ave NW, Washington DC 20008, USA. Tel: (202) 588-1500. Fax: (202) 588-0697.

Turks and Caicos

Long-Form Name: The Turks and Caicos Islands
Capital: Grand Turk

■ GEOGRAPHY

Area: 430 sq. km; 30+ small cays, of which only 8 are inhabited
Climate: sunny, relatively dry, equable climate with moderating winds; occasional hurricanes
Land Use: 2% arable, 0% permanent crops, meadows, forests, 98% other
Location: West Indies (S Atlantic Ocean), SE of Bahamas

■ PEOPLE

Population: 16,249 (July 1998 est.)
Nationality: none (British citizens)
Ethnic Groups: black majority
Languages: English (official)

■ GOVERNMENT

Colony Territory of: Colony of the United Kingdom
Leader(s): Head of State: Queen Elizabeth II, Gov. John Kelly
Government Type: dependent territory of the United Kingdom
National Holiday: Constitution Day, Aug. 30

■ ECONOMY

Overview: fishing is the most important activity; exports include lobster, conch, other fish products; imports include food and drink, tobacco, maufactured goods; tourism; offshore banking; chief trading partner: US

■ FINANCE/TRADE

Currency: US currency is used

Canadian Embassy: c/o The Canadian High Commission, Macdonald House, 1 Grosvenor Square, London W1X 0AB, England, UK. Tel: (011-44-171) 258-6600. Fax: (011-44-171) 258-6333.
Representative to Canada: c/o British High Commission, 80 Elgin St, Ottawa ON K1P 5K7. Tel: (613) 237-1530. Fax: (613) 237-7980.

Tuvalu

Long-Form Name: Tuvalu
Capital: Funafuti

■ GEOGRAPHY

Area: 26 sq. km
Coastline: 24 km
Climate: tropical; moderated by easterly trade winds (Mar. to Nov.); westerly gales and heavy rain (Nov. to Mar.)

Environment: severe tropical storms are rare; no natural safe drinking water resources
Terrain: very low-lying and narrow coral atolls
Land Use: the 9 coral atolls have just enough soil to allow for subsistence agriculture; there are also coconut groves
Location: S Pacific Ocean, NE of Australia

■ PEOPLE

Population: 10,444 (July 1998 est.)
Nationality: Tuvaluan
Age Structure: 0-14 yrs: 35%; 15-64: 60%; 65+: 5% (1998 est.)
Population Growth Rate: 1.4% (1998 est.)
Net Migration: 0 migrants/1,000 population (1998 est.)
Ethnic Groups: 96% Polynesian
Languages: Tuvaluan, English
Religions: 97% Congregationalist (Church of Tuvalu), 1.4% Seventh Day Adventists, 1% Baha'i, 0.6% other
Birth Rate: 22.6/1,000 population (1998 est.)
Death Rate: 8.62/1,000 population (1998 est.)
Infant Mortality: 26.23 deaths/1,000 live births (1998 est.)
Life Expectancy at Birth: 62.72 years male, 65.09 years female (1998 est.)
Total Fertility Rate: 3.11 children born/woman (1998 est.)
Literacy: less than 50%

■ GOVERNMENT

Leader(s): Queen Elizabeth II/Gov. Gen. Sir Tomasi Puapua, Prime Min. Ionatana Ionatana
Government Type: constitutional monarchy with a parliamentary democracy
Administrative Divisions: none
Nationhood: Oct. 1, 1978 from UK (formerly known as Ellice Islands)
National Holiday: Independence Day, Oct. 1

■ ECONOMY

Overview: scattered group of 9 coral atolls with poor soil; a small economy, no known mineral resources and few exports; receives money from the sale of stamps and coins and worker remittances as well as an international trust fund; subsistence farming and fishing are the primary economic activities
GDP: $7.8 million, per capita $800; real growth rate 8.7% (1995)
Inflation: n.a.
Industries: fishing, tourism, copra
Labour Force: n.a.
Unemployment: n.a.
Agriculture: coconuts, copra
Natural Resources: fish

■ FINANCE/TRADE

Currency: Australian dollar ($A) or Tuvaluan dollar ($T) = 100 cents
International Reserves Excluding Gold: n.a.
Gold Reserves: n.a.
Budget: n.a.
Defence Expenditures: n.a.
Education Expenditures: n.a.
External Debt: n.a.
Exports: n.a.; commodities: copra; partners: Fiji, Australia, New Zealand
Imports: n.a.; commodities: food, animals, fuels, machinery, manufactures; partners: Fiji, Australia, New Zealand

■ COMMUNICATIONS

Daily Newspapers: 0 (1996)
Televisions: 13.2/1,000 inhabitants (1996)
Radios: 400/1,000 inhabitants (1996)
Telephones: n.a.

■ TRANSPORTATION

Motor Vehicles: n.a.
Roads: 8 km gravel roads
Railway: none
Air Traffic: n.a.
Airports: 1; no paved runway (1997 est.)

Canadian Embassy: The Canadian High Commission to Tuvalu, c/o The Canadian High Commission, 61 Molesworth St, 3rd Fl, Thorndon, Wellington; mailing address: P.O. Box 12-049, Thorndon, Wellington, New Zealand. Tel: (011-64-4) 473-9577. Fax: (011-64-4) 471-2082.
Embassy in Canada: c/o New Zealand High Commission, Metropolitan House, 99 Bank St, Ste 727, Ottawa, ON K1P 6G3. Tel: (613) 238-5991. Fax: (613) 238-5707.

U.S. Virgin Islands

Long-Form Name: Virgin Islands of the United States
Capital: Charlotte Amalie

■ GEOGRAPHY

Area: 352 sq. km
Climate: subtropical, tempered by easterly trade winds, relatively low humidity, little seasonal temperature variation; rainy season May to Nov.
Land Use: 15% arable; 6% permanent; 26% meadows; 6% forest; 47% other
Location: Caribbean islands

■ PEOPLE

Population: 118,211 (July 1998 est.)
Nationality: Virgin Islander
Ethnic Groups: 74% West Indian (45% born in the Virgin Islands and 29% born elsewhere in the West Indies), 13% US mainland, 5% Puerto Rican, 8% other (80% black, 15% white, 5% other); 14% of Hispanic origin
Languages: English (official), but Spanish and Creole are widely spoken

■ GOVERNMENT

Colony Territory of: Dependent Territory of the United States
Leader(s): Head of State William Clinton (USA), Gov. Roy L. Schneider
Government Type: organized, unincorporated territory of the US
National Holiday: Transfer Day, Mar. 31 (1917, from Denmark to the US)

■ ECONOMY

Overview: tourism is the primary economic activity accounting for more than 70% of GDP and 70% of employment; some manufacturing; small agricultural sector (most food is imported); international business and financial services are a small but growing sector

■ FINANCE/TRADE

Currency: US dollar ($) = 100 cents

Canadian Embassy: c/o The Canadian Embassy, 501 Pennsylvania Ave NW, Washington DC 20001, USA. Tel: (202) 682-1740. Fax: (202) 456-7726.
Representative to Canada: c/o Embassy of the United States of America, 100 Wellington St, Ottawa ON K1P 5A1. Tel: (613) 238-5335. Fax: (613) 238-5720.

Uganda

Long-Form Name: Republic of Uganda
Capital: Kampala

■ GEOGRAPHY

Area: 236,040 sq. km
Coastline: none: landlocked
Climate: tropical; generally rainy with two dry seasons (Dec. to Feb., June to Aug.); semi-arid in northeast
Environment: straddles equator; deforestation; overgrazing; soil erosion; widespread poaching
Terrain: mostly plateau with rim of mountains

Land Use: 25% arable; 9% permanent crops; 9% permanent pastures; 28% forest; 29% other
Location: EC Africa

■ PEOPLE

Population: 22,167,195 (July 1998 est.)
Nationality: Ugandan
Age Structure: 0-14 yrs: 51%; 15-64: 47%; 65+: 2% (1998 est.)
Population Growth Rate: 2.85% (1998 est.)
Net Migration: -1.8 migrants/1,000 population (1998 est.)
Ethnic Groups: 17% Baganda, 12% Karamojong, 8% Basogo, 8% Iteso, 6% Langi, 6% Rwanda, 5% Bagisu, 4% Acholi, 4% Lugbara, 3% Bunyro, 27% other
Languages: English (official); Luganda and Swahili widely used; other Bantu and Nilotic languages
Religions: 33% Roman Catholic, 33% Protestant, 16% Muslim, rest indigenous beliefs
Birth Rate: 49.21/1,000 population (1998 est.)
Death Rate: 18.95/1,000 population (1998 est.)
Infant Mortality: 92.86 deaths/1,000 live births (1998 est.)
Life Expectancy at Birth: 41.81 years male, 43.41 years female (1998 est.)
Total Fertility Rate: 7.09 children born/woman (1998 est.)
Literacy: 61.8% (1997 est.)

■ GOVERNMENT

Leader(s): Pres. Yoweri Kaguta Museveni, Prime Min. Apollo Nsibambi
Government Type: republic
Administrative Divisions: 39 districts
Nationhood: Oct. 9, 1962 (from UK)
National Holiday: Independence Day, Oct. 9

■ ECONOMY

Overview: despite substantial natural resources, the economy has been ruined by years of political instability, mismanagement and civil war; the government has started a reform program which is partly aimed at lowering high inflation and increasing export earnings; agriculture is the most important economic sector
GDP: adjusted for purchasing power parity: $34.6 billion, per capita $1,700; real growth rate 5% (1997 est.)
Inflation: -1.2% (June 1998)
Industries: accounts for 13% of GDP; sugar, brewing, tobacco, cotton textile, cement
Labour Force: 10.1 million (1997 est.); 85.9% agriculture, 4.4% industry, 9.7% services
Unemployment: n.a.

Agriculture: accounts for 49% of GDP and 86% of labour force; coffee, tea and tobacco are the main export crops
Natural Resources: copper, cobalt, limestone, salt

■ FINANCE/TRADE

Currency: Ugandan shilling (USh) = 100 cents
International Reserves Excluding Gold: $682 million (Jan. 1999)
Gold Reserves: n.a.
Budget: revenues $869 million; expenditures $985 million, including capital expenditures of $69 million (1995-96)
Defence Expenditures: 2.4% of GDP (1996)
Education Expenditures: n.a.
External Debt: $3.674 billion (1996)
Exports: $474.7 million (1998 est.); commodities: coffee 97%, cotton, tea; partners: US 25%, UK 18%, France 11%, Spain 10%
Imports: $1.443 billion (1998 est.); commodities: petroleum products, machinery, cotton piece goods, metals, transportation equipment, food; partners: Kenya 25%, UK 14%, Italy 13%

■ COMMUNICATIONS

Daily Newspapers: 2 (1996)
Televisions: 15/1,000 inhabitants (1996)
Radios: 123/1,000 inhabitants (1996)
Telephones: 0.2/100 inhabitants (1996 est.)

■ TRANSPORTATION

Motor Vehicles: 51,000; 24,400 passenger cars (1997 est.)
Roads: n.a.
Railway: 1,241 km
Air Traffic: 100,000 passengers carried (1996)
Airports: 29; 5 have paved runways (1997 est.)

Canadian Embassy: The Canadian High Commission to Uganda, c/o The Canadian High Commission, Comcraft House, Hailé Sélassie Ave, Nairobi; mailing address: The Canadian High Commission, P.O. Box 30481, Nairobi, Kenya. Tel: (011-254-2) 21-48-04. Fax: (011-254-2) 22-69-87.
Embassy in Canada: High Commission for the Republic of Uganda, 231 Cobourg St, Ottawa ON K1N 8J2. Tel: (613) 789-7797. Fax: (613) 789-8909.

Ukraine

Long-Form Name: Ukraine
Capital: Kiev

■ GEOGRAPHY

Area: 603,700 sq. km

Coastline: 2,782 km
Climate: temperate continental; subtropical on southern Crimean coast; moderate rainfall in north; drier in southern regions
Environment: air and water pollution, unsafe drinking water, deforestation, radiation contamination around Chernobyl nuclear power plant
Terrain: Carpathian mountains in west, marshy in north, remainder flat fertile plains (steppes) and plateaux
Land Use: 58% arable, 2% permanent crops, 13% meadows and pastures, 18% forest, 9% other, includes 4% irrigated
Location: E Europe, bordering on Black Sea

■ PEOPLE

Population: 50,125,108 (July 1998 est.)
Nationality: Ukrainian
Age Structure: 0-14 yrs: 19%; 15-64: 67%; 65+: 14% (1998 est.)
Population Growth Rate: -0.64% (1998 est.)
Net Migration: 0.43 migrants/1,000 population (1998 est.)
Ethnic Groups: 73% Ukrainian, 22% Russian, 1% Jewish, 4% other
Languages: Ukrainian, Russian, Romanian, Polish
Religions: predominantly Eastern Orthodox and Roman Catholic; Uniate Church re-legalized in 1991; also, Autocephalous Orthodox Church, Greek rite Catholic
Birth Rate: 9.53/1,000 population (1998 est.)
Death Rate: 16.31/1,000 population (1998 est.)
Infant Mortality: 21.8 deaths/1,000 live births (1998 est.)
Life Expectancy at Birth: 60.08 years male, 71.89 years female (1998 est.)
Total Fertility Rate: 1.35 children born/woman (1998 est.)
Literacy: 98% (1997 est.)

■ GOVERNMENT

Leader(s): Pres. Leonid Kuchma, Premier Valery Pustovoitenko
Government Type: republic
Administrative Divisions: 24 oblasts, 1 autonomous republic, 2 municipalities with oblast status
Nationhood: Dec. 1, 1991 (from Soviet Union)
National Holiday: Independence Day, Aug. 24

■ ECONOMY

Overview: mining and heavy industry, with very strong agricultural sector; food surplus area of former USSR; internal political disputes are hobbling economic progress

GDP: $124.9 billion, per capita $2,500; real growth rate -3.2% (1997 est.)
Inflation: 9.9% (1997)
Industries: accounts for 30% of GDP and 33% of labour force; industries include: mining, manufacturing of machinery, food processing, chemicals, electric and electronic equipment, coal, electric power, food processing (esp. sugar)
Labour Force: 24.9 million (1997 est.); 32% industry and construction, 24% agriculture and forestry, 17% health and cultural services, 27% other
Unemployment: 2.6% (Dec. 1997) officially registered, but there is extensive unregistered unemployment or underemployment
Agriculture: accounts for about 14%; corn, wheat, sugar beets, sunflower seeds, barley, tobacco; livestock includes cattle, pigs, goats, sheep, vegetables, milk, sugar beets
Natural Resources: coal, manganese, oil, gypsum, iron, lead, zinc, titanium, natural gas, oil, salt, sulphur, graphite

■ **FINANCE/TRADE**

Currency: hryvnia (pl. hryvni), as of Sept. 2, 1996; 1 hryrnia = 100,000 karbovantsi (old currency)
International Reserves Excluding Gold: $602 million (Jan. 1999)
Gold Reserves: 0.117 million fine troy ounces (Jan. 1999)
Budget: revenues $18 billion; expenditures $21 billion, including capital expenditures n.a. (1997 est.)
Defence Expenditures: less than 2% of GDP (1996 est.)
Education Expenditures: 7.7% of GNP (1995)
External Debt: $9.335 billion (1996)
Exports: $14.441 billion (1996): minerals, agricultural products, heavy machinery, vehicles, airplanes
Imports: $18.639 billion (1996): machinery and equipment, chemicals, textiles, energy

■ **COMMUNICATIONS**

Daily Newspapers: 44 (1996)
Televisions: 349/1,000 inhabitants (1996)
Radios: 872/1,000 inhabitants (1996)
Telephones: 16.5/100 inhabitants (1996 est.)

■ **TRANSPORTATION**

Motor Vehicles: n.a.
Roads: 172,565 km; 163,937 km paved
Railway: 23,350 km
Air Traffic: 1,600,000 passengers carried (1997 est.)

Airports: 706; 163 have paved runways (1997 est.)
Canadian Embassy: The Canadian Embassy, 31 Yaroslaviv Val St, Kiev 252034, Ukraine. Tel: (011-380-44) 464-1144. Fax: (011-380-44) 464-1133.
Embassy in Canada: Embassy of Ukraine, 310 Somerset St W, Ottawa ON K2P 0J9. Tel: (613) 230-2961. Fax: (613) 230-2400.

United Arab Emirates

Long-Form Name: United Arab Emirates
Capital: Abu Dhabi

■ **GEOGRAPHY**

Area: 82,880 sq. km
Coastline: 1,318 km along Persian Gulf and Gulf of Oman
Climate: desert; cooler in eastern mountains
Environment: frequent dust and sand storms; lack of natural freshwater resources being overcome by desalination plants; desertification
Terrain: flat, barren coastal plain; desert wasteland; mountains in east
Land Use: 2% permanent pastures; 98% other
Location: SW Asia (Middle East), bordering on Persian Gulf

■ **PEOPLE**

Population: 2,303,088 (July 1998 est.)
Nationality: Emiri
Age Structure: 0-14 yrs: 32%; 15-64: 66%; 65+: 2% (1998 est.)
Population Growth Rate: 1.78% (1998 est.)
Net Migration: 2.25 migrants/1,000 population (1998 est.)
Ethnic Groups: 19% Emiri, 23% other Arab, 50% South Asian (fluctuating), 8% other expatriates (includes Westerners and East Asians); less than 20% of the population are United Arab Emirates citizens
Languages: Arabic (official); Farsi and English widely spoken in major cities; Hindi, Urdu
Religions: 96% Muslim (16% Shi'a); 4% Christian, Hindu and other
Birth Rate: 18.61/1,000 population (1998 est.)
Death Rate: 3.06/1,000 population (1998 est.)
Infant Mortality: 14.77 deaths/1,000 live births (1998 est.)
Life Expectancy at Birth: 73.5 years male, 76.44 years female (1998 est.)
Total Fertility Rate: 3.56 children born/woman (1998 est.)
Literacy: 79.2% (1997 est.)

■ GOVERNMENT

Leader(s): Pres. Zayid bin Sultan Al Nuhayyan, V. Pres. and Prime Min. Maktum bin Rashid al-Maktum

Government Type: federation with specified powers delegated to the United Arab Emirates central government and other powers reserved to member emirates

Administrative Divisions: 7 emirates

Nationhood: Dec. 2, 1971 (from UK; formerly known as Trucial States)

National Holiday: National Day, Dec. 2

■ ECONOMY

Overview: has an open economy tied to the world prices for oil and gas; currently has a high standard of living; crude oil reserves should last for over 100 years at present levels of production. The government is encouraging privatization measures

GDP: $54.2 billion, per capita $24,000; real growth rate 5% (1997 est.)

Inflation: n.a.

Industries: accounts for 55% of GDP; petroleum, fishing, petrochemicals, construction materials, some boat building, handicrafts, pearling

Labour Force: 1 million (1997 est.): 38% industry, 4.5% agriculture, 57.3% services

Unemployment: n.a.

Agriculture: accounts for 3% of GDP and 6% of labour force; cash crop: dates; food products: vegetables, watermelons, poultry, eggs, dairy, fish; only 25% self-sufficient in food

Natural Resources: crude oil and natural gas

■ FINANCE/TRADE

Currency: Emirian dirham (Dh) = 100 fils

International Reserves Excluding Gold: $9.077 billion (Dec. 1998)

Gold Reserves: 0.795 million fine troy ounces (Dec. 1998)

Budget: revenues $5.1 billion; expenditures $5.4 billion, including capital expenditures n.a. (1997 est.)

Defence Expenditures: 5.2% of GDP (1996)

Education Expenditures: 1.8% of GNP (1995)

External Debt: $14 billion (1996 est.)

Exports: n.a.; commodities: crude oil 75%, natural gas, re-exports, dried fish, dates; partners: US, European Community, Japan, Singapore, Korea

Imports: $29.952 billion (1997); commodities: food, consumer and capital goods; partners: European Community, Japan, US

■ COMMUNICATIONS

Daily Newspapers: 7 (1996)

Televisions: 133/1,000 inhabitants (1996)

Radios: 354/1,000 inhabitants (1996)

Telephones: 29.0/100 inhabitants (1996 est.)

■ TRANSPORTATION

Motor Vehicles: 400,000; 320,000 passenger cars (1997 est.)

Roads: 4,835 km, all paved

Railway: none

Air Traffic: 4,200,000 passengers carried (1997 est.)

Airports: 40; 22 have paved runways (1997 est.)

Canadian Embassy: The Canadian Embassy, Villa No. 440, 26th St, Rowdah District, Abu Dhabi; mailing address: P.O. Box 6970, Abu Dhabi, UAE. Tel: (011-971-2) 456-969. Fax: (011-971-2) 458-787.

Embassy in Canada: c/o Embassy of the United Arab Emirates, 747 Third Ave, 36th Flr, New York NY 10017, USA. Tel: (212) 371-0480. Fax: (212) 371-4923.

United Kingdom

Long-Form Name: United Kingdom of Great Britain and Northern Ireland

Capital: London

■ GEOGRAPHY

Area: 244,820 sq. km

Coastline: 12,429 km along English Channel, North Sea, North Atlantic Ocean, Irish Sea

Climate: temperate; moderated by prevailing southwest winds over the North Atlantic Current; more than half of the days are overcast

Environment: pollution control measures improving air, water quality; because of heavily indented coastline, no location is more than 125 km from tidal waters

Terrain: mostly rugged hills and low mountains; level to rolling plains in east and southeast

Land Use: 25% arable; negligible permanent crops; 46% meadows; 10% forest; 19% other

Location: NW Europe, bordering on North Sea, Atlantic Ocean

■ PEOPLE

Population: 58,970,119 (July 1998 est.)

Nationality: British

Age Structure: 0-14 yrs: 19%; 15-64: 65%; 65+: 16% (1998 est.)

Population Growth Rate: 0.25% (1998 est.)

Net Migration: 1.2 migrants/1,000 population (1998 est.)

Ethnic Groups: 81.5% English, 9.6% Scottish, 2.4% Irish, 1.9% Welsh, 1.8% Ulster, 2.8% West Indian, Indian, Pakistani and other

Languages: English, Welsh (about 26% of population of Wales), Scottish form of Gaelic (about 60,000 in Scotland)
Religions: 73% Anglican, 23% Roman Catholic, 3% Muslim, 0.1% Sikh, 0.2% Presbyterian, 0.5% Methodist, 0.2% Jewish
Birth Rate: 12.01/1,000 population (1998 est.)
Death Rate: 10.72/1,000 population (1998 est.)
Infant Mortality: 5.87 deaths/1,000 live births (1998 est.)
Life Expectancy at Birth: 74.57 years male, 79.97 years female (1998 est.)
Total Fertility Rate: 1.7 children born/woman (1998 est.)
Literacy: 99% (1997 est.)

■ GOVERNMENT

Leader(s): Queen Elizabeth II, Prime Min. Tony Blair
Government Type: constitutional monarchy
Administrative Divisions: 47 counties, 7 metropolitan counties, 26 districts, 9 regions and 3 island areas; dependent areas include: Anguilla, Bermuda, British Antarctic Territory (uninhabited except for variable population of research stations – about 300 persons), British Indian Ocean Territory, British Virgin Islands, Cayman Islands, Channel Islands, Falkland Islands, Gibraltar, Guernsey, Hong Kong, Isle of Man, Jersey, Montserrat, Pitcairn, Saint Helena, South Georgia (uninhabited except for scientific station and 500 persons in a whaling/sealing settlement), South Sandwich Islands (uninhabited), Turks and Caicos Islands
Nationhood: Jan. 1, 1801, United Kingdom established
National Holiday: Celebration of the Birthday of the Queen, second Saturday in June

■ ECONOMY

Overview: economy is essentially capitalist; intensive agricultural practices produce 60% of domestic food needs with only 1% of the labour force; strong service sector; industry is declining in importance
GDP: $1.242 trillion, per capita $21,200; real growth rate 3.5% (1997 est.)
Inflation: 3.7% (June 1998)
Industries: accounts for 31% of GDP and 25% of labour force; machinery and transportation equipment, metals, food processing, paper and paper products, textiles, chemicals, clothing, other consumer goods, motor vehicles, aircraft, shipbuilding, petroleum, coal
Labour Force: 26,292,000 (1997); 62.8% services, 1.2% agriculture, 1.9% energy, 25% manufacturing and construction, 9.1% government

Unemployment: 4.6% (Dec. 1998)
Agriculture: accounts for only 1.8% of GDP; highly mechanized and efficient farms; wide variety of crops and livestock products produced; about 60% self-sufficient in food and feed needs
Natural Resources: coal, crude oil, natural gas, tin, limestone, iron ore, salt, clay, chalk, gypsum, lead, silica

■ FINANCE/TRADE

Currency: pound sterling (£ or £ stg) = 100 pence
International Reserves Excluding Gold: $32.212 billion (Dec. 1998)
Gold Reserves: 23.00 million fine troy ounces (Dec. 1998)
Budget: revenues $421.5 billion; expenditures $474.9 billion, including capital expenditures n.a. (1996 est.)
Defence Expenditures: 3.1% of GDP (1995–96)
Education Expenditures: 4.94% of total govt. expenditure (1995)
External Debt: n.a.
Exports: $270.476 billion (1998); commodities: manufactured goods, machinery, fuels, chemicals, semifinished goods, transport equipment; partners: European Community 50.4% (Germany 11.7%, France 10.2%, Netherlands 6.8%), US 13%, Communist countries 2.3%
Imports: $313.119 billion (1998); commodities: manufactured goods, machinery, semifinished goods, foodstuffs, consumer goods; partners: European Community 52.5% (Germany 16.6%, France 8.8%, Netherlands 7.8%), US 10.2%, Communist countries 2.1%

■ COMMUNICATIONS

Daily Newspapers: 99 (1996)
Televisions: 516/1,000 inhabitants (1996)
Radios: 1,445/1,000 inhabitants (1996)
Telephones: 51.3/100 inhabitants (1996 est.)

■ TRANSPORTATION

Motor Vehicles: 28,800,000; 25,000,000 passenger cars (1997 est.)
Roads: 372,000 km, all paved
Railway: 16,878 km
Air Traffic: 65,000,000 passengers carried (1997 est.)
Airports: 497; 356 have paved runways (1997 est.)

Canadian Embassy: The Canadian High Commission, Macdonald House, 1 Grosvenor Square, London W1X OAB, England, UK. Tel: (011-44-171) 258-6600. Fax: (011-44-171) 258-6333.

Embassy in Canada: British High Commission, 80 Elgin St, Ottawa ON K1P 5K7. Tel: (613) 237-1530. Fax: (613) 237-7980.

United States

Long-Form Name: United States of America
Capital: Washington, D.C.

■ GEOGRAPHY

Area: 9,629,091 sq. km; includes only the 50 states and District of Columbia
Coastline: 19,924 km North Atlantic Ocean, Gulf of Mexico, North Pacific Ocean
Climate: mostly temperate, but varies from tropical (Hawaii) to arctic (Alaska); arid to semi-arid in west with occasional warm, dry chinook wind
Environment: pollution control measures improving air and water quality; acid rain; agricultural fertilizer and pesticide pollution; management of sparse natural water resources in west; desertification; tsunamis, volcanoes and earthquake activity around Pacific; permafrost in Alaska
Terrain: vast central plain, mountains in west, hills and low mountains in east; rugged mountains and broad river valleys in Alaska; rugged, volcanic topography in Hawaii
Land Use: 19% arable; negligible permanent crops; 25% meadows; 30% forest; 26% other, includes 2% irrigated
Location: North America, bordering on Pacific Ocean, Atlantic Ocean

■ PEOPLE

Population: 270,311,756 (July 1998 est.)
Nationality: American
Age Structure: 0-14 yrs: 22%; 15-64: 66%; 65+: 12% (1998 est.)
Population Growth Rate: 0.87% (1998 est.)
Net Migration: 3.0 migrants/1,000 population (1998 est.)
Ethnic Groups: 83.4% white, 12.4% black, 3.3% Asian, 0.7% other
Languages: predominantly English; sizable Spanish-speaking minority
Religions: 56% Protestant (including 21% Baptist, 12% Methodist, 8% Lutheran, 4% Presbyterian, 3% Episcopalian), 28% Roman Catholic, 2% Jewish, 4% other, 10% none
Birth Rate: 14.4/1,000 population (1998 est.)
Death Rate: 8.81/1,000 population (1998 est.)
Infant Mortality: 6.44 deaths/1,000 live births (1998 est.)
Life Expectancy at Birth: 72.85 years male, 79.58 years female (1998 est.)

Total Fertility Rate: 2.07 children born/woman (1998 est.)
Literacy: 97% (1997 est.)

■ GOVERNMENT

Leader(s): Pres. William Jefferson Clinton, V. Pres. Albert Arnold Gore
Government Type: federal republic
Administrative Divisions: 50 states and 1 district; dependent areas include: American Samoa, Baker Island, Federated States of Micronesia, Guam, Howland Island, Jarvis Island, Johnston Atoll, Kingman Reef, Marshall Islands, Midway Islands (inhabited by U.S. military personnel), Northern Marianas, Palau, Palymyra Atoll, Puerto Rico (for details see Puerto Rico entry), Virgin Islands (for details see Virgin Islands entry), Wake Island (military base)
Nationhood: July 4, 1776 (from England)
National Holiday: Independence Day, July 4

■ ECONOMY

Overview: market-oriented economy with a very large private sector; a powerful and diversified economy, with high per capita GNP; problems include the significant budget and trade deficits, large medical costs for the aging population and inadequate investment in industry and infrastructure
GDP: $8.083 trillion, per capita $30,200; real growth rate 3.89% (1997 est.)
Inflation: 1.7% (July 1998)
Industries: accounts for 23% of GDP and 25.3% of labour force; highly diversified industry; petroleum, steel, motor vehicles, aerospace, telecommunications, chemicals, electronics, food processing, consumer goods, fishing, lumber, mining
Labour Force: 129,972,000 (1997); 35.5% community, social and business services, 20.8% trade and tourism, 16.4% industry
Unemployment: 4.4% (Mar. 1999)
Agriculture: accounts for 2% of GDP and 2.8% of labour force; favourable climate and soils support a wide variety of crops and livestock production; world's second largest producer and top exporter of grain; surplus food producer; fish catch of 4.4 million metric tons
Natural Resources: coal, copper, lead, molybdenum, phosphates, uranium, bauxite, gold, iron, mercury, nickel, potash, silver, tungsten, zinc, crude oil, natural gas, timber

■ FINANCE/TRADE

Currency: US dollar ($ or $US) = 100 cents
International Reserves Excluding Gold: $69.629 billion (Jan. 1999)

Gold Reserves: 261.657 million fine troy ounces (Jan. 1999)
Budget: revenues $1.579 trillion; expenditures $1.601 trillion, including capital expenditures n.a. (1997)
Defence Expenditures: 15.71% of govt. expenditure (1997)
Education Expenditures: 1.76% of govt. expenditure (1997)
External Debt: $862 billion (1995 est.)
Exports: $682.572 billion (1998); commodities: capital goods, automobiles, industrial supplies and raw materials, consumer goods, agricultural products; partners: Canada 22.9%, Japan 11.8%
Imports: $944.557 billion (1998); commodities: crude and partly refined petroleum, machinery, automobiles, consumer goods, industrial raw materials, food and beverages; partners: Japan 19.6%, Canada 19.1%

■ COMMUNICATIONS

Daily Newspapers: 1,520 (1996)
Televisions: 805/1,000 inhabitants (1996)
Radios: 2,115/1,000 inhabitants (1996)
Telephones: 65.0/100 inhabitants (1996 est.)

■ TRANSPORTATION

Motor Vehicles: 212,000,000; 137,000,000 passenger cars (1997 est.)
Roads: 6,420,000 km; 3,903,360 km paved
Railway: 247,440 km
Air Traffic: 600,000,000 passengers carried (1997 est.)
Airports: 14,574; 5,167 have paved runways (1997 est.)

Canadian Embassy: The Canadian Embassy, 501 Pennsylvania Ave, NW, Washington DC 20001, USA. Tel: (202) 682-1740. Fax: (202) 682-7726.
Embassy in Canada: Embassy of the United States of America, 100 Wellington St, Ottawa ON K1P 5A1. Tel: (613) 238-5335. Fax: (613) 238-5720.

Uruguay

Long-Form Name: Oriental Republic of Uruguay
Capital: Montevideo

■ GEOGRAPHY

Area: 176,220 sq. km
Coastline: 660 km along South Atlantic Ocean
Climate: warm temperate; freezing temperatures almost unknown
Environment: subject to seasonally high winds, droughts, floods; industrial pollution from Brazil

Terrain: mostly rolling plains and low hills; fertile coastal lowland
Land Use: 7% arable; negligible permanent crops; 77% meadows; 6% forest; 10% other
Location: SE South America, bordering on Atlantic Ocean

■ PEOPLE

Population: 3,284,841 (July 1998 est.)
Nationality: Uruguayan
Age Structure: 0-14 yrs: 24%; 15-64: 63%; 65+: 13% (1998 est.)
Population Growth Rate: 0.71% (1998 est.)
Net Migration: -0.91 migrants/1,000 population (1998 est.)
Ethnic Groups: 88% white, 8% mestizo, 4% black
Languages: Spanish, Brazilero
Religions: 66% nominally Roman Catholic, 2% Protestant, 2% Jewish, 30% other
Birth Rate: 16.92/1,000 population (1998 est.)
Death Rate: 8.89/1,000 population (1998 est.)
Infant Mortality: 14.11 deaths/1,000 live births (1998 est.)
Life Expectancy at Birth: 72.39 years male, 78.84 years female (1998 est.)
Total Fertility Rate: 2.29 children born/woman (1998 est.)
Literacy: 97.3% (1997 est.)

■ GOVERNMENT

Leader(s): Pres. Julio Maria Sanguinetti, V. Pres Hugo Fernandez Faingold
Government Type: republic
Administrative Divisions: 19 departments
Nationhood: Aug. 25, 1828 (from Brazil)
National Holiday: Independence Day, Aug. 25

■ ECONOMY

Overview: a small economy with favourable climate, good soils and considerable hydropower potential; problems include high inflation rates, a large domestic debt and frequent strikes; growth in the agriculture and fishing sectors has spurred recovery; inflation continues to drop but unemployment is on the rise and hobbles economic progress
GDP: $29.1 billion, per capita $8,900; real growth rate 5.1% (1997 est.)
Inflation: 10.2% (June 1998)
Industries: accounts for 27% of GDP and 19% of labour force; meat packing, oil refining, manufacturing, foodstuffs, engineering, transport equipment, sugar, textiles, leather apparel, tires
Labour Force: 1 million (1997 est.); 36.6% community, social and business services, 21.1%

industry, 17.9% trade and tourism, 15.3% agriculture

Unemployment: 10.3% (Dec. 1997)

Agriculture: accounts for 11% of GDP and 11% of labour force; meat processing, wool and hides, sugar, textiles, footwear, leather apparel, tires, cement, fishing, petroleum refining, wine, wheat, rice, corn, sorghum; self-sufficient in most basic foods

Natural Resources: soil, hydropower potential, minor minerals

■ FINANCE/TRADE

Currency: new peso (N$Ur) = 100 centesimos

International Reserves Excluding Gold: $2.073 billion (Dec. 1998)

Gold Reserves: 1.783 million fine troy ounces (Dec. 1998)

Budget: revenues $4 billion; expenditures $4.3 billion, including capital expenditures of $385 million (1997 est.)

Defence Expenditures: 4.42% of total govt. expenditure (1997)

Education Expenditures: 7.22% of govt. expenditure (1997)

External Debt: $5.899 billion (1996)

Exports: $2.726 billion (1997); commodities: hides and leather goods 17%, beef 10%, wool 9%, fish 7%, rice 4%; partners: Brazil 17%, US 15%, Germany 10%, Argentina 10%

Imports: $3.716 billion (1997); commodities: fuels and lubricants 15%, metals, machinery, transportation equipment, industrial chemicals; partners: Brazil 24%, Argentina 14%, US 8%, Germany 8%

■ COMMUNICATIONS

Daily Newspapers: 36 (1996)

Televisions: 242/1,000 inhabitants (1996)

Radios: 610/1,000 inhabitants (1996)

Telephones: 20.6/100 inhabitants (1996 est.)

■ TRANSPORTATION

Motor Vehicles: 525,000; 475,000 passenger cars (1997 est.)

Roads: n.a.; 7,578 km paved

Railway: 2,998 km

Air Traffic: 504,000 passengers carried (1996)

Airports: 64; 15 have paved runways (1997 est.)

Canadian Embassy: The Canadian Embassy, Edifio Torre Libertad, Plaza Cagancha, 1335, off. 1105, 11100 Montevideo, Uruguay. Tel: (011-598-2) 902-20-30. Fax: (011-598-2) 902-20-29.

Embassy in Canada: Embassy of the Eastern Republic of Uruguay, 130 Albert St, Ste 1905, Ottawa ON K1P 5G4. Tel: (613) 234-2727. Fax: (613) 233-4670.

Uzbekistan

Long-Form Name: Republic of Uzbekistan

Capital: Tashkent

■ GEOGRAPHY

Area: 447,400 sq. km

Coastline: landlocked; 420 km coastline along Aral Sea

Climate: dry continental; warm to hot summers; cool to cold winters; semi-arid grassland in east

Environment: drying up of the Aral Sea is resulting in increasing concentrations of chemical pesticides and natural salts; water and soil pollution

Terrain: flat to rolling deserts and semideserts, mountains, shrinking Aral Sea in west

Land Use: 9% arable, 1% permanent crops, 46% meadows and pastures, 3% forest, 41% other, includes 9% irrigated

Location: C Asia

■ PEOPLE

Population: 23,784,321 (July 1998 est.)

Nationality: Uzbek

Age Structure: 0-14 yrs: 38%; 15-64: 57%; 65+: 5% (1998 est.)

Population Growth Rate: 1.33% (1998 est.)

Net Migration: -2.68 migrants/1,000 population (1998 est.)

Ethnic Groups: 80% Uzbek, 5.5% Russian, 1.5% Tartars, 5% Tajiks, 3% Kazakhs, 2.5% Kara-Kalpaks, 2.5% other

Languages: 74.3% Uzbek (official), 14.2% Russian, 4.4% Tajik, 7.1% other

Religions: predominantly Sunni Muslim and Eastern Orthodox

Birth Rate: 23.69/1,000 population (1998 est.)

Death Rate: 7.68/1,000 population (1998 est.)

Infant Mortality: 71.04 deaths/1,000 live births (1998 est.)

Life Expectancy at Birth: 60.49 years male, 67.91 years female (1998 est.)

Total Fertility Rate: 2.87 children born/woman (1998 est.)

Literacy: 97% (1997 est.)

■ GOVERNMENT

Leader(s): Pres. Islam A. Karimov, Prem. Otkir Sultonov

Government Type: republic

Administrative Divisions: 12 "wiloyatlar," 1 autonomous republic, 1 city

Nationhood: Aug. 31, 1991 (from Soviet Union)

National Holiday: Independence Day, Sept. 1

ECONOMY

Overview: despite the need for irrigation, agriculture is the predominant economic sector; small industrial sector, mining. Inflation is skyrocketing and economic problems are numerous. More than 60% of the population is living in overcrowded rural villages
GDP: $60.7 billion, per capita $2,500; real growth rate 2.4% (1997 est.)
Inflation: 7.7% per month (Oct. 1995 est.)
Industries: accounts for 27% of GDP, chemicals and gas, machine building, metalmaking, textile manufacture, clothing, butter, preserves, vegetable oil, textiles
Labour Force: 9.2 million (1997 est.); 39% agriculture and forestry, 24% industry and construction, 37% other
Unemployment: 5% (Dec. 1996); also large numbers of underemployed
Agriculture: accounts for 26% of GDP, vegetables, cotton, grains, almonds, fruit, livestock; 97% of all crops are grown on irrigated land
Natural Resources: gold, nonferrous metals, coal, natural gas, petroleum, uranium, silver, copper

FINANCE/TRADE

Currency: som
International Reserves Excluding Gold: n.a.
Gold Reserves: n.a.
Budget: n.a.
Defence Expenditures: 7% of GDP (1996)
Education Expenditures: 9.5% of GNP (1995)
External Debt: $2.319 billion (1996)
Exports: $4.388 billion (1997): cotton, agricultural products, machinery
Imports: $4.523 billion (1997): foodstuffs, machinery, consumer products

COMMUNICATIONS

Daily Newspapers: 3 (1996)
Televisions: 269/1,000 inhabitants (1996)
Radios: 452/1,000 inhabitants (1996)
Telephones: 8.2/100 inhabitants (1996 est.)

TRANSPORTATION

Motor Vehicles: n.a.
Roads: 81,600 km; 71,237 km hard-surfaced
Railway: 3,380 km, plus industrial lines
Air Traffic: 1,566,000 passengers carried (1996)
Airports: 3; all have paved runways (1997 est.)

Canadian Embassy: c/o The Canadian Embassy, 23 Starokonyushenny Pereulok, Moscow 121002, Russia. Tel: (011-7-095) 956-6666. Fax: (011-7-095) 232-9948.
Embassy in Canada: c/o The Embassy of the

Republic of Uzbekistan, 1746 Massachusetts Ave. NW, Washington, DC 20036. Tel: (202) 887-5300. Fax: (202) 293-6804.

Vanuatu

Long-Form Name: Republic of Vanuatu
Capital: Port Vila

GEOGRAPHY

Area: 14,760 sq. km
Coastline: 2,528 km
Climate: tropical; moderated by southeast trade winds
Environment: subject to tropical cyclones or typhoons (Jan. to Apr.); volcanism causes minor earthquakes; lack of safe drinking water
Terrain: mostly mountains of volcanic origin; narrow coastal plains
Land Use: 2% arable; 10% permanent crops; 2% meadows; 75% forests and woodlands; 11% other
Location: South Pacific Ocean, E of Australia

PEOPLE

Population: 185,204 (July 1998 est.)
Nationality: Ni-Vanuatu
Age Structure: 0-14 yrs: 39%; 15-64: 58%; 65+: 3% (1998 est.)
Population Growth Rate: 2.07% (1998 est.)
Net Migration: 0 migrants/1,000 population (1998 est.)
Ethnic Groups: 94% indigenous Melanesian, 4% French, remainder Vietnamese, Chinese and various Pacific Islanders
Languages: English and French (both official); pidgin (known as Bislama or Bichelama)
Religions: 36.7% Presbyterian, 15% Anglican, 15% Catholic, 7.6% indigenous beliefs, 6.2% Seventh-Day Adventist, 3.8% Church of Christ, 15.7% other
Birth Rate: 29.18/1,000 population (1998 est.)
Death Rate: 8.44/1,000 population (1998 est.)
Infant Mortality: 61.27 deaths/1,000 live births (1998 est.)
Life Expectancy at Birth: 59.02 years male, 63.07 years female (1998 est.)
Total Fertility Rate: 3.74 children born/woman (1998 est.)
Literacy: 53% (1997 est.)

GOVERNMENT

Leader(s): Pres. John Bani, Prime Min. Donald Kalpokas
Government Type: republic
Administrative Divisions: 6 provinces
Nationhood: July 30, 1980 (from France and UK;

formerly known as New Hebrides)
National Holiday: Independence Day, July 30

■ ECONOMY

Overview: economy is based on subsistence farming, fishing and tourism; few mineral deposits; a small light industry sector sees to local needs; tax revenues come largely from import duties
GDP: $231 million, per capita $1,300; real growth rate 3% (1997 est.)
Inflation: 2.8% (Mar. 1998)
Industries: accounts for 13% of GDP; food and fish freezing, meat canning, wood processing
Labour Force: n.a.; 65% agriculture, 32% services, 3% industry
Unemployment: n.a.
Agriculture: accounts for 23% of GDP and 65% of labour force; export crops: cocoa, coffee and fish; subsistence crops: copra, taro, yams, coconuts, fruit and vegetables
Natural Resources: manganese, hardwood forests, fish

■ FINANCE/TRADE

Currency: vatu (VT) = 100 centimes
International Reserves Excluding Gold: $20 million (July 1998)
Gold Reserves: n.a.
Budget: revenues $94.4 million; expenditures $99.8 million, including capital expenditures of $30.4 million (1996 est.)
Defence Expenditures: negligible
Education Expenditures: 4.6% of GNP (1995)
External Debt: $47 million (1996)
Exports: $35 million (1997); commodities: copra 37%, cocoa 11%, meat 9%, fish 8%, timber 4%; partners: Netherlands 34%, France 27%, Japan 17%, Belgium 4%, New Caledonia 3%, Singapore 2%
Imports: $94 million (1997); commodities: machines and vehicles 25%, food and beverages 23%, basic manufactures 18%, raw materials and fuels 11%, chemicals 6%; partners: Australia 36%, Japan 13%, New Zealand 10%, France 8%, Fiji 5%

■ COMMUNICATIONS

Daily Newspapers: 0 (1996)
Televisions: 13/1,000 inhabitants (1996)
Radios: 345/1,000 inhabitants (1996)
Telephones: 2.6/100 inhabitants (1996 est.)

■ TRANSPORTATION

Motor Vehicles: 6,300; 4,000 passenger cars (1997 est.)
Roads: 1,070 km; 256 km paved

Railway: none
Air Traffic: 73,000 passengers carried (1996)
Airports: 31; 2 have paved runways (1997 est.)

Canadian Embassy: The Canadian High Commission to Vanuatu, c/o The Canadian High Commission, Commonwealth Ave, Canberra A.C.T. 2600, Australia. Tel: (011-61-2) 6273-3844. Fax: (011-61-2) 6273-3285.
Embassy in Canada: c/o Australian High Commission, 50 O'Connor St, Ste 710, Ottawa, ON K1P 6L2. Tel: (613) 236-0841. Fax: (613) 236-4376.

Vatican City

Long-Form Name: State of the Vatican City, or the Holy See
Capital: Vatican City

■ GEOGRAPHY

Area: 0.438 sq. km
Coastline: none: landlocked
Climate: temperate; mild, rainy winters (Sept. to mid-May) with hot, dry summers (May to Sept.)
Environment: urban
Terrain: low hill
Land Use: 100% built-up
Location: S Europe (W Italy)

■ PEOPLE

Population: 860 (July 1998 est.)
Nationality: n.a.
Age Structure: n.a.
Population Growth Rate: 1.15% (1998 est.)
Net Migration: n.a.

Ethnic Groups: primarily Italians and Swiss but also many other nationalities
Languages: Italian, Latin and various other languages
Religions: Roman Catholic
Birth Rate: n.a.
Death Rate: n.a.
Infant Mortality: n.a.
Life Expectancy at Birth: n.a.
Literacy: 100%

■ GOVERNMENT

Leader(s): Head, Roman Catholic Church, Pope John Paul II (Karol Wojtyla)
Government Type: monarchical-sacerdotal state
Administrative Divisions: none
Nationhood: Feb. 11, 1929 (from Italy)
National Holiday: Installation Day of the Pope (John Paul II), Oct. 22; also Christmas, Easter, Feast of Saints Peter and Paul (June 29), and other holy days of obligation

■ ECONOMY

Overview: economy is supported financially by contributions (known as Peter's Pence) from Roman Catholics throughout the world, the sale of postage stamps, tourist mementos, fees for admission to museums and the sale of publications

GDP: n.a.

Inflation: n.a.

Industries: printing and production of a small amount of mosaics and staff uniforms; worldwide banking and financial activities

Labour Force: approximately 1,500 Vatican City employees divided into three categories: executives, office workers, salaried employees

Unemployment: n.a.

Agriculture: none

Natural Resources: none

■ FINANCE/TRADE

Currency: Vatican Lira (Lit) = 100 centesimi (at par with Italian lira)

International Reserves Excluding Gold: n.a.

Gold Reserves: n.a.

Budget: n.a.

Defence Expenditures: defence is the responsibility of Italy

Education Expenditures: n.a.

External Debt: n.a.

Exports: n.a.

Imports: n.a.

■ COMMUNICATIONS

Daily Newspapers: 1 (1996)

Televisions: n.a.

Radios: n.a.

Telephones: n.a.

■ TRANSPORTATION

Motor Vehicles: n.a.

Roads: no highways, all city streets

Railway: 862 m

Air Traffic: none

Airports: none

Canadian Embassy: The Canadian Embassy, Via Zara, 00198 Rome, Italy. Tel. (011-39-06) 445981. Fax: (011-39-06) 445 98912.

Embassy in Canada: Apostolic Nunciature, 724 Manor Ave, Rockcliffe Park, Ottawa ON K1M 0E3. Tel: (613) 746-4914. Fax: (613) 746-4786.

Venezuela

Long-Form Name: Republic of Venezuela

Capital: Caracas

■ GEOGRAPHY

Area: 912,050 sq. km

Coastline: 2,800 km along Caribbean Sea

Climate: tropical; hot, humid; more moderate in highlands

Environment: subject to floods, rockslides, mud slides; periodic droughts; increasing industrial pollution in Caracas and Maracaibo

Terrain: Andes Mountains and Maracaibo lowlands in northwest; central plains (llanos); Guyana highlands in southwest

Land Use: 4% arable; 1% permanent crops; 20% meadows; 34% forest; 41% other

Location: N South America, bordering on Caribbean Sea

■ PEOPLE

Population: 22,803,409 (July 1998 est.)

Nationality: Venezuelan

Age Structure: 0-14 yrs: 34%; 15-64: 62%; 65+: 4% (1998 est.)

Population Growth Rate: 1.77% (1998 est.)

Net Migration: -0.27 migrants/1,000 population (1998 est.)

Ethnic Groups: 67% mestizo, 21% white, 10% black, 2% Indian

Languages: Spanish (official); Indian dialects spoken by approximately 200,000 Amerindians in the remote interior

Religions: 96% nominally Roman Catholic, 2% Protestant, 2% other

Birth Rate: 22.96/1,000 population (1998 est.)

Death Rate: 4.98/1,000 population (1998 est.)

Infant Mortality: 27.52 deaths/1,000 live births (1998 est.)

Life Expectancy at Birth: 69.68 years male, 75.87 years female (1998 est.)

Total Fertility Rate: 2.7 children born/woman (1998 est.)

Literacy: 91% (1997 est.)

■ GOVERNMENT

Leader(s): Pres. Lt. Col. Hugo Chavez Frias

Government Type: republic

Administrative Divisions: 22 states, 1 federal district and 1 federal dependency

Nationhood: July 5, 1811 (from Spain)

National Holiday: Independence Day, July 5

■ ECONOMY

Overview: petroleum is the backbone of the economy, accounting for 27% of GDP, 78% of total exports and more than half of government revenue. It is likely to become even more important as the state petroleum company plans to double its production over the next 10 years.

GDP: $185 billion, per capita $8,300; real growth rate 5% (1997 est.)

Inflation: 39.6% (Apr. 1998)
Industries: accounts for 63% of GDP; petroleum, iron-ore mining, construction materials, food processing, textiles, steel, aluminum, motor vehicle assembly
Labour Force: 9.3 million (1997 est.); 27.5% community, social and business services, 22.2% trade and tourism, 15.5% industry (1993)
Unemployment: 11.5% (1997 est.)
Agriculture: accounts for 4% GDP; products: corn, sorghum, sugar cane, rice, bananas, vegetables, coffee, beef, pork, milk, eggs, fish; not self-sufficient in food other than meat
Natural Resources: crude oil, natural gas, iron ore, gold, bauxite, other minerals, hydropower, diamonds

■ FINANCE/TRADE

Currency: bolívar (Bs) = 100 centimos
International Reserves Excluding Gold: $11.418 billion (Jan. 1999)
Gold Reserves: 9.720 million fine troy ounces (Jan. 1999)
Budget: revenues $11.99 billion; expenditures $11.48 billion, including capital expenditures of $2.3 billion (1996 est.)
Defence Expenditures: 1.4 % of GDP (1996)
Education Expenditures: 5.2% of GNP (1995)
External Debt: $35.344 billion (1996)
Exports: $21.075 billion (1997); commodities: petroleum 81%, bauxite and aluminum, iron ore, agricultural products, basic manufactures; partners: US 50.3%, Germany 5.3%, Japan 4.1%
Imports: $14.578 billion (1997); commodities: foodstuffs, chemicals, manufactures, machinery and transport equipment; partners: US 44%, Germany 8.5%, Japan 6%, Italy 5%, Brazil 4.4%

■ COMMUNICATIONS

Daily Newspapers: 86 (1996)
Televisions: 179/1,000 inhabitants (1996)
Radios: 471/1,000 inhabitants (1996)
Telephones: 11.5/100 inhabitants (1996 est.)

■ TRANSPORTATION

Motor Vehicles: 2,025,000; 1,500,000 passenger cars (1997 est.)
Roads: 84,300 km; 33,214 km paved
Railway: 584 km
Air Traffic: 4,487,000 passengers carried (1996)
Airports: 377; 126 have paved runways (1997 est.)

Canadian Embassy: The Canadian Embassy, 6a Av. Entre 3a y 5a, Transv. de Altamira, Altamira, Edificio Omni, Caracas, Venezuela. mailing address: Apartado 62302, Caracas 1060A, Venezuela. Tel: (011-58-2) 264-0833. Fax: (011-58-2) 261-8741.
Embassy in Canada: Embassy of the Republic of Venezuela, 32 Range Rd, Ottawa ON K1N 8J4. Tel: (613) 235-5151. Fax: (613) 235-3205.

Vietnam

Long-Form Name: Socialist Republic of Vietnam
Capital: Hanoi

■ GEOGRAPHY

Area: 329,560 sq. km
Coastline: 3,444 km (excluding islands) along the South China Sea (Gulf of Tonkin and Gulf of Thailand)
Climate: tropical in south; monsoonal in north with hot, rainy season (mid-May to mid-Sept.) and warm, dry season (mid-Oct. to mid-Mar.)
Environment: occasional typhoons (May to Jan.) with extensive flooding; soil deterioration; inadequate supply of safe drinking water
Terrain: low, flat delta in south and north; central highlands; hilly, mountainous far north and northwest
Land Use: 17% arable; 4% permanent crops; 1% meadows; 30% forest; 48% other, includes 5.5% irrigated
Location: SE Asia, bordering on South China Sea

■ PEOPLE

Population: 76,236,259 (July 1998 est.)
Nationality: Vietnamese
Age Structure: 0-14 yrs: 35%; 15-64: 60%; 65+: 5% (1998 est.)
Population Growth Rate: 1.43% (1998 est.)
Net Migration: -0.54 migrants/1,000 population (1998 est.)
Ethnic Groups: 85–90% predominantly Vietnamese; 3% Chinese; more than 60 ethnic minorities including Muong, Thai, Meo, Khmer, Man, Cham; other mountain tribes
Languages: Vietnamese (official), French, Chinese, English, Khmer, tribal languages (Mon-Khmer and Malayo-Polynesian)
Religions: Buddhist, Confucian, Taoist, Roman Catholic, indigenous beliefs, Islamic, Protestant
Birth Rate: 21.55/1,000 population (1998 est.)
Death Rate: 6.69/1,000 population (1998 est.)
Infant Mortality: 36.02 deaths/1,000 live births (1998 est.)
Life Expectancy at Birth: 65.37 years male, 70.25 years female (1998 est.)

Total Fertility Rate: 2.5 children born/woman (1998 est.)
Literacy: 93.7% (1997 est.)

■ GOVERNMENT

Leader(s): Pres. Tran Duc Luong, Prime Min. Phan Van Khai
Government Type: communist state
Administrative Divisions: 50 provinces, 3 municipalities
Nationhood: Sept. 2, 1945 (from France)
National Holiday: Independence Day, Sept. 2

■ ECONOMY

Overview: centrally planned, developing economy with extensive government ownership and control of production facilities; dependent on foreign aid; high rate of population growth and high unemployment combine to form the economy's most serious problem
GDP: $128 billion, per capita $1,700; real growth rate 8.5% (1997 est.)
Inflation: 14% (1995)
Industries: accounts for 30% of GDP; food processing, textiles, machine building, mining, cement, chemical fertilizer, glass, tires, oil, fishing
Labour Force: 38.9 million (1997 est.); 65% agriculture, 11.8% industry, 20.7% services
Unemployment: 25% (1995 est.)
Agriculture: accounts for 28% of GDP; rice, corn, potatoes make up 50% of farm output; commercial crops (rubber, soybeans, coffee, tea, bananas) and animal products other 50%; not self-sufficient in rice
Natural Resources: phosphates, coal, manganese, bauxite, chromate, offshore oil deposits, forests

■ FINANCE/TRADE

Currency: dong (pl. dong) (D) = 100 xu
International Reserves Excluding Gold: $1.411 billion (Mar. 1998)
Gold Reserves: n.a.
Budget: adjusted for purchasing power parity: revenues $5.6 billion; expenditures $6 billion, including capital expenditures $1.7 billion (1996 est.)
Defence Expenditures: 2.7% of GDP (1995)
Education Expenditures: 2.7% of GNP (1995)
External Debt: $26.764 billion (1996)
Exports: $7.256 billion (1996); commodities: agricultural and handicraft products, coal, minerals, ores; partners: former USSR countries, Eastern Europe, Japan, Singapore
Imports: $11.144 billion (1996); commodities: petroleum, steel products, railroad equipment, chemicals, medicines, raw cotton, fertilizer, grain; partners: former USSR countries, Eastern Europe, Japan, Singapore

■ COMMUNICATIONS

Daily Newspapers: 10 (1996)
Televisions: 47/1,000 inhabitants (1996)
Radios: 106/1,000 inhabitants (1996)
Telephones: 1.5/100 inhabitants (1996 est.)

■ TRANSPORTATION

Motor Vehicles: 178,000; 80,000 passenger cars (1997 est.)
Roads: n.a.; 23,418 km paved
Railway: 2,835 km
Air Traffic: 2,108,000 passengers carried (1996)
Airports: 48; 36 have paved runways (1997 est.)

Canadian Embassy: The Consulate General of Canada, 10th Floor, The Metropolitan, 235 Doung Khoi St, District 1, Ho Chi Minh City, Vietnam. Tel: (011-84-4) 823-5500. Fax: (011-84-8) 829-4528.
Embassy in Canada: Embassy of the Socialist Republic of Vietnam, 470 Wilbrod St, Ottawa, ON KIN 6M8. Tel: (613) 236-0772. Fax: (613) 236-2704.

Wallis and Futuna

Long-Form Name: Territory of the Wallis and Futuna Islands
Capital: Mata-Utu

■ GEOGRAPHY

Area: 274 sq. km
Climate: tropical maritime, rainy season (Nov. to April); cool, dry season (May to Oct.)
Land Use: 5% arable, 20% permanent crops, 0% meadows and pasture, 0% forests, 75% other
Location: SW Pacific Ocean

■ PEOPLE

Population: 14,974 (July 1998 est.)
Nationality: Wallisian, Futunan, or Wallis and Futuna Islanders
Ethnic Groups: Polynesians, and descendants of French settlers
Languages: Wallisian, Futunian (Polynesian languages), French

■ GOVERNMENT

Colony Territory of: Overseas Territory of France
Leader(s): Head of State: Jacques Chirac (France); Prefect Christian Dors
Government Type: overseas territory of France
National Holiday: n.a.

■ ECONOMY

Overview: agriculture includes copra, cassava, yams, taro roots, bananas; livestock includes pigs and goats; considerable imports, negligible exports

■ FINANCE/TRADE

Currency: CFP franc = 100 centimes

Canadian Embassy: c/o The Canadian Embassy, 35-37 avenue Montaigne, 75008, Paris, France. Tel: (011-33-1) 44-43-29-00. Fax: (011-33-1) 44-43-29-99.
Representative to Canada: c/o Embassy of France, 42 Sussex Dr, Ottawa ON K1M 2C9. Tel: (613) 789-1795. Fax: (613) 562-3735.

Western Sahara

Long-Form Name: Western Sahara
Capital: none

■ GEOGRAPHY

Area: 266,000 sq. km
Coastline: 1,110 km
Climate: Mediterranean to arid; hot, dry desert; rain is rare; cold offshore air currents produce fog and heavy dew
Environment: desertification, sparse water and arable land; hot and dry and dust/sand-laden sirocco wind; harmattan haze
Terrain: mostly barren rocky desert; small mountains in south and northeast
Land Use: 19% arable; 24% permanent crops, 0% permanent pastures, 47% forests, 10% other
Location: NW Africa, bordering on Atlantic Ocean

■ PEOPLE

Population: 233,730 (July 1998 est.)
Nationality: Sahrawi, Sahraoui
Age Structure: n.a.
Population Growth Rate: 2.4% (1998 est.)
Net Migration: -4.78 migrants/1,000 population (1998 est.)
Ethnic Groups: Arabs, Berbers
Languages: Hassaniya Arabic, Moroccan Arabic
Religions: Islam (almost 100% Sunni Muslim)
Birth Rate: 45.78/1,000 population (1998 est.)
Death Rate: 17.05/1,000 population (1998 est.)
Infant Mortality: 139.74 deaths/1,000 live births (1998 est.)
Life Expectancy at Birth: 47.32 years male, 49.83 years female (1998 est.)
Total Fertility Rate: 6.75 children born/women (1998 est.)
Literacy: n.a.

■ GOVERNMENT

Leader(s): under de facto control of Morocco
Government Type: under Moroccan occupation; legal status and matters of sovereignty remain unresolved
Administrative Divisions: none (under de facto control of Morocco)
Nationhood: n.a.
National Holiday: n.a.

■ ECONOMY

Overview: economy severely disrupted by Moroccan occupation and ongoing guerrilla warfare; poor in natural resources and with inadequate rainfall, most food must be imported; all aspects of the economy are controlled by the Moroccan government
GDP: n.a.
Inflation: n.a.
Industries: phosphate mining, fishing, handicrafts
Labour Force: 12,000; 50% of the people are engaged in subsistence farming and animal husbandry
Unemployment: n.a.
Agriculture: limited to subsistence agriculture; some grain production, livestock (esp. sheep, goats, camels); cash economy exists largely for the garrison forces
Natural Resources: rich phosphate deposits, iron ore

■ FINANCE/TRADE

Currency: Moroccan dirham (DH) = 100 centimes
International Reserves Excluding Gold: n.a.
Gold Reserves: n.a.
Budget: n.a.
Defence Expenditures: n.a.
Education Expenditures: n.a.
External Debt: n.a.
Exports: phosphates main export product
Imports: fuel for fishing fleet; most of the country's food supply must be imported

■ COMMUNICATIONS

Daily Newspapers: n.a.
Televisions: 24/1,000 inhabitants (1996)
Radios: 211/1,000 inhabitants (1996)
Telephones: n.a.

■ TRANSPORTATION

Motor Vehicles: n.a.
Roads: 6,200 km; 1,350 km surfaced
Railway: none
Air Traffic: n.a.
Airports: 12; 3 have paved runways (1997 est.)

Canadian Embassy: none
Embassy in Canada: none

Yemen

Long-Form Name: Republic of Yemen
Capital: Sana'a (political capital); Aden (commercial capital)

■ GEOGRAPHY

Area: 527,970 sq. km
Coastline: 1,906 km
Climate: hot, dry desert in the south to temperate in central region and north; harsh desert in the east
Environment: desertification, overgrazing, lack of natural fresh water, soil erosion, summer dust and sand storms
Terrain: narrow coastal plain; western mountains, northern desert interior
Land Use: 3% arable land; 0% permanent crops; 30% meadows and pasture; 4% forest and woodland; 63% other
Location: SW Asia (Middle East), bordering on Red Sea

■ PEOPLE

Population: 16,387,963 (July 1998 est.)
Nationality: Yemeni
Age Structure: 0-14 yrs: 48%; 15-64: 49%; 65+: 3% (1998 est.)
Population Growth Rate: 3.31% (1998 est.)
Net Migration: 0 migrants/1,000 population (1998 est.)
Ethnic Groups: predominantly Arab; Afro-Arab, Indian, Somali and European minorities
Languages: Arabic
Religions: predominantly Muslim; Christian and Hindu minorities in the south
Birth Rate: 43.36/1,000 population (1998 est.)
Death Rate: 10.27/1,000 population (1998 est.)
Infant Mortality: 72.2 deaths/1,000 live births (1998 est.)
Life Expectancy at Birth: 57.71 years male, 61.32 years female (1998 est.)
Total Fertility Rate: 7.14 children born/women (1998 est.)
Literacy: 38% (1997 est.)

■ GOVERNMENT

Leader(s): Pres. Ali Abdallah Salih, Prime Min. Abd al-Karim Iryani
Government Type: republic
Administrative Divisions: 17 governorates
Nationhood: May 22, 1990
National Holiday: Proclamation of the Republic, May 22

■ ECONOMY

Overview: future economic level depends heavily on Western assistance. North: low level of domestic industry once self-sufficient in food but now dependent on imports; South: economic growth among the slowest of all Arab countries
GDP: adjusted for purchasing power parity: $31.8 billion, per capita $2,300; real growth rate 5% (1997 est.)
Inflation: 5.4% (1997)
Industries: accounts for 39% of GDP; petroleum, cotton, textiles, leather goods, food processing, handicrafts, cement, small aluminum products factory
Labour Force: 5.2 million (1997 est.)
Unemployment: 27% (1996 est.)
Agriculture: in the north, agriculture accounts for 15% GDP; main crops include fruit (grapes) and cotton; in the south, agriculture accounts for 17% GDP and 45% of the labour force; the main agricultural product is livestock (cattle, camels, sheep, goats, poultry)
Natural Resources: salt deposits, petroleum, fish, marble, coal, gold, lead

■ FINANCE/TRADE

Currency: Yemeni rial (YR)
International Reserves Excluding Gold: $949 million (Oct. 1998)
Gold Reserves: 0.050 million fine troy ounces (Oct. 1998)
Budget: revenues $2.6 billion; expenditures $2.7 billion, including capital expenditures of $1.1 billion (1998 est.)
Defence Expenditures: 17.37% of total govt. expenditure (1998)
Education Expenditures: 18.22% of govt. expenditure (1998)
External Debt: $8 billion (1996)
Exports: $2.503 billion (1997); crude oil, cotton, coffee, vegetables, cotton, animal hides, fish; partners: US, Japan, Singapore
Imports: $1.919 billion (1997); textiles and other manufactured consumer goods, petroleum products, sugar, grain, flour, other foodstuffs, cement, grain, consumer goods, crude oil, machinery, chemicals; partners: nations of the former Soviet Union, UK, Ethiopia

■ COMMUNICATIONS

Daily Newspapers: 3 (1996)
Televisions: 29/1,000 inhabitants (1996)
Radios: 64/1,000 inhabitants (1996)
Telephones: 1.2/100 inhabitants (1996 est.)

■ TRANSPORTATION

Motor Vehicles: 516,000; 230,000 passenger cars (1997 est.)

Roads: 64,725 km; 5,243 km paved
Railway: none
Air Traffic: 588,000 passengers carried (1996)
Airports: 48; 11 have paved runways (1997 est.)

Canadian Embassy: The Canadian Embassy to Yemen, c/o Canadian Embassy, Diplomatic Quarter, P.O. Box 94321, Riyadh 11693, Saudi Arabia. Tel: (011-966-1) 488-2288. Fax: (011-966-1) 488-1997.
Embassy in Canada: Embassy of the Republic of Yemen, 788 Island Park Drive, Ottawa ON K1Y OC2. Tel: (613) 729-6627. Fax: (613) 729-8915

Yugoslavia

Long-Form Name: Federal Republic of Yugoslavia
Capital: Belgrade (Serbia), Podgorica (Montenegro)

■ GEOGRAPHY

Area: 102,350 sq. km (Serbia 88,412 sq. km, Montenegro 13,938 sq. km)
Coastline: 199 km (Montenegro 199 km, Serbia 0 km)
Climate: continental in north; continental and Mediterranean in central region; south—Adriatic climate along coast, hot and dry summers, relatively cold winters, with heavy snowfall inland
Environment: coastal water pollution from sewage outlets, esp. in tourist-related areas; air and water pollution; subject to earthquakes
Terrain: varied: rich fertile plain in north, limestone ranges and basins in east, mountains and hills in southeast, high shoreline with no islands in southwest
Land Use: 30% arable, 5% permanent crops, 20% meadows and pastures, 25% forests, 20% other
Location: S Europe, bordering Adriatic Sea

■ PEOPLE

Population: 11,206,039 (July 1998 est.)
Nationality: Serb, Montenegrin
Age Structure: Serbia: 0-14 yrs: 20%; 15-64: 67%; 65+: 11% (1998 est.) Montenegro 0-14 yrs: 22%; 15-64: 68%; 65+: 10% (1997 est.)
Population Growth Rate: Serbia: -0.02% Montenegro: 0.07% (1998 est.)
Net Migration: Serbia: -3.1 migrants/1,000 population (1998 est.) Montenegro: -5.43 migrants/1,000 population (1998 est.)
Ethnic Groups: 63% Serb, 14% Albanian, 6% Montenegrin, 4% Hungarian, 13% other
Languages: 95% Serbo-Croatian, 5% Albanian

Religions: 65% Orthodox, 19% Muslim, 4% Roman Catholic, 1% Protestant, 11% other
Birth Rate: 12.62/1,000 population (Serbia); 13.55/1,000 population (Montenegro) (1998 est.)
Death Rate: 9.67/1,000 population (Serbia); 7.40/1,000 population (Montenegro) (1998 est.)
Infant Mortality: 17.11 deaths/1,000 live births (Serbia); 11.24 deaths/1,000 live births (Montenegro) (1998 est.)
Life Expectancy at Birth: 70.77 years male, 75.76 years female (Serbia); 72.67 years male, 79.92 years female (Montenegro) (1998 est.)
Total Fertility Rate: 1.75 children born/woman (Serbia); 1.76 children born/woman (Montenegro) (1998 est.)
Literacy: n.a.

■ GOVERNMENT

Leader(s): Federal President: Slobodan Milosevic, Premier Momir Bulatovic
Government Type: republic
Administrative Divisions: 2 republics and 2 nominally autonomous provinces
Nationhood: April 11, 1992 (from Yugoslavia)
National Holiday: St. Vitus Day, June 28

■ ECONOMY

Overview: bloody ethnic warfare has caused destabilization of republic boundaries and the break-up of important inter-republic trade connections; economic situation is complicated by the continuation in office of a communist government whose primary interest lies in political and military mastery rather than economic reform, as well as by the imposition of economic sanctions by the UN
GDP: $24.3 billion, per capita $2,280; real growth rate 7% (1997 est.)
Inflation: n.a.
Industries: accounts for 50% of GDP; machine building, metallurgy, mining, consumer goods, electronics, petroleum products, chemicals, pharmaceuticals
Labour Force: n.a.; 41% industry, 35% services, 12% trade and tourism, 7% transportation and communication, 5% agriculture
Unemployment: more than 40% (1995 est.)
Agriculture: accounts for 25% of GDP; cereals, cotton, oilseed plants, chicory, fodder crops, fruit, vegetables, tobacco, olives, citrus, rice, livestock (sheep, goats)
Natural Resources: oil, gas, coal, antimony, copper, lead, gold, chrome

■ FINANCE/TRADE

Currency: Yugoslav New Dinar (YD) = 100 paras

International Reserves Excluding Gold: $2.549 billion (Jan. 1998)
Gold Reserves: n.a.
Budget: n.a.
Defence Expenditures: 6% of GDP (1998 est.)
Education Expenditures: n.a.
External Debt: $13.439 billion (1996)
Exports: $2.368 million (1997) (adjusted for purchasing power parity); manufactured goods, food, live animals, raw materials; partners: Russia, Italy, Germany
Imports: $4.799 million (1997) (adjusted for purchasing power parity); machinery, transport equipment, fuels and lubricants, manufactuerd goods, chemicals, food, live animals, raw materials; partners: Germany, Italy, Russia

■ COMMUNICATIONS

Daily Newspapers: 18 (1996)
Televisions: 262/1,000 inhabitants (1996)
Radios: 143/1,000 inhabitants (1996)
Telephones: 19.4/100 inhabitants (1996 est.)

■ TRANSPORTATION

Motor Vehicles: 1,333,000; 1,002,000 passenger cars (1997 est.)
Roads: 49,525 km; 28,873 km paved
Railway: 3,987 km
Air Traffic: n.a.
Airports: 48; 18 have paved runways (1997 est.)

Canadian Embassy: The Canadian Embassy, 75 Kneza Milosa, 11000 Belgrade, Serbia and Montenegro. Tel: (011-381-11) 64-46-66. Fax: (011-381-11) 64-14-80.
Embassy in Canada: Embassy of the Federal Republic of Yugoslavia, 17 Blackburn Ave, Ottawa ON K1N 8A2. Tel: (613) 233-6289. Fax: (613) 233-7850.

Zaire

see Democratic Republic of Congo

Zambia

Long-Form Name: Republic of Zambia
Capital: Lusaka

■ GEOGRAPHY

Area: 752,610 sq. km
Coastline: none; landlocked
Climate: tropical; modified by altitude; rainy season (Oct. to Apr.)
Environment: deforestation; soil erosion; desertification; air pollution and resultant acid rain; tropical storms are a natural hazard from Nov. to Apr.
Terrain: mostly high plateau with some hills and mountains
Land Use: 7% arable; 0% permanent crops; 40% meadows; 39% forest; 14% other
Location: SC Africa

■ PEOPLE

Population: 9,460,736 (July 1998 est.)
Nationality: Zambian
Age Structure: 0-14 yrs: 49%; 15-64: 48%; 65+: 3% (1998 est.)
Population Growth Rate: 2.13% (1998 est.)
Net Migration: -0.8 migrants/1,000 population (1998 est.)
Ethnic Groups: 98.7% African, 1.1% European, 0.2% other
Languages: English (official); about 70 indigenous languages
Religions: 50–75% Christian, 24–49% Muslim and Hindu, remainder indigenous beliefs
Birth Rate: 44.6/1,000 population (1998 est.)
Death Rate: 22.55/1,000 population (1998 est.)
Infant Mortality: 92.57 deaths/1,000 live births (1998 est.)
Life Expectancy at Birth: 36.81 years male, 37.33 years female (1998 est.)
Total Fertility Rate: 6.41 children born/woman (1998 est.)
Literacy: 78.2% (1997 est.)

■ GOVERNMENT

Leader(s): Pres. Frederick Chiluba, V. Pres. Christon Tembo
Government Type: republic
Administrative Divisions: 9 provinces
Nationhood: Oct. 24, 1964 (from UK; formerly known as Northern Rhodesia)
National Holiday: Independence Day, Oct. 24

■ ECONOMY

Overview: economy continues to decline due to a sustained drop in copper production and ineffective economic policies; problems include a high inflation rate, high population growth and severe drought
GDP: $8.8 billion, per capita $950; real growth rate 3.5% (1997 est.)
Inflation: 19.1% (Jan. 1998)
Industries: accounts for 40% of GDP; copper mining and processing, transport, construction, foodstuffs, beverages, chemicals, textiles and fertilizer
Labour Force: 4.1 million (1997 est.); 37.9% agriculture, 7.8% industry, 54.9% services
Unemployment: n.a.

Agriculture: accounts for 23% of GDP and 85% of labour force; food production is insufficient for country's needs; crops: corn (food staple), sorghum, rice, peanuts, sunflower, tobacco, cotton, sugar cane, cassava; cattle, goats, beef, eggs produced; marginally self-sufficient in corn
Natural Resources: copper, cobalt, zinc, lead, coal, emeralds, gold, silver, uranium, hydropower potential

■ FINANCE/TRADE

Currency: kwacha (K) = 100 ngwee
International Reserves Excluding Gold: $185 million (Feb. 1998)
Gold Reserves: n.a.
Budget: revenues $888 million; expenditures $835 million, including capital expenditures of $110 million (1995 est.)
Defence Expenditures: 4.81% of govt. expenditure (1996)
Education Expenditures: 17.74% of govt. expenditure (1996)
External Debt: $7.113 billion (1996)
Exports: $901 million (1997); commodities: copper, zinc, cobalt, lead, tobacco; partners: European Community, Japan, South Africa, US
Imports: $806 million (1997); commodities: machinery, transportation equipment, foodstuffs, fuels, manufactures; partners: European Community, Japan, South Africa, US

■ COMMUNICATIONS

Daily Newspapers: 3 (1996)
Televisions: 42/1,000 inhabitants (1996)
Radios: 121/1,000 inhabitants (1996)
Telephones: 0.8/100 inhabitants (1996 est.)

■ TRANSPORTATION

Motor Vehicles: 215,500; 142,000 passenger cars (1997 est.)
Roads: 39,700 km; 7,265 km paved
Railway: 2,164 km
Air Traffic: 249,000 passengers carried (1995 est.)
Airports: 111; 12 have paved runways (1997 est.)

Canadian Embassy: The Canadian High Commission, 5199 United Nations Ave, Lusaka; mailing address: P.O. Box 31313, 10101 Lusaka, Zambia. Tel: (011-260-1) 25-08-33. Fax: (011-260-1) 25-41-76.
Embassy in Canada: High Commision for the Republic of Zambia, c/o Embassy of Zambia, 2419 Massachusetts Ave NW, Washington DC 20008, USA. Tel: (202) 265-9717. Fax: (202) 332-0826.

Zimbabwe

Long-Form Name: Republic of Zimbabwe
Capital: Harare

■ GEOGRAPHY

Area: 390,580 sq. km
Coastline: none: landlocked
Climate: tropical; moderated by altitude; rainy season (Nov. to Mar.)
Environment: recurring droughts; floods and severe storms are rare; deforestation; soil erosion; air and water pollution; desertification; poaching has significantly reduced the black rhinoceros population, which was once the largest concentration of the species anywhere in the world
Terrain: mostly high plateau with higher central plateau (high veld); mountains in east
Land Use: 7% arable; less than 1% permanent crops (coffee plantations); 13% meadows; 23% forest and woodland; 57% other
Location: SC Africa

■ PEOPLE

Population: 11,044,147 (July 1998 est.)
Nationality: Zimbabwean
Age Structure: 0-14 yrs: 44%; 15-64: 54%; 65+: 2% (1998 est.)
Population Growth Rate: 1.12% (1998 est.)
Net Migration: n.a.
Ethnic Groups: 98% African (71% Shona, 16% Ndebele, 11% other), 1% white, 1% mixed and Asian
Languages: English (official); Shona and Sindebele, numerous minor tribal dialects
Religions: 50% syncretic (part Christian, part indigenous beliefs), 25% Christian, 24% indigenous beliefs, a few Muslim
Birth Rate: 31.32/1,000 population (1998 est.)
Death Rate: 20.09/1,000 population (1998 est.)
Infant Mortality: 61.75 deaths/1,000 live births (1998 est.)
Life Expectancy at Birth: 39.12 years male, 39.19 years female (1998 est.)
Total Fertility Rate: 3.86 children born/woman (1998 est.)
Literacy: 85% (1997 est.)

■ GOVERNMENT

Leader(s): Exec. Pres. Robert Mugabe, V. Pres. Simon Vengai Muzenda, V.Pres. Joshua Nkomo
Government Type: parliamentary democracy
Administrative Divisions: 8 provinces and 2 cities with provincial status
Nationhood: Apr. 18, 1980 (from UK; formerly known as Southern Rhodesia)
National Holiday: Independence Day, Apr. 18

■ ECONOMY

Overview: severe droughts have adversely affected this agriculture-based economy in recent years. The government is working to consolidate earlier progress in developing a market-oriented economy.

GDP: $26.4 billion, per capita $2,340; real growth rate 5.5% (1996)

Inflation: 16.4% (1997)

Industries: accounts for 35% of GDP; mining (minerals and metals account for 40% of exports), steel, clothing and footwear, chemicals, foodstuffs, fertilizer, beverages, transportation equipment, wood products

Labour Force: 5.1 million (1997 est.); 29.9% community, social and business services, 25.9% agriculture, 15.1% industry (1992)

Unemployment: n.a.

Agriculture: accounts for approximately 18% of GDP; 40% of land area divided into 4,500 large commercial farms and 42% in communal lands; crops: corn (food staple), cotton, tobacco, wheat, coffee, sugar cane, peanuts; livestock: cattle, sheep, goats, pigs; self-sufficient in food

Natural Resources: coal, chromium ore, asbestos, gold, nickel, copper, iron ore, vanadium, lithium, tin

■ FINANCE/TRADE

Currency: Zimbabwean dollar ($Z) = 100 cents

International Reserves Excluding Gold: $119 million (Jan. 1999)

Gold Reserves: 0.602 million fine troy ounces (Jan. 1999)

Budget: revenues $2.5 billion; expenditures $2.9 billion, including capital expenditures of $29 million (1997 est.)

Defence Expenditures: 3.4% of GDP (1995–96)

Education Expenditures: 8.5% of GNP (1995)

External Debt: $5.005 billion (1996)

Exports: $2.464 billion (1997); commodities: agriculture 34% (tobacco 21%, other 13%), manufactures 19%, gold 11%, ferrochrome 11%, cotton 6%; partners: Europe 55% (European Community 41%, Netherlands 6%, other 8%), Africa 22% (South Africa 12%, other 10%), US 8%, Japan 4%

Imports: $3.068 billion (1997); commodities: machinery and transportation equipment 37%, other manufactures 22%, chemicals 16%, fuels 15%; partners: European Community 31%, Africa 29% (South Africa 21%, other 8%), US 8%, Japan 4%

■ COMMUNICATIONS

Daily Newspapers: 2 (1996)

Televisions: 31/1,000 inhabitants (1996)

Radios: 96/1,000 inhabitants (1996)

Telephones: 1.5/100 inhabitants (1996 est.)

■ TRANSPORTATION

Motor Vehicles: 358,000; 250,000 passenger cars (1997 est.)

Roads: n.a.

Railway: 2,759 km (1995)

Air Traffic: 654,000 passengers carried (1996)

Airports: 468; 20 have paved runways (1997 est.)

Canadian Embassy: The Canadian High Commission, 45 Baines Ave, Harare; mailing address: P.O. Box 1430, Harare, Zimbabwe. Tel: (011-263-4) 73-38-81. Fax: (011-263-4) 73-29-17.

Embassy in Canada: High Commission for the Republic of Zimbabwe, 332 Somerset St W, Ottawa ON K2P 0J9. Tel: (613) 237-4388. Fax: (613) 563-8269.

World Internet Links for Students

*T*he World Bank Group, with help from corporate and government partners, has sponsored a learning web site in English, French and Spanish. Called World Links For Development (WorLD), the program links secondary school students and teachers in developing countries with their counterparts in industrialized countries. During the period from 1997 to 2001, the WorLD program hopes to connect 1,200 secondary schools in 40 developing countries with partner schools in Australia, Canada, Europe, Japan and the U.S.

As of late 1999, 280 pilot schools were connected in 18 developing countries and partnered with schools in 24 other countries. Canadian students at Don Mills Collegiate Institute and St. Patrick's High School were partnered with students in South Africa and Uganda in a dialogue which examined and compared respective living conditions and environment. Students at Univeristy of Toronto Schools and École secondaire des Sources joined in a dialogue with students in Ghana, Senegal and the U.S. about the world in the 21st century; Canada's SchoolNet played a large role in co-ordinating this project.

For more information about WorLD program (or to join a project), visit http://www.worldbank.org/worldlinks

Astronomy has taught us that the universe is more complex than the ancients thought. Though less dependent on the "patterns" in the sky, we continue the exploration. The skies act not simply as a guide, but also as a frontier to be explored.

The Solar System

The solar system consists of the sun, at least nine planets and smaller bodies such as asteroids, comets and moons. The dominant member of this family is the sun, our nearest star. The sun is an enormous ball of hot, glowing gas, mostly hydrogen and helium. Its powerful pull of gravity holds the planets, asteroids and comets in orbit around it.

The planets have been known since people first turned their gaze skyward. The ancient Greeks called them "wanderers" because they moved through the sky relative to the fixed stars. Five planets can be seen without a telescope: Mercury, Venus, Mars, Jupiter and Saturn. They are visible because they reflect the light of the sun.

Until March 1999, in order of distance from the sun, the planets are Mercury, Venus, Earth, Mars, Jupiter, Saturn, Uranus, Pluto and Neptune. Pluto is *usually* the most remote planet, over seven billion kilometres from the sun at its maximum distance, but from 1979 to 1999, its strange orbit brings it closer to the sun than Neptune.

All the planets revolve (orbit) around the sun in the same counter clockwise direction. The closer to the sun, the greater their speed. Except for Pluto, all the orbits lie in nearly the same plane in space, like marbles rolling on a table top.

Our Place in the Universe Although the solar system seems enormous, it is quite small compared to the whole universe. Our sun is only one star among the hundreds of billions that make up our spiral-shaped galaxy, the **Milky Way**. It takes our sun, with planets in tow, about 250 million years to orbit around the Milky Way just once. All the stars that we see at night are in a small, nearby portion of our galaxy. There may be billions of galaxies in the universe, each containing billions of stars of its own.

The Birth of the Solar System Approximately 4.6 billion years ago, (billions of years after the galaxies were formed), astronomers believe that a vast cloud of gas and dust collapsed and formed a spinning disk. Gravitation compacted so much material in the centre that extremely high pressures and temperatures lit a nuclear fire—our sun began to shine. Meanwhile, any remaining lumps of hot solids and gases slowly collected to become the planets, moons, asteroids and comets.

Our Solar System The planets of the solar system can be divided into two groups. The inner planets, Mercury, Venus, Earth and Mars, are the **terrestrial**, or Earth-like, planets. These are small rocky worlds with metal cores and thin atmospheres, except for airless Mercury. Jupiter, Saturn, Uranus and Neptune make up the realm of the **gas giants**. These planets do not have a solid surface, but are made up of layers of gases and clouds, possibly with rocky cores the size of Earth. The gas giants are huge: a thousand Earths could easily fit inside Jupiter. Saturn's rings may be the most famous feature of the solar system but rings are also found around Jupiter, Uranus and Neptune.

Pluto is unique and does not fit into either of these two groups. It is a tiny world of rock and ice, smaller than the Earth's moon, and with an extremely thin atmosphere.

Separating the terrestrial planets from the gas giants is the **asteroid belt**, a region of space between Mars and Jupiter where as many as 50,000 rocky objects may orbit the sun. Asteroids, often called minor planets, range from gravel-size, or smaller, to the 1,000-km-wide Ceres. They may be the remains of a small, shattered planet.

Over 50 moons, or satellites, are found in the solar system. All the planets, except for Mercury and Venus, have at least one moon orbiting them. Some of these moons are fascinating worlds in their own right: **Phobos** and **Deimos**, the moons of Mars, may be captured asteroids; **Io**, one of Jupiter's moons, has many active volcanoes; **Europa**, another one of Jupiter's moons, may have a subterranean ocean; **Titan**, a moon of Saturn, has an atmosphere thicker than

Earth's. Jupiter with its 16 known moons, Saturn with its 18 and Uranus with its 17 are like miniature solar systems.

Exploring the Solar System Most of the planets have been visited by space probes from Earth: Mercury was visited in 1974 by *Mariner 10*, Soviet *Venera* spacecraft landed on Venus several times in the 1970s while *Viking 1* and *2* landed on Mars in 1976. The best spacecraft views of Jupiter and Saturn were obtained by *Voyager 1* and *2* in 1979 and 1980/81 respectively. *Voyager 2* went on to Uranus in 1986 and Neptune in August 1989. These spacecraft made discoveries not possible from the Earth: craters on Mercury, volcanoes and great valleys on Mars, Jupiter's ring and 10 new moons of Uranus were only a few.

Recent missions include the *Ulysses* mis-sion, launched in 1990, which finished its second orbit of the sun in 1997-8. The spacecraft will do a south polar pass of the sun from Sept. 2000 to Jan. 2001. The combined NASA/ESA (European Space Agency) *Cassini* mission to Saturn was launched in October 1997. *Cassini* will enter orbit around Saturn July 2004.

On Dec. 4, 1996 the Pathfinder mission to Mars was launched, and made a spectacularly successful landing on July 4, 1997, sending back data and pictures. In Sept. 1997 the Mars Global Surveyor was launched on a mapping and photography mission. The actual mapping began in March 1999 and is scheduled to continue for 687 days—a Martian year. The Surveyor is equipped to study the composition of surface minerals as well as map topography. By July, researchers knew that Mars has a pear-like shape, with a mountainous south half over three kilometres higher than the north.

Solar System at a Glance

	Distance from Sun (million km)	Equatorial diameter (km)	Gravity (Earth=1)	Mass (Earth=1)	Period of Orbit about the Sun	Period of Rotation on Axis (days)	Number of known Moons
Sun	—	1 392 000	27.90	332 830	—	25.38	—
Mercury	57.9	4 878	0.38	0.06	88.0 days	58.60	0
Venus	108.2	12 104	0.91	0.8	224.7 days	243.00	0
Earth	149.6	12 756	1.00	1.0	365.3 days	0.99	1
Mars	227.9	6 787	0.38	0.1	1.88 years	1.02	2
Jupiter	778.4	142 800	2.54	317.8	11.86 years	0.41	16
Saturn	1 423.8	120 000	1.08	95.2	29.63 years	0.42	18
Uranus	2 868.7	51 200	0.91	14.5	83.97 years	0.45	17
Neptune	4 492.1	48 680	1.19	17.2	164.80 years	0.67	8
Pluto	5 926.5	2 300	0.06	0.002	248.63 years	6.30	1

Source: *Global Atlas, Gage Educational Publishing Co.; Observer's Handbook, 1991, The Royal Astronomical Society of Canada*

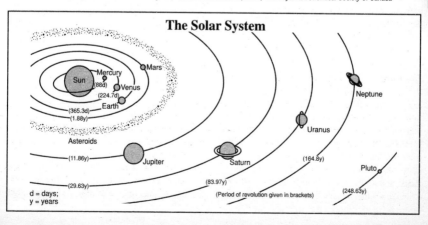

The Solar System

Mercury (88d)
Venus (224.7d)
Earth (365.3d) (1.88y)
Mars
Asteroids
Jupiter (11.86y)
Saturn (29.63y)
Uranus (83.97y)
Neptune (164.8y)
Pluto (248.63y)

d = days; y = years
(Period of revolution given in brackets)

Planet Profiles:

Saturn and Jupiter will be close together in the sky in 2000

SATURN is a giant sphere—120,660 km in diameter—over 90% of its upper atmosphere is composed of hydrogen, 7% is helium, both in liquid form. Below this "ocean" may lie a rocky core twice the size of Earth. Floating in this atmosphere are clouds which are largely hidden from view due to high altitude haze. Saturn produces more heat in its interior that it receives from the Sun. Scientists speculate that this may be caused by a slow sinking of helium through the hydrogen. (Saturn is less dense than water.)

Saturn's atmosphere is characterised by high winds—at the equator they blow at 500 m/sec. or 1800 km/hr. At higher latitudes wind speed decreases evenly. Measurements taken by the *Voyager* spacecraft found temperatures ranging from -156°C to -94°C at various depths of the atmosphere.

Saturn is most famous for the beautiful rings which surround it. Although Jupiter, Uranus and Neptune also have rings, Saturn's are the most impressive. They are made of hundreds of thousands of ringlets, each composed of millions of individual particles in their own orbit. These particles are mostly chunks of ice and ice-covered rock ranging from snowflake-size to pieces tens of metres in diameter. The rings are very wide (they would reach most of the way from the Earth to the moon), but are extremely thin, no more than a few metes thick.

The outermost bright ring, Ring A, extends 76,500 km above Saturn's cloud tops. Next, there is a 2,600 k m gap named the Cassini Division, after the astronomer who discovered it in 1675. This gap is not completely empty; it contains about twenty thin bands of material. Ring B, the widest and brightest, is next. It is followed by the fainter ring C, the Crepe Ring. In 1979, *Pioneer* discovered F-ring; it is made up of three separate twisted or braided strands.

Astronomers do not know how these rings were formed. One idea is that the particles in the rings are left over from the formation of Saturn and its moons. Another theory is that a moon travelled too close to Saturn and was torn apart by the planet's powerful gravity.

Saturn takes just 10 hours, 39 minutes and 24 seconds Earth time to complete a rotation, but 29.46 Earth years to complete a revolution around the Sun.

There are eighteen known moons orbiting Saturn—the last was found in 1990 using data from a Voyager flyby mission ten years earlier. The largest is **Titan** (5,150 km in diameter), the second largest moon in the solar system. Not only is Titan larger than the planet Mercury, but it is unique among moons in that it possesses of a thick atmosphere. This predominantly nitrogen atmosphere contains ten times more gas above every square metre of Titan's surface than Earth's atmosphere does. Thick orange clouds hide this surface from our view.

The other 17 moons range in size from 25 to 1,500 km. Although most are made of ice and have numerous craters, each is a unique world. **Mimas** (390 km) has a crater on its surface almost one-third the width of the moon itself. The crater walls a 9 km high—higher than Mount Everest. **Enceladus** (500 km) has a surface covered in long grooves while **Hyperion**, at 260 by 410 km, is shaped like a hockey puck. One hemisphere of **Ipatus**, 1,460 km in diameter) is white and the other black.

Saturn was visited by several of the same spaceprobes that flew past Jupiter. The first was *Pioneer* 11 in 1979. *Pioneer* proved that a spacecraft could pass close to the debris surrounding a ringed planet and survive. *Voyager 1* visited Saturn in 1980, followed by *Voyager 2* the following year.

JUPITER, the largest planet in the solar system, is a massive, colourful world composed mostly of hydrogen and helium in liquid form. It contains two-thirds of the planetary mass of the solar system; its diameter is eleven times that of the Earth. Despite this huge size, Jupiter is not big enough to be a star—theories of star formation suggest it would need to be 80 times larger before it would ignite. (Ignition occurs when internal gravitational collapse raises such a body's internal temperature to combustible levels. Jupiter's "cool centre" is only 30,000°C. This tremendous heat is left over from the time of the planet's formation.)

The observable face of Jupiter is really just the top of its atmosphere. Jupiter is covered by three dense layers of clouds; the outermost is made of ammonia ice crystals, the second of ammonium-hydrogen sulfide and the third—the lowest—of water ice and perhaps liquid water. Some 25,000 km below the clouds, the pressure is equivalent to three million Earth atmospheres and the temperature is just 11,000°C. At the top of the clouds, the temperature is -70°C.

The planet rotates quickly, once every ten hours, and this rapid motion drives its orange, red, white and brown clouds into turbulent, colourful belts that run parallel to its equator. These belts are constantly moving, with winds reaching 540 km/hour—twice as fast as the most severe hurricanes on Earth. The swirling colour of the layers may also be the result of plumes of warmer gases rising from further inside the planet. The colour themselves are likely the result of the chemical content of the gases; they could also be made of organic compounds, sulfur or phosphorus.

This cloud-layer of atmosphere is full of lightning, auroras and huge storm systems. One of the largest (and possibly oldest) of the storm systems is known as the Great Red Spot. It is estimated to be between 100 and 300 years old. The Spot is the size of three Earths side-by-side. As a storm, it's not a fixed feature on the planet, through the years its shape, colour and position have changed. It has even faded from view on occasion.

Beneath the three layers, the "surface" of Jupiter is thought to be covered by a sluggish ocean of liquid metallic hydrogen, something not found on the Earth. Underneath this layer, it's suggested that instead of a solid mass at the centre, the temperature and pressure conditions actually sustain a core with a liquid or slushy density. Scientists speculate that the internal pressure here,

generated by the weight of Jupiter's massive atmosphere and liquid hydrogen is 100 million times the surface pressure on Earth.

Jupiter has an immense magnetic field, first studied when *Pioneer 10* visited in December 1973. The tremendous electrical energy that pours from Jupiter sends billions of watts into Earth's atmosphere on a daily basis. This energy could be coming from the layer of liquid metallic hydrogen, which is capable of conducting huge amounts of electrical currents; in addition to the planet's strong magnetic field, Jupiter's atmosphere emits persistent radio noise.

Jupiter has at least 16 known moons. The four largest are planet-size, while the remaining twelve are mostly less than 100 km in diameter.

Io (3,630 km in diameter—Earth is 12,756) has no visible craters. Instead, it has at least seven volcanoes that are continually venting sulfur dioxide, giving this moon its unique orange, red and black colour. Sulfur lakes may also be present.

Europa (3,140 km) was the subject of the Galileo Europa Mission, a 14-month study of that moon. (Galileo then turned its attention to Io.) In 1996 and 1997, Galileo sent back evidence of an ionosphere (a layer of charged particles—electrons and ions—that exists at the top of an atmosphere), meaning that the moon, described as "icy," also has an atmosphere. In 1998, the Hubble Space Telescope observed oxygen emissions on Europa, another indicator that an atmosphere may exist.

Ganymede (5,268 km) is larger than the Mercury and Pluto, making it the largest moon in the solar system. It was first thought that this moon was a mixture of ice and rock, however evidence gathered during Galileo flybys indicates the existence of a magnetic field around Ganymede, meaning it is likely to have a metallic core. The surface is composed of ice and silicates, with a crust assumed to be a thick layer of frozen water.

Callisto (4,800 km) has a composition similar to Ganymede.

Source: *NASA; http://www.jpl.nasa.gov/galileo/Jovian.html*

Some Astronomical Terms

Asteroid Any of the thousands of small, rocky objects that orbit the Sun. Some pass closer to the Sun than Earth does and others have orbits that take them well beyond Jupiter. The largest asteroid is one called Ceres.

Big Bang The primeval explosion that most astronomers think gave rise to the universe as we see it today, in which clusters of galaxies are moving apart from one another. Astronomers calculate the Big Bang happened about 15 to 20 billion years ago.

Black Hole An object whose gravitational pull is so strong that—within a certain distance of it— nothing can escape, not even light. Black holes are thought to result from the collapse of certain very massive stars, but other kinds have been postulated as well: **mini black holes,** for example, which might have been formed in the turbulence shortly after the Big Bang. **Supermassive black holes**—with masses millions of times the Sun's—may exist in the cores of large galaxies.

Comet A small chunk of ice, dust and rocky material (a few kilometres across) which, when it comes close enough to the Sun, can develop a tenuous "tail." The tail of a comet is made of gas and dust that have been driven off the comet's surface by the Sun's energy. The tail always points away from the Sun (no matter in what direction the comet is moving).

Eclipse The blocking of all or part of the light from one object by another.

Galaxy A large assemblage of stars (and sometimes interstellar gas and dust), typically containing millions to hundreds of billions of member stars. A galaxy is held together by the gravitational attraction of its member stars (and other material) to one another.

Light-Year The distance light travels in one year in a vacuum. Since light travels at a speed of about 300 000 km per second, a light-year is roughly 9.5 trillion km long.

Magnitude A way of expressing the brightness of astronomical objects, inherited from the Greeks. In the magnitude system, a lower number indicates a brighter object (for example, a 1st-magnitude star is brighter than a 3rd-magnitude star). Each step in magnitude corresponds to a brightness difference of about 2.5. Stars of the 6th magnitude are the faintest the unaided human eye can see.

Meteor A bit of solid debris from space, burning up in the Earth's atmosphere because of friction with the air. Before entering Earth's atmosphere, the body is called a meteoroid. If any of the object survives its fiery passage through the air, the parts that hit the ground are called **meteorites.**

Milky Way Galaxy A spiral galaxy, with a disk approximately 100 000 light-years across, containing roughly 400 billion stars. Our Sun is in the disk about two-thirds of the way from the centre. It takes about 200 million years to orbit the centre of the Milky Way once.

Neutron Star A crushed remnant left over when a very massive star explodes. Some neutron stars are known to spin very rapidly, at least at the beginning, and can be detected as **pulsars**: rapidly flashing sources of radio radiation or visible light. The pulses are produced by the spinning of a neutron star, much as a lighthouse beacon appears to flash off, on and off.

Nova A star that abruptly and temporarily increases its brightness by a factor of hundreds of thousands.

Orbit The path of one body around another (such as the Moon around the Earth) or around the centre of gravity of a number of objects (such as the Sun's 200-million-year path around the centre of our galaxy).

Planet A major object that orbits around a star.

Quasar One of a class of very distant (typically billions of light years away), extremely bright, and very small objects. Quasar means "quasistar"— that is, something that looks like a star but can't actually be a star.

Red Giant A very large distended, and relatively cool star in the final stages of its life.

Solar System The Sun and all things orbiting it, including the nine major planets, their satellites, and all the asteroids and comets.

Supernova An explosion that marks the end of a very massive star's life. When it occurs, the star can outshine all the other stars in a galaxy in total for several days, and may leave behind a crushed core (perhaps a neutron star or a black hole).

White Dwarf The collapsed remnant of a relatively low-mass star (roughly one and a half times the Sun's mass and less), which has exhausted the fuel for its nuclear reactions and shines only by radiating its stored up heat.

Source: *The Astronomical Society of the Pacific, San Francisco, CA*

The Sky in 2000

*Prepared by Ian G. McGregor, Science &
Astronomy Educator, Royal Ontario Museum*

■ The Sun

Solar activity has been steadily rising over
the past year. Every eleven years the sun
reaches a peak of activity called the "solar
maximum" when there are many sunspots on
the face of the sun, powerful explosions
called flares and ejections of mass from the
sun. All of these affect communications,
orbiting satellites, and weather on the earth.
The current solar cycle, Cycle #23 since
records began, is now predicted to peak late
this year or early in 2001. For solar observers
with proper observing equipment, there will
be many sunspots and sunspot groups, which
can be observed to slowly cross the face of
the sun this year.

■ The Planets

Mercury: The closest planet to the sun is
never observed far from the sun and is
therefore usually seen in the west just after
sunset or in the east just before sunrise. But
most of the year the planet is lost in the sun's
glare and not observable at all. When the
planet is at its greatest angular separations
from the sun, properly called elongations, for
about a week on either side of the elongation
date the planet can be observed. This year
there are six elongations of Mercury—3 in
the evening sky (February 15, June 9 and
October 6) and 3 in the morning sky (March
28, July 27 and November 15). The best
elongations and best chance to see the planet
occur in the evening in the spring (June 9)
and in the morning in the autumn (Nov. 15).

Venus: The brightest object in the sky after
the sun and moon begins the year as a
brilliant morning star in the east before
sunrise. As the winter and spring months pass
the planet gradually overtakes the sun and
disappears into the sun's glare in late April.
On June 11, Venus is in superior conjunction
and on the far side of the sun to the earth.
The planet reappears in the west after sunrise
in late July and for the rest of the year is an
increasingly dominant "Evening Star". By
November, it will set about three hours after

sunset. Watch for some pretty pairings of
Venus and crescent moon in the autumn,
especially December 29.

Mars: The "Red Planet" begins the year
appearing as a rather ordinary "star" in the
constellation of Aquarius. Last year was a big
year for the planet as it reached opposition
and a minimum distance from the earth and it
was extremely bright. This year, the planet
rapidly wanders through the constellations of
the zodiac. In the spring, it joins the slower
moving Jupiter and Saturn in Aries. April is
the big month with all three planets closely
clustered together in the dim constellation of
Aries. The last time these three planets were
as close was in 1921. Mars is however
overtaken by the sun late in the April.
Conjunction with the sun is on July 1. It is
not until late August the planet moves out of
the sun's glare to appear in the eastern sky
before sunrise in Leo. Mars ends the year as a
bright "star" in Virgo.

Jupiter and Saturn: This year the two planets
will be very close together in the sky all year
long and a spectacular sight in the evening
sky during the winter and early spring period,
and again from mid-summer to year end in
the morning sky. Both of these giant planets
move very slowly relative to the background
stars but every 20 years the slightly faster-
moving Jupiter catches up to Saturn. Around
the time of their oppositions, which occur
within nine days of each other this year
(Jupiter November 28; Saturn November 19)
these very bright, star-like objects are a treat
for naked-eye, binocular, and telescope
observers. In the late autumn this pair of gas
giant planets rise in the east as the sunset and
set in the west at sunrise.

Uranus, Neptune and Pluto: This trio of
planets is always rather unimpressive for
earth-bound observers. Uranus is at the limit
of naked-eye visibility but you have to know
where to look for it and with binoculars,
good sky conditions, keen eyesight and good
star maps it can be found. Neptune is
definitely a telescope object and faint Pluto
requires a good instrument to be spotted. The
best time to look for them is around the time
of opposition when they are at their
minimum distance from the earth for the
year. Uranus is at opposition on August 11
(Capricornus), Neptune on July 27
(Capricornus), and Pluto on June 1
(Ophiuchus).

Predicting Solar Storms

*S*torms on the sun are far away, but they can have an impact on Earth. In May 1998, a solar storm knocked out the electronic pagers of 45 million users across North America when it shorted out an Earth-orbiting communications satellite. The frequency of such storms is expected to reach an 11-year peak between January and April 2000.

The most violent solar storms are caused by eruptions known as coronal mass ejections (CMEs)—huge bubbles of gas explode off the surface of the sun and send waves of charged particles into space. When the "solar tsunami" hits the Earth's atmosphere, it can destroy satellites or black out cities. In early 1999, NASA announced that it may be able to predict these eruptions and give warnings that will enable satellite and power grid operators to try to protect their systems. The key is huge, S-shaped twists of plasma, known as sigmoids, that appear on the surface of the sun. The explosions usually happen a few days after the sigmoid is spotted, and the wave of energy takes another four days to reach the Earth, giving ample time for Earthlings to take evasive action (or astronauts to cancel their walk).

Phases of the Moon, 2000

(Eastern Standard Time)

New Moon	First Quarter	Full Moon	Last Quarter
Jan 6 - 1:14 pm	Jan 14 - 8:34 am	Jan 20 - 11:41 pm	Jan 28 - 2:58 am
Feb 5 - 8:04 am	Feb 12 - 6:21 pm	Feb 19 - 11:27 am	Feb 26 - 10:55 pm
Mar 6 - 12:18 am	Mar 13 - 1:59 am	Mar 19 - 11:44 pm	Mar 27 - 7:23 pm
Apr 4 - 1:13 pm	Apr 11 - 8:30 am	Apr 18 - 12:41 pm	Apr 26 - 2:32 pm
May 3 - 11:13 pm	May 10 - 3:01 pm	May 18 - 2:34 am	May 26 - 6:56 am
Jun 2 - 7:15 am	Jun 8 - 10:29 pm	Jun 16 - 5:27 pm	Jun 24 - 8:01 pm
Jul 1 - 2:20 pm	Jul 8 - 7:53 am	Jul 16 - 8:56 am	Jul 24 - 6:03 am
Jul 30 - 9:25 pm	Aug 6 - 8:02 pm	Aug 15 - 12:14 am	Aug 22 - 1:51 pm
Aug 29 - 5:20 am	Sep 5 - 11:28 am	Sep 13 - 2:38 pm	Sep 20 - 8:29 pm
Sep 27 - 2:53 pm	Oct 5 - 5:59 am	Oct 13 - 3:54 am	Oct 20 - 3:00 am
Oct 27 - 2:58 am	Nov 4 - 2:26 am	Nov 11 - 4:16 pm	Nov 18 - 10:26 am
Nov 25 - 6:12 pm	Dec 3 - 10:55 pm	Dec 11 - 4:04 am	Dec 17 - 7:43 pm
Dec 25 - 12:23 pm			

Daylight Saving Time (Summer Time) is kept in most places across Canada. It starts at 2 a.m. on Sunday, April 2, 2000 when clocks go forward one hour. Clocks return to Standard Time at 2 a.m. on Sunday, October 29 when clocks go back one hour. To get wristwatch time in the Eastern Time Zone between April 2 and October 29 *add* one hour to the times listed.

Across Canada, there are six Standard Time Zones. To adjust to wristwatch time in another time zone, add or subtract the following to the times listed in the table: Newfoundland (+1hr 30m), Atlantic (+1hr), Central (-1hr), Mountain (-2hr), Pacific (-3hr).

Organizations

Canadian Astronomical Society:
An organization of professional astronomers. Contact: Serge Demers, CASCA Secretary, Département de Physique, Université de Montréal, Montreal, Quebec H3C 3J7.
e-mail: http://www.casca@astro.queensu.ca/~casca

Royal Astronomical Society of Canada (RASC):
The Society is an organization of amateur and professional astronomers open to anyone interested in astronomy. The Society publishes the annual *Observer's Handbook* as well as other publications. It has over 3 000 members in 23 clubs across Canada. National Headquarters is located at 136 Dupont Street, Toronto, Ontario M5R 1V2 Tel: (416) 924-7973. http://www.rasc.ca

Events in the 2000 Sky

January

3	Earth at perihelion (closest point to sun for year) — 147.1 million km.
4	Peak of Quadrantid meteor shower.
10-15	Moon near Mars, Jupiter and Saturn.
20-21	Total lunar eclipse visible from all of North and South America. (See Eclipses page 562)

February

2	Waning crescent moon very close to Venus in east before sunrise.
5	Partial solar eclipse (See Eclipses page 562)
8-11	Waxing crescent moon near Mars, Jupiter and Saturn.
15	Mercury at greatest angular separation from sun for evening apparition of planet in west after sunset.

March

8-10	Waxing crescent moon near Mars, Jupiter, and Saturn.
20	Sun reaches the March (or vernal) equinox at 2:35 a.m. EST. First day of spring in northern hemisphere.
28	Mercury at greatest angular separation from sun for morning apparition of planet in east before sunrise.

April

2	Daylight Savings Time begins at 2 a.m.; clocks are advanced by one hour.
6	Waxing crescent Moon a pretty sight with Saturn, Mars and Jupiter after sunset in west.
13-15	Jupiter, Saturn and Mars in a very compact grouping (five degrees wide) in west after sunset.
21	Peak of Lyrid meteor shower. Moonlight interferes.

May

3	Peak of Eta Aquarid meteor shower. (No interference from moonlight)
3-4	Sun, Moon, Mercury, Venus, Jupiter and Saturn gathered in a grouping about two hand spans (27 degrees) wide in the sky. Unfortunately, because the Sun is in the middle of the grouping, most of the planets are not visible.
17	Sun and planets in closer grouping (20 degrees) than on May 3-4 as Moon has left this area of the sky.

June

1	Pluto at opposition
9	Mercury at greatest angular separation from sun for evening apparition of planet in west after sunset.
11	Venus in superior conjunction.
20	Sun reaches June solstice at 9:48 p.m. EDT. Official start of summer in northern hemisphere.
28	Jupiter, Saturn and waning crescent Moon form a line in east before sunrise.

July

1	Partial solar eclipse (See Eclipses page 562)
3	Earth at aphelion (furthest point from sun for year) — 152.1 million kilometres.
16	Total lunar eclipse (See Eclipses page 562)
27	Neptune at opposition
27	Mercury at greatest angular separation from sun for morning apparition of planet in east before sunrise.
30	Partial solar eclipse (See Eclipses page 562)
31	Very young crescent moon very close to Venus in western sky just after sunset.

August

11	Uranus at opposition
12	Peak of Perseid meteor shower. Moonlight interferes this year.
27	Mercury at greatest angular separation from sun for evening apparition of planet in east before sunrise.
30	Waxing crescent moon near Venus low in west after sunset.

September

18-19	Waning gibbous Moon forms attractive pattern with Jupiter, Saturn and star Aldebaran.
21	Sun reaches the September equinox at 1:27 p.m. Official start of the autumn season in the northern hemisphere.
29	Venus below and to left of waxing crescent moon in west after sunset.

October

6	Mercury at greatest angular separation from sun for evening apparition of planet in west after sunset.
15-16	Gibbous Moon near Jupiter, Saturn and the star Aldebaran.
20	Peak of Orion meteor shower. Moonlight interferes this year.
29	Eastern Standard Time begins. Clocks go back one hour at 2 a.m.

November

11-12	Moon near Saturn, Jupiter and bright star Aldebaran.
15	Mercury at greatest angular separation from sun for morning apparition of planet in east before sunrise.
17	1st peak of Leonid meteor shower (11 p.m.)
18	2nd peak of Leonid meteor shower (3 a.m.)
19	Saturn in opposition.
27	Jupiter at opposition.
29	Waxing crescent Moon near Venus in west in early evening.

December

8-10	Moon near Saturn, Jupiter and star Aldebaran.
13	Peak of Geminid meteor shower. Moonlight interferes this year.
21	The Sun reaches the December solstice at 8:38 a.m. Eastern Standard Time. The winter season officially begins in the Northern Hemisphere.
25	Partial solar eclipse visible over most of Canada and the United States. (See Eclipses page 562)
29	Waxing crescent Moon near Venus in west in early evening.

Source: *Royal Ontario Museum, Toronto*

Eclipses in 2000

The year features four partial eclipses of the Sun and two total eclipses of the Moon. Of the six, the January 20-21 total lunar eclipse and the December 25 partial solar eclipse promise to be of most interest to North American observers.

January 20-21

Total Lunar Eclipse: This is the best lunar eclipse visible from all of North America and South America since 1996. The shadow of the earth crossing the face of the moon will become visible shortly after 10 p.m. Mid-eclipse is at 11:43 p.m. The best part of the eclipse ends at 1:26 a.m. No equipment is needed to observe this event.

February 5

Partial Solar Eclipse: The first of four partial solar eclipses is only visible from the southern Atlantic Ocean and Antarctica.

July 1

Partial Solar Eclipse: The second partial solar eclipse of the year is only visible in the southeastern Pacific Ocean and the extreme south end of South America.

July 15-16

Total Lunar Eclipse: The second total lunar eclipse of the year is best seen in Australia and over the western Pacific Ocean. Early partial phases of the eclipse will be visible from western North America.

July 31

Partial Solar Eclipse: The third partial solar eclipse of the year occurs over the high Canadian Arctic, Alaska, and northern Russia. It is visible from western Canada in the mid-afternoon.

December 25

Partial Solar Eclipse: The best eclipse of the sun this year is visible across all of North America. The eclipse starts at 10:26 a.m. EST, mid-eclipse is at 2:25 p.m. EST, and the event ends at 2:43 p.m. EST.

> **WARNING: SPECIAL PRECAUTIONS MUST BE TAKEN TO OBSERVE THE SUN AT ALL TIMES. AT NO TIME DURING A PARTIAL SOLAR ECLIPSE CAN THE SUN BE OBSERVED SAFELY WITH THE UNPROTECTED HUMAN EYE.**

Source: *Royal Ontario Museum, Toronto*

Space Information on the World Wide Web

NASA Home Page   http://www.nasa.gov
NASA provides links to the massive amount of information the agency has placed on the Web, as well as links to other space-related sites in the United States and other countries.

Space Telescope Science Institute   http://www.stsci.edu
This is the site for the Hubble Telescope.

Mars Global Surveyor   http://mars.jpl.gov/mgs   *Images, press releases, student activities.*

Canadian Space Agency (see page 563) has a home page dedicated to our Space Science Program, including an overview that goes back to our first observatory in 1839, and details of current work being done in Space Life Sciences, Atmospheric Sciences, Space Astronomy, Microgravity Sciences and Solar Terrestrial Relations. Review news releases, research opportunities, the special student section or the image gallery. Each program page includes links to major projects and advisory committees (visit the Meteorite and Impacts Advisory Committee) and newsletters. The Microgravity site includes a guide to Microgravity Science. http://www.science.sp-agency.ca is the home of the Space Science Program.

The Canadian Space Agency (CSA)

The CSA was created by an act of Parliament on December 14, 1990; its mission is to "promote the peaceful use and development of space for the social and economic benefit of Canadians." Its more immediate job is to co-ordinate Canada's space programs and manage our space-related activities.

Canadian experience in space predates the creation of the CSA: Canadians designed and built the first Canadian satellite in time for a launch on Sept. 9, 1962. *Alouette I* made us the third country in space (after Russia and the US), and was the first satellite to return useful information on the ionosphere, (the layer of the upper atmosphere that affects long-distance radio transmissions).

In 1972, Canada launched *Anik A1* and became the first country to have a commercial communications satellite network. It made nation-wide, real-time television possible. It also brought reliable telephone service to the North for the first time. *Anik E-2* still provides services to television networks and telephone systems, and facilitates activities such as the transmission of newspaper copy to five printing plants across the country.

In 1976, Canada and the United States launched a joint venture communications satellite, *Hermes*, which became the prototype for direct broadcast satellites. In 1981, the Canadian-designed and built Remote Manipulator System or Canadarm, was used on the Space Shuttle *Colombia*. Operated by two hand controls from the comfort of the space shuttle's cabin, the Canadarm allows astronauts to take satellites from the cargo bay and position them in space; it is also designed to snare satellites already in orbit and place them into the cargo bay for a return to Earth.

The Canadian Astronaut Program has been in operation since 1983; see page 564 for details.

Canada and the International Space Station: Canada's contribution is the Mobile Servicing System (MSS), consisting of equipment and facilities on the ISS and on the ground. A very sophisticated "space arm" is part of this system, as is a robotic hand (known formally as a Special Purpose Dexterous Manipulator or SPDM). These pieces and the Canadarm will be used for assembly and maintenance tasks on the space station. The arm, together with the hand, can manipulate delicate objects; the Canadarm can work with large objects. The CSA is working on a Canadian Space Vision System to assist those using the equipment. Ground support for the devices will be at CSA headquarters in St. Hubert, Quebec. Training, logistics support and other resources will be used to monitor the condition of the equipment and train personnel to use it.

RadarSat, launched in 1995, is the country's first Earth Observation satellite. This remote sensing satellite is in a near-polar orbit 800 km above the Earth. RadarSat produces images of the Earth's surface using a microwave Synthetic Aperture Radar (SAR) system. (Similar devices use optical sensors; unlike them, Radarsat can function night or day, and through clouds, fog or smoke.)

RadarSat II, to be launched in 2001, will be an advanced SAR satellite. Personnel in fields as diverse as ice navigation, cartography, geological exploration, maritime surveillance, disaster relief operations, and agriculture and forestry surveillance will be able to use the data images as the markets served by RadarSat I expand. Visit http://www.space.gc.ca/ENG/About/Radarsat for updates on Canada's Earth Observation technology.

Canadian Space Agency

Canadian Space Agency (CSA)   http://www.space.gc.ca
Information on Canada's contribution to space research and Canada's astronauts, including regular updates on the International Space Station

Canadian Astronaut Office   http://www.astro.space.gc.ca

Canada's Astronauts

The Canadian Astronaut Program began in 1983 when Canada was invited to send an astronaut on the U.S. space shuttle. A permanent corps of Canadian astronauts who could co-ordinate and conduct Canadian experiments in space was created as a result.

The first recruiting drive for the astronaut program resulted in 4,300 applications. Six were successful. In 1992, a second invitation for recruits went out and another 5,000 applications poured in. Four more candidates were selected, based on a combination of academic background, professional experience, health and communication skills.

The first Canadian astronaut to fly in space was **Dr. Marc Garneau**. He conducted a set of experiments in space science, space technology, and life sciences during Mission 41-G, from October 5-13, 1984, aboard the Space Shuttle *Challenger*. **Dr. Steve MacLean** was scheduled to fly in 1987 and conduct a second set of such experiments, but was rescheduled following the *Challenger* tragedy. Dr. MacLean and the payload finally flew on the Space Shuttle mission STS-52, aboard *Columbia*, from October 22 to November 1, 1992.

January 22-30, 1992, **Dr. Roberta Bondar** flew aboard *Discovery* during Mission STS-42. She served as the prime Canadian Payload Specialist for the first International Microgravity Laboratory mission; she conducted more than 43 experiments on behalf of 13 countries.

In November 1995, **Col. Chris Hadfield** was the first Canadian Mission Specialist to participate in a Space Shuttle mission as a crew member and the first Canadian on board the Russian Space Station *Mir* when he flew aboard *Atlantis* during Mission STS-74, from November 12-20, 1995.

In May 1996, **Dr. Marc Garneau** made his second space flight, this time as a Mission Specialist aboard Space Shuttle *Endeavor*. This Mission, STS-77, was a rendezvous and proximity mission using the SPARTAN-207 satellite. Once again, the CANADARM played a large role in this run-up to the assembly of the International Space Station (ISS). This mission also carried the commercial SPACEHAB module and two Canadian experiments, one in material processing and one in biology.

Dr. Robert Thirsk flew as a Payload Specialist on Mission STS-78, also known as the Life and Microgravity Spacelab flight, launched on June 20, 1996. During the 17-day mission aboard the Space Shuttle *Columbia*, Dr. Thirsk conducted a series of 43 life and microgravity experiments aboard the Spacelab—a fully-equipped international space laboratory carried in the Shuttle's cargo bay.

On August 7, 1997, **Bjarni Tryggvason** was Payload Specialist for flight on STS-85. He focussed on further testing of the Microgravity Vibration Isolation Mount (MIM) and performing material science and fluid physics experiments designed to examine sensitivity to spacecraft vibrations. This work was directed at developing better understanding of the need for systems such as the MIM on the International Space Station (ISS) and on the effect of vibrations on the many experiments to be performed on the ISS.

The CSA's **Dr. Dave Williams** was one of seven astronauts to participate in the STS-90 mission on-board the Space Shuttle *Columbia* from April 17 to May 3, 1998. Dr. Williams and his fellow crew members conducted a total of 26 life science experiments designed to study the effects of microgravity on the brain and other parts of the central nervous system.

During this mission Williams served as official crew medical officer. On July 21, 1998, Dr. Williams was appointed Director of the Space and Life Sciences Directorate at NASA's Johnson Space Centre in Houston.

Julie Payette was selected as an astronaut by the CSA in June 1992 and underwent basic training in Canada. Once selected for work on the International Space Station (ISS), Payette studied Russian in addition to her other flight training. In August 1996, she began mission specialist training at the Johnson Space Centre, working for the Astronaut Office's Robotics branch. Initial astronaut training was completed in April 1999; Payette visited the ISS in May 1999 as part of STS-96, a 10-day logistics and resupply mission.

Source: *Canadian Space Agency* http://www.space.gc.ca

Constellations

Astronomers have divided the sky into 88 well-defined areas called constellations. They are named after people, animals or objects. The pattern of bright stars in some constellations (such as Orion or Scorpius) resembles the person, animal, or object they are named after but in most constellations it is difficult to see a pattern among the stars. The largest constellation is Hydrus, followed by Virgo and Ursa Major. The smallest is Crux.

Constellation	Meaning
Andromeda	Daughter of Cassiopeia
Antlia	The Air Pump
Apus	Bird of Paradise
Aquarius	The Water-bearer
Aquila	The Eagle
Ara	The Altar
Aries	The Ram
Auriga	The Charioteer
Bootes	The Herdsman
Caelum	The Chisel
Camelopardalis	The Giraffe
Cancer	The Crab
Canes Venatici	The Hunting Dogs
Canis Major	The Big Dog
Canis Minor	The Little Dog
Capricornus	The Horned Goat
Carina	The Keel
Cassiopeia	The Queen
Centaurus	The Centaur
Cepheus	The King
Cetus	The Whale
Chamaeleon	The Chameleon
Circinus	The Compasses
Columba	The Dove
Coma Berenices	Berenice's Hair
Corona Australis	The Southern Crown
Corona Borealis	The Northern Crown
Corvus	The Crow
Crater	The Cup
Crux	The Cross
Cygnus	The Swan
Delphinus	The Dolphin
Dorado	The Goldfish
Draco	The Dragon
Equuleus	The Little Horse
Eridanus	A River
Fornax	The Furnace
Gemini	The Twins
Grus	The Crane (bird)
Hercules	The Son of Zeus
Horologium	The Clock
Hydra	The Water Snake (f)
Hydrus	The Water Snake (m)
Indus	The Indian

Constellation	Meaning
Lacerta	The Lizard
Leo	The Lion
Leo Minor	The Little Lion
Lepus	The Hare
Libra	The Balance
Lupus	The Wolf
Lynx	The Lynx
Lyra	The Lyre
Mensa	Table Mountain
Microscopium	The Microscope
Monoceros	The Unicorn
Musca	The Fly
Norma	The Square
Octans	The Octant
Ophiuchus	The Serpent-bearer
Orion	The Hunter
Pavo	The Peacock
Pegasus	The Winged Horse
Perseus	Rescuer of Andromeda
Phoenix	The Phoenix
Pictor	The Painter
Pisces	The Fishes
Piscis Austrinus	The Southern Fish
Puppis	The Stern
Pyxis	The Compass
Reticulum	The Reticle
Sagitta	The Arrow
Sagittarius	The Archer
Scorpius	The Scorpion
Sculptor	The Sculptor
Scutum	The Shield
Serpens	The Serpent
Sextans	The Sextant
Taurus	The Bull
Telescopium	The Telescope
Triangulum	The Triangle
Triangulum Australe	The Southern Triangle
Tucana	The Toucan
Ursa Major	The Great Bear[1]
Ursa Minor	The Little Bear[2]
Vela	The Sails
Virgo	The Maiden
Volans	The Flying Fish
Vulpecula	The Fox

(1) Commonly known as the Big Dipper. (2) Commonly known as The Little Dipper

Observatories in Canada

■ Maritime Region:

Burke-Gaffney Observatory: Saint Mary's University, Halifax, NS B3H 3C3. Open: Nov. to Mar. at 7 pm and April to June at 9 pm, every 1st and 3rd Sat. From June to Sept. open every Sat. Tel: (902) 496-8257.

Web site: http://mnbsun.stmarys.ca/bgo/bgo.html

University of New Brunswick: Brydon Jack Observatory Museum, P.O. Box 4400, Fredericton, NB E3A 5A3. Oldest observatory in Canada, 1851. No charge. Summer (by appointment).

■ Central Canada:

David Dunlap Observatory: Richmond Hill, Ont. L4C 4Y6. Open Wednesday mornings from 10 to 11:30 am. From April to Sept. Open also on Saturday evenings. Reservations required. Tel: (905) 884-2112.

Web site: http://www.astro.utoronto.ca/ddo-home.html

Helen B. Hogg Observatory: National Museum of Science and Technology. 1867 St. Laurent Blvd. Ottawa, Ont. K1A 0M8. Open: Oct.-June. Group tours Mon.-Thurs., Public visits Fri. (in French 2nd Fri.); Jul.-Aug.: Public visits: Tues. (French), Wed., Thurs. (English). Eve. tours by appt only. Tel: (613) 991-3073.

Hume Cronyn Memorial Observatory: University of Western Ontario, London, Ont. N6A 3K7. late Oct. to early April by reservation. From June to Aug. on Saturday evenings at 8:30 pm. Tel: (519) 661-3183

Web site:

http://phobos.astro.uwo.ca/~dfgray/pub-nit.html

Science North Solar Observatory: 100 Ramsey Lake Rd., Sudbury, Ont. P3A 2K3. Viewing of the solar spectrum and the Sun in hydrogen-alpha and white light in a darkened theatre. Open most days. Tel: (705) 522-3701.

■ **Western Canada:**

Climenhaga Observatory: Dept. of Physics and Astronomy, University of Victoria, Victoria, BC V8W 2H2. Tel: (604) 388-0001. Open daily.

Web site: http://astrowww.phys.uvic.ca/climenhaga/obs/ telescope.html

Rothney Astrophysical Observatory: Physics and Astronomy Dept., University of Calgary, Calgary, Alta. T2N 1N4. Tel: (403) 220-5385.

Web site: http://www.ucalgary.ca/~milone/rao.html

Dominion Astrophysical Observatory: 5071 West Saanich Rd., Victoria, BC V8X 4M6. Open throughout the year Mon. to Fri. 9:15 am to 4:30 pm. In summer, May to Aug., open from 9:00 am until 8 pm Sun. to Fri., as well as on Sat from 9:30 am to 11:00 pm. Tel: (604) 363-0030

Web site:http://dao.nrc.ca/DAO/homepage.html

Dominion Radio Astrophysical Observatory: Penticton, BC V2A 6K3. Conducted tours. Sun., July-Aug. only, 2-5 pm. Visitors' centre open year-round during daytime. Tel: (604)497-5321.

Gordon MacMillan Southam Observatory: 1100 Chestnut St., Vancouver, B.C. V6J 3J9. Open Fri.-Sun., and statutory holidays 12 pm- 5 pm and 7 pm-11 pm, weather and volunteer staff permitting. Tel: (604) 738-2855.

Devon Observatory: Dept. of Physics, University of Alberta, Edmonton, Alta. T6G 2J1.

University of Saskatchewan Observatory: Saskatoon, Sask. S7N 0W0. Tel.: (306) 966-6434.

University of British Columbia Observatory: 2219 Main Mall, Van., BC V6T 1W5. Free public observing on clear Sat. eve. Tel: (604) 224-6186 (observing) or (604) 228-2802 (tours).

Planetariums

■ **Maritime Region:**

Burke-Gaffney Planetarium: Saint Mary's University, Department of Astronomy, Halifax, NS B3H 3C3.

The Halifax Planetarium: The education section of the Nova Scotia Museum of Natural History. Summer St., Halifax, NS B3H 3A6. Tel: (902) 429-1610. Located in the Sir James Dunn Building, Dalhousie Univeristy. The education section of the Nova Scotia Museum of Natural History. Open on Tuesday evenings at 7 pm. Free. Tel: (902) 424-7353.

Web site: http://apwww.stmarys.ca/rasc/hp/hp.html

■ **Central Canada:**

Doran Planetarium: Laurentian University, Ramsey Lake Rd., Sudbury, Ont. P3E 2C8. tel: (705) 675-1151, ext. 2222.

Web site: http://www.laurentian.ca/

Planetarium de Montréal: 1000 St. Jacques St. W., Montreal, Que. H3C 1G7. Tel: (514) 872-4530. Live shows in French and English. Open daily.

Web site: http://www.planetarium.montreal.qc.ca/ (Please note: web site in French only.)

McLaughlin Planetarium: Royal Ontario Museum: 100 Queen's Park, Toronto, Ont. M5S 2C6. Tel: (416) 586-5549 (switchboard). The McLaughlin Planetarium was closed in December 1995. On-going astronomy program using STARLAB planetariums for school and public programming. Phone (416) 586-5801 for information. Recorded astronomy information line (416) 586-5736.

William J. McCallion Planetarium: Department of Physics and Astronomy, McMaster University, 1280 Main Street, Hamilton, ON L8S 4M1. Tel: (905) 525-9140

■ **Western Canada:**

Calgary Centennial Planetarium: Alberta Science Centre, 701-11 St. S.W., P.O. Box 2100, Stn. M. Calgary, Alta. T2P 2M5. Tel: (403) 221-3700

Web site: http://www.supernet.ab.ca/Communities/Calgary/space.html

Edmonton Space Sciences Centre: Coronation Park, 1121-142 St., Edmonton. Alta T5M 4A1. Tel: (403) 451-7722 or 452-9100. Features planetarium Star Theatre, IMAX film theatre, exhibit galleries, telescope shop and bookstore. Open daily.

H.R. MacMillan Planetarium: 1100 Chestnut St., Vancouver, B.C. V6J 3J9. Tel: (604) 738-7827

Web site: http://pacific-space-centre.bc.ca/

Manitoba Planetarium: Museum of Man and Nature. 190 Rupert Ave., Winnipeg, Man. R3B 0N2. Tel: (204) 956-2830 (switchboard). Shows daily except some Mondays. Museum gift shop has scientific books and equipment.

Web site:

http://portal.mbnet.mb.ca/Manitoba Museum

Also worth a visit is the web site of the Manitoba Centre for UFO Studies

http://portal.mbnet.mb.ca/ManitobaMuseum/ufocases.html

EARTH SCIENCES

The earth sciences include **geology** (the study of earth's origin and composition), **oceanography** (the study of ocean water, currents, life-forms and the ocean floor), **paleontology** (the study of fossils and ancient life-forms), and **meteorology** (the study of earth's atmosphere, including weather and climate). This section includes material on geology and paleontology. Meteorology can be found in the section on Climate (pp.11-31).

The Geological Survey of Canada

The Geological Survey of Canada (GSC) is Canada's first scientific agency, and one of the first of its kind in the world. The agency was created to survey and map mineral deposits in Canada's nearly 1 million square kilometres of land and freshwater lakes, and more than 6 million square kilometres of coastal boundaries.

The Survey began life in Montreal in 1842. Under the first director William Edmond Logan, a Canadian businessman turned geologist, its initial task was a search for coal, the main industrial fuel at the time. The search, throughout Upper and Lower Canada, was unsuccessful, but Logan did find mineable deposits of copper and other metallic minerals.

Soon Survey geologists were undertaking expeditions westward. In the 1880s another director, George Mercer Dawson, became a noted ethnologist in Western Canada, as well as pioneer geologist. His reports included observations of the Haida people of British Columbia. During his expeditions he took many photographs of settlements and totem poles, capturing a glimpse of a vanishing landscape.

In 1992 the Geological Survey marked its 150th anniversary. While the task of mapping Canada's geology remains its central focus, the computerized Survey of the 1990s is very different from the one started by Sir William Logan. The Survey now undertakes an ever-expanding range of research—from exploring questions related to global change to those concerning natural hazards such as earthquakes, landslides, volcanoes, floods and ground instability.

For more information on the Geological Survey and its programs, contact: Communications Office, Geological Survey of Canada, 601 Booth Street, Ottawa, Ontario K1A OE8.

Geological Cyberspace Connections

http://www.nrcan.gc.ca will get you to Natural Resources Canada's web site; add /gsc and you will find the Geoscience Information Centre. http://www.atlas.gc.ca will take you to the National Atlas of Canada Online, where the 6th edition of The National Atlas of Canada *is available.*

EarthNet is a web site being developed by the Atlantic Geoscience Society, the Canadian Geological Foundation, Canada's Geoscience Education Network, the Canadian Society of Petroleum Geologists and the Geological Survey of Canada. It is hoped this will become our national earth science communication gateway. Check it out at http://agcwww.bio.ns.ca/schools/esrc/esr-home.html

Common Geological Terms

Continental shelf: Submerged edge of continent, extending to depths of less than 200 metres, and largely made up of sedimentary rock.

Earthquake: A sudden motion or trembling in the earth caused by the release of slowly accumulated strain along a fault line or through volcanic activity.

Echo Sounding: A determination of water depth by measuring the time required for a sonic or ultrasonic signal to travel to the bottom of a body of water and back to the ship emitting the signal.

Epicentre: Point on the earth's surface directly above the focus of an earthquake, usually the location of the most severe damage.

Erosion: Breakdown and wearing away of rocks on the earth's surface by the action of water, waves, glaciers, wind and underground water.

▶

▶ **Fault:** a fracture in the earth's crust along which there has been displacement of the rock on either side, relative to one another.

Geothermal energy: energy that can be extracted from the earth's internal heat, usually in the form of emissions of hot water, steam, and gas.

Glacier: a large ice mass formed on land by recrystallisation of compacted snow.

Ice Field: An extensive area of interconnected glaciers. An ice field is known as pack ice when floating on the sea.

Igneous Rock: Rock formed when a mass of molten magma cools and solidifies on or below earth's surface. One of three main classes of rock.

Magma: Molten rocky material (mostly silica) beneath the earth's surface. Reaching the surface red hot through volcanic activity, it cools and becomes lava.

Metamorphic Rock: Rock formed when preexisting rocks are altered by marked changes in temperature, pressure, or shearing stress. One of three major rock groups.

Sedimentary rock: Rock formed from the accumulation of loose material deposited by water, wind and ice, and solidified by compaction.

Seismograph: a device that records the seismic vibrations of an earthquake. The wave disturbances caused by earthquakes have different speeds and require different lengths of time to reach the surface.

Tectonic plates: Rigid outer layer of the earth's crust consists of about ten large plates, which "float" horizontally across the denser inner crust. The boundaries of these plates are zones of intense activity, and give rise to mountain building, volcanoes, changes in the ocean floor, and earthquakes.

Tsunami: Particular form of ocean wave produced by an earthquake in the ocean floor, noted for its destructive force.

Volcano: A vent in the earth's crust through which magma, rock fragments, dust, gases, and ash are ejected from below earth's surface.

Composition of the Earth

Core: The earth's core lies about 2,900 km below the surface, and consists of two layers: a solid inner core and an outer liquid layer. The inner core is a solid mass, 3,200 km in diameter, probably composed of compressed iron with small amounts of other metals such as nickel. The outer core (the only liquid layer) is about 3,470 km in radius and gives rise to earth's magnetic fields.

Mantle: Accounting for about 82% of earth's volume, the mantle is denser than the crust, and probably increases in density close to the core. The mantle extends from the core to about 90 km below the higher mountains, and to about 5 km beneath parts of the ocean crust.

Crust: The outside crust of planet earth ranges in thickness from 5 to 50 km. The relatively light, granite-like rock forming the continents overlies a thinner magnesium-iron layer that makes up the ocean floor. The continental blocks "float" on the denser layer forming the ocean bed.

Hydrosphere: A layer of water covering over 70% of the earth's crust, including all water on or near the surface of the planet.

Atmosphere: The lightest part of earth is the atmosphere, a gaseous envelope surrounding the planet. The atmosphere consists of nitrogen, oxygen, water vapour and argon. Less than 0.1% is composed of other gases. Gases have weight, so the atmosphere is densest near earth's surface, and thins towards the vacuum of space.

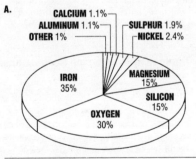

A. CALCIUM 1.1% — SULPHUR 1.9%
ALUMINUM 1.1% — NICKEL 2.4%
OTHER 1%
IRON 35%
MAGNESIUM 15%
SILICON 15%
OXYGEN 30%

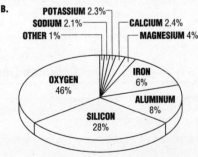

B. POTASSIUM 2.3% — CALCIUM 2.4%
SODIUM 2.1% — MAGNESIUM 4%
OTHER 1%
OXYGEN 46%
IRON 6%
ALUMINUM 8%
SILICON 28%

▲

Relative abundance of elements by weight of elements in the whole earth (A) and in the earth's crust (B).

Earthquakes

Although the earth's surface seems completely stable, it is constantly moving and changing. Layers of rock in the earth's crust, called plates, push and pull each other until they bend or stretch.

Vibrations or "seismic waves" emanate from the source of the breakage out through the earth, causing the planet to quiver or ring like a tuning fork. The waves can be so minor that the quake will not be felt by humans, or so severe it will change the physical landscape of the area.

Earthquakes can happen all over the world, but they tend to reoccur along weaknesses in the crust, called faults. By studying the patterns of earthquakes, scientists determine the areas at greatest risk and compile the information in seismic zoning maps. In this way, building regulations can be applied to earthquake zones to minimize possible damage.

The most common method of measuring an earthquake's magnitude is the Richter Scale. It estimates the force from recordings of seismic waves taken by an instrument called a seismometer. the scale is logarithmic, so that each numeric reading is ten times greater in recorded amplitude.

The intensity of an earthquake can also be measured through the Modified Mercalli Scale. In addition to mechanical recordings, it uses witness accounts to describe the effects of an earthquake.

Measuring Earthquakes

Richter		Modified Mercalli	
2.5	Generally felt, but not recorded.	I	Not felt except by a very few
		II	Felt only by a few persons at rest, especially on upper floors of buildings
3.5	Felt by many people.	III	Felt noticeably indoors. Standing cars may rock slightly. Most people do not recognize.
		IV	During daytime felt by many indoors, outdoors by a few. Dishes, windows and doors disturbed; walls creak. At night, some awaken. Sensation like a heavy truck passing.
		V	Felt by nearly everyone; many awakened. Some dishes and windows broken; some objects over-turned. Trees, poles and other tall objects disturbed.
4.5	Some local damage may occur.	VI	Felt by all, many run outdoors. Heavy furniture moves; occasionally plaster falls and chimneys damaged. Overall damage slight.
		VII	Everyone runs outdoors. Well-built structures suffer negligible damage; slight to moderate damage in well-built homes; poorly constructed buildings suffer considerable damage. Noticed by people in moving cars.
6.0	A destructive earthquake	VIII	Damage slight in specially designed structures; considerable in ordinary substantial buildings, with partial collapse; great in poorly-built structures. Chimneys fall. Heavy furniture overturned. Disturbs people driving cars. Sand and mud ejected in small amounts.
		IX	Damage to specially designed structures considerable. Buildings shifted off foundations. Conspicuous ground cracks. Underground pipes broken.

▶

Richter			Modified Mercali
7.0	A major earthquake, about 10 occur each year	X	Some well-built wooden structures destroyed; most masonry and frame structures destroyed. Ground badly cracked. Rails bent. Landslides considerable.
8.0	Great earthquake, occurs once every five to 10 years	XI	Few masonry structures remain standing. Bridges destroyed. Broad fissures in ground. Underground pipelines out of service. Earth slumps, and land slips in soft ground.
		XII	Damage total. Waves seen on ground surface. Lines of sight and levels distorted. Objects thrown upward into air.

World's Major Earthquakes

Date		Location	Deaths	Magnitude
1902	Dec. 16	Turkestan	4 500	—
1905	Apr. 4	India, Kangra	19 000	8.6
1905	Sep. 8	Italy, Calabria	2 500	7.9
1906	Aug. 17	Chile, Santiago	20 000	8.6
1907	Oct. 21	Central Asia	12 000	8.1
1908	Dec. 28	Italy, Messina	83 000	7.5
1915	Jan. 13	Italy, Avezzano	29 980	7.5
1920	Dec. 16	China, Gansu	200 000	8.6
1923	Sep. 1	Japan, Kwanto-Tokyo-Yokohama	143 000	8.3
1925	Mar. 16	China, Yunnan	5 000	7.1
1927	Mar. 7	Japan, Tango	3 020	7.9
1927	May 22	China, near Xining	200 000	8.3
1929	May 1	Iran	3 300	7.4
1932	Dec. 25	China, Gansu	70 000	7.6
1933	Mar. 2	Japan, Sanriku	2 990	8.9
1934	Jan. 15	India, Behar-Nepal	10 700	8.4
1935	Apr. 20	Formosa	3 280	7.1
1935	May 30	Pakistan, Quetta	30 000	7.6
1939	Jan. 25	Chile, Chillan	28 000	8.3
1939	Dec. 26	Turkey, Erzincan	30 000	7.6
1948	June 28	Japan, Fukui	5 390	7.3
1949	Aug. 5	Ecuador, Ambato	6 000	6.8
1960	Feb. 29	Morocco, Agadir	15 000	5.9
1960	May 22	Chile	5 000	7.3
1966	Aug. 19	Turkey, Varto	2 520	7.1
1968	Aug. 31	Iran	20 000	7.3
1969	July 25	Eastern China	3 000	5.9
1970	May 31	Peru	66 000	7.8
1972	Apr. 10	Southern Iran	5 054	7.1
1972	Dec. 23	Nicaragua, Managua	5 000	6.2
1974	Dec. 28	Pakistan	5 300	6.2
1976	Feb. 4	Guatemala	23 000	7.5
1976	June 30	Westirian, Indonesia	5 000	7.1
1976	July 27	China, Tangshan	255 000	8.0
1976	Aug. 16	Philippines, Mindanao	8 000	7.9
1976	Nov. 24	Turkey	4 000	7.3
1978	Sep. 16	Iran	25 000	7.8
1980	Oct. 10	Algeria	4 500	7.7
1980	Nov. 23	Southern Italy	4 800	7.2
1981	June 11	Southern Iran	3 000	6.9
1985	Sep. 19	Mexico, Michoacan	15 000	8.1
1988	Dec. 7	Turkey-USSR	25 000	7.0
1990	June 20	Western Iran	50 000	7.7
1993	Sept. 30	India	9 500	6.4
1995	Jan. 17	Kobe, Japan	6 000	7.2
1998	Feb. 1	Afghanistan	5,000	6.9
1999	Aug. 17	Turkey	12,000	7.4

Source: *Energy, Mines and Resources Canada; Swiss Re, sigma no 2/1996*

Earthquakes in Canada

Scientists estimate that more than 1,000 earthquakes are recorded in Canada each year. Most measure less than 3 on the Richter scale. The southwest corner of British Columbia is the most active earthquake region (more than 200 every year). Other active regions include coastal BC, the southern Yukon, the Mackenzie Valley in the Northwest Territories, the Arctic Islands, and parts of Ontario and Québec (especially the Ottawa and St Lawrence valleys).

Date		Location	Magnitude
1918	6 Dec.	Vancouver Island	7.0
1925	1 March	Charlevoix-Kamouraska region,Québec	6.7
1929	6 May	Off Queen Charlotte Islands	7.0
1929	18 Nov.	Atlantic Ocean. South of Newfoundland	7.2
1933	20 Nov.	Baffin Bay	7.3
1935	1 Nov.	Québec-Ontario border	6.2
1946	23 June	Vancouver Island	7.3
1949	22 August	Off Queen Charlotte Islands	8.1
1958	10 July	Alaska-BC border	7.9
1970	24 June	South of Queen Charlotte Islands	7.4
1976	20 Dec.	West of Vancouver Island	6.8
1979	28 Feb.	Yukon-Alaska border	7.5
1980	17 Dec.	West of Vancouver Island	6.8
1985	23 Dec.	Mackenzie region, NWT	6.9
1988	25 Nov.	Saguenay region, Quebec	6.0
1989	25 Dec.	Northern Quebec	6.1
1992	6 April	West of Vancouver Island	6.8

Source: *Geological Survey of Canada*

For more information on earthquakes, contact the Geological Survey of Canada.

Geophysics Division
1 Observatory Crescent
Ottawa K1A 0Y3
Phone (24 hrs): 613-995-5558

Pacific Geoscience Centre
PO Box 6000
9860 West Saanich
Sidney, BC V8L 4B2
Phone (24 hrs): 604-363-6500

Geological Time Periods

The story of planet earth is one of continuous change. Fossils, rock records and radioactive dating show three marked changes in the patterns of plant and animal life. These times of change in the most recent 570 million years of the earth's history are divided by geologists into three eras: Paleozoic (ancient life); Mesozoic (age of reptiles); and Cenozoic (age of mammals). The more than 4 billion years before the start of the Paleozoic era are referred to as Precambrian time. Each geological unit is divided further: the eras into periods, the periods into epochs.

The names of the time periods are taken either from the geographic locality where the fossil information was best displayed or first studied, or from some characteristic of the geological formations. For example, the Jurassic period is named from the Jura Mountains of France and Switzerland, and the Carboniferous is named from the coal-bearing sedimentary rocks.

Era	Period	Epoch	Years Ago	Changes and Characteristics
Precambrian Time			4.5 bil.?	Cooling and melting of the earth's crust. Evidence of bacteria, the first known living things, about 3.5 billion years ago.
Paleozoic	Cambrian		575 mil.	Seas spread across North America. First fishes appear. Greatest development of invertebrates.
	Ordovician		480 mil.	Floods sometimes cover two-thirds of North America. Jawless fish appear. Algae become plentiful.
	Silurian		435 mil.	Coral reefs are formed. First amphibians and forests of fernlike trees appear.
	Devonian		405 mil.	Gas and oil are formed. Many kinds of fish in seas and fresh water. First insects appear.
	Carboniferous —Mississippian		350 mil.	Warm, moist climate produces great forests that later become coal beds. Fish and amphibians plentiful.
	—Pennsylvanian		310 mil.	Appalachian Mountains are formed. Large amounts of coal are formed. First reptiles appear.
	Permian		270 mil.	Ural Mountains are formed. Glaciers in southern hemisphere melt. Gas, oil and salt are formed. Reptiles developing.
Mezozoic	Triassic		225 mil.	Reptiles dominate the earth. First mammals appear.
	Jurassic		180 mil.	Shallow seas invade continents. Dinosaurs reach their largest size. First birds appear.
	Cretaceous		130 mil.	Seas spread over the land. Flowering plants appear. Dinosaurs die out. Most chalk deposits are made.
Cenozoic	Tertiary	Paleocene	65 mil.	Mountains become higher. Climates less uniform. Mammals, flowering plants become common.
		Eocene	50 mil.	Climate mild. Seas flood shores of continents. Primitive apes, early horses and elephants appear.
		Oligocene	38 mil.	Climate mild. Alps and Himalayas begin to rise. Many volcanoes. Oil and natural gas are formed.
		Miocene	27 mil.	Climate mild. Rocky Mountains and Sierra Nevadas forming. Flowering plants and trees resemble modern kinds.
		Pliocene	10 mil.	Climate cooling. Mountains rising in western Canada. Many volcanoes. Birds and mammals spread around the world. Humans appear near end of epoch.
	Quaternary	Pleistocene	1.5 mil.	Great ice sheets cover northern hemisphere. Climate cool. Mountains continue to rise in North America. Early humans reach Europe and North America.
		Recent, or Holocene	10 000	Glaciers melt and Great Lakes are formed. Climate warm. Humans live in most parts of the earth, develop agriculture, use metals, domesticate animals.

LITHOPROBE

(by Horst Heise, Communications Adviser)

When European explorers called North America the "New World" they reversed geological time. In reality, our ancestral continent, Laurentia, formed long before the forces of plate tectonics shaped their building blocks into Eurasia, South America and Africa.

Tracing our continent's dramatic assembly is the purpose of Canada's national Lithoprobe project (a probe or study of the lithosphere—the Earth's crust), our biggest earth-science undertaking ever and the first of its kind. More than 750 specialists (including over 400 post-graduate and post-doctoral students) from the various branches of the earth sciences have joined the project. Since 1984, Lithoprobe scientists have been constructing a "moving" image of what North America has gone through during the last four billion years, and published about 1,000 technical papers on the subject.

From its beginning, Lithoprobe has included experts from all earth science specialties, including geologists, geophysicists and geochemists, as well as the whole geoscience community. The project has been funded by the Natural Sciences and Engineering Research Council of Canada and the Geological Survey of Canada, and supported by provincial agencies, and mining and oil companies when operating in their spheres of interest.

In hard-rock mining areas Lithoprobe showed that seismic reflection surveys could provide good lithological and structural leads. Given Canada's reliance on mineral resources, this technique is of fundamental importance to existing as well as future mining communities.

The project intends to trace the growth of our continent from its beginning until today. Canada's four-billion-year-old rocks belong to a piece of old continental crust which then became part of the Slave Province.

The Slave Province (a geological designation) is one of six "original" microcontinents or **cratons** of the Archean age which eventually drifted into each other to form the heart of the Canadian Shield. The other cratons have been named Rae, Hearne, Wyoming, Superior and Nain. Whatever land had been in the oceans between the craton, even the ocean floor itself, was squeezed into a series of mountain belts (**orogens**) in the biggest, most widely spread round of continental collision the world has ever known, accompanied by an enormous outpouring of magma, which formed a brand new crust.

This giant welding process occurred in the **Early Proterozoic** period and the new mountain belts created included ranges that exist today as only eroded remains that look like welds uniting the Archean pieces.

Rifting turned into continent splitting in the west where a wide continental slope received the sediments on which the prairies now produce grain, and oil and gas reserves are found. The same happened in the east a while later, when a massive supercontinent resulted from an earlier orogen split (roughly where the St. Lawrence River is today) and a wide ocean developed. It in turn was pushed out of existence in a series of tectonic squeezes which ended with the creation of the Appalachians. Comparatively recently, the Atlantic opened, and is still widening today. Out west, the Rockies formed during the Early Tertiary, while tectonic processes have kept BC growing westward since Jurassic times.

■ Tracking the Canadian Mosaic

Many bits and pieces have become part of the "Canadian mosaic" during the continent's long geologic past, including portions of old and new continents, islands or ocean floor which have drifted in from many parts of the world. Depending on where in Canada we live, its underground once may be been in tropical seas (parts of Saskatchewan, for instance) or shivered at Himalayan heights (large portions of Ontario and Quebec) or, in geological terms, not existed until fairly recently. Piecing the geological story of our continent together is like having to choose from a pile of not one but several jigsaw puzzles of various ages in which individual pieces likely were reshaped before they occupied their present positions. They may have come from various depths in the crust, or been newly formed during tectonic activity; developed long ago or more recently, either here or far away.

Earth's geologic history began with our planet's cooling 4.6 billion years ago, leading to the formation of the planet's outer crust, which became a patchwork of individual, moving pieces or "plates." Our own continent, North America, currently is moving westward at a fairly good pace, about 4 or 5 cm per year, about as fast as one's fingernails grow. That translates into 4,000 to 5,000 km in 100 million years—a small portion of Earth's lifetime (comparable to just 31 minutes of a 24-hour day).

The North American continent grew through a progressive sticking together, or **accretion**, of smaller into bigger pieces of land. But there were also continental breakups that involved huge supercontinents. As well, the flowing magma created new lithosphere that was added to the continents and the ocean floors.

As crustal plates meet, one may slip below the other, for instance the heavier oceanic plates slide under lighter continental crust. This tectonic action is called **subduction**. Portions of a subducted plate may become attached to the underside of the overlying crustal pate, but most of the subduction plate will be recycled into the mantle, where it melts, perhaps to enter into another cycle of melting, outpouring and cooling.

Such a subduction zone was discovered under Vancouver Island in 1984, when a first geophysical test section proved the feasibility of the Lithoprobe project. This survey across Vancouver Island sounded the underground with seismic reflection signals. It showed conclusively how a portion of the Pacific Ocean seafloor was vanishing under Vancouver Island and on into the depths of Earth, causing a trail of earthquakes and tremors and, farther inland, volcanoes to line up parallel to the west coast. This investigation, and Lithoprobe's subsequent work there, was the first major earth-science investigation to cross an ocean-continent-subduction zone.

◼ A Growing Continent

All of the Canadian Cordillera (with the exception of the volcanoes along the west coast), from the foothills in the east to the offshore in the west, is not where it used to be. All of it has been pushed, crunched or extended. The eastern portions are thrusted packages of sediments which previously had been laid down on the continental slope of the older North American continent. Part of this package still lies mostly undisturbed east of the Rockies in Alberta and in northeastern BC, and in the Western Canada Sedimentary Basin, which harbours western Canada's huge reserves of oil and gas.

Lithoprobe's west coast experiment was followed by an 1100-km long transect study and cross section all the way from the Juan de Fuca Ridge west of Vancouver Island to southwestern Alberta. This Southern Cordillera transect provided earth scientists with a rich record of how plate tectonics have worked in the recent past, and what the results of these processes look like.

Farther east, Lithoprobe looked at the Superior Province, in the heart of the Canadian Shield. Its age is Archean, the eon which comprises almost half of Earth's history, and the major period of its crustal formation. Archean rocks of the world, although a relatively small fraction of the

exposed continental crust, contain a disproportionate amount of the world's mineral wealth, including more than half of the world's gold and significant base metal reserves. Also, the vast majority of useful diamond deposits come from deep lithospheric roots beneath Archean cratons and in some parts beneath the Superior craton.

The oldest rocks known on Earth, just over 4 billion years old, are in the Slave geological province, in the western Northwest Territories. The Slave contains rocks formed between 4 and 2.5 billion years ago; it is a relatively small member of the Archean family of microcontinents.

The Slave craton is significantly different from the much larger Superior Province. It has different rock compositions; the type, setting and timing of gold and base metal mineralization is different. More of the Slave's volcanic rocks are somewhat lighter, and a greater precentage of sedimentary rocks is present. Oldest rocks in the Slave craton are much older than in the Superior Province; still, the Slave Province appears to be a fragment of a yet earlier and bigger craton. Structures also differ, intensifying the quest for tectonic evidence from our oldest geological past.

Other revelations from Lithoprobe include evidence that the area from South Dakota, through the exposed shield in Saskatchewan-Manitoba and across Hudson Bay to northern Quebec was once part of a vast ocean—more than 5,000 kms wide—and scattered tropical islands and archipelagoes like those in the southwest Pacific. (Try to picture yourself on Bali while digging out from the next Saskatchewan blizzard.) The clues are geological markers such as the origin of the rocks and the time markers imprinted by various, mostly tectonic, processes. Saskatchewan's and Manitoba's South Sea remnants began to form after a previous continent split, which created an initial rift, comparable to the present Red Sea-Gulf of Aden area. This water body, comparable to the Pacific Ocean, was in the area where wheat fields now sway in the breeze.

Lithoprobe is scheduled to continue until 2003. Visit the project's web site at http://www.litho. ucalgary.ca for an introduction, a look at the transects and archival data. A visit to the home page of the Lithoprobe Seismic Atlas of Canada at the site will give you a tutorial on Lithoprobe techniques and a project overview. The program also has a set of slides and other materials available for educational use; for more information contact the Lithoprobe Secretariat at the Unversity of British Columbia, Vancouver, BC V6T 1Z4

Minerals

Minerals are all around us—everything from ice on the sidewalk in winter to the salt you sprinkle on French fries. Each mineral species has a definite chemical composition and a crystal structure.Therefore, ice is mineral because it is solid, but water is not because it is liquid. Sea shells are not minerals because, although they are solid, they are organic—formed by living creatures.

The physical properties of minerals—their form and hardness—are easy to recognize. Specimens may be composed of large showy crystals or millions of tiny crystals fused together. The external shape (or habit) is determined by the internal arrangement of atoms. The atoms are joined together in a framework to form minute building blocks. Called the crystal structure, the arrangement of atoms is unique for each mineral. The habit is also partly the result of the environment in which a mineral grows. If there is enough space during growth, the mineral develops smooth external crystals. However, conditions are seldom ideal and more often than not, minerals grow together as masses of fibres, grains, plates or spheres. The hardness of a mineral—its resistance to scratching—is measured by the Mohs scale.

The optical properties of minerals—lustre, colour and transparency—are easily observed by the unaided eye; other optical properties are determined with microscopes. Lustre is the quality of light reflected from the surface of a mineral. For instance, the highly reflective surfaces of pyrite produce the metallic lustre characteristics of most sulphide minerals. Many silicates, carbonates and otherminerals have a softer, but still bright, glassy or vitreous lustre. Minerals with surfaces that reflect light more diffusely, such as serpentine asbestos or cyanotrichite, are said to have silky or earthly lustres. Lustre is reliable means of distinguishing minerals.

Colour can also be very distinctive, but is not always reliable in identifying most minerals because even minerals of the same species can occur in many colours. Quartz, which is quite common, can be as clear as water or the deepest purple because of flaws in the mineral's crystal structure. Colour can also be affected by the presence of major elements in the mineral: copper in azurite produces an intense azure blue; arsenic makes realgar appear red; and curite is coloured orange by uranium. Colour can also be produced by physical structure. When light strikes very thin layers within the structure of labradorite, the mineral glows with iridescent colours, an effect much like that of sunlight striking a film of gasoline on a puddle, causing a rainbow of colour.

Determining the chemical composition and crystal structure of minerals requires laboratory techniques and tools such as the electron microbe, a reliable tool for analysing chemical composition. Crystal structure is determined using an X-ray diffractometer. Other mineral properties such as magnetism, fluorescence and radioactivity are more easily detected: magnetite and pyrrhotite are noticeably magnetic; some minerals, such as scheelite, fluoresce strongly in ultra-violet light; and all uranium and thorium-bearing minerals are radioactive. The radiation can easily be detected with a Geiger counter or scintillometer.

Mohs Scale of Hardness

Mohs scale indicates the relative hardness of minerals. Each mineral listed is hard enough to scratch a smooth surface of those below it. On this scale, a polymer-like polyethylene would have a hardness of about 1, a finger nail 2.5, a penny 5, window glass 5.5, and the blade of a pocket knife 6.5 Tool steel has a hardness of about 7, and easily cuts glass.

10	Diamond	5	Apatite
9	Corundum	4	Fluorite
8	Topaz	3	Calcite
7	Quartz	2	Gypsum
6	Orthoclase	1	Talc

Source: *Geological Survey of Canada*

Earth Sciences Museums

Maritime Region:

☐ **St. Lawrence Miner's Museum**
St. Lawrence, Nfld A0E 2V0. (709) 873-2222. No charge. Open in summer.

☐ **Fundy Geological Museum**
4028 Eastern Avenue, Parrsboro, NS B0M 1S0. (902) 254-3814. Entrance fee. Open June to Oct. from 9:30 am to 5:30 pm daily, Nov. to May from Tues. to Sat. 9:00 am to 5:00 pm.
Web site: http://www.ednet.ns.ca/educ/museum/fundy.html

☐ **Inverness Miner's Museum**
Lower Railway Street, Inverness, NS B0E 1N0. (902) 258-2097. Entrance fee. Open all year.

☐ **Springhill Miner's Museum**
Black River Road, Springhill, NS B0M 1X0. B0M 1X0 (902) 597-3449. Entrance fee. Open spring, summer and fall.

Central Canada:

☐ **Alcan Museum**
1188 Sherbrooke Street West, Montreal, Quebec H3A 3G2. (514) 848-8187. No charge. Open all year.

☐ **Canadian Museum of Nature,**
Viola Macmillan Mineral Gallery
McLeod St. at Metcalfe, Ottawa, ON K1P 6P4. (613) 566-4730. Entrance fee. Closed Monday (Oct.-Apr.), Christmas Day and New Year's Day.

☐ **Logan Hall**
Geological Survey of Canada, 601 Booth Street, Ottawa, ON K1A 0E8. (613)995-4261. No charge. Open all year. Closed on weekends and holidays.

☐ **Musée de Géologie**
Laval University, Pavillon Pouliot, 4th floor, Sainte Foy, Quebec G1K 7P4. (418) 656-2193. No charge. Open all year.

☐ **Musée mineralogique et minier de la Région de l'amiante**
671 Smith Blvd. South, Thetford Mines, Quebec G6G 5T3. Entrance fee. Open all year.

☐ **Musée régional mines de Malartic**
650 rue da la Paix, Abitibi East, Malartic, Quebec J0Y 1Z0. (819) 757-4677. Entrance fee. Open all year.

☐ **Earth Sciences Museum**
University of Waterloo, Waterloo, Ontario N2L 3G1. (519) 885-1211, ext. 2469. No charge. Open weekdays from 8:30 am to 4:30 pm.
Web site:http://www.science.uwaterloo.ca/earth/museum/museum.html

☐ **Miller Museum of Geology and Minerology**
Queen's University, Dept. of Geological Sciences, Miller Hall, Kingston, Ontario K7L 3N6. (613) 545-2597. No charge. Open all year.

☐ **Oil Museum of Canada**
Oil Springs, 35 km southeast of Sarnia, Ontario N0N 1P0. (519) 834-2840. Entrance fee. Open in summer and fall. Tours all year.

☐ **The Petrolia Discovery Foundation**
Blind Line, Petrolia, Ontario N0N 1R0. (519) 882-0897. Entrance fee. Open in summer and fall.

☐ **Royal Ontario Museum,**
INCO Gallery of Earth Sciences (to open May 30, 1999)
100 Queen's Park, Toronto, ON M5S 2C6. (416) 586-5549. Entrance fee. Closed Christmas and New Year's Day only.

☐ **Timmins Museum**
70 Legion Drive, South Porcupine, Ontario P4N 1B3. (705) 235-5066. No charge. Open all year.

Western Canada:

☐ **Stonewall Quarry Park**
299 North Main Street, Stonewall, Manitoba R0C 2Z0. (204) 467-5354. Entrance fee. Open all year.

☐ **Geological Museum**
University of Saskatchewan, Geological Sciences Building, Saskatoon, Saskatchewan S7N 0W0. (306) 966-5683. No charge. Open all year.

☐ **Frank Slide Interpretive Centre**
1 km north of Frank, Alberta T0K 0E0. (403) 562-7388. No charge. Open all year.

☐ **Museum of Geology**
University of Alberta, basement of Earth Sciences Building, Edmonton Alberta T6G 2E3. (403) 492-3265. No charge. Open all year.

☐ **Royal Tyrrell Museum of Palaeontology**
Midland Provincial Park, Drumheller, Alberta T0Y 0Y0. (403) 823-7707. Entrance fee. Open all year.
Web site::http://www.tyrrell.com/

☐ **Field Station of the Tyrrell Museum**
Dinosaur Provincial Park, Patricia, Alberta T0J 2K0. (403) 378-4342. No charge. Open all year.

☐ **British Columbia Museum of Mining**
PO Box 188, Britannia Beach, BC V0N 1J0. Tel (604) 688-8735. Entrance fee. Open in summer and fall. All year for groups.

☐ **Manson Creek-Omenica Museum**
General Delivery, Manson Creek, BC V0J 2H0. Radio telephone only. No charge. Open all year.

☐ **M.Y. Williams Geological Museum**
University of British Columbia, 6339 Stores Road, Vancouver BC V6T 2B4. Tel (604) 228-5586. No charge. Open all year.

☐ **Princeton and District Museums**
167 Vermilion Street, Princeton BC V0X 1W0. Tel (604) 285-7588. No charge. Summer (30 June - 31 August)

☐ **Keno City Mining Museum**
Keno City, Yukon Y0B 1J0. (403) 995-2792. No charge. Open in summer.

PHYSICAL SCIENCES

Physics and chemistry constitute the physical sciences. **Chemistry** concerns itself with the composition, properties, and reactions of substances. Organic chemistry, one of the two main branches of chemistry, specializes in the composition, properties, and reactions of hydrocarbon compounds. The other branch, inorganic chemistry, deals primarily with the elements and compounds that do not include hydrocarbons. **Physics** concerns itself with universal aspects of nature—forces, energy, structure of matter, and their interactions. Some of its particular fields are: plasma physics, optics and quantum optics, particle physics, geophysics, biophysics, and acoustics. As basic sciences, physics and chemistry permeate all sciences and technologies.

Common Chemistry Terms

Acid: a substance that in liquid form will turn blue litmus paper red, react with alkalis (bases) to form salts, and dissolve metals to form salts.

Alkali: Any compound that has chemical qualities of a base, such as reacting with acid to form salts.

Atomic Weight (Mass): The relative mass of an atom, based on a scale in which a specific carbon atom is assigned a mass value of 12.

Base: an alkaline substance, either molecular or ionic in form, that will accept or receive a proton from another chemical unit.

Catalyst: a substance that accelerates a chemical reaction without becoming a part of the end product of the reaction.

Compound: A substance formed by the combination of two or more chemical elements that cannot be separated from the combination by physical means. The constituent atoms, however, can usually be separated by means of chemical reactions.

Electron: A negatively-charged particle that moves in orbit about the nucleus of an atom.

Element: A substance composed of atoms with the same atomic number or the same number of protons in their nuclei.

Isotope: One of two or more atoms having the same atomic number, but a different mass number.

Mass Number: the atomic weight of an isotope, calculated from the number of protons and neutrons in the nucleus.

Matter: Anything that has weight or fills space, such as a solid, liquid, or gas.

Polymer: a huge molecule composed of repeating units of the same molecule.

Valence: a number that represents the combining power of an element, ion, or radical.

Common Physics Terms

Acceleration: the rate of change of velocity with respect to time.

Anode: The positive terminal of an electric current flow. In a vacuum tube, electrons flow from the cathode to the anode.

Cathode: The negative terminal of an electric current system. In vacuum tube, the filament serves as the source electrons.

Conduction: the transfer of heat by molecular motion from a source of high temperature to a region of lower temperature, tending towards a result of equalized temperatures.

Convection: The mechanical transfer of heated molecules of a gas or liquid from a source to another area, as when a room is warmed by the movement of air molecules heated by a radiator.

Electromotive Force: The force that causes the movement of electrons through an electrical circuit.

Energy: the ability to perform work. Energy may be changed from one form to another, as from heat to light, but normally it cannot be created or destroyed.

Force: the influence on a body that causes it to accelerate.

Heat: A form of energy that results from the disordered motion of molecules. As the motion becomes more rapid and disordered, the amount of heat is increased.

Mass: a measure of the amount of matter. Near the surface of earth, it is roughly equivalent to weight.

Momentum: the mathematical product of the mass of a moving object and its velocity.

Velocity: The speed with which an object travels over a specified distance during a measured amount of time.

Weight: The force on a body produced by the downward pull of gravity on it.

Basic Laws of Physics

■ Newton's Laws of Motion

Newton's laws apply to objects in a vacuum, and are difficult to observe in the "real" world where forces such as friction affect all objects.

First Law: Any object at rest tends to stay at rest, and a body in motion will continue that motion with a constant velocity unless acted upon by some external unbalanced force.

Second Law: The acceleration of an object is directly proportional to the force acting upon it, and is inversely proportional to the mass of the object.

Third Law: Every action generates an equal and opposite reaction.

■ Gravity

When an object is dropped near the surface of the earth, it increases in speed as it falls. By rolling balls down inclined planes Galileo discovered that acceleration due to gravity is the same for all objects, independent of their weight (mass). For example, if you drop this book and a brick simultaneously, they will reach to floor at the same time. You can try the same experiment with a heavy book and a single sheet of paper. The paper is affected by the resistance of the air. Then crumple the paper, and try again.

Gravity is the force that tends to attract objects to the centre of a cellestial body, such as the earth, the moon or Mars. The weight of an object at the earth's surface is mainly due to the force of gravity between the earth and the object. The force exerted by the earth varies with the object's distance from the centre of the earth. Therefore the weight of an object is not the same at the earth's surface as it is on the moon or in space.

■ Laws of Thermodynamics

Sadi Carnot (1796-1832) stated in his work *Reflections on the Motive Power of Fire* that mechanical energy could be produced by the simple transfer of heat.

First Law: In a closed system, energy appears to be conserved in all but nuclear reactions and other extreme conditions.

Second Law: In a closed system, heat never travels from a low to a higher temperature in a self sustaining process. In a closed system, entropy (disorder) always increases.

■ Two Basic Laws of Quantum Physics

Heisenberg's Uncertainty Principle: It is impossible to specify completely the position and momentum of a particle, such as an electron.

Pauli's Exclusion Principle: No two electrons of the same atom can have identical values for all four quantum numbers: at least one quantum number must be different.

Loudness of Sounds

Sound is measured in decibels. A decibel is a unit for measuring the relative intensity of a sound, equal to one-tenth of a bel. A bel indicates the amount of energy in the form of sound transmitted to one sq cm of the ear. The bel was named after Alexander Graham Bell.

The decibel scale advances geometrically instead of arithmetically. Twenty decibels represents not twice as much noise as ten, but 10 times as much. The 80-decibel level of a pneumatic drill is 100 times as noisy as the 60-decibel level of a quiet motor.

Source: *Dictionary of Science, Barnhardt, American Heritage Series*

Intensity (decibels)	Loudness
0	Threshold of hearing
10 (1 bel)	Virtual silence
20	Quiet room
30	Watch ticking at 1 m
40	Quiet street
50	Quiet conversation
60	Quiet motor at 1 m

Intensity (decibels)	Loudness
70	Loud conversation
80	Door slamming
90	Busy typing room
100	Near loud motor horn
110	Pneumatic drill
120	Near airplane engine
130	Threshold of pain

The International System of Units (SI)

The Systeme Internationale (SI) or metric system was developed in France in 1799. By 1880 many European countries and much of South America had adopted the system as a common language of measurements.

The pressures of global trade have persuaded many of the English-speaking countries to adopt a uniform international standard of measure. Canada adopted the metric system in 1970.

Name	Symbol	Quantity
■ SI Base Units		
metre	m	length
kilogram	kg	mass
second	s	time
ampere	A	electric current
kelvin	K	thermodynamic temperature
mole	mol	amount of substance
candela	cd	luminous intensity
■ SI Supplementary Units		
radian	rad	plane angle
steradian	sr	solid angle
■ Common SI Derived Units With Special Names		
hertz	Hz	frequency
pascal	Pa	pressure, stress
watt	W	power, radiant flux
volt	V	electric potential, electromotive force
newton	N	force
joule	J	energy, work
coulomb	C	electric charge
ohm	Ω	electric resistance
farad	F	electric capacitance
■ Common Units Used With the SI		
litre	L	volume or capacity (= 1 dm^3)
degree Celsius	°C	temperature (= 1 K; 0°C = 273.2 K)

hectare	ha	area (= 10 000 m^2)
tonne	t	mass (= 1000 kg)
electronvolt	eV	energy (= 0.160 aJ)
nautical mile	M	distance (navigation) (= 1852 m)
knot	kn	speed (navigation) (= 1 M/h)
standard atmosphere	atm	atmospheric pressure (= 101.3 kPa)

■ SI Prefixes

Name	Symbol	Multiplying Factor*
exa-	E	10^{18}
peta-	P	10^{15}
tera-	T	10^{12}
giga-	G	10^9
mega-	M	10^6
kilo-	k	10^3
hecto-	h	10^2
deca-	da	10
deci-	d	10^{-1}
centi-	c	10^{-2}
milli-	m	10^{-3}
micro-	μ	10^{-6}
nano-	n	10^{-9}
pico-	p	10^{-12}
femto-	f	10^{-15}
atto-	a	10^{-18}

*10^2 = 100; 10^3 = 1 000; 10^{-1} = 0.1; 10^{-2} = 0.01; Thus, 2 km = 2 x 1 000 = 2 000 m ; 3 cm = 3 x 0.01 = 0.03 m

Source: *Gage Canadian Dictionary*

Large Numbers

1 thousand	= 1 000
1 million	= 1 000 000 or 10^6
1 milliard: used in Europe, USSR, former French possessions	= 1 000 000 000 or 10^9
1 billion:	= 1 000 000 000 000 or 10^{12}
—Canada, the United States and France	= 1 000 000 000 or 10^9
1 trillion:	= 1 000 000 000 000 000 000 or 10^{18}
—Canada and the United States	= 1 000 000 000 000 or 10^{12}

Source: *World Weights and Measures*

The Elements

(listed by name, symbol and atomic number)

An element is a substance composed of atoms that are chemically alike—each atom has an identical number of protons in its nucleus. Furthermore, there is no known process to break these elements down into more fundamental substances.

actinium	Ac	89	hafnium	Hf	72	promethium	Pm	61
aluminum	Al	13	hassium	Hs	108	protactinium	Pa	91
americium	Am	95	helium	He	2	radium	Ra	88
antimony	Sb	51	holmium	Ho	67	radon	Rn	86
argon	Ar	18	hydrogen	H	1	rhenium	Re	75
arsenic	As	33	indium	In	49	rhodium	Rh	45
astatine	At	85	iodine	I	53	rubidium	Rb	37
barium	Ba	56	iridium	Ir	77	ruthenium	Ru	44
berkellum	Bk	97	iron	Fe	26	rutherfordium	Rf	104
beryllium	Be	4	krypton	Kr	36	samarium	Sm	62
bismuth	Bi	83	lanthanum	La	57	scandium	Sc	21
bohrium	Bh	107	lawrencium	Lr	103	seaborgium	Sg	106
boron	B	5	lead	Pb	82	selenium	Se	34
bromine	Br	35	lithium	Li	3	silicon	Si	14
cadmium	Cd	48	lutetium	Lu	71	silver	Ag	47
calcium	Ca	20	magnesium	Mg	12	sodium	Na	11
californium	Cf	98	manganese	Mn	25	strontium	Sr	38
carbon	C	6	meitnerium	Mt	109	sulfur	S	16
cerium	Ce	58	mendelevium	Md	101	tantalum	Ta	73
cesium	Cs	55	mercury	Hg	80	technetium	Tc	43
chlorine	Cl	17	molybdenum	Mo	42	tellurium	Te	52
chromium	Cr	24	neodymium	Nd	60	terbium	Tb	65
cobalt	Co	27	neon	Ne	10	thallium	Tl	81
copper	Cu	29	neptunium	Np	93	thorium	Th	90
curium	Cm	96	nickel	Ni	28	thulium	Tm	69
dubnium	Db	105	niobium	Nb	41	tin	Sn	50
dysprosium	Dy	66	nitrogen	N	7	titanium	Ti	22
einsteinium	Es	99	nobelium	No	102	tungsten	W	74
erbium	Er	68	osmium	Os	76	uranium	U	92
europium	Eu	63	oxygen	O	8	vanadium	V	23
fermium	Fm	100	palladium	Pd	46	xenon	Xe	54
fluorine	F	9	phosphorus	P	15	ytterbium	Yb	70
francium	Fr	87	platinum	Pt	78	yttrium	Y	39
gadolinium	Gd	64	plutonium	Pu	94	zinc	Zn	30
gallium	Ga	31	polonium	Po	84	zirconium	Zr	40
germanium	Ge	32	potassium	K	19			
gold	Au	79	praseodymium	Pr	59			

What is the Periodic Table?

*T*he Periodic Table of Elements (shown opposite) has its roots in the 19th century when chemists calculated how much one atom of an element weighed in comparison to another. The resulting weight was known as the atomic mass and measured in atomic mass units (amu). (An amu is a mass equal to 1/12 of the mass of the most common form of carbon atom.) As the list of elements was compiled and ranked in order of mass, chemists noted that every seven or eight elements had similar properties.

By 1869 Dimitri Mendeleyev was confident enough to rearrange the list of elements to group those with similar properties and leave blanks for the missing ones that would make up the eight. Mendeleyev only had 63 elements but the periodic table now has 109 elements and still conforms to his 1869 rearrangement.

Early in the 20th century, the table was further refined when atoms were found to be made up of protons and electrons. The number of protons and electrons are equal in one atom and this number was designated the element's atomic number. The table now shows the elements in order according to their atomic number and their atomic mass.

Periodic Table of Elements

gases

non-metals

transition metals

other metals

rare earth elements

1	2	3	4	5	6	7	8	9	10	11	12	13	14	15	16	17	18
1 **H** 1.00																	2 **He** 4.00
3 **Li** 6.94	4 **Be** 9.01											5 **B** 10.81	6 **C** 12.01	7 **N** 14.01	8 **O** 15.99	9 **F** 18.99	10 **Ne** 20.17
11 **Na** 22.98	12 **Mg** 24.30											13 **Al** 26.98	14 **Si** 28.08	15 **P** 30.97	16 **S** 32.06	17 **Cl** 35.45	18 **Ar** 39.94
19 **K** 39.09	20 **Ca** 40.08	21 **Sc** 44.95	22 **Ti** 47.88	23 **V** 50.94	24 **Cr** 51.99	25 **Mn** 54.93	26 **Fe** 55.84	27 **Co** 58.93	28 **Ni** 58.69	29 **Cu** 63.54	30 **Zn** 65.39	31 **Ga** 69.72	32 **Ge** 72.59	33 **As** 74.92	34 **Se** 78.96	35 **Br** 79.90	36 **Kr** 83.80
37 **Rb** 85.46	38 **Sr** 87.62	39 **Y** 88.90	40 **Zr** 91.22	41 **Nb** 92.90	42 **Mo** 95.94	43 **Tc** (98)	44 **Ru** 101.07	45 **Rh** 102.90	46 **Pd** 106.42	47 **Ag** 107.87	48 **Cd** 112.41	49 **In** 114.82	50 **Sn** 118.71	51 **Sb** 121.75	52 **Te** 127.60	53 **I** 126.90	54 **Xe** 131.29
55 **Cs** 132.90	56 **Ba** 137.33	57 **La** 138.90	72 **Hf** 178.49	73 **Ta** 180.94	74 **W** 183.85	75 **Re** 186.20	76 **Os** 190.2	77 **Ir** 192.22	78 **Pt** 195.08	79 **Au** 196.96	80 **Hg** 200.59	81 **Tl** 204.38	82 **Pb** 207.2	83 **Bi** 208.98	84 **Po** (209)	85 **At** (210)	86 **Rn** (222)
87 **Fr** (223)	88 **Ra** 226.02	89 **Ac** 227.02	104 **Rf** 261	105 **Db** 262	106 **Sg** 263	107 **Bh** 264	108 **Hs** 265	109 **Mt** 266	110 (271)	111 (272)	112 (277)	113 (282)					

58 **Ce** 140.12	59 **Pr** 140.90	60 **Nd** 144.24	61 **Pm** (145)	62 **Sm** 150.36	63 **Eu** 151.96	64 **Gd** 157.25	65 **Tb** 158.93	66 **Dy** 162.50	67 **Ho** 164.93	68 **Er** 167.26	69 **Tm** 168.93	70 **Yb** 173.04	71 **Lu** 174.96
90 **Th** 232.03	91 **Pa** 231.03	92 **U** 238.02	93 **Np** 237.04	94 **Pu** (244)	95 **Am** (243)	96 **Cm** (247)	97 **Bk** (247)	98 **Cf** (251)	99 **Es** (252)	100 **Fm** (257)	101 **Md** (258)	102 **No** (259)	103 **Lr** (260)

This is a table which shows the properties of the elements, in the order of their atomic mass or number, and arranged in horizontal rows (periods) and vertical columns (groups) to illustrate the occurence of similarities in the structure of their atoms. When the elements are arranged in this order, their chemical and physical properties show repeatable trends. This pattern in properties occurs periodically; that is, the pattern is repeated in an orderly manner over time.

The order of the elements is that of their atomic numbers, the integers which are equal to the positive electrical charges of the atomic nuclei expressed in electronic units.

Science Centres and Museums

Maritime Region:

☐ **Discovery Centre**
Halifax Nova Scotia. Entrance fee. Open daily. Tel:
(902) 492-4422.
Web site:
www.cfn.cs.dal.ca/Science/DiscCentre/DC_Home.html

☐ **Electrical Engineering Museum**
University of New Brunswick, Dept. of Electrical
Engineering, Head Hall, Fredericton, NB No charge.
Open winter, spring and fall.

☐ **Nova Scotia Museum of Industry**
147 Foord Street, Stellarton, NS B0K 1S0. Entrance
fee. Open daily. Tel: (902) 755-5425.
Web site: http://www.ednet.ns.ca/educ/museum/moi.html

Central Canada:

☐ **Museum of Visual Science and Optometry**
University of Waterloo, Optometry Building, Columbia
Street, Waterloo, Ontario N2L 3G1. Tel (519) 885-
1211, ext. 3405. No charge. Open all year.

☐ **Hamilton Museum of Steam and Technology**
900 Woodward Avenue, Hamilton, Ontario L8H 7N2.
Tel (416) 549-5225. Entrance fee. Open all year.

☐ **National Museum of Science and Technology**
1867 St. Laurent Blvd., Ottawa, Ontario K1G 5A3. Tel
(613) 998-4566 Entrance fee. Open all year.
Web site: http://science-tech.nmstc.ca/

☐ **Ontario Science Centre**
770 Don Mills Road, Toronto, Ontario M3C 1T3.
Tel (416) 429-4100. Open daily (except Christmas Day)
Web site: http://www.osc.on.ca/

☐ **Science North**
100 Ramsay Lake Road, Sudbury, Ontario P3E 5S9.
Tel (705) 522-3700 Entrance fee. Open all year.

Western Canada:

☐ **Alberta Science Centre**
701-11 Street SW, Calgary, Alberta T2P 2M5.
Tel(403) 221-3700 No charge. Open all year.

☐ **Edmonton Space and Science Centre**
11211-142 Street, Edmonton, Alberta T5M 4A1.
Tel(403) 452-9100 Entrance fee. Open all year.
Web site: http://www.ee.ualberta.ca/essc

☐ **Energeum**
640-5th Avenue S.W., Main Floor, Energy Resources
Building, Calgary, Alberta T2P 3G4. Tel (403) 297-
4293 No charge. Open all year.

☐ **Pacific Geoscience Centre**
9860 West Saanich Road, Sidney, BC V8L4B2.
Tel(604) 363-6500 No charge. Open all year.

☐ **Saskatchewan Science Centre**
Wascana Drive, Regina. Entrance fee. Open all year.
Web site: http://www.sciencecentre.saskweb.com/

☐ **Science World**
1455 Quebec Street, Vancouver, BC V6A 3Z7. Tel
(604) 687-8414   Entrance fee. Open daily, except
Christmas Day.

Sudbury Neutrino Observatory (SNO)

*T*he joint Canada-US-UK observatory had the heavy water installed in the neutrino detector
and the ordinary water that surrounds the vessel also in place as of May 1999. Calibration
devices were being installed, and the detector had been turned on and was being tested.
   The SNO will be taking data that will provide insight into the properties of neutrinos and
the core of the sun where they originate. The observatory is a heavy-water Cherenkov detector
that uses 1,000 tonnes of heavy water in a 12-metre acrylic sphere. Neutrinos, which can pass
through matter (the SNO is over 2,000m below ground), react with the heavy water to produce
flashes of light called Cherenkov radiation. An array of 9,600 photomultiplier tubes
surrounding the heavy water vessel will be able to detect those flashes. The rock surrounding
the cavity that houses the observatory will protect it from interference from cosmic rays. The
laboratory itself must be kept extremely clean in order to reduce background radiation signals
which would mask the very weak signal from the neutrinos.
   Visit http://www.sno.phy.queensu.ca for the latest updates or an artist's rendering of the
detector.

SCIENCE AT WORK

This section takes a selective look at science as it is applied in industry and everyday life. Individual Canadians have been awarded recognition in the ranks of the world's pre-eminent scientists and researchers, as our lists of Nobel Prize winners and the Canadian Engineering and Science Hall of Fame both show.

Canadian Nobel Laureates in Science and Medicine

1923	Dr. Frederick G. Banting Dr. J.J.R. Macleod	Medicine and Physiology	for the discovery of insulin
1971	Dr. Gerhard Herzberg	Chemistry	for his contributions to the knowledge of electronic structure and geometry of molecules, particularly free radicals
1986	Dr. John Polyani	Chemistry	for contributions concerning the dynamics of elementary chemical reactions
1993	Dr. Michael Smith	Chemistry	co-winner for work on genetic codes
1994	Bertram Brockhouse	Physics	co-winner for study on atoms

Canadian Science and Engineering Hall of Fame

Twenty Canadians have been inducted into the Canadian Science and Engineering Hall of Fame. The inductees are outstanding researchers, inventors, and innovators who have won worldwide recognition for their accomplishments. The Hall of Fame portrait gallery is located at the National Research Council laboratories on Sussex Drive in Ottawa. Inductees are announced each October. The Hall of Fame web site can be accessed at http://www.nrc.ca

The Inductees

Maude Abbott (1869-1940)   - pathologist and specialist in congenital heart disease

Sir Frederick Banting (1891-1941)   - co-discoverer of insulin and Nobel laureate

Alexander Graham Bell (1847-1922)   - inventor of the telephone

J. Armand Bombardier (1907-1964)   - inventor of the snowmobile

Bertram Brockhouse (1918–)   - physicist who pioneered use of neutron scattering in study of atoms

Reginald Fessenden (1866-1932)   - pioneer in the development of the radio

Sir Sandford Fleming (1827-1915)   - architect of the transcontinental railway and inventor of standard time

Gerald Heffernan (1919–)   - for innovation in steel production, developer of the environment-friendly "mini-mill"

Gerhard Herzberg (1904- 99)   - astrophysicist and Nobel laureate

George J. Klein (1904-92)   - design engineer, the most productive inventor in 20th century Canada

Hugh LeCaine (1914-77)   - physicist; designed the first musical synthesizer

Sir William Logan (1798-1875)   - first director of the Geological Survey of Canada

Elizabeth "Elsie" MacGill (1905-80)   - aeronautical engineer, oversaw WWII production of Hawker Hurricane fighter aircraft

Frère Marie-Victorin (1885-1944)   - botanist, author and teache

Andrew G.L. MacNaughton (1887-1966)   - inventor of cathode-ray detection finder and military leader

Margaret Newton (1887-1971)   - plant pathologist, who developed techniques to combat wheat rust

Joseph-Alphonse Ouimet (1908-88)   - inventor, engineer and CBC president

Wilder Penfield (1891-1976)   - neurosurgeon who developed surgical treatments for epilepsy

John Polanyi (1929–)   - Nobel laureate whose work contributed to the development of laser chemistry

Michael Smith (1932–)   - chemistry researcher, genetic codes and DNA

Edgar William Richard Steacie (1900-62)   - researcher (free radical chemistry), educator and former president of the National Research Council

Wallace Turnbull (1870-1954)   - inventor of the variable pitch propeller

Canadian Invention

Undersea Cable Frederick Gisbourne developed a method of insulating wire to make it saltwater resistant. Then in 1852, he successfully laid the first undersea telegraph cable in North America, linking New Brunswick and Prince Edward Island. Gisbourne also proposed a cable linking North America and Europe. With the financial backing of American industrialist Cyrus Field, the Atlantic Cable, connecting Ireland and Newfoundland, was completed in 1866.

Standard Time In 1878, Sir Sandford Fleming, Canada's foremost railway surveyor and construction engineer, realized the new national railroad made local timekeeping obsolete. He devised a method whereby the world is divided into 24 time zones. His system of Standard Time was adopted by the International Prime Meridian Conference in Washington, DC, in 1884, and is still used today.

First Radio Voice Message Reginald Fessenden, from East Bolton, Quebec, discovered a way to send actual sounds via radio waves. In 1906, he transmitted the world's first radio broadcast from his transmitter at Brant Rock, Massachusetts. Sailors aboard ships of the United Fruit Company in the Caribbean found themselves listening to a Christmas Eve broadcast of music and voice. Fessenden produced the program himself, and even sang and played carols on his violin.

Gas Mask In 1915, Dr. Cluny Macpherson designed the first gas mask to protect troops from gas attacks during World War I.

The Snowmobile Fifteen-year-old Armand Bombardier built a prototype snowmobile in 1922 at his home in Valcourt, Quebec. Over the years, he refined the design and was granted a patent in 1937. At first he produced commercial vehicles, but in 1959 Bombardier perfected a sports model, the Ski-doo.

The First AC Radio Tube In 1925, Ted Rogers, a Torontonian, introduced the world's first batteryless radio. Gone were the days when programs faded away as batteries "died." The modern "plug in" radio was born. Rogers also built the world's first all-electric, batteryless broadcast station, CFRB.

The Variable Pitch Propeller Wallace Turnbull, an aeronautical engineer, worked on the variable pitch propeller in his home workshop in Rothesay, New Brunswick. This propeller was the first that could be adjusted in the air and adapted to the differing aerodynamic conditions of takeoff, climbing and diving. Pilots could adjust the propeller's blades for takeoff and again during flight. It was successfully tested by the RCAF at Camp Borden in 1927.

The Bush Plane The world's first bush aircraft was designed and built in Montreal by Robert Noorduyn in 1935. Norseman aircraft are noted for their performance in rugged terrain, and were known as "workhorses" of the North. Some are still in use.

Electronic Synthesizer In 1945, the world's first electronic synthesizer, the Sackbut, was designed and built by Hugh Le Caine in his home studio. A research physicist with the National Research Council, Le Caine was also a composer. His piece "Dripsody," using only the sound of single drop of water, is recognized as an electronic music classic.

Cobalt Bomb In 1951, Dr. Harold Johns, working with others, created the "Cobalt-60 bomb" for the treatment of cancer. Cobalt radiation therapy units have revolutionized cancer treatment worldwide.

Laser Sailboat The Laser sailboat was designed and built in 1970 by three Canadian Olympic sailors: Bruce Kirby, Hans Fogh and Ian Bruce. A stable, small pleasure craft, the Laser has given thousands of people their first introduction to sailing. The craft is now used throughout the world.

Flat Electric Wall Plug In 1989, Bob Dickie of King City, Ontario invented a revolutionary wall plug—it's flat. The first major change to wall plugs in 75 years, the FlatPlug extends only one-quarter inch from the wall. The power cord exits and travels parallel to the wall. Dickie was motivated to create a safer plug while watching his two-year-old daughter at play.

Panoramic Camera John Connor of Elora, Ontario invented the world's first panoramic camera in 1887. The camera had the capability of photographing an entire circle at one exposure.

Infant Evacuation Stretcher Motivated by television images of rescuers scrambling to evacuate babies from the 1985 Mexico City earthquake, Toronto researcher Wendy Murphy developed the world's first stretcher for taking infants from disaster areas.

1998 Nobel Prize Winners

Each October the Swedish academies for physics, chemistry and medicine announce the winners of the Nobel Prizes in science. The awards are named after Alfred Nobel, the Swedish-born chemist and businessman who invented dynamite and smokeless gunpowder. The science prizes, as well as a prize for literature and one for peace are financed by an

endowment from Nobel's estate. The prize for economics is financed by the Swedish national bank. Portugal's José Saramago won the Nobel Prize for Literature; David Trimble and John Hume won the Peace Prize for their efforts to bring peace to Northern Ireland. Amartya Sen of India won the economics prize for his contributions to welfare economics.

The 1998 **Chemistry** prize was awarded for pioneering contributions in developing methods that can be used for theoretical studies of the properties of molecules and the chemical processes in which they are involved. The prize was divided equally between: Walter Kohn for his development of the density-functional theory and John A. Pople for his development of computational methods in quantum chemistry.

The 1998 prize for **Physiology and Medicine** was awarded jointly to Robert F. Furchgott, Louis J. Ignarro and Ferid Murad for their discoveries concerning nitric oxide as a signalling molecule in the cardiovascular system.

The 1998 **Physics** prize was awarded jointly to Robert B. Laughlin, Horst L. Stormer and Daniel C. Tsui for their discovery of a new form of quantum fluid with fractionally charged excitations.

> The offical web site of the Nobel Foundation can be found at http://www. nobel.se The site offers information on The Nobel Foundation, the various institutions that award the prizes and an Electronic Nobel Museum Project that allows browsers to look into a searchable database of all the prizes and winners; take a virtual tour of some Nobel facilities and access a library of related books and papers.
>
> There is also a Nobel Internet Archive (not affiliated with The Nobel Foundation) that can be searched by category, year or name. Winners biographies can also be accessed at this site. It can be found at http://www.nobelprizes.com

1998 Manning Award Winners

The Manning Awards were established to recognize and encourage innovation in Canada by honouring individuals who have created and promoted a new concept, process or product which is beneficial to Canada and society.

Administered by the Calgary-based Ernest C. Manning Foundation, the awards are presented annually. For the 1999 winners, visit http://www.manningawards.ca

PRINCIPAL AWARD
Dr. Jim Cavers of Vancouver, BC, developed a new technology to increase the capacity of data transmission in digital communications systems. This means that cell phone users are less likely to experience busy signals, pager users can receive and send more information, and the device should reduce the costs of the personal communication systems.

AWARD OF DISTINCTION
Claude Coache, **Denis Jacob** and **Fabien Miller** of the Montreal area collaborated to develop the Cavity Monitoring System, a laser mining instrument that can provide three-dimensional representations of underground cavities, increasing safety and efficiency.

INNOVATION AWARDS
Cliff Devine and **Dan O'Connell** of BC developed a safe and efficient robotic arm which allows hydro workers to handle live, high-voltage power transmission lines more safely and efficiently. The device, known as the LineMaster, allows an operator to work by remote control.

Ontario's **Paul Paglericcio** won the second Innovation Award for developing a humane device to teach dogs to stop barking.

YOUNG CANADIAN INNOVATION AWARDS
Dilnaz Panjwani, Etobicoke, Ontario, for work on the pathophysiological basis of Chronic Fatigue Syndrome; **Janet Nielsen**, Kingston, Ontario, for an instrument to evaluate the severity of curvature of the forefoot in infants; **Julian Brazeau** and **Jean-Sebastien Ledoux**, Ottawa, Ontario, for work on a bacteria that will help plants resist salt damage; **Leslie Chambers** and **Keri McFarland**, Vernon, BC, for defining practical and beneficial uses for Russian Knapweed.

Source: *The Manning Awards*

FOCUS ON...

Science at Work in 1999

■ A Hybrid Car

By late 1999, Toyota had had 18,000 units of a "hybrid" car on Japanese roads for twelve months, evaluating performance and customer satisfaction. The model, known as Prius, combines a super-efficient gasoline engine with a powerful electric motor. The car also has a built-in system for recharging the batteries while the car is being driven so there is no need to plug into outside sources for re-charging.

Gas mileage in the city was twice that of conventional cars while emissions were one-tenth their level.

■ Artifical Bone

In September 1999, Israeli doctors announced the successful use of coral in bone replacement procedures. Tests were carried out on dogs, and the procedure was expected to be tested on humans within a year. Pure coral, with all the organic material removed, acts as a biodegradable frame that new bone can grow on. It is this growth of new bone tissue that has provided the breakthrough. Dr. Dan Atar and his team reported that "the coral merges with the bone and disappears. It is as strong as steel; it can't be broken." Furthermore, the coral is not rejected—a common problem during bone transplants—due to the similarity between coral and human bone. The coral used grows in abundance off the coast of Australia.

If the new technique is successful in humans, it would eliminate the need for more than one operation (in the case of bone grafts) as well as the need for repeat operations in cases such as hip replacement, necessary when the current type of replacement materials wear out.

■ Artificial Muscles

In an effort to build equipment that can function in remote and hostile places (like Mars), using very little power and weighing next to nothing, the U.S. National Aeronautics and Space Administration (NASA) has set out to build artificial muscles.

The latest models of NASA spacecraft are tiny (described as "basketball-sized") and so is the hardware that goes with them. The first task for the artificial muscles was to wipe dust from the windshield of an even smaller ("palm-sized")

rover that will be sent on the spacecraft to explore asteroid 4660 Nereus in 2003. The first "artificial muscle" was unveiled in March 1999 at the International Symposium on Smart Structures and Materials, and it was up to the job. Made of ploymer strips that bend in response to electrical charges, each strip of muscle weighed a fraction of an ounce and needed only four volts of power to operate.

Polymer gels—dubbed "Jell-O Jacks"—have also been developed to help raise and lower small objects during space missions. The development of artificial muscles that could help a human lift heavy objects is still years down the road.

■ The International Symposium on Smart Structures and Materials

Sponsored by The International Society for Optical Engineering (SPIE), the symposium issues a call for abstracts and then papers; later gathering participants to review the submissions. (Student papers are welcome.)

On the agenda of the 1999 conference was a demonstration and discussion of Electroactive Polymer Actuators and Devices—NASA's little muscles. In March 2000 a dual symposium will be held with a busy agenda concerning Smart Structures and Materials, and a second symposium scheduled to look at Nondestructive Evaluation and Health Monitoring of Aging Infrastructure.

The SPIE also sponsors an award for Smart Structures Product Implementation, hoping to move the ideas presented from paper stage to products with industrial and commercial potential. The 1999 winner was PhotoSense, Inc. and Boston University Photonics Centre for a device that would make air bags in cars much smarter. The Distributed Smart Skin Seat Sensor is able to calculate real-time measurement of the weight, stature and position of the passenger occupying the seat and relay the information to the airbag deployment control computer. The computer can then decide whether to fire the air bag, turn it off (in the case of an infant) or reduce the intensity of the deployment.

For more information about SPIE, visit http://www.spie.org or http://www.spie.org/info/ss for information about the symposiums.

Patents

If you have an idea for a new gizmo, what is required to have it patented? The Patent Office judges the idea based the following criteria:

1) the gizmo must be the first of its kind in the world;
2) the gizmo must be useful, and most importantly, it must work;
3) the gizmo must be obviously ingenious to others familiar with the field.

A patent gives you the right to exclude others from making, using or selling an invention from the day the patent is granted until 20 years after filing. Patents also provide useful technical information to the public. Although individual inventors still apply for patents, the majority of applications now come from large corporations. Patents are granted by individual countries; so the protection of a Canadian patent extends throughout Canada alone. Patent rights in the United States or elsewhere must be applied for separately in the individual countries.

A Canadian patent application can be filed from any Canada Post outlet across the country. Detailed information on the application procedure for Patents, Trademarks, Copyrights and Industrial and Integrated Circuits Designs can be obtained from the Canadian Intellectual Property Office in Hull, Québec. (819) 953-7620.

There are now a number of World Wide Web sites that are of interest to inventors. These include:

The Canadian Intellectual Property Office (CIPO)
http://cipo.gc.ca
CIPO's web site has information on Canadian Patents, Trademarks, Copyrights, Industrial Designs and Integrated Circuit Topographies. Trademarks can now be filed on line.

The Canadian Innovation Centre
http://www.innovationcentre.ca
The Canadian Innovation Centre is a not-for-profit corporation dedicated to helping Canadians commercialize their technological innovations. (The Centre issues a publication, *Eureka!*, quarterly.)

Canadian Technology Network
http://www.nrc.ca/ctn
Part of the National Reseearch Council site, CTN gives small and medium-sized technology businesses access to a cross-country network of expert advisors.

US Patent and Trademark Office
http://www.uspto.gov/
General information about US Patents and Trademarks is available, and the site has direct links to other national patent offices.

The Centre for Networked Information Discovery and Retrieval (CNIDR-US Patent Project)
http://patents.cnidr.org
You can access the US Patent Classifications Database at this site. You can also access the patent database and do a search for existing patents.

Contact the Women Inventors Project

*T*he Women Inventors Project is a non-profit organization founded in 1986 to provide education, advice and encouragement to innovators. A variety of activities and programs have been developed particularly to encourage girls and women to pursue careers in science, engineering and mathematics. Programs include resource materials, workshops, seminars, videos and presentations for entrepreneurs, teachers and members of service delivery ogranizations. Fledgling inventors have received assistance in everything from design to marketing.

The organization is located at 107 Holm Crescent, Thornhill, Ontario L3T 5J4.

ATMOSPHERIC SCIENCE

A Glossary of Weather Terms

air mass: an extensive body of air with a fairly uniform distribution of moisture and temperature throughout

Alberta clipper: named after the clipper sailing ships, which at one time were the fastest vessels on the seas. These storms zip along at 64 km/h, preceded by about 5 cm of light, powdery snow and followed by violent winds capable of reaching 100 km/h. This often results in severe blowing and drifting with blizzard conditions that can leave many roads impassable.

atmosphere: the envelope of air surrounding the earth. Most weather events are confined to the lower 10 km of the atmosphere.

atmospheric pressure: the force exerted on the earth by the weight of the atmosphere

blizzard: severe winter weather condition characterized by low temperatures, strong winds above 40 km/h, and visibility of less than 1 km due to blowing snow; condition lasts three hours or more

blowing snow: snow lifted from the earth's surface by the wind to a height of two metres or more. Blowing snow is higher than drifting snow.

bright sunshine: sunshine intense enough to burn a mark on recording paper mounted in the Campbell-Stokes sunshine recorder. The daily period of bright sunshine is less than that of visible sunshine because the sun's rays are not intense enough to burn the paper just after sunrise, near sunset and under cloudy conditions.

Chinook (also snow-eater): a dry, warm, strong wind that blows down the eastern slopes of the Rocky Mountains in North America. The warmth and dryness are due principally to heating by compression as the air descends the mountain slope.

cold wave: an occurrence of dangerous cold conditions, when temperatures often dip below -18°C, that usually lasts longer than a few days

crepuscular rays: clouds to excite any sky photographer. Crepuscular rays are caused by streaks or beams of sunlight shining through openings in large cumulonimbus clouds on the horizon. The beams reach down and outward from behind the clouds. If they focus upward, toward a point in the sky opposite the sun, they are called anticrepuscular rays. Sometimes they are called sun beams crossing the sky or Jacob's ladder. Sailors refer to them as "the sun drawing water." The dark bands you see crossing the sky are the shadows from clouds.

cyclone: a generic term that describes all classes of storms from local thunderstorms and tiny dust devils to monstrous hurricanes and typhoons. It comes from the Greek word, *kyklon*, meaning cycle, circle or coil of a snake and refers to all circular wind systems.

deep low: used to describe the central barometric pressure of a low [usually when it is about 975 millibars (97.50 kPa or less)]. Often has winds of gale to storm force around the low.

developing low: a low in which the central pressure is decreasing with time. Winds would normally increase as the low deepens.

dew point temperature: the temperature at which air becomes saturated, allowing condensation of water vapour as frost, fog, dew, mist or precipitation.

drizzle: precipitation consisting of numerous minute water droplets which appear to float; the droplets are much smaller than in rain.

El Niño: Near the end of most years, the normally cold Peru Current that sweeps northward along the South American coast from southern Chile to the equator is replaced by a warm southward flowing coastal current. Centuries ago the local fishermen named this the "Christ child current," because it appeared around the Christmas season. Every few years it was unusually intense and over time the term El Niño became more closely associated with occasional intense warmings.

filling low: a low in which the central pressure is increasing with time., i.e. the low is gradually weakening

flash floods: a very rapid rise of water with little or no advance warning, most often when an intense thunderstorm drops a huge rainfall on a fairly small area in a very short space of time.

fog: a cloud based at the earth's surface consisting of tiny water droplets or, under very cold conditions, ice crystals or ice fog; generally found in calm or low wind conditions. Under foggy conditions, visibility is reduced to less than one km.

Frazil ice: [French Canadian] during the freeze-up period ice forms on the river surface and ice crystals or frazil develop within the river, especially in open turbulent water slightly below 0°C. Frazil ice is very common in rapids.

freezing precipitation: supercooled water drops of drizzle, or rain which freeze on impact to form a coating of ice upon the ground or any objects they strike

front: the boundary between two different air masses which have originated from widely separated regions. A cold front is the leading edge of an advancing cold air mass, while a warm front is the trailing edge of a retreating cold air mass.

frost: the deposit of ice crystals that occurs when the air temperature is at or below the freezing point of water. The term frost is also used to describe the icy deposits of water vapor that may form on the ground or on other surfaces like car windshields, which are colder than the surrounding air and which have a temperature below freezing.

gale: a strong wind. A gale warning is issued for expected winds of 65 to 100 km/h (34 to 47 knots).

gust: a sudden, brief increase in wind speed, for generally less than 20 seconds

heat wave: a period with more than three consecutive days of maximum temperatures at or above 32°C

high pressure: a term for an area of high (maximum) pressure with a closed, clockwise (in the Northern Hemisphere) circulation of air

humidex: a measure of what hot weather "feels like." Air of a given temperature and moisture content is equated in comfort to air with a higher temperature and that of negligible moisture content. At a humidex of 30°C some people begin to experience discomfort. [*see* chart on p. 591.]

hurricanes: tropical systems are classed into several categories depending on maximum strength, usually measured by maximum sustained wind speed. A *tropical disturbance* is simply a moving area of thunderstorms in the tropics that maintains its identity for 24 hours or more. A *tropical depression* is a cyclonic system originating over the tropics with a highest sustained wind speed of up to 61 km/h. A *tropical storm* has a highest sustained wind speed of between 62 and 117 km/h. A *hurricane* has wind speeds of 118 km/h or more.

ice pellets: precipitation consisting of fragments of ice, 5 mm or less in diameter, that bounce when hitting a hard surface, making a sound upon impact

inversion: the term refers to a temperature increase with height, where the usual pattern is a decrease in temperature within increasing height.

isobar: a line on a weather map or chart connecting points of equal pressure. The large concentric lines on television or newspaper weather maps are isobars.

killing frost: a frost severe enough to end the growing season, usually when the air temperature falls below -2°C

land breeze: a small-scale wind set off when the air temperature over water is warmer than that over adjacent land. The land breeze develops at night and blows from the land out to the sea or onto the lake. Its counterpart is the sea or lake breeze.

low pressure: an area of low (minimum) atmospheric pressure that has a closed counter-clockwise circulation in the Northern Hemisphere

peak wind (gust): the highest instantaneous wind speed recorded for a specific time period

plough winds: these belong to a family of strong, straight-line downburst winds found in thunderstorms. These winds rush to the ground with great force, maybe 100 to 150 km/h and occasionally even higher. Damage usually covers an area less than 3 km across. Plough winds are capable of toppling trees, lifting roofs, and ripping apart houses and other structures.

precipitation: any and all forms of water, whether liquid or solid, that fall from the atmosphere and reach the earth's surface. A day with measurable precipitation is a day when the water equivalent of the precipitation is equal to or greater than 0.2 mm.

probability of precipitation (POP): subjective numerical estimates of your chances of encountering measurable precipitation at some time during the forecast period. For example, a 40% probability of rain means there are four chances in 10 of getting wet. They cannot be used to predict when, where or how much precipitation will occur.

relative humidity: the ratio of water vapour in the air at a given temperature to the maximum which could exist at that temperature. It is usually expressed as a percentage.

ridge: an elongated area of high pressure extending from the centre of a high pressure region; the opposite of a trough.

sea breeze: a small-scale wind set off when the air temperature over land is greater than that over the adjacent sea. The sea breeze develops during the day and blows from the sea to the land. Its counterpart is the land breeze.

sleet: is not what you think. In the United States, sleet is frozen raindrops that bounce when they hit the surface. It is not as treacherous to drive on as is freezing rain. What Americans call sleet a Canadian would call ice pellets or frozen raindrops. They are spherical or irregular shapes with a diameter of 5 mm or less. Pellets do not stick to trees or wires. On the other hand, sleet to a British weather watcher is a mix of rain and partly melted snowflakes.

small craft warning: issued when winds over the coastal marine areas are expected to reach and maintain speeds of 20 to 33 knots

snow: precipitation consisting of white or translucent ice crystals and often agglomerated into snowflakes. A day with measurable snow is a day when the total snowfall is at least 0.2 cm.

squall: a strong, sudden wind which generally lasts a few minutes then quickly decreases in speed. Squalls are generally associated with severe thunderstorms.

storm track: the path taken by a low-pressure centre

storm warning: the wind warning that is issued to mariners when winds are expected to be 48 to 63 knots

thunderstorm: a local storm, usually produced by a cumulonimbus cloud, and always accompanied by thunder and lightning. A thunderstorm day is a day when thunder is heard or when lightning is seen (rain and snow need not have fallen).

tornado (also twister): a violently rotating column of air that is usually visible as a funnel cloud hanging from dark thunderstorm clouds. It is one of the least extensive of all storms, but in violence, it is the most destructive.

trough: an elongated area of low pressure extending from the centre of a low pressure region; the opposite of a ridge

tsunami: also known (incorrectly) as a tidal wave. "Tsunami" comes from Japanese and means "harbour wave." It is a wave set in motion by an undersea movement such as an earthquake or a landslide. These waves can travel up to 1,000 km/h over long distances, hitting the shore with tremendous force.

typhoon: a severe tropical cyclone in the Western Pacific Ocean, counterpart of the Atlantic hurricane

virga: streaks of falling rain that evaporate before reaching the ground

watches and warnings: Environment Canada alerts Canadians to severe storms by issuing weather watches and warnings. Usually the first message is the severe thunderstorm watch. If a watch is issued in your area, maintain your routine, but keep an eye skyward for threatening weather, and listen to radio and television for further weather information. When severe local storms are building, or have actually been sighted or detected by radar, then warnings are issued and updated. These may be either severe thunderstorm warnings or tornado warnings. Warnings mean you should be on the alert.

waterspout: A waterspout is not really a waterspout. Often called a tornado over water, the actual water spray involved does not extend from the surface to the cloud, but 3 to 10 metres above the water surface. Like the tornado, the waterspout is very brief. Sailors believed one way of breaking up a waterspout was to fire a cannon through it.

Weatheradio: this is the name of Environment Canada's weather information broadcast network. The network has transmitters in every region and listeners need a receiver, which can be purchased from electronic equipment dealers, to pick up the broadcasts. Weatheradio signals warnings of severe weather automatically to receivers equipped with special alarm devices for that purpose.

westerlies (west-wind belt): the pronounced west-to-east motion of the atmosphere centred over middle latitudes from about 35 to 65° latitude.

willy-willies: refers to small, circular winds such as dust devils or whirlwinds in Australia, not very hazardous. Before 1950, willy-willies referred to much larger, more destructive typhoons or hurricanes.

wind chill: a simple measure of the chilling effect experienced by the human body when strong winds are combined with freezing temperatures. The larger the wind chill, the faster the rate of cooling. The wind chill factor is expressed in watts per square metre or in °C (an equivalent temperature). [*see* chart on p. 590, formula on p. 595.]

wind direction: the direction from which the wind is blowing

Source: *Environment Canada*

Weather Records

	Canada	United States	World
Highest maximum air temperature	45.0° Midale and Yellowgrass, Sask. July 5, 1937	56.7° Death Valley, CA July 10, 1913	58.0° Al'azizyah, Libya Sept. 13, 1922
Lowest minimum air temperature	-63.0° Snag, YT Feb. 3, 1947	-62.1° Prospect Creek Camp, AK Jan. 23, 1971	-89.6° Vostok, Antarctica July 21, 1983
Coldest month	-47.9° Eureka, NWT Feb. 1979		
Highest sea-level pressure	107.95 kPa Dawson, YT Feb. 2, 1989	107.86 kPa Northway, AK Jan. 31, 1989	108.38 kPa Agata, Siberia USSR Dec. 31, 1968
Lowest sea-level pressure	94.02 kPa St. Anthony, Nfld Jan. 20, 1977	89.23 kPa Matecumbe Key, FL Sept. 2, 1935	87 kPa in eye of Typhoon Tip (Pacific Ocean) Oct. 12, 1979
Greatest precipitation in 24hrs	489.2 mm Ucluelet Brynnor Mines, BC Oct. 6, 1967	1 090 mm Alvin, TX	1 869.9 mm Cilaos, La Réunion Is. March 15, 1952
Greatest precipitation in one month	2 235.5 mm Swanson Bay, BC Nov. 1917	2 717.8 mm Kukui, HI March 1942	9 300 mm Cherrapunji, India July 1861
Greatest precipitation in one year	9 341.1 mm Henderson Lake, BC 1998	17 902.7 mm Kukui, HI 1982	26 461.2 mm Cherrapunji, India Aug. 1860-July 1861
Greatest average annual precipitation	7 m Henderson Lake, BC	11 684 mm Mt. Waialeaie, Kauai, HI	11 684 mm Mt. Waialeaie, Kauai, HI
Least annual precipitation	13.6 mm Arctic Bay, NWT 1949	0.0 Bagdad, CA Oct. 3, 1912 to Nov. 8, 1914	0.0 Arica, Chile—no rain for 14 years
Greatest average annual snowfall	1 518 cm Glacier Mt. Fidelity, BC	1 461 cm Rainer Paradise Ranger Station, WA	
Greatest snowfall in one season	2 446.5 cm Revelstoke/Mt. Copeland, BC 1971-72	2 850 cm Rainer Paradise Ranger Station, WA 1971-72	
Greatest snowfall in one month	535.9 cm Haines Apps. No 2, BC Dec. 1959	990.6 cm Tamarack, CA Jan. 1911	
Greatest snowfall in one day	118.1 cm Lakelse Lake, BC Jan. 17, 1974	196.6 cm Montague, N.Y. Jan. 11-12, 1997	
Highest average annual number of thunderstorm days	36 days London, Ont.	96 days Fort Meyers, FL	322 days Bogor, Indonesia
Heaviest hailstone	290 g Cedoux, Sask. Aug. 27, 1973	758 g Coffeyville, KS Sept. 3, 1970	15 000 g Guangdong province of China April 19, 1995
Highest average annual wind speed	36 km/h Cape Warwick, Resolution Island, NWT	56.3 km/h Mt. Washington, NH	
Highest wind speed for 1 hr	201.1 km/h Cape Hopes Advance (Quaqtaq), Que. Nov. 18, 1931	362.0 km/h Mt. Washington, NH April 12, 1934	
Highest average hours of fog	1 890 hrs Argentia, Nfld	2 552 hrs Cape Disappointment, WA	

Source: *Environment Canada*

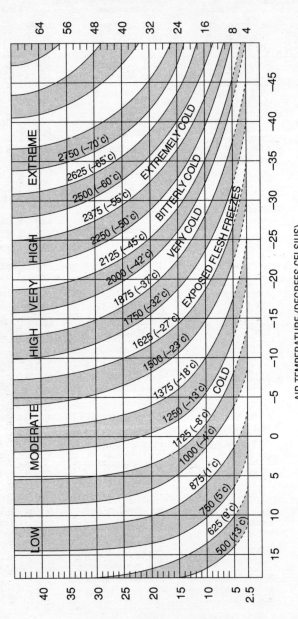

Wind Chill Factor

Watts Per Square Metre (equivalent temperature °C)

WIND SPEED (KILOMETRES PER HOUR)

64 56 48 40 32 24 16 8 4

EXTREME   HIGH   VERY   HIGH   MODERATE   LOW

EXTREMELY COLD
BITTERLY COLD
VERY COLD
EXPOSED FLESH FREEZES
COLD

2750 (-70°C)
2625 (-65°C)
2500 (-60°C)
2375 (-55°C)
2250 (-50°C)
2125 (-45°C)
2000 (-42°C)
1875 (-37°C)
1750 (-32°C)
1625 (-27°C)
1500 (-23°C)
1375 (-18°C)
1250 (-13°C)
1125 (-8°C)
1000 (-4°C)
875 (1°C)
750 (5°C)
625 (9°C)
500 (13°C)

-45 -40 -35 -30 -25 -20 -15 -10 -5 0 5 10 15

AIR TEMPERATURE (DEGREES CELSIUS)

40 35 30 25 20 15 10 5 2.5

WIND SPEED (MILES PER HOUR)

■ To determine the wind chill factor, follow the temperature across and the wind speed up until the two lines intersect. The value of the wind chill factor can be interpolated using the labeled wind chill factor curves. ■ For example, at -10°C with a wind speed of 20 miles per hour, the point of intersection lies between 1500 (-23°C) and 1625 (-27°C), or approximately 1570 (-25°C).

■ It is not recommended that wind chill factors be calculated for wind speeds below 8 km an hour and above 80 km an hour, since it is difficult to determine wind chill factors at these wind speeds.

Humidex

Relative Humidity (%)

Dry Bulb Temp (°C)	20	25	30	35	40	45	50	55	60	65	70	75	80	85	90	95	100
43	47	49	51	54	56												
42	46	48	50	52	54	56	56	57									
41	44	46	48	50	52	54	54	54	56	56	57						
40	43	44	47	49	51	52	53	52	54	53	55	57	58				
39	41	43	45	47	49	51	51	50	51	51	53	54	56	57	58		
38	40	42	43	46	47	49	49	48	50	49	51	52	54	56	57	58	58
37		40	42	43	45	47	47	47	48	48	49	51	52	53	55	57	55
36		38	40	42	43	45	45	45	47	46	47	48	50	51	52	54	52
35		37	38	41	42	43	43	43	44	43	45	46	47	49	50	51	50
34		36	37	39	41	42	42	41	42	41	43	44	45	46	48	49	48
33		34	36	37	38	40	39	39	40	40	41	42	43	44	46	47	46
32		33	34	36	37	38	38	37	38	38	39	41	42	43	44	45	43
31		31	33	34	35	36	36	36	37	36	37	38	39	41	41	42	41
30		31	31	33	34	35	34	34	35	34	35	36	37	38	39	40	39
29			30	31	32	33	33	32	33	32	33	34	35	36	37	38	37
28			28	29	31	32	31	31	31	31	32	33	33	34	35	36	35
27			28	28	29	30	29	29	30	29	30	31	32	33	33	34	33
26				27	28	28	28	28	28	27	28	29	30	31	32	32	31
25				26	27	27	27	26	27	26	26	27	28	28	29	29	29
24				25	26	26	25	24	24	24	26	26	27	27	28	29	
23					23	24	23	23	24								
22						23	23										
21						22											

DRY BULB TEMPERATURE (DEGREES CELSIUS)

Humidex (°C)	Degree of Comfort
20 - 29	Comfortable
30 - 39	Varying degrees of discomfort
40 - 45	Almost everyone uncomfortable
46 and over	Many types of labour must be restricted

■ In hot weather, our bodies regulate core temperature by using our sweat glands to shed water. Sweating doesn't cool the body, but the evaporation of sweat on your skin removes heat because it takes energy (heat) to change the liquid on your skin to vapour in the air. However, when it's humid, the air itself is already full of moisture and it can't absorb the moisture we are trying to shed, making us sticky and uncomfortable.

Ultra-Violet Index

Ultra-violet radiation is short-wavelength radiation that is part of the spectrum, just beyond visible violet light. These waves can harm both plant and animal life—the shorter of the UV wavelengths, known as UV-B, can cause sunburn, skin cancer and cataracts in humans and animals, and can also reduce agricultural productivity.

These rays are usually blocked by the protective ozone layer in the stratosphere, found between 10 and 50 km above the Earth. Ozone is a form of oxygen that has thee atoms instead of two and is created when ordinary oxygen interacts with ultraviolet radiation from the sun. Ozone can be destroyed by chemicals released into the air—most notably by the breakdown of chlorofluorocarbons (CFCs). CFCs have been used in air-conditioning, refrigeration and in some plastics manufacturing and CFC molecules are stable enough to last 100 years in the atmosphere—long enough to drift into the stratosphere where UV-B rays can break them down to produce free chlorine atoms. It is the chlorine atoms that destroy ozone.

In the 1970s, scientists had a theory that the chemicals drifting in the atmosphere could destroy the ozone layer. In the winter of 1985 NASA discovered a hole in the ozone layer over Antarctica. In recent years the continuing depletion of the ozone layer has resulted its general thinning, and in holes of varying sizes at the poles from time to time. Various attempts have been made to phase out the use of ozone-depleting chemicals all over the world, particularly at the Earth Summit in Rio de Janeiro in June 1992. While progress has been made, it is important to realize that more UV-B rays are getting through the atmosphere and there is a higher risk of UV-B generated health problems.

In May 1992, Canada's weather service launched a daily ultraviolet index as part of the forecast, the first country in the world to do so. The purpose of the index is to warn people about the dangers of over-exposure to the sun. Several other countries, including Australia, New Zealand, the Netherlands, Germany, Great Britain and the United States, have now started their own programs closely modelled on the Canadian UV index.

The amount of UV-B is measured on a scale of 0 to 10, with 10 being a typical amount you would receive on a summer day in the tropics. The higher the number, the faster you'll sunburn. (Sunburn times are for light untanned skin; times would be somewhat longer for those with darker skin.)

UV Index	Category	Sunburn Time
over 9	extreme	less than 15 minutes
7 - 9	high	about 20 minutes
4 - 7	moderate	about 30 minutes
0 - 4	low	more than one hour

Source: *Environment Canada*

Calculating Wind Chill

You can calculate the wind chill equivalent temperature in degrees Celsius (°C) or the wind chill factor in watts per square metre for your own values of air temperature (°C) and wind speed in kilometres per hour, by using the following equations:

Wind Chill Equivalent Temperature [WET] in °C:

$$WET = 33 - ((12.1 + 6.12\sqrt{W} - 0.32 \times W)\ (33 - T)/27.8)$$

Wind Chill Factor [WCF] in watts per square metre:

$$WCF = (12.1 + 6.12\sqrt{W} - 0.32 \times W)\ (33 - T)$$

T = ambient air temperature in °C	W = wind speed in kilometres per hour

This calculation gives meaningful values of WET and WCF for any air temperature lower than 5°C, and for any wind speed between 8 and 80 kilometres per hour.

The Beaufort Wind Scale

Beaufort forces range from 0 in calm conditions, to 12 in a hurricane. Rear-Admiral Sir Francis Beaufort of the British Royal Navy devised the scale in 1805. It originally referred to the amount of sail a full-rigged ship could carry in specific wind conditions. In light air, just one sail would be taken in; in a moderate gale, seven would come down; and in a heavy storm the number would be eleven, therefore Beaufort force 11. The Beaufort scale has been modified and modernized several times. Basically though, the idea is to estimate wind speed by watching the effects of wind on such things as flags, trees, smoke, water surface and even people. The scale is still widely used today.

Beaufort Wind Force	Wind Speed (km/h)	Wind Type	Descriptive Effects
0	0–1	calm	smoke rises vertically
1	2–5	light air	smoke drifts slowly
2	6–11	light breeze	leaves rustle; wind vanes move
3	12–19	gentle breeze	leaves and twigs in constant motion
4	20–29	moderate breeze	small branches move; raises dust and loose paper moves along
5	30–38	fresh breeze	small trees sway
6	39–50	strong breeze	large branches in continuous motion; telephone wires whistle
7	51–61	near gale	whole trees in motion; wind affects walking
8	62–74	gale	twigs and small branches break off trees
9	75–87	strong gale	branches break; shingles blow from roofs
10	88–101	storm	trees snap and uproot; some damage to buildings
11	102–117	violent storm	property damage widespread
12	118—	hurricane	severe and extensive damage

Source: *Environment Canada*

Tornado Intensity Scale

Tornadoes are classified by the destruction they leave behind. They are rated from F0 to F5, F standing for Fujita, one of the world's leading experts on tornadoes.

F-Scale	Winds (km/h)	Length (km)	Width	Damage
0 (very weak)	under 116	< 1.5	under 15m	light damage; minor roof, tree, chimney, antenna and sign damage
1 (weak)	117-180	1.6-5	50m	moderate damage; barns torn apart; mobile homes pushed off foundations; trees snapped; cars pushed off roads; sheet metal buildings destroyed
2 (strong)	181-252	5.1-15.9	160m	considerable damage; roofs torn off schools, homes and businesses; debris from barns scattered; trailers disintegrated; large trees uprooted; concrete block buildings destroyed
3 (severe)	253-332	16-50	161-500m	severe damage; roofs and walls of schools, homes and buildings blown away; large trees uprooted; weaker homes completely disappear
4 (devastating)	333-419	51-159	0.5-1.4km	interior and exterior walls of all homes blown apart; cars thrown more than 300m in the air
5 (incredible)	420-512	160-507	1.5-16km	strongly built homes completely blown away; bizarre phenomena such as straw driven through fence posts

Source: *Environment Canada*

The Saffir-Simpson Hurricane Intensity Scale

Category	Maximum Sustained Wind Speed (km/h)	Minimum Surface Pressure (kPa)	Storm Surge (m)	Remarks
1 (minimal)	119-153	>=98.0	1.0-1.7	Damage to trees and signs. Low-lying flooding. Small craft torn from mooring.
2 (moderate)	154-177	97.9 - 96.5	1.8-2.6	Trees blown down; damage to mobile homes and roofs. Marinas flooded; evacuation of shores.
3 (extensive)	178-209	96.4 - 94.5	2.7-3.8	Some structural damage to small buildings; serious coastal flooding;mobile homes destroyed.
4 (extreme)	210-249	94.4 - 92.0	3.9-5.6	Extensive damage: doors, roofs, windows; major damage to lower floors of buildings near shore. Major beach erosion.Massive evacuation from shore possible.
5 (catastrophic)	>250	<92.0	>5.6	Small buildings blown away; complete destruction of mobile homes; massive evacuation within 10 to 20 km of shore possible.

Source: *H.S. Saffir, P.E. and Dr. R. Simpson*

Hurricane Names in 2000

*T*he designated names for Atlantic Ocean, Gulf of Mexico and Caribbean Sea tropical storms are: *Alberto, Beryl, Chris, Debby, Ernesto, Florence, Gordon, Helene, Isaac, Joyce, Keith, Leslie, Michael, Nadine, Oscar, Patty, Rafael, Sandy, Tony, Valerie, William.*

The designated names for Eastern Pacific tropical storms (east of 140(W) are: *Aletta, Bud, Carlotta, Daniel, Emilia, Fabio, Gilma, Hector, Ileana, John, Kristy, Lane, Miriam, Norman, Olivia, Paul, Rosa, Sergio, Tara, Vicente, Willa, Xavier, Yolanda, Zeke.*

Retired Atlantic Hurricane Names

Names of great Atlantic hurricanes dropped from the rotating list of names are: Agnes, Allen, Andrew, Audrey, Betsy, Bob, Camille, Carla, Carol, Cleo, Connie, David, Diana, Diane, Donna, Dora, Edna, Elena, Eloise, Flora, Frederic, Gilbert, Gloria, Gracie, Hazel, Hilda, Hugo, Janet, Joan and Klaus.

Hurricane Season 1998-9

The North Atlantic received an unusually high number of tropical storms in the fall of 1998. The hurricane season started out slowly, but hit with a fury. By Sept. 25 four hurricanes (Georges, Ivan, Jeanne, and Karl) were swirling together in the Atlantic and the Caribbean. The three catastrophic storms were Danielle, Georges and Mitch. But it was Mitch, which struck Central America in late October that will be remembered as the deadliest hurricane in the Western Hemisphere in 200 years after causing 22,000 deaths, putting hundreds of thousands out of their homes and causing serious environmental damage.

The 1999 season to mid-fall was "highlighted" by Hurricane Floyd, which sparked the largest mass evacuation in U.S. history after forecasters suggested that the storm would go up the eastern seaboard "like a weed-eater."

Weather Symbols

Meteorologists in Canada, China and Croatia—in fact, all around the world—use a standard set of symbols in constructing detailed weather maps. Here are some samples of these universal weather symbols:

Dust or Sandstorm

Smoke

Haze

Drizzle

Thunderstorms (with hail)

Freezing Rain (moderate or heavy)

Fog

Hail

Cumulonimbus clouds

Cirrus clouds

Dust devil

Funnel cloud

50 knot wind

Sky obscured

Snow

Drifting Snow

Source: *Environment Canada*

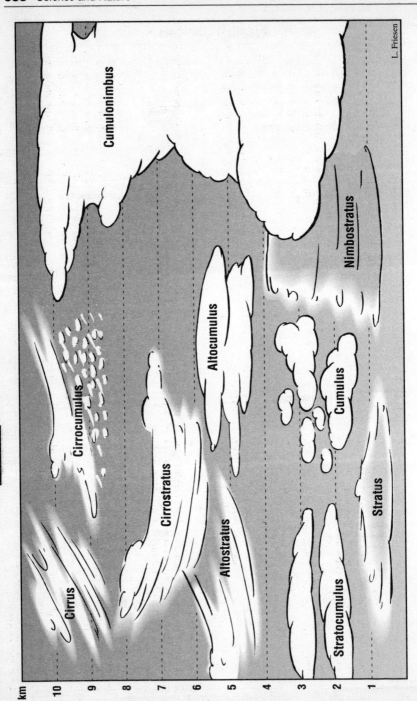

L. Friesen

Ten Basic Cloud Types

1. Cirrus
Thin wispy small white clouds that often occur as feathery filaments or long streamers stretching across the sky. Often their ends are swept by strong winds giving it the look of a mare's tail.

2. Cirrostratus
White uniform veil of thin transparent cloud. Sky still appears bright with a halo around the sun. Cloud sheets are small or extensive.

3. Cirrocumulus
Thin bands of either continuous or patchy small clouds, white or pale grey in colour. Cloud base occurs above 6,000 m.; ripple or rib pattern gives it a look of fish-scales, referred to as a "mackerel sky."

4. Altocumulus
Either patchy or continuous middle cumulus cloud with a dappled or rippled appearance. Thicker and lower version of cirrocumulus that is associated with changeable weather and perhaps rain.

5. Alto stratus
Grey pale uniform layer of cloud in which the sun may appear weakly. Too thick and low for halos to be seen, however, through the overcast, the sun can be seen weakly. A sign of precipitation within a few hours.

6. Stratocumulus
Low layers of grey or whitish clouds with occasional dark patches that have a well-defined rounded or undulating appearance. May

have a few breaks, but usually total cloud cover extends for hundreds of kilometres.

7. Stratus
A grey uniform low blanket of cloud that may be continuous or patchy, often producing light drizzle. The base is between the surface and 300 m, often obscuring hill tops and tall buildings. Looks like high drifting fog or making for a dull, grey day.

8. Nimbostratus
A thick low level (600 m) deck of cloud providing continuous rain or snow. Usually covers the entire sky and completely hides the sun.

9. Cumulus
White puffy clouds that often form by day and disappear by night. Well-defined base begins at 600 to 1,200 m; upper parts are cauliflower-like. Associated with fair weather, blue sky and no precipitation.

10. Cumulonimbus
Giant impressive cumulus clouds with dark base and a smooth anvil-shaped top. Called the kings of the sky, they are the biggest of all clouds, often towering in excess of 10 km. Often associated with severe thunderstorms and sometimes hail or tornadoes. In heavy rain, cumulonimbus clouds have a dark ominous base and a curtain of rain.

Source: *Environment Canada*

LIFE SCIENCES

The life sciences consist of diverse disciplines that share a knowledge base centered around the same fundamental question, "What is life?" Beginning with biology (the study of living organisms), the life sciences soon included: zoology (the study of animals), botany (the study of plants), and taxonomy (the study of the classification of living things).

Over this century, an ever increasing variety of subdisciplines and approaches to studying life have arisen: microbiology (the study of microorganisms), genetics (the study of heredity), biochemistry (the study of chemical compounds and reactions in living organisms), ecology (the study of the relationships between living things and their environment), and ethology (the study of animal behaviour); and most recently have been joined by biotechnology (the study and use of organisms or their components for the manufacture or production of commercial substances, aided by techniques of genetic manipulation).

Common Life Sciences Terms

Aerobic: Life processes that depend on the presence of oxygen.

Algae: Simple rootless plants that grow in bodies of water in relative proportion to the amount of nutrients available.

Allergen: Any of various sorts of material that as a result of coming into contact with appropriate tissues induce a state of sensitivity and/or resistance to infection or toxic substances.

Anaerobic: Life processes that occur in the absence of oxygen.

Animal: A vertebrate (having a bony skeleton or one made of cartilage) or invertebrate (lacking a spine or skeleton) species including, but not limited to, humans and other mammals, birds, fish, and shellfish.

Bacteria: Single cell microorganisms that possess cell walls. Some cause disease and some are beneficial.

Baleen: Horny plates with fringed inner edges attached to the upper jaw of Mysticeti type whales, such as right and blue whales. The baleen are used to filter plankton and other food from water.

Biodiversity: The total diversity within an ecosystem, including genetic variation among species, diversity of life forms, and ecosystem diversity.

Biomass: The amount of living matter in a given unit of the environment.

Biosphere: The portion of Earth (upwards at least to a height of 10,000 m and downward to the ocean floor and a 100 km below the planet's surface) and the atmosphere surrounding it that supports life.

Bloom: A seasonal, dense growth of small marine plants, i.e., phytoplankton.

Coniferous: Refers to a softwood, cone bearing tree.

Deciduous: Refers to a hardwood, leaf dropping tree.

Effluent Waste: Material discharged into the environment, treated or untreated.

Flood Tide: Interim period of tide between low and high water; a rising tide.

Lagoon: Shallow pond where sunlight, bacterial action and oxygen work to purify waste water.

Marsh: Wet, soft, low-lying land that provides a natural habitat for many plants and animals.

Molt: The periodic casting off or shedding of the outerbody covering (feathers, hair, skin, or cuticle) by birds, mammals, and reptiles.

Nutrients: Elements or compounds essential to growth and development of living things: carbon, oxygen, nitrogen, potassium, and phosphorus.

Osmosis: Tendency of a fluid to pass through a permeable membrane, such as the wall of a living cell, into a less concentrated solution, so as to equalize concentrations on both sides of the membrane.

Photosynthesis: A process of biochemical change in which plant cells, using light as an energy source, manufacture simple sugars from oxygen and carbon dioxide.

Regeneration (forests): The renewal of a forest by natural processes (self-sown seed or root suckers), as well as by sowing or planting new tree stock.

Synthesis: Production of a substance by the union of elements or simpler chemical compounds.

Tailings: Residue of raw materials or waste separated out during the processing of wood or minerals products.

Tidal Marsh: Low, flat marshlands crossed by interlaced channels and tidal sloughs, and subject to tidal inundation from the ocean, normally, the only vegetation present is salt-tolerant rushes and grasses.

Tide: Alternate rising and falling of water levels twice each lunar day, due to gravitational attraction of the moon and the sun in conjunction with the Earth's rotational force.

Major Groups of Living Organisms

All life forms are classified in a hierarchical series of groups. Taxonomy, the science of such classification, was introduced by Swedish scientist, Carolus Linneaus (1707-78).

The purpose of classification is to provide each plant or animal on the planet with a unique name by which it is known; to describe it so it may be recognized by anyone; and to place it within a system that shows its relationship to other plants and animals.

The system is flexible, allowing updating as more is learned about individual species and their history.

Naming

The scientific naming of species involves two Latin names. The first word in the species name denotes the Genus the species belongs to. For example, the first word in the scientific name of the Monarch butterfly is *Danaus*. The Monarch belongs to the Genus Danaus.

The second word in the scientific name is particular to a species and can be quite arbitrary. Sometimes species names refer to a person, a country, a particular feature of the animal or plant, or a food source. The second word in the scientific name for the Monarch is plexippus. Thus, the scientific name of the Monarch is *Danaus plexippus*.

A species usually also has a common or more familiar name. For example, people seldom refer to the Monarch butterfly as Danaus plexippus.

Species

The basic level in the system is species. The interpretation of differences and similarities between species is often subjective; so the number and name of a species may change. Also new species are still being found and identified.

Genus

Species with a number of common features are grouped together in Genera. The number of different species in a genus can vary from one to several hundred. Again identification is subjective and the number of genera is not fixed.

Family

Genera are further grouped into Families. Butterfly genera are broadly divided into four major families: 1) Papilionidae (swallowtails); 2) Pierodae (whites and sulphurs); 3) Nymphalidae (brush-footed); and 4) Lycaenidae (hairstreaks, coppers, and blues).

Order

Families that share major characteristics are grouped into Orders. For example, butterflies, along with moths, belong to the Order Lepidoptera or insects with scales. The word comes from the Greek words *lepis* (scale) and *pteron* (wing). Classification at this level can be a very complex structure of orders, sub-orders, and sub-sub-orders.

Class

Further up the hierarchy, all Orders belong to a Class. Members of each class show characteristics indicating a common evolutionary descent.

Phylum

At the next level, butterflies, for example, are members of the Phylum Arthropoda, along with millipedes, spiders, and crustaceans, among others. The word Phylum comes from the Greek *phulon* or race.

Kingdom

At the highest level of the hierarchy, butterflies along with other living creatures, including humans, are members of the Animal Kingdom.

Extinct and Endangered Species in Canada, 1999

The following list has been prepared by the Committee on the Status of Endangered Wildlife in Canada.

The "Extinct" category refers to any species that was indigenous to Canada that no longer exists anywhere in the world. The "Extirpated" category refers to any species that no longer exists in the wild but does occur elsewhere. The "Endangered" category refers to any species threatened with imminent extinction or extirpation throughout all or most of its Canadian range.

For more information, visit http://www. speciesatrisk.gc. ca

SPECIES	HABITAT	YEAR DOCUMENTED
EXTINCT CATEGORY		
MAMMALS		
Caribou, Woodland (since 1920s)	(Queen Charlotte Islands population) BC	1984
Mink, Sea (since 1894)	NB, NF	1986
BIRDS		
Auk, Great (since 1844)	NB, NF, NS, QC	1985
Duck, Labrador (since 1875)	NB, NF, NS, QC	1985
Pigeon, Passenger (since 1914)	MB, NB, NS, ON, PE, QC, SK	1985
FISH		
Cisco, Deepwater (since 1952)	ON	1988
Cisco, Longjaw (since 1975)	ON	1985
Dace, Banff Longnose (since 1986)	AB	1987
Stickleback, Hadley Lake (benthic, limnetic)	BC	1999
Walleye, Blue (since 1965)	ON	1985
MOLLUSCA		
Limpet, Eelgrass (since 1929)	NF, NS, QC	1996
EXTIRPATED CATEGORY		
MAMMALS		
Bear, Grizzly (since 1880s)	(Prairie population) AB, MB, SK	1991
Ferret, Black-footed (since 1974)	AB, MB, SK	1978
Walrus, Atlantic (since 1850)	(Northwest Atlantic population)	1987
Whale, Gray (prior to 1800)	Atlantic population	1987
BIRDS		
Grouse, Sage (since 1960s)	BC population	1997
Prairie-Chicken, Greater (since 1987)	AB, MB, ON, SK	1990
REPTILES		
Lizard, Pygmy Short-horned (last rep. 1898)	BC population	1992
FISH		
Chub, Gravel (last rep. 1958)	ON	1987
Paddlefish (since 1917)	ON	1987
LEPIDOPTERA		
Butterfly, Karner Blue (last rep. 1991)	ON	1997
Elfin, frosted	ON	1999
Island Marble	BC	1999
PLANTS		
Blue-eyed Mary (last rep. 1954)	ON	1987
Trefoil, Illinois Tick (last rep. 1888)	ON	1991
ENDANGERED CATEGORY		
MAMMALS		
Caribou, Peary	(Banks Island population) NT	1991
Caribou, Peary	(High Arctic population) NT	1991
Fox, Swift	AB, SK	1998
Marmot, Vancouver Island	BC	1997
Marten	(Newfoundland population) NF	1996
Whale, Bowhead	(Eastern Arctic population)	1980
Whale, Bowhead	(Western Arctic population)	1986
Whale, Right	(Atlantic and Pacific Oceans)	1990
Whale, White (Beluga)	(St. Lawrence River population) QC	1997

Whale, White (Beluga)	(Ungava Bay population) NT	1988
Whale, White (Beluga)	(Southeast Baffin Island - Cumberland Sound population) NT	1990
Wolverine	(Eastern population) QC, NF (Labrador)	1989

BIRDS

Crane, Whooping	NT	1978
Curlew, Eskimo	NT	1978
Bobwhite, Northern	ON	1994
Duck, Harlequin	(Eastern population) NB, NF, NS, QC	1990
Flycatcher, Acadian	ON	1994
Grouse, Sage	AB, SK; prairie population	1998
Owl, Barn	ON, QC	1999
Owl, Burrowing	AB, BC, MB, SK	1995
Owl, Spotted	BC	1986
Plover, Mountain	AB, SK	1987
Plover, Piping	AB, MB, NB, NF, NS, ON, PE, QC, SK	1985
Rail, King	ON	1994
Shrike, Loggerhead	(Eastern population) MB, ON, QC	1991
Sparrow, Henslow's	ON	1993
Tern, Roseate	NS, QC	1999
Thrasher, Sage	AB, BC, SK	1992
Warbler, Kirtland's	ON, QC	1979
Warbler, Prothonotary	ON	1996

AMPHIBIANS

Frog, Northern Cricket[1]	ON	1990
Frog, Norther Leopard	Southern mountain population	1998

REPTILES

Snake, Blue Racer	ON	1991
Snake, Lake Erie Water	ON	1991
Snake, Sharp-tailed	BC	1999
Turtle, Leatherback	Atlantic and Pacific Oceans	1981

FISH

Dace, Nooksack	BC	1996
Sucker, Salish	BC	1986
Trout, Aurora	ON	1987
Whitefish, Acadian	NS	1984

MULLUSCS

Northern Riffleshell	ON	1999
Physa, Hotwater	north central BC	1998
Rayed Bean	ON	1999
Wavy-rayed hampmussel	ON	1999

LEPIDOPTERA

Butterfly, Maritime Ringlet	NB	1997

PLANTS

Agalinis, Gattinger's	ON	1988
Agalinis, Skinner's	ON	1988
Ammania, Scarlet	BC, ON	1999
Balsamroot, Deltoid	BC	1006
Bluehearts	southern ON	1998
Braya, Long's	NF	1997
Buttercup, Water-plantain	BC	1996
Cactus, Eastern Prickly Pear	ON	1998
Clover, Slender Bush	ON	1986
Coreopsis, Pink	NS	1984
Cryptanthe, Tiny	AB, SK	1998
Cucumber Tree	ON	1999
Fern, Southern Maidenhair	BC	1998
Gentian, White Prairie	ON	1991
Ginseng, American	ON, QC	1999
Goldenrod, Showy	ON	1999
Lady's-slipper, Small White	ON, MB	1981
Lotus, Seaside Birds-foot	BC	1996
Lousewort, Furbish's	NB	1998
Lupine, Prairie	BC	1996
Milkwort, Pink	ON	1998
Mint, Hoary Mountain	ON	1998
Mountain Avens, Eastern	NS	1986
Mouse-ear-cress, Slender	AB, SK	1992
Mulberry, Red	ON	1999
Orchid, Western Prairie White Fringed	MB	1993
Owl-Clover, Bearded	SW Vancouver Island	1998
Plantain, Heart-leaved	ON	1998
Pogonia, Large Whorled	ON	1998
Pogonia, Nodding	ON	1999

Pogonia, Small Whorled	ON	1998
Poppy, Wood	ON	1993
Quillwort, Engelmann's	ON	1992
Sedge, Juniper	ON	1999
Sundew, Thread-leaved	NS	1991
Thistle, Pitcher's	ON	1999
Toothcup	BC, ON	1999
Trillium, Drooping	ON	1996
Twayblade, Purple	ON	1999
Wintergreen, Spotted	ON	1998
LICHENS		
Seaside Centipede	BC	1996

Source: *Committee on Status of Endangered Wildlife in Canada*
(1) Formerly listed as Blanchard's Cricket Frog (*Acris crepitans blanchardi*)

Zoos and Aquariums*

Maritime Region:

☐ **Aquarium and Marine Centre**
2nd Avenue, Shippigan, NB E0B 2P0. Tel: (506) 336-4771. Entrance fee. Open May to September.

☐ **Cherry Brook Zoo**
Saint John, NB E2L 3W2. Tel: (506) 634-1440. Entrance fee. Open all year.

Central Canada:

☐ **Aquarium du Québec**
1675, avenue du Parc, Sainte-Foy, Quebec G1W 4S3 Tel: (418) 659-5266. Entrance fee. Open all year.

☐ **The Biodôme de Montréal**
An environmental museum. 4777, avenue Pierre-de-Coubertin, Montréal, Quebec H1V 1B3. Entrance fee. Open all year.

☐ **Jardin Zoologique de Québec**
8191, avenue du Zoo, Charlesbourg, Quebec G1G 4G4. Tel: (418) 622-0313. Entrance fee. Open all year.

☐ **Parc safari Africain**
823 Rt. 202, Hemmingford, Quebec J0L 1H0 Tel: (514) 247-2727. Entrance fee. Open mid-May to Labour Day.

☐ **Société Zoologique de Granby**
347, rue Bourget, Granby, Quebec J2G 1E8. Tel: (514) 372-9113. Entrance fee. Open May to September.

☐ **African Lion Safari**
R.R#1, Cambridge, Ontario N1R 5S2. Tel: (519) 623-2620. Entrance fee. Open summer.

☐ **Jungle Cat World**
R.R.#1, Orono, Ontario L0B 1M0. Tel: (416) 983-5016. Entrance fee. Open March to November.

☐ **Metro Toronto Zoo**
Meadowvale Road, Scarborough, Ontario M1E 4R5. Tel; (416) 392-5900. Entrance fee. Open all year.

☐ **Riverview Park and Zoo**
Peterborough, Ontario K9J 6Z5. Tel: (705) 748-9300 No charge. Open all year.

Western Canada:

☐ **Assiniboine Park Zoo**
2355 Corydon Avenue, Winnipeg, Manitoba R3P 0R5. Tel: (204) 986-6921. Entrance fee. Open all year.

☐ **Forestry Farm Zoo**
Saskatoon, Saskatchewan S7N 2H0. Tel: (306) 975-3382. Entrance fee. Open all year.

☐ **Calgary Zoo, Botanical Garden and Prehistoric Park**
1300 Z00 Road, Calgary, Alberta T2E 7V6. Tel: (403) 232-9300. Entrance fee. Open all year.

☐ **Valley Zoo**
Edmonton, Alberta T5J 2R7. Tel: (403) 496-6911. Entrance fee. Open all year.

☐ **Crystal Garden**
713 Douglas Street, Victoria, BC V8W 1N8. Tel: (604) 386-1356. Entrance fee. Open all year.

☐ **Kamloops Wildlife Park**
East Trans Canada Highway, Kamloops, BC V2C 5L7. Tel: (604) 573-3242. Entrance fee. Open all year.

☐ **Okanagan Game Farm**
Kaleden, BC V2A 6J9. Tel: (604) 497-5405. Entrance fee. Open all year.

☐ **Vancouver Game Farm**
5048, 264 Street, Aldergrove, BC V0X 1A0. Tel: (604) 856-6825. Entrance fee. Open all year.

☐ **Vancouver Public Aquarium**
Stanley Park, Vancouver, BC V6B 3X8. Tel: (604) 268-9900. Entrance fee. Open all year.

*Accredited by the Canadian Association of Zoological Parks and Aquariums

ARTS AND ENTERTAINMENT

Canada may well have been one of the best kept secrets on the world's arts and entertainment scene, but the secret is getting harder and harder to keep as artists like David Cronenberg, Alannis Morissette, Robert LePage, and Carol Shields make their mark. Historically, the small size and scattered nature of the Canadian market made dissemination of Canadian works of art and entertainment products difficult. But the years following World War II saw an explosion of activity in every sector, fuelled by public institutions such as the CBC, the Canada Council for the Arts, and the National Film Board and similar provincial and local agencies. Canadian content requirements for broadcasters and tax and investment measures favouring Canadian publishers have also helped foster successful, if fragile, publishing and recording industries. In 1996 all levels of government devoted $5.8 billion to culture (this includes federal support for the CBC and provincial and local support for public libraries). Restraints on public spending over the past two decades have caused emphasis to be placed on private investment and on production for foreign markets. During the 1990s, Film and TV production saw a 200 percent increase in foreign investment and a 33 percent increase in private sector Canadian investment. At the same time Canadian authors, agents and publishers found the sale of foreign rights to be a lucrative stream of revenue in a world hungry to read the work of writers such as Shields, Michael Ondaatje, Anne Michaels and Anne-Marie MacDonald.

MAJOR ARTS COUNCILS

The Canada Council: 350 Albert St, Box 1047, Ottawa, Ont., K1P 5V8; tel: (613) 566-4414 (toll-free:1-800-263-5588); fax: (613) 566-4390; e-mail: [employee name]@*canadacouncil.ca* (see personnel directory at website);website: *www.canadacouncil.ca*.

Alberta Foundation for the Arts: Alberta Community Development, 901 Standard Life Centre, 10405 Jasper Ave, Edmonton, Alta, T5J 4R7; tel: (780) 427-9968; fax: (780)422-9132; e-mail: *afa@mcd.gov.ab.ca*; Website: *http://www.affta.ab.ca*

British Columbia Arts Council: Box 9819, Stn. Prov. Govt., Victoria, BC, V8W 9W3; tel: (250) 356-1718; fax: (250) 387-4099; e-mail: csbinfo@tbc.gov.bc.ca; Website: *www.bcartscouncil.gov.bc.ca*

Manitoba Arts Council: 525-93 Lombard Avenue, Winnipeg, Man., R3B 3B1; tel: (204) 945-2237; fax: 945-5925; website: *www.gov.mb.ca/cgi-bin/print_hit_bold.pl/chc/archives/MAC/mac.html?Manitoba+Arts+Council#first_hit*

New Brunswick Arts Board: P.O. Box 6000, Fredericton, NB, E3B-5H1; tel: (506) 453-4307; fax (506) 453-6043; e-mail: *artsboard@gov.nb.ca*

Newfoundland and Labrador Arts Council: Box 98, St. John's, Nfld, A1C 5H5; tel: (709) 726-2212; fax: (709)726-0619; e-mail: *nlacmail@newcomm.net*; website: *www.nlac.nf.ca*

Northwest Territories Arts Council: Department of Education, Culture and Employment, Government of the Northwest Territories, Box 1320, Yellowknife, NWT, X1A 2L9; phone: (867) 920-3103; fax: (867) 873-0205

Nova Scotia Arts Council: P.O. Box 1559, CRO, Halifax, NS, B3J-2Y3; phone: (902) 422-1123; fax (902) 422-1445; e-mail: *nsartscouncil@ns.sympatico.ca*

Ontario Arts Council: 151 Bloor St. W., Toronto, ON M5S 1T6; phone: (416) 961-1660; fax: (416) 961-7796 (Toll-free: 1-800-387-0058); e-mail: *info@arts.on.ca*; website: *www.arts.on.ca*

P.E.I. Council of the Arts: tel:(902) 368-4410

Conseil des arts et des lettres du Quebec: Quebec bureau: 79, boulevard René-Lévesque Est, bureau 320, Quebec, G1R 5N5; tel: (418) 643-1707, (Toll-free) 1-800-897-1707; fax: (418) 643-4558; Montreal bureau: 500, Place d'Armes, 15e étage, Montréal, QC, H2Y 2W2; tel: (514) 864-3350, (Toll-free)1-800-608-3350; fax: (514) 864-4160; e-mail. *affaires.publiques@calq.gouv.qc.ca*; website: *www.calq.gouv.qc.ca/fr/index.htm*

Saskatchewan Arts Board: 3rd Floor, 3475 Albert Street Regina, Saskatchewan S4S 6X6; tel: (306) 787-4056, (Toll-free, Saskatchewan only)1-800-667-7526; fax: (306) 787-4199; e-mail: *sab@artsboard.sk.ca*

Yukon Tourism, Arts Branch: Box 2703, Whitehorse, Yukon,Y1A 2C6; tel: (867) 667-8589, (Toll-free within Yukon) 1-800-661-0408; fax: (867) 393-6456. e-mail: *arts@gov.yk.ca*; website: *www.artsykon.com*

TELEVISION

Television first reached Canada in the 1940s from border stations in the United States. The Canadian Broadcasting Corporation's TV services were launched in 1952. The launch in English Canada was less than auspicious; the first image to appear on the screen was the CBC logo presented upside down. The CBC recovered its poise and the network grew rapidly opening stations across the country and broadcasting its programs on affiliated private stations.

CBC TV was joined by the private Canadian Television Network in 1961. The CanWest/Global system began in the 1970s and has become Canada's third major television network. Through the 1980s and 1990s the CRTC has licensed dozens of specialty cable services to ensure that Canadian services offer viewers a full range of choices.

While the most-watched television programs in Canada continue to be American dramas and situation comedies, Canadian broadcasters have scored considerable success with programs such as *Wojek*, *The King of Kensington*, *Street Legal*, and *Due South*. Canadian producers have been particularly successful with children's programs such as *Mr. Dressup* and with sketch comedy programs including *The Wayne and Shuster Comedy Hour*, *This Hour Has 22 Minutes*, and *SCTV*.

Today the television market accounts for 70 percent of the 14,000 film projects undertaken in Canada each year. Much of that production is destined for air in the United States and other countries as international coproduction becomes an increasingly popular way of funding television programs around the world.

The Gemini Awards, 1998

The Gemini Awards were established in 1986 to honor outstanding contributions to the Canadian television industry. Given out annually by the Academy of Canadian Cinema and Television, the Geminis grew out of the former ACTRA Awards, last presented in 1985. These awards were presented Oct. 2, 1998. The 14th Geminis will be given out Nov. 5-7, 1999.

Dramatic series .... *Traders*
Comedy series .... *This Hour Has 22 Minutes*, Series V
TV movie .... *The Sleep Room*
Actor (dramatic series) .... Patrick McKenna, *Traders*, "In Vacuo"
Actor (dramatic program) .... Nicholas Campbell, *Major Crime*
Supporting actor (dramatic program or mini-series)—Diego, Matamoros, *The Sleep Room* ....
Supporting actor (dramatic series) .... Kris Lemche, *Emily of New Moon*, "Falling Angels"
Actress (dramatic series) .... Sheila McCarthy, *Emily of New Moon*, "The Enchanted Doll"
Actress (dramatic program) .... Liisa Repo-Martell, *Nights Below Station Street*
Supporting actress (dramatic program or mini-series) .... Nicky Guadagni, *Major Crime*
Supporting actress (dramatic series) .... Kim Huffman, *Traders*, "Hope Chasers"
Guest performance in a series by an actress .... Wendy Crewson, *Due South*, "Bounty Hunter"
Guest performance in a series by actor .... Brent Carver, *Due South*, "I Coulda Been a Defendant"
Performance (performing arts program or series) .... Yo-Yo Ma, *Yo-Yo Ma Inspired by Bach: Falling Down Stairs*
Performance (comedy program or series) Steve Smith, Patrick McKenna, *The New Red Green Show VII*, "The Movie"
Performance (variety program or series) .... Brent Carver, *Young At Heart*
Animated program or series .... *Stickin' Around*
Children's or Youth program or series .... *Ready or Not*
Documentary series .... *The Nature of Things With David Suzuki*
Lifestyle information series .... *Moving On*
Sports program .... *Sports Journal*
Information series .... *Undercurrents*
Performing arts program .... Yo-Yo Ma Inspired by Bach: Falling Down Stairs
Short dramatic program .... Yo-Yo Ma Inspired by Bach: Sarabande
Science, technology, nature and environment documentary program .... *Before Their Time*

Source: *Academy of Canadian Cinema and Television*

The Most–Watched Television Programs in Canada

(by adults 18+; Sept. 1, 1998–May 17, 1999)

Top 10 Regularly Scheduled Programs (Series)

1. NHL Playoffs (CBC)
2. *E.R.* (CTV)
3. *Ally McBeal* (CTV)
4. NHL Playoffs (CBC)
5. Celine Dion (CTV)
6. *L.A. Doctors* (CTV)
7. *Law and Order* (CTV)
8. *Bank of Montreal Figure Skating* (CTV)
9. World Skating Championships Prime (CTV)
10. *Royal Canadian Air Farce* (CBC)

Top 10 Programs

1. Academy Awards (CTV)
2. Academy Awards Pre-show (CTV)
3. Grammy Awards (CTV)
4. Grey Cup Game (CBC)
5. Emmy Awards (CTV)
6. Golden Globe Awards (CTV)
7. NHL Playoffs (CBC)
8. *E.R.* (CTV)
9. *Ally McBeal* (CTV)
10. *Barbara Walters* (CTV)

Source: *Nielsen Media Research*

The Prime-Time Emmy Awards, 1998–99

OUTSTANDING DRAMA SERIES ....*The Practice,* ABC

Actor (drama series) ....Dennis Franz, *NYPD Blue,* ABC

Actress (drama series) ....Edie Falco, *The Sopranos,* HBO

Supporting actor (drama series) ....Michael Badalucco, *The Practice,* ABC

Supporting actress (drama series)...Holland Taylor, *The Practice,* ABC

Directing (drama series) ....Paris Barclay, "Hearts And Souls," *NYPD Blue,* ABC

Writing (drama series)...............................James Manos, Jr., David Chase, "College," *The Sopranos,* HBO

OUTSTANDING COMEDY SERIES...*Ally McBeal,* FOX

Actor (comedy series) ....John Lithgow, *3rd Rock From The Sun,* NBC

Actress (comedy series) ....Helen Hunt, *Mad About You,* NBC

Supporting actor (comedy series) ....David Hyde Pierce, *Frasier,* NBC

Supporting actress (comedy series) ....Kristen Johnston, *3rd Rock From The Sun,* NBC

Directing (comedy series) ....Thomas Schlamme, pilot, *Will & Grace,* NBC

Writing (comedy series).............................Jay Kogen, "Merry Christmas, Mrs. Moskowitz," *Frasier,* NBC

OUTSTANDING MINISERIES...*Horatio Hornblower,* A&E

Actor (miniseries or movie) ....Stanley Tucci, *Winchell,* HBO

Actress (miniseries or movie) ....Helen Mirren, *The Passion Of Ayn Rand,* Showtime

Supporting actor (miniseries or movie).........................Peter O'Toole, *Joan Of Arc,* CBS

Supporting actress (miniseries or movie).........................Anne Bancroft, *Deep In My Heart,* CBS

Directing (miniseries or movie) ....Allan Arkush, *The Temptations,* NBC

OUTSTANDING VARIETY, MUSIC OR COMEDY SERIES ....*Late Show with David Letterman,* CBS

OUTSTANDING VARIETY, MUSIC OR COMEDY SPECIAL ....*The 1998 Tony Awards,* CBS

Directing (variety or music) ....Paul Miller, *1998 Tony Awards,* CBS

Writing (variety or music) ....Tom Agna, Vernon Chatman, Louis CK, Lance Crouther, Gregory Greenberg, Ali LeRoi, Steve O'Donnell, Chris Rock, Frank Sebastiano, Chuck Sklar, Jeff Stilson, Wanda Sykes-Hall, Mike Upchurch, *The Chris Rock Show,* HBO

OUTSTANDING TV MOVIE ....*Don King: Only in America,* HBO

Source: *Academy of Television Arts and Science*

Television Networks and Cable Services

Arts & Entertainment Network (A&E): 235 E 45th St, New York, NY 10017. (212) 210-1328

Atlantic Television System & Atlantic Satellite Network: Box 1653, 2885 Robie St, Halifax, N.S. B3K 4P5. (902) 453-4000.

Bravo!: 299 Queen St W, Toronto, Ont. M5V 2Z5 (416) 591-5757

C-SPAN (Cable Satellite Public Affairs Network): 400 N. Capitol St. NW, Suite 650, Washington, DC 20001. (202) 737-3220

Cable News Network (CNN): 1 CNN Centre, Box 105366, Atlanta, GA 30348-5366. (404) 827-1700

Canadian Broadcasting Corporation (CBC): Box 500 Stn. A, Toronto, Ont. M5W 1E6. (416) 205-3311

Canal Famille: 2100 Sainte-Catherine ouest, Bureau 800, Montreal, Que. H3H 2T3. (514) 939-3150

CanWest/Global Communications Corp.: 201 Portage Ave, 31st Flr, TD Centre, Winnipeg, Man. R3B 3L7. (204) 956-2025

Capital Cities/ABC, Inc.: 77 W 66th St, New York, NY 10023-6298. (212) 456-7777

CHUM Limited: 1331 Yonge St, Toronto, Ont. M4T 1Y1. (416) 925-6666.

Columbia Broadcasting System (CBS): 51 W 52nd St, New York, NY 10019. (212) 975-4321

Country Music Television: 2806 Opreyland Dr., Nashville, TN 37214. (615) 871-5830

CTV Television Network Ltd.: Box Stn. O, 9 Channel Ct., Toronto, Ont. M4A 2M9. (416) 595-4100

Discovery Channel: 2225 Sheppard Ave E, Suite 100, Toronto, Ont. M2J 5C2

The Family Channel Inc.: BCE Place, 181 Bay St., Box 787, Toronto, Ont. M5J 2T3. (416) 956-2030

Fox Broadcasting Co.: P.O. Box 900, Beverly Hills, CA 90213-0900. (310) 369-1000

Global Television Network: 81 Barber Greene Rd, Don Mills, Ont. M3C 2A2 (416) 446-5311

Inuit Broadcasting Corporation: 217 Laurier Ave W, Ste 703, Ottawa, Ont. K1P 5J6. (613) 235-1892

Life Network: 1155 Leslie St, Toronto, Ont. M3C 2J6. (416) 444-9494

Maclean Hunter Limited: 777 Bay St, Toronto, Ont. M5W 1A7. (416) 596-5103

The Movie Network/First Choice: BCE Place, 181 Bay St., Box 787, Toronto, Ont. M5J 2T3. (416) 956-2010

MuchMusic Network: 299 Queen St W, Toronto, Ont. M5V 2Z5. (416) 591-5757

MusiquePlus: 1355 Sainte-Catherine est, Montreal, Que. H3B 1A5. (514) 284-7587

National Broadcasting Company (NBC): 30 Rockefeller Plaza, New York, NY 10112. (212) 664-4444

Premier Choix TVEC Inc.: 2100 Sainte-Catherine ouest, #800 Montreal, Que. H3H 2T3. (514) 939-3150

Public Broadcasting Service (PBS): 1320 Braddock Place, Alexandria, VA 22314-1698. (703) 739-5000

Le Reseau des Sports: 1755 Boul. René-Lévesque est, Bur. 300, Montreal, Que. H2K 4P6. (514) 599-2244

Rogers Broadcasting Ltd.: 36 Victoria St, Toronto, Ont. M5C 1H3. (416) 864-2000

Showcase Television Inc.: 121 Bloor St E, #200, Toronto, Ont. M4W 1B9 (416) 967-2473

Société de radio-télévision du Quebec (Radio-Quebec): 800, rue Fullum, Montreal, Que. H2K 3L7. (514) 521-2424

The Sports Network (TSN): 2225 Sheppard Ave E, Suite 100, Willowdale, Ont. M2J 5C2. (416) 494-1212

Telelatino Network Inc.: 5125 Steeles Ave W, Weston, Ont. M9L 1R5. (416) 744-8200

TVOntario (TVO): Box 200, Stn Q, Toronto, Ont. M4T 2T1. (416) 484-2600

Vision TV: 80 Bond St, Toronto, Ont. M5B 1X2. (416) 368-3194

The Weather Channel: 1 Robert Speck Parkway, Ste 1600, Mississauga, Ont. L4Z 4B3. (905) 566-9511

Women's Television Network: 300-1661 Portage Ave, Winnipeg, Man. R3J 3T7. (204) 783-5116

YTV Canada Inc.: 64 Jefferson Ave, Unit 18, Toronto, Ont. M6K 3H3. (416) 534-1191

POPULAR MUSIC

The watershed year in the Canadian music industry was 1971, when the federal government imposed Canadian content regulations on the country's radio stations. These regulations helped build a domestic recording industry that has produced several generations of world-class pop stars including Bryan Adams, Céline Dion, Sarah MacLauchlan and Shania Twain.

Montreal, Toronto, and Vancouver have consistently served as centres for the Canadian popular music industry. But other cities have served as hotbeds at various periods. Winnipeg in the 1960s was dubbed the Liverpool of Canada for a scene that launched the careers of Neil Young and

the Guess Who. The Ottawa Valley has long been a place of musical ferment owing to the interaction of the its Irish, Scottish, and French settlers. Bruce Cockburn and Alannis Morrissette are two of the National Capital Region's best known alumni.

Nova Scotia and Newfoundland have historically been home to vibrant Celtic folk traditions and the 1990s saw the rise of Atlantic Canada as a major centre for music production in Canada. Those traditions have been parlayed into commercial success for artists such as The Rankins, singer Rita MacNeil, and folk/rock fiddlers Ashley MacIsaac and Natalie McMaster.

The Juno Awards, 1989–99

The Juno Awards were established in 1975 to honor achievement in the Canadian recording industry. The name was chosen to honor Pierre Juneau, former head of the Canadian Radio-television and Telecommunications Commission (CRTC) which instituted "Canadian content" requirements in the nation's broadcast industry.

Nominations for most major Juno categories are determined by record sales, although the actual

winners are selected by a vote of members of the Canadian Academy of Recording Arts & Sciences.

There were no awards presented in 1988. Following the Nov. 1987 awards, the presentation of the Junos was moved from the fall to the spring so that the next awards were presented in the spring of 1989. The 1989 awards cover 1988 releases.

The 1999 awards were announced   , 1999.

Canadian Entertainer of the Year

1989	Glass Tiger
1990	The Jeff Healey Band
1991	The Tragically Hip
1992	Bryan Adams
1993	The Tragically Hip
1994	The Rankin Family
1995	The Tragically Hip
1996	Shania Twain

International Achievement Award

1997	Celine Dion/Alanis Morissette/Shania Twain

Album of the Year

1989	*Robbie Robertson*, Robbie Robertson
1990	*Alannah Myles*, Alannah Myles
1991	*Unison*, Celine Dion
1992	*Mad Mad World*, Tom Cochrane
1993	*Ingenue*, k.d. lang
1994	*Harvest Moon*, Neil Young
1995	*Colour of My Love*, Celine Dion
1996	*Jagged Little Pill*, Alanis Morissette
1997	*Trouble at the Henhouse*, The Tragically Hip
1998	*Clumsy*, Our Lady Peace
1999	*Let's Talk About Love*, Celine Dion

Single of the Year

1989	"Try," Blue Rodeo
1990	"Black Velvet," Alannah Myles
1991	"Just Came Back," Colin James
1992	"Life Is a Highway," Tom Cochrane
1993	"Beauty and the Beast," Celine Dion/Peabo Bryson
1994	"Fare Thee Well I ove," The Rankin Family
1995	"Could I Be Your Girl," Jann Arden
1996	"You Oughta Know," Alanis Morissette
1997	"Ironic," Alanis Morissette
1998	"Building a Mystery," Sarah McLachlan
1999	"One Week," Barenaked Ladies

Female Vocalist of the Year

1989	k.d. lang
1990	Rita MacNeil
1991	Celine Dion
1992	Celine Dion
1993	Celine Dion
1994	Celine Dion
1995	Jann Arden
1996	Alanis Morissette
1997	Celine Dion
1998	Sarah McLachlan
1999	Celine Dion

Male Vocalist of the Year

1989	Robbie Robertson
1990	Kim Mitchell
1991	Colin James
1992	Tom Cochrane
1993	Leonard Cohen
1994	Roch Voisine
1995	Neil Young
1996	Colin James
1997	Bryan Adams ▶

▶ 1998 . . . . Paul Brandt
1999 . . . . Jim Cuddy

Group of the Year
1989 . . . . Blue Rodeo
1990 . . . . Blue Rodeo
1991 . . . . Blue Rodeo
1992 . . . . Crash Test Dummies
1993 . . . . Barenaked Ladies
1994 . . . . The Rankin Family
1995 . . . . The Tragically Hip
1996 . . . . Blue Rodeo
1997 . . . . The Tragically Hip
1998 . . . . Our Lady Peace
1999 . . . . Barenaked Ladies

Songwriter of the Year
1989 . . . . Rita MacNeil, Tom Cochrane (tie)
1990 . . . . Greg Keelor and Jim Cuddy
1991 . . . . David Tyson
1992 . . . . Tom Cochrane
1993 . . . . k.d. lang
1994 . . . . Leonard Cohen
1995 . . . . Jann Arden
1996 . . . . Alanis Morissette (with Glen Ballard)
1997 . . . . Alanis Morissette (with Glen Ballard)
1998 . . . . Sarah McLachlan/Pierre Marchand
1999 . . . . Bryan Adams,(w' co-songwriter)
Phil Thornalley "On A Day Like Today;"
(w' co-songwriter) Eliott Kennedy,"When You're Gone"

Best New Solo Artist
1994 . . . . Jann Arden
1995 . . . . Susan Aglukark
1996 . . . . Ashley MacIsaac
1997 . . . . Terri Clark
1998 . . . . Holly McNarland
1999 . . . . Melanie Doane

Best New Group
1994 . . . . The Waltons
1995 . . . . Moist
1996 . . . . The Philosopher Kings
1997 . . . . The Killjoys
1998 . . . . Leahy
1999 . . . . Johnny Favourite Swing Orchestra

Best Selling Francophone Album
1994 . . . . *Album de Peuple: Tome 2*
1995 . . . . *Coup de tête*
1996 . . . . *D'eux*
1997 . . . . *Live À Paris*
1998 . . . . Marie Michèle Desrosiers
Chante Les Classiques de Noël
1999 . . . . . . *S'il Suffisait D'Aimer*, Celine Dion

Country Female Vocalist of the Year
1989 . . . . k.d. lang
1990 . . . . k.d. lang
1991 . . . . Rita MacNeil
1992 . . . . Cassandra Vasik
1993 . . . . Michelle Wright
1994 . . . . Cassandra Vasik

1995 . . . . Michelle Wright
1996 . . . . Shania Twain
1997 . . . . Shania Twain
1998 . . . . Shania Twain
1999 . . . . Shania Twain

Country Male Vocalist of the Year
1989 . . . . Murray McLauchlan
1990 . . . . George Fox
1991 . . . . George Fox
1992 . . . . George Fox
1993 . . . . Gary Fjellgaard
1994 . . . . Charlie Major
1995 . . . . Charlie Major
1996 . . . . Charlie Major
1997 . . . . Paul Brandt
1998 . . . . Paul Brandt
1999 . . . . Paul Brandt

Country Group or Duo of the Year
1989 . . . . The Family Brown
1990 . . . . The Family Brown
1991 . . . . Prairie Oyster
1992 . . . . Prairie Oyster
1993 . . . . Tracey Prescott & Lonesome Daddy
1994 . . . . The Rankin Family
1995 . . . . Prairie Oyster
1996 . . . . Prairie Oyster
1997 . . . . The Rankin Family
1998 . . . . Farmer's Daughter
1999 . . . . Leahy

Best Hard Rock Album
1991 . . . . *Presto*, Rush
1992 . . . . *Roll the Bones*, Rush
1993 . . . . *Doin' the Nasty*, Slik Toxik
1994 . . . . *Dig*, I. Mother Earth
1995 . . . . . *Suffersystem*, Monster Voodoo Machine
1996 . . . . *Jagged Little Pill*, Alanis Morissette

Best Alternative Album
1991 . . . . *One Chord to Another*, Sloan
1998 . . . . *Glee*, Bran Van 3000
1999 . . . . *Rufus Wainwright*, Rufus Wainwright

Best Rap Recording
1991 . . . . "Symphony in Effect," Maestro Fresh-Wes
1992 . . . . "My Definition of a Boombastic Jazz Style,"
Dream Warriors
1993 . . . . *Keep It Slammin'*, Devon
1994 . . . . *One Track Mind*, TBTBT
1995 . . . . *Certified*, Ghetto Concept
1996 . . . . *E-Z On Tha Motion*, Ghetto Concept
1997 . . . . *What It Takes*, Choclair
1998 . . . . *Cash Crop*, Rascalz
1999 . . . . *Northern Touch*, Rascalz featuring
Choclair, Kardinal Offishall, Thrust and Checkmate

Best Dance Recording
1990 . . . . "I Beg Your Pardon (I Never Promised You a
Rose Garden)," Kon Kan
1991 . . . . "Don't Wanna Fall in Love," Jane Child ▶

▶ 1992........ "Everyone's a Winner (Chocolate Movement
Mix)," Bootsauce
1993 . "Love Can Move Mountains (Club Mix)," Celine Dion
1994 .... "Thankful (Raw Club Mix)," Red Light
1995 .... "Higher Love (Club Mix)," Capital Sound
1996 .. "A Deeper Shade of Love (Extended Mix)," Camille
1997 .... "Astroplane" (City of Love Mix), BKS
1998 ..... "Euphoria" (Rabbit in the Moon Mix), Delerium
1999...................... Broken Bones, Love Inc.

Best Contemporary Jazz Album

1989 .... Looking Up, The Hugh Fraser Quintet
1990 .... Skydance, Jon Ballantyne Trio featuring Joe
Henderson
1991 .... Two Sides, Mike Murley
1992................... For the Moment, Renee Rosnes;
In Transition, Brian Dickinson; The Brass Is Back,
Rob McConnell and The Boss Brass
1993........................... My Ideal, P.J. Perry
1994 .... Don't Smoke in Bed, Holly Cole Trio
1995 .. The Merlin Factor, Jim Hillman & The Merlin Factor
1996 .... NOJO, Neufeld-Occhipinti Jazz Orchestra
1997 .... Africville Suite, Joe Sealy
1998...................... Metalwood, Metalwood
1999..................... Metalwood 2, Metalwood

Best Mainstream Jazz Album

1994 . Fables and Dreams, Dave Young/Phil Dwyer Quartet
1995...................... Free Trade, Free Trade
1996 ...., Vernal Fields, Ingrid Jensen
1997 .... Ancestors, Renee Rosnes
1998 .... In the Mean Time, The Hugh Fraser Quintet
1999 .... The Atlantic Sessions, Kirk MacDonald

Best R&B/Soul Recording

1989 .... "Angel," Erroll Star
1990................. "Spellbound," Billy Newton-Davis
1991 .... "Dance to the Music (Work Your Body),"
Simply Majestic Featuring B. Kool
1992................... "Call My Name," Love & Sas
1993 .... "Once in a Lifetime," Love & Sas
1994 .... "The Time is Right,"Rupert Gayle
1995........ "First Impressions for the Bottom Jigglers,"
Bass is Base
1996 .... "Deborah Cox," Deborah Cox
1997 .... "Feelin' Alright," Carlos Morgan
1998 .... Things Just Ain't the Same, Deborah Cox
1999 .... One Wish, Deborah Cox

Best Blues/Gospel Album

1994 .... South at Eight/North at Nine, Colin Linden
1995 .... Joy to the World Jubilation V,
Montreal Jubilation Gospel Choir
1996 .... That River, Jim Byrnes
1997 .... Right To Sing The Blues, Long John Baldry

Best Blues Album

1998................... National Steel, Colin James
1999.................... Blues Weather, Fathead

Best Gospel Album

1998 .... Romantics and Mystics, Steve Bell
1999 .... Life Is, Sharon Riley & Faith Chorale

Best Reggae/Calypso Recording

1989................. Conditions Critical, Lillian Allen
1990............ Too Late To Turn Back Now, Sattalites
1991 .... Soldiers We Are All, Jayson & Friends
1994 .... Informer, Snow
1995 .... Class and Credential, Carla Marshall
1996 .... Now and Forever, Sattalites
1997 .... Nana Maclean, Nana Maclean
1998 .... Catch de Vibe, Messenjah
1999 .... Vision, Frankie Wilmot

Best Global Album

1992 .... The Gathering, Various Artists
1993 .... Spirits of Havana, Jane Bunnett
1994 .... El Camino Real, Ancient Cultures
1995+.......................... Africa+, Eval Manigat
1996 .... Music From Africa, Takadja
1997 .... Africa Do Brasil, Paulo Ramos Group
1998 .... La Llorona, Lhasa
1999 .... La Llorona, Lhasa

Best Roots and Traditional Album

1989...... The Return of the Formily Brothers, The Amos
Garrett, Doug Sahm, Gene Taylor Band
1990 ..... Je Voudrais Changer D'Chapeau, La Bottine
Souriante
1991 .... Dance & Celebrate, Bourne & MacLeod
1992..... Saturday Night Blues, Various Artists; The Visit,
Loreena McKennitt
1993..... Jusqu'aux P'tites Heures, La Bouttine Souriante
1994 .... My Okios, Jamoo Koolaghan
1995 .... The Mask and Mirror, Loreena McKennitt
1996 ... Hi: How Are You Today?, Ashley MacIsaac (solo);
Gypsies & Lovers, The Irish Descendants (group)
1997............ drive-in movie, Fred Eaglesmith (solo);
Matapedia, Kate & Anna McGarrigle (group)
1998 .... Other Songs, Ron Sexsmith (solo)
Molinos, The Paperboys (group)
1999 .... Heartstrings, Willie P. Bennett (solo)
The McGarrigle Hour, Kate & Anna McGarrigle (group)

Instrumental Artist(s) of the Year

1989 .... David Foster
1990 .... Manteca
1991 .... Ofra Harnoy
1992 .... Shadowy Men on a Shadowy Planet
1993 .... Ofra Harnoy
1994 .... Ofra Harnoy
1995 .... André Gagnon
1996 .... Liona Boyd
1997 .... Ashley MacIsaac
1998 .... Leahy

Best Instrumental Album

1999 ...... My Roots Are Showing, Natalie MacMaster

Best Classical Album (solo or chamber ensemble)

1989........ Schubert: Arpeggione Sonata, Ofra Harnoy
1990 .... 20th Century Original Piano Transcriptions,
Louis Lortie
1991 .. Schafer: Five String Quartets, Orford String Quartet
1992 ..... Franz Liszt: Années de Pelerinage, Louis Lortie ▶

▶ 1993 . . . . *Beethoven: Piano Sonatas*, Louis Lortie
1994 . . . . *Beethoven: Piano Sonatas, Op. 10, No. 1-3*,
Louis Lortie
1995 . . . . *Erica Goodman Plays Canadian Harp Music*,
Erica Goodman
1996. *Aikan: Grande Sonate/Sonatine*, Marc-André Hamelin
1997 . . . . *Scriabin: The Complete Piano Sonatas*,
Marc-Andre Hamelin
1998 . . . . *Marc-André Hamelin plays Franz Liszt*,
Marc-André Hamelin
1999 . . . . *Bach: Well-Tempered Clavier - Book 1*,
Angela Hewitt

Best Classical Album (large ensemble)
1989 . . . . *Bartok: Concerto for Orchestra; Music for
Strings, Percussion and Celesta*, Montreal
Symphony and Orchestra, Charles Dutoit
1990   *Boccherini: Cello Concertos and Symphonies*,
Tafelmusik Baroque Orchestra
1991 . . . . *Debussy: Images, Nocturnes*, Orchestre
. . . . Symphonique de Montréal, Charles Dutoit
1992 . . . . *Debussy: Pelleas et Melisande*, Orchestre
Symphonique de Montréal, Charles Dutoit
1993 . . . . . *Handel: Excerpts from Floridante*, Tafelmusik
1994 . . *Handel: Concerti Grossi, Op. 3, No. 1-6*, Tafelmusik
1995 . . *Bach: Brandenburg Concertos Nos. 1-6*, Tafelmusik
1996 . . . . *Shostakovich: Symphonies 5 & 9, Orchestra
Symphonique de Montréal*
1997 . . . . *Ginastera/Villa-Lobos/Evangelista*,
I Musici de Montreal
1998 . . . . *Mozart Horn Concertos*, James Sommerville,
CBC Vancouver Orchestra, Mario Bernardi
1999 . . . . *Handel: Music For The Royal Fireworks*,
Tafelmusik, Jeanne Lamon (Musical Director)

Best Classical Album (vocal or choral performance)
1995 . . . . *Berlioz: Les Troyens*, Vocal Soloists,
Choeur et Orchestre symphonique de Montréal
1995 . . *Ben Heppner Sings Richard Strauss*, Ben Heppner,
Toronto Symphony Orchestra, Andrew Davis, conductor
1997 . . *Berlioz: La Damnation de Faust*, Choeur et Orchestre
symphonique de Montreal, Charles Dutoit, Conductor
1998 . . . . . *Soirée Francaise*, Michel Schade, Russel Braun,
Canadian Opera Company Orchestra,
Richard Bradshaw
1999 . . . . *Songs Of Travel*, Gerald Finley (baritone),
Stephen Ralls (piano)

Best Classical Composition
1989 . . . . *Songs of Paradise*, Alexina Louie
1990 . . . . *Concerto For Harp and Chamber Orchestra/
Morawetz Harp Concertos*, Oskar Morawetz
1991 . . . . *String Quartet No. 5 'Rosalind'*
R. Murray Schafer
1992 . . . . *Concerto For Piano & Chamber Orchestra*,
Michael Conway Baker
1993 . . . . *Concerto for Flute and Orchestra*,
R. Murray Schafer
1994 . . . . *Among Friends*, Chan Ka Nin

1995 . . . . *Sketches From Natal*, Malcolm Forsyth
1996 . . . . *Concerto For Violin and Orchestra*,
Andrew P. MacDonald
1997 . . . . *Picasso Suite*, Harry Somers
1998 . . . . *Electra Rising*, Malcolm Forsyth
1999 . . . . . *Concerto For Wind Orchestra*, Colin McPhee

Best Children's Album
1989 . . . . *Fred Penner's Place*, Fred Penner; *Lullaby
Berceuse*, Connie Kaldor & Carmen Campagne
1990 . . . . . . *Beethoven Lives Upstairs*, Susan Hammond &
Barbara Nichol
1991 . . . . *Mozart's Magic Fantasy*, Susan Hammond/
Classical Kids
1992 . . . . *Vivaldi's Ring of Mystery*, Susan Hammond/
Classical Kids
1993 . . . . *Waves of Wonder*, Jack Grunsky
1994 . . . . *Tchaikovsky Discovers America*,
SusanHammond/Classical Kids
1995 . . . . *Bananaphone*, Raffi
1996 . . . . *Celery Stalks at Midnight*, Al Simmons
1997 . . . . *Songs From the Treehouse*, Martha Johnson
1998 . . . . *Livin' in a Shoe*, Judy & David
1999 . *Mozart's Magnificent Voyage*, Susan Hammond's
Classical Kids

Producer of the Year
1989 . . . . Daniel Lanois and Robbie Robertson
1990 . . . . Bruce Fairbairn
1991 . . . . David Tyson
1992 . . . . Bryan Adams
1993 . . . . . . k.d. lang/Ben Mink (Greg Penny, co-producer)
1994 . . . . Steve MacKinnon/Marc Jordan
(Greg Penny, co-producer)
1995 . . . . Robbie Robertson
1996 . . . . Michael-Phillip Wojewoda
1997 . . . . Garth Richardson
1998 . . . . Pierre Marchand
1999 . . . . Colin James (co-producer, Joe Hardy)

Best Video of the Year
1989 . . . . *Try* (Blue Rodeo), Michael Buckley
1990 . . . . . *Boomtown* (Andrew Cash), Cosimo Cavallaro
1991 . . . . *Drop the Needle* (Maestro Fresh-Wes), Joel
Goldberg
1992 . . . . *Into the Fire* (Sarah McLachlan), Phil Kates
1993 . . . . . *Closing Time* (Leonard Cohen), Curtis Wehrfritz
1994 . . . . *I Would Die For You* (Jann Arden), Jeth Weinrich
1995 . . . . *Tunnel of Trees* (Gogh Van Go), Lyne Charlebois
1996 . . . . *Good Mother* (Jann Arden), Jeth Weinrich
1997 . . . . *Burned Out Car* (Junkhouse), Jeth Weinrich
1998 . . . . *Gasoline* (Moist), Javier Aguilera
1999 . . . . Javier Aguilera, *Forestfire* (David Usher)

Best Music of Aboriginal Canada Recording
1995 . . . . Susan Aglukark
1996 . . . . Jerry Alfred & The Medicine Beat
1997 . . . . Buffy Ste. Marie

Source: *Canadian Academy of Recording Arts & Sciences*

Canadian Country Music Awards, 1998

Awards and citations from the CCMA were presented September 13, 1999 during Country Music Week. These were the eighteenth annual awards, the sixth to be broadcast in the US and Europe.

FANS' CHOICE AWARD:	Shania Twain
FEMALE ARTIST OF THE YEAR	Shania Twain
MALE ARTIST OF THE YEAR	Paul Brandt
SINGLE OF THE YEAR	"26 Cents," The Wilkinsons
ALBUM OF THE YEAR	*Nothing But Love*, The Wilkinsons
VOCAL DUO OR GROUP OF THE YEAR	The Wilkinsons
MUSIC VIDEO OF THE YEAR	"That Don't Impress Me Much," Shania Twain
SONG OF THE YEAR	Steve Wilkinson and William Wallace, "26 Cents"
VOCAL/INSTRUMENTAL COLLABORATION	Shania Twain and Bryan White, "From This Moment On"
RISING STAR	The Wilkinsons

Source: *Canadian Country Music Awards*

Top 50 Albums in Canada, 1998

1. *Titanic*, Various Artists
2. *Now! 3*, Various Artists
3. *Big Shiny Tunes 2*, Various Artists
4. *Spice World*, Spice Girls
5. *Aquarium*, Aqua
6. ***Let's Talk About Love*, Celine Dion**
7. *Savage Garden*, Savage Garden
8. *City of Angels*, Various Artists
9. *Romanza*, Andrea Bocelli
10. *Ray of Light*, Madonna
11. *Backstreet's Back*, Backstreet Boys
12. *Armageddon*, Various Artists
13. *Never Say Never*, Brandy
14. ***Come On Over*, Shania Twain**
15. ***Surfacing*, Sarah McLachlan**
16. *Hello Nasty*, Beastie Boys
17. *Notre Dame de Paris*, Various Artists
18. *N'Sync*, N'Sync
19. *Women In Song*, Various Artists
20. *Hit Zone 4*, Various Artists
21. *All Saints*, All Saints
22. ***Phantom Power*, The Tragically Hip**
23. *Yourself or Someone Like You*, Matchbox 20
24. *Big Willie Style*, Will Smith
25. *Much Dance 1997*, Various Artists
26. *Spice*, Spice Girls
27. *Left of the Middle*, Natalie Imbruglia
28. *Groove Station 4*, Various Artists
29. *Godzilla*, Various Artists
30. *Bullworth*, Various Artists
31. *Urban Hymns*, The Verve
32. ***On a Day Like Today*, Bryan Adams**
33. ***Unplugged*, Bryan Adams**
34. *The Velvet Rope*, Janet Jackson
35. ***These Are Special Times*, Celine Dion**
36. *Yield*, Pearl Jam
37. ***Supposed Former Infatuation Junkie*, Alanis Morissette**
38. *Adore*, The Smashing Pumpkins
39. *The Miseducation of Lauryn Hill*, Lauryn Hill
40. ***The Book of Secrets*, Loreena McKennitt**
41. *The Wedding Singer*, Various Artists
42. *The Boy Is Mine*, Monica
43. *Love Inc.*, Love Inc.
44. *Harlem World*, Mase
45. *Best Of*, U2
46. *Pilgrm*, Eric Clapton
47. *Hellbilly Deluxe*, Rob Zombie
48. ***Clumsy*, Our Lady Peace**
49. *My Own Prison*, Creed
50. *Hits 1981-1990*, Phil Collins

Source: *RPM Weekly*

*Canadian artists set in bold face

The Grammy Awards, 1988–98

Grammy winners are selected annually by the 6,000 voting members of The Recording Academy, based on artistic and/or technical excellence. The titles for song of the year are followed by the names of the songwriters. The 1998 Grammy winners were announced Feb. 24, 1999.

Best Record

1988 "Don't Worry, Be Happy," Bobby McFerrin

1989 "Wind Beneath My Wings," Bette Midler

1990 "Another Day In Paradise," Phil Collins

1991 "Unforgettable," Natalie Cole (with Nat King Cole)

1992 "Tears in Heaven," Eric Clapton

1993 "I Will Always Love You," Whitney Houston

1994 "All I Wanna Do,' Sheryl Crow

1995 "Kiss From A Rose," Seal

1996 "Change the World," Eric Clapton

1997 "Sunny Came Home," Shawn Colvin

1998 "My Heart Will Go On," Celine Dion

Best Album

1988 *Faith,* George Michael

1989 *Nick of Time*, Bonnie Raitt

1990 *Back On The Block*, Quincy Jones

1991 *Unforgettable*, Natalie Cole

1992 *Unplugged*, Eric Clapton

1993 *The Bodyguard–Original Soundtrack Album*, Whitney Houston

1994 *MTV Unplugged*, Tony Bennett

1995 *Jagged Little Pill*, Alanis Morissette

1996 *Falling Into You*, Celine Dion

1997 *Time Out Of Mind*, Bob Dylan

1998 *The Miseducation of Lauryn Hill,* Lauryn Hill

Best Song

1988 "Don't Worry, Be Happy," Bobby McFerrin

1989 "Wind Beneath My Wings," Larry Henley, Jeff Silbar

1990 "From A Distance," Julie Gold

1991 "Unforgettable," Irving Gordon

1992 "Tears in Heaven," Eric Clapton, Will Jennings

1993 "A Whole New World (Aladdin's Theme)," Alan Menken, Tim Rice

1994 "Streets of Philadelphia," Bruce Springsteen

1995 "Kiss From A Rose," Seal

1996 "Change the World," Eric Clapton, Wynonna

1997 "Sunny Came Home," Shawn Colvin

1998 "My Heart Will Go On," James Harper, Will Jennings

Best Male Pop Vocal

1988 "Don't Worry, Be Happy," Bobby McFerrin

1989 "How Am I Supposed to Live Without You," Michael Bolton

1990 "Oh, Pretty Woman," Roy Orbison

1991 "When a Man Loves a Woman," Michael Bolton

1992 "Tears in Heaven," Eric Clapton

1993 "If I Ever Lose My Faith in You," Sting

1994 "Can You Feel the Love Tonight," Elton John

1995 "Kiss From A Rose," Seal

1996 "Change the World," Eric Clapton

1997 "Candle in the Wind 1997," Elton John

1998 "My Father's Eyes," Eric Clapton

Best Female Vocal

1988 "Fast Car," Tracy Chapman

1989 "Nick of Time," Bonnie Raitt

1990 "Vision Of Love," Mariah Carey

1991 "Something to Talk About," Bonnie Raitt

1992 "Constant Craving," k.d. lang

1993 "I Will Always Love You," Whitney Houston

1994 "All I Wanna Do," Sheryl Crow

1995 "No More 'I Love You's'," Annie Lennox

1996 "Un-Break My Heart," Toni Braxton

1997 "Building A Mystery," Sarah McLachlan

1998 "My Heart Will Go On," Celine Dion

Best New Artist

1988 Tracy Chapman

1989[1] Withdrawn

1990 Mariah Carey

1991 Mark Cohn

1992 Arrested Development

1993 Toni Braxton

1994 Sheryl Crow

1995 Hootie & The Blowfish

1996 LeAnn Rimes

1997 Paula Cole

1998 Lauryn Hill

Source: *National Academy of Recording Arts & Sciences*

(1) Initially awarded to Milli Vanilli who later admitted they had not performed on any of their recordings.

Canadian Music Hall of Fame

The Canadian Academy of Recording Arts and Sciences instituted a Hall of Fame Award in 1978 to honour Canadians who have contributed to the greater international recognition of Canadian artists and music.

■ Winners

1978	Guy Lombardo	1986	Gordon Lightfoot		Domenic Troiano
	Oscar Peterson	1987	The Guess Who		John Kay
1979	Hank Snow	1989	The Band		Zal Yanovsky
1980	Paul Anka	1990	Maureen Forrester	1997	Lenny Breau
1981	Joni Mitchell	1991	Leonard Cohen		Gil Evans
1982	Neil Young	1992	Ian & Sylvia		Maynard Ferguson
1983	Glenn Gould	1993	Anne Murray		Moe Kauffman
1984	The Crewcuts	1994	Rush		Rob McConnell
	The Diamonds	1995	Buffy Sainte-Marie	1998	David Foster
	The Four Lads	1996	David Clayton-Thomas		
1985	Wilf Carter		Denny Doherty		

1999 INDUCTEE

■ Luc Plamondon

Best known for his international success with the rock opera *Starmania*, Luc Plamondon was born and raised on a farm in Quebec. During the 1960s, while attending college, he began writing songs and plays. He always dreamed of Paris and New York. In the seventies, after spending time in California, he returned to Montreal where he met his favourite singer, Diane Dufresne. In 1978, with Michel Berger, Plamondon created *Starmania*, which was first produced as an album in French, featuring Ms. Dufresne. The English version of the record was produced in 1992 with Tim Rice providing the English lyrics. *Starmania* was first brought to the stage in 1979, at the Palais des Congres in Paris, where Tom O'Horgan directed it. In 1993, *Starmania* returned to Paris, to the Theatre Mogador, this time directed by Lewis Furey. Over the years, Plamondon has written numerous #1 hit singles for various Quebec and French artists such as Julien Clerc and Robert Charlebois. Plamondon's newest success, *Notre Dame de Paris*, opened in Paris on September 16, 1998 and subsequently played sold out engagements in France, Belgium and Canada.

Source: *Canadian Academy of Recording Arts and Sciences*   http://www.juno-awards.ca/caras/

The Canadian Academy of Recording Arts and Sciences (CARAS)

T his organization was originally created to administer and promote the Juno Awards. It has since expanded its mandate to link members of the Canadian music community and members of the public interested in the Canadian music and recording industry. The Junos themselves remain the centrepiece, to recognize (and reward) outstanding achievement in recorded music. The broadcast of the Junos brings singers, musicians, songwriters, producers and other creative talent together and to the attention of both a national audience and foreign markets.

CARAS uses a website to achieve its goals beyond the awards: a home page for the Canadian Music Hall of Fame has biographies, photos and sound clips from the inductees. In addition, CARAS is building a database containing information about Canadian music, and all of its artists and creators. Known as JAMA (Juno Awards Music Archive), the site boasted almost 2,000 entries in March of 1998 and is still growing. Browsers can access biographies, images, discographies and audio clips of Canadian artists. Check it out at http://www.juno-awards.ca

Top 50 Hit Tracks, 1998

1. "Torn," Natalie Imbruglia
2. "Crush," Jennifer Page
3. **"My Heart Will Go On," Celine Dion**
4. "The Way," Fastball-Make Your Mama Proud
5. "3 AM," Matchbox
6. "Truly Madly Deeply," Savage Garden
7. "Boy Is Mine," Brandy and Monica
8. "Want You Back," N'Sync
9. **"Back To You," Bryan Adams**
10. **"Adia," Sarah McLachlan**
11. "Together Again," Janet Jackson
12. "Iris," Goo Goo Dolls
13. "Sex And Candy," Marcy Playground
14. "Too Close," Next
15. "Frozen," Madonna
16. "Ray of Light," Madonna
17. "Real World," Matchbox 20
18. "Get Jiggy With It," Will Smith
19. **"Uninvited," Alanis Morissette**
20. **"Uninvited," Alanis Morissette**
21. "Walkin' On the Sun," Smash Mouth
22. "Kiss The Rain," Billie Myers
23. **"Sweet Surrender," Sarah McLachlan**
24. "All My Life," K-Ci and Jo Jo
25. "Are You My Jimmy Ray?" Jimmy Ray
26. "As Long As You Love Me," Backstreet Boys
27. "One Week," Barenaked Ladies.
28. "Tearin' Up My Heart," N'Sync
29. "Go Deep," Janet Jackson
30. **"You're Still the One," Shania Twain**
31. "Never Ever," All Saints
32. "Hurts To Love You," Philosopher Kings
33. "Closing Time," Samisonic
34. "Bittersweet Symphony," The Verve
35. "I Do," Lisa Loeb
36. "Stop," Spice Girls
37. "You Make Me Wanna," Usher
38. **"Cry," Philosopher Kings**
39. "Fly," Sugar Ray
40. "Cruel Summer," Ace of Base
41. "Show Me Love," Robyn
42. "My Father's Eyes," Eric Clapton
43. "Tumbthumping," Chumbawamba
44. "Broken Bones," Love Inc.
45. **"Everywhere," Bran Van 3000**
46. "(You're a) Superstar," Love Inc.
47. "I'll Be There," The Moffatts
48. "If You Could Read My Mind," Stars on 54
49. "Searchin' My Soul," Vonda Shepard
50. "Ghetto Superstar," Pras Michael Feat. Ol' Dirty Bastard

Source: *RPM Weekly*

Canadian artists set in bold type.

MTV Video Music Awards, 1999

BEST VIDEO OF THE YEAR	"Doo Wop (That Thing)," Lauryn Hill
BEST ROCK VIDEO	"Freak on a Leash," Korn
BEST R&B VIDEO	"Doo Wop (That Thing)," Lauryn Hill
VIEWER'S CHOICE	"I Want It That Way," Backstreet Boys
BEST RAP VIDEO	"Can I Get A…," Jay-Z (featuring Ja Rule and Amil-Lion)
BEST DIRECTION	"Praise You," Fatboy Slim
BEST FEMALE VIDEO	"Doo Wop (That Thing)," Lauryn Hill
BEST POP VIDEO	"Livin' La Vida Loca," Ricky Martin
BEST VIDEO FROM A FILM	"Beautiful Stranger," Madonna
BEST NEW ARTIST	"My Name Is," Eminem
BEST GROUP VIDEO	"No Scrubs," TLC
BEST MALE VIDEO	"Miami," Will Smith
BEST DANCE VIDEO	"Livin' La Vida Loca," Ricky Martin
BEST BREAKTHROUGH VIDEO	"Praise You," Fatboy Slim
BEST ART DIRECTION	"Doo Wop (That Thing)," Lauryn Hill
SPECIAL EFFECTS	"Special," Garbage
BEST EDITING	"Freak on a Leash," Korn
BEST CHOREOGRAPHY	"Praise You," Fatboy Slim
BEST CINEMATOGRAPHY	"The Dope Show," Marilyn Manson

Source: *MTV: Music Television*

The MuchMusic Video Awards, 1999

Best Rock Video ...."Hang Ten," Edwin
Best Pop Video..."Steal My Sunshine," Len
Best Editing...Jef Renfroe, "Sky's Love Song"
Best Cinematography...Noble Jones, "Why"
Best Video ...."Steal My Sunshine," Len
Best Director ....Alanis Morissette, "Unsent"
Best Rap Video ...."Take a Look," Infinite
Best Soul/R and B Video ...."Thinkin' About You," 2Rude featuring Latoya and Miranda
Best Independent Video ...."Take a Look," Infinite
Best Dance Video ...."Squeeze Toy," The Boomtang Boys featuring Kim Esty
Best International Video ...."Let Forever Be," The Chemical Brothers
MuchMoreMusic Award ....Shania Twain
Best Performance In A Video ....Poets, The Tragically Hip
Best French Video ...."Les Djinns," Lili Fatale
VideoFACT Award ...."If I Were a Planet," Black Katt
Eye Popper Award ...."Praise You," Fatboy Slim
New Technology Award...The Watchmen
People's choice, favourite Canadian artist: ....Sarah McLachlan
People's choice, favourite Canadian group: ....The Moffatts
People's choice, favourite Canadian video: ...."Steal My Sunshine," Len
People's choice, favourite international artist: ....Britney Spears
People's choice, favourite international group: ....Backstreet Boys

Source: *MuchMusic Network*

Recording Industry Sales, 1998-99[1]

These two charts examine the amount–and dollar value–of music purchased in a variety of forms in 1999, and compares those figures to the prior sales year. Sales information is supplied by members of the Canadian Recording Industry Association. Units and dollar amounts are expressed in the thousands.

Units Shipped (000s)	1999	1998	% change
Music Video . . .	879	629	40%
Cassette Single .	0	-1	
Other Singles . .	375	332	13%
Total Singles . . .	*375*	*331*	*13%*
Cassette	2231	3209	-30%
CD	22 173	22 484	-1%
Total Albums . .	*24 404*	*25 693*	*-5%*
Grand Total . . .	**25 658**	**26 653**	**-4%**

Net Value of Sales ($000s)	1999	1998	% change
Music Video . . .	7 630	6 700	14%
Cassette Single .	0	-2	
Other Singles . .	2057	1 829	12%
Total Singles . . .	*2057*	*1829*	*13%*
Cassette	13516	19771	-32%
CD	263 454	263 454	0%
Total Albums . .	*276 832*	*283 225*	*-2%*
Grand Total . . .	**$2286,519**	**291 752**	**-2%**

Source: *Canadian Recording Industry Association*

(1) For the period ending June 30th.

The Rock and Roll Hall of Fame

The Rock and Roll Hall of Fame was established in 1984 to preserve and enhance the status of rock and roll as an art form. The Rock and Roll Hall of Fame and Museum, opened in September 1995 in Cleveland, Ohio.

The members, chosen by a group of pop music experts, are listed below, followed by the years in which they were elected.

■ **ARTISTS**
The Allman Brothers Band (1995)
The Animals (1994)
LaVern Baker (1991)
Hank Ballard (1990)
The Band (1994)
The Beach Boys (1988)
The Beatles (1988)
The Bee Gees (1997)
Chuck Berry (1986)
Bobby "Blue" Bland (1992)
Booker T. & The MG's (1992)

Buffalo Springfield (1997)
David Bowie (1996)
James Brown (1986)
Ruth Brown (1993)
The Byrds (1991)
Johnny Cash (1992)
Ray Charles (1986)
The Coasters (1987)
Eddie Cochran (1987)
Sam Cooke (1986)
Cream (1993)
Creedence Clearwater Revival (1993)

▶

▶ Crosby, Stills and Nash (1997)
Bobby Darin (1990)
Bo Diddley (1987)
Dion (1989)
Fats Domino (1986)
The Doors (1993)
The Drifters (1988)
Bob Dylan (1988)
The Eagles (1998)
Duane Eddy (1994)
The Everly Brothers (1986)
Fleetwood Mac (1998)
The Four Seasons (1990)
The Four Tops (1990)
Aretha Franklin (1987)
Marvin Gaye (1987)
Grateful Dead (1994)
Al Green (1995)
Bill Haley (1987)
Buddy Holly (1986)
The Jimi Hendrix Experience (1992)
John Lee Hooker (1991)
The Impressions (1991)
The Isley Brothers (1992)
Etta James (1993)
Jefferson Airplane (1996)
Billy Joel (1999)
Elton John (1994)
Janis Joplin (1995)
B.B. King (1987)
The Jackson Five (1997)
The Kinks (1990)
Gladys Knight and the Pips (1996)
Led Zeppelin (1995)
Lloyd Price (1998)
John Lennon (1994)
Jerry Lee Lewis (1986)
Little Richard (1986)
Little Willie John (1996)
Frankie Lyman and the Teenagers (1993)
The Mamas and the Papas (1998)
Bob Marley (1994)
Martha and the Vandellas (1995)
Curtis Mayfield (1999)
Paul McCartney (1999)
Joni Mitchell (1997)
Clyde McPhatter (1987)
Van Morrison (1993)
Ricky Nelson (1987)
Roy Orbison (1987)
Parliament Funkadelic (1997)
Carl Perkins (1987)
Wilson Pickett (1991)
Pink Floyd (1996)
The Platters (1990)
Elvis Presley (1986)
Otis Redding (1989)
Jimmy Reed (1991)
Smokey Robinson (1987)
The Rolling Stones (1989)
Sam & Dave (1992)
Santana (1998)
Del Shannon (1999)
The Shirelles (1996)
Simon and Garfunkel (1990)
Sly and the Family Stone (1993)
Dusty Springfield (1999)
Bruce Springsteen (1999)
Rod Stewart (1994)
The Supremes (1988)
The Staple Singers (1999)
The Temptations (1989)
Ike and Tina Turner (1991)

Big Joe Turner (1987)
Gene Vincent (1998)
The Velvet Underground (1996)
Muddy Waters (1987)
The Who (1990)
Jackie Wilson (1987)
Stevie Wonder (1989)
The Yardbirds (1992)
The Young Rascals (1997)
Neil Young (1995)
Frank Zappa (1995)

■ NON-PERFORMERS
Paul Ackerman (1995)
Dave Bartholomew (1991)
Ralph Bass (1991)
Leonard Chess (1987)
Dick Clark (1993)
Tom Donahue (1996)
Lamont Dozier, Brian Holland & Eddie Holland (1990)
Ahmet Ertegun (1987)
Leo Fender (1992)
Alan Freed (1986)
Milt Gabler (1993)
Gerry Goffin & Carole King (1990)
Berry Gordy, Jr. (1988)
Bill Graham (1992)
Jerry Leiber & Mike Stoller (1987)
George Martin (1999)
Syd Nathan (1997)
Johnny Otis (1994)
Sam Phillips (1986)
Doc Pomus (1992)
Phil Spector (1989)
Allen Toussaint (1998)
Jerry Wexler (1987)

■ LIFETIME ACHIEVEMENT AWARDS
Willie Dixon (1994)
Nesuhi Ertegun (1991)
John Hammond (1986)

■ EARLY INFLUENCES
Louis Armstrong (1990)
Charles Brown (1999)
Charlie Christian (1990)
Willie Dixon (1994)
Woody Guthrie (1988)
Howlin' Wolf (1991)
The Ink Spots (1989)
Mahalia Jackson (1997)
Elmore James (1992)
Robert Johnson (1986)
Louis Jordan (1987)
Lead Belly (1988)
Bill Monroe (1997)
Jelly Roll Morton (1998)
The Orioles (1995)
Les Paul (1988)
Professor Longhair (1992)
Ma Rainey (1990)
Jimmie Rodgers (1986)
Pete Seeger (1996)
Bessie Smith (1989)
The Soul Stirrers (1989)
T-Bone Walker (1987)
Dinah Washington (1993)
Hank Williams (1987)
Bob Wills & His Texas Playboys (1999)
Jimmy Yancey (1986)

Source: *Rock and Roll Hall of Fame Foundation*

MOVIES

Canada has been a world leader in documentary filmmaking, producing renowned artists such as Donald Brittain and Harry Rasky primarily through the National Film Board of Canada. The film board has also helped bring Canada to prominence as a producer of animation, and short subjects. Canadians have made an enormous contribution to the Hollywood feature film industry, from film mogul Louis B. Mayer to acclaimed director Norman Jewison to stars including Mary Pickford, Dan Ackroyd, Michael J. Fox, John Candy and Keanu Reeves. The Department of Canadian Heritage estimates that 20 percent of those employed in the Hollywood film industry are Canadian and that about 60 percent of the software used in U.S. film productions was developed by Canadians. Made-in-Canada features by filmmakers such as Denys Arcand, David Cronenburg, Atom Egoyan, and Patricia Rozema have enjoyed considerable critical and "art house" success around the world. In the 1990s, Canadian features have twice won the Special Grand Jury Prize at the Cannes Film Festival. However, with U.S. distribution houses controlling 85 percent of the theatrical market, only one in twenty features gaining commercial release in Canada is produced in Canada.

■ Norman Jewison: 1999 Winner of the Irving G. Thalberg Memorial Award

It is the highest award that Hollywood can bestow in recognition of outstanding lifetime achievement in motion pictures. At the 1999 Oscars, it went to Canadian producer and director Norman Jewison. Jewison began his career at the Canadian Broadcasting Corporation in the 1950s and moved to Hollywood a decade later. His films have won 10 Academy Awards and 45 nominations. Jewison's *In the Heat of the Night* won the Oscar for Best Picture in 1967. His other films include *Moonstruck, A Soldier's Story, The Russians Are Coming!...The Russians Are Coming!* and *Fiddler On the Roof.*

The National Film Board: Origins

*O*n May 2, 1999, the National Film Board of Canada celebrated its 60th anniversary. It was established to improve Canadian Government Motion Picture Bureau productions and to increase their distribution in England. Canadian public servants working in London suggested that British documentary filmmaker John Grierson be invited to Canada to assess the film industry. Grierson submitted his report in June 1938, recommending that a coordinating body be established for Canadian film production.

A law was passed in May 1939, creating a National Film Commission (soon to be known as the National Film Board) to work alongside the Government Motion Picture Bureau. Its initial mandate was to make and distribute films designed to help Canadians in all parts of Canada understand each other's lives and problems. It was also responsible for coordinating the film activities of government departments.

Canada entered the war in September 1939, leading to a shift in film production towards patriotic propaganda. In October 1939, John Grierson became the first Government Film Commissioner. The NFB signed an agreement with The March of Time to distribute its films in the U.S., while Famous Players of Canada agreed to show NFB films in its 800 theatres.

Source: *The National Film Board of Canada*

Genie Awards, 1988–98

The Genie Awards have been presented since 1980 by the Academy of Canadian Cinema and Television to honor achievement in the Canadian film industry. Awards apply to films released in the previous year. Voting is conducted in a two-step process whereby the winners are chosen by all academy members from among the five nominees selected in each category by their respective craft branches. The 1998 awards were presented Feb. 4, 1999

1988

Picture . . . . *Un Zoo la nuit*
Actor . . . . Roger Le Bel, *Un Zoo la nuit*
Actress . . . . Sheila McCarthy, *I've Heard the Mermaids Singing*
Sup. Actor . . . . Germaine Houde, *Un Zoo la nuit*
Sup. Actress . . . . Paule Baillargeon, *I've Heard the Mermaids Singing*
Director . . . . Jean-Claude Lauzon, *Un Zoo la nuit*

1989

Picture . . . . *Dead Ringers*
Actor . . . . Jeremy Irons, *Dead Ringers*
Actress . . . . Jackie Burroughs, *A Winter Tan*
Sup. Actor . . . . Remy Girard, *Les Portes tournantes*
Sup. Actress . . . . Colleen Dewhurst, *Obsessed*
Director . . . . David Cronenberg, *Dead Ringers*

1990

Picture . . . . *Jesus de Montréal*
Actor . . . . Lothaire Bluteau, *Jesus de Montréal*
Actress . . . . Rebecca Jenkins, *Bye Bye Blues*
Sup. Actor . . . . Remy Girard, *Jesus de Montréal*
Sup. Actress . . . . Robyn Stevan, *Bye Bye Blues*
Director . . . . Denys Arcand, *Jesus de Montréal*

1991

Picture . . . . *Black Robe*
Actor . . . . Remy Girard, *Amoureux fou*
Actress . . . . Pascale Montpetit, *H*
Sup. Actor . . . . August Schellenberg, *Black Robe*
Sup. Actress . . . . Danielle Proulx, *Amoureux fou*
Director . . . . Bruce Beresford, *Black Robe*

1992

Picture . . . . *Naked Lunch*
Actor . . . . Tony Nardi, *La Sarrasine*
Actress . . . . Janet Wright, *Bordertown Café*
Sup. Actor . . . . Michael Hogan, *Solitaire*
Sup. Actress . . . . Monique Mercure, *Naked Lunch*
Director . . . . David Cronenberg, *Naked Lunch*

1993

Picture . . . . *Thirty-Two Short Films about Glenn Gould*
Actor . . . . Tom McCamus, *I Love A Man in Uniform*
Actress . . . . Sheila McCarthy, *The Lotus Eaters*
Sup. Actor . . . . Kevin Tighe, *I Love A Man in Uniform*
Sup. Actress . . . . Nicola Cavendish, *The Grocer's Wife*
Director . . . . François Girard, *Thirty-Two Short Films about Glenn Gould*

1994

Picture . . . . *Exotica*
Actor . . . . Maury Chaykin, *Whale Music*
Actress . . . . Sandra Oh, *Double Happiness*
Sup. Actor . . . . Don McKellar, *Exotica*
Sup. Actress . . . . Martha Henry, *Mustard Bath*
Director . . . . Atom Egoyan, *Exotica*

1995

Picture . . . . *Le Confessionnal*
Actor . . . . David La Haye, *L'Enfant D'Eau*
Actress . . . . Helena Bonham Carter, *Margaret's Museum*
Sup. Actor . . . . Kenneth Welsh, *Margaret's Museum*
Sup. Actress . . . . Kate Nelligan, *Margaret's Museum*
Director . . . . Robert Lepage, *Le Confessionnal*

1996

Picture . . . . *Lilies*
Actor . . . . . William Hutt, *Long Day's Journey Into Night*
Actress . . . Martha Henry, *Long Day's Journey Into Night*
Sup. Actor . . . . Peter Donaldson, *Long Day's Journey Into Night*
Sup. Actress . . . . Martha Burns, *Long Day's Journey Into Night*
Director . . . . David Cronenburg, *Crash*

1997

Picture . . . . *The Sweet Hereafter*
Actor . . . . Ian Holm, *The Sweet Hereafter*
Actress . . . . Molly Parker, *Kissed*
Sup. Actor . . . . Peter MacNeill, *The Hanging Garden*
Sup. Actress . . . . . Seana McKenna, *The Hanging Garden*
Director . . . . Atom Egoyan, *The Sweet Hereafter*

1998

Picture . . . . *The Red Violin*
Actor . . . . Roshan Seth, *Such a Long Journey*
Actress . . . . Sandra Oh, *Last Night*
Sup. Actor . . . . Callum Keith Rennie, *Last Night*
Sup. Actress . . . . Monique Mercure, *Conquest*
Director . . . . François Girard, *The Red Violin*
Original Screenplay . . . . . Don McKellar, François Girard, *The Red Violin*
Cinematography . . . . Alain Dostie, *The Red Violin*
Film Editing . . . . Jeff Warren, *Such a Long Journey*
Art Direction . . . . François Séguin, *The Red Violin*
Costume Design . . . . Renée April, *The Red Violin*
Overall Sound . . . . Claude La Haye, Jo Caron, Bernard Gariepy Strobl, Hans Peter Strobl, *The Red Violin*
Sound Editing . . . . David Evans, Rick Cadger, Donna Powell, Paul Shikata, Phong Tran, Clive Turner, *Such a Long Journey*
Music Score . . . . John Corigliano, *The Red Violin*
Best Feature Length Documentary . . . . Betsy Carson, Kirk Tougas, Nettie Wild, *A Place Called Chiapas.*
Best Short Documentary . . . . Anita Herczeg, Brenda Longfellow, *Shadow Maker: Gwendolyn MacEwan, Poet*
Best Live Action Short Drama . . . . Mary Lewis, *When Ponds Freeze Over*

Motion Picture Academy Awards (Oscars™), 1988–98

1988

Picture . . . . *Rain Man*, United Artists
Actor . . . . Dustin Hoffman, *Rain Man*
Actress . . . . Jodie Foster, *The Accused*
Sup. Actor . . . . Kevin Kline, *A Fish Called Wanda*
Sup. Actress . . . . Geena Davis, *The Accidental Tourist*
Director . . . . Barry Levinson, *Rain Man*

1989

Picture . . . . *Driving Miss Daisy*, Warner Bros.
Actor . . . . Daniel Day Lewis, *My Left Foot*
Actress . . . . Jessica Tandy, *Driving Miss Daisy*
Sup. Actor . . . . Denzel Washington, *Glory*
Sup. Actress . . . . Brenda Fricker, *My Left Foot*
Director . . . . Oliver Stone, *Born on the Fourth of July*

1990

Picture . . . . *Dances With Wolves*, Orion
Actor . . . . Jeremy Irons, *Reversal of Fortune*
Actress . . . . Kathy Bates, *Misery*
Sup. Actor . . . . Joe Pesci, *Good Fellas*
Sup. Actress . . . . Whoopi Goldberg, *Ghost*
Director . . . . Kevin Costner, *Dances With Wolves*

1991

Picture . . . . *The Silence of the Lambs*, Orion
Actor . . . . Anthony Hopkins, *The Silence of the Lambs*
Actress . . . . Jodie Foster, *The Silence of the Lambs*
Sup. Actor . . . . Jack Palance, *City Slickers*
Sup. Actress . . . . Mercedes Ruehl, *The Fisher King*
Director . . . . . Jonathan Demme, *The Silence of the Lambs*

1992

Picture . . . . *Unforgiven*, Clint Eastwood, producer
Actor . . . . Al Pacino, *Scent of A Woman*
Actress . . . . Emma Thompson, *Howards End*
Sup. Actor . . . . Gene Hackman, *Unforgiven*
Sup. Actress . . . . Marisa Tomei, *My Cousin Vinny*
Director . . . . Clint Eastwood, *Unforgiven*

1993

Picture . . . . *Schindler's List*, Steven Spielberg,
Gerald R. Molen, Branko Lustig, producers
Actor . . . . Tom Hanks, *Philadelphia*
Actress . . . . Holly Hunter, *The Piano*
Sup. Actor . . . . Tommy Lee Jones, *The Fugitive*
Sup. Actress . . . . Anna Paquin, *The Piano*
Director . . . . Steven Spielberg, *Schindler's List*

1994

Picture . . . . *Forrest Gump*, SteveTisch,
Wendy Finerman, Steve Sharkey, producers
Actor . . . . Tom Hanks, *Forrest Gump*
Actress . . . . Jessica Lange, *Blue Sky*
Sup. Actor . . . . Martin Landau, *Ed Wood*
Sup. Actress . . . . Dianne Wiest, *Bullets Over Broadway*
Director . . . . Robert Zemeckis, *Forrest Gump*

1995

Picture . . . . . . *Braveheart*, Mel Gibson, Alan Ladd, Jr., and
Bruce Davey, producers
Actor . . . . Nicolas Cage, *Leaving Las Vegas*
Actress . . . . Susan Sarandon, *Dead Man Walking*
Sup. Actor . . . . Kevin Spacey, *The Usual Suspects*
Sup. Actress . . . . Mira Sorvino, *Mighty Aphrodite*
Director . . . . Mel Gibson, *Braveheart*

1996

Picture . . . . . *The English Patient*, Saul Zaentz, producer
Actor . . . . Geoffrey Rush, *Shine*
Actress . . . . Frances McDormand, *Fargo*
Sup. Actor . . . . Cuba Gooding, Jr., *Jerry Maguire*
Sup. Actress . . . . . Juliette Binoche, *The English Patient*
Director . . . . Anthony Minghella, *The English Patient*

1997

Picture . . . . *Titanic*, James Cameron,
Jon Landau, producers
Actor . . . . Jack Nicholson, *As Good as It Gets*
Actress . . . . Helen Hunt, *As Good as It Gets*
Sup. Actor . . . . Robin Williams, *Good Will Hunting*
Sup. Actress . . . . Kim Basinger, *L.A. Confidential*
Director . . . . James Cameron, *Titanic*

1998

Picture . . . . *Shakespeare in Love*, Donna Gigliotti,
Marc Norman, David Parfitt, Harvey Weinstein,
Edward Zwick, producers
Actor . . . . Roberto Benigni, *Life is Beautiful*
Actress . . . . . . Gwyneth Paltrow, *Shakespeare in Love*
Sup. Actor . . . . James Coburn, *Affliction*
Sup. Actress . . . . Judi Dench, *Shakespeare in Love*
Director . . . . Steven Spielberg, *Saving Private Ryan*
Foreign-Language Film . . . . . *Life is Beautiful*, Italy
Original Screenplay . . . . . Marc Norman , Tom Stoppard,
Shakespeare in Love
Screenplay Adaptation . . . . Bill Condon,
Gods and Monsters
Cinematography . . . . Janusz Kaminski,
Saving Private Ryan
Editing . . . . Michael Kahn, *Saving Private Ryan*
Original Score (Dramatic) . . . . Nicola Piovani,
Life is Beautiful
Original Song . . Stephen Schwartz, "When You Believe,"
The Prince of Egypt
Art Direction . . . . . . Martin Childs, *Shakespeare in Love*
Costume Design . . . Sandy Powell, *Shakespeare in Love*
Sound . . . . Ronald Judkins, *Saving Private Ryan*
Sound Effects Editing . . . . Richard Hymns,
Gary Rydstrom, *Saving Private Ryan*
Makeup . . . . Jenny Shircore Pio, *Elizabeth*
Visual Effects . . . . Nicholas Brooks , Joel Hynek,
Kevin Mack, Stuart Robertson,
What Dreams May Come
Documentary Feature . . . . Ken Lipper, James Moll,
The Last Days
Documentary Short Subject . . . Keiko Ibi, *The Personals:
Improvisations on Romance in the Golden Years*

1998 Oscar™ Nominations

Picture: *Elizabeth, Life is Beautiful, Saving Private Ryan, Shakespeare in Love, The Thin Red Line*

Actor: Roberto Benigni, *Life is Beautiful;* Tom Hanks, *Saving Private Ryan;* Ian McKellen, *Gods and Monsters;* Nick Nolte, *Affliction;* Edward Norton, *American History X*

Actress: Cate Blanchett, *Elizabeth;* Fernanda Montenegro, *Central Station;* Gwyneth Paltrown, *Shakespeare in Love;* Meryl Streep, *One True Thing;* Emily Watson, *Hilary and Jackie*

Supporting Actor: James Coburn, *Affliction;* Robert Duvall, *A Civil Action;* Ed Harris, *The Truman Show;* Geoffrey Rush, *Shakespeare in Love;* Billy Bob Thornton, *A Simple Plan*

Supporting Actress: Kathy Bates, *Primary Colours;* Brenda Blethyn, *Little Voice;* Judi Dench, *Shakespeare in Love;* Rachel Griffiths, *Hilary and Jackie;* Lynn Redgrave, *Gods and Monsters*

Director: Roberto Benigni, *Life is Beautiful;* Steven Spielberg, *Saving Private Ryan;* John Madden, *Shakespeare in Love;* Terrence Malick, *The Thin Red Line;* Peter Weir, *The Truman Show*

Foreign-Language Film: *Central Station,* Brazil; *Children of Heaven,* Iran; *The Grandfather,* Spain; *Life is Beautiful,* Italy; *Tango,* Argentina.

Original Screenplay: Warren Beatty, Jeremy Pikser, *Buworth;* Roberto Benigni, Vincenzo Cerami, *Life is Beautiful;* Robert Rodat, *Saving Private Ryan;* Marc Norman, Tom Stoppard, *Saving Private Ryan;* Andrew Niccol, *The Truman Show*

Screenplay Adaptation: Bill Condon, *Gods and Monsters;* Scott Frank, *Out of Sight;* Elaine May, *Primary Colours;* Scott B. Smith, *A Simple Plan;* Terrence Malick, *The Thin Red Line*

Cinematography: Conrad L. Hall, *A Civil Action;* Remi Adefarasin, *Elizabeth;* Janusz Kaminski, *Saving Private Ryan;* Richard Greatrex, *Shakespeare in Love;* John Toll, *The Thin Red Line*

Original Song: Diane Warren, "I Don't Want to Miss a Thing," *Armageddon;* Carole Bayer Sager and David Foster, Tony Renis and Alberto Testa, "The Prayer," *Quest for Camelot;* Allison Moorer and Gwil Owen, "A Soft Place to Fall," *The Horse Whisperer;* Randy Newman, "That'll Do," *Babe: Pig in the City;* Stephen Schwartz, "When You Believe," *The Prince of Egypt*

Source: © Academy of Motion Picture Arts and Sciences

The Cannes Film Festival Awards, 1988–98

1988
Best Film . . . . *Pelle The Conqueror* (Denmark)
Special Grand Jury Prize . . . . . *A World Apart* (Great Britain)
Best Director . . . . Fernando E. Solanas, *The South*
Best Actor . . . . Forest Whitaker, *Bird*
Best Actress .Barbara Hershey, Jodhi May and Linda Mvusi, *A World Apart*

1989
Best Film . . . . *sex, lies and videotape* (USA)
Special Grand Jury Prize . . . . . *Trop Belle Pour Toi* (France); *Cinema Paradiso* (Italy)
Best Director . . . . Emir Kusturica, *Time of the Gypsies*
Best Actor . . . . James Spader, *sex, lies and videotape*
Best Actress . . . . Meryl Streep, *A Cry In The Dark*

1990
Best Film . . . . *Wild at Heart* (USA)
Special Grand Jury Prize . . . *Tilaï* (Burkina Faso); *The Sting of Death* (Japan)
Best Director . . . . Pavel Loungine, *Taxi Blues*
Best Actor . . . . Gerard Depardieu, *Cyrano de Bergerac*
Best Actress . . . . Krystyna Janda, *Interrogation*

1991
Best Film . . . . *Barton Fink* (USA)
Special Grand Jury Prize . . . . *La belle noiseuse* (France)
Best Director . . . . Joel Coen & Ethan Coen, *Barton Fink*
Best Actor . . . . John Turturro, *Barton Fink*
Best Actress . . . . . Irène Jacob, *The Double Life of Veronica*

1992
Best Film . . . . *The Best Intentions* (Switzerland)
Special Grand Jury Prize . . . . *Il Ladro di Bambini* (Italy)
Best Director . . . . Robert Altman, *The Player*
Best Actor . . . . Tim Robbins, *The Player*
Best Actress . . . . Pernilla August, *The Best Intentions*

1993
Best Film . . (tie) *The Piano,* (New Zealand), *Farewell To My Concubine* (China)
Special Grand Jury Prize . . . *Faraway, So Close!* (Germany)
Best Director . . . . Mike Leigh, *Naked*
Best Actor . . . . David Thewlis, *Naked*
Best Actress . . . . Holly Hunter, *The Piano*

1994
Best Film . . . . *Pulp Fiction,* (USA)
Special Grand Jury Prize . . . *Burnt by the Sun* (Russia) and *To Live!* (China)
Best Director . . . . Nanni Moretti, *Journal intime*
Best Actor . . . . Ge You, *To Live!*
Best Actress . . . . Virna Lisi, *la Reine Margot*

1995
Special Grand Jury Prize . . . . *Crash* (Canada)
Best Director . . . . Joel Coen, *Fargo* (U.S.)
Best Actor . . . . (tie) Daniel Autueil & Pascal Duquenne, *The Eighth Day* (France)
Best Actress . . . . Brenda Blethyn, *Secrets and Lies* (UK)
Palme d'Or . . . . *Secrets and Lies* (UK)

1996

Special Grand Jury Prize.... *The Sweet Hereafter* (Canada)
Best Director.... Wong Kar-Wai, *Happy Together* (Hong Kong)
Best Actor .... Sean Penn, *She's So Lovely* (U.S)
Best Actress .... Kathy Burke, *Nilby Mouth* (U.K)
Palme d'Or .... (tie) *Unagi* (The Eel) (Japan)
The Taste of Cherry (Iran)

1997

Grand Jury Prize .... *La Vita e Bella* (Italy)
Special Jury Prize .... *La Classe de Neige* (France);
Festen (Denmark)
Best Director ... John Boorman, *The General* (Great Britain)
Best Actor .... Peter Mullan, *My Name is Joe*
(Great Britain)

Best Actress ...... Elodie Bouchez and Natacha Regnier,
La Vie Revee des Anges (France)
Palme d'Or ...... *Eternity and a Day*, Theo Angelopoulos
(Greece)

1998

Grand Jury Prize .... *L'humanité* (France)
Jury Prize .... *A Carta* (Portugal)
Best Director .... Pedro Almodovar, *Todo Sobre
Mi Madre* (Spain)
Best Actor ..... Emmanuel Schotté, *L'humanité* (France)
Best Actress ..... Séverine Cancele, *L'humanité* (France)
and Emilie Dequenne, *Rosetta* (Belgium)
Palme d'Or .... *Rosetta*, Luc and Jean-Pierre
Dardenne (Belgium)

Source: *The Cannes Film Festival*

(1) The Cannes Festival Jury is not obliged to select a winner in any category except that of Best Film.

Toronto International Film Festival, 1999

The 24th annual festival was held Sept. 9 to 18 in 1999, showing 319 films from over 50 countries.

This is widely regarded as North America's major film festival.

lPeople's Choice Award .... *American Beauty* (Sam Mendes)

Discovery Award .... *Goat on Fire and Smiling* (Kevin Jordan)

Fipresci Award .... *Shower* (Zhang Yang)

Best Canadian First Feature .... ***Just Watch Me: Trudeau and the 70s Generation* (Catharine Annau)**

Best Canadian Feature Film .... ***The Five Senses* (Jeremy Podeswa)**

Best Canadian Short Film .... ***Décharge* (Patrick Demers)**

Source: *Toronto International Film Festival*

Montreal World Film Festival, 1999

The 23rd annual Festival des Films du Monde was held from Aug. 27th to Sept. 6th, 1999.

Grand Prix of the Americas .... *The Colour of Paradise* (Iran)

Special Grand Prix of the Jury (tie) .... *Not of this World* (Italy), *The Minus Man* (U.S.A.)

Best Director .... Louis Bélanger (Canada), *Post Mortem*

Best Actress .... Nina Hoss, *Der Vulkan*, (Germany)

Best Actor .... Ken Takakura, *Poppoya*, Yasuo Furuhata (Japan)

Best Screenplay .... Pierre Jolivet and Simon Michaël, *My Little Business*, (France)

Best Short Film .... *Just in Time*, (Germany)

People's Choice Award .... *Postmen in the Mountains*, (China)

Source: *Montreal World Film Festival*

GOVERNOR GENERAL'S PERFORMING ARTS AWARDS

The Governor General's Performing Arts Awards were inaugurated in 1992 to pay tribute to the lifetime achievements of outstanding artists in a variety of creative fields. The motto of the awards, "The Arts Engage and Inspire Us," reflects the cultural contribution made by recipients chosen from theatre, dance, classical music/opera, popular music, film and broadcasting. The awards are presented annually in November by the Governor General and are administered by the Governor General's Performing Arts Awards Foundation.

■ Winners

1993

Ludmilla Chiriaeff, dancer
Leonard Cohen, poet/singer/songwriter
Don Haig, film producer
Lois Maxwell, singer
Monique Mercure, actor
Gilles Vigneault, poet

1994

Frédéric Back, animator/designer/artist
Robert Charlebois, popular singer
Celia Franca, dancer/artistic director of
    National Ballet
Frances Hyland, actor/director
Jean Papineau-Couture, composer/educator/
    musical administrator
Neil Young, musician/singer/songwriter

1995

Denys Arcand, writer/director
Maureen Forrester, opera singer
Peter Gzowski, writer/broadcaster

Paul Hébert, actor/director
Anne Murray, singer
Jeanne Renaud, dancer/choreographer

1996

Francois Barbeau, artist/designer/teacher
Michel Brault, cameraman/director
Martha Henry, actor/director
Joni Mitchell, singer/songwriter
Luc Plamondon, songwriter
Grant Strate, dancer/choreographer/teacher
Martha Lou Henley, arts volunteer/benefactor
Jon Kimura Parker, pianist

1998

Paul Buissoneau, theatre director/actor/writer
Bruce Cockburn, singer-songwriter
Rock Demers, film producer
The Royal Canadian Air Farce, comedians
Arnold Spohr, dancer/choreographer
Jon Vickers, opera singer
Joseph H. Shoctor, arts volunteer/benefactor
Denis Marleau, theatre director

1999 WINNERS

■ David Cronenberg

In his explorations of biological terror, technology and sexual dread, filmmaker David Cronenberg draws into view the uncertainties and dark visions we all carry.

His work is characterized by a keen originality. Unlike many who claim the title, he is a true "auteur–director" with a uniquely personal body of work. Using shocking special effects and, today, a more subtle exploration of character and motivation, his films invariably reflect his longstanding fascination with the darker side of human psychology and behaviour.

From his biggest hit, *Scanners* (telepathic powers of an underground society) to the controversial *Crash* (car crashes and eroticism) to the acclaimed *Naked Lunch* (how dangerous writing can affect the writer), his films have garnered awards and critical acclaim worldwide.

■ Denise Filiatrault

"Her essence is energy!" Actress, writer and director, Denise Filiatrault, with her zest for "doing", has fashioned a long and fascinating career in all the entertainment media. Her love of life, her gusto, and her passionate pursuit of the future characterize this wonderful artist.

Raised in the same milieu as Michel Tremblay, she has performed in many of his works, part of the cadre of artists who have explored together every aspect of that world that formed the basis of their own lives.

Mistress of that most difficult art, making people laugh, she is known first as a comic actress but has also directed widely, winning many awards, most recently for her magnificent stagings of works as diverse as *Les Leçons de Maria Callas* and *Le Bourgeois Gentilhomme*. All the main French–language stages in the country have been home for her productions, and she has directed all the French–language mainstage productions of Montreal's "Just for Laughs" comedy festival. Today, again using the words and scenes of Tremblay, she has achieved a lifetime dream: directing her first feature film to huge box-office success: *C't'à ton tour, Laura Cadieux*. She is already embarked on its sequel.

Officer of the Order of Canada, a Gemini Award and the Victor–Morin Prize, both for lifetime achievement, are among her many honours.

■ Mavor Moore

"Master of all arts", Mavor Moore is a passionate creator who has been a life force in Canadian culture. Actor, writer, producer, director, librettist, critic, essayist, arts administrator and teacher, there is nothing—with the possible exception of ballet dancing—that he has not done.

Author of many dramatic works in various media, including opera, he has served the most important and interesting stories in our history. As co–writer/producer he presented the stage production of what's become the longest–running story in Canadian drama, *Anne of Green Gables*.

He is the founder of a vast range of artistic projects. Many of them became Canadian institutions, such as *Spring Thaw*, the Charlottetown Festival, the Canadian Theatre Centre and Toronto's St. Lawrence Centre.

His life has been a cornucopia of ideas and actions poured out in the cause of making the arts in Canada matter. Coupled with his

talents has been his generosity to others and his ability, indeed his insistence, on bringing out the best in them.

The first artist to chair the Canada Council, he is a Companion of the Order of Canada and a Member of the Order of British Columbia. The Molson Prize and seven doctorates are also among his many honours.

■ Louis Quilico

"The purest of baritones", both in quality of voice and spirit, opera singer Louis Quilico has had a distinguished forty–five–year career. He has sung throughout Canada and on all the great stages of Europe and the U.S., including 25 consecutive years at New York's Metropolitan Opera.

Numbered among the greatest singers of our time, he's performed with Corelli, Domingo, Sutherland, Tebaldi, Price and many others. No one in the highly–charged world of opera could outsing him. An admiring Pavarotti said, "When you sing with him you never worry that he won't be up to standard!"

His singing has an unaffected assurance based on his fundamental understanding of the physicality that produces his robust and beautiful sound. Talking of one of the world's most difficult art forms, he makes the complicated interplay between "vocal cords, breath, and muscle" sound easy: "The sound is just a natural result of what you're trying to do." His many great roles, among them Scarpia, Renato, and his signature role, Rigoletto (which he performed 510 times), are infused with an instinctive understanding of the deep complexities of human emotions.

Innumerable distinguished awards include Companion of the Order of Canada, an honorary doctorate from l'Université du Québec, and a street in Montreal named after him.

■ Ginette Reno

A true star of the Canadian and international music scene for over three decades, singing with equal ease in both French and English, "La Reno" is one of Canada's most popular and best-loved singers. Her candour, simplicity and warmth are reflected not only in her art but in her life.

Attributing her talent to "a gift my mother prayed for", she began singing at age six or seven, bringing her tapes (and fibbing about her age) to Montreal radio stations. Over fifty albums later, with appearances across North America, Britain and France with some of the greatest names in show business—Johnny

Carson, Roger Whittaker, Dinah Shore—, she is a star who still believes that "it's angels" and not her own hard work and dedication which have brought her such enormous success.

Life for her resides in "a passion for doing things". Her latest projects include a proposed musical comedy, perhaps destined some day for Broadway, and she has launched a secondary career as an actress in films such as *C't'à ton tour, Laura Cadieux*, for which she earned a Genie Award nomination for Best Actress.

Juno and Felix awards for best albums and best singer are among her many trophies, and she is an Officer of the Order of Canada.

■ Michel Tremblay

Canada's most widely-produced playwright, Michel Tremblay burst onto the scene in 1968 with *Les Belles Sœurs*. It gave voice to ordinary people who had not been heard from before. Drawing on their Montreal working-class lives and using their own

means of expression, "joual", Tremblay identified the universal themes found in their stories. His plays, grounded in their world, have been translated and performed in more than twenty languages.

At the height of the Sixties, his role was crucial, challenging the domination and censorship of the clergy in the intellectual life of Quebec, championing the place of women in society and signaling the first stirrings of nationalism in Quebec political life. He opened the way for others to follow, while his own work has continued to explore questions of identity, both cultural and sexual.

Today, the vastness of his enterprise—plays, films scripts, novels, adaptations, musicals and operas—is "Balzacian" in its scope, with many of his characters appearing and reappearing across the range of his works. In the same fashion, the work of colleagues and friends—actors, directors, other writers—has become intertwined with his, his vision and creativity providing an ever–lowing resource for others.

Eight Chalmers Awards, four honorary doctorates and Officer of France's Ordre des Arts et des Lettres are among his many honours.

Ramon John Hnatyshyn Award for Voluntarism in the Performing Arts
■ Sam Sniderman

Time and circumstance took Sam Sniderman into business but he is a man driven by a passion for art. Deeply romantic and sensitive, he has hidden behind a jesting and gregarious façade—"Well, I made money too, you know!"—while channeling his love of music into the selfless support of others.

He sold his first records in 1937. By the early sixties his store, "Sam the Record Man", had become legendary. He stocked everything, but his heart was behind young and rising Canadian talent. Anne Murray, Gordon Lightfoot, Buffy Sainte–Marie, Joni

Mitchell are among the hundreds he helped, attending their concerts, promoting their records, ensuring Canadian music lovers bought Canadian artists. He came to symbolize the birth and evolution of the Canadian music industry and had a significant hand in the crafting of "CanCon" regulations which allowed Canadian artists to

be heard in their own land.

He established the Sniderman Sound Recording Archive at the University of Toronto's School of Music, making it "as big as possible!", and continues to add material yearly. He also continues to volunteer his support for innumerable projects such as First Nations music, and is President of Canada's Audio–Visual Heritage. Member of the Order of Canada, he has an honorary doctorate from Ryerson Polytechnic University.

National Arts Centre Award
■ Mario Bernardi

Mario Bernardi embodies an extraordinary combination of musicality and discipline. He is "the compleat musician", from chamber music all the way to his beloved opera and work with singers. Always he is guided by his own well-researched judgment and his musical inner ear, a man who serves music and not vice versa.

With many international engagements, he's put his greatest effort into music in Canada. One of his greatest gifts to the country has been the creation of the National Arts Centre Orchestra. As founding conductor, he played the pivotal role in creating its unique voice. Through his courage and foresight hiring its first players and through thirteen years of leadership, he laid a foundation which has endured for thirty years.

Many Canadian composers have seen their new work premiered under his baton. "Often we get a good piece and I feel such joy that I helped start it!"

THEATRE

Toronto is now considered the third largest production centre of live theatre in the English speaking world (following New York, and London, England). The English Canadian theatre scene has undergone exponential growth since the birth the Stratford Shakespearean Festival at Stratford, Ont. in 1954. The alternative theatre movement that swept English Canada in the 1970s established producers of Canadian drama in every large centre. Diminishing government support in the 1980s and 1990s led to more emphasis on commercial Canadian productions of British, French and American "megamusicals" while development of new and experimental work has passed increasingly to independent artists

often appearing at a cross-Canada network of"fringe" festivals.

Theatrical activity in French Canada burgeoned in the 1950s and 1960s as playwrights such as Marcel Dubé (Un Simple Soldat) and Gratien Gélinas (`Tit Coq) explored the social and moral issues confronting Québecers in their own dialect. This movement reached its apex in the work of Michel Tremblay in the early 1970s. More recently, Quebec theatre has also excelled in less verbal forms of theatre such as the spectacles produced by Cirque du Soleil, while the "total theatre" productions of Quebec City writer/performer/director Robert LePage have garnered critical acclaim around the world.

Dora Awards, 1999

The Doras, honoring excellence in Toronto theatrical productons, were first handed out in 1981. Named for Dora Mavor Moore, a teacher and director who helped establish

professional theatre in Canada in the 1930s and 1940s, the awards are annually chosen from over 200 productions.

Outstanding New Play or Musical ....*The Drawer Boy* by Michael Healey

Outstanding New Musical ....*The Nutmet Princess* by Richardo Keens-Douglas

Outstanding Production of a Play ....*The Drawer Boy*, Theatre Passe Muraille

Outstanding Production of a Musical ....*Norma*, Canadian Opera Company

Outstanding Direction of a Play ....Sheil Parsa, *Aurash*, Miles Potter, *The Drawer Boy*

Outstanding Direction of a Musical ....Stephen Wadsworth, *Xerxes*

Outstanding Performance by a Male in a Principle Role-Play ....David Fox, *The Drawer Boy*

Outstanding Performance by a Female in a Principal Role-Play ....Nancy Beatty, *Risk Everything*

Outstanding Performance by a Male in a Principal Role-Musical..................Colm Wilkinson, *Les Miserables*

Outstanding Performance by a Female in a Principal Role-Musical........................Irina Mishura, *Il Trovatore*

Outstanding Performance in a Featured Role-Play or Musical ....Gerard Parkes, *Kilt*

Outstanding Production for Young Audiences ....*Dib and Bob and the Journey Home*, Roseneath Theatre

Independent Theatre

Outstanding New Play or Musical ....*Easy Lenny Lazmon and the Great Western Ascension*, Anton Piatigorsky

Outstanding Production..*Easy Lenny Lazmon and the Great Western Ascension*, Moriah Productions in association with Go Chicken Go

Outstanding Direction ....Chris Abraham, *Easy Lenny Lazmon and the Great Western Ascension*

Outstanding Performance by a Female ....Waneta Storms, *Coyote Ugly*

Outstanding Performance by a Male ....Graeme Somerville, *Lenz*

Source: *Toronto Theatre Alliance*

Jessie Awards, 1999

Named for professional theatre pioneer Jessie Richardson, these awards honour excellence in and raise awareness of professional theatre in Vancouver. Winners of the 17th annual awards were announced June 13, 1999.

Small Theatre

Outstanding Original Production of a Play or Musical .... Ruby Slippers, Touchstone Theatre & Vancouver Moving Theatre, *The Good Person of Setzuan*

Outstanding Performance by an Actress in a Lead Role .... Gian Chiarelli, *Agnes of God*

Outstanding Performance by an Actor in a Lead Role .... Jonathon Young, *The Good Person of Setzuan*

Outstanding Performance by an Actress in a Supporting Role .... Lois Anderson, *Devil Box Cabaret*

Outstanding Performance by an Actor in a Supporting Role .... Ian Ross McDonald, *The Ruby Cabaret*

Outstanding Costume Design .... Mara Gottler, *The Life of Galileo*

Outstanding Set Design of a Play .... João Cartos d'Almeida, David C. Jones & Michelle Porter— *A Twisted Christmas Carol*

Outstanding Lighting Design .... Eduardo Meneses, *Reading Hebron*

Outstanding Sound Design or Original Composition .... David Rhymer, *Devil Box Cabaret*

Large Theatre

Outstanding Production of a Play or Musical .... *Problem Child*, Green Thumb Theatre

Larry Lillo Award for Outstanding Direction .... Patrick McDonald, *Problem Child*

Outstanding Performance by an Actress in a Lead Role .... Jillian Fargey, *Problem Child*

Outstanding Performance by an Actor in a Lead Role .... Lorne Kennedy, *Moon Over Buffalo*

Outstanding Performance by an Actress in a Supporting Role .... Patti Allan, *Hamlet*

Outstanding Performance by an Actor in a Supporting Role .... Dean Paul Gibson, *Problem Child*

Outstanding Set Design of a Play or Musical .... David Roberts, *Adult Entertainment* and *Problem Child*

Outstanding Lighting Design of a Play or Musical .... Susann Hudson, *Problem Child*

Outstanding Sound Design or Original Composition .... Jeff Comess & Mark Ferris, *Hamlet*

Outstanding Costume Design of a Play or Musical .... Nancy Bryant, *Hamlet*

Source: *Jessies Richardson Society*

Theatre Highlights for 2000

The Vancouver Playhouse, Vancouver B.C.

The Overcoat, an award-winning production conceived and directed by Morris Panych and Wendy Gorling launches a national tour from the Playhouse, January 24 to February 5. Through a dynamic mix of music, movement and physical theatre reminiscent of a silent movie, *The Overcoat* tells the captivating story of The Man whose beautiful new overcoat changes his life in ways he never imagined. After a production of Oliver Goldsmith's comedy of manners *She Stoops to Conquer*, the Playhouse presents *Patience*, by Canadian playwright Jason Sherman, from March 15 to April 15. Sherman uses black humour and dialogue to give a new twist to the Book of Job. *Patience* is followed, from April 24 to May20 by the world premiere of *The Bachelor Brothers On Tour*, by Bill Dow & Martin Kinch, based on the novels by popular CBC broadcaster Bill Richardson. When the local cemetery is once again threatened by the ever-expanding golf course, the Bachelor Brothers decide to capitalize on their fame and save the peace and tranquility of their gulf island community.

Tickets and performance information can be obtained by calling (604)873-3311.

Neptune Theatre,
Halifax, Nova Scotia

From January 21 to February 21, Neptune presents *The Memory of Water* by British playwright Shelagh Stephenson. The season continues with the professional World Premiere of *Rough Waters*, by Melissa Mullen, February 25 to March 19. Set in a coastal community in Nova Scotia, this is the story of Gordon O'Neill, who is doggedly follows in his late father's footsteps as an inshore fisherman, but now finds his livelihood threatened. *The Government Inspector* by Nikolai Gogol continues the season from March 31 to April 23, running simultaneously with *Wingfield Unbound* by Ontario's Dan Needles. The final chapter in Needles' Wingfield Cycle chronicling the uproarious saga stockbroker-turned-farmer Walt Wingfield.

Tickets and information can be obtained by calling (902) 429-7300, 1-800-565-7345.

Theatre Calgary,
Calgary, Alberta

The new year begins with *Gaslight,* by Patrick Hamilton which runs from January 18 to February 5, 2000. It describes the torment of a young bride slowly going insane in the gaslit rooms of her Victorian home. The season continues from February 15 to March 4 with *A Fitting Confusion*, a delightful French farce by Georges Feydau .Philip Barry's *Holiday* (March 21 to April 8, 2000) tells the story of the young and successful Johnny Case and his struggle with the high society family of Julia Seton, the woman of his dreams. Theatre Calgary concludes the 1999-2000 season between April 25 and May 13 with *Berlin to Broadway with Kurt Weill— A Musical Voyage!*, a tour of musical theatre history that takes the German composer from the avant garde theatre of 1920s Berlin to the acclaim of Broadway in the 1930s and 1940s. **Tickets and information can be obtained by calling (403) 294-7440.**

Summer Theatre in Canada

Blyth Festival: P.O. Box 10, Blyth, Ont. N0M 1H0

Charlottetown Festival: Confederation Centre of Arts, 145 Richmond St., Charlottetown, P.E.I. C1A 1J1)

Huron Country Playhouse: R.R. #1, Grand Bend, Ont. N0M 1T0

Kawartha Summer Theatre: P.O. Box 161, 2 Lindsay St. S, Lindsay, Ont. K9V 4S1

Lighthouse Festival Theatre: P.O. Box 1208, Port Dover, Ont. N0A 1N0

Nanaimo Festival: P.O. Box 626, Nanaimo, B.C. V9R 5L9 (Michael McLaughlin)

Port Credit Summer Theatre: 161 Lakeshore Road W., Mississauga, Ont. L5H 1G3

Red Barn Theatre: P.O. Box 291, Jackson's Point, Ont. L0E 1L0

Shaw Festival Theatre: P.O. Box 774, Niagara-on-the-Lake, Ont. L0S 1J0

Stephenville Festival: 149 Montana Dr., Stephenville, Nfld. A2N 2T4

Stratford Shakespearean Festival: P.O. Box 520, Stratford, Ont. N5A 6V2

Theatre Orangeville: 87 Broadway, Orangeville Opera House, Orangeville, Ont. L9W 1K1)

Thousand Islands Playhouse: Box 241, Gananoque, Ont. K7G 2T8

Upper Canada Playhouse: P.O. Box 852, Morrisburg, Ont. K0C 1X0

Sources Include: *The Professional Association of Canadian Theatres*

Major Theatre Companies in Canada

MARITIMES

Mermaid Theatre of Nova Scotia: Box 2697, Windsor, N.S. B0N 2T0

Mulgrave Road Co-op Theatre: Box 219, Guysborough, N.S. B0H 1N0

Neptune Theatre Foundation: #B24, 1903 Barrington St., Halifax, N.S. B3J 3L7

Ship's Company Theatre: P.O. Box 275, Parrsboro, N.S. B0M 1S0

Theatre New Brunswick: Box 566, Fredericton, N.B. E3B 5A6

CENTRAL CANADA

Buddies in Bad Times: 12 Alexander St, Toronto, Ont. M5R 1E8

Canadian Stage Company: 26 Berkeley St, Toronto, Ont. M5A 2W3

Centaur Theatre Company: 453, rue Saint-François-Xavier, Montreal, Que. H2Y 2T1

La Compagnie Jean Duceppe: 1400 rue Saint-Urbain, Montreal, Que. H2X 2M5

Company of Sirens: 736 Bathurst St, Toronto, Ont. M5S 2R4

Factory Theatre: 125 Bathurst St, Toronto, Ont. M5V 2R2

Grand Theatre Company (Theatre London): 471 Richmond St, London, Ont. N6A 3E4

Great Canadian Theatre Company: 910 Gladstone Ave, Ottawa, Ont. K1R 6Y4

Gryphon Theatre: Box 454, Barrie, Ont. L4M 4T7

Magnus Theatre Company: The Central School Bldg., 10 South Algoma St, Thunder Bay, Ont. P7B 3A7

National Arts Centre: Box 1534, Stn. B, Ottawa, Ont. K1P 5W1

Native Earth Performing Arts: 503-720 Bathurst St, Toronto, Ont. M5S 2R4

Nightwood Theatre: 6000-317 Adelaide St W, Toronto, Ont. M5V 1T2

The Piggery: Box 390, North Hatley, Que. J0B 2C0

Princess of Wales Theatre: 300 King St W, Toronto, Ont. M5V 1J2

Royal Alexandra Theatre: 260 King St W, Toronto, Ont. M5V 1H9

Saidye Bronfman Centre for the Arts: 5170 Chemin de la Côte, Ste.-Catherine, Montreal, Que. H3Y 1M7

Sudbury Theatre Centre: Box 641, Stn. B, Sudbury, Ont. P3E 4P8

Tarragon Theatre: 30 Bridgman Ave, Toronto, Ont. M5R 1X3

Theatre Aquarius: 190 King William St., Hamilton, Ont. L8R 1A8

Théâtre de la Bordée: 1105, rue Saint-Jean, #201, Quebec, Que. G1R 1S3

Théâtre du Nouveau Monde: 137, Saint-Ferdinand, #201, Montreal, Que. H4C 2S7

Théâtre du Rideau Vert: 269 Rene Levesque G, Que., Que. G1R 2B3

Le Théâtre du Trident: 580, ave Grande-Allée est, #20, Quebec, Que. G1R 2K2

Theatre Passe Muraille: 16 Ryerson Ave, Toronto, Ont. M5T 2P3

Young People's Theatre: 165 Front St E, Toronto, Ont. M5A 3Z4

WESTERN CANADA

Alberta Theatre Projects: 220-9th Ave SE, Calgary, Alta. T2G 5C4

Arts Club Theatre: 1585 Johnson St, Vancouver, B.C. V6H 3R9

Belfry Theatre: 1291 Gladstone Ave, Victoria, B.C. V8T 1G5

Citadel Theatre: 9828-101A Ave, Edmonton, Alta. T5J 3C6

Globe Theatre: 1801 Scarth St, Regina, Sask. S4P 2G9

Manitoba Theatre Centre: 174 Market Ave, Winnipeg, Man. R3B 0P8

Manitoba Theatre for Young People: 89 Princess St, Winnipeg, Man. R3B 2X5

New Bastion Theatre Company: 625 Superior Ave, Victoria, BC V8V 1V1

Nightcap Productions: Box 1646, Saskatoon, Sask. S7K 3R8

Persephone Theatre: 2802 Rusholme Rd, Saskatoon, Sask. S7L 0H2

Popular Theatre Alliance of Manitoba: 2-413 Selkirk Ave, Winnipeg, Man. R2W 2M4

Prairie Theatre Exchange: 389 Portage Ave, Portage Place, Unit Y300, Winnipeg, Man. R3B 3H6

Tamahnous Theatre Workshop Society: 222-275 Woodland Dr, Vancouver, B.C. V5L 3S7

Theatre Calgary: 220-9th Ave. SE, Calgary, Alta. T2G 5C4

Theatre Network Society: 10708-124th St, Edmonton, Alta. T5M 0H1

25th Street Theatre: 420 Duchess St, Saskatoon, Sask. S7K 0R1

Vancouver Playhouse: 160 West 1st Ave, Vancouver, B.C. V5Y 1A4

Western Canada Theatre Company: Box 329, Kamloops, BC V2C 5K9

Sources Include: *The Professional Association of Canadian Theatres*

DANCE

Canada is home to strong traditions in both classical and contemporary dance. Founded in 1938, The Royal Winnipeg Ballet is the second oldest company in North America and was the first in the Commonwealth to receive a Royal charter. Since 1951, the Toronto-based National Ballet of Canada has provided a home to major talents including prima ballerinas Karen Kain and Veronica Tennant. It has also been a favoured stopping place for international greats such as the late Rudolph Nureyev. The National Ballet was instrumental in facilitating the 1979 defection of Russia's Mikhail Barishnykov in Toronto. Barishnykov danced his first performances as a free man with the National Ballet, an event whose anniversary was marked in 1999 with the presentation of an honorary doctorate to Baryshnikov at the University of Toronto.

Major Ballet Companies

Alberta Ballet: 141-18th Avenue SW, Calgary , AB, T2S 0B8

Ballet British Columbia: #102, 1101 West Broadway, Vancouver, B.C. V6H 1G2

Ballet Jorgen: 213B Glebeholme Blvd., Toronto, Ont., M4J 1S8

Ballet North: 12245-131 St., Edmonton, Alta. T5L 1M8

Les Grands Ballets Canadiens: 4816 rue Rivard, Montreal, Que. H2J 2N6

Royal Winnipeg Ballet: 380 Graham Ave., Winnipeg, Man. R3C 4K2

The National Ballet of Canada: The Walter Carson Centre, 470 Queen's Quay W, Toronto, Ont. M5V 3K4

Major Contemporary and Jazz Dance Companies

Les Ballets Jazz de Montréal: 3450 rue St-Urbain, Montreal, Que. H2X 2N5

Contemporary Dancers Canada: 109 Pulford St., Winnipeg, Man. R3L 1X8

Dancemakers: 927 Dupont St., Toronto, Ont. M6H 1Z1

Decidedly Jazz Danceworks: 1514 - 4 St. SW, Calgary, Alta. T2R 0Y4

Desrosiers Dance Theatre: 103-219 Broadview Ave., Toronto, Ont. M4M 2G3

Fortier Danse Création: Box 605, Stn. C., Montreal, Que. H2L 4L5

Margie Gillis Dance Foundation: 502-3575 boul. St. Laurent, #502, Montreal, Que. H2X 2T7

Danny Grossman Dance Company: 511 Bloor St. W., Toronto, Ont. M5S 1Y4

LaLaLa Human Steps: #206, 5655 av. du Parc, Montreal, Que. H2V 4H2

Le Groupe de la Place Royale: 2 Daly Ave., Ste. 2, Ottawa, Ont. K1N 6E2

Karen Jamieson Dance Company: 221 E. 16th Ave., Vancouver, B.C. V5T 2T5

Kompany!: #810, 10136-100th St., Edmonton, Alta. T5J 0P1

Mascall Dance: 1130 Jervis St., Vancouver, B.C. V6E 2C7

O Vertigo Danse: 4455 rue de Rouen, Montreal, Que. H1V 1H1

La Fondation Jean-Pierre Perreault: 2022 Rue Sherbrooke Est, Montreal, Que. H2K 1B9

Gina Lori Riley Dance Enterprises: 3277 Sandwich St., Windsor, Ont. N9C 1A9

Toronto Dance Theatre: 80 Winchester St., Toronto, Ont. M4X 1B2

Canadian Children's Dance Theatre: 509 Parliament St. Toronto, Ont. M4X 1P3

Compagnie Marie Chouinard: #615-3981 boul. St.-Laurent, Montreal, Wue. H2W 1Y5

Dance Arts Vancouver: #402-873 Beatty St. Vancouver, BC V6B 2M6

Source: *Dance Umbrella of Ontario*

BOOKS, MAGAZINES, NEWSPAPERS

The 326 Canadian-owned publishers account for half of all book sales in Canada, but they publish between 80 and 90 percent of new Canadian books. Canadian Heritage's most recent study (for 1994-1995) puts total revenues for Canadian publishers at $1.8 billion plus annually. Magazine publishing in Canada is an $866 million business in which domestic magazines take a 30 percent share of the market. The magazine industry was dealt a serious blow this year as the federal government was forced by the World Trade Organization to abandon tax measures aimed at protecting the advertising market from nominally Canadian "split run" editions of U.S. magazines. Canadian newspapers continue to enjoy increased profitability after advertising revenues slumped in the early 1990s. 1999 saw a major shift in newspaper ownership as Montreal-based Québecor Inc. took control of the Sun newspaper chain. The year also saw the emergence of a new national newspaper, Southam Inc.'s *National Post*, giving Southam and its owner, Conrad Black, a foothold in the lucrative and influential Toronto market and offering national competition to the *Globe and Mail*.

The Governor General's Literary Awards, 1988–98

The Governor General's Literary Awards, Canada's foremost literary prizes, are presented annually to recognize and reward Canadian writers. The awards were initiated in 1937 by the Canadian Authors' Association with the agreement of Governor General Baron Tweedsmuir (novelist John Buchan), and were administered by the Association until 1958.

The Awards are now administered by the Canada Council which appoints juries composed of literary specialists who select the best English and French-language works in each of 6 best categories: drama, fiction, poetry, non-fiction, and beginning in 1987, children's literature (text and illustration) and translation. The juries review all books by Canadian authors, illustrators and translators published in Canada or abroad during the previous year (Oct. 1— Sept. 30). In the case of translation, the original work must also be a Canadian-authored title. Winners receive a medal from the Governor General, $10,000 and a specially-bound copy of their award-winning book. The 1998 winners were announced Nov. 17, 1998.

English

—1988—

Fiction	*Nights Below Station Street*, David Adams Richards
Non-fiction	*In the Sleep Room*, Anne Collins
Poetry	*Furious*, Erin Mouré
Drama	*Nothing Sacred*, George F. Walker
Translation	*Second Chance*, Philip Stratford
Children's Literature (Illustration)	*Amos's Sweater*, Kim LaFave
Children's Literature (Text)	*The Third Magic*, Welwyn Wilton Katz

—1989—

Fiction	*Whale Music*, Paul Quarrington
Non-fiction	*Willie: The Life of W. Somerset Maugham*, Robert Calder
Poetry	*The Word for Sand*, Heather Spears
Drama	*The Other Side of the Dark*, Judith Thompson

Translation . . . . *On the Eighth Day*, Wayne Grady
Children's Literature (Illustration) . . . . *The Magic Paintbrush*, Robin Muller
Children's Literature (Text) . . . . *Bad Boy*, Diana Wieler

—1990—

Fiction . . . . *Lives of the Saints*, Nino Ricci
Non-fiction . . . . *Trudeau and Our Times*, Stephen Clarkson
Poetry . . . . *No Time*, Margaret Avison
Drama . . . . *Goodnight Desdemona (Good Morning Juliet)*, Ann-Marie MacDonald
Translation . . . . *Yellow-Wolf and Other Tales
of the Saint Lawrence*, Jane Brierley
Children's Literature (Illustration) . . . . *The Orphan Boy*, Paul Morin
Children's Literature (Text) . . . . *Redwork*, Michael Bedard

—1991—

Fiction . . . . *Such a Long Journey*, Rohinton Mistry
Non-fiction . . . . *Occupied Canada*, Robert Hunter and Robert Calihoo
Poetry . . . . *Night Field*, Don McKay
Drama . . . . *Amigo's Blue Guitar*, Joan MacLeod
Translation . . . . *A Dictionary of Literary Devices*, Albert W. Halsall
Children's Literature (Illustration) . . . . *Doctor Kiss Says Yes*, Joanne Fitzgerald
Children's Literature (Text) . . . . *Pick-Up Sticks*, Sarah Ellis

—1992—

Fiction . . . . *The English Patient*, Michael Ondaatje
Non-fiction . . . . *Revenge of the Land: A century of greed, tragedy
and murder on a Saskatchewan Farm*, Maggie Siggins
Poetry . . . . *Inventing the Hawk*, Lorna Crozier
Drama . . . . *Possible Worlds, A Short History of Night*, John Mighton
Translation . . . . *Imagining the Middle East*, Fred A. Reed
Children's Literature (Illustration) . . . . *Waiting for the Whales*, Ron Lightburn
Children's Literature (Text) . . . . *Hero of Lesser Causes*, Julie Johnston

—1993—

Fiction . . . . *The Stone Diaries*, Carol Shields
Non-fiction . . . . *Touch the Dragon*, Karen Connelly
Poetry . . . . *Forest of the Medieval World*, Don Coles
Drama . . . . *Fronteras Americanas*, Guillermo Verdecchia
Children's Literature (Illustration) . . . . *Sleep Tight*, Mireille Levert
Children's Literature (Text) . . . . *Some of the Kinder Planets*, Tim Wynne-Jones

—1994—

Fiction . . . . *A Discovery of Strangers*, Rudy Wiebe
Non-fiction . . . . *Rogue Primate: An Exploration of Human Domestication*, John A. Livingston
Poetry . . . . *Cantos from a Small Room*, Robert Hilles
Drama . . . . *The Ends of the Earth*, Morris Panych
Translation . *The Lyric Generation: The Life and Times of the Baby Boomers*, Donald Winkler
Children's Literature (Illustration) . . . . *Josepha: A Prairie Boy's Story*, Murray Kimber
Children's Literature (Text) . . . . *Adam and Eve and Pinch-Me*, Julie Johnston

—1995—

Fiction..*The Roaring Girl*, Greg Hollingshead
Non-fiction..........*Shadow Maker: The Life of Gwendolyn MacEwen*, Rosemary Sullivan
Poetry...Voice, Anne Szumigalski
Drama.........................*Three in the Back, Two in the Head*, Jason Sherman
Translation......................*Why Must a Black Writer Write About Sex?* David Homel
Children's Literature (Illustration)..........*The Last Quest of Gilgamesh*, Ludmila Zeman
Children's Literature (Text)..............................*The Maestro*, Tim Wynne-Jones

—1996—

Fiction......................................*The Englishman's Boy*, Guy Vanderhaeghe
Non-fiction..........................*The Unconscious Civilization*, John Raulston Saul
Poetry.............................*Apostrophes: Woman at a Piano*, E.D. Blodgett
Drama...*The Monument*, Colleen Wagner
Translation..*Stone and Ashes*, Linda Gaboriau
Children's Literature (Illustration).....................Eric Beddows, *The Rooster's Gift*
Children's Literature (Text)..*Ghost Train*, Paul Yee

—1997—

Fiction..*The Underpainter*, Jane Urquhart
Non-fiction..............*Drumblair-Memories of an American Childhood*, Rachel Manley
Poetry.......................................*Land to Light On*, Dionne Brand
Drama...*fareWel*, Ian Ross
Translation..*The Eugelion*, Howard Scott
Children's Literature (Illustration)..............................*The Party*, Barbara Reid
Children's Literature (Text)..........................*Awake and Dreaming*, Kit Pearson

—1998—

Fiction..*Forms of Devotion*, Diane Schoemperlen
Non-fiction.....................*Lines on the Water—A Fisherman's Life on the Miramichi*,
David Adams Richards
Poetry.................................*White Stone: The Alice Poems,* Stephanie Bolster
Drama...*Harlem Duet*, Djanet Sears
Translation..*Bambi and Me*, Shelia Fischman
Children's Literature (Illustration)..................*A Child's Treasury of Nursery Rhymes*,
Kady MacDonald Denton
Children's Literature (Text)..................................*The Hollow Tree*, Janet Lunn

French

—1988—

Fiction..............................*Le Silence ou le Parfait Bonheur*, Jacques Folch-Ribas
Non-fiction.................................*Écrire dans la maison du père*, Patricia Smart
Poetry...*Papiers d'épidémie*, Marcel Labine
Drama..*Le Chien*, Jean Marc Dalpé
Translation...*Nucléus*, Didier Holtzwarth
Children's Literature (Illustration).....................*Les Jeux de Pic-mots*, Philippe Béha
Children's Literature (Text)...............................*Cassiopée ou L'été polonais*,
Michèle Marineau

—1989—

Fiction . . . . *La Rage*, Louis Hamelin
Non-fiction . . . . *L'Intolérance : une problématique générale*, Lise Noël
Poetry . . . . *Monème*, Pierre Desruisseaux
Drama . . . . *Mademoiselle Rouge*, Michel Garneau
Translation . . . . *Les Âges de l'amour*, Jean Antonin Billard
Children's Literature (illustration) . . . . *Benjamin et la saga des oreillers*, Stéphane Poulin
Children's Literature (Text) . . . . *Temps mort*, Charles Montpetit

—1990—

Fiction . . . . *La Mauvaise Foi*, Gérald Tougas
Non-fiction . . . . *Dans l'oeil de l'aigle*, Jean François Lisée
Poetry . . . . *Les Cendres bleues*, Jean-Paul Daoust
Drama . . . . *Le Voyage magnifique d'Emily Carr*, Jovette Marchessault
Translation . . . . *Le Second Rouleau*, Charlotte and Robert Melançon
Children's Literature (Illustration) . . . . *Les fantaisies de l'oncle Henri*,
Pierre Pratt
Children's Literature (Text) . . . . *La Vraie Histoire du chien de Clara Vic*,
Christiane Duchesne

—1991—

Fiction . . . . *La Croix du Nord*, André Brochu
Non-fiction . . . . *Le Jaguar et le Tamanoir*, Bernard Arcand
Poetry . . . . *Chant pour un Québec lointain*, Madeleine Gagnon
Drama . . . . *Mon oncle Marcel qui vague vague près du métro Berri*, Gilbert Dupuis
Translation . . . . *Les Enfants d'Aataentsic: l'histoire du peuple huron*,
Jean-Paul Sainte-Marie and Brigitte Chabert Hacikyan
Children's Literature (Illustration) . . . . *Un champion*, Sheldon Cohen
Children's Literature (Text) . . . . *Deux heures et demie avant Jasmine*,
François Gravel

—1992—

Fiction . . . . *L'enfant chargé de songes*, Anne Hébert
Non-fiction . . . . *La Radissonie. Le pays de la baie James*, Pierre Turgeon
Poetry . . . . *Andromède attendra*, Gilles Cyr
Translation . . *La mémoire postmoderne. Essai sur l'artcanadien contemporain*, Jean Papineau
Children's Literature (Illustration) . . . . *Simon et la ville de carton*, Gille Tibo
Children's Literature (Text) . . . . *Victor*, Christiane Duchesne

—1993—

Fiction . . . . *Cartique des Plaines*, Nancy Huston
Non-fiction . . . . *Le littérature de l'exiguité*, François Paré
Poetry . . . . *Le Saut de L'ange*, Denise Desautels
Translation . . . . *L'oeuvre du Gallois*, Marie Josée Thariault
Children's Literature (Illustration) . . . . *Le monde salon jean de...*, Stéphane Jorisch
Children's Literature (Text) . . . . *La Route de Chlifa*, Michele Marineau
Drama . . . . *Celle-la*, Daniel Danis

—1994—

Fiction .... *Le Petit Aigle à tête blanche*, Robert Lalonde
Non-fiction .... *Du sida*, Chantal Saint-Jarre
Poetry .... *Aknos*, Fulvio Caccia
Translation .... *Le mythe du sauvage*, Jude des Chênes
Children's Literature (Illustration) .... *Mon chien est un éléphant*, Pierre Pratt
Children's Literature (Text) .... *Une belle journée pour mourir*, Suzanne Martel
Drama .... *French Town*, Michel Ouellette

—1995—

Fiction .... *Les Oiseaux de Saint-John Perse*, Nicole Houde
Non-fiction .... *Louis-Antoine Dessaulles*, Yvan Lamonde
Poetry .... *Pour orchestre et poète seul*, Émile Martel
Translation .... *Entre l'ordre et la liberté*, Hervé Juste
Children's Literature (Illustration) ... *Sho et les dragons d'eau*, Annouchka Gravel Galouchko
Children's Literature (Text) .... *Comme une peau de chagrin*, Sonia Sarfati
Drama .... *Les Quatre Morts de Marie*, Carole Fréchette

—1996—

Fiction .... *Soifs*, Marie-Claire Blais
Non-fiction .... *Le Naufrage de l'universite-Et autres essais d'epistemologie politique*
Poetry .... *Le Quator de l' errance, La traversee du desert*
Drama .... *Le Passage de L'Indiana,* Normand Charette
Children's Literature (Illustration) .... no award
Children's Literature (Text) .... *Noemie-Le Secret de Madame Lumbago*, Gilles Tibo

—1997—

Fiction .... *Cet imperceptible mouvement*, Aude
Non-fiction .... *Enfants du néant et mangeurs d'âmes-Guerre,*
culture et société en Iroquoisie ancienne, Roland Viau
Poetry .... *Romans-fleuves*, Pierre Nepveu
Drama .... *Dits et Inédits*, Yvan Bienvenue
Translation .... *Arracher les montagnes*, Marie José Thériault
Children's Literature (Illustration) .... *Poil de serpent, dent d'araignée*, Stéphane Poulin
Children's Literature (Text) .... *Pien*, Michel Noël

—1998—

Fiction .... *La Terre ferme*, Christiane Frenette
Non-fiction .... *Intérieurs du nouveau monde: essais dur les littératures du*
Québec et des Amériques, Pierre Nepveu
Poetry .... *Le Part de feu/Le Deuil de la rancune*, Suzanne Jacob
Drama .... *15 secondes*, François Archambault
Translation .... Charlotte Mclançon, *Les Sources du moi- La Formation de l'identité moderne*
Children's Literature (Illustration) .... *Monsieur Ilétaitunefois*, Pierre Pratt
Children's Literature (Text) .... *Variations sur un même &laqnot'aime*, Angèle Delaunois

Source: *The Canada Council*

Bestselling Books in Canada, 1998

(Canadian books in bold type)

Fiction

1. ***Fugitive Pieces*, by Anne Michaels**
2. ***Barney's Version*, by Mordecai Richler**
3. *Wizard And Glass: Dark Tower IV*, by Stephen King
4. *Tara Road*, by Maeve Binchy
5. ***The Underpainter*, by Jane Urquhart**
6. *The Street Lawyer*, by John Grisham
7. *The Path Of Daggers*, by Robert Jordan
8. *I Know This Much Is True*, by Wally Lamb
9. *Rainbow Six*, by Tom Clancy
10. *A Widow For One Year*, by John Irving

Non-fiction

1. *Angela's Ashes*, by Frank McCourt
2. ***The Ice Storm*, by Mark Abley**
3. *The Man Who Listens To Horses*, by Monty Roberts
4. *Talking To Heaven*, by James Van Praagh
5. ***Boom Bust & Echo*, by David K. Foot with Daniel Stoffman**
6. *Conversations With God*, Book I, by Neale Donald
7. ***The Morningside Years*, by Peter Gzowski**
8. ***James Cameron's Titanic*, by Ed Marsh, Douglas Kirkland and James Cameron**
9. ***No Holds Barred: My Life In Politics*, by John C. Crosbie**
10. **The Canadian Oxford Dictionary, edited by Katherine Barber**

Source: *The Globe and Mail*

Canadian books set in bold type.

The Booker Prize, 1988–98

The Booker Prize recognizes the best work of English fiction published in the Commonwealth, South Africa and Ireland. It is sponsored by Booker McConnell Ltd., an international food and agriculture business, and administered by the Booker Prize Book Trust, a British educational charity. Since 1984, the value of the Booker Prize has been £15,000.

Year	Author	Title
1988	Peter Carey	*Oscar and Lucinda*
1989	Kazuo Ishiguro	*The Remains of the Day*
1990	A.S. Byatt	*Possession*
1991	Ben Okri	*The Famished Road*
1992 (joint winners)	Michael Ondaatje	*The English Patient*
	Barry Unsworth	*Sacred Hunger*
1993	Roddy Doyle	*Paddy Clarke Ha Ha Ha*
1994	James Kelman	*How Late it Was, How Late*
1995	Pat Barker	*The Ghost Road*
1996	Graham Swift	*Last Orders*
1997	Arundhati Roy	*God of Small Things*
1998	Ian McEwan	*Amsterdam*

Pulitzer Prizes, 1998

The winners of these annual American literary awards were announced on April 14, 1999.

Fiction ....Michael Cunningham, *The Hours*

Non-fiction ....John McPhee, *Annals of the Former World*

Poetry ....Mark Strand, *Blizzard of One*

Drama ....Margaret Edson, *Wit*

Biography ....A. Scott Berg, *Lindbergh*

History ....Edwin G. Burrows and Mike Wallace, *Gotham: A History of New York City to 1898*

Music ....Melinda Wagner, *Concerto for Flute, Strings and Percussion*

Special Award ....Edward Kennedy "Duke" Ellington

National Magazine Awards, 1998

These annual awards were given June 4, 1999 by the National Magazine Awards Foundation. In 1997 there were gold and silver awards in 33 categories, including writing, design and photography.

One-of-a-Kind Articles . . . . .Patricia Pearson, "Death Becomes Her," *Saturday Night*

Humour . . . . .Caitlin Kelly, "Yak Attack.," *Elm Street*

Business . . . . .Trevor Cole, "The Empire Builders," *Report on Business Magazine*

Science, Health and Medicine . . . . .Yanick Villedieu "Portrait de famille," *L'Actualité*

Still-Life Photography . . . . .George Whiteside, "Precious Metals," *President's Choice Magazine*

Fashion . . . . .Denis Desro, Raphael Mazzucco, Isabelle Long, "Impact," *Elle Québec*

Politics . . . . .André Lachance, "Du mauvais côté de la Baie James," *L'Actualité*

Investigative Reporting . . . . .Jane O'Hara, "Rape in the Military," *Maclean's*

Fiction . . . . .Alice Munro, "Jalarata," *Saturday Night*

Arts and Entertainment . . . . .Anne Kingston, "Lolita Writes Back," *Saturday Night*

Environments . . . . .George Whiteside, "Objects of Desire," *Canadian House & Home*

Sports and Recreation .Ian Brown, "Thirteen Ways of Learning at a Rapid," *Outdoor Canada*

Photojournalism . . . . .William DeKay, "Double Take," *Canadaian Geographic*

Personal journalism . . . . .Moira Johnston, "The Raven's Last Journey," *Saturday Night*

Portrait Photography . . . . .Tom Feiler, "Picture Perfect," *Shift*

Columns . . . .Jean Paré, "Dossier 25506: Chirurgie à la tronconneuse 50%…C'est trop peu. Et c'est trop!" *L'Actualité*

Service . . . . .Jamie Maw, Ninth Annual Restaurant Awards, *Vancouver Magazine*

Travel . . . . .Carole Beaulieu, "Au Pays des superbranches," *L'Actualité*

Spot Illustration . . . . .Barbar Klunder, "Guide to World Music," *Shift*

How-To . . . . .John Sillaots, "The Ultimate Shop," *Canadian Home Workshop*

Essays . . . . .Jay Teitel, "The Road Not Taken," *Toronto Life*

Profiles . . . . .Sarah Hampson, "Toth, He Went a Courtin'," *Saturday Night*

Poetry . . . . .Julie Bruck, "Drive," *Carousel*

Art Direction for a Single Article . . . . .Carmen Dunjko, Malcolm Brown, "Picture Perfect," *Shift*

Editorial Package . . . . .Ann Dowsett and *Maclean's* staff , "Measuring Excellence," *Maclean's*

Words and Pictures . . . . .Harvey Chan, Ken Hewitt-White, *Cottage Life* staff, "Legends in the Sky," *Cottage Life*

Social Affairs . . . . .Pierre Lacerte, "Rien ne va plus," *L'Actualité*

Magazine Covers . . . . .Carmen Dunjko, Malcolm Brown, "Bran Man 3000," *Shift*

President's Medal . . . . .Jane O'Hara, *Maclean's*

Magazine of the Year . . . .*Adbusters*

Best New Magazine . . . .*Gardening Life*

Alexander Ross Award for Best New Magazine Writer . . . . .Hal Niedviecki

Foundation Award for Outstanding Achievement . . . . .Lynn Cunningham

Source: *National Magazine Awards Foundation*

Bill C-55: "Split Run" Magazines in Canada

anada-U.S. relations were strained through the first half of 1999 by the threatened passage into law of Bill C-55 by the federal government. The bill would have made it illegal for Canadian advertisers to purchase space in American "split run" magazines (magazines produced in the United States with small additions of Canadian content and beamed via satellite into Canada for printing). In 1998, the World Trade Organization overturned the tax measures that Canada had used to protect the domestic advertising market after a complaint from the American government. Bill C-55 was intended as a replacement for the disallowed tariffs. It was passed by the federal parliament in March, causing American Trade Officials to threaten retaliation in key trade sectors including steel, wood products and textiles. Before the bill was given royal assent, an agreement was reached, allowing certain split runs to sell up to 18 percent of their advertizing space to Canadian advertisers provided they meet yet-to-be agreed on quotas for Canadian content. Some Canadian industry spokespersons saw the agreement as a major blow to the financial viability of Canadian magazines. Others spoke of a future in which Canadian magazines might either adopt a more intensely local focus, or seek U.S. production partners to keep competitive.

Top Canadian Paid–Circulation Magazines, 1998

Magazine	Circulation
Reader's Digest (Canadian English edition)	1 090 036
Chatelaine (English language edition)	788 861
TV Guide	678 611
Canadian Living	555 118
Maclean's	503 497
Time (Canadian edition)	315 298
Séléction du Reader's Digest (Canadian French edition)	240 010
Canadian Geographic	229 420
TV Hebdo	209 025
Châtelaine (French language edition)	187 913
L'Actualité	181 201
Flare	169 626
Coupe de Pouce	157 212
7 Jours	142 151

Source: *CARD: Media Information Network*

The Stephen Leacock Award for Humour

tephen Butler Leacock was born in England in 1869. His education included Upper Canada College, a B.A. at U of T, and a Ph.D from the University of Chicago. He taught at UCC, and later lectured in political science at McGill. His literary output included works in history, economics and political science, although by far the most popular were his humour books. By the time of his death in 1944, he was the best-known humourist in the English-speaking world.

Canada's highest award for humour is named in Leacock's honour and is given annually at a ceremony in his hometown of Orillia, Ontario. The 1999 winner was Stuart McLean for Home From the Vinyl Café.

Top Canadian Daily Newspapers, 1999

Newspaper	Circulation[1]		
	Daily[2]	Weekend	
Toronto Star (m)	467 651	708,815 (Sat.)	474 299 (Sun.)
Globe and Mail (m)(3)	317 826 (Mon.-Fri.);		
330 679 (Mon-Sat.)	381 783 (Sat.)		
Journal de Montreal (m)	273 990	337 642(Sat.)	284 741 (Sun.)
Toronto Sun (m)	240 674	189 198 (Sat.)	405 163 (Sun.)
Vancouver Sun (m)	190 414 (Mon-Thu.)		285 940 (Sat.)
	230 125 (Fri.)		
La Presse (m)	178 359	291 134 (Sat.)	188 100 (Sun.)
Vancouver Province (m)	156 826		195 824 (Sun.)
Edmonton Journal (m)	148 946 (Mon.-Th./Sat.);		145 133 (Sun.)
	177 221 (Fri.)		
Montreal Gazette (m)	143 329	198 738 (Sat.)	134 062 (Sun.)
Ottawa Citizen (m)	139 618	185 704 (Sat.)	129 983 (Sun.)
Winnipeg Free Press (m)	129 542	194 000 (Sat.)	146 107 (Sun.)
Calgary Herald (m)	117 514 (Mon-Th.);	137 511 (Sat.)	120 018 (Sun.)
	161 159 477 (Fri.)		
Hamilton Spectator (m)	109 175	132 356 (Sat.)	
London Free Press (m)	101 705	131 196 (Sat.)	
Le Journal de Quebec (m)	97 861	128 681 (Sat.)	99 612 (Sun.)
Halifax Chronicle Herald (m)	123 323 (comb.)		
	91 545 (m)		
	31 778 (e)		58 829 (Sun.)
Victoria-Times Columnist (m)	75 709 (Mon.-Sat.)		75 154 (Sun.)
Windsor Star (m)	74 927	88 155 (Sat.)	
Edmonton Sun (m)	75 073 (Mon.-Sat.)		113 783

Sources: *CARD Media Information Network*
(1) Average total circulation for most recently reported 6 month period as of July 1999. (2) Monday to Friday unless otherwise indicated (m) morning (e) evening

National Newspaper Awards, 1998

These annual awards were announced in Toronto on May 8, 1999.

Editorial Writing ....Murdoch Davis, *Edmonton Journal.*
Spot News Photography ....Ryan Remiorz, Canadian Press.
Feature Photography ....Julie Oliver, *Ottawa Citizen.*
Spot News Reporting ....Canadian Press, Halifax Bureau.
International Reporting ....Christina Spencer, *Ottawa Citizen.*
Sports Writing ....Damien Cox, *Toronto Star.*
Feature Writing ....Shelley Page, *Ottawa Citizen.*
Columns ....Marcus Gee, *Globe and Mail.*
Sports Photography ....Jeff MacIntosh, *Calgary Herald.*
Enterprise Reporting ....Peter Cheney, *Toronto Star/Globe and Mail.*
Critical Writing ....Doug Saunders, *Globe and Mail.*
Layout and Design ....Gayle Grin, *Montreal Gazette.*
Editorial Cartooning ....Roy Peterson, *Vancouver Sun.*
Business Reporting ....David Bains, Adrian du Plessis, *Vancouver Sunl.*
Special Projects ....*Vancouver Sun.*
Local Reporting ....*New Brunswick Telegraph Journal*

Source: *Canadian Newspaper Association*

GALLERIES AND MUSEUMS

Canadian art is a time-honoured tradition with the oldest surviving work of prehistoric First Nations carving dating back to 5,000 B.C. European traditions were slow to take hold in the colonnial regime. Bishop Laval established the country's first school of art near Quebec in 1675 and religious art dominated the Canadian scene until the 19th century when Paul Kane and Cornelius Krieghoff became the country's first genre painters, rendering scenes of native and settler life respectively. After the establishment of major art institions such as the Royal Canadian Academy of Art (1880) and the Ontario College of Art (1875), landscape became the dominant form of Canadian painting, a trend that peaked with the formation of the Group of Seven in 1920 (see article below). Abstract art reached Canada in the 1940s and gained its first domestic expression in the work of Montreal's automatiste painters, lead by Jean Paul Riopelle and Paul-Emile Borduas, working under the influence of cubism and the French surreallists. Art in English Canada remained under the sway of the Group of Seven and that of British representational trends in portraiture and urban landscape until the formation in 1954 and subsequent international success of Painters Eleven in Toronto. This group which featured Jack Bush, Kazuo Nakamura, Jock MacDonald, William Ronald, and Harold Town drew heavily on the abstract expressionist movement in the United States for inspiration and its members scored success in New York critical circles of the period. Leadership reverted to Montreal in the 1960s with the emergence of painters devoted to the op art school focussing on experiments in visual effects and surface dynamics. While magic realist painters such as Nova Scotia's Alex Colville, and Newfoundland's Christopher Pratt and Manitoba-born naïve painter William Kurelek kept representational painting popular through the 1970s, a new generation of artists such as Michael Snow, Greg Curnoe, General Idea, and Iain Baxter followed the international trend away from painting into conceptual art exploring new media such as film, photography, performance and installation art. The 1980s saw a rebirth in interest in representational painting with the emergence of neo-expressionist influenced work from groups such as Vancouver's New Romantics and Toronto's ChromaZone Collective. Today the Canadian art scene features artists working in every conceivable medium and genre. Their work is shown in artist run collectives, commercial galleries and larger public galleries in every major centre.

Group of Seven

The Group of Seven held its first exhibition at the Art Gallery of Toronto in May 1920. The original members included J.E.H. MacDonald, Lawren Harris, A.Y. Jackson, Arthur Lismer, F.H. Varley, Frank Johnston and Franklin Carmichael.

In 1924, Johnston resigned from the Group and, in 1926, A.J. Casson was invited to join. In the later years of the Group, two new members, Edwin Holgate and Lionel Lemoine FitzGerald, were added. The Group held its final exhibition in Dec. 1931 and disbanded in 1932.

Tom Thomson, who drowned in 1917, was never a member of the Group of Seven, though his boldly-colored works depicting the rugged landscape of northern Ontario became associated with its style of painting.

By breaking with the traditional, European, painting style popular in Canada in the 1920s,

The Group of Seven made a huge impact on Canadian art. Although originally reviled by critics, the Group had gained wide acceptance and popularity by the 1930s. Today, the Group's paintings are exhibited in every major gallery in Canada.

J.E.H. **MacDonald** (1873–1932)

Lawren **Harris** (1885–1970)

Alexander Young (A.Y.) **Jackson** (1882–1974)

Arthur **Lismer** (1885–1969)

Frederick Horsman **Varley** (1881–1969)

Frank Hans **Johnston** (1888–1949)

Frank **Carmichael** (1890–1945)

Alfred Joseph (A.J.) **Casson** (1898–1992)

Edwin **Holgate** (1892–1977)

Lionel Lemoine **FitzGerald** (1890–1956)

Tom **Thomson** (1877–1917)

Source: *Looking at Landscape,* Dwight Siegner, The McMichael Canadian Art Collection

Gallery and Museum Highlights, 2000

Glenbow Museum, Calgary

The dawn of the new millenium will find the Glenbow exploiting its French connections, first *Toulouse-Lautrec: The Baldwin M. Baldwin Collection,* October 16, 1999 to January 2, 2000. The exhibition will comprise 108 drawings, prints, and paintings which chart the extraordinary life and art of Henri Toulouse-Lautrec. An aristocratic and bohemian artist who immersed himself in the nightlife of Paris, Toulouse-Lautrec provides a look into Paris at the end of the 19th century: its night life, cafes, dance halls, theatres, and brothels. His graphic works portray the essence of this era. Organized and circulated by the San Diego Museum of Art. The Parisian theme will be given a Canadian twist in *Canadian Artists in Paris and The French Influence* which will run simultaneously.The works of Canadian artists who left Canada for Paris around the turn of the last century will be highlighted, including celebrated painters Emily Carr, A.Y. Jackson and James Wilson Morrice. The millenium itself is the subject of Glenbow's first show of 2000. From January 29, 2000 to May 22, 2000, the museum will present *Face Forward: 6 Canadians Confron the Millenium* in which six prominent Western Canadians who have made a contribution in politics, sports or the arts – will curate an exhibit on six different themes, from heroes to communications and the media,; from the environment to the universal search for home.

Montreal Museum of Fine Art, Montreal

The Museum of Fine Art proposes to offer a visit to sunny Mexico as an antidote to those blustery Montreal winters with *Modern Mexican Art 1900-1950,* a show organized in cooperation with the National Gallery of Canada which runs from November 4, 1999 to February 6, 2000. An exhibition on the birth and flourishing of modernism in Mexico during the first half of the twentieth century, a

time when several overlapping generations of painters, sculptors and photographers inspired by the Mexican Revolution provoked a "Renaissance" of the arts. The show features 280 paintings, sculptures, prints and photographs by a wide range of renowned artists, including Rivera, Orozco, Siqueiros, Kahlo, Tamayo, Izquierdo and Ruiz. Rare and captivating seventeenth- to early eighteenth-century architectural models, drawings and paintings from all over Europe make up *Triumphs of the Baroque,* which runs December 9, 1999, to April 9, 2000. Models of opulent pontifical and private sites by Bernini, Pierre de Cortone and Borromi will reveal the heart of modern Rome, while the works of Italian architects then working abroad at the time demonstrate the introduction of new styles elsewhere. Landscape gardening, which burgeoned in this period in conjunction with the construction of palaces and villas, will also be a feature.

Art Gallery of Ontario, Toronto

An opportunity to visit the roots of representational painting in Canada will be offered with *Krieghoff: Images of Canada* running from November 26, 1999 to March 5, 2000.

Cornelius Krieghoff is considered the earliest Canadian genre painter to focus on scenes of the everyday lives of Canadian settlers in the nineteenth century. Also running through 2000 is *Treasures of a Collector: European Works of Art, 1100 to 1800,* from the Thomson Collection. The more than 350 objects in this exhibition form one of the world's finest collections of early European decorative art treasures. For the first time in any museum, these works —personally acquired over five decades by Kenneth Thomson—add an exciting dimension to the Gallery's European Arts holdings.

Major Public Art Galleries in Canada

Art Gallery of Greater Victoria: 1040 Moss St., Victoria, B.C. V8V 4P1 (604) 384-4101

Art Gallery of Nova Scotia: P.O. Box 2262, Halifax, N.S. B3J 3C8 (902) 424-7542

Art Gallery of Ontario: 317 Dundas St. W., Toronto, Ont. M5T 1G4 (416) 979-6648

Art Gallery of Windsor: 3100 Howard Ave., Windsor, Ont. N8X 3Y8 (519) 258-7111

Beaverbrook Art Gallery: P.O. Box 605, Fredericton, N.B. E3B 5A6 (506) 458-8545

Confederation Centre Art Gallery and Museum: 145 Richmond St., Charlottetown, P.E. C1A 1J1 (902) 628-6111

Dunlop Art Gallery: P.O. Box 2311, Regina, Sask. S4P 3Z5 (306) 777-6040

Edmonton Art Gallery: 2 Sir Winston Churchill Sq., Edmonton, Alta. T5J 2C1 (403) 422-6223

McMichael Canadian Art Collection: 10365 Islington Ave., Kleinburg, Ont. L0J 1C0 (905) 893-1121

Montreal Museum of Fine Arts: 1379-1380 Sherbrooke St. W., P.O. Box 3000, Stn. H, Montreal, Que. H3G 2T9 (514) 285-1600

Musee d'Art Contemporain de Montreal: 185 St. Catherine St. W, Montreal, Que. H2X 1Z8 (514) 847-6212

Musée du Québec: Parc des Champs de Bataille, 1, rue Wolfe/Montcalm, Quebec, Que. G1R 5H3 (418) 643-2150

National Gallery of Canada: 380 Sussex Dr., Ottawa, Ont. K1N 9N4 (613) 990-1985

Thunder Bay Art Gallery: P.O. Box 1193, Station F, Thunder Bay, Ont. P7C 4X9 (807) 577-6427

Vancouver Art Gallery: 750 Hornby St., Vancouver, B.C. V6Z 2H7 (604) 662-4700

Winnipeg Art Gallery: 300 Memorial Blvd., Winnipeg, Man. R3C 1V1 (204) 786-6641

Major Public Museums in Canada

Canadian Centre for Architecture: 1920 rue Baile, Montreal, Que. H3A 1E9 (514) 939-7000

Canadian Museum of Civilization: 100 Laurier St., Box 3100, Stn B, Hull, Que. J8X 4H2 (819) 776-7000

Canadian Museum of Contemporary Photography: 1 Rideau Canal, P.O. Box 465, Station A, Ottawa, Ont. K1N 9N6 (613) 990-8257

Canadian Museum of Nature: P.O. Box 3443, Station D, Ottawa, Ont. K1P 6P4 (613) 566-4700

Canadian War Museum: 330 Sussex Dr., Ottawa, Ont. K1A 0M8 (613) 996-1420

Glenbow-Alberta Institute: 130-9th Ave. SE, Calgary, Alta. T2G 0P3 (403) 268-4100

Manitoba Museum of Man and Nature: 190 Rupert Ave., Winnipeg, Man. R3B 0N2 (204) 956-2830

Maritime Museum of the Atlantic: 1675 Lower Water St., Halifax, N.S. B3J 1S3 (902) 429-7490

McCord Museum of Canadian History: 690, rue Sherbrooke ouest, Montreal, Que. H3A 1E9 (514) 398-7100

Musée de la Civilisation: 85, rue Dalhousie, C.P. 155, Succursale B, Quebec, Que. G1K 7A6 (418) 643-2158

New Brunswick Museum: 277 Douglas Ave., Saint John, N.B. E2K 1E5 (506) 643-2300

Newfoundland Museum: 285 Duckworth St., P.O. Box 8700, St. John's, Nfld. A1B 4J6 (709) 729-2329

Nova Scotia Museum: 1747 Summer St., Halifax, N.S. B3H 3A6 (902) 424-6471

Prince of Wales Northern Heritage Centre: P.O. Box 1320, Yellowknife, N.W.T. X1A 2L9 (867) 873-7551

Provincial Museum of Alberta: 12845-102nd Ave., Edmonton, Alta. T5N 0M6 (403) 453-9100

Royal British Columbia Museum: P.O. Box 9815, Stn. Prov. Govt., Victoria, B.C. V8W 9W2 (250) 387-3701

Royal Ontario Museum: 100 Queen's Park, Toronto, Ont. M5S 2C6 (416) 586-8000

Royal Saskatchewan Museum: Wascana Park, College and Albert, Regina, Sask. S4P 3V7 (306) 787-2815

Vancouver Museum: 1100 Chestnut St., Vancouver, B.C. V6J 3J9 (604) 736-4431

Prince Edward Island Museum and Heritage Foundation: 2 Kent St., Charlottetown, PEI C1A 1M6 (902) 368-6600

Festivals and Major Entertainment Events, 2000

This listing provides a taste of some of the major seasonal festivals and entertainment events which take place each year across Canada. Most exact dates had not been set for 2000 at press time, however, more details can be obtained by calling the information numbers, provincial tourism bureaus (numbers listed below) or visiting the websites shown.

■ WESTERN CANADA

BRITISH COLUMBIA

Feb: **Polar Carnival**, Logan Lake, (604) 523-6225

Apr: **18th TerriVic Jazz Party**, Victoria, (604) 953-2011

Apr: **48th Annual Square Dance Jamboree**, Trail, (250) 368-3144

May: **Okanagan Spring Wine & Food Festival**, Kelowna, (250) 861-6654

May: **Cathedral Lakes Pow Wow**, Keremeos, (250) 499-5528

May: **Canadian Northern Children's Festival**, Prince George, (250) 562-3700

May: **Dixieland Jazz Festival**, Chilliwack, (604) 795-3600

May: **Cloverdale Rodeo**, Cloverdale (Surrey), (604) 576-9461

May: **Seabird Island Indian Festival**, Hope, (604) 796-2177

June: **JazzFest International**, Victoria, (250) 953-2023

June/July. **International Dragon Boat Festival**, Vancouver, (604) 688-2382

July: **Kimberley International Old Time Accordion Championships**, Kimberley, (250) 427-4547

July: **Folkfest Celebrations,** Port Alberni, (250) 723-6023

July: **Nanaimo Marine Festival,** Nanaimo, (250) 753-7223

July: **Harrison Festival of the Arts,** Harrison Hot Springs, (604) 796-3664

July/Aug: **Filberg Festival**, Comox, (250) 334-9242

Aug: **Festival of the Written Arts**, Sechelt, (604) 885-9631

Aug: **Kamloopa Pow Wow Days**, Kamloops, (604) 828-9700

Aug: **Penticton Peach Festival**, Penticton, (250) 975-9642

Sept: **Agassiz Fall Fair and Corn Festival**, Agassiz, (604) 796-3246

Sept/Oct: **Fall Wine Festival**, Okanagan Valley, (250) 861-6654

Oct: **Wine Tasting Festival**, Nanaimo, (250) 758-1131

Dec: **Candlelight Parade**, Mission, (604) 826-6914

Dec/Jan: **Festival of Lights**, Ladysmith, (250) 245-5888

For more details about BC events, call 1 (800) Hello BC or visit http://www.gov.bc.ca

YUKON

Jan: **17th Annual Champagne & Aishihik First Nations Bonspiel,** Haines Junction, (867) 634-2288

Feb: **Yukon Quest Sled Dog Race,** Whitehorse, (867) 668-4711

Feb: **Yukon Sourdough Rendezvous Festival**, Whitehorse, (867) 667-2148

Feb: **Frostbite Music Festival**, Whitehorse, (867) 668-4921

Mar: **Thaw-Di-Gras Spring Carnival**, Dawson City, (867) 993-5575

2000 Arctic Winter Games

March 5-11 Whitehorse will host the circumpolar region's most prestigious multi-sport and cultural event. More than 1,750 young people from Yukon, Alaska, NWT, Nunavut, Greenland, Northern Alberta and Siberia will participate.

Mar: **Snowmobile Rodeo at Pine Lake**, Haines Junction, (867) 634-2432

Apr: **Celebration of Swans**, Whitehorse, (867) 668-8291

May: **International Gold Show**, Dawson City, (867) 993-6720

June: **Alsek Music Festival**, Dawson City, (867) 634-2520

June: **Gathering of the Clans and Celtic Festival**, Whitehorse, (867) 667-7715

June: **Yukon International Storytelling Festival**, Whitehorse, (867) 633-7550

June: **Mayo Midnight Marathon,** Mayo, (867) 996-2368

July: **Yukon Gold Panning Championships**, Dawson City, (867) 993-5575

July: **Dawson City Music Festival**, Dawson City, (867) 993-5584

July: **Commissioner's Potlach**, Whitehorse (867) 667-7698

Aug: **Discovery Days 2000**, Dawson City, (867) 993-7400

Aug: **Klondyke Harvest Fair**, Whitehorse, (867) 668-6864

Sept: **Great Klondike International Outhouse Race**, Dawson City (867) 993-5575

For more details about Yukon events , call (867) 667-3053 or visit http://www.gov.yk.ca

NORTHWEST TERRITORIES

Jan: **Sunrise Festival**, Inuvik, (867) 777-2607

Mar: **Beavertail Jamboree**, Fort Simpson, (867) 695-3300

Mar: **Kamba Winter Carnival**, Hay River, (867) 874-6701

Mar: **Caribou Carnival**, Yellowknife, (867) 873-4262

Apr: **Muskrat Jamboree**, Inuvik, (867) 777-3813

Apr: **Beluga Jamboree**, Tuktoyaktuk, (867) 977-2286

June: **Kingalik Jamboree**, Holman, (867) 376-3511

June: **Raven Mad Daze**, Yellowknife, (867) 873-3912

July: **12th Annual Great Northern Arts Festival**, Inuvik, (867) 777-3536

July: **Festival of the Midnight Sun**, Yellowknife, (867) 873-4262

July: **Folk on the Rocks**, Yellowknife, (867) 920-7806

July: **Midway Lake Festival**, Fort McPherson, (867) 952-2330

Aug: **South Slave Friendship Festival**, Fort Smith, (867) 872-2014

Aug: **Deninoo Days**, Slave Lake (Fort Resolution), (867) 394-4556

Aug: **Ikhalukpik Jamboree**, Paulatuk, (867) 580-3531

Aug: **Pehdzeh Dene Daze**, Wrigley, (867) 581-3410

Aug/Sept: **Aklavik Dizzy Daze**, Aklavik, (867) 978-2351

Nov: **GeoScience Forum**, Yellowknife, (867) 873-5281

Nov: **Far North Film Festival**, Yellowknife, (867) 873-4262

For more details about NWT events , call (800) 661-0788 or visit http://www.gov.nt.ca

ALBERTA

June: **International Native Awareness Week**, Calgary, (403) 296-2227

June: **Heritage Days**, Raymond, (403) 752-3322

June: **The Works: A Visual Arts Celebration**, Edmonton, (780) 426-2122

June: **Aboriginal Day Festival**, Edmonton, (780) 453-9100

July: **Ukrainian Pysanka Festival**, Vegreville, (780) 632-2777

July: **Jasper Heritage Folk Festival**, Jasper, (780) 852-5781

July: **Riverboat Daze**, Fort MacLeod, (403) 849-5711

July: **Midnight Days Indoor Rodeo and Cowboy Poetry**, Fort Macleod, (403) 553-3123

Aug: **Hayshaker Days**, Calgary, (403) 259-1900

Aug: **Bentley and District Annual Fair**, Bentley, (780) 748-2358

Aug: **Alberta in Bloom**, Drayton Valley, (780) 339-2360

Aug: **Alberta Hot-Air Balloon Championships**, Grande Prairie, (780) 539-1589

Aug: **Old Tyme Fair**, Cochrane, (403) 932-7279

Aug: **Afrikadey!**, Calgary, (403) 234-9110

Sept: **Storytelling Festival**, Edmonton, (780) 496-8787

Oct: **Festival of Eagles**, Canmore, (403) 678-1878

Oct: **Scarecrow Festival**, Edmonton, (780) 436-6851

Nov: **Canadian Finals Rodeo**, Edmonton, (780) 471-7210

Nov: **Farmfair International**, Edmonton, (780) 471-7210

For more details about Alberta events , call (800) 661-8888 or visit http://www.gov.ab.ca

SASKATCHEWAN

Jan: **Sask 100 Snowmobile Rally**, Candle Lake, (306) 929-2236

Feb: **Carrot River Winter Festival**, Carrot River, (306) 768-3833

Feb: **Love's 27th Annual Valentine Winter Fest**, Love, (306) 276-2380

Feb: **Battlefords Winter Festival/Frechette Commemorative Mail Run**, Battlefords, (306) 445-5876

Mar: **Regina Beach Classic Ice Fishing Derby**, Regina Beach, (603) 729-4471

Mar: **Saskatchewan Music Festival Concerto Competition**, Saskatoon, (306) 757-1722

Mar: **Flicks: Saskatchewan International Children's Film Festival**, Saskatoon, (306) 956-3456

Apr: **Moose Jaw Hometown Rodeo**, Moose Jaw, (306) 692-2723

Apr: **Saskatchewan Indian Federated College Powwow**, Regina, (306) 779-6267

May: **"Syttende Mai Fest,"** Weldon, (306) 749-3559

June: **Saskatchewan Music Festival 92nd Anniversary Final**, Regina, (306) 757-1722

June/Oct: **Nipawin Pike Festival**, Nipawin, (306) 862-9866

July: **Ness Creek Festival**, Big River, (306) 652-6377

Aug: **Standing Buffalo Indian Powwow**, Fort Qu'Appelle, (306) 332-4685

Sept: **Threshing Day**, Balcarres, (306) 334-2318

Oct: **Western Canada Amateur Old Tyme Fiddling Championship**, Swift Current, (306) 773-8924

Nov: **Quill Lake Goose Fest**, Quill Lake, (306) 383-2512

Dec-Jan: **Sundog Handcraft Faire**, Saskatoon, (306) 384-7364

For more details about Saskatchewan events, call (877)-2 ESCAPE or visit www.sasktourism.com

MANITOBA

Feb: **Festival du Voyageur**, Winnipeg, (204) 237-7692

Mar/Apr: **Royal Manitoba Winter Fair**, Brandon, (204) 726-3590

June: **Winnipeg International Children's Festival**, Winnipeg, (204) 958-4730

June: **Winnipeg International Air Show**, Winnipeg, (204) 257-8400

June: **Jazz Winnipeg Festival**, Winnipeg, (204) 989-4656

June: **Scottish Heritage Festival**, Winnipeg, (204) 888-9380

June: **Nickel Days**, Thompson, (204) 677-7952

June/July: **Red River Ex**, Winnipeg, (204) 772-9464

July: **Winnipeg Folk Festival**, Winnipeg, (204) 231-0096

July: **Triple S Fair and Rodeo**, Selkirk, (204) 482-4822

July: **Winnipeg Fringe Festival**, Winnipeg, (204) 956-1340

July: **Manitoba Stampede and Exhibition**, Morris, (204) 746-2552

Aug: **Folkorama**, Winnipeg, (800) 665-0234

Aug: **Canada's National Ukrainian Festival**, Dauphin, (204) 638-5645

Aug: **Islendingadagurinn** (Icelandic Festival of Manitoba), Gimli, (204) 338-3014

Sept: **Oktoberfest**, Winnipeg, (204) 957-4516

Nov: **Manitoba Fall Fair**, Brandon, (204) 726-3590

Nov: **Manitoba Christmas Craft Sale**, Winnipeg, (888) 773-4444

For more details on Manitoba events, call (800) 665-0040 or visit http://www.travel manitoba.com

■ CENTRAL CANADA

ONTARIO

May: **Sportcard and Memorabilia Spring Expo '98**, Mississauga, (416) 674-4636

May: **Timeless Treasures Quilt Show**, St. Catharines, (905) 682-4952

May: **Kingston Potters' Guild Spring Show and Sale**, Kingston, (613) 546-1437

May: **Northumberland Scottish Country Dancers**, Cobourg, (905) 349-3401

May: **Prince Edward County Birding Festival**, Picton, (613) 476-5072

June: **Niagara Film Festival**, Niagara Falls, (905) 353-9565

June: **Franco-Ontarian Festival**, Ottawa, (613) 239-5000

July: **Muskoka Pioneer Power Show**, Bracebridge, (705) 645-9357

July: **Festival of Arts and Crafts**, Goderich, (519) 357-3155

July: **Fiddle and Stepdance Festival**, Stratford, (519) 271-6115

July: **Grand River Champion of Champions Powwow**, Ohsweken, (519) 758-5444

Aug: **Natural Life Festival**, St. George, (519) 448-4001

Aug: **13th Annual Antique Show and Sale**, Lakefield, (705) 292-8228

Aug: **Hamilton Chapter Ikenobo Ikebana Society Flower Exhibition**, Burlington (Hamilton), (905) 385-2155

Sept: **Fine Art Fine Wine,** Kingsville, (800) 597-3533

Sept: **Children's Arts Festival**, Toronto, (416) 395-7350

Sept: **Nipigon Fall Fishing Festival**, Nipigon, (807) 887-1070

Oct: **The Woodstock Wood Show Inc.**, Woodstock, (519) 539-7772

Oct: **Ontario Cavy Club Guinea Pig Show**, Ruthven, (519) 326-3287

Oct: **Harvest Festival-Come Feel the Farm**, Gananoque, (613) 382-7531

For more information on Ontario events, call 1-800-ONTARIO or visit http://www.gov.on.ca

QUEBEC

Jan: **Laval International Synchronized Skating Competition**, Laval
Jan: **Cinoche Film Festival**, Baie-Comeau
Jan: **Freestyle Skiing World Cup**, Mont-Tremblant
Jan: **Rendezvous TELEMARK**, Petite-Riviere-Saint-Francois
Jan/Feb: **Quebec Winter Carnival**, Quebec City
Jan/Feb: **Festi-Glace**, Joliette
Jan/Feb: **Fete des Neiges**, Montreal
Feb: **Winterlude**, Hull (Ouatouais)
Feb: **Festival de la Saint-Valentin**, Saint-Valentin (Monteregie)
Feb: **Carnaval Souvenir**, Chicoutimi
Feb: **Salon du livre** (Book fair), Sept-Iles
Feb: **Fete d'hiver**, Rouyn Noranda
Mar: **Fete des joues rouges** (Red Cheeks Festival), Sept-Iles
Mar: **Mi-Careme a l'Isle-aus-Grues**, (Costume event) Ile aux Grues
Apr: **L'Effleure Printemps**, Laval
Oct/Nov: **Salon vins, bieres, et gastronomie**, Quebec City
Oct/Nov: **Abitibi-Temiscamingue International Film Festival**, Rouyn-Noranda
Nov: **Coup de coeur francophone** (rendezvous for French singers), Montreal
Nov: **Patriots Festival** (Fêtes des Patriotes), Saint-Denis
Nov: **Creche Exhibition**, Riviere-Eternite
Dec: **Old Quebec in the Snow**, Quebec City
Dec/Apr: **Week-end blancs**, Saint-Donat
Dec/Apr: **Tomcod Carnival**, Sainte-Anne-de-la-Perade
For more details on Quebec events, call (800) 363-7777 or visit http://www.gov.qc.ca

■ ATLANTIC CANADA

NEW BRUNSWICK

May 4-6: **Salon de la Forêt**, Edmundston, (506) 737-5238
May 14-16: **Annual Big Tex Trout Derby**, Miramichi, (506) 622-1780
July 1-9: **Shediac Lobster Festival**, Shediac (506) 532-1122
July 2-9: **Festival Provincial de la Tourbe (Peat Moss Festival)**, Lamèque, (506) 344-3222
July 8-16: **Festival des Pêches et de l'Aquaculture du N.B.**, Shippagan, (506) 336-8726
July 13-16: **Canada's Irish Festival on the Miramichi**, Miramichi, (506) 778-8810
July 22-29: **Woodstock Old Home Week**, Woodstock, (506) 328-4277 (seasonal)
July 15-23: **Festival Western de Saint-Quentin**, Saint-Quentin, (506) 235-1999
July 28-30: **New Brunswick Highland Games & Scottish Festival**, Fredericton, 1 (888) 368-4444 or (506) 450-2065
July 21-23: **Buskers Festival**, Saint John, (506) 658-3606
July 28-August 6: **Festival Bon Ami Get Together Inc.**, Dalhousie, (506) 684-5395
July 30-August 6: **Belledune Days**, Belledune, (506) 237-3200
August 2-6: **La Foire Brayonne Inc.**, Edmundston, (506) 739-6608
July 29-August 7: **Lamèque International Festival of Baroque Music**, Lamèque, (506) 344-5846, (800) 320-2276
August 7-11: **Chocolate Festival**, St. Stephen, (506) 465-5616
August 7-11: **Miramichi Folk Song Festival**, Miramichi, (506) 622-1780
August 4 -15: **Festival Acadien de Caraquet**, Caraquet, (506) 727-6515
August 11-19: **Festival By The Sea Inc.**, Saint John, (506) 632-0086
August 18-20: **Antique Auto Flea Market**, Sussex, (506) 363-5105
August 12-13: **Victoria Park Arts & Craft Fair**, Moncton, (506) 853-3595
Sept 3-6: **Demi-Marathon Festival**, Saint-François-de-Madawaska, (506) 992-2747
September 4 -10: **Fredericton Exhibition**, Fredericton, (506) 458-9819
September 13-17: **Harvest Jazz and Blues Festival**, Fredericton, (506) 454-2583
Sept 8-10: **Atlantic Balloon Fiesta**, Sussex, (506) 432-9444
For more information about tourism and events, call 1-800 561-0123 or visit http://www.gov.nb.ca

NOVA SCOTIA

May: **Truro International Tulip Festival**, Truro
June/July: **Stan Rogers Folk Festival**, Canso
June/July: **Nova Scotia Internationl Tattoo**, Halifax
July: **Atlantic Jazz Festival**, Halifax
May/June: **Annapolis Valley Apple Blossom Festival,** Windsor to Digby

---

Tall Ships 2000

July 19-24, Halifax will be welcoming 5,000 young visitors and an expected 700,000 visitors to commemorate the city's pionneering role in the sport of tall ships racing. Celebrations will include numerous public events, including a concert on Halifax's historic Citadel Hill, a fireworks display and parades.

June/Sept: **Atlantic Theatre Festival,**
Wolfville
June/Sept: **Windsor County Fair,** Windsor
July/Aug: **King's Theatre Summer Festival,**
Annapolis Royal
July: **Festival Acadien,** Ste. Anne du
Ruisseau
July: **Antigonish Highland Games,**
Antigonish
July/Aug: **Granville Green Concert Series,**
Port Hawkesbury
July: **Yarmouth Seafest,** Yarmouth
July: **Nova Scotia Bluegrass & Old Time
Music Festival,** Ardoise
Aug: **Western Nova Scotia Exhibition,**
Yarmouth
Aug: **Wooden Boat Festival,** Mahone Bay
Sept: **Berwick Gala Days,** Berwick
Sept: **Bridgetown Ciderfest,** Bridgetown
Oct: **Celtic Colours,** Cape Breton Island
Oct: **Harvest Wine Fest,** Falmouth
Oct: **Pumpkin Festival,** Windsor
Nov: **A Dicken's Storybook Weekend,**
Wolfville
Dec: **Christmas Home Tours and Yuletide
Tea,** Yarmouth
*For more details on Nova Scotia events, call
(800) 565-0000 or visit http://exploreNS.com*

PRINCE EDWARD ISLAND

June/July: **Indian River Festival,** Indian
River, (902) 836-3733
June/Oct: **The Charlottetown Festival,**
Charlottetown 1 (800) 565-0278
June: **Highland Gathering and Military
Tattoo,** Summerside, (902) 436—5377
June/July: **Festival of Lights,** Charlottetown,
(902)629-1864
June/July: **22nd Annual PEI Street Rod
Association Show'n'Shine,** Lobster Shanty,
Montague (902)962-4140
July: **PEI Bluegrass and Oldtime Music
Festival,** Rollo Bay, (902)569-4501
July: **24th Annual Rollo Bay Fiddlers
Festival,** Rollo Bay, (902) 687-2584/3464
July: **Emerald Junction Irish Festival,**
Emerald, (902) 886-2400
Aug: **St. Peter's Wild Blueberry Festival,**
St. Peter's Park, (902) 961-2880
Aug: **7th Annual Lucy Maud Montgomery
Festival,** (902)963-2149
Sept: **Festival of the Fathers,** Charlottetown,
(902) 629-1864
Sept: **Evangeline Area Agriculture
Exhibition and Acadian Festival,** (902)
854-2869
Sept: **Prince Edward Island Storytelling
Festival,** island-wide, (902) 368-4410
Sept: **The PEI Shellfish Festival,**

Charlottetown, (902) 566-9748
Sept: **3rd Annual 70 Mile Coastal Yard
Sale,** Wood Islands and area, (902)962-3242
Oct: **Trailfest 2000,** island-wide, (902) 583-
2662
*For more details on PEI events, call (888)
PEI-PLAY or visit http://www.gov.pe.ca*

NEWFOUNDLAND AND LABRADOR

Vikings! 1000 Years
1000 years ago the Vikings guided their
open plank ships, down the coast of
Labrador and crossed the Strait of Belle
Isle to Newfoundland. They were the
first Europeans to plough the waves of
the rich coastal waters off North
America's northeast coast.
Newfoundland and Labrador celebrate
this important anniversary with
festivals, exhibitions and special events
throughout the year including:

June-August (St. John's), Sept-Nov
(Corner Brook): **Full Circle—First
Contact: Vikings and Skraelings in
Newfoundland and Labrador**
July 22-28th: Viking **Sail 2000,**
Cartwright, Wonderstrand, Southern
Labrador, and L'Anse aux Meadows
July 28-August 21: **Islendingur,**
L'Anse aux Meadows and other
Newfoundland ports
July 17-September 8: **Grand
Encampment,** L'Anse aux Meadows
June and August: **The Snorri Explores
Vinland,** viking ship replica will appear
at various local festivals

Feb: **Winterlude 2000,** Grand Falls-
Windsor, (709)789-0450
Mar: **Grand Bank Winter Carnival,** Grand
Bank, (709) 832-2617
May: **Western Newfoundland Heritage
Fair,** Corner Brook, (709) 634-5831
July: **Festival 500 Sharing The Voices**
(choral music) Corner Brook, (709) 738-6013
July: **Robinson's Great Lobster Boil,**
Robinsons, (709) 645-2770
July: **Emile Benoit Festival** (French music
and culture), Black Duck Brook, (709) 642-
5254
*For more details on Newfoundland and
Labrador events, call (800) 563-6353 or visit
http://www.gov.nfca*

The following list is not meant to be exhaustive, but rather a listing of prominent Canadians, and those whose reputations are inextricably linked with Canada, from all fields.

A

ABBOTT, John Joseph Caldwell (Sir), politics. St Andrews, Lower Canada, 1821-93. Canada's third prime minister.

ABBOTT, Maude Elizabeth Seymour, medicine. St Andrews, Que., 1869-1940. Specialist in congenital heart disease. *History of Medicine in the Province of Quebec.*

ABBOTT, Roger, performing arts. Eng., 1946. Actor and co-producer of CBC's *Royal Canadian Air Farce*; noted for impersonation of Jean Chrétien.

ABEL, Sidney Gerald (Sid), sports. Melville, Sask., 1918. Hockey player;1949-52 considered best offensive unit when centred with Gordie Howe and Ted Lindsay (Detroit Red Wings); four-time all-star.

ABERDEEN, Ishbel Maria Marjoribanks Gordon (Lady), reformer. Eng., 1857-1939. Helped create National Council of Women, Victorian Order of Nurses.

ABERHART, William "Bible Bill", politics. Hibbard Twp, Ont., 1878-1943. Founded Social Credit party; Alberta premier 1935-43.

ACORN, Milton, literary arts. Charlottetown, PEI, 1923-86. Radical poet. "The Island Means Minago."

ADAMS, Bryan, performing arts. Kingston, Ont., 1959. Singer/songwriter; rock star. *Reckless.*

ADAMS, Ian, literary arts. Tanzania, 1937. Novelist, nonfiction writer. *S, Portrait of a Spy; The Trudeau Papers.*

ADAMS, Thomas, city planner. Scot., 1871-1940. Father of the Canadian Planning Movement.

AFFLECK, Raymond Tait, visual arts. Penticton, BC, 1922-89. Architect; designed Place Ville Marie, Place Bonaventure.

AGLUKARK, Susan, performing arts. Arviat, NWT, 1966. Singer/songwriter; first Inuit recording artist.

AIRD, John Black, politics. Toronto, Ont., 1923-95. Liberal senator; Ontario lieutenant-governor 1980-85.

AISLIN (b. Christopher Terry Mosher), visual arts. Ottawa, Ont., 1942. *Montreal Gazette* cartoonist; sports caricaturist.

AITKEN, William Maxwell (Lord Beaverbrook), literary arts. Maple, Ont., 1879-1964. Publisher; newspaper magnate; British Conservative cabinet minister.

AKEEAKTASHUK, visual arts. Hudson Bay, Ont., 1898-1954. Sculptor; first important Inuit carver.

ALBANI, Emma (b. Louise Cecile Emma Lajeunesse), performing arts. Chambly, Que., 1847-1930. Opera singer; grand diva excelled in Wagnerian opera, popular in Britain and US.

ALEXANDER, Lincoln MacCauley, politics. Toronto, Ont., 1922. First Black in Parliament; Ont. lieutenant-governor 1985-91.

ALLAN, Hugh (Sir), business. Scot., 1810-82. Railway promoter; suspected of electoral bribery for soliciting favours in Pacific Scandal (1873).

ALLAN, Ted (b. Allan Herman), performing arts. Montreal, Que., 1916-95. Author; screenwriter. *Lies My Father Told Me; Bethune: The Making of a Hero.*

ALLEN, Charlotte Vale, literary arts. Toronto, Ont., 1941. Writer, lecturer on child abuse. *Daddy's Girl.*

ALLEN, John F. (Jack), science. Winnipeg, Man., 1908. Co-discoverer of superfluidity in liquid helium.

ALLEN, Montagu (Sir), sports. Montreal, Que., 1860-1951. Financier and sportsman who donated Allen Cup in 1908 for senior amateur competition in Canada.

ALLEN, Ralph, literary arts. Winnipeg, Man., 1913-66. Influential *Maclean's* editor (1946-60).

ALMOND, Paul, performing arts. Montreal, Que., 1931. Film director. *Act of the Heart.*

ALTMAN, Sidney, science. Montreal, Que., 1939. Microbiologist; 1989 Nobel Prize in chemistry for role in research into chemical cell reactions.

AMIEL, Barbara, media. Eng., 1940s. Journalist; conservative political and social columnist.

AMOS, Beth (b. Bessie Rymer), performing arts. St Catharines, Ont., 1915-95. Actor. *Jake and the Kid; Miracle at Indian Creek; Canadian Bacon.*

ANDERSON, Doris Hilda, literary arts. Toronto, Ont., 1921. Writer; feminist; editor,*Chatelaine* 1958-77.

ANDERSON, Pamela Denise, performing arts. Ladysmith, BC, 1967. Voluptuous actress who has starred in *Baywatch, Barb Wire.*

ANDRE, Brother (b. Alfred Bissette), religion. St Gregoire d'Iberville, Lower Canada, 1845-1937. Mystic; built Montreal's St Joseph's Oratory.

ANGILIK, Paul Apak, performing arts. Hall Beach, NWT, 1954-98. Documentary filmmaker of Inuit life; adventurer; contributor to Inuit Broadcasting Corporation.

ANKA, Paul Albert, performing arts. Ottawa, Ont., 1941. Singer/songwriter; composed more than 400 songs. "My Way."

APPLEBAUM, Louis, performing arts. Toronto, Ont., 1918. Composer; writer of opera, concerts, film scores.

APPLEYARD, Peter, performing arts. Eng., 1928. Jazz musician; vibraphonist; TV personality. "Swing Fever."

APPS, Charles Joseph Sylvanus (Syl), sports. Paris, Ont., 1915-98. Hockey player; Toronto Maple Leafs (1936-48); 3-time all-star; pole vault contender in 1936 Olympics; 1937 Canadian Athlete of the Year.

AQUIN, Hubert, literary arts. Montreal, Que., 1929-77. Novelist; modernist writer. *Neige Noire.*

ARCAND, Denys, performing arts. Deschambault, Que., 1941. Film director. *Decline of the American Empire.*

ARCHAMBAULT, Louis, visual arts. Montreal, Que., 1915. Sculptor; his work is in many museum collections.

ARDEN, Jann (b. Jann Arden Richards), performing arts. Calgary, Alta, 1962. Juno-award winning pop singer, songwriter. *Happy?; Time for Mercy.*

ARTHUR, Eric Ross, visual arts. New Zealand, 1898-1982. Architectural conservancy advocate; writer. *Toronto: No Mean City; The Barn:A Vanishing Landmark in North America.*

ASPER, Israel Harold, business. Minnedosa, Man., 1932. Financier; founder Global-TV; columnist; author.

ATHANS, George S. Jr., sports. Kelowna, BC, 1952. Three-time world water ski champion.

ATKINSON, Joseph, media. Newcastle, Ont., 1865-1948. Journalist; built *Toronto Star* into nation's largest newspaper.

ATWOOD, Margaret Eleanor, literary arts. Ottawa, Ont., 1939. Prolific novelist with international following. *The Handmaid's Tale, Alias Grace.*

AUBERT de GASPE, Philippe-Ignace François, literary arts. Quebec City, Que., 1814-41. Novelist; wrote first French-Cdn novel. *L'influence d'un livre* (1837).

AUF DER MAUR, Nick, journalism. Montreal, Que., 1942-98. Long-time columnist for *Montreal Gazette;* co-wrote biography of Brian Mulroney: *The Boy from Baie Comeau.*

AUGUSTYN, Frank Joseph, performing arts. Hamilton, Ont., 1953. Former principal dancer, National Ballet of Canada; director, Ottawa Ballet.

AVERY, Oswald, science. Halifax, NS, 1877-1955. First person to show agent responsible for transferring genetic information was DNA, not a protein as previously thought.

AXWORTHY, Norman Lloyd, politics. North Battleford, Sask., 1939. Liberal Minister of External Affairs.

AYKROYD, Daniel Edward (Dan), performing arts. Ottawa, Ont., 1952. Actor/comedian. *Saturday Night Live, Ghostbusters.*

B

BACHMAN, Randy, performing arts. Winnipeg, Man., 1946. Rock musician; guitarist for Guess Who, Bachman-Turner Overdrive. *American Woman.*

BAETZ, Reuben, politics. Chelsey, Ont., 1923-96. Executive director of Canadian Council on Social Development; proponent of national unemployment insurance program.

BAFFIN, William, exploration and discovery. Eng., 1584-1622. Made two Arctic voyages in search of the Northwest Passage; first to conclude Hudson Bay did not lead westward; explored Baffin Island.

BAILEY, Donovan, sports. Jamaica, 1967. Track star who won 100 m race at world record time, 9.84, at 1996 Olympics in Atlanta.

BAKER, Carroll, performing arts. Bridgewater, NS, 1949. Singer; country music star.

BALDWIN, Robert, politics. York, Ont., 1804-58. Proponent of responsible government; co-premier (with LaFontaine) of Upper Canada.

BALLARD, Harold Edwin, sports. Toronto, Ont., 1903-90. Sports capitalist; irascible owner of Toronto Maple Leafs, Hamilton Tiger Cats.

BANTING, Sir Frederick Grant, medicine. Alliston, Ont., 1891-1941. Medical researcher; co-discoverer of insulin; Nobel Prize for medicine, 1923.

BARBEAU, Charles Marius, ethnologist. St-Marie-de-Beauce, Que., 1883-1969. Eminent folklorist.

BARFOOT, Joan Louise, literary arts. Owen Sound, Ont., 1947. Novelist. *Dancing in the Dark; Family News; Charlotte and Claudia Keeping in Touch.*

BARKER, William George (Billy), military. Dauphin, Man., 1894-1930. Fighter pilot awarded Victoria Cross for 60 solo combat missions against German aircraft during WWI.

BARLOW, Maude Victoria, politics. Toronto, Ont., 1947. Political/human rights activist, author. Chair, Council of Canadians.

BARR, Murray Llewellyn, medicine. Belmont, Ont., 1908. Anatomist; developed chromosome analysis to diagnose genetic disorders.

BARRY, James (b. Miranda Stewart), medicine. Eng., 1795-1865. In 1857 appointed inspector general of military hospitals in Province of Canada; as a woman disguised as a man, was the first woman doctor to work in Canada.

BASINSKI, Zbigniew Stanislaw, science. Poland, 1928. Outstanding metal physics researcher.

BASSETT, John White Hughes, media. Ottawa, Ont., 1915-98. Media executive.

BASSETT-SEGUSO, Carling Kathrin, sports. Toronto, Ont., 1967. Top-ranked Canadian tennis player.

BATA, Sonja Ingrid, public service. Switzerland, 1926. Founder of the Bata Shoe Museum in Toronto; wife of shoe retailing entrepreneur Thomas Bata.

BATA, Thomas John, business. Czech., 1914. Industrialist; chairman, Bata Shoes; in over 70 countries.

BATEMAN, Robert McLellan, visual arts. Toronto, Ont., 1930. Painter; major international wildlife artist.

BAUER, Father David William, sports. Kitchener, Ont., 1925-88. Hockey coach; father of Cdn Olympic hockey.

BAUMANN, Alexander (Sasha), sports. Czech., 1964. Swimmer; gold medals in 200 m, 400 m individual medley, 1984 Olympics; 1984 top male athlete.

BEARDY, Quentin Pickering Jackson, visual arts. Island Lake, Man., 1944-84. Graphic stylist using Cree legends.

BEATTY, Henry Perrin, politics. Toronto, Ont., 1950. President of CBC, 1995-98; former PC cabinet minister.

BECK, Sir Adam, business. Baden, Canada W, 1857-1925. Hydro commissioner; built Ontario Hydro.

BECKER, Abigail, military. Frontenac Cty, UC, 1831-1905. Heroine; saved men shipwrecked on Lake Erie.

BECKWITH, John, literary arts/performing arts. Victoria, BC, 1927. Composer; writer; critic. *The Shivaree.*

BEDARD, Myriam, sports. Loretteville, Que., 1969. Biathlete; two gold medals, biathlon, '94 Olympics.

BEDDOES, Dick, media. Daysland, Alta, 1926-91. Colourful sportswriter, broadcaster, hockey commentator with the Vancouver *Sun, Globe & Mail,* Edmonton *Bulletin;* broadcaster on CFRB radio in Toronto.*Pal Hal,* a profile of Harold Ballard.

BEECROFT, Norma Marian, performing arts. Oshawa, Ont., 1934. Composer; avant-garde musician. "From Dreams of Brass."

BEERS, William George, medicine/sports. Montreal, Que., 1843-1900. Popularized lacrosse; Dean, Canada's first dental college.

BEGIN, Monique, politics. Italy, 1936. First Quebec woman in Commons; health minister.

BELANGER, Michel, business. Lévis, Que., 1929-97. President of Quebec's National Bank; 1991-92 was co-chairman of Belanger-Campeau Commission which examined constitutional concerns in Quebec.

BELIVEAU, Jean Arthur, sports. Trois-Rivières, Que., 1931. Hockey player; stylish Montreal Canadiens centre, 1953-71; 507 goals.

BELL, Alexander Graham, invention. Scot., 1847-1922. Invented telephone; worked on iron lung, phonograph, seawater desalination.

BELL, George Maxwell (Max), business. Regina, Sask., 1912-72. Industrialist; principal, FP Publications and sportsman.

BELL, Marilyn, sports. Toronto, Ont., 1937. First person to swim Lake Ontario (1954).

BELL, Robert Edward, science. Ladner, BC, 1918-92. Nuclear physicist; discovered proton radioactivity.

BELLOW, Saul, literary arts. Lachine, Que., 1915. Nobel Prize for Literature. *Herzog.*

BELZBERG, Samuel, business. Calgary, Alta., 1928. Financier; developed real estate financing in W Canada; founder, First City Trust.

BENNETT, Richard Bedford, first Viscount, politics. Hopewell Hill, NB, 1870-1947. Prime minister of Canada 1930-35.

BENNETT, William Andrew Cecil (W.A.C.), politics. Hastings, NB, 1900-79. Social Credit premier of BC, 1952-72.

BENNETT, William Richards, politics. Kelowna, BC, 1932. Social Credit premier of BC, 1975-86.

BENOIT, Jehane, media. Montreal, Que., 1904-87. Food expert; cookbook writer; featured on TV; authority on Cdn/Québécois cooking.

BENY, Roloff (b. Wilfred Roy), visual arts. Medicine Hat, Alta., 1924-84. Photographer; lavish travel books. *India.*

BERBICK, Trevor, sports. Jamaica, 1952. Boxer; Canadian heavyweight champion (1978-85); WBC world heavyweight champion (1986).

BERESFORD-HOWE, Constance Elizabeth, literary arts. Montreal, Que., 1922. Novelist. *Night Studies.*

BERGER, Thomas Rodney, politics. Victoria, BC, 1933. Jurist; proponent of aboriginal rights; commissioner, Mackenzie Valley Pipeline Inquiry.

BERNARDI, Mario, performing arts. Kirkland Lake, Ont., 1930. Conductor, Calgary Philharmonic.

BERNIER, Sylvie, sports. Quebec City, Que., 1964. Diver; gold medal, 3 m springboard,1984 Olympics.

BERTON, Pierre, literary arts. Whitehorse, YT, 1920. Popular historian; author and media personality. *The Last Spike.*

BESSETTE, Gerard, literary arts. Ste-Anne-de-Sabrevois, Que., 1920. Novelist, poet, literary critic. *Mes romans et moi.*

BEST, Charles Herbert, medicine. USA, 1899-1978. Physiologist; co-discoverer of insulin.

BETHUNE, Henry Norman, medicine. Gravenhurst, Ont., 1890-1939. Surgeon; hero in China, where he died helping revolutionary army.

BEY, Salome, performing arts. USA, 1938?. Singer, songwriter, actress. Noted for jazz, blues, spirituals. Wrote and starred in *Indigo,* a history of blues. *Shimmytime.*

BIG BEAR, politics. Ft. Carlton, Sask., 1825-88. Cree leader; opposed treaties on grounds they would destroy Cree way of life.

BIGELOW, Dr. Wilfred Gordon, medicine. Brandon, Man., 1913. Surgeon; developed first cardiac pacemaker.

BILLES, Alfred Jackson, business. Toronto, Ont., 1902-95. Co-founder in 1922 of Canada-wide chain Canadian Tire Corporation.

BILLES, John William, business. Toronto, Ont., 1896-1956. Original founder of Canadian Tire chain of hardware stores.

BIRNEY, Alfred Earle, literary arts. Calgary, Alta., 1904-1995. Narrative poet and professor. *David and Other Poems.*

BISHOP, William Avery (Billy), military. Owen Sound, Ont., 1894-1956. WWI flying ace; downed 72 enemy planes.

BISSELL, Keith, performing arts. Meaford, Ont., 1912-92. Composer of choral, vocal, organ, orchestral and chamber music; folksong arrangements for piano and voice; commissioned by Lois Marshall, Charles Peaker and others.

BISSOONDATH, Neil Devindra, literary arts. Trinidad, 1955. Novelist, short story writer. *A Casual Brutality.*

BLACK, Conrad Moffat, business. Montreal, Que., 1944. Press baron; owner of Hollinger Inc. newspaper empire.

BLAIS, Marie-Claire, literary arts. Quebec City, Que., 1939. Influential novelist. *Une Saison dans la vie d'Emmanuel.*

BLAISE, Clark Lee, literary arts. USA, 1940. Writer; explorer of the displaced person. *Resident Alien.*

BLAKE, Hector "Toe", sports. Victoria Mines, Ont., 1912-95. Hockey player; coached Montreal Canadiens to eight Stanley Cups, 1955-68.

BLAKENEY, Allan Emrys, politics. Bridgewater, NS, 1925. NDP premier of Saskatchewan 1971-82.

BLISS, John William Michael, politics. Leamington, Ont., 1941. Author, history commentator. *Right Honorable Men: The Descent of Canadian Politics from Macdonald to Mulroney.*

BLOHM, Hans Ludwig, visual arts. Germany, 1927. Photographer; author of many photography books. *The Beauty of the Maritimes.*

BLONDIN-ANDREWS, Ethel, politics. Fort Norman, NWT, 1951. In 1988, first native woman elected to Parliament, for Western Arctic (Lib).

BLUMENFELD, Hans, city planner. Germany, 1892-1988. Urban planner; author. *The Modern Metropolis.*

BLYTHE, Dominic, performing arts. Eng., 1947. Actor with Stratford Festival, Ont.

BOCHNER, Lloyd, performing arts. Toronto, Ont., 1924. Character actor who has appeared in TV series *Dynasty* and *Santa Barbara* and in movies. *Naked Gun 2 1/2.*

BODOGH, Marilyn, sports. Toronto, Ont., 1955. Curling. Two-time world champion (skip) in women's curling; member of Team Canada.

BOGGS, Jean Sutherland, visual arts. Peru, 1922. Art curator; National Gallery curator, 1966-76.

BOLDT, Arnie, sports. Osler, Sask., 1957. One-legged high jumper holds disabled world record (2.08 m).

BOLT, Carol, literary arts. Winnipeg, Man., 1941. Playwright; socially conscious writer. *One Night Stand.*

BOMBARDIER, Joseph Armand, invention. Valcourt, Que., 1908-64. Inventor; developer of snowmobiles.

BONDAR, Roberta Lynn, science. Sault Ste Marie, Ont., 1945. Astronaut; first Canadian woman in space.

BORDEN, Sir Robert Laird, politics. Grand Pré, NS, 1854-1937. Canada's prime minister throughout WWI (1911-20).

BORDUAS, Paul-Emile, visual arts. St-Hilaire, Que., 1905-60. Painter; founded Automatistes. *L'etoile noire.*

BORSOS, Phillip, performing arts. Tasmania, 1954-95. Filmmaker. *The Grey Fox* (winner of Best Picture and Best Director, 1982 Genie Awards); *Bethune.*

BOSSY, Michael, sports. Montreal, Que., 1957. Hockey player; NY Islanders winger; nine 50-goal seasons.

BOTSFORD, Sara, performing arts. Dobie, Ont., 1952. Stage, film and TV actress. *Bay Boy; E.N.G.*

BOTTERELL, Edmund Henry, science. Vancouver, BC, 1906-97. Neurosurgeon who initiated program into spinal chord injury research; during WWII devoted to rehabilitation of veterans.

BOUCHARD, Lucien, politics. St-Coeur-de-Marie, Que., 1938. Founder and leader of Bloc Québécois; leader of Parti Québécois; premier of Quebec, 1996-.

BOUCHER, Gaetan, sports. Charlesbourg, Que., 1958. Speedskater; two gold medals (1000 m,1500 m) and a bronze medal (500 m) 1984 Winter Olympics.

BOUEY, Gerald Keith, business. Axford, Sask., 1920. Banker; governor.

BOURASSA, Henri, politics. Montreal, Que., 1868-1952. Federalist; founded *Le Devoir* newspaper.

BOURASSA, Jocelyne, sports. Shawinigan-Sud, Que., 1947. Golf champion, winner of many awards, including La Canadienne 1973 LPGA event; Golf Personality of the Year, Golf Canada, 1972.

BOURASSA, Robert, politics. Montreal, Que., 1933-96. Quebec premier 1970-76, 1985-93.

BOURGEOYS, Marguerite, religion. France, 1620-1700. Religious educator; canonized, 1982.

BOURGET, Ignace, religion. Lauzon, Que., 1799-1885. Catholic bishop of Montreal; avid ultra-Montanist opposed secular Quebec.

BOURNE, Shae-Lynn, sports. Chatham, Ont., 1976. Ice dancing; with Victor Kraatz won Canadian title, 1993-96; third in World Championships, 1996.

BOURQUE, James, politics. Wandering River, Alta, 1935-96. Aboriginal activist appointed to Privy Council, 1992. Co-director of policy for Royal Commission on Aboriginal Peoples, 1994.

BOURQUE, Raymond, sports. Montreal, Que., 1960. Hockey player; Boston Bruins defenceman; four-time Norris Trophy winner.

BOWELL, Sir Mackenzie, politics. Eng., 1823-1917. Canada's fifth prime minister (1894-96).

BOWER, John William (Johnny), sports. Prince Albert, Sask., 1924 Hockey player. Long-time goalkeeper for New York Rangers, Toronto Maple Leafs; led Leafs to four Stanley Cup wins.

BOWERING, George Harry, literary arts. Penticton, BC, 1935. Prolific poet and prose writer. "Burning Water."

BOWMAN, Scotty, sports. Montreal, Que., 1933. Hockey coach; won six Stanley Cups; five with Montreal.

BOYD, Liona, performing arts. Eng., 1950. Acclaimed classical guitarist. *The Guitar-Liona Boyd.*

BOYLE, Joseph Whiteside, exploration and discovery. Toronto, Ont., 1867-1923. Adventurer "Klondike Joe"; mining entrepreneur; national hero in Romania.

BOYLE, Willard S., invention. Amherst, NS, 1924. Physicist who co-invented the charge-coupled device for camcorders and telescopes.

BRACKEN, John, politics. Ellisville, Ont., 1883-1969. Cons. Manitoba premier 1922-42.

BRAITHWAITE, Max, literary arts. Nokomis, Sask., 1911-95. Prairie novelist noted for autobiographical novel *Why Shoot the Teacher?*

BRAND, Oscar, performing arts. Winnipeg, Man., 1920. Folksinger; recorded 80 albums; author folk song collections. *Squid Jiggin' Ground.*

BRANT, Joseph (b. Thayendanegea), politics/religion. USA, 1742-1807. Mohawk leader; British loyalist during American Revolution; translated Bible into Mohawk.

BRASSARD, Jean-Luc, sports. Valleyfield, Que., 1972. Skier; gold medal moguls 1994 Olympics.

BRASSEUR, Isabelle, sports. Kingsbury, Que., 1970. Skater; with Lloyd Eisler won 1993 pairs world title, two Olympic bronze medals (1992).

BRAULT, Jacques, literary arts. Montreal, Que., 1933. Poet; playwright; novelist. *Agonie.*

BREAU, Lenny, performing arts. USA, 1941-84. Guitarist, singer, composer of jazz, country, folk and pop; aired on CBC radio in 1940s and 1950s.

BREBEUF, Jean de, religion. France, 1593-1649. Jesuit martyr; missionary at Sainte Marie among the Hurons.

BRILL, Debbie, sports. Mission, BC, 1953. High jumper; originated "Brill bend" jumping style.

BRITTAIN, Donald, visual arts. Ottawa, Ont., 1928-89. Documentary filmmaker. *On Guard for Thee.*

BROADBENT, John Edward (Ed), politics. Oshawa, Ont., 1936. National leader, NDP 1975-89.

BROADFOOT, Dave, performing arts. Toronto, Ont., 1925. Comedian; Sergeant Renfrew character on *Royal Canadian Air Farce.*

BROCK, Sir Isaac, military. Eng., 1769-1812. Soldier; War of 1812 hero; died at Queenston Heights.

BROCKHOUSE, Bertram Neville, science. Lethbridge, Alta., 1918. Pioneer of use of thermal neutrons to study aspects of behaviour of condensed matter systems at atomic level. Won 1994 Nobel Prize for physics.

BRONFMAN, Charles Rosner, business. Montreal, Que., 1931. Industrialist; chairman, Cemp Investments Ltd; former owner, Montreal Expos.

BRONFMAN, Edgar M., business. Montreal, Que., 1929. Industrialist; CEO, Seagram's Ltd; president, World Jewish Congress.

BRONFMAN, Samuel, business. Brandon, Man., 1891-1971. Capitalist; distiller (Seagram Co. Ltd) and philanthropist.

BROSSARD, Nicole, literary arts. Montreal, Que., 1943. Formalist poet. "Mecanique jongleuse suivi de masculin grammaticale."

BROWN, Arthur Royal "Roy", military. Carleton Place, Ont., 1893-1944. On April 21, 1918, shot down Germany's Red Baron, Manfred von Richthofen.

BROWN, George, media/politics. Scot., 1818-80. Journalist; founded *Toronto Globe* (1844); as Reformer, played major role in Confederation.

BROWN, John George "Kootenai", exploration and discovery. Ire., 1839-1916. Adventurer; army official; prospector; whisky trader; established Waterton Lakes Natl Park.

BROWN, Rosemary, politics. Jamaica, 1930. Activist; head, Ontario Human Rights Assn; former NDP leadership candidate.

BROWNING, Kurt, sports. Rocky Mountain House, Alta, 1966. World figure skating champion, 1989-91, 1993.

BRUHN, Erik Belton Evers, performing arts. Denmark, 1928-86. Dancer; choreographer; guiding figure for National Ballet.

BRULE, Etienne, exploration and discovery. France, 1592-1633. Explorer; first known European to reach Lake Superior.

BRZOZOWICZ, Czelaw Peter, engineering. Poland, 1911-97. Structural engineer consulted on Toronto's original subway line, Niagara Falls Skylon Tower and CN Tower in Toronto.

BUCHAN, John, first Baron Tweedsmuir, literary arts. Scot., 1875-1940. Thriller novelist, wrote *The 39 Steps*; governor general, 1935-40.

BUCHANAN, John MacLennan, politics. Sydney, NS, 1931. Conservative premier of NS.

BUCK, Tim, politics. Eng., 1891-1973. Radical politician; led Canadian Commmunist Party, 1929-61.

BUCKE, Richard Maurice, medicine. Eng., 1837-1902. Physician; writer; advocate for the mentally ill; spiritual writer. *Cosmic Consciousness.*

BUCZYNSKI, Walter, performing arts. Toronto, Ont., 1933. Pianist and composer of orchestral, chamber, vocal and piano music; soloist internationally in 1960s and 1970s. *Songs of War, Ressurrection II.*

BUJOLD, Geneviève, performing arts. Montreal, Que., 1942. Actress; international star. *Dead Ringers.*

BULL, Gerald Vincent, invention. North Bay, Ont., 1928-90. Inventor; weapons designer; murdered mysteriously.

BURKA, Petra, sports. Holland, 1946. Figure skater; women's world champion, 1965.

BURNS, Tommy (b. Noah Brusso), sports. Hanover, Ont., 1881-1955. Boxer; world heavyweight champion, 1906-08.

BURR, Raymond William Stacy, performing arts. New Westminster, BC, 1917-93. Actor; TV's Perry Mason, 1957-66, 1985-93.

BURROUGHS, Jackie, performing arts. Eng., 1942. Actress; versatile performer; Hetty in *Road to Avonlea.*

BUSH, John Hamilton (Jack), visual arts. Toronto, Ont., 1909-77. Abstract artist. "Bridge Passage."

BUTALA, Sharon Annette, literary arts. Nipawin, Sask., 1940. Novelist, short story writer, playwright. *Coming Attractions; The Fourth Archangel.*

BY, John, military. Eng., 1779-1836. Engineer; built Rideau Canal, Quebec fortifications.

BYNG, Julian Hedworth George, first Viscount, military. Eng., 1862-1935. Soldier; governor general, 1921-26.

C

CABOT, John (b. Giovanni Caboto), exploration and discovery. Italy, c. 1450-99. First N American landing since the Vikings.

CABOT, Sebastian, performing arts. Eng., 1918-76. Portly, bearded character actor in film and television. *The Captain's Paradise, The Beachcombers, Family Affair.*

CAIN, Larry, sports. Toronto, Ont., 1963. Canoeist; gold (500 m) and silver (1000 m) medals, 1984 Olympics.

CALDER, Frank Arthur, politics. Nass Harbour, BC, 1915. Native politician; Nishga leader; BC MLA.

CALDWELL, Zoe, performing arts. Australia, 1933. Actor, director. *The Prime of Miss Jean Brodie.*

CALLAGHAN, Barry, literary arts. Toronto, Ont., 1937. Founder of *Exile: A Literary Quarterly*; novelist, journalist; son of Morley Callaghan.

CALLAGHAN, Morley Edward, literary arts. Toronto, Ont., 1903-90. Novelist; memoirist. *The Loved and the Lost.*

CALLBECK, Catherine, politics. Central Bedeque, PEI, 1939. First woman to be elected premier. Liberal premier of PEI 1993-96.

CALLWOOD, June, public service. Chatham, Ont., 1924. Journalist; civil libertarian, AIDS activist.

CAMERON, Elspeth MacGregor, literary arts. Toronto, Ont., 1943. Biographer. *Robertson Davies: An Appreciation; Hugh MacLennan: A Writer's Life; Irving Layton: A Portrait.*

CAMERON, James, literary arts. Eng., 1910. Philosopher; essayist; poet. "Images of Authority."

CAMERON, James, performing arts. Kapuskasing, Ont., 1954. Hollywood-based director of action movies including *Terminator* series, *Aliens, True Lies, Titanic.*

CAMERON, Michelle, sports. Calgary, Alta, 1962. Gold medalist in sychronized swimming with Carolyn Waldo, 1988 Olympics.

CAMERON, Silver Donald, literary arts. Toronto, Ont., 1937. Novelist, critic, editor, playwright. *Dragon Lady; Wind, Whales and Whisky: A Cape Breton Voyage.*

CAMERON, Thomas Wright Moir, medicine. Scot., 1894-1947. Parasitologist; pioneered study of parasitic worms.

CAMP, Dalton Kingsley, politics. Woodstock, NB, 1920. PC consultant; newspaper columnist.

CAMPBELL, Alexander (Sir), politics. Eng., 1822-92. Tory leader; Father of Confederation.

CAMPBELL, Avril Phaedra "Kim", politics. Port Alberni, BC, 1947. First woman prime minister of Canada, June 1993-December 1993.

CAMPBELL, Clarence, sports. Fleming, Sask., 1905-84. Sports administrator; headed NHL, 1946-77.

CAMPBELL, Douglas, performing arts. Scot., 1922. Actor at Stratford Festival, Ont. Co-founder of Canadian Players.

CAMPBELL, Norman Kenneth, performing arts. USA, 1924. Music producer; innovative developer of ballet and musicals.

CAMPEAU, Robert, business. Sudbury, Ont., 1923. Financier; exemplar of 1980s expansionist business mania; developer; retail store magnate.

CANDY, John Franklin, performing arts. Toronto, Ont., 1950-94. Actor; comedian; bearish *SCTV* regular (Johnny LaRue, William B.); film star. *Uncle Buck.*

CARDINAL, Douglas Joseph, visual arts. Red Deer, Alta., 1934. Métis architect; Canadian Museum of Civilization.

CARDINAL, Tantoo, performing arts. Fort McMurray, Alta, 1951. Native actress who has appeared in films, *Big Bear, Smoke Signals, Black Robe* and CBC's *North of 60.*

CARLE, Gilles, visual arts. Maniwaki, Que., 1929. Film director. *La Vrai Nature de Bernadette.*

CARLETON, Guy (Sir), first Baron Dorchester, politics. Ire., 1724-1808. Quebec governor, 1768-78, 1785-95; supporter of French traditions.

CARMAN, William Bliss, literary arts. Fredericton, NB, 1861-1929. Poet; journalist. "The Pipes of Pan."

CARMICHAEL, Franklin, visual arts. Orillia, Ont., 1890-1945. Group of Seven founding member.

CARR, Emily, visual arts. Victoria, BC, 1871-1945. Painter of NW coastal Indians and nature.

CARR, Shirley, politics. Niagara Falls, Ont., First Woman to lead CUPE, Canada's largest union. President Emeritus, Canadian Labour Congress.

CARREY, James (Jim), performing arts. Jackson's Point, Ont., 1962. Comedic actor. *Ace Ventura; The Mask; Batman Forever.*

CARRIER, Roch, literary arts. Beauce, Que., 1937. Novelist; playwright. *La Guerre, Yes Sir!*

CARSON, John Elmer (Jack), performing arts. Carman, Man., 1910-63. Square-jawed film actor. *Mildred Pierce.*

CARTER, Cardinal Emmett, religion. Montreal, Que., 1912. As Toronto Cardinal, helped get full funding for Catholic schools.

CARTER, Wilf, performing arts. Port Hilford, NS, 1904-96. Singer; father of Canadian country music.

CARTIER, Georges-Etienne (Sir), politics. St Antoine, UC, 1814-73. Father of Confederation; joint premier of United Canada, 1857-62.

CARTIER, Jacques, exploration and discovery. France, 1491-1557. Credited with European discovery of Canada; first explorer of St. Lawrence River.

CARVER, Humphrey Stephen Mumford, politics. Engl., 1902-95. Key figure in Central Mortgage and Housing Corporation 1950s-60s; formed Co-operative Commonwealth Federation, forerunner of NDP.

CASGRAIN, Thérèse,, politics. Montreal, Que., 1896-1981. Won Quebec women the right to vote (1940) and hold provincial office; leader of Quebec's CCF party in 1951.

CASSON, Alfred Joseph (A.J.), visual arts. Toronto, Ont., 1898-1992. Member, Group of Seven. "Country Store."

CATHERWOOD, Ethel, sports. Haldimand Cty, Ont., 1909. High jumper; gold in high jump, 1928 Olympics.

CAVOUKIAN, Artin and Lucie, visual arts. Egypt, Armenia, 1915-95, 1923-95. Clientele of photographer Artin with wife Lucie included world leaders.

CHALMERS, Floyd Sherman, public service. USA, 1898-1993. Instituted Floyd S. Chalmers Foundation funding for arts in Canada.

CHAMPLAIN, Samuel de, exploration and discovery. France, 1567-1635. Explorer; important cartographer/geographer; "Father of New France."

CHANG, Thomas Ming Sui, medicine/science. China, 1933. Physiologist; expert on artificial cells and organs.

CHAPMAN, John Herbert, science. London, Ont., 1921-79. Physicist; lead role in Canada's satellite program.

CHAPUT-ROLLAND, Solange, media. Montreal, Que., 1919. Writer; broadcaster; Québécoise federalist.

CHAREST, Jean J., politics. Sherbrooke, Que., 1958. Led PC rump after '93 federal electoral debacle.

CHARLEBOIS, Robert, performing arts. Montreal, Que., 1945. Singer/songwriter. "Solidaritude."

CHARLEVOIX, Pierre François Xavier de, literary arts. France, 1682-1761. Historian; first complete history of New France.

CHAYKIN, Maury, performing arts. Mystery, Alaska, 1949. Prolific actor has appeared in *Jacob Two-Two Meets the Hooded Fang; Dances With Wolves.*

CHERRY, Don, sports. Kingston, Ont., 1934. Hockey coach; commentator; feisty nationalist.

CHEVALIER, Leo, business. Montreal, Que., 1934. Fashion designer of international lines.

CHIPMAN, Ward, law. St John, NB, 1787-1851. Jurist; chief justice of NB; noted abolitionist.

CHIRAEFF, Ludmilla, performing arts. Latvia, 1924. Choreographer; founder, Les Grands Ballets Canadiennes.

CHISHOLM, George Brock, medicine. Oakville, Ont., 1896-1971. Psychiatrist; early opponent of pollution, nuclear arms; first head of World Health Org

CHONG, Rae Dawn, performing arts. Vancouver, BC, 1962. Film actress. *Quest for Fire.*

CHONG, Thomas (Tommy), performing arts. Edmonton, Alta., 1938. Actor; half of Cheech and Chong comedy team. *Cheech and Chong's Nice Dreams.*

CHOUART DES GROSEILLIERS, Medard, exploration and discovery. France, 1618-90. Explorer; fur trader; with Radisson opened western fur trade.

CHOUINARD, Josée, sports. Rosemont, Que., 1969. Three-time Canadian figure skating champion.

CHRETIEN, Joseph Jacques Jean, politics. Shawinigan, Que., 1934. Became prime minister of Canada, general election 1993.

CHRISTIE, Robert Wallace, performing arts. Toronto, Ont., 1920-96. Played at Ontario's Stratford Festival; Old Vic in London, Eng.; famous for portrayal of John A. MacDonald.

CHRISTIE, William Mellis, business. Scot., 1829-1900. Biscuit manufacturer; Christie Biscuits founder.

CHUVALO, George, sports. Toronto, Ont., 1937. Boxer; fought three world champions; never knocked down. Anti-drug crusader.

CLAIR, Frank, sports. USA, 1917. Football coach; 174 wins (Ottawa Rough Riders) tops CFL coaches.

CLANCY, Francis Michael "King", sports. Ottawa, Ont., 1903-86. Hockey player; defenceman, Ottawa Senators, Toronto Maple Leafs; lively raconteur.

CLARK, Charles Joseph (Joe), politics. High River, Alta., 1939. Prime minister of Canada 1979-80.

CLARK, Greg, literary arts. Toronto, Ont., 1892-1977. Journalist and humorist, winner of Leacock Award for Humour.

CLARK, Susan, performing arts. Sarnia, Ont., 1940. Actress who has appeared in Hollywood movies, television. *Murder by Decree; Coogan's Bluff: Webster.*

CLARKE, Austin Chesterfield, literary arts. Barbados, 1934. Novelist; short story writer. *Proud Empires; Nine Men Who Laughed.*

CLARKSON, Adrienne Louise, media/politics. Hong Kong, 1939. Broadcaster; long-time CBC host. *Appointed governor general in 1999.*

CLAYTON-THOMAS, David, performing arts. Eng., 1941. Singer; member, Blood, Sweat and Tears. *Spinning Wheel.*

COCHRANE, Tom, performing arts. Lynn Lake, Man., 1953. Singer, songwriter, guitarist. Led Toronto-based quintet, Tom Cochrane and Red Rider, formed in 1976. *Breaking Curfew.* Went solo in 1991 with *Mad, Mad World.* "Life is a Highway."

COCKBURN, Bruce, performing arts. Ottawa, Ont., 1945. Singer/songwriter; politically conscious performer. *Dancing in the Dragon's Jaws.*

COE-JONES, Dawn, sports. Lake Cowichan, BC, 1961. Golfer; leading pro; 1993 LPGA title.

COHEN, Leonard, literary arts/performing arts. Montreal, Que., 1934. Poet; singer. *Flowers for Hitler, I'm Your Man.*

COHEN, Matt, literary arts. Kingston, Ont., 1942. Short story writer, novelist, translator. *The Colour of War; Living on Water; Freud: The Paris Notebooks.*

COHEN, Morris (Moishe) Abraham "Two-Gun", military. Eng., 1889-1970. China hand; confidant of Sun Yat-sen; general in Chinese army.

COHEN, Samuel Nathan, literary arts. Sydney, NS, 1923-71. Critic; Canada's first serious drama critic.

COHON, George, business. USA, 1937. CEO, Cdn McDonald's restaurants; philanthropist.

COLDWELL, Major James William, politics. Eng., 1888-1974. CCF founder; leader, 1942-60.

COLE, Jack, business. Toronto, Ont., 1920-97. With brother Carl started Coles chain of bookstores in Toronto, which later became national; created Coles Notes, study booklets for students, in 1947.

COLEMAN, Kathleen Blake (Kit), media. Toronto, Ont., 1864-1915. First woman war correspondent.

COLICOS, John, performing arts. Toronto, Ont., 1928. Stage actor; Stratford Festival regular.

COLLIP, James Bertram, medicine. Belleville, Ont., 1892-1965. Biochemist; co-discoverer of insulin.

COLOMBO, John Robert, literary arts. Kitchener, Ont., 1936. Anthologist; prolific compiler of reference books. *Colombo's Canadian Quotations.*

COLVILLE, Alexander, visual arts. Toronto, Ont., 1920. Realistic painter; designed centennial coins.

COMFORT, Charles Fraser, visual arts. Scot., 1900-94. Artist, graphic designer, created murals for Toronto Stock Exchange, director of National Gallery of Canada 1960-65.

CONACHER, Lionel Pretoria, sports. Toronto, Ont., 1901-54. Canada's Athlete of the Half-Century (1900-1950).

CONNOR, Ralph (b. Charles William Gordon), literary arts. West Indian Lands, Glengarry County, Canada West 1860-1937. Popular novelist, preacher of "red-blooded" Christianity. *The Sky Pilot.*

CONNORS, Charles Thomas "Stompin' Tom", performing arts. Saint John, NB, 1936. Country singer; nationalist performer. *Across This Land with Stompin' Tom.*

COOK, George Ramsay, literary arts. Alameda, Sask., 1931. Prolific historian. *Canada: A Modern Study; The Maple Leaf Forever.*

COOK, James, exploration and discovery. Eng., 1728-79. Navigator; explored Newfoundland and Northwest coasts.

COOKE, Jack Kent, business. Hamilton, Ont., 1912-97. Capitalist; flamboyant owner of newspapers, radio stations, sports teams (Washington Redskins).

COOMBS, Ernest Arthur (Ernie), performing arts. USA, 1927. Children's entertainer; CBC's "Mr. Dressup."

COPP, Harold, science. Toronto, Ont., 1915. Physiologist; discovered calcitonon, hormone that regulates calcium in blood.

COPPS, Sheila Maureen, politics. Hamilton, Ont., 1952. Liberal deputy prime minister.

CORMIER, Ernest, visual arts. Montreal, Que., 1885-1980. Architect; designed University of Montreal.

CORRIGAL, Jim, sports. Barrie, Ont., 1946. Football player. Lineman with Toronto Argonauts 1970-81; four-time CFL all-star.

COSENTINO, Frank, sports. Hamilton, Ont., 1937. Football player; CFL quarterback, 1960-69; sports history writer; prof., physical education.

COSTAIN, Thomas Bertram, literary arts. Brantford, Ont., 1885-1965. Historical novelist. *High Towers.*

COUGHTRY, Graham, visual arts. St Lambert, Que., 1931-99. Abstract figurative painter; exhibited in New York's Guggenheim Museum, Museum of Modern Art, as well as across Canada.

COULTHARD, Jean, performing arts. Vancouver, BC, 1908. Composer. "The Pines of Emily Carr."

COUPLAND, Douglas Campbell, literary arts. Germany, BC, 1961. Novelist; humorist. *Generation X.*

COURNOYEA, Nellie J., politics. Aklavik, NWT, 1940. First woman aboriginal leader of Northwest Territories.

COWAN, Garry, sports. Kitchener, Ont., 1938. Golfer; twice US amateur champion (1966, 1971).

CRANSTON, Toller, sports. Hamilton, Ont., 1949. Skater; brought innovation and artistry to men's figure skating.

CRAWLEY, Frank Radford "Budge", visual arts. Ottawa, Ont., 1911-87. Film producer. *The Rowdyman.*

CREIGHTON, Donald Grant, literary arts. Toronto, Ont., 1902-79. Historian; developed literary side of history.

CREMAZIE, Claude Joseph Olivier "Octave", literary arts. Quebec City, Que., 1827-79. Father of French Canadian poetry. "Le Drapeau de Carillon."

CROLL, David Arnold, politics. Russia, 1900-91. Liberal MLA in 1934; first Jewish cabinet minister (1955).

CROMBIE, David Edward, politics. Toronto, Ont., 1936. Civic reformer; Toronto mayor 1973-78.

CRONENBERG, David, visual arts. Toronto, Ont., 1943. Film director; inventive horror; science fiction filmmaker. *Videodrome, Crash.*

CRONYN, Hume (b. Hume Blake), performing arts. London, Ont., 1911. Stage actor; film character player. *Cocoon.*

CROSBIE, John Carnell, politics. St John's, Nfld, 1931. PC minister of fisheries and oceans; international trade; justice.

CROTHERS, William, sports. Markham, Ont., 1940. Runner; silver medal (800 m), 1964 Olympics.

CROW, John William, business. Eng., 1937. Economist; governor of Bank of Canada, 1987-94.

CROWFOOT, military. Belly R, Alta, 1830-90. Blackfoot Chief, diplomat.

CUDDY, James Gordon (Jim), performing arts. Toronto, Ont., 1955. Lead singer for rock group Blue Rodeo.

CUMMINGS, Burton, performing arts. Winnipeg, Man., 1947. Rock singer; lead singer, The Guess Who; later solo artist. *My Own Way to Rock.*

CUNARD, Sir Samuel, business. Halifax, NS, 1787-1865. Shipowner; founded Cunard Line forerunner.

CURNOE, Gregory Richard, visual arts. London, Ont., 1936-92. Fine artist whose paintings often incorporated written words; also created collages, drawings, prints.

CURRIE, Sir Arthur William, military. Strathroy, Ont., 1875-1933. Commander, Canadian corps, WWI.

CURRIE, Philip, science. Toronto, Ont., 1948. Curator of dinosaurs for Alberta's Royal Tyrrel Museum in Drumheller and world leader in paleontology; recently discovered a feathered dinosaur that proved birds were dinosaurs.

CURTOLA, Robert Allen (Bobby), performing arts. Thunder Bay, Ont., 1944. Singer; early teen idol. "Fortune Teller."

CYR, Louis, sports. Napierville, Que., 1863-1912. World's strongest man, 1880-1990.

D

DAFOE, Allan Roy, medicine. Madoc, Ont., 1883-1943. Small-town physician who delivered the Dionne quintuplets, 28 May 1934; later faced accusations of exploiting the sisters.

DAFOE, John Wesley, media. Combermere, Ont., 1866-1944. Journalist; influential editor,*Winnipeg Free Press*.

DAIR, Carl, visual arts. Welland, Ont., 1912-67. Internationally recognized designer, topographer; created Cartier, first modern Canadian typeface. *Design with Type* .

DANBY, Kenneth Edison (Ken), visual arts. Sault Ste Marie, Ont., 1940. Painter of realistic sports figures.

DAVEY, Keith, politics. Toronto, Ont., 1926. Long-time Liberal Party strategist.

DAVIES, Robertson William, literary arts. Thamesville, Ont., 1913-95. Novelist; playwright. *Fifth Business.*

DAVIS, Andrew, performing arts. Eng., 1944. Conductor of Toronto Symphony Orchestra 1975-88; participated in 1978 TSO visit to People's Republic of China.

DAVIS, Donald, performing arts. Newmarket, Ont., 1928-98. Distinguished Shakespearean actor, played Ontario's Stratford Festival; also appeared in TV roles: *Mission Impossible*. Co-founder of Toronto's Crest Theatre.

DAVIS, Fred, media. Toronto, Ont., 1921-96. Broadcaster and host of long-running CBC panel show "Front Page Challenge" (1957-95).

DAVIS, Victor, sports. Guelph, Ont., 1964-89. Swimmer; three medals 1984 Olympics; gold in 200 m breaststroke.

DAVIS, Warren, performing arts. Peterborough, Ont., 1926-95. CBC newsman. *The National; This Hour Has Seven Days.*

DAVIS, William Grenville, politics. Brampton, Ont., 1929. PC premier of Ontario, 1971-85.

DAWSON, George Mercer, science. Pictou, NS, 1849-1901. Geologist; surveyed much of northern and western Canada.

DAWSON, Sir John William, science. Pictou, NS, 1820-99. Geologist; made McGill a leading university; founded Royal Society of Canada.

DAY, James, sports. Thornhill, Ont., 1946. Equestrian; team gold medal, 1968 Olympics.

DE CARLO, Yvonne (b. Peggy Yvonne Middleton), performing arts. Vancouver, BC, 1924. Actress; film/TV star. *The Munsters.*

DE LA ROCHE, Mazo (b. Maisie Roche), literary arts. Newmarket, Ont., 1879-1961. Prolific popular novelist. *Jalna.*

de VILLIERS, Priscilla, politics. Pretoria, S. Africa, 1942. Activist and founder of CAVEAT, Canadians Against Violence Everywhere Advocating Its Termination.

DEL GRANDE, Louis, performing arts. USA, 1942. Actor, producer, writer. Starred in CBC TV series *Seeing Things.*

DENNYS, Louise, literary arts. Egypt, 1948. Vice-president and publisher at Knopf Canada.

DESCHENES, Jules, law. Montreal, Que., 1923. Jurist; Que. chief justice; chairman, Inquiry of War Criminals in Canada.

DESJARDINS, Alphonse, business. Lévis, Que., 1854-1920. Banker; established first Caisse populaire (credit union) in 1900.

DESMARAIS, Paul, business. Sudbury, Ont., 1927. Industrialist; chairman of Power Corp., controlling trust, insurance and paper companies.

DESMOND, Trudy, performing arts. USA, 1946-99. Ballad and jazz singer, appeared in 1970 revue Spring Thaw. *My One and Only Love,* a tribute to Gershwin.

DEWAR, Marion, politics. Montreal, Que., 1928. Mayor, Ottawa, 1978-85; NDP MP.

DEWDNEY, Christopher, literary arts. London, Ont., 1951. Eclectic poet. *The Immaculate Perception: The Recent Artifacts from the Institute of Applied Fiction.*

DEWHURST, Colleen, performing arts. Montreal, Que., 1926-91. Actress who cultivated an earth-mother persona; noted for TV and film roles and performances in Albee and O'Neill plays. *Annie Hall; Murphy Brown.*

DICKENS, Francis Jeffrey, military. Eng., 1844-86. Policeman; novelist's son; inspector in NWMP.

DICKINS, Clennell Haggerston "Punch", exploration and discovery. Portage la Prairie, Man., 1899-1995. Adventurer. First to fly length of MAckenzie River and above Arctic Circle.

DICKSON, Robert George Brian, law. Yorkton, Sask., 1916-98 Chief justice of Canada, 1984-90.

DIEFENBAKER, John George, politics. Neustadt, Ont., 1895-1979. Prime minister of Canada 1957-63. (PC)

DION, Celine, performing arts. Montreal, Que., 1968. Popular Quebec chanteuse. "Unison."

DION, Stéphane, politics. Quebec City, Que., 1955. Political scientist; Liberal Minister of Intergovernmental Affairs 1996-.

DIONNE, Marcel, sports. Drummondville, Que., 1951. Hockey player; centre; 731 goals, third all-time.

DIONNE sisters, medicine. Corbeil, Ont., 1934. Annette, Emilie (d. 1954), Yvonne, Cecile and Marie (d. 1970), identical quintuplets born to poor rural family, became tourist attraction through government exploitation.

DMYTRYK, Edward, visual arts. Grand Forks, BC, 1908-99. Film director; film noir specialist. One of Hollywood Ten during McCarthy era. *Detour.*

DOBBS, Kildare Robert Eric, literary arts. India, 1923. Short story writer, essayist. *Coastal Canada; Historic Canada.*

DOHERTY, Denny, performing arts. Halifax, NS, 1941. Pop singer; founding member, The Mamas and the Papas.

DONKIN, Eric Albert, performing arts. Eng., 1930-98. Classical actor who played 26 seasons at Ontario's Stratford Festival.

DOUGHTY, Sir Arthur George, archivist. Eng., 1860-1936. Established Public Archives of Canada.

DOUGLAS, Sir James, politics. British Guiana, 1803-77. Administrator; governor of BC, 1858-64.

DOUGLAS, Robert John Wilson, science. Southampton, Ont., 1920. Geologist; famous for geographical survey of structure of Rockies and foothills of southern Alberta.

DOUGLAS, Thomas Clement (Tommy), politics. Scot., 1904-86. Eloquent socialist; Sask. premier, 1944-61; NDP federal leader, 1961-71.

DRABINSKY, Garth Howard, performing arts. Toronto, Ont., 1948. Impresario; Cineplex founder, theatrical producer. *Show Boat.*

DRAPEAU, Jean, politics. Montreal, Que., 1916-99. Montreal mayor for 29 years; brought city Expo 67, 1976 Olympics, Montreal Expos.

DRESSLER, Marie (b. Leila von Koerber), performing arts. Cobourg, Ont., 1869-1934. Actress; oversize film star. *Min and Bill.*

DRYDEN, Kenneth Wayne, sports. Hamilton, Ont., 1947. Hockey goaltender; six-time all-star for Montreal; also lawyer and writer. *The Game.*

DUCKWORTH, Henry Edmison, science. Brandon, Man., 1915. With associates constructed highy accurate mass spectrometers for determination of atomic masses.

DUDEK, Louis, literary arts. Montreal, Que., 1918. Socially aware poet; critic. "East of the City."

DUGUID, Don, sports. Winnipeg, Man., 1935. Curler; Canadian and world champion, 1970, 1971.

DUMONT, Fernand, politics. Montmorency, Que., 1927-97. Quebec sovereigntist named deputy minister of cultural development for PQ in 1976; drafter of Bill 101, French Language Charter.

DUMONT, Gabriel, military. Red River, Sask., 1837-1906. Métis leader; guerrilla leader in NW Rebellion.

DUNNING, George, performing arts. Toronto, Ont., 1920. Animator and director; creator of Beatles *Yellow Submarine* film animation.

DUPLESSIS, Maurice Le Noblet, politics. Trois-Rivières, Que., 1890-1959. Powerful premier of Quebec, 1936-39, 1944-59.

DURBIN, Deanna (b. Edna Mae Durbin), performing arts. Winnipeg, Man., 1921. Actress; singer; teenage movie star. *3 Smart Girls.*

DURELLE, Yvon, sports. Baie Ste Anne, Que., 1929. Canadian middleweight boxing title 1953; light heavyweight 1953-54; British empire light heavyweight champion 1957.

DURHAM, John George Lambton, first Earl of, politics. Eng., 1792-1840. Statesman; "Radical Jack" urged union of English and French Canada.

DURNAN, William Arnold (Bill), sports. Toronto, Ont., 1915-72. Hockey goaltender; six-time Vezina Trophy winner for Montreal Canadiens.

DUTOIT, Charles Edouard, performing arts. Switz., 1936. Conductor of Montreal Symphony Orchestra.

DWAN, Allan, visual arts. Toronto, Ont., 1885-1981. Film director from silent era, made over 200 Hollywood films. *Sands of Iwo Jima.*

EATON, Cyrus Stephen, business. Pugwash, NS, 1883-1979. Financier; promoter of international peace.

EATON, Fredrik Stefan, business. Toronto, Ont., 1938. Retailer; former chairman, T. Eaton Co.

EATON, Timothy, business. Ire., 1834-1907. Retailer; innovative founder of T. Eaton Co. in 1867.

EDWARDS, Robert Chambers (Bob), media. Scot., 1864-1922. Journalist; published satirical *Calgary Eye Opener.*

EGOYAN, Atom, visual arts. Egypt, 1960. Film director; guitarist; playwright. *The Sweet Hereafter.*

EISLER, Lloyd, sports. Seaforth, Ont., 1963. Figure skater; with Isabelle Brasseur won world pairs title, 1993; Olympic bronze medals.

ELDER, Jim, sports. Toronto, Ont., 1934. Equestrian; team gold medal, 1968 Olympics.

ELGAARD, Ray, sports. Edmonton, Alta., 1959. Football player; Sask. Roughriders star wide receiver.

ELGIN, James Bruce, eighth Earl of, politics. Eng., 1811-63. Governor general, 1847-54.

EMERY, Victor, sports. Montreal, Que., 1933. Bobsledder; piloted 1964 Olympic gold medal team.

ENGEL, Howard, literary arts. Toronto, Ont., 1931. Mystery writer. *Murder See the Light.*

ENGEL, Marian, literary arts. Toronto, Ont., 1933-85. Novelist. *Bear.*

ERASMUS, Georges Henry, politics. Ft Rae, NWT, 1948. Dene leader; former head, Assembly of First Nations.

ERICKSON, Arthur Charles, visual arts. Vancouver, BC, 1924. Architect; Simon Fraser University (Burnaby, BC).

ESPOSITO, Phillip Anthony (Phil), sports. Sault Ste Marie, Ont., 1942. Hockey player; Boston centre; 717 goals, fourth all-time.

ESTEY, Willard Zebedee "Bud", law. Saskatoon, Sask., 1919. Supreme Court justice, 1977-88; headed several royal commissions.

ETROG, Sorel, visual arts. Romania, 1933. Monumental sculptor; designer. "Ritual Head."

EVANGELISTA, Linda, media. St Catharines, Ont., 1965. International top model.

EVANS, Gil, performing arts. Toronto, Ont., 1912-88. Composer, arranger, pianist. Played free jazz, rock and funk. Gil Evans Orchestra.

EVANS, James, education. Eng., 1801-46. English Methodist missionary, invented Cree syllabic writing system. *Cree Syllabic Hymn Book.*

EVANSHEN, Terrance Anthony (Terry), sports. Montreal, Que., 1944. Football player; outstanding CFL receiver.

EYTON, Trevor, business. Quebec City, Que., 1934. Executive; president, Brascan Ltd; many corporate boards.

FACKENHEIM, Emil Ludwig, literary arts. Germany, 1916. Philosopher; works on religion and the Holocaust. *Quest for Past and Future.*

FAIRCLOUGH, Ellen Louks, politics. Hamilton, Ont., 1905. First woman Cabinet minister (1957).

FAIRFIELD, Robert, visual arts. St Catharines, Ont., 1918-95. Designed Stratford Festival Theatre, Ont.; Ontario pavilion at Expo 67.

FAIRLEY, Barker, visual arts. Eng., 1887-1986. Critic; essential Goethe scholar; portrait painter.

FAITH, Percy, performing arts. Toronto, Ont., 1908-76. Bandleader; top music arranger. "Canadian Sunset."

FALONEY, Bernie, sports. USA, 1932. Football player; long-time star QB for Edmonton, Hamilton.

FEINBERG, Rabbi Abraham (b. Abraham Nisselevicz, aka Anthony Frome), politics. USA, 1899-1986. Peace activist; champion of radical causes.

FERGUSON, Don, performing arts. Montreal, Que., 1946. Actor, writer, director of CHC documentaries; on team of CBC's *Royal Canadian Air Farce.* Impersonates Lucien Bouchard, Preston Manning.

FERGUSON, Ivan Graeme, invention. Toronto, Ont., 1929. Inventor; developed IMAX and OMNIMAX film systems.

FERGUSON, James Francis, performing arts. Ire., 1940-97. Founder, with George Millar, of the Irish Rovers, a singing group that popularized Irish pub music from the sixties on; appeared on CBC television.

FERGUSON, Max "Rawhide", media. Eng., 1924. Broadcaster; popular host of CBC Radio's *Rawhide.*

FERGUSON, Maynard, performing arts. Verdun, Que., 1928. Jazz trumpeter; versatile stylist made 50 albums.

FERRON, Jacques, literary arts/politics. Louiseville, Que., 1921-85. Playwright, *Contes du pays incertain*; Rhinoceros Party founder.

FESSENDEN, Reginald Aubrey, invention. Milton-Est, Canada E, 1866-1932. Inventor; transmitted world's first radio broadcast (1906).

FIELDING, Joy, literary arts. Toronto, Ont., 1945. Novelist, journalist, scriptwriter. *Tell Me No Stories.*

FILION, Herve, sports. Angers, Que., 1940. Harness driver; all-time leader in victories; 12,000+.

FILMON, Gary Albert, politics. Winnipeg, Man., 1942. PC Manitoba premier since 1988.

FINDLEY, Timothy, literary arts. Toronto, Ont., 1930. Novelist; versatile writer. *The Wars.*

FITZ-JONES, Philip Chester, science. Vancouver, BC, 1920. Researched structure and chemical nature of bacterial spores.

FITZGERALD, Lionel LeMoine, visual arts. Winnipeg, Man., 1890-1956. Impressionist turned to abstracts. "Doc Snider's House."

FLAVELLE, Sir Joseph Wesley, business. Peterborough, Ont., 1858-1939. Financier; executive for Canada Packers, Bank of Commerce, National Trust.

FLEMING, Sir Sandford, invention. Scot. 1827-1915. Engineer; developed standard time; designed Canada's first postage stamp; built railways.

FOLLOWS, Megan, performing arts. Toronto, Ont., 1969. Actor who portrayed Anne of Green Gables in CBC TV series. *Silver Bullet.*

FONYO, Stephen Charles (Steve), sports. Montreal, Que., 1965. Handicapped runner; "Journey for Lives" raised funds for cancer research, 1985.

FORD, Glenn (b. Gwyllyn Samuel Newton Ford), performing arts. Quebec City, Que., 1916. Noted American actor of the 1940s and 1950s. *Gilda, Teahouse of the August Moon.*

FORRESTER, Helen, literary arts. Eng., 1919. Novelist. Wrote semiautobiographical Liverpool series: *Twopence to Cross the Mersey; Liverpool Miss; By the Waters of Liverpool; Lime Street at Two.*

FORRESTER, Maureen, performing arts. Monteal, Que., 1930. Operatic contralto; Canada's prima diva.

FORSEY, Eugene Alfred, politics. Grand Bank, Nfld, 1904-91. Intellectual; commentator on public affairs; social radical; strong federalist.

FORTIER, L. Yves, politics. Quebec City, Que., 1935. Former Canadian ambassador to the United Nations.

FOSTER, David Walter, performing arts. Victoria, BC, 1949. Musician; produced many major acts (Chicago, Barbra Streisand); 12 Grammy awards.

FOSTER, Sir George Eulas, politics. Carleton, NB, 1847-1931. Statesman; central in Cdn political life; acting PM during Borden's illness (1920).

FOTHERINGHAM, Allan, media. Hearne, Sask., 1932. Journalist; popular political columnist.

FOWKE, Edith Margaret, literary arts. Lumsden, Sask., 1913-96. Music ethnologist, published traditional Canadian folksongs. *Penguin Book of Canadian Folksongs; Sally Go Round the Sun.*

FOX, Michael James (J.), performing arts. Edmonton Alta., 1961. Actor; diminutive leading man. *Back to the Future.*

FOX, Terrance Stanley (Terry), sports. Winnipeg, Man., 1958-81. Began "Marathon of Hope" cross-Canada run to raise funds for cancer research; Lou Marsh Trophy as Canada's top athlete, 1980.

FRANCA, Celia (b. Celia Franks), performing arts. Eng., 1921. Choreographer; founder of National Ballet of Canada.

FRANCK, Albert Jacques, visual arts. Holland, 1899-1973. Painter especially noted for his depiction of old houses and back lanes in the old city of Toronto.

FRANKLIN, John (Sir), exploration and discovery. Eng., 1786-1847. Bold, doomed Arctic explorer.

FRANKS, Wilbur Rounding, invention. Weston, Ont., 1901-86. Inventor; devised pressure suit for airplane pilots.

FRAPPIER, Armand, science. Valleyfield, Que., 1904-91. Influential microbiologist.

FRASER, Anna, sports. Ottawa, Ont., 1963. Free-style skier; World Cup Aerial Champion (1986).

FRASER, John Anderson, literary arts. Montreal, Que., 1944. Author; former editor of *Saturday Night* magazine; master of Massey College, Toronto. *The Chinese: A Portrait of a People.*

FRASER, Simon, exploration and discovery. USA, 1776-1862. First white man to explore Fraser River.

FRASER, Sylvia Lois, literary arts. Hamilton, Ont., 1935. Novelist. *Pandora; Berlin Solstice; My Father's House; The Emperor's Virgin.*

FRECHETTE, Sylvie, sports. Laval, Que., 1967. Received post-event gold medal in synchronized swimming, 1992 Olympics.

FRENCH, David, literary arts. Coley's Point, Nfld, 1939. Playwright. *Salt-Water Moon; Jitters; Leaving Home.*

FREUND, Kurt, medicine. Czech., 1914-96. Psychiatrist; noted researcher into human sexuality.

FROBISHER, Martin (Sir), exploration and discovery. Eng., 1539-94. Mariner; discovered Frobisher Bay.

FRONTENAC ET PALLUAU, (Louis de Buade) Comte de, politics. France, 1622-98. Gov. gen, New France, 1672-82, 1689-98.

FROST, Leslie Miscampbell, politics. Orillia, Ont., 1895-1973. PC premier of Ontario, 1949-61.

FRUM, Barbara Ruth, media. USA, 1937-92. Broadcaster; interviewer. *As It Happens; The Journal.*

FRUM, David, literary arts. Toronto, Ont., 1960. Journalist of "new right."

FRYE, Herman Northrop, literary arts. Sherbrooke, Que., 1912-91. Canada's most influential literary critic. *Anatomy of Criticism.*

FULFORD, Robert Marshall Blount, media. Ottawa, Ont., 1932. Journalist; former editor, *Saturday Night*; columnist.

FUNG, Donna Lori, sports. Vancouver, BC, 1963. Rhythmic gymnast; gold medal, 1984 Olympics.

FURST, Judith, performing arts. New Westminster, BC, 1943. Opera singer; internationally renowned diva.

G

GABEREAU, Vicki Frances, media. Vancouver, BC, 1946. Broadcaster, author. Host of CBC Radio's *Gabereau,* 1988-97. Host of TV talk show on Baton Broadcasting.

GABRIEL, Tony, sports. Hamilton, Ont., 1948. Football player; CFL tight end; held record 138 straight games with receptions until 1995.

GAGNON, André, performing arts. Saint-Pacôme-de-Kamouraska, Que., 1942. Pianist; composer. "Le Saint-Laurent."

GAGNON, André Phillipe, performing arts. Loretteville, Que., 1961. Comedian, impressionist, noted for one-man shows.

GALBRAITH, John Kenneth, business/literary arts. Iona Station, Ont., 1908. Economist; author; influential intellectual. *The Affluent Society.*

GALLANT, Mavis Leslie, literary arts. Montreal, Que., 1922. Author of more than 100 short stories. "A Fairly Good Time."

GALLEY, Harry A., invention. Montreal, Que., 1903-95. Inco employee; designer of first mass-produced stainless steel sink.

GALLIVAN, Danny, sports. Montreal, Que., 1917-93. Hockey announcer; voice of the Montreal Canadiens.

GALT, Alexander Tilloch, politics. Eng., 1817-93. Railway promoter; proposed union of all British colonies.

GARNEAU, François Xavier, literary arts. Quebec City, Que., 1809-66. Writer; early historian. *Histoire du Canada.*

GARNEAU, Hector de Saint Denys, literary arts. Montreal, Que., 1912-43. Poet. "Regards et jeux dans l'espace."

GARNEAU, Marc, science. Quebec City, Que., 1949. First Canadian astronaut (1984) to achieve liftoff.

GARNER, Hugh, literary arts. Eng., 1913-79. Working class novelist. *Cabbagetown.*

GASCON, Jean, performing arts. Montreal, Que., 1921-88. Actor; director; influential man of the theatre; headed Stratford Festival, Natl Arts Centre.

GAYFORD, Thomas Franklin, sports. Toronto, Ont., 1928. Equestrian; won gold medal Prix des Nations in 1968 Olympics.

GEDGE, Pauline, literary arts. New Zealand, 1945. Novelist. *Scroll of Saqqara; The Twelfth Transforming; The Covenant.*

GEHRY, Frank, visual arts. Toronto, Ont., 1929. Internationally recognized architect. Guggenheim Museum in Bilbao, Spain; Art and Teaching Museum, University of Minnesota.

GELBER, Arthur Ellis, public service. Toronto, Ont., 1915-98. Philanthropist who was prominent on arts boards, including National Arts Centre, National Ballet of Canada and the Ontario Arts Council.

GELINAS, Gratien, performing arts. St Tite, Que., 1909-99. Actor; director; playwright; crucial to modern Quebec theatre.

GEOFFRION, Joseph André Bernard "Boom Boom", sports. Montreal, Que., 1931. Hockey player; right-winger, Montreal Canadiens (1950-64), noted for strength and speed.

GEORGE, Dan (Teswahno), performing arts. Burrard Reserve, BC, 1899-1981. Actor; helped redefine image of Aboriginal peoples in media. *Little Big Man.*

GERUSSI, Bruno, performing arts. Medicine Hat, Alta., 1928-95. Actor; regular on *The Beachcombers.*

GESNER, Abraham, invention. Cornwallis, NS, 1797-1864. Inventor of kerosene oil.

GETTY, Donald Ross, politics/sports. Montreal, Que., 1933. Edmonton Eskimos quarterback; PC premier of Alberta, 1985-92.

GHIZ, Joseph Atallah, politics. Charlettetown, PEI, 1945-97. Liberal premier of PEI 1986-93. Avid supporter of Meech Lake Accord and Charlettetown Accord.

GIAUQUE, William Francis, science. Niagara Falls, Ont., 1895-1982. Chemist who won 1949 Nobel Prize in chemistry for studies of properties of substances at temperatures near absolute zero.

GIBSON, George "Mooney", sports. London, Ont., 1880-1967. Baseball player; pro catcher, 1905-18.

GIBSON, Graeme C., literary arts. London, Ont., 1934. Novelist. *Five Legs; Perpetual Motion.*

GIBSON, William, literary arts. USA, 1948. Science fiction writer, pioneered "Cyberpunk" paradigm; novel *Neuromancer* won Hugo and Nebula awards; wrote screenplay for *Johnny Mnemonic.*

GILMOUR, Clyde, media. Calgary, Alta., 1912-97. Journalist; arts radio broadcaster. *Gilmour's Albums.*

GIMBY, Bobbie (Robert Stead), performing arts. Cabri, Sask., 1918-98. Trumpeter, songwriter. Appeared in CBC radio series *The Happy Gang.* Composed "CA-NA-DA" in 1967 for centennial celebrations.

GISBORNE, Frederick Newton, invention. Eng., 1824-92. Inventor; developed undersea telegraph cable (1852).

GIVENS, Philip, politics. Toronto, Ont., 1922-95. Mayor of Toronto 1964-66; responsible for acquisition of Henry Moore's *The Archer* sculpture at Toronto's New City Hall.

GOLDSMITH, Robert, literary arts. St Andrews, NB, 1794-1861. First Canadian-born poet to write in English: *The Rising Village* described Acadian experience.

GOMEZ, Avelino, sports. Cuba, 1928-80. Jockey; over 4,000 career wins, including four Queen's Plates.

GOODMAN, Henry George, business. USA, 1907-97. Philanthropist, volunteer and lawyer who helped initiate and served as president of the Jewish Children's Aid Society in Toronto.

GOODYEAR, Scott, sports. Toronto, Ont., 1959. Indy car driver; winner of Canadian Racing Drivers Association Driver of the Year award; first Canadian to win oval race.

GORDON, Charles William, literary arts. Glengarry Cty., Canada W, 1860-1937. Presbyterian minister who wrote western-style novels, *The Sky Pilot; The Prospector,* as well as *Glengarry School Days.*

GORDON, Donald, business. Scot., 1901-69. Executive; controversial head of CNR, 1950-66.

GORDON, Walter Lockhart, politics. Toronto, Ont., 1906-87. Economic nationalist; inspired creation of Committee for an Independent Canada.

GORMAN, Charles, sports. Saint John, NB, 1897-1940. Speed skater; held seven world records.

GOTLIEB, Allan Ezra, politics. Winnipeg, Man., 1928. Career public servant; Canadian ambassador to US 1981-89.

GOTLIEB, Phyllis Fay, literary arts. Toronto, Ont., 1926. Poet, science fiction writer. *Heart of Red Iron; The Kingdom of the Cats.*

GOTLIEB, Sondra, literary arts. Winnipeg, Man., 1936. Newspaper columnist with *Washington Post, Globe and Mail.* Writer: *"Wife Of": An Irreverent Account of Life in Washington; True Confections.*

GOUIN, Jean-Lomer (Sir), politics. Canada E, 1861-1929. Liberal premier of Quebec, 1905-20.

GOULD, Glenn Herbert, performing arts. Toronto, Ont., 1932-82. Classical pianist; *Goldberg Variations* stand out in brilliant, eccentric career.

GOULET, Robert Gerard, performing arts. USA, 1933. Singer/actor, noted for romantic male leads. *South Pacific; Camelot.*

GOUZENKO, Igor Sergeievich, military. USSR, 1919-82. Spy; defector exposed Soviet espionage network.

GOVIER, Katherine Mary, literary arts. Edmonton, Alta, 1948. Novelist, short story writer. *Random Descent; Angel Walk.*

GOWAN, Elsie Park, literary arts. Scot., 1905-99. Internationally recognized playwright for radio and stage. *Beeches from Bond Street; The Building of Canada.*

GOWDY, Barbara, literary arts. Windsor, Ont., 1950. Editor, writer. *Through the Green Valley; We So Seldom Look on Love.*

GOY, Luba, performing arts. Germany, 1946. Comedian on *Royal Canadian Air Farce;* impersonations include Sheila Copps, Pamela Wallin.

GRANT, Charles, law. Toronto, Ont., 1902-80. Activist; fought anti-Semitism, racism, bigotry.

GRANT, George Parkin, literary arts. Toronto, Ont., 1918-88. Philosopher; influential pessimistic thinker and nationalist. *Lament for a Nation.*

GRAY, George R., sports. Canada W, 1865-1933. Shot putter; world record holder during 1880s.

GRAY, James Henry, literary arts. Whitemouth, Man., 1906-98. Social historian whose works reflected Western Canadian society. *The Winter Years,* a story about the Depression; *The Boy From Winnipeg.*

GREENE, Graham, performing arts. Six Nations Reserve, Ont., 1952. Film/TV actor. *Dances with Wolves.*

GREENE, Lorne Hyman, performing arts. Ottawa, Ont., 1915-87. Actor; Ben Cartwright on TV's *Bonanza* for 14 years.

GREENE, Nancy Catherine, sports. Ottawa, Ont., 1943. Skier; World Cup winner, 1967, 1968; gold and silver slalom medals.

GREENOUGH, Gail, sports. Edmonton, Alta., 1960. Equestrian; 1986 world champion, individual show jumping.

GREENSPAN, Edward Leonard, law. Niagara Falls, Ont., 1944. Distinguished criminal lawyer.

GRENFELL, Sir Wilfred Thomason, medicine. Eng., 1865-1940. Medical missionary; builder of hospitals in Nfld

GRETZKY, Wayne, sports. Brantford, Ont., 1961. Hockey player; all-time leading NHL scorer.

GREY OWL (b. Archibald Stansfield Belaney), literary arts. Eng., 1888-1938. Writer; conservationist who identified with Aboriginal peoples. *Pilgrims of the Wild.*

GRIERSON, John, visual arts. Scot., 1898-1972. Documentarist; creator of National Film Board.

GRIFFITH, Linda, performing arts. Toronto, Ont., 1953. Film, TV and stage actress. *Maggie and Pierre.*

GROSS, Paul, performing arts. Calgary, Alta, 1959. Actor, playwright; starred in TV series *Due South.*

GROSSMAN, Lawrence S. (Larry), politics. Toronto, Ont., 1943-97. High-profile minister in Bill Davis's Ontario PC government, ran unsuccessfully as Tory leader against David Peterson in 1975.

GROULX, Lionel Adolphe, religion. Vaudreuil, Que., 1878-1967. Historian; Quebec religious nationalist.

GROVE, Frederick Philip, literary arts. Prussia, 1879-1948. Writer. *In Search of Myself.*

GUERIN, Gertrude Ettershank (Klaw Law We Leth), politics. Mission Reserve, N. Vancouver, BC, A Musqueam chief, considered to be the first native woman to hold such a high-ranking position.

GUILLET, Dr. James Edwin, invention. Toronto, Ont., 1927. Inventor of biodegradable plastics.

GUSTAFSON, Ralph Barker, literary arts. Lime Ridge, Que., 1909-95. Founder of League of Canadian Poets. Governor General's Award, 1974. *Fire and Stone.*

GWYN, Sandra (Alexandra) Jean Fraser, literary arts. St John's, Nfld. 1935. Governor General's Award, 1984. *The Private Capital; Tapestry of War.*

GWYNNE, Horace "Lefty", sports. Toronto, Ont., 1912. Boxer; bantamweight gold medal, 1932 Olympics.

GZOWSKI, Peter, media. Toronto, Ont., 1934. Broadcaster; author; long-time radio host. *Morningside.*

GZOWSKI, Sir Casimir Stanislaus, exploration and discovery. Russia, 1813-98. Engineer; built roads, bridges, and railroads.

H

HACKNER, Allan, sports. Nipigon, Ont., 1954. Curler; Canadian and world champion, 1982, 1985.

HADFIELD, Chris Austin, science. Sarnia, Ont., 1959. Astronaut, first Canadian mission specialist on space shuttle, 1996.

HAILEY, Arthur, literary arts. Eng., 1920. Writer; produced string of best-sellers. *Airport.*

HAIM, Corey, performing arts. Toronto, Ont., 1972. Actor, producer. *Demolition High; Life 101.*

HALDER, Walter (Wally), sports. Toronto, Ont., 1925-94. Leading goal scorer on Canada's gold medallist team at 1948 Olympic Winter Games.

HALIBURTON, Thomas Chandler, literary arts. Windsor, NS, 1796-1865. Writer; social satirist. *The Clockmaker.*

HALL, Emmett Matthew, public service. Saint-Columban, Que., 1898-1995. Chief Justice of Saskatchewan; co-author of Ontario's 1966 Hall-Dennis education report.

HALL, Glenn Henry, sports. Humboldt, Sask., 1931. Hockey goaltender; 11-time all-star; record 502 consecutive games.

HALL, Monty, performing arts. Winnipeg, Man., 1925. Long-time TV host of *Let's Make a Deal* show.

HAMEL, Theophile, visual arts. Ste-Foy, LC, 1817-70. Painted life-like official portraits.

HAMILTON, Barbara, performing arts. Toronto, Ont., 1926-96. Veteran screen and stage actor. *Anne of Green Gables; Crazy for You.*

HANLAN, Edward (Ned), sports. Toronto, Ont., 1855-1908. World champion oarsman, 1880-84.

HANSEN, Rick, sports. Port Alberni, BC, 1957. Wheelchair athlete; "Man in Motion" tour raised $20M for medical research.

HANSON, Melvin "Fritzie", sports. USA, 1912. Football player; led Winnipeg to first western Grey Cup (1935).

HARCOURT, Michael Franklin, politics. Edmonton, Alta., 1943. NDP Premier of BC 1991-96.

HARDY, Hagood, performing arts. USA, 1937-97. Pop/jazz pianist and composer; Juno award-winner. "The Homecoming"; scores for *Anne of Green Gables, Road to Avonlea.*

HARE, Frederick Kenneth, science. Eng., 1919. Environmentalist; expert on climate change, greenhouse effect.

HARNOY, Ofra, performing arts. Israel, 1965. International virtuoso cellist.

HARPER, Elijah, politics. Red Sucker L, Man., MLA in Manitoba legislature who blocked passage of Meech Lake Accord.

HARPER, J. Russell, visual arts. Caledonia, Ont., 1914-83. Art historian; pioneered study of art history.

HARRINGTON, Michael Francis, performing arts. St John's, Nfld, 1916-99. Supporter of an independent Newfoundland prior to 1949 confederation, Harrington hosted popular 1940s Newfoundland radio program *The Barrelman;* co-edited complete National Convention debates.

HARRIS, Lawren Stewart, visual arts. Brantford, Ont., 1885-1970. Founder of Group of Seven; noted for stark landscapes. *Above Lake Superior.*

HARRIS, Micheal Deane, politics. Toronto, Ont., 1945. PC premier of Ontario 1995-.

HARRIS, Mike, sports. Georgetown, Ont., 1967. Skip of the silver-medal-winning curling team during the 1998 winter Olympics in Nagano, Japan.

HARRIS, Wayne, sports. USA, 1938. Football player; outstanding Calgary Stampeders linebacker.

HARRON, Donald (Don), performing arts. Toronto, Ont., 1924. Actor; comedian; host of *Morningside* 1977-82; also noted for portraying farmer Charlie Farquharson.

HART, Corey Mitchell, performing arts. Montreal, Que., 1962. Pop singer; teen heartthrob. *Boy in the Box.*

HART, Evelyn Anne, performing arts. Toronto, Ont., 1956. Prima ballerina, Royal Winnipeg Ballet.

HARTMAN, Grace, business. Toronto, Ont., 1918. Labour leader; first woman to head Canadian Union of Public Employees (1975-83).

HARVEY, Douglas N. (Doug), sports. Montreal, Que., 1924-90. Hockey player; Montreal Canadiens defenceman; won seven Norris Trophies.

HARWOOD, Vanessa Clare, performing arts. Eng., 1947. National Ballet soloist.

HATFIELD, Richard Bennett, politics. Woodstock, NB, 1931-91. PC premier of NB, 1970-87.

HAWKINS, Ronald "Rompin' Ronnie", performing arts. USA, 1935. Pop/country singer; pioneer of Canadian rock. "Mary Lou."

HAWLEY, Sanford Desmond (Sandy), sports. Oshawa, Ont., 1949. Jockey; winner of more than 6,000 races.

HAYDEN, Melissa (b. Mildred Herman), performing arts. Toronto, Ont., 1923. Virtuoso with New York City Ballet.

HEALEY, Jeff, performing arts. Toronto, Ont., 1966. Pop singer; blind blues guitarist. "See the Light."

HEARNE, Samuel, exploration and discovery. Eng., 1745-92. Explorer; *A Journey from Prince of Wales's Fort in Hudson's Bay to the Northern Ocean* is one of the great travel narratives.

HEATH, John Geoffrey "Jeff", sports. Ft William, Ont., 1915-75. Baseball player; hit .293 in 14-year career.

HEBB, Donald Olding, science. Chester, NS, 1904-85. Psychologist; developmental work showed importance of environmental stimulation.

HEBERT, Anne, literary arts. Ste-Catherine-de-Fossambault, Que., 1916. Novelist. *Kamouraska.*

HEBERT, Louis-Philippe, visual arts. Megantic, Que., 1850-1917. Commemorative sculptor of many public monuments. *Queen Victoria.*

HEDDLE, Kathleen, sports. Vancouver, BC, 1965. With Marnie McBean won women's double sculls rowing medals: two golds in 1992 at Barcelona Olympics; one gold, one bronze in 1996 Olympics in Atlanta.

HEES, George Harris, politics. Toronto, Ont., 1910-96. PC cabinet minister for John Diefenbaker and Brian Mulroney.

HEGGTVEIT, Anne, sports. Ottawa, Ont., 1939. Skier; Canada's first Olympic gold medal in skiing; women's slalom, 1960.

HELLSTROM, Brig-Gen Sheila Anne, military. Bridgewater, NS, 1935. Soldier; first Cdn woman general.

HELWIG, David Gordon, literary arts. Toronto, Ont., 1938. Poet; novelist. "Figures in a Landscape."

HENLEY, Garney, sports. USA, 1935. Football player; Hamilton star CFL's most versatile player.

HENNING, Douglas, performing arts. Ft Garry, Man., 1947. Magician; co-founder, Natural Law Party.

HENRY, Martha, performing arts. USA, 1938. TV/film actress; Stratford regular. *The Wars.*

HENSON, Josiah, politics. USA, 1789-1883. Black leader; escaped slave; model for *Uncle Tom's Cabin.*

HEPBURN, Doug, sports. Vancouver, BC, 1926. Weight lifter; world heavyweight title, 1953.

HEPBURN, Mitchell Frederick, politics. St Thomas, Ont., 1896-1953. Liberal Ontario premier, 1934-42.

HEPPNER, Ben, performing arts. Murrayville, BC, 1956. Tenor opera singer, Metropolitan debut in 1991.

HERBERT, Paul, performing arts. Thetford Mines, Que., 1924. Actor; screenwriter; director.

HERIOT, George, visual arts. Scot., 1759-1839. Watercolourist. *Lake St Charles Near Quebec.*

HEROUX, Denis, visual arts. Montreal, Que., 1940. Film producer. *Atlantic City.*

HERZBERG, Gerhard, medicine. Germany, 1904-99. Physicist; molecular analyst; Nobel Prize, chemistry, 1971.

HEWITT, Foster William, sports. Toronto, Ont., 1903-85. Hockey announcer; voice of Toronto Maple Leafs.

HIGHWAY, Tomson, literary arts. Brochet, Man., 1951. Playwright. *Dry Lips Oughta Move to Kapuskasing.*

HILL, Arthur, performing arts. Melfort, Sask., 1922. Stage and film performer. *The Ugly American.*

HILL, Dan Jr, performing arts. Toronto, Ont., 1954. Ballad singer and composer. "Sometimes When We Touch."

HILL, Daniel Grafton Sr, politics. USA, 1923. Reformer; human rights; black history activist and writer.

HILL, James Jerome, business. Rockwood, Ont., 1838-1916. In 1890 consolidated vast railway holdings into the Great Northern Railway Co., also was integral in the building of the Canadian Pacific Railway.

HILLER, Arthur Garfin, visual arts. Edmonton, Alta., 1923. Filmmaker/director. *Love Story.*

HILLIER, James, invention. Brantford, Ont., 1915. Inventor; pioneered electron microscopes.

HIRSCH, John Stephen, performing arts. Hungary, 1930-89. Stage director; founded Manitoba Theatre Centre; headed Stratford Festival, CBC TV drama.

HITSCHMANOVA, Lotta, politics. Czech., 1909-80. Activist; founding director, Unitarian Service Committee of Canada development agency.

HNATYSHYN, Ramon John, politics. Saskatoon, Sask., 1934. Governor general of Canada 1990-95.

HODGINS, Jack Stanley, literary arts. Comox, BC, 1938. Novelist. *The Resurrection of Joseph Bourne.*

HODGSON, George Ritchie, sports. Montreal, Que., 1893-1983. Swimmer; first Canadian Olympic gold medals in swimming; 400 m, 1500 m freestyle in 1912.

HOFFMAN, Abigail (Abbie), sports. Toronto, Ont., 1947. Sports feminist; director of Sport Canada.

HOGG-PRIESTLY, Helen Battles, science. USA, 1905-93. Astronomer; star clusters expert; asteroid named for her.

HOHL, Elmer, sports. Wellesley, Ont., 1919-87. Horseshoe pitcher; world champion, 1965-87.

HOLGATE, Edwin, visual arts. Allandale, Ont., 1892-1977. Group of Seven artist, noted for portraiture; member of Royal Canadian Academy of Arts.

HOLLINGSHEAD, Gregory Albert Frank, literary arts. Toronto, Ont., 1947. Governor General's Award for fiction, 1995, *The Roaring Girl.*

HOMME, Robert, performing arts. USA, 1919. Portrayed the Friendly Giant on long-running CBC children's program of same name.

HOOD, Hugh John Blagdon, literary arts. Toronto, Ont., 1928. Novelist; essayist. *The Swing in the Garden.*

HORTON, Miles Gilbert "Tim", sports. Cochrane, Ont., 1930-74. Toronto Maple Leaf hockey player, five Stanley Cup wins; founder of national doughnut chain.

HOSPITAL, Janette Turner, literary arts. Australia, 1942. Winner of the Seal first Novel Award, 1982, *The Ivory Swing.* *Isobars.*

HOUSSER, Yvonne McKague, visual arts. Toronto, Ont., 1898-1996. Group of Seven-influenced paintings: National Art Gallery; Art Gallery of Ontario; McMichael Gallery.

HOUSTON, Heather, sports. Thunder Bay, Ont., 1959. Curler; skip of 1989 world championship team; Canadian championships 1988, 1989.

HOUSTON, James Archibald, literary/visual arts. Toronto, Ont., 1921. In the 1950s became a major buyer and supporter of Inuit art. *White Dawn; Confessions of an Igloo Dweller.*

HOWARD, Russ, sports. Penetanguishene, Ont., 1955. Curler; Canadian and world champion, 1987, 1993.

HOWE, Clarence Decatur (C.D.), business/politics. USA, 1886-1960. Foremost grain elevator builder of his day, Howe was a Liberal minister of transport; helped create Trans-Canada Airlines, forerunner of Air Canada.

HOWE, Gordon (Gordie), sports. Floral, Sask., 1928. Hockey player; Detroit Red Wings great; 801 NHL goals.

HOWE, Joseph, politics. Halifax, NS, 1804-73. Led fight against Nova Scotia entry into Confederation; later joined cabinet.

HUBEL, David Hunter, science. Windsor, Ont., 1926. Winner of 1981 Nobel Prize in medicine and physiology for research in processing the visual system.

HUGGINS, Charles Brenton, science. Halifax, NS, 1901. Won Nobel Prize for medicine in 1966 for discoveries concerning hormonal treatment of prostate cancer.

HULL, Robert Marvin, sports. Pte Anne, Ont., 1939. Hockey player; "Golden Jet," left winger for Chicago and Winnipeg; 610 NHL goals.

HUMPHREY, John Peters, public service. Hampton, NB, 1905-95. Principal author of the Universal Declaration of Human Rights; founder of the Canadian Human Rights Foundation and Amnesty International (Can.).

HUNGERFORD, George William, sports. Vancouver, BC, 1944. Rower; gold medal, coxless pairs, 1964 Olympics.

HUNTER, Thomas James (Tommy), performing arts. London, Ont., 1937. Country singer; *Tommy Hunter Show* on CBC, 1965-92.

HUNTSMAN, Archibald Gowanlock, science. Tintern, Ont., 1883-1973. Biologist; pioneered fisheries science.

HURTIG, Melvyn (Mel), literary arts. Edmonton, Alta., 1932. Publisher; Canadian nationalist. *The Canadian Encyclopedia*.

HUSTON, Walter (b. Walter Houghston), performing arts. Toronto, Ont., 1884-1960. Actor. *Treasure of the Sierra Madre*.

HUTCHISON, William Bruce, literary arts. Prescott, Ont., 1901-92. Political historian; biographer of W. L. Mackenzie King, *The Incredible Canadian*.

HUTT, William Ian deWitt, performing arts. Toronto, Ont., 1920. Stage actor; distinguished Stratford leading player.

HYLAND, Francis, performing arts. Regina, Sask., c. 1932. Actor with Stratford Festival, Ont.

IBERVILLE, Pierre Le Moyne, Sieur d', military. Montreal, Que., 1661-1706. soldier; daring, often cruel, adventurer.

IDE, Thomas Ranald (Ran), media. Ottawa, Ont., 1919-96. Appointed in 1966 to set up TVOntario, an innovative education network.

IGNATIEFF, George, politics. Russia, 1913-89. Diplomat; expert in East-West relations; UN ambassador.

IGNATIEFF, Michael, literary arts/media. Toronto, Ont., 1947. Writer; broadcaster. *The Russian Album*.

IMLACH, George "Punch", sports. Toronto, Ont., 1918-87. Hockey coach and manager; during 11 seasons with Toronto Maple Leafs won four Stanley Cups.

INNIS, Harold Adams, politics. Otterville, Ont., 1894-1952. Political economist; communications theorist. *Empire and Communications*.

IRELAND, John, performing arts. Vancouver, BC, 1914. Actor; often played a heavy. *Red River*.

IRVIN, Dick Sr, sports. Limestone Ridge, Ont., 1892-1957. Hockey executive; innovative coach/mgr of Montreal Canadiens, Toronto Maple Leafs.

IRVING, Kenneth Colin (K.C.), business. Buctouche, NB, 1899-1992. Industrialist; founder of NB business empire, from oil to broadcasting.

ISELER, Elmer Walter, performing arts. Port Colbourne, Ont., 1927-98. Choral conductor who founded Festival Singers of Canada; from 1964 to 1997 conductor of the Toronto Mendelssohn Choir; also founded the Elmer Iseler Singers.

ISRAEL, Werner, science. Germany, 1931. Physicist; pioneered study of black holes, gravitation.

ISSAJENKO, Angella (Taylor), sports. Jamaica, 1958. Sprinter; many medals in 100 m races.

JACKS, Terry, performing arts. Winnipeg, Man., 1944. Singer; founding member, the Poppy Family.

JACKSON, Alexander Young (A.Y.), visual arts. Montreal, Que., 1882-1974. Painter; landscape artist; member, Group of Seven. *Barns*.

JACKSON, Donald, sports. Oshawa, Ont., 1940. Figure skater; men's world champion, 1962.

JACKSON, Roger, sports. Toronto, Ont., 1942. Rower; gold medal, coxless pairs, 1964 Olympics.

JACKSON, Russell Stanley (Russ), sports. Hamilton, Ont., 1936. Football player; Ottawa quarterback; 3-time Schenley Award winner as CFL top player.

JACKSON, Tom, performing arts. Winnipeg, Man., Native actor and singer, has appeared on CBC's *North of 60; Medicine River; The Diviners*.

JACOBS, "Indian" Jack, sports. USA, 1920-74. Football player; fiery quarterback for Winnipeg Blue Bombers; helped popularize CFL.

JACOBS, Jane, literary arts. USA, 1916. Urban critic; major urban thinker. *Systems of Survival*.

JAMES, Gerry, sports. Regina, Sask., 1934. Football/hockey player; rare pro double; Winnipeg Blue Bombers, Toronto Maple Leafs.

JANES, Percy Maxwell, literary arts. St John's, Nfld, 1922-99. Newfoundland writer whose gritty works depicted the reality of life on the island. *House of Hate*.

JELINEK, Otto John, sports/politics. Czech., 1940. PC minister; with sister Maria won world pairs figure skating title (1972).

JENKINS, Ferguson Arthur, sports. Chatham, Ont., 1943. Baseball pitcher; only Canadian in Hall of Fame, 284 career wins.

JENNESS, Diamond, literary arts. New Zealand, 1886-1969. Anthropologist; author; expert on native Canadians. *The People of the Twilight*.

JENNINGS, Peter Charles, media. Toronto, Ont., 1938. Broadcaster; anchorman, *ABC Evening News*.

JEROME, Harry Winston, sports. Prince Albert, Sask., 1940-82. Sprinter; one-time world record holder in 100 m.

JEWISON, Norman Frederick, visual arts. Toronto, Ont., 1926. Film director; founded Canadian Film Centre in Toronto. *In the Heat of the Night*.

JOHANSSON, Herman Smith "Chief Jackrabbit", sports. Norway, 1875-1986. Skier; popularizer of cross-country skiing.

JOHNS, Dr Harold Elford, medicine. China, 1915. Physician; developed cobalt bomb for treating cancer.

JOHNSON, Ben, sports. Jamaica, 1961. Sprinter; stripped of 100 m world record time gold medal in 1988 Olympics for using banned drug.

JOHNSON, Daniel, politics. Montreal, Que., 1944. Liberal opposition leader in Quebec 1994-98.

JOHNSON, Edward, performing arts. Guelph, Ont., 1878-1959. Opera singer, performed at Metropolitan Opera in New York; later chairman of board of Royal Conservatory of Music in Toronto.

JOHNSON, Emily Pauline "Tekahionwake", literary arts. Six Nations Reserve, UC, 1861-1913. Her poetry celebrated Canada and her native heritage. "Flint and Feather."

JOHNSTON, Francis Hans (Franz), visual arts. Toronto, Ont., 1888-1949. Early Group of Seven member. *Batchawana Falls.*

JOHNSTON, Lynn, visual arts. Collingwood, Ont., 1947. Cartoonist; creator, "For Better or For Worse."

JOHNSTON, Rita Margaret, politics. Melville, Sask., 1935. First woman premier in Canada (BC) in 1991, succeeded Bill Vander Zalm.

JOLIAT, Aurele, sports. Ottawa, Ont., 1908-86. Hockey player; left winger for Montreal Canadiens.

JOLLIET, Louis, exploration and discovery. Quebec City, Que., 1645-1700. Co-discoverer of the Mississippi R.

JONAS, George, literary arts. Hungary, 1935. Poet, writer, scriptwriter. Script for CBC's *The Scales of Justice; Vengeance; By Persons Unknown: The Strange Death of Christine Demeter.*

JONES KONIHOWSKI, Diane, sports. Vancouver, BC, 1951. Canadian pentathlon record holder.

JORY, Victor, performing arts. Yukon, 1902-82. Actor; Hollywood villain. *Huckleberry Finn.*

JUCKES, Gordon, sports. Watrous, Sask., 1914-95. Hockey and Sports Hall of Fame member, established national team program.

JULIEN, Pauline, performing arts. Trois-Rivières, Que., 1928-98. Quebec singer, political activist, separatist and feminist, Julien embodied the spirit of Quebec through songs of her own composition as well as Kurt Weill, Bertolt Brecht and Gilles Vigneault.

JULIETTE (b. Juliette Augustina Sysak), performing arts. Winnipeg, Man., 1927. Singer; early TV star; own show, 1954-66.

JUNEAU, Pierre, business. Verdun, Que., 1922. Broadcast executive; headed CRTC, 1968-75.

JUTRA, Claude, visual arts. Montreal, Que., 1930-87. Film director. *Mon Oncle Antoine.*

K

KAIN, Karen, performing arts. Hamilton, Ont., 1951. Prima ballerina, National Ballet of Canada.

KANE, Lori, sports. Charlottetown, PEI, 1964. Golfer: member of Canadian Inernational Team 1989-92; member of Commonwealth Team in 1991; 1992 Canadian World Amateur Team; 1997, Canadian Athlete of the Year.

KANE, Paul, visual arts. Ire., 1810-71. Painter of the Canadian West and native peoples.

KARPIS, Alvin (b. Albin Karpowicz). Montreal, Que., 1908-79. Barker Gang member; US Public Enemy No. 1.

KARSH, Yousuf, visual arts. Armenia, 1908. Photographer; portraitist of the famous, e.g., Churchill.

KEELER, Ruby (b. Ethel Keeler), performing arts. Halifax, NS, 1909-93. Actress; dancer. *42nd Street.*

KEITH, Vicki, sports. Winnipeg, Man., 1961. Swam all five Great Lakes in 1988.

KELESI, Helen Mersi, sports. Victoria, BC, 1969. Tennis player; Canadian women's championship 1987-90.

KELLY, Leonard "Red", sports. Simcoe, Ont., 1927. Hockey player; star defenceman with Detroit and Toronto; two-time Liberal MP.

KELLY, Milton Terrence (M.T.), literary arts. Toronto, Ont., 1947. Poet, playwright, novelist. *A Dream Like Mine.*

KELSO, John Joseph, politics. Ire., 1864-1935. Reformer; founded Toronto Humane Society, Children's Aid.

KENOJUAK Ashevak, visual arts. Baffin Island, NWT, 1927. Artist noted for bird graphics.

KEON, David Michael, sports. Noranda, Que., 1940. Hockey player with Toronto Maple Leafs 1960-75. Team Canada member 1977. Winner of Conn Smythe trophy, 1967.

KHORANA, Har Gobind, science. India, 1922. Chemist; Nobel Prize in medicine (1968) for DNA research.

KIDD, Bruce, sports. Ottawa, Ont., 1943. Runner; many wins at various distances; outstanding athlete in Canada, 1961 and 1962.

KIDDER, Margot, performing arts. Yellowknife, NWT, 1948. Actress; Hollywood star. *Superman.*

KIERANS, Eric William, politics. Montreal, Que., 1914. Economist; outspoken nationalist.

KILBOURN, William, literary arts. Toronto, Ont., 1926-95. Writer; historian; biographer of C.D. Howe.

KILLAM, Isaac Walton, business. Yarmouth, NS, 1885-1955. Industrialist; built business empire; known for philanthropy.

KING, Allan Winton, visual arts. Vancouver, BC, 1930. Filmmaker; documentarist. *Warrendale.*

KING, Thomas, literary arts. USA, 1943. Aboriginal writer, novelist. Creator of "Dead Dog Café" on CBC radio programs *Morningside* and *This Morning. Medicine River.*

KING, William Lyon Mackenzie, politics. Kitchener, Ont., 1874-1950. Prime minister of Canada during WWII.

KINSELLA, William Patrick (W. P.), literary arts. Edmonton, Alta., 1935. Writer; known for poetic baseball fiction. *Shoeless Joe.*

KIRKE, David (Sir), exploration and discovery. France, 1597-1654. First governor of Nfld, 1637.

KLEIN, Abraham Moses, literary arts. Ukraine, 1909-72. Poet of Jewish themes. "The Rocking Chair."

KLEIN, George John, invention. Hamilton, Ont., 1904-92. Productive inventor: wind tunnels, gearing systems, Canadarm gear design.

KLEIN, Ralph Philip, politics. Calgary, Alta, 1942. PC premier of Alberta, 1992-.

KNOTT, Elsie Marie, politics. Curve Lake, Ont., 1922-95. First native woman in Canada to be elected chief, at Ojibwa reserve near Peterborough, Ont.

KNOWLES, Stanley Howard, politics. USA, 1908-97. A founder of the New Democratic Party; represented Winnipeg North Centre riding 1942-81. Admired for his support of old-age pensions; president of Canadian Labour Congress 1958-62.

KNUDSON, George, sports. Winnipeg, Man., 1937-89. Golfer; Canada's top pro; 12 PGA tour victories.

KOFFLER, Murray Bernard, business. Toronto, Ont., 1924. Entrepreneur; made Shopper's Drug Mart Canada's largest pharmacy chain.

KOFFMAN, Morris (Moe), performing arts. Toronto, Ont., 1928. Jazz flautist. "Swinging Shepherd Blues."

KOGAWA, Joy Nozomi, literary arts. Vancouver, BC, 1935. Writer. *Obasan; Itsuka.*

KOTCHEFF, William Theodore (Ted), visual arts. Toronto, Ont., 1931. Film director. *The Apprenticeship of Duddy Kravitz.*

KRAATZ, Victor, sports. Germany, 1971. Ice dancing; with Shae-Lynn Bourne won Canadian title, 1993-96; third in World Championships, 1996.

KREINER, Kathy, sports. Timmins, Ont., 1957. Skier; gold medal, giant slalom, 1976 Olympics.

KREVER, Horace, law. Montreal, Que., 1929 Judge who led Royal Commission of Inquiry on the Blood System in Canada, 1997-97.

KRIEGHOFF, Cornelius David, visual arts. Holland, 1815-72. Known for paintings of Quebec life. *The Habitant Farm.*

KROL, Joseph "Joe King", sports. Hamilton, Ont., 1919. Football player; Toronto Argos star; top athlete, 1946.

KUERTI, Anton Emil, performing arts. Austria. 1938. Leading pianist; composer; Beethoven specialist.

KURELEK, William (Wasyl), visual arts. Whitfield, Alta., 1927-77. Symbolist religious painter.

KUWABARA, Bruce, visual arts. Hamilton, Ont., 1949. Partner with Toronto-based architecture firm Kuwabara Payne McKenna Blumberg; award-winning designer of Kitchener, Ont., City Hall; City Hall in Richmond, BC.

LA SALLE, Rene Robert Cavelier, Sieur de, exploration and discovery. France, 1643-87. Became commandant of Fort Frontenac in present-day Kingston, Ont., 1673.

LA VERENDRYE, Pierre Gaultier de Varennes, Sieur de, exploration and discovery. Trois-Rivières, Que., 1685-1749. Explorer of W Canada.

LAFLEUR, Guy Damien, sports. Thurso, Que., 1951. Hockey player; Canadiens star right winger; 560 goals.

LAFONTAINE, Sir Louis Hippolyte, politics. Boucherville, LC, 1807-64. In effect, Canada's first PM, 1848-51.

LALONDE, Donny, sports. Kitchener, Ont., 1960. Boxer; WBC light heavyweight champion (1987-88).

LALONDE, Edouard Charles, sports. Cornwall, Ont., 1887-1970. In 1950 named as one of Canada's outstanding lacrosse player of the half-century; played NHL Montreal Canadiens, scoring 124 goals in 98 games 1913-18.

LAMBERT, Natalie, sports. Montreal, Que., 1963. Speed skater; short track title, 500 m, 1993.

LAMBERTS, Heath, performing arts. Toronto, Ont., 1941 Actor at Stratford Festival, Ont. *Glengarry Glen Ross; Cyrano de Bergerac.*

LAMER, Antonio, law. Montreal, Que., 1933. Chief justice of the Supreme Court 1990-99.

LAMPMAN, Archibald, literary arts. Morpeth, Canada W, 1861-99. Nature poet. "Lyrics of Earth."

LANCASTER, Ron, sports. USA, 1938. Football player; coach; quarterback set 30 CFL records.

LANDRY, G. Yves, business. Thetford Mines, Que., 1938-98. Died while chairman, president and CEO of Chrysler Canada; co-chairman of Automotive Advisory Committee to the Minister of Industry Canada.

LANG, Katherine Dawn (k.d.), performing arts. Consort, Alta., 1961. Country-torch singer; vegetarian activist. *Shadowlands.*

LANGFORD, Sam, sports. Weymouth Falls, NS, 1886-1956. Boxer; great fighter; denied title shot.

LANOIS, Daniel, performing arts. Hamilton, Ont., 1953. Singer; producer of Peter Gabriel's "Sledgehammer" and with Brian Eno U2's *Joshua Tree.*

LANTOS, Robert, visual arts. Hungary, 1949. Film producer; CEO, Alliance Communications. *Black Robe.*

LAPIERRE, Laurier L., media. Megantic, Que., 1929. TV personality, author; co-host, *This Hour Has Seven Days.*

LASKIN, Bora, law. Ft William, Ont., 1912-84. Chief justice of Canada, 1973-84.

LASTMAN, Melvin Douglas (Mel), politics. Toronto, Ont., 1933. Elected mayor of the amalgamated City of Toronto in 1997; formerly long-time mayor of North York, a satellite "city" of the former Metropolitan Toronto.

LAUMANN, Silken, sports. Toronto, Ont., 1964. Rower; braved broken leg for bronze medal in 1992 Olympics; Athlete of the Year 1991, 1992.

LAURE, Carole (b. Carol Champagne), performing arts. Montreal, Que., 1949. Actress; screen star. *Maria Chapdelaine.*

LAURENCE, Jean Margaret, literary arts. Neepawa, Man., 1926-87. Writer; created fictional setting of Manawaka. *The Diviners.*

LAURENDEAU, Joseph-Edmond-André, politics. Montreal, Que., 1912-68. Co-chairman of Royal Commission on Bilingualism and Biculturalism 1963-68; editor of Montreal's *Le Devoir* 1958-68.

LAURIER, Sir Wilfrid, politics. St-Lin, Canada E, 1841-1919. Canada's first French-speaking prime minister.

LAURIN, Camille, politics. Charlemagne, Que., 1922-99. Drafted Bill 101, Quebec's French Language Charter; joined Quebec National Assembly in 1970, member of Parti Québécois.

LAVAL, François de, religion. France, 1623-1708. First bishop of Quebec (1674-88).

LAVALLEE, Calixa, performing arts. Verchères, Canada E, 1842-1891. Composer of "O Canada."

LAW, Andrew Bonar, politics. Rexton, NB, 1858-1923. Prime Minister of Britain 1922-23; signed Treaty of Versailles on behalf of Great Britain in 1919.

LAYTON, Irving Peter, literary arts. Romania, 1912. Prolific, flamboyant poet. "A Red Carpet for the Sun."

LE CAINE, Hugh, performing arts/science. Port Arthur, Ont., 1914-77. Physicist; composer; designed the sackbut, the first musical synthesizer.

LEACOCK, Stephen Butler, literary arts. Eng., 1869-1944. Humorist. *Sunshine Sketches of a Little Town.*

LEBLANC, Romeo, politics. Memramcook, NB, 1927. Governor-General of Canada 1994-99; former Liberal MP.

LEBLOND, Charles Philippe, science. France, 1910. Anatomist; pioneer in cell biology.

LECLERC, Felix, performing arts. La Tuque, Que., 1914-88. Singer/songwriter; influential chansonnier and Quebec nationalist.

LEE, Dennis Beynon, literary arts. Toronto, Ont., 1939. Poet, children's writer. *Alligator Pie; Garbage Delight.*

LEE, Geddy, performing arts. Toronto, Ont., 1953. Singer/songwriter; lead singer for Rush. *Moving Pictures.*

LEE-GARTNER, Kerrin, sports. Trail, BC, 1966. Skier; gold medal, women's downhill, 1992 Olympics.

LEGER, Gabrielle Carmel, politics. Montreal, Que., 1916-98. Wife of the late governor general Jules Leger; acted for her husband when he suffered a stroke shortly after taking office.

LEGER, Jules, politics. St-Anicet, Que., 1913-80. Canada's governor general, 1974-79.

LEGER, Paul-Emile, religion. Valleyfield, Que., 1904-91. Cardinal; eloquent, compassionate religious leader; became missionary in Africa.

LEMELIN, Roger, literary arts. Quebec City, Que., 1919-92. Writer; creator of the popular Plouffe family.

LEMIEUX, Jean-Paul, visual arts. Quebec City, Que., 1904-90. Landscape painter. *Le Visiteur du Soir; Lazare.*

LEMIEUX, Mario, sports. Montreal, Que., 1965. Hockey player; Pittsburgh Penguins centre, one of two players to average two points per game.

LEONARD, Stanley, sports. Vancouver, BC, 1915. Golfer; won many Canadian titles; three US tour wins.

LESAGE, Jean, politics. Montreal, Que., 1912-80. Liberal premier of Quebec, 1960-66.

LETHEREN, Carol Anne, sports. Toronto, Ont., 1942. Chief executive of Canadian Olympic Association.

LEVESQUE, Jean-Louis, business. Nouvelle, Que., 1911. Financier; co-founder of Levesque Beaubien Inc., Quebec's largest brokerage house.

LEVESQUE, René, politics. New Carlisle, Que., 1922-87. Led Parti Québécois; Quebec premier 1976-85.

LEVY, Eugene, performing arts. Hamilton, Ont., 1946. Actor; comedian; *SCTV* regular (Earl Camembert, Bobby Bitman).

LEWIS, David, politics. Russia, 1909-81. Federal NDP leader, 1971-75; eloquent speaker.

LEWIS, Lennox, sports. Eng., 1965. Boxer; super heavyweight gold medal, 1988 Olympics.

LEWIS, Stephen Henry, politics. Ottawa, Ont., 1937. Ont. NDP leader; Cdn UN ambassador.

LEWIS, Wilfrid Bennett, science. Eng., 1908-87. Physicist; prime role in developing CANDU reactor.

LEYRAC, Monique, performing arts. Montreal, Que., 1928. Actress; popular Quebec chanteuse.

LIGHTFOOT, Gordon Meredith, performing arts. Orillia, Ont., 1938. Singer/songwriter; popular vocalist with many hits. "Canadian Railroad Trilogy."

LILLIE, Beatrice Gladys, performing arts. Toronto, Ont., 1894-1989. Stage comedienne. *Auntie Mame.*

LINDER, Cec, performing arts. Poland, 1921-92. Television, stage and film character actor. *Goldfinger; A Touch of Class; The Edge of Night.*

LINDROS, Eric, sports. London, Ont., 1973. Hockey player; centre for Philadelphia Flyers; winner of Hart Trophy, 1995.

LINDSAY, Robert Blake Theodore (Ted), sports. Renfrew, Ont., 1925. Hockey player; left winger 17 seasons with Detroit and Chicago.

LINKLETTER, Art (b. Arthur Brown), performing arts. Moose Jaw, Sask., 1912. Radio/TV host. *People Are Funny.*

LISMER, Arthur, visual arts. Eng., 1885-1969. Painter; Group of Seven founding member. *September Gale.*

LITTLE, Richard Carruthers (Rich), performing arts. Ottawa, Ont., 1938. Impersonator; night club and television performer.

LIVESAY, Dorothy, literary arts. Winnipeg, Man., 1909-96. Poet; sensitive feminist writer. *Poems for People.*

LOATES, Glen Martin, visual arts. Toronto, Ont., 1945. Wildlife artist; painter and naturalist.

LOCKHART, Gene, performing arts. London, Ont., 1891-1957. Character actor appeared in *Miracle on 34th Street, Carousel,* and on Broadway. Father of actress June Lockhart.

LOGAN, William Edmond (Sir), science. Montreal, Que., 1798-1875. Geologist; first head of Geological Survey of Canada; first to map Laurentian Shield.

LOMBARDO, Gaetano Alberto "Guy", performing arts. London, Ont., 1902-77. Bandleader; his Royal Canadians most popular band in N America; 300 million records sold.

LONGBOAT, Thomas Charles, sports. Brantford, Ont., 1887-1949. Runner; set record in 1907 Boston Marathon.

LONGDEN, John (Johnny), sports. Eng., 1910. Jockey; first N American with 4,000 winners (career: 6,032).

LORTIE, Louis, performing arts. Montreal, Que., 1959. Pianist; five-time winner of Canadian Music Competition, 1968-72, 1990 Juno for Best Classical Album.

LOUGHEED, Edgar Peter, politics. Calgary, Alta., 1928. PC premier of Alberta, 1971-85; played strong role in federal politics.

LOVELL, Jocelyn, sports. Eng., 1950. Canada's leading cyclist 1970-83; winner of 1000 m silver medal in 1978 world championships; paralysed in training accident 1983.

LOWRY, (Clarence) Malcolm, literary arts. Eng., 1909-57. British novelist whose powerful novels reflected his turbulent life; lived in BC 1937-54. *Under the Volcano.*

LUBA (b. Luba Kowalchyk), performing arts. Montreal, Que., 1958. Pop singer-songwriter. "Between the Earth and Sky"; "All or Nothing."

LUND, Alan, performing arts. Toronto, Ont., 1927-92. Dancer/choreographer. With wife Blanche Harris performed as an Astaire/Rogers-style dancing team; Stratford Festival, Charlettetown Festival.

M

MacDONALD, Flora Isabel, politics. Sydney, NS, 1926. First woman to hold senior cabinet post; external affairs in Clark govt (1979).

MacDONALD, James Edward Hervey (J.E.H.), visual arts. Eng., 1874-1932. Landscape painter; Group of Seven founder. *Mist Fantasy.*

MacDONALD, James Williamson Galloway (Jock), visual arts. Scot., 1897-1960. Early abstract painter; member, Painters Eleven.

MACDONALD, Sir John Alexander, politics. Scot., 1815-91. Canada's first official prime minister.

MacEWEN, Gwendolyn, literary arts. Toronto, Ont., 1941-87. Poet. *The Shadow-Maker.*

MacGILL, Elizabeth "Elsie" Muriel Gregory, science. Vancouver, BC, 1905-80. Designer of Maple Leaf Trainer aircraft during WWII; designed winterized version of Hawker Hurricane fighter plane.

MacGREGOR, Roy, literary arts. Whitney, Ont., 1948. Novelist, columnist. *Home Game: Hockey and Life in Canada; The Last Season.*

MacGUIGAN, Mark Rudolph, politics. Charlettetown, PEI, 1931-98. Liberal politician who served with Pierre Trudeau, ran unsuccessfully for leader in 1984, later appointed judge of the Federal Court of Appeal. Founding member of the Canadian Civil Liberties Association.

MacISAAC, Ashley, performing arts. Antigonish, NS, 1975. Eclectic musician who blends pop music with traditional Celtic sound. *How Are You Today?; Fine Thank You Very Much.*

MACKENZIE, Alexander, politics. Scot., 1822-1892. Canada's second prime minister.

MacKENZIE, Alexander (Sir), exploration and discovery. Scot., 1764-1820. Charted MacKenzie R. (1789); crossed from L. Athabasca to Pacific Ocean (1793).

MacKENZIE, Maj.-Gen. Lewis W., military. Truro, NS, 1940. Soldier; led UN soldiers from 33 nations (incl. Canada) in opening Sarajevo airport for delivery of humanitarian aid during Bosnian civil war.

MacKENZIE, William Lyon, politics. Scot., 1795-1861. Led 1837 rebellion for reform in Upper Canada; Toronto's first mayor.

MACLEAN, John Bayne, media. Crieff, Ont., 1862-1950. Founder of *Maclean's* magazine in 1905; also of *Financial Post, Chatelaine.*

MacLEAN, Steven Glenwood, science. Ottawa, Ont., 1954. Laser physicist who trained with NASA's astronaut program, specializes with NASA's robotics branch.

MacLENNAN, John Hugh, literary arts. Glace Bay, NS, 1907-90. Respected Canadian novelist. *The Watch That Ends the Night.*

MacLEOD, John James Rickard, medicine. Scot., 1876-1935. Medical researcher, co-winner with Drs. Banting and Best of Nobel Prize in 1923 for discovery of insulin.

MacMILLAN, Sir Ernest Campbell, performing arts. Mimico, Ont., 1893-1973. Renowned conductor, composer, arranger; championed Canadian works.

MacMILLAN, Harvey Reginald (H.R.), business. Newmarket, Ont., 1885-1976. Industrialist; established forerunner of logging giant MacMillan Bloedel.

MacNAUGHTON, Andrew George Latta, military. Moosomin, NWT, 1887-1966. Soldier; led Cdn army in WWII; endorsed Dieppe raid; diplomat; UN Atomic Energy Assn.

MacNEIL, Rita, performing arts. Big Pond, NS, 1944. Cape Breton country singer; star of CBC's *Rita MacNeil Show.*

MacNEIL, Robert Breckenridge Ware, media. Toronto, Ont., 1932. TV host, newscaster, reporter, co-hosted public television series in USA, *MacNeil-Lehrer Newshour.*

MacNUTT, Walter, performing arts. Charlettetown, PEI, 1910-96. Composer of orchestral, chamber, choral, vocal, and keyboard music; noted for compositions for Anglo-Catholic service.

MACPHAIL, Agnes Campbell, politics. Proton Twp., Ont., 1890-1954. Only woman MP in 1921 (first women's vote); founded Elizabeth Fry Society.

MacPHERSON, Cluny, invention. St John's, Nfld, 1879-1966. Invented the gas helmet.

MacPHERSON, Duncan, visual arts. Toronto, Ont., 1925-93. Long-time *Toronto Star* cartoonist.

MAGEE, Helen Gagan, journalism. Toronto, Ont., 1908-98. Author and food writer for the Toronto *Globe and Mail* and former *Telegram.*

MAGNUSSEN, Karen Diane, sports. North Vancouver, BC, 1952. Figure skater; world champion, 1973.

MAHOVLICH, Francis William, sports. Timmins, Ont., 1938. Toronto Maple Leaf hockey player, 1957-68; winner of Calder Trophy, 1958.

MAILLET, Antonine, literary arts. Buctouche, NB, 1929. Novelist of Acadian life. Winner of France's *La Prix Goncourt. La Sagouine.*

MAISONNEUVE, Paul de Chomedey, Sieur de, politics. France, 1612-76. Founder of Montreal, 1642.

MAITLAND, (Herbert) Alan, performing arts. Lilburn, Ont., 1920-99. Long-running CBC radio host noted for his rich, resonant voice; appeared on *Maitland Manor, Read to Me* and most notably, *As It Happens,* with co-hosts Barbara Frum and Michael Enright, among others, from 1974-93.

MAK, Tak Wah, medicine. China, 1946. Research led him to discover the T-cell receptor, crucial to understanding the human immune system.

MANDEL, Howie, performing arts. Toronto, Ont., 1955. Manic comic and TV actor. *St Elsewhere.*

MANGUEL, Alberto Adrian, literary arts. Argentina, 1948. Critic, anthologist, novelist. *News from a Foreign Country; The Oxford Book of Canadian Ghost Stories.*

MANLEY, Elizabeth, sports. Belleville, Ont., 1965. Figure skater; silver medal, 1988 Olympics.

MANNING, Ernest Charles, politics. Carnduff, Sask., 1908-96. Alberta's Social Credit premier 1943-68; father of Reform Party leader Preston Manning.

MANNING, Ernest Preston, politics. Edmonton, Alta., 1942. Led Reform Party to breakthrough in 1993 federal election.

MANNING, Thomas Henry, exploration and discovery. Eng., 1911-98. Mapmaker who charted vast territories of the Arctic; also biologist and naturalist focusing on Arctic environment.

MANSBRIDGE, Peter, media. Eng., 1948. Broadcaster; anchorman, CBC national news.

MANSOURI, Lotfallah (Lotfi), performing arts. Iran, 1929. Former general director of Canadian Opera Company; creator of "surtitles," English translations of opera house librettos screened above stage.

MARCHAND, Leonard Stephen, politics. Vernon, BC, 1933. Native politician; first native federal cabinet minister.

MARCUS, Egerton, sports. Guyana, 1919-65. Boxer; silver medalist, middleweight category in 1988 Olympics.

MARCUS, Rudolph A., science. Montreal, Que., 1923. Winner of 1992 Nobel Prize in chemistry for work on electron transfer reactions in chemical systems.

MARGISON, Richard, performing arts. Victoria, BC, 1953. Tenor opera singer whose repertoire includes Verdi, Puccini and Bizet; international reputation.

MARIE-VICTORIN, Frère, science. Kingsley Falls, Que., 1885-1944. Distinguished botanist, author of *Croquis laurentiens; Les filicinée de Québec.*

MARK, J. Carson, science. Lindsay, Ont., 1913-97. Head of theoretical division of Los Alamos Scientific Library, influence in creation of hydrogen bomb.

MARQUETTE, Jacques, exploration and discovery. France, 1637-75. Jesuit priest explored North America with Louis Jolliet; served at Sault Ste Marie, 1666.

MARSHALL, Amanda, performing arts. Toronto, Ont., 1964. Singer, songwriter with powerful voice. "Birmingham."

MARSHALL, Donald, law. Sydney, NS, 1953. Acquitted of murder after serving 11 years in prison.

MARSHALL, Lois Catherine, performing arts. Toronto, Ont., 1924-97. Soprano, career began with Sir Ernest MacMillan's Bach's *St Matthew's Passion* with Mendelssohn Choir and Toronto Symphony; Toronto Arts Award for Music, 1989.

MARSHALL, Phyllis, performing arts. Barrie, Ont., 1921-96. Jazz singer; pioneer among black Canadian performers; performed with Cab Calloway, Percy Faith; 1949-52 on CBC radio's *Blues for Friday.*

MARTIN, Andrea, performing arts. USA, 1947. Stage, television and film actor particularly well known for comic roles in *SCTV* series.

MARTIN, Clara Brett, law. Toronto, Ont., 1874-1923. First woman lawyer in British Empire.

MARTIN, Paul Edgar Philippe, politics. Windsor, Ont., 1938. Liberal minister of finance.

MARTIN, Paul Joseph James, politics. Ottawa, Ont., 1903-92. Long-time Liberal cabinet minister.

MARTINI, Paul, sports. Weston, Ont., 1960. Figure skater; world pairs champion (with Barbara Underhill), 1984.

MASON, Roger Burford, literary arts. Eng., 1943-98. Editor and writer, short stories: *The Beaver Picture & Other Stories;* biography of John Evans, who devised a Cree alphabet (*Travels in the Shining Island*), and a biography of artist Franz Johnson.

MASSEY, Charles Vincent, politics. Toronto, Ont., 1887-1967. First Canadian-born governor general, 1952-59.

MASSEY, Hart Almerrin, business. Haldemand Twp, Ont., 1823-96. Capitalist; developed Massey-Ferguson Ltd.

MASSEY, Raymond Hart, performing arts. Toronto, Ont., 1896-1983. Craggy-faced actor often played Lincoln. *Dr. Kildare.*

MASSON, Henri Leopold, visual arts. Belgium, 1907-96. Paintings of city and landscapes in the 1940s; National Gallery.

MAXWELL, Lois (b. Lois Ruth Hooker), performing arts. Kitchener, Ont., 1927. Actress, columnist. Played character Moneypenny in James Bond movie series from 1963-83. Former columnist for *Toronto Sun.*

MAYER, Louis B. (Burt) (b. Eliezer Mayer), performing arts. Russia, 1885-1957. Grew up in Saint John, NB; with Samuel Goldwyn formed MGM movie studio in 1924; co-founded the Academy of Motion Picture Arts and Sciences in 1927.

McBEAN, Marnie, sports. Toronto, Ont., 1968. With Kathleen Heddle won women's double sculls rowing medals: two gold in 1992 Barcelona Olympics; one gold, one bronze in 1996 Olympics in Atlanta.

McBRIDE, Robert Bruce (Bob), performing arts. Toronto, Ont., 1946-98. Juno-award-winning lead singer of the 1970s rock band Lighthouse.

McCAIN, H. Harrison, business. Florenceville, NB, 1927. Industrialist; turned potato-processing plant into international firm.

McCARTHY, Doris, visual arts. Calgary, Alta, 1910. Artist, calligrapher, more than 90 solo exhibitions.

McCLELLAND, John Gordon (Jack), literary arts. Toronto, Ont., 1922. Publisher; his McClelland & Stewart nurtured Canadian writing; over 5,000 Canadian titles.

McCLUNG, Nellie Letitia, law. Chatsworth, Ont., 1873-1951. Reformer; fought for women's suffrage.

McCONNELL, Robert Murray Gordon, performing arts. London, Ont., 1935. Jazz musician; founded Boss Brass, major big band.

McCRAE, John, literary arts. Guelph, Ont., 1872-1918. Poet; physician who wrote "In Flanders Field."

McCURDY, Howard Douglas, politics. London, Ont., 1932. Black activist; also biologist.

McCURDY, John Alexander Douglas, exploration and discovery. Baddeck, NS, 1886-1961. Pilot; first airplane flight in British Empire in Silver Dart (1909).

McDERMOTT, Dennis, business. Eng., 1922. Labour leader; former president, Canadian Labour Congress.

McDONALD, Bruce, performing arts. Kingston, Ont., 1959. Film director. *Roadkill; Highway 61; Dance Me Outside.*

McDOUGALL, Barbara Jean, politics. Toronto, Ont., 1937. PC External Affairs minister 1991-93; political commentator and journalist.

McELCERAN, William, visual arts. Hamilton, Ont., 1927-99. Internationally renowned sculptor; designer of ACTRA's Nellie award; famous for bronze "Everyman" sculptures depicting burly businessmen in striking poses.

McEWEN, Jean Albert, visual arts. Montreal, Que., 1923-99. "Nonfigurative" artist inspired by Riopelle, French Impressionists and American abstract artists.

McFARLANE, Leslie (F. W. Dixon), literary arts. Ottawa, Ont., 1903-77. Author of *Hardy Boys* adventure series.

McGARRIGLE, Anna and Kate, performing arts. Montreal, Que., 1944, 1946. Songwriters/ singers. Unique duo sings folk, own compositions. "Love Over and Over."

McGEE, Thomas D'Arcy, politics. Ire., 1825-68. Eloquent proponent of Confederation; assassinated 1868.

McGIBBON, Pauline Emily, politics. Sarnia, Ont., 1910. Cda's first woman lieutenant-governor (Ont., 1974).

McINTOSH, John, invention. USA, 1777-1845. Inventor; breeder of McIntosh apple.

McKENNA, Frank Joseph, politics. Apolaqui, NB, 1948. Liberal premier of NB since 1987.

McKENNA, Patrick Ivan Peter, performing arts. Hamilton, Ont., 1960. Comic actor plays Harold on *Red Green Show.* Also appears on drama series *Traders.*

McKENNITT, Loreena, performing arts. Morden, Man., 1957. Singer; harpist; Celtic music repertoire.

McKENZIE, Robert Tait, visual arts. Almonte, Ont., 1867-1938. Sculptor, orthopedic surgeon; designer of war memorials, sculptures.

McKINNON, Catherine, performing arts. Saint John, NB, 1944. Singer, actress. Appeared in CBC's *Don Messer's Jubilee;* Spring Thaw revue; *The Catherine MacKinnon Show;* Charlottetown Festival. Married to actor/humorist Don Harron.

McKOY, Mark, sports. Guyana, 1961. Hurdler; gold medal, 110 m hurdles, 1992 Olympics.

McLACHLAN, Sara, performing arts. Halifax, NS, 1968. Singer-songwriter of pop music. *Surfacing.*

McLAREN, Norman, visual arts. Scot., 1914-87. Filmmaker; innovative NFB animator. *Pas de deux.*

McLARNIN, Jimmy, sports. Ire., 1907. Boxer; world welterweight champion, 1933-35.

McLAUCHLAN, Murray Edward, performing arts. Scot., 1948. Country performer; *Swingin' on a Star,* CBC Radio (1990); seven-time Juno award winner.

McLAUGHLIN, Audrey, politics. Dutton, Ont., 1936. NDP national leader 1989-95. First woman to lead a national party.

McLAUGHLIN, Col. Robert Samuel, business. Enniskillen, Ont., 1871-1972. Industrialist; founded firm that became General Motors of Canada.

McLEAN, Stuart, media. Montreal, Que., 1948. Broadcaster on CBC's *Morningside; Vinyl Café;* author of *Welcome Home: Travels in Small Town Canada.*

McLUHAN, Herbert Marshall, media. Edmonton, Alta., 1911-80. Media theorist; developed theory about "hot" and "cool" media. *The Gutenburg Galaxy.*

McMURTRY, Roland Roy, politics. Toronto, Ont., 1932. Chief Justice of Ontario Court of Justice.

McNAUGHTON, Andrew George Latta, military. Moosomin, NWT, 1887-1966. Army officer, scientist, as chief of general staff of Armed Forces 1929-35 began modernization of nonpermanent militia; 1935-39 president of National Research Council of Canada.

McNAUGHTON, Duncan Anderson, sports. Cornwall, Ont., 1910. High jumper; 1932 Olympic high jump gold medal.

McPHERSON, Aimee Semple, religion. Ingersoll, Ont., 1890-1944. Controversial evangelist.

McPHERSON, Donald, sports. Windsor, Ont., 1945. World professional champion figure skater, 1965.

MEAGHER, Blanche Margaret, public service. Halifax, NS, 1911-99. Canada's first woman ambassador beginning in 1942, Meagher was posted in various locations: Mexico, Israel, Sweden, Uganda and London.

MEIGHEN, Arthur, politics. Anderson, Ont., 1874-1960. Succeeded Sir Robert Borden as prime minister of Canada.

MEILLEUR, Marie Louise Febronie Chasse, Kamouraska, Que., 1880-1998. Recognized in 1997 as the world's oldest person, lived in rural Ontario for most of her life.

MERCER, Ruby, performing arts. USA, 1906-99. Former opera singer who debuted at New York's Metropolitan Opera in 1936, Mercer was instrumental in the development of Canadian opera; founder of *Opera Canada* magazine, Canadian Children's Opera Chorus and host of CBC radio's *Opera Time* and *Opera in Stereo.*

MERCREDI, Ovide William, politics. Grand Rapids, Man., 1946. National chief of the Assembly of First Nations 1991.

MERRIL, Judith, literary arts. USA, 1923-97. Science fiction writer, novelist, editor, short story writer, critic. *Survival Ship and Other Stories; Daughters of the Earth and Other Stories.*

MESSER, Donald Charles Frederick (Don), performing arts. Tweedside, NB, 1909-73. Bandleader; popular maker of traditional fiddle and dance music. *Don Messer's Jubilee.*

METCALF, John Wesley, literary arts. Eng., 1938. Essayist; short story writer. *Going Down Slow; Private Parts: A Memoir; Adult Entertainment.*

MICHAELS, Lorne (b. Lorne Lipowitz), media. Toronto, Ont., 1945. TV producer; founding producer, *Saturday Night Live.*

MICHENER, Daniel Roland, politics. Lacombe, Alta., 1900-91. Governor general of Canada, 1967-74.

MIKITA, Stan (b. Stanislaus Gvoth), sports. Czech., 1940. Hockey player; centre with Chicago Blackhawks (1959-80); first Czech to play in NHL.

MILLAR, Ian D., sports. Halifax, NS, 1947. Eight-time Canadian show-jumping champion, Cdn Athlete of the Year, 1987, 1989.

MILLAR, Margaret, literary arts. Kitchener, Ont., 1915. Thriller writer. *Beast in View.*

MILNE, David Brown, visual arts. Paisley, Ont., 1882-1953. Versatile painter. *Raspberry Jam.*

MILNER, Brenda, science. Eng., 1915. Neuropsychologist; ground-breaking brain researcher.

MINER, John Thomas (Jack), science. USA, 1865-1944. Conservationist; pioneered bird sanctuaries, migratory banding.

MIRVISH, Edwin (Ed) (b. Yehudi Mirvish), business. USA, 1914. Entrepreneur; retailer (Honest Ed's) and theatre owner.

MISTRY, Rohinton, literary arts. India, 1952. Novelist, short story writer. *Such a Long Journey; A Fine Balance.*

MITCHELL, Joni (b. Roberta Joan Anderson), performing arts. Ft Macleod, Alta., 1943. Singer/songwriter; influential lyricist. *Court and Spark.*

MITCHELL, Ray, sports. Peace River, Alta, 1931. Bowler; winner of 1972 Canadian and world 10-pin championship.

MITCHELL, William Ormond (W.O.), literary arts. Weyburn, Sask., 1914-98. Prairie novelist. *Who Has Seen the Wind?*

MOLSON, John, business. Eng., 1764-1836. Founded Molson brewery; built railroads.

MONTCALM DE SAINT VERAN, Louis Joseph de Montcalm Grozon, military. France, 1712-59. Soldier; French commander in Seven Years War; died on Plains of Abraham.

MONTGOMERY, Lucy Maud, literary arts. Clifton, PEI, 1874-1942. Writer; creator of *Anne of Green Gables.*

MONTGOMERY, Robert Douglas, performing arts. Bradford, Ont., 1908-66. Movie actor, played Laurie in 1933 version of *Little Women* opposite Katharine Hepburn.

MOODIE, Susanna, literary arts. Eng., 1803-85. Writer; pioneer author of *Roughing It in the Bush.*

MOORE, Brian, literary arts. N Ire., 1921-99 Prolific novelist; winner of two Governor General's Awards. *The Luck of Ginger Coffey; Black Robe.*

MOORE, James Mavor, literary arts. Toronto, Ont., 1919. TV producer; librettist; columnist; critic.

MOORES, Frank Duff, politics. Carbonear, Nfld, 1933. PC premier of Newfoundland, 1972-79.

MORANIS, Rick, performing arts. Toronto, Ont., 1953. Comedian; actor; *SCTV* regular. *Ghostbusters.*

MORAWETZ, Oskar, performing arts. Czech., 1917. Composer. *From the Diary of Anne Frank.*

MORENZ, Howarth Williams (Howie), sports. Mitchell, Ont., 1902-37. Hockey player; centre; Canada's player of half century (CP), 1950; died of on-ice injuries.

MORGAN, John, performing arts. Wales. Comedian who appears on CBC's *Royal Canadian Air Farce,* roles include Jock McBile and Mike from Canmore.

MORGENTALER, Henry, medicine. Poland, 1923. Physician; challenge of abortion laws led to Supreme Court ruling them unconstitutional.

MORISSETTE, Alanis Nadine, performing arts. Ottawa, Ont., 1974. Singer-songwriter. Juno award winner 1996 for *Jagged Little Pill* (Best Album) and Female Vocalist of the Year; Grammy Award winner, 1996.

MORIYAMA, Raymond, visual arts. Vancouver, BC, 1929. Architect; Ontario Science Centre.

MORRICE, James Wilson (J.W.), visual arts. Montreal, Que., 1864-1924. Artist; early modernist. *The Ice Bridge.*

MORRIS, Alwyn, sports. Montreal, Que., 1957. With Hugh Fisher won gold medal in 1000 m and bronze in 500 m kayak doubles at 1984 Olympics.

MORRIS, Joseph (Joe), politics. Eng., 1913-96. Former president of Canadian Labour Congress; chairman of International Labour Organization.

MORRISSEAU, Norval, visual arts. Sand Point Reserve, Ont., 1932. Ojibway artist originated pictographic style.

MORSE, Barry, performing arts. Eng., 1918. Stage/film/TV actor; regular on *The Fugitive.*

MORTON, William Lewis (W.L.), literary arts. Gladstone, Man., 1908-80. Historian. *Manitoba: A History.*

MOWAT, Claire Angel, literary arts. Toronto, Ont., 1933. Graphic artist, fiction writer, wife of writer Farley Mowat. *The Girl From Away; The Outport People; The French Isles.*

MOWAT, Farley McGill, literary arts. Belleville, Ont., 1921. Controversial, popular naturalist writer. *A Whale for the Killing.*

MOWAT, Sir Oliver, politics. Kingston, UC, 1820-1903. Ontario premier, 1872-96; lieutenant-governor, 1897-1903.

MUKHERJEE, Bharati, literary arts. India, 1940. Novelist, *The Middleman and Other Stories; Jasmine.*

MULRONEY, Brian Martin, politics. Baie Comeau, Que., 1939. Prime minister of Canada 1984-93.

MUNK, Peter, business. Hungary, 1927. Capitalist; CEO, American Barrick Resources gold mining company.

MUNRO, Alice, literary arts. Wingham, Ont., 1931. Short story writer. Winner of 1998 Giller prize. *Lives of Girls and Women.*

MUNSCH, Robert, literary arts. USA, 1945. Children's writer. *The Paper Bag Princess; Love You Forever.*

MURPHY, Emily Cowan, law. Cookstown, Ont., 1868-1933. Legal reformer; first woman magistrate in British Empire; fought for women's rights.

MURPHY, Rex media. Carbonear, Nfld, 1947. CBC news journalist with acerbic style. *Cross Country Checkup.*

MURRAY, Anne, performing arts. Springhill, NS, 1945. Singer; Canada's most successful performer; many Junos and Grammys. "Snowbird."

MURRAY, George Henry, politics. Grand Narrows, NS, 1861-1929. Lib. premier of NS, 1896-1923.

MURRAY, John Wilson, law. Scot., 1840-1906. Detective; pioneered scientific crime detection.

MURRAY, Margaret Teresa "Ma", media. USA, 1888-1982. Journalist; pungent editorialist in own magazines.

MURRAY, Robert George Everitt, science. Eng., 1919. With Philip Fitz-Jones, researched structure and chemical nature of bacterial spores.

MUSGRAVE, Susan, literary arts. USA, 1951. Poet, novelist, children's writer. *The Embalmer's Art: Poems; The Charcoal Burners.*

MUSTARD, James Fraser, medicine. Toronto, Ont., 1927. Physician; medical humanitarian; found connection between aspirin and blood clotting.

MUSTARD, William, medicine. Clinton, Ont., 1914-87. Physician; beloved children's surgeon developed operations for blue babies, polio cripples.

MYERS, Mike, performing arts. Toronto, Ont., 1963. Comic actor has appeared in movies *Austin Powers; It's a Dog's Life; Wayne's World,* also appeared on *Saturday Night Live.*

MYLES, Alannah, performing arts. Toronto, Ont., 1958. Pop singer/composer of hard rock, ballads. "Lover of Mine"; *Black Velvet; Al-Lan-Nah.*

NAISMITH, James A., sports. Almonte, Ont., 1861-1939. Physician; invented basketball in 1891.

NAMARO, James (Jimmy), performing arts. USA, 1913-98. A member of the CBC's *Happy Gang,* the longest-running program on the radio network; also led his own jazz band.

NASH, Cyril Knowlton, media. Toronto, Ont., 1927. Broadcaster; former anchorman, CBC national news.

NATTRASS, Susan Marie, sports. Medicine Hat, Alta., 1950. Shooter; six women's world trapshooting titles.

NAULT, Fernand (b. Fernand-Noel Boissonneault), performing arts. Montreal, Que., 1921. Dancer; choreographer, Les Grands Ballets Canadiens.

NELLIGAN, Emile, literary arts. Montreal, Que., 1879-1941. Romantic poet. "Romance du Vin."

NELLIGAN, Kate, performing arts. London, Ont., 1951. Actor; appears on both stage and film. *Eleni.*

NEMETZ, Nathaniel "Sonny", law. Winnipeg, Man., 1913-97. Chief Justice of British Columbia 1979-88, leading judicial administrator in BC.

NEVILLE, John, performing arts. Eng., 1925. Actor, director. Stratford Festival, Ont.; director of Stratford's The Young Company.

NEWMAN, Peter Charles, media. Austria, 1929. Journalist; popular historian. *The Canadian Establishment; Maclean's* editor, 1971-82.

NEWTON, Margaret, science. Montreal, Que., 1887-1971. Plant pathologist; first scientist to research rust in wheat.

NICHOL, Barrie Phillip (bp), literary arts. Vancouver, BC, 1944-88. Concrete and sound poet, novelist. *Journeying and Returns; Love: A Book of Remembrance.*

NICHOL, Dave, business. Chatham, Ont., 1940. Made Loblaws stores market leader with President's Choice label.

NICHOLAS, Cynthia (Cindy), sports. Toronto, Ont., 1957. Marathon swimmer; first woman to swim English Channel both ways.

NICOL, Eric, media. Kingston, Ont., 1919. Humour columnist. "Girdle Me a Globe."

NIELSEN, Erik Hersholt, politics. Regina, Sask., 1924. PC MP elected in Yukon 1957, served as deputy prime minister in Mulroney government.

NIELSEN, Leslie, performing arts. Regina, Sask., 1926. Deadpan film/TV comedian. *Naked Gun.*

NORQUAY, John, politics. St Andrews, Man., 1841-89. Manitoba premier of mixed European and native ancestry, 1878-87.

NORTHCOTT, Ronald Charles, sports. Innisfail, Alta., 1935. Curler; skipped three Brier and world champion rinks.

NOWLAN, Alden, literary arts. Windsor, NS, 1933-83. Poet. "Bread, Wine and Salt."

O

O'BRIEN, Mary, public service. Scot., 1926-98. Midwife, philosopher; founding member of the Feminist Party of Canada, wrote *The Politics of Reproduction; Reproducing the World.*

ODJIG, Daphne, visual arts. Manitoulin Island, Ont., 1919. Blends western and native styles. *The Indian in Transition.*

O'HARA, Catherine, performing arts. Toronto, Ont., 1954. Actor; comedian; *SCTV* regular (Lola Heatherton).

OKALIK, Paul, politics. Pangnirtung, NWT, 1964. First premier of 19-member Legislative Assembly for Nunavit in the Eastern Arctic, created in 1999.

OLCOTT, Sidney, performing arts. Toronto, Ont., 1873-1949. Director of Hollywood silent films, pioneered locations shots, westerns. *Ben Hur.*

OLIPHANT, Betty, performing arts. Eng., 1918. Founded National Ballet School.

ONDAATJE, Christopher, business/literary arts. Sri Lanka, 1933. Financier; author. *Leopard in the Afternoon.*

ONDAATJE, Michael, literary arts. Sri Lanka, 1943. Poet; editor; novelist. *The English Patient* (Booker Prize).

O'NEILL, James Edward "Tip", sports. Canada W, 1859-1918. Baseball player; batted .326 in 10-year career.

ORR, Robert Gordon (Bobby), sports. Parry Sound, Ont., 1948. Hockey player; spectacular offensive defenceman; won eight consecutive Norris trophies.

ORSER, Brian Ernest, sports. Belleville, Ont., 1961. Figure skater; 1987 world champion, twice Olympic silver medallist (1984, 1988).

ORTON, George W., sports. Strathroy, Ont., 1873-1958. Runner; Canada's first Olympic gold medallist, winning for USA in 1900 (2500 m steeplechase).

OSLER, Sir William, medicine. Bond Head, UC, 1849-1919. Physician; renowned medical educator; writer of authoritative textbooks.

OTTENBRITE, Anne, sports. Whitby, Ont., 1966. Swimmer; gold medal, 200 m, 1984 Olympics.

OUIMET, Joseph Alphonse, media. Montreal, Que., 1908-88. TV executive; designed first Canadian TV receiver; CBC president, 1958-67.

P

PACE, Kate, sports. North Bay, Ont., 1969. Skier; World Cup downhill champion, 1993.

PACHTER, Charles, visual arts. Toronto, Ont., 1942. Painter famous for flag series; 1973 acrylic sketch titled *Queen on Moose.*

PAGE, Patricia Kathleen, (P.K.), literary arts. Eng., 1916. Poet; novelist; artist. "The Metal and the Flower."

PANNETON, Philippe (Ringuet), literary arts. Trois-Rivières, Que., 1895-1960. Man of letters; acclaimed Quebec writer. *Trente Arpents.*

PAPINEAU, Louis Joseph, politics. Montreal, Que., 1786-1871. Led political reform movement in Lower Canada.

PARIS, Erna, literary arts. Toronto, Ont., 1938. Writer. *The Garden and the Gun; End of Days.*

PARIZEAU, Jacques, politics. Montreal, Que., 1930. Leader, Parti Québécois 1987-95.

PARKER, Jackie, sports. USA, 1932. Football player; coach; Edmonton Eskimos star quarterback; named CFL outstanding player three times.

PARKER, Jon Kimura, performing arts. Vancouver, BC, 1959. Concert pianist, performed for Queen, prime ministers, and at Carnegie Hall.

PARROT, Jean-Claude, business. Montreal, Que., 1936. Labour leader; leader of militant postal union.

PARTRIDGE, Edward Alexander, business. Canada W, 1862-1931. Farm reformer; visionary in grain industry fought monopolies, started growers' cooperative.

PASSAGLIA, Lui, sports. Vancouver, BC, 1954. Football player; kicker with BC Lions; CFL's all-time scoring leader.

PATRICK, Lester, sports. Drummondville, Que., 1883-1960. Hockey executive; NHL builder.

PATTISON, James Allen, business. Saskatoon, Sask., 1928. Industrialist; developed car dealership into business empire; chairman, Expo 86.

PAUL, Robert, sports. Toronto, Ont., 1937. Figure skater; with Barbara Wagner, won four pairs titles, 1960 Olympic gold.

PAYETTE, Julie, science. Montreal, Que., 1963. Astronaut and mission specialist on crew of STS-96 Atlantis, a 10-day logistics and resupply mission that launched in May 1999.

PEAKER, Charles, performing arts. Eng., 1899-1978. Organist, choirmaster, writer. Foremost concert organist in Canada. Edited *Organ Music of Canada.*

PEARSON, Lester Bowles, politics. Newtonbrook, Ont., 1897-1972. Prime minister of Canada 1963-1968; awarded Nobel Peace Prize in 1957.

PECKFORD, Alfred Brian, politics. Whitbourne, Nfld, 1942. PC premier of Nfld, 1979-89.

PEEL, Paul, visual arts. London, Ont., 1860-92. Painter famous for *After the Bath,* which depicts two children warming themselves before a fireplace. *The Tired Model; Good News, Toronto.*

PELADEAU, Pierre, media. Outremont, Que., 1925-97. Publisher; head of newspaper giant Quebecor.

PELLAN, Alfred, visual arts. Quebec City, Que., 1906-88. Painter; cubist and surrealist artist.

PELLATT, Sir Henry Mill, military. Kingston, Canada W, 1860-1939. Soldier; builder of eccentric Toronto mansion, Casa Loma.

PELLETIER, Gerard, politics. Victoriaville, Que., 1919-97. Chief editor for *La Presse* (1961-65); federal deputy minister for Montreal riding of Hochelaga 1965-75. Later ambassador for Canada in Paris and for United Nations.

PENFIELD, Dr Wilder Groves, medicine. USA, 1891-1976. Neurologist; writer; pioneered mapping of brain functions; founded Montreal Neurological Inst.

PENNELL, Nicholas, performing arts. Eng., 1938-95. Former actor at Stratford Festival; starred in British TV series *The Forsyte Saga.*

PEPIN, Jean-Luc, politics. Drummondville, Que., 1924-95. Longtime Liberal cabinet minister; served on Anti-Inflation Board, co-chairman of 1977 unity task force.

PERCY, Karen, sports. Edmonton, Alta., 1966. Skier; won two bronze medals, 1988 Olympics.

PERRAULT, Pierre, visual arts. Montreal, Que., 1927. Filmmaker; realist director. *L'Acadie, L'Acadie.*

PETERSON, Eric, politics. Indian Head, Sask., 1946. Actor. *Billy Bishop Goes to War;* CBC's *Street Legal* series.

PETERSON, Oscar Emmanuel, performing arts. Montreal, Que., 1925. Jazz pianist; "Canadiana Suite"; over 90 albums.

PETRIE, Daniel, performing arts. Glace Bay, NS, 1920. Film director, won Genie award for *Bay Boy; A Raisin in the Sun.*

PEZER, Vera, sports. Melfort, Sask., 1939. Curler; Canadian women's champion, 1971-73.

PFLUG, Christiane, visual arts. Germany, 1936-72. Painter of melancholy landscapes and domestic scenes. *Cottingham School After the Rain; Kitchen Door with Esther.*

PHILLIPS, Robin, performing arts. Eng., 1942. Director, Stratford Festival, 1975-80, 1986-87.

PICKFORD, Mary (b. Gladys Smith), performing arts. Toronto, Ont., 1893-1979. Actress; "America's Sweetheart" was early movie star. *Sparrows.*

PIDGEON, Walter, performing arts. E Saint John, NB, 1897-1984. Leading man. *Mrs. Miniver.*

PINSENT, Gordon Edward, performing arts. Grand Falls, Nfld, 1930. Versatile actor. *The Rowdyman; Due South.*

PITSEOLAK Ashoona, visual arts. NWT, 1904-83. Artist of Inuit myth and legend.

PITSEOLAK, Peter, visual arts. NWT, 1902-73. Photographer; recorded passing of traditional Inuit life.

PLAMONDON, Antoine, visual arts. Lorette, Que., 1804-95. Portraitist and religious painter.

PLAMONDON, Luc, performing arts. St Raymond-de-Portneuf, Que., 1945. Lyricist; wrote rock opera *Starmania;* collaborated with Britain's Tim Rice; has written songs for Celine Dion.

PLANTE, Jacques, sports. Mt Carmel, Que., 1929-86. Hockey goaltender; seven-time Vezina winner; originated face mask.

PLUMMER, Arthur Christopher Orme, performing arts. Toronto, Ont., 1929. Stage and film star. *Murder By Decree.*

POCKINGTON, Peter H., business. Regina, Sask., 1941. Entrepreneur; owner of Edmonton Oilers.

POCOCK, Nancy Meek, philanthropy. USA, 1911-98. Quaker and pacifist, an antiwar and refugee advocate; won the Medal of Friendship from Socialist Republic of Vietnam.

PODBORSKI, Steve, sports. Toronto, Ont., 1957. Skier; world downhill champion, 1982.

POLANYI, John Charles, science. Germany, 1929. Chemist; Nobel Prize (1986) for work on infrared chemiluminescence.

POLLEY, Sarah, performing arts. Toronto, Ont., 1979. Actress; *The Road to Avonlea; The Sweet Hereafter.*

POLLOCK, Sam, sports. Montreal, Que., 1925. Hockey executive; built Montreal Canadiens dynasty.

POLLOCK, Sharon, literary arts. Fredericton, NB, 1936. Playwright; writer of conscience. *Blood Relations.*

PONTIAC, military. USA, 1720?-69. Ottawa Indian chief who formed alliance with various Indian federations to attack English, including a fort at Point Pelee, Ont.; in 1765 key signer of peace treaties with the English.

PORTER, Anna Maria, literary arts. Hungary. Publisher, author. CEO and director of Key Porter Books; mystery writer. *The Bookfair Murders; Mortal Sins.*

POST, Sandra, sports. Oakville, Ont., 1943. Golfer; Canada's first woman touring professional.

POTTS, Jerry (b. Ky-yo-Kosi), military. USA, 1840-96. Native scout; Blackfoot became NWMP special constable.

POTVIN, Dennis, sports. Ottawa, Ont., 1953. Hockey player; as defenceman with New York Islanders (1973-88) all-time leader in goals and assists.

POWELL, Marion, medicine. Toronto, Ont., 1923-97. Former president of Planned Parenthood in Toronto; a pioneer in introducing birth control information in the 1960s.

PRATT, Edwin James (E.J.), literary arts. Western Bay, Nfld, 1883-1964. Leading pre-WWII poet. "Newfoundland Verse."

PRATT, John Christopher, visual arts. St John's, Nfld, 1935. Artist; developed style of "conceptual realism."

PRIESTLEY, Jason Bradford, performing arts. Vancouver, BC, 1969. Popular actor noted for his brooding looks. *Beverly Hills, 90210.*

PURDY, Alfred Wellington, literary arts. Wooler, Ont., 1918. Working-class poet. "The Cariboo Horses."

Q

QUARRINGTON, Paul Lewis, literary arts. Toronto, Ont., 1953. Governor General's Award for Fiction, 1990. *Home Game; Whale Music.*

QUILICO, Louis, performing arts. Montreal, Que., 1925. Operatic baritone; appeared with most major companies.

R

RADDAL, Thomas Head, literary arts. Eng., 1903-94. Governor General's Award winning historical novelist. *The Pied Piper of Dipper Creek and Other Tales; His Majesty's Yankees.*

RADISSON, Pierre Esprit, exploration and discovery. France, 1636-1710. Explorer; fur trader; important in early history of Hudson's Bay Co as guide and advisor.

RAE, Robert Keith (Bob), politics. Ottawa, Ont., 1948. NDP premier of Ontario 1990-95.

RAFFI (b. Raffi Cavoukian), performing arts. Egypt, 1948. Singer. *Baby Beluga.*

RASKY, Harry, performing arts. Toronto, Ont., 1928. Filmmaker; noted documentarist. *The Dispossessed: The War Against the Indians.*

RASMINSKY, Louis, business. Montreal, Que., 1908-98. Governor, Bank of Canada, 1961-72.

RAYNER, Gordon, visual arts. Toronto, Ont., 1935. Realist, abstract painter, landscapes and cityscapes; northern Ontario landscapes. *Magnetawan No. 2.*

READ, Ken, sports. 1955. Skier; winner of five World Cup downhill victories (1975-80).

REANEY, James Crerar, literary arts. Easthope, Ont., 1926. Playwright; poet; critic. "A Suit of Nettles."

REBICK, Judy, politics. USA, 1945. Former head, Natl Action Committee on Status of Women.

REED, George Robert, sports. USA, 1939. Football player; running back with Sask. Roughriders; 44 CFL records.

REEVES, Keanu, performing arts. Lebanon, 1965. Actor. *Bill and Ted's Excellent Adventure; My Own Private Idaho.*

REGAN, Gerald Augustine, politics. Windsor, NS, 1928. Liberal premier of NS, 1970-78.

REICHMANN, Paul, business. Austria, 1930. Developer; philanthropist; with brothers Albert and Ralph, built Olympia & York into world's largest real estate developers in 1980s.

REID, Daphne Kate, performing arts. Eng., 1930-93. Primarily stage actress; Stratford mainstay.

REID, Fiona, politics. Eng., 1951. Dramatic and comedic actor. CBC's *King of Kensington* series; Stratford Festival, Ont.

REID, William Ronald (Bill), visual arts. Victoria, BC, 1920-98. Noted artist who promoted Northwest Coast native carving; also a sculptor whose works appear in major galleries and buildings.

REITMAN, Ivan, visual arts. Czech., 1946. Film director; producer; went from exploitation movies to blockbusters. *Ghostbusters.*

RICCI, Nino Pio, literary arts. Leamington, Ont., 1959. Novelist, recipient of Governor General's Award for Fiction, 1990, for *Lives of the Saints.*

RICHARD, Joseph Henry Maurice "Rocket", sports. Montreal, Que., 1921. Hockey player; legendary right winger; hockey's first 50-goal, 500-goal scorer.

RICHARDSON, Ernie, sports. Stoughton, Sask., 1931. Curler; skipped four Brier and world title rinks.

RICHARDSON, James Armstrong, business. Kingston, Ont., 1885-1939. Financier; founded family grain business and investment house.

RICHLER, Mordecai, literary arts. Montreal, Que., 1931. Novelist; essayist; acerbic comic writer. *St Urbain's Horseman.*

RIDOUT, Godfrey, performing arts. Toronto, Ont., 1918-94. Composer of chamber, symphonic and religious choral works.

RIEL, Louis, politics. St Boniface, Man., 1844-85. Métis leader; led North West Rebellion, 1870 and 1885; hanged for treason; rehabilitated and recognized as a founder of Manitoba in 1992.

RIOPELLE, Jean-Paul, visual arts. Montreal, Que., 1923. Acclaimed painter, sculptor. *Autrich.*

RITCHIE, Charles Stewart Almon, politics. Halifax, NS, 1906-95. Diplomat post-WWII; author of a number of books. *The Siren Years.*

ROBARTS, John Parmenter, politics. Banff, Alta., 1917-82. PC premier of Ontario, 1961-71.

ROBERTS, Charles George Douglas (Sir), literary arts. Douglas, NB, 1860-1943. Poet; animal story writer. *Eyes of the Wilderness.*

ROBERTSON, Heather Margaret, literary arts. Winnipeg, Man., 1942. Novelist, critic. *More Than a Rose: Prime Ministers, Wives and Other Women.*

ROBERTSON, Jaime Robbie, performing arts. Toronto, Ont., 1944. Singer/songwriter; founding member of The Band; later soloist. *Music from Big Pink.*

ROBERTSON, John Ross, business. Toronto, Ont., 1841-1918. Financier; publisher and philanthropist.

ROBERTSON, Lloyd, media. Stratford, Ont., 1934. Broadcaster; chief anchor, CTV news.

ROBICHAUD, Louis Joseph, politics. St-Antoine, NB, 1925. Liberal premier of NB, 1960-70.

ROBINETTE, John Josiah (J.J.), law. Toronto, Ont., 1906-96. Lawyer; prominent in criminal and constitutional law.

ROBINSON, Svend J., politics. USA, 1952. NDP MP, British Columbia; social activist, gay rights.

ROBLIN, Dufferin (Duff), politics. Winnipeg, Man., 1917. PC premier of Manitoba, 1958-67.

ROBLIN, Sir Rodmond Palen, politics. Sophiasburg, Canada W, 1853-1937. PC premier of Manitoba, 1900-15.

ROCK, Allan Michael, politics. Ottawa, Ont., 1947. Liberal MP made minister of justice and attorney general in 1993, introduced major changes in Young Offender's Act and gun control legislation, minister of health in Chrétien government.

RODRIGUEZ, Sue, public service. Winnipeg, Man., 1959-94. Lou Gehrig's disease victim who championed right to die.

ROGERS, Edward S. (Ted), business. Toronto, Ont., 1933. Cable TV executive; runs Canada's largest cable system; 1994 take-over of Maclean Hunter.

ROGERS, Edward Samuel, invention. Toronto, Ont., 1900-39. Radio inventor; perfected alternating current radio tube, revolutionizing the industry.

ROGERS, Shelagh, media. Ottawa, Ont., 1956. CBC radio personality. Co-host of CBC's *Morningside; Take Five* with *Shelagh Rogers.*

ROGERS, Stan, performing arts. Hamilton, Ont., 1949-83. Folk singer/songwriter. "Between the Breaks."

ROHMER, Richard, literary arts. Hamilton, Ont., 1924. Writer. *Triad, Red Arctic, Death by Deficit.*

ROLPH, John, medicine. Eng., 1793-1870. Physician; ran medical school; constitutional reformer.

ROMAN, Stephen Boleslav, business. Slovakia, 1921-88. Industrialist; founded Denison Mines Ltd.

ROMANOW, Roy John, politics. Saskatoon, Sask., 1939. NDP premier of Sask. since 1991.

RONALD, William (b. William Smith), visual arts. Stratford, Ont., 1926-98. Abstract artist; host, *As It Happens.*

ROOKE, Leon, literary arts. USA, 1934. Short story writer, novelist, playwright. *Krokodile; Shakespeare's Dog; How I Saved the Province; A Bit of White Cloth.*

ROSE, Fred (b. Fred Rosenburg), politics. Poland, 1907-83. Only Canadian Communist MP (1945); jailed as spy.

ROSENFELD, Fanny "Bobbie", sports. Russia, 1905-69. Track star; Canada's female athlete of half century.

ROSS, Anne Glass, medicine. Ukraine, 1911-98. Executive director of Winnipeg's Mount Carmel community health clinic, the first of its kind in Canada; birth control advocate. *Pregnant and Alone; Clinic with a Heart.*

ROSS, James Sinclair, literary arts. Shellbrook, Sask., 1908-96. Novelist. *As for Me and My House.*

ROTHSTEIN, Aser, science. Vancouver, BC, 1918. Physiologist; introduced radioisotopes in biology.

ROULEAU, Joseph, performing arts. Matane, Que., 1929. Operatic bass; internationally famous singer.

ROUX, Jean-Louis, performing arts/politics. Montreal, Que., 1923. Actor, playwright with successful career was rejected as proposed lieutenant governor of Quebec in 1997 due to youthful support of Nazi regime during WWII; appointed head of Canada Council in 1998.

ROY, Gabrielle, literary arts. St Boniface, Man., 1909-83. Popular novelist. *The Tin Flute.*

ROY, Patrick, sports. Quebec City, Que., 1965. Hockey player with Montreal Canadiens, youngest ever to win Conn Smythe trophy; in 1989-92 considered to be one of best goalies in the world.

ROZEMA, Patricia, politics. Kingston, Ont., 1958. Filmmaker; *I've Heard the Mermaids Singing, White Room.*

RUBES, Jan, performing arts. Czech., 1920. Singer; actor; operatic bass; TV host; film actor.

RUBINEK, Saul, performing arts. Toronto, Ont., 1948. Versatile character player. *The Quarrel.*

RUBINSKY, Yuri, business. Lebanon, 1952-96. Founder of Banff Publishing Workshop; co-director of SoftQuad Inc.; software designer.

RULE, Jane Vance, literary arts. USA, 1931. Novelist, short story writer. *Desert of the Heart; After the Fire; Contract With the World.*

RUSSELL, Loris Shano, science. USA, 1904. Paleontologist; suggested dinosaurs might be warm-blooded.

RUTHERFORD, Ann, performing arts. Toronto, Ont., 1917. Actress who appeared as Andy Hardy's girlfriend, Polly Benedict, in 12 Hardy films. *Secret Life of Walter Mitty.*

RUTHERFORD, Ernest (Rutherford of Nelson), science. NZ, 1871-1937. Physicist; much of his seminal work done at McGill University.

RYAN, Pat, sports. Winnipeg, Man., 1955. Curler; skip of world championship team in 1989; Canadian championship 1988, 1989.

RYAN, Thomas F. (Tommy), business. Guelph, Ont., 1872-1961. Entrepreneur; invented five-pin bowling (1909).

RYBCZYNSKI, Witold, literary arts/visual arts. Scot., 1943. Architect; critic; writer. *Paper Heroes.*

RYERSON, Adolphus Egerton, politics. Norfolk County, UC, 1803-82. Leading figure in 19th century politics and education.

RYGA, George, literary arts. Deep Creek, Alta, 1932-87. Playwright, novelist. *Ecstasy of Rita Joe; Night Desk.*

S

SABIA, Laura Louise, public service. Pembroke, Ont., 1916-96. Headed Royal Commission on the Status of Women in 1960s; became president of National Action Commitee on the Status of Women 1973.

SAFDIE, Moshe, visual arts. Israel, 1938. Architect; Habitat; National Gallery of Canada.

SAFER, Morley, media. Toronto, Ont., 1931. Broadcaster; co-host, *60 Minutes* since 1971.

SAHL, Mort, performing arts. Montreal, Que., 1926. Comedian; delivered political satire in monologues.

SAINTE-MARIE, Buffy, performing arts. Craven, Sask., 1941. Native singer. "Soldier Blue."

SALABERRY, Charles Michel D'Irumberry de, military. Beauport, Que., 1778-1829. Soldier; repelled American force in Battle of Chateaugay (1813).

SALTZMAN, Harry, performing arts. Saint John, NB, 1915-94. Co-producer of James Bond films. *The Man With the Golden Gun; The Ipcress File.*

SALUTIN, Rick, literary arts. Toronto, Ont., 1942. Playwright, columnist; leftist commentator. *Marginal Notes; Challenges to the Mainstream; Globe and Mail* columnist.

SARLOS, Andrew, business. Hungary, 1931-97. Financial trader with Toronto Stock Exchange. Realized $22 million profit from Hiram-Walker-Consumer's Gas merger.

SARRAZIN, Michael, performing arts. Quebec City, Que., 1940. Leading man. *They Shoot Horses, Don't They?*

SAUL, John Ralston, literary arts. Ottawa, Ont., 1947. Novelist, essayist. *The Paradise Eater; Voltaire's Bastards: The Dictatorship of Reason in the West.*

SAUNDERS, Sir Charles Edward, science. London, Ont., 1867-1937. Agriculturalist; introduced Marquis wheat to W Canada.

SAUVE, Jeanne Mathilde, politics. Prud'homme, Sask., 1922-93. Governor general, 1984-89.

SAWCHUK, Terrence Gordon, sports. Winnipeg, Man., 1929-70. Hockey goaltender; all-time shutouts leader (103).

SAWYER, Robert, literary arts. Ottawa, Ont., 1960. Science fiction writer, winner of US Nebula award, awards in Japan, France, Spain *Flashforward; Factoring Humanity.*

SCHAEFER, Carl Fellman, visual arts. Hanover, Ont., 1903-95. Painter of rural Ontario landscapes, director of Ontario College of Art.

SCHAFER, Raymond Murray, performing arts. Sarnia, Ont., 1933. Composer of contemporary music, first recipient of Glenn Gould Award in 1987.

SCHALLY, Andrew Victor, science. Poland, 1926. Winner of 1977 Noble Prize in medicine and physiology, for research into understanding peptide hormones in the brain.

SCHAWLOW, Arthur, science. USA, 1921-99. Canadian educated scientist, winner of 1964 Nobel Prize with Charles Hand Townes, co-patented the laser.

SCHLESINGER, Joe, media. Austria, 1928. Journalist; longtime CBC foreign correspondent.

SCHMIRLER, Sandra Marie, sports. Biggar, Sask., 1963. Skip of the gold-medal-winning curling team at the 1998 Winter Olympics in Nagano, Japan.

SCHNARRE, Monika, performing arts. Toronto, Ont., 1971. Won 1986 Face of the 1980s modeling award; acting career includes role on *The Bold and the Beautiful.*

SCHOLES, Myron, economics. Timmins, Ont., 1941. Stanford University-based co-winner (with Harvard academic Robert Merton) of Nobel Prize for economics, for developing a mathematical formula for estimating values in the worldwide market of derivatives, known as the Black-Scholes formula.

SCHREYER, Edward Richard, politics. Beausejour, Man., 1935. NDP premier of Man., 1969-77; governor general of Canada, 1979-84.

SCOTT, Barbara Ann, sports. Ottawa, Ont., 1928. Figure skater; women's world champion, 1947-48; Olympic gold medal, 1948.

SCOTT, Duncan Campbell, literary arts. Ottawa, Ont., 1862-1947. Poet. "New World Lyrics and Ballads."

SCOTT, Francis (Frank) Reginald, literary arts. Quebec City, Que., 1899-1985. Poet. "Collected Poems."

SCOTT, Jack, performing arts. Windsor, Ont., 1936. Singer; 1950s rockabilly star. "My True Love."

SCRIVEN, Joseph Medlicott, religion. Ire., 1819-86. Hymn writer; wrote "What a Friend We Have in Jesus."

SECORD, Laura, military. USA, 1775-1868. Heroine; warned British of American attack (1813).

SEGAL, Hugh, politics. Montreal, Que., 1950. Back-room PC advisor to Robert Stanfield, William Davis and Brian Mulroney.

SELKIRK, George, sports. Huntsville, Ont., 1899-1987. Baseball player; outfielder on several NY Yankee champions; replaced Babe Ruth in 1934.

SELKIRK, Thomas Douglas, fifth Earl of, exploration and discovery. Scot., 1771-1820. Colonizer; established Red River settlement in Manitoba.

SELYE, Hans, medicine. Austria, 1907-82 Endocrinologist; author; pioneer in stress research. *The Stress of Life.*

SENNETT, Mack (b. Mikail Sinnott), visual arts. Danville, Que., 1880-1960. Producer; silent comedy pioneer; Keystone Kops.

SERVICE, Robert William, literary arts. Eng., 1874-1958. Poet of the Yukon, "Songs of a Sourdough."

SETON, Ernest Thompson, literary arts. Eng., 1860-1946. Naturalist; writer. *Wild Animals I Have Known.*

SHADBOLT, John Leonard (Jack), visual arts. Eng., 1909-98. BC artist noted for nature and native Canadian influenced work.

SHANNON, Kathleen, performing arts. Vancouver, BC, 1935-98. Founder of National Film Board's Studio D in 1974, which provided female filmmakers an opportunity to create documentaries with a feminist perspective. *If You Love This Planet; Not a Love Story.*

SHATNER, William, performing arts. Montreal, Que., 1931. Actor; Capt. Kirk on TV/movies *Star Trek.*

SHAVER, Helen, performing arts. St Thomas, Ont., 1951. Actress appeared in *The Amityville Horror; Bethune: the Making of a Hero.*

SHEARER, Douglas, performing arts. Westmount, Que., 1899-1971. Sound recording technician, 40 years with MGM; won 12 Academy Awards; brother of actress Norma Shearer. *The Great Caruso; The Big House.*

SHEARER, Norma, performing arts. Edmonton, Alta., 1900-83. Actress; Hollywood star. *Romeo and Juliet.*

SHEBIB, Donald, visual arts. Toronto, Ont., 1939. Acclaimed filmmaker. *Goin' Down the Road; Heartaches.*

SHIELDS, Carol, literary arts. USA, 1935. Writer; won 1993 Booker and Pulitzer prizes for *The Stone Diaries.*

SHORE, Eddie, sports. Ft Qu'Apelle, Sask., 1902-85. Hockey player; Boston defenceman; four-time Hart Trophy winner.

SHORT, Martin, performing arts. Toronto, Ont., 1951. Comedian; TV/film star; *SCTV*'s Ed Grimley. *3 Amigos.*

SHULMAN, Dr Morton, business/medicine. Toronto, Ont., 1925. Investor; physician; author; stock promoter; introduced anti-Parkinson's disease drug into Canada.

SHUSTER, Frank, performing arts. Toronto, Ont., 1918. Comedian; straighter half of Wayne & Shuster team.

SHUSTER, Joe, visual arts. Toronto, Ont., 1914-92. Cartoonist; co-creator of Superman.

SIBERRY, Jane, performing arts. Ottawa, Ont., 1955. Singer, songwriter, guitarist. Contemporary folk style. *Jane Siberry; No Borders Here.*

SIFTON, Sir Clifford, politics. Arva, Canada W, 1861-1929. Promoted immigration to settle western Canada.

SILVERHEELS, Harold Jay Smith, performing arts. Six Nations Reserve, Ont., 1919-80. Actor; played Tonto in Lone Ranger.

SIMARD, René, performing arts. Chicoutimi, Que., 1961. Quebec pop singer began as boy soprano turned international pop star. *The René Simard Show* on CBC.

SIMCOE, John Graves, politics. Eng., 1752-1806. Upper Canada's first lieutenant-governor, 1792-96.

SIMPSON, Allan John, public service. Ottawa, Ont., 1939-98. Co-founder of Canadians with Disabilities and the Canadian Association of Independent Living Centres; created first Pan-Am Wheelchair Games and Canadian Wheelchair Sports Association. Lobbied to have disabled included in Charter of Rights and Freedoms.

SIMPSON, Sir George, business. Scot., 1787-1860. Financier; governor, Hudson's Bay Co., 1820-60.

SINCLAIR, Gordon Allan, media. Toronto, Ont., 1900-84. Journalist; feisty commentator; long-time *Front Page Challenge* panelist.

SITTLER, Darryl Glen, sports. St Jacob's, Ont., 1950. Hockey player; with Toronto Maple Leafs set NHL record 10 points in one game.

SKVORECKY, Josef, literary arts. Czech., 1924. Intellectual writer; novelist; critic. *The Engineer of Human Souls.*

SLADE, Bernard (b. Bernard Slade Newbound), performing arts. St Catharines, Ont., 1930. Sitcom pilot writer for *The Flying Nun; The Partridge Family; Bridget loves Bernie.* Wrote screenplay for *Same Time Next Year.*

SLOCUM, Joshua, literary arts. Wilmot Twp, NS, 1844-1909. Sailor; wrote classic *Sailing Alone Around the World.*

SMALLWOOD, Joseph Roberts (Joey), politics. Gambo, Nfld. 1900-92. Led Newfoundland into Confederation, 1949; premier 1949-72.

SMART, Elizabeth, literary arts. Ottawa, Ont., 1913-86. Novelist. *By Grand Central Station I Sat Down and Wept.*

SMELLIE, Elizabeth Lawrie, medicine. Port Arthur, Ont., 1884-1968. Nurse; builder, Victorian Order of Nurses.

SMITH, Alexis, performing arts. Penticton, BC, 1921-93. Film and television actress appeared in *Marcus Welby; Rhapsody in Blue; Of Human Bondage.*

SMITH, Donald Graham, sports. Edmonton, Alta., 1958. Swimmer; six gold medals, 1978 Commonwealth Games.

SMITH, Lois Irene, performing arts. Vancouver, BC, 1929. National Ballet's first prima ballerina.

SMITH, Michael, science. Eng., 1932. Biochemist; 1993 Nobel Prize winner in chemistry.

SMITH, Michael, sports. Kenora, Ont., 1967. Decathlete; silver medal, 1991 world championships.

SMITH, Stephen Richard (Steve), performing arts. Toronto, Ont., 1945. Comedian who stars in *Red Green Show,* also plays stand-up comedy.

SMITS, Sonja, performing arts. Sudbury, Ont., 1958. Star of CBC series *Street Legal;* CBC's *The Diviners.* Appeared in stage production of *Nothing Sacred.*

SMYTH, Constantine Falkland Cary (Conn), sports. Toronto, Ont., 1895-1980. Hockey executive; owner of Toronto Maple Leafs, 1930-61.

SNIDERMAN, Sam, business. Toronto, Ont., 1920. Retailer; established Sam the Record Man; 130 stores.

SNOW, Clarence Eugene "Hank", performing arts. Liverpool, NS, 1914. Country music singer. "I'm Movin' On."

SNOW, Michael James Aleck, visual arts. Toronto, Ont., 1929. Painter; sculptor; filmmaker; photographer.

SOBEY, Frank, business. Lyons Brook, NS, 1902-85. Industrialist; turned family grocery business into a major industry.

SOMERS, Harry Stewart, performing arts. Toronto, Ont., 1925-99. Composer of opera, orchestral, vocal and ballet music, acclaimed for operas *Louis Riel* and *The Fool;* commissioned by Yehudi Menuhin to write *Music for Solo Violin.*

SOPINKA, John, law/sports. Broderick, Sask., 1933-97. Supreme Court justice; former CFL player.

SOUSTER, Raymond Holmes, literary arts. Toronto, Ont., 1921. Poet; editor. "The Colour of the Times."

SOUTHAM, William, media. Montreal, Que., 1843-1932. Publisher; founded Southam newspaper dynasty.

SPICER, Keith, media. Toronto, Ont., 1934. Civil servant; chairman, Canadian Radio-Television and Telecommunications Commission.

SPOHR, Arnold, performing arts. Rhein, Sask., 1927. Ballet teacher; led Royal Winnipeg Ballet to world fame.

ST LAURENT, Louis Stephen, politics. Compton, Que., 1882-1973. Prime minister of Canada 1948-57; one of the architects of NATO.

STAEBLER, Edna, media. Kitchener, Ont., 1906. Journalist, cookbook writer, specializing in Mennonite cuisine. *Food That Really Schmecks; Whatever Happened to Maggie?*

STANFIELD, Robert Lorne, politics. Truro, NS, 1914. PC premier of NS, 1956-67; as federal PC leader, lost three elections to Trudeau.

STANLEY, George Frances Gillman, literary arts. Westmount, Que., 1907. Historian; proposed basic design of Maple Leaf flag in 1965.

STARYK, Steven, performing arts. Toronto, Ont., 1932. Violinist; virtuoso performer and teacher.

STEACIE, Edgar William Richard, science. Montreal, Que., 1900-62. Chemist; authority on free radical kinetics.

STEELE, Sir Samuel Benfield, military. Purbrook, Canada W, 1849-1919. NWMP and WWI officer.

STEFANSSON, Vilhjalmur, exploration and discovery. Arnes, Man., 1879-1962. Controversial Arctic explorer. Wrote *My Life With the Eskimo; The Friendly Arctic.*

STEINBERG, David (b. Duddy Steinberg), performing arts. St Boniface, Man., 1942. Stand-up comic; talk show host.

STEINBERG, Samuel, business. Hungary, 1905-78. Retailer; turned family grocery into supermarket empire.

STEPHENSON, Sir William Samuel, military. Winnipeg, Man., 1896-1989. Spy; "Intrepid," head of British counter-espionage during WWII; invented wirephotos.

STOJKO, Elvis, sports. Newmarket, Ont., 1972. Figure skater; silver medal, 1994 Olympics; world champion, 1995.

STOWE, Emily Howard, medicine. Norwich, UC, 1831-1903. Physician; first Canadian woman to practice medicine; had to obtain degree in US.

STRACHAN, John, religion. Scot., 1778-1867. Anglican bishop; strove to keep Upper Canada British.

STRATAS, Teresa (b. Anastasia Stratakis), performing arts. Toronto, Ont., 1938. Opera soprano; diva with strong stage presence.

STRATHCONA, Sir Donald Alexander Smith, first Baron, politics. Scot., 1820-1914. Politician, businessman, diplomat; drove the Last Spike.

STRATTON, Dorothy (b. Dorothy Ruth Hoogstratten), performing arts. Vancouver, BC, 1960-80. *Playboy* model; murdered by estranged husband. Her story was told in film *Star 80,* starring Mariel Hemingway.

STREIT, Marlene Stewart, sports. Cereal, Alta., 1934. Golfer; won many international titles. Canadian Athlete of the Year 1951, 1956.

STRONACH, Frank, business. Austria, 1954. Industrialist; chairman, Magna Intl; built machine company into global enterprise.

STRONG, Lori, sports. Toronto, Ont., 1972. Gymnast; winner of four gold medals at 1990 Commonwealth Games.

STRONG, Maurice Frederick, business. Oak Lake, Man., 1929. Headed Canadian International Development Agency; secretary-general of UN Conference in the Human Environment; head of Petro-Canada and Ontario Hydro; Canadian Ambassador to the UN.

SULLIVAN, Kevin Roderick, performing arts. Toronto, Ont., 1955. Producer; made *Anne of Green Gables;* launched popular *Road to Avonlea* TV series.

SUNG, Alfred (b. Sung Wang Moon), business. Toronto, Ont., 1948. Fashion designer; top designer of the 1980s.

SURIN, Bruny, sports. Haiti, 1967. Sprinter; world 100 m outdoor champion, 1993.

SUTHERLAND, Donald, performing arts. Saint John, NB, 1934. Versatile actor of Hollywood and Canadian films. *Murder by Decree; Don't Look Now.*

SUTHERLAND, Kiefer, performing arts. Eng., 1964. Actor. *Bay Boy, Flatliners, Stand By Me.*

SUZUKI, David Takayoshi, media/science. Vancouver, BC, 1936. Geneticist; promoter of environmental causes; columnist; host of CBC's *The Nature of Things.*

SWAN, Anna Haining, performing arts. Mill Brook, NS, 1846-88. Giantess; at 7 ft. 6 in., 352 lbs; was P.T. Barnum star.

SWAN, Susan, literary arts. Midland, Ont., 1945. Novelist. *Women of the World; The Last of the Golden Girls.*

SYDOR, Alison, sports. Vancouver, BC, 1966. Champion mountain biker; won 1996 Olympics silver award, three-time World MTB champion, 1994, 1995, 1996.

SZNAJDER, Andrew, sports. Toronto, Ont., 1968. Four-time Canadian singles tennis champ.

TALON, Jean-Baptiste, politics. France, 1625-94. Governor; as intendant, sought to diversify economy of New France with minerals, timber, farming.

TANNER, Elaine, sports. Vancouver, BC, 1951. Canada's best woman swimmer by age 15; world records in individual medley and butterfly; won silver and bronze medals in 1968 Olympics.

TASCHEREAU, Louis-Alexandre, politics. Quebec City, Que., 1867-1952. Liberal premier of Quebec, 1920-36; anti-nationalist leader.

TAUBE, Henry, science. Neudorf, Sask., 1915. Nobel Prize winner in 1983 in chemistry for research into electron transfer reactions, especially in metal complexes.

TAYLOR, Edward Plunket (E.P.), business. Ottawa, Ont., 1901-89. Industrialist; founded Argus Corp; notable horseman.

TAYLOR, Fred "Cyclone", sports. Tara, Ont., 1883-1979. Hockey's first great star.

TAYLOR, Kenneth Douglas, politics. Calgary, Alta., 1934. Diplomat; engineering freedom for six US hostages in Iran made him an instant celebrity in 1980.

TAYLOR, Richard Edward, science. Medicine Hat, Alta., 1929. Physicist; nuclear accelerator pioneer; 1990 Nobel Prize in physics.

TAYLOR, Ronald, medicine/sports. Toronto, Ont., 1937. Major league relief pitcher (1962-72) and sports medicine pioneer.

TECUMSEH, military. USA, 1768?-1813. Chief of Shawnee Indians, ally of Britain and Canada during the War of 1812.

TEMPLETON, Charles Bradley, media. Toronto, Ont., 1915. Author, broadcaster, playwright, evangelist, journalist; wrote controversial *Act of God*.

TENNANT, Veronica, performing arts. Eng., 1947. Prima ballerina, National Ballet of Canada.

TEWKSBURY, Mark, sports. Calgary, Alta., 1968. Swimmer; gold medal, 100 m backstroke, 1992 Olympics.

THERIAULT, Yves, literary arts. Quebec City, Que., 1915-83. Novelist, dramatist. *Contes pour un homme seul; Agaguk.*

THICKE, Alan (b. Alan Jeffery), performing arts. Kirkland Lake, Ont., 1948. Actor and talk show host; host of TV game show *Pictionary,* formerly host of talk show *Thicke of the Night.*

THIRSK, Robert Brent (Bob), science. New Westminster, BC, 1953. In 1996 flew a 17-day journey on space shuttle Columbia, conducting experiments on space sickness and researching other areas.

THOM, Linda, sports. Hamilton, Ont., 1943. Shooter; gold medal, women's sports pistol, 1984 Olympics.

THOM, Ronald James, visual arts. Penticton, BC, 1923. Architect; Shaw Festival Theatre, Toronto Zoo.

THOMAS, Dave, performing arts. Toronto, Ont., 1953. Comedic actor noted for roles on *SCTV,* portrayed with Rick Moranis one of the McKenzie Brothers in *Strange Brew.*

THOMPSON, David, exploration and discovery. Eng., 1770-1857. Charted Columbia River.

THOMPSON, Sir John Sparrow David, politics. Halifax, NS, 1845-94. Canada's fourth prime minister, 1892-94; largely responsible for establishment of the Criminal Code.

THOMSON, David Kenneth Roy, business. Toronto, Ont., 1923. Businessman; art collector; chairman, Thomson Newspapers Ltd.

THOMSON, Roy Herbert (R. H.), performing arts. Toronto, Ont., 1947. Stage and television actor. *Charlie Grant's War; Cry from the Heart; Ticket to Heaven.*

THOMSON, Roy (Lord Thomson of Fleet), media. Toronto, Ont., 1894-1976. Publisher; owned major newspapers in English-speaking world.

THOMSON, Thomas John (Tom), visual arts. Claremont, Ont., 1877-1917. Influential painter. *Autumn Foliage.*

THORBURN, Clifford Charles Devlin, sports. Victoria, BC, 1948. Snooker player; world champion, 1980.

TILLY, Jennifer, performing arts. USA, 1959. Actress, appeared in Woody Allen's *Bullets Over Broadway.*

TILLY, Margaret (Meg), performing arts. Texada Is., BC, 1960. Actress whose winsome face appeared in *The Body Snatchers; The Big Chill.*

TIMMINS, Noah Anthony, business. Mattawa, Ont., 1867-1936. Mining operator; developed N America's largest gold mine; town named for him.

TOBIN, Brian Vincent, politics. Stephenville, Nfld, 1954. Began "cod war" with Spain while serving as Liberal Minister of Fisheries and Oceans, 1995; premier of Nfld, 1996-.

TORGOV, Morley Edward, literary arts. Sault Ste Marie, Ont., 1927. Story writer. *The Abramsky Variations; The Outside Chance of Maximilian Glick.*

TORY, Henry Marshall, educator. Pt Shoreham, NS, 1864-1947. University founder: UBC, Carleton.

TOTH, Jerry (Jaroslav), performing arts. Windsor, Ont., 1929-99. Saxophonist, clarinetist, arranger, conductor and producer, Toth was responsible for the *Hockey Night in Canada* theme on CBC, as well as many other network productions: *Wayne and Shuster; Parade.* Member of Boss Brass ensemble for 20 years.

TOWN, Harold Barling, visual arts. Toronto, Ont., 1924-90. Influential painter, sculptor, writer.

TOWNSEND, Eleanor, performing arts. Goderich, Ont., 1944-98. Fiddling champion who was first woman to win North American Fiddle Championship at Shelburne, Ont.; member of both Canada's and US Fiddling Halls of Fame.

TRACY, Paul, sports. Scarborough, Ont., 1968. Auto racer; winner of three Indy titles in 1993.

TRAILL, Catharine Parr, literary arts. Eng., 1802-99. Writer. *The Backwoods of Canada.*

TREBEK, Alex, performing arts. Sudbury, Ont., 1940. TV host of *Jeopardy* quiz show.

TREMBLAY, Jean-Claude, sports. Bagotville, Ont., 1939-94. Star defenceman for Montreal Canadiens in 1960s.

TREMBLAY, Michel, literary arts. Montreal, Que., 1942. Playwright; novelist. *Le Vrai Monde.*

TROIANO, Dominic, performing arts. Italy, 1946. Rock guitarist collabortated with the Mandalas, The Guess Who; wrote for CBC TV. *Night Heat; Diamonds.*

TRUDEAU, Pierre Elliott, politics. Montreal, Que., 1919. Prime minister of Canada 1968-79, 1980-84.

TRYGGVASON, Bjarni V., science. Iceland, 1945. Astronaut who flew aboard the Discovery in 1997 for 11 days to test Canadian-made equipment at zero gravity.

TSUI, Dr Lap-Chee, science. China, 1950. Geneticist; identified gene carrying cystic fibrosis.

TUPPER, Sir Charles, politics. Amherst, NS, 1821-1915. Appointed as Canada's sixth prime minister, 1896.

TURCOTTE, Ron, sports. Drummond, NB, 1941. Jockey; long-time leading jockey rode Secretariat to Triple Crown (1973).

TURNBULL, Wallace, invention. Saint John, NB, 1870-1954. Inventor of variable pitch propeller in 1927, contributed to improved flying safety.

TURNER, John Napier, politics. Eng., 1929. Prime minister of Canada June 1984-July 1984.

TUROFSKY, Riki, performing arts. Toronto, Ont., 1944. Debuted in 1972 at New York City Opera in *Carmen;* host of CBC's *Summer Festival* in 1978; *Festival Today* in 1984.

TWAIN, Shania (b. Eileen Regina Edwards), performing arts. Windsor, Ont., 1965. Winner of Country Music of the Year Award (US) 1995. *The Woman in Me.*

TYRRELL, Joseph Burr, science. Weston, Canada W, 1858-1957. Geologist; discovered S Alberta dinosaur beds.

TYSON, Ian Dawson, performing arts. Victoria, BC, 1933. Singer/songwriter; half of Ian and Sylvia. "Four Strong Winds."

TYSON, Sylvia Fricker, performing arts. Chatham, Ont., 1940. Singer; half of Ian and Sylvia. "You Were on My Mind."

U

UNDERHILL, Barbara Ann, sports. Pembroke, Ont., 1963. Figure skater; world pairs champion (with Paul Martini), 1984.

UNGER, James, visual arts. Eng., 1937. Cartoonist; creator of popular "Herman" cartoon strip.

V

VAILLANCOURT, Armand J. R., visual arts. Black L., Que., 1932. Sculpts in aid of social activism.

VALDY, (b. Vladimir Horsdal), performing arts. Ottawa, Ont., 1946. Country-folk singer-songwriter, guitarist. "Rock and Roll Song"; *Valdy; Notes from Places.*

VALLIERES, Pierre, politics. Montreal, Que., 1938-98. Journalist and former leader of Front de Libération de Québec (FLQ); author of *White Niggers of America,* which compared Québécois with American Blacks; fell out with FLQ after murder of labour minister Pierre Laporte.

VAN HERK, Aritha, literary arts. Wetaskiwin, Alta, 1954. Novelist. *Judith; No Fixed Address; Places Far from Ellesmere.*

VAN HORNE, Sir William Cornelius, business. USA, 1843-1915. Driving force behind Canadian Pacific Railroad.

VAN VOGT, Alfred Elton (A.E.), literary arts. Winnipeg, Man., 1912. Writer; science fiction standout. *Slan.*

VANCOUVER, George, exploration and discovery. Eng., 1757-98. Navigator; surveyor of BC coastline.

VANDER ZALM, William Nick, politics. Holland, 1934. Social Credit premier of BC 1986-91, proponent of free trade.

VANDERBURG, Helen, sports. Calgary, Alta., 1959. Synchronized swimmer; dominated sport in 1979.

VANDERHAEGHE, Guy Clarence, literary arts. Esterhazy, Sask., 1951. Novelist, won 1982 Governor General's Award for *Man Descending. My Present Age; Homesick.*

VANIER, Georges Phileas, politics. Montreal, Que., 1888-1967. Governor general, 1959-67.

VANIER, Jean, public service. Switz., 1928. Spiritual leader; man of great moral conviction established homes for handicapped around the world.

VANNELLI, Gino, performing arts. Montreal, Que., 1954. Pop singer. *Brother to Brother; Nightwalker.*

VARLEY, Frederick Horsman, visual arts. Eng., 1881-1969. Member, Group of Seven. *Vera.*

VEREGIN, Peter Vasilevich, religion. Russia, 1859-1924. Charismatic Doukhobor leader.

VERNON, John, performing arts. Montreal, Que., 1931. TV and film actor. *Wojeck.*

VEZINA, Georges, sports. Chicoutimi, Que., 1887-1926. Hockey goalie; NHL trophy named for him.

VICKERS, Jonathan Stewart (Jon), performing arts. Prince Albert, Sask., 1926. Tenor; operatic star; Wagner specialist.

VICKREY, William, economics. Victoria, BC, 1914-96. Winner of Nobel Prize in economics in 1996. Worked with United Nations on tax issues in African countries.

VIGNEAULT, Gilles, performing arts. Natashquan, Que., 1928. Beloved poet and cultural icon of Québécois. "Mon Pays."

VILLENEUVE, Gilles, sports. St-Jean, Que., 1950-82. Auto racer; won six Grand Prix titles.

VILLENEUVE, Jacques, sports. St-Jean, Que., 1971. Winner of Indianapolis 500 in 1995; Lou Marsh trophy for Canadian Athlete of the Year, 1995.

VINCENT, Anthony Gustave, public service. Eng., 1939. Canadian ambassador to Peru when, in December 1996, Tupac Amaru guerrillas stormed Japanese ambassador's residence in Lima, taking 575 hostages. Vincent attempted negotiations with leader Nestor Cerpa; the remaining hostages were freed when troops stormed residence in April 1997.

W

WAGNER, Barbara Aileen, sports. Toronto, Ont., 1938. Figure skater; with Robert Paul, won four pairs titles and 1960 Olympic gold.

WALDO, Carolyn, sports. Montreal, Que., 1964. Synchronized swimmer; two gold medals, 1988 Olympics.

WALKER, Larry, sports. Maple Ridge, BC, 1966. Baseball player; star outfielder for Montreal Expos, Colorado Rockies. NL MVP, 1997. NL batting champion, 1998.

WALLIN, Pamela, media. Wadena, Sask., 1953. Longtime CBC journalist and independent newsmagazine host. *Pamela Wallin.*

WALLS, Earl, sports. Puce, Ont., 1928-96. Canadian heavyweight boxing champion, 1952.

WALTERS, Angus, exploration and discovery. Lunenburg, NS, 1882-1968. *Bluenose* captain; skipper of celebrated schooner.

WARD, Maxwell William, business. Edmonton, Alta., 1921. Capitalist; charter flights pioneer; founded Wardair.

WARNER, Jack L., performing arts. London, Ont., 1892-1978. Head of production at Warner Brothers in 1927; launched talkies with *The Jazz Singer,* starring Al Jolson.

WATKINS, Melville Henry, business. Toronto, Ont., 1932. Economist; founded left-wing Waffle Movement.

WATSON, Homer Ransford, visual arts. Doon, Canada W, 1855-1936. Landscape painter. *The Pioneer Mill.*

WATSON, John, literary arts. Scot., 1847-1939. Philosopher; metaphysician. "Kant and His English Critics."

WATSON, Ken, sports. Minnedosa, Man., 1904-86. Curler; three-time Brier winner; curling teacher.

WATSON, Patrick, media. Toronto, Ont., 1929. TV host; actor; writer; producer.

WATSON, Sheila Doherty, literary arts. New Westminster, BC, 1909-98. Author of *Double Hook,* considered to be the first modern Canadian novel; also *Deep Hollow Creek.* Described experiences as schoolteacher in central BC in the 1930s.

WATSON, William "Whipper Billy", sports. Toronto, Ont., 1917-1990. Wrestler; twice world pro champion.

WAXMAN, Albert Samuel (Al), performing arts. Toronto, Ont., 1935. Movie and TV performer. *King of Kensington.*

WAYNE, John Louis (Johnny), performing arts. Toronto, Ont., 1918-90. Comedian; wilder half of Wayne and Shuster comedy team.

WEBSTER, Donald Colin "Ben", invention. Montreal, Que., 1928-97. Founder of high-tech Helix Investments (Canada), credited with introduction of the fastening material Velcro.

WEBSTER, John Edgar (Jack), media. Scot., 1918-99. Broadcaster; journalist on Vancouver *Sun.* Noted for outspoken opinions.

WEINZWEIG, John Jacob, performing arts. Toronto, Ont., 1913. Influential composer using 12-tone technique. "Red Ear of Corn."

WEIR, Robert Stanley, literary arts. Hamilton, Ont., 1856-1926. Jurist; author; wrote English lyrics of National Anthem, "O Canada."

WELLS, Clyde Kirby, politics. Buchans Junction, Nfld, 1937. Newfoundland premier 1989-96.

WELSH, Kenneth, politics. Edmonton, Alta, 1942. Versatile actor noted for roles in *Empire Inc.; And Then You Die; The Tar Sands.*

WESTON, Hilary M., politics. Ire., 1942. Appointed lieutenant governor of Ontario in 1997, wife of grocery magnate Galen Weston.

WESTON, W. Galen Gordon, business. Eng., 1940. Industrialist; Canadian head for George Weston Ltd.

WESTON, Willard Garfield, business. Toronto, Ont., 1893-1978. Industrialist; pioneer in food retailing.

WHEELER, Anne, visual arts. Edmonton, Alta., 1946. Filmmaker. *A Change of Heart; Bye Bye Blues.*

WHEELER, Lucille, sports. Montreal, Que., 1935. Skier; first N American to win world title, downhill and slalom (1958).

WHITE, Bob, business. Ire., 1935. Labour leader; first head of Canadian Auto Workers' Union.

WHITTON, Charlotte Elizabeth, politics. Renfrew, Ont., 1896-1975. Reformer; outspoken Ottawa mayor.

WIEBE, Rudy Henry, literary arts. Speedwell, Sask., 1934. Mennonite novelist. *Temptations of Big Bear.*

WILLAN, James Healey, performing arts. Eng., 1880-1968. Classical composer and musician. "O Lord, Our Governour" sung at Queen Elizabeth II's coronation in Westminster Abbey.

WILLIAMS, Daffyd (Dave) Rhys, science. Saskatoon, Sask., 1954. Astronaut, flew on 16-day Spacelab flight aboard Space Shuttle Columbia in 1998; coordinator of Canadian Astronaut Program Space Unit Life Simulation (CAPSULS) project.

WILLIAMS, Percy Alfred, sports. Vancouver, BC, 1908-82. Sprinter; Olympic gold in 100 m and 200 m, 1928.

WILSON, Bertha, law. Scot., 1923. First woman named to Supreme Court of Canada (1982).

WILSON, Cairine Reay, politics. Montreal, Que., 1885-1962. Canada's first woman senator, 1930 (Lib.).

WILSON, Sir Daniel, educator. Scot., 1816-92. Darwinian opposed idea of natural selection; energetic administrator, author, scholar.

WILSON, Ethel Davis, literary arts. S Africa, 1888-1980. BC novelist. *Swamp Angel.*

WILSON, John Tuzo, science. Ottawa, Ont., 1908-93. Geophysicist; pioneered plate tectonics theory.

WILSON, Michael Holcombe, politics. Toronto, Ont., 1937. PC minister of industry, science and technology; international trade; finance minister (1984-91).

WISEMAN, Adele, literary arts. Winnipeg, Man., 1928-92. Novelist, poet. *The Sacrifice; Crackpot.*

WISEMAN, Joseph, performing arts. Montreal, Que., 1918. Actor; title role in James Bond movie, *Dr. No.*

WOLFE, James, military. Eng., 1727-59. Soldier; took Quebec for British; died on Plains of Abraham.

WONG, Celia Jan, media. Montreal, Que., 1952. *Globe and Mail* correspondant in China, 1988-94. *Red China Blues.*

WOOD, Elizabeth Wyn, visual arts. Orillia, Ont., 1903-66. Sculptor; fountains and panels for Rainbow Bridge Gardens, monument to King George VI, Niagara Falls.

WOODCOCK, George, literary arts. Winnipeg, Man., 1912-95. Historian; journalist; activist. *Anarchism.*

WOODSWORTH, James Shaver, politics. Etobicoke, Ont., 1874-1942. Founder Cooperative Commonwealth Federation (later NDP).

WRAY, Fay, performing arts. Medicine Hat, Alta., 1910. Famous as screaming heroine in *King Kong.*

WRIGHT, Eric Stanley, literary arts. Eng., 1929. Mystery writer. *A Senstive Case; Final Cut.*

WRIGHT, Michelle, performing arts. Merlin, Ont., 1960. Sultry country songstress. "Now and Then."

YANOVSKY, Zal, performing arts. Toronto, Ont., 1944. Singer; member of folk-rock group, Lovin' Spoonful.

YOST, Elwy, performing arts. Toronto, Ont., 1925. Affable and knowledgeable host of TVOntario's popular *Saturday Night at the Movies.*

YOUNG, Neil Percival, performing arts. Toronto, Ont., 1945. Singer/songwriter; seminal rocker. *After the Gold Rush.*

YOUNG, Scott Alexander, literary arts. Glenboro, Man., 1918. Novelist, short story writer, children's writer, biographer. *The Boys of Saturday Night; Power Play.*

YOUVILLE, Marie Marguerite d', religion. Varennes, Que., 1701-71. First Canadian to be beatified by Pope; founded Grey Nuns.

ZEIDLER, Eberhard Heinrich, visual arts. Germany, 1936. Award-winning architect of Toronto Eaton Centre, Toronto's Queen's Quay Terminal, Ontario Place.

ZNAIMER, Moses, business. Toronto, Ont., 1942. TV executive; founder of CITY-TV, Much Music.

ZOLF, Larry, media. Winnipeg, Man., 1934. Broadcaster; journalist; writer. CBC's *Fifth Estate.*

ZUCKERMAN, Mortimer, business. Montreal, Que., 1937. Financier; developer, magazine publisher.

BASEBALL

American League Final Standings, 1999

Eastern Division					Central Division					Western Division				
Club	W	L	Pct	GB	Club	W	L	Pct	GB	Club	W	L	Pct	GB
New York	98	64	.605	-	Cleveland	97	65	.599	-	Texas	95	67	.586	-
Boston*	94	68	.580	4	Chicago	75	86	.466	21	Oakland	87	75	.537	8
Toronto	84	78	.518	14	Detroit	69	92	.429	27	Seattle	79	83	.488	16
Baltimore	78	84	.481	20	Kansas City	64	97	.398	32	Anaheim	70	92	.432	25
Tampa Bay	69	93	.426	29	Minnesota	63	97	.394	33					

Source: *Canadian Press*   *-won wild-card berth

American League Leaders, 1999

Batting

Batting Average		On-Base Pct		Runs	
Nomar Garciaparra, Bos	.357	Edgar Martinez, Sea	.447	Roberto Alomar, Cle	138
Derek Jeter, NYY	.349	Manny Ramirez, Cle	.442	**Shawn Green, Tor**	**134**
Bernie Williams, NYY	.342	Derek Jeter, NYY	.438	Derek Jeter, NYY	134
Edgar Martinez, Sea	.337	Bernie Williams, NYY	.435	Manny Ramirez, Cle	131
Manny Ramirez, Cle	.333	**Tony Fernandez, Tor**	**.427**	Ken Griffey Jr., Sea	123

Hits		Runs Batted In		Doubles	
Derek Jeter, NYY	219	Manny Ramirez, Cle	165	**Shawn Green, Tor**	**45**
B.J. Surhoff, Bal	207	Rafael Palmeiro, Tex	148	Jermaine Dye, KC	44
Bernie Williams, NYY	202	**Carlos Delgado, Tor**	**134**	Mike Sweeney, KC	44
Randy Velarde, Oak	200	Ken Griffey Jr., Sea	134	Nomar Garciaparra, Bos	42
Ivan Rodriguez, Tex	199	Juan Gonzalez, Tex	128	**Tony Fernandez, Tor**	**41**

Triples		Home Runs		Slugging Average	
Jose Offerman, Bos	11	Ken Griffey Jr., Sea	48	Manny Ramirez, Cle	.663
Johnny Damon, KC	9	Rafael Palmeiro, Tex	47	Rafael Palmeiro, Tex	.630
Carlos Febles, KC	9	**Carlos Delgado, Tor**	**44**	Nomar Garciaparra, Bos	.603
Derek Jeter, NYY	9	Manny Ramirez, Cle	44	Juan Gonzalez, Tex	.601
Four tied with four		**Shawn Green, Tor**	**42**	**Shawn Green, Tor**	**.588**

Stolen Bases		Walks		Total Bases	
Brian Hunter, Sea	44	Jim Thome, Cle	127	Shawn Green, Tor	361
Omar Vizquel, Cle	42	Jason Giambi, Oak	105	Rafael Palmeiro, Tex	356
Tom Goodwin, Tex	39	Albert Belle, Bal	101	Ken Griffey Jr., Sea	349
Shannon Stewart, Tor	**37**	John Jaha, Oak	101	Derek Jeter, NYY	346
Roberto Alomar, Cle	37	Bernie Williams, NYY	100	Manny Ramirez, Cle	346 ▶

▶

Pitching

Wins

					Earned Run Average	
Pedro Martinez, Bos	23-4	Orlando Hernandez, NYY	17-9		Pedro Martinez, Bos	2.07
Bartolo Colon, Cle	18-5	**David Wells, Tor**	**17-10**		David Cone, NYY	3.44
Mike Mussina, Bal	18-7	Charles Nagy, Cle	17-11		Mike Mussina, Bal	3.50
Aaron Sele, Tex	18-9	Kevin Appier, Oak	16-14		Brad Radke, Min	3.75
Freddy Garcia, Sea	17-8				Jose Rosado, KC	3.85

Strikeouts / Saves / Shutouts

Strikeouts		Saves		Shutouts	
Pedro Martinez, Bos	313	Mariano Rivera, NYY	45	Scott Erickson, Bal	3
Chuck Finley, Ana	200	Roberto Hernandez, T.B.	43	Eric Milton, Min	2
Aaron Sele, Tex	186	John Wetteland, Tex	43	Brian Moehler, Det	2
Cone, NY	177	Mike Jackson, Cle	39	Aaron Sele, Tex	2
Dave Burba, Cle	174	Jose Mesa, Sea	33	Bobby Witt, T.B.	2

Innings Pitched / Games / Complete Games

Innings Pitched		Games		Complete Games	
David Wells, Tor	**231.2**	Buddy Groom, Oak	76	**David Wells, Tor**	**7**
Scott Erickson, Bal	230.1	Bob Wells, Min	76	Scott Erickson, Bal	6
Jamie Moyer, Sea	228.0	Mike Trombley, Min	75	Sidney Ponson, Bal	6
Dave Burba, Clev	220.0	**Graeme Lloyd, Tor**	**74**	Pedro Martinez, Bos	5
Rick Helling, Tex	219.1	Derek Lowe, Bos	74	Jose Rosado, KC	5

Source: *Canadian Press*

National League Final Standings, 1999

Eastern Division					Central Division					Western Division				
Club	W	L	Pct	GB	Club	W	L	Pct	GB	Club	W	L	Pct	GB
Atlanta	103	59	.63	-	Houston	97	65	.599	-	Arizona	100	62	.617	-
New York*	97	66	.595	6	Cincinnati	96	67	.589	1	San Francisco	86	76	.531	14
Philadelphia	77	85	.475	26	Pittsburgh	78	83	.484	18	Los Angeles	77	85	.475	23
Montreal	68	94	.420	35	St. Louis	75	86	.466	21	San Diego	74	88	.457	26
Florida	64	98	.395	39	Milwaukee	74	87	.460	22	Colorado	72	90	.444	28
					Chicago	67	95	.414	30					

Source: *Canadian Press*   *-won wild-card berth. New York beat Cincinnati 5-0 in a playoff for the wild-card berth

National League Leaders, 1999

Batting

Batting Average		On-Base Pct		Runs	
Larry Walker, Col	.379	Larry Walker, Col	.458	Jeff Bagwell, Hou	143
Luis Gonzalez, Ari	.336	Jeff Bagwell, Hou	.454	Jay Bell, Ari	132
Bobby Abreu, Phi	.335	Bobby Abreu, Phi	.446	Edgardo Alfonzo, NY	123
Sean Casey, Cin,	.332	Chipper Jones, Atl	.441	Craig Biggio, Hou	123
Jeff Cirillo, Mil	.326	John Olerud, NY	.427	Bobby Abreu, Phi	118

▶

Hits		Runs Batted In		Doubles	
Luis Gonzalez, Ari	206	Mark McGwire, StL	147	Craig Biggio, Hou	56
Doug Glanville, Phi	204	Matt Williams, Ari.	142	Luis Gonzalez, Ari.	45
Jeff Cirillo, Mil	198	Sammy Sosa, Chi	141	Jose Vidro, Mtl	45
Sean Casey, Cin	197	Dante Bichette, Col	133	Mark Grace, Chi	44
Vladimir Guerrero, Mtl	**193**	**Vladimir Guerrero, Mtl**	**131**	Geoff Jenkins, Mil	43

Triples		Home Runs		Slugging Average	
Bobby Abreu, Phi	11	Mark McGwire, StL	65	Larry Walker, Col	.710
Neifi Perez, Col	11	Sammy Sosa, Chi	63	Mark McGwire, StL	.697
Steve Finley, Ari	10	Chipper Jones, Atl	45	Sammy Sosa, Chi	.635
Tony Womack, Ari	10	Greg Vaughn, Cin	45	Chipper Jones, Atl	.633
Mark Kotsay, Fla	9	**Vladimir Guerrero, Mtl**	**42**	Brian Giles, Pit	.614

Stolen Bases		Walks		Total Bases	
Tony Womack, Ari	72	Jeff Bagwell, Hou	149	Sammy Sosa, Chi	397
Roger Cedeno, NY	66	Mark McGwire, StL	133	**Vladimir Guerrero, Mtl**	**366**
Eric Young, LA	51	Chipper Jones, Atl	126	Mark McGwire, StL	363
Luis Castillo, Fla	50	John Olerud, NY	125	Chipper Jones, Atl	359
Pokey Reese, Cin	38	Bobby Abreu, Phi	109	Chad Helton, Col	339

Pitching

Wins-Loss Record				Earned Run Average	
Mike Hampton, Hou	22-4	Kevin Brown, LA	18-9	Randy Johnson, Ari	2.48
Jose Lima, Hou	21-10	Russ Ortiz, SF	18-9	Kevin Millwood, Atl	2.68
Greg Maddux, Atl	19-9	Randy Johnson, Ari	17-9	Mike Hampton, Hou	2.90
Kent Bottenfield, StL	18-7	Pedro Astacio, Col	17-11	Kevin Brown, LA	3.00
Kevin Millwood, Atl	18-7			John Smoltz, Atl	3.19

Strikeouts		Saves		Shutouts	
Randy Johnson, Ari	364	Ugueth Urbina, Mtl	41	Andy Ashby, SD	3
Kevin Brown, LA	221	Tervor Hoffman, SD	40	Mike Hampton, Hou	2
Pedro Astacio, Col	210	Billy Wagner, Hou	39	Pete Harnisch, Cin	2
Kevin Millwood, Atl	205	John Rocker, Atl	38	Jose Jimenez, StL	2
Shane Reynolds, Hou	197	Rob Nen, SF	37	Randy Johnson, Ari	2

Innings Pitched		Games		Complete Games	
Randy Johnson, Ari	271.2	**Steve Kline, Mtl**	**82**	Randy Johnson, Ari	12
Kevin Brown, LA	252.1	Turk Wendell, NY	80	Curt Schilling, Phi	8
Jose Lima, Hou	246.1	Scott Sullivan, Cin	79	Pedro Astacio, Col	7
Mike Hampton, Hou	239.0	**Anthony Telford, Mtl**	**79**	Kevin Brown, LA	5
Tom Glavine, Atl	234.0	Armando Benitez, NY	77	Four tied with four	

Source: *Canadian Press*

Directory of Selected Baseball Organizations in Canada

Canadian	*Major League*	*Montreal Expos*	*Toronto Blue Jays*
Federation of	*Baseball*	*Baseball Club*	*The Skydome*
Amateur Baseball	*350 Park Ave*	*PO Box 500, Station M*	*300 The Esplanade*
1600 James	*New York, NY 10022*	*Montreal, Que*	*West, Suite 3200*
Naismith Dr.	*Tel: (212)339-7800*	*H1V 3P2*	*Toronto, Ont.*
Gloucester, Ont.	*www.majorleague*	*Tel: (514)253-3434*	*M5V 3B3*
K1B 5N4	*baseball.com*	*Fax: (514)253-8282*	*Tel: (416)341-1000*
Tel: (613)748-5606		*www.montrealexpos.*	*www.bluejays.ca*
Fax: (613(748-5706		*com*	

Major League Pennant Winners, 1901–98

National League

Year	Winner	Won	Lost	Pct.
1901	Pittsburgh	90	49	.647
1902	Pittsburgh	103	36	.741
1903	Pittsburgh	91	49	.650
1904	New York	106	47	.693
1905	New York	105	48	.686
1906	Chicago	116	36	.763
1907	Chicago	107	45	.704
1908	Chicago	99	55	.643
1909	Pittsburgh	110	42	.724
1910	Chicago	104	50	.675
1911	New York	99	54	.647
1912	New York	103	48	.682
1913	New York	101	51	.664
1914	Boston	94	59	.614
1915	Philadelphia	90	62	.592
1916	Brooklyn	94	60	.610
1917	New York	98	56	.636
1918	Chicago	84	45	.651
1919	Cincinnati	96	44	.686
1920	Brooklyn	93	61	.604
1921	New York	94	59	.614
1922	New York	93	61	.604
1923	New York	95	58	.621
1924	New York	93	60	.608
1925	Pittsburgh	95	58	.621
1926	St. Louis	89	65	.578
1927	Pittsburgh	94	60	.610
1928	St. Louis	95	59	.617
1929	Chicago	98	54	.645
1930	St. Louis	92	62	.597
1931	St. Louis	101	53	.656
1932	Chicago	90	64	.584
1933	New York	91	61	.599
1934	St. Louis	95	58	.621
1935	Chicago	100	54	.649
1936	New York	92	62	.597
1937	New York	95	57	.625
1938	Chicago	89	63	.586
1939	Cincinnati	97	57	.630
1940	Cincinnati	100	53	.654
1941	Brooklyn	100	54	.649
1942	St. Louis	106	48	.688
1943	St. Louis	105	49	.682
1944	St. Louis	105	49	.682
1945	Chicago	98	56	.636
1946	St. Louis	98	58	.628
1947	Brooklyn	94	60	.610

American League

Year	Winner	Won	Lost	Pct.
1901	Chicago	83	53	.610
1902	Philadelphia	83	53	.610
1903	Boston	91	47	.659
1904	Boston	95	59	.617
1905	Philadelphia	92	56	.622
1906	Chicago	93	58	.616
1907	Detroit	92	58	.613
1908	Detroit	90	63	.588
1909	Detroit	98	54	.645
1910	Philadelphia	102	48	.680
1911	Philadelphia	101	50	.669
1912	Boston	105	47	.691
1913	Philadelphia	96	57	.627
1914	Philadelphia	99	53	.651
1915	Boston	101	50	.669
1916	Boston	91	63	.591
1917	Chicago	100	54	.649
1918	Boston	75	51	.595
1919	Chicago	88	52	.629
1920	Cleveland	98	56	.636
1921	New York	98	55	.641
1922	New York	94	60	.610
1923	New York	98	54	.645
1924	Washington	92	62	.597
1925	Washington	96	55	.636
1926	New York	91	63	.591
1927	New York	110	44	.714
1928	New York	101	53	.656
1929	Philadelphia	104	46	.693
1930	Philadelphia	102	52	.662
1931	Philadelphia	107	45	.704
1932	New York	107	47	.695
1933	Washington	99	53	.651
1934	Detroit	101	53	.656
1935	Detroit	93	58	.616
1936	New York	102	51	.667
1937	New York	102	52	.662
1938	New York	99	53	.651
1939	New York	106	45	.702
1940	Detroit	90	64	.584
1941	New York	101	53	.656
1942	New York	103	51	.669
1943	New York	98	56	.636
1944	St. Louis	89	65	.578
1945	Detroit	88	65	.575
1946	Boston	104	50	.675
1947	New York	97	57	.630

National League					American League			
Year	**Winner**	**Won**	**Lost**	**Pct.**	**Year**	**Winner**	**Won**	**Lost**	**Pct.**
1948	Boston	91	62	.595	**1948**	Cleveland	97	58	.626
1949	Brooklyn	97	57	.630	**1949**	New York	97	57	.630
1950	Philadelphia	91	63	.591	**1950**	New York	98	56	.636
1951	New York	98	59	.624	**1951**	New York	98	56	.636
1952	Brooklyn	96	57	.627	**1952**	New York	95	59	.617
1953	Brooklyn	105	49	.682	**1953**	New York	99	52	.656
1954	New York	97	57	.630	**1954**	Cleveland	111	43	.721
1955	Brooklyn	98	55	.641	**1955**	New York	96	58	.623
1956	Brooklyn	93	61	.604	**1956**	New York	97	57	.630
1957	Milwaukee	95	59	.617	**1957**	New York	98	56	.636
1958	Milwaukee	92	62	.597	**1958**	New York	92	62	.597
1959	Los Angeles	88	68	.564	**1959**	Chicago	94	60	.610
1960	Pittsburgh	95	59	.617	**1960**	New York	97	57	.630
1961	Cincinnati	93	61	.604	**1961**	New York	109	53	.673
1962	San Francisco	103	62	.624	**1962**	New York	96	66	.593
1963	Los Angeles	99	63	.611	**1963**	New York	104	57	.646
1964	St. Louis	93	69	.574	**1964**	New York	99	63	.611
1965	Los Angeles	97	65	.599	**1965**	Minnesota	102	60	.630
1966	Los Angeles	95	67	.586	**1966**	Baltimore	97	63	.606
1967	St. Louis	101	60	.627	**1967**	Boston	92	70	.568
1968	St. Louis	97	65	.599	**1968**	Detroit	103	59	.636
1969	New York	100	62	.617	**1969**	Baltimore	109	53	.673
1970	Cincinnati	102	60	.630	**1970**	Baltimore	108	54	.667
1971	Pittsburgh	97	65	.599	**1971**	Baltimore	101	57	.639
1972	Cincinnati	95	59	.617	**1972**	Oakland	93	62	.600
1973	New York	82	79	.509	**1973**	Oakland	94	68	.580
1974	Los Angeles	102	60	.630	**1974**	Oakland	90	72	.556
1975	Cincinnati	108	54	.667	**1975**	Boston	95	65	.594
1976	Cincinnati	102	60	.630	**1976**	New York	97	62	.610
1977	Los Angeles	98	64	.605	**1977**	New York	100	62	.617
1978	Los Angeles	95	67	.586	**1978**	New York	100	63	.613
1979	Pittsburgh	98	64	.605	**1979**	Baltimore	102	57	.642
1980	Philadelphia	91	71	.562	**1980**	Kansas City	97	65	.599
1981	Los Angeles	63	47	.573	**1981**	New York	59	48	.551
1982	St. Louis	92	70	.568	**1982**	Milwaukee	95	67	.586
1983	Philadelphia	90	72	.556	**1983**	Baltimore	98	64	.605
1984	San Diego	92	70	.568	**1984**	Detroit	104	58	.642
1985	St. Louis	101	61	.623	**1985**	Kansas City	91	71	.562
1986	New York	108	54	.667	**1986**	Boston	95	66	.590
1987	St. Louis	95	67	.586	**1987**	Minnesota	85	77	.525
1988	Los Angeles	94	67	.584	**1988**	Oakland	104	58	.642
1989	San Francisco	92	70	.568	**1989**	Oakland	99	63	.611
1990	Cincinnati	91	71	.562	**1990**	Oakland	103	59	.636
1991	Atlanta	94	68	.580	**1991**	Minnesota	95	67	.586
1992	Atlanta	98	64	.605	**1992**	**Toronto**	**96**	**66**	**.593**
1993	Philadelphia	97	65	.599	**1993**	**Toronto**	**95**	**67**	**.586**
***1994**	no winner				***1994**	no winner			
1995	Atlanta	90	54	.625	**1995**	Cleveland	100	44	.694
1996	Atlanta.	96	66	.593	**1996**	New York.	92	70	.569
1997	Florida.	92	70	.568	**1997**	Cleveland	86	75	.534
1998	San Diego	98	64	.605	**1998**	New York.	114	48	.704

* Players strike Aug. 12, 1994; owners suspended season, Sept. 14, 1994

World Series Results, 1903–98

Year	Champion	Final Opponent	Series Result
1903	Boston Red Sox, AL	Pittsburgh Pirates, NL	5-3
1904	No series		
1905	New York Giants, NL	Philadelphia Athletics, AL	4-1
1906	Chicago White Sox, AL	Chicago Cubs, NL	4-2
1907	Chicago Cubs, NL	Detroit Tigers, AL	4-0; 1 tie
1908	Chicago Cubs, NL	Detroit Tigers, AL	4-1
1909	Pittsburgh Pirates, NL	Detroit Tigers, AL	4-3
1910	Philadelphia Athletics, AL	Chicago Cubs, NL	4-1
1911	Philadelphia Athletics, AL	New York Giants, NL	4-2
1912	Boston Red Sox, AL	New York Giants, NL	4-3; 1 tie
1913	Philadelphia Athletics, AL	New York Giants, NL	4-1
1914	Boston Braves, NL	Philadelphia Athletics, AL	4-0
1915	Boston Red Sox, AL	Philadelphia Phillies, NL	4-1
1916	Boston Red Sox, AL	Brooklyn Dodgers, NL	4-1
1917	Chicago White Sox, AL	New York Giants, NL	4-2
1918	Boston Red Sox, AL	Chicago Cubs, NL	4-2
1919	Cincinnati Reds, NL	Chicago White Sox, AL	5-3
1920	Cleveland Indians, AL	Brooklyn Dodgers, NL	5-2
1921	New York Giants, NL	New York Yankees, AL	5-3
1922	New York Giants, NL	New York Yankees, AL	4-0; 1 tie
1923	New York Yankees, AL	New York Giants, NL	4-2
1924	Washington Senators, AL	New York Giants, NL	4-3
1925	Pittsburgh Pirates, NL	Washington Senators, AL	4-3
1926	St. Louis Cardinals, NL	New York Yankees, AL	4-3
1927	New York Yankees, AL	Pittsburgh Pirates, NL	4-0
1928	New York Yankees, AL	St. Louis Cardinals, NL	4-0
1929	Philadelphia Athletics, AL	Chicago Cubs, NL	4-1
1930	Philadelphia Athletics, AL	St. Louis Cardinals, NL	4-2
1931	St. Louis Cardinals, NL	Philadelphia Athletics, AL	4-3
1932	New York Yankees, AL	Chicago Cubs, NL	4-0
1933	New York Giants, NL	Washington Senators, AL	4-1
1934	St. Louis Cardinals, NL	Detroit Tigers, AL	4-3
1935	Detroit Tigers, AL	Chicago Cubs, NL	4-2
1936	New York Yankees, AL	New York Giants, NL	4-2
1937	New York Yankees, AL	New York Giants, NL	4-1
1938	New York Yankees, AL	Chicago Cubs, NL	4-0
1939	New York Yankees, AL	Cincinnati Reds, NL	4-0
1940	Cincinnati Reds, NL	Detroit Tigers, AL	4-3
1941	New York Yankees, AL	Brooklyn Dodgers, NL	4-1
1942	St. Louis Cardinals, NL	New York Yankees, AL	4-1
1943	New York Yankees, AL	St. Louis Cardinals, NL	4-1
1944	St. Louis Cardinals, NL	St. Louis Browns, AL	4-2
1945	Detroit Tigers, AL	Chicago Cubs, NL	4-3
1946	St. Louis Cardinals, NL	Boston Red Sox, AL	4-3
1947	New York Yankees, AL	Brooklyn Dodgers, NL	4-3
1948	Cleveland Indians, AL	Boston Braves, NL	4-2
1949	New York Yankees, AL	Brooklyn Dodgers, NL	4-1
1950	New York Yankees, AL	Philadelphia Phillies, NL	4-0
1951	New York Yankees, AL	New York Giants, NL	4-2
1952	New York Yankees, AL	Brooklyn Dodgers, NL	4-3
1953	New York Yankees, AL	Brooklyn Dodgers, NL	4-2
1954	New York Giants, NL	Cleveland Indians, AL	4-0
1955	Brooklyn Dodgers, NL	New York Yankees, AL	4-3
1956	New York Yankees, AL	Brooklyn Dodgers, NL	4-3
1957	Milwaukee Braves, NL	New York Yankees, AL	4-3
1958	New York Yankees, AL	Milwaukee Braves, NL	4-3
1959	Los Angeles Dodgers, NL	Chicago White Sox, AL	4-2
1960	Pittsburgh Pirates, NL	New York Yankees, AL	4-3

▶

▶ 1961 . . . . New York Yankees, AL   Cincinnati Reds, NL 4-1
1962 . . . . New York Yankees, AL   San Francisco Giants, NL. 4-3
1963 . . . . Los Angeles Dodgers, NL   New York Yankees, AL. 4-0
1964 . . . . St. Louis Cardinals, NL   New York Yankees, AL. 4-3
1965 . . . . Los Angeles Dodgers, NL   Minnesota Twins, AL. 4-3
1966 . . . . Baltimore Orioles, AL   Los Angeles Dodgers, NL. 4-0
1967 . . . . St. Louis Cardinals, NL   Boston Red Sox, AL 4-3
1968 . . . . Detroit Tigers, AL   St. Louis Cardinals, NL 4-3
1969 . . . . New York Mets, NL   Baltimore Orioles, AL 4-1
1970 . . . . Baltimore Orioles, AL   Cincinnati Reds, NL 4-1
1971 . . . . Pittsburgh Pirates, NL   Baltimore Orioles, AL 4-3
1972 . . . . Oakland Athletics, AL   Cincinnati Reds, NL 4-3
1973 . . . . Oakland Athletics, AL   New York Mets, NL. 4-3
1974 . . . . Oakland Athletics, AL   Los Angeles Dodgers, NL. 4-1
1975 . . . . Cincinnati Reds, NL   Boston Red Sox, AL 4-3
1976 . . . . Cincinnati Reds, NL   New York Yankees, AL. 4-0
1977 . . . . New York Yankees, AL   Los Angeles Dodgers, NL. 4-2
1978 . . . . New York Yankees, AL   Los Angeles Dodgers, NL. 4-2
1979 . . . . Pittsburgh Pirates, NL   Baltimore Orioles, AL 4-3
1980 . . . . Philadelphia Phillies, NL   Kansas City Royals, AL 4-2
1981 . . . . Los Angeles Dodgers, NL   New York Yankees, AL. 4-2
1982 . . . . St. Louis Cardinals, NL   Milwaukee Brewers, AL 4-3
1983 . . . . Baltimore Orioles, AL   Philadelphia Phillies, NL 4-1
1984 . . . . Detroit Tigers, AL   San Diego Padres, NL 4-1
1985 . . . . Kansas City Royals, AL   St. Louis Cardinals, NL 4-3
1986 . . . . New York Mets, NL   Boston Red Sox, AL 4-3
1987 . . . . Minnesota Twins, AL   St. Louis Cardinals, NL 4-3
1988 . . . . Los Angeles Dodgers, NL   Oakland Athletics, AL 4-1
1989 . . . . Oakland Athletics, AL   San Francisco Giants, NL. 4-0
1990 . . . . Cincinnati Reds, NL   Oakland Athletics, AL 4-0
1991 . . . . Minnesota Twins, AL   Atlanta Braves, NL 4-3
1992 . . . . **Toronto Blue Jays,** AL   Atlanta Braves, NL 4-2
1993 . . . . **Toronto Blue Jays,** AL   Philadelphia Phillies, NL 4-2
1994 . . . . No World Series: season suspended Sept. 15, 1994
1995 . . . . Atlanta Braves, NL   Cleveland Indians, AL 4-2
1996 . . . . New York, AL   Atlanta, NL. 4-2
1997 . . . . Florida, NL   Cleveland, AL. 4-3
1998 . . . . New York Yankees, AL   San Diego, NL. 4-0

World Series MVPs

1955	Johnny Podres, Bklyn
1956	Don Larsen, New York (AL)
1957	Lew Burdette, Mil
1958	Bob Turley, NY (AL)
1959	Larry Sherry, LA
1960	Bobby Richardson, NY (AL)
1961	Whitey Ford, NY (AL)
1962	Ralph Terry, NY (AL)
1963	Sandy Koufax, LA
1964	Bob Gibson, StL
1965	Sandy Koufax, LA
1966	Frank Robinson, Bal
1967	Bob Gibson, StL
1968	Mickey Lolich, Det
1969	Donn Clendenon, NY (NL)
1970	Brooks Robinson, Bal
1971	Roberto Clemente, Pgh
1972	Gene Tenace, Oak
1973	Reggie Jackson, Oak
1974	Rollie Fingers, Oak
1975	Pete Rose, Cin
1976	Johnny Bench, Cin
1977	Reggie Jackson, NY (AL)
1978	Bucky Dent, NY (AL)
1979	Willie Stargell, Pgh
1980	Mike Schmidt, Pha
1981	Ron Cey, LA
1981	Pedro Guerrero, LA
1981	Steve Yeager, LA
1982	Darrell Porter, StL
1983	Rick Dempsey, Bal
1984	Alan Trammell, Det
1985	Bret Saberhagen, KC
1986	Ray Knight, NY (NL)
1987	Frank Viola, Min
1988	Orel Hershiser, LA
1989	Dave Stewart, Oak
1990	Jose Rijo, Cin
1991	Jack Morris, Min
1992	**Pat Borders, Tor**
1993	**Paul Molitor, Tor**
1994	No award
1995	Tom Glavine, Atl
1996	John Wetteland, NY
1997	Livan Hernandez, Fla
1998	Scott Brosius, NY

Cy Young Award Winners, 1956–98[1]

Year		Player, club	Year		Player, club
1956[1]		Don Newcombe, Brooklyn Dodgers	1980	(NL)	Steve Carlton, Philadelphia Phillies
1957[1]		Warren Spahn, Milwaukee Braves		(AL)	Steve Stone, Baltimore Orioles
1958[1]		Bob Turley, New York Yankees	1981	(NL)	Fernando Valenzuela, Los Angeles Dodgers
1959[1]		Early Wynn, Chicago White Sox		(AL)	Rollie Fingers, Milwaukee Brewers
1960[1]		Vernon Law, Pittsburgh Pirates	1982	(NL)	Steve Carlton, Philadelphia Phillies
1961[1]		Whitey Ford, New York Yankees		(AL)	Pete Vuckovich, Milwaukee Brewers
1962[1]		Don Drysdale, Los Angeles Dodgers	1983	(NL)	John Denny, Philadelphia Phillies
1963[1]		Sandy Koufax, Los Angeles Dodgers		(AL)	LaMarr Hoyt, Chicago White Sox
1964[1]		Dean Chance, California Angels	1984	(NL)	Rick Sutcliffe, Chicago Cubs
1965[1]		Sandy Koufax, Los Angeles Dodgers		(AL)	Willie Hernandez, Detroit Tigers
1966[1]		Sandy Koufax, Los Angeles Dodgers	1985	(NL)	Dwight Gooden, New York Mets
1967	(NL)	Mike McCormick, San Francisco Giants		(AL)	Bret Saberhagen, Kansas City Royals
	(AL)	Jim Lonborg, Boston Red Sox	1986	(NL)	Mike Scott, Houston Astros
1968	(NL)	Bob Gibson, St. Louis Cardinals		(AL)	Roger Clemens, Boston Red Sox
	(AL)	Dennis McLain, Detroit Tigers	1987	(NL)	Steve Bedrosian, Philadelphia Phillies
1969	(NL)	Tom Seaver, New York Mets		(AL)	Roger Clemens, Boston Red Sox
	(AL)	Dennis McLain, Detroit Tigers	1988	(NL)	Orel Hershiser, Los Angeles Dodgers
	(AL)	Mike Cuellar, Baltimore Orioles		(AL)	Frank Viola, Minnesota Twins
1970	(NL)	Bob Gibson, St. Louis Cardinals	1989	(NL)	Mark Davis, San Diego Padres
	(AL)	Jim Perry, Minnesota Twins		(AL)	Bret Saberhagen, Kansas City Royals
1971	(NL)	Ferguson Jenkins, Chicago Cubs	1990	(NL)	Doug Drabek, Pittsburgh Pirates
	(AL)	Vida Blue, Oakland A's		(AL)	Bob Welch, Oakland A's
1972	(NL)	Steve Carlton, Philadelphia Phillies	1991	(NL)	Tom Glavine, Atlanta Braves
	(AL)	Gaylord Perry, Cleveland Indians		(AL)	Roger Clemens, Boston Red Sox
1973	(NL)	Tom Seaver, New York Mets	1992	(NL)	Greg Maddux, Chicago Cubs
	(AL)	Jim Palmer, Baltimore Orioles		(AL)	Dennis Eckersley, Oakland A's
1974	(NL)	Mike Marshall, Los Angeles Dodgers	1993	(NL)	Greg Maddux, Atlanta Braves
	(AL)	Jim (Catfish) Hunter, Oakland A's		(AL)	Jack McDowell, Chicago White Sox
1975	(NL)	Tom Seaver, New York Mets	1994	(NL)	Greg Maddux, Atlanta Braves
	(AL)	Jim Palmer, Baltimore Orioles		(AL)	David Cone, Kansas City Royals
1976	(NL)	Randy Jones, San Diego Padres	1995	(NL)	Greg Maddux, Atlanta Braves
	(AL)	Jim Palmer, Baltimore Orioles		(AL)	Randy Johnson, Seattle Mariner
1977	(NL)	Steve Carlton, Philadelphia Phillies	1996	(NL)	John Smoltz, Atlanta Braves
	(AL)	Sparky Lyle, New York Yankees		**(AL)**	**Pat Hentgen, Toronto Blue Jays**
1978	(NL)	Gaylord Perry, San Diego Padres	1997	**(NL)**	**Pedro Martinez, Montreal Expos**
	(AL)	Ron Guidry, New York Yankees		**(AL)**	**Roger Clemens, Toronto Blue Jays**
1979	(NL)	Bruce Sutter, Chicago Cubs	1998	(NL)	Tom Glavine, Atlanta Braves
	(AL)	Mike Flanagan, Baltimore Orioles		**(AL)**	**Roger Clemens, Toronto Blue Jays**

(1) One award, 1956–66

Most Valuable Player, 1931–98

	National League	American League
1931[1]	Frank Frisch, St. Louis Cardinals	Lefty Grove, Philadelphia Athletics
1932	Chuck Klein, Philadelphia Phillies	Jimmie Foxx, Philadelphia Athletics
1933	Carl Hubbell, New York Giants	Jimmie Foxx, Philadelphia Athletics
1934	Dizzy Dean, St. Louis Cardinals	Mickey Cochrane, Detroit Tigers
1935	Gabby Hartnett, Chicago Cubs	Hank Greenberg, Detroit Tigers
1936	Carl Hubbell, New York Giants	Lou Gehrig, New York Yankees
1937	Joe Medwick, St. Louis Cardinals	Charley Gehringer, Detroit Tigers
1938	Ernie Lombardi, Cincinnati Reds	Jimmie Foxx, Boston Red Sox
1939	Bucky Walters, Cincinnati Reds	Joe DiMaggio, New York Yankees
1940	Frank McCormick, Cincinnati Reds	Hank Greenberg, Detroit Tigers
1941	Dolph Camilli, Brooklyn Dodgers	Joe DiMaggio, New York Yankees
1942	Mort Cooper, St. Louis Cardinals	Joe Gordon, New York Yankees
1943	Stan Musial, St. Louis Cardinals	Spud Chandler, New York Yankees
1944	Marty Marion, St. Louis Cardinals	Hal Newhouser, Detroit Tigers
1945	Phil Cavarretta, Chicago Cubs	Hal Newhouser, Detroit Tigers
1946	Stan Musial, St. Louis Cardinals	Ted Williams, Boston Red Sox
1947	Bob Elliott, Boston Braves	Joe DiMaggio, New York Yankees
1948	Stan Musial, St. Louis Cardinals	Lou Boudreau, Cleveland Indians
1949	Jackie Robinson, Brooklyn Dodgers	Ted Williams, Boston Red Sox
1950	Jim Konstanty, Philadelphia Phillies	Phil Rizzuto, New York Yankees
1951	Roy Campanella, Brooklyn Dodgers	Yogi Berra, New York Yankees
1952	Hank Sauer, Chicago Cubs	Bobby Shantz, Philadelphia Athletics
1953	Roy Campanella, Brooklyn Dodgers	Al Rosen, Cleveland Indians
1954	Willie Mays, New York Giants	Yogi Berra, New York Yankees
1955	Roy Campanella, Brooklyn Dodgers	Yogi Berra, New York Yankees
1956	Don Newcombe, Brooklyn Dodgers	Mickey Mantle, New York Yankees
1958	Ernie Banks, Chicago Cubs	Jackie Jensen, Boston Red Sox
1959	Ernie Banks, Chicago Cubs	Nelson Fox, Chicago White Sox
1960	Dick Groat, Pittsburgh Pirates	Roger Maris, New York Yankees
1961	Frank Robinson, Cincinnati Reds	Roger Maris, New York Yankees
1962	Maury Wills, Los Angeles Dodgers	Mickey Mantle, New York Yankees
1963	Sandy Koufax, Los Angeles Dodgers	Elston Howard, New York Yankees
1964	Ken Boyer, St. Louis Cardinals	Brooks Robinson, Baltimore Orioles
1965	Willie Mays, San Francisco Giants	Zoilo Versalles, Minnesota Twins
1966	Roberto Clemente, Pittsburgh Pirates	Frank Robinson, Baltimore Orioles
1967	Orlando Cepeda, St. Louis Cardinals	Carl Yastrzemski, Boston Red Sox
1968	Bob Gibson, St. Louis Cardinals	Denny McLain, Detroit Tigers
1969	Willie McCovey, San Francisco Giants	Harmon Killebrew, Minnesota Twins
1971	Joe Torre, St. Louis Cardinals	Vida Blue, Oakland Athletics
1972	Johnny Bench, Cincinnati Reds	Dick Allen, Chicago White Sox
1975	Joe Morgan, Cincinnati Reds	Fred Lynn, Boston Red Sox
1976	Joe Morgan, Cincinnati Reds	Thurman Munson, New York Yankees
1979	Keith Hernandez, St. Louis Cardinals; Willie Stargell, Pittsburgh Pirates	Don Baylor, California Angels
1980	Mike Schmidt, Philadelphia Phillies	George Brett, Kansas City Royals
1981	Mike Schmidt, Philadelphia Phillies	Rollie Fingers, Milwaukee Brewers
1982	Dale Murphy, Atlanta Braves	Robin Yount, Milwaukee Brewers
1983	Dale Murphy, Atlanta Braves	Cal Ripken, Jr., Baltimore Orioles
1984	Ryne Sandberg, Chicago Cubs	Willie Hernandez, Detroit Tigers
1985	Willie McGee, St. Louis Cardinals	Don Mattingly, New York Yankees
1986	Mike Schmidt, Philadelphia Phillies	Roger Clemens, Boston Red Sox

	National League	**American League**
1987	André Dawson, Chicago Cubs	**George Bell, Toronto Blue Jays**
1988	Kirk Gibson, Los Angeles Dodgers	Jose Canseco, Oakland Athletics
1989	Kevin Mitchell, San Francisco Giants	Robin Yount, Milwaukee Brewers
1990	Barry Bonds, Pittsburgh Pirates	Rickey Henderson, Oakland Athletics
1991	Terry Pendleton, Atlanta Braves	Cal Ripken, Jr., Baltimore Orioles
1992	Barry Bonds, Pittsburgh Pirates	Dennis Eckersley, Oakland A's
1993	Barry Bonds, San Francisco Giants	Frank Thomas, Chicago White Sox
1994	Jeff Bagwell, Houston Astras	Frank Thomas, Chicago White Sox
1995	Barry Larkin, Cincinnati Reds	Mo Vaughn, Boston Red Sox
1996	Ken Caminiti, San Diego Padres	Juan Gonzalez, Texas Rangers
1997	Larry Walker, Colorado Rockies	Ken Griffey Jr., Seattle Mariners
1998	Sammy Sosa, Chicago Cubs	Juan Gonzalez, Texas Rangers

Batting Champions, 1925–99

Year	National League Player/Club	Pct	Year	American League Player/Club	Pct
1924	Rogers Hornsby, St. Louis	**.424**	1924	Babe Ruth, New York	**.378**
1925	Rogers Hornsby, St. Louis	**.403**	1925	Harry Heilmann, Detroit	**.393**
1926	Eugene Hargrave, Cincinnati	**.353**	1926	Heinie Manush, Detroit	**.377**
1927	Paul Waner, Pittsburgh	**.380**	1927	Harry Heilmann, Detroit	**.398**
1928	Rogers Hornsby, Boston	**.387**	1928	Goose Goslin, Washington	**.379**
1929	Lefty O'Doul, Philadelphia	**.398**	1929	Lew Fonseca, Cleveland	**.369**
1930	Bill Terry, New York	**.401**	1930	Al Simmons, Philadelphia	**.381**
1931	Chick Hafey, St. Louis	**.349**	1931	Al Simmons, Philadelphia	**.390**
1932	Lefty O'Doul, Brooklyn	**.368**	1932	Dale Alexander, Detroit-Boston	**.367**
1933	Charles Klein, Philadelphia	**.368**	1933	Jimmie Foxx, Philadelphia	**.356**
1934	Paul Waner, Pittsburgh	**.362**	1934	Lou Gehrig, New York	**.363**
1935	Arky Vaughan, Pittsburgh	**.385**	1935	Buddy Myer, Washington	**.349**
1936	Paul Waner, Pittsburgh	**.373**	1936	Luke Appling, Chicago	**.388**
1937	Joe Medwick, St. Louis	**.374**	1937	Charlie Gehringer, Detroit	**.371**
1938	Ernie Lombardi, Cincinnati	**.342**	1938	Jimmie Foxx, Boston	**.349**
1939	John Mize, St. Louis	**.349**	1939	Joe DiMaggio, New York	**.381**
1940	Debs Garms, Pittsburgh	**.355**	1940	Joe DiMaggio, New York	**.352**
1941	Pete Reiser, Brooklyn	**.343**	1941	Ted Williams, Boston	**.406**
1942	Ernie Lombardi, Boston	**.330**	1942	Ted Williams, Boston	**.356**
1943	Stan Musial, St. Louis	**.357**	1943	Luke Appling, Chicago	**.328**
1944	Dixie Walker, Brooklyn	**.357**	1944	Lou Boudreau, Cleveland	**.327**
1945	Phil Cavarretta, Chicago	**.355**	1945	George Stirnweiss, New York	**.309**
1946	Stan Musial, St. Louis	**.365**	1946	Mickey Vernon, Washington	**.352**
1947	Harry Walker, Philadelphia	**.363**	1947	Ted Williams, Boston	**.343**
1948	Stan Musial, St. Louis	**.376**	1948	Ted Williams, Boston	**.369**
1949	Jackie Robinson, Brooklyn	**.342**	1949	George Kell, Detroit	**.343**
1950	Stan Musial, St. Louis	**.346**	1950	Billy Goodman, Boston	**.354**
1951	Stan Musial, St. Louis	**.355**	1951	Ferris Fain, Philadelphia	**.344**

National League			American League		
Year	Player/Club	Pct	Year	Player/Club	Pct
1952	Stan Musial, St. Louis	.336	1952	Ferris Fain, Philadelphia	.327
1953	Carl Furillo, Brooklyn	.344	1953	Mickey Vernon, Washington	.337
1954	Willie Mays, New York	.345	1954	Roberto Avila, Cleveland	.341
1955	Richie Ashburn, Philadelphia	.338	1955	Al Kaline, Detroit	.340
1956	Hank Aaron, Milwaukee	.328	1956	Mickey Mantle, New York	.353
1957	Stan Musial, St. Louis	.351	1957	Ted Williams, Boston	.388
1958	Richie Ashburn, Philadelphia	.350	1958	Ted Williams, Boston	.328
1959	Hank Aaron, Milwaukee	.355	1959	Harvey Kuenn, Detroit	.353
1960	Dick Groat, Pittsburgh	.325	1960	Pete Runnels, Boston	.320
1961	Roberto Clemente, Pittsburgh	.351	1961	Norm Cash, Detroit	.361
1962	Tommy Davis, Los Angeles	.346	1962	Pete Runnels, Boston	.326
1963	Tommy Davis, Los Angeles	.326	1963	Carl Yastrzemski, Boston	.321
1964	Roberto Clemente, Pittsburgh	.339	1964	Tony Oliva, Minnesota	.323
1965	Roberto Clemente, Pittsburgh	.329	1965	Tony Oliva, Minnesota	.321
1966	Matty Alou, Pittsburgh	.342	1966	Frank Robinson, Baltimore	.316
1967	Roberto Clemente, Pittsburgh	.357	1967	Carl Yastrzemski, Boston	.326
1968	Pete Rose, Cincinnati	.335	1968	Carl Yastrzemski, Boston	.301
1969	Pete Rose, Cincinnati	.348	1969	Rod Carew, Minnesota	.332
1970	Rico Carty, Atlanta	.366	1970	Alex Johnson, California	.329
1971	Joe Torre, St. Louis	.363	1971	Tony Oliva, Minnesota	.337
1972	Billy Williams, Chicago	.333	1972	Rod Carew, Minnesota	.318
1973	Pete Rose, Cincinnati	.338	1973	Rod Carew, Minnesota	.350
1974	Ralph Garr, Atlanta	.353	1974	Rod Carew, Minnesota	.364
1975	Bill Madlock, Chicago	.354	1975	Rod Carew, Minnesota	.359
1976	Bill Madlock, Chicago	.339	1976	George Brett, Kansas City	.333
1977	Dave Parker, Pittsburgh	.338	1977	Rod Carew, Minnesota	.388
1978	Dave Parker, Pittsburgh	.334	1978	Rod Carew, Minnesota	.333
1979	Keith Hernandez, St. Louis	.344	1979	Fred Lynn, Boston	.333
1980	Bill Buckner, Chicago	.324	1980	George Brett, Kansas City	.390
1981	Bill Madlock, Pittsburgh*	.341	1981	Carney Lansford, Boston	.336
1982	**Al Oliver, Montreal**	.331	1982	Willie Wilson, Kansas City	.332
1983	Bill Madlock, Pittsburgh	.323	1983	Wade Boggs, Boston	.361
1984	Tony Gwynn, San Diego	.351	1984	Don Mattingly, New York	.343
1985	Willie McGee, St. Louis	.353	1985	Wade Boggs, Boston	.368
1986	**Tim Raines, Montreal**	.334	1986	Wade Boggs, Boston	.357
1987	Tony Gwynn, San Diego	.370	1987	Wade Boggs, Boston	.363
1988	Tony Gwynn, San Diego	.313	1988	Wade Boggs, Boston	.366
1989	Tony Gwynn, San Diego	.336	1989	Kirby Puckett, Minnesota	.339
1990	Willie McGee, St. Louis	.335	1990	George Brett, Kansas City	.329
1991	Terry Pendleton, Atlanta	.319	1991	Julio Franco, Texas	.341
1992	Gary Sheffield, San Diego	.330	1992	Edgar Martinez, Seattle	.343
1993	Andres Galarraga, Colorado	.370	1993	**John Olerud, Toronto**	.363
1994	Tony Gwynn, San Diego*	.394	1994	Paul O'Neill, New York*	.359
1995	Tony Gwynn, San Diego	.368	1995	Edgar Martinez, Seattle	.356
1996	Tony Gwynn, San Diego	.353	1996	Alex Rodriguez, Seattle	.358
1997	Tony Gwynn, San Diego	.372	1997	Frank Thomas, Chicago	.347
1998	Larry Walker, Colorado	.363	1998	Bernie Williams, New York	.339
1999	Larry Walker, Colorado	.379	1999	Nomar Garciaparra, Boston	.357

* strike abbreviated season

Individual Earned Run Average Leaders, 1901–99

National League

Year	Player/Team	ERA	Year	Player/Team	ERA	Year	Player/Team	ERA
1901	Jesse Tannehill, Pgh	2.18	1934	Carl Hubbell, NY	2.30	1967	Phil Niekro, Atl	1.87
1902	Jack Taylor, Chi	1.33	1935	Cy Blanton, Pgh	2.58	1968	Bob Gibson, StL	1.12
1903	Sam Leever, Pgh	2.06	1936	Carl Hubbell, NY	2.31	1969	Juan Marichal, SF	2.10
1904	Joe McGinnity, NY	1.61	1937	Jim Turner, Bos	2.38	1970	Tom Seaver, NY	2.81
1905	Christy Mathewson, NY	1.27	1938	Bill Lee, Chi	2.66	1971	Tom Seaver, NY	1.76
1906	Three Finger Brown, Chi	1.04	1939	Bucky Walters, Cin	2.29	1972	Steve Carlton, Pha	1.97
1907	Jack Pfiester, Chi	1.15	1940	Bucky Walters, Cin	2.48	1973	Tom Seaver, NY	2.08
1908	Christy Mathewson, NY	1.43	1941	Elmer Riddle, Cin	2.24	1974	Buzz Capra, Atl	2.28
1909	Christy Mathewson, NY	1.14	1942	Mort Cooper, StL	1.78	1975	Randy Jones, SD	2.24
1910	George McQuillan, Pha	1.60	1943	Howie Pollet, StL	1.75	1976	John Denny, StL	2.52
1911	Christy Mathewson, NY	1.99	1944	Ed Heusser, Cin	2.38	1977	John Candelaria, Pgh	2.34
1912	Jeff Tesreau, NY	1.96	1945	Hank Borowy, Chi	2.13	1978	Craig Swan, NY	2.43
1913	Christy Mathewson, NY	2.06	1946	Howie Pollet, StL	2.10	1979	J.R. Richard, Hou	2.71
1914	Bill Doak, StL	1.72	1947	Warren Spahn, Bos	2.33	1980	Don Sutton, LA	2.21
1915	Grover Alexander, Pha	1.22	1948	Harry Brecheen, StL	2.24	1981	Nolan Ryan, Hou	1.69*
1916	Grover Alexander, Pha	1.55	1949	Dave Koslo, NY	2.50	1982	**Steve Rogers, Mtl**	**2.40**
1917	Grover Alexander, Pha	1.86	1950	Jim Hearn, StL/NY	2.49	1983	Atlee Hammaker, SF	2.25
1918	Hippo Vaughn, Chi	1.74	1951	Chet Nichols, Bos	2.88	1984	Alejandro Pena, LA	2.48
1919	Grover Alexander, Chi	1.72	1952	Hoyt Wilhelm, NY	2.43	1985	Dwight Gooden, NY	1.53
1920	Grover Alexander, Chi	1.91	1953	Warren Spahn, Mil	2.10	1986	Mike Scott, Hou	2.22
1921	Bill Doak, StL	2.59	1954	Johnny Antonelli, NY	2.30	1987	Nolan Ryan, Hou	2.76
1922	Rosy Ryan, NY	3.01	1955	Bob Friend, Pgh	2.83	1988	Joe Magrane, StL	2.18
1923	Dolf Luque, Cin	1.93	1956	Lew Burdette, Mil	2.70	1989	Scott Garrelts, SF	2.28
1924	Dazzy Vance, Brooklyn	2.16	1957	Johnny Podres, Brooklyn	2.66	1990	Danny Darwin, Hou	2.21
1925	Dolf Luque, Cin	2.63	1958	Stu Miller, SF	2.47	1991	**Dennis Martinez, Mtl**	**2.39**
1926	Ray Kremer, Pgh	2.61	1959	Sam Jones, SF	2.83	1992	Bill Swift, S	2.08
1927	Ray Kremer, Pgh	2.47	1960	Mike McCormick, SF	2.70	1993	Greg Maddux, Atl.	2.36
1928	Dazzy Vance, Brooklyn	2.09	1961	Warren Spahn, Mil	3.02	1994	Greg Maddux, Atl	1.56*
1929	Bill Walker, NY	3.09	1962	Sandy Koufax, LA	2.54	1995	Greg Maddux, Atl	1.63
1930	Dazzy Vance, Brooklyn	2.61	1963	Sandy Koufax, LA	1.88	1996	Kevin Brown, Fla	1.89
1931	Bill Walker, NY	2.26	1964	Sandy Koufax, LA	1.74	1997	**Pedro Martinez, Mtl**	**1.90**
1932	Lon Warneke, Chi	2.37	1965	Sandy Koufax, LA	2.04	1998	Greg Maddux, Atl.	2.22
1933	Carl Hubbell, NY	1.66	1966	Sandy Koufax, LA	1.73	1999	Randy Johnson, Ari	2.48

* strike abbreviated season   ▶

American League

	Player/Team	ERA		Player/Team	ERA		Player/Team	ERA
1901	Cy Young, Bos	1.62	1934	Lefty Gomez, NY	2.33	1967	Joel Horlen, Chi	2.06
1902	Ed Siever, Det	1.91	1935	Lefty Grove, Bos	2.70	1968	Luis Tiant, Cle	1.60
1903	Earl Moor, Cle	1.77	1936	Lefty Grove, Bos	2.81	1969	Dick Bosman, Wash	2.19
1904	Addie Joss, Cle	1.59	1937	Lefty Gomez, NY	2.33	1970	Diego Segui, Oak	2.56
1905	Rube Waddell, Pha	1.48	1938	Lefty Grove, Bos	3.08	1971	Vida Blue, Oak	1.82
1906	Doc White, Chi	1.52	1939	Lefty Grove, Bos	2.54	1972	Luis Tiant, Bos	1.91
1907	Ed Walsh, Chi	1.60	1940	Bob Feller, Cle	2.61	1973	Jim Palmer, Bal	2.40
1908	Addie Joss, Cle	1.16	1941	Thornton Lee, Chi	2.37	1974	Catfish Hunter, Oak	2.49
1909	Harry Krause, Pha	1.39	1942	Ted Lyons, Chi	2.10	1975	Jim Palmer, Bal	2.09
1910	Ed Walsh, Chi	1.27	1943	Spud Chandler, NY	1.64	1976	Mark Fidrych, Det	2.34
1911	Vean Gregg, Cle	1.81	1944	Dizzy Trout, Det	2.12	1977	Frank Tanana, Cal	2.54
1912	Walter Johnson, Wash	1.39	1945	Al Newhouser, Det	1.81	1978	Ron Guidry, NY	1.74
1913	Walter Johnson, Wash	1.09	1946	Al Newhouser, Det	1.94	1979	Ron Guidry, NY	2.78
1914	Dutch Leonard, Bos	1.01	1947	Spud Chandler, NY	2.46	1980	Rudy May, NY	2.47
1915	Smoky Joe Wood, Bos	1.49	1948	Gene Bearden, Cle	2.43	1981	Steve McCatty, Oak	2.32*
1916	Babe Ruth, Bos	1.75	1949	Mel Parnell, Bos	2.77	1982	Rick Sutcliffe, Cle	2.96
1917	Eddie Cicotte, Chi	1.53	1950	Early Wynn, Cle	3.20	1983	Rick Honeycutt, Tex	2.42
1918	Walter Johnson, Wash	1.27	1951	Saul Rogovin, Det/Chi	2.78	1984	Mike Boddicker, Bal	2.79
1919	Walter Johnson, Wash	1.49	1952	Allie Reynolds, NY	2.06	1985	**Dave Stieb, Tor**	**2.48**
1920	Bob Shawkey, NY	2.45	1953	Ed Lopat, NY	2.42	1986	Roger Clemens, Bos	2.48
1921	Red Faber, Chi	2.48	1954	Mike Garcia, Cle	2.64	1987	**Jimmy Key, Tor**	**2.76**
1922	Red Faber, Chi	2.80	1955	Billy Pierce, Chi	1.97	1988	Allan Anderson, Min	2.45
1923	Stan Coveleski, Cle	2.76	1956	Whitey Ford, NY	2.47	1989	Bret Saberhagen, KC	2.16
1924	Walter Johnson, Wash	2.72	1957	Bobby Shantz, NY	2.45	1990	Roger Clemens, Bos	1.93
1925	Stan Coveleski, Wash	2.84	1958	Whitey Ford, NY	2.01	1991	Roger Clemens, Bos	2.62
1926	Lefty Grove, Pha	2.51	1959	Hoyt Wilhelm, Bal	2.19	1992	Roger Clemens, Bos	2.41
1927	Wilcy Moore, NY	2.28	1960	Frank Baumann, Chi	2.67	1993	Kevin Appier, KC	2.56
1928	Garland Braxton, Wash	2.51	1961	Dick Donovan, Wash	2.40	1994	Steve Ontiveras, Oak	2.65*
1929	Lefty Grove, Pha	2.81	1962	Hank Aguirre, Det	2.21	1995	Randy Johnson, Sea	2.48
1930	Lefty Grove, Pha	2.54	1963	Gary Peters, Chi	2.33	1996	**Juan Guzman, Tor**	**2.93**
1931	Lefty Grove, Pha	2.06	1964	Dean Chance, LA	1.65	1997	**Roger Clemens, Tor**	**2.05**
1932	Lefty Grove, Pha	2.84	1965	Sam McDowell, Cle	2.18	1998	**Roger Clemens, Tor**	**2.65**
1933	Monte Pearson, Cle	2.33	1966	Gary Peters, Chi	1.98	1999	Pedro Martinez, Bos	2.07

Source: *The Baseball Encyclopedia*   * strike abbreviated season

Home Run Derby II

*A*fter breaking Roger Maris's home run record in 1998, Mark McGwire and Sammy Sosa continued their assault on the record books in 1999, becoming the first players to post back-to-back 60-homer seasons.

Sosa reached the 60-homer plateau first, but he was later passed by McGwire, who ended up with 65 homers as he won his second straight home run title. Sosa finished with 63.

"I am a happy man, not disappointed," said Sosa. "I had a great year."

McGwire and Sosa's exploits continued the magic of their home run derby of 1998, when they broke baseball's most cherished record, Roger Maris's 61 homers in a season. McGwire smacked 70 in '98 and Sosa hit 66 homers, the two highest totals in baseball history.

"I'm pretty proud of myself as far as I overcame a lot of things and put up the numbers I put up this year," McGwire said.

Still, neither McGwire nor Sosa could lead their clubs into the playoffs.

Only four players have hit 60 or more homers in a season—McGwire, Sosa, Maris and Babe Ruth.

Source: *Canadian Press*

Greatest Home Run Seasons

Player/Team	HR	Year	Player/Team	HR	Year	Player/Team	HR	Year
Mark McGwire, StL	70	1998	Hack Wilson, Chi Cubs	56	1930	Mark McGwire, Oak	52	1996
Sammy Sosa, Chi Cubs	66	1998	Ken Griffey Jr., Sea	56	1998	Ralph Kiner, Pit	51	1947
Mark McGwire, StL	65	1999	Ken Griffey Jr., Sea	56	1997	Johnny Mize, NY Giants	51	1947
Sammy Sosa, Chi Cubs	63	1999	Babe Ruth, NYY	54	1920	Willie Mays, NY Giants	51	1955
Roger Maris, NYY	61	1961	Babe Ruth, NYY	54	1928	Cecil Fielder, Det	51	1990
Babe Ruth, NYY	60	1927	Ralph Kiner, Pit	54	1949	Jimmie Foxx, Bos	50	1938
Babe Ruth, NYY	59	1921	Mickey Mantle, NYY	54	1961	Albert Belle, Cle	50	1995
Jimmie Foxx, Phi Athletics	58	1932	Mickey Mantle, NYY	52	1956	Brady Anderson, Bal	50	1996
Hank Greenberg, Det	58	1938	Willie Mays, SF	52	1965	Greg Vaughn, SD	50	1998
Mark McGwire, Oak/ StL	58	1997	George Foster, Cin	52	1977			

Source: *Canadian Press*

Baseball and Basketball

Baseball Canada
www.baseball.ca

Baseball scores and recaps, plus other sports
CNN Sports Illustrated
www.cnnsi.com

Sports Network
www.tsn.ca

TESPN
espn.go.com

National Basketball Association
www.nba.com
all you need to know about the NBA

Basketball Canada
http://users.worldgate.com/~imckay/
info on national teams

See also pages 683, 701, 727

Canadian Players in Major League Baseball, 1999

Player	Avg	OBA	AB	R	H	2B	3B	HR	RBI	BB	SO	SB	CS	E
Larry Walker, Col	.379	.458	438	108	166	26	4	37	115	57	52	11	4	4
Matt Stairs, Oak	.258	.366	531	94	137	26	3	38	102	89	124	2	7	5
Corey Koskie, Min	.310	.387	342	42	106	21	0	11	58	40	72	4	4	8
Rob Ducey, Pha	.261	.383	188	29	49	10	2	8	33	38	57	2	1	0
Rob Butler, Tor	.143	.250	7	1	1	0	0	0	1	0	0	0	0	0

Pitcher	W	L	ERA	G	GS	Sv	IP	H	R	ER	HR	BB	SO
Ryan Dempster, Fla	7	8	4.71	25	25	0	147	146	77	77	21	93	126
Paul Quantrill, Tor	3	2	3.33	41	0	0	48.2	53	19	18	5	17	28
Paul Spoljaric, Tor ...	2	2	4.65	37	2	0	62	62	41	32	9	32	63
Jeff Zimmerman, Tex ..	9	3	2.36	65	0	3	87.2	50	24	23	9	23	67
Steve Sinclair, Tor/Sea ..	0	1	6.52	21	0	0	19.1	22	16	14	5	14	18
John Zimmerman, Sea ..	0	0	7.88	12	0	0	8.0	14	8	7	0	4	3

Source: *Canadian Press*

Career Records of Some Canadian Major League Players of the Past

Player	G	AB	R	H	2B	3B	HR	RBI	BA	OBA	SA
Jeff Heath, 1936–49	1 383	4 937	777	1 447	279	102	194	887	.293	.370	.509
Terry Puhl, 1977–90	1 531	4 855	676	1 361	226	56	62	435	.280	.350	.388
George Gibson, 1905–18 ..	1 213	3 776	295	893	142	49	15	335	.236	.294	.312
Tip O'Neill, 1883–92	1 054	4 255	880	1 386	222	92	52	435	.326	.392	.458
Pete Ward, 1962–70	973	3 060	345	776	136	17	98	427	.254	.342	.405
George Selkirk 1934–42....	046	2 790	503	810	131	41	108	576	.290	.400	.483
Jack Graney 1908–22	1 402	4 705	706	1 178	219	79	18	420	.250	.354	.342
Frank O'Rourke 1917–31 ...	1 131	4 069	547	1 032	196	42	15	430	.254	.315	.333

Pitcher	W	L	Pct.	G	ShO	Sv	IP	H	BB	SO	ERA
Ferguson Jenkins, 1965–83	284	226	.557	664	49	7	4 498	4 142	997	3 192	3.34
Reggie Cleveland, 1969–81 .	105	106	.498	203	12	25	1 809	1813	543	930	4.01
Russ Ford, 1909–15	99	71	.582	199	15	9	1 487	1 318	376	710	2.59
Phil Marchildon, 1942–50[1]	68	75	.476	185	6	2	1 214	1084	684	4 81	3.93
Oscar Judd, 1941–48	40	51	.440	161	4	7	770	744	397	304	3.90
John Hiller 1965–80	87	76	.534	545	6	125	1 242	1040	535	1 036	2.83
Dick Fowler 1941–52......	66	79	.455	221	11	4	1 303	1367	578	382	4.11
Ron Taylor 1962–72	45	43	.511	491	0	72	800	794	209	464	3.93

G: Games played. **AB:** At bats. **R:** Runs. **H:** Hits. **2B:** Doubles. **3B:** Triples. **HR:** Home runs. **RBI:** Runs batted in. **BA:** Batting average. **OBA:** On-base percentage. **SA:** Slugging average.

W: Wins. **L:** Losses. **Pct.:** Percentage. **G:** Games pitched. **ShO:** Shutouts. **Sv:** Saves. **IP:** Innings pitched. **H:** Hits allowed. **BB:** Walks. **K:** Strikeouts. **ERA:** Earned run average.

(1) Marchildon was in Canadian Armed Forces in 1943–44

Montreal Expos Year-By-Year Record

Year	Won	Lost	Pct.	Pos.	GB	Home Attendance	Manager
1969 52	110	.321	6th	48	1 212 608	Gene Mauch
1970 73	89	.451	6th	16	1 424 683	Gene Mauch
1971 71	90	.441	5th	25 1/2	1 290 963	Gene Mauch
1972 70	86	.449	5th	26 1/2	1 142 145	Gene Mauch
1973 79	83	.488	4th	3 1/2	1 246 863	Gene Mauch
1974 79	82	.491	4th	8 1/2	1 019 134	Gene Mauch
1975 75	87	.463	5th	17 1/2	908 292	Gene Mauch
1976 55	107	.340	6th	46	646 704	K. Kuehl/C. Fox
1977 75	87	.463	5th	26	1 433 757	Dick Williams
1978 76	86	.469	4th	14	1 427 007	Dick Williams
1979 95	65	.594	2nd	8	2 102 173	Dick Williams
1980 90	72	.556	2nd	1	2 208 175	Dick Williams
1981 60	48	.556	—	—	1 534 564	Dick Williams/Jim Fanning
1982 86	76	.531	3rd	6	2 318 292	Jim Fanning
1983 82	80	.506	3rd	8	2 320 651	Bill Virdon
1984 78	83	.484	5th	18	1 606 531	Bill Virdon/Jim Fanning
1985 84	77	.522	3rd	16 1/2	1 502 494	Buck Rodgers
1986 78	83	.484	4th	29 1/2	1 128 981	Buck Rodgers
1987 91	71	.562	3rd	4	1 850 324	Buck Rodgers
1988 81	81	.500	3rd	20	1 478 659	Buck Rodgers
1989 81	81	.500	4th	12	1 783 533	Buck Rodgers
1990 85	77	.525	3rd	10	1 421 388	Buck Rodgers
1991 70	91	.441	6th	26 1/2	978 045	Buck Rodgers/Tom Runnells
1992 87	75	.537	2nd	9	1 731 566	Tom Runnells/Felipe Alou
1993 94	68	.580	2nd	3	1 641 437	Felipe Alou
1994 74	40	.649	1st[a]	6	1 276 250	Felipe Alou
1995 66	78	.458	5th	24	1 309 618	Felipe Alou
1996 88	74	.543	2nd	8	1 618 573	Felipe Alou
1997 78	84	.481	4th	22	1 175 000	Felipe Alou
1998 65	97	.401	4th	41	914 909	Felipe Alou
1999 68	94	.420	4th	35	773 277	Felipe Alou

(a) Eastern Division: first year with three divisions

Montreal Expos Individual Statistics, 1999

Batters

	Avg	OBA	AB	R	H	2B	3B	HR	RBI	BB	SO	SB	CS	E
Vladimir Guerrero	.316	.378	610	102	193	37	5	42	131	55	62	14	7	19
Rondell White	.312	.359	539	83	168	26	6	22	64	32	85	10	6	11
Jose Vidro	.304	.346	494	67	150	45	2	12	59	29	51	0	4	11
Marty Barrett	.293	.345	433	53	127	32	3	8	52	32	39	0	2	14
Wilton Guerrero	.292	.324	315	42	92	15	7	2	31	13	38	7	6	12
Brad Fullmer	.277	.321	347	38	96	34	2	9	47	22	35	2	3	7
Terry Jones	.270	.303	63	4	17	1	1	0	3	3	14	1	2	0
Orlando Merced	.268	.353	194	25	52	12	1	8	26	26	27	2	1	5
Trace Coquillette	.265	.333	49	2	13	3	0	0	4	4	7	1	0	1
Chris Widger	.264	.325	383	42	101	24	1	14	56	28	86	1	4	6
James Mouton	.262	.364	122	18	32	5	1	2	13	18	31	6	2	1
Fernando Seguignol.	.257	.328	105	14	27	9	0	5	10	5	33	0	0	2
Orlando Cabrera	.254	.293	382	48	97	23	5	8	39	18	38	2	2	10
Manny Martinez	.245	.279	331	48	81	12	7	2	26	17	51	19	6	8
Peter Bergeron	.244	.370	45	12	11	2	0	0	1	9	5	0	0	1
Geoff Blum	.241	.327	133	21	32	7	2	8	18	17	25	1	0	10
Darron Cox	.240	.296	25	2	6	1	0	1	2	0	5	0	0	2
Mike Mordecai	.235	.297	226	29	53	10	2	5	25	20	31	2	5	7
Ryan McGuire	.221	.347	140	17	31	7	2	2	18	27	33	1	1	2
Jose Fernandez	.208	.240	24	0	5	2	0	0	1	1	7	0	0	2
Robert Machado	.182	.250	22	3	4	1	0	0	0	2	6	0	0	0
Shane Andrews	.181	.287	281	28	51	8	0	11	37	43	88	1	0	14

Source: *Canadian Press*

AVG = batting average; OBA = on base average; AB = times at bat; R = runs; H = hits; 2B = doubles; 3B = triples; HR = home runs; RBI = runs batted in; BB = walks; SO = strikeouts; SB = stolen bases; CS = caught stealing; E = errors.

Pitchers

	W	L	ERA	G	GS	SV	IP	H	R	ER	HR	BB	SO
Guillermo Mota	2	4	2.93	51	0	0	55.1	54	24	18	5	25	27
Bobby Ayala	1	6	3.68	53	0	0	66	60	36	27	6	34	64
Ugueth Urbina	6	6	3.69	71	0	41	75.2	59	35	31	6	36	100
Steve Kline	7	4	3.75	82	0	0	69.2	56	32	29	8	33	69
Anthony Telford	5	4	3.94	79	0	2	96	112	52	42	3	38	69
Mike Thurman	7	11	4.05	29	27	0	146.2	140	84	66	17	52	85
Dustin Hermanson	9	14	4.20	34	34	0	216.1	225	110	101	20	69	145
Scott Strickland	0	1	4.50	17	0	0	18	15	10	9	3	11	23
Jeremy Powell	4	8	4.73	17	17	0	97	113	60	51	14	44	44
Miguel Batista	8	7	4.88	39	17	1	134.2	146	88	73	10	58	95
Javier Vazquez	9	8	5.00	26	26	0	154.2	154	98	86	20	52	113
J.D. Smart	0	1	5.02	29	0	0	52	56	30	29	4	17	21
Carl Pavano	6	8	5.63	19	18	0	104	117	66	65	8	35	70
Dan Smith	4	9	6.02	20	17	0	89.2	104	64	60	12	39	72
Ted Lilly	0	1	7.61	9	3	0	23.2	30	20	20	7	9	28

Source: *Canadian Press*

W = games won; L = games lost; ERA = earned run average; G = games played in; GS = games started; SV = saves; IP = innings pitched; H = hits allowed; R = runs allowed; ER = earned runs; HR = home runs allowed; BB = walks allowed; SO = strikeouts.

Montreal Expos Team Records up to 1999 season

Batting

Single Season

Batting Average: Tim Raines, 1986, .334; Moises Alou, 1994, .339 (106g)
At Bats: Warren Cromartie, 1979, 659
Games: Rusty Staub, 1971, 162; Ken Singleton, 1973, 162;
  Warren Cromartie, 1980, 162
Hits: Al Oliver, 1982, 204
Runs: Tim Raines, 1983, 133
Singles: Tim Raines, 1986, 140
Doubles: Mark Grudzielanek, 1997, 54
Triples: Rodney Scott, 1980, 13; Tim Raines, 1985, 13; Mitch Webster, 1986, 13
Home Runs: Vladimir Guerrero, 1999, 42
Runs Batted In: Vladimir Guerrero, 1999, 131
Total Bases: Andre Dawson, 1983, 341
Slugging Average: Moises Alou, 1994, .592 (106g); Andre Dawson, 1981, .553
On-Base Average: Tim Raines, 1987, .431
Stolen Bases: Ron LeFlore, 1980, 97
Strikeouts: Andres Galarraga, 1990, 169
Walks: Ken Singleton, 1973, 123
Hit By Pitch: Ron Hunt, 1971, 50
Hitting Streak: Vladimir Guerrero, 1999, 31
Pinch Hits: Jose Morales, 1976, 25

Career Leaders

Batting Average: Al Oliver, .315
At Bats: Tim Wallach, 6 529
Games: Tim Wallach, 1 767

Hits: Tim Wallach, 1 694
Runs: Tim Raines, 934
Singles: Tim Raines, 1,148
Doubles: Tim Wallach, 360
Triples: Tim Raines, 81
Home Runs: Andre Dawson, 225
Runs Batted In: Tim Wallach, 905
Total Bases: Tim Wallach, 2,728

Stolen Bases: Tim Raines, 634
Strikeouts: Tim Wallach, 1,008
Walks: Tim Raines, 775

Pitching

Single Season

Games: Mike Marshall, 1973, 92
Games Started: Steve Rogers, 1977, 40
Complete Games: Bill Stoneman, 1971, 20
Innings Pitched: Steve Rogers, 1977, 302
Wins: Ross Grimsley, 1978, 20
Losses: Steve Rogers, 1974, 22
Saves: John Wetteland, 1993, 43
Earned Run Average: Ugueth Urbina, 1998, 1.30
Strikeouts: Pedro Martinez, 1991, 305

Career Leaders

Games: Tim Burke, 425
Games Started: Steve Rogers, 393
Complete Games: Steve Rogers, 129
Innings Pitched: Steve Rogers, 2 839
Wins: Steve Rogers, 158
Losses: Steve Rogers, 152
Saves: Jeff Reardon, 152
Earned Run Average: Dennis Martinez, 2.93

Source: *Canadian Press*

Montreal Expos Player of the Year

1969	Rusty Staub	**1977**	Gary Carter	**1984**	Gary Carter	**1992**	Larry Walker
1970	Carl Morton	**1978**	Ross Grimsley	**1985**	Tim Raines	**1993**	Marquis Grissom
1971	Ron Hunt	**1979**	Larry Parrish	**1986**	Tim Raines	**1994**	Moises Alou
1972	Mike Marshall	**1980**	Gary Carter	**1987**	Tim Wallach	**1995**	David Segui
1973	Mike Marshall	**1981**	Andre Dawson	**1988**	Andres Galarraga	**1996**	Hank Rodriguez
1974	Willie Davis	**1982**	Al Oliver	**1989**	Tim Wallach	**1997**	Pedro Martinez
1975	Gary Carter	**1983**	Andre Dawson;	**1990**	Tim Wallach	**1998**	Vladimir Guerrero
1976	Woodie Fryman		Tim Raines (tie)	**1991**	Dennis Martinez		

Directory of Sports Organizations

A number of Canadian amateur sports organizations can be reached at 1600 James Naismith Drive, Gloucester, Ontario K1B 5N4. These include:

Other sports organizations include:

Basketball Canada
(613)748-5607
www.cdnsport.cu/basketball

Canadian Amateur Boxing Assn
Tel: (613)748-5611
Fax: (613)748-5740
www.boxing.ca/cuba.html

Canadian Amateur Diving Assn
Tel: (613)748-5631

Canadian Amateur Hockey Association
Tel: (613)748-5613
Fax: (613)748-5709

Canadian Curling Association
Tel: (613)748-5628
Fax: (613)748-5713
www.curling.ca

Canadian Cycling Assn
Tel: (613)748-5629
Fax: (613)748-5692
www.canadian-cycling.com

Canadian Federation of Amateur Baseball
Tel: (613)748-5606
Fax: (613)748-5706

Canadian Figure Skating Association
Tel: (613)748-5635
Fax: (613)748-5718
www.cfsa.ca

Canadian Interuniversity Athletic Union
Tel: (613)748-5619
Fax: (613)748-5764
www.ciau.ca

Canadian Soccer Association
Tel: (613)748-5667
Fax: (613)745-1938

Canadian Track and Field Assn
Tel: (613)748-5678
Fax: (613)748-5645

Canadian Volleyball Assn
Tel: (613)748-5681

Football Canada
Tel: (613)748-5636
Fax: (613)748-5702

Rowing Canada
Tel: (613)748-5656
Fax: (613)748-5712

Softball Canada
Tel: (613)748-5668
home.sprynet.com/sprynet/softball.ca

Swimming Canada
Tel: (613)748-5673
Fax: (613)748-5715
www.swimming.ca

Canadian Automobile Sports Clubs
Tel: (905)667-9500
Fax: (905)667-9555
www3.sympatico.ca/case.or

Canadian Trotting Assn
2150 Meadowvale Blvd
Mississauga, Ont.
L5N 6R6
Tel: (905)858-3060
Fax: (905)858-3111

Royal Canadian Golf Association
1333 Dorval Dr.
Oakville, Ont.
L6J 4Z3
Tel: (416)849-9700
Fax: (416)845-7040
www.rcga.org

Toronto Blue Jays Year-By-Year Record

Year	Won	Lost	Pct.	Pos.	GB	Home Attendance	Manager
1977	54	107	.335	7th	45½	1 701 052	Roy Hartsfield
1978	59	102	.366	7th	50	1 562 585	Roy Hartsfield
1979	53	109	.327	7th	50½	1 431 651	Roy Hartsfield
1980	67	95	.414	7th	36	1 400 327	Bob Mattick
1981	37	69	.349	—	—	755 083	Bob Mattick
1st half	16	42	.276	7th	19	—	
2nd half	21	27	.438	7th	7½	—	
1982	78	84	.481	6th[1]	17	1 275 978	Bobby Cox
1983	89	73	.549	4th	9	1 930 415	Bobby Cox
1984	89	73	.549	2nd	15	2 110 009	Bobby Cox
1985	99	62	.615	1st	+2	2 468 925	Bobby Cox
1986	86	76	.531	4th	9½	2 455 477	Jimy Williams
1987	96	66	.593	2nd	2	2 778 459	Jimy Williams
1988	87	75	.537	3rd	2	2 595 175	Jimy Williams
1989	89	73	.549	1st	+2	3 375 573	Williams/Cito Gaston
1990	86	76	.531	2nd	2	3 885 284	Cito Gaston
1991	91	71	.562	1st	+7	4 001 526	Cito Gaston
1992	96	66	.593	1st	+4	4 028 318	Cito Gaston
1993	95	67	.586	1st	+7	4 057 947	Cito Gaston
1994	55	60	.476	3rd[2]	16	2 907 933	Cito Gaston
1995	56	88	.389	5th	30	2 826 483	Cito Gaston
1996	74	88	.457	4th	18	2 559 563	Cito Gaston[3]
1997	76	86	.469	5th	22	2 589 297	Cito Gaston[3]
1998	88	74	.543	3rd	26	2 454 303	Tim Johnson
1999	84	78	.518	3rd	14	2 163 473	Jim Fregosi

(1) Tied. (2) Eastern Division: first year with three divisions (3) Gaston was fired with five games remaining in the 1997 season.

Toronto Blue Jays Individual Statistics, 1999

Batters

	Avg	OBA	AB	R	H	2B	3B	HR	RBI	BB	SO	SB	CS	E
Craig Grebeck	.363	.443	113	18	41	7	0	0	10	15	13	0	0	5
Tony Fernandez	.328	.427	485	73	159	41	0	6	75	77	62	6	7	18
Homer Bush	.320	.353	485	69	155	26	4	5	55	21	82	32	8	16
Shawn Green	.309	.384	614	134	190	45	0	42	123	66	117	20	7	1
Shannon Stewart	.304	.371	608	102	185	28	2	11	67	59	83	37	14	5
Dave Segui	.298	.355	440	57	131	27	3	14	52	40	60	1	2	4
Alex Gonzalez	.292	.370	154	22	45	13	0	2	12	16	23	4	2	4
Darrin Fletcher	.291	.339	412	48	120	26	0	18	80	26	47	0	0	2
Tony Batista	.285	.328	375	61	107	25	1	26	79	22	79	2	0	12
Carlos Delgado	.272	.377	573	113	156	39	0	44	134	86	141	1	1	14
Pat Kelly	.267	.318	116	17	31	7	0	6	20	10	23	0	1	6
Pat Borders	.265	.286	34	3	9	0	1	1	6	1	5	0	1	2
Vernon Wells	.261	.293	88	8	23	5	0	1	8	4	18	1	1	0
Jose Cruz Jr.	.241	.358	349	63	84	19	3	14	45	64	91	14	4	3
Willis Otanez	.237	.293	207	28	49	11	0	7	24	15	46	0	0	6
Jacob Brumfield	.235	.307	170	25	40	8	3	2	19	19	39	1	2	3
Dave Hollins	.222	.260	99	12	22	5	0	2	6	5	22	0	0	0
Mike Matheny	.215	.271	163	16	35	6	0	3	17	12	37	0	0	2
Willie Greene	.204	.266	226	22	46	7	0	12	41	20	56	0	0	1
Brian McRae	.195	.340	82	11	16	3	1	3	11	16	22	0	1	0
Geronimo Berroa	.194	.315	62	11	12	3	0	1	6	9	15	0	0	0
Rob Butler	.143	.250	7	1	1	0	0	0	1	0	0	0	0	0

Source: *Canadian Press*

AVG = batting average; OBA = on base average; AB = times at bat; R = runs; H = hits; 2B = doubles; 3B = triples; HR = home runs; RBI = runs batted in; BB = walks; SO = strikeouts; SB = stolen bases; CS = caught stealing; E = errors.

▶

Pitchers

	W	L	ERA	G	GS	SV	IP	H	R	ER	HR	BB	SO
Paul Quantrill	3	2	3.33	41	0	0	48.2	53	19	18	5	17	28
Billy Koch	0	5	3.39	56	0	31	63.2	55	26	24	5	30	57
John Frascatore	7	1	3.41	33	0	1	37	42	16	14	5	9	22
Graeme Lloyd	5	3	3.63	74	0	3	72	68	36	29	11	23	47
Roy Halladay	8	7	3.92	36	18	1	149.1	156	76	65	19	79	82
Chris Carpenter	9	8	4.38	24	24	0	150	177	81	73	16	48	106
Paul Spoljaric	2	2	4.65	37	2	0	62	62	41	32	9	32	63
Pat Hentgen	11	12	4.79	34	34	0	199	225	115	106	32	65	118
David Wells	17	10	4.82	34	34	0	231.2	246	132	124	32	62	169
Kelvim Escobar	14	11	5.69	33	30	0	174	203	118	110	19	81	129
Pete Munro	0	2	6.02	31	2	0	55.1	70	38	37	6	23	38
Joey Hamilton	7	8	6.52	22	18	0	98	118	73	71	13	39	56
Dan Plesac	0	3	8.34	30	0	0	22.2	28	21	21	4	9	26

Source: *Canadian Press*

W = games won; L = games lost; ERA = earned run average; G = games played in; GS = games started; SV = saves; IP = innings pitched; H = hits allowed; R = runs allowed; ER = earned runs; HR = home runs allowed; BB = walks allowed; SO = strikeouts.

Toronto Blue Jays Team Records up to 1999 season

Batting

Single Season

Batting Average: John Olerud, 1993, .363

At Bats: Tony Fernandez, 1986, 687

Games: Tony Fernandez, 1986, 163

Hits: Tony Fernandez, 1986, 213

Runs: Paul Molitor, 1993, 121

Singles: Tony Fernandez, 1986, 161

Doubles: John Olerud, 1993, 54

Triples: Tony Fernandez, 1990, 17

Home Runs: George Bell, 1987, 47

Runs Batted In: George Bell, 1987, 134; Carlos Delgado, 1999, 134

Total Bases: George Bell, 1987, 369

Slugging Average: George Bell, 1987, .605

On-Base Average: John Olerud, 1993, .473

Stolen Bases: Dave Collins, 1984, 60

Strikeouts: José Canseco, 1998, 154

Walks: Fred McGriff, 1989, 119

Hit By Pitch: Ed Sprague, 1996, 18

Hitting Streak: Shawn Green ,1999, 27

Career Leaders

Batting Average: Roberto Alomar, .310

At Bats: Lloyd Moseby, 5,124

Games: Lloyd Moseby, 1,392

Hits: Tony Fernandez, 1,406

Runs: Lloyd Moseby, 768

Singles: Tony Fernandez, 1,035

Doubles: Tony Fernandez, 246

Triples: Tony Fernandez, 72

Home Runs: Joe Carter, 203

Runs Batted In: George Bell, 740

Total Bases: George Bell, 2,201

Slugging Average: Fred McGriff, .530

On-Base Average: Fred McGriff, .391

Stolen Bases: Lloyd Moseby, 255

Strikeouts: Lloyd Moseby, 1,015

Walks: Lloyd Moseby, 547

Hit By Pitch: Lloyd Moseby, 50

▶

Pitching

Single Season	Career Leaders
Games: Mark Eichhorn, 1987, 89	**Games:** Tom Henke, 446
Games Started: Jim Clancy, 1982, 40	**Games Started:** Dave Stieb, 408
Complete Games: Dave Stieb, 1982, 19	**Complete Games:** Dave Stieb, 103
Innings Pitched: Dave Stieb, 1982, 288.1	**Innings Pitched:** Dave Stieb, 2 872.1
Wins: Jack Morris, 1992, 21	
Roger Clemens, 1997, 21	**Wins:** Dave Stieb, 175
Losses: Jerry Garvin, 1977, 18; Phil Huffman, 1979, 18	**Losses:** Jim Clancy, 140
Saves: Duane Ward, 1993, 45	**Saves:** Tom Henke, 217
Earned Run Average: Roger Clemens, 1997, 2.05	**Earned Run Average:** Tom Henke, 2.48
Shutouts: Dave Stieb, 1982, 5	**Shutouts:** Dave Stieb, 30
Strikeouts: Roger Clemens, 1997, 292	**Strikeouts:** Dave Stieb, 1 658
Walks: Jim Clancy, 1980, 128	**Walks:** Dave Stieb, 1 020
Home Runs Allowed: Woody Williams, 1998, 36	**Home Runs Allowed:** Jim Clancy, 219
Hit Batsmen: Dave Stieb, 1986, 15	**Hit Batsmen:** Dave Stieb, 129

Source: *Canadian Press*

Toronto Blue Jays Player of the Year

1977	Bob Bailor	**1984**	Dave Collins	**1991**	Roberto Alomar
1978	Bob Bailor	**1985**	Jesse Barfield	**1992**	Roberto Alomar
1979	Alfredo Griffin	**1986**	Jesse Barfield	**1993**	Paul Molitor
1980	John Mayberry	**1987**	George Bell	**1994**	Joe Carter
1981	Dave Stieb	**1988**	Fred McGriff	**1995**	Roberto Alomar
1982	Damaso Garcia	**1989**	George Bell	**1996**	Ed Sprague
1983	Lloyd Moseby	**1990**	Kelly Gruber	**1997**	Carlos Delgado
				1998	Carlos Delgado

Still Surfing for Sports Info?

Football

Canadian Football League
www.cfl.ca
all you need to know about the CFL

National Football League
www.nfl.com
all the information you want on the NFL

Canadian Junior Football League
www.cjfl.ca
scores, standings and stats

Hockey
Canadian Hockey League
www.canoe.ca/CHL/
info on Canadian junior hockey with links to various leagues

Ontario Hockey League
www.ontariohockeyleague.com
scores, standings, game recaps and news

American Hockey League
www.theahl.com
stats, rosters and team info

The Hockey News
www.thn.com
news and stats

www.hockeysfuture.com
learn about the stars of tomorrow today

See also pages 683, 694, 727

BASKETBALL

National Basketball Association, 1998–99

Final Standings

Eastern Conference

■ Atlantic Division

	W	L	Pct	GB
Miami Heat	33	17	.660	-
Orlando Magic	33	17	.660	-
Philadelphia 76ers	28	22	.560	5
New York Knicks	27	23	.540	6
Boston Celtics	19	31	.380	14
Washington Wizards	18	32	.360	15
New Jersey Nets	16	34	.320	17

■ Central Division

	W	L	Pct	GB
Indiana Pacers	33	17	.660	-
Atlanta Hawks	31	19	.620	2
Detroit Pistons	29	21	.580	4
Milwaukee Bucks	28	22	.560	5
Charlotte Hornets	26	24	.520	7
Toronto Raptors	**23**	**27**	**.460**	**10**
Cleveland Cavaliers	22	28	.440	11
Chicago Bulls	13	37	.260	20

Western Conference

■ Midwest Division

	W	L	Pct	GB
San Antonio Spurs	37	13	.740	-
Utah Jazz	37	13	.740	-
Houston Rockets	31	19	.620	6
Minnesota Timberwolves	25	25	.500	12
Dallas Mavericks	19	31	.380	18
Denver Nuggets	14	36	.280	23
Vancouver Grizzlies	**8**	**42**	**.160**	**29**

■ Pacific Division

	W	L	Pct	GB
Portland Trailblazers	35	15	.700	-
Los Angeles Lakers	31	19	.620	4
Sacramento Kings	27	23	.540	8
Phoenix Suns	27	23	.540	8
Seattle Supersonics	25	25	.500	10
Golden State Warriors	21	29	.420	14
Los Angeles Clippers	9	41	.180	26

(1) Prior to this season, Washingtons NBA team was known as the Bullets.

NBA Playoff Results, 1998–99

Eastern Conference

First Round (best-of-5)
New York defeated Miami 3-2
Indiana defeated Milwaukee 3-0
Philadelphia defeated Orlando 3-1
Atlanta defeated Detroit 3-2

Semifinals (best-of-7)
Indiana defeated Philadelphia 4-0
New York defeated Atlanta 4-0

Western Conference

First Round (best-of-5)
San Antonio defeated Minnesota 3-1
Portland defeated Phoenix 3-0
Utah defeated Sacramento 3-2
L.A. Lakers defeated Houston 3-1

Semifinals (best-of-7)
San Antonio defeated L.A. Lakers 4-0
Portland defeated Utah 4-2

Conference finals (best-of-7)
East – New York defeated Indiana 4-2
West – San Antonio defeated Portland 4-0

Final (best-of-7)
San Antonio defeated New York 4-1

Source: *Canadian Press*

1998–99 NBA Season Review

The San Antonio Spurs were the champions of the NBA season that nearly never was.

At the precipice of becoming the first major sports league to cancel an entire season, the NBA owners and players' association signed an agreement to end a 204-day lockout and save the 1998-99 season.

The teams played a 50-game schedule and for the first time in a few years, somebody other than the Chicago Bulls had a shot at winning it all.

With Michael Jordan's retirement and the free-agent defections of Scottie Pippen and Dennis Rodman, the Bulls turned to chumps from champions. Their 13-37 record was the third-worst in the NBA.

The Spurs cruised through the playoffs to claim their first-ever NBA championship. They lost only twice in the playoffs, beating the surprise New York Knicks 4-1 in the final.

The Knicks, who battled the Toronto Raptors and Charlotte Hornets for the final playoff berth in the East, stunned Miami in the first round and kept on advancing despite an injury to Patrick Ewing.

The Raptors made an impressive turnaround from a dismal 1997-98, making a run at their first playoff spot and .500 season. Led by rookie of the year Vince Carter and veterans Charles Oakley and Kevin Willis, the Raptors finished 23-27.

In Vancouver, things continued to get worse for the Grizzlies. They finished last in the NBA at 8-42 and aside from Shareef Abdur-Rahim, there were no real bright spots.

NBA Statistical Leaders, 1998–99

■ Scoring

	FG	Pts	Avg
Allen Iverson, Phi	435	1284	26.8
Shaquille O'Neal, LAL	510	1289	26.3
Karl Malone, Utah	393	1164	23.8
Shareef Abdur-Rahim, Van	386	1152	23.0
Keith Van Horn, NJ	322	916	21.8
Tim Duncan, SA	418	1084	21.7
Gary Payton, Sea	401	1084	21.7
Stephon Marbury, NJ	378	1044	21.3
Antonio McDyess, Den	415	1061	21.2
Grant Hill, Det	384	1053	21.1

■ Field Goal Percentage

	FG	FGA	Pct
Shaquille O'Neal, LAL	510	885	.576
Otis Thorpe, Mia	240	440	.545
Hakeem Olajuwon, Hou	373	525	.514
Alonzo Mourning, Mia	324	634	.511
David Robinson, SA	268	527	.509
Rasheed Wallace, Por	242	476	.508
Bison Dele, Det	216	431	.501
Tim Duncan, SA	418	845	.495
Danny Fortson, Bos	191	386	.495
Vitaly Potapenko, Bos	204	412	.495

■ Rebounds

	Def	Total	Avg
Chris Webber, Sac	396	545	13.0
Charles Barkley, Hou	349	516	12.3
Dikembe Mutombo, Atl	418	610	12.2
Danny Fortson, Bos	371	581	11.6
Tim Duncan, SA	412	571	11.4
Alonzo Mourning, Mia	341	507	11.0
Antonio McDyess, Den	369	537	10.7
Shaquille O'Neal LAL	338	525	10.7
Kevin Garnett, Min	323	489	10.4
Vlade Divac, Sac	361	501	10.0

■ Free Throw Percentage

	FT	FTA	Pct
Reggie Miller, Ind	226	247	.915
Chauncey Billups, Den	157	172	.913
Darrell Armstrong, Orl	161	178	.904
Ray Allen, Mil	176	195	.903
Hersey Hawkins, Chi	119	132	.902
Jeff Hornacek, Utah	125	140	.893
Chris Mullin, Ind	80	92	.870
Glenn Robinson, Mil	140	161	.870
Mario Elie, SA	103	119	.866
Eric Piatkowski, LAC	88	102	.863

■ Assists

	G	Ast	Avg
Jason Kidd, Pho	50	539	10.8
Rod Strickland, Was	44	434	9.9
Stephon Marbury, Min	49	437	8.9
Gary Payton, Sea	50	436	8.7
Terrell Brandon, Min	36	309	8.6
Mark Jackson, Ind	49	386	7.9
Brevin Knight, Cle	39	302	7.7
John Stockton, Utah	50	374	7.5
Avery Johnson, SA	50	369	7.4
Nick Van Exel, Den	50	368	7.4

■ Steals

	G	Steals	Avg
Kendall Gill, NJ	50	134	2.68
Eddie Jones, Cha	50	125	2.50
Allen Iverson, Phi	48	110	2.29
Jason Kidd, Pho	50	114	2.28
Doug Christie, Tor	**50**	**113**	**2.26**
Anfernee Hardaway, Pho	50	111	2.22
Gary Payton, Sea	50	109	2.18
Darrell Armstrong, Orl	50	108	2.16
Eric Snow, Phi	48	100	2.08
Mookie Blaylock, Atl	48	99	2.06

■ 3-Point Field Goal Percentage

	3FG	3FGA	Pct
Dell Curry, Mil (Now with Tor)	69	145	.476
Chris Mullin, Ind	73	157	.465
Hubert Davis, Dal	65	144	.451
Walt Williams, Por	63	144	.438
Michael Dickerson, Hou	71	164	.433
Dale Ellis, Mil	94	217	.433
Jeff Hornacek, Utah	34	81	.420
Clifford Robinson, Pho	58	139	.417
George McCloud, Den	69	166	.416
Jud Buechler, Det	61	148	.412

■ Blocked Shots

	G	Blocks	Avg
Alonzo Mourning, Mia	46	180	3.91
Shawn Bradley, Dal	49	159	3.24
Theo Ratliff, Phi	50	149	2.98
Dikembe Mutombo, Atl	50	147	2.94
Greg Ostertag, Utah	48	131	2.73
Patrick Ewing, NY	38	100	2.63
Tim Duncan, SA	50	126	2.52
Hakeem Olajuwon, Hou	50	123	2.46
David Robinson, SA	49	119	2.43
Antonio McDyess, Den	50	115	2.30

Source: *Canadian Press*

All-Time NBA Statistical Leaders

(as of the end of the 1998–99 season)

	Scoring Average (400 games or 10 000 points minimum)				
	G	FGM	FTM	Points	Avg
Michael Jordan	930	10 962	6 798	29 277	31.5
Wilt Chamberlain	1 045	12 681	6 057	31 419	30.1
Elgin Baylor	846	8 693	5 763	23 149	27.4
Shaquille O'Neal*	455	4 940	2 462	12 343	27.1
Jerry West	932	9 016	7 160	25 192	27.0
Bob Pettit	792	7 349	6 182	20 880	26.4
George Gervin	791	8 045	4 541	20 708	26.2
Karl Malone*	1 110	10 683	7 511	28 946	26.1
Oscar Robertson	1 040	9 508	7 694	26 710	25.7
Dominique Wilkins	1 047	9 913	6 002	26 534	25.3

Most Games Played, Career	Most Points, Career	Most Minutes, Career	Field Goals, Career
Robert Parish 1 611	Kareem Abdul-Jabbar 38 387	Kareem Abdul-Jabbar 57 446	Kareem Abdul-Jabbar 15 837
Kareem Abdul-Jabbar .1 560	Wilt Chamberlain 31 419	Elvin Hayes 50 000	Wilt Chamberlain 12 681
Moses Malone 1 329	Michael Jordan 29 277	Wilt Chamberlain 47 859	Elvin Hayes 10 976
Buck Williams 1 307	Karl Malone 28 946	John Havlicek 46 471	Michael Jordan 10 962
Elvin Hayes 1 303	Moses Malone 27 409	Robert Parish 45 704	Alex English 10 659

Source: *Canadian Press*

*active player

Toronto Raptors 1998–99 Statistics

Player	G	FG	FG-PCT	3-pt FG	FT	PCT	REB	AST	STL	PTS	AVG
Vince Carter	.50	345	.450	204	.761	19	283	149	55	913	18.3
Doug Christie	.50	252	.388	207	.841	49	207	187	113	760	15.2
Kevin Willis	.42	187	.418	130	.839	0	350	67	28	504	12.0
Dee Brown	.49	187	.378	40	.727	135	103	143	56	549	11.2
Tracy McGrady	.49	168	.436	114	.726	8	278	113	52	458	9.3
John Wallace	.48	153	.432	105	.700	0	171	46	12	411	8.6
Charles Oakley	.50	140	.428	67	.807	1	374	168	46	348	7.0
Alvin Williams	.50	95	.401	44	.846	14	82	130	51	248	5.0
John Thomas	.39	71	.577	27	.563	0	134	15	17	169	4.3
Reggie Slater	.30	31	.383	53	.624	0	70	5	3	115	3.8
Michael Stewart	.42	22	.415	17	.680	0	99	5	4	61	1.5
Sean Marks	.8	5	.625	1	.500	0	1	0	1	11	1.4
Negele Knight	.6	3	.375	2	.500	0	6	8	1	8	1.3
Michael Williams	.2	1	.200	0	—	0	1	0	0	2	1.0

Source: *Canadian Press*
G= games played; FG = field goals; FG PCT = field goal percentage; 3-pt FG = three-point field goals; FT = free throws; FT PCT = free throw percentage; REB = rebounds; AST = assists; STL = steals; PTS = points; AVG = scoring average.

Vancouver Grizzlies 1998–99 Statistics

Player	G	FG	FG-PCT	3-pt FG	FT	PCT	REB	AST	STL	PTS	AVG
Shareef Abdur-Rahim	.50	386	.432	369	.841	11	374	172	69	1152	23.0
Mike Bibby	.50	260	.430	127	.751	15	136	325	78	662	13.2
Tony Massenburg	.43	189	.487	103	.665	0	257	23	26	481	11.2
Bryant Reeves	.25	102	.406	67	.578	0	138	37	13	271	10.8
Felipe Lopez	.47	169	.446	87	.644	12	166	62	49	437	9.3
Doug West	.14	31	.477	19	.760	0	25	19	16	81	5.8
Cherokee Parks	.48	118	.429	30	.545	0	243	36	28	266	5.5
Michael Smith	.48	77	.535	76	.594	0	350	48	46	230	4.8
De Juan Wheat	.46	73	.378	40	.727	22	45	102	26	208	4.5
Pete Chilcutt	.46	63	.366	14	.824	26	117	30	22	166	3.6
Rodrick Rhodes	.13	13	.250	16	.640	1	17	11	5	43	3.3
J.R. Henderson	.30	35	.365	25	.556	2	47	22	9	97	3.2
Terry Dehere	.26	31	.365	5	.714	16	24	27	7	83	3.2
Lee Mayberry	.9	7	.368	4	.800	2	3	23	7	20	2.2
Makhtar Ndiaye	.4	1	.250	3	.750	0	5	1	0	3	0.75

Source: *Canadian Press*
G= games played; FG = field goals; FG-PCT = field goal percentage; 3-pt FG = three-point field goals; FT = free throws; FT PCT = free throw percentage; REB = rebounds; AST = assists; STL = steals; PTS = points; AVG = scoring average.

FOOTBALL

Canadian Football League

(1998 Standings)

Team	W	L	T	F	A	Pts
East Division						
Hamilton Tiger-Cats 12	5	1	503	351	25	
Montreal Allouettes 12	5	1	470	435	25	
Toronto Argonauts 9	9	0	452	410	18	
Winnipeg Blue Bombers ..3	15	0	399	588	6	

Team	W	L	T	F	A	Pts
West Division						
Calgary Stampeders 12	6	0	558	397	24	
Edmonton Eskimos 9	9	0	396	450	18	
B.C. Lions 9	9	0	394	427	18	
Saskatchewan Roughriders 5	13	0	411	525	10	

Divisional Semi-finals:
Montreal 41, Toronto 28
Edmonton 40, B.C. 33

Divisional Finals:
Hamilton 22, Montreal 20
Calgary 33, Edmonton 10

Grey Cup:
Calgary 26, Hamilton 24

Source: *Canadian Football League*

Canadian Football League All-Stars, 1998

(voted by Football Reporters of Canada)

Offence

Quarterback: Jeff Garcia, Calgary
Running Back: Kelvin Anderson, Calgary
Running Back: Mike Pringle, Montreal
Slotback: Derrell Mitchell, Toronto
Slotback: Allen Pitts, Calgary
Wide Receiver: Don Narcisse, Saskatchewan
Wide Receiver: Terry Vaughn, Calgary
Centre: Carl Coulter, Hamilton
Guard: Fred Childress, Calgary
Guard: Pierre Vercheval, Toronto
Tackle: Moe Elewonibi, B.C.
Tackle: Uzooma Okeke, Montreal
Punter: Tony Martino, Calgary
Kicker: Paul Osbaldiston, Hamilton
Specialty Teams: Eric Blount, Winnipeg

Defence

Tackle: Joe Fleming, Winnipeg
Tackle: Johnny Scott, B.C.
End: Elfrid Payton, Montreal
End: Joe Montford, Hamilton
Linebacker: Calvin Tiggle, Hamilton
Linebacker: Alondra Johnson, Calgary
Linebacker: Willie Pless, Edmonton
Cornerback: Eric Carter, Hamilton
Cornerback: Steve Muhammad, B.C.
Defensive back: Gerald Vaughn, Hamilton
Defensive back: Orlando Steinauer, Hamilton
Safety: Dale Joseph, B.C.

Source: *Canadian Football League.*

The Grey Cup

The Grey Cup was donated in 1909 by Governor General Earl Grey for the "Rugby Football Championship of Canada." Since 1954, only teams in the Canadian Foot-ball League have challenged for the trophy, with the winners of the East and West divisions meeting in the championship game.

1909 ....U. of Toronto 26, Parkdale 6
1910 ....U. of Toronto 16, Ham. Tigers 7
1911 ....U. of Toronto 14, Toronto 7
1912 ....Ham. Alerts 11, Toronto 4
1913 ....Ham. Tigers 44, Parkdale 2
1914 ....Toronto 14, U. of Toronto 2
1915 ....Ham. Tigers 13, Tor. R.A.A. 7
1916–19 ....No games held.
1920 ....U. of Toronto 16, Toronto 3
1921 ....Toronto 23, Edmonton 0
1922 ....Queen's U. 13, Edmonton 1
1923 ....Queen's U. 54, Regina 0
1924 ....Queen's U. 11, Balmy Beach 3
1925 ....Ott. Senators 24, Winnipeg 1
1926 ....Ott. Senators 10, U. of Toronto 7
1927 ....Balmy Beach 9, Ham. Tigers 6
1928 ....Ham. Tigers 30, Regina 0
1929 ,........Ham. Tigers 14, Regina 3
1930 ....Balmy Beach 11, Regina 6
1931 ....Mtl. A.A.A. 22, Regina 0
1932 ....Ham. Tigers 25, Regina 6
1933 ....Toronto 4, Sarnia 3
1934 ....Sarnia 20, Regina 12
1935 ....Winnipeg 18, Ham. Tigers 12
1936 ....Sarnia 26, Ott. R.R. 20
1937 ....Toronto 4, Winnipeg 3
1938 ....Toronto 30, Winnipeg 7
1939 ....Winnipeg 8, Ottawa 7
1940[1] ....Ottawa 12, Balmy Beach 5
    Ottawa 8, Balmy Beach 2
1941 ....Winnipeg 18, Ottawa 16
1942 ....Tor. R.C.A.F. 8, Win. R.C.A.F. 5
1943 ....Ham. F. Wild 23, Win. R.C.A.F. 14
1944 ....Mtl. St. H.D. Navy 7, Ham. F. Wild 6
1945 ....Toronto 35, Winnipeg 0
1946 ....Toronto 28, Winnipeg 6
1947 ....Toronto 10, Winnipeg 9
1948 ....Calgary 12, Ottawa 7
1949 ....Mtl. Als. 28, Calgary 15
1950 ....Toronto 13, Winnipeg 0
1951 ....Ottawa 21, Saskatchewan 14
1952 ....Toronto 21, Edmonton 11
1953 ....Hamilton 12, Winnipeg 6

1954 ....Edmonton 26, Montreal 25
1955 ....Edmonton 34, Montreal 19
1956 ....Edmonton 50, Montreal 27
1957 ....Hamilton 32, Winnipeg 7
1958 ....Winnipeg 35, Hamilton 28
1959 ....Winnipeg 21, Hamilton 7
1960 ....Ottawa 16, Edmonton 6
1961 ....Winnipeg 21, Hamilton 14
1962 ....Winnipeg 28, Hamilton 27
1963 ....Hamilton 21, BC 10
1964 ....BC 34, Hamilton 24
1965 ....Hamilton 22, Winnipeg 16
1966 ....Saskatchewan 29, Ottawa 14
1967 ....Hamilton 24, Saskatchewan 1
1968 ....Ottawa 24, Calgary 21
1969 ....Ottawa 29, Saskatchewan 11
1970 ....Montreal 23, Calgary 10
1971 ....Calgary 14, Toronto 11
1972 ....Hamilton 13, Saskatchewan 10
1073 ....Ottawa 22, Edmonton 18
1974 ....Montreal 20, Edmonton 7
1975 ....Edmonton 9, Montreal 8
1976 ....Ottawa 23, Saskatchewan 20
1977 ....Montreal 41, Edmonton 6
1978 ....Edmonton 20, Montreal 13
1979 ....Edmonton 17, Montreal 9
1980 ....Edmonton 48, Hamilton 10
1981 ....Edmonton 26, Ottawa 23
1982 ....Edmonton 32, Toronto 16
1983 ....Toronto 18, BC 17
1984 ....Winnipeg 47, Hamilton 17
1985 ....BC 37, Hamilton 24
1986 ....Hamilton 39, Edmonton 15
1987 ....Edmonton 38, Toronto 36
1988 ....Winnipeg 22, B.C. 21
1989 ....Saskatchewan 43, Hamilton 40
1990 ....Winnipeg 50, Edmonton 11
1991 ....Toronto 36, Calgary 21
1992 ....Calgary 24, Winnipeg 10
1993 ....Edmonton 33, Winnipeg 23
1994 ....BC 26, Baltimore 23
1995 ....Baltimore 37, Calgary 20
1996 ....Toronto 43, Edmonton 37
1997 ....Toronto 47, Saskatchewan 23
1998 ....Calgary 26, Hamilton 24

Source: *Canadian Press*

(1) A 2-game total point series.

CFL Individual Player Records

(up to the end of the 1998 season)

Most games played: .... **372, Lui Passaglia**, BC (1976-98)

Most career points: .... **3 668, Lui Passaglia**, BC (1976-98)

Most points one season: .... **236, Lance Chomyc**, Tor, 1991

Most points one game: .... **36, Bob McNamara**, Wpg, Wpg at BC, Oct. 13, 1956

Most touchdowns one season: .... **22, Cory Philpot**, BC, 1995

Most touchdowns one game: .... **6, Bob McNamara**, Wpg, Wpg at BC, Oct. 13, 1956
Eddie James, Wpg, Wpg St Johns at Wpg, Garrison, Sept 28, 1932

Most touchdown passes one season: .... **48, Doug Flutie**, Cal, 1994

Most touchdown passes one game: .... **8, Joe Zuger**, Ham, Sask at Ham, Oct. 15, 1962

Most touchdowns scored rushing one season: .... **18, Gerry James**, Wpg, 1957; Jim Germany, Edm, 1981

Most touchdowns scored rushing one game: .... **5, Earl Lunsford**, Cal, Edm at Cal, Sept. 3, 1962,
Martin Paton, Shrev, Wpg at Shrev, Aug. 5, 1995

Most touchdowns on pass receptions one season: .... **21, Allen Pitts**, Cal, 1994

Most touchdowns on pass receptions one game: .... **5, Ernie Pitts**, Wpg, Wpg at Sask, Aug. 29, 1959

Most passes attempted one season: .... **770, Kent Austin**, Sask, 1992

Most passes attempted one game: .... **65, Kent Austin**, Sask, Edm at Sask, Sept. 15, 1991

Most passes completed one season: .... **466, Doug Flutie**, BC, 1991

Most passes completed one game: .... **41, Dieter Brock**, Wpg, Wpg at Ott, Oct. 3, 1981;
Kent Austin, Sask, Sask at Tor, Oct. 31, 1993

Most yards passed one season: .... **6 619, Doug Flutie**, BC, 1991

Most yards passed one game: .... **713, Matt Dunigan**, Edm at Wpg, July 14, 1994

Most consecutive pass completions: .... **18, Joe Paopao**, BC, Tor at BC, Sept. 22, 1979

Longest pass: .... **109 yds, Sam Etcheverry to Hal Patterson**, Mtl, Ham at Mtl, Sept. 22, 1956;
Jerry Keeling to Terry Evanshen, Cal, Cal at Wpg, Sept. 27, 1966

Most yards rushing one season: .... **2065, Mike Pringle**, Mtl, 1998

Most yards rushing one game: .... **287, Ron Stewart**, Ott, Ott at Mtl, Oct. 10, 1960

Longest rushing plays: .... **109 yds, George Dixon**, Mtl, Ott at Mtl, Sept. 2, 1963;
.... **Willie Fleming**, BC, BC at Edm, Oct. 17, 1964

Most carries one season: .... **347, Mike Pringle**, Mtl, 1975

Most carries one game: .... **37, Doyle Orange**, Tor, Ham at Tor, Aug. 13, 1975

Most pass reception yardage one season: .... **2036, Allen Pitts**, Cal, 1994

Most pass reception yardage one game: .... **338, Hal Patterson**, Mtl, Mtl at Ham, Sept. 29, 1956

Most pass receptions one season: .... **160, Derrell Mitchell**, Tor, 1998

Most pass receptions one game: .... **16, Terry Greer**, Tor, Tor at Ott, Aug. 19, 1983
Brian Wiggins, Cal, Cal at Sask, Oct 23, 1993
Derrell Michell, Tor, Tor at Edm, Sept. 26, 1998

Most combined yards one game: .... **401, Raghib Ismail**, Tor, Tor at Ott, July 9, 1992

Most field goals one season: .... **59, Dave Ridgway**, Sask, 1990

Most field goals one game: .... **8, Dave Ridgway**, Sask, Sask At Ott, July 29, 1984;
Dave Ridgway, Sask, Edm at Sask, July 23, 1988;
Mark McLoughlin, Cal, Sask at Cal, Aug. 5, 1996;
Paul Osbaldiston, Ham, Ham at Ott, Sept. 22, 1996

Longest field goal: .... **60 yds, Dave Ridgway**, Sask, Wpg at Sask, Sept. 6, 1987

Longest punt: .... **108 yds, Zenon Andrusyshyn**, Tor, Tor at Edm, Oct. 23, 1977

Best punting average one season: .... **50.2, Lui Passaglia**, BC, 1983

Most punt return yardage one season: .... **1 440, Henry Williams**, Edm, 1991

Most interceptions one game: .... **5, Rod Hill**, Wpg, Ham at Wpg, Sept 9, 1990

Most interceptions one season: .... **15, Al Brenner**, Ham, 1972

Most quarterback sacks one season: .... **26.5, James Parker**, BC, 1984

Most defensive tackles one season: .... **129, Calvin Tiggle**, Tor, 1994

Source: *Canadian Football League*

All-Time Leading CFL Players

(up to the end of the 1998 season)

Touchdowns

	TD	Seasons		TD	Seasons
George Reed, Sask	137	13 (1963-75)	Ray Elgaard, Sask	78	13 (1983-95)
Allen Pitts, Cal	101	9 (1990-98)	Matt Dunigan, Edm/BC/Tor/Wpg/Bir/Ham	77	14 (1983-96)
Brian Kelly, Edm	97	9 (1979-87)	Hal Patterson, Mtl/Ham	75	14 (1954-67)
Dick Shatto, Tor	91	12 (1954-65)	Leo Lewis, Wpg	75	12 (1955-66)
Tom Scott, Wpg/Edm/Cal	91	11 (1974-84)	Donald Narcisse, Sask	74	12 (1987-98)
Jackie Parker, Edm/Tor/BC	88	13 (1954-68)	Tony Gabriel, Ham/Ott	72	11 (1971-81)
Craig Ellis, Wpg/Cal/Sask/Tor/Edm	88	9 (1982-92)	Johnny Bright, Cal/Edm	71	13 (1952-64)
Earl Winfield, Ham	87	11 (1987-97)	Jim Germany, Edm	71	7 (1977-83)
Willie Fleming, BC	86	8 (1959-68)	Bob Simpson, Ott	70	13 (1950-62)
Normie Kwong, Cal/Edm	83	13 (1948-60)	Jeff Boyd, Wpg/Tor	70	9 (1983-91)
Michael Clemons, Tor	83	10 (1989-98)	Jim Young, BC	68	13 (1967-79)
Terry Evanshen, Mtl/Cal/Ham/Tor	80	14 (1965-78)	Jim Sandusky, Edm	68	11 (1984-96)
Virgil Wagner, Mtl	79	9 (1946-54)	Ron Stewart, Ott	67	12 (1959-70)
David Williams, BC/Ott/Edm/Tor/Wpg	79	8 (1988-95)			

Points

	Points	TD	Con	FG	Sing	Seasons
Lui Passaglia, BC	3 668	1	956	805	291	23 (1976-98)
Dave Ridgway, Sask	2 374	0	541	574	111	14 (1982-95)
Dave Cutler, Edm	2 237	0	627	464	218	16 (1969-84)
Paul Osbaldiston, BC/Wpg/Ham	2 129	0	486	477	212	13 (1986-98)
Mark McLoughlin, Cal	2 126	0	603	469	116	11 (1988-98)
Trevor Kennerd, Wpg	1 840	0	509	394	149	12 (1980-91)
Bernie Ruoff, Wpg/Ham	1 772	0	401	384	219	14 (1975-88)
Lance Chomyc, Tor	1 498	0	412	337	75	9 (1985-93)
Gerry Organ, Ott	1 462	2	391	318	105	12 (1971-83)
John T. Hay, Ott/Cal	1 411	0	363	308	124	11 (1978-88)
Terry Baker, Sask/Ott/Tor/Mtl	1 352	0	342	290	140	12 (1987-98)
Don Sweet, Mtl/Ham	1 342	0	327	314	73	14 (1972-85)
Troy Westwood, Wpg	1 313	1	348	298	65	8 (1991-98)
Sean Fleming, Edm	1 208	0	333	262	89	7 (1992-98)
Larry Robinson, Cal	1 030	9	362	171	101	14 (1961-74)
Zenon Andrusyshyn, Tor/Ham/Edm/Mtl	1 010	0	222	215	143	12 (1971-86)
Tommy Joe Coffey, Edm/Ham/Tor	971	65	204	108	53	14 (1959-73)
Dean Dorsey, Tor/Ott	951	0	244	219	50	8 (1982-91)
Jack Abendschan, Sask	863	0	312	159	74	11 (1965-75)
George Reed, Sask	823	137	0	0	1	13 (1963-75)
Jackie Parker, Edm-Tor-BC	750	88	103	40	19	13 (1954-68)

Rushing

	Yards	Carries	Avg	Long	TD	Seasons
George Reed, Sask	16 116	3 243	5.0	71	134	13	(1963-75)
Johnny Bright, Cal/Edm	10 909	1 969	5.5	90	69	13	(1952-64)
Normie Kwong, Cal/Edm	9 022	1 745	5.2	60	78	13	(1948-60)
Mike Pringle, Edm/Sac/Bal/Mtl	8 923	1 481	6.0	86	56	7	(1992-98)
Leo Lewis, Wpg	8 861	1 351	6.6	92	48	11	(1955-66)
Dave Thelen, Ott/Tor	8 463	1 530	5.5	77	47	9	(1958-66)
Tracy Ham, Edm/Tor/Bal/Mtl	7 832	1 015	7.7	80	59	12	(1987-98)
Damon Allen, Edm/Ott/Ham/Mem/BC	7 612	1 071	7.1	51	64	13	(1985-97)
Jim Evenson, BC/Ott	7 060	1 460	4.8	68	37	7	(1968-74)
Earl Lunsford, Cal	6 994	1 199	5.8	85	55	6	(1956-63)
Dick Shatto, Tor	6 958	1 322	5.3	67	39	12	(1954-65)

Passing
(ranked by total yards)

	Attempts	Comp	Yards	Pct	Avg[1]	Int	TD	Seasons
Ron Lancaster, Ott/Sask	6 233	3 384	50 535	54.3	14.9	396	333	19 (1960-78)
Matt Dunigan, Edm/BC/Tor/Wpg/Bir/Ham	5 476	3 057	43 857	55.8	14.3	211	306	14 (1983-96)
Damon Allen, Edm/Ott/Ham/Mps/BC	5 434	2 949	41 730	54.3	14.2	190	231	14 (1985-98)
Doug Flutie, BC/Cal/Tor	4 854	2 975	41 355	61.3	13.9	155	270	8 (1990-97)
Tom Clements, Ott/Sask/Ham/Wpg	4 657	2 807	39 041	60.3	13.9	214	252	12 (1975-87)
Tracy Ham, Edm/Tor/Bal	4 731	2 542	38 605	53.7	15.2	161	273	12 (1987-98)
Kent Austin, Sask/BC/Tor/Wpg	4 700	2 709	36 030	57.6	13.3	191	198	10 (1987-96)
Dieter Brock, Wpg/Ham	4 535	2 602	34 830	57.4	13.4	158	210	11 (1974-84)
Tom Burgess, Ott/Sask/Wpg	4 034	2 118	30 308	50.3	14.3	191	190	10 (1986-95)
Sam Etcheverry, Mtl	2 829	1 630	25 582	57.6	15.7	163	183	7 (1953-60)
Condredge Holloway, Ott/Tor/BC	3 013	1 710	25 193	56.8	14.7	94	155	13 (1975-87)
Russ Jackson, Ott	2 530	1 356	24 592	53.6	18.1	125	185	12 (1958-69)
Bernie Faloney, Edm/Ham/Mtl/BC	2 876	1 493	24 264	51.9	16.3	201	151	12 (1954-66)
Roy Dewalt, BC/Wpg/Ott	3 130	1 803	24 147	57.6	13.4	96	132	9 (1980-88)
Danny McMannus, Wpg/BC/Edm/Ham	2 988	1 589	23 998	53.2	15.1	131	118	9 (1990-98)
Danny Barrett, Cal/Tor/BC/Ott	3 078	1 656	23 419	53.8	14.1	93	133	14 (1984-97)

(1) Yards per pass completed. (2) Did not play in 1988 or 1989.

Pass Receiving

	Rec	Yards	Avg	TD	Seasons
Don Narcisse, Sask	872	11 766	13.5	77	12 (1987-98)
Ray Elgaard, Sask	819	13 098	16.0	78	13 (1983-95)
Allen Pitts, Cal	792	12 397	15.7	101	9 (1990-98)
Rocky DiPietro, Ham	706	9 762	13.8	45	14 (1978-91)
Darren Flutie, BC/Edm/Ham	665	9 949	15.0	45	8 (1991-98)
Tommy Joe Coffey, Edm/Ham/Tor	650	10 320	15.9	63	14 (1959-73)
Tom Scott, Wpg/Edm/Cal	649	10 837	16.7	88	11 (1974-84)

▶ Michael Clemons, Tor	630	6 554	10.4	44	10 (1989-98)
Tony Gabriel, Ham/Ott	614	9 832	16.0	69	11 (1971-81)
Terry Evanshen, Mtl/Cal/Ham/Tor	600	9 697	16.2	80	14 (1965-78)
Craig Ellis, Wpg/Cal/Sask/Tor/Edm	580	7 759	13.4	58	10 (1982-93)
Brian Kelly, Edm	575	11 169	19.4	97	9 (1979-87)

Source: *Canadian Football League*

CFL Outstanding Player Awards[1]

Outstanding player

1954 Sam Etcheverry, Mtl	**1969** Russ Jackson, Ott	**1984** Willard Reaves, Wpg
1955 Pat Abbruzzi, Mtl	**1970** Ron Lancaster, Sask	**1985** Mervyn Fernandez, BC
1956 Hal Patterson, Mtl	**1971** Don Jonas, Wpg	**1986** James Murphy, Wpg
1957 Jackie Parker, Edm	**1972** Garney Henley, Ham	**1987** Tom Clements, Wpg
1958 Jackie Parker, Edm	**1973** George McGowan, Edm	**1988** David Williams, BC
1959 Johnny Bright, Edm	**1974** Tom Wilkinson, Edm	**1989** Tracy Ham, Edm
1960 Jackie Parker, Edm	**1975** Willie Burden, Cal	**1990** Mike Clemons, Tor
1961 Bernie Faloney, Ham	**1976** Ron Lancaster, Sask	**1991** Doug Flutie, BC
1962 George Dixon, Mtl	**1977** Jimmy Edwards, Ham	**1992** Doug Flutie, Cal
1963 Russ Jackson, Ott	**1978** Tony Gabriel, Ott	**1993** Doug Flutie, Cal
1964 Lovell Coleman, Cal	**1979** David Green, Mtl	**1994** Doug Flutie, Cal
1965 George Reed, Sask	**1980** Deiter Brock, Wpg	**1995** Mike Pringle, Bal
1966 Russ Jackson, Ott	**1981** Deiter Brock, Wpg	**1996** Doug Flutie, Tor
1967 Peter Liske, Cal	**1982** Condredge Holloway, Tor	**1997** Doug Flutie, Tor
1968 Bill Symons, Tor	**1983** Warren Moon, Edm	**1998** Mike Pringle, Mtl

Outstanding Canadian

1954 Gerry James, Wpg	**1969** Russ Jackson, Ott	**1984** Nick Arakgi, Mtl
1955 Normie Kwong, Edm	**1970** Jim Young, BC	**1985** Paul Bennett, Ham
1956 Normie Kwong, Edm	**1971** Terry Evanshen, Mtl	**1986** Joe Poplawski, Wpg
1957 Gerry James, Wpg	**1972** Jim Young, BC	**1987** Scott Flagel, Wpg
1958 Ron Howell, Ham	**1973** Gerry Organ, Ott	**1988** Ray Elgaard, Sask
1959 Russ Jackson, Ott	**1974** Tony Gabriel, Ham	**1989** Rocky DiPietro, Ham
1960 Ron Stewart, Ott	**1975** Jim Foley, Ott	**1990** Ray Elgaard, Sask
1961 Tony Pajaczkowski, Cal	**1976** Tony Gabriel, Ott	**1991** Blake Marshall, Edm
1962 Harvey Wylie, Cal	**1977** Tony Gabriel, Ott	**1992** Ray Elgaard, Sask
1963 Russ Jackson, Ott	**1978** Tony Gabriel, Ott	**1993** Dave Sapunjis, Cal
1964 Tommy Grant, Ham	**1979** Dave Fennell, Edm	**1994** Gerald Wilcox, Wpg
1965 Zeno Karcz, Ham	**1980** Gerry Dattilio, Mtl	**1995** Dave Sapunjis, Cal
1966 Russ Jackson, Ott	**1981** Joe Poplawski, Wpg	**1996** Leroy Blugh, Edm
1967 Terry Evanshen, Cal	**1982** Rocky DiPietro, Ham	**1997** Sean Millington, BC
1968 Ken Nielson, Wpg	**1983** Paul Bennett, Wpg	**1998** Mike Morreale, Ham ▶

▶

Outstanding defensive player

1955 Tex Coulter, Mtl	1970 Wayne Harris, Cal	1985 Tyrone Jones, Wpg
1956 Kaye Vaughan, Ott	1971 Wayne Harris, Cal	1986 James Parker, BC
1957 Kaye Vaughan, Ott	1972 John Helton, Cal	1987 Gregg Stumon, BC
1958 Don Luzzi, Cal	1973 Ray Nettles, BC	1988 Grover Covington, Ham
1959 Roger Nelson, Edm	1974 John Helton, Cal	1989 Danny Bass, Edm
1960 Herb Gray, Wpg	1975 Jim Corrigall, Tor	1990 Greg Battle, Wpg
1961 Frank Rigney, Wpg	1976 Bill Baker, BC	1991 Greg Battle, Wpg
1962 John Barrow, Ham	1977 Dan Kepley, Edm	1992 Willie Pless, Edm
1963 Tom Brown, BC	1978 Dave Fennell, Edm	1993 Jearld Baylis, Sask
1964 Tom Brown, BC	1979 Ben Zambiasi, Ham	1994 Willie Pless, Edm
1965 Wayne Harris, Cal	1980 Dan Kepley, Edm	1995 Willie Pless, Edm
1966 Wayne Harris, Cal	1981 Dan Kepley, Edm	1996 Willie Pless, Edm
1967 Ed McQuarters, Sask	1982 James Parker, Edm	1997 Willie Pless, Edm
1968 Ken Lehmann, Ott	1983 Greg Marshall, Ott	1998 Joe Montford, Ham
1969 John LaGrone, Edm	1984 James Parker, BC	

Outstanding offensive lineman

1975 Charlie Turner, Edm	1983 Rudy Phillips, Ott	1991 Jim Mills, BC
1976 Dan Yochum, Mtl	1984 John Bonk, Wpg	1992 Rob Smith, Ott
1977 Al Wilson, BC	1985 Nick Bastaja, Wpg	1993 Chris Walby, Wpg
1978 Jim Coode, Ott	1986 Roger Aldag, Sask	1994 Shar Pourdanesh, Bal
1979 Mike Wilson, Edm	1987 Chris Walby, Wpg	1995 Mike Withycombe, Bal
1980 Mike Wilson, Edm	1988 Roger Aldag, Sask	1996 Mike Kiselak, Tor
1981 Larry Butler, Wpg	1989 Rod Connop, Edm	1997 Mike Kiselak, Tor
1982 Rudy Phillips, Ott	1990 Jim Mills, BC	1998 Fred Childress, Cal

Outstanding rookie

1972 Chuck Ealey, Ham	1981 Vince Goldsmith, Sask	1990 Reggie Barnes, Ott
1973 Johnny Rodgers, Mtl	1982 Chris Isaac, Ott	1991 Jon Volpe, BC
1974 Sam Cvijanovich, Tor	1983 Johnny Shepherd, Ham	1992 Mike Richardson, Wpg
1975 Tom Clements, Ott	1984 Dwaine Wilson, Mtl	1993 Michael O'Shea, Ham
1976 John Sciarra, BC	1985 Michael Gray, BC	1994 Matt Goodwin, Bal
1977 Leon Bright, BC	1986 Harold Hallman, Cal	1995 Shalon Baker, Edm
1978 Joe Poplawski, Wpg	1987 Gill Fenerty, Tor	1996 Kelvin Anderson, Cal
1979 Brian Kelly, Edm	1988 Orville Lee, Ott	1997 Derrell Mitchell, Tor
1980 William Miller, Wpg	1989 Stephen Jordan, Ham	1998 Steve Muhammad, BC

Source: *Canadian Football League*

(1) Winners are chosen by a vote of the Football Reporters of Canada; prior to 1989 they were known as the Schenley Awards.

Canadian Football Hall of Fame

(only players listed, (year of election))

Player / Year Elected / Team(s)

Ah You, Junior (1997) Mtl
Atchison, Ron, (1978) Sask
Bailey, Byron (1975) BC
Baker, Bitt (1994) Sask/BC
Barrow, John (1976) Ham
Batstone, Harry (1963) Tor/Queen's
Beach, Ormond (1963) Sarnia
Benecick, Al (1996) Sask
Box, Ab (1965) Balmy Beach/Tor
Breen, Joseph (1963) U of Toronto/Tor
Bright, Johnny (1970) Edm/Cal
Brock, Ralph Dieter (1995) Wpg/Ham
Brown, Tom (1984) BC
Campbell, Jerry "Soupy" (1996) Cal/Ott
Casey, Tom (1964) Wpg
Charlton, Ken (1992) Ott/Sask
Clements, Tom (1994) Ott/Sask/Ham/Wpg
Clark, Bill (1996) Sask
Coffey, Tommy Joe (1977) Edm/Cal
Conacher, Lionel (1963) Tor
Copeland, Royal (1988) Tor
Corrigal, Jim (1990) Tor
Cox, Ernest (1963) Ham
Craig, Ross (1964) Ham
Cronin, Carl (1967) Wpg
Cutler, Dave (1998) Edm
Cutler, Wes (1968) Tor
Dalla Riva, Peter (1993) Mtl
Dipietro, Rocky (1997) Ham
Dixon, George (1974) Mtl
Eliowitz, Abe (1969) Ott/Mtl
Emerson, Eddie (1963) Ott
Etcheverry, Sam (1969) Mtl
Evanshen, Terry (1984) Mtl/Cal/Ham/Tor
Faloney, Bernie (1974) Edm/Ham
Fear, Cap (1967) Tor/Mtl/Ham
Fennell, Dave (1990) Edm
Ferraro, John (196)6 Ham/Mtl
Fieldgate, Norm (1979) BC
Fleming, Willie (1982) BC
Gabriel, Tony (1984) Ham/Ott
Gaines, Geve (1994) Mtl/Ott
Gall, Hugh (1963) U of Toronto
Golab, Tony (1964) Ott
Grant, Tom (1995) Ham/Wpg
Gray, Herb (1983) Wpg
Griffing, Dean (1965) Sask/Cal
Hanson, Fritz (1963) Wpg
Harris, Dickie (1998) Mtl
Harris, Wayne (1976) Cal

Harrison, Herman (1993) Cal
Helton, John (1985) Cal/Wpg
Henley, Garney (1979) Ham
Hinton, Tom (1991) BC
Holloway, Condredge (1998) O /Tor/BC
Huffman, Dick (1987) Wpg/Cal
Isbister, Bob (1965) Ham
Jackson, Russ (1973) Ott
Jacobs, Jack (1963) Wpg
James, Eddie (1963) Wpg/Reg
James, Gerry (1981) Wpg
Kabat, Greg (1966) Wpg
Kapp, Joe (1984) Cal/BC
Keeling, Jerry (1989) Cal/Ott/Ham
Kelly, Brian (1991) Edm
Kelly, Ellison (1992) Edm/Ham
Kepley, Dan (1996) Edm
Krol, Joe (1963) Tor/Ham
Kwong, Normie (1969) Cal/Edm
Lawson, Smirle (1963) U. of Toronto
Leadlay, Frank (1963) Queen's/Ham
Loar, Loc (1074) Wpg/Cal
Lewis, Leo (1973) Wpg
Lunsford, Earl (1983) Cal
Luster, Marv (1990) Mtl/Tor
Luzzi, Don (1985) Cal
McCance, Chester (1976) Wpg/Mtl
McGill, Frank (1965) Mtl
McQuarters, Ed (1988) Sask
Miles, Rollie (1980) Edm
Morrio, Frank (1983) Tor/Edm
Morris, Ted (1964) Tor
Mosca, Angelo (1987) Ham
Nelson, Roger (1985) Edm
Neumann, Peter (1979) Ham
O'Quinn, Red (1981) Mtl
Pajaczkowski, Tony (1988) Cal/Mtl
Parker, Jackie (1971) Edm/Tor/BC
Patterson, Hal (1971) Mtl/Ham
Perry, Gordon (1970) Mtl
Perry, Norman (1963) Sarnia
Ploen, Ken (1975) Wpg
*****Poplawski,** Joe (1998) Wpg
Quilty, Silver (1966) U. of Ottawa
Rebholz, Russ (1963) Wpg
Reed, George (1979) Sask
Reeve, Ted (1963) Tor
Rigney, Frank (1984) Wpg
*****Robinson,** Larry (1998) Cal
Rodden, Michael (1964) Queen's/Tor

►

▶ **Rowe,** Paul (1964) Cal
Ruby, Martin (1974) Sask
Russel, Jeff (1963) Ott
*****Scott,** Tom (1998) Wpg/Edm
Scott, Vince (1982) Ham
Shatto, Dick (1975) Tor
Simpson, Benjamin (1963) Ham
Simpson, Bob (1976) Ott
Sprague, David (1963) Ham/Ott
Stevenson, Art (1969) Wpg
Stewart, Ron (1977) Ott
Stirling, Bummer (1966) Sarnia
Sutherin, Don (1992) Ham/Ott
Symons, Bill (1997) BC/Tor
Thelen, Dave (1989) Ott/Tor

Timmis, Brian (1963) Ham/Ott
Tinsley, Buddy (1982) Wpg
Tommy, Andrew (1989) Ott/Tor
Trawick, Herb (1975) Mtl
Tubman, Joe (1968) Ott
Tucker, Whit (1993) Ott
Urness, Ted (1989) Sask
Vaughn, Kaye (1978) Ott
Wagner, Virgil (1980) Mtl
Welch, Huck (1964) Ham/Mtl
Wilkinson, Tom (1987) Edm
Wilson, Al (1997) BC
Wylie, Harvey (1980) Cal
Young, Jim (1991) BC
Zock, William (1984) Tor/Edm

Source: *Canadian Football League*

*new inductee

NFL Final Standings, 1998

American Conference

■ Eastern Division

	W	L	T	Pct	Pts	OP
New York Jets	12	4	0	.750	416	266
Miami*	10	6	0	.625	321	265
Buffalo*	10	6	0	.625	400	333
New England*	9	7	0	.563	337	329
Indianapolis	3	13	0	.188	310	444

■ Central Division

	W	L	T	Pct	Pts	OP
Jacksonville	11	5	0	.688	392	338
Tennessee	8	8	0	.500	330	320
Pittsburgh	7	9	0	.438	263	303
Baltimore	6	10	0	.375	269	335
Cincinnati	3	13	0	.188	268	452

■ Western Division

	W	L	T	Pct	Pts	OP
Denver	14	2	0	.875	501	309
Oakland	8	8	0	.500	288	356
Seattle	8	8	0	.500	372	310
Kansas City	7	9	0	.438	327	363
San Diego	5	11	0	.313	241	342

National Conference

■ Eastern Division

	W	L	T	Pct	Pts	OP
Dallas	10	6	0	.625	381	275
Arizona*	9	7	0	.563	325	378
New York Giants	8	8	0	.500	287	309
Washington	6	10	0	.375	319	421
Philadelphia	3	13	0	.188	161	344

■ Central Division

	W	L	T	Pct	Pts	OP
Minnesota	15	1	0	.938	556	296
Green Bay*	11	5	0	.688	408	319
Tampa Bay	8	8	0	.500	314	295
Detroit	5	11	0	.313	306	378
Chicago	4	12	0	.250	276	368

■ Western Division

	W	L	T	Pct	Pts	OP
Atlanta	14	2	0	.875	442	289
San Francisco*	12	4	0	.750	479	328
New Orleans	6	10	0	.375	305	359
Carolina	4	12	0	.250	336	413
St. Louis	4	12	0	.250	285	378

* Wild card playoff qualifier.

Playoffs

■ NFC Wild Card
Phoenix 20, Dallas 7
San Francisco 30, Green Bay 27

■ AFC Wild Card
Miami 24, Buffalo 17
Jacksonville 25, New England 10

■ NFC Divisional Playoffs
Atlanta 20, San Francisco 18
Minnesota 41, Arizona 21

■ AFC Divisional Playoffs
Denver 38, Miami 3
N.Y. Jets 34, Jacksonville 24

■ NFC Championship
Atlanta 30, Minnesota 27 (OT)

■ AFC Championship
Denver 23, N.Y. Jets 10

■ Super Bowl XXXII
(at Miami, Florida)
Denver 34, Atlanta 19

■ AFC-NFC Pro Bowl
(at Honolulu, Hawaii)
AFC 23, NFC 10

Source: *National Football League*

All-Time Pro Football Records

(all conferences; up to the start of the 1999 season)

Leading Lifetime Scorers

	Yrs	TD	PAT	FG	Total		Yrs	TD	PAT	FG	Total
George Blanda	26	9	943	335	2 002	Mark Moseley	16	0	482	300	1 382
Gary Anderson	18	0	585	420	1 845	Jim Bakken	17	0	534	282	1 380
Morten Andersen	17	0	558	401	1 761	Fred Cox	15	0	519	282	1 365
Nick Lowery	18	0	562	383	1 711	Al Del Greco	15	0	463	263	1 360
Jan Stenerud	19	0	580	373	1 699	Lou Groza	17	1	641	234	1 349
Norm Johnson	17	0	613	348	1 657	Jim Breech	14	0	517	243	1 246
Eddie Murray	19	0	521	337	1 532	Chris Bahr	14	0	490	241	1 213
Pat Leahy	18	0	558	304	1 470	Kevin Butler	13	0	413	265	1 208
Jim Turner	16	1	521	304	1 439	Gino Cappelletti	11	42	350	176	1 130
Matt Bahr	17	0	322	310	1 422	Ray Wersching	15	0	456	222	1 122

Most points, one season .... **176, Paul Hornung, GB**, 1960 (15 TD, 41 PAT, 15 FG)

Most points, one game .... **40, Ernie Nevers,** Chi Cardinals vs. Chi Bears, Nov. 28, 1929 (6 TD, 4 PAT)

Most touchdowns, career .... **175, Jerry Rice**, SF, 1985–98

Most touchdowns, one season .... **25, Emmitt Smith,** Dal, 1995 (25 rushing)

Most touchdowns, one game .... **6, Ernie Nevers,** Chi Cardinals vs. Chi Bears, Nov. 28, 1929 (6 rushing)

.... **Dub Jones,** Cle vs. Chi Bears, Nov. 25, 1951 (4 rushing, 2 pass receptions)

.... **Gale Sayers,** Chi Bears vs. SF, Dec. 12, 1965 (4 rushing, 1 pass reception, 1 punt return)

Most points after touchdown, one season .... **66, Uwe von Schamann,** Mia, 1984

Most points after touchdown, career .... **943, George Blanda,** 4 teams, 1949–75

Most consecutive points after touchdown .... **276, Norm Johnson,** Atl, 1991–94; Pit 1995-98

Most field goals, one game .... **7, Jim Bakken,** StL vs. Pit, Sept. 24, 1967

....**Rich Karlis,** Min vs. LA Rams, Nov. 5, 1989

....**Chris Boniol,** Dal vs. GB, Nov. 18, 1996

Most field goals, one season .... **37 John Kasay,** Car, 1996

Most field goals, career .... **420, Gary Anderson,** 3 teams, 1982–98

Most consecutive field goals .... **40, Gary Anderson,** SF 1997, Min 1998

Longest field goal .... **63 yds, Tom Dempsey,** NO vs. Det, Nov. 8, 1970

....**Jason Elam,** Den vs. Jack, Oct. 25, 1998

Pass Interceptions

Most passes had intercepted, one game .... **8, Jim Hardy**, Chi Cardinals vs. Phi, Sept. 24, 1950 (39 attempts)

Most passes had intercepted, one season .... **42, George Blanda,** Hou, 1962

Most passes had intercepted, career .... **277, George Blanda,** 4 teams, 1949–75;

Most consecutive passes attempted without interception .... **308, Bernie Kosar,** Cle, 1990–91

Most interceptions by, one season .... **14, Dick (Night Train) Lane,** LA Rams, 1952

Most interceptions by, career .... **81, Paul Krause,** Wash, 1964–67; Min, 1968–79 ▶

Punting

Most punts, one game .... **16, Leo Arguaz,** Oak vs. SD, Oct. 11, 1998
Most punts, career .... **1 154, Dave Jennings,** NY Giants, 1974–84; NY Jets, 1985–87
Most punts, season .... **114, Bob Parsons,** Chi Bears, 1981
Highest punting average, season (20 punts) .... **51.40, Sam Baugh,** Wash, 1940 (35 punts)
Longest punt .... **98 yds, Steve O'Neal,** NY Jets vs. Den, Sept. 21, 1969

Miscellaneous Records

Most fumbles, one season .... **21, Tony Banks,** StL, 1996
Most fumbles, one game .... **7, Len Dawson,** KC vs. SD, Nov. 15, 1964
Most sacks, career .... **192.5, Reggie White,** Phi, 1985–92; GB, 1993-98
Most sacks, season .... **22, Mark Gastineau,** NY Jets, 1984
Highest punt return average, season .... **23.00 yards, Herb Rich,** Bal, 1950
Highest punt return average, career .... **13.64 yards, Darrien Gordon,** SD, 1993-94; 1996; Den, 1997
Highest kickoff return average, season .... **41.06 yards, Travis Williams,** GB, 1967
Highest kickoff return average, career .... **30.56 yards, Gale Sayers,** Chi Bears, 1965–71
Most consecutive games played, career .... **282, Jim Marshall,** Cle, 1960; Min, 1961–79
Most seasons played .... **26, George Blanda,** Chi Bears, 1949–58; Bal, 1950; Hou, 1960–66; Oak, 1967–75

Leading Lifetime Rushers

	Yrs	Att	Yards	Avg		Yrs	Att	Yards	Avg
Walter Payton	13	3 838	16 726	4.4	O.J. Anderson	14	2 562	10 273	4.0
Barry Sanders	10	3 062	15 269	5.0	Earl Campbell	8	2 187	9 407	4.3
Eric Dickerson	11	2 996	13 259	4.4	Jim Taylor	10	1 941	8 597	4.4
Tony Dorsett	12	2 936	12 739	4.3	Joe Perry	14	1 737	8 378	4.8
Emmitt Smith	9	2 914	12 566	4.3	Earnest Byner	14	2 095	8 261	3.9
Jim Brown	9	2 359	12 312	5.2	Herschel Walker	12	1 954	8 225	4.2
Marcus Allen	16	3 022	12 243	4.1	Roger Craig	11	1 991	8 189	4.1
Franco Harris	13	2 949	12 120	4.1	Gerald Riggs	10	1 989	8 188	4.1
Thurman Thomas	11	2 813	11 786	4.2	Larry Csonka	11	1 891	8 081	4.3
John Riggins	14	2 916	11 352	3.9	Freeman McNeil	12	1 798	8 074	4.5
O.J. Simpson	11	2 404	11 236	4.7					

Most yards gained, one season .... **2 105, Eric Dickerson,** LA Rams, 1984
Most yards gained, one game .... **275, Walter Payton,** Chi Bears vs. Min, Nov. 20, 1977
Most touchdowns rushing, career .... **125, Emmitt Smith,** Dal, 1990-98
Most touchdowns rushing, one season .... **25, Emmitt Smith,** Dal, 1995
Most touchdowns rushing, one game .... **6, Ernie Nevers,** Chi Cardinals vs. Chi Bears, Nov. 8, 1929
Most rushing attempts, one season .... **410, Jamal Anderson,** Atl, 1998
Most rushing attempts, one game .... **45, Jamie Morris,** Wash vs. Cin, Dec. 17, 1988
Longest run .... **99 yds, Tony Dorsett,** Dal vs. Minn, Jan. 3, 1983

Leading Lifetime Receivers

	Yrs	No.	Yards	Avg		Yrs	No.	Yards	Avg
Jerry Rice	14	1 139	17 612	15.5	Andre Rison	10	681	9 381	13.8
Art Monk	16	940	12 725	13.5	Tim Brown	11	680	9 600	14.1
Andre Reed	14	889	12 559	14.1	Ozzie Newsome	13	662	7 980	12.1
Cris Carter	12	834	10 447	12.5	Charley Taylor	13	649	9 110	14.0
Steve Largent	14	819	13 089	16.0	Drew Hill	14	634	9 831	13.5
Henry Ellard	16	809	13 691	16.9	Don Maynard	15	633	11 834	18.7
Irving Fryar	15	784	11 983	15.3	Raymond Berry	13	631	9 275	14.7
James Lofton	16	764	14 804	18.3	Herman Moore	8	610	8 467	13.9
Charlie Joiner	18	750	12 146	16.2	Anthony Miller	10	595	9 148	15.4
Michael Irvin	11	740	11 737	15.9	Sterling Sharpe	7	595	8 134	13.7 ▶
Gary Clark	11	699	10 856	15.5					

▶ Most yards gained, one season ....**1 848, Jerry Rice,** SF, 1995
Most yards gained, one game ....**336, Willie Anderson,** LA Rams vs. NO, Nov. 26, 1989
Most pass receptions, one season ....**123, Herman Moore,** Det, 1995
Most pass receptions, one game ....**18, Tom Fears,** LA Rams vs. GB, Dec. 3, 1950 (189 yds)
Most consecutive games, pass receptions .... **193, Jerry Rice,** SF, 1985–98
Most touchdown passes, career .... **164, Jerry Rice,** SF, 1985–98
Most touchdown passes, one season .... **22, Jerry Rice,** SF, 1987
Most touchdown passes, one game .... **5, Bob Shaw,** Chi Cardinals vs. Bal, Oct. 2, 1950;
Kellen Winslow, SD vs. Oak, Nov. 22, 1981; **Jerry Rice,** SF vs. Atl, Oct. 14, 1990

Leading Lifetime Passers
(Minimum 1 500 attempts)

	Rtg[1]	Yrs	Att	Comp	Yards		Rtg[1]	Yrs	Att	Comp	Yards
Steve Young	97.6	14	4 065	2 622	32 678	Ken Anderson	81.9	16	4 475	2 654	32 838
Joe Montana	92.3	15	5 391	3 409	40 551	Bernie Kosar	81.8	12	3 365	1 994	23 301
Brett Favre	89.0	8	3 757	2 318	26 803	Danny White	81.7	13	2 950	1 761	21 959
Dan Marino	87.8	16	7 989	4 763	58 913	Dave Krieg	81.5	18	5 290	3 093	37 948
Jim Kelly	84.4	11	4 779	2 874	35 467	Warren Moon	81.2	15	6 786	3 972	49 097
Roger Staubach	83.4	11	2 958	1 685	22 700	Boomer Esiason	81.1	14	5 205	2 969	37 920
Neil Lomax	82.7	8	3 153	1 817	22 771	Jeff Hostetler	80.5	14	2 338	1 357	16 430
Sonny Jurgensen	82.6	18	4 262	2 433	32 224	Neil O'Donnell	80.5	9	2 862	1 650	19 026
Len Dawson	82.6	19	3 741	2 136	28 711	Bart Starr	80.5	16	3 149	1 808	24 718
Troy Aikman	82.3	10	4 011	2 479	28 346	Ken O'Brien	80.4	10	3 602	2 110	25 094

Most yards gained, one season .... **5 084, Dan Marino,** Mia, 1984
Most yards gained, one game ....**554, Norm Van Brocklin,** LA Rams vs. NY Giants, Sept. 28, 1951
Most touchdowns passes, career .... **408, Dan Marino,** Mia, 1983–98
Most touchdowns passing, one season .... **48, Dan Marino,** Mia, 1984
Most touchdowns passing, one game .... **7, Sid Luckman,** Chi Bears vs. NY Giants, Nov. 14, 1943;
Adrian Burk, Phi vs. Was, Oct. 17, 1954; **George Blanda,** Hou vs. NY Titans, Nov. 19, 1961;
Y.A. Tittle, NY Giants vs. Was, Oct. 28, 1962; **Joe Kapp,** Min vs. Bal, Sept. 28, 1969
Most passing attempts, one season .... **691, Drew Bledsoe,** NE, 1994
Most passing attempts, one game ....**70, Drew Bledsoe,** NE vs. Min, Nov 13, 1994 (OT)
Most passes completed, one season .... **404, Warren Moon,** Hou, 1991
Most passes completed, one game .... **45, Drew Bledsoe,** NE vs. Min, Nov 13, 1994 (OT)

Source: *National Football League*

(1) Rating based on performance standards for completion percentage, interception percentage, touchdown percentage and average gains.

Super Bowl Results, 1967–99

Date	Results	MVP
Jan. 15, 1967	Green Bay 35, Kansas City 10	Bart Starr, Green Bay
Jan. 14, 1968	Green Bay 33, Oakland 14	Bart Starr, Green Bay
Jan. 12, 1969	N.Y. Jets 16, Baltimore 7	Joe Namath, N.Y. Jets
Jan. 11, 1970	Kansas City 23, Minnesota 7	Len Dawson, Kansas City
Jan. 17, 1971	Baltimore 16, Dallas 13	Chuck Howley, Dallas
Jan. 16, 1972	Dallas 24, Miaml 3	Roger Staubach, Dallas
Jan. 14, 1973	Miami 14, Washington 7	Jake Scott, Miami
Jan. 13, 1974	Miami 24, Minnesota 7	Larry Csonka, Miami
Jan. 12, 1975	Pittsburgh 16, Minnesota 6	Franco Harris, Pittsburgh
Jan. 18, 1976	Pittsburgh 21, Dallas 17	Lynn Swann, Pittsburgh
Jan. 9, 1977	Oakland 32, Minnesota 14	Fred Biletnikoff, Oakland
Jan. 15, 1978	Dallas 27, Denver 10	Randy White, Harvey Martin, Dallas
Jan. 21, 1979	Pittsburgh 35, Dallas 31	Terry Bradshaw, Pittsburgh

▶

▶ Jan. 20, 1980 . . . . Pittsburgh 31, L.A. Rams 19 — Terry Bradshaw, Pittsburgh
Jan. 25, 1981 . . . . Oakland 27, Philadelphia 10 — Jim Plunkett, Oakland
Jan. 24, 1982 . . . . San Francisco 26, Cincinnati 21 — Joe Montana, San Francisco
Jan. 30, 1983 . . . . Washington 27, Miami 17 — John Riggins, Washington
Jan. 22, 1984 . . . . L.A. Raiders 38, Washington 9 — Marcus Allen, L.A. Raiders
Jan. 20, 1985 . . . . San Francisco 38, Miami 16 — Joe Montana, San Francisco
Jan. 26, 1986 . . . . Chicago 46, New England 10 — Richard Dent, Chicago
Jan. 25, 1987 . . . . N.Y. Giants 39, Denver 20 — Phil Simms, N.Y. Giants
Jan. 31, 1988 . . . . Washington 42, Denver 10 — Doug Williams, Washington
Jan. 22, 1989 . . . . San Francisco 20, Cincinnati 16 — Jerry Rice, San Francisco
Jan. 28, 1990 . . . . San Francisco 55, Cincinnati 10 — Joe Montana, San Francisco
Jan. 27, 1991 . . . . N.Y. Giants 20, Buffalo 19 — Ottis Anderson, N.Y. Giants
Jan. 26, 1992 . . . . Washington 37, Buffalo 24 — Mark Rypien, Washington
Jan. 31, 1993 . . . . Dallas 52, Buffalo 17 — Troy Aikman, Dallas
Jan. 30, 1994 . . . . Dallas 30, Buffalo 13 — Emmitt Smith, Dallas
Jan. 29,.1995 . . . . San Francisco 49, San Diego 26 — Steve Young, San Francisco
Jan. 28, 1996 . . . . Dallas 27, Pittsburgh 17 — Larry Brown, Dallas
Jan. 26, 1997 . . . . Green Bay 35, New England 21 — Desmond Howard, Green Bay
Jan. 25, 1998 . . . . Denver 31, Green Bay 24 — Terrell Davis, Denver
Jan. 31, 1999 . . . . Denver 34, Atlanta 19 — John Elway, Denver

Source: *National Football League*

Note: Canadian Rugby Union, 1908–46; Canadian Amateur Football Association, 1947–74; Leader Post Trophy to winner. Canadian Junior Football League, 1975– ; Armadale Cup 1975–88; Canadian Bowl 1989– .

Top Ten NFL Rushers, 1998

Player	Attempts	Yards	Average	Player	Attempts	Yards	Average
Terrell Davis, Den	392	2008	5.1	Marshall Faulk, Ind . . .	324	1319	4.1
Jamal Anderson, Atl . .	410	1846	4.5	Eddie George, Ten	348	1294	3.7
Garrison Hurst, SF . . .	310	1570	5.1	Curtis Martin, NYJ . . .	369	1287	3.5
Barry Sanders, Det . . .	343	1491	4.3	Ricky Watters, Sea . . .	319	1239	3.9
Emmit Smith, Dal	319	1332	4.2	F Taylor, Jax	264	1223	4.6

Source: *Canadian Press*

Top Ten NFL Receivers, 1998

Player	Number	Yards	Average	Player	Number	Yards	Average
A Freeman, GB	84	1424	17.0	T Martin, Atl	66	1181	17.9
Eric Moulds, Buf	67	1368	20.4	Jerry Rice, SF	82	1157	14.1
Randy Moss, Min	69	1313	19.0	F Sanders, Ari	89	1145	12.9
R Smith, Den	86	1222	14.2	T. Mathis, Atl	64	1136	17.8
Jimmy Smith, Jax	78	1182	15.2	K Johnson, NYJ	83	1131	13.6

Source: *Canadian Press*

HOCKEY

Final Standings

Eastern Conference

■ **Northeast Division**

	W	L	T	GF	GA	Pts
Ottawa	44	23	15	239	179	103
Toronto	45	30	7	268	231	97
Boston	39	30	13	214	181	91
Buffalo	37	28	17	207	175	91
Montreal	32	39	11	184	209	75

■ **Atlantic Division**

	W	L	T	GF	GA	Pts
New Jersey	47	24	11	248	196	105
Philadelphia	37	26	19	231	196	93
Pittsburgh	38	30	14	242	225	90
NY Rangers	33	38	11	217	227	77
NY Islanders	24	48	10	194	244	58

■ **Southeast Division**

	W	L	T	GF	GA	Pts
Carolina	34	30	18	210	201	86
Florida	30	34	18	210	228	78
Washington	31	45	6	200	218	68
Tampa Bay	19	54	9	179	292	47

Western Conference

■ **Central Division**

	W	L	T	GF	GA	Pts
Detroit	43	32	7	245	202	93
St. Louis	37	32	13	237	209	87
Chicago	29	41	12	202	248	70
Nashville	28	47	7	190	261	63

■ **Pacific Division**

	W	L	T	GF	GA	Pts
Dallas	51	19	12	236	168	114
Phoenix	39	31	12	205	197	90
Anaheim	35	34	13	215	206	83
San Jose	31	33	18	196	191	80
Los Angeles	32	45	5	189	222	69

■ **Northwest Division**

	W	L	T	GF	GA	Pts
Colorado	44	28	10	239	205	98
Edmonton	33	37	12	230	226	78
Calgary	30	40	12	211	234	72
Vancouver	23	47	12	192	258	58

Source: *Canadian Press*

1998–99 NHL Season Review

Wayne Gretzky retires, NHL hockey thrives in Nashville and the Stanley Cup comes home to Dallas.

The 1998-99 NHL season was definitely a bizarre one.

After 20 seasons in the NHL, the Great One called it a career holding every record of importance in the league. Saying that it was time, Gretzky, the game's greatest scorer, leaves the NHL without a dominant marquee player.

Jaromir Jagr, however, has begun making a strong case. The Czech star led the league in scoring for the third time in 98-99 and began to dominate the game the way Gretzky and another recently retired superstar—Mario Lemieux—had.

Gretzky's popularity helped build the game in the southern United States and part of the credit for the birth of the Predators in the country music heartland should go to the Great One. Nashville opened its arms to the Predators who, at 28-47-7, didn't prey on very many NHL opponents. But with a solid foundation the future appears bright for hockey in Nashville.

For inspiration, Nashville need only to look to Dallas, who won the franchise's first Stanley Cup. Despite winning on a controversial goal, the Stars were deserving champions, having compiled the season's best record.

The Toronto Maple Leafs surprised many by finishing third in the Eastern Conference and advancing to the conference final. It was there they met their demise, when a gritty Buffalo Sabres team knocked them out to reach the final.

The Ottawa Senators, who compiled the second best record in the East, were first-round victims of the Sabres. After years of dismal hockey, the Senators have finally turned the corner and can be considered among the NHL's elite.

But like their poor cousins in Edmonton and Calgary, money remains a problem. Canadian teams made as many headlines with their pleas for tax relief as they did for their play on the ice.

A lack of scoring remained a problem for the NHL and a new problem, too many ties, emerged.

The NHL changed the regular-season overtime format in 1999-2000 to 4-on-4 with each team getting at least a point in hopes of deciding more games that go past regulation. A winning team will receive a second point.

The NHL was also pleased with its two-referee experiment. The number of games officiated under the two-referee system will increase to 700 this season, from 270.

NHL Playoff Results, 1998-99

■ Eastern Conference

Teams, Result

Pittsburgh	1	at	New Jersey	3
Pittsburgh	4	at	New Jersey	1
New Jersey	2	at	Pittsburgh	4
New Jersey	4	at	Pittsburgh	2
Pittsburgh	3	at	New Jersey	4
New Jersey	2	at	Pittsburgh	3*
Pittsburgh	4	at	New Jersey	2

Pittsburgh wins series 4-3

Buffalo	2	at	Ottawa	1
Buffalo	3**	at	Ottawa	2
Ottawa	0	at	Buffalo	3
Ottawa	3	at	Buffalo	4

Buffalo wins series 4-0

Boston	2	at	Carolina	0
Boston	2	at	Carolina	3*
Carolina	3	at	Boston	2
Carolina	1	at	Boston	4
Boston	4**	at	Carolina	3
Carolina	0	at	Boston	2

Boston wins series 4-2

Philadelphia	3	at	Toronto	0
Philadelphia	1	at	Toronto	2
Toronto	2	at	Philadelphia	1
Toronto	2	at	Philadelphia	5
Philadelphia	1	at	Toronto	2*
Toronto	1	at	Philadelphia	0

Toronto wins series 4-2

■ Western Conference

Teams, Result

Edmonton	1	at	Dallas	2
Edmonton	2	at	Dallas	3
Dallas	3	at	Edmonton	2
Dallas	3***	at	Edmonton	2

Dallas wins series 4-0

San Jose	1	at	Colorado	3
San Jose	1	at	Colorado	2*
Colorado	2	at	San Jose	4
Colorado	3	at	San Jose	7
San Jose	2	at	Colorado	6
Colorado	3*	at	San Jose	2

Colorado wins series 4-3

Anaheim	3	at	Detroit	5
Anaheim	1	at	Detroit	5
Detroit	4	at	Anaheim	2
Detroit	3	at	Anaheim	0

Detroit wins series 4-0

St. Louis	3	at	Phoenix	1
St. Louis	3	at	Phoenix	4*
Phoenix	5	at	St. Louis	4
Phoenix	2	at	St. Louis	1
St. Louis	2	at	Phoenix	1
Phoenix	3	at	St. Louis	5
St. Louis	1*	at	Phoenix	0

St. Louis wins series 4-3

■ Eastern Conference Semifinals

Teams, Result

Pittsburgh	2	at	Toronto	0
Pittsburgh	2	at	Toronto	4
Toronto	3	at	Pittsburgh	4
Toronto	3*	at	Pittsburgh	2
Pittsburgh	1	at	Toronto	4
Toronto	4*	at	Pittsburgh	3

Toronto wins series 4-2

Buffalo	2	at	Boston	4
Buffalo	3	at	Boston	1
Boston	2	at	Buffalo	3
Boston	0	at	Buffalo	3
Buffalo	3	at	Boston	5
Boston	2	at	Buffalo	3

Buffalo wins series 4-2

Source: *Canadian Press*

■ Eastern Conference Final

Teams, Result

Buffalo	5	at	Toronto	4
Buffalo	3	at	Toronto	6
Toronto	2	at	Buffalo	4
Toronto	2	at	Buffalo	5
Buffalo	4	at	Toronto	2
Buffalo wins series 4-1				

■ Western Conference Semifinals

Teams, Result

St. Louis	0	at	Dallas	3
St. Louis	4	at	Dallas	5*
Dallas	2	at	St. Louis	3*
Dallas	2	at	St. Louis	3*
St. Louis	1	at	Dallas	3
Dallas	2	at	St. Louis	1
Dallas wins series 4-2				

Detroit	3	at	Colorado	2
Detroit	4	at	Colorado	0
Colorado	5	at	Detroit	3
Colorado	6	at	Detroit	2
Detroit	0	at	Colorado	3
Colorado	5	at	Detroit	2
Colorado wins series 4-2				

■ Western Conference Final

Teams, Result

Colorado	2	at	Dallas	1
Colorado	2	at	Dallas	4
Dallas	3	at	Colorado	0
Dallas	2	at	Colorado	3*
Colorado	7	at	Dallas	5
Dallas	4	at	Colorado	1
Colorado	1	at	Dallas	4
Dallas wins series 4-3				

■ Stanley Cup Final

Teams, Result

Buffalo	3*	at	Dallas	2
Buffalo	2	at	Detroit	4
Dallas	2	at	Buffalo	1
Dallas	1	at	Buffalo	2
Buffalo	0	at	Dallas	2
Dallas	2***	at	Buffalo	1
Dallas wins cup 4-2				

*Overtime-number of stars indicates number of overtime periods.

Crease Rule

When Brett Hull scored the Stanley Cup winning goal in triple overtime, the NHL was faced with its worst nightmare.

The Dallas Stars had poured off the bench and were celebrating their Cup win as the Buffalo Sabres complained that the goal should not count because Hull's toe preceded the puck into the crease.

Video replays clearly showed this, but the goal, which the Sabres argue shouldn't have counted, stood.

Two days later, the NHL board of governors eliminated the video goal judge review for man-in-the-crease violations.

Commissioner Gary Bettman said the rule change had nothing to do with Hull's Game 6 goal that won the Cup.

In the 1999-2000 season, on-ice officials will have the final say on crease violations

The rule, which sparked endless controversy, was designed to protect goaltenders from player interference. It forced numerous goals to be called back when video goal judges detected a player who had entered the crease before the puck.

The problem was on several occasions, a player with a toe in the opposite end of the crease would cost his team a goal, even though he wasn't interfering with the goalie.

Video review will still be used to determine whether a puck crosses the goal-line; whether a puck crosses the goal-line before the net is dislodged or before time ends; if a puck is pushed or kicked in; if a puck deflects in off an official; if a puck is deflected in by a high stick; and to determine time on the game clock.

As for Hull's goal, the official response from the league was that it didn't matter that Hull had his skate in the crease, but that he had full control of the puck. Director of officiating Brian Lewis said officials looked at the play probably six or eight times.

Buffalo coach Lindy Ruff said after the game that to reverse a goal that decided the title would be a "nightmare" for the league.

Wayne Gretzky Retires

For the first time since 1977-78, the NHL is without Wayne Gretzky.

After 20 seasons, the Great One ended the most prolific career in hockey history at the end of the 1998-99 season.

"It's time" he said.

Urged by many to keep playing—including Prime Minister Jean Chretien—Gretzky decided that the wear and tear of his storied career had taken enough of a toll on his slight body.

"It's going to kill me not to play," he said at his retirement news conference. "But time does something to you and it's time."

Gretzky, who set up more goals than anyone else had points, leaves the game holding an astonishing 61 records. He won four Stanley Cups, two Canada Cups and 37 trophies.

But as great as his accomplishments were on the ice—and they were spectacular—what he did for the game off the ice cannot be overlooked.

His tenure with the Los Angeles Kings is credited with saving hockey in California and setting the stage for the success of the San Jose Sharks and Anaheim Mighty Ducks in that state, as well as the Panthers and Lightning in Florida, the Stars in Dallas and the Coyotes in Phoenix.

Gretzky's personality and charisma helped the game grow in areas where hockey was non-existent 10 years ago. Perhaps the greatest ambassador the game has ever had, Gretzky's presence off the ice will be missed as much as his magic on it.

And Gretzky's talents were most certainly magical.

"Nobody could figure out how to stop Gretzky," said Bobby Clarke.

He will be predominantly remembered as an outstanding playmaker for his ability to make the impossible pass, to see the play before it happens, to find the open man through a maze of sticks and skates and to feed Jari Kurri from his office behind the net.

"His greatest strength was that he could convince the other team of what he had no intention of doing whatsoever," said Harry Sinden.

Gretzky's great passing ability—he had 1963 assists in his career—overshadowed his scoring touch, which faded later in his career.

But Gretzky retires as the greatest sniper to ever play the game. He scored a record 894 goals and in 1981-82, scored an astonishing 92 goals.

"He makes us all look like bums," Marcel Dionne, No. 3 on the NHL's all-time points list, once said.

The Hockey Hall of Fame waived the mandatory three-year waiting period, allowing Gretzky to be inducted in 1999.

The Great One's retirement leaves a gaping hole in the NHL. Many expect Jaromir Jagr to step up and become the game's most dominant player both on and off the ice. Other hopes include Paul Kariya, Eric Lindros, Peter Forsberg and Teemu Selanne.

But none of them will be able to replace The Great Gretzky.

Wayne Gretzky's Trophy Case

NHL

Hart Memorial Trophy (regular season, most valuable player), 1980, 81, 82, 83, 84, 85, 86, 87, 89

Art Ross Trophy (regular season scoring champion), 1981, 82, 83, 84, 85, 86, 87, 90, 91, 94

Conn Smythe Trophy (Stanley Cup playoffs most valuable player), 1985, 88

Lester B. Pearson Award (outstanding player, selected by the players), 1982, 83, 84, 85, 87)

Lady Byng Memorial Trophy (most gentlemanly player), 1980, 91, 92, 94, 99

Emery Edge Award (best plus minus-rating), 1984, 1985, 1987

Chrysler-Dodge (NHL performer of the year), 1985, 86, 87

Lionel Conacher Award (given out by CP for male athlete of the year), 1980, 81, 82, 83, 85, 89

Lester Patrick trophy (outstanding service to hockey in the U.S.), 1994

Post-Season All-Star

First Team, 1981, 82, 83, 84, 85, 86, 87, 91

Second Team, 1980, 88, 89, 90, 94, 97, 98, 99

Stanley Cup, 1984, 85, 87, 88

Canada Cup All-Star Team, 1984, 87, 91

NHL All-Star Game Appearances, 1980, 81, 82, 83, 84, 85, 86, 88, 89, 90, 91, 92, 94, 97, 97, 98

WHA

Second All-Star Team, 1979

Lou Kaplan Trophy (Rookie of the Year), 1979

World Junior Championships

All-Star Team, 1978

Best Forward, 1978

Junior Hockey

OHA Second All-Star Team, 1978

Wayne Gretzky's Career Statistics

Regular Season Season, Team	GP	G	A	Pts	Playoffs Season, Team	GP	G	A	Pts
1979-80, Edm	79	51	86	137	1979-80, Edm	3	2	1	3
1980-81, Edm	80	55	109	164	1980-81, Edm	9	7	14	21
1981-82, Edm	80	92	120	212	1981-82, Edm	5	5	7	12
1982-83, Edm	80	71	125	196	1982-83, Edm	16	12	26	38
1983-84, Edm	74	87	118	205	1983-84, Edm	19	13	22	35
1984-85, Edm	80	73	135	208	1984-85, Edm	18	17	30	47
1985-86, Edm	80	52	163	215	1985-86, Edm	10	8	11	19
1986-87, Edm	79	62	121	183	1986-87, Edm	21	5	29	34
1987-88, Edm	64	40	109	149	1987-88, Edm	18	12	31	43
1988-89, LA	78	54	114	168	1988-89, LA	11	5	17	22
1989-90, LA	73	40	102	142	1989-90, LA	7	3	7	10
1990-91, LA	78	41	122	163	1990-91, LA	12	4	11	15
1991-92, LA	74	31	90	121	1991-92, LA	6	2	5	7
1992-93, LA	45	16	49	65	1992-93, LA	24	15	25	40
1993-94, LA	81	38	92	130	1995-96, StL	13	2	14	16
1994-95, LA	48	11	37	49	1996-97, NYR	15	10	10	20
1995-96, LA	46	13	54	67	**Totals**	**208**	**122**	**260**	**382**
StL	18	8	13	21					
1996-97, NYR	82	25	72	97					
1997-98, NYR	82	23	67	90					
1998-99, NYR	70	9	53	62					
Totals	**1487**	**894**	**1963**	**2857**					

NHL Records Owned or Shared by Wayne Gretzky

Career

Regular Season: NHL goals – 894; Assists – 1,963; Points – 2,857 (894 goals, 1,963 assists); Goals by a centre – 894; Points by a centre – 2,857; Assists by a centre – 1,963; Assists-per-game average (300-or-more assists) – 1.32; Games, three-or-more assists – 50; Overtime assists – 15; Goals, including regular season and playoffs, 1,016 (894 regular season, 122 playoff); Assists, including playoffs – 2,223 (1,963 regular season, 260 playoff); Points, including playoffs – 3,239 (2,857 regular season and 382 playoff); Hat tricks – 50; 40-or-more goal seasons – 12; 50-or-more goal seasons – 9; 60-or-more goal seasons – 5; 100-or-more point seasons – 15; Consecutive 40-or-more goal seasons – 12; Consecutive 60-or-more goal seasons – 4; Consecutive 100-or-more point seasons – 13.

Playoffs: Points – 382 (122 goals, 260 assists in 208 games); Goals – 122; Assists – 260; Game-winning goals – 24; Three-or-more goal games – 10;

Single Season: Goals – 92 in 1981-82; Assists – 163 in 1985-86; Points – 215 in 1985-86; Goals by a centre – 92 in 1981-82; Assists by a centre – 163 in 1985-86; Points by a centre – 215 in 1985-86; Three-or-more goal games – 10 in 1981-82, 1983-84; Goals per-game average – 1.18 in 1983-84 (87 goals in 74 games); Assists per-game average – 2.04 in 1985-86; Point-per-game average – 2.77 in 1983-84; Goals, including play-offs – 100 in 1983-84; Assists, including playoffs – 174 in 1985-86; Points, including playoffs – 255 in 1984-85; Goals, minimum 50 games, from start of a season – 61 in 1981-82, 1983-84; Consecutive point-scoring streak – 51 games in 1983-84; Consecutive point-scoring streak from the start of a season – 51 games in 1983-84; Consecutive assist-scoring streak – 23 games in 1990-91 (48 assists); Fastest 50 goals from start of season – 39 games in 1981-82.

Single Game: Goals, one period – 4 vs. St. Louis, Feb. 18, 1981; Assists, one game – 7 (vs. Washington, Feb. 15, 1980; at Chicago, Dec. 11, 1985; vs. Quebec, Feb. 14, 1986); Assists, road game – 7 at Chicago, Dec. 11, 1985; Assists by a player in his first NHL season – 7, vs. Washington, Feb. 15, 1980.

Playoffs

Single Year: Points – 47 in 1985 (17 goals, 30 assists); Assists – 31 in 1988; Short-handed goals – 3 in 1983. **Single Series**: Points, one final series – 13 in 1988 vs. Boston; Assists in final series – 10 in 1988 vs. Boston; Assists in one series – 14 in 1985 Conference final vs. Chicago. **Single Game**: Short-handed goals – 2, April 6, 1983 vs. Winnipeg; Assists – 6, April 9, 1987 vs. Los Angeles. **Single Period**: Assists – 3 (five times); Points – 4 (one goal, three assists, 3rd period), April 12, 1987 vs. Los Angeles.

All-Star Games: (16 games) Goals, one period – 4 in 1983 at Uniondale, N.Y.; Goals, career – 13. Shares Record: Goals, one game – 4 in 1983 at Uniondale, N.Y.; Points, one period – 4 in 1983 at Uniondale, N.Y.; Points, career – 25.

Stanley Cup Champions, 1918–99

The Stanley Cup, the oldest trophy competed for by professional athletes in North America, was donated by Frederick Arthur, Lord Stanley of Preston, in 1893. Originally presented to the amateur hockey champions of Canada, it has been awarded to the top professional team since 1910 and, since 1926, has been competed for only by NHL teams.

Year	Champion	Final Opponent	Series Result	Winning Coach	Winning Manager
1918	Toronto Arenas	Vancouver	3-2	Dick Carroll	Charlie Querrie
1919[1]	No decision				
1920	Ottawa Senators	Seattle	3-2	Pete Green	Tommy Gorman
1921	Ottawa Senators	Vancouver	3-2	Pete Green	Tommy Gorman
1922	Toronto St. Pats	Vancouver	3-2	Eddie Powers	Charlie Querrie
1923[2]	Ottawa Senators	Vancouver; Edm.	3-1; 2-0	Pete Green	Tommy Gorman
1924[3]	Montreal Canadiens	Vancouver; Calgary	2-0; 2-0	Leo Dandurand	Leo Dandurand
1925	Victoria Cougars	Montreal	3-1	Lester Patrick	Lester Patrick
1926	Montreal Maroons	Victoria	3-1	Eddie Gerard	Eddie Gerard
1927	Ottawa Senators	Boston	2-0	Dave Gill	Dave Gill
1928	New York Rangers	Montreal	3-2	Lester Patrick	Lester Patrick
1929	Boston Bruins	New York	2-0	Cy Denneny	Art Ross
1930	Montreal Canadiens	Boston	2-0	Cecil Hart	Cecil Hart
1931	Montreal Canadiens	Chicago	3-2	Cecil Hart	Cecil Hart
1932	Toronto Maple Leafs	New York	3-0	Dick Irvin	Conn Smythe
1933	New York Rangers	Toronto	3-1	Lester Patrick	Lester Patrick
1934	Chicago Black Hawks	Detroit	3-1	Tommy Gorman	Tommy Gorman
1935	Montreal Maroons	Toronto	3-0	Tommy Gorman	Tommy Gorman
1936	Detroit Red Wings	Toronto	4-0	Jack Adams	Jack Adams
1937	Detroit Red Wings	New York	3-2	Jack Adams	Jack Adams
1938	Chicago Black Hawks	Toronto	4-1	Bill Stewart	Bill Stewart
1939	Boston Bruins	Toronto	4-1	Art Ross	Art Ross
1940	New York Rangers	Toronto	4-2	Frank Boucher	Lester Patrick
1941	Boston Bruins	Detroit	4-0	Cooney Weiland	Art Ross
1942	Toronto Maple Leafs	Detroit	4-3	Hap Day	Conn Smythe
1943	Detroit Red Wings	Boston	4-0	Jack Adams	Jack Adams
1944	Montreal Canadiens	Chicago	4-0	Dick Irvin	Tommy Gorman
1945	Toronto Maple Leafs	Detroit	4-3	Hap Day	Conn Smythe
1946	Montreal Canadiens	Boston	4-1	Dick Irvin	Tommy Gorman
1947	Toronto Maple Leafs	Montreal	4-2	Hap Day	Conn Smythe
1948	Toronto Maple Leafs	Detroit	4-0	Hap Day	Conn Smythe
1949	Toronto Maple Leafs	Detroit	4-0	Hap Day	Conn Smythe
1950	Detroit Red Wings	New York	4-3	Tommy Ivan	Jack Adams
1951	Toronto Maple Leafs	Montreal	4-1	Joe Primeau	Conn Smythe
1952	Detroit Red Wings	Montreal	4-0	Tommy Ivan	Jack Adams
1953	Montreal Canadiens	Boston	4-1	Dick Irvin	Frank Selke
1954	Detroit Red Wings	Montreal	4-3	Tommy Ivan	Jack Adams
1955	Detroit Red Wings	Montreal	4-3	Jimmy Skinner	Jack Adams
1956	Montreal Canadiens	Detroit	4-1	Toe Blake	Frank Selke
1957	Montreal Canadiens	Boston	4-1	Toe Blake	Frank Selke

▶	1958	Montreal Canadiens	Boston	4-2	Toe Blake	Frank Selke
	1959	Montreal Canadiens	Toronto	4-1	Toe Blake	Frank Selke
	1960	Montreal Canadiens	Toronto	4-0	Toe Blake	Frank Selke
	1961	Chicago Black Hawks	Detroit	4-2	Rudy Pilous	Tommy Ivan
	1962	Toronto Maple Leafs	Chicago	4-2	Punch Imlach	Punch Imlach
	1963	Toronto Maple Leafs	Detroit	4-1	Punch Imlach	Punch Imlach
	1964	Toronto Maple Leafs	Detroit	4-3	Punch Imlach	Punch Imlach
	1965	Montreal Canadiens	Chicago	4-3	Toe Blake	Sam Pollock
	1966	Montreal Canadiens	Detroit	4-2	Toe Blake	Sam Pollock
	1967	Toronto Maple Leafs	Montreal	4-2	Punch Imlach	Punch Imlach
	1968	Montreal Canadiens	St. Louis	4-0	Toe Blake	Sam Pollock
	1969	Montreal Canadiens	St. Louis	4-0	Claude Ruel	Sam Pollock
	1970	Boston Bruins	St. Louis	4-0	Harry Sinden	Milt Schmidt
	1971	Montreal Canadiens	Chicago	4-3	Al MacNeil	Sam Pollock
	1972	Boston Bruins	New York	4-2	Tom Johnson	Milt Schmidt
	1973	Montreal Canadiens	Chicago	4-2	Scotty Bowman	Sam Pollock
	1974	Philadelphia Flyers	Boston	4-2	Fred Shero	Keith Allen
	1975	Philadelphia Flyers	Buffalo	4-2	Fred Shero	Keith Allen
	1976	Montreal Canadiens	Philadelphia	4-0	Scotty Bowman	Sam Pollock
	1977	Montreal Canadiens	Boston	4-0	Scotty Bowman	Sam Pollock
	1978	Montreal Canadiens	Boston	4-2	Scotty Bowman	Sam Pollock
	1979	Montreal Canadiens	New York	4-1	Scotty Bowman	Irving Grundman
	1980	N.Y. Islanders	Philadelphia	4-2	Al Arbour	Bill Torrey
	1981	N.Y. Islanders	Minnesota	4-1	Al Arbour	Bill Torrey
	1982	N.Y. Islanders	Vancouver	4-0	Al Arbour	Bill Torrey
	1983	N.Y. Islanders	Edmonton	4-0	Al Arbour	Bill Torrey
	1984	Edmonton Oilers	New York	4-1	Glen Sather	Glen Sather
	1985	Edmonton Oilers	Philadelphia	4-1	Glen Sather	Glen Sather
	1986	Montreal Canadiens	Calgary	4-1	Jean Perron	Serge Savard
	1987	Edmonton Oilers	Philadelphia	4-3	Glen Sather	Glen Sather
	1988	Edmonton Oilers	Boston	4-0	Glen Sather	Glen Sather
	1989	Calgary Flames	Montreal	4-2	Terry Crisp	Cliff Fletcher
	1990	Edmonton Oilers	Boston	4-1	John Muckler	Glen Sather
	1991	Pittsburgh Penguins	Minnesota	4-2	Bob Johnson	Craig Patrick
	1992	Pittsburgh Penguins	Chicago	4-0	Scotty Bowman	Craig Patrick
	1993	Montreal Canadiens	Los Angeles	4-1	Jacques Demers	Serge Savard
	1994	New York Rangers	Vancouver	4-3	Mike Keenan	Neil Smith
	1995	New Jersey Devils	Detroit	4-0	Jacques Lemaire	Lou Lamoriello
	1996	Colorado Avalanche	Florida	4-0	Marc Crawford	Pierre Lacroix
	1997	Detroit Red Wings	Philadelphia	4-0	Scotty Bowman	Scotty Bowman
	1998	Detroit Red Wings	Washington	4-0	Scotty Bowman	Ken Holland
	1999	Dallas Stars	Buffalo	4-2	Ken Hitchcock	Bob Gainey

Source: *National Hockey League*

(1) The series between Montreal Canadiens and Seattle Metropolitans was halted by Spanish influenza epidemic with the series tied at 2 wins each. (2) Ottawa also met and defeated Edmonton Eskimos, champions of the WCHL. (3) Because of an agreement between the NHL and the 2 western leagues (WCHL and PCHA), Canadiens had to play the champions of each league. ▶

NHL Scoring Leaders, 1998–99

Player	GP	G	A	Pts	+/-	PIM	PP	SH	S	Pct
Jaromir Jagr, Pit	81	44	83	127	17	66	9	1	343	12.8
Teemu Selanne, Ana	75	47	59	106	18	30	25	0	280	16.8
Paul Kariya, Ana	82	39	62	101	17	40	11	1	429	9.1
Peter Forsberg, Col	78	30	67	97	27	108	9	2	217	13.8
Joe Sakic, Col	73	41	55	96	23	29	12	5	255	16.1
Alexei Yashin, Ott	82	44	50	94	19	54	19	0	336	13.1
Theoren Fleury, Cal/Col	75	40	53	93	26	86	7	3	301	13.3
Eric Lindros, Phi	71	40	53	93	36	130	10	1	246	16.3
John Leclair, Phi	76	43	48	91	36	30	16	0	245	17.6
Pavol Demitra, StL	82	37	52	89	13	16	14	0	259	14.3
Mats Sundin, Tor	82	31	52	83	23	58	4	0	207	15.0
Martin Straka, Pit	80	35	47	82	12	26	5	4	177	19.8
Mike Modano, Dal	77	34	47	81	27	44	6	4	224	15.2
Jason Allison, Bos	82	23	54	77	5	66	5	1	158	14.6
Tony Amonte, Chi	82	44	31	75	0	60	14	3	256	17.2
Luc Robitaille, LA	82	39	35	74	-1	54	11	0	292	13.4
Steve Yzerman, Det	80	29	45	74	8	42	13	2	231	12.6
Rod Brind'Amour, Phi	82	24	50	74	4	47	10	0	190	12.6
Steve Thomas, Tor	78	28	45	73	27	33	11	0	209	13.4
Petr Sykora, NJ	80	29	43	72	16	22	15	0	222	13.1
Jeremy Roenick, Pho	78	24	48	72	6	125	4	0	202	11.9

Source: *Canadian Press*

GP = Games played; G = Goals; A = Assists; Pts = Points; +/- = Plus/minus statistic, which shows the number of even-strength and shorthanded goals scored by a player's team, minus those scored against, while he is on the ice; PIM = Penalties in minutes; PP = Power play goals; SH = Shorthanded goals; S = Shots on goal; Pct = Percentage of shots that score goals.

NHL Playoff Scoring Leaders, 1998–99

Player	GP	G	A	Pts	+/-	PIM	PP	SH	S	Pct
Peter Forsberg, Col	19	8	16	24	7	31	1	1	54	14.82
Mike Modano. Dal,	23	5	18	23	6	16	1	1	83	6.03
Joe Nieuwenduk, Dal	23	11	10	21	7	19	3	0	72	15.3
Joe Sakic, Col	19	6	13	19	2	8	1	1	56	10.75
Jamie Langenbrunner, Dal	23	10	7	17	7	16	4	0	46	21.7
Theoren Fleury, Col	18	5	12	17	2	20	2	0	56	8.97
Mats Sundin, Tor	17	8	8	16	2	16	3	0	44	18.28
Brett Hull, Dal	22	8	7	15	3	4	3	0	86	9.39
Martin Straka, Pit	13	6	9	15	0	6	1	0	27	22.22
Jason Woolley, Buf	21	4	11	15	0	10	2	0	43 9	4311
Alexei Zhitnik, Buf	21	4	11	15	6	52	4	0	58	6.912
Claude Lemieux, Col	19	3	11	14	5	26	1	0	69	4.313
Jere Lehtinen, Dal	23	10	13	8	2	1	1	0	55	18.21
Steve Yzerman, Det	10	9	4	13	2	0	4	0	41	22.01
Curtis Brown, Buf	21	7	6	13	3	10	3	0	34	20.62
Michael Peca, Buf,	21	5	8	13	1	18	2	1	37	13.52
Pierre Turgeon, StL	13	4	9	13	3	6	0	0	42	9.52
Sergei Zubov, Dal	23	1	12	13	13	4	0	0	46	2.22

Source: *Canadian Press*

NHL Individual Records

(up to the end of the 1997–98 season)

Most seasons . . . . **26, Gordie Howe,** Det, 1946/47 through 1970/71; Htfd, 1979/80

Most games . . . . **1 767, Gordie Howe,** Det, 1946/47 through 1970/71; Htfd, 1979/80

Most goals . . . . **894 Wayne Gretzky,** Edm, LA, StL, NYR in 19 seasons, 1 487 games

Most assists . . . . **1 963, Wayne Gretzky,** Edm, LA, StL, NYR in 19 seasons, 1 487 games

Most points . . . . **2 857, Wayne Gretzky,** Edm, LA, StL, NYR in 19 seasons, (885 goals, 1 910 assists), 1 487 games

Most penalty minutes . . . . **3 966, Dave Williams,** Tor, Vcr, Det, LA, Htfd, in 14 seasons, 962 games

Most consecutive games . . . . **964, Doug Jarvis,** Mtl, Wash, Htfd from Oct. 8, 1975 through Oct. 10, 1987

Most games appeared in by a goaltender, career . . . . **971, Terry Sawchuk,** Det, Bos, Tor, LA, NYR (1949–70)

Most consecutive complete games by a goaltender . . . . **502, Glenn Hall,** Det, Chi.

> Played 502 games from beginning of 1955/56 season through first 12 games of 1962/63. In his 503rd straight game, Nov. 7, 1962, at Chicago, Hall was removed from the game against Boston with a back injury in the first period.

Most shutouts by a goaltender, career . . . . **103, Terry Sawchuk,** Det, Bos, Tor, LA, NYR, in 20 seasons

Most 50-or-more goal seasons . . . . **9, Mike Bossy,** NYI; **Wayne Gretzky,** Edm, LA

Most goals, one season . . . . **92, Wayne Gretzky,** Edm, 1981/82 (80 games)

Most assists, one season . . . . **163, Wayne Gretzky,** Edm, 1985/86 (80 games)

Most goals, one season, by a defenceman . . . . **48, Paul Coffey,** Edm, 1985/86 (79 games)

Most goals, one season, by a centre . . . . **92, Wayne Gretzky,** Edm, 1981/82 (80 games)

Most goals, one season, by a right winger . . . . **86, Brett Hull,** StL, 1990/91 (80 games)

Most goals, one season, by a left winger . . . . **63, Luc Robitaille,** LA, 1992/93 (84 games)

Most goals, one season, by a rookie . . . . **76, Teemu Selanne,** Win, 1992/93 (84 games)

Most points, one season, by a defenceman . . . . **139, Bobby Orr,** Bos, 1970/71 (78 games)

Most points, one season by a centre . . . . **215, Wayne Gretzky,** Edm, 1985/86 (80 games)

Most points, one season, by a right winger . . . . **149, Jaromir Jagr,** Pitt, 1995/96 (82 games)

Most points, one season, by a left winger . . . . **125, Luc Robitaille,** LA, 1992/93 (84 games)

Most points, one season, by a rookie . . . . **132,Teemu Selanne,** Win, 1992/93 (84 games)

Most power-play goals, one season . . . . **34, Tim Kerr,** Phi, 1985/86 (76 games)

Most penalty minutes, one season . . . . **472, Dave Schultz ,** Phi, 1974/75 (80 games)

Most shutouts, one season . . . . **22, George Hainsworth,** Mtl, 1928/29 (44 games)

Source: *Canadian Press*

Directory of Selected Hockey Organizations

Hockey Hall of Fame	**National Hockey League**	**National Hockey League Players' Association**
30 Yonge St	1155 Metcalfe St, Suite 960	777 Bay St., Suite 2400
Toronto, Ont.	Montreal, Que.	Toronto, Ont.
M5E 1X8	H3B 2W2	M5G 2C8
Tel: (416)360-7735	Tel: (514)871-9220	Tel: (416)408-4040
Fax: (416)360-1501	http://www.nhl.com	Fax: (416)408-3685
http://www.hhof.com		http://nhlpa.medius.com

Regular Season NHL Scoring Champions, 1917–99

Season	Player, Team	GP	G	A	Pts	Season	Player, Team	GP	G	A	Pts
1917–18[1]	Joe Malone, Mtl	20	44	—	44	1947–48	Elmer Lach, Mtl	60	30	31	61
1918–19	Newsy Lalonde, Mtl	17	23	9	32	1948–49	Roy Conacher, Chi	60	26	42	68
1919–20	Joe Malone, Que	24	39	6	45	1949–50	Ted Lindsay, Det	69	23	55	78
1920–21	Newsy Lalonde, Mtl	24	33	8	41	1950–51	Gordie Howe, Det	70	43	43	86
1921–22	Punch Broadbent, Ott	24	32	14	46	1951–52	Gordie Howe, Det	70	47	39	86
1922–23	Babe Dye, Tor	22	26	11	37	1952–53	Gordie Howe, Det	70	49	46	95
1923–24	Cy Denneny, Ott	21	22	1	23	1953–54	Gordie Howe, Det	70	33	48	81
1924–25	Babe Dye, Tor	29	38	6	44	1954–55	Bernie Geoffrion, Mtl	70	38	37	75
1925–26	Nels Stewart, Mtl Maroons	36	34	8	42	1955–56	Jean Béliveau, Mtl	70	47	41	88
1926–27	Bill Cook, NYR	44	33	4	37	1956–57	Gordie Howe, Det	70	44	45	89
1927–28	Howie Morenz, Mtl	43	33	18	51	1957–58	Dickie Moore, Mtl	70	36	48	84
1928–29	Ace Bailey, Tor	44	22	10	32	1958–59	Dickie Moore, Mt l	70	41	55	96
1929–30	Cooney Weiland, Bos	44	43	30	73	1959–60	Bobby Hull, Chi	70	39	42	81
1930–31	Howie Morenz, Mtl	39	28	23	51	1960–61	Bernie Geoffrion, Mtl	64	50	45	95
1931–32	Harvey Jackson, Tor	48	28	25	53	1961–62	Bobby Hull, Chi	70	50	34	84
1932–33	Bill Cook, NYR	48	28	22	50	1962–63	Gordie Howe, Det	70	38	48	86
1933–34	Charlie Conacher, Tor	42	32	20	52	1963–64	Stan Mikita, Chi	70	39	50	89
1934–35	Charlie Conacher, Tor	48	36	21	57	1964–65	Stan Mikita, Chi	70	28	59	87
1935–36	Dave Schriner, NY Americans	48	19	26	45	1965–66	Bobby Hull, Chi	65	54	43	97
1936–37	Dave Schriner, NY Americans	48	21	25	46	1966–67	Stan Mikita, Chi	70	35	62	97
1937–38	Gordie Drillon, Tor	48	26	26	52	1967–68	Stan Mikita, Chi	72	40	47	87
1938–39	Toe Blake, Mtl	48	24	23	47	1968–69	Phil Esposito, Bos	74	49	77	126
1939–40	Milt Schmidt, Bos	48	22	30	52	1969–70	Bobby Orr, Bos	76	33	87	120
1940–41	Bill Cowley, Bos	46	17	45	62	1970–71	Phil Esposito, Bos	78	76	76	152
1941–42	Bryan Hextall, NYR	48	24	32	56	1971–72	Phil Esposito, Bos	76	66	67	133
1942–43	Doug Bentley, Chi	50	33	40	73	1972–73	Phil Esposito, Bos	78	55	75	130
1943–44	Herbie Cain, Bos	48	36	46	82	1973–74	Phil Esposito, Bos	78	68	77	145
1944–45	Elmer Lach, Mtl	50	26	54	80	1974–75	Bobby Orr, Bos	80	46	89	135
1945–46	Max Bentley, Chi	47	31	30	61	1975–76	Guy Lafleur, Mtl	80	56	69	125
1946–47	Max Bentley, Chi	60	29	43	72	1976–77	Guy Lafleur, Mtl	80	56	80	136
						1977–78	Guy Lafleur, Mtl	78	60	72	132
						1978–79	Bryan Trottier, NYI	76	47	87	134
						1979–80	Marcel Dionne, LA	80	53	84	137
						1980–81	Wayne Gretzky, Edm	80	55	109	164

► **1981–82** Wayne Gretzky, Edm 80 92 120 212

1982–83 Wayne Gretzky, Edm 80 71 125 196

1983–84 Wayne Gretzky, Edm . . . 74 87 118 205

1984–85 Wayne Gretzky, Edm . . . 80 73 135 208

1985–86 Wayne Gretzky, Edm . . . 80 52 163 215

1986–87 Wayne Gretzky, Edm . . . 79 62 121 183

1987–88 Mario Lemieux, Pitt 77 70 98 168

1988–89 Mario Lemieux, Pitt 76 85 114 199

1989–90 Wayne Gretzky, LA 73 40 102 142

1990–91 Wayne Gretzky, LA 78 41 122 163

1991–92 Mario Lemieux, Pitt 64 44 87 131

1992–93 Mario Lemieux, Pitt 60 69 91 160

1993–94 Wayne Gretzky, LA 81 38 92 130

1994–95 Jaromir Jagr[2], Pitt . . . . 48[3] 32 38 70

1995–96 Mario Lemieux, Pitt 70 69 92 161

1996–97 Mario Lemieux, Pitt 76 50 72 122

1997–98 Jaromir Jagr, Pitt 77 35 67 102

1998–99 Jaromir Jagr, Pitt 81 44 83 127

Source: *National Hockey League*
(1) Number of assists not recorded. (2) Jagr tied with Lindros (Phi); awarded title based on most goals scored. (3) Season shortened to 48 games due to owner/player dispute.

Top 25 All-Time NHL Point-Scoring Leaders

(to the end of the 1998/99 season; active players in bold type)

Player/Teams	Seasons	Games	Goals	Assists	Points	Points/Game
Wayne Gretzky, Edm/LA/StL/NYR	20	1487	894	1963	2857	1.92
Gordie Howe, Det/Hfd	26	1767	801	1049	1850	1.05
Marcel Dionne, Det/LA/NYR	18	1348	731	1040	1771	1.31
Mark Messier, Edm/NYR/Van	20	1413	610	1050	1660	1.19
Phil Esposito, Chi/Bos/NYR	18	1282	717	873	1590	1.24
Mario Lemieux, Pitt	12	745	613	881	1494	2.01
Paul Coffey, Edm/Pitt/LA/Det/Hfd/Phi	19	1322	385	1102	1487	1.16
Ron Francis, Hfd, Pitt	18	1329	449	1035	1484	1.15
Steve Yzerman, Det	15	1178	592	891	1483	1.28
Ray Bourque, Bos	20	1453	385	1082	1467	1.03
Stan Mikita, Chi	22	1394	541	926	1467	1.05
Bryan Trottier, NYI/Pitt	18	1279	524	901	1425	1.11
Dale Hawerchuk, Wpg/Buf/StL/Phi	16	1188	518	891	1409	1.19
Jari Kurri, Edm/LA/NYR/Ana/Col	17	1251	601	797	1398	1.12
John Bucyk, Det/Bos	23	1540	556	813	1369	.889
Guy Lafleur, Mtl/NYR/Que	17	1126	560	793	1353	1.20
Denis Savard, Chi/Mtl/TB	17	1196	473	865	1338	1.12
Mike Gartner, Was/Min/NYR/Tor/Pho	19	1432	708	627	1335	.932
Gilbert Perreault, Buf	17	1191	512	814	1326	1.11
Alex Delvecchio, Det.	24	1549	456	825	1281	.827
Jean Ratelle, NYR, Bos	21	1281	491	776	1267	.989
Peter Stasny, Que/NJ/StL	15	977	450	789	1239	1.27
Doug Gilmour, StL,/Cal/Tor/NJ/Chi	**16**	**1197**	**397**	**835**	**1232**	**1.03**
Norm Ullman, Det/Tor	20	1410	490	739	1229	.872
Jean Beliveau, Mtl	20	1125	507	712	1219	1.08

Source: *National Hockey League* (1) Did not play 1994/95

►

Top Ten NHL Draft Selections, 1993–99

(Teams selected by in parentheses)

	1994	1995	1996
1	Ed Jovanovski, Fla	Bryan Berard, Ott	Chris Phillips, Ott
2	Oleg Tverdovsky, Ana	Wade Redden, NYI	Andrei Zyuzin, SJ
3	Radek Bonk, Ott	Aki-Petteri Berg, LA	Jean-Pierre Dumont, NYJ
4	Jason Bonsignore, Edm	Chad Kilger, Ana	Alexandre Volchkov, Wash
5	Jeff O'Neill, Htfd	Daymond Langkow, TB	Richard Jackman, Dal
6	Ryan Smith, Edm	Steve Kelly, Edm	Boyd Devereaux, Edm
7	Jamie Storr, LA	Shane Doan, Wpg	Erik Rasmussen, Buf
8	Jason Weimer, TB	Terry Ryan, Mtl	Johnathan Aitken, Bos
9	Brett Lindros, NYI	Kyle McLaren, Bos	Ruslan Salei, Ana
10	Nolan Baumgartner, Wash	Radek Dvorak, Fla	Lance Ward, NJ
	1997	**1998**	**1999**
1	Joe Thornton, Bos	Vincent Lecavalier, TB	Patrik Stefan, Atl[1]
2	Patrick Marleau, SJ	David Legwand, Nas	Daniel Sedin, Van
3	Olli Jokinen, LA	Brad Stuart, SJ	Henrik Sedin, Van
4	Roberto Luongo, NYI	Bryan Allen, Van	Pavel Brendl, NYR
5	Eric Brewer, NYI	Vitaly Vishnevsky, Ana	Tim Connolly, NYI
6	Daniel Tkaczuk, Cal	Rico Fata, Cal	Brian Finley, Nas
7	Paul Mara, TB	Manny Malhotra, NYR	Kris Beech, Was
8	Sergei Samsonov, Bos	Mark Bell, Chi	Taylor Pyatt, NYI
9	Nicholas Boynton, Ott	Michael Rupp, NYI	Jamie Lundmark, NYR
10	Brad Ference, Van	Nikolai Antropov, Tor	Branislav Mezei, NYI

Source: *Canadian Press*   (1) The Atlanta Thrashers begin play in the 1999-2000 season.

NHL All-Star Teams, 1993–99[1]

First Team	Second Team	First Team	Second Team
1994		**1997**	
Dominik Hasek, Buf, g	John Vanbiesbrovek, Fla, g	Dominik Hasek, Buf, g	Martin Brodeur, NJ, g
Raymond Bourque, Bos, d	Al MacInnis, Cal, d	Sandis Ozolinsh, Col, d	Chris Chelios, Chi, d
Scott Stevens, NJ, d	Brian Leetch, NYR, d	Brian Leetch, NYR, d	Scott Stevens, NJ, d
Sergei Federov, Det, c	Wayne Gretzky, Bos, rw	Mario Lemieux, Pitt, c	Wayne Gretzky, NYR, c
Pavel Bure, Van, rw	Cam Neely, Bos, rw	Teemu Selanne, Ana, rw	Jaromir Jagr, Pitt, rw
Brendan Shanahan, SH, lw	Adam Graves, NYR, lw	Paul Kariya, Ana, lw	John LeClair, Phi, lw
1995		**1998**	
Dominik Hasek, Buf, g	Jim Carey, Wash, g	Dominik Hasek, Buf, g	Martin Brodeur, NJ, g
Chris Chelios, Chi, d	Raymond Bourque, Bos, d	Rob Blake, LA, d	Raymond Bourque, Bos, d
Paul Coffey, Det, d	Larry Murphy, Pitt, d	Nicklas Lidstrom, Det, d	Chris Pronger, StL, d
Eric Lindros, Phi, c	Alexei Zhamnov, Wpg, c	Peter Forsberg, Col, c	Wayne Gretzky, NYR, c
Jaromir Jagr, Pitt, rw	Theoren Fleury, Cal, rw	Jaromir Jagr, Pitt, rw	Teemu Selanne, Ana, rw
John Leclair, Phi, lw	Keith Tkachuk, Wpg, lw	John LeClair, Phi, lw	Keith Tkachuk, Pho, lw
1996		**1999**	
Jim Carey, Wash, g	Chris Osgood, Det, g	Dominik Hasek, Buf, g	Byron Dafoe, Bos, g
Chris Chelios, Chi, d	Brian Leetch, NYR, d	Al MacInnis, StL, d	Raymond Bourque, Bos, d
Raymond Bourque, Bos, d	Vladimir Konstantinov, Det, d	Nicklas Lidstrom, Det, d	Eric Desjardins, Pha, d
Mario Lemieux, Pitt, c	Eric Lindros, Phi, c	Peter Forsberg, Col, c	Alexei Yashin, Ott, c
Jaromir Jagr, Pitt, rw	Alexander Mogilny, Van, rw	Jaromir Jagr, Pit, rw	Teemu Selanne, Ana, rw
Paul Kariya, Ana, lw	John Leclair, Phi, lw	Paul Kariya, Ana, lw	John LeClair, Phi, lw

Source: *Canadian Press*   (1) As selected by members of the Professional Hockey Writers' Association.

NHL Individual Award Winners, 1950–99

Hart Trophy (Most Valuable Player)[1]

1950 Charlie Rayner, NYR	**1967** Stan Mikita, Chi	**1983** Wayne Gretzky, Edm
1951 Milt Schmidt, Bos	**1968** Stan Mikita, Chi	**1984** Wayne Gretzky, Edm
1952 Gordie Howe, Det	**1969** Phil Esposito, Bos	**1985** Wayne Gretzky, Edm
1953 Gordie Howe, Det	**1970** Bobby Orr, Bos	**1986** Wayne Gretzky, Edm
1954 Al Rollins, Chi	**1971** Bobby Orr, Bos	**1987** Wayne Gretzky, Edm
1955 Ted Kennedy, Tor	**1972** Bobby Orr, Bos	**1988** Mario Lemieux, Pitt
1956 Jean Béliveau, Mtl	**1973** Bobby Clarke, Phi	**1989** Wayne Gretzky, LA
1957 Gordie Howe, Det	**1974** Phil Esposito, Bos	**1990** Mark Messier, Edm
1958 Gordie Howe, Det	**1975** Bobby Clarke, Phi	**1991** Brett Hull, StL
1959 Andy Bathgate, NYR	**1976** Bobby Clarke, Phi	**1992** Mark Messier, NYR
1960 Gordie Howe, Det	**1977** Guy Lafleur, Mtl	**1993** Mario Lemieux, Pitt
1961 Bernie Geoffrion, Mtl	**1978** Guy Lafleur, Mtl	**1994** Sergei Fedorov, Det
1962 Jacques Plante, Mtl	**1979** Bryan Trottier, NYI	**1995** Eric Lindros, Phi
1963 Gordie Howe, Det	**1980** Wayne Gretzky, Edm	**1996** Mario Lemieux, Pitt
1964 Jean Béliveau, Mtl	**1981** Wayne Gretzky, Edm	**1997** Dominik Hasek, Buf
1965 Bobby Hull, Chi	**1982** Wayne Gretzky, Edm	**1998** Dominik Hasek, Buf
1966 Bobby Hull, Chi		**1999** Jaromir Jagr, Pitt

Calder Trophy (Best Rookie)[1]

1950 Jack Gelineau, Bos	**1967** Bobby Orr, Bos	**1983** Steve Larmer, Chi
1951 Terry Sawchuk, Det	**1968** Derek Sanderson, Bos	**1984** Tom Barrasso, Buf
1952 Bernie Geoffrion, Mtl	**1969** Danny Grant, Min	**1985** Mario Lemieux, Pit
1953 Lorne Worsley, NYR	**1970** Tony Esposito, Chi	**1986** Gary Suter, Cal
1954 Camille Henry, NYR	**1971** Gilbert Perreault, Buf	**1987** Luc Robitaille, LA
1955 Ed Litzenberger, Chi	**1972** Ken Dryden, Mtl	**1988** Joe Nieuwendyk, Cal
1956 Glenn Hall, Det	**1973** Steve Vickers, NYR	**1989** Brian Leetch, NYR
1957 Larry Regan, Bos	**1974** Denis Potvin, NYI	**1990** Sergei Makarov, Cal
1958 Frank Mahovlich, Tor	**1975** Eric Vail, Atl	**1991** Ed Belfour, Chi
1959 Ralph Backstrom, Mtl	**1976** Bryan Trottier, NYI	**1992** Pavel Bure, Vcr
1960 Bill Hay, Chi	**1977** Willi Plett, Atl	**1993** Teemu Selanne, Wpg
1961 Dave Keon, Tor	**1978** Mike Bossy, NYI	**1994** Martin Brodeur, NJ
1962 Bobby Rousseau, Mtl	**1979** Bobby Smith, Min	**1995** Peter Forsberg, Que
1963 Kent Douglas, Tor	**1980** Raymond Bourque, Bos	**1996** Daniel Alfredsson, Ott
1964 Jacques Laperrière, Mtl	**1981** Peter Stastny, Que	**1997** Bryan Berard, NYI
1965 Roger Crozier, Det	**1982** Dale Hawerchuk, Wpg	**1998** Sergei Samsonov, Bos
1966 Brit Selby, Tor		**1999** Chris Drury, Col

▶

James Norris Trophy (Best Defenceman)[1]

1954 Red Kelly, Det	**1969** Bobby Orr, Bos	**1984** Rod Langway, Wash
1955 Doug Harvey, Mtl	**1970** Bobby Orr, Bos	**1985** Paul Coffey, Edm
1956 Doug Harvey, Mtl	**1971** Bobby Orr, Bos	**1986** Paul Coffey, Edm
1957 Doug Harvey, Mtl	**1972** Bobby Orr, Bos	**1987** Raymond Bourque, Bos
1958 Doug Harvey, Mtl	**1973** Bobby Orr, Bos	**1988** Raymond Bourque, Bos
1959 Tom Johnson, Mtl	**1974** Bobby Orr, Bos	**1989** Chris Chelios, Mtl
1960 Doug Harvey, Mtl	**1975** Bobby Orr, Bos	**1990** Raymond Bourque, Bos
1961 Doug Harvey, Mtl	**1976** Denis Potvin, NYI	**1991** Raymond Bourque, Bos
1962 Doug Harvey, NYR	**1977** Larry Robinson, Mtl	**1992** Brian Leetch, NYR
1963 Pierre Pilote, Chi	**1978** Denis Potvin, NYI	**1993** Chris Chelios, Chi
1964 Pierre Pilote, Chi	**1979** Denis Potvin, NYI	**1994** Raymond Bourque, Bos
1965 Pierre Pilote, Chi	**1980** Larry Robinson, Mtl	**1995** Paul Coffey, Det
1966 Jacques Laperrière, Mtl	**1981** Randy Carlyle, Pitt	**1996** Chris Chelios, Chi
1967 Harry Howell, NYR	**1982** Doug Wilson, Chi	**1997** Brian Leetch, NYR
1968 Bobby Orr, Bos	**1983** Rod Langway, Wash	**1998** Rob Blake, LA
		1999 Al MacInnis, Stl

Vezina Trophy (Best Goalkeeper)[2]

1950 Bill Durnan, Mtl	**1968** Lorne Worsley, Mtl	**1981** Richard Sevigny, Mtl
1951 Al Rollins, Tor	Rogie Vachon, Mtl	Denis Herron, Mtl
1952 Terry Sawchuk, Det	**1969** Jacques Plante, StL	Michel Larocque, Mtl
1953 Terry Sawchuk, Det	Glenn Hall, StL	**1982** Bill Smith, NYI
1954 Harry Lumley, Tor	**1970** Tony Esposito, Chi	**1983** Pete Peeters, Bos
1955 Terry Sawchuk, Det	**1971** Ed Giacomin, NYR	**1984** Tom Barrasso, Buf
1956 Jacques Plante, Mtl	Gilles Villemure, NYR	**1985** Pelle Lindbergh, Phi
1957 Jacques Plante, Mtl	**1972** Tony Esposito, Chi	**1986** John Vanbiesbrouck, NYR
1958 Jacques Plante, Mtl	Gary Smith, Chi	**1987** Ron Hextall, Phi
1959 Jacques Plante, Mtl	**1973** Ken Dryden, Mtl	**1988** Grant Fuhr, Edm
1960 Jacques Plante, Mtl	**1974** Bernie Parent, Phi	**1989** Patrick Roy, Mtl
1961 Johnny Bower, Tor	Tony Esposito, Chi	**1990** Patrick Roy, Mtl
1962 Jacques Plante, Mtl	**1975** Bernie Parent, Phi	**1991** Ed Belfour, Chi
1963 Glenn Hall, Chi	**1976** Ken Dryden, Mtl	**1992** Patrick Roy, Mtl
1964 Charlie Hodge, Mtl	**1977** Ken Dryden, Mtl	**1993** Ed Belfour, Chi
1965 Terry Sawchuk, Tor	Michel Larocque, Mtl	**1994** Dominik Hasek, Buf
Johnny Bower, Tor	**1978** Ken Dryden, Mtl	**1995** Dominik Hasek, Buf
1966 Lorne Worsley, Mtl	Michel Larocque, Mtl	**1996** Jim Carey, Wash
Charlie Hodge, Mtl	**1979** Ken Dryden, Mtl	**1997** Dominik Hasek, Buf
1967 Glenn Hall, Chi	Michel Larocque, Mtl	**1998** Dominik Hasek, Buf
Denis Dejordy, Chi	**1980** Bob Suavé, Buf	**1999** Dominik Hasek, Buf
	Don Edwards, Buf	

Lady Byng Trophy (Most Sportsmanlike)[1]

► **1950** Edgar Laprade, NYR	**1966** Alex Delvecchio, Det	**1982** Rick Middleton, Bos
1951 Red Kelly, Det	**1967** Stan Mikita, Chi	**1983** Mike Bossy, NYI
1952 Sid Smith, Tor	**1968** Stan Mikita, Chi	**1984** Mike Bossy, NYI
1953 Red Kelly, Det	**1969** Alex Delvecchio, Det	**1985** Jari Kurri, Edm
1954 Red Kelly, Det	**1970** Phil Goyette, StL	**1986** Mike Bossy, NYI
1955 Sid Smith, Tor	**1971** John Bucyk, Bos	**1987** Joe Mullen, Cal
1956 Earl Reibel, Det	**1972** Jean Ratelle, NYR	**1988** Mats Naslund, Mtl
1957 Andy Hebenton, NYR	**1973** Gilbert Perreault, Buf	**1989** Joe Mullen, Cal
1958 Camille Henry, NYR	**1974** John Bucyk, Bos	**1990** Brett Hull, StL
1959 Alex Delvecchio, Det	**1975** Marcel Dionne, Det	**1991** Wayne Gretzky, LA
1960 Don McKenney, Bos	**1976** Jean Ratelle, NYR/Bos	**1992** Wayne Gretzky, LA
1961 Red Kelly, Tor	**1977** Marcel Dionne, LA	**1993** Pierre Turgeon, NYI
1962 Dave Keon, Tor	**1978** Butch Goring, LA	**1994** Wayne Gretzky, LA
1963 Dave Keon, Tor	**1979** Bob MacMillan, Atl	**1995** Ron Francis, Pitt
1964 Ken Wharram, Chi	**1980** Wayne Gretzky, Edm	**1996** Paul Kariya, Ana
1965 Bobby Hull, Chi	**1981** Rick Kehoe, Pitt	**1997** Paul Kariya, Ana
		1998 Ron Francis, Pitt
		1999 Wayne Gretzky, NYR

Conn Smythe Trophy (Most Valuable in Playoffs)[3]

1965 Jean Béliveau, Mtl	**1977** Guy Lafleur, Mtl	**1988** Wayne Gretzky, Edm
1966 Roger Crozier, Det	**1978** Larry Robinson, Mtl	**1989** Al MacInnis, Cal
1967 Dave Keon, Tor	**1979** Bob Gainey, Mtl	**1990** Bill Ranford, Edm
1968 Glenn Hall, StL	**1980** Bryan Trottier, NYI	**1991** Mario Lemieux, Pitt
1969 Serge Savard, Mtl	**1981** Butch Goring, NYI	**1992** Mario Lemieux, Pitt
1970 Bobby Orr, Bos	**1982** Mike Bossy, NYI	**1993** Patrick Roy, Mtl
1971 Ken Dryden, Mtl	**1983** Bill Smith, NYI	**1994** Brian Leetch, NYR
1972 Bobby Orr, Bos	**1984** Mark Messier, Edm	**1995** Claude Lemieux, NJ
1973 Yvan Cournoyer, Mtl	**1985** Wayne Gretzky, Edm	**1996** Joe Sakic, Col
1974 Bernie Parent, Phi	**1986** Patrick Roy, Mtl	**1997** Mike Vernon, Det
1975 Bernie Parent, Phi	**1987** Ron Hextall, Phi	**1998** Steve Yzerman, Det
1976 Reggie Leach, Phi		**1999** Joe Nieuwendyk, Dal

Frank J. Selke Trophy (Best Defensive Forward)[1]

1978 Bob Gainey, Mtl	**1985** Craig Ramsay, Buf	**1992** Guy Carbonneau, Mtl
1979 Bob Gainey, Mtl	**1986** Troy Murray, Chi	**1993** Doug Gilmour, Tor
1980 Bob Gainey, Mtl	**1987** Dave Poulin, Phi	**1994** Sergei Fedorov, Det
1981 Bob Gainey, Mtl	**1988** Guy Carbonneau, Mtl	**1995** Ron Francis, Pitt
1982 Steve Kasper, Bos	**1989** Guy Carbonneau, Mtl	**1996** Sergei Fedorov, Det
1983 Bobby Clarke, Phi	**1990** Rick Meagher, StL	**1997** Mike Peca, Buf
1984 Doug Jarvis, Wash	**1991** Dirk Graham, Chi	**1998** Jere Lehtinen, Dal
		1999 Jere Lehtinen, Dal ►

Jack Adams Trophy (Coach of the Year)

▶ **1975** Bob Pulford, L.A.

1976 Don Cherry, Bos.

1977 Scotty Bowman, Mtl.

1978 Bobby Kromm, Det.

1979 Al Arbour, N.Y.I.

1980 Pat Quinn, Phi.

1981 Red Berenson, StL.

1982 Tom Watt, Wpg.

1983 Orval Tessier, Chi.

1984 Bryan Murray, Wsh.

1985 Mike Keenan, Phi.

1986 Glen Sather, Edm.

1987 Jacques Demers, Det.

1988 Jacques Demers, Det.

1989 Pat Burns, Mtl.

1990 Bob Murdoch, Wpg.

1991 Brian Sutter, StL.

1992 Pat Quinn, Van.

1993 Pat Burns, Tor.

1994 Jacques Lemaire, N.J.

1995 Marc Crawford, Que.

1996 Scotty Bowman, Det.

1997 Ted Nolan, Buf.

1998 Pat Burns, Bos

1999 Jacques Martin, Ott

Source: *Canadian Press*

(1) As selected at the end of the regular season by members of the Professional Hockey Writers' Association in the NHL cities. (2) Since the 1981–82 season, Vezina Trophy winners have been selected by general managers of the NHL clubs. In earlier seasons the trophy was awarded to the goalkeeper(s) of the team allowing the fewest goals during the regular season. (3) As selected by members of the Professional Hockey Writers' Association at the end of the last game of the Stanley Cup finals.

Men's World Hockey Championship, 1999

(Oslo, Hamar, Lillehammer Norway)

Gold Medal match
Czech Republic 3, Finland 1
Finland 4, Czech Republic 1
Tiebreaker
Czech Republic 1, Finland 0

Bronze Medal match
Sweden 3, Canada 2
Champions:
1999- Czech Republic
1998 - Sweden
1997 - Canada

1996 - Czech Republic
1995 - Finland
1994- Canada
1993 - Russia
1992 - Sweden
1991 - Sweden

Source: *Canadian Press*

World Junior Hockey Tournament, 1999

(Winnipeg)

Semifinals
Canada 6, Sweden 1
Russia 3, Slovakia 2

Bronze Medal match
Slovakia 5, Sweden 4

Gold Medal match
Russia 3, Canada 2 (OT)

Source: *Canadian Press*

Previous World Junior Hockey Tournament Winners

1977 . . . . Soviet Union

1978 . . . . Soviet Union

1979 . . . . Soviet Union

1980 . . . . Soviet Union

1981 . . . . Sweden

1982 . . . . **Canada**

1983 . . . . Soviet Union

1984 . . . . Soviet Union

1985 . . . . **Canada**

1986 . . . . Soviet Union

1987 . . . . Finland

1988 . . . . **Canada**

1989 . . . . Soviet Union

1990 . . . . **Canada**

1991 . . . . **Canada**

1992 . . . . C.I.S. (former Soviet Union)

1993 . . . . **Canada**

1994 . . . . **Canada**

1995 . . . . **Canada**

1996 . . . . **Canada**

1997 . . . . **Canada**

1998 . . . . Finland

1999 . . . . Russia

Source: *Canadian Press*

Women's World Hockey Championships, 1999

(Espoo, Finland)

Semifinals
Canada 4, Sweden 1
United States 3, Finland 1

Bronze Medal match
Finland 8, Sweden 2

Gold Medal match
Canada 3, United States 1

Source: *Canadian Press*

(1) Next competition in March 1999, in Espoo, Finland.

Memorial Cup Winners, 1919–99

(Canadian Junior Hockey Champions)

1919	University of Toronto Schools	**1959**	Winnipeg Braves
1920	Toronto Canoe Club	**1960**	St. Catharines Tee Pees
1921	Winnipeg Falcons	**1961**	St. Michael's Majors
1922	Fort William War Veterans	**1962**	Hamilton Red Wings
1923	University of Manitoba—Winnipeg	**1963**	Edmonton Oil Kings
1924	Owen Sound Greys	**1964**	Toronto Marlboros
1925	Regina Pats	**1965**	Niagara Falls Flyers
1926	Calgary Canadians	**1966**	Edmonton Oil Kings
1927	Owen Sound	**1967**	Toronto Marlboros
1928	Regina Monarchs	**1968**	Niagara Falls Flyers
1929	Toronto Marlboros	**1969**	Montreal Jr. Canadiens
1930	Regina Pats	**1970**	Montreal Jr. Canadiens
1931	Winnipeg Elmwoods	**1971**	Quebec Ramparts
1932	Sudbury	**1972**	Cornwall Royals
1933	Newmarket	**1973**	Toronto Marlboros
1934	Toronto St. Michael's	**1974**	Regina Pats
1935	Winnipeg Monarchs	**1975**	Toronto Marlboros
1936	West Toronto Redmen	**1976**	Hamilton Fincups
1937	Winnipeg Monarchs	**1977**	New Westminster Bruins
1938	St. Boniface Seals	**1978**	New Westminster Bruins
1939	Oshawa Generals	**1979**	Peterborough Petes
1940	Oshawa Generals	**1980**	Cornwall Royals
1941	Winnipeg Rangers	**1981**	Cornwall Royals
1942	Portage La Prairie	**1982**	Kitchener Rangers
1943	Winnipeg Rangers	**1983**	Portland Winter Hawks
1944	Oshawa Generals	**1984**	Ottawa 67's
1945	Toronto St. Michael's	**1985**	Prince Albert Raiders
1946	Winnipeg Monarchs	**1986**	Guelph Platers
1947	Toronto St. Michael's	**1987**	Medicine Hat Tigers
1948	Port Arthur West End Bruins	**1988**	Medicine Hat Tigers
1949	Montreal Royals	**1989**	Swift Current Broncos
1950	Montreal Canadiens	**1990**	Oshawa Generals
1951	Barrie Flyers	**1991**	Spokane Chiefs
1952	Guelph Biltmores	**1992**	Kamloops Blazers
1953	Barrie Flyers	**1993**	Sault Ste. Marie Greyhounds
1954	St. Catharines Tee Pees	**1994**	Kamloops Blazers
1955	Toronto Marlboros	**1995**	Kamloops Blazers
1956	Toronto Marlboros	**1996**	Granby Predateurs
1957	Flin Flon Bombers	**1997**	Hull Olympiques
1958	Ottawa-Hull Canadiens	**1998**	Portland Winterhawks
		1999	Ottawa 67s

Source: *Canadian Amateur Hockey Association*

Memorial Cup Tournament, 1999

(Ottawa)

Team	Wins	Losses	Pts	GF	GA
Calgary Hitmen	2	1	4	11	7
Ottawa 67s	2	1	4	13	9
Belleville Bulls	2	1	4	10	4
Acadie-Bathurst Titan	0	3	0	3	12

• Semi-Final: Ottawa 4, Belleville 2   • Final: Ottawa 7, Calgary 6 (OT)

Source: *Canadian Press*

The Hockey Hall of Fame and Museum

(Toronto, Ont.)

(players only; year of election to the Hall indicated in brackets)

Abel, Sid (1969)

Adams, Jack (1959)

Apps, Syl (1961)

Arbour, Al (1996)

Armstrong, George (1975)

Bailey, Ace (1975)

Bain, Dan (1945)

Baker, Hobey (1945)

Barber, Bill (1990)

Barry, Marty (1965)

Bathgate, Andy (1978)

Béliveau, Jean (1972)

Benedict, Clinton (1965)

Bentley, Doug (1964)

Bentley, Max (1966)

Blake, Toe (1966)

Boivin, Leo (1986)

Boon, Dickie (1952)

Bossy, Mike (1991)

Bouchard, Butch (1966)

Boucher, Frank (1958)

Boucher, Buck (1960)

Bower, Johnny (1976)

Bowie, Russell (1945)

Brimsek, Frank (1966)

Broadbent, Punch (1962)

Broda, Turk (1967)

Bucyk, Johnny (1981)

Burch, Billy (1974)

Cameron, Harry (1962)

Cheevers, Gerry (1985)

Clancy, King (1958)

Clapper, Dit (1945)

Clarke, Bob (1987)

Cleghorn, Sprague (1958)

Colville, Neil (1967)

Conacher, Charlie (1961)

Conacher, Lionel (1994)

Connell, Alex (1958)

Cook, Bill (1952)

Cook, Bun (1995)

Coulter, Art (1974)

Cournoyer, Yvan (1982)

Cowley, William (1968)

Crawford, Rusty (1962)

Darragh, Jack (1962)

Davidson, Scotty (1950)

Day, Hap (1961)

Delvecchio, Alex (1977)

Denneny, Cy (1959)

Dionne, Marcel (1992)

Drillon, Gordie (1975)

Drinkwater, Charles (1950)

Dryden, Ken (1983)

Dumart, Woody (1992)

Dunderdale, Thomas (1974)

Durnan, Bill (1964)

Dutton, Red (1958)

Dye, Babe (1970)

Esposito, Phil (1984)

Esposito, Tony (1988)

Farrell, Arthur (1965)

Flaman, Fern (1990)

▶

▶ **Foyston,** Frank (1958)

Frederickson, Frank (1958)

Gadsby, Bill (1970)

Gainey, Bob (1992)

Gardiner, Chuck (1945)

Gardiner, Herb (1958)

Gardner, Jimmy (1962)

Geoffrion, Boom Boom (1972)

Gerard, Eddie (1945)

Giacomin, Ed (1987)

Gilbert, Rod (1982)

Gilmour, Billy (1962)

Goheen, Moose (1952)

Goodfellow, Ebbie (1963)

*****Goulet,** Michel (1998)

Grant, Mike (1950)

Green, Shorty (1962)

Gretzky, Wayne (1999)

Griffis, Si (1950)

Hainsworth, George (1961)

Hall, Glenn (1975)

Hall, Joe (1961)

Harvey, Doug (1973)

Hay, George (1958)

Hern, Riley (1962)

Hextall, Bryan (1969)

Holmes, Hap (1972)

Hooper, Tom (1962)

Horner, Red (1965)

Horton, Tim (1977)

Howe, Gordie (1972)

Howell, Syd (1965)

Howell, Harry (1979)

Hull, Bobby (1983)

Hutton, Bouse (1962)

Hyland, Harry (1962)

Irvin, Dick (1958)

Jackson, Busher (1971)

Johnson, Moose (1952)

Johnson, Ching (1958)

Johnson, Tom (1970)

Joliat, Aurel (1947)

Keats, Duke (1958)

Kelly, Red (1969)

Kennedy, Teeder (1966)

Keon, Dave (1986)

Lach, Elmer (1966)

Lafleur, Guy (1988)

Lalonde, Newsy (1950)

Laperrière, Jacques (1987)

Lapointe, Guy (1993)

Laprate, Edgar (1993)

Laviolette, Jack (1962)

Lehman, Hugh (1958)

Lemaire, Jacques (1984)

Lemieux, Mario (1997)

LeSueur, Percy (1961)

Lewis, Herbie (1989)

Lindsay, Ted (1966)

Lumley, Harry (1980)

Mackay, Mickey (1952)

Mahovlich, Frank (1981

Malone, Joe (1950)

Mantha, Sylvio (1960)

Marshall, Jack (1965)

Maxwell, Steamer (1962)

McDonald, Lanny (1992)

McGee, Frank (1945)

McGimsie, Billy (1962)

McNamara, George (1958)

Mikita, Stan (1983)

Moore, Dickie (1974)

Moran, Paddy (1958)

Morenz, Howie (1945)

Mosienko, Bill (1965)

Nighbor, Frank (1947)

Noble, Reg (1962)

O'Connor, Buddy (1988)

O'Neill, Brian (1994)

Oliver, Harry (1967)

Olmstead, Bert (1985)

Orr, Bobby (1979)

Parent, Bernie (1984)

Park, Brad (1988)

Patrick, Lynn (1980)

Patrick, Lester (1947)

Perreault, Gilbert (1990)

Phillips, Tommy (1945)

Pilote, Pierre (1975)

Pitre, Didier "Pit" (1962)

Plante, Jacques (1978)

Potvin, Denis (1991)

Pratt, Babe (1966)

Primeau, Joe (1963)

Pronovost, Marcel (1978)

Pulford, Bob (1991)

Pulford, Harvey (1945)

Quackenbush, Bill (1976)

Rankin, Frank (1961)

Ratelle, Jean (1985)

Rayner, Chuck (1973)

Reardon, Ken (1966)

Richard, Henri (1979)

Richard, Maurice "Rocket" (1961)

Richardson, George (1950)

Roberts, Gordon (1971)

Robinson, Larry (1995)

Ross, Art (1945)

Russel, Blair (1965)

Russell, Ernest (1965)

▶

▶ **Ruttan,** Jack (1962)

Sabetski, Dr. Gunther (1995)

Salming, Borje, (1996)

Savard, Serge (1986)

Sawchuk, Terry (1971)

Scanlan, Fred (1965)

Schmidt, Milt (1961)

Schriner, Sweeney (1962)

Seibert, Earl (1963)

Seibert, Oliver (1961)

Shore, Eddie (1947)

Shutt, Steve (1993)

Siebert, Babe (1964)

Simpson, Bullet Joe (1962)

Sittler, Darryl (1989)

Smith, Alfred (1962)

Smith, Bill (1993)

Smith, Clint (1991)

Smith, Hooley (1972)

Smith, Thomas (1973)

Stanley, Allan (1981)

Stanley, Barney (1962)

*****Stasny,** Peter (1998)

Stewart, Black Jack (1964)

Stewart, Nels (1962)

Stuart, Bruce (1961)

Stuart, Hod (1945)

Taylor, Cyclone (1947)

Thompson, Tiny (1959)

Torrey, Bill (1995)

Tretiak, Vladislav (1989)

Trihey, Harry (1950)

Trottier, Bryan (1997)

Ullman, Norm (1982)

Vezina, Georges (1945)

Walker, Jack (1960)

Walsh, Marty (1962)

Watson, Harry (1994)

Watson, Moose (1962)

Weiland, Cooney (1971)

Westwick, Harry (1962)

Whitcroft, Fred (1962)

Wilson, Phat (1962)

Worsley, Lorne "Gump" (1980)

Worters, Roy (1969)

Source: *Canadian Press*

* New inductees

The NHL $4-Million Dollar Club for the 1999-2000 Season

(as of Sept. 1, 1999. All figures in U.S. dollars)

Player	Club		Salary
Jaromir Jagr	PIT	R	$10,359,852
Paul Kariya	ANA	L	$10,000,000
Peter Forsberg	COL	C	$9,000,000
Theoren Fleury	NYR	R	$8,500,000
Eric Lindros	PHI	C	$8,500,000
Pavel Bure	FLA	R	$8,000,000
Patrick Roy	COL	G	$7,500,000
Dominik Hasek	BUF	G	$7,000,000
Mats Sundin	TOR	C	$7,000,000
Brian Leetch	NYR	D	$6,680,000
Curtis Joseph	TOR	G	$6,150,000
Raymond Bourque	BOS	D	$6,000,000
Doug Gilmour	CHI	C	$6,000,000
Valeri Kamensky	NYR	L	$6,000,000
Nicklas Lidstrom	DET	D	$6,000,000
Mark Messier	VAN	C	$6,000,000
Mike Modano	DAL	C	$6,000,000
Brett Hull	DAL	R	$5,500,000
Teemu Selanne	ANA	R	$5,450,000
Rob Blake	LA	D	$5,267,500
Ron Francis	CAR	C	$5,000,000
Zigmund Palffy	LA	R	$5,000,000
Mark Recchi	PHI	R	$5,000,000
Mike Richter	NYR	G	$5,000,000
Pierre Turgeon	STL	C	$5,000,000
Steve Yzerman,	DET	C	$4,975,000
Al MacInnis	STL	D	$4,763,802
Alexander Mogilny	VAN	R	$4,600,000
Guy Hebert	ANA	G	$4,500,000
Mike Vernon	SJ	G	$4,378,007
Keith Tkachuk	PHO	L	$4,300,000
Doug Weight	EDM	C	$4,300,000
John Vanbiesbrouck	PHI	G	$4,289,756
Jeremy Roenick	PHO	C	$4,200,000
Scott Stevens	NJ	D	$4,152,579
Martin Brodeur	NJ	G	$4,130,687
Uwe Krupp	DET	D	$4,100,000
Sandis Ozolinsh	COL	D	$4,000,000
Brendan Shanahan	DET	L	$4,000,000

Source: *National Hockey League Player's Association*

OLYMPICS

Summer Olympics

Year	Location	Date of competition	Competitors Men	Women	Nations Represented	Unofficial Winners
1896	Athens, Greece	Apr. 6–15	311	0	13	United States
1900	Paris, France	May 20–Oct. 28	1 319	11	22	United States
1904	St. Louis, United States	July 1–Nov. 23	681	6	12	United States
1906[1]	Athens, Greece	Apr. 22–May 2	877	7	20	United States
1908	London, England	Apr. 27–Oct. 31	1 999	36	23	United States
1912	Stockholm, Sweden	May 5–July 22	2 490	57	28	United States
1916	Cancelled because of World War I					
1920	Antwerp, Belgium	Apr. 20–Sept. 12	2 543	64	29	United States
1924	Paris, France	May 4–July 27	2 956	136	44	United States
1928	Amsterdam, Netherlands	May 17–Aug. 12	2 724	290	46	United States
1932	Los Angeles, United States	July 30–Aug. 14	1 281	127	37	United States
1936	Berlin, Germany	Aug. 1–16	3 738	328	49	Germany
1940	Cancelled because of World War II					
1944	Cancelled because of World War II					
1948	London, England	July 29–Aug. 14	3 714	385	59	United States
1952	Helsinki, Finland	July 19–Aug.3	4 407	518	69	United States
1956	Melbourne, Australia[2]	Nov. 22–Dec. 8	2 958	384	67	USSR
1960	Rome, Italy	Aug. 25–Sept. 11	4 738	610	83	USSR
1964	Tokyo, Japan	Oct. 10–24	4 457	683	93	United States
1968	Mexico City, Mexico	Oct. 12 27	4 750	781	112	United States
1972	Munich, West Germany	Aug. 26–Sept. 10	5 848	1 299	122	USSR
1976	Montreal, Canada	July 17–Aug. 1	4 834	1 251	92[3]	USSR
1980	Moscow, USSR	July 19–Aug. 3	4 265	1 088	81	USSR
1984	Los Angeles, United States	July 28–Aug. 12	5 458	1 620	141	United States
1988	Seoul, South Korea	Sept. 17–Oct. 2	7 105	2 476	160	USSR
1992	Barcelona, Spain	July 25–Aug. 9	7 555	3 008	172	Unified Team
1996	Atlanta, United States	July 19–Aug. 4	7 000	3 800	197	United States
2000	Sydney, Australia	Sept. 16-Oct. 1				
2004	Athens, Greece					

Source: *Canadian Olympic Association*

(1) 1906 Games were not recognized by the International Olympic Committee. (2) The equestrian events were held in Stockholm, Sweden, June 10–17, 1956. (3) Most sources list this figure as 88. Cameroon, Egypt, Morocco and Tunisia all boycotted the 1976 Olympics; however, their athletes had already competed before the boycott was officially announced. (n.a.) not available.

Final Medal Standings of the Summer Olympics, 1996

(Atlanta, Georgia, July 21-August 4, 1996)

Country	Gold	Silver	Bronze	Total	Country	Gold	Silver	Bronze	Total
United States	43	32	25	100	Algeria	2	0	1	3
Germany	20	18	27	65	Ethiopia	2	0	1	3
Russia	26	21	16	63	Iran	1	1	1	3
China	16	22	12	50	Slovakia	1	1	1	3
Australia	9	9	22	40	Argentina	0	2	1	3
France	15	7	15	37	Austria	0	1	2	3
Italy	13	10	12	35	Armenia	1	1	0	2
South Korea	7	15	5	27	Croatia	1	1	0	2
Cuba	9	8	8	25	Portugal	1	0	1	2
Ukraine	9	2	12	23	Thailand	1	0	1	2
Canada	**3**	**8**	**11**	**22**	Namibia	0	2	0	2
Hungary	7	4	10	21	Slovenia	0	2	0	2
Romania	4	7	9	20	Malaysia	0	1	1	2
Netherlands	4	5	10	19	Moldova	0	1	1	2
Poland	7	5	5	17	Uzbekistan	0	1	1	2
Spain	5	6	6	17	Georgia	0	0	2	2
Bulgaria	3	7	5	15	Morocco	0	0	2	2
United Kingdom	1	8	6	15	Trinidad & Tobago	0	0	2	2
Belarus	1	6	8	15	Burundi	1	0	0	1
Japan	3	6	5	14	Costa Rica	1	0	0	1
Brazil	3	2	9	14	Ecuador	1	0	0	1
Czech Republic	4	3	4	11	Hong Kong	1	0	0	1
Kazakhstan	3	4	4	11	Syria	1	0	0	1
Greece	4	4	0	8	Azerbaijan	0	1	0	1
Kenya	1	4	3	8	Bahamas	0	1	0	1
Sweden	2	4	2	8	Latvia	0	1	0	1
Switzerland	4	3	0	7	Philippines	0	1	0	1
Norway	2	2	3	7	Taiwan	0	1	0	1
Denmark	4	1	1	6	Tonga	0	1	0	1
Turkey	4	1	1	6	Zambia	0	1	0	1
New Zealand	3	2	1	6	India	0	0	1	1
Belgium	2	2	2	6	Israel	0	0	1	1
Nigeria	2	1	3	6	Lithuania	0	0	1	1
Jamaica	1	3	2	6	Mexico	0	0	1	1
South Africa	3	1	1	5	Mongolia	0	0	1	1
North Korea	2	1	2	5	Mozambique	0	0	1	1
Ireland	3	0	1	4	Puerto Rico	0	0	1	1
Finland	1	2	1	4	Tunisia	0	0	1	1
Indonesia	1	1	2	4	Uganda	0	0	1	1
Yugoslavia	1	1	2	4					

Source: *Canadian Olympic Association*

Canada's Olympic Gold Medalists, 1900–96

■ Winter Olympic Games

1920 Winnipeg Falcons, Ice Hockey (Although the Olympic Winter Games did not begin until 1924, ice hockey was an official event at the 1920 Olympic Games.)

1924 Toronto Granites, Ice Hockey

1928 University of Toronto Graduates, Ice Hockey

1932 Winnipeg Hockey Team, Ice Hockey

1948 Barbara Ann **Scott,** Women's Figure Skating; **RCAF Flyers,** Ice Hockey

1952 Edmonton Mercurys, Ice Hockey

1960 Anne **Heggtveit,** Alpine Skiing, Women's Slalom; Barbara **Wagner** & Robert **Paul,** Pairs Figure Skating

1964 Vic **Emery,** John **Emery,** Douglas **Anakin** & Peter **Kirby,** Four-Man Bobsled

1968 Nancy **Greene,** Alpine Skiing, Women's Giant Slalom

1976 Kathy **Kreiner,** Alpine Skiing, Women's Giant Slalom

1984 Gaetan **Boucher,** Speed Skating, Men's 1 000 m; Gaetan **Boucher,** Speed Skating, Men's 1 500 m

1992 Kerrin **Lee-Gartner,** Alpine Skiing, Women's Downhill; Sylvie **Daigle,** Nathalie **Lambert,** Annie **Perreault,** Angela **Cutrone,** Speed Skating, Women's Short Track Relay; Philippe **Laroche,** Freestyle Skiing, Men's Aerials (demonstration)

1994 Jean-Luc **Brassard,** Freestyle Skiing, Men's Alpine; Myriam **Bedard,** Biathlon, Women's 7.5 km Sprint; Myriam **Bedard,** Biathlon, Women's 15 km

1998 Pierre **Lueders** and Dave **MacEachern,** Bobsled (Two-man); Sandra **Schmirler,** Jan **Betker,** Joan **McCusker,** Marcia **Gudereit** and Atina **Ford,** Curling (Women); Ross **Rebagliati,** Snowboarding (Giant Slalom); Catriona **Le May Doan,** Speed Skating, Long Track (500 metres); Annie **Perreault,** Speed Skating, Short Track (500 metres); Eric **Bedard,** Derrick **Campbell,** Francois **Drolet,** and Marc **Gagnon,** Speed Skating, Short Track (5,000-metre relay).

■ Summer Olympic Games

1900 George **Orton,** 2 500 Steeplechase (Although a Canadian citizen, he represented the University of Pennsylvania; Canada did not officially appear at the Olympics until 1904.)

1904 Étienne **Desmarteau,** 56-pound Weight Throw; George **Lyon,** Golf; **The Galt Association Football Club,** Football (Soccer); **The Winnipeg Shamrocks Lacrosse Club,** Lacrosse 190; William **Sherring,** Marathon (The 1906 Games are not officially recognized by the I.O.C.)

1908 Walter **Ewing,** Trapshooting; Robert **Kerr,** Men's 200 m Run; **The All Canadas,** Lacrosse

1912 George **Goulding,** 10 000 m Walk; George **Hodgson,** Swimming, Men's 400 m Freestyle; George **Hodgson,** Swimming, Men's 1 500 m Freestyle

1920 Albert **Schneider,** Boxing, Welterweight; Earl **Thomson,** Men's 110 m Hurdles

1928 Ethel **Catherwood,** Women's High Jump; Percy **Williams,** Men's 100 m Run; Percy **Williams,** Men's 200 m Run; Women's Relay Team (Fanny **Rosenfeld,** Ethel **Smith,** Florence **Bell** & Myrtle **Cook**), Women's 4 x 100 m Relay

1932 Horace **Gwynne,** Boxing, Bantamweight; Duncan **McNaughton,** Men's High Jump

1936 Francis **Amyot,** Canoeing, Canadian Singles 1 000 m

1952 George **Genereux,** Trapshooting

1956 Gerald **Ouellette,** Small-Bore Rifle (Prone); University of British Columbia Team (Archibald **McKinnon,** Lorne **Loomer,** Walter **D'Hondt** & Donald **Arnold,** Rowing, Four-Oared Shell without Coxswain

1964 George **Hungerford** & Roger **Jackson,** Rowing, Pair-Oared Shell without Coxswain

1968 Equestrian Team (James **Elder,** James **Day** & Thomas **Gayford**), Grand Prix (Jumping)

1984 Alex **Baumann,** Swimming, Men's 200 m Individual Medley; Alex **Baumann,** Swimming, Men's 400 m Individual Medley; Sylvie **Bernier,** Women's Spring-board Diving; Larry **Cain,** Canoeing, Canadian Singles 500 m; Victor **Davis,** Swimming, 200 m Breaststroke; Hugh **Fisher** & Alwyn **Morris,** Canoeing, Kayak Pairs 1 000 m; Lori **Fung,** Rhythmic Gymnastics, All-Around; Anne **Otten-brite,** Swimming, Women's 200 m Breast-stroke; Linda **Thom,** Women's Sport Pistol; National Team (Patrick **Turner,** Kevin **Neufeld,** Mark **Evans,** Grant **Main,** Paul **Steele,** J. Michael **Evans,** Dean **Crawford,** Blair **Horn** & Brian **McMahon**), Eight-Oared Shell with Coxswain

1988 Lennox **Lewis,** Boxing, Super heavyweight; Carolyn **Waldo,** Synchronized Swimming, Solo; Carolyn **Waldo** & Michelle **Cameron,** Synchronized Swimming, Duet

1992 Marnie **McBean** and Kathleen **Heddle,** Rowing, Women's Pairs; Mark **McKoy,** Track, Men's 110 m Hurdles; Mark **Tewksbury,** Swimming, Men's 100 m Backstroke; Women's Fours, Rowing (Kirsten **Barnes,** Brenda **Taylor,** Jessica **Monroe,** Kay **Worthington**); Men's Eights, Rowing (John **Wallace,** Bruce **Robertson,** Michael **Forgeron,** Darren **Barber,** Robert **Marland,** Michael **Rascher,** Andy **Crosby,** Derek **Porter,** Terry **Paul**); Women's Eights, Rowing (Kirsten **Barnes,** Brenda **Taylor,** Megan **Delehanty,** Shannon **Crawford,** Marnie **McBean,** Kay **Worthington,** Jessica **Monroe,** Kathleen **Heddle,** Lesley **Thompson**); Sylvie **Frechette,** synchronized swimming

1996 Donovan **Bailey,** Track, Men's 100m; Donovan **Bailey,** Bruny Surin, Glenroy **Gilbert,** Robert **Esmie,** Carlton **Chambers,** Men's 4x100 Relay; Marnie **McBean** and Kathleen **Heddle,** Rowing, Women's Double Sculls.

Source: *Canadian Press*

Canadians to Watch in Sydney

Track and field: Bruny Surin; Donovan Bailey; Mark Boswell; Graham Hood; Joel Bourgeois; Philomenah Mensah; Jason Tunks.

Rowing: Marnie McBean; Emma Robinson; Derek Porter.

Swimming: Jessica Deglau; Joanne Malar; Laura Nicholls; Marianne Limpert; Kelly Stefanyshyn; Curtis Myden; Morgan Knabe; Yannick Lupien; Mark Versfeld.

Squash: Jonathan Power; Melanie Jans.

Cycling: Tanya Dubnicoff; Linda Jackson; Alison Sydor; Clara Hughes.

Equestrian: Ian Millar; Eric Lamaze; Beth Underhill.

Diving: Alexander Despatie; Eryn Bulmer; Anne Montimy; Myriam Boileau.

Men's and Women's Basketball teams.

Men's Field Hockey Team.

Boxing: Mike Strange; Benoit Gaudet; Troy Ross; Jeremy Moliter; Mark Simmons.

2000 Olympic Games Schedule

For the latest information, visit http: www.sydney.olympic.org, the official web site for the Summer Games.

(With Results from the 1996 Olympic Games in Atlanta. Sept 13-October 1, Sydney, Australia)
(*Olympic record; **Olympic and world record)
(Schedule subject to change)

	Event	Date	1996 Results
Men's Athletics	100-Metre	Sept. 22, 23	1. Donovan Bailey, Oakville, Ont. 9.84*
			2. Frankie Fredericks, Namibia 9.89
			3. Ato Bolden, Trinidad and Tobago, 9.90
	200-metre	Sept. 27, 28	1. Michael Johnson, United States, 19.32**
			2. Frankie Fredericks, Namibia, 19.68
			3. Ato Boldon, Trinidad and Tobago, 19.80
	400-metre	Sept. 22, 23, 24, 25	1. Michael Johnson, United States, 43.49*
			2. Roger Black, Britain, 44.41
			3. Davis Kamoga, Uganda, 44.53
	800-metre	Sept. 22, 23, 24, 27	1. Vebjoern Radal, Norway, 1:42.58 *
			2. Hezikiel Sepeng, South Africa, 1:42.74
			3. Fred Onyancha, Kenya, 1:42.79
	1 500-metre	Sept. 25, 28, 30	1. Noureddine Morceli, Algeria, 3:35.78
			2. Fermin Cacho, Spain, 3:36.40
			3. Stephen Kipkorir, Kenya, 3:36.72
	5 000-metre	Sept. 27, 28, 30	1. Venuste Niyonbgabo, Burundi, 13:07.96
			2. Paul Bitok, Kenya, 13:08.16
			3. Khalid Boulami, Morocco, 13:08.37
	10 000-metre	Sept. 23, 25	1. Haile Gebrselassie, Ethiopia, 27:07.34*
			2. Paul Tergat, Kenya,
			3. Salah Hissau, Morocco
	110-metre Hurdles	Sept. 24. 25	1. Allen Johnson, United States, 12.95*
			2. Mark Crear, United States, 13.09
			3. Florian Schwarthoff, Germany, 13.17
	400-metre hurdles	Sept. 25, 27, 28	1. Derrick Adkins, United States, 47.54
			2. Samuel Matete, Zambia, 47.78
			3. Calvin Davis, United States, 47.96
	3 000-metre steeplechase	Sept. 24, 25, 27	1. Joseph Keter, Kenya, 8:07.12
			2. Moses Kiptanui, Kenya, 8:08.33
			3. Alessandro Lambruschini, Italy, 8:11.28
	20K walk	Sept. 22	1. Jefferson Perez, Ecuador,1:20.07
			2. Llya Markov, Russia,1:20.16
			3. Bernardo Sugura, Mexico,1:20.23

Event	Date	1996 Results
50-Kilometre walk	Sept. 29	1. Robert Korzeniowski, Poland, 3:43.30 2. Mikhail Shchennikov, Russia, 3:43.46 3. Valentin Massana, Spain, 3:44.19
4x100 Relay	Sept. 29, 30	**1. Canada, Robert Esmie, Sudbury (Final), Carlton Chambers, Mississauga, Ont(Semi); Glenroy Gilbert, Ottawa; Bruny Surin, Montreal; Donovan Bailey, Oakville, 37. 69** 2. United States, 38.05 3. Brazil, 38.41
4x400 Relay	Sept. 29, 30	1. United States,2:55.89 2. Britain, 2:56.60 3. Jamaica, 2:59.42
Decathalon	Sept. 27, 28	1. Dan O'Brien, United States, 8824 2. Frank Busemann, Germany, 8706 3. Tomas Dvorak, Czech Republic, 8664
High Jump	Sept.22, 24	1. Charles Austin, United States, 2.39* 2. Artur Partyka, Poland 3. Steve Smith, Britain
Long Jump	Sept. 25, 28	1. Carl Lewis, United States, 8.50 2. James Beckford, Jamaica, 8.29 3. Joe Greene, United States, 8.24
Triple Jump	Sept. 23, 25	1. Kenny Harrison, United States, 18.09* 2. Jonathan Edwards, Britain, 17.88 3. Yaelbi Quesada, Cuba, 17.44
Discus	Sept. 27, 29	1. Lars Riedel, Germany, 69.40* 2. Vladimir Dubrovshcick, Belarus, 66.60 3. Vasiliy Kaptyukh, Belarus, 65.80
Hammer	Sept. 23, 24	1. Balazs Kiss, Hungary, 81.24 2. Lance Deal, United States, 81.12 3. Alexandr Krykun, Ukraine, 80.20
Javelin	Sept. 22, 23	1. Jan Zelezmy, Czech Republic, 88.16 2. Steve Backley, Britian, 87.44 3. Seppo Rati, Finland, 86.98
Pole Vault	Sept. 23, 27, 20	1. Jean Galfione, 5.92* 2. Igor Tradenkov, Russia, 5.92* 3. Andrei Tivontchik, Germany, 5.92*
Shot Put	Sept. 22, 29	1. Randy Barnes, United States, 21.62 2. John Godina, United States, 20.79 3. Oleksander Bagach, Ukraine, 20.75
Marathon	Sept. 24	1. Josia Thugwane, South Africa, 2:12.36 2. Lee Bang-ju, South Horea, 2:12.39 3. Eric Wainaina, Kenya, 2:12.44
Women's Athletics **100-Metre**	Sept. 22, 23	1. Gail Devers, United States, 10.94 2. Merlene Ottey, Jamaica, 10.94 3. Gwen Torrence, United States, 10.96
200-metre	Sept. 27, 28	1. Marie-Jose Perec, France, 22.12 2. Merlene Ottey, Jamaica, 22.24 3. Mary Onyall, Nigeria, 22.38
400-metre	Sept. 22, 23, 25	1. Marie-Jose Perec, France, 48.25* 2. Cathy Freeman, Australia, 48.63 3. Falilat Ogukoya, Nigeria, 49.10
800-metre	Sept. 22, 23, 24	1. Svetelena Masterkova, Russia, 1:57.73

Event	Date	1996 Results
		2. Ana Quirot Fidelia, Cuba, 1:58.11
		3. Maria Mutola Lurdes, Mozambique, 1:58.71
1 500-metre	Sept. 27, 28, 30	1. Svetelena Masterkova, Russia, 4:00.83
		2. Gabriela Szabo, Romania, 4:01.54
		3. Theresia Kiesl, Australia, 4:03.02
5 000-metre	Sept. 22, 24	1. Wang Junxia, China
		2. Pualine Konga, Kenya
		3. Roberta Bruney, Italy
10 000-metre	Sept. 27, 29	1. Fernanda Ribiero, Portugal, 31:01.63
		2. Wang Junxia, China, 31:02.58
		3. Gete Wami, Ethiopia, 31:06.55
100-metre Hurdles	Sept. 25, 27	1. Ludmilla Enquist, Sweden, 12.58
		2. Brigita Bukovec, Slovenia, 12.59
		3. Patricia Girard-Leno, France, 13.04
400-metre hurdles	Sept. 23, 24, 25	1. Deon Hemmings, Jamaica, 52.82**
		2. Kim Batten, United States, 53.08
		3. Tonja Buford-Bailey, United States, 53.22
10K Walk		Not contested in 2000 Olympics
		1. Yelena Nikolayeva, Russia 41:49*
		2. Elisabetta Perrone, Italy, 42:12
		3. Wang Yan, China, 42:19
20K walk	Sept. 28	Not contested in 1996 Olympics
4x100 Relay	Sept. 29, 30	1. Unites States, 41.95
		2. Bahamas, 42.14
		3. Jamaica, 42.24
4x400 Relay	Sept. 29, 30	1. United States, 3:20.91
		2. Nigeria, 3:21.04
		3. Germany, 3:21.14
Heptathalon	Sept. 23, 24	1. Gahda Shouaa, Syria
		2. Natasha Sazanovich, Belarus
		3. Denise Lewis, Britain
High Jump	Sept. 28, 30	1. Stefka Kostadinova, Bulgaria, 2.05*
		2. Niki Bakogianni, Greece, 2.03
		3. Inha Babakova, Ukraine, 2.01
Long Jump	Sept. 28, 29	1. Chioma Ajunwa, Nigeria, 7.12
		2. Fiona May, Italy, 7.02
		3. Jackie Joyner-Kersee, United States, 7.00
Triple Jump	Sept. 22, 24	1. Inessa Kravets, Ukraine, 15.33
		2. Inna Lasovskaya, Russia, 14.98
		3. Sarka Kasparkova, Czech Republic, 14.98
Discus	Sept. 24, 25	1. Ilke Wyludda, Germany,
		2. Natalya Sadova, Russia
		3. Elya Zvereva, Belarus
Hammer	Sept. 25, 27	
Javelin	Sept. 29, 30	1. Heli Rantanin, Finland, 67.94
		2. Louise Mcpaul, Australia, 65.54
		3. Trine Hattestad, Norway, 64.98
Pole Vault	Sept. 23, 25	Not contested in 1996 Olympics
Shot Put	Sept. 28, 29	1. Astrid Kumbernuss, Germany, 20.56
		2. Xinmei Sui, China, 19.88
		3. Zrina Khudorozhkina, Russia, 19.35
Marathon	Sept. 24	1. Fatuma Roba, Ethiopia, 2:26.05

	Event	Date	1996 Results
			2. Valentina Yegorova, Russia, 2:28.05
			3. Yuko Arimori, Japan, 2:28.39
Men's Rowing	**Single sculls**	Sept. 17, 19, 21, 22, 23	1. Xeno Mueller, Switzerland, 6:44.85
			2. Derek Porter, Victoria, 6:47.45
			3. Thomas Lange, Germany, 6:47.72
	Double sculls	Sept. 17, 19, 21, 22, 23	1. Italy, 6:16.98
			2. Norway, 6:18.42
			3. France, 6:19.85
	Coxless pair	Sept. 17, 19, 21, 22, 23	1. Britain, 6:20.09
			2. Australia, 6:21.02
			3. France, 6:22.15
	Coxless fours	Sept. 17, 19, 21, 22, 23	1. Australia, 6:06.37
			2. France, 6:07.03
			3. Britain, 6:07.28
	Lightweight double sculls	Sept. 18, 20, 22, 23, 24	1. Switzerland, 6:23.47
			2. Netherlands, 6:26.48
			3. Australia, 6:26.69
	Lightweight four	Sept. 18, 20, 22, 23, 24	1. Denmark, 6:09.58
			2. Canada (Jeffery Lay, Mississauga, Ont; David Boyes, St. Catharines, Ont; Gavin Hassett, Victoria; Brian Peaker, London, Ont) 6:10. 13
			3. United States, 6:12. 29
	Quad sculls	Sept. 18, 20, 22, 23, 24	1. Germany, 5:56.93
			2. United States, 5:59.10
			3. Australia, 6:01.65
	Eights	Sept. 18, 20, 23, 24	1. Netherlands, 5:42.74
			2. Germany, 5:44.58
			3. Russia, 5:45.77
Women's Rowing	**Single sculls**	Sept. 17, 19, 21, 22, 23	1. Yekaterina Khodotovitch, Belarus, 7:32.21
			2. Silken Lauman, Victoria, 7:35.15
			3. Trine Hanson, Denmark, 7:37.20
	Double sculls	Sept. 17, 19, 22, 23	**1. Canada (Marnie Mcbean, Toronto; Kathleen Heddle, Vancouver) 6:56.84**
			2. China, 6:58.35
			3. Netherlands, 6:58.72
	Coxless pair	Sept. 17, 19, 22, 23	1. Australia, 7:01.39
			2. United States, 7:01.78
			3. France, 7;03.82
	Lightweight double sculls	Sept. 18, 20, 22, 23, 24	1. Romania, 7:12.78
			2. United States, 7:14.65
			3. Australia, 7:16.56
	Quad sculls	Sept. 18, 20, 23, 24	1. Germany, 6:27.44
			2. Ukraine, 6:30.36
			3. Canada (Laryssa Biesenthal, Walkerton, Ont; Marnie Mcbean, Toronto; Diane O'Grady, North Bay, Ont; Kathleen Heddle, Vancouver)
	Eights	Sept. 18, 20, 24	1. Romania, 6:19.73
			2. Canada (Heather Mcdermid and Tosha Tsang, Both Calgary; Maria Maunder, St. Johns; Alison Korn, Nepean, Ont; Emma Robinson, Winnipeg; Anna van der Kamp, Port Hardy, B. C. ; Jessica Monroe, N. Vancouver; Theresa Luke 100

	Event	Date	1996 Results
			Mile House, B. C. ; Lesley Thompson, London, Ont) **6:24.05** 3. Belarus, 6:24.44
Men's Gymnastics	Men's Qualifications rounds 1, 2, and 3 take place on Sept. 16		
	All-around	Sept. 20	1. Li Xiaoshuang, China 2. Alexei Nemov, Russia 3. Vitaly Scherbo, Belarus
	Team Medal Event	Sept. 18	1. Russia 2. China 3. Ukraine
	Floor	Sept. 24	1. Loannis Melissandis, Greece 2. Li Xiaoshaung, China 3. Alexei Nemov, Russia
	Horizontal Bar	Sept. 25	1. Andreas Wecker, Germany 2. Krasimir Dounev, Bulgaria 3. Vitaly Scherbo, Belarus & Alexei Nemov, Russia & Fan Bin, China
	Parallel Bar	Sept. 25	1. Rustam Sharipov, Ukraine 2. Jair Lynch, United States 3. Vitaly Scherbo, Belarus
	Pommel Horse	Sept. 24	1. Donghua Li, Switzerland 2. Marius Urzica, Romania 3. Alexei Nemov, Russia
	Rings	Sept. 24	1. Yuri Chechi, Italy 2. Dan Burinca, Romania and Szilveszter Csollany, Hungary
	Vault	Sept. 25	1. Alexei Nemov, Russia 2. Hong-Chul Yeo, China 3. Vitaly Scherbo, Belarus
Women's Gymnastics	Women's qualifications rounds 1, 2, 3, and 4 take place on Sept. 17		
	All-around	Sept 21	1. Lilia Podkopayeva, Ukraine, 39.255 2. Gina Gogean, Romania, 39.075 3. Simona Amanar and Lavinia Milosovici, Romania, 39.067
	Team Medal Event	Sept. 19	1. United States, 389.225 2. Russia, 388.404 3. Romania, 388.246
	Balance Beam	Sept. 25	1. Shannon Miller, United States, 9.862 2. Lilia Podkopayeva, Ukraine, 9.825 3. Gina Gogean, Romania, 9.787
	Floor	Sept. 25	1. Lilia Podkopayeva, Romania, 9.887 2. Simona Amanar, Romania, 9.850 3. Domonique Dawes, United States, 9.837
	Vault	Sept. 24	1. Simona Amanar, Romania 2. Mo Huilan, China 3. Gina Gogean, Romania
	Uneven Bars	Sept. 24	1. Svetlana Chorkina, Russia 2. Bi Wenjing, China 3. Amy Chow, United states
Men's Archery	**Individual**	Sept. 18, 20	1. Justin Huish, United States 2. Magnus Pettersson, Sweden 3. Oh Kyo-moon, South Korea
	Team	Sept. 22	1. United States

	Event	Date	1996 Results
			2. South Korea
			3. Italy

Note: South Korea set a world record of 2 031 in the 216 arrow ranking round.

	Event	Date	1996 Results
Women's Archery	Individual	Sept. 17, 19	1. Kim Kyung-Wook, South Korea
			2. He Ying, China
			3. Olena Sadovnycha, Ukraine
	Team	Sept. 21	1. South Korea
			2. Germany
			3. Poland

Note: Lina Herasymenko of the Ukraine tied a world record of 673 in the 72 arrow ranking round.

	Event	Date	1996 Results
Men's Badminton	Singles	Sept. 17, 18, 19, 20, 22, 23,	1. Poul-Erik Hoyer-Larson, Denmark
			2. Dong Jiong, China
			3. Rashid Sidak, Malaysia
	Doubles	Sept. 16, 17, 18, 20, 21	1. Indonesia
			2. Malaysia
			3. Indonesia
Women's Badminton	Singles	Sept. 16, 17, 18, 19, 21, 22	1. Bang Soo-hyun, South Korea
			2. Mia Audina, Indonesia
			3. Susi Susanti, Indonesia
	Doubles	Sept. 18, 19, 20, 22, 23	1. China
			2. South Korea
			3. China
	Mixed Doubles	Sept. 16, 17, 18, 20, 21	1. South Korea
			2. South Korea
			3. China
	Baseball	Sept. 17, 18, 19, 20, 22, 23, 24, 26, 27	1. Cuba
			2. Japan
			3. United States
	Men's Basketball	Sept. 17, 19, 21, 23, 25, 26, 28, 29, 30, Oct. 1	1. United States
			2. Yugoslavia
			3. Lithuania
	Women's Basketball	Sept. 16, 18, 20, 22, 24, 26, 27, 29, 30	1. United States
			2. Brazil
			3. Australia
	Men's Beach Volleyball	Sept. 17, 19, 22, 24, 26	1. Karch Kiraly, Kent Steffes, US
			2. Mike Dodd, Mike Whitmrash, US
			3. **Mark Heese, John Child, Toronto**
	Women's Beach Volleyball	Sept. 16, 18, 21, 23, 25	1. Jackie Silva, Sandra Pires, Brazil
			2. Monica Rodrigues, Adriana Samuel, Brazil
			3. Natalie Cook, Kerri Ann, Australia
Boxing	Light flyweight	Sept. 17, 22, 26, 28, 30	1. Daniel Petrov, Bulgaria
			2. Mansueto Velasco, Phillipines
			3. Oleg Kiryukhin, Ukraine, and Rafael Lozano, Spain
	Flyweight	Sept. 19, 24, 27, 29, Oct. 1	1. Maikro Romero, Cuba
			2. Bolat Djumadilov, Kazakhstan
			3. Albert Pakeev, Russia, and Zoltan Lunka, Germany
	Bantamweight	Sept. 16, 21, 26, 28, 30	1. Istvan Kovacs, Hungary
			2. Arnaldo Mesa, Cuba
			3. Raimkul Malakhbekov, Russia, and Vichairachanon Khadpo, Thailand
	Featherweight	Sept. 18, 23, 27, 29, Oct. 1	1. Somiuck Kansing, Thialand
			2. Serafim Todorov, Bulgaria

	Event	Date	1996 Results
			3. Pablo Chacon, Argentina; Floyd Mayweather, US
	Lightweight	Sept. 17, 22, 26, 28, 30	1. Hocine Soltani, Algeria
			2. Tontch Tontchev, Bulgaria
			3. Terrance Cauthen, United States; Leonard Doroftei, Romania
	Light welterweight	Sept. 20, 24, 27, 29, Oct. 1	1. Hector Vinent, Cuba
			2. Oktay Urkal, Germany
			3. Bolat Niyazymbetov, Kazakhstan; Fethi Missaoui, Tunisia
	Welterweight	Sept. 16, 21, 26, 28, 30	1. Oleg Saitov, Russia
			2. Juan Hernandez, Cuba
			3. Marian Simion, Romania; Daniel Santos, Porto Rico
	Light Middleweight	Sept. 19, 23, 27, 29, Oct. 1	1. David Reid, United States
			2. Alfredo Duvergel, Cuba
			3. Karim Tulaganov, Uzbekestan; Ermekhan Ibraimov, Kazakhstan
	Middleweight	Sept. 18, 22, 26, 28, 30	1. Ariel Hernandez, Cuba
			2. Malik Beyleroglu, Turkey
			3. Rhoshil Wells, United States; Mohamad Bahari, Algeria
	Light Heavyweight	Sept. 20, 24, 29, Oct. 1	1. Vassili Jirov, Kazakhstan
			2. Lee Sueng-boo, South Korea
			3. Antonio Tarver United States; Thomas Urlich, Germany
	Heavyweight	Sept. 21, 26, 28, 30	1. Felix Savon, Cuba
			2. David Defiagbon, Halifax
			3. Nate Jones, United States; Luan Krasniqi, Germany
	Super Heavyweight	Sept. 23, 27, 29, Oct. 1	1. Vladimir Kitchko, Ukraine
			2. Paea Wolfgramm, Tonga
			3. Alexei Lezin, Russia; Duncan Dokiwari, Nigeria
Men's Canoe-Kayak	**Canoe Single 500**	Sept. 27, 29, Oct. 1	1. Martin Doktor, Czech Republic
			2. Slavomir Knazovicky, Slovakia
			3. Imre Pulai, Hungary
	Single 1000	Sept. 26, 28, 30	1. Martin Doktor, Germany
			2. Ivan Klementyev, Latvia
			3. Gyorgy Zala, Hungary
	Double 500	Sept. 27, 29, Oct.1	1. Gyorgy Kolonics, Csaba Harvath, Hungary
			2. Moldova
			3. Romania
	Double 1000	Sept. 26, 28, 30	1. Andreas Dittmer, Gunar Kirchbach, Germany
			2. Romania
			3. Hungary
	Kayak Single 500	Sept. 27, 29, Oct. 1	1. Antonio Rossi, Italy
			2. Knut Holmann, Norway
			3. Piotr Mariewicz, Poland
	Single 1000	Sept. 26, 28, 30	1. Knut Holmann, Norway
			2. Beniamino Bonomi, Italy
			3. Clint Robinson, Australia
	Double 500	Sept. 27, 29, Oct. 1	1. Kay Bluhm, Torsten Gutsche, Germany
			2. Italy
			3. Australia
	Double 1000	Sept. 26, 28, 30	1. Antonio Rossi, Daniele Scarpa, Italy
			2. Germany
			3. Bulgaria

	Event	Date	1996 Results
	Kayak Fours 1000	Sept. 26, 28, 30	1. Germany
			2. Hungary
			3. Russia
Women's Canoe-Kayak	**Kayak single 500**	Sept. 27, 29, Oct. 1	1. Rita Koban, Hungary
			2. Caroline Brunet, Lac Beauport, Que
			3. Josefa Idem, Italy
	Double 500	Sept. 27, 29, Oct. 1	1. Sweden
			2. Germany
			3. Australia
	Fours 500	Sept. 26, 28, 30	1. Germany
			2. Switzerland
			3. Sweden
Men's Slalom	**Canoe Singles**	Sept. 17, 18	1. Michal Martikan, Slovakia
			2. Lukas Pollert, Czech Republic
			3. Patrice Estanguet, France
	Doubles	Sept. 19, 20	1. France
			2. Czech Republic
			3. Germany
	Kayak Singles	Sept. 19, 20	1. Oliver Fix, Germany
			2. Andraz Vehovar, Slovenia
			3. Thomas Becker, Germany
Women's Slalom	**Kayak Singles**	Sept. 17, 18	1. Stepanka Hilgertova, Czech Republic
			2. Dana Chiadek, United States
			3. Myriam Fox-Jerusalami
	Men's Olympic sprint	Sept. 17	Not contested in 1996 Olympics
	Men's Keirin	Sept. 21	Not contested in 1996 Olympics
	Men's Madison	Sept. 21	Not contested in 1996 Olympics
Men's Cycling	**Sprint**	Sept. 18, 19, 20	1. Jens Fiedler, Germany
			2. Marty Nothstein, United States
			3. **Curt Harnett, Thunder Bay, Ont.**
	Note:Gary Neiwand of Australia set an Olympic record of 10. 129 in his heat.		
	Points Race	Sept. 20	1. Silvio Martinello, Italy
			2. Brian Walton, North Delta, B. C.
			3. Stuart O'Grady, Australia
	Individual Pursuit	Sept. 16, 17	1. Andrea Collinelli, Italy**
			2. Phillippe Ermanault, France
			3. Bradley McGee, Australia
	Road Race	Schedule TBA (To be announced)	1. Pascal Richard, Switzerland
			2. Rolf Sorenson, Denmark
			3. Maximillian Sciandri, Britain
	Individual Time Trial	Schedule TBA (To be announced)	1. Miguel Indurain, Spain
			2. Abraham Olano, Spain
			3. Chris Boardman, Britain
	Mountain Bike	Sept. 23	1. Bart Jan Brentjens, Netherlands
			2. Thomas Frischknecht, Switzerland
			3. Miguel Martinez, France
	1km Time Trial	Sept. 16	1. Florian Rousseau, France*
			2. Erin Hartwell, United States
			3. Takanobu Jumanji, Japan
	Team Pursuit	Sept. 18, 19	1. France*
			2. Russia

	Event	Date	1996 Results
			3. Australia
Women's Cycling	**Sprint**	Sept. 18, 19, 20	1. Fellicia Ballanger, France
			2. Michelle Ferris, Australia
			3. Ingrid Haringa, Netherlands
	Points Race	Sept. 21	1. Nathalie Lancien, France
			2. Ingrid Haringa, Netherlands
			3. Lucy Tyler Sharman, Australia
	Individual Pursuit	Sept. 17, 18	1. Antonella Bellutti, Italy
			2. Marion Clignet, France
			3. Judith Arndt, Germany
	Road Race	Schedule TBA	1. Jeannie Longo-Ciperlli, France
			2. Imelda Chiappa, Italy
			3. Clara Hughs, Winnipeg
	Individual Time Trial	Schedule TBA	1. Zulfiya Zabirova, Russia
			2. Jeannie Longo-Ciperlli, France
			3. Clara Hughs, Winnipeg
	Mountain Bike	Sept. 23	1. Paolo Pezzo, Italy
			2. Alison Sydor, N. Vancouver
			3. Susan Demattei, United States
Men's Swimming	**50-metre free style**	Sept. 21, 22	1. Aleksandr Popov, Russia, 22.13
			2. Gary Hall Jr. , United States, 22.26
			3. Fernando Scherer, Brazil, 22.29
	100-metre free style	Sept. 19, 20	1. Aleksander Popov, Russia, 48.74
			2. Gary Hall Jr. , United States, 48.81
			3. Gustavo Borges, Brazil, 49.02
	200-metre free style	Sept. 17, 18	1. Danyon Loader, New Zealand, 1:47.63
			2. Gustavo Borges, Brazil, 1:48.08
			3. Daniel Kowalski, Australia, 1:48.25
	400-metre free style	Sept. 16	1. Danyon Loader, New Zealand, 3:47.97
			2. Paul Palmer, Britain, 3:49.00
			3. Daniel Kowalski, Australia, 3:49.39
	1,500-metre free style	Sept. 22, 23	1. Kieren Perkins, Australia, 14:56.40
			2. Daniel Kowalski, Australia, 15:02.43
			3. Graeme Smith, Britain, 15:02.48
	100-metre back stroke	Sept. 17, 18	1. Jeff Rouse, United States, 54.10
			2. Rodolfo Falcon Cabrera, Cuba, 54.98
			3. Neisser Bent, Cuba, 55.02
	200-metre back stroke	Sept. 20, 21	1. Brad Bridgewater, United States, 1:58.54
			2. Tripp Schwenk, United States, 1:58.99
			3. Emanuele Merisi, Italy, 1:59.08
	100-metre breast stroke	Sept. 16, 17	1. Fred Deburghgraeve, Belgium, 1:00.65
			2. Jeremy Linn, United States,1:00.77
			3. Mark Warnecke, Germany, 1:01.33

Note:Deburghgraeve set a world record of 1:00.60 in his heat.

	200-metre breast stroke	Sept. 19, 20	1. Norbert Rozsa, Hungary, 2:12.57
			2. Karoly Guttler, Hungary, 2:13.03
			3. Andrey Korneyev, Russia, 2:13.17
	100-metre butterfly	Sept. 21, 22	1. Denis Pankratov, Russia, 52.27
			2. Scott Miller, Australia, 52.53
			3. Vladislav Kulikov, Russia, 53.13
	200-metre butterfly	Sept. 18, 19	1. Denis Pankratov, Russia, 1:56.51
			2. Tom Malchow, United States, 1:57.54

Event	Date	1996 Results
		3. Scott Goodman, Australia, 1:57.48
200-metre **individual medley**	Sept. 20, 21	1. Attila Czene, Hungary, 1:59.91
		2. Jani Sievinen, Finland, 2:00.13
		3. **Curtis Myden, Calgary, 2:01.13**
400-metre **individual medley**	Sept. 17	1. Tom Dolan, United States, 4:14.90
		2. Eric Namesnik, United States, 4:15.25
		3. **Curtis Myden, Calgary, 4:16.28**
400-metre free **style relay**	Sept. 16	1. United States, 3:15.41
		2. Russia, 3:17.06
		3. Germany, 3:17.20
4x200-metre **free style relay**	Sept. 19	1. United States, 7:14.84
		2. Sweden, 7:17.84
		3. Germany, 7:17.56
400-medley **relay**	Sept. 22, 23	1. United States, 3:34.85
		2. Russia, 3:37.55
		3. Australia, 3:39.56
Women's Swimming 50-metre **free style**	Sept. 22, 23	1. Amy van Dyken, United States, 24.87
		2. Le Jingyi, China, 24.90
		3. Sandra Volker, Germany, 25.14
100-metre **free style**	Sept. 20, 21	1. Jingyi Le, China, 54:50
		2. Sandra Volker, Germany, 54.88
		3. Angel Martino, United States, 54.93
200-metre **free style**	Sept. 18, 19	1. Claudia Poll, Costa Rica, 1:58.16
		2. Franziska van Almsick, Germany, 1:58.57
		3. Dagmar Hase, Germany, 1:59.56
400-metre **free style**	Sept. 17	1. Michelle Smith, Ireland, 4:07.25
		2. Dagmar Hase, Germany, 4:08.30
		3. Kristen Vlieghuis Netherlands, 4:08.70
800-metre **free style**	Sept. 21, 22	1. Brooke Bennett, United States, 8:27.89
		2. Dagmar Hase, Germany, 8:29.91
		3. Kristen Vlieghuis, Netherlands, 8:30.84
100-metre **back stroke**	Sept. 17, 18	1. Beth Botsford, United States, 1:01.19
		2. Whitney Hedgepath, United states, 1:01.47
		3. Marianne Kriel, South Africa, 1:02.12
200-metre **back stroke**	Sept. 21, 22	1. Krisztina Egerszegi, Hungary, 2:07.83
		2. Whitney Hedgepeth, United States, 2:11.98
		3. Cathleen Rund, Germany, 2:12.06
100-metre **breast stroke**	Sept. 17, 18	1. Penelope Heyns, South Africa, 1:07.73
		2. Amanda Beard, United States, 1:08.09
		3. Samantha Riley, Australia, 1:09.18
Note: Heyns set a world record of 1:07.02 in her heat		
200-metre **breast stroke**	Sept. 20, 21	1. Penelope Heyns, South Africa, 2:25.41
		2. Amanda Beard, United States, 2:25.75
		3. Agnes Kovacs, Hungary, 2:26.57
100-metre **butterfly**	Sept. 16, 17	1. Amy van Dyken, United States, 59.13
		2. Liu Limin, China, 59.14
		3. Angel Martino, United States, 59.23
200-metre **butterfly**	Sept. 19, 20	1. Susan O'Neill, Australia, 2:07.76
		2. Petria Thomas, Australia, 2:09.82
		3. Michelle Smith, Ireland, 2:09.91
200-metre **individual medley**	Sept. 18, 19	1. Michelle Smith, Ireland, 2:13.93
		2. **Marianne Limpert, Fredricton, 2:14.35**

	Event	Date	1996 Results
			3. Lin Li, China, 2:14.74
			4. Joanne Malar, Hamilton, 2:15.30
	400-metre Individual medley	Sept. 16	1. Michelle Smith, Ireland, 4:39.18
			2. Allison Wagner, United States, 4:42.03
			3. Krisztina Egerszegi, Hungary, 4:42.53
	400-metre free style relay	Sept. 16	1. United States, 3:39.29
			2. China, 3:40.48
			3. Germany, 3:40.48
	4x200-metre free style relay	Sept. 20	1. United States, 7:59:87
			2. Germany, 8:01.55
			3. Australia, 8:05.47
	400-metre medley relay	Sept. 22, 23	1. United States, 4:02.88
			2. Australia, 4:05.08
			3. China, 4:07.34
Men's Diving	Platform	Sept. 29, 30	1. Dimitry Sautin, Russia
			2. Jan Hempel, Germany
			3. Xiao Hailiang, China
	Springboard	Sept. 25, 26	1. Xiong Ni, China
			2. Yu Zhoucheng, China
			3. Mark Lenzi, United States
Women's Diving	Platform	Sept. 22, 24	1. Fu Minxia, China
			2. Annika Walter, Germany
			3. Mary Ellen Clark, United States
	Springboard	Sept. 27, 28	1. Fu Minxia, China
			2. Irina Lashko, Russia
			3. Annie Pelletier, Montreal
Men's Platform Synchronized		Sept. 23	Not contested in 1996 Olympics
Women's Platform Synchronized		Sept. 28	Not contested in 1996 Olympics
Women's Springboard Synchronized		Sept. 23	Not contested in 1996 Olympics
Equestrian	Individual Dressage	Sept. 29, 30	1. Isabell Werth, Germany
			2. Anky Van Grunsven, Netherlands
			3. Sven Rothenburger, Netherlands
	Individual Jumping	Sept. 25, 28, Oct. 1	1. Urlich Krichoff, Germany
			2. Willi Mellige, Switzerland
			3. Alexandra Ledermann, France
	Individual Three Day Event	Sept. 20, 21, 22	1. Blyth Tait, New Zealand
			2. Sally Clark, New Zealand
			3. Kerry Millikin, United States
	Team Dressage	Sept. 26, 27	1. Germany
			2. Netherlands
			3. United States
	Team Jumping	Sept. 28	1. Germany
			2. United States
			3. Brazil
	Team Three Day Event	Sept. 16, 17, 18, 19	1. Australia
			2. United States
			3. New Zealand
Men's Fencing	Individual Epee	Sept. 16	1. Aleksandr Beketov, Russia
			2. Ivan Tevejo Perez, Cuba
			3. Geza Imre, Hungary
	Individual Foil	Sept. 20	1. Allesandro Puccini, Italy
			2. Lionel Plumnail, France

	Event	Date	1996 Results
			3. Frank Boidin, France
	Individual Sabre	Sept. 21	1. Stanislav Pozdnyakov, Russia
			2. Sergey Sharikov, Russia
			3. Damien Touya, France
	Team Epee	Sept. 18	1. Italy
			2. Russia
			3. France
	Team Foil	Sept. 22	1. Russia
			2. Poland
			3. Cuba
	Team Sabre	Sept. 24	1. Russia
			2. Hungary
			3. Italy
Women's Fencing	Individual Epee	Sept. 17	1. Laura Flessel, France
			2. Valerie Barlois, France
			3. Gyoengyi Szalay, Hungary
	Individual Foil	Sept. 21	1. Laura Badea, Romania
			2. Valentina Vezzali, Italy
			3. Giovanna Trillini, Italy
	Team Epee	Sept. 19	1. France
			2. Italy
			3. Russia
	Team Foil	Sept. 23	1. Italy
			2. Romania
			3. Germany
Men's Field Hockey		Sept. 16-21, 23-30	1. Netherlands
			2. Spain
			3. Australia
Women's Field Hockey		Sept. 16-22, 24, 25, 27, 29	1. Australia
			2. South Korea
			3. Netherlands
Men's Judo	Extra Lightweight	Sept. 16	1. Tadahiro Nomura, Japan
			2. Girolamo Giovanazzo, Italy
			3. Richard Trautman, Germany; Dorjpalam Narmandakh, Mongolia
	Half-Lightweight	Sept. 17	1. Udo Quellmaiz, Germany
			2. Yukimasa Nakamura, Japan
			3. Israel Hernandez, Cuba; Henrique Guimares, Brazil
	Lightweight	Sept. 18	1. Kenzo Nakomura, Japan
			2. Kwak Dae-sung, South Korea
			3. Jimmy Pedro, United States; Cristophe Gagliano, France
	Half-Middleweight	Sept. 19	1. Djamel Bouras, France
			2. Toshihiko Koga, Japan
			3. Soso Liparteliani, Georgia; Cho In-Chui, South Korea
	Middleweight	Sept. 20	1. Jeon Ki-young, South Korea
			2. Armen Bagdasarov, Uzbekestan
			3. Marko Spittka, Germany; Mark Huizenga, Netherlands
	Half-Heavyweight	Sept. 21	1. Pawel Nastula, Poland
			2. Kim Min-soo, South Korea
			3. Stephane Traineau, France; Miguel Fernandes, Brazil
	Heavyweight	Sept. 22	1. David Douillet, France
			2. Ernesto Perez, Spain

	Event	Date	1996 Results
			3. Harry van Barneveld, Belgium; Frank Moeller, Germany
Women's Judo	Extra Lightweight	Sept. 16	1. Kye Sun, North Korea
			2. Ryoko Tamura, Japan
			3. Yolanda Soler, Spain; Amarilis Savon, Cuba
	Half-Lightweight	Sept. 17	1. Marie-Claire Restoux, France
			2. Hyun Sook-hee, South Korea
			3. Noriko Sagawara, Japan; Legan Verdecia, Cuba
	Lightweight	Sept. 18	1. Driulis Gonzalez, Cuba
			2. Jun Sun-yong, South Korea
			3. Isabel Fernandez, Spain; Marisbel Lomba, Belgium
	Half-Middleweight	Sept. 19	1. Yuko Emoto, Japan
			2. Gella Vn de Caveye, Belgium
			3. Jung Sung-sook, South Korea; Jenny Gal, Netherlands
	Middleweight	Sept. 20	1. Cho Min-sun, South Korea
			2. Aneta Szczepanska, Poland
			3. Wang Xianbo, China; Claudia Zweirs, Netherlands
	Half-Heavyweight	Sept. 21	1. Ulla Werbrouk, Belgium
			2. Yako Tanabe, Japan
			3. Ylenia Scapin, Italy; Diadenis Luna, Cuba
	Heavyweight	Sept. 22	1. Sun Fuming, China
			2. Estela Rodriguez, Cuba
			3. Johanna Hogn, Germany; Christine Cicot, France
Modern Pentathalon	Men's Pentathlon events take place on Sept. 30th. Women's Pentathlon events take place on Oct. 1st		1. Aleksandr Parygin, Kazakhstan
			2. Eduard Zenovka, Russia
			3. Janos Martinek, Hungary
Rhythmic Gymnastics	Individual		1. Yekaterina Serebryanskaya, Ukraine
			2. Lanina Batyrchina, Russia
			3. Yelena Vitrichenko, Ukraine
	Team		1. Spain
			2. Bulgaria
			3. Russia
Men's Shooting	Air Pistol	Sept. 16	1. Rebert Di Donna, Italy
			2. Wang Yifu, China
			3. Tano Kriakov, Bulgaria
	Free Pistol	Sept. 19	1. Boris Kokorev, Russia*
			2. Igor Basinski, Belarus
			3. Reberto Di Donna, Italy
	Rapid Fire Pistol	Sept. 20, 21	1. Ralf Schuman, Germany
			2. Emil Milev, Bulgaria
			3. Vladimer Vokhmyanin, Kazakhstan
	Running Target	Sept. 21, 22	1. Yang Ling, China*
			2. Xiao Jun, China
			3. Miroslav Janas, Czech Republic
	Air Rifle	Sept. 18	1. Artem Khadzhibekov, Russia*
			2. Wolfram Waibel Jr. , Austria
			3. Jean-Pierre Amat, France
	Small-Bore Rifle Prone	Sept. 21	1. Christain Klees, Germany**
			2. Sergey Beliaev, Kazakhstan
			3. Jozef Gonci, Slovakia
	Small-Bore Rifle 3-Position	TBA (To be announced)	1. Jean-Pierre Amat, France
			2. Sergey Beliaev, Kazakhstan*
			3. Wolfram Waibel Jr. , Austria

	Event	Date	1996 Results
	Trap	Sept. 16, 17	1. Michael Diamond, Australia
			2. Josh Lakotos, United States
			3. Lance Bade, United States
	Double Trap	Sept. 20	1. Russell Mark, Australia
			2. Albeno Pera, Italy
			3. Zhang Bing, China
	Skeet	Sept. 22, 23	1. Ennio Falco, Italy
			2. Marislaw Rzepkowski, Poland
			3. Andrea Benelli, Italy
	Free Rifle	Sept. 23	Not contested in 1996 Olympics
Women's Shooting	**Air Pistol**	Sept. 17	1. Olga Klochneva, Russia*
			2. Marina logvinenko, Russia
			3. Mariya grozdeva, Bulgaria
	Air Rifle	Sept. 16	1. Renata Mauer, Poland
			2. Petra Horneber, Germany
			3. Aleksandr Ivaosev, Yugoslavia
	Sport Pistol	Sept. 22	1. Li Duihong, China*
			2. Diana Yorgova, Bulgaria
			3. Marina Logvinenko, Russia
	Small-Bore Rifle	TBA	1. Aleksandra Ivosev, Yugoslavia*
	3-Position	(To be announced)	2. Irina Geresimenok, Russia
			3. Renata Mauer, Poland
	Double Trap	Sept. 19	1. Kim Rhode, United States
			2. Susanne Kiermayer, Germany
			3. Deserie Huddleston, Australia
	Sport rifle	Sept. 20	Not contested in 1996 Olympics
	Trap	Sept. 18	Not contested in 1996 Olympics
	Skeet	Sept. 21	Not contested in 1996 Olympics
Men's Soccer		Sept. 13, 14, 16, 17, 19, 20, 23, 26, 29, 30	1. Nigeria
			2. Argentina
			3. Brazil
Women's Soccer		Sept. 13, 14, 16, 17, 19, 20, 24, 28	1. United States
			2. China
			3. Norway
Women's Softball		Sept. 17-26	1. United States
			2. China
			3. Australia
Synchronized Swimming			1. United States
			2. Canada (Karen Clark, Calgary; Christine Larson, Coquitium, B. C.; Janice Bremner, Vancouver; Sylvie Frechette, Laval, Que. ; Valerie Hould-Marchand, Quebec City; Karen Fonteyne, Calgary; Kasia Kulesza, Laval; Carl Read, Calgary; Erin Woodly, Toronto; Lisa Alexander, Mississauga, Ont.)
			3. Japan
	Team	Sept. 28, 29	
	Duet	Sept. 24, 25, 26	
Men's Table Tennis	**Singles**	Sept. 17, 18, 19, 21, 22, 23, 24, 25	1. Liu Guoliang, China
			2. Wang Too, China
			3. Joerg Rosskopf, Germany
	Doubles	Sept. 16, 18, 20, 21, 22, 23	1. China
			2. China

	Event	Date	1996 Results
			3. South Korea
Women's Table Tennis	Singles	Sept. 17, 18, 19, 20, 21, 22, 23, 24	1. Deng Yaping, China
			2. Cheng Jin, Taiwan
			3. Qiau Hong, China
	Doubles	Sept. 16, 18, 20, 21, 22	1. China
			2. China
			3. South Korea
Men's Team Handball		Sept. 16, 18, 20, 22, 24, 26, 29, 30	1. Croatia
			2. Sweden
			3. Spain
Women's Team Handball		Sept. 17, 19, 21, 23, 25, 28, 29, 30, 31	1. Denmark
			2. South Korea
			3. Hungary
Men's Tennis	Singles	Sept. 19-28	1. Andre Agassi, United States
			2. Sergi Brugera, Spain
			3. Leander Paes, India
	Doubles	Sept. 21-28	1. Woodbridge and Woodforde, Australia
			2. Broad and Henman, Britain
			3. Goellner and Prinosil, Germany
Women's Tennis	Singles	Sept. 19-27	1. Lindsay Davenport, United States
			2. Arantxa Sanches Vicario, Spain
			3. Jana Novotna, Czech Republic
	Doubles	Sept. 21-28	1. Gigi Fernandez and Mary Joe Fernandez, United States
			2. Novotna and Sokova, Czech Republic
			3. Vicario and Martinez, Spain
Men's Volleyball		Sept. 17, 19, 21, 23, 25, 27, 28, 29, Oct. 1	1. Netherlands
			2. Italy
			3. Yugoslavia
Women's Volleyball		Sept. 16, 18, 20, 22, 24, 26, 27, 28, 30	1. Cuba
			2. China
			3. Brazil
Water Polo			1. Spain
			2. Croatia
			3. Italy
	Men's Water Polo	Sept. 23, 24, 25, 26, 27, 29, 30, Oct. 1	
	Women's Water Polo	Sept. 16, 17, 18, 19, 20, 22, 23	
Weightlifting	54-kg		1. Halil Mulu, Turkey**
			2. Zhang Xiangsen, China
			3. Sevdalin Minchev, Bulgaria
	59-kg		1. Tang Ningsheng, China**
			2. Leonidas Sabanis, Greece
			3. Nikolay Pechalov, Bulgaria
	64-kg		1. Naim Suleymanoglu, Turkey**
			2. Valerios Leonidis, Greece
			3. Xiao Jiangang, China

**Note: World records in both clean and jerk and total.

	70-kg		1. Zhan Xugang, China**
			2. Kim Myong-nam, North Korea
			3. Attila Feri, Hungary

**Note: Xugang broke world records in the snatch, the clean and jerk, and the total.

	Event	Date	1996 Results
	76-kg		1. Pablo Lara, Cuba
			2. Yoto Yotov, Bulgaria
			3. Jon Chol, North Korea
	83-kg		1. Pyros Dimus, Greece**
			2. Marc Huster, Germany
			3. Anderzei Cofalik, Poland

**Note: Dimus Broke world records in the snatch and the total.
**Note: Huster broke world record in the clean and jerk.

	Event	Date	1996 Results
	91-kg		1. Aleksey Petrov, Russia**
			2. Leonadis Kokas, Greece
			3. Oliver Caruso, Germany
	99-kg		1. Akakide Kakhiashivilis, Greece**
			2. Anatoly Khrapaty, Kazakhstan
			3. Denis Gotfrid, Ukraine

** Note: Kakhiashivilis broke world records in both clean and jerk and total.

	Event	Date	1996 Results
	108-kg		1. Timur Talmazov, Ukraine**
			2. Sergey Syrtsov, Russia
			3. Nicu Vlad, Romania
	108-kg plus		1. Andrey Chemerkin, Russia**
			2. Ronny Weller, Germany
			3. Stefan Botev, Australia
Men's Weightlifting	56-kg	Sept. 16	
(Weight classes	62-kg	Sept. 17	
changed)	69-kg	Sept. 20	
	77-kg	Sept. 22	
	85-kg	Sept. 23	
	94-kg	Sept. 24	
	105-kg	Sept. 25	
	105-kg plus	Sept. 26	
Women's Weightlifting			(Not contested in 1996 Olympics)
	48-kg	Sept. 17	
	53-kg	Sept. 18	
	58-kg	Sept. 18	
	63-kg	Sept. 19	
	69-kg	Sept. 19	
	75-kg	Sept. 20	
	75-kg plus	Sept. 22	
Freestyle Wrestling	48-kg		1. Kim Il, North Korea
			2. Armen Mkrttchian, Armenia
			3. Alexis Vila, Cuba
	52-kg		1. Valentin Jordanov, Bulgaria
			2. Namik Abdullaev, Azerbaijan
			3. Maulen Mamirov, Kazakhstan
	57-kg		1. Kendall Cross, United States
			2. Gia Sissauri, Montreal
			3. Ri Yong Sam, North Korea
	62-kg		1. Tom Brands, United States
			2. Jang Jae-sung, South Korea
			3. Elbrus Tedeev, Ukraine
	68-kg		1. Vadim Boglev, Russia
			2. Townsend Saunders, United States
			3. Zoza Zazirov, Ukraine
	74-kg		1. Bouvaisa Satiev, Russia
			2. Park Jang-soon, South Korea

	Event	Date	1996 Results
			3. Takuya Ota, Japan
	82-kg		1. Khadzhimurad Magomedov, Russia
			2. Yang Hyunma, South Korea
			3. Amir Reza Khadem, Iran
	90-kg		1. Rasul Khadem, Iran
			2. Makharbek Khadartsev, Russia
			3. Eldari Kurtanidze, Georgia
	100-kg		1. Kurt Angle, United States
			2. Abbas Jadidi, Iran
			3. Arawat Sabejew, Germany
	130-kg		1. Mahmut Demir, Turkey
			2. Alexei Medvedev, Belarus
			3. Bruce Baumgartner, United States
Freestyle Wrestling	54-kg	Sept. 28, 29, 30	
(Weight classes	58-kg	Sept. 29, 30, Oct. 1	
changed)	63-kg	Sept. 28, 29, 30	
	69-kg	Sept. 29, 30, Oct.1	
	76-kg	Sept. 28, 29, Oct. 1	
	85-kg	Sept. 30, Oct. 1	
	97-kg	Sept. 28, 29, 30	
	130-kg	Sept. 29, 30, Oct. 1	
Greco-Roman Wrestling	48-kg		1. Sim Kwon-ho, South Korea
			2. Alexander Povtov, Belarus
			3. Zafar Gulyov, Russia
	52-kg		1. Arman Nazaryan, Armenia
			2. Brandon Paulson, United States
			3. Andriy Kalashnikov, Ukraine
	57-kg		1. Yuri Melnichenko, Kazakhstan
			2. Dennis Hall, United States
			3. Sheng Zetlan, China
	62-kg		1. Wlodzimierz Zawadzki, Poland
			2. Juan Luis Maren, Cuba
			3. Mahmet Pirim, Turkey
	68-kg		1. Ryszard Wolny, Poland
			2. Ghani Yolouz, France
			3. Alexander Tretyakov, Russia
	74-kg		1. Feliberto Ascuy, Cuba
			2. Marko Asell, Finland
			3. Josef Tracz, Poland
	82-kg		1. Hamza Yerlikya, Turkey
			2. Thomas Zander, Germany
			3. Valery Tsilent, Belarus
	90-kg		1. Vyacheslav Oleynyk, Ukraine
			2. Jacek Fafinski, Poland
			3. Maik Bullmann, Germany
	100-kg		1. Anderzei Wronski, Poland
			2. Sergei Lishtvan, Belarus
			3. Mikael Ljunberg, Sweden
	130-kg		1. Alexander Karelin, Russia
			2. Matt Ghaffari, United States
			3. Sergei Moureiko, Moldova
Greco-Roman Wrestling	54-kg	Sept. 24, 25, 26	
	58-kg	Sept. 25, 26, 27	

	Event	Date	1996 Results
(Weight classes changed)	**63-kg**	Sept. 24, 25, 26	
	69-kg	Sept. 25, 26, 27	
	76-kg	Sept. 24, 25, 26	
	85-kg	Sept. 25, 26, 27	
	97-kg	Sept. 24, 25, 26	
	130-kg	Sept. 25, 26, 27	
Open Yachting	**Laser**	Sept. 20, 21, 23, 26, 28, 29	1. Robert Scheidt, Brazil 2. Ben Ainslie, Germany 3. Peer Moberg, Denmark
	Sailing	TBA (To be announced)	1. Germany 2. Russia 3. United States
	Star	Sept. 23, 25, 26, 27, 28	1. Brazil 2. Sweden 3. Australia
	Tornado	Sept. 18, 19, 21, 22, 24	1. Spain 2. Australia 3. Brazil
	Three Person Keelboat (Soling)	Sept. 17, 18, 19, 25, 27, 29	Not contested in 1996
	High Performance Dinghy (49er)	Sept. 18, 19, 20, 22, 23, 25	Not contested in 1996
Men's Yachting	**Finn**	Sept. 23, 25, 26, 27, 28, 30	1. Mateusz Kusnierewicz, Poland 2. Sebastian Godefroid, Belgium 3. Roy Heiner, Netherlands
	Mistral	Sept. 17, 18, 19, 20, 21, 22, 24, 25, 27	1. Nikolaus Kaklamanakis, Greece 2. Carlos Espinola, Argentina 3. Gal Fridman, Israel
	470	TBA (To be announced)	1. Ukraine 2. Britain 3. Portugal
Women's Yachting	**Europe**	Sept. 20, 21, 23, 26, 28, 29	1. Kristine Roug, Denmark 2. Margriet Matthijsse, Netherlands 3. Courtenay Becker-Dey, United States
	Mistral	Sept. 17, 18, 19, 21, 22, 24	1. Lee Lai-shan, Hong Kong 2. Barbara Kendell, New Zealand 3. Alessandra Sensini, Italy
	470	Sept. 20, 21, 22, 24, 25, 27	1. Spain 2. Japan 3. Ukraine
Trampoline Gymnastics	**Women's**	Sept. 22	Not contested in 1996
	Men's	Sept. 23	Not contested in 1996
Rythmic Gymnastics	**Group**	Sept. 28, 30	Not contested in 1996
	Individual	Sept. 28, 29, 30	Not contested in 1996
Men's Taekwondo	**less than 58-kg**	Sept. 27	Not contested in 1996
	58-68 kg	Sept. 28	Not contested in 1996
	68-80 kg	Sept. 29	Not contested in 1996
	Over 80 kg	Sept. 30	Not contested in 1996
Women's Taekwondo	**Less than 49 kg**	Sept. 27	Not contested in 1996
	49-57 kg	Sept. 28	Not contested in 1996
	57-67 kg	Sept. 29	Not contested in 1996
	Over 67 kg	Sept. 30	Not contested in 1996
Men's Triathlon		Sept. 16	Not contested in 1996
Women's Trialthlon		Sept. 17	Not contested in 1996

(*Olympic record; **Olympic and world record)

Winter Olympics

Year	Location	Date of Competition	Competitors Men	Competitors Women	Nations Represented	Unofficial Winners
1924	Chamonix, France	Jan. 25–Feb. 4	281	13	16	Norway
1928	St. Moritz, Switzerland	Feb. 11–19	468	27	25	Norway
1932	Lake Placid, United States	Feb. 4–15	274	32	17	United States
1936	Garmisch-Partenkirchen, Germany	Feb. 6–16	675	80	28	Norway
1940	Cancelled because of World War II					
1944	Cancelled because of World War II					
1948	St. Moritz, Switzerland	Jan. 30–Feb. 8	636	77	28	Sweden
1952	Oslo, Norway	Feb. 14–25	623	109	30	Norway
1956	Cortina d'Ampezzo, Italy	Jan. 26–Feb. 5	686	132	32	U.S.S.R.
1960	Squaw Valley, United States	Feb. 18–28	521	144	30	U.S.S.R.
1964	Innsbruck, Austria	Jan. 29–Feb. 9	986	200	36	U.S.S.R.
1968	Grenoble, France	Feb. 6–18	1 081	212	37	Norway
1972	Sapporo, Japan	Feb. 3–13	1 015	217	35	U.S.S.R.
1976	Innsbruck, Austria	Feb. 4–15	900	228	37	U.S.S.R.
1980	Lake Placid, United States	Feb. 14–23	833	234	37	East Germany
1984	Sarajevo, Yugoslavia	Feb. 7–19	1 180	409	49	U.S.S.R.
1988	Calgary, Canada	Feb. 13–28	1 128	317	57	U.S.S.R.
1992	Albertville, France	Feb. 8–23	1 545	602	64	Germany
1994	Lillehammer, Norway	Feb. 12–27	1216	521	67	Norway
1998	Nagano, Japan	Feb. 7-22			70	Germany
2002	Salt Lake City	Feb. 8-24				

Source: *Canadian Press*

1998 Winter Olympics Medal Standings by Country

Country	Gold	Silver	Bronze	Total
Germany	12	9	8	29
Norway	10	10	5	25
Russia	9	6	3	18
Austria	3	5	9	17
Canada	**6**	**5**	**4**	**15**
United States	6	3	4	13
Finland	2	4	6	12
Netherlands	5	4	2	11
Japan	5	1	4	10
Italy	2	6	2	10
France	2	1	5	8
China	0	6	2	8

Country	Gold	Silver	Bronze	Total
Switzerland	2	2	3	7
Korea	3	1	2	6
Czech Republic	1	1	1	3
Sweden	0	2	1	3
Belarus	0	0	2	2
Kazakhstan	0	0	2	2
Bulgaria	1	0	0	1
Denmark	0	1	0	1
Ukraine	0	1	0	1
Britain	0	0	1	1
Australia	0	0	1	1
Belgium	0	0	1	1

Source: *(CP)*

Canadian medal winners at the 1998 Winter Olympics

(Nagano, Japan)

■ Gold (6)

Bobsled (two-man)
Pierre Lueders, Edmonton, and Dave MacEachern, Charlottetown

Curling (women)
Skip – Sandra Schmirler; Third – Jan Betker; Second – Joan McCusker; Lead – Marcia Gudereit and spare Atina Ford, all Regina

Snowboarding (giant slalom)
Ross Rebagliati, Whistler, B.C.

Speed Skating, long track (500 metres)
Catriona Le May Doan, Saskatoon

Speed Skating, short track (500 metres)
Annie Perreault, Rock Forest, Que.

Speed Skating, short track (5,000-metre relay)
Eric Bedard, Ste-Thecle, Que.; Derrick Campbell, Cambridge, Ont.; Francois Drolet, Quebec City; Marc Gagnon, Chicoutimi, Que.

■ Silver (5)

Curling (Men)
Skip – Mike Harris; Third – Richard Hart; Second – Collin Mitchell; Lead – George Karrys and spare Paul Savage, all Toronto.

Figure Skating (men's singles)
Elvis Stojko, Richmond Hill, Ont.

Hockey (women)
Women's team.

Speed Skating, long track (500 metres)
Jeremy Wotherspoon, Red Deer, Alta.

Speed Skating, long track (500 metres)
Susan Auch, Winnipeg.

■ Bronze (4)

Speed Skating, long track (500 metres)
Kevin Overland, Kitchener, Ont.

Speed Skating, long track (1,000 metres)
Catriona Le May Doan, Saskatoon

Speed Skating, short track (1,000 metres)
Eric Bedard, Ste-Thecle, Que.

Speed Skating, short track (3,000-metre relay)
Chritine Boudrias, Montreal; Isabelle Charest, Montreal; Annie Perreault, Rock Forrest, Que., and Tania Vicent, Laval, Que.

Source: *Canadian Olympic Association*

Scandal hits the IOC

Scandal hit the International Olympic Committee in late 1998-early-1999, when it was discovered that organizers for the 2002 Winter Olympic Games in Salt Lake City had bribed Olympic officials for their votes.

An IOC report into the bidding process for the 2002 Games found that IOC members had accepted more than $1 million US worth of inducements from Salt Lake City organizers. Everything from cash to scholarships, free trips and Super Bowl tickets were given to voters. IOC members are not allowed to accept gifts worth more than $150.

The corruption scandal plunged the IOC into the worst crisis of its 105-year history.

As part of its effort to clean up its tattered image, the IOC expelled six members, 10 received warnings and four resigned.

As well, the bidding process rules were changed in the hopes of preventing another bribery scandal. IOC members were banned from visiting bid cities and a "selection college" of eight members would narrow the field of contenders to two, before the entire membership would vote.

In the first vote using the new process, Sion, Switzerland and Turin, Italy were chosen as the finalists for the 2006 Winter Games from a group that also included Helsinki, Finland; Klagenfurt, Austria; Poprad-Tatry, Slovakia; and Zakopane, Poland.

In the final, Turin, a northern industrial town of 2.2 million, beat out Sion to earn the right to host the 2006 Winter Olympic Games.

OTHER SPORTS

Canadian Curling Champions

Men

Year	Skip, Province	Year	Skip, Province	Year	Skip, Province
1927	Murray Macneill, N.S.	1952	Billy Walsh, Man.	1974	Hector Gervais, Alta.
1928	Gordon Hudson, Man.	1953	Ab Gowanlock, Man.	1975	Bill Tetley, N. Ont.
1929	Gordon Hudson, Man.	1954	Matt Baldwin, Alta.	1976	Jack MacDuff, Nfld.
1930	Howard Wood, Man.	1955	Garnet Campbell, Sask.	1977	Jim Ursel, Que.
1931	Bob Gourley, Man.	1956	Billy Walsh, Man.	1978	Ed Lukowich, Alta.
1932	Jim Congalton, Man.	1957	Matt Baldwin, Alta.	1979	Barry Fry, Man.
1933	Cliff Manahan, Alta.	1958	Matt Baldwin, Alta.	1980	Rick Folk, Sask.
1934	Leo Johnson, Man.	1959	Ernie Richardson, Sask.	1981	Kerry Burtnyk, Man.
1935	Gordon Campbell, Ont.	1960	Ernie Richardson, Sask.	1982	Al Hackner, N. Ont.
1936	Ken Watson, Man.	1961	Hec Gervais, Alta.	1983	Ed Werenich, Ont.
1937	Cliff Manahan, Alta.	1962	Ernie Richardson, Sask.	1984	Mike Riley, Man.
1938	Ab Gowanlock, Man.	1963	Ernie Richardson, Sask.	1985	Al Hackner, N. Ont.
1939	Bert Hall, Ont.	1964	Lyall Dagg, B.C.	1986	Ed Lukowich, Alta.
1940	Howard Wood, Man.	1965	Terry Braunstein, Man.	1987	Russ Howard, Ont.
1941	Howard Palmer, Alta.	1966	Ron Northcott, Alta.	1988	Pat Ryan, Alta.
1942	Ken Watson, Man.	1967	Alf Phillips, Jr., Ont.	1989	Pat Ryan, Alta.
1946	Billy Rose, Alta.	1968	Ron Northcott, Alta.	1990	Ed Werenich, Ont.
1947	Jimmy Welsh, Man.	1969	Ron Northcott, Alta.	1991	Kevin Martin, Alta.
1948	Frenchy D'Amour, B.C.	1970	Don Duguid, Man.	1992	Vic Peters, Man.
1949	Ken Watson, Man.	1971	Don Duguid, Man.	1993	Russ Howard, Ont.
1950	Tom Ramsay, N. Ont.	1972	Orest Meleschuk, Man.	1994	Rick Folk, BC
1951	Don Oyler, N.S.	1973	Harvey Mazinke, Sask.	1995	Kerry Burtnyk, Man
				1996	Jeff Stoughton, Man
				1997	Kevin Martin, Alta.
				1998	Wayne Middaugh, Ont.
				1999	Jeff Stoughton, Man.

Women

Year	Skip, Province	Year	Skip, Province	Year	Skip, Province
1961	Joyce McKee, Sask.	1973	Vera Pezer, Sask.	1984	Connie Laliberte, Man.
1962	Ina Hansen, B.C.	1974	Emily Farnham, Sask.	1985	Linda Moore, B.C.
1963	Mabel DeWare, N.B.	1975	Lee Tobin, Que.	1986	Marilyn Darte, Ont.
1964	Ina Hansen, B.C.	1976	Lindsay Davie, B.C.	1987	Pat Sanders, B.C.
1965	Peggy Casselman, Man.	1977	Myrna McQuarrie, Alta.	1988	Heather Houston, Ont.
1966	Gail Lee, Alta.	1978	Cathy Pidzarko, Man.	1989	Heather Houston, Ont.
1967	Betty Duguid, Man.	1979	Lindsay Sparkes, B.C.	1990	Alison Goring, Ont.
1968	Hazel Jamieson, Alta.	1980	Marj Mitchell, Sask.	1991	Julie Sutton, B.C.
1969	Joyce McKee, Sask.	1981	Susan Seitz, Alta.	1992	Connie Laliberte, Man.
1970	Dorenda Schoenhais, Sask.	1982	Colleen Jones, N.S.	1993	Sandra Peterson, Sask.
1971	Vera Pezer, Sask.	1983	Penny LaRocque, N.S.	1994	Sandra Peterson, Sask
1972	Vera Pezer, Sask.			1995	Connie Laliberte, Man.
				1996	Marilyn Bodogh, Ont.
				1997	Sandra Schmirler, Sask.
				1998	Cathy Borst, Alta.
				1999	Colleen Jones, N.S.

Source: Canadian Press

The Women's World Cup

The third Women's World Cup of Soccer was an undeniable success. Smashing attendance records for women's sporting events, the Women's World Cup drew the attention of not only soccer-mad countries, but of also host nation United States.

The American team, a co-favourite before the tournament with defending champion Norway and China, won the heart of American fans with their skill, personality and looks. Debate raged over whether Americans really cared about their team or whether they were attractive marketing comodities.

It is likely fans were drawn by both, as the tournament's lasting image will be that of American Brandi Chastain on her knees, waving her jersey over her head, sporting only a sports bra after her penalty kick clinched the title. That photo keys a Nike marketing campaign for sports bras.

Nonetheless the championship game, score-less between the United States and China after 120 minutes and won by the Americans 5-4 on penalty kicks, was a classic. The crowd of 90,185 was the largest to ever watch a women's sporting event.

At the 1995 World Cup, only 17,158 watched Norway defeat Germany 2-0 in Stockholm. In 1991, the U.S. won the inaugural championship by defeating Norway 2-1 before 65,000 in Guangzhou, China.

Canada's woes on the soccer field continued in the '99 tournament. Canada failed to make it out of the first round, finishing with an 0-2-1 record. That included dismal losses to Russia and Norway and a disappointing tie with Japan. The tournament ended with star striker Charmaine Hooper sniping publicly at head coach Neil Turnbull, who was later fired.

Canada finished 0-2-1 in the '95 tournament and failed to qualify in '91.

1999 Women's World Cup Standings

■ First Round

Group A	W	L	D	P
x-United States	3	0	0	9
x-Nigeria	2	1	0	6
North Korea	1	2	0	3
Denmark	0	3	0	0

Group B	W	L	D	P
x-Brazil	2	0	1	7
x-Germany	1	0	2	5
Italy	1	1	1	4
Mexico	0	3	0	0

Group C	W	L	D	P
x-Norway	3	0	0	9
x-Russia	2	1	0	6
Japan	0	2	1	1
Canada	**0**	**2**	**1**	**1**

Group D	W	L	D	P
x-China	3	0	0	9
x-Sweden	2	1	0	6
Australia	0	2	1	1
Ghana	0	2	1	1

x-advances to quarter-final

Quarter-finals
United States 3, Germany 2
Brazil 4, Nigeria 3
China 2, Russia 0
Norway 3, Sweden 1

Semifinals
United States 2, Brazil 0
China 5, Norway 0

Third Place
Brazil 0, Norway 0
(Brazil wins 5-4 on penalty kicks)

Final
United States 0, China 0
(United States wins 5-4 on penalty kicks)

Canadian Interuniversity Athletic Union Champions

Men

	Basketball	Football	Ice Hockey	Soccer	Swimming	Volleyball	Track & Field
1975/76	Manitoba	Ottawa	Toronto	Alberta	Toronto	B.C.	—
1976/77	Acadia	Western	Toronto	Concordia	Waterloo	Winnipeg	—
1977/78	St. Mary's	Western	Alberta	York	Waterloo	Manitoba	—
1978/79	St. Mary's	Queen's	Alberta	Manitoba	Waterloo	Saskatchewan	—
1979/80	Victoria	Acadia	Alberta	Alberta	Toronto	Manitoba	—
1980/81	Victoria	Alberta	Moncton	New Brunswick	Toronto	Alberta	Toronto
1981/82	Victoria	Acadia	Moncton	McGill	Calgary	Calgary	Toronto
1982/83	Victoria	B.C.	Saskatchewan	McGill	Calgary	B.C.	York
1983/84	Victoria	Calgary	Toronto	Laurentian	Calgary	Manitoba	York
1984/85	Victoria	Guelph	York	B.C.	Calgary	Manitoba	Toronto
1985/86	Victoria	Calgary	Alberta	B.C.	Toronto	Winnipeg	Toronto
1986/87	Brandon	B.C.	Trois-Rivières	B.C.	Calgary	Winnip eg	Saskatchewan
1987/88	Brandon	McGill	York	Victoria	Calgary	Manitoba	Manitoba
1988/89	Brandon	Calgary	York	Toronto	Calgary	Calgary	Manitoba
1989/90	Concordia	Western	Moncton	B.C.	Calgary	Laval	Manitoba/Toronto
1990/91	Western	Saskatchewan	Trois-Rivières	B.C.	Calgary	Manitoba	Windsor
1991/92	Brock	Wilfrid Laurier	Alberta	B.C.	Toronto	Laval	Manitoba
1992/93	St. Francis Xavier	Queen's	Acadia	B.C.	Toronto	Calgary	Windsor
1993/94	Alberta	Toronto	Lethbridge	Sherbrooke	Toronto	Laval	Manitoba
1994/95	Alberta	Western	Moncton	B.C.	Calgary	Manitoba	Manitoba
1995/96	Brandon	Calgary	Acadia	Dalhousie	Calgary	Manitoba	Manitoba
1996/97	Victoria	Saskatchewan	Guelph	Victoria	Calgary	Alberta	Sherbrooke
1997/98	Bishop's	B.C.	New Brunswick	McGill	B.C.	Winnipeg	Sherbrooke
1998/99	St Mary's	Saskatchewan	Alberta	Western	B.C.	Saskatchewan	Sherbrooke

Women

	Basketball	Field Hockey	Swimming	Track & Field	Volleyball	Soccer	Ice Hockey
1975/76	Laurentian	Toronto	—	—	Western		
1976/77	Laurentian	Dalhousie	Acadia	—	B.C.		
1977/78	Laurentian	Toronto	Acadia	—	B.C.		
1978/79	Laurentian	B.C.	Toronto	—	Saskatchewan		
1979/80	Victoria	Toronto	Toronto	—	Saskatchewan		
1980/81	Victoria	B.C.	Toronto	Western	Saskatchewan		
1981/82	Victoria	Toronto	Toronto	Western	Dalhousie		
1982/83	Bishop's	B.C.	Toronto	Western	Winnipeg		
1983/84	Bishop's	B.C.	Toronto	York	Winnipeg		
1984/85	Victoria	Victoria	B.C.	Alta. & Sask.	Winnipeg		
1985/86	Toronto	Toronto	B.C.	Saskatchewan	Winnipeg		
1986/87	Victoria	Toronto	Toronto	Calgary	Winnipeg		
1987/88	Manitoba	Victoria	Toronto	York	Winnipeg	B.C.	
1988/89	Calgary	Toronto	Toronto	Toronto	Calgary	Queen's	
1989/90	Laurentian	Victoria	Toronto	York	Manitoba	Alberta	
1990/91	Laurentian	B.C.	Toronto	Calgary	Manitoba	Acadia	
1991/92	Victoria	Victoria	Toronto	Windsor	Manitoba	McMaster	
1992/93	Winnipeg	Victoria	Toronto	Windsor	Winnipeg	Laurier	
1993/94	Winnipeg	Toronto	B.C.	Windsor	Calgary	B.C.	
1994/95	Winnipeg	Victoria	B.C.	Windsor	Alberta	Dalhousie	
1995/96	Manitoba	Victoria	B.C.	Windsor	Alberta	Laurier	
1996/97	Manitoba	Toronto	Toronto	Toronto	Alberta	Ottawa	
1997/98	Victoria	Victoria	B.C.	Toronto	Alberta	Alberta	
1998/99	Alberta	B.C.	B.C.	Windsor	Alberta	Calgary	Concordia

Source: *Canadian Interuniversity Athletic Union.*

Association of Tennis Professionals–1999 Grand Slam Events

	Date	Winner		Date	Winner
Australian Open	Jan. 18-31	Yevgeny Kafelnikov	Wimbledon	June 21-July 4	Pete Sampras
French Open	May 24-June 6	Andre Agassi	U.S. Open	Aug. 30-Sept. 12	Andre Agassi

Men's ATP Rankings

(as of September 13, 1999, including top Canadians)

1. Andre Agassi
2. Yevgeny Kafelnikov
3. Pete Sampras
4. Todd Martin
5. Gustavo Kuerten
6. Tim Henman
7. Greg Rusedski
8. Marcelo Rios

9. Richard Krajicek
10. Tommy Haas
58. **Daniel Nestor**
94. **Sebastien Lareau**
290. **Frederic Niemeyer**
472. **Bobby Kokavec**
494. **Simon Larose**
609. **Emin Agaev**

Lareau wins Canada's first Grand Slam

Sebastien Lareau made Canadian tennis history in September 1999, teaming with Texan partner Alex O'Brien to win the U.S. Open doubles crown and become the first Canadian to secure a Grand Slam title.

The win ended a 12-match losing streak for Canadians in Grand Slam finals.

The 11th-seeded duo of Lareau and O'Brien won the winners' cheque of some $500,000 Cdn by knocking off top-seeded Mahesh Bhupathi and Leander Paes of India 7-6 (9-7), 6-4 in one hour 50 minutes.

"This is the culmination of a lot of work," said Lareau. "It's great."

Lareau, from Boucherville, Que., now has 11 career doubles titles, four of which have come this year.

No Canadian had ever won a Grand Slam title at the senior level although five players had combined for 12 previous cracks at a Grand Slam championship.

Lareau an O'Brien also reached the final of the 1996 and 1997 Australian Opens.

Toronto's Daniel Nestor, Glenn Michibata, Jill Hetherington and Grant Connell have also played in a Grand Slam doubles final.

Women's Tennis Association–1999 Grand Slam Events

	Date	Winner		Date	Winner
Australian Open	Jan. 18-31	Martina Hingis	Wimbledon	June 21-July 4	Lindsay Davenport
French Open	May 24-June 6	Steffi Graf	U.S. Open	Aug. 30-Sept. 12	Serena Williams

Women's Final WTA Rankings

(as of September 13, 1999, including top Canadians)

1. Martina Hingis
3. Lindsay Davenport
5. Venus Williams
7. Serena Williams
9. Monica Seles
6. Mary Pierce
7. Barbara Schett
8. Julie Halard-Decugis

17. Amanda Coetzer
10. Nathalie Tauziat
47. **Maureen Drake**
75. **Jana Nejedly**
129. **Sonya Jeyaseelan**
177. **Renata Kolbovic**
188. **Vanessa Webb**
277. **Martina Nejedly**

Source: *Canadian Press*

Canadian Long Course Swimming Records

(as of August 30, 1999)

Men

Event	Time	Swimmer	Location and Date
50 Free style	22.81	Mark Andrews	Indianapolis, April 10, 1988
100 Free style	49.94	Yannick Lupien	Sydney, Aug. 26, 1999
200 Free style	1:49.71	Turlough O'Hare	Perth, Jan. 7, 1991
400 Free style	3:50.49	Peter Szmidt	Etobicoke, July 16, 1980
800 Free style	8:00.22	Chris Bowie	Etobicoke, Aug. 2
1500 Free style	15:12.63	Harry Taylor	Auckland, Jan. 30, 1990
100 Back stroke	53.98	Mark Tewksbury	Barcelona, July 30, 1992
200 Back stroke	1:59.39	Mark Versfeld	Perth, Jan. 18, 1998
100 Breast stroke	1:01.99	Victor Davis	Los Angeles, July 29
200 Breast stroke	2:13.34	Victor Davis	Los Angeles, Aug. 2, 1984
100 Butterfly	53.33	Stephen Clarke	Atlanta, July 24, 1996
200 Butterfly	1:58.14	Tom Ponting	Montreal, May 31, 1988
200 Individual Medley	2:00.38	Curtis Myden	New York, July 31, 1998
400 Individual Medley	4:15.52	Curtis Myden	Winnipeg, Aug. 3, 1999

Women

Event	Time	Swimmer	Location and Date
50 Free style	25.86	Laura Nicholls	Victoria, Mar. 19, 1999
100 Free style	55.94	Laura Nicholls	Sydney, Aug. 27, 1999
200 Free style	2:00.21	Jessica Deglau	Winnipeg, Aug. 3, 1999
400 Free style	4:12.64	Joanne Malar	Winnipeg, Aug. 4, 1999
800 Free style	8:36.24	Debbie Wurzburger	Seoul, Sept. 23
1500 Free style	16:40.60	Elissa Purvis	Los Altos, July 13, 1986
100 Back stroke	1:02.14	Kelly Stefanyshyn	Winnipeg, Aug. 4, 1999
200 Back stroke	2:13.24	Kelly Stefanyshyn	Winnipeg, Aug. 7, 1999
100 Breast stroke	1:08.86	Lauren Van Oosten	Perth, Jan. 13, 1998
200 Breast stroke	2:27.27	Allison Higson	Montreal, May 29, 1988
100 Butterfly	1:00.24	Jessica Amey	Atlanta, Aug. 12, 1995
200 Butterfly	2:09.64	Jessica Deglau	Winnipeg, Aug. 7, 1999
200 Individual Medley	2:14.18	Joanne Malar	Winnipeg, Aug. 6, 1999
400 Individual Medley	4:38.46	Joanne Malar	Winnipeg, Aug. 2, 1999

Source: *Swim Canada*

Relay Records

Men

Event	Time	Swimmer	Location and Date
4x100 Medley	3:39.28	Olympic Team (Mark Tewksbury, Victor Davis, Tom Ponting, Sandy Goss)	Seoul, Sept. 25, 1988
4x100 Freestyle	3:20.73	Pan Pacific Team (Yannick Lupien, Craig Hutchinson, Steele, Dulhie)	Sydney, Aug. 22, 1999
4x200 Freestyle	7:22.74	World Championship Team (Eddie Parenti, Paul Szekula, Darren Ward, Turlough O'Hare)	Perth, Jan. 8, 1991

Women

Event	Time	Swimmer	Location and Date
4x50 Medley	1:55.16	Pan Pacific Team (Lori Melien, Keltie Duggan, Debbie Gaudin, Kristin Topham)	Tokyo, Aug. 17, 1989
4x100 Medley	4:08.13	Pan Pacific Team (Julie Howard, Guylaine Cloutier, Jessica Amey, Shannon Shakespeare)	Seoul, Sept. 25, 1988
4x100 Freestyle	3:44.50	Pan Pacific Team (Laura Nicholls, Marianne Limpert, Jessica Deglau, Lydall)	Sydney, Aug. 22, 1999
4x200 Freestyle	8:05.59	World Champs Team (Joanne Malar, Shannon Shakespeare, Jessica Deglau, Laura Nicholls)	Perth, Jan. 17, 1998

Source: *Swim Canada*

Canadian Alpine Skiing Champions, 1980–99

Men

	Downhill	Slalom	Giant Slalom	Super Giant Slalom
1980	Ken Read	Peter Monod	Peter Monod	—
1981	Robin McLeish	Peter Monod	Peter Monod	—
1982	Urs Raeber (SUI)	Peter Monod	Jim Read	—
1983	Steve Podborski	Francois Jodoin	Mike Tommy	—
1984	Steve Podborski	Mike Tommy	Jim Read	Jim Read
1985	Steven Lee (AUS)	Gordon Perry	Jim Read	Mike Brown (USA)
1986	Don Stevens	Jim Read	Jim Read	Derek Trussler
1987	Brian Stemmle	Alain Villiard	Alain Villiard	Jim Read
1988	Steven Lee (AUS)	Jack Miller (USA)	Tiger Shaw (USA)	Leonard Stock (AUT)
1989	Mike Carney	Alain Villiard	Alain Villiard	Felix Belczyk
1990	Felix Belczyk	Rob Crossan	Robbie Parisien	David Duchesne
1991	Edi Podivinsky	Eric Villiard	Eric Villiard	Rob Boyd
1992	Reggie Crist (USA)	Rob Crossan	Thomas Grandi	Reggie Crist (USA)
1993	John Mealey	Rob Crossan	Thomas Grandi	Eric Villiard
1994	Ralf Socher	Stanley Hayer	Christopher Pickett (US)	Ralf Socher
1995	Edi Podivinsky	Stanley Hayer	Thomas Grandi	Brian Stemmle
1996	Edi Podivinsky	Stanley Hayer	Thomas Grandi	(cancelled)
1997	Graydon Oldfield	Thomas Grandi	Thomas Grandi	Ryan Oughtred
1998	Daimion Applegath	Thomas Grandi	Thomas Grandi	Darin McBeath
1999	Kevin Wert	Munroe Hunsicker	Vincent Lavoie	Brian Stemmle

Women

	Downhill	Slalom	Giant Slalom	Super Giant Slalom
1980	Laurie Graham	Lynn Lacasse	Ann Blackburn	—
1981	Gerry Sorensen	Josée Lacasse	Diana Haight	—
1982	Dianne Lehodey	Lynn Lacasse	Lynn Lacasse	—
1983	Gerry Sorensen	Lynn Lacasse	Liisa Savijarvi	—
1984	Diana Haight	Andréa Bedard	Liisa Savijarvi	Laurie Graham
1985	Laurie Graham	Andréa Bedard	Liisa Savijarvi	Karen Percy
1986	Karen Percy	Josée Lacasse	Josée Lacasse	Karen Percy
1987	Liisa Savijarvi	Julie Klotz	Josée Lacasse	Karen Percy
1988	Laurie Graham	Josée Lacasse	Karen Percy	Karen Percy
1989	Lucie LaRoche	Sonja Rusch	Karen Percy	Kendra Kobelka
1990	Lucie LaRoche	Josée Lacasse	Josée Lacasse	Nancy Gee
1991	Kerrin Lee-Gartner	Sonja Rusch	Annie Laurendeau	Michelle McKendry
1992	Kerrin Lee-Gartner	Annie Laurendeau	Michelle McKendry	Michelle McKendry
1993	Kerrin Lee-Gartner	Nanci Gee	Melanie Turgeon	Michelle Ruthven*
1994	Kate Pace	Katarina Tichy (Czech)	Edith Rozsa	Michelle Ruthven
1995	Lindsey Roberts	Edith Rozsa	Melanie Turgeon	Melanie Turgeon
1996	Kate Pace	Melanie Turgeon	Melanie Turgeon	(cancelled)
1997	Kate Pace Lindsay	Edith Rozsa	Allison Forsyth	Melanie Turgeon
1998	Jennifer Mickelson	Allison Forsyth	Allison Forsyth	Emily Brydon
1999	Emily Brydon	Amy Prohal	Allison Forsyth	Allison Forsyth

Source: *Ski Canada*　　　　　　　　　*Michelle McKendry's married name is Ruthven

Figure Skating Champions, 1953–99

	Canadian Champions		World Champions	
	Men	**Women**	**Men**	**Women**
1953	Peter Firstbrook	Barbara Gratton	Hayes Jenkins, U.S.	Tenley Albright, U.S.
1954	Charles Snelling	Barbara Gratton	Hayes Jenkins, U.S.	Gundi Busch, W. Germany
1955	Charles Snelling	Carole Jane Pachl	Hayes Jenkins, U.S.	Tenley Albright, U.S.
1956	Charles Snelling	Carole Jane Pachl	Hayes Jenkins, U.S.	Carol Heiss, U.S.
1957	Charles Snelling	Carole Jane Pachl	Dave Jenkins, U.S.	Carol Heiss, U.S.
1958	Charles Snelling	Margaret Crosland	Dave Jenkins, U.S.	Carol Heiss, U.S.
1959	Donald Jackson	Margaret Crosland	Dave Jenkins, U.S.	Carol Heiss, U.S.
1960	Donald Jackson	Wendy Griner	Alain Giletti, France	Carol Heiss, U.S.
1961	Donald Jackson	Wendy Griner	none[1]	none[1]
1962	Donald Jackson	Wendy Griner	Don Jackson, Canada	Sjoukje Dijkstra, Neth.
1963	Donald McPherson	Wendy Griner	Don McPherson, Canada	Sjoukje Dijkstra, Neth.
1964	Charles Snelling	Petra Burka	Manfred Schnelldorfer, W. Germany	Sjoukje Dijkstra, Neth.
1965	Donald Knight	Petra Burka	Alain Calmat, France	Petra Burka, Canada
1966	Donald Knight	Petra Burka	Emmerich Danzer, Austria	Peggy Fleming, U.S.
1967	Donald Knight	Valerie Jones	Emmerich Danzer, Austria	Peggy Fleming, U.S.
1968	Jay Humphry	Karen Magnussen	Emmerich Danzer, Austria	Peggy Fleming, U.S.
1969	Jay Humphry	Linda Carbonetto	Tim Wood, U.S.	Gabriele Seyfert, E. Germany
1970	David McGillivray	Karen Magnussen	Tim Wood, U.S.	Gabriele Seyfert, E. Germany
1971	Toller Cranston	Karen Magnussen	Ondrej Nepela, Czech.	Beatrix Schuba, Austria
1972	Toller Cranston	Karen Magnussen	Ondrej Nepela, Czech.	Beatrix Schuba, Austria
1973	Toller Cranston	Karen Magnussen	Ondrej Nepela, Czech.	Karen Magnussen, Canada
1974	Toller Cranston	Lynn Nightingale	Jan Hoffman, E. Germany	Christine Errath, E. Germany
1975	Toller Cranston	Lynn Nightingale	Sergei Volkov, USSR	Dianne de Leeuw, Neth.-U.S.
1976	Toller Cranston	Lynn Nightingale	John Curry, Gr. Brit.	Dorothy Hamill, U.S.
1977	Ron Shaver	Lynn Nightingale	Vladimir Kovalev, USSR	Linda Fratianne, U.S.
1978	Brian Pockar	Heather Kemkaran	Charles Tickner, U.S.	Anett Poetzsch, E. Germany
1979	Brian Pockar	Janet Morrisey	Vladimir Kovalev, USSR	Linda Fratianne, U.S.
1980	Brian Pockar	Heather Kemkaran	Jan Hoffmann, E. Germany	Anett Poetzsch, E. Germany
1981	Brian Orser	Tracey Wainman	Scott Hamilton, U.S.	Denise Biellmann, Switzerland
1982	Brian Orser	Kay Thomson	Scott Hamilton, U.S.	Elaine Zayak, U.S.
1983	Brian Orser	Kay Thomson	Scott Hamilton, U.S.	Rosalyn Sumners, U.S.
1984	Brian Orser	Kay Thomson	Scott Hamilton, U.S.	Katarina Witt, E. Germany
1985	Brian Orser	Elizabeth Manley	Alexandre Fadeev, USSR	Katarina Witt, E. Germany
1986	Brian Orser	Tracey Wainman	Brian Boitano, U.S.	Debi Thomas, U.S.
1987	Brian Orser	Elizabeth Manley	Brian Orser, Canada	Katarina Witt, E. Germany
1988	Brian Orser	Elizabeth Manley	Brian Boitano, U.S.	Katarina Witt, E. Germany
1989	Kurt Browning	Karen Preston	Kurt Browning, Canada	Midori Ito, Japan
1990	Kurt Browning	Lisa Sargeant	Kurt Browning, Canada	Jill Trenary, U.S.
1991	Kurt Browning	Josée Chouinard	Kurt Browning, Canada	Kristi Yamaguchi, U.S.
1992	Michael Slipchuk	Karen Preston	Victor Petrenko, Russia	Kristi Yamaguchi, U.S.
1993	Kurt Browning	Josée Chouinard	Kurt Browning, Canada	Oksana Baiul, Ukraine
1994	Elvis Stojko	Josée Chouinard	Elvis Stojko, Canada	Yuka Sato, Japan
1995	Sebastien Britten	Netty Kim	Elvis Stojko, Canada	Lu Chen, China
1996	Elvis Stojko	Jennifer Robinson	Todd Eldredge, U.S.	Michelle Kwan, U.S.
1997	Elvis Stojko	Susan Humphreys	Elvis Stojko, Canada	Tara Lapinski, U.S.
1998	Elvis Stojko	Angela Derochie	Alexei Yagudin, Russia	Michelle Kwan, U.S.
1999	Elvis Stojko	Jennifer Robinson	Alexei Yagudin, Russia	Maria Butyrskaya, Russia

Source: *Canadian Figure Skating Association*

(1) The 1961 world championships were cancelled after an air crash killed the entire U.S. team travelling to the competition.

Lacrosse—The Mann Cup

The Mann Cup was presented by the late Sir Donald Mann, builder of the Canadian Northern Railway, for the Senior Amateur Championship of Canada and was originally a challenge cup.

1910	Young Torontos, Toronto, Ontario
1911	Vancouver Athletic Club, Vancouver, B.C.
1912	Vancouver Athletic Club, Vancouver, B.C.
1913	Vancouver Athletic Club, Vancouver, B.C.
1914	Vancouver Athletic Club, Vancouver, B.C.
1915	Salmonbellies, New Westminster, B.C.
1916	Salmonbellies, New Westminster, B.C.
1917	Salmonbellies, New Westminster, B.C.
1918	Coughlans, Vancouver, B.C.
1919	Foundation Club, Vancouver, B.C.
1920–1925	Salmonbellies, New Westminster, B.C.
1926	Westonmen, Weston, Ontario
1927	Salmonbellies, New Westminster, B.C.
1928	Emmets, Ottawa, Ontario
1929	Generals, Oshawa, Ontario
1930	Excelsiors, Brampton, Ontario
1931	Excelsiors, Brampton, Ontario
1932	Mountaineers, Mimico, Ontario
1933	Tigers, Hamilton, Ontario
1934	Terriers, Orillia, Ontario
1935	Terriers, Orillia, Ontario
1936	Terriers, Orillia, Ontario
1937	Salmonbellies, New Westminster, B.C.
1938	Athletics, St. Catharines, Ontario
1939	Adanacs, New Westminster, B.C.
1940	Athletics, St. Catharines, Ontario
1941	Athletics, St. Catharines, Ontario
1942	Combines, Mimico/Brampton, Ontario
1943	Salmonbellies, New Westminster, B.C.
1944	Athletics, St. Catharines, Ontario
1945	Burrards, Vancouver, B.C.
1946	Athletics, St. Catharines, Ontario
1947	Adanacs, New Westminster, B.C.
1948	Tigers, Hamilton, Ontario
1949	Burrards, Vancouver, B.C.
1950	Crescents, Owen Sound, Ontario
1951	Timbermen, Peterborough, Ontario
1952	Timbermen, Peterborough, Ontario
1953	Timbermen, Peterborough, Ontario
1954	Timbermen, Peterborough, Ontario
1955	Shamrocks, Victoria, B.C.
1956	Timbermen, Nanaimo, B.C.
1957	Shamrocks, Victoria, B.C.
1958	Salmonberries, New Westminster, B.C.
1959	O'Keefes, New Westminster, B.C.
1960	Sailors, Port Credit, Ontario
1961	Burrards, Vancouver, B.C.
1962	O'Keefes, New Westminster, B.C.
1963	Carlings, Vancouver, B.C.
1964	Carlings, Vancouver, B.C.
1965	Salmonbellies, New Westminster, B.C.
1966	Lakers, Peterborough, Ontario
1967	Carlings, Vancouver, B.C.
1968	Redmen, Brooklin, Ontario
1969	Redmen, Brooklin, Ontario
1970	Salmonbellies, New Westminster, B.C.
1971	Warriors, Brantford, Ontario
1972	Salmonbellies, New Westminster, B.C.
1973	Lakers, Peterborough, Ontario
1974	Salmonbellies, New Westminster, B.C.
1975	Burrards, Vancouver, B.C.
1976	Salmonbellies, New Westminster, B.C.
1977	Burrards, Vancouver, B.C.
1978	Red Oaks, Peterborough, Ontario
1979	Shamrocks, Victoria, B.C.
1980	Excelsiors, Brampton, Ontario
1981	Salmonbellies, New Westminster, B.C.
1982	Lakers, Peterborough, Ontario
1983	Payless, Victoria, B.C.
1984	Lakers, Peterborough, Ontario
1985	Redmen, Brooklin, Ontario
1986	Salmonbellies, New Westminster, B.C.
1987	Redmen, Brooklin, Ontario
1988	Redmen, Brooklin, Ontario
1989	Salmonbellies, New Westminster, B.C.
1990	Redmen, Brooklin, Ontario
1991	Salmonbellies, New Westminster, B.C.
1992	Excelsiors, Brampton, Ontario
1993	Excelsiors, Brampton, Ontario
1994	Chiefs, Six Nations, Ontario
1995	Chiefs, Six Nations, Ontario
1996	Chiefs, Six Nations, Ontario
1997	Shamrocks, Victoria, B.C.
1998	Excelsiors ,Brampton, Ontario
1999	Shamrocks, Victoria, B.C.

Source: *Canadian Lacrosse Association*

Auto Racing

Molson Indy

Toronto

1986: Bobby Rahal	**1993:** Paul Tracy*
1987: Emerson Fittipaldi	**1994:** Michael Andretti
1988: Al Unser Jr.	**1995:** Michael Andretti
1989: Michael Andretti	**1996:** Adrian Fernandez
1990: Al Unser Jr.	**1997:** Mark Blundell
1991: Michael Andretti	**1998:** Alex Zanardi
1992: Michael Andretti	**1999:** Dario Franchitti

Vancouver

1990: Al Unser Jr.	**1997:** Alex Zanardi
1991: Michael Andretti	**1998:** Dario Franchitti
1992: Michael Andretti	**1999:** Juan Montoya
1993: Al Unser Jr.	
1994: Al Unser Jr.	
1995: Al Unser Jr.	
1996: Michael Andretti	

* Canadian

Source: *Canadian Press*

Championship Auto Racing Teams (CART), 1999

	Date	Winner
Marlboro Grand Prix of Miami	Mar. 21	**Greg Moore**
Firestone Firehawk 500	Apr. 10	Adrian Fernandez
Toyota Grand Prix of Long Beach	Apr. 19	Juan Montoya
Bosch Spark Plug Grand Prix	Apr. 27	Juan Montoya
GP Telemar Rio 400	May 15	Juan Montoya
Motorolla 300	May 29	Michael Andretti
Miller Lite 225	June 6	**Paul Tracy**
Budweiser/G.I. Joe's 200	June 20	Gil de Ferran
Medic Drug Grand Prix of Cleveland	June 27	Juan Montoya
Texaco/Havoline 200	July 11	Christian Fittipaldi
Molson Indy	**July 18**	**Dario Franchitti**
U.S. 500	July 25	Tony Kanaan
Tenneco Automotive Grand Prix of Detroit	Aug. 8	Dario Franchitti
Miller Lite 200 of Mid-Ohio	Aug. 15	Juan Montoya
Target Grand Prix	Aug. 22	Juan Montoya
Vancouver Molson Indy	**Sept. 5**	**Juan Montoya**
Honda Grand Prix of Monterey	Sept. 12	Bryan Herta

Source: *Canadian Press*

Formula One, 1999

	Date	Winner
Australian Grand Prix	Mar. 7	Eddie Irvine
Brazilian Grand Prix	April 11	Mika Hakkinen
San Marino Grand Prix	May 2	Michael Schumacher
Monaco Grand Prix	May 16	Michael Schumacher
Spanish Grand Prix	May 30	Mika Hakkinen
Canadian Grand Prix	**June 13**	**Mika Hakkinen**
French Grand Prix	June 27	Heinz-Harald Frentzen
British Grand Prix	July 11	David Coulthard
Austrian Grand Prix	July 25	Eddie Irvine
German Grand Prix	Aug. 1	Eddie Irvine
Hungarian Grand Prix	Aug. 15	Mika Hakkinen
Belgian Grand Prix	Aug. 29	David Coulthard
Italian Grand Prix	Sept. 12	Heinz-Harald Frentzen

Source: *Canadian Press*

Canadian Open Golf Tournament, 1904–99

	Winner	Score		Winner	Score		Winner	Score
1904	J.H. Oke	156	1938	Sam Snead	277	1970	Kermit Zarley	279
1905	George Cumming	146	1939	Harold McSpaden	282	1971	Lee Trevino	275
1906	Charles Murray	170	1940	Sam Snead	281	1972	Gay Brewer	275
1907	Percy Barrett	306	1941	Sam Snead	274	1973	Tom Weiskopf	278
1908	Albert Murray	300	1942	Craig Wood	275	1974	Bobby Nichols	270
1909	Karl Keffer	309	**1943–1944** No Tournament			1975	Tom Weiskopf	274
1910	Daniel Kenny	303	1945	Byron Nelson	280	1976	Jerry Pate	267
1911	Charles Murray	314	1946	George Fazio	278	1977	Lee Trevino	280
1912	George Sargent	299	1947	Robert Locke	268	1978	Bruce Lietzke	283
1913	Albert Murray	295	1948	C.W. Congdon	280	1979	Lee Trevino	281
1914	Karl Keffer	300	1949	E.J. Dutch Harrison	271	1980	Bob Gilder	274
1915–1918 No Tournament			1950	Jim Ferrier	271	1981	Peter Oosterhuis	280
1919	J. Douglas Edgar	278	1951	Jim Ferrier	273	1982	Bruce Lietzke	277
1920	J. Douglas Edgar	298	1952	John Palmer	263	1983	John Cook	277
1921	W.H. Trovinger	293	1953	Dave Douglas	273	1984	Greg Norman	278
1922	Al Watrous	303	1954	Pat Fletcher[1]	280	1985	Curtis Strange	279
1923	C.W. Hackney	295	1955	Arnold Palmer	265	1986	Bob Murphy	280
1924	Leo Diegel	285	1956	Doug Sanders	273	1987	Curtis Strange	276
1925	Leo Diegel	295	1957	George Bayer	271	1988	Ken Green	275
1926	Macdonald Smith	283	1958	Wesley Ellis Jr.	267	1989	Steve Jones	271
1927	T.D. Armour	288	1959	Doug Ford	276	1990	Wayne Levi	278
1928	Leo Diegel	282	1960	Art Wall Jr.	269	1991	Nick Price	273
1929	Leo Diegel	274	1961	Jacky Cupit	270	1992	Greg Norman	280
1930	T.D. Armour	277	1962	Ted Kroll	278	1993	David Frost	279
1931	Walter Hagen	292	1963	Doug Ford	280	1994	Nick Price	275
1932	Harry Cooper	290	1964	Kel Nagle	277	1995	Mark O'Meara	274
1933	Joe Kirkwood	282	1965	Gene Littler	273	1996	Dudley Hart	202[2]
1934	T.D. Armour	287	1966	Don Massengale	280	1997	Steve Jones	275
1935	Gene Kunes	280	1967	Bill Casper	279	1998	Billy Andrade	275
1936	Lawson Little	271	1968	Bob Charles	274	1999	Hal Sutton	275
1937	Harry Cooper	285	1969	Tommy Aaron	275			

Source: *Canadian Press*   (1) Last Canadian winner.   (2) Held to 54 holes by bad weather.

Du Maurier Ltd. Women's Golf Classic, 1975–99

	Winner	Score		Winner	Score		Winner	Score
1975[1]	JoAnne Carner	214	1983	Hollis Stacy	277	1992	Sherri Steinhauer	277
1976[1]	Donna Caponi Young	212	1984	Juli Inkster	274	1993	Brandie Burton[2]	277
1977[1]	Judy T. Rankin	212	1985	Pat Bradley	278	1994	Martha Nause	279
1978	JoAnne Carner	278	1986	Pat Bradley	276	1995	Jenny Lidback	280
1979	Amy Alcott	285	1987	Jodi Rosenthal	272	1996	Laura Davies	277
1980	Pat Bradley	277	1988	Sally Little	279	1997	Colleen Walker	278
1981	Jan Stephenson	278	1989	Tammie Green	279	1998	Brandie Burton	270[3]
1982	Sandra Haynie	280	1990	Cathy Johnston	276	1999	Karrie Webb	277
			1991	Nancy Scranton	279			

Source: *Canadian Press*   (1) Three rounds only. (2) Won on first playoff hole vs. Betsy King. (3) Tournament Record

PGA Major Tournaments

	Date	Winner
The Masters	Apr. 8-11, 1999	Jose Maria Olazabal
U.S. Open Championship	June 17-20, 1999	Payne Stewart
British Open Championship	July 15-18, 1999	Paul Lawrie
PGA Championship	Aug. 12-15, 1999	Tiger Woods

Source: *Canadian Press*

Top-10 PGA Money Leaders and Canadians

(as of September 12, 1999)

	Events	Money		Events	Money
Tiger Woods	18	$4,266,585	Carlos Franco	20	$1,732,884
David Duval	19	$3,471,206	Chris Perry	25	$1,602,540
Payne Stewart	19	$2,077,950	**24. Mike Weir**	24	**$1,120,914**
Vijay Singh	25	$1,961,750	**141. Stephen Ames**	12	**$210,625**
Hal Sutton	21	$1,906,511	**238. Richard Zokol**	4	**$27,022**
Jeff Maggert	20	$1,861,112	**307. Craig Matthew**	2	**$5,475**
Davis Love III	20	$1,771,728	**310. Dave Barr**	4	**$5,375**
Justin Leonard	24	$1,742,634			

Source: *Canadian Press*

LPGA Major Tournaments

	Date	Winner
Nabisco Dinah Shore	Mar. 25-28, 1999	Dottie Pepper
LPGA Championship	June 24-27, 1999	Juli Inkster
U.S. Open Championship	June 3-6, 1999	Juli Inkster
Du Maurier Canadian Open	July 29-Aug. 1, 1999	Karrie Webb

Source: *Canadian Press*

Top-10 LPGA Money Leaders

(as of September 12, 1999)

	Events	Money		Events	Money
Karrie Webb	21	$1,391,360	Rosie Jones	19	$525,187
Juli Inkster	20	$1,143,703	Kelli Kuehne	19	$456,652
Se Ri Pak	21	$681,603	Rachel Hetherington	23	$448,314
Lorie Kane	24	**$656,883**	Mi Hyun Kim	25	$409,080
Annika Sorenstam	17	$649,921	Mardi Lunn	26	$392,099
Sherri Steinhauer	25	$603,055	Janice Moodie	24	$368,294
Meg Mallon	20	$589,687	Kelly Robbins	21	$366,384
Dottie Pepper	20	$577,875			

Source: *Canadian Press*

Canadian LPGA Money Winners

(as of September 12, 1999)

	Events	Money		Events	Money
4. Lorie Kane	24	$656,883	125. Liz Earley	21	$33,645
57. Dawn Coe-Jones	20	$137,595	143. Tina Tombs	14	$23,019
61. A.J. Eathorne	22	$123,997	170. Barb Bunkowsky Scherbak	9	$9,822
64. Gail Graham	22	$111,030	174. Kim Brozer	10	$ 8,465
124. Nancy Harvey	23	$33,882			

Source: *Canadian Press*

World Track and Field Records

(as of August 30, 1999)
Men

Event	Record	Holder/Country	Date	Where Made
■ Running				
100 Metres	9.79	Maurice Greene, US	June 16, 1999	Athens
200 Metres	19.32	Michael Johnson, US	Aug. 8, 1996	Atlanta
400 Metres	43.18	Michael Johnson, US	Aug. 26, 1999	Seville
800 Metres	1:41.11	Wilson Kipketer, Den	Aug. 24, 1997	Cologne
1000 Metres	2:11.96	Noah Ngeny, Ken	Sept. 5, 1999	Rieti
1500 Metres	3:26.00	Hicham El Guerrouj, Mor	July 14, 1998	Rome
1 Mile	3:43.13	Hicham El Guerrouj, Mor	July 7, 1999	Rome
2000 Metres	4:44.79	Hicham El Guerrouj, Mor	Sept. 7, 1999	Berlin
3000 Metres	7:20.67	Daniel Komen, Ken	Sept. 1, 1996	Rieti
5000 Metres	12:39.36	Haile Gebrselassie, Eth	June 13, 1998	Helsinki
10000 Metres	26:22.75	Haile Gebrselassie, Eth	June 1, 1998	Hengelo
20000 Metres	56:55.6	Arturo Barrios, Mex	March 3, 1991	La Fleche
25000 Metres	1:13:55.8	Toshihiko Seko, Jpn	March 22, 1981	Christchurch
30000 Metres	1:29:18.8	Toshihiko Seko, Jpn	March 22, 1981	Christchurch
3000 Metres Steeplechase	7:55.72	Bernard Barmasai, Ken	Sept. 24, 1997	Cologne
Marathon	2:06:05	Ronaldo da Costa, Bra	Sept. 20, 1998	Berlin
■ Hurdles				
110 Metre Hurdles	12.91 0.5	Colin Jackson, Bri	Aug. 20, 1993	Stuttgart
400 Metre Hurdles	46.78	Kevin Young, US	Aug. 06, 1992	Barcelona
■ Field Events				
High Jump	2.45	Javier Sotomayor, Cuba	July 27, 1993	Salamanca
Long Jump	8.95	Mike Powell, US	Aug. 8, 1991	Tokyo
Triple Jump	18.29	Jonathan Edwards, Br	Aug. 7, 1995	Goteborg
Pole Vault	6.14	Sergey Bubka, Ukr	July 31, 1994	Sestriere
Shot Put	23.12	Randy Barnes, US	May 20, 1990	Westwood
Discus Throw	74.08	Jurgen Schult Ger	June 6, 1986	Brandenburg
Hammer Throw	86.74	Yuriy Sedykh USSR	Aug. 30, 1986	Stuttgart
Javelin	98.48	Jan Zelezny, Cze	May 25, 1996	Jena
Decathlon	8994	Tomas Dvorak, Cze	July 4, 1999	Praha
■ Relay Races				
4x100 Metres	37.40	United States	Aug. 8, 1992	Barcelona
	37.40	United States	Aug. 21, 1993	Stuttgart
4x200 Metres	1:18.68	United States	April 17, 1994	Walnut
4x400 Metres	2:54.20	United States	July 22, 1998	Uniondale
4x800 Metres	7:03.89	Great Britain	Aug. 30, 1982	London
4x1500 Metres	14:38.8	Germany	Aug. 17, 1977	Cologne

▶

Women

Event	Record	Holder/Country	Date	Where Made
■ Running				
100 Metres	10.49	Florence Griffith-Joyner, US	July 16, 1988	Indianapolis
200 Metres	21.34	Florence Griffith-Joyner, US	Sept. 29, 1988	Seoul
400 Metres	47.60	Marita Koch, Ger	Oct. 6, 1985	Canberra
800 Metres	1:53.28	Jarmila Kratochvilova, Cze	July 26, 1983	Munich
1000 Metres	2:28.98	Svetlana Masterkova, Rus	Aug. 23, 1996	Brusells
1500 Metres	3:50.46	Yunxia Qu, Chi	Sept. 11, 1993	Beijing
1 Mile	4:12.56	Svetlana Masterkova, Rus	Aug. 14, 1996	Zurich
2000 Metres	5:25.36	Sonia O'Sullivan, Ire	July 8, 1994	Edinburgh
3000 Metres	8:06.11	Junxia Wang, Chi	Sept. 13, 1993	Beijing
5000 Metres	14:28.09	Bo Jiang, Chi	Oct. 23, 1997	Shanghai
10000 Metres	29:31.78	Junxia Wang, Chi	Sept. 8, 1993	Beijing
20000 Metres	1:06:48.8	Izumi Maki, Jpn	Sept. 19, 1993	Amagasaki
25000 Metres	1:29:29.2	Karolina Szabo, Hun	April 22, 1988	Budapest
30000 Metres	1:47:05.6	Karolina Szabo, Hun	April 22, 1988	Budapest
Marathon	2:21:06	Ingrid Kristiansen, Nor	April 21, 1985	London
■ Hurdles				
100 Metre Hurdles	12.21	Yordanka Donkova, Bul	Aug. 20, 1988	Stara Zagora
400 Metre Hurdles	52.61	Kim Batten, US	Aug. 11, 1995	Goteborg
■ Field Events				
High Jump	2.09	Stefka Kostadinova, Bul	Aug. 30, 1987	Rome
Long Jump	7.52	Galina Chistyakova, Rus	June 11, 1988	Leningrad
Triple Jump	15.50	Inessa Kravets, Ukr	Aug. 10, 1995	Goteborg
Pole Vault	4.60	Emma George, Aus	Feb. 20, 1999	Sydney
	4.60	Stacy Dragila, US	Aug. 21, 1999	Seville
Shot Put	22.63	Natalya Lisovskaya, USSR	June 7, 1987	Moscow
Discus Throw	76.80	Gabriele Reinsch, Ger	July 9, 1988	Brandenburg
Hammer Throw	76.07	Mihaela Melinte, Rom	Aug. 29, 1999	Rudlingen
Javelin Throw	68.19	Trine Solberg-Hattestad, Nor	July 28, 1999	Bergen
Heptathlon	7291	Jackie Joyner-Kersee, US	Sept. 24, 1988	Seoul
■ Relay Races				
4x100 Metres	41.37	Germany	Oct. 6, 1985	Canberra
4x200 Metres	1:28.15	Germany	Aug. 9, 1980	Jena
4x200 Metres	3:15.17	Soviet Union	Oct. 1, 1988	Seoul
4x800 Metres	7:50.17	Soviet Union	Aug 5, 1984	Moscow

Source: *IAAF*

(1) Record set at high altitude. (*) Pending ratification.

The Queen's Plate, 1920–99

The Queen's Plate, first run in 1860, is North America's oldest annual sports event. The race for 3-year-olds foaled in Canada, is run at Toronto's Woodbine Race Track in late June or July.

	Winner	Jockey	Time[1]		Winner	Jockey	Time[1]
1920	St. Paul	Roxy Romanelli	2:09	1959	New Providence	Robert Ussery	2:04.4
1921	Herendesy	Jimmy Butwell	2:10	1960	Victoria Park	Avelino Gomez	2:02
1922	South Shore	Kenny Parrington	2:12	1961	Blue Light	Hugo Dittfach	2:05
1923	Flowerful	Terry Wilson	2:11	1962	Flaming Page	Jim Fitzsimmons	2:04.3
1924	Maternal Pride	George Walls	1:57.3	1963	Canebora	Manuel Ycaza	2:04
1925	Fairbank	Chick Lang	1:56.2	1964	Northern Dancer	Bill Hartack	2:02.1
1926	Haplite	Henry Erickson	1:59.3	1965	Whistling Sea	Tak Inouye	2:03.4
1927	Troutlet	Francis Horn	1:55.4	1966	Titled Hero	Avelino Gomez	2:03.3
1928	Young Kitty	Lester Pichon	1:57	1967	Jammed Lovely	Jim Fitzsimmons	2:03
1929	Shorelint	Jaydee Mooney	1:57.3	1968	Merger	Wayne Harris	2:05.2
1930	Aymond	Henry Little	1:57.1	1969	Jumpin Joseph	Avelino Gomez	2:04.1
1931	Froth Blower	Frank Mann	1:59.1	1970	Almoner	Sandy Hawley	2:04.4
1932	Queensway	Frank Mann	1:55.1	1971	Kennedy Road	Sandy Hawley	2:03
1933	King O'Connor	Eddie Legere	1:56.2	1972	Victoria Song	Robin Platts	2:03.1
1934	Horometer	Frank Mann	1:54.1	1973	Royal Chocolate	Ted Colangelo	2:08
1935	Sally Fuller	Herb Lindberg	1:55.1	1974	Amber Herod	Robin Platts	2:09.1
1936	Monsweep	Danny Brammer	1:55	1975	L'Enjoleur	Sandy Hawley	2:02.3
1937	Goldlure	Sterling Young	1:55.2	1976	Norcliffe	Jeffrey Fell	2:05
1938	Bunty Lawless	John Bailey	1:54.2	1977	Sound Reason	Robin Platts	2:06.3
1939	Archworth	Sydney D. Birley	1:54.2	1978	Regal Embrace	Sandy Hawley	2:02
1940	Willie the Kid	Ronnie Nash	1:55.4	1979	Steady Growth	Brian Swatuk	2:06.3
1941	Budpath	Bobby Watson	1:56.4	1980	Driving Home	Bill Parsons	2:04.1
1942	Ten to Ace	Charlie Smith	1:57.4	1981	Fiddle Dancer Boy	David Clark	2:04.4
1943	Paolita	Pat Remillard	2:02.3	1982	Son of Briartic	John-Paul Souter	2:04.3
1944	Acara	Bobby Watson	1:54.4	1983	Bompago	Larry Attard	2:04.1
1945	Uttermost	Bobby Watson	1:53.4	1984	Key to the Moon	Robin Platts	2:03.4
1946	Kingarvie	Johnny Dewhurst	1:55.3	1985	La Lorgnette	David Clark	2:04.3
1947	Moldy	Colin McDonald	1:54.1	1986	Golden Choice	Vince Bracciale	2:07.1
1948	Last Mark	Howard Bailey	1:52	1987	Market Control	Ken Skinner	2:03.2
1949	Epic	Chris Rogers	1:52.1	1988	Regal Intention	Jack Lauzon	2:06.1
1950	McGill	Chris Rogers	1:52.2	1989	With Approval	Don Seymour	2:03
1951	Major Factor	Alf Bavington	1:53	1990	Izvestia	Don Seymour	2:01.4
1952	Epigram	Gil Robillard	1:58.3	1991	Dance Smartly	Pal Day	2:03.2
1953	Canadiana	Eddie Arcaro	1:52.1	1992	Alydeed	Craig Perret	2:04.6
1954	Collisteo	Chris Rogers	1:52	1993	Peteski	Craig Perret	2:04.2
1955	Ace Marine	George Walker	1:52.2	1994	Basqueian	Jack Laron	2:03.4
1956	Canadian Champ	Dave Stevenson	1:55	1995	Regal Discovery	Todd Kabel	2:03.4
1957	Lyford Cay	Avelino Gomez	2:02.3	1996	Victor Cooley	Emke Ramsammy	2:03.8
1958	Calendon Beau	Al Coy	2:04.1	1997	Awesome Again	A.E. Smith	2:04
				1998[2]	Archer's Bay	Kent Desormeaux	2:02.1
				1999	Woodcarver	Mickey Walls	2:03

Source: *Ontario Jockey Club*

(1) Fractions of a second are in fifths. (2) Held June 21, 1998.

Thoroughbred Racing

	Date	Winner
Triple Crown		
Kentucky Derby	May 1, 1999	Charismatic
Preakness Stakes	May 15, 1999	Charismatic
Belmont Stakes	June 5, 1999	Lemon Dropkid

Source: *Canadian Press*

Prince of Wales Stakes, 1960–99

	Winner	Jockey	Time[1]		Winner	Jockey	Time[1]
1960	Bulpamiru	Hugo Dittfach	2:19.4	**1979**	Mass Rally	George Ho Sang	2:33.2
1961	Song of Even	Jim Fitzsimmons	2:29.0	**1980**	Allan Blue	Joe Belowus	2:34.4
1962	King Gorm	Hugo Dittfach	2:21.1	**1981**	Cadet Corps	Robin Platts	2:34.4
1963	Canebora	Hugo Dittfach	2:30.3	**1982**	Runaway Groom	Robin Platts	2:38.2
1964	Canadillis	Avelino Gomez	2:35.0	**1983**	Archdeacon	Vince Bracciale	2:32.0
1965	Good Old Mort	S. McComb	2:22.4	**1984**	Val Dansant	John LeBlanc	2:48.3
1966	He's A Smoothie	Hugo Dittfach	2:19.0	**1985**	Imperial Choice	Irwin Driedger	2:34.3
1967	Battling	Hugo Dittfach	2:21.0	**1986**	Golden Choice	Vince Bracciale	2:44.2
1968	Rouletabille	Richard Grubb	2:18.3	**1987**	Coryphee	Brian Swatuk	2:39.3
1969	Sharp-Eyed Quillo	H. Gustines	2:16.3	**1988**	Regal Classic	Sandy Hawley	2:00.1
1970	Almoner	Sandy Hawley	2:19.4	**1989**	With Approval	Don Seymour	1:56.4
1971	New Pro	Jim Kelly	2:15.1	**1990**	Izvestia	Don Seymour	1:56.2
1972	Presidial	John LeBlanc	2:16.3	**1991**	Dance Smartly	Pal Day	1:56.3
1973	Tara Road	Sandy Hawley	2:16.4	**1992**	Benburb	Larry Attard	1:57.2
1974	Rushton's Corsair	Jim Kelly	2:23.2	**1993**	Peteski	Dave Penna	1:34.4
1975	L'Enjoleur	Sandy Hawley	2:32.2	**1994**	Bruce's Mill	Craig Perret	1:53.4
1976	Norcliffe	Jeff Fell	2:30.1	**1995**	Kiridashi	Larry Attard	1:55.0
1977	Dance in Time	Gary Stahlbaum	2:31.4	**1996**	Stephanotis	Mickey Walls	1:55.2
1978	Overskate	Robin Platts	2:34.2	**1997**	Cryptocloser	W. Martinez	1:56
				1998[2]	Archer's Bay	Robert Landry	1:55.1
				1999	Gandria	Constant Montpellier	1:56.4

Source: *Ontario Jockey Club*   (1) Fractions of a second are in fifths. (2) Held July 25, 1999.

Breeders Stakes, 1960–99

Year	Winner	Jockey	Time[1]	Year	Winner	Jockey	Time[1]
1960	Hidden Treasure	Al Coy	2:34.2	**1979**	Bridle Path	Sandy Hawley	2:29.3
1961	Song of Even	Jim Fitzsimmons	2:31.3	**1980**	Ben Fab	Gary Stahlbaum	2:31.3
1962	Crafty Lace	Ron Turcotte	2:52	**1981**	Social Wizard	George Ho Sang	2:48.4
1963	Canebora	Manuel Ycaza	2:32.1	**1982**	Runaway Groom	Robin Platts	2:32.1
1964	Artic Hills	R. Armstrong	2:33.3	**1983**	Kingsbridge	Robin Platts	2:32.2
1965	Good Old Mort	P. Kallai	2:43	**1984**	Bounding Away	David Clark	2:32.3
1966	Titled Hero	Avelino Gomez	2:31.2	**1985**	Crowning Honors	Brian Swatuk	2:50
1967	Pine Point	Avelino Gomez	2:32.1	**1986**	Carotene	Richard Dos Ramos	2:32.3
1968	No Parando	John LeBlanc	2:30	**1987**	Hangin On a Star	Dave Penna	2:30
1969	Grey Whiz	John LeBlanc	2:29	**1988**	King's Deputy	Sandy Hawley	2:30.3
1970	Mary of Scotland	Richard Grubb	2:38.2	**1989**	With Approval	Don Seymour	2:29
1971	Belle Geste	Noel Turcotte	2:28	**1990**	Izvestia	Don Seymour	2:33.2
1972	Nice Dancer	Sandy Hawley	2:35.4	**1991**	Dance Smartly	Pal Day	2:31.2
1973	Come In Dad	Wayne Green	2:33.3	**1992**	Blitzer	Don Seymour	2:35.3
1974	Haymaker's Jig	Robin Platts	2:30.4	**1993**	Peteski	Craig Perret	2:30.4
1975	Momigi	Gary Melanson	2:38.1	**1994**	Basquean	Jack Lauzon	2:47.4
1976	Tiny Tinker	Sandy Hawley	2:31.1	**1995**	Charlie's Dewan	Craig Perret	2:26.4
1977	Dance in Time	Gary Stahlbaum	3:01.3	**1996**	Chief Bearheart	Mickey Walls	2:28.3
1978	Overskate	Robin Platts	2:29.2	**1997**	John The Magician	Steven Bahen	2:35
				1998[2]	Pinafore Park	Robert Landry	2:30.1
				1999	Free Vacation	Laurie Gulas	2:28.4

Source: *Ontario Jockey Club*   (1) Fractions of a second are in fifths. (2) August 15, 1999.

Canadian Sports Hall of Fame

(living members as of October 1999)

Anakin, Douglas, bobsled
Arnold, Don, rowing
Athans, George, Jr., water skiing
Balding, Al, golf
Baldwin, Matt, curling
Baumann, Alex, swimming
Bedard, Bob, tennis
Bédard, Myriam, biathlon
Béliveau, Jean, hockey
Bell, Florence, track relay
Bell, Marilyn, marathon swimming
Bernier, Sylvie, diving
Bionda, Jack, lacrosse
Boldt, Arnie, field high jump
Boucher, Gaetan, speed skating
Box, Ab, football
Boys, Bev, diving
Brasseur, Isabelle, figure skating
Brooks, Lela, speed skating
Brouillard, Lou, boxing
Browning, Kurt, figure skating
Burka, Ellen, skating coach
Burka, Petra, figure skating
Burka, Sylvia, speed skating
Cain, Larry, canoeing
Callura, Jackie, boxing
Cameron, Michelle, synchro swimming
Chuvalo, George, boxing
Cliff, Leslie, swimming
Clifford, Betsy, skiing
Coleman, Jim, sports journalism
Côté, Gérard, marathon swimming
Cowan, Gary, golf
Cranston, Toller, figure skating
Crothers, Bill, track mid-distance
D'hondt, Walter, rowing
Dafoe, Frances, figure skating
Day, James, equestrian
Dexter, Glen, yachting
Dionne, Marcel, hockey
Dojack, Paul, football official
Drake, Clare, hockey builder
Drayton, Jerome, marathon running
Dryden, Ken, hockey
Duguid, Don, curling
Dunnell, Milt, all-around builder
Durrelle, Yvon, boxing
Eagleson, Alan, hockey builder
Eisler, Lloyd, figure skating
Elder, James, equestrian
Emery, Dr. John, bobsled
Emery, Victor, bobsled
Esaw, Johnny, all-around builder
Esposito, Phil, hockey
Filion, Hervé, harness racing
Fogh, Hans, yachting
Fortier, Sylvie, synchro swimming
Gabriel, Tony, football
Gainey, Bob, hockey
Galbraith, Sheldon, figure sk. builder
Gate, George, swimming builder
Gaudaur, Jake, Jr., football builder
Gayford, Tom, equestrian
Geoffrion, Bernard "Boom Boom," hockey

Golab, Tony, football
Graham, Laurie, skiing
Greene, Nancy, skiing
Grenier, Jean, speed skating builder
Gwynne, Horace, boxing
Hall, Glenn, hockey
Hanson, Fritz, football
Hartman, Barney, skeet shootin
Hawley, Sandy, horse racing
Heddle, Kathleen, rowing
Heggtveit, Anne, skiing
Henderson, Paul, hockey
Hepburn, Doug, weightlifting
Hildebrand, Ike, lacrosse
Hoffman, Abigal, track and field
Howe, Gordie, hockey
Hull, Bobby, hockey
Hungerford, George W., rowing
Huot, Jules, golf
Hutton, Ralph, swimming
Jackson, Donald, figure skating
Jackson, Dr. Roger, rowing
Jackson, Russ, football
Jelinek, Maria, figure skating
Jelinek, Otto, figure skating
Jenkins, Ferguson, baseball
Josenhans, Andreas, yachting
Juckes, Gordon, hockey builder
Kelly, Leonard (Red), hockey
Kidd, Bruce, track mild-distance
Kirby, Kirby, bobsled
Kreiner, Kathy, skiing
Krol, Joe, football
Kwong, Norm, football
Lafleur, Guy, hockey
Lancaster, Ron, football
Laumann, Silken, rowing
Le cavelier, Rene, broadcasting
Lee-Gartner, Kerrin, skiing
Lemieux, Mario, hockey
Leonard, Stan, golf
Lessard, Lucille, archery
Lévesque, Jean-Louis, equestrian
Lidstone, Dorothy, archery
Loney, Don, football builder
Longden, Johnny, horse racing
Loomer, Lorne, rowing
Lovell, Jocelyn, cycling
Luftspring, Sammy, boxing
MacDonald, Irene, diving
MacDonald, Noel, basketball
McKinnon, Archie, rowing
MacKinnon, Lt. Col. Dan, harness racing builder
McLarnin, Jimmy, boxing
MacMillan, Sandy, yachting
McBean, Marnie, rowing
McNaughton, Duncan, field high jump
McPherson, Donald, figure skating
Magnussen, Karen, figure skating
Mahovlich, Frank, hockey
Marchildon, Phil, baseball
Martini, Paul, figure skating
Miles, John C., marathon swimming
Millar, Ian, equestrian

▶

▶ **Mitchell,** Ray, bowling
Muir, Debbie, synchro swim coach
Nattrass, Susan, trap shooting
Nicholas, Cindy, marathon swimming
Northcott, Ron, curling
O'Donnell, Bill, harness racing
Orr, Robert (Bobby), hockey
Orser, Brian, figure skating
Ottenbrite, Anne, swimming
Parker, Jackie, football
Paul, Robert, figure skating
Peden, Doug, multi-sport
Percy, Karen, skiing
Perry, Gordon, football
Podborski, Steve, skiing
Pollock, Sam, hockey builder
Porter, R.A. (Bobby), multi-sport
Post, Sandra, golf
Presley, Gerald, bobsled
Primrose, John, trap shooting
Ramage, Pat, skiing builder
Read, Ken, skiing
Reed, George, football
Richard, Henri, hockey
Richard, Maurice (Rocket), hockey
Richardson, Arnold, curling
Richardson, Ernie, curling
Richardson, Garnet, curling
Richardson, Wes, curling
Robertson, Bruce, swimming
Robinson, Graydon, bowling
Rogers, Doug, judo
Saunders, Claude, rowing builder
Schmidt, Milt, hockey
Schneider, Bert, boxing
Scott, Barbara Ann, figure skating

Seller, Peggy, synchro swimming
Shedd, Marjory, badminton
Smith, Graham, swimming
Sorensen, Gerry, skiing
Steen, Dave, decathlon
Stewart, Marlene, golf
Stewart, Nels, hockey
Stewart, Ron, football
Stirling, Hugh, football
Storey, R.A. (Red), all-around
Stukus, Annis, football builder
Sullivan, Jack, sports journalism
Tanner, Elaine, swimming
Taylor, Ron, baseball
Tewksbury, Mark, swimming
Thom, Linda, shooting
Thompson, James, speedboating builder
Townsend, Cathy, bowling
Trifunov, James, wrestling
Turcotte, Ron, horse racing
Underhill, Barbara, figure skating
Vanderburg, Helen, synchro swimming
Van Vliet, Maury, builder
Wagner, Barbara, figure skating
Waldo, Carolyn, synchro swimming
Waples, Keith, harness racing
Watson, Ken J., curling
Weslock, Nick, golf
Wheeler, Lucille, skiing
Whitaker, Brig. Gen. Denis, equestrian builder
Wilson, Harold A., speed boating
Worrall, Jim, builder
Young, Michael, bobsled

Source: *Canadian Sports Hall of Fame*

* New members in 1997

Canadian Press Athlete of the Year

	Male (Lionel Conacher Award)	Female (Bobbie Rosenfeld Award)
1932	**Somerville,**Sandy, golf	No award
1933	**Komonen,** Dave, track and field	**Mackenzie,** Ada, golf
1934	**Webster,** Harold, track and field	**Dewar,** Phyllis, swimming
1935	**Rankine,**Robert (Scotty), track and field	**Meagher,** Aileen, track and field
1936	**Edwards,** Phil, track and field	**Taylor,** Betty, track and field
1937	**Apps,** Syl, hockey	**Higgins,** Robina, track and field
1938	**Stirling,**Hugh (Bummer), football	**Macdonald,** Noel, basketball
1939	**Hanson,** Fritz, football	**Thacker,** Mary Rose, figure skating
1940	**Cote,** Gerard, track and field	**Walton,** Dorothy, badminton
1941	**Golab,** Tony, football	**Thacker,** Mary Rose, figure skating
1946	**Krol,** Joe, football	**Scott,** Barbara Ann, figure skating
1947	**Krol,** Joe, football	**Scott,** Barbara Ann, figure skating
1948	**O'Connor,** Buddy, hockey	**Scott,** Barbara Ann, figure skating
1949	**Filchock,** Frank, football	**Strong,** Irene, swimming
1950	**Conacher,** Lionel named athlete of the half century (no athlete of the year)	**Rosenfeld,** Bobbie, track and field, named athlete of the half century (no athlete of the year)
1952	**Richard,** Maurice, hockey	**Stewart,** Marlene, golf
1953	**Hepburn,** Doug, weightlifting	**Stewart,** Marlene, golf
1954	**Ferguson,** Rich, track and field	**Bell,** Marilyn, swimming
1955	**Kwong,** Normie, football	**Bell,** Marilyn, swimming
1956	**Beliveau,** Jean, hockey	**Stewart,** Marlene, golf
1957	**Richard,** Maurice, hockey	**Stewart,** Marlene, golf
1958	**Richard,** Maurice, hockey	**Wheeler,** Lucile, skiing
1959	**Jackson,** Russ, football	**Heggtveit,** Anne, skiing
1960	**Stewart,** Ron, football	**Heggtveit,** Anne, skiing
1961	**Kidd,** Bruce, track and field	**Stewart,** Mary, swimming

1962	**Kidd,** Bruce, track and field	**Stewart,** Mary, swimming
1963	**Howe,** Gordie, hockey	**Stewart Streit,** Marlene, golf
1964	**Crothers,** Bill, track and field	**Burka,** Petra, figure skating
1965	**Hull,** Bobby, hockey	**Burka,** Petra, figure skating
1966	**Hull,** Bobby, hockey	**Tanner,** Elaine, swimming
1967	**Jenkins,** Ferguson, baseball	**Greene,** Nancy, skiing
1968	**Jenkins,** Ferguson, baseball	**Greene,** Nancy, skiing
1969	**Jackson,** Russ, football	**Boys,** Beverley, diving
1970	**Orr,** Bobby, hockey	**Boys,** Beverley, diving
1971	**Jenkins,** Ferguson, baseball	**Van Kiekebelt,** Debbie, track and field;
		Brill, Debbie, track and field (tie)
1972	**Esposito,** Phil, hockey	**Bourassa,** Jocelyn, golf
1973	**Esposito,** Phil, hockey	**Magnussen,** Karen, figure skating
1974	**Jenkins,** Ferguson, baseball	**Cook,** Wendy, swimming
1975	**Clarke,**Bobby, hockey	**Garapick,** Nancy, swimming
1976	**Joy,** Greg, track and field	**Kreiner,** Kathy, skiing
1977	**Lafleur,** Guy, hockey	**Nicholas,** Cindy, swimming
1978	**Smith,** Graham, swimming	**Jones-Konihowski,** Diane, track and field
1979	**Villeneuve,** Gilles, auto racing	**Post,** Sandra, golf
1980	**Gretzky,** Wayne, hockey	**Post,** Sandra, golf
1981	**Gretzky,** Wayne, hockey	**Wainman,** Tracey, figure skating
1982	**Gretzky,** Wayne, hockey	**Sorensen,** Gerry, skiing
1983	**Gretzky,** Wayne, hockey	**Bassett,** Carling, tennis
1984	**Baumann,** Alex, swimming	**Bernier,** Sylvie, diving
1985	**Gretzky,** Wayne, hockey	**Bassett,** Carling, tennis
1986	**Johnson,** Ben, track and field	**Graham,** Laurie, skiing
1987	**Johnson,** Ben, track and field	**Waldo,** Carolyn, synchronized swimming
1988	**Lemieux,** Mario, hockey	**Waldo,** Carolyn, synchronized swimming
1989	**Gretzky,** Wayne, hockey	**Kelesi,** Helen, tennis
1990	**Browning,** Kurt, figure skating	**Kelesi,** Helen, tennis
1991	**Browning,** Kurt, figure skating	**Laumann,** Silken, rowing
1992	**Tewksbury,** Mark, swimming	**Laumann,** Silken, rowing
1993	**Lemieux,** Mario, hockey	**Pace,** Kate, skiing
1994	**Stojko,** Elvis, figure skating	**Bedard,** Myriam, biathlon
1995	**Villeneuve,** Jacques, auto racing	**Auch,** Susan, speed skating
1996	**Bailey,** Donovan, track	**Sydor,** Alison, cycling
1997	**Villeneuve,** Jacques, auto racing	**Kane,** Lorie, golf
1998	**Walker,** Larry, baseball	**LeMay Doan,** Catriana, speed skating

Source: *Canadian Press*

The 13th Pan American Games

The 13th Pan American Games in Winnipeg lasted 18 days, featured a record 196 Canadian medals, eight drug suspensions and seven Cuban defections. The Games were a fantastic experience for many of the 5,000 athletes and estimated 100,000 visitors. The Games ran very smoothly, thanks to an army of 20,000 volunteers. Canada finished second in the medal standings behind perennial champion United States (296). Cuba was third with 156, but the island nation did have more golds (69) than Canada (64). It was the first time since the Pan Am Games were last held in Winnipeg in 1967 that Canada had finished anywhere other than third in the overall standings.

Not all countries sent their top athletes. In swimming, the U.S. won the most medals—37 to Canada's 32—despite sending second- and third-tier athletes. As host country, Canada sent most of its best.

There were a record 41 sports contested in Winnipeg, six more than the Olympics.

"There will probably be no more than 28 or 30 (sports)" at the 2003 Games in Santo Domingo, Dominican Republic, said organizing committee president Joaquin Puello. Cuban defections were prominent and the attention paid to the defectors and the presence of sports agents targeting Cuban baseball players infuriated Cuban leader Fidel Castro, who lashed out at Canada.

The Games were run with a $140 million budget—more than $100 million of that from the three levels of government.

Source: *Canadian Press*

1999 Pan American Games Medal Standings

Country	Gold	Silver	Bronze	Total	Country	Gold	Silver	Bronze	Total
United States	106	110	80	296	Guatemala	2	1	1	4
Canada	64	52	80	196	Uruguay	0	1	3	4
Cuba	69	40	47	156	Bahamas	2	0	1	3
Brazil	25	32	44	101	Bermuda	1	2	0	3
Argentina	25	19	28	72	Surinam	1	0	1	2
Mexico	11	16	30	57	Barbados	0	1	1	2
Colombia	7	17	18	42	Panama	0	1	1	2
Venezuela	7	16	17	40	Netherlands Antilles	1	0	0	1
Jamaica	3	4	6	13	Cayman Islands	0	1	0	1
Puerto Rico	1	3	9	13	Honduras	0	1	0	1
Chile	1	3	7	11	Costa Rica	0	0	1	1
Dominican Republic	1	3	5	9	El Salvador	0	0	1	1
Ecuador	1	2	5	8	Trinidad & Tobago	0	0	1	1
Peru	0	2	6	8					

Source: *Canadian Press*

Canadian Medalists at the 13th Pan American Games

GOLD:

Men's Canoe: Steve Giles, Lake Echo, N.S., *C-1 1,000;*

Women's Kayak: Marie-Josee Gibeau-Ouimet, Lachine, Que., Liza Racine, Lac Sergent, Que., Karen Furneaux, Waverley, N.S., Carrie Lightbound, Mississauga, Ont., *K-4 500;*
Karen Furneaux, Waverley, N.S., *K1 500;*
Marie-Josee Gibeau-Ouimet, Lachine, Que., Carrie Lightbound, Mississauga, Ont., *K2 500.*

Women's Gymnastics: Yvonne Tousek, Cambridge, Ont., Lise Leveille, Burnaby, B.C., Michelle Conway, Toronto, Kate Richardson, Coquitlam, B.C., Emilie Fournier, Iberville, Que., Julie Beaulieu, Montreal, *Team Competition.*
Yvonne Tousek, Cambridge, Ont., *Uneven Bars.*
Lise Leveille, Burnaby, B.C., *Balance beam.*
Yvonne Tousek, Cambridge, Ont., *Floor exercises.*

Men's Gymnastics: Alexander (Sasha) Jeltkov, Montreal, *High Bar.*

Women's Triathlon: Sharon Donnelly, Ottawa.

Men's Cycling Individual Time Trial: Eric Wohlberg, Levack, Ont.

Women's Cycling 500 Time Trial: Tanya Dubnicoff, Winnipeg.

3000 steeplechase: Joel Bourgeois, Grand-Digue, N.B.

Women's Rowing: Theresa Luke, Forest Grove, B.C., Emma Robinson, Winnipeg, *Coxless pairs.*
Marnie McBean, Toronto, *Single Sculls.*
Laryssa Biesenthal, Walkerton, Ont., and Jenn Browett, Victoria, *Double Sculls.*

Men's Rowing: Derek Nesbitt-Porter, Victoria, *Single Sculls.*

Badminton: Brent Olynyk, West Vancouver, B.C., and Iain Sydie, Toronto, *Men's Doubles Final.*
Sydie and Denyse Julien, Calgary, *Mixed Doubles.*
Robbyn Hermitage, Kitchener, Ont., and Milaine Cloutier, Calgary, *Women's Doubles Final.*

Women's Diving: Eryn Bulmer, Edmonton, *3-Metre Springboard.*
Emilie Heymans, Greenfield Park, Que., *Platform.*

Men's Wrestling: Guivi Sissaouri, Montreal, *58 kg.*

Women's Air Pistol: Kim Eagles, Maple Ridge, B.C.

Women's Cycling: Tanya Dubnicoff, Winnipeg.

Men's High Jump: Mark Boswell, Brampton, Ont., and Kwaku Boateng, Montreal.

Men's 1,500-metres: Graham Hood, Burlington, Ont.

Women's Water Polo Team.

Men's Sailing: Richard Clarke, Toronto, *Finn Final.*
Oskar Johansson, Burlington, Ont., *Singlehand Sunfish Open Final.*

Women's Sailing: Kelly Hand, Carman, Man., *Laser Radial Final.*

Swimming: Laura Nicholls, Waterloo, Ont., *Women's 100 Freestyle.*
Joanne Malar, Hamilton, Ont., *Women's 400 Medley.*
Jessica Deglau, Vancouver, Malar, Marianne Limpert, Fredericton, Nicholls, *Women's' 4x200 Freestyle Relay.*
Curtis Myden, Calgary, *Men's 400 Individual Medley.*
Jessica Deglau, Vancouver, *Women's 200 Freestyle.*
Lauren van Oosten, Nanaimo, B.C., *200 Breaststroke.*
Kelly Stefanyshyn, Winnipeg, *Women's 100 Backstroke.*
Jessica Deglau, Vancouver, Marianne Limpert, Fredericton, Sarah Evanetz, Vancouver, Laura Nicholls, Waterloo, Ont.), *Women's 4x100 Freestyle.*
Morgan Knabe, Edmonton, *Men's 200 Breaststroke.*
Shamek Pietucha, Edmonton, *Men's 200 Butterfly.*
Joanne Malar, Hamilton, *Women's 200 Individual Medley.*
Curtis Myden, Calgary, *Men's 200 Individual Medley.*
Jessica Deglau, Vancouver, *Women's 200 Butterfly.*

Men's Judo: Nicolas Gill, Montreal, 100 kg.

Men's Beach Volleyball: Jody Holden, Shelburne, N.S. and Conrad Leinemann, Kelowna, B.C.

Men's Road Race: Brian Walton, North Delta, B.C.

Men's Field Hockey Team.

Squash: Graham Ryding, Toronto, *Men's Singles.*
Melaine Jans, Toronto, *Women's Singles.*
Graham Ryding, Toronto, Kelly Patrick, Edmonton, Jamie Crombie, Calgary, *Men's Team.*
Melanie Jans, Toronto, Marnie Baizley and Carolyn Russell, Winnipeg, *Women's Team.*

Women's Combined Clean & Jerk and Snatch: Maryse Turcotte, Brossard, Que., *58 kg.*
Miel McGerrigle, Vancouver, *63 kg.*

Synchronized Swimming: Claire Carver-Dias, Mississuaga, Ont. and Fanny Letourneau, Deux-Montagnes, Que., *Duet Free.*

Synchronized Swimming: *Team Free.*

Men's Softball Team.

Fencing: Even Gravel, Montreal, Michel Boulos,

Candiac, Que., Marc Hassoun, Montreal, *Men's Team Sabre*.
Women's Taekwondo: Roxanne Forget, Crabtree, Que., *49 kg*.
Men's Water Ski Slalom: Andrew Ross, Belleville, Ont.
Men's Water Ski Tricks: Jaret Llewellyn, Innisfail, Alta.
Men's Water Ski Jump: Jaret Llewellyn, Innisfail, Alta.
Rhythmic Gymnastics: Emilie Livington, Toronto, *Individual All-Around*.
Equestrian: Ian Millar, Perth, Ont., *Individual Stadium Jump*.

SILVER:

Women's Canoe: Attila Buday and Tamas Buday Jr., Mississauga, Ont., *C-2 1,000*.
Men's Canoe-Kayak : Steve Giles, Lake Echo, N.S., *C1 500*;
Maxime Boilard, Lac-Beauport, Que., Howard Pellerin, Halifax, *C2 500*.
Men's 5000 metres: Jeffrey Schiebler, New Westminister, B.C.
Women's Cycling Individual Time Trial: Lyne Bessette, Knowlton, Que.
Men's Gymnastics: Alexander Jeltkov, Montreal, *Individual All-Around*.
Women's Gymnastics: Michelle Conway, Toronto, *Individual All-Around*.
Julie Beaulieu, Montreal , *Uneven Bars*.
Michelle Conway, Toronto , *Floor exercises*.
Women's Rowing: Tracy Duncan, Saskatoon, Sask., *Lightweight single scull*.
Men's Shooting: Wayne Sorensen, Calgary, *50-metre prone free rifle*.
Women's Table Tennis: Women: Lijuan Geng, Ottawa, Chris Xu, Vancouver, Petra Cada, Ottawa.
Men's Rowing: Andrew Bordon, Toronto, and Kyle Warrington, Oakville, Ont., *Lightweight Double Sculls*.
Badminton: Charmaine Reid, Fort Erie, Ont., *Women's Singles Final*.
Charmaine Reid, Denyse Julien, Calgary, *Women's Doubles Final*.
Stuart Arthur, Mississauga, Ont., *Men's Singles*.
Brent Olynyk, West Vancouver, and Robbyn Hermitage, Kitchener, Ont., *Mixed Doubles*.
Women's 1,500 metres: Leah Pells, Langley, B.C.
Men's Wrestling: Paul Ragusa, Kingston, Ont., *54 kg*.
Gary Holmes, Thornhill, Ont., *85 kg*.
Equestrian: Shannon Oldham-Dueck, Langley, B.C., (on Korona), *Individual Dressage*.
Women's Diving: Blythe Hartley, Vancouver, *Platform*.
Racquetball: Lori-Jane Powell, Prince Albert, Sask., and Deborah Ward, Prince George, B.C., *Women's Doubles*.
Christie Van Hees, Kelowna, B.C., *Singles*.
Roger Harripersad, Calgary, and Kelly Kerr, North Vancouver, B.C., *Men's Doubles*.
Women's Air Rifle: Sharon Bowes, Waterloo, Ont.
Table Tennis: Lijuan Geng, Ottawa, *Women's Singles*.
Men's 4x100 relay: Donovan Bailey, Oakville, Ont., Glenroy Gilbert, Ottawa, Brad McCuaig, Calgary, Trevino Betty, London, Ont.
Women's Sailing: Caroll-Ann Alie, Gracefield, Que., *Mistal Final*.
Women's Moutain Bike: Alison Sydor, Victoria.
Swimming: Morgan Knabe, Edmonton, *Men's 100 Breastroke*.
Shamek Pietucha, Edmonton, *Men's 100 Butterfly*.
Jessica Deglau, Vancouver, *Women's 100 Butterfly*.
Kelly Stefanyshyn, Winnipeg, Lauren Van Oosten, Nanaimo, B.C., Jessica Deglau, Vancouver, Laura Nicholls, Waterloo, Ont., *Women's 4 x 100 Medley Relay*.

Jennifer Button, Waterloo, Ont., *Women's 200 Butterfly*.
Women's Judo: Niki Jenkins, Selkirk, Man., *78 kg*.
Men's Cycling: Gord Fraser, Nepean, Ont.
Men's Tenpin Bowling: Mathieu Chouinard, Quebec City, Marc Doi, Toronto, Alan Tone, Hamilton, Jean-Sebastien Lessard, Quebec City, *Team of Four*.
Women's Combined Clean & Jerk and Snatch: Nancy Niro, Greenfield Park, Que., *58 kg*.
Women's Team Fencing: Sherraine Schalm, Brooks, Alta., Heather Landymore, Halifax, Monique Kavelaars, Toronto.
Boxing: Dana Laframboise, Regina, *60 kg*.
Zaya Younan, Hamilton , *57 kg*.
Jeremy Molitor, Sarnia, Ont., *67 kg*.
Scott MacIntosh, Sydney, N.S., *71 kg*.
Mark Simmons, Toronto, *91 kg*.
Women's Taekwondo: Barbara Pak, Edmonton, *Women's 67 kg*.
Women's Basketball Team.
Women's Softball Team.
Men's Water Skiing: Kreg Llewellyn, Innisfail, Alta.
Women's Water Ski Slalom: Susan Graham, Kitchener, Ont.
Men's Archery Team.
Women's Handball Team.

BRONZE:

Men's Kayak: Adrian Richardson, Burritts Rapids, Ont., *K-1 1,000*.
Men's Gymnastics: Darin Good, Fredericton, N.B., Richard Ikeda, Abbotsford, B.C., Alexander Jeltkov, Montreal, Kristan Burley, Truro, N.S., Roshawn Amendra, Toronto, *Team Competition*.
Kristan Burley, Truro, N.S., *Vault*.
Men's Triathlon: Simon Whitfield, Kingston, Ont.
Men's Shot Put: Bradley Snyder, Windsor, Ont.
Women's Triathlon: Carol Montgomery, Sechelt, B.C.
Women's Hammer Throw: Caroline Wittrin, Vancouver.
Women's Shooting: Christina Ashcroft, Waterloo, Ont.
Men's Trap Shooting: George Leary, Newmarket, Ont.
Men's Skeet: Clayton Miller, Kelowna, B.C.
Men's 50-metre prone free rifle: Henry Gerow, Winnipeg.
3000 steeplechase: Jean-Nicolas Duval, Trois-Rivieres, Que.
800 metres: Zachary Whitmarsh, Victoria.
Men's Pole Vault: Jason Pearce, Richmond, B.C.
Men's Greco-Roman Wrestling: Colbie Bell, Edmonton, *97 kg*.
Men's Rowing: Phil Graham, Corner Brook, Nfld., Kevin White, Victoria, *Coxless pairs*.
Phil Graham, Corner Brook, N.S., Kevin White, Victoria, Ken Kozel, Thorold, Ont., Andrew Hoskins, Edmonton, *Coxless Fours*.
Women's Rowing: Katrina Scott, Toronto and Nathalie Benzing, Toronto , *Lightweight Double Sculls*.
Renata Troc, London, Ont., Tracy Duncan, Saskatoon, Sask., Katrina Scott, Toronto, Nathalie Benzing, Toronto, *Lightweight Quadruple Sculls*.
Women's Karate: Btissima Es-Sadiqi, Aylmer, Que., *Up to 53 kg*.
Lisa Ling, Kitimat, B.C., *Up to 60 kg*.
Men's Table Tennis: Xavier Therien, Sherbrooke, Que., Pradeeban Peter-Paul, Ottawa, Horatio Pintea, Gatineau, Que.
Badminton: Denyse Julien, Calgary, *Women's Singles*.
Denyse Julien, Calgary, and Charmaine Reid, Fort Erie, Ont., *Women's Doubles*.
Mike Beres, Mt. Pleasant, and Bryan Moody, Pointe-Claire, Que., *Men's Doubles*.
Men's Cycling 1-km time trial: Douglas Baron, Calgary.

Men's Diving: Blythe Hartley, Vancouver, *3-Metre Springboard*.
Women's Discus: Jason Tunks, London, Ont.
Women's 10,000: Tina Connelly, Port Coquitlam, B.C.
Men's Wrestling: Marty Calder, St. Catherines, Ont., *63 kg*.
Daniel Igali, Surrey, B.C., *69 kg*.
Dean Schmeichel, Prince Albert, Sask., *97 kg*.
Wayne Weathers, Oshawa, Ont., *130 kg*.
Roller Sports Artistic: Ron Woods, and Sherri Bint, Caledonia, Ont., *Pairs*.
Men's Air Rifle: Wayne Sorenson, Calgary.
Table Tennis: Petra Čada, Ottawa, *Women's Singles*.
Men's Water Polo Team.
Men's Sailing: David Sweeney and Kevin Smith, Toronto, *Catam Hobie 16 Open Final*.
Mixed Sailing: Larry MacDonald, Hamilton, Ont., Trevor Born, Toronto, Julie-Marie Innes-MacDonald, Carlisle, Ont., *Three Hand Lightning Open Final*.
Women's Modern Pentathlon: Kara Grant, Charlottetown, P.E.I.
Men's Baseball Team.
Men's Volleyball Team.
Men's Mountain Bike: Chris Sheppard, Kamloops, B.C.
Swimming: Mark Johnston, St. Catharines, Ont., *Men's 200 Freestyle*.
Marianne Limpert, Frederiction, *Women's 100 Freestyle*.
Owen von Richter, Mississauga, Ont., *Men's 400 Individual Medley*.
Mark Johnston, St. Catharines, Ont., Brian Johns, Richmond, B.C., Yannick Lupien, Aylmer, Que., Richard Say, Salmon Arm, B.C., *Men's 4x200 Freesytle Relay*.
Joanne Malar, Hamilton, *Women's 400 Freestyle*.
Richard Say, Salmon Arm, B.C., *Men's 400 Freestyle*.
Karine Chevrier, Montreal, *Women's 100 Butterfly*.
Lauren van Oosten, *Women's 100 Breaststroke*.
Marianne Limpert, Fredericton, *Women's 200 Individual Medley*.

Lindsay Beavers, Orangeville, Ont., *Women's 800 Freestyle*.
Owen von Richter, Mississauga, Ont., *Men's 200 Individual Medley*.
Mark Versfeld, Fort McMurray, Alta., Morgan Knabe, and Shamek Pietucha, Edmonton, Yannick Lupien, Aylmer, Que., *Men's 4x100 Medley Relay*.
Laura Nicholls, Waterloo, Ont., *Women's 50 Freestyle*.
Kelly Stefanyshyn, Winnipeg, *Women's 200 Backstroke*.
Women's Judo: Luce Baillargeon, Montreal, *52 kg*.
Brigitte Lastrade, Montreal, *57 kg*.
Men's Judo: Keith Morgan, Calgary, *90 kg*.
Maxime Roberge, Montreal, *81 kg*.
Women's Field Hockey Team.
Fencing: Laurie Shong, Vancouver, *Men's Individual Epee*.
Julie Mahoney, Montreal, *Women's Individual Foil*.
Michel Boulos, Candiac, Que., *Men's Individual Sabre*.
Women's Tennis: Renata Kolbovic, Vancouver and Aneta Soukup, Kitchener, *Doubles*.
Equestrian: Beth Underhill, Schomberg, Ont., Ian Millar, Perth, Ont., Eric Lamaze, Schomberg, Ont., Jill Henselwood, Oxford Mills, Ont., *Team Stadium Jump*.
Women's Taekwondo: Gael Texier, Montreal, *57 kg*.
Dominique Bosshart, Landmark, Man., *67 kg*.
Men's Taekwondo: Raymond Mourad, Laval, Que., *58 kg*.
Darrell Henegan, Montreal, *80 kg*.
Men's Combined Clean & Jerk and Snatch: Jean Lassen, Whitehorse, *75 kg*.
Boxing: Troy Ross, Brampton, Ont., *81 kg*.
Tenpin Bowling: Marc Doi, Toronto, *Men's Individual Masters*.
Jennifer Willis, Duncan, B.C., *Women's Individual Masters*.
Women's Water Ski Jump: Kim De Macedo, Shawnigan Lake, B.C.
Rhythmic Gymnastics: *Groups*.

Source: *Canadian Press*

QUICK REFERENCE

Temperature Equivalents

(Celsius and Fahrenheit)

°C	°F	°C	°F	°C	°F	°C	°F	°C	°F
-50	-58	-30	-22	-10	14	10	50	30	86
-49	-56.2	-29	-20.2	-9	15.8	11	51.8	31	87.8
-48	-54.4	-28	-18.4	-8	17.6	12	53.6	32	89.6
-47	-52.6	-27	-16.6	-7	19.4	13	55.4	33	91.4
-46	-50.8	-26	-14.8	-6	21.2	14	57.2	34	93.2
-45	-49	-25	-13	-5	23	15	59	35	95
-44	-47.2	-24	-11.2	-4	24.8	16	60.8	36	96.8
-43	-45.4	-23	-9.4	-3	26.6	17	62.6	37	98.6
-42	-43.6	-22	-7.6	-2	28.4	18	64.4	38	100.4
-41	-41.8	-21	-5.8	-1	30.2	19	66.2	39	102.2
-40	-40	-20	-4	0	32	20	68	40	104
-39	-38.2	-19	-2.2	1	33.8	21	69.8	41	105.8
-38	-36.4	-18	-0.4	2	35.6	22	71.6	42	107.6
-37	-34.6	-17	1.4	3	37.4	23	73.4	43	109.4
-36	-32.8	-16	3.2	4	39.2	24	75.2	44	111.2
-35	-31	-15	5	5	41	25	77	45	113
-34	-29.2	-14	6.8	6	42.8	26	78.8	50	122
-33	-27.4	-13	8.6	7	44.6	27	80.6	100	212
-32	-25.6	-12	10.4	8	46.4	28	82.4	150	302
-31	-23.8	-11	12.2	9	48.2	29	84.2	200	392

Canadian Imperial and Metric Measures

Name	Abbrev.	Equivalent in Related Units	Metric Equivalent
■ Length			
inch	in.	—	2.54 cm
foot	ft.	12 in.	30.48 cm
yard	yd.	3 ft.; 36 in.	0.91 m
mile	mi.	1 760 yd.; 5 280 ft.	1.609 km
■ Mass (Weight)			
grain	gr.	—	0.06 g
dram	dr.	27.343 gr.	1.77 g
ounce	oz.	16 dr.	28.35 g
pound	lb.	16 oz.	0.453 kg
hundredweight			
(short)	cwt.	100 lb.	45.36 kg
(long)	cwt.	112 lb.	50.80 kg
ton (short)	—	2 000 lb.	0.907 t
ton (long)	—	2 240 lb.	1.016 t
■ Volume and Capacity			
fluid dram	fl. dr.	0.22 cu. in.	3.55 cm^3
fluid ounce	fl. oz.	8 fl. dr.; 1.7 cu. in.	28.41 cm^3
pint	pt.	20 fl. oz.; 34.7 cu. in.	568.3 cm^3
quart	qt.	2 pt.; 69.4 cu. in.	1.14 dm^3
gallon	gal.	4 qt.; 277 cu. in.	4.55 dm^3
peck	pk.	2 gal.; 555 cu. in.	9.09 dm^3
bushel	bu.	4 pk.; 2 219 cu. in.	36.37 dm^3
barrel (oil)	bbl	35 gal.	0.159 m^3
cubic foot	ft.^{3}	1 728 in.^{3}	0.028 m^3
cubic yard	yd.^{3}	27 ft.^{3}	0.765 m^3
■ Area			
square foot	ft.^{2}	144 sq. in.	0.09 m^2
square yard	yd.^{2}	9 sq. ft.	0.836 m^2
acre	—	4 840 sq. yd.	4 047 m^2
square mile	sq. mi.	640 acres	2.590 km^2

Source: *Gage Canadian Dictionary*

Roman Numerals

I	1	VII	7	XX	20	C	100
II	2	VIII	8	XXX	30	CC	200
III	3	IX	9	XL	40	CD	400
IV	4	X	10	L	50	D	500
V	5	XI	11	LX	60	CM	900
VI	6	XIX	19	XC	90	M	1 000

$\overline{V}$	5 000
$\overline{X}$	10 000
$\overline{L}$	50 000
$\overline{C}$	100 000
$\overline{D}$	500 000
$\overline{M}$	1 000 000

Canada's Food Guide To Healthy Eating[1]

Canada's Food Guide, revised in November of 1992, recognizes that the amount of food each Canadian needs every day from the four food groups and other foods depends on age, body size, activity level, whether the individual is male or female, and if the individual is pregnant or breast-feeding. That's why the Food Guide gives a range of possible servings for each food group—young children can choose the lower number of recommended servings from a particular group, while male teenagers can go to the higher number. Most other people can choose servings somewhere in between.

Canada's Food Guide recommends, every day:

■ 5 to 12 servings from the grain products group. An example of one serving would be one slice of bread; 30 g of cold cereal or 175 mL of hot cereal. Two servings would be a bagel, pita or bun; or 250 mL of rice or pasta.

■ 5 to 10 servings of vegetables and fruit.

One serving would be one medium size vegetable or fruit; 125 mL of fresh, frozen or canned vegetables or fruit; 250 mL of salad; or 125 mL of juice.

■ 2 to 3 servings of meat or alternatives. One serving would be 50-100 g of meat, poultry or fish; 1-2 eggs; 125-250 mL of beans; 100 g of tofu; or 30 mL of peanut butter.

■ Recommended servings of milk products vary according to age: 2-3 servings for children aged 4-9; 3-4 servings for young people aged 10-16; 2-4 servings for adults; and 3-4 servings for pregnant or breast-feeding women. Examples of one serving would be 250 mL of milk, 50 g of cheese or 175 g of yogurt.

Taste and enjoyment can also come from other foods and beverages that are not part of the four food groups. Some of these foods are higher in fat or calories, so it is recommended that these foods be used in moderation. The important things to remember are: enjoy a variety of foods from each group every day and choose lower-fat foods more often.

Source: Health and Welfare Canada

(1) For people four years and over.

Functions of Nutrients

Calcium aids in the formation and maintenance of strong bones and teeth; promotes healthy nerve function and normal blood clotting.

Carbohydrate supplies energy; assists in the utilization of fats.

Fat supplies energy; aids in the absorption of fat-soluble vitamins.

Fibre provides undigestible bulk, which encourages the normal elimination of body wastes.

Folacin (folic acid) aids red blood cell formation.

Iodine aids in function of the thyroid gland.

Iron combines with protein to form hemoglobin, the red blood cell constituent that transports oxygen and carbon dioxide.

Magnesium aids in formation and maintenance of strong bones and teeth; aids in energy metabolism and tissue formation.

Phosphorus aids in formation and maintenance of strong bones and teeth.

Protein builds and repairs body tissues; builds antibodies, the blood components that fight infection.

Riboflavin (vitamin B_2) maintains healthy skin and eyes; maintains a normal nervous system; releases energy to body cells during metabolism.

Thiamin (vitamin B_1) releases energy from carbohydrate; aids normal growth and appetite.

Vitamin A aids normal bone and tooth development; promotes good night vision; maintains the health of skin and membranes.

Vitamin B_{12} (cobalamin) aids in red blood cell formation; maintains healthy nerve and gastrointestinal tissues.

Vitamin C (ascorbic acid) maintains healthy teeth and gums; maintains strong vessel walls.

Vitamin E (tocopherol)protects the fat in body tissues from oxidation.

Zinc aids in energy and metabolism and tissue formation.

Source: *Canada's Food Guide Handbook*

Health Canada   Santé Canada

CANADA'S
Food Guide
TO HEALTHY EATING

Enjoy a variety
of foods from each
group every day.

Choose lower-
fat foods
more often.

Grain Products
Choose whole grain
and enriched
products more
often.

Vegetables & Fruit
Choose dark green and
orange vegetables and
orange fruit more often.

Milk Products
Choose lower-fat
milk products more
often.

Meat & Alternatives
Choose leaner meats,
poultry and fish, as well
as dried peas, beans and
lentils more often.

Canadä

CANADA'S
Food Guide
TO HEALTHY EATING
FOR PEOPLE FOUR YEARS AND OVER

Different People Need Different Amounts of Food

The amount of food you need every day from the 4 food groups and other foods depends on your age, body size, activity level, whether you are male or female and if you are pregnant or breast-feeding. That's why the Food Guide gives a lower and higher number of servings for each food group. For example, young children can choose the lower number of servings while male teenagers can go to the higher number. Most other people can choose servings somewhere in between.

Grain Products
5-12
SERVINGS PER DAY

1 Serving — 1 Slice — Cold Cereal 30 g — Hot Cereal 175 mL 3/4 cup

2 Servings — 1 Bagel, Pita or Bun — Pasta or Rice 250 mL 1 cup

Vegetables & Fruit
5-10
SERVINGS PER DAY

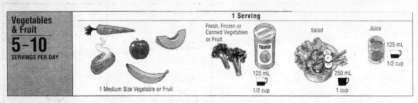

1 Serving — 1 Medium Size Vegetable or Fruit — Fresh, Frozen or Canned Vegetables or Fruit 125 mL 1/2 cup — Salad 250 mL 1 cup — Juice 125 mL 1/2 cup

Milk Products
SERVINGS PER DAY
Children 4–9 years: 2–3
Youth 10–16 years: 3–4
Adults: 2–4
Pregnant & breast-feeding
Women: 3–4

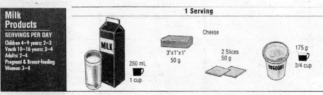

1 Serving — MILK 250 mL 1 cup — Cheese 3"x1"x1" 50 g — 2 Slices 50 g — YOGURT 175 g 3/4 cup

Other Foods

Taste and enjoyment can also come from other foods and beverages that are not part of the 4 food groups. Some of these foods are higher in fat or Calories, so use these foods in moderation.

Meat & Alternatives
2-3
SERVINGS PER DAY

1 Serving — Meat, Poultry or Fish 50-100 g — Fish 1/3–2/3 Can 50–100 g — 1-2 Eggs — Beans 125-250 mL — TOFU 100 g 1/3 cup — Peanut Butter 30 mL 2 tbsp

Enjoy eating well, being active and feeling good about yourself. That's VITALITÉ

© Minister of Supply and Services Canada 1992   Cat. No. H39-252/1992E   No changes permitted. Reprint permission not required.
ISBN 0-662-19648-1

Laundry Care Symbols

The Canadian Care Labelling Program is a voluntary one that provides consumer information on the care of textiles, usually clothing. It uses five basic symbols, illustrated in the conventional "traffic light" colours. The program takes into consideration the fabric's colourfastness (i.e. whether the dye will bleed into the water and other clothing); whether it will shrink or stretch; how bleach will affect the garment; and how it may be ironed safely.

This labelling program does not apply to upholstered furniture, mattresses, carpets, leather, fur, or yarn.

The basic symbols represent washing, bleaching, drying, ironing and drycleaning, and the colours represent stop/do not (red), be careful (yellow), and go ahead (green). The red/crossed out symbol is only used when the procedure would damage the article.

Symbol	Red	Yellow	Green
	Stop	**Be careful**	**Go ahead**
Washing	Do not wash	Hand wash in cool water; Machine wash in cool water at a gentle setting—reduced agitation (30°C); Machine wash in lukewarm water at a gentle setting—reduced agitation (40°C); Machine wash in warm water at a gentle setting—reduced agitation (50°C)	Machine wash in warm water at a normal setting (50°C); Machine wash in hot water at a normal setting (70°C)
Bleaching	Do not use chlorine bleach (Cl)	Use chlorine bleach with care (Cl)	
Drying		Dry flat (–); Tumble dry at low temperature	Tumble dry at medium to high temperature; Hang to dry; Drip dry
Ironing	Do not iron	Iron at low setting (110°C) or; Iron at medium setting (150°C) or	Iron at high setting (200°C) or
Dry Cleaning	Do not dry clean	Dry clean—with caution	Dry clean

Source: *Industry Canada*

Product Safety Symbols

Health Canada has devised a set of safety symbols for containers of household chemicals and other materials. These symbols indicate possible hazards associated with various products such as cleaning liquids and powders, paint thinners, drain cleaners, windshield washer fluids and polishes, as well as some glues and treatments for household surfaces such as brick and metal, and garden chemicals.

The symbols indicate the type of danger and are contained in a frame that indicates the degree of danger—the more sides the frame has, the more dangerous the product is. In addition to the symbols, the labels on most of these containers include a safety warning. Learn the symbols opposite and handle the materials with care, especially if children live in the home or visit often.

Follow these steps to Safety:

• Teach children that the symbols mean Danger! Do Not Touch!
• Chemical product containers, even if sealed or empty, are not toys. Never let children play with them.
• If there is anything in the label instructions that you don't understand, ask for help. Make sure the symbols and labels on containers are not removed or covered up.
• Keep household chemicals in their original containers. Never mix them together. Some mixtures can produce harmful gases.
• Close the cap on the container tightly, even if you set it down for just a moment. Make sure that child-resistant containers are working.
• Keep all chemical products out of sight and out of reach of children.

Corrosive: the product can burn skin or eyes, and if swallowed, will damage the throat and stomach.

Explosive: the container can explode if heated or punctured. Flying pieces of metal or plastic from the container can cause serious injury, especially to the eyes.

Flammable: the product or its vapous will catch fire easily if it is near heat, flames or sparks

Poison: if the product is swallowed, licked or even, in some cases inhaled, it can cause sickness or death

---

If someone is injured:

• Call your doctor or the Poison Control Centre immediately.
• Give the information from the label to the person answering.
• Take the container with you when you go for help.

October 1, 1998–September 30, 1999

APAK ANGILIK, Paul, 44. Celebrated Inuit filmmaker, Apak made pioneering documentaries on Inuit life; he produced films for the Inuit Broadcasting Corporation and documented his 3000 km journey to Greenland from Baffin Island, and a voyage across the Bering Strait on a traditional Inuit skin boat. December 31, 1998.

APPS, Charles Joseph Sylvanus (Syl), 83. Two-time Canadian champion pole-vaulter and British Empire champion in 1934; placed sixth in Berlin Olympics in 1936. Apps joined the Toronto Maple Leafs in 1936 and became the leading scorer, winning Calder Trophy; was team captain for most of his career and retired in 1947-48 season. Served as PC MPP from 1963-74. December 24, 1998.

ARMSTRONG, Jane, 84. Journalist who covered Allied forces in World War II for the *Montreal Standard*; also worked for the *Globe and Mail* and *Toronto Telegram*. June 17, 1999.

AUTRY, Gene, 91. One of Hollywood's "singing cowboys," Autry appeared in 95 films, starting in the 1930s and culminating in a TV show in the 1950s. His business interests in broadcasting and sports (he was original owner of California Angels baseball team) led him to become one of the richest men in America. October 2, 1998.

BENNETT, Peter Hally, 85. As director of Canada's national historic sites and monuments, Bennett was instrumental in having Newfoundland's archeological site L'Anse aux Meadows declared a World Heritage Site. Bennett achieved similar recognition for a Haida village in the Queen Charlotte Islands, Wood Buffalo National Park in Alberta, and the Yukon wilderness area, Kluane National Park. August 30, 1999.

BOLGER, Clarence Martin, 76. Appointed chairman of the Canadian Metric Commission in 1977, Bolger was instrumental in initiating the metric system to a reluctant audience. June 5, 1999.

BURT, Jim, 51. CBC creative head since 1975, Burt was responsible for network miniseries

such as *Conspiracy of Silence*, *The Boys of St. Vincent*, *The Diviners* and *Million Dollar Babies*. January 2, 1999.

CASTELLI, Leo, 91. New York art dealer who during his 40-year career nurtured the course of modern art, giving such artists as Jasper Johns, Robert Rauschenberg, Roy Lichenstein and Frank Stella their first solo exhibitions. August 21, 1999.

CHIASSON, Steve, 32. Barrie, Ont.-born hockey defenceman for the Carolina Hurricanes, died in a single-passenger auto accident after playoff loss. Also played with Detroit Red Wings, Calgary Flames and Hartford Whalers, and participated in 1997 with Canada's gold-medal championship team. May 3, 1999.

COHEN, Shaughnessy, 50. Died shortly after sufferering a brain hemorrhage in the House of Commons, Liberal party MP (Ontario's Windsor-St. Clair riding) Cohen was chair of Commons Justice committee. December 9, 1998.

CONRAD, Charles Peter (Pete), 69. Astronaut who became the third person to walk on the moon in 1969 on the Apollo 12 mission with the spacecraft *Intrepid*; he flew two *Gemini* missions in the 1960s and was commander of the 1973 Skylab flight. July 8, 1999.

COUCHTRY, Graham, 67. Highly regarded abstract figurative painter, Coughtry taught at the Ontario College of Art and worked in the graphics department at the CBC. He exhibited his work at Toronto's Isaacs Gallery; his paintings were also shown at New York's Guggenheim Museum and the Museum of Modern Art. Played trombone in Artists Jazz Band. January 14, 1999.

DAVID, Paul P., 79. Retired senator and founder of the Montreal Institute of Cardiology, David was a pioneer in cardiovascular surgery; under his direction, Canada's first heart transplant was carried out in 1968. April 5, 1999.

DESMOND, Trudy, 53. American-born jazz and ballad singer appeared in 1970 revue *Spring Thaw*, and continued to perform both in Toronto and New York; was music director of Toronto's Church Street Café; cut several CDs later in her career. "Make Me Rainbows." February 19, 1999.

DICKSON, Robert George Brian, 82. As Supreme Court Chief Justice (1984-90) was instrumental in applying Charter of Rights and Freedoms to the practical concerns of Canadians. He supported native treaty rights, opposed the Sunday shopping ban and declared abortion laws were contrary to the rights of women. October 17, 1998.

DIMAGGIO, Joseph Paul (Joe), 84. Celebrated not only for his outstanding baseball career with the New York Yankees, DiMaggio was also revered as the quintessential gentleman and remembered for his marriage to movie siren Marilyn Monroe. Born in 1914 to Sicilian immigrant parents, DiMaggio won the MVP designation in 1939, '41 and '47; between May 15 and July 17, 1941, he had a 56-game hitting streak, a record that remained unbroken for 40 years; played in nine World Series, the Yankees winning all but one, in 1942. He retired in 1951. March 8, 1999.

DRAPEAU, Joseph Jean, 83. Longtime mayor (1954-86) of Montreal, Drapeau worked to rid the city of organized crime; built the city's subway system; hosted Expo 67 and the 1976 Summer Olympics; and brought the Expos, Canada's first major-league team, to the city. August 12, 1999.

DUECK, Tyrell, 13. Saskatchewan cancer patient who made headlines when his parents refused conventional medical treatment for his disease and instead followed their religious faith and sought out alternative cure in Mexico. June 30, 1999.

EHRLICHMAN, John, 73. With H. R. Haldeman, was a domestic affairs advisor to Richard Nixon and imprisoned for eighteen months as a result of the 1972 Watergate scandal for obstruction of justice. He later pursued writing and art as a career. February 14, 1999.

ETIDLOOIE, Sheojuk, 70. Inuit artist whose works comprised a major part of the 1998 annual Cape Dorset art collection; although her short career spanned only her last six years, her simple prints and drawings were sold internationally. May 17, 1999.

FAIRBAIRN, Bruce, 49. Juno Award-winning producer of hard-rock bands, including Kiss, Aerosmith, Loverboy, Prism and Bon Jovi. May 17, 1999.

FAULDER, Stanley, 61. Albertan convicted of the murder of an elderly Texan heiress; brain-damaged when young and denied access to Canadian authorities, he became the subject of an international controversy when he was executed by Texas authorities for his crime after serving 22 years on death row. June 17, 1999.

FISHER, Orville Norman, 88. Fisher studied art at the Vancouver School of Art under Lawren Harris and Fred Varley, becoming a "war artist" during the Second World War. His famous *D-Day: The Assault* recorded the action in Normandy in the aftermath of D-Day. After the war he founded the graphic arts department at Vancouver's Emily Carr Institute of Art. July 13, 1999.

FLETT, Bill, 55. "Cowboy Bill" Flett began his hockey career with the L.A. Kings after the 1967 expansion of the NHL and later played with Toronto, Atlanta and Edmonton; he was renowned for his keen competitiveness, flamboyant style and goal-scoring prowess. July 12, 1999.

GALLAGHER, John Patrick, 82. Geologist who founded Dome Petroleum, he was a pioneer of oil exploration in the Arctic. December 16, 1998.

GÉLINAS, Gratien, 89. An actor and playwright, Gélinas celebrated Quebec culture, convincing the province that its own culture stood up to that of the rest of the world's. His last work, the 1986 play *The Passion of Narcisse Mondoux*, in which he portrayed an elderly man, toured for five years; he also received acclaim for the dramatic *Bousille et les justes*, *Tit-Coq* and *Yesterday the Children Were Dancing*, which portrayed a family split by conflicts between separatism and federalism. Gélinas served as chairman of the Canadian Film Development Corporation from 1969-78. March 16, 1999.

GODDEN, Margaret Rumer, 91. British author of 70 novels, children's books, biographies and poetry collections. Black Narcissus and The River were both made into films. Her work was often set in India, the home of her youth. November 8, 1998.

GORBACHEV, Raisa, 67. Wife of the last president of the USSR, Mikhail Gorbachev. Gorbachev's public image was unpopular with many Soviet citizens—her glamour and assertiveness grabbed the media spotlight. September 20, 1999.

GOWAN, Elsie Park Young, 93. Scottish-born playwright in radio and theatre, Gowan flourished in Western Canada, where she wrote stage plays (*Beeches From Bond Street, The Jasper Story*) and radio plays (*New Lamps for Old, The Building of Canada*). Her work has been produced internationally. January 23, 1999.

GRAHAM, James Wesley, 67. Pioneer in the computer industry and professor at Ontario's University of Waterloo, Graham developed the first WATFOR (Waterloo Fortran) program that corrected computer errors; it was widely used in universities around the world; also designed computer curriculums for the Ministry of Education and co-wrote textbooks. August 23, 1999.

GRAY, James Henry, 92. Popular social historian whose books reflected life in Western Canada. Gray's *The Winter Years,* a chronicle of the Depression years in the West, was published in 1966, followed by Men Against the Desert, *The Boy From Winnipeg, Red Lights on the Prairies* and *Booze.* Winner of Pierre Berton Award. November 12, 1998.

HARRINGTON, Michael Francis, 82. Host of Newfoundland's popular radio show *The Barrelman* in the 1940s, Harrington was a fervent supporter of independence for Newfoundland and Labrador prior to 1949; he co-edited a complete collection of National Convention debates, published in 1995. March 13, 1999.

HARRIS, Walter, 94. Former Liberal MP for Grey-Bruce in Ontario, responsible for introduction of registered retirement savings plan. Served as minister of citizenship and immigration, and of finance. January 10, 1999.

HASSAN II, King (b. Moulay Hassan ben Mohammed), 70. King Hassan, spent 38 years on the Moroccan throne, surpassing all other Arab monarchs, despite many attempts on his life. Responsible for the imprisonment of leftist opponents and accused of abusing human rights, Hassan released many political prisoners and participated in the Middle East peace process in the 1990s. July 23, 1999.

HERZBERG, Gerhard, 94. German-born scientist who was a world leader in molecular spectroscopy, which led to a better understanding of the structure of molecules and how they absorbed and reflected light. In 1971 Herzberg won the Nobel Prize for chemistry. He joined the National Research Council in 1948, retiring at age 90. The NRC's Herzberg Institute of Astrophysics was named after him. March 4, 1999.

HEWGILL, Roland, 69. Stratford Festival actor who first appeared in 1954, playing 35 roles in plays that included *Death of a Salesman, Oedipus Rex, Merchant of Venice* and *Alice Through the Looking Glass.* Also appeared in film: *Beautiful Dreamers*; *John and the Missus*; *Airwaves.* November 9, 1998.

HORNING, Ted, 58. Bridge expert and columnist for the *Toronto Star*, Horning became Canada's first syndicated bridge columnist. He played in the Blue Ribbon Pairs championships in 1978, placing second, and helped found the Canadian National Team championships. He later participated in tournaments representing Canada in Stockholm and New Orleans. July 19, 1999.

HUGHES, Ted, 68. Britain's poet laureate since 1984, Hughes was an accomplished poet and author of children's books. Hughes recently published *Birthday Letters*, a collection of poems that shed light on his relationship with his late wife Sylvia Plath. October 29, 1998.

HUNTER, Jim "Catfish", 53. Hunter was the first baseball "free agent" to demand a multimillion-dollar contract, in 1974; he received $3.75 million (US) to pitch with the Yankees in a five-year deal. His pitching career saw five World Series wins with both the Oakland Athletics and the Yankees. Hunter died of Lou Gehrig's disease. September 9, 1999.

HUSSEIN, King (b. Hussein bin Tal Abdullah al-Hashem), 63. British-educated Hussein, King of Jordan, was much celebrated for his lifelong quest for peace in the Middle East. For 46 years he ruled Jordan as head of the Hashemite dynasty, and in 1994 signed a peace accord with Israel. His liberal policies, such as successfully supporting multiparty elections in Jordan, gained him admiration to the end of his life. February 7, 1999.

IRWIN, William Arthur, 102. Became editor of *Maclean's* magazine in 1945, responsible for its increasing success by hiring preeminent authors such as Pierre Berton, June Callwood and Ralph Allen; headed National Film Board for three years; served as a Canadian diplomat in Australia, Brazil, Mexico and Guatemala. August 9, 1999.

ISRAEL, Charles, 78. Prolific screenwriter and novelist, Israel wrote documentaries for the National Film Board, for CBC (*The Open Grave*) and for American television (*Marcus Welby M.D.*; *The Mayflower Madam*). While serving on the United Nations Relief and Rehabilitation Administration in Germany, was instrumental in the repatriation of Czech children who had been sent to Germany after their parents had been killed by the Nazis. August 7, 1999.

JANES, Percy Maxwell, 76. Newfoundland author whose novels and poetry reflected the island's unique character. His acclaimed novel House of Hate depicted the tribulations of a Newfoundland family damaged by the father's violent rages. February 19, 1999.

JULIEN, Pauline, 70. Quebec singer, political activist and fervent separatist and feminist, Julien was jailed briefly during the War Measures Act of 1970, which was invoked to counter the FLQ-inspired October Crisis. Julien was an adherent of the music of Kurt Weill and Bertolt Brecht, also sang songs by Quebec's Gilles Vigneault and those of her own composition. October 1, 1998.

KENNEDY, John Fitzgerald Jr., 38. Son of former US president John F. Kennedy, he was the co-founder and editor of the political satire magazine *George*. An enthusiast of extreme sports, he died while piloting his Piper Saratoga airplane. Also killed were his wife, Carolyn Bessette Kennedy, and her sister Lauren Bessette. July 16, 1999.

KUBRICK, Stanley, 70. Acclaimed film director whose movie themes varied widely, from the surreal *A Clockwork Orange* to the sci-fi blockbuster *2001: A Space Odyssey*. He is regarded as one of the world's great modern filmmakers. March 7, 1999.

LAURIN, Camille, 76. A psychiatrist who turned to politics, Laurin drafted Quebec's controversial French Language Charter, known as Bill 101. He joined the Quebec National Assembly in 1970 and was a long-time member of the Parti-Québécois. March 11, 1999.

LECAVALIER, René, 81. Formerly a host of cultural programs on Radio-Canada, Lecavalier became, in 1952, the French-language sportscaster for the National Hockey League and continued his career for more than 30 years; he was recognized as one of the best in the business. September 6, 1999.

MACKASEY, Bryce Stuart, 78. Mackasey joined the House of Commons as a Liberal representative for Verdun; in 1968 he became labour minister in the Trudeau government, and later a minister for Manpower and Immigration, where he raised unemployment insurance to a then-princely $100 a week. He later served as postmaster general and minister of consumer and corporate affairs. September 5, 1999.

MACLEAN, Lennox Allister, 73. Labour lawyer who oversaw the Canadian Auto Workers union split from the American United Auto Workers in 1984. September 5, 1999.

MACNAUGHTON, Alan A., 95. Speaker of the House of Commons 1963-66; served 1949-66 as Liberal MP for Mount Royal; founder and first chairman of the Canadian branch of the World Wildlife Fund. July 16, 1999.

MACPHERSON, Kathleen (Kay) Margaret, 86. Activist, humanitarian and feminist who was a founder of Voice of Women and Women for Political Action; past-president of the National Action Committee for the Status of Women. August 19, 1999.

MAITLAND, Herbert Alan, 78. Maitland, a long-time CBC announcer, joined the network in 1947 and went on to host programs including *Maitland Manor* and *Read to Me*. In 1974 he began a long stint on *As It Happens*, co-hosting with Barbara Frum, Elizabeth Gray, Denis Trudeau and Michael Enright, and retiring in 1993. February 11, 1999.

MANNING, Thomas Henry, 86. Arctic mapmaker who, with a British-Canadian team, charted vast territories of the Arctic, beginning in 1936 and continuing after World War II; also a keen observer of Arctic wildlife and natural environment. November 8, 1998.

MASON, Roger Burford, 54. Author and free-lance journalist, published short story collections *Telling Bees & Other Stories* (1980) and *The Beaver Picture & Other Stories* (1992); also wrote *Travels in the Shining Island*, about James Evans, the missionary who devised a Cree alphabet. Other works included a biography of Canadian painter Franz Johnson and travel pieces. October 4, 1998.

MATURE, Victor John, 83. American actor who starred in a string of epic movies, often based on Old Testament and Roman Empire themes; his good looks and expansive chest made him a favourite among screen idols. Samson and Delilah; No, No, Nanette; My Darling Clementine; After the Fox. August 4, 1999.

McDOWALL, Roderick Andrew Anthony Jude (Roddy), 70. British-born actor who became a Hollywood success in theatre, televison and movies, starred in 1941 How Green Was My Valley, the story of Welsh coal miners; co-starred with Elizabeth Taylor in Lassie Come Home; and appeared in many other films, including Cleopatra and Planet of the Apes, and in several television dramas. October 3, 1998.

McELCHERAN, William, 71. Sculptor whose works won him international recognition, McElcheran designed the Nellie ACTRA award, and is the creator of many works in Canadian cities and around the world. His striking bronze businessmen are a common theme, representing the "Everyman" in today's society. February 13, 1999.

MEAGHER, Margaret Blanche, 88. Canada's first woman ambassador, Meagher joined the Department of External Affairs in 1942 and was posted to Mexico in 1945. During her career she held diplomatic positions in Israel, Sweden, Kenya, Uganda, London and Vienna. February 25, 1999.

MENUHIN, Sir Yehudi, 82. Menuhin combined his virtuoso ability at the violin with many other talents: as a conductor, a teacher and a writer. His extensive recordings included works by Beethoven, Mozart and Bach, and he also collaborated with the late jazz violinist Stéphane Grappelli and Indian sitar player Ravi Shankar. He won a plethora of awards and honours, including the 1990 Glenn Gould Prize, and hosted the CBC television documentary *The Music of Man*. March 12, 1999.

MERCER (POR), Ruby, 92. Former opera singer who sang with the Metropolitan Opera, Mercer came to Canada in 1958 and founded *Opera Canada* magazine and instituted the Canadian Children's Opera Chorus in 1968; she appeared on CBC radio on *Opera Time* and *Opera in Stereo*, and wrote a biography of the Guelph tenor Edward Johnson. January 26, 1999.

MOORE, Brian, 77. Irish-born novelist won two Governor General Awards: for *The Luck of Ginger Coffey*, 1961, and *The Great Victorian Collection*, 1976, and was short-listed three times for the Booker Prize. Moore came to Canada in 1948 and worked as a feature writer for the *Montreal Gazette*. He launched his career as a novelist with the publication of *The Lonely Passion of Judith Hearne* in 1955. *Black Robe* told of seventeenth-century Jesuits in Canada. In 1967 he moved to Malibu, Calif., with his wife Jean Denney, though he retained his Irish and Canadian connections for the rest of his life. January 10, 1999.

MURDOCH, Dame Jean Iris, 79. British novel-ist whose 27 novels were internationally praised. She won the Whitbread Prize for *The Sacred and Profane Love Machine* and the Booker Prize for *The Sea, The Sea*. Her multicharactered nov-els encompassed a range of human emotion and dark secrets: suicide, murder, adultry and incest among them. Murdoch also wrote nonfiction: *Sartre: Romantic Rationalist* and *Metaphysics as a Guide to Morals*. February 8, 1999.

NYKOMO, Joshua, 82. Nicknamed the "father of Zimbabwe," Nykomo formed an uneasy alliance with Robert Mugabe, as his vice presi-dent, in 1985, after years of exile and imprison-ment; seen as a unifying influence on the coun-try. July 1, 1999.

O'BRIEN, Mary, 72. A feminist, midwife and philosopher, O'Brien wrote *The Politics of Reproduction*. She supported the Toronto branch of Women Against Violence Against Women, was a founding member of the Feminist Party of Canada and taught at the Ontario Institute for Studies in Education and at the University of Toronto. October 17, 1998.

PAPADOPOULOS, George, 80. Greek dictator who led a coup against King Constantine's gov-ernment in 1967; his rule ended when he was arrested for high treason in 1974; he died while still in prison. June 27, 1999.

PATERSON, Jennifer, 71. Paterson starred with Clarissa Dickson Wright on the British television cooking program *Two Fat Ladies*; she delighted in preparing rich, decadent recipes and admonishing her audience to avoid diets. August 10, 1999.

PUDDY, Bill, 82. Canadian 300-yard relay swim team gold medallist in 1934 British Empire Games; bronze medal winner in the 200-yard breaststroke; took part in the 1936 Berlin Olympics. June 23, 1999.

PUZO, Mario, 78. American novelist whose *Godfather* series of books brought him international fame. An accomplished screenwriter, Puzo also wrote *Fools Die*, *The Fourth K* and *The Last Don*; his last book, *Omerta*, is to be published posthumously. July 2, 1999.

RAE, Saul F., 84. Member of Canadian Foreign Service from 1940-79, served as Canadian Ambassador to the United Nations in Geneva, later to Mexico, Guatemala, the United Nations in New York and the Netherlands. In his early days, he played vaudeville with brother Jack and sister Grace, as the "Three Little Raes of Sunshine." Father of former NDP premier of Ontario, Bob Rae and bandleader Jackie Rae. January 9, 1999.

RODRIGO, Joaquin, 97. Internationally renowned Spanish composer; his Concierto de Aranjuez for guitar and orchestra, written in 1939, remains a classical favourite. July 6, 1999.

ST. CYR, Lili (b. Willis Marie Van Schaack), 81. Burlesque queen in Montreal during the 1940s and '50s, American-born St. Cyr was arrested in 1951 for obscenity but was acquitted. January 29, 1999.

SCHAWLOW, Arthur Leonard, 77. American-born physicist who attended the University of Toronto, Schawlow did research, with Charles Townes, into early laser technology, and in 1981 won the Nobel Prize for Physics for contributions to laser spectroscopy research. April 28, 1999.

SCOTT, George C., 71. Crusty American actor famous for his sympathetic portrayal of General George S. Patton in the 1970 film *Patton*; also appeared in stage and film roles, including *Death of a Salesman, The Hustler, Plaza Suite* and *Anatomy of a Murder*. September 23, 1999

SEABORG, Glenn Theodore, 86. The discoverer of plutonium, Seaborg won, in 1951, the Nobel Prize for Physics; in 1942 he joined the Manhattan Project; his ability to isolate plutonium for the atomic bomb led to the destruction of Nagasaki, Japan, in 1945. February 25, 1999.

SEMON, Waldo Lonsbury, 100. Chemist and inventor, in 1926, of vinyl, while working for B. F. Goodrich in Akron, Ohio; also developed a number of synthetic materials, such as Ameripol, a synthetic rubber used in the construction of modern automobile tires. May 26, 1999.

SHADBOLT, Jack, 89. Acclaimed BC-based artist whose powerful work was influenced by West Coast native mythical themes as well as those from the natural world in his multimedia works. In addition to his more than 70 solo exhibitions, Shadbolt taught at the Vancouver School of Art, and with wife Doris, herself an art scholar, founded the Vancouver Institute of the Visual Arts. November 22, 1998.

SIMPSON, Allan, 59. Disabled himself from contracting polio as a child, Simpson was a co-founder of the Council of Canadians with Disabilities and the Canadian Association of Independent Living Centres; also created the first Pan-Am Wheelchair Games, then known as the Canadian Wheelchair Sport Association. December 26, 1998.

SISKEL, Gene, 53. Movie critic with Roger Ebert since 1982 on public television: known for their "thumbs-up" and "thumbs-down" ratings. Also a critic with the *Chicago Tribune* since 1969. February 20, 1999.

SOMERS, Harry Stewart, 73. Prolific composer of opera, orchestral, chamber, vocal and ballet music, Somers was acclaimed for his operas *Louis Riel* and *The Fool* and was commissioned by Yehudi Menuhin to write *Music for Solo Violin*; his *Five Songs for Dark Voice* was performed by Maureen Forrester. March 9, 1999.

STEINBERG, Saul, 84. Noted cartoonist whose work appeared regularly in the New Yorker; well known for his 1976 New Yorker cover drawing of Manhattan dominating the world. His clean, evocative drawings were compared to those of Miró and Picasso. May 12, 1999.

STIKEMAN, H. (Harry) Heward, 85. Co-founder in 1952 of Stikeman Elliott, one of the largest law firms in Canada with branches worldwide; leading tax lawyer; in 1990 founded the Heward Stikeman Fiscal Institute, which studied issues in Canadian tax law. June 12, 1999.

STRATFORD, Philip, 71. Poet and English translator of French literary works: Félix Lecleric fiction; memoirs of René Lévesque; and Diane Hébert's *Second Chance*, which described her heart-lung replacement surgery and won Stratford a Governor General's Award. Also translated Antonine Maillet's *Pélagie*. April 23, 1999.

THOMPSON, Patricia, 71. Founder and editor of the *Film Canada Yearbook*, a sourcebook for Canada's burgeoning film and television industry; also co-founded (with Gerald Pratley) the Ontario Film Institute. June 27, 1999.

TOTH, Jerry (Jaroslav), 70. Arranger, conductor and producer for CBC orchestras, Toth, a saxophonist and clarinetist, created orchestrations for CBC productions: *Once Upon a Brothers Grimm*, *A Place to Stand* and *Hockey Night in Canada*. Recordings include *The Twelve Sides of Jerry Toth* and *The Classic Jerry Toth*. March 31, 1999.

TOWERS, Gordon, 79. For 16 years, a PC member of Parliament in Alberta, appointed the province's lieutenant-governor in 1991 and served till 1996. Known as a populist politician, Towers was also affectionately regarded as the "poet laureate" of the House of Commons. June 8, 1999.

TOWNSEND, Eleanor Reed, 54. In 1979 was the first and only woman to win the North American Fiddle Championship at Shelburne, Ont., as well as becoming champion woman fiddler several times. Both she and her husband, champion Graham Townsend, were inducted into the U.S. Fiddling Hall of Fame and Canada's National Fiddling Hall of Fame. Townsend died in a house fire with her granddaughter a month after her husband's death. December 31, 1998.

TRUDEAU, Michel Charles-Emile, 23. Son of former prime minister Pierre Trudeau, Trudeau died near Nelson, BC, when an avalanche swept him into a mountain lake in Kokanee Glacier

Provincial Park. Trudeau was an avid backcountry skier. November 13, 1998.

TURE, Kwame (b. Stokely Carmichael), 57. In the 1960s, as Stokely Carmichael, was a leading black activist; later prime minister of the Black Panther Party, leading marches in Mississippi and participating in "freedom rides," aimed at desegregating public transportation. In 1969 moved to Guinea to lead the socialist All-African People's Revolutionary Party. November 15, 1998.

VALLIERES, Pierre, 60. Journalist and former leader of the Front de Libération de Québec (FLQ), Vallières authored *White Niggers of America*, postulating that the French in Quebec were an oppressed people. He severed his ties with the FLQ after the kidnapping and murder of then labour minister Pierre Laporte, and served a one-year sentence for his part in the FLQ terrorist activities. December 22, 1998.

VISZMEG, Joseph, 42. Edmonton filmmaker whose documentary In *My Own Time: Diary of a Cancer Patient* won a Genie award for best director. That documentary, and its successor, *My Healing Journey: Seven Years with Cancer*, were first aired by CBC and later across the world. June 22, 1999.

WEBSTER, Jack, 80. A crusty broadcaster known for his acerbic wit and strong Scottish brogue, the outspoken Webster appeared on BC radio and television as well as CBC's *This Hour Has Seven Days* and frequently on *Front Page Challenge*. His notorious radio hot-line show began on BC's CJOR; he later moved moved to BCTV. March 2, 1999.

WELLS, "Cactus" Jack, 88. Winnipeg sports broadcaster was CBC's first sportscaster in Winnipeg when television arrived in 1954. Noted for his fervent support of the city's sports teams, Wells enjoyed a lifelong sportcasting career that ended only a few weeks before his death. May 24, 1999.

WHELAN, Peter, 65. After a career in journalism at Toronto's *Globe and Mail*, Whelan authored his bird-watching column for more than 20 years; his easy style earned him the respect of the birding community as well as novice ornithologists. August 14, 1999.

NEWS EVENTS OF 1998–99

October 1, 1998 to September 30, 1999

(*See also* A Canadian Sports Chronology pp. 675-82, and Obituaries pp. 781-88.)

October

INTERNATIONAL

Bosnia and Herzegovina: On Oct. 8, the largest mass grave found to date in Bosnia was unearthed near Glumina; the site contained the bodies of 274 Muslims probably killed early in the 1992-95 war. **China:** On Oct. 6-10, British Prime Min. Tony Blair visited China–the first visit by a British PM since 1991–and praised Prem. Zhu Rongji for China's economic reforms. **Indonesia:** On Oct. 28, thousands of students demonstrated outside the House of Representatives in Jakarta and in five other cities in the biggest protest since the fall of Pres. Suharto in May; the protesters demanded the resignation of Pres. B.J. Habibie. Earlier, on Oct. 11-12, thousands demonstrated in Dili, East Timor, against Indonesia's rule in the formerly independent territory. **Iran:** On Oct. 23, elections were held for the Assembly of Experts; left-wing candidates were barred from running and conservatives retained control of the assembly. **Iraq:** On Oct. 31, the government announced its decision to stop cooperating with the United Nations Special Commission (UNSCOM); on Aug. 5, Iraq had decided to suspend UNSCOM inspections of weapons sites. **Japan:** After the Diet passed bills to reform indebted banks, the government nationalized the Long Term Credit Bank of Japan on Oct. 23; the bank had debts of 340 billion yen. **Northern Ireland:** On Oct. 16, political leaders John Hume and David Trimble won the 1998 Nobel Peace Prize for their peace efforts. **Philippines:** On Oct. 6, the Supreme Court acquitted Imelda Marcos, widow of former Pres. Ferdinand Marcos, of corruption; a lower court had sentenced her to 12 years in prison in 1993. **Russia:**

Poor health forced Pres. Boris Yeltsin to abandon or cut short foreign trips. On Oct. 31, the government approved measures aimed at controlling inflation. **Rwanda:** On Oct. 2, the International Criminal Tribunal for Rwanda sentenced Jean-Paul Akeyesu to three life terms in prison for genocide. **South Africa:** On Oct. 29, Archbishop Desmond Tutu gave Pres. Nelson Mandela the final report of the Truth and Reconciliation Commission on crimes committed during the apartheid era; the report chronicled past abuses by National Party governments, the African National Congress (ANC), the Inkatha Freedom Party and others. **United Kingdom:** On Oct. 16, authorities arrested former Chilean dictator Augusto Pinochet in London; the arrest followed a Spanish request for his extradition to answer charges of genocide and terrorism committed during his rule (1973-90). **United Nations:** On Oct. 5, China signed the International Covenant on Civil and Political Rights. On Oct. 14, the General Assembly called for an end to the USA's Cuban embargo by a record vote of 157-2 with 12 abstentions. **United States:** On Oct. 8, the House of Representatives authorized its judiciary committee to begin an impeachment inquiry against Pres. Bill Clinton for his role in the Monica Lewinsky affair. On Oct. 15, Pres. Clinton began nine days of talks with Israeli Prime Min. Binyamin Netanyahu and Palestinian Pres. Yasser Arafat in Wye, Md.; the talks broke a 19-month impasse in Israeli-Palestinian relations over the West Bank. On Oct. 12, Matthew Shepard, a gay student, died after a beating in Wyo.; his death prompted calls for tougher anti-hate laws. **Yugoslavia:** Pres. Slobodan Milosevic and the West negotiated Yugoslavia's withdrawal of troops from Kosovo–a Yugoslav territory populated mostly by Albanians. NATO threatened air strikes to force withdrawal while Milosevic slowly withdrew troops. On Oct. 12, Milosevic agreed for the first time to the presence of an international observer force in Kosovo. On Oct. 17, the Albanian Kosovo Liberation Army (UCK) ended a ceasefire with the Serbs.

CANADA

Bombardier won a record CDN$1.5 billion contract to build 50 jets over 10 years (Oct. 1). On Oct. 2, an RCMP probe into skirmishes between the Mounties and demonstrators at the 1997 Asia-Pacific Economic Co-operation (APEC) summit opened in Vancouver. Finance Min. Paul Martin urged the need to restore confidence in the global economy on Oct. 6 after talking with International Monetary Fund and G-7 officials in Washington. All federal Opposition parties condemned a Liberal government proposal to spend a CDN$20 billion surplus in Employment Insurance (Oct. 6). Canada won a seat on the United Nations (UN) Security Council (Oct. 8). Merchant navy veterans ended an 11-day protest in Ottawa over benefits denied to them since World War II (Oct. 9). Finance Min. Martin rejected big tax cuts and increases in health spending for his next budget because of the slumping world economy (Oct. 14). Ottawa confirmed plans to slash the West Coast commercial salmon fleet by half within three years (Oct. 14). The public learned that Ward Elcock, director of the Canadian Security Intelligence Service (CSIS), told a Senate committee in June that Canada was a haven for foreign terrorists (Oct. 14). Dia Met Minerals of Kelowna, BC and BHP of Australia opened the Ekati Diamond Mine in NWT (Oct. 14). The Toronto Stock Exchange announced plans to become a publicly owned company (Oct. 15). The military grounded 30 aging Sea King helicopters on Oct. 15 after a crash killed six people on Oct. 2 at Marsoui, Que. Jon Gerrard became Man. Liberal leader (Oct. 17). NB Conservative leader Bernard Lord and a colleague defeated the Liberals in two provincial by-elections (Oct. 19). Edmonton-based Telus Corp. and BC Tel agreed to merge (Oct. 19). Statistics Canada said the nation's inflation rate had fallen to 1960s levels (Oct. 21). NS Prem. Russell MacLellan promised CDN$1.8 million in severance pay to 147 Westray employees six years after a deadly blast and mine closure cost them their jobs (Oct. 22). The *National Post* appeared on newsstands for the first time (Oct. 27). Toronto City Council declared homelessness a national disaster (Oct. 28). The Ont. government passed the Energy Competition Act to end Ontario Hydro's 90-year monopoly on power in 2000 (Oct. 29).

November

INTERNATIONAL

Argentina: On Nov. 2-14, delegates from over 160 countries met in Buenos Aires for a UN-sponsored conference on climate change; the delegates disagreed over who should bear the costs of stopping emissions of greenhouse gases to slow global warming. On Nov. 24, former Adml. Eduardo Emilio Massera, a member of the military junta in 1976-78, was arrested for ordering the past kidnapping and torture of civilians. **Burundi:** In early Nov., the Tutsi-dominated army massacred at least 100 Hutu civilians at Mutambu. **Central America:** On Nov. 1, Hurricane Mitch ended six days of devastation, killing more than 10,000 people, wrecking tens of thousands of homes and leaving as many as two million homeless; winds reaching speeds of almost 300 km/h wiped out running water, roads, power and crops, and displaced landmines. **China:** On Nov. 11, the government condemned US Pres. Clinton's meeting with Tibet's exiled Dalai Lama at the White House. On Nov. 22-25, Pres. Jiang Zemin met pneumonia-stricken Russian Pres. Yeltsin in a hospital in Moscow. On Nov. 25-30, Pres. Jiang became the first Chinese head of state to pay an official visit to Japan. **Colombia:** On Nov. 4, government soldiers recaptured Mit three days after guerrillas of the

Revolutionary Armed Forces of Colombia (FARC) seized the city; about 150 troops and police were killed. **European Union:** On Nov. 22, finance ministers from 11 centre-left governments launched "The New European Way," a manifesto for a socialist Europe with more harmonized taxes, closely shared economic policies and higher public spending. **Indonesia:** On Nov. 13, at least 16 people were killed in Jakarta in clashes between police and student demonstrators outside the People's Consultative Assembly (MPR). Meanwhile the MPR passed decrees repealing many repressive laws from the Suharto era. **Iraq:** On Nov. 15, Pres. Saddam Hussein allowed UNSCOM weapons inspectors to return to work after two weeks of American and British threats of air and missile strikes from naval forces in the Persian Gulf. By Nov. 20, Iraqi officials were refusing to hand over documents to UNSCOM. **Korea (North):** On Nov. 18, after three days of talks in Pyongyang, the government refused US access to a suspected underground nuclear site at Yangbon. **Korea (South):** On Nov. 20-22, US Pres. Clinton and Pres. Kim Dae Jung discussed Yangbon; addressing US troops near Seoul, Clinton called upon N. Korea to dismantle its nuclear weapons and to stop making chemical and biological weapons. **Malaysia:** On Nov. 14-18, the leaders of 21 countries attended the annual APEC conference in Kuala Lumpur. On Nov. 16, US V. Pres. Al Gore offended his hosts by backing the reform movement of imprisoned former government minister Anwar Ibrahim. **Netherlands:** On Nov. 16, the UN Criminal Tribunal for the Former Yugoslavia at The Hague convicted three men of war crimes against Bosnian Serbs in 1992. **Russia:** On Nov. 5, the Russian Constitutional Court ruled Pres. Yeltsin could not seek a third term. On Nov. 6, the USA agreed to send US$600 million in food and food credits after a poor Russian harvest; the EU agreed to send another US$500 million in food aid. On Nov. 20, Galina Starovoitova, a deputy in the Russian State Duma and human rights activist, was murdered in St. Petersburg.

On Nov. 23, Yeltsin entered hospital again with pneumonia. **Space:** On Nov. 7, US Sen. John Glenn, 77, the oldest person to enter space, and the crew of the US space shuttle *Discovery* returned to earth after nine days in orbit. **United States:** On Nov. 3, the results of mid-term elections boosted the fortunes of Pres. Clinton and the Democratic Party. Minn. elected Jesse Ventura, a former wrestler, as governor. On Nov. 6, Speaker Newt Gingrich announced his resignation from the House of Representatives. On Nov. 13, Pres. Clinton agreed to pay US$850,000 to Paula Jones to settle her sexual harassment suit. On Nov. 19, Independent Prosecutor Kenneth Starr appeared for 12 hours before the house judiciary committee to present his case against Pres. Clinton in the Lewinsky affair and to answer questions about his investigations. **Yugoslavia:** Killings among Serbs and Albanians in Kosovo threatened to destroy the ceasefire between Pres. Milosevic and the Western powers. On Nov. 5, Yugoslavia stopped investigators with the International Criminal Tribunal for the Former Yugoslavia from entering Kosovo. On Nov. 6, the first unarmed international peacekeepers arrived in Kosovo under the command of the Organisation for Security and Co-operation in Europe (OSCE). **Zimbabwe:** On Nov. 26, the High Court in Harare found former Pres. Canaan Banana (1980-87) guilty of sodomy and indecent assault; in the previous week, Banana had fled to Botswana.

CANADA

Pierre Bourque won a landslide victory in Montreal's mayoralty race (Nov. 1). TransCanada Pipelines announced up to 600 layoffs (Nov. 2) after its CDN$15.6 billion merger with Nova Corp. Auditor Erik Peters slammed the Ont. government for spending CDN$180 million on private consultants hired to cut the province's welfare budget; Peters also warned of major fraud in the Ontario Hospital Insurance Plan (Nov. 3). A month-long strike of support workers ended at Toronto

International Airport (Nov. 8). Sask. Prem. Roy Romanow asked Prime Min. Jean Chrétien for emergency farm aid (Nov. 10). The Nisga'a Indians voted to ratify their treaty with the BC government (Nov. 12). The Supreme Court of Canada ruled that step-parents cannot avoid child support payments when their marriages fail (Nov. 12). In Charlottetown, PEI, federal Industry Min. John Manley unveiled a plan to tackle Canada's CDN\$4 billion telemarketing fraud problem (Nov. 13). Michel Trudeau, son of former Prime Min. Pierre Trudeau, died when an avalanche swept him into BC's Kokanee Lake (Nov. 13). Former Prime Min. Joe Clark resumed control of the federal Conservative party (Nov. 14). Canada pledged CDN\$100 million in hurricane relief to Central America over the next four years (Nov. 15). Prime Min. Chrétien attended the APEC summit in Malaysia (Nov. 16-18). Auditor-General Denis Desautels said the federal Liberals had understated their budget surplus for 1997-98 by CDN\$2.5 billion (Nov. 17). On Nov. 20, the Ont. government announced plans to shed 13,000 civil servants on top of the 16,500 employees let go or retired since 1995. Forestry workers at Abitibi-Consolidated returned to work after voting for a new contract and ended a five-month strike (Nov. 20). On Nov. 23, Ont. Health Min. Elizabeth Witmer pledged CDN\$10,000 per person for Ont.'s 20,000 residents who contracted hepatitus C through Canada's tainted blood supply but who were ineligible for federal compensation. Federal Solicitor-General Andy Scott resigned on Nov. 23 following weeks of criticism over his comments about the pepper-spraying of demonstrators at the 1997 APEC conference in Vancouver and allegations that he prejudged an RCMP inquiry. The Sask. Court of Appeal ruled Robert Latimer must serve at least 10 years in prison for the 1993 killing of his disabled daughter (Nov. 23). Mourners at the funeral of slain newspaper publisher Tara Singh Hayer in Vancouver demanded an end to violence among Canada's Sikhs (Nov. 28). Environment Canada declared 1998 the warmest year globally in 130-140 years (Nov. 30). Prem. Lucien Bouchard led the Parti Québécois to another majority government (Nov. 30).

December

INTERNATIONAL

Algeria: Terrorist violence surged across the country before Ramadan; on Dec. 8-9, in the month's worst incident, radical Muslims killed 45 people in a village west of Algiers. On Dec. 9, security officials confirmed the discovery of a well containing at least 100 murder victims. **Angola:** An upsurge in fighting in the country's 23-year-old civil war forced the government to concede territory to the rebel National Union for the Total Independence of Angola (UNITA) and, on Dec. 8, to withdraw soldiers from the war in the Democratic Republic of Congo. **Democratic Republic of Congo:** On Dec. 5, French TV said Pres. Laurent-Désiré Kabila's troops killed more than 1,000 rebels at Moba. On Dec. 30, about 500 people were massacred at Makobola. **Guatemala:** Three ex-paramilitaries were sentenced to death for taking part in the killings of at least 269 people; the convictions were the first for massacres committed during the nation's 36-year civil war. **Iraq:** On Dec. 16-20, the US and UK carried out air strikes to "degrade" Pres. Saddam Hussein's military forces; the attacks, prompted by Iraq's refusal to cooperate with UNSCOM, lacked support from the UN Security Council. **Korea:** On Dec. 18, S. Korean air and sea forces sank a suspected N. Korean spy vessel at sea after an exchange of gunfire. **Russia:** On Dec. 7, Pres. Yeltsin dismissed four senior aides, including Valentin Yumashev, head of the presidential administration. **South Africa:** On Dec. 6, Pres. Mandela ruled out a general amnesty for crimes committed during the apartheid era but repeated that amnesties were possible for those who applied for them. **Thailand:** At Surat Thani, a Thai Airways jet crashed while landing in heavy rain; 45 of 146 passengers survived. **United States:** On Dec. 18, the House of Representatives approved two articles of impeachment against Pres. Clinton. **Yugoslavia:** Clashes between Serbs and the Albanian UCK in Kosovo threatened a ceasefire.

CANADA

Federal Justice Min. Anne McLellan officially launched Canada's new gun control law on Dec. 1, three years after Parliament passed the law. The International Court of Justice rejected Spain's attempt to haul Canada into court for seizing one Spanish turbot fishing ship in 1995 (Dec. 4). Gerald Morin stepped down as head of the inquiry into the 1997 APEC affair after weathering charges of bias and claiming interference by the RCMP Public Complaints Commission (Dec. 4). Hundreds of angry American farmers met at the border to block trucks bearing Canadian livestock and grain from entering the US (Dec. 6). Que. Prem. Bouchard promised another referendum on the province's sovereignty (Dec. 7). NS Labour Min. Russell MacKinnon reneged on the pledge to compensate Westray workers (Dec. 8); NS Prem. MacLellan shuffled his cabinet three days later. The Ont. government pledged CDN$100 million to hospitals running deficits (Dec. 10) after cutting CDN$800 million from health care within two years. Jim Antoine was elected NWT's premier (Dec. 10). The federal government offered CDN$18 million in tax-free compensation to Canadian soldiers who were captured and brutalized by the Japanese after the fall of Hong Kong in World War II (Dec. 11). Federal Finance Min. Martin closed the door on Canadian bank mergers (Dec. 14), forcing four banks to abandon planned merges. Martin said mergers would concentrate too much economic power in bankers' hands and reduce competition in banking. Que. Prem. Bouchard introduced his new cabinet; nine of 28 members were women (Dec. 15). On the same day, Nfld Prem. Brian Tobin shuffled his cabinet. The BC Supreme Court overturned the Surrey school board's ban on elementary school books depicting same-sex couples (Dec. 16). BC Prem. Glen Clark testified before the BC Supreme Court, defending his 1996 dismissal of BC Hydro executives who invested in a joint-venture power project in Pakistan without Clark's knowledge (Dec. 17). On the same day, BC approved three new casinos. A Halifax jury acquitted Gerald Regan, a former premier, of eight sex-related charges (Dec. 18). Guy Belanger, a former Que. Liberal MNA, was found guilty of defrauding the Que. government of CDN$66,000 in 1990-92 (Dec. 18). Ted Hughes took over the APEC inquiry (Dec. 21). An Ont. court ruled the province's Game and Fish Act was unconstitutional, giving Ont. Métis the same rights as status Indians to hunt and fish for food (Dec. 21).

January

INTERNATIONAL

Argentina: On Jan. 21, Gen. Reynaldo Bignone, the last of the junta presidents (in 1982-83), was arrested for theft and the kidnapping of babies born to imprisoned mothers during the "dirty war" of 1976-83; Bignone was the eighth former military chief held for stealing babies. **Colombia:** An earthquake rocked the city of Armenia, killing more than 900 people and leaving at least 200,000 homeless (Jan. 25). **European Union:** On Jan. 1, the euro, the new European single currency, was launched in 11 countries; Germany took over the six-month presidency of the EU from Austria. **Indonesia:** On Jan. 19-23, Muslim-Christian rioting killed 50 people and injured more than 100 on Ambon. **Mexico:** On Jan. 21, Raoul Salinas de Gortari, brother of former Pres. Carlos Salinas de Gortari, was sentenced to 50 years in prison for ordering the 1994 murder of José Francisco Ruiz Massieu, then general secretary of the ruling Institutional Revolutionary Party. **Pakistan:** On Jan. 3, a bomb intended for Prime Min. Nawaz Sharif killed four people near Lahore;

Sharif and his family escaped unharmed. **Romania:** On Jan. 22, Miron Cosma led 20,000 striking miners on a march to Bucharest; the miners broke through roadblocks and injured 170 people (mostly police). **Russia:** On Jan. 31, Prime Min. Yevgeny Primakov announced an anti-crime campaign against "oligarchs." **Sierra Leone:** Fighting between troops loyal to Pres. Ahmed Tejan Kabbah and the rebel Revolutionary United Front caused about 3,000 deaths in Freetown. **Space:** On Jan. 3, an American rocket carrying the *Polar Lander* spacecraft took off for Mars. **Switzerland:** On Jan. 23-24, the International Olympic Committee (IOC) in Lausanne, facing allegations of corruption in its selection of host cities, suspended six of its members. In late Jan., four IOC members resigned. **United States:** On Jan. 19, Pres. Clinton delivered his sixth State of the Union Address, concentrating on social security, education and health care. **Yugoslavia:** On Jan. 15, the bodies of 45 Albanians were found in Racak; NATO and OSCE officials blamed Serbs for the massacre; the Serbs denied responsibility. On Jan. 18, Yugoslav border guards prevented Canadian judge Louise Arbour, the UN war crimes prosecutor, from entering Kosovo.

CANADA

An avalanche of snow crashed into a school, killing nine people and injuring 25 more, in Kangiqsualujjuak, Que. (Jan. 1). Prime Min. Chrétien created an unprecedented caucus task force to find out why the Liberal party is unpopular in Western Canada (Jan. 7). Taras Sokolyk, Man. Prem. Gary Filmon's former chief of staff, admitted lying to investigators about his role in a scheme to split votes in three ridings in the 1995 provincial election (Jan. 11). Bell Canada unloaded 2,400 jobs by selling its telephone-operator division to US-based Excell Global Services (Jan 11). Canada and Mexico pledged to push for a worldwide ban on landmines and to help mine victims in Central America (Jan. 11).

A Senate report on immigration announced that Ottawa lost track of more than 5,000 former refugee claimants facing deportation (Jan. 14). Health Canada announced it would not approve the use of rBST, a hormone that boosts milk production in cows (Jan. 14); some scientists had warned of high risks to cows' health. Toronto's task force on homelessness, chaired by Anne Golden, reported that the fastest growing groups of homeless people were youths under age 18 and families with children (Jan. 14). The next day, snowfall in Toronto surpassed 120 cm for Jan. and broke an 1871 record for snowfall in one month; businesses, schools and some public transit shut down while 400 soldiers helped dig out the city. In BC, Supreme Court Justice Duncan Shaw ruled that a ban on possessing child pornography violated freedom of thought and expression guarantees in the Canadian Charter of Rights and Freedoms (Jan. 15). BC Prem. Clark pledged to preserve more than 250,000 ha. of new parkland (Jan. 25). Ombudsman Daniel Jacoby released a report saying biker gangs and drug traffickers controlled some Que. jails (Jan. 25). Al McLean, former speaker of the Ont. legislature, said he would pay back the CDN$130,000 that the Ont. government gave him to pay his legal bills in a sexual harassment suit; McLean also promised not to run in Ont.'s next election (Jan. 26). Statistics Canada said the number of self-employed and part-time workers steadily grew in the 1990s (Jan. 27). Former judge Lawrence Poitras released a report condemning Que.'s police for habitual intimidation, secrecy and abuse of authority (Jan. 28). Ottawa pulled the plug on the Cape Breton Development Corp., announcing the closure of the Phalen coal mine by the year 2000 while putting a second mine up for sale (Jan. 28). Gordon Wilson abandoned his party, the Progressive Democratic Alliance, for an NDP cabinet post in BC (Jan. 29). At the World Economic Forum in Davos, Switzerland, Prime Min. Chrétien rejected the idea of a Canadian-US dollar (Jan 29).

February

INTERNATIONAL

Australia: Queensland's worst floods in a century killed at least seven people. **France:** On Feb. 6-23, under threat of NATO air strikes, Yugoslavian Serbs and Albanian Kosovars met in Rambouillet for unsuccessful talks aimed at ending the fighting in Kosovo. **Guatemala:** On Feb. 25, the Historical Clarification Commission published a report on the country's 36-year civil war in which 200,000 people died; the report blamed the army for 90 percent and leftist guerillas for three percent of the atrocities committed during the war. **Indonesia:** Throughout the month Muslim-Christian riots in the eastern Spice Islands caused 150 deaths. **Iraq:** On Feb. 19, Grand Ayatollah Mohammed Sadeq al-Sadr, one of the highest-ranking Shi'ite clerics in Iraq, and his two sons were assassinated in Najaf. **Israel:** On Feb. 14, about 200,000 ultra-Orthodox Jews prayed near the Supreme Court in Jerusalem to protest against the court's alleged religious persecution of them. **Lebanon:** On Feb. 22-23, the Hezbollah ambushed and killed three Israeli officers in the western Bekaa; on Feb. 28, another Hezbollah ambush killed four Israelis, including a general, inside the Israeli security zone. **Romania:** On Feb. 15, the Supreme Court sentenced Miron Cosma to 18 years in prison for fomenting miners' riots in 1991. **Turkey:** On Feb. 15, Turkish authorities captured Abdullah Ocalan, leader of the Kurdistan Workers' Party (PKK), in Kenya; Ocalan's return to Turkey sparked Kurdish protests around the world. **United Kingdom:** On Feb. 22, George Robertson, secretary of state for defence, announced the British army had destroyed its stock of two million landmines. **United States:** On Feb. 12, after five weeks of deliberation, the Senate acquitted Pres. Clinton of perjury and obstruction of justice charges stemming from the Paula Jones sexual harassment case and the Lewinsky scandal.

CANADA

Prime Min. Chrétien got nine premiers to agree to a social union accord after promising more health care funding for the provinces but failed to secure Que.'s signature (Feb. 4). The Supreme Court of NS ruled against a couple seeking medicare payments for their infertility treatments (Feb. 5). Man. Prem. Filmon shuffled his cabinet (Feb. 5). Que. Prem. Bouchard warned that Canada could lose a future referendum on national unity over signing the social union accord without Que.'s consent (Feb. 8). Prime Min. Chrétien paid his respects to the Jordanian ambassador in Ottawa (Feb. 9) after missing the state funeral of King Hussein the previous day. Prem. Tobin's Liberal party won a reduced majority in the Nfld election (Feb. 9). Alta Prem. Ralph Klein said he felt vindicated (Feb. 10) after Auditor General Peter Valentine concluded a six-month investigation into the CDN$420 million public refinancing of the West Edmonton Mall in 1994 and found no evidence of undue political influence. BC Finance Min. Joy MacPhail said the province's deficit for the fiscal year ended Mar. 31 would be nearer CDN$500 million than the original target of CDN$95 million (Feb. 10). Voters in the eastern Arctic elected 19 members to the first assembly of Nunavut (Feb. 15) before the new territory appeared on the map. In his federal budget address, Finance Min. Martin promised an CDN$11.5 billion boost in health-care transfers to the provinces over the next five years (Feb. 16). Alta. Prem. Klein declared future Alta budget surpluses will be split 75 percent for debt payment and 25 percent for new spending (Feb. 16). The *Free Press* of Regina and Saskatoon declared bankruptcy (Feb. 17). In Ottawa, Kurds hurled a gasoline bomb at a police line outside the Turkish Embassy, setting one officer ablaze (Feb. 17); in Montreal, police and about 100 Kurds–some of whom were armed–clashed outside the Israeli consulate (Feb 22). Matthew Barrett resigned as chief executive of the Bank of Montreal (Feb. 23). Reform party leader Preston

Manning declared his willingness to lead a new national right-wing party if such a party emerged from "United Alternative" talks between Reformers and Conservatives (Feb. 24). The boards of the Crown-owned BC Ferry Corp. and Catamaran Ferries Inc. resigned hours after an accountant's report said the government's fast ferry project was CDN$235 million over budget (Feb. 24). Ottawa and all provinces except NS offered CDN$1.5 billion in relief to 45,000 farm families facing financial hardship caused by falling international grain and hog markets (Feb. 24). Sen. Eric Berntson became the 15th Conservative convicted in Sask.'s long-running expense fraud scandal ((Feb. 25).

March

INTERNATIONAL

Argentina: On Mar. 10, during a state visit to Buenos Aires, the UK's Prince Charles upset his hosts when he spoke of the Falkland Islands' right to self determination; earlier the prince had placed a wreath at a memorial to the Argentine soldiers who died in the 1982 Falklands War. **Commonwealth of Independent States (CIS):** On Mar. 4, Russian Pres. Yeltsin, acting as chairman of the heads of state of the CIS, dismissed Executive Secretary Boris Berezovsky for overstepping his authority. **Cuba:** On Mar. 15, a court in Havana imposed prison sentences on four dissidents convicted of sedition. **European Union:** On Mar. 16, the executive 20-member European Commission resigned en masse after an independent committee set up by the European Parliament found the commission guilty of fraud, nepotism and mismanagement. **India:** In Dharmsala, on the 40th anniversary of a Tibetan uprising against Chinese rule, the Dalai Lama told 4,000 supporters that he sought autonomy but not independence for Tibet. **Iraq:** US and UK aircraft hammered Iraqi air defences while patrolling "no-fly zones." Periodic air strikes continued throughout 1999. **Italy:** On Mar. 9-11, Iranian Pres. Mohammad Khatami became the first Iranian leader to visit the West since 1979 during a visit to Italy and the Vatican. **NATO:** On Mar. 12, NATO admitted three former Warsaw Pact states as members: Poland, Hungary and the Czech Republic. **Northern Ireland:** On Mar. 15, Rosemary Nelson, a human rights lawyer, was killed by a car bomb in Armagh; Ulster loyalists claimed responsibility. **Paraguay:** On Mar. 23, V. Pres. Ferraro was shot dead by three men in military uniforms in Asuncion. **Russia:** On Mar. 30, during a major address to the Federal Assembly, Pres. Yeltsin condemned NATO air strikes against Yugoslavia; days earlier he withdrew Russian representatives from NATO. **United States:** On Mar. 26, Jack Kevorkian, an advocate of physician-assisted suicide, was convicted in Mich. for the murder of Thomas Youk, a terminally ill man. **Yugoslavia:** On Mar. 24, after the failure of peace talks in Paris, NATO began launching air strikes against Yugoslavia to force Pres. Milosevic to compromise over Kosovo. Serbian forces in Kosovo stepped up the "ethnic cleansing" of Albanian Kosovars, creating tens of thousands of refugees.

CANADA

The RCMP raided the home of BC Prem. Clark, searching for evidence that he had helped a friend apply for a casino license in exchange for backyard decks at Clark's home and cottage (Mar. 2). Health Min. Allan Rock approved medical studies on the benefits of marijuana use (Mar. 3). Ont. Education Min. Dave Johnson reformed the province's high school curriculum by adding required credits for graduation and emphasizing math and science (Mar. 4). The Liberal government moved to bar federal Crown corporations from donating to political parties (Mar. 5) after an Opposition MP revealed that the Liberals had received money from Atomic Energy of Canada, Canada Post and the Business Development Bank of Canada in 1995-96. Ottawa passed a law transferring control of reserve lands to band councils; the law granted councils the power to expropriate land and to divide property after divorces (Mar. 8). The Canadian Wheat Board and the Canadian Pacific Railway settled their dispute over who was to blame for the disastrous 1996-97 grain shipping season (Mar. 8); the settlement ended the board's CDN$45 million law suit and resulted in CDN$15 million in compensation for Prairie farmers. Canadian Communists won a victory in court for smaller political parties when a judge struck down sections in the Canada Elections Act that required parties to field minimum numbers of candidates to be registered (Mar 11). Prime Min. Chrétien condemned Cuba's conviction of four dissidents (Mar. 15). Canada's four stock exchanges announced major reforms, including the merger of the Vancouver and Alta exchanges (Mar. 15). The Progressive Democratic Alliance, the BC party founded by Gordon Wilson in 1993, disbanded (Mar. 20). Atlantic Canada's four telephone companies agreed to merge into AtlanticCo (Mar. 22). Opposition MPs continued criticizing Prime Min. Chrétien for securing CDN$2.3 million in public money for two hotel owners with histories of legal and financial problems in Chrétien's riding (Mar. 23). Canadian CF-18 fighter-bombers began taking part in NATO air strikes against Yugoslavia (Mar. 24); in Toronto, Serbs threw rocks, paint and Molotov cocktails at the US consulate and police (Mar. 24-25). In Man., an inquiry led by Alfred Monnin reported that senior Tories illegally recruited and backed supposedly independent aboriginal candidates in the 1995 provincial election to split popular support for the NDP (Mar. 29). For the first time in Canada, Mohawks on Que.'s Kahnawake reserve won the right to collect tax-like levies from non-natives on reserves (Mar. 30). Canada's first legal strike by prison guards ended when Ottawa legislated them back to work (Mar. 30). Nfld celebrated the 50th anniversary of its entry into Canada (Mar. 31). MPs from all federal parties endorsed Canadian participation in NATO's air campaign against Yugoslavia (Mar. 31).

April

INTERNATIONAL

China: On Apr. 25, 10,000 practitioners of Falun Gong, a spiritual movement, held a vigil in Beijing to protest persecution by police. **India:** On Apr. 17, the Bharatiya Janata Party's coalition government lost a confidence motion in the lower house by a vote of 270-269, causing the fall of Prime Min. A.B. Vajpayee's government. **Malaysia:** On Apr. 14, a court declared former Deputy Prime Min. Anwar Ibrahim guilty of corruption and sentenced him to six years in prison. **Niger:** On Apr. 9, Pres. Ibrahim Barre Mainassara was assassinated in Niamey. **Northern Ireland:** On Apr. 1, British Prime Min. Blair and Irish Prime Min. Bertie Ahern published the Hillsborough Declaration, aimed at disarming terrorists and bringing Sinn Féin into the power-sharing executive. **Pakistan:** On Apr. 15, former Prime Min. Benazir Bhutto was convicted in absentia of corruption and sentenced to five years in prison. **Space:** On Apr. 15, US astronomers announced the first discovery of a solar system outside our own orbiting the star Upsilon Andromeda. **Switzerland:** On Apr. 30, a military court in Lausanne sentenced Fulgence Niyonteze, a former Rwandan mayor, to life imprisonment for war crimes in Rwanda. **United Kingdom:** On Apr. 1, Anthony Sawoniuk became the first person convicted in the UK for Nazi war crimes committed in World War II. In late Apr., three bombs exploded in London; the first two injured 45 people in ethnic communities and the third caused three deaths and 65 injuries in a gay pub. **United States:** On Apr. 6-14, Chinese Prem. Zhu paid his first visit to the US. On Apr. 12, a judge in Little Rock, Ark., declared that Pres. Clinton had lied in his deposition of Jan. 17, 1998, in the Paula Jones case; Clinton thus became the first sitting president to be found in contempt of court. On Apr. 14, former V. Pres. Dan Quayle announced his bid for the Republican leadership in the presidential election in 2000. On Apr. 20, students Eric Harris and Dylan Klebold attacked Columbine High School in Littleton, Col., killing 13 people before killing themselves. **Yugoslavia:** NATO continued its bombing campaign. **Zambia:** A High Court judge stripped ex-Pres. Kenneth Kaunda of his citizenship and said he had ruled illegally for 27 years.

CANADA

Nunavut became Canada's newest territory; Paul Okalik became its first premier (Apr. 1). In Man., hundreds of protesters disrupted the opening of the legislature; they demanded jobs, better housing and an apology for the government's attempt at rigging votes in aboriginal ridings in 1995 (Apr. 6). The Federal Court of Canada quashed Ottawa's approval for an open-pit coal mine near the edge of Jasper National Park (Apr. 8). Ont. sold Highway 407 to a Que.-led consortium for CDN$3.1 billion in the biggest privatization in Canadian history to date (Apr. 13). Statistics Canada reported that the average household was no richer than it was 20 years ago (Apr. 14). Wayne Gretzky played his last professional hockey game (Apr. 18). The Ont. Court, general division, was renamed the Superior Court of Justice; the Ont. Court, provincial division, was renamed the Ont. Court of Justice (Apr. 19). Chinese Prem. Zhu ended a visit to Canada (Apr. 20); protesters condemned China's human rights record in six cities. The Supreme Court of Canada said the courts put too many offenders behind bars, making Canada's incarceration rate one of the highest in the world (Apr. 23). A VIA Rail train crashed in Thamesville, Ont., killing two people (Apr. 23). Prime Min. Chrétien announced the departure of 800 soldiers to Macedonia to join a larger NATO force for training exercises (Apr. 27). BC Prem. Clark signed the Nisga'a Treaty after invoking closure on debate (Apr. 27); the treaty gave the Nisga'a about 2,000 sq. km of land, fishing and hunting rights and some self-government. About 1,000 teachers picketed Alta Prem. Klein's office in Calgary to protest the government's postponement of their strike (Apr. 27). Federal Information Commissioner John Reid condemned excessive secrecy in six departments: Revenue, Defence, Health, Citizenship and Immigration, the Privy Council Office and Foreign Affairs (Apr. 28). A 14-year-old killed one student and wounded another in shootings at the W.R. Myers High School in Taber, Alta (Apr. 28). Nfld's legislature unanimously voted to change the province's official name to Newfoundland and Labrador (Apr. 29).

May

INTERNATIONAL

Angola: In early May, the government launched a major offensive in the north against UNITA rebels. **Cambodia:** On May 9, a government spokesman said Kang Kek Leu, the former Khmer Rouge chief of security and commandant of Tuol Sleng prison camp, had been arrested after admitting responsibility for mass murder. **China:** The authorities detained about 130 dissidents to prevent the commemoration of the 10th anniversary on June 4 of the massacre at Tiananmen Square in Beijing. **Guinea-Bissau:** On May 7, a military coup overthrew Pres. Joao Bernardo Vieira. **India:** On May 26, for the first time since 1971, Indian fighter jets attacked Islamic guerrillas in Jammu and Kashmir. **Israel:** On May 17, in prime ministerial elections, Ehud Barak defeated incumbent Binyamin Netanyahu. **Korea (North):** On May 8, officials said thousands of people had died from famine since 1995. On May 20-24, US officials inspected a suspected nuclear weapons site at Kumchangri, finding it empty. **Netherlands:** On May 19, the entire cabinet resigned over a proposal to allow voter referendums to overturn government decisions. **Pakistan:** On May 27, the government shot down two Indian aircraft during fighting over the border; on May 28, Pakistan shot down an Indian helicopter gunship. **Russia:** On May 12, Pres. Yeltsin dismissed the government of Prime Min. Primakov; Sergei Stepashin became prime minister. **Sri Lanka:** At least 86 people died in fighting between the army and Tamil militants. **United Kingdom:** On May 6, in elections to the new Scottish Parliament and Welsh Assembly, Labour emerged as the largest party in both legislatures without winning majorities. **United States:** On May 3, Japanese Prime Min. Keizo Obuchi and Pres. Clinton held a summit meeting. On May 17, Secretary of State Madeleine Albright announced food aid for N. Korea. On May 20, a 15-year-old boy shot and wounded six students at a high school in Conyers, Ga. On May 25, the House of Representatives released the Cox report on China's alleged espionage in US nuclear weapons labs. **Yugoslavia:** All month NATO air forces hit targets in Serbia and Montenegro; on May 7, NATO mistakenly bombed the Chinese Embassy in Belgrade, prompting anti-NATO protests in China. Yugoslav troops infiltrated Albania to attack the UCK.

CANADA

In early May, Albanian Kosovar refugees began arriving in Canada. American Family Publishers, a Montreal-based tele-marketing firm, was fined CDN$1 million for fraud (May 5); in Mar., its telemarketers became the first in Canada to get prison sentences. Horseback riders in historic uniforms began a 1,500-km ride west from Fort Dufferin, Man., to recreate the first trek of the North-West Mounted Police across the Prairies in 1874 (May 8). A court found John Roby, a former usher at Toronto's Maple Leaf Gardens, guilty of 35 counts of child abuse (May 9). Alta's Whaleback landscape, a region with distinct windswept ridges, won protection from drilling, logging and mining (May 11). After a two-year probe, the RCMP said crimes occurred at Bre-X Minerals Ltd, but lack of evidence prevented the laying of charges (May 12). Ottawa approved the construction of a dry storage site for used nuclear fuel at Ont.'s Bruce Nuclear Power Development (May 14). A month-long strike by 9,500 Bell Canada

workers ended (May 15). David Milgaard, who spent 22 years in prison for a murder he did not commit, got a record CDN$10 million in compensation from the Sask. and federal governments (May 17). The Canadian Radio-television and Telecommunications Commission said it would not regulate the Internet or impose Canadian content rules (May 17). Que. Prem. Bouchard returned from Mexico with at least CDN$51 million in contracts for Que. firms (May 19). The Supreme Court of Canada ruled that the Ont. Family Law Act's definition of spouse–which applies only to heterosexual couples–is unconstitutional because it discriminates against gays; the Court also opened band elections to off-reserve natives for the first time (May 20). Alta Prem. Klein shuffled his cabinet (May 26). Ottawa unanimously passed a law giving victims more voice in the criminal justice system (May 28). Ottawa agreed to liberalize trade with five Andean countries (May 31).

June

INTERNATIONAL

Belgium: Two separate health scares caused bans on Coca-Cola in Belgium and bans on Belgian livestock across Europe. **Chile:** On June 9, police arrested five senior military men–the "caravan of death"–for kidnapping 72 people after the 1973 coup. **China:** On June 4, more than 70,000 people in Hong Kong commemorated the 1989 massacre in Tiananmen Square in Beijing. **Colombia:** On June 22-23, at least 68 people died when FARC attacked a paramilitary stronghold belonging to the United Self Defence Forces of Colombia. **India:** The army won territory back from Islamic guerrillas backed by Pakistani troops in Kashmir and Jammu. **Korea:** On June 15, the North and South Korean navies fought a battle in the Yellow Sea; S. Korea sank one N. Korean torpedo boat and hit five other N. Korean vessels. **Latvia:** On June 17, Vaira Vike-Freiberga, a former psychology professor in Canada, was elected president.

Lebanon: On June 7, two gunmen killed four judges and injured about 50 bystanders in a court in Sidon. On June 24, Israel carried out air strikes against the Hezbollah. **Mexico:** On June 15, an earthquake hit south-central Mexico, killing about 19 people. **Nigeria:** On June 10, Pres. Olusegun Obasanjo removed more than 150 senior military officers who had held political power in 1985-99 to consolidate civilian rule. **Northern Ireland:** On June 22, Patrick Magee, the IRA bomber who almost killed British former Prime Min. Margaret Thatcher in 1984, was freed from prison under the Good Friday Agreement. **Poland:** On June 5-17, Pope John Paul II made his longest trip abroad since his election as pope in 1978. On June 5, he spoke to 700,000 people near Gdansk. **South Africa:** On June 2, the ANC won landslide victories in the National Assembly and in provincial assemblies; on June 16, Pres. Thabo Mbeki was sworn into office, succeeding Mandela. **Space:** On June 6, the crew of the space shuttle *Discovery*, carrying Canadian astronaut Julie Payette, returned to earth after a 10-day mission. **Turkey:** On June 29, a court sentenced Abdullah Ocalan to death for leading the PKK's war against the Turkish state. **United Kingdom:** On June 19, Prince Edward and Sophie Rhys-Jones wed at Windsor. **United States:** On June 12, George W. Bush, governor of Texas and son of ex-Pres. George Bush, declared his bid for the Republican presidential nomination. On June 16, V. Pres. Al Gore declared his second bid for the Democratic presidential nomination. On June 17, Stanley Faulder became the first Canadian to be executed in the US since 1952. On June 18, a gun control bill failed in the House of Representatives. On June 30, Charles Ng was sentenced to death for 11 sex murders in Calif. in 1984-85; Ng fled to Canada in 1985 and fought extradition for six years. **Yugoslavia:** On June 3, Pres. Milosevic accepted NATO's peace terms. On June 10, NATO's bombing campaign stopped. On June 11-13, NATO K-For and Russian troops entered Kosovo as peacekeepers.

By June 20, Yugoslav troops had left Kosovo; NATO soon found evidence that as many as 10,000 people had been slaughtered there.

CANADA

MTS, Man.'s telephone company, locked out 1,400 unionized employees over fears that a labour dispute was affecting emergency calls (June 3). Prem. Mike Harris's Conservatives won a reduced majority in Ont.'s election (June 3). Ont. provincial court judges won a phased-in 30 percent pay hike, raising annual salaries to CDN$170,000 per judge (June 3). In Kingston, Ont., the grave of Prime Min. John A. Macdonald was designated a national historical site (June 6). Bernard Lord's Conservatives won a landslide victory over the Liberals in NB's election (June 7). The House of Commons passed a Reform party motion saying marriage is a union between man and woman (June 8). The federal NDP disciplined Svend Robinson (June 9) for presenting a petition in the House of Commons calling for the removal of God from the Constitution (June 8). In NS, Fred Kaufman's review of Crown prosecutors concluded that they suffered from overwork, poor supervision, poor morale and relatively low pay (June 9). Health Canada opened a new high-security lab in Winnipeg to study the deadliest human and animal diseases in the world (June 11). Defence Min. Art Eggleton announced the departure of another 500 peacekeepers to Kosovo (June 11), two days after Western generals and Yugoslavia signed a peace accord. BC's NDP repaid some of the money (CDN$118,000) stolen from charities during the bingo scandal of 1983-84 (June 11). The Supreme Court of Canada ruled that children's organisations can be liable for charges of sexual abuse if their workplaces make employees' sex crimes easier to commit (June 17). In BC, a judge awarded CDN$600,000 to John Sheehan, former head of BC Hydro, in his wrongful dismissal suit against the province (June 17). BC announced plans to halt the expansion of gambling facilities (June 17). US forestry giant Weyerhaeuser Co. announced its intention to buy MacMillan Bloedel Ltd for CDN$3.6 billion (June 20). In Sask. by-elections, the right-wing Saskatchewan Party won its first seat in Cypress Hills; the NDP won two more (June 28).

July

INTERNATIONAL

Bangladesh: Floods caused by monsoons displaced almost one million people and killed at least 19. **China:** Throughout July, emergency workers tried to contain the flooding Yangtze River and its tributaries; about 1.84 million people were evacuated from floodplains and hundreds died. On July 15, the military announced it had neutron bombs and, referring to Taiwan, threatened to smash "attempts at separatism." On July 21, police arrested about 30,000 members of Falun Gong in 30 cities. **Colombia:** On July 8-12, after twice-postponed peace talks with the government, FARC attacked 15 towns; about 200 people died in the fighting. **Democratic Republic of Congo:** Following the collapse of a ceasefire signed by six African states, the rebel Congolese Rally for Democracy launched a new offensive and drove tens of thousands of refugees into Tanzania. **Indonesia:** On July 15, officials confirmed the victory of Megawati Sukarnopurti's Indonesian Democratic Party in the June 7 parliamentary elections, the first held in 44 years. **Iran:** On July 8-9, police and Ansar-e Hezbollah radicals broke up a student rally in Tehran, killing and wounding an unknown number of students. More student protests and arrests followed; on July 27, Ayatollah Khatami condemned the initial raid. **Netherlands:** On July 15, the International Criminal Tribunal for the Former Yugoslavia at The Hague reclassified the 1992-95 Bosnian war as an international (not an "internal") conflict; the ruling opened the way for tougher prosecutions against Balkan war criminals.

Northern Ireland: On July 15, David Trimble's Ulster Unionists boycotted a special session of the new assembly, saying they couldn't work with Sinn Féin until its military wing, the IRA, began disarming. **Romania:** On July 15, a court sentenced two Communist generals to 15 years in prison for trying to suppress the 1989 revolution against Pres. Nicolai Ceausescu. **Russia:** In mid-month, the army conducted manoeuvres near the Baltic states. On July 20, a naval court cleared Captain Grigory Pasko of treason and espionage charges for publicizing the Pacific Fleet's dumping of nuclear waste into the sea. **Sierra Leone:** On July 7, the government agreed to share power with the rebel Revolutionary United Front, ending an eight-year war. **Spain:** On July 20, the nation's highest court quashed the convictions of 23 former political leaders of ETA, the Basque separatist group. **United States:** On July 16, John Kennedy, Jr, and two family members died in a plane crash off the coast of Mass. On July 19, Carleton Fiorina became president of Hewlett-Packard Co., the first woman to lead a firm listed in the Dow industrial average. On July 29, Mark Barton, a stock market trader who had lost US$105,000 within two months, killed 12 people in Atlanta, Ga., before shooting himself.

CANADA

Party leaders in the NS election squared off in a TV debate (July 14). Graeme Bowbrick, parliamentary secretary to BC Prem. Clark, resigned (July 14). Joy MacPhail resigned as BC's finance minister; Gordon Wilson replaced her (July 16). In Toronto, a fire in a Bell Canada switching room knocked out bank machines and 100,000 telephone lines for a day (July 16). About 200 farmers on tractors on the Trans-Canada Highway in Sask. and Man. protested against lack of aid in the face of low grain prices and waterlogged fields (July 16). Sue Hammell, BC's minister for women's equality, resigned (July 19). The Coast Guard intercepted a cargo ship filled with 123 Chinese illegal immigrants off

Vancouver Island (July 20). Canadian Pacific Railway announced 1,900 layoffs by the end of 2000 (July 21). Statistics Canada reported that Canada's crime rate fell for the seventh year in a row and hit a 19-year low (July 21). Que. nurses ended a four-week strike for higher pay (July 26). John Hamm led Conservatives to victory over the Liberals in the NS election (July 27). Bell Canada announced its decision to buy back a 35 percent stake in BCE Mobile Communications for CDN$1.6 billion (July 30).

August

INTERNATIONAL

Austria: On Aug. 25, police arrested Gen. Momir Talic, chief of staff of the Bosnian Serb army, in Vienna for war crimes committed in Bosnia in 1992-95. **Germany:** On Aug. 9, Berlin replaced Bonn as the nation's capital. **Honduras:** On Aug. 8, officials said they found secret graves at El Aguacate, a base built by the US in 1983 and used by Nicaraguan Contras in the 1980s. **India:** On Aug. 2, two trains collided in West Bengal, killing at least 285 people. **Indonesia:** On Aug. 30, 78% of East Timorese voted for independence after years of Indonesian repression. **Northern Ireland:** On Aug. 15, more than 10,000 Catholics and Protestants united in Omagh to mark the anniversary of Ulster's worst IRA bombing, in which 29 people died and hundreds were wounded. **Philippines:** Heavy rains throughout southeast Asia triggered mudslide in Manila that killed nearly 80; the estimated death toll in the region due to flooding was over 1,000. **Russia:** On Aug. 8, Russian troops launched attacks on Islamic rebels in Dagestan. On Aug. 9, Pres. Yeltsin dismissed Prime Min. Stepashin and his cabinet and appointed Vladimir Putin as prime minister. **Sierra Leone:** On Aug. 8-9, rebels released hostages, including one Canadian serving with the UN. **Turkey:** On Aug. 17, an earthquake measuring 7.4 on the Richter scale shook Izmit; at least 12,000 people died, 30,000 people were

injured and 200,000 were left homeless. **United States:** On Aug. 2, Pres. Clinton said a two-week heat wave had claimed the lives of 190 people across the nation. On Aug. 10, a neo-Nazi gunman shot and wounded five people at a Jewish centre in Los Angeles. **Venezuela:** On Aug. 30, to override lawmakers' opposition to his new constitution and anti-corruption campaign, Pres. Hugo Chavez stripped Congress of its last powers. **Yugoslavia:** On Aug. 19, between 100,000 and 150,000 people in Belgrade peacefully demanded the resignation of Pres. Milosevic. In Kosovo, returning Albanian Kosovars killed Serbs in revenge for alleged Serbian atrocities.

CANADA

Canadian goaltender Steve Vézina tested positive for banned stimulants at the Pan American Games; his roller hockey team was stripped of its gold medals (Aug. 1). The World Trade Organization gave Canada 90 days to scrap or radically change Technology Partnerships Canada, Ottawa's biggest high-technology development program (Aug. 2). In Sarnia, Ont., the grave of Alexander Mackenzie, Canada's second prime minister, was designated a national historical site (Aug. 2). Prime Min. Chrétien shuffled the cabinet (Aug. 3). Toronto-Dominion Bank announced plans to buy Canada Trust for CDN$7.85 billion (Aug. 3). In Winnipeg, the Pan American Games closed after Canadian athletes won 196 medals, 64 of them gold. Five Cuban athletes defected (Aug. 8). Explosions rocked an oil recycling plant in Calgary; the sky filled with black smoke, five people were injured and 2,000 people fled their homes and businesses (Aug. 9). The premiers met in Quebec City for their annual conference; although divided, they called for tax cuts and the restoration of federal funds for health and postsecondary education (Aug. 9-10). A second cargo ship dumped 131 Chinese illegal immigrants in the Queen Charlotte Islands (Aug. 11). Bill Matthews, a Conservative MP in Nfld, crossed the floor to join the federal Liberals (Aug. 13). The Reform party expelled Man.

MP Jake Hoeppner from caucus for opposing "United Alternative" talks (Aug 13). After 130 years, Eaton's filed for bankruptcy protection and announced plans to close its stores (Aug. 20). BC Prem. Clark resigned following the revelation that he was under criminal investigation for awarding a casino license to a friend (Aug. 21). Onex Corp. unveiled a CDN$1.8 billion bid to buy Air Canada and Canadian Airlines International (Aug. 24). Dan Miller became BC's new premier (Aug. 25). The NDP met for a national convention in Ottawa; Alexa McDonough won support for a policy of balanced budgets and moderate tax cuts (Aug.27-29). The Canadian Forces, RCMP and Coast Guard rescued Chinese immigrants aboard a third ship near Vancouver Island (Aug. 31).

September

INTERNATIONAL

China: Tropical storm Wendy, billed as the worst storm in a century, battered eastern China, killing 200 and doing over $277 million in damage. **Colombia:** On Sept. 1, 1.5 million unionized workers ended a two-day strike to protest the government's austerity measures. **Ecuador:** On Sept. 11, 12 foreigners, including eight Canadians, were kidnapped by guerrillas; the kidnapping was the first ever of Canadians in Ecuador. **France:** Pres. Jacques Chirac said France would not recognize Que. immediately after a Yes vote in a referendum (Sept. 1). **Greece:** On Sept. 7, an earthquake measuring 5.9 on the Richter scale hit Athens, leaving thousands homeless. **Indonesia:** Pro-Jakarta militias stepped up attacks on East Timorese. By mid-month, the Indonesian army had withdrawn at least 3,500 troops from the territory while 8,000 UN troops under Australian command to arrived on Sept. 20 to restore order. Jakarta handed control of East Timor to the peacekeepers on Sept. 27. Pro-Jakarta militias threatened to attack UN troops. **Israel:** On Sept. 5, three Arab citizens of Israel died in suicide car bombings in Tiberias and Haifa; Israeli-Arab leaders condemned the attacks. **Japan:** A nuclear fission reaction accident on Sept. 30 left 310 000 residents in Tokaimura trapped in their homes as officials issued a radiation advisory. **Mexico:** Southern Mexico was rocked by a 7.5 earthquake that left 27 dead and 122 injured. **Russia:** Early in the month, a series of bombings in Moscow and other cities killed more than 300 people; authorities blamed Islamic rebels from Dagestan and Chechnya. A retaliatory bombing campaign against the republic of Chechnya began on Sept. 23. **Taiwan:** On Sept. 20, an earthquake estimated to be between 7.3 and 8.1 on the Richter struck central Taiwan, killing at least 1,700 and injuring thousands more. **United States:** On Sept. 8, after campaigning for months, Democratic Sen. Bill Bradley declared his candidacy for the presidency. On Sept. 15, a gunman killed seven people and himself in a Baptist Church in Fort Worth, Tex. On Sept. 15-17, Hurricane Floyd battered the east coast, forcing three million people to flee, killing 68 and leaving 6,000 homeless.

CANADA

The Aboriginal Peoples Television Network aired for the first time (Sept. 1). Seven people died in a 63-vehicle crash on Ont.'s Highway 401 (Sept. 3). A BC court sentenced Dave Stupich, a provincial finance minister in the 1980s, to two years in prison for stealing hundreds of thousands of dollars from an NDP fundraising society in Nanaimo (Sept. 3). In NS, the Speaker of the House refused to name an Official Opposition because the Liberals and the NDP won 11 seats apiece in the July election (Sept. 8). Ottawa imposed a ban on military equipment sales to Indonesia (Sept. 13). Cape Breton's Phalen coal mine shut down ahead of schedule; 400 workers lost their jobs (Sept. 13). Louise Arbour was sworn in as the newest justice on the Supreme Court of Canada (Sept. 15). In Sask., Prem. Romanow was re-elected to a third term, but his NDP government fell to minority status; the new Saskatchewan Party became the Opposition (Sept. 16). Donald Marshall won a victory in the Supreme Court of Canada defending historic Micmac fishing rights (Sept. 17). NDP leader Gary Doer led his party to a majority victory in the Sept. 21 Manitoba provincial election.

Index

1999

JANUARY
S	M	T	W	T	F	S
					[1]	2
3	4	5	6	7	8	9
10	11	12	13	14	15	16
17	18	19	20	21	22	23
24	25	26	27	28	29	30
31						

FEBRUARY
S	M	T	W	T	F	S
	1	2	3	4	5	6
7	8	9	10	11	12	13
14	15	16	17	18	19	20
21	22	23	24	25	26	27
28						

MARCH
S	M	T	W	T	F	S
	1	2	3	4	5	6
7	8	9	10	11	12	13
14	15	16	17	18	19	20
21	22	23	24	25	26	27
28	29	30	31			

APRIL
S	M	T	W	T	F	S
				1	[2]	3
4	5	6	7	8	9	10
11	12	13	14	15	16	17
18	19	20	21	22	23	24
25	26	27	28	29	30	

MAY
S	M	T	W	T	F	S
						1
2	3	4	5	6	7	8
9	10	11	12	13	14	15
16	17	18	19	20	21	22
23	[24]	25	26	27	28	29
30	31					

JUNE
S	M	T	W	T	F	S
		1	2	3	4	5
6	7	8	9	10	11	12
13	14	15	16	17	18	19
20	21	22	23	24	25	26
27	28	29	30			

JULY
S	M	T	W	T	F	S
				[1]	2	3
4	5	6	7	8	9	10
11	12	13	14	15	16	17
18	19	20	21	22	23	24
25	26	27	28	29	30	31

AUGUST
S	M	T	W	T	F	S
1	2	3	4	5	6	7
8	9	10	11	12	13	14
15	16	17	18	19	20	21
22	23	24	25	26	27	28
29	30	31				

SEPTEMBER
S	M	T	W	T	F	S
			1	2	3	4
5	[6]	7	8	9	10	11
12	13	14	15	16	17	18
19	20	21	22	23	24	25
26	27	28	29	30		

OCTOBER
S	M	T	W	T	F	S
					1	2
3	4	5	6	7	8	9
10	[11]	12	13	14	15	16
17	18	19	20	21	22	23
24	25	26	27	28	29	30
31						

NOVEMBER
S	M	T	W	T	F	S
	1	2	3	4	5	6
7	8	9	10	11	12	13
14	15	16	17	18	19	20
21	22	23	24	25	26	27
28	29	30				

DECEMBER
S	M	T	W	T	F	S
			1	2	3	4
5	6	7	8	9	10	11
12	13	14	15	16	17	18
19	20	21	22	23	24	25
26	[27]	[28]	29	30	31	

2001

JANUARY
S	M	T	W	T	F	S
	[1]	2	3	4	5	6
7	8	9	10	11	12	13
14	15	16	17	18	19	20
21	22	23	24	25	26	27
28	29	30	31			

FEBRUARY
S	M	T	W	T	F	S
				1	2	3
4	5	6	7	8	9	10
11	12	13	14	15	16	17
18	19	20	21	22	23	24
25	26	27	28			

MARCH
S	M	T	W	T	F	S
				1	2	3
4	5	6	7	8	9	10
11	12	13	14	15	16	17
18	19	20	21	22	23	24
25	26	27	28	29	30	31

APRIL
S	M	T	W	T	F	S
1	2	3	4	5	6	7
8	9	10	11	12	[13]	14
15	16	17	18	19	20	21
22	23	24	25	26	27	28
29	30					

MAY
S	M	T	W	T	F	S
		1	2	3	4	5
6	7	8	9	10	11	12
13	14	15	16	17	18	19
20	[21]	22	23	24	25	26
27	28	29	30	31		

JUNE
S	M	T	W	T	F	S
					1	2
3	4	5	6	7	8	9
10	11	12	13	14	15	16
17	18	19	20	21	22	23
24	25	26	27	28	29	30

JULY
S	M	T	W	T	F	S
[1]	2	3	4	5	6	7
8	9	10	11	12	13	14
15	16	17	18	19	20	21
22	23	24	25	26	27	28
29	30	31				

AUGUST
S	M	T	W	T	F	S
			1	2	3	4
5	6	7	8	9	10	11
12	13	14	15	16	17	18
19	20	21	22	23	24	25
26	27	28	29	30	31	

SEPTEMBER
S	M	T	W	T	F	S
						1
2	[3]	4	5	6	7	8
9	10	11	12	13	14	15
16	17	18	19	20	21	22
23	24	25	26	27	28	29
30						

OCTOBER
S	M	T	W	T	F	S
	1	2	3	4	5	6
7	[8]	9	10	11	12	13
14	15	16	17	18	19	20
21	22	23	24	25	26	27
28	29	30	31			

NOVEMBER
S	M	T	W	T	F	S
				1	2	3
4	5	6	7	8	9	10
11	12	13	14	15	16	17
18	19	20	21	22	23	24
25	26	27	28	29	30	

DECEMBER
S	M	T	W	T	F	S
						1
2	3	4	5	6	7	8
9	10	11	12	13	14	15
16	17	18	19	20	21	22
23	24	[25]	[26]	27	28	29
30	31					

2000 CALENDAR AND HOLIDAYS

JANUARY
S	M	T	W	T	F	S
						1
2	3	4	5	6	7	8
9	10	11	12	13	14	15
16	17	18	19	20	21	22
23	24	25	26	27	28	29
30	31					

FEBRUARY
S	M	T	W	T	F	S
		1	2	3	4	5
6	7	8	9	10	11	12
13	14	15	16	17	18	19
20	21	22	23	24	25	26
27	28	29				

MARCH
S	M	T	W	T	F	S
		1	2	3	4
5	6	7	8	9	10	11
12	13	14	15	16	17	18
19	20	21	22	23	24	25
26	27	28	29	30	31	

APRIL
S	M	T	W	T	F	S
						1
2	3	4	5	6	7	8
9	10	11	12	13	14	15
16	17	18	19	20	21	22
23	24	25	26	27	28	29
30						

MAY
S	M	T	W	T	F	S
	1	2	3	4	5	6
7	8	9	10	11	12	13
14	15	16	17	18	19	20
21	22	23	24	25	26	27
28	29	30	31			

JUNE
S	M	T	W	T	F	S
				1	2	3
4	5	6	7	8	9	10
11	12	13	14	15	16	17
18	19	20	21	22	23	24
25	26	27	28	29	30	

JULY
S	M	T	W	T	F	S
						1
2	3	4	5	6	7	8
9	10	11	12	13	14	15
16	17	18	19	20	21	22
23	24	25	26	27	28	29
30	31					

AUGUST
S	M	T	W	T	F	S
		1	2	3	4	5
6	7	8	9	10	11	12
13	14	15	16	17	18	19
20	21	22	23	24	25	26
27	28	29	30	31		

SEPTEMBER
S	M	T	W	T	F	S
					1	2
3	4	5	6	7	8	9
10	11	12	13	14	15	16
17	18	19	20	21	22	23
24	25	26	27	28	29	30

OCTOBER
S	M	T	W	T	F	S
1	2	3	4	5	6	7
8	9	10	11	12	13	14
15	16	17	18	19	20	21
22	23	24	25	26	27	28
29	30	31				

NOVEMBER
S	M	T	W	T	F	S
			1	2	3	4
5	6	7	8	9	10	11
12	13	14	15	16	17	18
19	20	21	22	23	24	25
26	27	28	29	30		

DECEMBER
S	M	T	W	T	F	S
					1	2
3	4	5	6	7	8	9
10	11	12	13	14	15	16
17	18	19	20	21	22	23
24	25	26	27	28	29	30
31						

New Year's Day (January 1), Good Friday (April 21), Victoria Day (May 22), Canada Day (July 1), Labour Day (September 4), Thanksgiving (October 9), Christmas Day and Boxing Day December 25 and 26.

Other Holidays and Holy Days

Government and bank holidays: April 24 (Easter Monday), November 11 (Remembrance Day).

Jewish Holy Days: Purim—March 21; Passover—April 20-21; Pesach—April 7-8; Shavuot—June 9-10; Rosh Hashanah—September 30-October 1; Yom Kippur—October 9; Sukkot—October 14-15; Simchat Torah—October 21-2; Hanukkah—December 22-29.

Islamic Holy Days: These are subject to the sighting of the moon. The key days are: Nuzulul Qur'an; Eidul Fitri; Eidul Adha; Islamic New Year; Ashoora; Maulid Nabi; Isra'and Miraj; First Day of Ramadhan.

Chinese New Year—Feb 5, 2000.